PRISON LAW

PRISON LAW

Third Edition

STEPHEN LIVINGSTONE

Professor of Human Rights Law, Queen's University, Belfast

TIM OWEN QC

Barrister, Matrix Chambers, London

ALISON MACDONALD

Barrister, Matrix Chambers, London
Fellow, All Souls College, Oxford

OXFORD
UNIVERSITY PRESS

OXFORD
UNIVERSITY PRESS

Great Clarendon Street, Oxford OX2 6DP

Oxford University Press is a department of the University of Oxford.
It furthers the University's objective of excellence in research, scholarship,
and education by publishing worldwide in

Oxford New York

Auckland Bangkok Buenos Aires Cape Town Chennai
Dar es Salaam Delhi Hong Kong Istanbul Karachi Kolkata
Kuala Lumpur Madrid Melbourne Mexico City Mumbai Nairobi
São Paulo Shanghai Taipei Tokyo Toronto

Oxford is a registered trade mark of Oxford University Press
in the UK and in certain other countries

Published in the United States
by Oxford University Press Inc., New York

First published 2003

© Stephen Livingstone, Tim Owen and Alison Macdonald 2003

The moral rights of the author have been asserted

Database right Oxford University Press (maker)

Third edition published 2003

Crown copyright material is reproduced under Class Licence Number C01P0000148 with
the permission of the Controller of HMSO and the Queen's Printer for Scotland

British Library Cataloguing in Publication Data
Data available

Library of Congress Cataloging in Publication Data
Data available

ISBN 0–19–925899–6

3 5 7 9 10 8 6 4 2

Typeset by Hope Services (Abingdon) Ltd.
Printed in Great Britain
on acid-free paper by
Biddles Ltd, King's Lynn, Norfolk

FOREWORD TO THE SECOND EDITION

The first edition of this book was a notable achievement. It comprehensively stated the law on prisons and prisoners as it stood in 1993. The authors also described the interwoven roles of history, political morality, countervailing policy considerations and principle in creating the mosaic of prison law. Rightly, the authors also examined the law critically, While tracing the progress since the 1970s towards an enlightened prison law the authors concluded that reform was mostly focused on the procedural rights of prisoners. The courts had proved hesitant to recognize minimum standards in the treatment of prisoners.

Now in the second edition the authors confront and describe a changed and changing landscape. It is true that the Prison Act of 1952 and the Prison Rules of 1964, together with non-statutory orders and instructions issued by the Home Secretary, still by and large remain the basic texts. But much has changed.

First, in parallel with the continuing development of public law judgments of the higher courts have developed prison law in ways which are broadly consistent with the principles of the European Convention on Human Rights. In respect of issues of jurisdiction, access to courts and other procedural matters the development has been extensive. When it comes to the positive rights of prisoners, such as the entitlement to proper medical care, and their negative rights, such as protection against ill treatment, the authors are right to insist that progress has been more limited. But gradually, even in respect of standards of treatment, prisoners' rights have been recognized. This is surely as it should be: at some point treatment must require objective justification.

Secondly, since 1993 the European Commission and the European Court of Human Rights have proved themselves more prepared than English courts to recognize and protect the rights of prisoners. Above all they have influenced English law by enunciating an explicit rights based philosophy. That process has slowly gathered pace since 1993.

Thirdly, there is the impending impact of the enactment of the Human Rights Bill. The principles of minimum standards of treatment, and actionable prisoners' rights, are now fully vindicated. Under the Act the courts will be required to adopt a fair and balanced approach: the rights of prisoners must be weighed against the need to secure stability and order in prisons in a civilized way. The practical effect of the Act will be pervasive. Most of the rules affecting prisoners stem from secondary legislation. The courts will now be required to examine the legitimacy of prison regulations far more closely than in the past. Indeed as the authors persuasively argue the Government may come to recognize the need for a new Prison Act to clarify the rights and duties of prisoners in primary legislation.

It is an opportune time for a new edition of *Prison Law*. The second edition is an indispensable book for all lawyers who are engaged on work concerned with prisons and prisoners. But it is much more. Prisons and prisoners have proved an important testing ground for the development of our public law. The new edition of this book is a valuable contribution to public law literature.

Johan Steyn

House of Lords
November 1998

FOREWORD TO THE FIRST EDITION

Frequently enough to carry conviction, a prisoner will recount how somebody in authority has said 'I'm the law here'. The sense of impotence and isolation the phrase creates is designedly chilling. In too many instances, moreover, the officer is right: he or she is in sole control and there is no recourse to any legal authority.

Such absolute power is the antithesis of the rule of law. Yet for an age the courts were either afraid or unwilling to take responsibility for the protection of citizens behind bars from unlawful treatment. It was not said, of course, that prisoners had no rights; only that the assurance of such rights as they had could safely be entrusted to their custodians. Behind this lay, I think, an assumption that in any contest the custodian would be stolidly in the right and the prisoner a mendacious troublemaker, so that nothing was to be gained by giving a prisoner a day in court.

The acquiescent attitude of the courts was not confined to prisons. With unimpressive exceptions it ran across the whole range of public administration. But when in the 1960s and 70s the judicial review of administrative action began to wake from its long sleep, the problem remained that prisoners who alleged that the power of their custodians over them had been abused were simply not going to be believed. It was the Hull prison riots which changed the story, aided by one of the peculiarities of the laborious bureaucracy of prison administration—the practice of recording disciplinary proceedings word for word in longhand. Departures from natural justice which no judge would have believed merely on a prisoner's say-so turned out to have been faithfully verified in manuscript and routinely filed. In consequence, in the landmark case of *St Germain* at the end of the 1970s, the Court of Appeal placed a judicial foot in the prison door, holding that judicial review lay to Boards of Visitors in their (then) disciplinary capacity.

The Court of Appeal's decision is hallmarked by the judgment of Lord Justice Shaw, who as Sebag Shaw QC had been not a public law practitioner but one of the country's leading criminal advocates. In a judgment which contains one of the handsomest prose passages in the modern law reports as well as one of the most far-sighted, Shaw spelt out the status of the prisoner as a citizen behind bars whose entitlement to the court's vigilance for those rights he or she retained was as great as any other citizen's.

I do not believe that it was a coincidence that this breakthrough occurred when and where it did. The Hull prison riots, like others since, were the product of a suppressed sense of grievance at unjust and sometimes inhuman treatment in our prisons. Although public law had independently begun to rediscover the doctrines and to develop within the law, it was the Hull riots which afforded not only the opportunity but—more important—the incentive to carry it through. The more recent syndrome of the 1990 prison riots followed by the radical and reforming Woolf Report is in many ways a replication of the *Hull-St Germain* sequence. This is not an argument for violent disorder: it is the case for proactive and vigilant courts of public law at the elbow of a conscientious and law-abiding public administration.

The other important dimension of these early developments lay in Strasbourg. Sidney Golder, a prisoner who was unable to obtain redress through the English courts for an injustice done to him in prison, established his claim under the European Convention of Human Rights. Those who have since practised in this field have been in little doubt that, while it was, until recently, impossible to cite the Convention as even an indirect source of law, the courts have consciously taken decisions on prisoners' rights designed at least in part to rescue the UK government from the prospect of further embarrassment in Strasbourg.

It should not be forgotten that it takes not only awareness but a degree of courage on a prisoner's part to take his or her custodians or their departmental superiors to court. The occasionally expressed judicial perception of disgruntled and devious prisoners sitting in their cells devising fresh ways of making life difficult for the authorities, even if partly true, has to yield to the fact that prisoners' challenges to the prison administration have been few in number but proportionately pretty successful by comparison with public law challenges in other fields.

Although there are now some useful books in this important field of law, none does the job that the present volume does. Stephen Livingstone and Tim Owen are unusually well equipped and qualified for the task. Stephen Livingstone, a distinguished academic lawyer in Belfast, has the invaluable touchstone of knowledge of the American penal system and of the rights litigation which it has generated. Tim Owen, one of the handful of barristers specializing in prison and inquest law, has in a succession of important cases moved outward the frontiers of legal protection for prisoners. The book they have written does something which, even today, few legal books accomplish: it combines an excellent and compendious account of the state of the law on prisons and prisoners with a historical and political analysis of where the present system has come from and where it is headed. They do not place a narrow meaning on 'law': they recognize that administrative rules and practices and non-legal avenues of redress are as important as substantive law and recourse to the courts, and they provide a full treatment of the European dimension which, acknowledged or not, is unquestionably influential.

The concluding chapter is an essay of distinct importance. It attempts an appraisal of the now historic meeting of the prison system and the courts. Legal scholarship is traditionally deficient in this vital appraisal of law, not as a thing in itself, but as an element in a many-faceted social process. The authors delineate the unevenness of judicial intervention, which has been powerful in relation to procedural norms of discipline but hesitant in relation to standards of treatment. Debate is needed as to whether the latter are best left to respected public invigilators, whose effect has been palpable, or whether at some point minimum standards must become justiciable too. Before lawyers acclaim the latter, a sober look is needed at the actual effect that the courts' pronouncements of legal principle have had on the day-to-day treatment of prisoners. Attention has also to be given to the view that it is from the Prison Service that concrete reform comes. My own view, and I think that of the authors, is that these are all moving parts of a constantly changing whole. Just as prison discontent has plainly catalysed judicial and administrative responses, so the setting of legal standards has concentrated administrative minds; and just as the Prison Service does the detailed work of devising and implementing reforms, so the public pressure generated by independent reports furnishes the political impetus under which many of its policy choices are actually made.

The rule of law will not, however, have finally permeated the prison system until the vocabulary of administration and discipline no longer contains the sentence 'I'm the law here', and that—as Stephen Livingstone and Tim Owen demonstrate—is still some distance from realization.

LONDON
May 1993

Stephen Sedley

PREFACE

Some four years have elapsed since the second edition of this book went to press. In the meantime the Human Rights Act 1998 (HRA) has come into force and we have acquired a third author, Alison Macdonald, a reflection perhaps of the increasing volume of prison law as well as the desirability of injecting fresh blood into the re-writing and revising process.

In the last edition we were able to do no more than predict the likely impact of the HRA on prison law. We pointed out that in a series of cases beginning with *Raymond v Honey* and ending in *Ex parte Simms*, the common law had already established an approach to the protection of a prisoner's fundamental rights (the principle of legality) that closely mirrors the jurisprudence of the European Convention on Human Rights, and we suggested that a sea change in the outcome of prison litigation under the HRA was unlikely. We also said that while the HRA would offer new avenues of redress for prisoners and their lawyers to pursue, and new norms for prison officials to take into account when designing policy and practice, it would leave much of the old law still relevant.

It is fair to say that both these predictions have proved to be true. The continuity of approach as between the common law principle of legality and the HRA was best illustrated by the outcome of *R (Daly) v Home Secretary*, a landmark case which has become the leading authority on the proportionality test to be applied in cases which engage Convention rights. There is, of course, nothing new about the boundaries of public law being reformulated or extended by prison litigation. *Ex parte Hague* marked an important extension of the High Court's judicial review jurisdiction. *Ex parte Doody* remains a landmark case about procedural fairness. And, as stated above, in *Leech (No 2), Pierson, and Simms* the common law principle of legality was articulated and developed so that, even before the coming into force of the Human Rights Act, Lord Hoffmann felt able in *Simms* to say (disingenuously perhaps) that the common law had fully anticipated its provisions. The fact is that the recognition by Lord Justice Shaw in the *St Germain* case that prisoners are to be regarded as citizens behind bars meant that prisoners' cases were thereafter destined to raise, in a most acute form, the question as to whether the judges would resist the Executive's assertion that in the absence of express Parliamentary approval all basic rights could be overridden by a process of necessary implication. The antiquated Prison Act 1952 provides no express authority whatsoever for the destruction of a prisoner's basic rights other than his right to liberty.

And so it came as no surprise that the facts of *Daly* (the legality of a cell-searching policy which excluded prisoners from their cells while prison staff searched all their belongings, including their legally privileged documents) provided an ideal opportunity to explore the difference between the traditional *Wednesbury* test and the proportionality test as required under the HRA. What was, perhaps, more remarkable was the Home Secretary's keenness to uphold a blanket policy affecting the fundamental right to legal privilege of all prisoners after his earlier attempt to justify the blanket exclusion of meetings between prisoners and journalists had met with such a singular lack of success in *Simms*. But out of Mr Straw's addiction to blanket policies good things have come. It is now clear, as Lord Steyn said in his important speech in *Daly*, that there is a material difference between the *Wednesbury/Smith* grounds of review and the approach of proportionality where Convention rights are at stake, although this will not necessarily result in radically different outcomes in all cases. The fact is that by applying the common law principle of legality, *Daly* would have been decided in precisely the same way by the House of Lords, regardless of the coming into force of the HRA. However, this is not to diminish its importance in finally marking the end of the traditional *Wednesbury* doctrine in cases which engage fundamental rights.

Away from the well-trodden area of access to courts, prisoners' correspondence and access to legal advice, the HRA case law has occasionally displayed an approach which is at odds even with the pre-HRA law. The decision of the Court of Appeal in the artificial insemination case of *R (Mellor) v Home Secretary*, for example, demonstrates a particularly regressive approach to prisoners' legal rights. Quite apart from its upholding of the paternalistic view that it is a wholly legitimate function of the State to act to prevent the birth of children in circumstances where it is known that they will be brought up in a one parent family (at least for some period of time), the reasoning of the Court of Appeal misstates what the House of Lords said in *Ex parte Simms* about the purpose of imprisonment. It was central to Lord Phillips MR's reasoning on the issue of justification/proportionality that it is necessary for a court to take into account the penal objective of deprivation of liberty when considering whether a particular restriction of a fundamental right is lawful. The result of this approach is an apparent refinement of the *Raymond v Honey* principle so that *all* fundamental rights asserted by prisoners are first subjected to a quality assessment as part and parcel of the application of the proportionality principle, and in the context of an assumption that imprisonment is meant to interfere with basic rights. Disappointingly, the House of Lords refused Mr Mellor's application for permission to appeal. However, his case is destined for the European Court of Human Rights, where it is to be hoped that a more imaginative approach to the Article 8 and 12 case law will emerge. In the meantime, perhaps the best domestic route through the apparent conflict between *Simms* and *Mellor* is to be found in the thoughtful (and unappealed) judgment of Elias J in *R (Hirst) v Home Secretary*, a case which declared unlawful the policy of denying prisoners the right to contact the media by telephone in order to comment on matters of legitimate public interest. In our view, Elias J's judgment correctly applies the reasoning in both *Simms* and *Daly* and demonstrates (without, of course, overruling) how the Court of Appeal went badly wrong in *Mellor*. The limited way in which some courts have approached the HRA reminds us of the need still to look to the role of the Strasbourg institutions in this area. In 2002 the Court handed down a major decision in *Ezeh and Connors v United Kingdom* which has significant implications for prison discipline and it has also delivered a number of other important rulings on prison conditions and suicide prevention.

Further Developments

The text seeks to reflect the state of the law on 1 October 2002, but we are able in this Preface to comment on some further developments in the law up to 15 January 2003. The most significant of these is undoubtedly the decision of the House of Lords in the mandatory lifer cases of *R (Anderson) v Home Secretary*[1] and *R (Lichniak and Pyrah) v Home Secretary*[2]. In *Anderson* (delivered on 25 November 2002) the House of Lords applied the reasoning of the ECtHR in *Stafford v UK* (which had already established that post-tariff mandatory lifers, like discretionary lifers, were entitled to an Article 5 (4) review of their suitability for release) to the issue of the compatibility of the Home Secretary's tariff-fixing power with the requirements of Article 6. A seven Law Lord Committee unanimously held that (i) Article 6(1) guarantees a criminal defendant a right to a fair trial by an independent and impartial tribunal; (ii) the imposition of a sentence is a part of a trial; (iii) the fixing of the tariff of a convicted murderer is legally indistinguishable from the imposition of a sentence; (iv) therefore the tariff should be fixed by an independent and impartial tribunal; (v) the Home Secretary is not an independent and impartial tribunal; (vi) therefore the Home Secretary's power to determine the tariff of convicted murderers is incompatible with Article 6. Their Lordships held that s 29 of the Crime (Sentences) Act 1997 could not be read compatibly with the Convention, and accordingly made a declaration of incompatibility under s 4 of the HRA.

---

[1] [2002] 3 WLR 1800.
[2] [2002] 3 WLR 1834.

After the Grand Chamber judgment in *Stafford* had been issued in Strasbourg earlier in 2002, an apparently incandescent Home Secretary Blunkett issued dark warnings that should *Stafford* lead to the removal of all his powers to control the time that convicted murderers would spend in prison he would somehow seek to derogate from the Convention on this issue. In the event, and no doubt heavily influenced by statements in *Anderson* upholding the legality of the whole life tariff, wiser counsels prevailed. Shortly after the ruling in *Anderson*, the Home Office issued a statement confirming that new legislation will be drafted to establish a clear set of principles within which judges will fix minimum tariffs in the future. Tariffs will be set in open court and the judge will be required to justify any term imposed that is inconsistent with these principles. It is anticipated that the new system will become law by autumn 2003. In the meantime, it has been made clear that pending the coming into force of the new legislation, the Home Secretary will not himself entertain any applications by prisoners whose tariffs have not yet expired and who have served more than the period recommended by the judiciary but less than the period fixed by the Home Secretary. Such prisoners will remain without an effective domestic remedy until the new legislation is in force.

Having accepted the Convention-based arguments in favour of full judicialization of the mandatory life sentence, the House of Lords proceeded in *Lichniak and Pyrah* to reject the argument that the existence of the mandatory life sentence was incompatible with Articles 3 and 5 of the Convention, precisely because they had concluded in *Anderson* that, like the discretionary life sentence, a mandatory life sentence is in fact partly punitive and partly preventative. In the light of this finding, their Lordships concluded (again unanimously) that the mandatory nature of the life sentence imposed on convicted murderers was not in reality arbitrary, disproportionate, or excessive to a point which would engage either Article 3 or Article 5.

A further development in the field of the mandatory life sentence since the main body of the text was completed has been the announcement of the interim arrangements to be applied to the review and release of mandatory life prisoners in the wake of *Stafford v UK*, pending the enactment of fresh primary legislation. In a Parliamentary answer dated 17 October 2002, the Minister of State (Lord Falconer of Thorodon) said that the arrangements apply to all prisoners whose next Parole Board review begins on or after 1 January 2003. The changes will mean that in most instances these prisoners' cases will be heard initially (as before) by the Parole Board on the papers and will result in a provisional recommendation. If prisoners wish to make representations about provisional recommendations it will be open to them to request an oral hearing before the Parole Board, at which they may have legal representation. They will normally receive full disclosure of all material relevant to the question of whether they should be released.

They will also be able to examine and cross-examine witnesses. Similarly the Secretary of State may also require an oral hearing of the Board in cases where he believes that further examination of the evidence is required. If, at the end of the review process, the Parole Board favours the release of a mandatory lifer once the minimum period has been served, the Home Secretary has stated that he will normally accept that recommendation.

Plainly, these significant developments in the nature and practical administration of the mandatory life sentence mean that the fundamental distinction between the mandatory and discretionary life sentences has disappeared, and with it the justification for dealing with the sentences in two distinct chapters (as we have done in Chapters 13 and 14 of this edition). Our decision to maintain the distinction was influenced by uncertainty as to the date when judgment would be delivered in *Anderson* as well as the uncertainty as to the likely reaction of the Home Secretary in the face of a decision stripping him of his powers to fix the tariffs of convicted murderers, and the possibility of further delay in clarifying the law should Mr Anderson be faced with the need to make the long haul to Strasbourg. Accordingly, we decided for both practical and principled reasons to maintain the distinction in a way which reflected the true distinction in domestic law at the time of writing. What we have done in Chapter 13 is anticipate (correctly, we believe) what the likely impact of *Stafford v UK* would be in terms of its effect on the outcome of *Anderson* and the likely legislative changes that would be needed to bring domestic law into line with the Convention. The final result, we hope, is to inform and remind the reader of the historical distinction between the two sentences, while providing sufficient guidance to ensure a smooth transition into the new legislative arrangements that will eventually apply (and which will have to await the fourth edition for full elucidation).

On 29 November 2002, Munby J delivered an important judgment affecting the nature of the duties owed by the State to children (ie young people under 18) detained in Prison Service institutions. In *R (on the application of the Howard League for Penal Reform) v Home Secretary* [3] the Administrative Court was asked to consider the legality of the Prison Service claim that the Children Act 1989 does not apply to under-18 year olds in prison establishments, and whether the policy adopted in Prison Service Order 4950 was satisfactory and complied with domestic and human rights law. Munby J's impressive analysis concluded that the Children Act 1989 did not confer or impose any functions, powers, duties or responsibilities or obligations on either the Prison Service or its staff or the Home Secretary, and in that sense the Act did not apply to the Prison Service or to Young

---

[3] [2002] EWHC 2497 Admin.

Offender Institutions. Nevertheless, he went on to hold that the duties which a local authority would otherwise owe to a child, either under s 17 or s 47 of the Children Act, did not cease to be owed merely because the child was in such an institution. In that sense, the Act *did* apply to children held in YOIs. However, a local authority's functions, powers, duties, and responsibilities under the Act took effect and operated subject to the necessary requirements of imprisonment. While generally complimenting the Prison Service on the content of its statement of policy towards the treatment of children in penal institutions, Munby J concluded by expressing serious concerns about whether this policy was yet being implemented in a satisfactory manner throughout the whole of the Prison Service juvenile estate. He pointed out that the Joint Chief Inspectors' report, *Safeguarding Children*, and various other reports by the Chief Inspector of specific Young Offender Institutions, indicated that the State 'appears to be failing, and in some instances failing very badly, in its duties to vulnerable and damaged children in YOIs'. He expressed the view that material in these reports suggested that some of these failings may be such as to give rise to actionable breaches of applicable human rights law.

Finally, in terms of fresh developments, the Home Office announced that, with effect from April 2003, the funding responsibility for prison health services in England is to be transferred from the Home Office to the Department of Health. This is said to be seen as the first step in a process over the next five years which will see prison health become part of the NHS. Primary Care Trusts will then become responsible for the commissioning and provision of health services to prisoners in their areas. It follows that references to the Health Care Service for Prisoners (HCSP) in Chapter 6 will soon become out of date as the much-anticipated abolition of a separate health care system for prisoners becomes a reality.

Many of those who assisted us in the preparation of the first two editions have continued to help us in producing the third. We would especially like to thank Simon Creighton (of Bhatt Murphy, solicitors) and Phillippa Kaufmann (barrister), both prison law experts who provided valuable comments on the chapters dealing with life sentence prisoners and the release of determinate sentence prisoners as well as more general ideas on the state and development of prison law. Steve Foster at Coventry University drew our attention to a number of developments, especially regarding prisoners' contact with the outside world. Many officials within the Prison Service responded promptly and helpfully to our various requests for information. Edward Fitzgerald QC was a continuing source of inspiration and ideas, especially in relation to the law governing life sentence prisoners. Professor Roger Hood and Professor Andrew Ashworth offered guidance and support throughout the revision process, particularly on issues of parole and the mandatory life sentence. Last, but not least, Annabel Macris, Michelle

Thompson and Becky Allen at OUP displayed patience and encouragement in equal measures, the hallmarks of good publishers. As always, all errors and omissions are our responsibility alone.

15 January 2003

Stephen Livingstone
Professor of Human Rights Law
Head of the School of Law
The Queen's University of Belfast
Belfast BT7 1NN

Tim Owen QC
Matrix Chambers
Griffin Building
Gray's Inn
London WC1R 5LN

Alison Macdonald
Matrix Chambers
Griffin Building
Gray's Inn
London WC1R 5LN

CONTENTS—SUMMARY

CONTENTS

Contents

Contents

Contents

TABLE OF CASES

Other jurisdictions
Canada

India

Inter-American Court of Human Rights

South Africa

United States

United Kingdom

United Nations Human Rights Committee

TABLE OF LEGISLATION

All references are to paragraph numbers apart from the Appendices which have page numbers following the Appendix number. Please note that any references in bold denote main mentions.

UK Acts

Administrative Guidance (Documents, Instructions, Standards and Rules)

UK Statutory Instruments

r 39(6) 7.12
r 41 ....1.61, 2.53, 5.15
    (1) 5.15
    (3) 11.05
r 42 ....2.53
r 43(21) 9.20
r 43A 10.42
r 45 ....1.20, 1.22, 1.35, 1.60, 2.19, 2.20, 2.35, 2.39, 2.40,
    2.43, 2.54, 2.80, 2.87, 2.89, 5.55, 5.56, 5.68, 6.09, 9.31, 9.33, 10.02,
    10.04, 10.05, 10.06, 10.08, 10.09, 10.10, 10.11, 10.12, 10.13,
    10.16, 10.17, 10.18, 10.19, 10.20, 10.23, 10.26, 10.29, 10.30,
    10.31, 10.32–10.38, 10.49, 10.65, 10.67, 11.06
    (1)...2.85, 10.06, 10.20, 10.32
    (2)...1.20, 2.85, 10.24, 10.32
    (3) 6.11
    (4)..10.42
r 46...1.22, 1.31, 4.19, 10.04, 10.10, 10.28, 10.42
    (1) 10.07, 10.39
    (2) 1.31
r 47...16.09
    (4) 9.19
    (6) 9.18
    (21)...1.30, 9.20, 10.17
r 48 ....1.35, 1.60, 4.19, 10.46, 10.49, 10.50, 10.52, 10.53, 10.54
r 49 ....1.35, 1.60, 10.46, 10.56
    (1) 10.53
    (3) 6.11
    (4) 1.20, 1.21
r 50 ....5.22, 6.30
    (7) 5.22
    (8) 5.22
r 50A 1.31
r 51 ....9.18
    (1) 9.11, 9.18
    (1A)...1.30, 9.18
    (3) 9.18
    (6) 9.18
    (9) 6.30, 9.19
    (12) 9.18
    (17) 9.18
    (17A)..1.30, 9.18
    (20A)..1.30, 8.18
    (21) 5.32, 9.18
    (22) 7.41, 9.20
    (24A)..1.30, 9.18
rr 51–55..1.60
rr 51–61..1.35, 9.08

Other jurisdictions

Canada

France

India

TABLE OF INTERNATIONAL CONVENTIONS, TREATIES, INSTRUMENTS AND STANDARDS

All references are to paragraph numbers except for the Appendices which have the page numbers following the Appendix Number. Please note that any references in bold denote main mentions.

TABLE OF ABBREVIATIONS

CAT	United Nations Convention Against Torture and Other Cruel, Inhuman or Degrading Treatment or Punishment
CI	Circular Instruction
CNA	certified normal accommodation
CPR	Civil Procedure Rules
CPS	Crown Prosecution Service
CPT	European Committee for the Prevention of Torture
CRC	United Nations Convention on the Rights of the Child
CSC	Close Supervision Centre
DCMF	'design, construct, manage and finance'
DfES	Department for Education and Skills
DLP	discretionary lifer panel
DRS	discretionary release scheme
DTO	detention and training order
ECHR	European Convention on Human Rights
ECtHR	European Court of Human Rights
ECPT	European Convention for the Prevention of Torture and Inhuman or Degrading Treatment or Punishment
ESCRC	Economic, Social and Cultural Rights Covenant
GOAD	good order and discipline
HCSP	Health Care Service for Prisoners
HDC	home detention curfew
HMP	Her Majesty's Pleasure
HRA	Human Rights Act 1998
HRC	United Nations Human Rights Committee
ICCPR	United Nations International Covenant on Civil and Political Rights
ICRC	International Committee of the Red Cross
IEP	incentives and earned privileges
IG	Instruction to Governors
IMR	Inmate Medical Record
LRC	Local Review Committee
LSP	life sentence plan
MDT	mandatory drug test
MQP	minimum qualifying period
NATFHE	National Association of Teachers in Further and Higher Education
NGO	non-governmental organization

OCA	observation, classification and allocation
PAS	Prisoners' Advice Service
PED	parole eligibility date
PRES	pre-release employment scheme
PSO	Prison Service Order
SED	sentence expiry date
SO	Standing Order
SOTP	Sex Offenders Treatment Programme
SSU	Special Secure Unit
YOI	Young Offenders Institution

Journal abbreviations

AJIL	American Journal of International Law
CLJ	Cambridge Law Journal
Crim LR	Criminal Law Review
ICLQ	International and Comparative Law Quarterly
ILJ	Industrial Law Journal
JR	Judicial Review
LQR	Law Quarterly Review
LS	Legal Studies
PL	Public Law

1

THE LEGAL FRAMEWORK AND ADMINISTRATIVE STRUCTURE OF THE PRISON SYSTEM

A. Introduction

History

Since 1877 prisons and prisoners in England and Wales have been subject to the **1.01** exclusive authority and jurisdiction of the Home Secretary. Until 1963 this was exercised via a managerial body of five Prison Commissioners but the passage of the Prison Commissioners Dissolution Order 1963 resulted in the absorption by the Home Office of all responsibility for administering the penal estate.[1] Thirty

---

[1] SI 1963/597. The Prison Service was and remains part of the Home Office. Agency status has not changed this and accordingly Prison Service staff remain civil servants employed by the Home Office.

1

years later in 1993, in a move intended to give greater autonomy to the administrators and greater freedom from day-to-day ministerial interference in the running of prisons, the Prison Service was made an Executive Agency. Agency status was subsequently confirmed in 1998.

1.02 Prior to 1877 there were two separate prison systems governed by separate administrative authorities—the local prison system and a much smaller number of prisons run by central government known as 'convict' prisons. Local prisons were run independently, with little or no central control, by local Justices of the Peace. The description 'local prison' embraced a variety of institutions—bridewells and houses of correction (which existed to encourage vagabonds, beggars, and the 'idle poor' in the ways of work but which also housed minor offenders), as well as small local gaols. The local gaol housed felons, misdemeanants, convicted or unconvicted, civil debtors, and, until 1867, those awaiting transportation to Australia.[2]

The First Government-owned Prisons

1.03 Towards the end of the 18th century, central government began to acquire its own penal institutions. So long as transportation was the normal method of dealing with the long-term prisoner, it was necessary to use the prisons only to hold offenders awaiting trial or the next transport, and local prisons were able to carry out this function adequately. The American War of Independence brought a temporary end to transportation in 1776 and so the Government invented the Hulks as an alternative. These were old ships taken out of commission, moored in rivers or estuaries and adapted to house convicts. In 1779 an Act was passed to authorize the punishment of 'hard labour' for offenders who would normally have been transported, the hard labour in question being cleansing and improving the navigation of the River Thames and any other navigable port.[3]

Transportation and After

1.04 The 1779 Act helped to establish imprisonment with hard labour as a standard punishment for felony. The 'discovery' of Australia by Cook led to the use of transportation to Australia, which began in 1787 and continued to be the mainstay of penal treatment for convicts up to 1857. But the 1779 Act resulted in an increasing growth of prisons for long sentence prisoners. In addition to the Hulks, a national penitentiary was built at Millbank in 1816 under the control of the Home Secretary. There followed a prison for juvenile convicts at Parkhurst (1839)

---

[2] Felony was the common law term employed to describe graver crimes below high treason and petty treason. Until 1827 all felonies were liable to be punished by death. Misdemeanours applied to all offences below felonies whether punishable on indictment or on summary conviction.

[3] Chap 74, Geo III. For an interesting summary of the development of the prison system in the late 18th and 19th centuries see Gordon Rose, *The Struggle for Penal Reform* (London, 1961) to which the current analysis is indebted.

and Pentonville (1842), which was intended to be a model prison for local prison authorities to emulate. Portland (1849) and Dartmoor (1850) were the precursors of what became an outbreak of government prison building following the creation of the Board of Directors of Convict Prisons in 1850. The new Board was soon able to abolish the use of the Hulks and the way was clear for the introduction of penal servitude which, by 1857, superseded transportation.

Reform

The 19th century saw a progressive movement towards greater central government intervention in the local prison system, a movement which culminated in the unified, centralized system achieved by the Prison Act 1877. The 1791 Gaols Act had authorized Justices to appoint a governor for gaols and houses of correction within their jurisdiction. It also authorized and required them 'to make such Rules and Orders for receiving, separating, classing, dieting, clothing, maintaining, employing, reforming, governing, managing, treating and watching all offenders during their respective confinement'. The Act was very much a response to the prison conditions described by John Howard's *State of the Prisons* (1776), which advocated that prisons should be sanitary and secure, the sexes should be effectively separated, the keeper should be a paid and responsible servant of the Justice, who, in turn, should exercise effective supervision.   **1.05**

The 1823 Gaols Act was a further attempt at reform. It consolidated the 23 pre-existing statutes on the subject of gaols and houses of correction. The aim was to provide for the safety of prisoners but also 'more effectually to preserve the health and to improve the morals of . . . prisoners'.[4] The means to achieve this end was to enforce a strict system of 'separation, superintendence, employment and instruction of prisoners'.[5] Section 10 set out a uniform code of 24 rules and regulations to be observed in every prison and gaol within the jurisdiction of Justices. Sidney and Beatrice Webb commented in their authoritative work *English Prisons under Local Government* that the code was 'the first measure of general prison reform to be framed and enacted on the responsibility of the national executive'.[6] The Act provided for regular reports to be made by Justices to the Home Secretary and for systematic inspections to be carried out by the Justices. But it had only a limited impact, in that it only applied to a minority of prisons in the country—the London debtors' prisons were excluded, as were 150 gaols in the boroughs. Furthermore, there was no system for enforcement or any national inspectorate to investigate whether standards were being maintained.   **1.06**

---

[4] Gaols Act 1823, s 1.
[5] Prison Act 1865, s 20.
[6] Quoted in Sir Louis Blom Cooper QC's article 'The Centralisation of Government Control of National Prison Services with special reference to the Prison Act 1877' contained in J Freeman (ed), *Prisons Past and Future* (London, 1978).

1.07 The 1835 Prisons Act changed this and empowered the Home Secretary to appoint prison inspectors to inspect on his behalf and report to him. It also required Justices to submit such rules as they had drafted to the Home Secretary for his approval and possible amendment.

The Prison Act 1865

1.08 The legislative reforms of the 1820s and 1830s did not, however, produce the desired results. The 1863 inquiry conducted by the Select Committee of the House of Lords on Prison Discipline revealed widespread discrepancies and anomalies in the administration of the local prison system. Of greatest concern was the fact that most prisons were failing to enforce the 'separate system' which had been introduced in 1838 following the recommendation of the original Inspectors of Prisons. The 1865 Prison Act was a consolidation of 13 other Acts of Parliament. It amalgamated the gaols and houses of correction into what were henceforth to be called local prisons. It also strengthened the Home Secretary's powers of control by incorporating in a Schedule to the Act detailed 'Regulations for Government of Prisons' which were binding on all prison authorities charged with administering the various penal institutions.[7]

1.09 The regulations placed a statutory duty on the governor to visit the whole prison every day and see each prisoner. Further specific duties were cast upon the prison doctor and chaplain. The Act also gave power to the Home Secretary to close any prison which failed to meet the requirements of the Act for four successive years. Although the 1865 Act succeeded in securing the closure of a large number of smaller prisons, too many local prisons remained. They were already expensive to run and to put them in a state where they could comply with the law and satisfy the Inspectors placed an intolerable burden on the county rates. Further, there remained wide variations in the method of enforcing the statutory code. As Sir Louis Blom-Cooper, QC, has commented, 'the situation was ripe for a national take-over'.[8]

The Prison Act 1877

1.10 The 1877 Prison Act led to the control of all local prisons vesting in the Home Secretary and the cost of their maintenance was transferred to public funds. Their general superintendence, subject to the overall political control of the Home Secretary, was vested in a Board of Prison Commissioners assisted by Inspectors, appointed by the Home Secretary, and a departmental staff. The rule-making power of Justices having passed to the Home Secretary, a new code of rules was issued in 1878, and from 1 April of that year all prisons, local and convict, fell under one central control and a single set of rules. For the first time, the local community ceased to have any statutory administrative function in respect of the prisons located in its midst.

---

[7] Prison Act 1865, s 20.
[8] 'The Centralisation of Government Control', 64.

The Prison Act 1898 and After

The Prison Act 1898 and the 1899 Rules made thereunder, together with the   **1.11**
(largely) unrepealed portions of the 1865 and 1877 Acts, formed the legal basis for
the administration of prisons until the passage of the Prison Act 1952.[9] And despite
the numerous inquiries into the state of the prisons, culminating in the publication
of the Woolf Report in 1991, the 1952 Act remains in force as the primary source
of legislative authority governing prisons and imprisonment. The detailed provisions of the Act and the Rules will be analysed in later chapters. Before descending
into the mire of statute, case law, and administrative guidance, however, it will be
helpful to stand back and examine the legislative framework which regulates life in
a prison. Having done that we will look at the administrative structure of the Prison
Service before, finally, we turn to the implications in both law and administrative
practice of the introduction of 'contracted-out' prisons.

B. The Legislative Framework

The Prison Act 1952

The Prison Act 1952 is a relatively brief statute and is expressed in remarkably   **1.12**
general terms given its subject matter.[10] As originally enacted it vested powers of
management of prisons in the Prison Commissioners subject to the overall control of the Home Secretary. In addition, an adjudicative power in relation to
prison disciplinary offences was divided between the Commissioners and visiting
Justices. The 1963 Order 'dissolving' the Commissioners meant that their functions of oversight became merged with those of the Home Secretary while the
adjudicative powers were distributed between the Home Secretary and the Boards
of Visitors.

Apart from identifying the Home Secretary as the source of power and authority   **1.13**
and providing for a central administration, a Chief Inspector of Prisons, a Board
of Visitors for each prison, as well as 'officers' to run the prisons, the Act is little
more than a series of enabling and deeming provisions designed to give the Home
Secretary maximum discretion in the organization of the prison system.[11] In effect

---

[9]   The full text of the Prison Act 1952 is to be found at Appendix 1 below.

[10]   Its 55 sections, with only 41 still in force, are six fewer than in the 1877 Act.

[11]   The personal responsibility of the Home Secretary for the running of the Prison Service does
not of course deny his wide powers of delegation; see eg *R v Home Secretary, ex p Oladehinde* [1991]
1 AC 254, in which the Home Secretary's ability to delegate his powers under the Immigration Act
1971 was considered. It is to be noted that the Prison Act makes no mention of the Director-
General as such, and his appointment as Chief Executive of the Prison Service is simply an example
of the Home Secretary's general discretion pursuant to ss 1 and 2 of the 1952 Act to manage the
penal system. The controversial debate during the Michael Howard era about the distinction

the Act simply calls upon the Home Secretary to create and police an internal regime for prisons. With one exception in relation to disciplinary proceedings against a prisoner, the Act creates no clear statutory rights for prisoners.[12] The details of prison life are left to be expressed in the Rules, which, by the rule-making power in s 47(1), require the Home Secretary to provide for the 'regulation and management of prisons and for the classification, treatment, employment, discipline and control of persons required to be detained therein'. Precisely because the Rules contain the 'meat' of prison law, most judicial attention has focused on their implications and effect, but certain aspects of the Act require analysis.

'Superintendence'

1.14 Section 4 is of some significance, particularly sub-sections (1) and (2) which state:

(1) The Secretary of State shall have the general superintendence of prisons and shall make the contracts and do the other acts necessary for the maintenance of prisons and the maintenance of prisoners.

(2) Officers of the Secretary of State duly authorised in that behalf shall visit all prisons and examine the state of the buildings, the conduct of officers, the treatment and conduct of prisoners and all other matters concerning the management of prisons and shall ensure that the provisions of this Act and of any Rules made under this Act are duly complied with.

Section 4(1) thus creates a general duty of 'superintendence' over prisons, which is cast upon the Home Secretary. (Its reference to a power 'to make the contracts' necessary for the maintenance of prisons and prisoners is to be distinguished from the power now contained in the Criminal Justice Act 1991 to 'contract out' the running of any prison.) Section 4(2) imposes a duty upon the Home Secretary, expressed in broad terms, to ensure compliance with both the 1952 Act and the Prison Rules. For several years prior to the decisions of the House of Lords in *R v Deputy Governor of Parkhurst, ex p Leech*[13] and *R v Deputy Governor of Parkhurst, ex p Hague*,[14] s 4(2) was relied upon by the Home Secretary, and accepted by the courts, as a form of ouster clause which prevented the High Court from exercising its supervisory jurisdiction to grant judicial review in respect of disciplinary and administrative decisions taken by prison governors. Underlying this approach was a powerful aversion to the courts becoming embroiled in the day-to-day decisions of prison life. Accordingly, it was sought to rationalize this concern by reference to

---

between 'operational' and 'policy' matters (which culminated in the dismissal of Derek Lewis, the former Director-General, for the alleged 'operational' failures identified in the Learmont Report (Cm 3020, 1995)) was always, in legal terms, a false one. In law, the Home Secretary is responsible for and, therefore, liable for the acts and omissions of the Prison Service.

[12] See s 47(2).
[13] [1988] 1 AC 533.
[14] [1992] 1 AC 58.

the public policy principle enshrined in s 4(2) whereby Parliament, it was argued, had made the Secretary of State uniquely responsible for ensuring that the prison regime was carried out according to law. Only his acts or omissions in carrying out that task were susceptible to judicial review. Governors were immune from direct challenge by way of judicial review in order, so it was believed, to ensure the smooth administration of the prison system.

This argument was accepted by the Court of Appeal in *R v Deputy Governor of* **1.15** *Camphill Prison, ex p King*,[15] in which a prisoner sought to quash a disciplinary adjudication conducted by a governor on the basis that he had misconstrued his powers in relation to a specific disciplinary charge. While accepting that, logically, no proper distinction could be drawn under the legislative scheme between the disciplinary powers of Boards of Visitors (which were subject to review[16]) and those of governors, the majority of the Court of Appeal in *King* pointed to s 4(2) as the justification for a different approach. Griffiths LJ said the section meant that:

> the court should, in the first instance, be prepared to assume that the Secretary of State will discharge the duty placed upon him by Parliament to ensure that the prison governor is doing his job properly. If it is shown that the Minister is not discharging this duty and allowing a prison governor to disregard the prison rules then judicial review will go to correct that situation by requiring the Minister to perform his statutory duty.

A different decision was reached by the Northern Ireland Court of Appeal in *R v Governor of the Maze Prison, ex p McKiernan*,[17] where it was accepted that jurisdiction to review governors' disciplinary decisions existed. But the Northern Ireland legislation had no equivalent to s 4(2).[18] In *Leech*, however, the House of Lords decisively rejected the Home Secretary's argument that s 4(2) had any relevance to the issue of jurisdiction. Dismissing as 'fundamentally fallacious' the argument that the court had jurisdiction to entertain an application for judicial review only where that jurisdiction was shown to be necessary in order to secure compliance with the law, Lord Bridge said that to invoke the Home Secretary's general duty to ensure compliance with prison legislation in order to oust the jurisdiction of the court in relation to governors' disciplinary powers 'is to stand the doctrine by which the limits of jurisdiction in this field are determined on its head'.[19] Furthermore, the mere fact that a prisoner could petition the Home Secretary under rule 56 asking him to remit a disciplinary award imposed by a governor and that the Home Secretary was obliged pursuant to s 4(2) to consider

---

[15] [1985] QB 735.
[16] See *R v Board of Visitors of Hull Prison, ex p St Germain* [1979] QB 425.
[17] (1985) 6 NIJB 6.
[18] See the Prison (Northern Ireland) Act 1953.
[19] [1988] 1 AC 533, 562B–D.

whether the governor had acted in accordance with the Rules did not constitute an alternative remedy which prevented an immediate challenge to the governor's decision.

1.16 Notwithstanding the decision in *Leech*, a further attempt to rely on s 4(2) as an ouster provision preventing the court from directly reviewing a governor's decision was made in *Hague*, which concerned a decision to segregate a prisoner under rule 43 (now rule 45). Applying the reasoning in *Leech*, the Divisional Court rejected this argument and it was not renewed on appeal. Accordingly, s 4(2) in no way inhibits the exercise of the High Court's supervisory jurisdiction in relation to the disciplinary or administrative decisions either of prison governors or their delegates.[20]

The Chief Inspector of Prisons

1.17 Section 5A of the 1952 Act provides for the appointment of a Chief Inspector of Prisons whose duty it is to inspect prisons in England and Wales and to report to the Home Secretary on his findings. He or she is required in particular to report on prison conditions and the treatment of prisoners.[21] The Home Secretary may refer specific matters connected with prisons and prisoners to the Chief Inspector and direct him to report on them.[22] An annual report must also be submitted to the Home Secretary to be laid before Parliament. The Chief Inspector before last, Sir Stephen Tumim, pursued a vigorous, well-publicized campaign over the impoverished regimes, poor conditions, and depressing, insanitary buildings which characterize prisons in England and Wales.[23] He also produced authoritative reports on specific issues, most significantly an investigation of suicide prevention policies in prisons in the wake of an alarming series of suicides particularly of young prisoners.[24] Sir Stephen's term of office came to an end in December 1995 and his successor, Sir David Ramsbotham, proved to be no less willing to make public his sometimes fierce criticisms of prison conditions and the pressures which overcrowding and limited resources bring to bear upon the Prison

---

[20] In *Hague* at 116A Taylor LJ was content to accept that the courts should approach the exercise of discretion in matters relating to prison administration/management 'with great caution', an observation which was perhaps unnecessary in the light of the great reluctance displayed by English judges to intervene with reckless enthusiasm in prison cases.

[21] Prison Act 1952, s 5A(3). The term 'prison' is negatively defined in s 53(1) as not including a naval, military, or air force prison. Until the publication of the May Committee Report (*Report of the Committee of Inquiry into the United Kingdom Prison Services*, Cm. 7673, 1980) the Inspectorate was an internal Prison Service body and did not lay a report before Parliament; see 983 House of Commons Report (5th series), 30 April 1980, col 1395.

[22] s 5A(4).

[23] Judge Tumim was co-author with Woolf LJ of the Woolf Report, *Prison Disturbances: April 1990* (Cm 1456, 1991).

[24] *Suicide and Self-Harm in Prison Service Establishments in England and Wales* (Cm 1383, 1990).

Service.[25] Sir David Ramsbotham was succeeded as Chief Inspector in August 2001 by Anne Owers, who has continued the tradition of independent and wide-ranging reporting.

The Chief Inspector's power to inspect does not extend to the conditions 'enjoyed' **1.18** by prisoners in police cells who might (albeit temporarily) be detained there pursuant to the Imprisonment (Temporary Provisions) Act 1980. In his 1992 Annual Report, Judge Tumim stated that police cells did not come within his 'lawful remit' and that 'it would be impracticable to inspect police cells without inspecting police stations, which would be wholly outside [my] duties'. This is strictly correct since the terms of s 6 of the 1980 Act expressly contrast detention in a 'prison, remand centre . . . or detention centre' with detention 'in the custody of a constable'. The Chief Inspector's statutory duty is to inspect 'prisons' and to report on the treatment of 'prisoners . . . in prisons'.[26]

The Board of Visitors

Sections 6–9 of the 1952 Act provide for the personnel necessary for the running **1.19** of every prison. Section 6 requires the Home Secretary to appoint a Board of Visitors for each prison and for rules to be made requiring individual Board members to pay frequent visits to the prison and to hear any complaints. The Board of Visitors is to be distinguished from individual prison visitors, whose role is to visit and befriend individual prisoners. The existence of official prison visitors is not

---

[25] The early termination of Judge Tumim's term of office, like the sacking of Derek Lewis and the clipping of the wings of the Prisons Ombudsman by narrowing his terms of reference, was another example of Michael Howard's determination to ensure that critical voices of his brand of penal policy ('prison works') were silenced. But the new Chief Inspector quickly proved himself to be equally independent and critical. Early in his term of office he and his team of inspectors walked out of Holloway prison midway through the inspection in protest at the appalling conditions they had encountered. Sir David's reports on individual prisons and his thematic reports on specific subjects, such as women in prison, have ensured that the Prison Inspectorate remains an important engine for reform and innovation in penal policy. His successor, Anne Owers, has already published several reports which have been critical of both prison conditions and penal policy. In a joint report with the Chief Inspector of Probation, she criticizes the widespread neglect of prisoners' needs, and the 'paper exercises', required by the prison bureaucracy, which often produce scanty results: *Through the Prison Gate: A Joint Thematic Review by HM Inspectorates of Prisons and Probation* (London, 2001).

[26] s 5A(2). The technical obstacle to the Chief Inspector's assumption of jurisdiction to inspect conditions in police cells is extremely unfortunate, since it prevents a complete assessment of the treatment of prisoners in England and Wales. When resort is had to the use of police cells, conditions for detainees are significantly worse than for other prisoners and, by not subjecting them to the same process of inspection as other prisons, a false impression is given of prison conditions in general. See Howard League, 12 July 2002: 'Prison crisis leads to use of police cells'. In *R v Commissioner of Police for the Metropolis, ex p Nahar,* The Times, 28 May 1983, two prisoners detained in police cells sought writs of habeas corpus on the basis of the conditions of their confinement. They failed, but the court accepted that minimum standards of confinement had to be complied with under the 1980 Act. For a strong criticism of the Chief Inspector's refusal to inspect police cells, see Rod Morgan, 'Prisons Accountability Revisited' [1993] PL 314.

dependent on any discrete statutory provisions and they have no statutory functions. Until 1992, Boards of Visitors had two distinct functions. First, they were (and still are) supposed to act as watchdogs of the daily life and regime in an individual prison. To assist them in this task, Boards have a statutory right of free access to every part of the prison and to every prisoner at any time.[27] Their second function was to act in an adjudicatory capacity within the prison disciplinary system. Their remit extended to those disciplinary cases which were regarded as too serious to be dealt with by the governor.

1.20 Since April 1992, Boards no longer play any role in the formal disciplinary process. This was a direct result of the Woolf Report which confirmed what many critics of the system had long felt, namely that the Boards' adjudicatory role impinged upon and undermined their watchdog functions. In particular, it was widely felt by prisoners that Boards were not truly independent of the prison authorities and were too easily persuaded to uphold the views and interests of staff in preference to those of prisoners. This partiality was especially obvious in disciplinary hearings, where too many Boards accepted the word of prison officers rather than that of the accused and handed out severe penalties for relatively minor disciplinary infractions.[28] The abolition of the disciplinary jurisdiction of Boards does not mean that they have no role to play in the informal disciplinary process. For example, it is still necessary for a governor who wishes to extend a prisoner's segregation on rule 45 beyond three days to obtain the approval of a member of the Board of Visitors.[29] Similarly, the use of a mechanical restraint (such as a body belt) on a prisoner for longer than 24 hours requires the written

---

[27] s 6(3). See also Prison Rules 1999, rr 74–80.

[28] The best example of the partiality of Boards of Visitors concerned their approach to the granting of legal representation to prisoners appearing before them in disciplinary hearings. After the extraordinary decision of the Court of Appeal in *R v Risley Board of Visitors, ex p Draper,* The Times, 24 May 1988, in which the Risley Board's refusal to grant legal representation to all prisoners who appeared before it following a two-day roof top protest was upheld, the grant of legal representation slowed to a trickle. It could hardly be said that standards of justice had improved to the extent that prisoners no longer required legal representation before Boards. Rather, it seemed to be the case that Boards were unduly discomfited by the presence of lawyers, regarding their presence as productive of delay and unnecessary 'legality' in what they liked to think of as an inquisitorial rather than adversarial process. The lawyer acting for a prisoner in such hearings tended to be regarded as a rather unwelcome guest who had to be tolerated through gritted teeth before being shown the door. See G Richardson and M Sunkin, 'Judicial Review: Questions of Impact' [1996] PL 79 where the authors observed that in 1988–89 Boards of Visitors granted legal representation in fewer than 50 cases.

[29] See r 45(2). In the case of prisoners under 21 the maximum single period of extension is 14 days, whereas for adults it is one month. In each case, the renewal is subject to further extension. The decision to authorize continued or extended segregation requires, as was pointed out by the Court of Appeal in *R v Deputy Governor of Parkhurst Prison, ex p Hague* [1992] 1 AC 58, a reasoned approach both as to the need for continued segregation at all and the period for which it might be necessary. There is very little hard evidence, but the impression is that Board members rarely disagree with the views of prison governors. An obvious weakness in the system is that if a governor knows that one particular Board member is too independently minded for his liking, he can simply approach another 'tame' member of the Board for the authorization needed to extend segregation.

authority of either a member of the Board of Visitors or an officer of the Secretary of State (rule 49(4)). The ending of their involvement in the disciplinary process gave Boards of Visitors a real opportunity to develop a distinct role as fearless, independent, public critics of the numerous aspects of the prison system which deserve such attention. But with some notable exceptions, most Boards seem to be content to pursue a low profile and somewhat cosy relationship with the prison authorities. So long as Boards have no statutory powers to change the decisions of prison staff, still less to alter policy at a higher level, it is difficult to see how they will be able to do more than create the appearance of being independent scrutineers of the system in action.[30]

The Statutory 'Officers' of a Prison

Section 7 demands that 'every prison shall have a governor, a chaplain and a medical officer and such other officers as may be necessary'. It follows that the term 'officer', which is not defined in the Act, embraces not merely uniformed prison officers (or discipline staff as they are described) but all the statutory officers who work in a prison and are, administratively, members of the Prison Service. They are to be distinguished from the Home Secretary's 'officers', whose duties are defined in s 4.[31] Since the pay and productivity agreement known as Fresh Start, the number of grades of officer between the basic grade officer and the 'number one' governor has been reduced to eight, of whom there can, in any one prison, be seven.[32] Consistent with the sketchy nature of the Act, there is no detailed exposition of the powers and duties of the various prison 'officers'. This is left to the Prison Rules, save in one respect. Section 8 states that 'every prison officer while acting as such shall have the powers, authority, protection and privileges of a constable'. The words 'while acting as such' limit the effect of the section to the actual discharge of a prison officer's duties. Accordingly, prison officers do not have the status of 'constable' at all times. It means, however, that prison officers, while acting as such, have the same powers of arrest as police officers and that an assault on a prison officer constitutes an assault on a constable in the execution of his duty. In 1994 prison officers at Preston prison sought to rely on s 8 of the 1952 Act as

1.21

---

[30] One of the last decisions of Kenneth Clarke's term of office as Home Secretary was to reject the Woolf Report's recommendation that there should be an independent President to oversee Boards of Visitors, who would drive forward organizational improvements and propose more effective methods for recruiting and training Board of Visitors members. The official explanation was that the consultation period revealed 'no strong consensus of opinion amongst Boards in favour of a President and some concern from them that their local, autonomous and voluntary nature might be compromised by such an appointment'. In fact the response rate to the consultation papers was very disappointing, with the majority of Boards not bothering to reply.

[31] See eg r 49(4).

[32] The Lygo Report on *The Management of the Prison Service* (London, 1991) commented that there were too many grades which 'made for a very long chain of command and inhibits career progress for the most able'.

authority for the proposition that it was an implied term of their contract with the Home Office that they were not obliged to carry out instructions which impinged on the exercise of their powers as constables to prevent a breach of the peace or, in the alternative, that it was a contractual term that any obligation to obey instructions was subject to s 8. The purpose of the claim was in effect to prevent the Home Secretary from moving any additional prisoners to the already over-crowded Preston prison on the basis that any extra prisoners might give rise to rioting or other forms of disturbance. The High Court held that the power of a constable given to a prison officer was designed to enable him to perform his duties as a prison officer as set out in the Prison Rules. Prominent amongst these duties was a duty to obey the governor's lawful instructions and, consequently, any conflict between a prison officer's exercise of discretion in the use of his powers as a constable had always to be exercised in the context of his duty to obey lawful instructions. Any apparent conflict between the two duties must be resolved in favour of the duty to obey the governor's lawful orders.[33]

1.22 The office of prison governor, it can be seen, is a creation of statute and although the exercise of his powers is governed by the Rules made pursuant to s 47, the powers themselves are original and are not derived from or exercised on behalf of the Home Secretary. The mere fact that content is given to the governor's functions and duties by the Rules drafted on behalf of the Home Secretary, who is thus able to decide what the extent of the governor's powers should be, does not derogate from the governor's discrete status under the Act. Accordingly, in *Leech* Lord Bridge dismissed the argument that, in exercising his disciplinary powers, the governor could somehow be distinguished from the Board of Visitors:

> A prison governor may in general terms be aptly described as the servant of the Secretary of State, but he is not acting as such when adjudicating upon a charge of a disciplinary offence. He is then exercising the independent power conferred on him by the rules. The Secretary of State has no authority to direct the governor, any more than the Board of Visitors, as to how to adjudicate on a particular charge or what

---

[33] *Home Secretary v Barnes,* The Times, 19 December 1994. The employment status of prison officers is now governed by the Criminal Justice and Public Order Act 1994, ss 126–128, which was designed to clarify what remained unresolved after the interlocutory decision in *Home Office v Prison Officers' Association,* The Times, 19 November 1993, in which the Home Office secured an injunction to restrain threatened strike action by the Prison Officers' Association on the basis that s 8 meant that prison officers were in 'police service' and that the Association was not a trade union enjoying ordinary trade union immunities from the consequences of industrial action. Section 126 gives prison officers the status of an employee/worker for the purposes of the Employment Rights Act 1996 and the Trade Union and Labour Relations (Consolidation) Act 1992, thereby giving officers equal rights with other workers in matters such as unfair dismissal, redundancy, maternity leave, and the right of access to industrial tribunals. Section 127 however effectively removes the right of a prison officer trade union to take industrial action by expressly conferring on the Home Secretary the right to compensation for any loss or damage caused as a result of inducing strike action by prison officers. This prohibition on inducing industrial action applies equally to private sector prison custody officers.

punishment should be awarded. If a Home Office official sought to stand behind the governor at a disciplinary hearing and tell him what to do, the governor would probably send him packing.[34]

For similar reasons the power given to 'the governor' in rule 45 to segregate a prisoner is confined to the governor of the prison in which a prisoner is, for the time being, detained. It follows that neither the Home Secretary, acting through his officers, nor the governor of any other prison may initiate the prisoner's segregation under rule 45.[35]

Place of Confinement and Lawful Custody

Sections 12 and 13 of the 1952 Act deal with the 'place' in which a prisoner may be lawfully confined and the legal custody of prisoners. Section 12(1) states that prisoners, whether convicted or on remand, 'may be lawfully confined in any prison'. In *Ex p Hague* the House of Lords held that this provision was not subject to any implied term making lawful confinement dependent on compliance with the Prison Rules.[36] Even gross or 'fundamental' breaches of the Rules could not therefore affect the lawfulness of a prisoner's confinement such that he could sue in false imprisonment. Both Lords Bridge and Jauncey in *Ex p Hague* concluded that the broad terms of s 12(1) would always provide a complete answer to any claim for false imprisonment against the governor or anyone acting on his authority.[37]   **1.23**

Section 12(2) gives the Home Secretary the power to transfer a prisoner from one prison to another during the course of his sentence.[38] This power can be delegated to a governor who may wish, for example, to transfer a prisoner in the interests of good order or discipline pursuant to Instruction to Governors 28/1993.[39] While the power to transfer is a broad one, it is susceptible to challenge by means of an application for judicial review. In *R v Home Secretary, ex p McAvoy*[40] the Divisional   **1.24**

---

[34] [1988] 1 AC 533, 563D. Boards of Visitors no longer have any adjudicatory role but the principle remains applicable to governors.

[35] *Ex p Hague* [1992] 1 AC 58, 105–108. Note however now that r 46 gives the Home Secretary the power to initiate the removal from association of any prisoner to a close supervision centre of a prison in the interests of good order or discipline or to ensure the safety of officers, prisoners, or others. The same rule enables the Secretary of State to extend such segregation from month to month with no requirement to consult any other body or person. On the face of it this enables the Home Secretary to circumvent the procedural safeguards in r 45. The vires of r 46 must be open to question.

[36] ibid, 163F.

[37] In reaching this conclusion both Lord Bridge and Lord Jauncey distinguished 19th century cases involving claims for false imprisonment (such as *Cobbett v Grey* (1850) 4 Exch 729 and *Osborne v Millman* (1887) 18 QBD 471) on the basis that there was no 19th century equivalent of s 12. This is not correct; see Prison Act 1877, s 25.

[38] But see also the Crime (Sentences) Act 1997, s 41, which provides for a comprehensive code governing the transfer of prisoners between the different prison jurisdictions in Great Britain, Northern Ireland and the Channel Islands.

[39] See per Taylor LJ, in *Ex p Hague* [1992] 1 AC 58, 107H.

[40] [1984] 1 WLR 1408.

Court said that a transfer decision reached without reference to a remand prisoner's 'right' to receive legal and family visits could 'in principle' be quashed as an unlawful exercise of discretion. Where a transfer has a serious impact on a prisoner's contact with his family, there may also be a claim under the Human Rights Act 1998 (HRA) for violation of Article 8 of the European Convention on Human Rights (ECHR).[41]

1.25 Section 13 deals with the formalities of the legal custody of a prisoner, and establishes two principles. First, a prisoner is deemed to be in the legal custody of 'the governor of the prison'.[42] This simply defines the legal responsibility or liability of the governor of the prison to which a prisoner has been allocated under s 12. In the event of a challenge to the legality of a prisoner's detention by means of an application for habeas corpus or a claim under s 7(1)(a) of the HRA, the governor, as legal custodian, is the proper respondent to the claim. Secondly, s 13(2) extends the concept of legal custody to include any period of time when the prisoner is being taken from one prison to another or is for any reason outside the prison in the custody or control of an officer of the prison.

Certification of Prison Accommodation

1.26 Section 14 of the 1952 Act is an important provision, since it is the only statutory provision which deals with the necessity for the Home Secretary to satisfy himself that 'in every prison sufficient accommodation is provided for all prisoners'.[43] The means by which the Home Secretary is to satisfy himself on matters such as the size, lighting, heating, ventilation, and fittings in cells is by a system of certification by an inspector of every cell. The certificate may specify the period of time during which a prisoner may be separately confined in the cell.[44] Since the Prison Commissioners Dissolution Order 1963, the reference to an 'inspector' is to be read as a reference to 'an officer (not being an officer of a prison) acting on behalf of the Secretary of State'.[45] It can readily be seen that, since s 14 permits no independent means of certifying the sufficiency of prison accommodation, the Act cannot itself act as a brake on overcrowding. If overcrowding places a strain on the system, making it impossible for the available cells to comply with their certificates, the Home Secretary merely has to alter the criteria for certification.[46] Since the one thing that all observers of the prison system agree upon is that for at least the last 15 years local prisons in England and Wales have been grossly over-

---

[41] Claims under the HRA are discussed further in Ch 2.
[42] s 13(1).
[43] s 14(1).
[44] s 14(3).
[45] SI 1963/597, Art 3(2). Such officers are appointed pursuant to Prison Act 1952, s 3(1).
[46] See r 26(2).

crowded, so that 'sufficient accommodation' has not been provided for all prisoners, it is hard to resist the conclusion that s 14 of the Prison Act 1952 is probably the most ineffective provision on the statute book.

Aside from the power to pass rules for the management of prisons, which we **1.27** examine below, the rest of the 1952 Act deals with a number of unconnected and largely uncontroversial matters which have rarely been the subject of litigation. These include provisions dealing with the temporary discharge of prisoners on grounds of ill health,[47] the maintenance and closure of prisons,[48] criminal offences such as assisting a prisoner to escape,[49] and provision for the payment of all expenses incurred under the Prison Act from money provided by Parliament.[50]

C. The Prison Rules

The important rule-making power is contained in s 47 of the Act: **1.28**

(1) The Secretary of State may make rules for the regulation and management of prisons . . . and for the classification, treatment, employment, discipline and control of persons required to be detained therein.
(2) Rules made under this section shall make provision for ensuring that a person who is charged with any offence under the rules shall be given a proper opportunity of presenting his case.

Section 52(1) of the Act requires that any power to make rules shall be exercisable by statutory instrument. Any rules made pursuant to s 47 are subject to the negative resolution procedure.[51] The Prison Rules may therefore be distinguished from, for example, the Immigration Rules, which are issued as House of Commons papers rather than by statutory instrument. In *Alexander v Immigration Appeal Tribunal*[52] the House of Lords held that the Immigration Rules are not to be construed with all the strictness applicable to the construction of a statutory instrument. Lord Roskill said that the rules 'give guidance to the various officers concerned and contain statements of general policy regarding the operation of the relevant immigration legislation'. The Prison Rules, by contrast, must be regarded as delegated legislation in the strict sense.

---

[47] s 28.
[48] ss 33–37.
[49] ss 39–42.
[50] s 51 and see also *Becker v Home Office* [1972] 2 QB 407.
[51] Criminal Justice Act 1967, s 66(4). This means that any statutory instrument containing rules under s 47(1) is subject to annulment by a resolution of either House of Parliament.
[52] [1982] 1 WLR 1076.

The Rules Analysed

1.29   The current Prison Rules[53] came into force on 1 April 1999, replacing the Prison Rules 1964. The current version of the Rules incorporates amendments made in 2000, many with a view to the coming into force of the HRA, and in 2002, to respond to the judgment of the European Court of Human Rights (ECtHR) in *Ezeh and Connors v UK*.[54] In the main, the new Rules simply consolidate and renumber the 1964 Rules. They do, however, contain several significant changes and additions. The detail of these changes is examined in the appropriate chapters. After highlighting the main changes, this section focuses on the structure of the Rules as a whole.

1.30   The 1999 Rules, as amended, introduce a new rule 73, which gives governors the power to ban visitors who smuggle drugs into prison, and add to rule 51 a new offence of receiving an article or controlled drugs during a visit. The notorious disciplinary offence of 'in any way offending against good order and discipline', contained in the old rule 47(21), has been removed. However, the Rules introduce four new disciplinary offences directed at protecting prisoners from racist abuse. Under the amended rule 51, a prisoner is guilty of an offence against discipline if he:

> (1A) commits any racially aggravated assault; . . .
> (17A) causes racially aggravated damage to, or destruction of, any part of a prison or any other property, other than his own; . . .
> (20A) uses threatening, abusive or insulting racist words or behaviour; . . .
> (24A) displays, attaches or draws on any part of a prison, or on any other property, threatening, abusive or insulting racist words, drawings, symbols or other material.

A new rule 51A sets out the definition of 'racist'. It remains to be seen whether these new offences will be fairly enforced, and whether they will have any practical effect in reducing racial victimization in prison.[55]

1.31   Rule 46 on allocation to Closed Supervision Centres also differs from the old rule 43A. Once a prisoner is subject to a direction to be removed from association and placed in a CSC, that direction 'shall continue to apply notwithstanding any

---

[53] The Prison Rules 1999, SI 1999/728, as amended by the Prison (Amendment) Rules 2000, SI 2000/1794, the Prison (Amendment) (No 2) Rules 2000, SI 2000/2641 and the Prison (Amendment) Rules 2002, SI 2002/2116.

[54] Applications 39665/98 and 40086/98 (2002) 35 EHRR 28.

[55] The seriousness of racism in prisons was admitted by Martin Narey, Director-General of the Prison Service, in his introduction to *HM Prison Service: Annual Reports and Accounts 2000–2001* (HC 29, 2001): 'We have to start with an acceptance that the Prison Service is an institutionally racist organisation, which reflects an institutionally racist white society. We have to add to this, our knowledge that there are pockets of blatant and malicious racism within the Service. It is time to face up to these things.'

transfer of a prisoner from one prison to another'.[56] Several references to 'proportionality' were introduced by the 2000 amendments, presumably in an effort to make the relevant rules Convention-compliant. Rule 34, on the interception of communications, has been amended so as to require any restriction on a prisoner's communications to be proportionate and justified by the pursuit of a legitimate aim. Of course, whether these requirements are in fact complied with in any particular case is still a matter for the courts. The mere mention of the Convention in rule 34 does not in itself legitimate restrictions on communication. New rule 50A provides that a governor may place a prisoner under constant supervision by means of an overt closed circuit television system if he considers it is necessary on specified grounds and is proportionate to that end. It is difficult to imagine when it would be proportionate to subject a prisoner to such a regime, save where the governor concludes that this is necessary to comply with the obligations under Article 2 of the Convention, which protects the right to life. New rules 35A, 35C and 35D implement European Community rules on telecommunications privacy, and the processing of personal data.[57]

The disciplinary part of the 1999 Rules was significantly altered in 2002 in response to the judgment of the ECtHR in *Ezeh and Connors v UK*. The Prison (Amendment) Rules 2002[58] introduce a new rule 53A, 'Determination of mode of inquiry', whereby the governor must decide whether a disciplinary charge is so serious that additional days should be awarded for the offence, if the prisoner is found guilty. If so, the governor must refer the charge to an independent adjudicator. Rule 54, as amended, now provides for prisoners to be legally represented in front of the adjudicator. In rule 55, the governor's power to award additional days as a punishment is removed, and a new rule 55A is inserted, providing for the award of such days by the adjudicator. A new rule 59A provides for the punishment of removal from a cell or living unit. These changes, and the decision in *Ezeh and Connors*, are considered in detail in Chapter 9.

1.32

The 1999 Rules are divided into six parts, one more than the 1964 Rules. However, the five substantive parts have the same titles as before, the only change being the addition of Part 1, which contains provisions on interpretation.[59] In an exemplary analysis of the Prison Rules 1964, Professor Graham Zellick described the Rules as falling into five broad categories.[60] This suggested structure remains a

1.33

---

[56] r 46(2). The new rule also enables the Secretary of State to designate as CSCs cells in prisons other than the two—Woodhill and Durham—which contain CSCs proper. The rules on CSCs are examined in detail in Ch 10 below.

[57] Council Directive (EC) 97/66 concerning the processing of personal data and the protection of privacy in the telecommunications sector [1998] OJ L024/1.

[58] SI 2002/2116.

[59] The Rules subdivide into 'Interpretation', 'Prisoners', 'Officers of Prisons', 'Persons Having Access To Prisons', 'Boards of Visitors', and 'Supplemental'.

[60] 'The Prison Rules and the Courts' [1981] Crim LR 602. See also 'The Prison Rules and the Courts: A Postscript' [1982] Crim LR 575.

helpful framework for understanding the five substantive sections of the 1999 Rules. Category one, in Professor Zellick's analysis, is 'rules of general policy objectives' which include the 'mission statement' of the Prison Service set out in rule 3, namely that 'the purpose of the training and treatment of convicted prisoners shall be to encourage and assist them to lead a good and useful life'.[61] Rule 6 sets out a broad principle in relation to the way in which good order and discipline are to be maintained ('with firmness, but with no more restriction than is required for safe custody and well ordered community life').

1.34 Category two is 'rules of a discretionary nature' which expressly leave a number of important matters within the discretion of the prison authorities. Examples include temporary release[62] and communications with the outside world.[63] Many rules use the words 'so far as reasonably practicable'[64] and 'subject to any directions of the Secretary of State',[65] which have a similar effect. Category three is the 'rules of general protection' which deal, broadly speaking, with health and welfare 'standards'. Thus rule 24(2) specifies that 'food provided shall be wholesome, nutritious, well prepared and served, reasonably varied and sufficient in quantity' and others deal with the provision of bedding and 'toilet articles necessary for . . . health and cleanliness'.[66]

1.35 Professor Zellick's fourth category was the 'rules as to institutional structure and administrative functions'. These he described as plainly designed to benefit prisoners but framed in such a way as to cast duties upon particular persons or bodies, including the governor, medical officer, chaplain and the Board of Visitors. Thus the governor is required to hear requests and complaints by prisoners every day[67] and the chaplain is required to make daily visits to prisoners belonging to the Church of England (and any others willing to see him) who are 'sick, under restraint or undergoing cellular confinement'.[68] The various duties of Boards of Visitors are set out in rules 74–80, and include an obligation to inquire into any

---

[61] To continue to describe r 3 as the Prison Service's mission statement is slightly misleading. History, and a 'new realism' about the reforming potential of prisons, has led to the Prison Service's Framework Document. The Statement of Purpose still proclaims that 'Her Majesty's Prison Service serves the public by keeping in custody those committed by the courts. Our duty is to look after them with humanity and help them lead law-abiding and useful lives in custody and after release.' However, the Prison Service Aim is now the 'effective execution of the sentence of the courts so as to reduce re-offending and protect the public', and its Objectives are 'to protect the public by holding in custody those committed by the Courts in a safe, decent, and healthy environment; to reduce crime by providing constructive regimes which address offending behaviour, improve educational and work skills and promote law abiding behaviour in custody and after release.'
[62] r 9.
[63] rr 34–35.
[64] r 19.
[65] r 33.
[66] rr 27 and 28.
[67] r 11(2).
[68] r 14(2).

report that a prisoner's health, mental or physical, is likely to be injuriously affected by any conditions of his imprisonment.[69] The fifth and final category covers 'rules of specific individual protection'. These include the disciplinary code to be found in rules 51–61 as well as non-disciplinary rules relating to good order or discipline such as rules 45, 48 and 49.

Professor Zellick's article was written at a time when a breach of the Rules was not   **1.36**
regarded as giving rise to a remedy in either public or private law, still less as amounting to a breach of Convention rights. Lord Denning's description of the Rules in *Becker v Home Office*[70] as 'regulatory directions only' seemed to suggest that they were not amenable to any form of judicial supervision. The purpose of the five-fold division was to support an argument that the courts had hitherto adopted an erroneous 'all or nothing' approach towards the Rules which failed to distinguish those rules which were plainly not intended to be 'actionable' (category one) from those in category five where the specific protective purpose required strict compliance by the prison authorities. As Professor Zellick pointed out, 'these provisions were hardly included in the rules so that the prison authorities could obey them or not as they preferred'. In his view 'strict compliance goes hand in hand with judicial oversight'.

Status

Since Professor Zellick's article was published the legal status of the Prison Rules   **1.37**
has changed significantly. There is no doubt but that individual rules are 'justiciable' in the sense that breaches may give rise to a public law remedy.[71] Further, since the Rules are not a piece of primary legislation, and are made under very broad powers contained in the Prison Act, the HRA also applies in full force to the Rules, and to all action taken under them. The complicated legal wranglings of the past, in which the courts tried to define the status of the Rules, are of far reduced significance since the HRA came into force. However, the status of the Rules remains relevant for some civil claims, and is also important in understanding the historical background to the present position.

In *Hague* the House of Lords finally ruled, after a period of some uncertainty, that   **1.38**
the Prison Rules are not 'actionable', in that they cannot in any circumstance give rise to a claim for breach of statutory duty.[72] The Woolf Report did not recommend

---

[69] r 78(3).
[70] [1972] 2 QB 407.
[71] See *Ex p McAvoy* [1984] 1 WLR 1408; *R v Home Secretary, ex p Hickling & JH (a minor)* [1986] 1 FLR 543; and, most importantly, *Ex p Hague* [1992] 1 AC 58.
[72] But see the different approaches of Lord Bridge and Lord Jauncey on whether the rule-making power in s 47 is broad enough to cover the enactment of rules which could create a private law right to damages. Lord Bridge said it was. Lord Jauncey disagreed. The remainder of their Lordships expressed no view on the matter.

any change in this area of prison law. So, for example, the Code of Accredited Standards, which was recommended as the means whereby an individual prison could move gradually towards 'accredited status' based on its ability to offer identified regime standards, would eventually be the subject of a Prison Rule 'and so enforceable by judicial review'.[73] Woolf did not favour the creation of private law rights in prisoners which would entitle them to sue for damages, an approach consistent with the prevalent mood of judicial distaste for such a remedy.[74]

1.39 The broad nature of the rule-making power contained in the 1952 Act and the fact that the House of Lords held in *Raymond v Honey*[75] that 'a convicted prisoner retains all civil rights which are not taken away expressly or by necessary implication' has led the Court of Appeal to strike down an individual prison rule as ultra vires, on the basis that it interfered with a prisoner's fundamental or constitutional right. In *R v Home Secretary, ex p Leech (No 2)*, the rule in question was rule 33(3) of the 1964 Rules, which purported to give a prison governor a general power to read every letter from a prisoner and to stop any letter which he considered to be objectionable or of inordinate length.[76] This power extended to letters passing between a prisoner and his lawyer unless they related to proceedings in which a writ had already been issued. In a complex and important judgment Steyn LJ (giving the judgment of the court) analysed the extent of the civil rights of prisoners before turning to the circumstances in which basic rights may be curtailed or extinguished by subordinate legislation. Concluding that unimpeded access to a solicitor for the purpose of receiving advice and assistance in connection with the possible institution of legal proceedings in the courts forms an inseparable part of a prisoner's fundamental right of access to the courts themselves, Steyn LJ went on to find that the terms of rule 33(3) created an impediment to the exercise of this

---

[73] Woolf Report, n 23 above, para 12.117.

[74] See *Ex p Hague* [1992] 1 AC 58 and *H v Home Office*, The Independent, 6 May 1992, in which the Court of Appeal held that a prisoner who had had to seek r 43 (now r 45) protection as a result of the negligence of prison staff could not, absent proof of injury, obtain damages for the distress and deprivation he had endured. More generally the courts have been anxious to close down the potential for private law claims for damages (whether in negligence or breach of statutory duty) arising from maladministration in the exercise of statutory functions: see eg *W (Minors) v Bedfordshire CC* [1995] 2 AC 633; *Stovin v Wise* [1996] AC 923; *Olotu v Home Office* [1997] 1 WLR 328; and *W v Home Office* [1997] Imm AR 302. The ECtHR has considered the issue in *Osman v UK* (1998) 29 EHRR 245 (exclusionary rule preventing negligence actions against the police found to be an unjustified restriction on the right of access to a court under Art 6 of the Convention), and *Z v UK* (2002) 34 EHRR 3 (strike-out proceedings in a negligence claim against a local authority constituted sufficient access to a court for the purposes of Art 6). See further R Clayton and H Tomlinson, *The Law of Human Rights* (Oxford, 2000); J Simor and B Emmerson, *Human Rights Practice* (London, 2000) 6.095.

[75] [1983] 1 AC 1.

[76] [1994] QB 198. Rule 34, the equivalent in the 1999 Rules, now explicitly directs governors to take into account the requirements of the ECHR, and to ensure that any restriction on a prisoner's Convention rights is necessary and proportionate.

basic right.[77] The issue which then arose was whether such interference was lawful. The Court of Appeal held it was not, and the route to this conclusion is highly significant.

Recognizing that s 47(1) did not *expressly* authorize interference with the right to **1.40** unimpeded access to legal advice, Steyn LJ held that in determining whether the right was restricted by *necessary implication* the more fundamental the right interfered with, and the more drastic the interference, the more difficult becomes the implication. Crucially, the test applicable in establishing whether the right is restricted by necessary implication is whether there is an objective, 'self-evident and pressing need' for the interference in question. If such a need is established, the authorized intrusion must be the 'minimum necessary to ensure that the need is met'. The court concluded on the evidence before it that although s 47(1) must be interpreted as conferring by necessary implication a power to screen some mail between solicitor and prisoner to ensure that it was bona fide, no objective need had been established for a rule drawn up in the broad terms of rule 33(3) which purported to sanction routine reading of prisoners' privileged correspondence. Accordingly, the then rule 33(3) was declared to be ultra vires in so far as it applied to correspondence between prisoners and solicitors.[78]

---

[77] He did so by adopting the reasoning of the Canadian Supreme Court in *Solosky v The Queen* (1979) 105 DLR (3d) 745, 760 in which Dickson J described the impact of a right to read a prisoner's correspondence as follows: '[n]othing is more likely to have a "chilling effect" upon the frank and free exchange and disclosure of confidences, which should characterise the relationship between inmate and counsel, than knowledge that what has been written will be read by some third person and perhaps used against the inmate at a later date'. Steyn LJ went on to state that 'an unrestricted right to read correspondence passing between a solicitor and a prisoner must create a considerable disincentive to a prisoner exercising his basic rights as expounded in *Raymond v Honey* and *Ex p Anderson* [1984] QB 778'.

[78] In *R v Home Secretary, ex p O'Dhuibhir* [1997] COD 315 (in which the Home Secretary's decision to impose closed legal and family visits on Exceptional Risk category A prisoners was challenged by two prisoners convicted of IRA offences) the Court of Appeal appeared to be alarmed at the implication of the *Leech* approach in the context of a case which engaged sensitive issues of prison security involving the (allegedly) most dangerous prisoners in the prison system. Its response was to confine *Leech* to a decision about the vires of a particular prison rule instead of accepting it as identifying the correct approach of the court whenever a fundamental right is interfered with without express Parliamentary approval either by a prison rule or by a policy decision contained in an Instruction to Governors. On this aspect of the case, *O'Dhuibhir* was clearly wrongly decided. In *R v Home Secretary, ex p Pierson* [1998] AC 539 the correctness of the *Leech* approach was implicitly accepted by Lord Browne-Wilkinson when he said '[a] power conferred by Parliament in general terms is not to be taken to authorise the doing of acts by the donee of the power which adversely affect the legal rights of the citizen or the basic principles on which the law of the United Kingdom is based unless the statute conferring the power makes it clear that such was the intention of Parliament'. See also the judgment of Laws J in *R v Lord Chancellor, ex p Witham* [1997] 2 All ER 779 and, most importantly, the decision of the House of Lords in *R v Home Secretary, ex p Simms and O'Brien* [2000] 2 AC 115.

1.41 Both the outcome and the reasoning in *Leech (No 2)* closely reflected the decision of the ECtHR in *Campbell v UK*,[79] in which a Scottish prisoner alleged that the practice of routine reading of prisoner/lawyer correspondence was in breach of Article 8 of the Convention.

1.42 In the important decision of *R (Daly) v Home Secretary*,[80] the House of Lords has made it clear that the appropriate standard of review of interferences with prisoners' rights is that set out in *Leech (No 2)*. The common law principle of legality, developed by the courts in cases before the coming into force of the HRA, has now been endorsed. The case concerned a challenge to the policy of cell searches, including searches through a prisoner's legal correspondence, carried out in the prisoner's absence. As well as stressing the importance of legal professional privilege in the prison context, the Committee took the opportunity in *Daly* to set out clearly the reasoning process by which infringements of fundamental rights must be scrutinized. The policy was set out in the Security Manual, a Prison Service Order, rather than the Rules themselves. However, it was clear that their Lordships considered that the same reasoning process should apply when assessing infringements of prisoners' rights, regardless of whether that infringement was authorized by the Rules or by less formal guidance. Lord Bingham, reaffirming the principles laid down in the series of important prisoners' rights decisions, from *Raymond v Honey* to *Leech (No 2)*, stated that:

> Any custodial order inevitably curtails the enjoyment, by the person confined, of rights enjoyed by other citizens. He cannot move freely and choose his associates as they are entitled to do. It is indeed an important objective of such an order to curtail such rights, whether to punish him or to protect other members of the public or both. But the order does not wholly deprive the person confined of all rights enjoyed by other citizens. Some rights, perhaps in an attenuated or qualified form, survive the making of the order. And it may well be that the importance of such surviving rights is enhanced by the loss or partial loss of other rights. Among the rights which, in part at least, survive are three important rights, closely related but free standing, each of them calling for appropriate legal protection: the right of access to a court; the right of access to legal advice; and the right to communicate confidentially with a legal adviser under the seal of legal professional privilege. Such rights may be curtailed only by clear and express words, and then only to the extent reasonably necessary to meet the ends which justify the curtailment.[81]

---

[79] (1993) 15 EHRR 137. The conclusion of the ECtHR at 161 was that 'the reading of a prisoner's mail . . . should only be permitted in exceptional circumstances when the authorities have reasonable cause to believe that that privilege is being abused in that the contents of the letter endanger prison security or the safety of others or are otherwise of a criminal nature. What may be regarded as "reasonable cause" will depend on all the circumstances but it presupposes the existence of facts or information which would satisfy an objective observer that the privileged channel of communication was being abused.' Steyn LJ commented that *Campbell* 'although not directly binding in England, reinforces a conclusion that we have arrived at in the light of the principles of our domestic jurisprudence'.

[80] [2001] 2 AC 532.

[81] ibid, para 5.

The remainder of the Committee all made it clear that the test of proportionality is to be applied whenever a prisoner's (or indeed any citizen's) rights have been interfered with: does the interference pursue a legitimate aim (security, order, etc), and does it constitute the minimum interference necessary to fulfil that aim? The Committee did not distinguish between violations flowing from the Rules or from other policies, showing that the same test is to be applied across the board. This represents a huge improvement on the days when prisoners' rights issues were not even considered justiciable (discussed further in Chapter 2). It was notable that Lord Bingham made it quite clear that the case was decided on traditional principles of English common law, although he would have come to the same conclusion by applying Article 8 of the Convention. The common law principle of legality has retained its full force in cases decided under the HRA.

D. Prison Service Orders and Instructions

The broad canvas created by the Prison Act 1952 and the Prison Rules is 'filled in' **1.43** by a plethora of administrative guidance and directions which, since January 1997, is contained in Prison Service Orders and Instructions. These are supplemented by a series of Prison Service Standards, which purport to ensure 'a consistent and high quality of service'.[82] The new system results from the Woodcock Report, which recommended that the Prison Service must provide a clear framework within which governors are expected to operate. This required that 'levels of autonomy, responsibility and accountability should be clearly published, making it plain which aspects of existing manuals and national instructions are mandatory, advisory or purely informative'.[83]

The old system of Standing Orders, Circular Instructions and Instructions and **1.44** Advices to Governors has thus been gradually replaced by a new one which is intended to ensure that current policy and practice are easily accessible to staff and, where relevant and appropriate for security reasons, to prisoners alike. Prison Service Instructions are short term documents intended to last no more than one year. Prison Service Orders, intended to last more than one year, together with their supporting guidance, are contained in separate Manuals

---

[82] Prison Service Standards Manual (PSO 0200): Foreword from the Director-General. See also PSI 19/2001, which introduces the most recent Standards. PSI 19/2001 acknowledges the strain placed on prison administrators by the deluge of paperwork emanating from Prison Service Headquarters: 'Due to the heavy demands placed on establishments as a result of the number of Standards issued in a short period of time these Standards are subject to audit nine months after issue.'

[83] The Woolf Report noted 'the confetti of instructions descending from Headquarters', an observation recently endorsed by Lord Laming of Tewin in the report *Modernising the Management of the Prison Service* (London, 2000) 3.

according to subject matter. Prison Service Standards are contained in their own Manual, arranged by subject matter. They aim to provide a concise, detailed statement of key details of the 'services' which should be provided. The system is managed by an Instructions Unit based in the Secretariat at Prison Service headquarters.

1.45 Despite their greater formality, Prison Service Orders, Instructions and Standards enjoy no greater legal status than the previous system of Standing Orders and Circular Instructions. In other words they have no legal status whatsoever, despite the fact that they contain massive detail relevant to the conduct of daily life in prison. Though several prison rules refer to the Secretary of State's power to make directions in regard to a particular matter,[84] the directions themselves have no legislative authority and are never debated by Parliament. Rather like the circulars issued by various government departments responsible for town and country planning, they are no more than non-statutory guidance to those charged with managing the prison system. Thus, SO 5, which dealt with prisoners' letters and visits, did not define the Secretary of State's power to interfere with a prisoner's right to communicate with the outside world. In *Raymond v Honey* the House of Lords considered the legality of Standing Orders issued in purported compliance with rules governing correspondence and access to legal advisers. The effect of the Standing Orders was to restrict access to the courts by a prisoner in respect of any complaint against a prison officer which had not been ventilated through the internal complaints system (the now abolished 'prior ventilation' rule). The House of Lords held that there was nothing in the Prison Act 1952 which was capable of conferring a power to make regulations which would deny, or interfere with, the right of a prisoner to have unimpeded access to a court. Section 47 of the Act was wholly insufficient to authorize hindrance or interference with so basic a right. Accordingly, neither rule 34 (now rule 35) nor rule 37A (now rule 39), and certainly not the Standing Orders, could sanction a decision by a prison governor to stop a prisoner from communicating with the courts. As Lord Wilberforce said:

> The standing orders, if they have any legislative force at all, cannot confer any greater powers than the [Rules] which, as stated, must themselves be construed in accordance with the statutory power to make them.[85]

This principle reflects the fact that any policy applied by the Prison Service will only be lawful to the extent that it is permitted by the Rules and the Act (and, of course, the HRA). Whether or not the Rules authorize the curtailment or abrogation of a prisoner's fundamental or constitutional rights depends on the applica-

---

[84] See eg r 35(1).
[85] [1983] 1 AC 1.

tion of the test set out by the Court of Appeal in *Leech (No 2)*,[86] and confirmed in *Simms* and *Daly*.[87]

Judicial Review

Of course, where advice contained in a Prison Service Order or Instruction leads **1.46** to unlawful administrative action, or where the application of the policy results in the violation of a prisoner's rights, there will be no difficulty in obtaining relief via an application for judicial review to correct the error. In *Gillick v West Norfolk Area Health Authority* Lord Bridge said that the question whether advice tendered in a non-statutory form such as a departmental circular is good or bad, reasonable or unreasonable, cannot, as a general rule, be subject to any form of judicial review.[88] But he concluded that there were exceptions and that:

> We must now say that if a government department, in a field of administration in which it exercises responsibility, promulgates in a public document, albeit non-statutory in form, advice which is erroneous in law, then the court, in proceedings in appropriate form commenced by an applicant or plaintiff who possesses the necessary locus standi, has jurisdiction to correct the error of law by an appropriate declaration.

Exactly such a result was achieved in *Ex p Hague*[89] when the court ruled that Circular Instruction 10/1974 was ultra vires rule 43 (now rule 45), and in *Daly*[90] when the House of Lords ruled that paras 17.69 to 17.74 of the Security Manual were ultra vires s 47 of the Prison Act 1952. In *Ex p Simms and O'Brien*,[91] the House of Lords held that, although paras 37 and 37A of SO 5 were not ultra vires in themselves, they could not be construed so as to justify the Home Secretary's indiscriminate ban on prisoners' interviews with journalists. The Standing Order itself was lawful, but its application constituted too great an infringement of

---

[86] [1994] QB 198. This book previously argued that, to the extent that the Court of Appeal in *Ex p O'Dhuibhir* [1997] COD 315 held that *Leech* was only relevant to determining the vires of a Prison Rule (as opposed to a policy introduced by Standing Order or an Instruction to Governors), it was clearly wrongly decided. In both *Raymond v Honey* [1983] 1 AC 1 and *Ex p Anderson* [1984] QB 778 the restriction on a prisoner's basic rights (access to the courts and to legal advice) were introduced by non-statutory Standing Orders and yet the 'Leech approach' was adopted. Why should less effective protection be afforded when a fundamental right is interfered with not by the express terms of subordinate legislation but, instead, by a non-statutory policy statement or circular said to derive its authority from subordinate legislation? (See also Tim Owen, 'Prisoners and Fundamental Rights' [1997] JR 81.) The House of Lords in *Simms* and *Daly* has subsequently affirmed the applicability of the approach in *Leech (No 2)* to all violations of prisoners' rights, regardless of their source of purported authority.

[87] [2000] 2 AC 115; [2001] 2 AC 532.

[88] [1986] 1 AC 112, 193A.

[89] [1992] 1 AC 58.

[90] [2001] 2 AC 532.

[91] [2000] 2 AC 115.

fundamental rights. The principle of legality applies with full force to Standing Orders, just as it applies to primary legislation. All these decisions demonstrate that, merely because Standing Orders and Instructions do not have the force of law, this does not mean that they are irrelevant to a consideration of what 'rights' prisoners enjoy. As we have seen, policies in any form may be challenged if they constitute too great an infringement of fundamental rights, either on their face or as applied in a particular case. Further, the issuing of guidance and advice may give rise to a legitimate expectation on the part of a prisoner that a particular administrative procedure will be followed, the denial of which will give rise to an application for judicial review.[92] Thus Instruction to Governors 28/1993, which deals with transfers in the interests of good order or discipline, states that 'inmates must be told the reasons for their transfer as far as is practicable, and as soon as possible'.[93] A refusal to give such reasons would, arguably, be susceptible to judicial review, although before IG 28/1993 was issued it had been held that a prisoner had no legal right to demand them.[94]

1.47 Access to and awareness of the content of non-statutory guidance and instructions to governors has in the past presented a problem for both prisoners and prison staff. Prison Rule 10 requires each prisoner within 24 hours of reception to be provided with written information about the Rules 'and other matters which it is necessary that he should know'. The Prison Service does not regard this as including the provision of copies of all Orders and current Instructions, though a refusal to

---

[92] After a period of uncertainty, the law on legitimate expectations is now fairly clear. Fordham's *Judicial Review Handbook* (3rd edn, 2001) 474 summarizes these as: substantive rights arising from representation/policy; interest in a benefit whose denial triggers basic duties of fairness and reasonableness; general interest in basic fairness; and special procedural entitlement. It is the first category which has generated most controversy, with different judges taking radically different approaches to the question whether legitimate expectation has hardened into a substantive, as opposed to procedural, basis for challenging a public law decision so that, in some circumstances, a public body will be prevented from changing its policy in a way which adversely affects the applicant—a form of public law estoppel. The judgment of Sedley J in *R v Ministry of Agriculture, Fisheries and Food, ex p Hamble Fisheries* [1995] 2 All ER 714 was the first judicial recognition of the substantive expectation doctrine, but it was condemned as 'heresy' by the Court of Appeal in the home leave case of *R v Home Secretary, ex p Hargreaves* [1997] 1 WLR 906, in which prisoners who had suffered as a result of the new home leave policy (introduced in 1995 by Michael Howard) failed in their attempt to 'hold' the Home Secretary to his former policy on the basis that they had entered into a compact which prevented an alteration to the home leave policy to their detriment. However, the Court of Appeal revisited the issue in *R v North and East Devon Health Authority, ex p Coughlan* [2001] QB 213, Lord Woolf MR, Mummery and Sedley LJJ. This case concerned a severely disabled patient who had been promised, when accepting a move from hospital to an NHS facility for the disabled, that this would be her 'home for life'. The Authority subsequently tried to shut the facility, and the Court of Appeal held that she had a substantive legitimate expectation that the Authority would keep to its promise. This legitimate expectation was not outweighed by the Authority's attempted justifications, and therefore the decision to close the facility amounted to an abuse of power and was unlawful. See the helpful analysis by Karen Steyn, 'Substantive Legitimate Expectations' [2001] JR 244.

[93] See paras 10.37–10.38 below.

[94] See *per* Taylor LJ, in *Hague* [1992] 1 AC 58, 112.

do so in the face of a direct request by a prisoner could be challenged by means of an application for judicial review. Prison Service Instruction 1/1997 states that 'as a general principle, prisoners will be allowed access, through libraries in Prison Service establishments, to all Orders and Instructions which affect them' although 'some parts . . . will, for security or similar reasons, not be accessible to prisoners'.

E. The Administrative Framework

While the Home Secretary remains personally accountable to Parliament for the **1.48** running of the Prison Service, the responsibility for administering the penal estate on a day-to-day basis rests with the Prison Service. Since 1990 the Service has been subject to almost continuous administrative restructuring and reform, culminating most significantly in April 1993 with the Prison Service becoming an Executive Agency. In a book devoted to explaining the nature of prison law, it is important to avoid becoming obsessed with the minutiae of these administrative changes. It is also important to stress that none of the radical alterations to the administrative structure have been accompanied by any changes to the legislative framework set out in the 1952 Act. Nor do the Prison Rules 1999 reflect the extensive administrative changes which have taken place since the passing of the 1964 Rules. Agency status does not mean that the administrators are no longer subject to the rule of law or that the basic legal ground rules regulating prisoners' lives have changed, either for worse or better. Nevertheless some understanding of the administrative structure is essential to a complete understanding of the operation of the prison service.

The Woolf Report

The current administrative system is largely the result of the recommendations of **1.49** the Woolf Report, which dealt in some detail with the managerial lessons to be drawn from the prison disturbances of spring 1990, and Sir Raymond Lygo's *Review of the Management of the Prison Service*. Woolf commented on 'a most remarkable dichotomy within the Prison Service' between 'the high calibre and deep commitment of the majority of Prison Service staff at all levels' and 'the dissension, division and distrust which exists between all levels of Prison Service staff. They labour under a blanket of depression. They lack confidence in the value of what they do. They harbour a deep sense of frustration that the effort which they are devoting to the Service is not appreciated.'[95] Woolf's answer was three-fold. First, there was a need for more visible leadership of the Prison Service with the appointment of a Director-General who is, and is seen to be, in day-to-day charge of the Service. Secondly, the relationship between the Prison Service and Home Office Ministers needed to be more clearly structured to allow the

---

[95] Woolf Report, n 23 above, para 12.1.

Director-General to exercise the leadership needed to run the Service. Ministers should establish policies, priorities and resources. The Director-General should then be allowed to 'get on with the job'. Woolf recommended that the mechanism for achieving the new relationship should be a new document drawn up by the Prison Service and approved by Ministers, setting out the tasks and objectives for the Service for the coming year and the available resources. The document would be laid before Parliament and would be, in effect, a 'compact' or 'contract' between the Director-General and the Secretary of State. Finally, the relationship between Prison Service Headquarters and governors needed to be reformed so that the latter had greater discretion in the implementation of Prison Service policy. Each prison should be able to decide, as far as possible, how its budget is spent. The Governor's contract with the Area Manager should set out specifically what his prison intends to provide for each prisoner as well as laying down the Service's obligation to provide the necessary resources.

The Lygo Report

1.50 The Lygo Report, commissioned by the Home Secretary in 1991 to provide a detailed managerial assessment of the working of the Service, endorsed many of Woolf's recommendations and concluded that agency status was the means whereby the necessary reforms could be achieved. Lygo commented that, since the absorption of the Prison Commissioners by the Home Office, numerous reports on the Prison Service had called for greater managerial independence for the Service from day-to-day Home Office control. Yet such independence remained illusory. While recognizing that the Home Secretary must remain politically accountable to Parliament for the Prison Service, Lygo said that:

> the need for greater managerial independence suggests a move away from the present arrangements and towards a much more independent Prison Service, clearly separate from the rest of the Home Office but having responsibility to the Home Secretary. In current Civil Service thinking, this would equate to 'agency status'.

He concluded that the critical factor in the success or failure of the new arrangement would be the ability of Ministers to allow the Prison Service to operate in an almost autonomous mode while retaining their responsibility to Parliament for the overall policy and conduct.

F. Agency Status

1.51 The Government accepted Lygo's basic recommendation, and since 1 April 1993 the Prison Service has been an Executive Agency.[96] Agency status was reaffirmed

---

[96] Agency status was a key feature of the Conservative Government's Next Steps programme. The Learmont Report, n 11 above, revealed that the Lygo Inquiry team sought clarification from

following a quinquennial review in 1998. The main features of an executive agency are that it is headed by a Chief Executive[97] directly accountable to the Secretary of State, that the agency has clearly defined aims and objectives agreed with Ministers and set out in a Framework Document, and that, while the agency remains part of its parent government department, it has a great deal of autonomy, particularly in financial and personnel matters. The Secretary of State decides on the agency's resources, is responsible for policy, and remains ultimately accountable to Parliament. The Chief Executive is responsible for day-to-day management of the agency and, in the case of the Prison Service, will be the Home Secretary's main policy adviser. In April 1993 a Framework Document for the Prison Service was published, a revised Framework Document was published following the 1998 quinquennial review, and a copy of this appears at Appendix 10.[98]

If it was hoped that agency status would free the Prison Service from day-to-day ministerial control and persistent interference in 'operational' matters, the reality between 1993 and 1996 proved otherwise. The spectacular escapes of high security prisoners from the Whitemoor Special Secure Unit and from Parkhurst prison made the management of the Prison Service a major political issue. The Woodcock and Learmont reports were savagely critical both of the events which led to the escapes and the entire managerial structure of the Prison Service. They triggered a highly contentious debate around the distinction drawn by the former Home Secretary, Michael Howard, between responsibility for policy and operational matters and eventually led to the dismissal of the Director-General, Derek Lewis. Though the political heat has, to some extent, cooled since the election of the Labour Government, the issue of political involvement in the management of the penal system remains a controversial matter.[99] As prison overcrowding

1.52

---

the Prime Minister's adviser on the Next Steps programme, Sir Robin Ibbs, about the appropriateness of agency status for an organization like the Prison Service. He confirmed that there was no conflict between agency status and the proposition that the Chief Executive should report to an 'owner' in the Home Office. The 'owner' would be responsible for guarding the independence of the agency. No doubt Sir Robin had not envisaged what might happen when the 'owner' turned out to be Michael Howard.

[97] In fact the 'Chief Executive' of the Prison Service has retained the old title of Director-General.

[98] In his Introduction to the new Framework Document, Jack Straw, the then Home Secretary, stresses the need 'to ensure proper Ministerial responsibility and accountability to Parliament for the work of the Prison Service', and to ensure that the 'roles of the principal players and bodies, including a Prison Service Strategy Board to be chaired by the Prisons and Probation Minister, are set out within a framework of responsibilities and accountabilities'. However, the structure of the Prison Service remains highly complex.

[99] A book such as this is not the appropriate place to discuss in detail the extraordinary sequence of events leading to the sacking of the Director-General and the later full frontal assault on Michael Howard's integrity by former Prisons Minister, Ann Widdecombe. For a (partial) but highly readable account of the story see Derek Lewis, *Hidden Agendas: Politics, Law and Disorder* (London, 1997). In his *Annual Report* April 1995–March 1996, the then Chief Inspector of Prisons added his

becomes extreme, one particularly sharp tension is that between the Labour Government's desire not to be seen as 'soft on crime', and to increase sentences, and the inability of the prison service to cope with ever increasing numbers of prisoners. However, Home Secretary David Blunkett's announcement in March 2002 that increased use would be made of electronic tagging to reduce prison overcrowding was greeted with concern by both the prison and probation service, who were not confident that they were equipped to carry out this initiative. The tension between political policies emanating from the Home Office and the administration which is to carry them out appears to transcend changes in the government.

G. Administrative Structure

1.53 The administrative structure of the Prison Service is based on a series of reforms beginning in September 1990 and continuing periodically ever since. The Director-General of the Prison Service is assisted by a Deputy Director-General. Beneath the Directors-General are seven Directorates: High Security, Security, Personnel, Corporate Affairs, Finance and Procurement, Resettlement, and Health. Each Director has responsibility for sub-groups with responsibility for specific issues, such as prisoner escorts, the running of close supervision centres, racial equality and drug strategy. Issues relating to parole, sentence management and release now fall within the remit of the newly created Director of Resettlement. The Deputy Director-General oversees the work of 13 Area Managers, each of whom is responsible for approximately eight penal establishments based on geographical divisions of England and Wales, a Manager of Women's prisons and Young Offender Institutions, and a Manager with responsibility for Juveniles.

1.54 At the level of policy formation, the Framework Document announced the formation of a Prison Service Strategy Board. The members include a Home Office Minister, the Director-General, and various directors of the Prison Service. The Board is intended to 'provide a forum for discussing the strategic direction of the Service and Prison Service plans and performance'.[100] This is part of a general move to integrate the Prison Service into the Home Office's framework of criminal justice policy, which can be seen either as a welcome move to 'joined-up'

---

voice to the criticisms in Lygo and Learmont about the management structure of the Prison Service, pointing out that the Director-General 'is, at one and the same time, required to be Chairman of the Prisons Board, Chief Executive of the Prison Service Agency, principal adviser to Ministers and professional head of the Prison Service'. He called for a drastic reappraisal of the composition of the Prisons Board and management structure of the Prison Service and said that consideration should be given to the early appointment of Directors of the Women's and Young Offender's estates.

[100] Framework Document, para. 3.4.

government, or as further evidence of the tendency to see prison policy as a means of crime control rather than, for example, rehabilitation.

H. Private Prisons

The Criminal Justice Act 1991 introduced a new dimension to the prison system **1.55** by giving the Home Secretary the power to 'contract out' the running of a prison.[101] In effect, the Act provides for the privatization of prisons.

The contracting-out provisions now extend to any kind of prison although the **1.56** power to include prisons catering for convicted as well as remand prisoners was added as a result of a back bencher's amendment, and consequently is achieved by a somewhat circuitous statutory route. Section 84(1) confines the power to contract out the running of a prison solely to remand prisons established after the commencement date of the section. Section 84(2) then enables the Home Secretary by statutory instrument (approved by both Houses of Parliament) to apply the provisions of s 84(1) to any prison—whether or not established after commencement and regardless of whether it holds remand or convicted prisoners or both. In July 1992 a statutory instrument (SI 1992/1656) was approved which enables the Home Secretary to contract out any new prison, holding remand or sentenced prisoners, which is established after the commencement date of s 84.[102] A subsequent statutory instrument removed even this limitation, enabling the Home Secretary to contract out existing prisons as well.[103]

Following these two amendments, s 84 of the Criminal Justice Act 1991 was then **1.57** rewritten entirely by s 96 of the Criminal Justice and Public Order Act 1994 which provided for the second phase of the contracting-out process to be embarked upon. Section 84 (as amended) provides for the Secretary of State to 'contract with another person for the provision or running (or the provision and running) by him, or (if the contract so provides) for the running by subcontractors of his, of any prison or any part of a prison'. This enables contractors to design, build and then run the new prisons. Such prisons are known as 'design, construct, manage and finance' or DCMF new prisons, and the government will identify and provide the site which will then be leased to the contractor.

---

[101] Criminal Justice Act 1991, ss 84–87. See also the Home Affairs Select Committee Report on the Management of the Prison Service 1996–97 (HC 57–1). For an Australian perspective on the privatization of the prison system, see P Moyle, 'Separating the allocation of punishment from its administration: theoretical and empirical observations' (2001) 41(1) British J of Criminology 77–100.

[102] Criminal Justice Act 1991 (Contracted Out Prisons) Order 1992, SI 1992/1656.

[103] Criminal Justice Act 1991 (Contracted Out Prisons) Order 1993, SI 1993/368 which came into effect in March 1993.

1.58   The first private prison opened in April 1992.[104] The Wolds was a new prison built to hold remand prisoners and is run by the private security firm Group 4 Remand Services. The Wolds was intended to be a pilot project evaluated over two years by the University of Hull, but apparently the Home Secretary was in a hurry and tenders were invited for Blakenhurst before the completion of the study. Not all the tender bids for 'contracted out' prisons have been won by private contractors. The contract to run Strangeways in Manchester, for instance, was won by the in-house team, which means that although it is a contracted out prison it still remains under direct Home Office control.[105]

Rank Structure of Contracted-out Prisons

1.59   The legal status of a contracted-out prison does to some extent have significant legal implications, particularly in the identification of the correct party to any litigation. Section 84(2) (as amended by the Criminal Justice and Public Order Act 1994) states that while a contract under this section is in force 'the prison or part shall be run subject to and in accordance with sections 85 and 86 below, the 1952 Act (as modified by section 87 below) and prison rules'. Section 85 creates three new officers to manage a contracted-out prison. Instead of a governor, each prison must have a 'director' who will be a 'prisoner custody officer appointed by the contractor and specially approved . . . by the Secretary of State'.[106] In addition to the director there must also be a 'controller' for each prison who is a Crown servant appointed by the Home Secretary.[107] Finally, instead of prison officers, 'every officer . . . who performs custodial duties shall be a prisoner custody officer who is authorised to perform such duties'.[108] Section 85 has been amended by s 97 of the Criminal Justice and Public Order Act 1994 to add 'a prison officer who is temporarily attached to the prison' to the category of persons authorized to perform custodial duties. This is to enable the contracted-out prison to draw on the support and assistance of other prisons in times of crisis which previously they had legally been barred from doing.

---

[104]   There are now two 'management-only' prisons (The Wolds and Doncaster), seven completed DCMF prisons (Parc, Altcourse, Lowdham Grange, Ashfield, Forest Bank, Rye Hill, and Dovegate) and two further planned (Ashford and Peterborough). The Times, 5 July 2002, reports that insurance companies are refusing to provide cover for the two planned prisons. The Wolds was ten years old in April 2002: for an in-depth examination of the arguments against the privatization of prisons, see *Howard League Magazine*, Special Edition, April 2002.

[105]   Although see the *Annual Report* of the Chief Inspector of Prisons April 1995–March 1996 (published 13 November 1996) for criticisms that the Prison Service is not honouring the service level agreement with the Strangeways management team and effectively they are being treated like any other public sector local prison. For a detailed study of the Wolds experience, see A James, A Bottomley, A Liebling, and E Clare, *Privatising Prisons: Rhetoric and Reality* (London, 1997) ch 4. See also R Harding, *Private Prison and Public Accountability* (London, 1997).

[106]   s 85(1)(a).

[107]   s 85(1)(b).

[108]   s 85(1).

Directors' and Controllers' Powers

The director has the same duties and functions as the governor of a State prison, **1.60**
save that he may not in any circumstance inquire into a disciplinary charge against
a prisoner under rules 51–55 nor may he conduct a disciplinary hearing or make,
remit, or mitigate any disciplinary award.[109] Furthermore, except in cases of
urgency, the director has no power to segregate a prisoner under rule 45, nor any
power to order confinement in a special cell under rule 48 nor power to apply any
restraint to a prisoner under rule 49. All these powers are to be exercised by the
controller by virtue of a new rule 98A (now rule 82) of the Prison Rules.[110] In addition the controller is under a duty to keep under review and report to the Home
Secretary on the running of the prison by or on behalf of the director and must
investigate and report on any allegations made against prisoner custody officers
performing custodial duties at the prison.[111] The potential for a conflict of interest in requiring a person both to perform the role of judging how the contractor
succeeds in keeping good order and also to be personally responsible for maintaining good order has not been addressed.

Prison Custody Officers

The powers and duties of prisoner custody officers are defined in s 86 of the 1991 **1.61**
Act. They include the power to search prisoners in accordance with the Prison
Rules[112] and any other person seeking to enter the prison.[113] This latter power is
confined, however, to requiring a visitor to remove an outer coat, jacket or gloves.
No intimate searching is authorized. Section 86(3) defines the duties of prisoner
custody officers as being to prevent the escape of prisoners; to prevent, detect, and
report on other unlawful acts by prisoners (including prison disciplinary offences
presumably); to ensure good order and discipline; and to attend to prisoners' well-
being. In carrying out these duties, prisoner custody officers are entitled to use reasonable force.[114] They do not, however, possess the powers of a constable under s
8 of the 1952 Act.[115] Accordingly, all prisoner custody officers must be approved
and certified by the Home Secretary to carry out both custodial duties and escort
functions.[116]

---

[109] s 85(3)(a).
[110] See s 85(4).
[111] ibid.
[112] See r 41.
[113] r 71. An abuse of the power to search, including a failure to conduct a search in a reasonably
seemly and decent manner, may give rise to an action for assault: see *Bayliss and Barton v Governor
of HM Prison Frankland*, Liverpool County Court, HH Judge Marshall Evans, February 1993 *Legal
Action* 16. See also *Wainwright v Home Office* [2001] EWCA 2081.
[114] s 86(4).
[115] s 87(3).
[116] s 89 and Sch 10.

Home Secretary's Intervention Powers

1.62 Section 88 of the 1991 Act provides for the Home Secretary to intervene in a contracted-out prison where it appears to him that the director has lost or is likely to lose effective control of the prison or any part of it and that it is necessary to appoint a Crown servant to act as governor of the prison in the interests of preserving the safety of any person or to prevent serious damage to property. Where such an appointment is made, the governor assumes the powers and functions of both the director and the controller, although the prison remains a 'contracted-out' prison despite the assumption of control. This emergency provision is plainly intended to reassure the public that, in the event of a major prison disturbance, the entire resources of the State will be available to deal with it. There is now no legal bar to contracted-out prisons borrowing Control and Restraint teams from other prisons, as currently occurs with an arrangement between neighbouring State prisons in times of need, and although the Act does not specifically provide for payment by the contractor to the public sector for the use of such resources it is envisaged that such arrangements will be made. Concern had been expressed regarding the manning levels at private prisons as the numbers of staff on duty tend to be fewer than in public sector prisons, which raised questions concerning their ability to cope with major incidents,[117] and this may be responsible for the removal of the bar. The sharing of staff resources is intended to be a two way process and s 91 of the 1994 Act inserts a new s 88A into the Criminal Justice Act 1991 which enables contractual arrangements to be made to allow for assistance from the private sector to the public sector and to give (private-sector) prison custody officers the power to act at a directly managed (public-sector) prison.

Standards

1.63 The key document which sets the standards for the running of a contracted-out prison is the contract concluded between the Home Secretary and the contractor. The Home Office refuses to publish any of the final contracts on the grounds of commercial confidentiality (although where the contractor is in a consortium with or part owned by a US company, such as UK Detention Services, the contracts can be obtained by applying to the US Securities and Exchange Commission) but the tender documents for contracted-out prisons have been published. It seems clear that they require regime standards far better than those provided by State prisons. For example, the tender documents for The Wolds laid down a minimum entitlement of 12 hours out of cell for each prisoner each weekday and ten and a half hours at weekends. In marked contrast to the dreary regime of the average State local prison, the tender document opines that '[i]deally, pris-

---

[117] See eg Gen Sir John Learmont, *Review of Prison Service Security in England and Wales and the Escape from Parkhurst Prison on Tuesday 3rd of January 1995* (Cm 3020, 1995).

oners should be free to leave their cells at the first unlocking in the morning and remain cell-free until final lock-up prior to the commencement of the night shift'. The documents identify 'performance criteria', for example an obligation to provide 24 hour on-call arrangements by a qualified doctor and daily medical visits. In the event of a failure to meet the agreed targets, stiff financial penalties are envisaged, but this sanction is only effective if the Home Secretary is prepared to act upon reported breaches. The reality appears to be that not only are the medical obligations not always fulfilled in every contracted-out prison but that neither the contractor nor the Home Office considers itself responsible for any negligence on the part of the doctor, thus multiplying the parties to any litigation.

The tender documents also make clear that, while the rules governing the management of the contracted-out prison will be the Prison Rules 1999, Prison Service policy as expressed in Prison Service Orders and Prison Service Instructions will not automatically apply. The contractor will, however, be obliged to comply with any policy and procedural decisions which the Home Secretary deems applicable to contracted-out prisons. An example of such a requirement is in the area of suicide prevention and other healthcare matters. The Wolds' tender documents stated that 'procedures for the identification of suicide risks and their prevention, and of known or identifiable mental or psychiatric disorder, and for the handling of AIDS and hepatitis cases must be carried out with standards at least consistent with those in the Prison Service'. Each contracted-out prison is to have a Board of Visitors appointed by the Home Secretary and is subject to inspection by the Chief Inspector of Prisons. **1.64**

Breach of Contract and Prisoners' Rights

For the purposes of claims under the HRA, the contractor of a private prison is clearly carrying out a 'public function'. The HRA focuses attention, not on the legal structure of an organization, but on the nature of the functions which it carries out. Imprisonment is obviously a paradigm example of the exercise of State power. Prisoners in private prisons can therefore bring claims under the HRA for breaches of their rights, in exactly the same way as those in State-run prisons.[118] Turning to cases not involving the HRA, the existence of a contract between the Home Secretary and a private contractor does not of course give any contractual rights to individual prisoners vis-à-vis the contractor. Basic principles of privity of contract would obviously prevent such claims. Prisoners' remedies in respect of unlawful **1.65**

---

[118] HRA, s 6(3)(b) brings within the scope of the Act 'any person certain of whose functions are functions of a public nature'. The courts are in the process of developing the definition of 'public functions': see *Poplar Housing and Regeneration Community Association Ltd v Donoghue* [2002] QB 48; *R (Heather) v Leonard Cheshire Foundation* [2002] UKHRR 883; *Parochial Church Council of the Parishes of Aston Cantlow and Wilmcote with Billesley Warwickshire v Wallbank* [2002] Ch 51. See also C McDougall, ' "The Alchemist's Search for the Philosopher's Stone": Public Authorities and the Human Rights Act (One Year On)' [2002] JR 23; J Johnston, 'The Meaning of "Public Authority" under the Human Rights Act' [2001] JR 250.

treatment in a contracted-out prison will remain the same as in a State prison,[119] although the nature of the allegation will define who is the correct defendant to any proceedings. But the better regime standards required by the contract should provide a basis for a prisoner to argue that the contract creates a legitimate expectation of their provision. A failure by the contractor to meet these standards, or the Home Secretary's failure to enforce them, could therefore lead to a successful challenge by means of an application for judicial review or, possibly, by a private law claim for negligence based on a standard of care defined by the contract.

1.66 The proper respondent in judicial review proceedings for failure to enforce the contract is likely to be the Home Secretary, although where the proceedings concern matters arising from the day to day running of the prison (other than matters which are the responsibility of the Controller) the correct respondent would be the private contractor, who would clearly be carrying out a sufficiently public law function to make this appropriate.[120] As discussed above, proceedings under the HRA can also be brought against the contractor directly, since most of their functions will be of a public nature for the purposes of s 6 of the Act. Procurement decisions in the field of contracting-out within the legal system however have been held not to be susceptible to judicial review on the basis that they lacked a sufficient public law element.[121] However the rationale that the government department was merely acting effectively in a private capacity when it dealt with bids for the court reporting service would not appear to be appropriate to the situation of a contractor carrying out the traditional State function of punishing through incarceration. Where the allegation is one of assault by a custody officer or negligence leading to a prisoner-on-prisoner assault then the appropriate defendant will be the private contractor, unless it is being alleged that it was negligent for the Home Secretary to have appointed the particular contractor (under the ordinary principles of liability for the negligence of an independent contractor). There is no authority on whether exemplary damages would be payable by the private contractor, and it could be argued that for these purposes the contractor operates as an agent of the Crown. It would be surprising if the safeguard of exemplary damages had been removed by the 1991 Act.

1.67 Legal advisers must therefore be astute to identify the nature of any claim and, accordingly, who the appropriate defendant or respondent should be. Particular care must be taken when dealing with allegations concerning the medical or dental services within a contracted out prison to identify whether they are provided by the Prison Health Service (for which the Home Office is responsible) or by a private contractor (which may well not be the same contractor as that which runs the prison).

---

[119] See Ch 2 for the scope of such remedies.
[120] Group 4, which runs a large number of immigration detention centres, has been the respondent in a number of claims relating to its running of the centres: see further Ch 15.
[121] *R v Lord Chancellor's Department, ex p Hibbit and Saunders* [1993] COD 326.

2

AVENUES OF REDRESS: DOMESTIC LAW

A. Introduction

The fact of imprisonment invariably means that prisoners cease to have responsi- **2.01** bility for, and control over, their environment. Living in a world governed almost entirely by the exercise of discretion naturally generates a wide range of grievances. The Woolf Report recognized this, pointing out that 'a prisoner, as a result of being in prison, is peculiarly vulnerable to arbitrary and unlawful action'.[1] Accordingly it is essential that prisoners have a number of avenues of redress open to them whereby the illegal exercise of power may be challenged, and by which compensation can be recovered for the infringement of such civil rights as survive in all prisoners notwithstanding their imprisonment.[2]

---

[1] Woolf Report, *Prison Disturbances: April 1990* (Cm 1456, 1991), para 14.293.
[2] A 1977 American Report claimed that 'elementary psychology and fundamental justice both dictate that, wherever large numbers of human beings are confined involuntarily in close quarters, there must be effective credible machinery to provide an outlet for their complaints and dissatisfaction': J Keating, *Grievance Mechanisms in Correctional Institutions* (National Institute of Law

2.02 Not all these avenues necessarily involve recourse to law. Indeed, as with life out-side, by no means every problem which arises in prison is capable of successful res-olution by legal means. In this chapter, therefore, we set out the range of remedies which are available to prisoners in order to redress the various grievances and com-plaints which arise most frequently in prison.

2.03 The extra-judicial options are largely those which are 'internal' to the prison sys-tem itself, though they include recourse to the Prisons and Probation Ombudsman, Members of Parliament, and the Parliamentary Commissioner for Administration. These will be dealt with first under the general heading 'com-plaints procedures'. The judicial options include three different forms of action—a civil action, usually involving a claim for damages for a civil wrong (a tort), a claim for judicial review in the High Court and a claim alleging an infringement of the Human Rights Act 1998. A fourth option, namely an application to the European Court of Human Rights (ECtHR) in Strasbourg, is dealt with in the following chapter.

2.04 We do not intend in this chapter to describe and analyze the detailed provisions of tort or administrative law as they apply in the prison context. Nor do we pretend that this book can be a substitute for specialist textbooks dealing with the sub-stantive law and procedure for both civil actions and claims for judicial review. Rather, our aim is to identify the appropriate means whereby the wide range of decisions and events which may affect prisoners can be challenged and the partic-ular features which distinguish legal actions by prisoners from other forms of liti-gation.

2.05 As will, in due course, be explained, the division between different avenues of redress is not a rigid one, because it will frequently be the case that pursuing a complaint via the internal complaints mechanism will give rise to a claim for judicial review, possibly combined with an application under the Human Rights Act 1998. Indeed, in many cases such internal recourse will be a wise, or indeed essential, prerequisite of mounting a successful challenge in the High Court.

B. Complaints Procedures

2.06 Under the Prison Rules, prisoners have the right to pursue a request or complaint connected to or arising from their imprisonment with the governor of the prison

---

Enforcement and Criminal Justice, Law Enforcement Assistance Administration, Washington, DC, US Government Printing Office, 1977).

or the Board of Visitors.[3] Though there is no longer any express reference to this in the Rules, it has long been accepted that in addition to these two avenues of redress, prisoners also have the right to complain to or petition the Secretary of State as the Minister with overall responsibility for the Prison Service and the care of prisoners.[4] In practice, of course, such petitions are dealt with by civil servants who act on behalf of the Home Secretary.[5]

In September 1990 a new system of dealing with prisoners' complaints/requests **2.07** was introduced by the Prison Service. The previous scheme, developed piecemeal over the previous 100 years, was generally regarded as unsatisfactory for a number of reasons. It was inefficient, slow, and lacking in coherence. The replies which were sent to prisoners, sometimes months after a complaint had been lodged, were almost always brief and wholly uninformative, thereby generating a complete lack of confidence in prisoners that their requests were taken seriously.[6] Furthermore, the system lacked any safeguards to ensure that complaints were not blocked by

---

[3] Prison Rules 1999, r 11, the main rule regarding prisoners' complaints, reproduces r 8 of the 1964 Rules. Rule 8 was brought into force by the Prison (Amendment) Rules 1990 and commenced on 25 September 1990. The effect of the amendment was to delete from the old r 7(1) any reference to the need to provide prisoners with information about how to petition the Secretary of State and to institute an entirely new machinery for dealing with prisoners' requests and complaints based on the recommendations in the Prison Service Working Group Report, 'An Improved System of Grievance Procedures for Prisoners' Complaints and Requests' (P3 Div, July 1989). The Working Group's Report was itself a response to the Chief Inspector's 1987 Report, *Prisoners' Complaints: A Review of the Procedures Used by Prisoners in Making Requests and Complaints* (Home Office, 1987). Both these reports provide a detailed and exhaustive analysis of the merits and demerits of various different methods of complaint/grievance resolution. PSO 2510, Ch 16 deals with external avenues of complaint, including petitions to Parliament, civil actions, the Criminal Cases Review Commission, the Criminal Injuries Compensation Authority, the ECHR and the Commission for Racial Equality. There appears to be no enforceable obligation to make prisoners aware of these remedies; Ch 16 simply states that '[s]taff need to be aware of other avenues through which prisoners may pursue a complaint'.

[4] The 'right' to petition the Secretary of State is not based on any express provision of the Prison Act or the Rules though SO 5C acknowledges its existence in para 1: 'Inmates have the right to make requests or complaints to the governor, the Board of Visitors or to the Secretary of State'. Strangely, the Secretary of State is not mentioned as one of the 'external avenues of complaint' in PSO 2510, Ch 16. Article 5 of the Bill of Rights 1688 states that 'it is the right of the subjects to petition the King and all commitments and prosecutions for such petitioning are illegal'. On the *Raymond v Honey* [1983] 1 AC 1 principle prisoners are no worse off than ordinary 'subjects'.

[5] Such civil servants were described as 'a faceless authority in Whitehall' by Lord Bridge in *R v Deputy Governor of Parkhurst Prison, ex p Leech* [1988] 1 AC 533, 568C.

[6] It was normal under the old complaints system for a prisoner to wait six months for a reply which, when it arrived, amounted to no more than a six-line statement informing the prisoner that his submissions had been considered carefully but that the original decision was upheld. This approach did not encourage confidence that a fearless, critical analysis had been conducted by the Whitehall bureaucracy. In her book *Bricks of Shame* (London, 1987), the former Director of NACRO, Vivien Stern, commented that 'in this country the only appeal against . . . decisions is by petition to the Home Secretary whose officials made the decision in the first place. So if you came to prison with the feeling that it is an unfair world, and with a certain amount of anger and bitterness, your stay may well increase it'.

staff, contrary to the requirement in the European Prison Rules that 'every prisoner shall be allowed to make a request or complaint, under confidential cover, to the central prison administration, the judicial authority or other proper authorities'.[7] Above all, the old system made no provision for independent review of action taken by the prison authorities. The sole power to remedy any complaint lay with the governor or the Home Secretary, who was, either personally or through an agent, the author of the matter giving rise to complaint. Boards of Visitors, while nominally independent, had no power to take action without the agreement of the prison authorities and were in any event not regarded by prisoners as truly independent, compromised as they were by their disciplinary functions.[8]

2.08 In turn, the system introduced in 1990 was subject to a major review in 1999–2000, which culminated in the issuing of a new Prison Service Order (PSO) on the subject.[9] The review considered that the 1990 system was better than before, but still had major defects, and had failed to dispel the culture of defensiveness surrounding the issue of complaints/requests. Before analyzing the extent to which the new scheme meets the criticisms levelled at the old one, we summarize the existing provisions as they appear in the Rules and administrative orders and regulations issued by the Prison Service.

Prison Rules

2.09 The statutory requirement to provide some mechanism for dealing with prisoners' complaints and requests is to be found in rules 11 and 78(1), which state:

> 11(1) A request or complaint to the governor or board of visitors relating to a prisoner's imprisonment shall be made orally or in writing by the prisoner
>   (2) On every day the governor shall hear any requests and complaints that are made to him under paragraph (1) above.
>   (3) A written request or complaint under paragraph (1) above may be made in confidence.
> 78(1) The board of visitors for a prison and any member of the board shall hear any complaint or request which a prisoner wishes to make to them or him.

---

[7] European Prison Rule 42(3).

[8] The Woolf Report stated (para 12.171) that '[w]e have no doubt whatsoever that the public and the Prison Service have cause to be indebted to the Boards of Visitors. The Boards should be preserved. We are conscious, however, that their endeavours on behalf of prisoners are inhibited by the fact that a substantial part of the prison population does not recognise the Boards' members as being as impartial as they in fact are.' Woolf recommended that the Boards' adjudicatory function be abolished and that organizational improvements be made to the Boards' structure including the appointment of a president, who would develop 'more effective methods for recruiting new members to Boards'. In May 1993, the Home Secretary announced that, following a period of consultation, it had been decided to reject this recommendation.

[9] PSO 2510, the requirements of which were due to be phased in during 2002, with all establishments applying the new system by October 2002.

There are a number of points to be noted about these provisions. First, rule 11 requires 'the governor' to be available to hear any requests or complaints every day. Rule 81 enables the governor to delegate any of his powers under the Rules to another officer of the prison where the leave of the Secretary of State is obtained, and SO 5C confirms that the Secretary of State has authorized governors to delegate to any of their staff the task of hearing complaints pursuant to rule 11. Accordingly a prisoner cannot demand to make his request/complaint to the 'Number 1' governor in charge of the prison and, so long as a system is arranged for a member of staff to be available to hear complaints or requests every day, then the requirements of rule 11 can be fulfilled.

Secondly, prisoners can make their requests/complaints either orally or in writing, **2.10** but if they wish to do so in confidence then the request/complaint must be made in writing. Rule 11 says nothing about the circumstances in which such a confidential complaint may be made and there is nothing in the Rules which fully equates with the requirement in European Prison Rule 42(2) that 'it shall be possible to make requests or complaints to an inspector of prisons during his inspection. The prisoner shall have the opportunity to talk to the inspector or to any other duly constituted authority entitled to visit the prison without the director or other members of staff being present.' Rule 79(2) states that a member of a Board of Visitors 'shall have access at any time to every part of the prison and to every prisoner, and he may interview any prisoner out of the sight and hearing of officers', but this is not the same as a right in the prisoner to demand that he be allowed to see the Board member in private and in confidence.

Thirdly, the requirement of daily availability to hear prisoners' requests/com- **2.11** plaints does not apply to Boards of Visitors as it does to the governor. Rule 79(1) requires the members of the Board to visit the prison frequently and to arrange a rota whereby at least one of the members visits the prison between meetings of the full Board. In practice most Boards ensure that one of their number visits at least three or four times each week. A prisoner who is dissatisfied with only seeing a single member of the Board can reasonably ask to have access to the full Board at one of their regular meetings.[10]

Finally, the Rules say nothing about time limits for responding to a prisoner's **2.12** request/complaint, although guidance is given in SO 5C, which complies with the requirement in European Prison Rule 42(4) that prison authorities deal with complaints 'promptly' and 'without undue delay' unless they are obviously

---

[10] The practice adopted by Boards for hearing prisoners' complaints varies from prison to prison. The three principal methods are: (1) an individual member seeing prisoners in the course of a routine visit; (2) one or more members holding a pre-arranged 'clinic'; and (3) the Board (in whole or in part) seeing prisoners when they convene for their regular meetings.

frivolous or groundless.[11] A failure to deal promptly with prisoners' complaints could therefore be challenged by an application for judicial review.

The Complaints Scheme in Practice

2.13   The previous complaints scheme envisaged a two-tier process for dealing with prisoners' written requests/complaints. The first tier sought to resolve the matter within the prison if it could properly be dealt with at local level. The second tier involved taking the matter to Prison Service Headquarters (in practice, the Prisoner Casework Unit based at Headquarters) either as an appeal against the decision reached at local level or because the subject matter of the complaint was a 'reserved subject' which could only be dealt with by Headquarters. The new PSO 2510 abolishes the Headquarters stage for ordinary complaints, leaving it in place only for reserved subjects and confidential access to the Area Manager. Instead, ordinary complaints are to be resolved in the prison in three stages. The first stage is a response by the prisoner's wing officer. If dissatisfied with that response, the prisoner can take the matter to someone at management level, and finally to the governing governor. After that, the prisoner can seek redress from the Prisons Ombudsman. The Ombudsman scheme is discussed in detail below.

2.14   In PSO 2510 the different ways of making a complaint or request are defined in more detail. The first change brought about by the Order is that requests and complaints are now to be dealt with separately. Paragraph 1.4.1 states that '[p]revious procedures have made no distinction between a request and a complaint. Failing to distinguish between the two can create a sense of grievance where none need exist. A complaints system should be a means of redressing grievances, not of meeting everyday needs.' Requests are therefore made using the informal wing applications, which also form the first tier of the complaints system. This first, informal, level involves making oral or written applications to wing staff, who should be available daily for this purpose, preferably in private. This informal procedure is intended to resolve the more mundane and trivial matters which arise in prison life: it is intended to be 'an intermediate process between simply speaking to an officer on the one hand and invoking the formal complaints procedure on the other'.[12] The second, formal, option itself divides into two stages or levels.[13] Level one (the wing stage) requires a prisoner to lodge a written complaint form

---

[11]   SO 5C, para 9. Further details about time limits for responding to complaints are given in PSO 2510.

[12]   PSO 2510, para 3.1.5.

[13]   PSO 2510, Ch 4 sets out ten principles underlying the formal complaints process: openness, simplicity, ease of access, timeliness, fairness, responding at an appropriate level, confidentiality, appropriate redress, freedom from penalty, and use of the system to provide management information. Prisoners who have tried to complain in the past, and those who have tried to help them complain, may well be sceptical about the extent to which these laudable aims will be achieved in the near future.

(form COMP1, COMP2 for confidential access complaints, or ADJ1 for appeals against adjudications) in a locked box on the wing. The boxes must be emptied each working day. The forms are required to be freely available without the prisoner having to request one. Lodging a form will result in the first instance in a written, reasoned[14] reply being supplied by a prison officer. Level two (the management stage) involves the prisoner submitting an appeal form (COMP1A), again in the locked box, usually within seven days of receiving the initial response. A member of senior management in the prison will respond in writing. If the prisoner remains unhappy with the response, he or she can appeal (on the same form) to the governing governor of the prison. This is the final level of appeal in the Prison Service, after which a complaint may be taken to the Ombudsman. The governor is required to consider speaking to the prisoner about the problem, or asking a senior member of staff to do so.

In addition to these options, PSO 2510 makes clear that, as a safeguard, all prisoners may take advantage of confidential access to the governor of the prison, the Chair of the Board of Visitors and/or the Area Manager by lodging a written complaint (on form COMP2) in a sealed envelope, which must not be opened until it reaches the person to whom it is addressed.[15] Finally, prisoners are entitled to make oral or written application to the Board of Visitors. Where none of these routes achieves a satisfactory resolution from the prisoners' point of view, PSO 2510 makes clear that staff must be able to inform prisoners of further avenues of complaint, including recourse to the Prisons Ombudsman (see below), MPs, MEPs, the police, petitioning the Queen or Parliament, the Commission for Racial Equality, the Criminal Injuries Compensation Authority, the ECtHR, individual legal advisers and organizations in the voluntary sector. **2.15**

PSO 2510 provides general guidance on how the internal complaints system should operate, leaving it to individual governors to work out in detail how to operate the scheme in each establishment. It is important to recognize, however, **2.16**

---

[14] Para 8.2.8 of the Order states that '[r]esponding to a written complaint is not simply a matter of correcting a problem or showing the prisoner that he or she is wrong. It is an opportunity for the establishment to demonstrate a positive commitment to fairness and to the welfare of prisoners in its care. The trouble taken in going beyond the minimum required to answer a complaint—and the tone in which this is done—can help to prevent prisoners from feeling that the prison system is unjust or repressive.' Those who have seen the answers to past complaints might feel that the tone of those answers might well lead prisoners to feel that the system is both unjust and repressive.

[15] 'Confidential access does not mean that the fact that a complaint has been made will necessarily be kept confidential, or that investigations will be carried out without the knowledge of the staff or prisoners involved, or that the complaint will necessarily remain confidential between the prisoner and the recipient alone, although there may be rare occasions when that would be right.' (PSO 2510, para 9.3.1.) On receipt of the form, the recipient may decide s/he is not the best person to deal with the matter and may refer it elsewhere for a response to be made. A prisoner who expressly wishes confidentiality to be maintained should explain why on the form although, even then, the Prison Service does not absolutely guarantee that this can be granted.

that neither the Order nor an individual governor's practice can override the requirements set out in the Rules themselves. Thus 'advice' about exhausting the various options in a particular order is merely advice. Accordingly, it would be unlawful for the Board of Visitors to require a prisoner first to have raised a complaint with a wing officer before approaching it, and equally the governor can make no such requirement before responding within seven days to a written complaint form addressed to him.

2.17 In 1997 the Prison Service introduced a time limit for lodging a request or complaint form. This requires prisoners to submit any request or complaint form within three months of the matter under complaint coming to light. Only in exceptional circumstances will a complaint be eligible for consideration when submitted outside that limit or where the prisoner can show good cause why it has been lodged out of time.[16]

2.18 PSO 2510 sets out time limits for each stage of the process:

- Stage 1 response: three weekdays.
- Stage 1 response to complaint against a member of staff: ten weekdays.
- Stage 1 response to complaint involving another establishment: ten weekdays.
- Stage 1 response by Race Relations Liaison Officer: five weekdays.
- Stage 1 response with racial aspect (not provided by Race Relations Liaison Officer): five weekdays.
- Re-submission by prisoner of complaint at stage 2: within one week of receipt of stage 1 response.
- Stage 2 response: seven weekdays.
- Stage 2 response to complaint against member of staff: ten weekdays.
- Stage 2 response to complaint involving another establishment: ten weekdays.
- Re-submission by prisoner of complaint at stage 3: within one week of receiving stage 2 response.
- Stage 3 response: seven weekdays.
- Stage 3 response to complaint against member of staff: ten weekdays.
- Stage 3 response to complaint involving another establishment: ten weekdays.
- Confidential access to governing governor: seven weekdays.
- Confidential access to Area Manager: six weeks.
- Submission of adjudication appeal by prisoner: within three months of the adjudication.
- Response to adjudication appeal: six weeks.
- Response to complaint about a reserved subject: six weeks.

---

[16] This time limit is now contained in PSO 2510, para 6.4.1.

As previously indicated, a prisoner who wishes to complain about a 'reserved sub-   **2.19**
ject' must write to Prison Service Headquarters where his/her complaint will be
dealt with by the Prisoner Casework Unit. 'Reserved subjects' are set out at Annex
H of PSO 2510. They are subjects which the relevant establishment has no power
to make a decision upon and include allegations against the governing governor,
parole for determinate sentenced prisoners, litigation against the Prison Service,
artificial insemination, repatriation, transfer to Scotland or Northern Ireland,
mother and baby unit placement appeals, special remission, and all
complaints where, respectively, category A or life sentence status is relevant to the
subject matter of the complaint.

Giving Reasons for Decisions

In the light of the Prison Service's clear commitment in numerous official docu-   **2.20**
ments to the giving of reasons for all decisions which affect prisoners, there can no
longer be any doubt that prisoners may rely on the doctrine of legitimate expectation as a basis for arguing that there is now a legal obligation on the Prison Service
to supply reasons for administrative decisions.[17] It is well established that where a
body is subject to a duty to give reasons for its decisions, it must satisfy a minimum
standard of clarity and explanation. It must also address the basic issues in dispute.
In *Save Britain's Heritage v Secretary of State for the Environment*[18] Lord Bridge
expanded on some earlier dicta that reasons must be proper, intelligible, and adequate, stating that:

> if the reasons given are improper they will reveal some flaw in the decision-making
> process which will be open to challenge on some ground other than failure to give
> reasons. If the reasons given are unintelligible, this will be equivalent to giving no
> reasons at all. The difficulty arises in determining whether the reasons given are

---

[17] In *R v Deputy Governor of Parkhurst Prison, ex p Hague* [1992] 1 AC 58, 112A, *per* Taylor LJ,
the Court of Appeal had held that a prisoner had no legal right to be given reasons for a decision to
segregate him under r 43 (now r 45), and this issue was not pursued in the House of Lords because
the point had become academic with the issue of CI 26/1990 which promised that, in future, written reasons would be given. Now the terms of PSO 2510, together with the Prison Service's
Framework Document issued in 1998 (which promises that 'prisoners will be treated with fairness,
justice and respect as individuals . . . they will be given reasons for decisions') clearly amount to the
kind of clear, unambiguous, and unqualified representation which is necessary before a legitimate
expectation can arise: see *R v Board of Inland Revenue, ex p MFK Underwriting Agencies Ltd* [1990]
1 WLR 1545, 1569, *per* Bingham LJ as approved in the Court of Appeal in *R v ITC, ex p TSW
Broadcasting*, The Times, 7 February 1992; *R v Home Secretary, ex p Duggan* [1994] 3 All ER 277,
where Rose LJ apparently accepted this argument; *R v Inland Revenue Commissioners, ex p Unilever*
[1996] STC 681; *R v Ministry of Agriculture, Fisheries and Foods, ex p Hamble Fisheries Ltd* [1995] 2
All ER 714; *R v Home Secretary, ex p Hargreaves* [1997] 1 WLR 906. The law of legitimate expectations was reviewed by the Court of Appeal in *R v North and East Devon Health Authority, ex p
Coughlan* [2001] QB 213. See also K Steyn, 'Substantive Legitimate Expectations' [2001] JR 244;
P Craig and S Schonberg, 'Substantive Legitimate Expectations after *Coughlan*' [2000] PL 684.
[18] [1991] 1 WLR 153, 165. See also *Re Poyser and Mills' Arbitration* [1964] 2 QB 467, 477–478
(approved in *Westminster City Council v Great Portland Estates plc* [1985] AC 661, 673).

adequate, whether they deal with the substantial points that have been raised or enable the reader to know what conclusion the decision-maker has reached on the principal controversial issues. What degree of particularity is required? I do not think that one can safely say more in general terms than that the degree of particularity required will depend entirely on the issues falling for decision.

Lord Bridge was speaking there in the context of a planning case, where the legislative framework required that reasons be given by the Secretary of State for his decision, but no different principle applies to the situation where a duty to give reasons arises at common law. Lord Bridge concluded that the reasons for a planning inspector's or the Secretary of State's decision in a planning question should enable a person who is entitled to contest the decision to make a proper assessment whether it should be challenged, but that the onus always lay upon the applicant to satisfy the court that he had been substantially prejudiced by the deficiency of the reasons. The more drastically a decision affects a prisoner's civil rights or liberties, the greater should be the obligation to explain or justify it.[19]

The Prisons and Probation Ombudsman

2.21 An important recommendation in the Woolf Report[20] was the creation of an independent Complaints Adjudicator. According to Woolf, the existing 'internal' avenues for complaints lacked a key feature, namely recourse to an independent person/body with power to review the decisions of the prison authorities. While the Association of Members of Boards of Visitors and the Parliamentary All-Party Penal Affairs Group supported the idea of a 'Prisons Ombudsman', the Prison

---

[19] For many years the decision of the Court of Appeal in *Payne v Lord Harris of Greenwich* [1981] 1 WLR 754 (which held that the duty to act fairly which was imposed on all administrative bodies by the rules of natural justice did not require that the Parole Board should provide reasons to a mandatory life sentence prisoner for refusing to recommend his release on parole) insulated the Prison Service from the general trend in public law in favour of an obligation to give reasons in an increasing number of situations. *Payne* was relied upon by Taylor LJ in *Ex p Hague* to deny a right to reasons for a decision to segregate a prisoner under r 43 (now r 45). Interestingly, only two years later, Taylor LJ was to refer in *R v Parole Board, ex p Wilson* [1992] QB 740 to *Payne* as a case 'decided in 1981 when established views on prisoners were very different from those of today' and ruled that it would be unjust to apply it to deny a discretionary lifer access to reports and other materials before the Parole Board considering his release on licence. Finally, in *Ex p Doody* [1994] 1 AC 531, *Payne* was overruled. Lord Mustill's speech is now the locus classicus in this area of law and establishes that the existence and extent of a duty to give reasons for a decision depend on the statutory and administrative framework in which it is taken and its effect upon the person concerned. See also *R v Higher Education Funding Council, ex p Institute of Dental Surgery* [1994] 1 All ER 651; *R v Newham LBC, ex p Dawson* (1994) 26 HLR 747 and *R v Kensington and Chelsea Royal LBC, ex p Grillo* (1996) 28 HLR 94; *Stefan v General Medical Council* [1999] 1 WLR 1293. For a valuable analysis on the 'reasons' debate see David Toube, 'Requiring Reasons at Common Law' [1997] JR 68. See also P Craig, 'Common Law, Reasons and Administrative Justice' [1994] CLJ 282 and P Robertshaw, 'Providing Reasons for Administrative Decisions' (1998) 27 Anglo-American L Rev 29.
[20] Cm 1456, 1991.

Service in its evidence to Woolf said that it was too soon to move to create such a post. It argued that until the new internal grievance procedures had had time to bed in, it was impossible to make a measured judgment on the need for a Prisons Ombudsman. The Woolf Report rejected this excessively cautious approach, concluding that:

> the presence of an independent element within the Grievance Procedure is more than just an 'optional extra'. The case for some form of independent person or body to consider grievances is incontrovertible. There is no possibility of the present system satisfactorily meeting this point even once it has bedded down. A system without an independent element is not a system which accords with proper standards of justice.[21]

Woolf went on to recommend that the Home Secretary should appoint a Complaints Adjudicator, and it was almost the last act of the outgoing Home Secretary, Kenneth Clarke, to announce the appointment of a Prisons Ombudsman.

Terms of Reference

The office of Prisons Ombudsman, which commenced work in October 1994, is **2.22** non-statutory, created in the exercise of the Home Secretary's general powers relating to prisons and prisoners.[22] Since 1 September 2001, the Ombudsman has also had jurisdiction over complaints relating to the probation system, hence the new title.[23] His office is independent of the Prison Service and the National Probation Service, and he reports directly to the Home Secretary. His function is to investigate complaints submitted by individual prisoners, or people on probation, who have failed to obtain satisfaction from the Prison or Probation Service

---

[21] Woolf Report, n 1 above, paras 14.342–14.363. There appears to be a constant tension between the aim of a just investigative system and one which is bureaucratically efficient. In his *Annual Report 2000-2001* (Cm 5170, July 2001), the current Ombudsman, Stephen Shaw, notes that he has come to 'wonder why the work of my office is exclusively attributed to Aim 4 of the Home Office ('Effective execution of the sentences of the courts . . .'). Aim 2 (Delivery of justice . . .) seems no less relevant.' He stresses the deep sense of injustice which can be caused by seemingly small events: 'Justice in prison can often concern matters which in the world at large we would treat as unforgiveably petty. A piece of property goes missing or is damaged. An envelope is opened in error. Somebody says a word out of turn. But what is trivial to the rest of us takes on more significance in prison. In a situation where prisoners exercise so little autonomy over their lives, my investigations into these affairs also take on a much greater importance. And some of my investigations go to the heart of human rights in prisons' (p 4).

[22] See Prison Act 1952, s 1. In his *Annual Report 1996*, the then Ombudsman, Sir Peter Woodhead, reviewed the debate which had raged over Michael Howard's decision to alter the Ombudsman's terms of reference and stated that he shared the view of the House of Commons Select Committee on the Parliamentary Commissioner for Administration that the present non-statutory framework for the Prisons Ombudsman's work is unsatisfactory: '[i]f the terms on which I am to operate are to be laid out precisely and if the confusion caused by sudden changes to them is to be avoided, my office needs to be established in statute'.

[23] Prison Service guidance on the Prison and Probation Ombudsman is contained in PSO 2520.

request and complaints system and who are eligible in all other respects.[24] The Ombudsman acts only on the basis of eligible complaints from prisoners or those on probation, and not on those from other individuals or organizations. His remit extends to consideration of the merits of matters complained of as well as procedural issues. In this respect he can offer a more wide ranging examination of a prisoner's complaint than can be achieved by an application for judicial review, which cannot (save in wholly exceptional circumstances) review the merits of a particular decision. But the Ombudsman may not overturn a decision himself. His powers are confined to the making of recommendations to the Director-General of the Prison Service, the Director of the National Probation Service or to the Chair of the Area Board, as appropriate.

2.23   The Ombudsman's current terms of reference extend to the investigation of all decisions relating to individual prisoners taken by Prison Service staff, people acting as agents of the Prison Service, other people working in prisons and members of a Board of Visitors with the exception of decisions involving the clinical judgment of doctors. Thus his remit includes contracted-out prisons, contracted-out services and the actions of people working in prisons but not employed by the Prison Service (for example, education staff).[25]

2.24   The following matters are expressly excluded from investigation by the Ombudsman: policy decisions taken personally by a Minister and the official advice to Ministers upon which such decisions are made; the merits of decisions taken by Ministers, save in cases which have been approved by Ministers for consideration; the personal exercise by Ministers of their function in the setting and review of tariff and the release of mandatory life sentenced prisoners;[26] actions and decisions outside the responsibility of the Prison Service such as issues about conviction or sentence; cases currently the subject of civil litigation or criminal proceedings; and the decisions and recommendations of outside bodies including the judiciary, the police, the Crown Prosecution Service, the Parole Board and its Secretariat.

---

[24] This discussion concentrates on the Ombudsman's functions in relation to complaints from prisoners, though it is likely that the extension of his remit will have an impact on the Probation Service. The current Ombudsman, Stephen Shaw, has noted that all the early complaints about probation services came from prisoners, probably because of the higher awareness of his existence among prisoners than among others on probation ('On the Case', Journal of the Prisons and Probation Ombudsman, Issue No 4, Autumn 2001, 1).

[25] In relation to probation services, the remit extends to 'individuals who are, or have been, under the supervision of the NPS or housed in NPS accommodation or who have had pre-sentence reports prepared on them by the NPS and who have failed to obtain satisfaction from the NPS complaints system and who are eligible in other respects'.

[26] This part of the terms of reference is clearly no longer applicable since the decision of the ECtHR in *Stafford v UK* Application 46295/99 (2002) 35 EHRR 32, discussed in detail in Ch 13.

The Koranke Case

The current terms of reference, issued in 2001, replace the previous terms of ref- **2.25**
erence, issued in May 1996. The 1996 terms of reference significantly limited the
original remit granted to the Ombudsman when he commenced office and
resulted from a major clash between Prison Service officials (backed by the Home
Secretary) and the Ombudsman's office over the investigation of a complaint by a
mandatory lifer, Edward Koranke, in 1995.[27] Mr Koranke had complained to the
Ombudsman about the Home Secretary's decision to move him from a Pre-release
Employment Hostel back to closed (category C) conditions following allegations
that he had breached hostel rules. The Ombudsman eventually agreed that
Koranke's complaint did fall within his terms of reference and he wrote to the
Prison Service seeking disclosure of the relevant papers. The Ombudsman's argument was that although his original terms of reference excluded the investigation
of decisions by Ministers on matters relating to the review and release of life sentence prisoners, Mr Koranke's complaint fell outside this excluded area. He was
not complaining about a decision whether he should be released on licence but
the decision to return him to closed conditions. The Director-General disagreed
with this interpretation, asserting that as the process of determining release dates
for mandatory lifers invariably involves an inextricably linked series of decisions,
all of which bear on release either presently or at some time in the future,
Koranke's complaint was excluded from investigation by the Ombudsman's
office. Thus, although the original terms of reference did not say this, the
Director-General claimed it had always been intended that any Ministerial decision should be outside the Ombudsman's remit.

Faced with a refusal by the Prison Service to co-operate with his efforts to investi- **2.26**
gate, the Ombudsman was unable to proceed. Mr Koranke applied for judicial
review of the Prison Service's decision, arguing that it was in breach of the
published policy (then embodied in IG 68/1994) and that it was irrational to conclude that a Ministerial decision to return a lifer to closed conditions was an exercise of a Minister's function in considering the release of a mandatory life sentence
prisoner. In the event, the Home Secretary backed down in Mr Koranke's specific
case, agreeing to allow the Ombudsman to investigate his complaint, but he went
on to publish the revised terms of reference which remain in force. Lest there be
any doubt about the matter, the new terms of reference concluded that 'the
Prisons Ombudsman is required to accept any change or modification to the
terms of reference which the Home Secretary may make' and 'the Home Secretary

---

[27] For a fuller account of this episode, see the Ombudsman's *Annual Report 1996*, ch 1, which
sets out a robust defence of the original terms of reference extended to the Prisons Ombudsman and
which graphically illustrates the sensitivity of both the Prison Service and Home Secretary Michael
Howard to the reality of independent scrutiny of Prison Service officials as well as Ministerial decisions which directly impact on prisoners.

will determine unresolved issues about the eligibility of a complaint or about the interpretation of these terms of reference'.[28]

2.27 Significantly, the 2001 terms of reference contain no such statements. They provide that '[t]he Ombudsman will examine complaints to consider whether they are eligible. To assist in this process, where there is some doubt or dispute as to the eligibility of a complaint, the Ombudsman will inform the Prison Service or the NPS area board of the nature of the complaint and, where necessary, the Prison Service or area board will then provide the Ombudsman with such documents or other information as the Ombudsman considers are relevant to considering eligibility.' This represents a major advance on the 1996 terms of reference, since the Ombudsman is now the arbiter of his own jurisdiction. However, the large list of excluded areas remains, making a complaint to the Ombudsman an ineffective tool for challenging policy decisions, whatever their effects on the individual prisoner.

2.28 The 1996 terms of reference also made clear that the Ombudsman's original power of 'unfettered access to Prison Service information, documents, establishments and individuals including classified information entrusted to the Prison Service by other organizations' was to be cut back. Under the new scheme, unfettered access to Prison Service documents exists only 'for the purpose of investigations within his terms of reference'.[29] This limitation is reproduced in the 2001

---

[28] As the then Ombudsman commented in his *Annual Report 1996*, there could be no doubt that the alteration of the terms of reference was significant and has had a harmful effect on his reputation as an independent arbiter of grievances. Sir Peter went on to say that the revised terms of reference showed two significant alterations, 'first my original terms of reference was inclusive: my remit extended to all matters affecting individual prisoners with certain explicit exclusions. The revised terms of reference, on the other had, give a limited account of what lies within my remit and states that "all other matters are excluded". Second, and more important in my mind, the original terms of reference only excluded from my remit "Ministers' exercise of their function in considering the release of mandatory life sentence prisoners". The revised terms of reference exclude all Ministerial decisions about whatever subject and all official advice to Ministers from civil servants.' In true 'Sir Humphrey' style, the Permanent Secretary to the Home Office had responded that 'the remit has not been changed: it has been confirmed in the form it was intended'. The original remit documents had, he said, been flawed. Parliament and the courts were the appropriate checks on Ministerial actions. According to the Permanent Secretary, it would be 'constitutionally strange' to have someone who was technically a civil servant reviewing Ministerial decisions!

[29] The Ombudsman requires access to documents for two purposes. First, to assess whether a complaint is eligible for investigation and, secondly, to carry out the investigation of eligible complaints. Under the new terms of reference, the Ombudsman remains the ultimate arbiter of whether a complaint is or is not eligible but he is no longer entitled to unfettered access to Prison Service documents to assist him in this task. The Prison Service is now only required to provide documents where it considers it to be necessary and only where there exists some doubt or dispute as to the eligibility of a complaint. The Ombudsman said in evidence to the Parliamentary Select Committee on the Parliamentary Commissioner for Administration in May 1996 that the fact that the Prison Service now has the power to select the documents it regards as relevant to an individual complaint means that it can exercise control over eligibility decisions. The Committee agreed with the Ombudsman's view and recommended that 'the Prisons Ombudsman be granted unfettered access to all papers he considers relevant to the investigation of a complaint'. The Home Secretary responded by asserting that the revised terms did provide the Ombudsman with unfettered access to papers 'relevant to the investigation of eligible complaints'.

terms of reference. However, the 2001 document gives the Ombudsman greater power to disclose information, stating that 'the Ombudsman will follow the Government's policy that official information should be made available unless it is clearly not in the public interest to do so'. Some such circumstances are suggested: when disclosure is against the interests of national security; likely to prejudice security measures designed to prevent the escape of particular prisoners or classes of prisoners; likely to put at risk a third party source of information; likely to be detrimental on medical or psychiatric grounds to the mental or physical health of a prisoner; likely to prejudice the administration of justice; and when the documents are capable of attracting legal professional privilege. Under the 1996 document, the Ombudsman could not reveal to prisoners or make public in any way documents which 'would not normally be disclosed'. The 2001 terms of reference reproduce the requirement that before issuing his final report on an investigation the Ombudsman must send a draft to the Director-General to allow the Prison Service to draw attention to points of factual accuracy, to confidential or sensitive material which is not disclosable and to enable any identifiable member of staff subject to criticism to make representations.[30] The limitations introduced in 1996, many of which are still in place, show that the Home Secretary was clearly motivated by a desire to muzzle what was becoming an effective and enthusiastic watchdog of the actions of the Prison Service. However, the 2001 terms of reference show some redress in the balance of power, particularly since the Ombudsman is now able to judge which material to disclose, and to determine the limits of his own jurisdiction.

Procedure for Investigating Complaints

Before putting a grievance to the Prison Ombudsman, a prisoner must first seek **2.29** redress through 'appropriate use' of the Prison Service complaints procedure. In practice, this means pursuing a complaint to level three within the prison, or to Headquarters in the case of a reserved subject.[31] Complaints will be considered for investigation by the Ombudsman if the prisoner is dissatisfied with the reply from the prison or receives no reply within six weeks to his complaint. Access to the Ombudsman is confidential.

---

[30] The Select Committee did not object in principle to this requirement but commented that 'the purpose of this new requirement is to give the Prison Service an opportunity to ensure that no sensitive information is in danger of being made public in the report. That is a legitimate concern. It is not intended as an opportunity for the department to question the Prisons Ombudsman's judgments. We expect, however, the Prisons Ombudsman to be robust enough to withstand any pressure to modify his judgments and recommendations unless he is convinced of the validity of the Agency's arguments.'

[31] In the year 2000–01, the Ombudsman received 2,176 complaints, 12% more than the previous year. 857 of those were identified as meeting the eligibility criteria, an increase of 53% on the previous year. The main cause for ineligibility was failure to exhaust the Prison Service complaints procedure.

2.30 All complaints to the Ombudsman must be submitted within one calendar month of receiving a substantive reply from the Prison Service. However, the Ombudsman will not normally accept complaints where there has been a delay of more than 12 months between the prisoner becoming aware of the relevant facts and submitting a complaint to the Ombudsman unless the delay has been the fault of the Prison Service. There is, however, a general discretion to disapply these time limits where good reason exists for the delay or where the issues raised are so serious as to override time factors.

2.31 The Ombudsman aims to give a substantive reply to the complaint within 12 weeks, or to give a progress report if a substantive reply is not possible in that time period.[32] As previously indicated, all reports are now required to be sent to the Director-General for comment or correction before being sent to the prisoner. Where a complaint is upheld a recommendation is made with a view to rectifying the matter in issue. This may extend to correcting an Instruction issued by the Prison Service or simply correcting a particular practice in one prison.[33]

C. Redress through the Courts

2.32 In many cases resort to the internal complaints system or the Prisons Ombudsman will fail to resolve a particular problem either because it cannot lead to an award of financial compensation or because the response to the complaint is itself unsatisfactory, giving rise to the possibility of a legal challenge. In that event consideration must be given to litigation and a basic question then arises: what is

---

[32] This marks a loosening of the time criteria—the 1996 terms of reference committed the Ombudsman to reporting within eight to 12 weeks, other than in exceptional circumstances. In his *Annual Report 1996* the Ombudsman commented that both the request/complaints system and the Ombudsman's service seemed to be working well with regard to complaints about relatively formal and non-urgent topics such as disciplinary adjudications and property losses and that prisoners were willing to wait while the lengthy complaint processes are worked through. The situation is however different for most other categories of complaints—assaults, closed visits, allegations of victimisation by staff—where prisoners want a much quicker resolution—'the relatively lengthy and formalised process of a complaint to the governor (taking a week plus), an appeal to Headquarters (taking at least 6 weeks) and an Ombudsman's investigation (taking up to 3 months and sometimes more) will not commend itself to a disaffected prisoner wanting immediate release.' In 1996, the Ombudsman issued 64% of his final reports within the target time of 12 weeks. In his 2001 Report, the Ombudsman notes that 'I regret to say that the growth in the number of cases has meant a deterioration in our performance against this 12 week target. Sixty-three per cent of cases were completed on time compared to 73 per cent a year earlier.' This shows that, despite the vastly growing workload of the Ombudsman in the last few years, there has not in fact been a deterioration in meeting time limits since 1996.

[33] In 2000–01, the Ombudsman made 251 recommendations to the Director-General, of which he had accepted 208 by the time of the Report, and was still considering others. He refused to accept the Ombudsman's recommendations in only five cases, which had no common subject matter.

the proper forum in which to commence proceedings? The answer to this question necessarily involves consideration of the difference between private law claims for damages and public law challenges to administrative decisions by means of an application for judicial review, as well as the remedies available under the Human Rights Act 1998.

D. Civil Actions

The decision of the House of Lords in *Ex p Hague/Weldon v Home Office*[34] clarified **2.33** the scope of the private law remedies which a prisoner may pursue in respect of any complaint which might arise from his treatment by the prison authorities. There are essentially three civil (tort) claims potentially available to cover the entire range of such complaints, namely actions for negligence, assault and battery, and misfeasance in public office.

Excluded from this list are potential claims for breach of statutory duty and false **2.34** imprisonment. It is perhaps surprising that it was not until *Ex p Hague/Weldon v Home Office* reached the House of Lords in 1991 that it was conclusively decided that neither of these actions could be pursued by a prisoner (at least, in the case of false imprisonment, not against the prison authorities). It is important to understand the reasoning behind this decision, since it has widespread implications for the potential of the law to remedy apparently wrongful conduct by the prison authorities.

The Decision in *Ex p Hague and Weldon v Home Office*

Christopher Hague, who pursued an application for judicial review and included **2.35** a claim for damages for false imprisonment and breach of statutory duty in his Form 86A,[35] had been held for 28 days in solitary confinement at Wormwood Scrubs in breach of rule 43 (now rule 45) under the administrative procedures set out in CI 10/74, the predecessor to IG 28/1993. Known by prisoners as the 'ghost train', a '10/74' was designed to transfer and segregate a supposedly 'subversive' prisoner. The Court of Appeal held this to be unlawful and, though the Home Office subsequently issued CI 37/90, which incorporated virtually all the procedural safeguards for which Hague had been arguing, it maintained the line in the House of Lords that he was not entitled to damages for his admittedly 'unlawful'

---

[34] [1992] 1 AC 58.
[35] Before the recent reforms to the civil justice system, Form 86A was the formal document to be used to make an application for judicial review. Such claims are now made on Form N461, under CPR Pt 54.

(ie ultra vires) confinement at Wormwood Scrubs in substantially worse conditions than he would have enjoyed had he remained on normal location at Parkhurst.[36]

2.36 Kenneth Weldon had pursued a private law claim for assault and false imprisonment in which he alleged that he had been beaten up by prison staff at Armley Prison and then dumped without authority inside a strip cell, where he was left naked overnight. The appeal reached the House of Lords as a striking-out application by the Home Office, which claimed that no cause of action for false imprisonment arose at the suit of a prisoner as against the prison authorities. The Court of Appeal had dismissed the Home Office's application, holding that the facts disclosed a 'clearly arguable case' of false imprisonment.[37] Accordingly, the two conjoined appeals raised two key questions: first, whether a breach of the Prison Rules could in any circumstance give rise to a claim for breach of statutory duty; secondly, whether a prisoner who was otherwise lawfully in prison could sue for false imprisonment in respect of an allegedly unlawful confinement.

Breach of Statutory Duty

2.37 Before *Ex p Hague* reached the House of Lords, a prisoner seeking to pursue a private law action for breach of the Prison Rules faced two Court of Appeal decisions which held that no such claim could be entertained by the courts. *Arbon v Anderson*[38] and *Becker v Home Office*[39] were both cases which reflected a judicial approach to prisoners' rights which today is almost unrecognizable. The common theme in the judgments of Lord Goddard in *Arbon* and Lord Denning in *Becker* was the fear that prison discipline would be fatally undermined if governors and prison officers had to perform their duties with the fear of legal action hanging over their heads.

2.38 The subsequent evolution of administrative law and decisions in the prison context such as *Ex p St Germain*,[40] *Ex p Tarrant*,[41] and *Ex p Leech*[42] destroyed the validity of this approach, and so the fact that both *Arbon* and *Becker* were approved by the House of Lords in *Ex p Hague* seems, at first sight, to mark a reversal of the *Raymond v Honey*[43] principle that prisoners retain all civil rights save those which

---

[36] The judgment of the Court of Appeal in *Ex p Hague* is at [1992] 1 AC 102.
[37] The judgment of the Court of Appeal in *Weldon v Home Office* is at [1992] 1 AC 130.
[38] [1943] KB 252.
[39] [1972] 2 QB 407. For an excellent critique of this decision, see AM Tettenborn, 'Prisoners' Rights' [1980] PL 74. Note however that the author wrongly states that the claimant in *Cobbett v Grey* (1850) 4 Exch 729 succeeded in his action and that the judgment of Denman J was reversed on appeal in *Osborne v Milman* (1886) 17 QBD 514.
[40] [1979] QB 425.
[41] [1985] QB 251.
[42] [1988] 1 AC 533.
[43] [1983] 1 AC 1.

are taken away by express statutory provision or by necessary implication from the fact of imprisonment. In fact no such reversal has occurred. Lords Bridge and Jauncey (who gave the main speeches in *Ex p Hague/Weldon v Home Office*) approached the question whether existing prison legislation gave rise to a cause of action for breach of statutory duty as, conventionally, one of legislative intention. Reviewing the leading authorities from *Groves v Lord Wimborne*[44] to *P v Liverpool Daily Post and Echo Newspapers PLC*[45] in the light of the provisions in rule 43 (now rule 45) designed to protect prisoners from unwarranted solitary confinement, Lord Jauncey concluded that the fact that a particular statutory provision was intended to protect certain individuals was not of itself sufficient to confer private law rights of action upon them. Something more was required to show that the legislature intended such conferment, namely some express reference enabling regulations to be made enforceable by a private law cause of action such as is to be found in s 76(2) of the Factories Act 1961.[46]

Lord Bridge, in similar vein, rejected the argument advanced on behalf of Hague   **2.39** that the 'ground rule' for ascertaining whether a claimant has a cause of action for breach of statutory duty is whether he belongs to a class of persons which the particular provision was intended to protect and has suffered damage in consequence of a breach of the duty of the kind from which the provision was intended to protect him—in Hague's case the requirement that only the governor of the prison in which he is located (and not the transferring governor) may decide to place him in rule 43 (now rule 45) segregation in the interests of good order or discipline. In Lord Bridge's view, such an approach was fallacious in the context of existing prison legislation, which differed fundamentally from, for example, the Factories Acts, where the sole purpose of the statutory duties imposed was to protect various persons from the risk of personal injury. The Prison Act 1952 was concerned with the management and administration of both prisons and prisoners and covered a wide range of matters wholly unconnected with the protection of prisoners from personal injury. Accordingly it was impossible to conclude that Parliament had intended to confer private law rights of action in respect of any of the matters covered by the Prison Rules.[47]

---

[44] [1898] 2 QB 402.

[45] [1991] 2 AC 370.

[46] In his stimulating article 'Liability in Tort for Breach of Statutory Duty' [1984] LQR 204, RA Buckley concluded that '[t]he fiction that liability depends exclusively on legislative intention should finally be abandoned. The courts should recognise that the decision whether or not to grant a civil action is ultimately one of policy for them.'

[47] In an article which retains its originality today, 'The Prison Rules and the Courts' [1981] Crim LR 602, Graham Zellick advocated an approach to the Prison Rules which divided them into five categories: rules of general policy objectives; rules of a discretionary nature; rules of general protection; rules as to institutional structure and administrative functions; and, finally, rules of specific individual protection including those dealing with discipline and segregation. Prof Zellick was writing before the 'new approach' signalled by *Raymond v Honey* and he was concerned to identify those

2.40 In one potentially important respect Lord Bridge and Lord Jauncey differed in their analysis. Lord Jauncey accepted the Home Office submission that the rule-making power contained in s 47 of the Prison Act did not authorize the creation of any private law rights in prisoners and thus any rule which expressly sought to do so would be ultra vires. Lord Bridge disagreed. In his view the power conferred by s 47, with its express reference to the creation of rules for the 'treatment' of prisoners, was broad enough to cover the enactment of rules providing a cause of action for breach of statutory duty. None of the existing rules, including rule 43 (now rule 45), did so provide but Lord Bridge's analysis leaves open the possibility of an amendment to the Rules without the need for fresh primary legislation. The vires point remains moot, however, since Lords Ackner, Goff, and Lowry stated that they agreed with both Lords Bridge and Jauncey without expressing any view on the specific issue which divided them.

False Imprisonment

2.41 Before *Hague/Weldon* reached the House of Lords there was no modern authority in which a prisoner had successfully sued the Home Office for damages for false imprisonment.[48] Indeed there were several which held that no such claim could be

---

rules whose breach should ipso facto entitle a prisoner to redress in the courts in the wake of Lord Denning's assertion of non-justiciability in *Becker v Home Office*. It was argued before the House of Lords in *Ex p Hague* that Prof Zellick's fifth category was a sensible basis for permitting a claim for damages for breach of statutory duty in some case of breaches of the Prison Rules. As he said, these rules 'are so concrete and precise in nature that it is inconceivable that any latitude should be left to the authorities in their implementation. Strict compliance goes hand in hand with judicial oversight.'

[48] A number of 19th century cases had suggested that a false imprisonment claim could be sustained by an otherwise lawfully imprisoned prisoner; see *Osborne v Angle* (1835) 2 Scott 500; *Yorke v Chapman* (1839) 10 Ad 38, E 210; *Cobbett v Grey* (1850) 4 Exch 729; *Osborne v Milman* (1887) 18 QBD 471. In *Hague/Weldon* these were described as cases which 'depended upon the strict classification of prisoners at the time and the statutory requirements as to where they should be confined dependent upon their classification' (*per* Lord Jauncey). The terms of s 12(1) of the Prison Act 1952 with its reference to the Home Secretary's power to confine a prisoner 'in any prison' demonstrated, according to Lord Jauncey, 'how different is the position today to that which prevailed in the 19th century'. It is submitted, with great respect, that this supposed difference is not soundly based. *Cobbett*, for example, did not turn on a simple statutory provision requiring prisoners in a particular class to be confined and only confined within a particular defined place. The 1842 Act in question simply required prisoners in the Queen's Prison to be divided into seven classes and empowered the Secretary of State to make separate rules for each class of prisoners and 'as far as the construction of the prison will allow thereof, prisoners of each class shall be separated from each other'. Debtors could be and were throughout the 19th century (and into the 20th) lawfully detained in prisons which also housed criminals—the Queen's Prison housed criminal prisoners as well as debtors. The issue in *Cobbett* was: on the assumption that Cobbett was confined in the 'right place', ie within a prison to which he could lawfully be sent, was there proof that he had been treated lawfully within the 'place'? The majority of the Court of Exchequer accepted that a breach of the Rules (ie a failure to satisfy the court that Cobbett had been dealt with in accordance with the Rules applicable to him) would give rise to an action for false imprisonment.

pursued.[49] In this sense *Hague/Weldon* did not represent a step backwards from the point of view of prisoners.

The House of Lords did, however, close the door on one potential basis for a false **2.42** imprisonment claim stemming from the decision of the Court of Appeal in *Middleweek v Chief Constable of Merseyside*,[50] namely one based on an allegation that the conditions of confinement were 'intolerable'. Current British prison conditions do not make such a claim remote or fanciful, and since false imprisonment carries with it the right to trial by jury, the ability to pursue such a remedy was potentially of some significance.

The facts of *Hague/Weldon* neatly raised two possible bases for a false imprison- **2.43** ment claim on the part of an otherwise lawfully detained prisoner. In *Hague* it was alleged that his segregation at Wormwood Scrubs, in breach of rule 43 (now rule 45) and in conditions identical to those on punishment, deprived him of his 'residual liberty' within the prison to associate with fellow prisoners and to have access to his possessions which he was entitled to retain unless deprived of it by a lawful order. He alleged that this wrongful interference with his residual liberty constituted the tort of false imprisonment. It was never argued that Hague was entitled to leave prison altogether, merely that his detention was tortious and gave rise to a claim for damages.[51]

Weldon's claim involved an allegation both that his detention in the strip cell **2.44** infringed his residual liberty and that his conditions of confinement in the strip cell were 'intolerable'. The idea that prisoners retained a 'residual liberty', the wrongful infringement of which might sound in damages, had received the

---

[49] See *Williams v Home Office (No 2)* [1981] 1 All ER 1211 and *R v Board of Visitors of Gartree Prison, ex p Sears*, The Times, 20 March 1985.

[50] Now reported as a Note at [1992] 1 AC 179. The 'intolerable conditions' analysis had been foreshadowed in an earlier decision, *R v Commissioner of Police for the Metropolis, ex p Nahar*, The Times, 28 May 1983, which arose from the conditions of confinement of two remand prisoners in police cells under the provisions of the Imprisonment (Temporary Provisions) Act 1980. *Nahar* was an application for habeas corpus. Stephen Brown J refused the applications but expressed the view that 'there must be some minimum standard to render detention lawful'. In *Middleweek* the Court of Appeal built on this approach and Ackner LJ said that 'it must be possible to conceive of hypothetical cases in which the conditions of detention are so intolerable as to render the detention unlawful and thereby provide a remedy to the prisoner in damages for false imprisonment. A person lawfully detained in a prison cell would, in our judgment, cease to be so lawfully detained if the conditions in that cell were such as to be so seriously prejudicial to his health if he continued to occupy it eg because it became and remained seriously flooded or contained a fractured gas pipe allowing gas to escape into the cell. We do not therefore accept as an absolute proposition that if detention is initially lawful it can never become unlawful by reason of changes in the conditions of confinement.' In *Hague/Weldon* Lord Ackner described his dictum as 'erroneous'.

[51] It was argued that just as in the Canadian case of *Cardinal and Oswald v Director of Kent Institution*, 24 DLR (4th) 44 the prisoner successfully sought habeas corpus with certiorari in aid to secure his release from the 'dissociation unit' into the general population of the prison, it was not necessary to hold that the availability of a remedy in damages for false imprisonment necessarily meant that a prisoner could achieve complete freedom from any kind of restraint.

support of Ralph Gibson LJ in his judgment in *Weldon* in the Court of Appeal.[52] Recognizing the need to define the nature of a prisoner's residual liberty, he held that the Prison Rules indicated the extent to which a prisoner may enjoy some freedom of movement within the prison, together with access to his permitted possessions and association with other prisoners. In his view, the Rules may be regarded as the detailed provisions designed to achieve the purpose stated in rule 1 ('encourage and assist to lead a good and useful life') and rule 2(1) ('treatment designed to encourage self-respect and sense of personal responsibility'). Against this background he concluded that:

> There is no reason apparent to me why the nature of the tort [of false imprison-ment], evolved by the common law for the protection of personal liberty, should be held to be such as to deny its availability to a convicted prisoner, whose residual lib-erty should, in my view, be protected so far as the law can properly achieve unless statute requires otherwise.[53]

Both the residual liberty ground and the intolerable conditions ground were rejected by the House of Lords. Lord Bridge expressed the view that to talk of 'residual liberty' as a species of freedom within prison enjoyed as a legal right which cannot lawfully be restrained by the prison authorities was 'quite illusory' since:

> The prisoner is at all times lawfully restrained within closely defined bounds and if he is kept in a segregated cell at a time when, if the rules had not been misapplied, he would be in the company of other prisoners . . . this is not the deprivation of his lib-erty of movement, which is the essence of the tort of false imprisonment, it is the substitution of one form of restraint for another.[54]

So far as the intolerable conditions ground was concerned, the House of Lords held that an otherwise lawful detention, such as committal to prison, could not be rendered unlawful by the fact that the conditions of confinement were intolerable partly because such a concept was too imprecise and partly also because, in the words of Lord Jauncey:

> a prisoner at any time has no liberty to be in any place other than where the regime permits [and so] he has no liberty capable of deprivation by the regime so as to con-stitute the tort of false imprisonment. An alteration of his conditions therefore deprives him of no liberty because he has none already.[55]

Accordingly the case of *Middleweek*, in so far as it suggested otherwise, was wrongly decided. The issue which concerned the Court of Appeal in *Weldon*,

---

[52] [1992] 1 AC 130.

[53] ibid, 139 D.

[54] ibid, 163 C.

[55] [1992] 1 AC 130, 177E. The same conclusion has been reached by the ECtHR in *Ashingdane v UK* Series A No 93 (1985) 7 EHRR 528 and following cases. The ECtHR has held that Art 5 does not apply to the conditions or type of detention: Art 5 deals only with the initial decision to detain. Prison conditions claims must therefore be brought under Art 3 of the Convention. *Ashingdane* rep-resents a major hurdle for claims to procedural rights in, for example, the security categorization process (see further Ch 4).

namely a concern to ensure that a prisoner held captive by a fellow prisoner (as happened for example during the Strangeways disturbance) should be entitled to sue for false imprisonment, also concerned the House of Lords. They dealt with it by distinguishing the Home Office's authority totally to restrain a prisoner's freedom of movement, derived from s 12(1) of the Prison Act, from that of a prisoner 'imprisoning' a fellow prisoner who had no such authority. Lacking the statutory defence provided by s 12(1), a prisoner or any other person would be liable in the ordinary way for false imprisonment. The quality of a prisoner's already attenuated liberty thus depends on the identity of the person who unlawfully attenuates or abuses it further!

False Imprisonment and Vicarious Liability

This led Lord Bridge to a somewhat startling conclusion, namely that a prison **2.45** officer who acts in bad faith by deliberately subjecting a prisoner to a restraint which he knows he has no authority to impose may render himself personally liable to an action for false imprisonment as well as committing the tort of misfeasance in public office. According to Lord Bridge, such an officer, lacking the authority of the governor, also lacks the protection of s 12(1) of the Prison Act, and by deliberately acting outside the scope of his authority 'he cannot render the governor or the Home Office vicariously liable for his tortious conduct'. This analysis therefore left open the possibility of actions for false imprisonment being pursued by prisoners, but only against fellow prisoners or individual prison officers in respect of whose actions no vicarious liability may attach to the Home Office.[56] But on this latter issue, Lord Bridge's remarks must now be read subject to the decision of the House of Lords in *Racz v Home Office*[57] where it was pointed out that bad faith was not expressly alleged in *Weldon* nor was the vicarious liability of the Home Office in issue. According to Lord Jauncey in *Racz*, Lord Bridge had been 'merely seeking to exemplify situations in which the Home Office might not be responsible for the actions of prison officers but was certainly not intending to lay down any general principle of law relevant to a matter which had never been argued before the House'.[58] Arguments about vicarious liability apart, it necessarily follows from the reasoning in *Weldon* that so long as a prison officer is acting within the scope of his authority neither he personally nor the Home Office can be successfully sued in false imprisonment because of the absolute protection provided by s 12 of the Prison Act.[59]

---

[56] [1992] 1 AC 130, 164D.

[57] [1994] 2 AC 45.

[58] ibid.

[59] s 12, however, only protects the Home Office from false imprisonment claims for the lawful length of a prisoner's sentence. In *R v Governor of HM Prison Brockhill, ex p Evans (No 2)* [2001] 2 AC 19 the House of Lords upheld the Court of Appeal's award of £5,000 damages for 59 days' loss of liberty where the applicant had been held in prison after her lawful release date because of an

2.46 These issues were revisited by the Court of Appeal in *Toumia v Evans*.[60] The claimant, a prisoner serving a life sentence, brought an action in false imprisonment and misfeasance against the defendant prison officer, sued as a representative of the Prison Officers' Association. He argued that he was locked in his cell without food on a morning when members of the Prison Officers' Association held a meeting, in the absence of which he would have been let out for breakfast and other activities. He argued that the officers' refusal to let him out of his cell was in contravention of orders, was without the governor's authority, and therefore constituted a false imprisonment. The defendant applied to have the action struck out, relying on *Hague/Weldon* in support of the proposition that a lawfully detained prisoner could not bring an action for false imprisonment. The Court of Appeal (Brooke and Clarke LJJ) refused to strike the action out, holding that such an action against a prison officer had not been ruled out by the House of Lords:

> In our judgment, it is at least arguable in the light of these dicta[61] that a prison officer who deliberately locks a prisoner in his cell contrary to the orders of the governor will be guilty of the tort of false imprisonment. In Lord Jauncey's words, he would be depriving the prisoner of such liberty as is permitted to him by the prison regime, and as Lord Bridge put it, he would be acting in bad faith by deliberately subjecting the prisoner to a restraint which he knew he had no authority to impose. Whether bad faith is relevant to the tort of false imprisonment (which we doubt) is not a question which arises for decision on this appeal, but if it is, it is at least arguable that a prison officer who acted in such a way would be acting in bad faith for the reasons given by Lord Bridge.[62]

Negligence

2.47 Negligence is a tort (a civil wrong) and has been described as 'the failure to exercise that care which the circumstances demand'.[63] What amounts to negligence will vary according to the facts of any given case. It can consist in failing to do something which ought to be done or in doing something which ought to be done either in a different manner or not at all. Where there is no duty to exercise care, the fact that a person may be said to have acted carelessly has no legal consequence.

---

erroneous interpretation of the Criminal Justice Act 1967. This is a particularly strong decision, since the governor in question was acting on an interpretation of the legislation given by the courts. However, their Lordships considered that the fact that the governor had acted in accordance with the law as it was (wrongly) thought to be at the time was no defence, since false imprisonment is a tort of strict liability. This judgment is of huge significance, given the complexity of calculating release dates and the potentially large numbers of prisoners who spend longer in prison than is lawful.

[60] Judgment of 12 March 1999, [1999] All ER (D) 262.
[61] The court had set out the dicta of Lord Bridge in *Hague/Weldon* at 164A–E, and of Lord Jauncey at 178E.
[62] para 43.
[63] *Halsbury's Laws of England* (4th edn, London, 1997), vol 33, para 601.

Where, however, there is a duty to exercise care, reasonable care must be taken to avoid acts or omissions which can be reasonably foreseen to be likely to cause injury to persons or property. Negligence, in order to give a cause of action, must be the neglect of some duty owed to the person who makes the claim—'negligence in the air will not do'.[64] The degree of care required in a particular case will vary according to the amount of risk to be encountered and to the magnitude of the prospective injury.

There is no general duty of care to prevent a third party from causing injury **2.48**
to another by the third party's own deliberate wrongdoing. There are, however, special circumstances where the law does impose an affirmative duty of care to prevent a third party from injuring others. One such example is where a special relationship exists between a person and a third party by virtue of which that person is responsible for controlling the third party.[65] This has some significance in the context of prison life, where the Home Office has complete control over and responsibility for the actions of prisoners in its custody.

The prison authorities owe a common law duty of care to prisoners to take rea- **2.49**
sonable care for their safety.[66] A breach of that duty may arise in a wide range of circumstances. The most common instances will be where a prisoner suffers injury either:

(1) as the direct result of the negligence of prison staff (for example prison medical staff);[67] or

(2) as a result of being required to work with dangerous equipment or in conditions injurious to health;[68] or

---

[64] *Haynes v Harwood* [1935] 1 KB 146, per Greer LJ.

[65] See *Home Office v Dorset Yacht Co Ltd* [1970] AC 1004 and *Smith v Littlewoods* [1987] AC 241.

[66] *Ellis v Home Office* [1953] 2 All ER 149, CA, 154, and more recently *Palmer v Home Office*, The Guardian, 31 March 1988, CA.

[67] See, however, *Knight v Home Office* [1990] 3 All ER 237, in which Pill J held that the standard of care provided for a mentally ill prisoner detained in a prison hospital was not required to be as high as the standard of care provided in a psychiatric hospital outside prison since psychiatric and prison hospitals performed different functions and the duty of care had to be tailored to the act and function to be performed. Garland J specifically refused to follow *Knight*—without overruling it— in the context of maternity care in *Brooks v Home Office* [1999] 2 FLR 33. Garland J rejected the claimant's case on the facts, but also rejected the Home Office argument that *Knight* was authority for the proposition that a pregnant woman in prison is not entitled to the same standard of care as one at liberty. All pregnant women are entitled to the same high standard of care, regardless of whether or not they are serving a prison sentence.

[68] *Pullen v Prison Commissioners* [1957] 3 All ER 470 and see also *Ferguson v Home Office*, The Times, 8 October 1977, in which a prisoner recovered £15,000 when his hand was badly mutilated as a result of inadequate instruction by prison staff in the use of a circular saw.

(3) as a result of the actions of fellow prisoners in circumstances where there was a failure to provide reasonable supervision or protection against such injury;[69] or

(4) as a result of defective or dangerous premises;[70] or

(5) as a result of being detained in 'intolerable conditions'.[71]

These examples are merely factual variations of the application of the general duty of care to prison life. In most negligence claims the problem is not in establishing the existence of the duty of care but rather in demonstrating that the action (or inaction) of prison staff fell below the standard of care which the law imposes upon them and that the injury in question was the reasonably foreseeable consequence of the breach of duty. Thus in negligence claims arising from an assault by a fellow prisoner, the courts have demonstrated a marked reluctance to impose too rigid a constraint on a governor's discretion to permit prisoners known or believed to be dangerous to mix freely with other prisoners and even to have access to potentially lethal weapons. In *Palmer v Home Office*,[72] for example, the claimant was stabbed in the stomach by a fellow prisoner who had been convicted of three murders as well as other serious offences of violence and who had been allowed to work in the tailor's workshop, where he had access to scissors. It was conceded in evidence by a governor grade officer that the assailant was 'very dangerous to anybody in the prison, staff and inmates'. None the less Neill LJ refused to characterize the decision to permit him to work in the tailor's shop as negligent, stating that:

> Those in charge of prisoners have a difficult task. Clearly, except in extreme cases, of which obviously there are some, those responsible for prisons cannot keep prisoners

---

[69] There are several examples of this kind of action including *D'Arcy v Prison Commissioners*, The Times, 17 November 1955, where damages of £190 were awarded to a prisoner in respect of an assault by fellow prisoners; *Egerton v Home Office* [1978] Crim LR 494; *Porterfield v Home Office*, The Independent, 9 March 1988; *Palmer v Home Office*, The Guardian, 31 March 1988; *Steele v Northern Ireland Office* (1988) 12 NIJB 1; *H v Home Office*, The Independent, 6 May 1992, CA; *Thompson v Home Office* [2001] EWCA Civ 331, The Independent, 16 March 2001. The European Committee for the Prevention of Torture has stressed that 'the duty of care which is owed by the prison authorities to prisoners in their charge includes the responsibility to protect them from other prisoners who might wish to cause them harm', and has recommended that 'current strategies to combat inter-prisoner violence be vigorously pursued, and that means of rendering them more effective be pursued': see *Report to the Government to the United Kingdom on the visit to the United Kingdom carried out by the European Committee for the Prevention of Torture and Inhuman or Degrading Treatment or Punishment from 4 to 16 February 2001*, paras 50–51.

[70] *Christofi v Home Office*, The Times, 31 July 1975, where a prisoner recovered damages for injuries caused by a fall on a broken step.

[71] Despite the dictum of Lord Bridge in *Hague/Weldon* [1992] 1 AC 58, 165H, which suggests that the basic principles of the tort of negligence might be stretched to accommodate a negligence action by a prisoner who suffers 'intolerable discomfort' as a result of detention in 'intolerable conditions', the better view is that unless a prisoner can prove some physical or mental injury ('nervous shock') he will not have a cause of action in negligence; see also *Calveley v Chief Constable of Merseyside* [1989] 1 AC 1228 and *Hicks v Chief Constable of South Yorkshire* [1992] 2 All ER 65.

[72] The Guardian, 31 March 1998.

permanently locked up or segregated from other prisoners. In addition it is necessary, or certainly desirable wherever possible, to provide suitable employment for
individual prisoners.

In *Thompson v Home Office*,[73] a prisoner who had been attacked with a razor blade **2.50**
by another inmate in HM Young Offenders Institution Swinfen Hall sued for
negligence. The Home Office argued that there had been no breach of duty, since
the system for issuing razor blades in Swinfen Hall at the time was reasonable, and
that the claimant had not proved causation. May LJ emphasized that 'prison governors, and especially those in charge of Young Offenders Institutions, have to
make balancing judgments between tight security and a regime aimed at rehabilitation in which the inmates are allowed to exercise responsibility.'[74] The court did
not consider that any deficiencies in the system would have caused the claimant's
injuries. This meant that, in order to succeed, he would have to show that the system itself was negligently adopted. On the facts, this high threshold had not been
met by the claimant.[75] This approach (the 'Hannibal Lecter' test, perhaps) reveals
an obvious and difficult conflict between a liberal, rehabilitative approach towards
all prisoners, even violent ones, and the desire to ensure that prisoners who are
injured while in prison through no fault of their own are not left without a remedy. This latter point is particularly important when it is remembered that prisoners with convictions for violence who are injured by fellow prisoners will rarely,
if ever, be able to recover compensation from the Criminal Injuries Compensation
Authority.[76]

Article 2 of the Convention

The protective and investigative obligations imposed by this Article are discussed **2.51**
in detail below, in the context of deaths in custody. In this section, we consider the
duty to protect prisoners from harm at the hands of fellow inmates. This was

---

[73] [2001] EWCA Civ 331; The Independent, 16 March 2001.

[74] para 25.

[75] It is important to note that the Court of Appeal specifically confined their reasoning to the particular facts. It is suggested that *Thompson* clearly does not require prisoners in every such case to
prove that the relevant system within the prison was negligently adopted. The facts of *Thompson*
were that the claimant was alleging that the only injuries was the existence of an inadequate policy on the control of razor blades. In cases where there is clear evidence that a system has
been negligently operated, or, for example, that staff were inadequately deployed or were not where
they were supposed to be at the time of the assault, the issue of negligent adoption of a system would,
it is argued, not come into play.

[76] *R v Criminal Injuries Compensation Board, ex p Thompstone* [1984] 1 WLR 1234. The Court
of Appeal held that the proper question for the Board (now the Authority) to ask itself is 'is the applicant an appropriate recipient of an ex gratia compensatory payment made at the public expense?'
and that there was nothing unlawful in the Board's decision that an applicant's previous convictions
for either dishonesty or violence disentitled him to an award. It was reasonable to withhold compensation or reduce it even where the applicant's conduct, character, or way of life had no ascertainable bearing on the occurrence of the injury or its aftermath. For the position in relation to
compensation for miscarriages of justice, see *R (Mullen) v Home Secretary* [2002] 1 WLR 1857.

examined by the ECtHR in *Edwards v UK*.[77] The applicants were the parents of a mentally ill prisoner who had been murdered by a fellow prisoner, also mentally ill, in HM Prison Chelmsford. The court considered that, in failing to appreciate the vulnerability of the applicants' son and the dangerousness of the other inmate, the prison service (as well as several other authorities who had dealt with that inmate throughout the criminal justice system) had violated Article 2. Article 2 requires not only effective systems to protect prisoners' right to life from threats from accidents, fellow inmates and officers, but thorough and effective investigations into deaths in custody. It therefore places on the State a more exacting standard than the law of negligence.

Lost Property Claims

2.52 Claims for lost property allegedly mislaid due to the negligence of the prison authorities are a regular source of litigation in the county court.[78] Many of them concern items of property which are not valuable in money terms but which may be of great sentimental or symbolic importance to the prisoner concerned. The majority of these claims will have to be conducted by prisoners themselves without the benefit of public funding under the small claims procedure. Whether or not a prisoner can successfully sue the Home Office for negligence in respect of lost or stolen property will depend on the status of the property in question and its location at the time of its disappearance.

2.53 Each prisoner's property is recorded on Property Record cards or sheets upon being received into prison custody. Each time a prisoner is transferred, the Property Record should record that fact and the prisoner's confirmation that his or her property has been transferred correctly. The basic distinction is between 'stored' and 'in-possession' property.[79] At the time when property is allocated to one or other category, prisoners are routinely required to sign a reception certificate and disclaimer. The purpose of this is, first, to certify that all the stored property has been correctly recorded and securely sealed for safekeeping by the prison and, secondly, to acknowledge that the Prison Service will not accept liability for the loss of or damage to property which is kept in the prisoner's possession.

2.54 Where property which has been listed as 'stored' goes missing there is little difficulty in fixing the Home Office with liability in negligence—in practice an *ex gratia* payment will usually be made. More difficult is the question of liability for property listed as being 'in-possession' but which goes missing at a time when the prisoner had no control over it. For example, a prisoner who is subject to a sudden

---

[77] (2002) 35 EHRR 19.

[78] At the time of writing, a PSO on prisoners' property and compensation is in preparation.

[79] See rr 41–42 for the provisions governing disposal of prisoners' property. See also the Prisoners' Property Service Standard.

transfer under IG 28/93 will have no opportunity to collect together his personal possessions from his cell. Indeed, for the whole period of the transfer, he will normally be kept in rule 45 conditions with no access to his property. If, when he is eventually reunited with his possessions, he discovers that items are missing it would hardly be reasonable for the Home Office to rely on the original signed disclaimer in order to evade liability. And what of the Rolex watch which goes missing from the supposedly secure wing office while the prisoner has gone to the gym? Will a notice in the office to the effect that 'any valuables left in the staff office are left at the owner's own risk' always relieve the Home Office of liability even where an officer has agreed to look after the items in question? Surely not, at least not in circumstances where it can be established that the loss was directly attributable to some act of carelessness on the part of a member of the prison staff rather than the criminal act of a third party.[80]

Assault and Battery

There are three forms of trespass to the person—assault, battery, and false impris- **2.55** onment. Each is concerned with a different form of interference with a person's liberty. As we have seen, the tort of false imprisonment is not available to a prisoner vis-à-vis his legal custodian, the governor, because he is deemed to have lost all his freedom of movement to the State by the fact of imprisonment. By an action for assault and battery, however, a prisoner is able to define the limitations on the State's right to interfere directly with his person. It is an assertion by the prisoner of his freedom from physical molestation save in accordance with the law.

---

[80] In *Nolan v Premier Prison Services Ltd* [2002] CL 492 (Northampton County Court), various items of the claimant's personal property had gone missing when he and his possessions had been moved to the segregation unit of the prison. The claimant had signed a disclaimer at the time, but argued that this did not apply since, in the circumstances, he had been physically unable to protect his property. The respondent argued that no duty of care arose: particular latitude should be given to the prison authorities in this context. District Judge Cernik accepted that, for the purposes of establishing a duty of care, it was foreseeable that the claimant's property was at high risk of going missing, and that there was sufficient proximity between the parties to create an obligation on the prison authorities to safeguard the claimant's property. However, he considered that, despite this, it was not fair and reasonable to impose a duty of care on the prison to safeguard the claimant's property. If prisons were to be held responsible for such losses, which occur frequently, the eventual effect would be to restrict the amount of property which prisoners are allowed to have. This is a very regrettable decision, which responds to the frequency of violation of prisoners' property rights by refusing any remedy. The assumption that the prison service would respond to judicial scrutiny of their care of prisoners' possessions by restricting the right rather than improving systems of protection may or may not be correct, but does not, it is submitted, provide any convincing reason for leaving prisoners without redress. Just as the undisputed duty of care to take reasonable care of prisoners has not led to a flood of negligence claims, so a duty of reasonable care towards their property ought not to prove too onerous. In any event, institutional issues can be dealt with at the stage of considering what is reasonable in the circumstances, rather than by the blunt instrument of refusing to impose any duty of care.

2.56 A battery is the actual infliction of unlawful force on another person, whereas an assault is an act which causes another person to apprehend the infliction of immediate, unlawful force on his person.[81] Thus, if force is actually applied, directly or indirectly, unlawfully or without the consent of the person assaulted, the assault becomes a battery however slight the force. In popular language the term 'assault' includes a 'battery' though a person may be guilty of an assault without being guilty of a battery.

2.57 An intention to injure is not a necessary ingredient of a battery. The deliberate use of force against another will not always amount to a battery. Apart from special justifications, such as self-defence, there are numerous examples in ordinary life where an intended contact or touching is not actionable as a trespass. These are not limited to those occasions where consent is actual or reasonably to be implied—such as shaking hands. They include the ordinary 'collisions' of everyday life, such as the knocking and pushing which occur in, for example, a crowded underground train. In this context it has been suggested that a hostile intent is not the crucial determinant of the existence of a battery but, rather, 'whether an absence of consent on the part of the plaintiff can be inferred'.[82] An unintentional trespass cannot, it would seem, be pursued by an action for assault and battery, but instead as a claim for negligence with proof of a want of reasonable care by the person who has caused injury.[83]

2.58 The circumstances in which force may be used by prison officers against prisoners are dealt with elsewhere. Suffice it to say that a claim for assault and battery may arise in the following circumstances:

(1) where a prisoner is deliberately attacked either by fellow prisoners or by staff;

(2) where excessive force is used to carry out an otherwise lawful order, such as forcibly removing a prisoner to the segregation unit following an order made pursuant to rule 45;[84]

---

[81] *Collins v Wilcock* [1984] 1 WLR 1172 and see also *Wilson v Pringle* [1987] QB 237.

[82] See eg *F v West Berkshire Health Authority* [1990] 2 AC 1.

[83] *Fowler v Lanning* [1959] 1 QB 426 and *Letang v Cooper* [1965] 1 QB 232.

[84] The use of control and restraint methods to force a prisoner to a segregation unit will only be justifiable if the prisoner is resisting such removal. In the case of *Russell v Home Office*, Daily Telegraph, 13 March 2001, three prisoners who escaped from the Special Secure Unit at HM Prison Whitemoor—whose escape was the subject of the Woodcock Report—sued for damages for excessive force used to recapture them. Crane J noted that '[s]ome people may take the view that if a group of armed prisoners escape from a prison, they should not be entitled to complain about any violence to them in the course of their recapture' (para 16). He made clear that the security category of the prisoner and the gravity of his or her criminal record is relevant to the degree of force which it is reasonable to use to recapture them (para 165). However, he also found that several of the prison officers' actions amounted to unlawful force (and degrading treatment or punishment, contrary to Art 3 of the Convention), in particular baton blows to the head of one of the claimants and the failure to provide prompt medical treatment. The court awarded aggravated damages, but held that exemplary damages were not appropriate, given the background to the assaults.

(3) where force is used to execute an unlawful order, for example the unauthorized, forcible removal of a prisoner to a strip cell by officers below the rank of senior officer or the imposition of a restraint without proper authority;[85]

(4) where a restraint is imposed for too long, ie after a prisoner has ceased to be a danger to himself or others.[86]

Aggravated and Exemplary Damages

A claimant who succeeds in a claim for an assault carried out by prison staff or for **2.59** misfeasance in a public office may be entitled to an award of aggravated and exemplary damages.[87] Aggravated damages are part of the award of compensatory damages. Their effect is to increase the level of damages above what would otherwise have been recovered, and they arise where the manner of commission of the tort 'was such as to injure the plaintiff's proper feelings of dignity and pride'.[88] As with claims against the police for assault, false imprisonment, and malicious prosecution, in which aggravated damages are frequently awarded, the circumstances in which a prisoner finds himself under attack from prison officers are likely to heighten his sense of injury or humiliation. From the defendant's perspective it appears that aggravated damages are designed to punish, but strictly they are made to compensate the claimant's injured feelings. Where a claimant has himself been guilty of some form of reprehensible conduct, this may be reflected in a reduced or nil award of aggravated damages.[89]

It is by an award of exemplary or punitive damages that the court is able to teach **2.60** the defendant that 'tort does not pay'. In effect the award of exemplary damages sends out a message to others and is meant to act as a deterrent against further

---

[85] Where there is no lawful justification for a prisoner's removal to a segregation unit or strip cell then all force used will be actionable as an assault. In this situation the prisoner who resists and is subjected to greater force in order to enforce an illegal segregation order will be in a better position than the prisoner who 'goes quietly', as a result of the decision in *Hague/Weldon* which holds that unlawful segregation does not, of itself, gives rise to a cause of action unless malice or conscious abuse of power can be established.

[86] *Rodrigues v Home Office*, February 1989 *LAG Bulletin* 14.

[87] For a comprehensive analysis of the law on aggravated and exemplary damages as well as proposals for reform, see Law Commission Report 247, *Aggravated, Exemplary and Restitutionary Damages* (HC 346, 1997).

[88] *Clerk and Lindsell on Torts* (17th edn, London, 1995), paras 27–66.

[89] *O'Connor v Hewitson* [1979] Crim LR 46. In *Russell v Home Office*, n84 above, the claimants argued that, despite the fact that they had been injured while escaping from prison, Art 3 of the Convention entitled them to aggravated and exemplary damages. They argued that the obligation under the Convention to ensure effective deterrence against inhuman and degrading treatment created an obligation on the State to enforce criminal sanctions against those who perpetrate such treatment. If, as in this case, no criminal proceedings were brought, the State should be penalized by the award of exemplary damages in civil proceedings brought by the victim. Crane J did not accept this, taking into account the claimants' conduct and the fact that the authorities had acted perfectly properly in having the matter investigated, albeit that a lack of evidence prevented the bringing of criminal charges (paras 204–205).

abuse of power. Exemplary damages may not be awarded in every case of tortious conduct, but only in those categories of cases identified in Lord Devlin's speech in *Rookes v Barnard*.[90] One such category includes 'oppressive, arbitrary or unconstitutional conduct by the servants of the Government', and this plainly includes members of the Prison Service. In *Burke v Home Office*,[91] a prisoner who was subjected to a quasi-sexual assault by prison staff in the aftermath of a riot at Brixton prison in April 1990 was awarded £12,000 in exemplary damages. A factor in the judge's award was that despite an extensive inquiry, no member of staff had admitted being involved in removing the claimant under control and restraint to the segregation unit (where the assault occurred), demonstrating a clear, organized attempt to cover up wrongdoing.

Misfeasance in Public Office[92]

2.61 A finding that a public body has been guilty of maladministration does not ordinarily give rise to any liability to pay damages at common law.[93] Where an unlawful administrative act involves the commission of a tort such as negligence, trespass, or nuisance then a private law claim for damages may arise on ordinary

---

[90] [1964] AC 1129. See also *Cassell v Broome* [1972] AC 1027. Actions which may be characterized as violent, cruel, threatening, or abusive will normally be regarded as 'oppressive or arbitrary' and, if there is evidence of such conduct, the issue of exemplary damages will be at large; see eg *Holden v Chief Constable of Lancashire* [1987] QB 380. The cause of action test formulated by the Court of Appeal in *AB v SW Water Services Ltd* [1993] QB 507 restricted the availability of exemplary damages to those causes of action for which exemplary damages had been awarded before *Rookes v Barnard*. In a detailed review of the law on exemplary damages, the House of Lords in *Kuddus v Chief Constable of Leicestershire* [2001] 2 WLR 1789 considered that this limitation was not justified. Lord Slynn stated that, 'I do not consider that the House is bound by a clear or unequivocal decision in *Broome v Cassell* [1972] AC 1027 to hold that the power to award exemplary damages is limited to cases where it can be shown that the cause of action had been recognised before 1964 as justifying an award of exemplary damages . . . I do not consider that in principle it should be so limited. In any event . . . I do not consider that courts should be required to undertake a trawl of the authorities in order to decipher whether awards of damages for misfeasance pre-1964 might have included an award for exemplary damages' (paras 21–22). Their Lordships questioned the desirability of awarding exemplary damages in cases where liability is vicarious—as will generally be the case in claims against the Home Office relating to the actions of prison officers—but did not rule on the issue. Exemplary damages are therefore still available in cases of vicarious liability. In *Russell v Home Office*, Crane J considered the relationship between Art 3 of the Convention and domestic law damages principles. For guidance on the level of exemplary damages appropriate in claims against the police for assault, false imprisonment, and malicious prosecution, see *Thompson v Commissioner of Police for the Metropolis* [1998] QB 498. There is no reason for different principles to apply to claims against prison staff in assault and misfeasance in a public office.

[91] [1996] CL 2160.

[92] The *Oxford English Dictionary* defines misfeasance as 'a transgression, trespass . . . the wrongful exercise of lawful authority or improper performance of a lawful act'.

[93] As Lord Woolf MR commented in *W v Home Office* [1997] Imm AR 302, '[i]n fact it is because there is no liability to pay damages for maladministration in the ordinary way that the Central and Local Government Ombudsmen are required to investigate maladministration and, where they find a complaint proved, to exercise their discretion as to whether to recommend the payment of compensation'.

principles. But what of the situation where a person holding a public office, such as a member of the Prison Service, commits a deliberate abuse of power without being liable in negligence (for want of inflicting personal injury) or without committing an act of trespass? An opportunity to recover damages in the event of such unlawful action is afforded by the tort of misfeasance in a public office. In *Dunlop v Woollahra Municipal Council*[94] Lord Diplock referred to misfeasance in public office as a 'well-established tort' and the existence of the tort was recognized by the Appellate Committee in *Jones v Swansea City Council*.[95] Until recently, there were very few examples of such claims being pursued through the English courts.[96] However, misfeasance has gained a new lease of life in recent years in a wide variety of civil claims against public authorities, particularly the police. Its importance as a remedy to prisoners has been reinforced by the decision of the House of Lords in *Hague/Weldon*, where it was expressly identified as the appropriate remedy for certain forms of unlawful action by prison staff.

In neither *Hague* nor *Weldon* was misfeasance in public office directly in issue by **2.62** the time the case reached the House of Lords. Hague had included a claim for damages for misfeasance in public office (as well as for false imprisonment and breach of statutory duty) in his application for judicial review of the compendious decisions to transfer and segregate him. The misfeasance claim was based on the allegation that he had been segregated deliberately for an improper motive, namely a desire to avoid the embarrassment of charging him with a disciplinary offence where he would have had an opportunity to defend himself. During a disciplinary hearing it would have become clear that prison officers had, at the very least, condoned Hague's alleged protest at the removal of exercise periods for category A prisoners at Parkhurst. The Divisional Court held that avoiding embarrassment to staff could be a proper reason not to lay a disciplinary charge and the misfeasance claim was abandoned before the Court of Appeal.

In Weldon's case it was alleged that his segregation in the strip cell had been done **2.63** maliciously (ie in bad faith) and with knowledge of the absence of authority for it by prison staff. But misfeasance had not been pleaded, only a claim for assault and false imprisonment. It is now clear that misfeasance in public office may be committed in one of two ways. A claimant must be able to prove either that a public officer has performed or omitted to perform an act with the object of injuring him (targeted malice) or that the official performed an act knowing he had no power so to do and that it would injure the claimant (recklessness being sufficient mens

---

[94] [1982] AC 158. The tort has been traced back to the reign of Henry V and includes malicious abuse of power, deliberate maladministration, and, possibly, other unlawful acts causing injury: see eg *Ashby v White* (1703) 2 Ld Raym 938.

[95] [1990] 1 WLR 1453.

[96] In Canada the tort seems better developed: see eg *Roncarelli v Duplessis* (1959) 16 DLR (2d) 689 and *McGillivray v Kimber* (1915) 26 DLR 164.

rea under this head).[97] It is thus clear that malice and the conscious abuse of power are alternative, not cumulative, requirements for the existence of the tort.

2.64 Where a claimant establishes (a) that the defendant intended to injure him or a person in a class of which he is a member (limb one) or that the defendant knew that he had no power to do what he did, or was recklessly indifferent to whether or not he had such power, and that the claimant or a person in a class of which the claimant is a member would probably suffer loss or damage (limb two) and (b) that the claimant has suffered loss as a result, the claimant has a sufficient right or interest to maintain an action for misfeasance in public office.[98]

2.65 For prisoners there will never be any difficulty in establishing that those who exercise immediate power over their lives are holding public office. All persons employed by the Prison Service, whether full time or part time, are discharging the powers of a public office while working in a prison and exercising authority over prisoners.[99] The need to prove 'damage' arises because misfeasance is a development of the action on the case.[100] It does not mean that personal injury or financial loss must be established. Rather the nature of the damage necessary to give rise to liability in misfeasance depends on the object and consequences of the power abused or unlawfully arrogated by the defendant. In most of the decided cases, including the leading decision of *Three Rivers v Bank of England,* the powers in question were intended to regulate economic interests, and accordingly the damage which completed the tort was necessarily financial. But the tort is not limited to financial interests. Indeed in *Weldon* Lords Bridge and Ackner accepted on the comparable assumed facts that prison officers who abuse their powers by impos-

---

[97] See the judgment of the House of Lords in *Three Rivers District Council v Bank of England (No 3)* [2000] 2 WLR 1220. The Committee held that the tort of misfeasance in public office involves an element of bad faith, and arises when a public officer exercises his or her power specifically intending to injure the claimant, *or* acts in the knowledge of, or reckless indifference to, the probability of causing injury to the claimant or to a class of which the claimant is a member. In relation to the second limb of the test, they made it clear that subjective recklessness—not caring whether or not the act is illegal or whether the consequences happened—is sufficient.

[98] For the purpose of establishing the requirement that the officer knew that his act would probably injure the claimant or a person in a class of which the claimant was a member, it was sufficient if the officer had actual knowledge that his act would probably damage the claimant or such a person or, in circumstances in which he believed or suspected that his act would probably damage the claimant or such a person, if he did not ascertain whether that was so or not or if he failed to make such inquiries as an honest and reasonable man would have made as to the probability of such damage. If the officer had such a state of mind, that amounted to recklessness sufficient to support liability even if it did not amount to actual knowledge.

[99] Prison officers are appointed by the Home Secretary pursuant to the Prison Act 1952, s 7(1). They have the status of Crown servants but are not engaged under a contract of employment—*R v Home Secretary, ex p Benwell* [1984] 3 All ER 854. By s 8 of the 1952 Act, prison officers while acting as such have 'all the powers, authority, protection and privileges of a constable'.

[100] *Beaurain v Scott* (1811) 3 Camp 387.

ing an unjustified restraint (in the case of Lord Ackner amounting to intolerable conditions) upon a prisoner may render themselves liable in misfeasance.[101]

Damages can be awarded to vindicate the claimant's rights, and substantial damages may be awarded for an injury to a person's dignity or for discomfort or inconvenience. A prisoner who is placed in adverse, punitive conditions of confinement maliciously or with knowledge that there is no authority for it under the Prison Rules would be able to recover damages for his experience. **2.66**

The most difficult element of the tort to prove will, of course, be the mental element of the alleged tortfeasor. Malice rarely exists on paper. It will almost always have to be inferred from other evidence. Precisely because it is so serious, the courts require cogent evidence before making a finding that someone exercising a public office has deliberately (or recklessly) inflicted injury on another. Furthermore, because the existing legislative framework vests prison officers and governors with such broad discretionary powers (for example 'to maintain good order and discipline') it will frequently be difficult to establish that an officer/governor has done something he knows is outwith his powers. Examples of such behaviour would be: a prison officer who deliberately places a prisoner in a special cell instead of an ordinary segregation cell because the ordinary cells are full up, and a governor who leaves a prisoner in segregation for more than three days without obtaining authorization from the Board of Visitors or the Secretary of State. A prison officer who fabricates a disciplinary charge resulting in wrongful conviction and punishment would also be liable in misfeasance, as would an officer who overtly condoned racial abuse carried out by prisoners.[102] **2.67**

Misfeasance and Vicarious Liability

There is now no doubt that the tort of misfeasance may give rise to vicarious liability on the part of the relevant government department on conventional principles. The elements of the tort are not inconsistent with the principle that an employer may be held responsible for the actions of an employee even where such actions are deliberate or even criminal. For a time the effectiveness of misfeasance **2.68**

---

[101] It is surely sensible that the nature of the injury/damage in respect of which damages may be awarded will depend on the nature of the power which has been abused. Where the power is the power to segregate prisoners (ie remove from normal association and access to privileges) or to place them in a special cell then damages will be designed to compensate for the deprivation and distress occasioned by the impoverished regime of segregation under r 45.

[102] *Thomas v Secretary of State for the Home Office*, 20 November 2000, CA, Otton LJ stressed that 'in order to establish a case of misfeasance in public office the Claimant has to go much further than merely proving that the prison officers having heard the racial abuse did nothing about it. They would have to commit some overt act which amounted to condonation of what was going on. The judge here found as a fact that there was no condonation and, accordingly, that is the end of the matter. It is always to be borne in mind that the other element of misfeasance in public office is that the defendant must have acted in bad faith' (para 19).

in public office as a remedy to prisoners in respect of consciously unlawful or malicious actions by prison staff had been seriously undermined by the decision of the Court of Appeal in *Racz v Home Office*.[103] The facts of the case were very similar to those in *Weldon*. Mr Racz alleged that while he was a prisoner at HM Prison Armley, in Leeds, he was assaulted by hospital officers in the hospital wing, stripped of his clothing and then dumped without authority inside a strip cell for two days, with only canvas clothing to wear. He claimed that he had to sleep on the floor with only a single blanket for warmth and that officers deliberately tipped his food on the floor and ordered him to clear it up. He sued the Home Office in assault, negligence, and misfeasance in public office. It was conceded that in respect of the two days spent in the strip cell and the associated mistreatment he could not succeed in a negligence claim since he could not prove the necessary physical or mental injury resulting from the experience.[104] Accordingly, his only remedy was in misfeasance in public office. The Home Office sought to strike out the misfeasance claim, arguing that it could not be held to be vicariously liable for a deliberate or malicious abuse of power by prison officers.

2.69   Basing itself on some remarks of Lord Bridge in *Hague/Weldon*, the Court of Appeal accepted the Home Office's argument and struck out the misfeasance claim. But on appeal the House of Lords held that Lord Bridge's remarks were obiter, and that he was not intending in any event to lay down a general principle of law to the effect that an allegation of misfeasance was inevitably inconsistent with vicarious liability, merely seeking to exemplify situations in which the Home Office might avoid liability for the wrongful acts of prison staff. The House of Lords accepted the submission that it would be a question of fact and degree in each case (only ascertainable after a trial) whether prison officers were engaged in a misguided and unauthorized method of performing their authorized duties or were engaged in what was tantamount to an unlawful frolic of their own.[105]

Misfeasance and Trial by Jury

2.70   But on the other issue raised by Racz, whether misfeasance gave rise to a right to trial by jury, the House of Lords agreed with the Court of Appeal that it did not. It had been argued that the discretion to order such mode of trial contained in the Supreme Court Act 1981, s 69(2), should be exercised in Mr Racz's favour for three reasons. First, his claim involved an allegation of arbitrary and oppressive behaviour by government servants, a matter traditionally appropriate for arbitration by judge and jury. Secondly, the possibility of an award of exemplary damages placed the claim in a category which the courts recognized as being influential in

---

[103]   The Times, 17 December 1992, CA.
[104]   See n 76 above.
[105]   [1994] 2 AC 45, HL.

the exercise of discretion under s 69(2). Finally, it was argued that a misfeasance claim was so similar to an action for malicious prosecution, where jury trial was a right, that it would be perverse to fail to exercise the court's discretion against jury trial. In effect, if the discretion was not exercised in favour of jury trial in a misfeasance claim it was hard to envisage any circumstances in which it would be appropriate to do so.

The House of Lords rejected these arguments, holding that Parliament's decision   **2.71** to retain a right to jury trial in the case of the four widely differing torts of libel, slander, malicious prosecution and false imprisonment was for historical rather than logical reasons. Thus the mere fact that misfeasance was capable of being similar to, say, malicious prosecution was not a relevant factor in determining, in the exercise of the court's discretion, whether it is appropriate to rebut the presumption against civil jury trial created by the Supreme Court Act 1981, s 69(3). As for the other factors, Lord Jauncey found no fault with the manner in which the Court of Appeal had exercised its discretion against jury trial, noting that Neill LJ considered that the case did not raise matters of constitutional importance, nor involve an allegation of grave injury or the actions of senior officials. It follows from this that Racz does not prevent future application for jury trial in cases of misfeasance. Where a claim does raise an issue of serious public interest or involve the actions of senior members of staff or where serious injury has been caused these may each be capable of rebutting the presumption against jury trial.[106]

Breach of the Bill of Rights

The Bill of Rights 1688 is a statute which prohibits the infliction of 'cruell and   **2.72** unusuall punishment'. As such it lays down a matter of fundamental importance protecting the rights and freedoms of the individual, but the statute does not specify a penalty for breach. Does a prisoner who can show that he is the victim of a 'cruell and unusuall punishment' have a private law cause of action for damages for breach of statutory duty or does his remedy lie exclusively in the public law realm? Recent authority suggests that a private law claim is highly unlikely, though the point has not been authoritatively decided.

In *Williams v Home Office (No 2)*[107] the claimant sued for damages for false impris-   **2.73** onment arising from his detention for 180 days in the notorious control unit at

---

[106] Salmond, *The Law of Torts* (15th edn). See also *General Engineering v Kingston Corporation* [1989] 1 WLR 64, 72A–G.

[107] [1981] 1 All ER 1211. The control unit regime was created against a background of widespread disruption in the prison system in 1972, the most prolific incident being a serious disturbance at Gartree Prison. A Home Office working party was set up to consider the question of control in dispersal prisons. It felt that existing segregation units were frequently inadequate to deal with certain 'hardcore, disruptive' prisoners because they were not sufficiently insulated or isolated from the main part of the prison. The working party therefore recommended that special control units be set up (in Wakefield and Wormwood Scrubs) which were physically separate and insulated from the

Wakefield Prison in 1974. A claim for breach of the Bill of Rights was not specifically pleaded (indeed counsel for the claimant expressly disavowed the existence of such a cause of action) but it was asserted that, because the control unit regime amounted to a breach of the 1688 statute, the Home Office could not seek to justify the claimant's detention by reference to rule 43 (now rule 45) of the Prison Rules or the Prison Act generally. It was submitted that the words 'cruell and unusuall' must be read disjunctively, with the result that the Act prohibits the infliction of cruel punishment and, separately, the infliction of unusual punishments. Any other reading would mean that it would be lawful to inflict a cruel punishment in present day England provided such a punishment was inflicted commonly, an absurd construction. Tudor Evans J dismissed the claim for false imprisonment (on grounds partly upheld by the House of Lords in *Hague/Weldon*), and in the process held that the Bill of Rights was clear in its meaning and showed an intention to prohibit punishments which are both cruel and unusual. On the facts he found the Wakefield regime to be neither cruel nor unusual.[108]

2.74 In *R v Home Secretary, ex p Herbage*[109] the applicant sought interlocutory relief in respect of his conditions of detention in Pentonville Prison, which he claimed amounted to the infliction of 'cruell and unusuall punishment'. He alleged that by reason of his gross obesity and resultant inability to walk more than 50 yards without resting he had been allocated a cell on the ground floor mental observation landing of the hospital wing close to severely mentally disturbed inmates. He had been held in solitary confinement there for seven months with no opportunity for exercise or association with others and the noise prevented him from sleeping. In support of his application for an injunction he claimed that he would have a private law cause of action based on a breach of the 1688 Bill. The Home Secretary submitted that the Bill of Rights did not create actionable claims either in public or private law. Herbage succeeded in obtaining leave to apply for judicial review and, when the Home Office appealed to the Court of Appeal against the grant of

main prison. Prisoners allocated to them should not come from the prison in which the unit was situated. The nature of the regime was set out in CI 35/1974 and was approved by the Secretary of State. After widespread concern about the coercive, punitive nature of the regime and its possible side-effects the units were closed down in 1975.

[108] This was a somewhat surprising conclusion. The control unit regime was divided into two stages, each intended to last 90 days. At stage one the prisoner did not associate with other prisoners save when he was allowed his one hour's exercise per day. He was not obliged to work, but if he did not he would not progress to stage two, when he would be allowed a degree of association with other prisoners during work, leisure, and education. If he failed to work during stage two or caused trouble, the prisoner reverted to stage one and was required to complete a continuous 90-day period of good behaviour before qualifying once more for stage two. If the prisoner completed a full 180–day period he would be allowed to return to normal association. Tudor Evans J said that 'judged by the standards of the English prison system, I do not think that the regime in the unit was cruel'!

[109] [1987] QB 872. The decision of the Court of Appeal is at [1987] QB 1077.

leave, there was some discussion of whether a claim based on breach of the Bill of Rights was justiciable. Purchas LJ described the prohibition on inflicting 'cruell and unusuall' punishment as:

> a fundamental right which, in my judgment, goes far beyond the ambit of the Prison Rules. For my part if it were established that a prison governor was guilty of such conduct it would be an affront to common sense that the court should not be able to afford relief under Order 53[110]. . . . Once the central issue is divested of the encumbrance of considerations of breaches of Prison Rules or duties under the Prison Act 1952 and is viewed as a case involving a breach of the Bill of Rights alone then the matter, in my judgment, becomes easier to comprehend. Two questions arise. The first is: what are the conditions in fact in which the applicant is presently detained at Pentonville? The second is: do these amount to 'cruel and unusual punishment'? By way of example, and not wishing to indicate any view of the actual conditions existing, it is generally held to be unacceptable that persons supposedly of normal mentality, should be detained in psychiatric conditions as is said to occur in certain parts of the world. Coming closer to the alleged facts of this case, if it were to be established that the applicant as a sane person was, for purely administrative purposes, being subjected in the psychiatric wing to the stress of being exposed to the disturbance caused by the behaviour of mentally ill and disturbed prisoners, this might well be considered as a 'cruel and unusual punishment' and one which was not deserved. This raises issues quite different from compliance or non-compliance with the Prison Rules although they may well involve breaches on the part of the Secretary of State of the Prison Act 1952.

The above passage is plainly not authority for the existence of a private law claim for breach of statutory duty since it was made in the context of an application for judicial review where no claim for damages was included in the relief sought. However, it is supportive of a submission that so fundamental a provision ought to give rise to a private law sanction where it is breached in the absence of any statutory remedy or penalty to secure its enforcement.[111] The matter is not purely academic either. While an applicant can include a claim for damages in the relief sought on an application for judicial review, this is only when it can be established that the applicant could have recovered damages had he brought an independent private

---

[110] Now CPR Pt 54.

[111] Recent authority has demonstrated that the tort of breach of statutory duty is ineffective as a means of securing compensation for unlawful action by a public body. In *Olotu v Home Office and Crown Prosecution Service* [1997] 1 WLR 328 the claimant sought damages for breach of statutory duty in respect of the CPS' failure to comply with its statutory duty under the Prosecution of Offences (Custody Time Limits) Regulations 1987, SI 1987/299, thereby resulting in the claimant's unlawful detention prior to her trial. Her claim was dismissed in reliance on the principles in *Ex p Hague* (as was her claim in false imprisonment against the Home Office). Although she had undoubtedly been detained longer than the custody time limit allowed, the court held that her only remedy in private law lay against her own solicitor in negligence. See also *W (Minors) v Bedfordshire CC* [1995] 2 AC 633, *Stovin v Wise* [1996] AC 923 and *Barrett v Enfield LBC* [2001] 2 AC 550. The exclusion in *W (Minors) v Bedfordshire CC* was upheld by the ECtHR in *Z v UK* (2002) 34 EHRR 3. The court was 'satisfied that the law of negligence as developed in the domestic courts since the case of *Caparo* . . . and as recently analysed in the case of *Barrett v Enfield LBC* . . . includes the fair, just and reasonable criterion as an intrinsic element of the duty of care and that

law action in respect of the matter sought to be challenged by judicial review.[112] If a breach of the Bill of Rights is not justiciable as a private law action then, even though declaratory relief might be available under Pt 54 of the Civil Procedure Rules, no compensation would be recoverable. In practice it is hard to see how the infliction of a 'cruel and unusual punishment' could fail to give rise to a claim for misfeasance in public office but the point remains moot.

Protection from Discrimination

2.75 Prisoners are entitled to the protection of a range of anti-discrimination legislation: the Race Relations Act 1976 (as amended by the Race Relations (Amendment) Act 2000), the Sex Discrimination Act 1977 and the Disability Discrimination Act 1995. Until the Race Relations (Amendment) Act 2000, which prohibits race discrimination by public authorities in carrying out any of their public functions, prisoners' protection from racial discrimination was confined to cases of discrimination in the provision of 'goods, facilities and services', since prisoners did not count as 'employees' for the purposes of the Act. The protection against race discrimination now extends to all aspects of prison life— for example, to decisions on discipline, segregation and access to facilities and privileges. Claims for compensation can be brought in the county court, with the possible support of the Commission for Racial Equality. Prisoners who have been discriminated against on the ground of disability may also have a claim under Pt III of the Disability Discrimination Act 1995. We consider the application of the Sex Discrimination Act 1977 in Chapter 11, in the context of women prisoners.[113]

E. Judicial Review

Jurisdiction to Intervene in Prison Life

2.76 Since the late 1970s there has been a steady but persistent change in favour of the view that the normal function of the courts is not ousted by the fact of imprison-

---

the ruling of law concerning that element in this case does not disclose the operation of an immunity. In the present case, the Court is led to the conclusion that the inability of the applicants to sue the local authority flowed not from an immunity but from the applicable principles governing the substantive right of action in domestic law' (para 96).

[112] Supreme Court Act 1981, s 31(4), and RSC Order 54, rr 7(1), 9(5). The effect of these provisions is that although damages (in contrast to an injunction or declaration) is not a specific form of relief by way of judicial review, where a decision gives rise to both a claim for judicial review and a claim for damages the two may be joined. If the application for judicial review fails, the claim for damages may be continued as a claim under Part 7 of the CPR. Where however the matter involves no public law element, it will be struck out if commenced by writ: *Guevara v Hounslow LBC*, The Times, 17 April 1987. Cf *An Bord Bainne Co-Operative Ltd (Irish Dairy Board) v Milk Marketing Board* [1984] 2 CMLR 584.

[113] For detailed coverage of the full range of remedies in the field of discrimination, see A McColgan (ed), *Discrimination Law Handbook* (London, 2002).

ment. This reversal of fortune from a prisoner's perspective can be traced through a number of landmark decisions which have finally established that the supervisory jurisdiction of the High Court extends to all decisions taken in pursuance of the Prison Rules.

In *R v Board of Visitors of Hull Prison, ex p St Germain*[114] the Court of Appeal held that the High Court had jurisdiction to review the disciplinary adjudications of Boards of Vi`sitors (although the majority of the court held that a governor's disciplinary powers were not susceptible to review). In *R v Home Secretary, ex p Anderson*[115] the Divisional Court held that the Prison Service's 'simultaneous ventilation' rule, whereby prisoners who wished to seek legal advice about any aspect of their treatment in prison were required as a condition of receiving such advice to lodge an internal complaint, was unlawful in that it placed an unwarranted fetter on a prisoner's right of access to legal advice, which was an inseparable aspect of the right to unimpeded access to the courts. In *R v Home Secretary, ex p McAvoy*[116] the Divisional Court held that a decision to transfer a prisoner from one prison to another pursuant to s 12 of the Prison Act was susceptible to review. In *R v Deputy Governor of Camphill Prison, ex p King,*[117] the 'forward march' of jurisdiction was temporarily halted when the Court of Appeal ruled that disciplinary adjudications conducted by governors were immune from judicial review. However in *R v Deputy Governor of Parkhurst Prison, ex p Leech*[118] the House of Lords overruled *King*, holding that jurisdiction did extend to governors' disciplinary functions as well as those exercised by Boards of Visitors. Finally, the Court of Appeal in *R v Deputy Governor of Parkhurst Prison, ex p Hague*[119] held that operational or managerial decisions affecting the transfer and segregation of prisoners were amenable to judicial review, thereby opening up all decisions affecting prisoners to challenge. **2.77**

The new-found willingness to extend the jurisdiction of the High Court in order potentially to grant relief against the abuse of power in prison was not, however, taken lying down. At each stage the Home Office sought to hold back the incoming tide, arguing that the intervention of the courts was inconsistent with running an efficient, secure prison system. It was entitled to believe that this argument had some validity. Until Shaw LJ declared in St Germain that 'the rights of a citizen, however circumscribed by a penal sentence or otherwise, must always be the concern of the Courts unless their jurisdiction is clearly excluded by some statutory **2.78**

---

[114] [1979] QB 425.
[115] [1984] QB 778.
[116] [1984] 1 WLR 1408.
[117] [1985] QB 735. In *R v Governor of the Maze Prison, ex p McKiernan* (1985) 6 NIJB 6 the Northern Ireland Court of Appeal refused to follow *King* and held that governors' adjudications were susceptible to judicial review.
[118] [1988] 1 AC 533.
[119] [1992] 1 AC 58. See also *R v Home Secretary, ex p Leech (No 2)* (1994) QB 198, CA.

provision', English judges found it impossible to accept that prisoners could assert any legitimate claim to be protected from arbitrary and unlawful action once the prison gate had closed behind them. Prisoners, so the reasoning went, had only 'privileges', which could be denied them without the need for justification, rather than rights or legitimate expectations which entitled them to legal remedies. And in the judgments of Lord Goddard and, more recently, Lord Denning and Lawton LJ, the harassed prison administrator found full support for the 'catastrophe' scenario—that security, good order, or discipline would irretrievably break down if governors and prison officers had to perform their duties with a judge looking over their shoulders.[120]

2.79 This consequentialist argument against extending the judicial review jurisdiction into prison life was maintained by the Home Office throughout the 1980s in the face of overwhelming evidence that the existence of legal recourse not only did not injure the good and efficient conduct of prison life but enhanced it. In *Leech* the Home Office sought to resist the extension of jurisdiction to include a governor's disciplinary powers by arguing that this would eventually mean that administrative or managerial decisions of the governor would be potential candidates for judicial review. It was submitted that this would entail the court directly interfering in the administration of the prison regime, a consequence so undesirable that the House of Lords must reject it.[121] Experience has shown that this fear was entirely without foundation. Each advance of the High Court's supervisory jurisdiction did not result in the Administrative Court list groaning under the strain of unmeritorious applications from 'disgruntled' prisoners with nothing better to do than spend their every waking hour drafting a stream of judicial review claim forms.

2.80 The Home Office (or perhaps more precisely the Prison Service) finally accepted this in the course of the *Hague* litigation. During argument before the Court of Appeal in March 1990 it abandoned its previous claim that the court lacked jurisdiction to review a rule 43 (now rule 45) decision and, six months later in September 1990, issued CI 37/1990. This provided for the future all the procedural safeguards for which Mr Hague had been arguing in his application,

---

[120] Lord Goddard's judgment in *Arbon v Anderson* [1943] KB 252, Lord Denning's judgment in *Becker v Home Office* [1972] 2 QB 407, and Lawton LJ's judgment in *Ex p King* make up a trio of highly conservative judges who despaired at the idea of prisoners being allowed to litigate their grievances in the courts. Lawton LJ's father had himself been a prison governor!

[121] In his speech in *Leech* Lord Bridge, in rejecting the 'floodgates' arguments of Treasury Counsel, said that 'Mr Laws held out the prospect as one which should make our judicial blood run cold, that opening the door to judicial review of governor's awards would make it impossible to resist an invasion by what he called the "tentacles of the law" of many other department of prison administration'. In argument before their Lordships in *Ex p Hague*, leading counsel for Mr Hague commented that the extension of jurisdiction to include decisions taken under r 43 (now r 45) showed that 'the octopus had breached the floodgates'.

notwithstanding the fact that he had failed to establish his entitlement to them as a matter of law before the Court of Appeal. Lord Bridge commented in his speech in *Hague* in the House of Lords that the course the litigation had taken had confirmed that the availability of judicial review as a means of questioning the legality of action taken pursuant to the Prison Rules was a 'beneficial and necessary jurisdiction'.

The Public/Private Law Distinction

In his seminal speech in the *GCHQ* case, Lord Diplock commented that: **2.81**

> for a decision to be susceptible to judicial review the decision maker must be empowered by public law (and not merely, as in arbitration, by agreement between private parties) to make decisions that, if validly made, will lead to administrative action or abstention from action by an authority endowed by law with executive powers.[122]

The necessity for there to be a 'public law' element to a decision before it can attract the judicial review jurisdiction does not however give rise to much (if any) difficulty in the prison context. All decisions taken in pursuance of the Prison Act or Rules and which affect the rights, privileges, interests, or legitimate expectations of prisoners are prima facie amenable to judicial review. Accordingly, the legal adviser concerned to ensure that procedural correctness is preserved need not be concerned with the more esoteric arguments which have arisen in other areas where the public/private law divide is altogether less clear.[123] Disciplinary decisions, segregation, transfer, security categorization, parole, the regulation of access to the outside world whether by visits or correspondence, indeed almost every conceivable aspect of a prisoner's life in prison, all lie within the public law net.

More difficult is the question when it will be an abuse of process for a prisoner to **2.82** proceed by way of a private law action, thereby evading the procedural rules which govern applications for judicial review. In a trilogy of cases in 1983–84, the House of Lords examined the implications of s 31 of the Supreme Court Act 1981 and the amended RSC Order 53 (now replaced by Pt 54 of the Civil Procedure Rules), which together define the scope of the High Court's supervisory jurisdiction.[124] One of these, *O'Reilly v Mackman*, was a prison case and arose from the serious disturbance at Hull Prison in September 1976. After it ended a number of prisoners were charged with disciplinary offences under the Prison Rules and

---

[122] *Council of Civil Service Unions v Minister for the Civil Service* [1985] AC 374.

[123] See eg *R v Panel on Take Overs and Mergers, ex p Datafin PLC* [1987] QB 699; *Roy v Kensington and Chelsea and Westminster Family Practitioner Committee* [1992] 1 AC 624; and *R v Football Association Ltd, ex p Football League Ltd* [1992] COD 52.

[124] *O'Reilly v Mackman* [1983] 2 AC 237; *Cocks v Thanet DC* [1983] 2 AC 286; *Davy v Spelthorne BC* [1984] AC 262.

appeared before the Board of Visitors in December 1976. All those convicted were awarded severe punishments of cellular confinement and loss of remission. In 1980 three prisoners issued statements of claim in the Queen's Bench Division of the High Court, and a fourth issued an originating summons in the Chancery Division joining as defendants the members of the Board of Visitors who had adjudicated upon them four years before. In each case the relief sought was confined to a declaration that the proceedings were void and of no effect on the ground that the Board had acted in breach of the Prison Rules and the rules of natural justice. The Board members applied to strike out the proceedings on the ground that they were an abuse of the process of the court. It was never contended on the prisoners' behalf that they could not have proceeded under RSC Order 53 with applications for judicial review. Rather, it was asserted that they were entitled to choose which form of proceeding to initiate since nothing in either s 31 of the Supreme Court Act or the amended version of Order 53 indicated that judicial review was an exclusive remedy in cases such as theirs.

2.83 The House of Lords upheld the Board's argument that, in proceeding by writ and originating summons rather than pursuing applications for judicial review, the prisoners had been guilty of an abuse of process, and all four sets of proceedings were struck out. Lord Diplock's important speech is of general application in the field of administrative law, but it also involved a particular analysis of the nature of the remedies available to each prisoner arising from his treatment at the hands of the Hull board. He pointed out that, under the Prison Rules, remission of a prisoner's sentence was a matter not of right but of indulgence. All a prisoner could assert was a legitimate expectation that he would be granted remission of one-third of his sentence in accordance with rule 5(2) so long as no disciplinary award of forfeiture of remission was made against him. In the circumstances none of the prisoners had any independent remedy in private law. In public law, however, their legitimate expectation gave each of them a sufficient interest to challenge the legality of the Board's exercise of its statutory powers on the grounds that it had acted in breach of the rules of natural justice and the Prison Rules.

2.84 Having described the procedural reforms to Order 53 brought about by the 1977 amendments (which permitted applications for a declaration or injunction as well as a claim for damages to be included in an application for judicial review), Lord Diplock concluded that:

> it would in my view as a general rule be contrary to public policy, and as such an abuse of the process of the court, to permit a person seeking to establish that a decision of a public authority infringed rights to which he was entitled to protection under public law to proceed by way of an ordinary action and by this means to evade the provisions of Order 53 for the protection of such authorities.[125]

---

125 [1983] 2 AC 237, 285D.

Lord Diplock went on, however, to make the point that this 'general rule' was subject to exceptions, and he gave as one example a case 'where the invalidity of the decision arises as a collateral issue in a claim for infringement of a right of the plaintiff arising under private law'.[126]

Abuse of Process

Where does this leave a prisoner who wishes to pursue a private law action for   **2.85** assault, negligence, or misfeasance in the course of which it may be necessary to analyze the legality of a decision purportedly taken in pursuance of the Prison Rules, a 'public law' decision? Take, for example, the case of a prisoner who is seg- regated pursuant to an initially valid order by a governor under rule 45(1). After three days no authority is obtained from either the Board of Visitors or the Secretary of State for his further segregation in breach of rule 45(2). On the fourth day the prisoner refuses to return to his segregation cell after an exercise period and force is used by officers to return him to the cell. Is it an abuse of process for him to commence an ordinary action in the county court for assault rather than proceed first by way of judicial review to quash the decision to continue his segre- gation?

The answer must surely be 'no'. It is not a condition precedent to the establish-   **2.86** ment of the prisoner's private law cause of action for the tort of assault that an appropriate public law decision be set aside. It is therefore quite different from the situation which arose in *Cocks v Thanet DC*,[127] where the House of Lords struck out an action commenced in the county court for declaratory relief and damages arising from an alleged breach by a local authority of its statutory duty to secure permanent accommodation for the claimant and his family imposed by the Housing (Homeless Persons) Act 1977. Lord Bridge explained that it was inher- ent in the scheme of the 1977 Act that an appropriate public law decision be taken by the local authority as a condition precedent to the establishment of any private law duty to house a homeless family which might then be enforced by an injunc- tion or give rise to a liability in damages. For example, the authority would have to decide if the family was in priority need or intentionally homeless, and only if the answers were favourable would a duty to house arise. Precisely because tor- tious liability depends on a successful application for judicial review, it is an abuse to proceed immediately with a private law claim.

In the example we are concerned with, however, the invalidity of the prisoner's   **2.87** continued segregation arises as a collateral issue. The claim form would plead the use of unlawful force by prison staff to enforce his segregation. By way of Defence the Home Office would plead (if it could) that all force used was

---

[126] ibid, 285F.
[127] [1983] 2 AC 286.

lawful either to enforce a valid rule 45 order or, more generally, to maintain good order or discipline in the face of defiance of a lawful order from prison staff. In reply, the claimant would plead that there was no lawful justification for his continued segregation because no valid authority had been obtained from the Board of Visitors or Secretary of State. This latter issue would necessarily have to be decided in order to determine liability. But the claimant's cause of action does not depend on such determination for its very existence. The essence of the claim is for breach of a private law right, that is, a claim for assault.[128]

Exhausting Alternative Remedies

2.88 In both *King* and, later, in *Leech* the Home Office had argued that the High Court had no jurisdiction to grant judicial review of a governor's disciplinary powers primarily because of the existence of alternative remedies within the statutory framework which regulates the prison system. Specifically, s 4(2) of the Prison Act 1952 had expressly imposed on the Home Secretary the duty to ensure compliance by his officers (including the governor) with the Act and the rules made thereunder. Accordingly, it was argued, there was no need for the High Court to intervene at any point short of a failure by the Secretary of State to perform that duty. And it was that failure which alone was susceptible to judicial review.

2.89 This argument was (as we have described) emphatically rejected by the House of Lords, with Lord Bridge stating that:

> The existence of an alternative remedy has never been sufficient to oust jurisdiction in judicial review and, in the last analysis, the reliance on section 4(2) of the Act of 1952, however ingeniously the argument is presented, amounts to no more than saying that the Secretary of State's statutory duty to ensure compliance with the law by the governor affords an alternative remedy for any public law wrong which a prisoner charged with an offence against discipline may suffer at the governor's hands.[129]

In *Hague* the Home Office renewed its objection to an extension of the High Court's supervisory jurisdiction to cover 'managerial' decisions such as segregation under rule 45. Before the Divisional Court it was argued once again that s 4(2) and the possibility of a prisoner petitioning the Home Secretary or complaining to the Board of Visitors meant that, for policy reasons, as well as on general principles concerning the availability of judicial review as a remedy, the court should not entertain applications for judicial review of transfer and segregation decisions. In effect it was sought to distinguish the principles set out in *Leech* on the ground that they were confined to disciplinary proceedings where there was a duty

---

[128] See *Lonrho PLC v Tebbit and the Department of Trade and Industry* [1991] 4 All ER 973, in which the Vice-Chancellor refused to strike out a private law action in respect of governmental delay in releasing Lonrho from its undertaking, restricting its ability to bid for shares in the House of Fraser, which owned Harrods.

[129] [1988] 1 AC 533, 562D.

to observe the rules of natural justice. This argument was again rejected, and by the time the case reached the Court of Appeal a new approach was suggested by the Home Office. It was conceded that jurisdiction existed but that the court should exercise the utmost circumspection in exercising it. The court should distance itself from operational/managerial decisions by only entertaining applications made *after* a prisoner had unsuccessfully complained to the Board of Visitors or had petitioned the Home Secretary in respect of the decision under challenge. In other words it was sought to establish a principle that unless a prisoner had exhausted such internal 'remedies' as exist under the Act and the Rules the court would be bound to exercise its discretion to refuse relief. The availability of judicial review would be policed not in terms of basic jurisdiction but rather by the court's power to withhold what is in any event always a discretionary remedy.

Fortunately this 'second stage' approach was also rejected by the Court of Appeal, **2.90** though Taylor LJ was willing to agree that when reviewing managerial decisions in the prison context the court should approach the exercise of discretion with great caution.

Exhausting Internal Remedies

In the light of *Leech* and *Hague*, is there any principle of law which demands or **2.91** suggests that before proceeding to challenge a decision, whether disciplinary or managerial, a prisoner should exhaust such internal remedies as exist such as complaint to the Board of Visitors or the Home Secretary or the Prisons and Probation Ombudsman? The answer is that there is no rule which requires such a step to be taken, but in many cases it may well be wise to use the internal mechanisms before proceeding by way of judicial review (so long as this does not give rise to the danger that the applicant will be out of time for lodging an application for leave for judicial review, as may well prove to be the case in relation to waiting for the outcome of the Ombudsman's investigation). Whether or not internal recourse should be attempted will depend on the nature of the decision under challenge and the kind of relief or remedy available via the various complaints mechanisms. The reasons are as follows.

Judicial review is a remedy of last resort.[130] The Administrative Court will not **2.92** generally grant permission to bring a claim for judicial review if an applicant has

---

[130] See *Re Preston* [1985] AC 835; *R v Chief Constable of Merseyside, ex p Calveley* [1986] QB 424; *R v Home Secretary, ex p Swati* [1986] 1 WLR 477; *R v Secretary of State of the Environment, Transport and the Regions, ex p Channel Tunnel Group Ltd* [2001] EWCA Civ 1185; Bradley, 'Judicial Review by Other Routes' [1988] PL 169; Lewis, 'The Exhaustion of Alternative Remedies in Administrative Law' [1992] CLJ 138; M Beloff QC and H Mountfield, 'There is no alternative' [1999] JR 143; K Olley, 'Alternative Remedies and the Permission Stage' [2000] JR 240. The cases (of which there are many) on this subject reveal an inconsistent approach. Though there are dicta in the House of Lords to the effect that alternative remedies must always be exhausted, in practice the courts are usually more generous in granting judicial review than these suggest. An applicant will not

not exhausted established appeal procedures, save in exceptional circumstances. But the right to petition or complain to the Home Secretary or a Board of Visitors or the Ombudsman is not an established appeals procedure, nor is it properly to be described as a 'remedy', although it may in some cases afford appropriate redress. In *Leech* Lord Bridge was scathing about the idea that the right to petition the Home Secretary in respect of a disciplinary adjudication could possibly be regarded as an adequate remedy, pointing out that:

> save perhaps in a case taken up by a Member of Parliament, the matter will come before a civil servant in the Home Office who will consider on the one hand the prisoner's petition, on the other hand the relevant records and reports supplied by the governor. If those disclose an issue of fact, I hope that it is not unduly cynical to suppose that in the majority of cases the civil servant is likely simply to believe the governor's account. But even if he wishes to resolve any issue of fact in a judicial way, he probably lacks the experience and certainly lacks the procedural machinery, including the power to require evidence on oath, enabling him to do so . . . If a prisoner has a genuine grievance arising from disciplinary proceedings unfairly conducted, his right to petition a faceless authority in Whitehall for a remedy will not be of much comfort to him.[131]

These are strong words, but it is important to recall that they were made in the context of a dismissal of the Home Office's argument that there was no jurisdiction to review a governor's disciplinary decision. Earlier Lord Bridge had wholeheartedly endorsed the judgment of Shaw LJ in *St Germain*, which included the following passage on the relevance of internal remedies to the availability of judicial review:

> The opportunity for a prisoner to seek from the Secretary of State redress for a grievance . . . does not amount to a right of appeal for review of an unwarranted decision by a board of visitors or a prison governor. The fact that such means of possible redress has not been pursued before application is made to the court may in some cases be regarded as a discretionary obstacle to the grant of relief by the courts; but it cannot be an absolute bar.[132]

The effect of these statements would seem to be that where it can be shown that a prisoner's complaint could be fully and properly dealt with by some internal avenue of complaint, both in terms of the machinery available to investigate it and the power to reverse, correct, vary, or quash the decision under challenge, then there is a real danger that a failure to pursue such 'alternative remedy' may lead to

---

be required to resort to another procedure if that other procedure is less convenient or otherwise less appropriate. It may, as the House of Lords held in *Leech* in relation to the Home Secretary's inability at that time to remove a disciplinary finding from a prisoner's record, lack the power fully to deal with the issue.

[131] [1988] 1 AC 533, 568B.
[132] ibid, 555E.

relief being refused by the court in the exercise of its discretion.[133] It is safer not to go beyond such a broad statement of principle save to say that Lord Bridge's speech in *Leech* makes clear that where a complaint involves disputed issues of fact, then the existing internal remedies available under the Act and the Rules will never be regarded as adequate or truly alternative to the court's function.

F. The Human Rights Act 1998

The major recent innovation with respect to the legal remedies available to pris-   **2.93**
oners is the enactment of the Human Rights Act 1998 (HRA). The idea that the
United Kingdom required a legal statement of fundamental rights gained
increasing support among opposition political parties and senior members of the
judiciary throughout the 1990s. However, not all of those who advocated a Bill
of Rights were agreed on what form it should take. For some, the Bill of Rights
should ideally be part of a new written constitution for the United Kingdom,
drafted after wide consultation and perhaps entrenched by a referendum or a
special procedure requiring a weighted majority in Parliament to overturn
any provisions of it. For others it seemed better to incorporate one of the
international human rights conventions that the United Kingdom was already
a party to, with a preference being for the United Nations International
Covenant on Civil and Political Rights 1966 as the most modern and desirable
model.[134]

The view which gained most widespread acceptance was that the United   **2.94**
Kingdom should incorporate the European Convention on Human Rights
(ECHR), a much better known Convention and one which had already, via decisions of the ECtHR at Strasbourg, had a significant influence on UK law. By the
time of the 1997 general election both Labour and Liberal Democrat parties were
pledged to incorporate the ECHR. Shortly after its electoral victory the new
Labour Government produced a White Paper on its incorporation intentions[135]
and introduced a Human Rights Bill to this effect. The Act came into force on
2 October 2000.

Deciding on an incorporated ECHR as the means to give greater protection to   **2.95**
human rights in UK law still left the Government with decisions to make about

---

[133] As a result of the 1990 amendment to the Prison Rules, r 61 now gives the Secretary of State power to 'quash any finding of guilt and [he] may remit any punishment or mitigate it either by reducing it or by substituting another award which is, in his opinion, less severe'. Under a previous rule he had no power to quash, only to remit or mitigate it.

[134] See Klug, Starmer, and Weir, *Three Pillars of Liberty* (London, 1996) as an example of this viewpoint.

[135] *Rights Brought Home: The Human Rights Bill* (Cm 3782, 1997).

how incorporation should take place.[136] In the end the Government opted for a model which falls somewhat short of a fully 'constitutional' Bill of Rights in that, while it enables courts (and tribunals) to give remedies in respect of the actions of public authorities which violate Convention rights, the most that can be done in respect of primary legislation which cannot be interpreted in conformity with the Convention is the making of a 'declaration of incompatibility' by a court (ie the House of Lords, the Court of Appeal, or the High Court). This, according to the White Paper, 'will almost certainly prompt the Government and Parliament to change the law' and the Act provides a fast track procedure for amending law so as to bring it into conformity with the Convention.[137]

2.96 In the prisons context this limitation on the effectiveness of the HRA has not proved to be of great consequence. As we demonstrate throughout this book, most of the rules affecting prisoners stem from secondary legislation (the Prison Rules 1999) and non-statutory administrative orders/instructions which themselves derive from the Home Secretary's broad rule-making power in the Prison Act 1952. It follows that all of these provisions can now be fully examined by the courts for their compatibility with the ECHR, rather than primary legislation. The Act requires courts and tribunals to take into account the judgments, decisions, declarations, and advisory opinions of the ECtHR, the opinions and decisions of the Commission of Human Rights and the decisions of the Committee of Ministers of the Council of Europe.[138]

2.97 However, if the courts do now exercise a closer scrutiny of prison regulations, the Government may become increasingly convinced of the need for a new Prison Act to clarify the rights and duties of prisoners. This was the case in Canada following a number of court decisions indicating that rules restricting fundamental rights as recognized under the Canadian Charter could not be based on secondary legislation or administrative guidance.[139] Were any new Prison Act to be introduced in

---

[136] See B Emmerson, 'This Year's Model: Options for Incorporation' [1997] European Human Rights L Rev 313 for a review of different possible forms of incorporation.

[137] Cm 3782, n 135 above, para 2.10.

[138] The relevance and status of the Strasbourg case law has been considered by the courts: see *R (Alconbury) v Secretary of State for the Environment, Transport and the Regions* [2001] 2 WLR 1389, *per* Lord Slynn: 'In the absence of some special circumstances it seems to me that the court should follow any clear and consistent jurisprudence of the European Court of Human Rights' (para 26); *per* Lord Hoffmann: if the decisions of the ECtHR 'compelled a conclusion fundamentally at odds with the distribution of powers under the British constitution, I would have considerable doubt as to whether they should be followed' (para 76); *R (M) v Commissioner of Police of the Metropolis* [2002] Crim LR 215, *per* Laws LJ, 'by force of the Act of 1998, not least s2, we are to fashion a municipal jurisprudence of human rights, in light of the decisions of the Court at Strasbourg. That is an endeavour which is by no means separate from the common law's own development.' See also, on the over-use of Convention case law, M Fordham, 'Convention Case-Law: Judicial Warnings' [2000] JR 139.

[139] For a discussion of these developments, see S Livingstone, 'Designing a New Framework for Prison Administration: The Experience of the Canadian Corrections and Conditional Release Act 1992' (1994) 24 Anglo-American L Rev 426, 438.

the United Kingdom, then issues concerning the courts' power to review primary legislation might become more pertinent in the prison context. Any such legislation, or indeed any other new primary legislation affecting prisons, must now be preceded by a statement by the relevant Minister to the effect that its provisions are compatible with the incorporated Convention rights.[140]

The Act, via its Sch 1, incorporates into UK law Articles 2 to 12 and Article 14 of **2.98** the ECHR and Articles 1 to 3 of the First Protocol (as read with Articles 16 to 18 of the Convention). This means that all of the substantive rights contained in the Convention now become actionable in UK law.[141] Article 13, the right to an effective remedy, has not been incorporated.[142] Under the Act it is unlawful for a public authority to act in any way which is incompatible with a Convention right unless such action is required by primary legislation which is itself incompatible. This provision opens up to challenge most actions of the Prison Service, as these are taken under discretionary powers and are not mandated by provisions of the Prison Act or other legislation. The definition of 'public authority' includes 'any person certain of whose functions are of a public nature'.[143] This would include

---

[140] HRA, s 19. Although the Act also allows the Minister to indicate that although he is unable to make a statement of compatibility the Government nevertheless wishes the House to proceed with the Bill. One hopes this will be reserved for complex but urgent legislation, such as Finance Bills, where not all the potential consequences can be foreseen in time, rather than legislation which the Government knows or believes is not in compliance. The latter would appear to breach obligations under Art 1 of the ECHR and would render it difficult for courts to follow their s 3 obligation to read legislation as being compatible.

[141] This is subject to any reservations to the Convention or derogations under Art 15 of the Convention at the time entered by the UK at the Council of Europe.

[142] The consequences of the non-incorporation of Art 13 have been debated: see R Clayton and H Tomlinson, *The Law of Human Rights* (Oxford, 2000). The extent to which judicial review satisfies the 'effective remedy' requirement in Art 13 is considered in I Leigh, 'Taking Rights Proportionately: Judicial Review, the Human Rights Act and Strasbourg' (2002) PL 265, 268. He argues that, even without Art 13 being incorporated, any statutory ambiguity still has to be resolved in a 'Convention-friendly' manner. 'Consequently, if there is a genuine conflict about the standard of review arising from ambiguity in the wording of section 6 [of the HRA], it must be resolved in favour of a standard of review which gives an effective remedy for claims of violations of the Convention, in its entirety.' See also I Leigh and L Lustgarten, 'Making Rights Real: the Courts, Remedies and the Human Rights Act' (1999) 58 CLJ 509.

[143] s 6(3). This section brings within the scope of the Act 'any person certain of whose functions are functions of a public nature'. The courts are in the process of developing the definition of 'public functions': see *Poplar Housing and Regeneration Community Association Ltd v Donoghue* [2002] QB 48; *R (Heather) v Leonard Cheshire Foundation* [2002] UKHRR 883; *Parochial Church Council of the Parishes of Aston Cantlow and Wilmcote with Billesley Warwickshire v Wallbank* [2002] Ch 51. See also C McDougall, '"The Alchemist's Search for the Philosopher's Stone": Public Authorities and the Human Rights Act (One Year On)' [2002] JR 23; J Johnston, 'The Meaning of "Public Authority" under the Human Rights Act' [2001] JR 250. In D Oliver, 'The Frontiers of the State: Public Authorities and Public Functions under the Human Rights Act' [2000] PL 476, the author identifies several features which she considers indicative of a public function: the existence of authority or coercive power, the provision of public funds, whether the body has a statutory basis, whether it has a role in the public interest or is democratically accountable. Private prisons are a very clear example of the first category.

the operators of private prisons as the function of imprisonment is one which is clearly public in nature.

2.99   Challenges to the actions of a public authority can be brought by anyone who is a victim of the challenged act, within the meaning of Article 34 of the ECHR.[144] This would clearly include prisoners who claim to have been adversely affected by actions of the prison authorities. It is envisaged that Convention points can normally be taken in proceedings which already exist (for example, judicial review, a criminal trial, or a civil action). If no such proceedings are available however it will be possible to bring a claim on Convention grounds alone.[145]

2.100   If the authority is found to be in violation of Convention rights then the court can order 'such relief or remedy or make such order, within its jurisdiction as it considers just and appropriate'.[146] The Act leaves untouched the remedies available to courts in judicial review applications. Such remedies may include an award of damages, but only by a court which has power to award damages (or to order a payment of compensation) in civil proceedings, and where, taking into account any other available remedies, the court feels an award of damages is necessary to afford just satisfaction. Even in making a damages award a court must take into account the principles developed by the ECtHR when awarding 'just satisfaction' under Article 41 of the Convention.[147] Given that these principles are not a model of clarity and have been less than generous when it comes to damages sought by prisoners,[148] those seeking redress for prisoners (where the facts offer them the choice) may still find it more useful to pursue their claims by way of a civil action alleging unlawful action at common law rather than breaches of the Convention.

---

[144] See Ch 3 for further discussion of this criterion in the ECHR context.

[145] See s 7(1)(a) and Cm 3782, n 135 above, para 2.3. The intention to impose a one year limitation period indicates that there is a specific cause of action arising under the Convention.

[146] s 8(1).

[147] For a table of Strasbourg 'just satisfaction' awards for the violation of each of the Convention articles, see J Simor and B Emmerson, *Human Rights Practice* (London, 2000), Appendix A9.

[148] See eg *Weeks v UK* (1988) 10 EHRR 293. It would be desirable for the courts to apply a more liberal causation test in relation to the award of damages for breach of the HRA than is applied in domestic tort law. The ECHR principle of 'lost opportunities' would be more appropriate than the stricter, domestic 'but for' test. It enables the court to make an award of compensation in circumstances where it is considered that pecuniary damage has resulted from a violation, but it is difficult to quantify or assess. It would also be necessary to review the types of injury which may result in an award of compensation under the HRA. The ECtHR has awarded non-pecuniary (moral) damages in relation to anxiety, distress, loss of employment prospects, feelings of injustice, deterioration of way of life, and various other forms of harm and suffering. A rigid application of domestic principles of tort damages would be incapable of providing a flexible, universal, discretionary remedy of compensation for breach of the HRA. As with the recent CA guideline decision on damages in police actions, the higher courts would be able to give guidance on appropriate tariffs for the various forms of breach of the HRA as the case law develops. It is unclear if exemplary damages are capable of application in respect of a breach of the HRA simpliciter, although in principle the award of such damages would be consistent with the purpose of exemplary damages, namely to mark out and to punish 'arbitrary, oppressive and unconstitutional' action on the part of a public authority.

Where a public authority claims that its actions are justified or required by a pro- **2.101**
vision of primary or subordinate legislation, different considerations arise. Section
3 of the Act indicates that all primary and subordinate legislation, whenever
enacted, must be read and given effect to in a way which is compatible with the
Convention rights unless it is impossible to do so. This is a wholly new interpretative principle. It means that the courts must construe statutory provisions in a way
which makes them compatible with Convention rights unless it is impossible to do
so because there is an express limitation of a fundamental right.[149] Instead of a court
having first to decide whether legislation is ambiguous before turning to the
Convention for guidance, it can assume that Parliament intended to legislate in
conformity with the ECHR and to prefer an interpretation of the legislation which
advances that aim over one that does not.[150] In the prison context, for example, it
can assume that when Parliament makes rules on matters such as searches or drug
tests it intends those rules to be in conformity with the ECHR. Any search not in
conformity with ECHR standards or even any Prison Rule requiring searches
which breach ECHR standards (for example if the Rules were to require more frequent searches of foreign nationals) would hence be ultra vires the Prison Act.

The courts are in the process of developing a body of case law on the extent and **2.102**
mode of operation of s 3.[151] The operation of that section was described by Lord
Woolf MR as follows:

> It is difficult to overestimate the importance of section 3. It applies to legislation
> passed both before and after the HRA came into force. Subject to the section not
> requiring the court to go beyond that which is possible, it is mandatory in its terms.
> In the case of legislation predating the HRA where the legislation would otherwise
> conflict with the Convention, section 3 requires the court now to interpret legisla-
> tion in a manner which it would not have done before the HRA came into force.
> When the court interprets legislation usually its primary task is to identify the inten-
> tion of Parliament. Now, when section 3 applies, the courts have to adjust their
> traditional role in relation to interpretation so as to give effect to the direction
> in section 3. It is as though legislation which predates the HRA and conflicts with
> the Convention has to be treated as being subsequently amended to incorporate the
> language of section 3.[152]

---

[149] The courts should interpret as consistent with the Convention not only those provisions
which are ambiguous in the sense that the language used is capable of two different meanings but
also those provisions where there is no ambiguity in that sense unless a clear limitation on a fundamental right is expressly spelled out.

[150] Cm 3782, n 135 above, para 2.13.

[151] See *Poplar Housing and Regeneration Community Association Ltd v Donoghue* [2002] QB 48,
per Lord Woolf MR at [75]; *R v A* [2002] 1 AC 45, *per* Lord Steyn and Lord Hope; *R (Fuller) v Chief
Constable of Dorset Constabulary* [2002] 3 All ER 57; *Re B (a minor)* [2002] 1 WLR 258;
International Transport Roth GmbH v Home Secretary [2002] 3 WLR 344; *R v Lambert* [2001] 3
WLR 206; *R (H) v Mental Health Review Tribunal, North and East London Region* [2002] QB 1. In
Re S (Minors) [2002] 2 AC 291.

[152] *Poplar Housing and Regeneration Community v Donoghue* [2002] QB 48, at [75]. For academic discussion of s 3, see F Bennion, 'What Interpretation is "Possible" under Section 3(1) of the

This is a powerful tool, which the courts have used in two main ways: 'reading in' words to a statute, in order to make it Convention compatible,[153] and 'reading down'. The latter technique involves confining a statute which has a range of application, some parts of which may violate the Convention, to a usage which is Convention compatible.[154]

2.103 However if, applying the new interpretative canon, the court cannot read the legislation as being compatible with the Convention, the HRA does not affect the validity, continuing operation, or enforcement of incompatible primary legislation or subordinate legislation which by reason of the related primary legislation cannot be interpreted as compatible. In such a case, the court may only make a 'declaration of incompatibility'.[155] This declaration has no effect in itself either on the status of the legislation or the rights of the parties.[156] It is then up to the Government whether to introduce legislation, by Order in Council if it desires, to amend the legislation which the courts have found incompatible with the Convention.[157] The Government resisted going for a fully fledged power of constitutional review by which the courts could strike down incompatible primary legislation, because it said this would erode traditions of Parliamentary sovereignty and bring the courts into conflict with Parliament in way few judges wished for.[158] It takes the view that such a declaration 'will almost certainly prompt the

Human Rights Act 1998?' [2000] PL 77; A Lester, 'The Art of the Possible—Interpreting Statutes under the Human Rights Act' [1998] European Human Rights L Rev 665; P Craig, 'The Courts, the Human Rights Act and Judicial Review' (2001) 117 LQR 589; D Manknell, 'The Interpretative Obligation under the Human Rights Act' [2000] JR 109; A Henderson, 'Readings and Remedies: Section 3(1) of the HRA and Rectifying Construction' [2000] JR 258; J Wadham, 'The Human Rights Act: One Year On' [2001] European Human Rights L Rev 620.

[153] The most notable example of this technique is *R v A* [2002] 1 AC 45, where the House of Lords read s 41(3)(c) of the Youth Justice and Criminal Evidence Act 1999, which prohibits a defendant charged with rape from leading evidence about the complainant's previous sexual history, other than in very narrowly defined circumstances, as containing an implied provision that 'evidence or questioning which is required to secure a fair trial under Article 6 of the Convention should not be treated as inadmissible' (para 45). But see now *In Re S (Minors)* [2002] 2 AC 291.

[154] One pre-HRA example of 'reading down' is, of course, *R v Home Secretary, ex p Simms and O'Brien* [2000] 2 AC 115, in which the House of Lords confined r 37A of the Prison Rules—although very broadly worded—to a mode of operation which complied with prisoners' rights to free expression in exposing miscarriages of justice. A notable early example of 'reading down' under the HRA is *R v Offen* [2001] 1 WLR 253, in which, as we discuss further in Ch 14, the Court of Appeal interpreted the automatic life sentence in s 2 of the Crime (Sentences) Act 1997 to apply only when the offender was a risk to the public.

[155] The first such declaration was granted by the Divisional Court in *R (Alconbury Ltd) v Secretary of State for the Environment, Transport and the Regions* [2001] 2 All ER 929, where it was held that certain aspects of the planning regime did not comply with Art 6. However, that decision was reversed by the House of Lords: [2001] 2 WLR 1389.

[156] For this reason, one commentator has described the s 4 declaration as a booby prize: G Marshall, 'Two Kinds of Compatibility: More about section 3 of the Human Rights Act 1998' [1999] PL 377.

[157] Under HRA, s 10.

[158] See n 135 above, para 2.10.

Government and Parliament to change the law'. The Act provides for a fast track procedure for amending the law so as to bring it into conformity with the Convention. The amendment can be made by order. This power of amendment applies not only where there has been a declaration of incompatibility but also where it appears to a Minister of the Crown having regard to a judgment of the ECtHR, that a provision of legislation is incompatible with a Convention obligation. However, the need to uphold Parliamentary sovereignty has long been given as a reason for not having a Bill of Rights at all. Having gone this far it might be argued that the Act only creates unnecessary confusion. Moreover the language of 'almost certainly' suggests that there will be some occasions when the Government will not want to introduce amending legislation or when Parliament will not approve such legislation. The inevitable result may then be that the case is taken on to Strasbourg where the ECtHR finds a violation. In such cases the court may well be inclined to find a violation not only of the substantive right in question but also of the Article 13 right to an effective remedy in domestic law for a Convention violation. Even without getting to this stage the present law is unsatisfactory, especially in criminal cases where it raises the possibility that someone can be validly convicted and imprisoned for breach of a law which the House of Lords finds to be incompatible with the ECHR. The defendant will then have to wait either for the Government to 'fast track' amending legislation or for the ECtHR to rule on the issue. This delay in giving effect to acknowledged rights is exactly what the HRA was meant to avoid.[159] The limited value of a declaration of incompatibility to the individual claimant has led Lord Steyn to stress that the making of such a declaration 'must be avoided unless it is impossible to do so'.[160]

The Prison Service considers, perhaps somewhat optimistically,[161] that it 'complies with the principles of the ECHR already, having been subject to numerous proceedings at Strasbourg, and that it does not need to modify its policies'. However, it acknowledges that 'there have been some challenges already and more are certain to follow'. The Act is clearly of potential significance in the field of prison law. Many of the sorts of legal challenges which have been pursued by way of judicial review or civil action may now be advanced by way of claiming a breach of the HRA. Given that hardly any of the decisions taken by the prison service in respect of individual prisoners will be mandated by primary legislation—the Prison Act 1952 is, as we have seen, very generalized—the courts will very rarely be precluded from quashing a decision which violates prisoners' fundamental

2.104

---

[159] In C Neenan, 'Is a Declaration of Incompatibility an Effective Remedy?' [2000] JR 247, the author argues that a declaration of incompatibility does not satisfy the 'effective remedy' requirements of Art 13 of the Convention, and would thus leave the UK vulnerable to challenge in Strasbourg.

[160] *R v A* [2002] 1 AC 45 at [44].

[161] HM Prison Service, *Annual Report and Accounts 2000–2001* (HC 29, 2001).

rights. In judicial review itself, there is now a fourth ground of challenge—incompatibility with the Convention—to add to illegality, irrationality, and procedural impropriety. In a case which raises a Convention issue, the *Wednesbury* test of lawfulness and reasonableness is no longer enough. The court must focus on the substance and not merely the form of the decision. This new approach is exemplified by the decision of the House of Lords in *R (Daly) v Home Secretary*.[162] Lord Cooke described *Wednesbury* as:

> an unfortunately retrogressive decision in English administrative law, in so far as it suggested that there are degrees of unreasonableness and that only a very extreme degree can bring an administrative decision within the legitimate scope of judicial invalidation. The depth of judicial review and the deference due to administrative discretion vary with the subject matter. It may well be, however, that the law can never be satisfied in any administrative field merely by a finding that the decision under review is not capricious or absurd.[163]

Although *Daly* involves a classic application of the principle of proportionality, Lord Bingham was keen to stress that the case was decided 'on an orthodox application of common law principles derived from the authorities and an orthodox domestic approach to judicial review'.[164] The fact that proportionality is now considered 'orthodox' suggests that the influence of the Convention may indeed be changing the structure of judicial reasoning (if not always the outcome of particular cases).[165]

2.105 *Daly* involved a challenge to the prison service policy on cell searching, as set out in the Security Manual. In relation to such challenges to Prison Rules and administrative instructions/orders, however, it can fairly be said that, even before the HRA came into force, the domestic courts had already established an interpretative approach—the common law principle of legality—which complied with Convention principles. The *Raymond v Honey* principle (that prisoners retain all

---

[162] [2001] 2 AC 532.

[163] ibid, at [32].

[164] ibid, at [23]. One case in which the HRA *did* undoubtedly make a difference is that of *R (P and Q) v Home Secretary* [2001] EWCA Civ 1151; [2001] 1 WLR 2002, where Lord Phillips MR said that '[b]efore the introduction of a rights-based culture into English public law these applications for judicial review would have been quite unarguable' (para 56).

[165] For further commentary on the standard of review under the HRA, see M Elliott, 'The HRA 1998 and the Standard of Substantive Review' (2001) 60 CLJ 301; J Jowell, 'Beyond the Rule of Law: Towards Constitutional Review' [2000] PL 671; M Fordham and T de la Mare, 'Identifying the Principles of Proportionality' in J Jowell and J Cooper (eds), *Understanding Human Rights Principles* (Oxford, 2001); P Craig, 'The Courts, the Human Rights Act and Judicial Review' (2001) 117 LQR 589; *R (Mahmood) v Home Secretary* [2001] 1 WLR 840, CA; *R (Alconbury Developments Ltd) v Secretary of State for the Environment, Transport and the Regions* [2001] 2 WLR 1389; *R v Home Secretary, ex p Samaroo* [2001] UKHRR 1150, where Dyson LJ considered that proportionality included a 'fair balance' test: for criticism of this approach, see I Leigh, 'Taking Rights Proportionately: Judicial Review, the Human Rights act and Strasbourg' [2002] PL 265, 277.

civil rights save those which are taken away expressly or by necessary implication) was the starting point for a series of decisions, culminating in *R v Home Secretary, ex p Leech (No 2)*,[166] which provide an approach to the protection of a prisoner's fundamental rights that closely mirrors the jurisprudence of the Convention.[167] *Leech (No 2)* was then followed by the House of Lords in *Ex p Simms and O'Brien*,[168] and was confirmed by the House of Lords in *Daly* to embody the correct approach to prisoners' rights issues even after the HRA. The courts will continue to debate the precise meaning of the proportionality test.[169] However, there can be no doubt that prisoners are now entitled to searching review of the purported justifications for infringements of their rights.[170]

Throughout the book, we comment on cases brought by prisoners via the HRA in a wide range of contexts. The HRA has brought some significant improvements in particular areas of prison life. However, it has not been revolutionary. As mentioned above, the courts have shown a marked preference for deciding cases on 'orthodox' principles of common law, with the Convention rights discussed almost as an afterthought. Very rarely has the Convention clearly been stated to differ from the common law. The application of the Strasbourg case law has often highlighted the limitations of that case law, particularly in the area of prison conditions.[171] However, it is to be hoped that the courts will gain in confidence.

2.106

---

[166] [1994] QB 198.

[167] See Tim Owen, 'Prisoners and Fundamental Rights' [1997] JR 81. The approach in *Leech (No 2)* closely mirrored the ECtHR's approach to prisoners' rights, first established in *Golder v UK* (1979–80) 1 EHRR 542.

[168] [2000] 2 AC 115.

[169] M Fordham and T de la Mare, 'Anxious Scrutiny, the Principle of Legality and the HRA' [2000] JR 48 state, with reference to *Simms*, that the HRA does not greatly change the standard of review, 'not because the 1998 Act is weak . . . but because . . . the common law is strong'.

[170] As I Leigh puts it, in 'Taking Rights Proportionately: Judicial Review, the Human Rights Act and Strasbourg' [2002] PL 265, 287, 'judicial inquiry under section 6 of the HRA begins and (in the absence of clear contrary legislation) ends also with a simple question: have the victim's Convention rights been contravened by the public authority? If the answer is affirmative all metaphors of balance, all territorial boundaries of executive competence, expertise and political accountability, all distinctions between law, fact and policy, all invocations of the separation of powers are, frankly, irrelevant.' The notion of 'due deference', developed by the courts in a series of cases, has been used to limit the intensity of review in some contexts, giving the government a 'discretionary area of judgment' into which the courts will not inquire: see *R v DPP, ex p Kebilene* [2000] 2 AC 326; *Brown v Stott* [2001] 2 WLR 817; *R v A* [2002] 1 AC 45; *R v Lambert* [2001] 3 WLR 206; *International Transport Roth GmbH v Home Secretary* [2002] EWCA Civ 158. However, J Jowell, in 'Due Deference under the Human Rights Act', paper given to the Justice seminar, *Delivering Rights? How the Human Rights Act is Working and For Whom*, 25 June 2002, argues that '[u]nder the Human Rights Act there is no reason why the courts should not appreciate the limits of their own capacity to decide certain questions best answered by the body being reviewed. The new constitutional review does not empower the courts to act as if they were in the shoes of the primary decision-maker. Nor, however, does it permit the courts to shirk their ultimate responsibility as guardians of the new constitutional order—irrespective of Parliament's power to defy that order.'

[171] Although it is notable that, at the time of writing, two of the most far-reaching prison law cases in the last year were decisions of the ECtHR, holding incompatible with the Convention two practices—governors' imposition of added days in disciplinary hearings (*Ezeh and Connors v UK*),

Jurisdictions such as Canada which have adopted written human rights instruments have found that it takes time to develop a strong body of constitutional jurisprudence. The English courts are not—as they sometimes seem to think—bound by the Strasbourg case law: it provides minimum standards, on which they may in time find the confidence to build.

2.107   However, it would be wrong to believe that the Act will ever subsume all legal channels of redress for prisoners. For one thing, as we have observed above, there may be remedial advantages in bringing a case through another route. For another, as we highlight at many points of this book, reliance on the Convention will offer no additional remedy or assistance in circumstances where domestic public law has already done so. The whole area of security classification is one example of this. The ECHR clearly offers no remedy to prisoners who feel they have been unfairly classified. Judicial review has established, however, that they have some rights to consultation before, or review after, a classification to category A. Even if the prison authorities have acted towards prisoners in a way which is consistent with human rights norms, it remains open to prisoners and their representatives to examine whether they have been treated fairly and reasonably. Hence while the HRA offers new avenues for prisoners and their lawyers to pursue, and new norms for prison administrators to take account of in designing policy and practice, much of the old law remains relevant.

G. The State's Obligation to Protect the Right to Life of Prisoners

2.108   The enactment of the HRA has significantly illuminated and extended the nature of the State's obligation to take active steps to prevent suicide and self-harm in custody, as well as the obligation to investigate those deaths in custody which raise arguable violations of the right to life and the right not to be subjected to inhuman and/or degrading treatment or punishment.[172] The right to life is often said to be the most fundamental of all human rights, the basic precondition of the enjoyment of other rights.[173] Variants of the ECHR right to life

---

and the Home Secretary's power of release of mandatory life sentence prisoners (*Stafford v UK*)—which the domestic courts had refused to hold incompatible with the Convention. It is to be hoped that Strasbourg's willingness to require reform will inspire the domestic courts.

[172] Prison Service policy in relation to suicide and self-harm in custody is discussed in detail in Ch 6.

[173] *Bugdaycay v Home Secretary* [1987] AC 514, 553 and, more recently, *R v Lord Saville of Newdigate, ex p A* [2000] 1 WLR 1855, 1877. In *Jordan v UK* Application 24746/94, 11 BHRC 1, the ECtHR emphasized the importance of Art 2, stating that it 'ranks as one of the most fundamental provisions in the Convention, to which in peacetime no derogation is permitted under Article 15. Together with Article 3, it also enshrines one of the basic values of the democratic societies making up the Council of Europe. The circumstances in which deprivation of life may be justified must therefore be strictly construed. The object and purpose of the Convention as an

are given equivalent prominent protection in other human rights instruments.[174] It is perhaps obvious that any constitutional bill of rights dedicated to the protection of individual human beings should have the right to life and the prohibition on torture and inhuman and degrading treatment as its most fundamental provisions. The ECHR deals with these rights in Articles 2 and 3 respectively. These articles are said to encompass the basic values of democratic societies.[175] In any consideration of cases involving either loss of life and/or torture and inhuman and degrading treatment in custody three overriding considerations must be borne in mind:

(1) The relevant provisions of Articles 2 and 3 should be applied so as to make their safeguards practical and effective.[176]

(2) Articles 2 and 3 admit no peacetime derogation under Article 15, therefore the level of a discretion afforded to a decision maker is far less than other Articles in the Convention.[177]

(3) Deprivations of life must be subject to the most careful scrutiny. Such scrutiny must focus upon not only those who were allegedly directly responsible for the death, but the State organization or operation that provided the context in which the death took place.[178]

There were a number of pre-HRA domestic cases that laid particular emphasis upon the special need for full and fearless inquiries in relation to custodial deaths.[179] The requirements of the Convention are however more exacting than

---

instrument for the protection of individual human beings also requires that Article 2 be interpreted and applied so as to make its safeguards practical and effective.' See also *State v Makwanyane* [1995] LRC 269, 313 in which the South African Constitutional Court recognized the right to life in the following statement of principle: '[t]he rights to life and dignity are the most important of all human rights, and the source of all personal rights. . . . By committing ourselves to a society founded on the recognition of human rights we are required to value these two rights above all others. And this must be demonstrated by the state in everything that it does . . .' (emphasis added)

[174] eg, a decision under Art 21 of the Indian Constitution has particularly emphasized that '[c]ustodial death is perhaps one of the worst crimes in a civilised society governed by the rule of law'—see *Basu v. State of West Bengal* [1997] 2 LRC 1, 12.

[175] *McCann v UK* (1996) 21 EHRR 97, 161–162, paras 146–150; *Andronicou and Constantinou v Cyprus* (1997) 25 EHRR 491, para 171. For similar considerations in relation to Art 3 see *Chahal v UK* (1997) 23 EHRR 413 and *Assenov v Bulgaria* (1998) 28 EHRR 652, para 93.

[176] *McCann*, paras 146–147; *Osman v UK* (2000) 29 EHRR 245, para 116.

[177] *Bugdaycay v Home Secretary* [1987] AC 514; *R v Lord Saville of Newdigate, ex p A* [2000] 1 WLR 1855.

[178] *McCann v UK*, paras 181 and 201; *Tomasi v France* (1992) 15 EHRR 1; *Ribitsch v Austria* (1995) 21 EHRR 573; *Andronicou and Constantinou v Cyprus* (1997) 25 EHRR 491, para 186; *Edwards v UK* (2002) EHRR 19, para 61.

[179] *Re Rapier* [1988] QB 26; *R v Southwark Coroner, ex p Hicks* [1987] 1 WLR 1624; *R v Coroner for North Humberside and Scunthorpe, ex p Jamieson* [1995] QB 1, 18 and 26; *R v HM Coroner for Wiltshire, ex p Clegg* 520 JP 521, 531; *R v HM Coroner for Western District of East Sussex, ex p Homber* 158 JP 357, 379H ; *R v HM Coroner for Inner South London District, ex p Lisa*

the pre-HRA domestic law and in the wake of the coming into force of the 1998 Act a series of cases both in Strasbourg and in the domestic courts have made more effective the range of remedies available to the bereaved relatives of persons who die in the custody of the State.

The State's Positive Obligation to Prevent a Real and Immediate Risk to Life

2.109 The first sentence of Article 2(1) emphasizes that a person's right to life 'shall be protected by law'. It has been held that this requirement enjoins the State not only to refrain from the intentional and unlawful taking of life, but also to take steps to safeguard the lives of those within its jurisdiction.[180] The use of the word 'protection' indicates a level of effective security that goes beyond the word 'respect' used elsewhere in the Convention. In addition the State is required to give appropriate training, instructions and briefing to its agents who are faced with situations where the deprivation of life may take place under their control or field of responsibility.[181]

2.110 The fact that the State is subject to a positive obligation to protect life has been recognized in a number of ECtHR cases, most notably *Osman v UK*.[182] In that case the Court was considering a situation in which the police had been alerted to the potential risk of violence to a father and son posed by an apparently deranged and obsessive teacher. The critical reasoning of the ECtHR is set out in para 116 of the judgment:

> In the opinion of the Court where there is an allegation that the authorities have violated their positive obligation to protect the right to life . . ., it must be established to its satisfaction that the authorities knew or ought to have known at the time of the existence of a real and immediate risk to the life of an identified individual or individuals . . . and that they failed to take measures within the scope of their powers which, judged reasonably, might have been expected to avoid that risk. The Court does not accept the Government's view that the failure to perceive the risk to life in the circumstances known at the time or to take preventive measures to avoid that

---

Douglas–Williams [1999] 1 All ER 345, 347–348; *R v DPP, ex p Manning and Melbourne* [2001] QB 330, at [33] and *R (Wright and Bennett) v Home Secretary* [2001] EWHC Admin 520, [2002] HRLR 1, at [63].

[180] *Osman v UK* 5 BHRC 293, para 115; *LCB v UK* (1998) 27 EHRR 212, para 36. See also *X v UK* 14 DR 31 (vaccine damages). In *R (Amin and Middleton) v Home Secretary* [2002] 3 WLR 505, the Court of Appeal summarized the requirements of Art 2 in the following way: 'Article 2 imposes two distinct but complementary obligations on the State. Putting the matter very shortly, the first is a substantive obligation not intentionally to take life and also to take reasonable preventative measures to protect an individual whose life is at risk whether from the criminal acts of others or suicide. The second is an adjectival, procedural obligation to investigate deaths where arguably there has been a breach of the substantive obligation.'

[181] *McCann v UK*, para 201; *Andronicou and Constantinou v Cyprus*, para 186.

[182] 5 BHRC 293.

risk must be tantamount to gross negligence or wilful disregard of the duty to protect life. Such a rigid standard must be considered to be incompatible with the
requirements of Article 1 of the Convention and the obligations of Contracting
States under that Article to secure the practical and effective protection of the rights
and freedoms laid down therein, including Article 2. For the Court, and having
regard to the nature of the right protected by Article 2, a right fundamental in the
scheme of the Convention, it is sufficient for an applicant to show that the authorities did not do all that could be reasonably expected of them to avoid a real and
immediate risk to life of which they have or ought to have knowledge. This is a question which can only be answered in the light of all the circumstances of any particular case.

The obligation to take positive steps to protect life is not limited to the taking of **2.111**
steps to prevent unlawful violence (whether by agents of the State or
private individuals against one another). The right has also been identified as
extending to the taking of positive steps to prevent environmental disasters[183] as
well as suicides by persons in State custody.[184] Thus, in *Keenan v UK*,[185] the
ECtHR acknowledged that the obligation under Article 2 extended to a duty to
prevent self-inflicted deaths in custody when the authorities were on notice of a
'real and immediate risk' to life.[186] A lack of proper medical treatment in a case
where a prisoner is suffering from an illness could in certain circumstances
amount to a violation of Articles 2 and 3.[187] Finally, the failures of the authorities
to communicate relevant and reasonably obtainable information will give rise to

---

[183] *LCB v UK* (1998) 27 EHRR 212.

[184] *Keenan v UK* (2001) 33 EHRR 38 (subsequently applied in *R (Amin and Middleton) v Home Secretary* [2001] EWHC 1043; [2002] 3 WLR 505, at [49].

[185] (2001) 33 EHRR 38.

[186] In *R (DF) v Chief Constable of Norfolk Police* [2002] EWHC 1738, Crane J considered the application of the *Osman/Keenan* threshold test of a real and immediate risk to life in the context of a refusal by the Prison Service to admit a life sentence prisoner to a Protected Witness Unit. He commented that 'it does not make it easy for those who have to take decisions, or for courts reviewing those decisions, if the search for a phrase encapsulating the threshold of risk is a chimaera' (para 33). He pointed to the difference between the situation in a prison as compared with the difficulties facing the police in terms of protecting an individual at large in the community in that the prison authorities will generally be aware that a prisoner who has helped the authorities is at risk, they are in a ready position to take steps to avoid any risk and they are less likely to be inhibited by restraints imposed on the scope of their actions by the need to respect the human rights of others since providing a protective regime is unlikely to affect the rights of others. On the issue of the 'immediacy' of the risk, he held that it should not be understood, in the context of admission to a protective regime, to mean that the threat will necessarily materialize in the very near future, rather 'the question to be asked is whether there is a real risk to the life of a prisoner if he is not admitted to a PWU, rather than some alternative regime, for whatever period is being considered. However immediacy requires that the risk must be present and continuing' (para 38).

[187] *McFeeley v UK* (1980) 3 EHRR 161; *Keenan v UK* (2001) 33 EHRR 38, para 110 and *R (Wright and Bennett) v Home Secretary* [2001] EWHC Admin 520, [2002] HRLR 1, at [54]–[57].

a violation of Article 2 if the subsequent information deficit leads to a person not being adequately cared for when they could have been.[188]

2.112   In judging what reasonable responses are required by the State to protect life it will be necessary to consider what other Convention rights are potentially jeopardized and which must therefore be put in the balance when considering whether the right to life has been violated. In *Osman*, the countervailing issues were the potential authorization of the arrest, detention and charge of the suspect at a premature stage, thereby giving rise to potential breaches of Article 5. Other Article 2 cases where countervailing considerations have been considered include the legitimacy of forced feeding,[189] banning smoking in public,[190] banning the sale of alcohol on an army base,[191] the organization of a rescue mission[192] and abortion.[193]

2.113   In considering the standard to be applied to 'operational failures' resulting in deprivation of an individual's right to life, the court in *Osman* rejected the 'gross dereliction or wilful disregard of duty' standard on the ground that it was over-rigid and incompatible with the duty to secure effective protection of Convention rights (see para 116). The lower threshold test of whether the State has taken steps which were adequate and appropriate to protect life is consistent with the 'due diligence' test adopted by the Inter-American Court of Human Rights in *Velasquez Rodriguez v Honduras*.[194] What is reasonable and appropriate will of course take account of all the factors in the individual case including the age and vulnerability of the victim.[195]

---

[188]   *Edwards v UK* (2002) 35 EHRR 19, para 61. In relation to the same principle in domestic law see *R v HM Coroner for Swansea and Gower, ex p Chief Constable of Wales* 164 JP 191; *R v HM Coroner for Coventry, ex p O'Reilly and O'Reilly* 160 JP 749.

[189]   *X v FRG* 7 EHRR 152; *Herczegfalvy v Austria* (1992) 15 EHRR 437, para 32.

[190]   *Wockel v Germany* Application 32165/96, 16 April 1998.

[191]   *Barrett v UK* [1997] EHRLR 546; (1997) 23 EHRR CD 185 where the Commission recognized that the absence of measures designed to discourage drinking alcohol to excess in State-provided facilities could raise issues under Art 2.

[192]   *Andronicou and Constantinou v Cyprus* (1997) 25 EHRR 491.

[193]   *Paton v UK* 19 DR 244 where it was indicated that a considerable margin of appreciation should be afforded to the individual States.

[194]   [1989] 28 ILM 291.

[195]   In *Keenan* (2001) 33 EHRR 38, the court was anxious to emphasize that Art 2 should not be read as imposing impossible burdens on State parties. Thus it said in para 89: '[b]earing in mind the difficulties in policing modern societies, the unpredictability of human conduct and the operational choices which must be made in terms of priorities and resources, the scope of the positive obligation must be interpreted in a way which does not impose an impossible or disproportionate burden on the authorities. Not every claimed risk to life therefore can entail for the authorities a Convention requirement to take operational measures to prevent that risk from materialising. For a positive obligation to arise, it must be established that the authorities knew or ought to have known at the time of the existence of the real and immediate risk to the life of an identified individual from the criminal acts of a third party and that they failed to take measures within the scope of their powers which, judged reasonably, might have been expected to avoid that risk. In this case, the Court has had to consider to what extent this applies where the risk to a person derives from self-harm.'

A careful or strict scrutiny approach implies that the actions or inactions of the **2.114** authorities will be closely examined to establish whether they meet the standards of adequate protection. Moreover, where the protection of the life of a recognized vulnerable person—such as a child or a mentally disturbed individual—is involved there is an increased standard of vigilance.[196]

A Free-standing Right to an Effective Investigation

The obligation to take positive steps to protect life also requires some form of **2.115** effective investigation where death has occurred in circumstances which engage either Articles 2 or 3 of the Convention.[197] The principle that a procedural right to an investigation into a death could be taken as a free-standing right under Article 2 was first identified in the case of *McCann v UK*. Thereafter a number of cases involving the lack of effective investigations into deaths in custody and missing persons in Turkey resulted in the court applying greater emphasis to the principle.[198]

In relation to deaths that result from State sponsored violence there is a far- **2.116** reaching requirement to consider the propriety of the activity.[199] Thus in *McCann* and *Andronicou* the inquiry deemed necessary by the court went significantly beyond an investigation of the means by which the victims came by their deaths and extended to the operational contexts in which the deaths took place. In *McCann* the inquest itself was held to be a sufficiently effective inquiry; not surprisingly so given that there was major international interest in the inquest and its subsequent aftermath and what resulted was clearly not an average coroner's inquest. The question of whether the inquest system in the United Kingdom amounted to an effective remedy in and of itself was left unconsidered.[200] However, the court emphasized in *McCann* that the protection conferred by Article 2(1):

> . . . would be ineffective, in practice, if there existed no procedure for reviewing the lawfulness of the use of force by State authorities. The obligation to protect the right to life under this provision read in conjunction with the State's general duty under

---

[196] *Herczegfalvy v Austria* (1993) 15 EHRR 437, para 82; *Keenan v UK* (2001) 33 EHRR 38.
[197] *McCann v UK* (1996) 21 EHRR 97, para 161.
[198] *Kaya v Turkey* (1999) 28 EHRR 1, para 86.
[199] The mere knowledge of the killing on the part of the authorities can give rise to an obligation under Art 2 to carry out an effective investigation into circumstances surrounding the death: *Ergi v Turkey* Application 66/1997/850/1057, 28 July 1998.
[200] In *Keenan v UK* (2001) 33 EHRR 38 it was accepted that an inquest could not in law determine the liability of the State in relation to a death which engaged Art 2 nor could it award damages/just satisfaction. It is now clear from *R (Amin and Middleton) v Home Secretary* [2002] EWCA Civ 390; [2002] 3 WLR 505 that an inquest may be capable of discharging the investigative obligation inherent in Art 2 albeit that other remedies may have to be pursued to secure the punishment of those criminally to blame and to secure non-pecuniary damages for the bereaved, thereby securing compliance with Art 13. See below at para 2.19 for a discussion of the inter-relationship between Arts 2 and 13.

> Article 1 of the convention to 'secure to everyone within their jurisdiction the rights and freedoms defined in [the] convention' requires by implication that there should be some form of effective official investigation when individuals have been killed as a result of the use of force by, inter alia, agents of the State.

It is now clear that the Strasbourg case law also demands that investigation into any loss of life that occurs within the custody or as a result of the actions of agents of the State in circumstances which engage Article 2 (or Article 3) must also be subject to the most careful scrutiny.[201]

2.117   At the time of writing there is an apparent conflict between the Strasbourg case law and domestic law in relation to the required scope of an effective Article 2 investigation. Thus, in both *Jordan v UK* and *Edwards v UK* the ECtHR held that in order to satisfy the requirements of Article 2, any investigation must be: independent from those implicated in the events; capable of leading to a determination of whether State agents are liable for the death, the identification of those responsible and, if appropriate, their punishment; prompt; must involve a sufficient element of public scrutiny; and must involve the next of kin in the investigative procedure to the extent necessary to protect his or her legitimate interests. The language of the court suggested that these were essential requirements of *any* effective investigation where an arguable violation of Article 2 had been made out.

In *R (Amin and Middleton) v Home Secretary*,[202] however, the Court of Appeal diluted the apparently clear Strasbourg requirements, holding that the investigative duty under Article 2 could not be defined by strict rules and that it was up to the domestic courts to decide what is sensibly required to support and vindicate Convention rights on a case by case basis. The *Amin* case arose from the vicious murder of a young Asian prisoner, Zahid Mubarak, in Feltham Young Offenders

---

[201] See *Edwards v UK* (2002) 35 EHRR 19, paras 69–73. In *R (Amin and Middleton) v Home Secretary* [2002] 3 WLR 505, the Government had originally sought to argue that the procedural obligation to investigate only arose if the relevant death occurred or is alleged to have occurred as a result of the use of force by State agents. Where a death resulted from a failure by the State to fulfil its positive duty to take steps to protect the life of someone in its care against a perceived risk—or a risk that should have been perceived—of death or serious injury at the hands of another, then the availability of the ordinary civil remedies in the domestic courts was said to suffice for Art 2 purposes. In the light of *Edwards* however the Government accepted that this distinction was unarguable and the Court of Appeal held at [44] that 'we should without hesitation have concluded that the procedural duty was engaged [on the facts of *Amin*] without the assistance of *Edwards*. A death in State custody, at the hands of another prisoner or (as in *Middleton*) at the deceased's own hands, excites very anxious public concern. The State owes a pressing duty to minimise the risk of such a calamity, even if it cannot be altogether extinguished. The common law would impose such a duty, if it could find an appropriate litigious framework within which to make it good. Now however it is enough to say that such a duty lies within the scope of Article 2. When such a death takes place, the procedural duty to investigate is in our judgment undoubtedly engaged.'
[202] [2002] 3 WLR 505.

Institution by his notoriously violent, racist cell mate. Though the cell mate was successfully prosecuted for murder in the criminal courts, no inquest, in which the culpability of the prison service for failing to protect the deceased's right to life might be examined, had taken place.

The Director-General of the Prison Service had promptly admitted that the Service had been at fault in a private letter to the deceased's family and an internal Prison Service inquiry had also taken place whose report had been disclosed to the family and its advisers but with a requirement that the report not be disclosed to anyone else. In addition, a private investigation into race discrimination in the Prison Service, being conducted by the Commission for Racial Equality, was specifically focusing on Feltham Young Offenders Institution and the circumstances in which Mr Mubarak was murdered. Faced with a situation in which there had been no public investigation of the acts and/or omissions of Prison Service personnel in which they had been able to participate meaningfully, the family of Mr Mubarak pressed the Home Secretary to hold a public inquiry. At first instance, the Home Secretary's refusal to accede to this request was quashed by Hooper J, who held that public scrutiny and the involvement of the next of kin were separate requirements of the Article 2 investigative duty and that accordingly an independent public investigation must be held to satisfy the requirements of the Convention. But the Home Secretary's appeal was allowed, with the Court of Appeal holding that public scrutiny and next of kin involvement are not separate, compulsory requirements of Article 2 and that the investigative duty had already been discharged on the facts of the case. Most significantly, the court held that 'the nature and scope of an adjectival duty, which by definition is not expressly provided for in the Convention, must expressly be fashioned by the judgment of the domestic courts as to what in their jurisdiction is sensibly required to support and vindicate the substantive Convention rights'.[203]

2.118 The court drew a clear distinction between a death which involves a credible accusation of murder or manslaughter by State agents and an allegation of negligence leading to death in custody. The former 'will call for an investigation of the utmost rigour, conducted independently for all to see' whereas the latter 'though grave enough in all conscience bears a different quality from a case where it is said the State has laid on lethal hands'. Rejecting the argument that there were fixed requirements of publicity and family participation uniformly applicable to every investigation, the Court of Appeal said that the means of fulfilling the aims of the procedural obligation (minimizing the risk of future like deaths, giving justice to the bereaved and assuaging public anxiety) cannot be reduced to a catechism of rules. Rather, 'what is required is a flexible approach, responsive to the dictates of

---

[203] ibid, at [61].

the facts case by case'.[204] In finding that the procedural obligation to investigate had been satisfied on the facts of the *Amin* case, the Court of Appeal said that it was necessary to take into account all the measures taken by public authorities to respond to and investigate the death, whether instituted by central government or otherwise, and form a pragmatic view 'in the round' as to whether the basket of actions taken was satisfactory in all the circumstances of the particular case.

2.119 The Strasbourg and post-HRA case law make clear that it is necessary to maintain a distinction between the free-standing Article 2 right to an effective investigation and the Article 13 right to an effective domestic law remedy which is capable of determining the liability of the State for a particular death and, if appropriate, awarding compensation or just satisfaction. In *Keenan v UK* it was accepted by all parties that the inquest into Mark Keenan's death could not in law determine issues of civil or criminal liability and thus did not furnish the applicant with the possibility of establishing the responsibility of the prison authorities or obtaining damages.[205] Moreover, as Mark Keenan had died before the coming into force of the HRA, his mother could not pursue a claim under ss 7(1)(a) and 8 of the 1998 Act in respect of his ill treatment and death in prison and, as he was over 18 when he died, nor was it practical for her to pursue any claim either under the Law Reform (Miscellaneous Provisions) Act 1934 or the Fatal Accidents Act 1976.[206] In these circumstances, the court found, in addition to the breach of Article 3, that Article 13 had also been violated, stating that it considered that 'in cases of a breach of Articles 2 and 3 of the Convention, which rank as the most fundamental provisions of the Convention, compensation for the non-pecuniary damage flowing from the breach should in principle be available as part of the range of

---

[204] ibid, at [62]–[63]. The Court of Appeal effectively overruled that aspect of the judgment of Jackson J in *R (Wright and Bennett) v Home Secretary* [2001] EWHC Admin 520; [2002] HRLR 1 in which he had held, applying *Jordan v UK*, that 'where the victim has died and it is arguable that there has been a breach of Article 2, the investigation should have the general features identified by the Court in *Jordan v. UK* at paras 106–109'.

[205] The court stated at para 127 that '[t]urning to the remedies available after Mark Keenan's death, it is common ground that the inquest, however useful a forum for establishing the facts surrounding Mark Keenan's death, did not provide a remedy for determining the liability of the authorities for any alleged mistreatment or for providing compensation'. As Jackson J correctly pointed out in his judgment in *R (Wright and Bennett) v Home Secretary* [2001] EWHC Admin 520; [2002] 1 HRLR 1, it was unnecessary in *Keenan* for the applicant to allege a freestanding breach of the Art 2 investigative obligation before the ECtHR as the substance of the complaint of a lack of an effective remedy in domestic law was addressed under Art 13.

[206] See the concurring opinion of the ad hoc UK judge, Sir Stephen Sedley, in which he analyzes the potential inadequacy of the HRA in terms of its ability to convert a coroner's inquest into an effective Art 13 remedy. In so far as his analysis is focusing on the inability of an inquest to award compensation/just satisfaction in relation to any breach of Arts 2 and/or 3 it is plainly correct but his analysis of the difficulty of deploying s 3 of the HRA to override the content of r 42 of the Coroners' Rules 1984 (which forbids the framing of a verdict in such a way as to appear to determine civil liability or a named person's criminal responsibility) must now be read in the light of *R (Amin and Middleton) v Home Secretary* [2002] 3 WLR 505, at [83]–[93].

possible remedies'.[207] The fact that an individual is potentially able to pursue a civil claim in relation to a death that engages Articles 2 and/or 3 will not of itself discharge the Article 2 investigative obligation. As the ECtHR commented in *Jordan v UK*:

> Civil proceedings would provide a judicial fact-finding forum, with the attendant safeguards and the ability to reach findings of unlawfulness, with the possibility of damages. It is however a procedure undertaken on the initiative of the applicant, not the authorities and it does not involve the identification or punishment of any alleged perpetrator. As such, it cannot be taken into account in the assessment of the State's compliance with its procedural obligations under Article 2 of the Convention.[208]

H. Disclosure: Documents to Watch For

In a private law action for damages, disclosure and inspection of documents are **2.120** automatic.[209] In an application for judicial review, disclosure is not automatic, but otherwise almost identical principles apply. In the words of Lord Diplock in *O'Reilly v Mackman*,[210] 'discovery is obtainable on application whenever, and to the extent that, the justice of the case requires'. Whether in a private law claim or an application for judicial review, the court will only order disclosure and inspection of documents where it is satisfied that the documents sought relate to any matter in question in the cause or matter and that the order is 'necessary either for disposing fairly of the cause or matter or for saving costs'.[211]

In prison cases more than most, disclosure and inspection is frequently a vital **2.121** stage in the process of establishing a winning claim. This is mainly because, until a prisoner obtains access to the documents in the hands of the prison authorities, he will have few, if any, contemporaneous records relating to the matter in dispute. In a claim for damages for personal injuries he may have been able to obtain an order for pre-action discovery of his medical records but, in other claims, no other documents will normally be available.[212]

---

[207] para 129.
[208] Application 24746/94, 11 BHRC 1.
[209] See CPR Pt 31.
[210] [1983] 2 AC 237.
[211] RSC Ord 24, r 13. Though see M Fordham, *Judicial Review Handbook* (3rd edn, Oxford, 2001) para 19.4.6: '[t]he test should now be approached with caution, as it does not feature expressly in CPR Part 31'.
[212] The Access to Health Records Act 1990, which by s 3 creates a statutory right of access to a health record on the part of the patient, applies to a health professional in the public service of the Crown (see s 2(4)). Accordingly prisoners who wish to pursue a claim where such records are going to be relevant should make an application to the holder of the record, ie the Director of the Prison Healthcare Service, whose address is Cleland House, Page Street, London SW1P 4LN.

2.122 The possibility of third-party disclosure under CPR 31.17 should not be over-looked. In cases where the police have been involved, for example to investigate claims of assault by officers on a prisoner, they will be in possession of interview transcripts and other investigative materials. The police authority may provide disclosure of these materials on a voluntary basis once the investigation is completed, either by a trial or a decision not to prosecute. Alternatively, the claimant can make an application to the court for disclosure of this material. The court may order disclosure if the material is (1) relevant, and (2) disclosure is necessary in the interests of fairness or efficient case management.[213]

2.123 In any civil litigation, it is essential to have a detailed understanding of the kind of documentation which a defendant is likely to have compiled and which will be relevant to the issues in dispute. Whether a claimant is considering an application for pre-action disclosure or scrutinizing a List of Documents at the stage of disclosure and inspection, an awareness of your opponent's record-keeping methods is a distinct advantage. It will enable a request to be made for specific documents and thus avoid the allegation that what is being pursued is a generalized fishing expedition in the hope that something may emerge.

2.124 This is particularly true in prison litigation. The Prison Service produces a bewildering array of forms, records, and documents, many of them overlapping. Below is a list of those documents which are likely to be most frequently relevant in claims for negligence, assault and misfeasance in public office as well as in applications for judicial review/Human Rights Act applications.

  1 *Prisoner's personal record (F2050)*—a loose-leaf file kept in a yellow cardboard wallet which is supposed to be a comprehensive record of a prisoner's time in prison. It should include details of his conviction, sentence, and earliest date of release. A History Sheet should record each transfer as well as any applications/petitions and governors' observations from prison to prison. A Medical Record should record the medical officer's view of the prisoner's state of health and work classification on each reception and a Medical History sheet should record the results of any reception medical examination. The prisoner's disciplinary record will be recorded and, on what is called page 24, 'Information of Special Importance' should be listed.[214] This includes security information (escapes, attempted escapes,

---

[213] In *Abbey v Home Office*, 3 May 2002, prison officers who had been interviewed by the police in relation to assaults on Mr Abbey objected to disclosure of their interview transcripts (in the course of a civil claim for damages) on the ground of confidentiality. HHJ Collins in the Central London County Court held that, although some confidentiality did attach, it was outweighed by the public interest in the administration of justice, particularly since the claim involved very serious allegations of assault.

[214] The selection of p 24 for this information remains a mystery since it bears no relation to the logical sequence of page numbering within the record itself.

suspicious circumstances connected with visits/correspondence) as well as suicide attempts/concerns or special medical problems. Any periods of time in segregation or good order and discipline transfers should also be logged on page 24.

2   *Continuous Inmate Medical Record*—the IMR should record all entries by prison doctors relevant to a prisoner's medical history in prison. It is a loose-leaf folder inside an orange cardboard wallet. The IMR is different from the Medical Record and Medical History sheets which are kept in the F2050.

3   *Hospital case papers/Kardex*—if a prisoner is located in a prison hospital, a separate set of records will normally be kept. Any treatment/drugs pre-scribed will be recorded on special Treatment Cards.

4   *Suicide prevention*—each prisoner should be screened for suicide risk on reception and at each transfer by a hospital officer and a doctor using Form F2169, the Reception Assessment Form. If any member of staff is con-cerned at any time that a prisoner is or may be suicidal, a Self Harm At Risk Form (F2052SH) should be completed to ensure an assessment of risk by the medical officer.[215]

5   *Disciplinary proceedings*—these give rise to a number of different records. They include the original memoranda compiled by staff (usually done on an F1384), the Report to the Governor of Alleged Offence by Inmate (F254), the Notice of Report (F1127), and the Record of Adjudication (F256).

6   *Use of Force Reports*—whenever a member of staff uses force against a pris-oner he or she should give a brief factual report explaining why force was necessary.

7   *Report of Injury to an Inmate* (F213)—this is self-explanatory. It should be filled in by the medical officer whenever it is believed that a prisoner has been injured. It includes a diagram of the human body for the sites of any injuries to be recorded.

8   *Rule 45* segregation—whenever a prisoner is segregated the authority for it and the reasons should be recorded on Form F1299A. Any authority for its continuance obtained from either the Board of Visitors or the Secretary of State should also be logged.

9   *Register of Non-Medical Restraints (F2323)*—this is the form used whenever a prisoner is placed in any form of mechanical restraint or is ordered to be located in a special cell under rule 48. The reason for it must be recorded and approved by the medical officer as well as the time the restraint or loca-tion commenced and the time it ended.

10   *Property cards*—these should record the property which is retained by the prisoner in his personal possession and that which is kept by the prison as

---

[215] For a full understanding of the detailed procedures governing suicide prevention in prisons, see IG 1/1994 and IG 79/1994.

'stored property'. Cell clearance sheets should be made up whenever a prisoner is 'ghosted' from one prison to another pursuant to IG 28/1993 for reasons of good order or discipline and he has no opportunity to collect his property from his cell.

11 *Miscellaneous wing records*—every wing should keep some form of diary/record of significant events. This may include staff rosters, though in many cases these are kept separately. The segregation unit and hospital wing will always have a more detailed form of record-keeping than a normal wing. Most prisons have a Gatekeeper's Daily Occurrence book to record movements in and out of the main gate. In some prisons there seems to be a practice of compiling Incident Reports (sometimes designated as Forms LP 180) to record significant incidents such as escape attempts or mass disturbances.

I. Preparing Evidence in Prison Actions

2.125 As the preceding section has shown, the prison authorities begin with a distinct advantage in any kind of civil litigation, in that they have access to a wide range of contemporaneous documents compiled in respect of almost every conceivable event within a prison. A prisoner-claimant who has been assaulted or been the victim of negligent medical treatment has, by contrast, many disadvantages. He has no legal right of access to an independent doctor unless and until litigation has been commenced. Given the delays in obtaining legal aid, this may be many months or even years after the incident which has given rise to the complaint. By then a medical examination may be useless. Obtaining statements from witnesses may cause special difficulties. Fellow prisoners may be transferred to a different prison or released. Alternatively, the prisoner-claimant may be placed in solitary confinement after the incident which has given rise to the claim and thus find it impossible to contact potential witnesses.

2.126 In these circumstances it is essential that a prisoner who believes that he or she is the victim of any form of injustice should take as many steps as possible to strengthen any subsequent legal action by following a number of basic rules:

1 Take steps at the earliest moment to write a clear, chronological account of the relevant incident or sequence of events. If a prisoner has difficulty in reading or writing he should seek assistance from a fellow prisoner or sympathetic member of staff. Sign and date the statement and ask someone (preferably a member of the prison staff such as a probation officer or the chaplain) to countersign and date it. If the statement is made sufficiently soon after the incident in dispute, it can be used as a memory-refreshing document in court. It will be bound to be more reliable than a statement given

to a solicitor many months later. Make sure that the statement is not vague and generalized. It is no good in an assault claim merely to say 'Prison officers X and Y viciously attacked me'. The statement must record, as much as is possible, who did what, giving details of what blows were landed where, whether they were kicks or punches, and how many were delivered. Where the identity of any assailant is unknown, give as detailed a description as possible ('Officer 1 was six feet tall, blond haired, bearded with a Welsh accent').

2 Establish at the earliest possible moment the identities of any witnesses and try to obtain written statements from them while memories are fresh. These too should be dated, signed, and preferably countersigned. Where the prison authorities make it difficult to obtain such statements, make a formal complaint and keep a record of it. Follow up the complaint with a letter to an MP if this does not produce results.

3 Where any injury whatsoever is sustained, demand access to any medical report compiled by the prison medical officer. If it does not fully record all the complaints made and the injuries sustained ask for the report to be amended. If this is refused, ask that the request is formally recorded. Failing this, make an immediate complaint about the quality of the medical report and follow it up with a letter to an MP. In actions for assault, the prison medical officer's report will normally be the only one available to support (or destroy) the prisoner's claim and now that a medical report which supports all injuries pleaded must be served at the time that any claim for personal injuries is commenced, it is obviously vital that it is as full as possible. A complaint two years after the incident that the medical report is inaccurate will carry far less weight than an immediate, formal objection to its content.[216]

4 Where the complaint relates to a lengthy course of conduct such as persistently poor medical treatment or long-term segregation in intolerable conditions, keep a contemporaneous diary of events (preferably countersigned each day). Such a document can be a vital weapon in establishing credibility, accuracy, and reliability as well as being an important counter to the records maintained by the prison authorities.

---

[216] If a prisoner has complained to prison healthcare staff after being injured by staff (or other prisoners), the injuries should be recorded in the IMR. However, there are numerous examples of such injuries going unrecorded. In its *Report to the Government to the United Kingdom on the visit to the United Kingdom carried out by the European Committee for the Prevention of Torture and Inhuman or Degrading Treatment or Punishment from 4 to 16 February 2001*, the Committee stressed that 'the record made of the medical examination of an inmate following a violent episode in prison should contain (i) a full account of the statements made by the person concerned which are relevant to the medical examination (including the description of his/her state of health and any allegations of ill-treatment), (ii) a full account of objective medical findings based on a thorough examination, and (iii) the doctor's conclusions in light of (i) and (ii)' (para 43).

5 Contact a solicitor as soon as possible whenever legal action is contemplated. A solicitor will be able to provide advice on how to preserve and collect evidence relevant to the claim but he or she cannot remedy any failures to follow steps (1)–(4) above, which all rest on immediate action by the potential prisoner-claimant.

3

INTERNATIONAL LAW AVENUES
OF REDRESS

A. Introduction

In the previous chapter we surveyed the ways in which prisoners can pursue claims **3.01** relating to their conditions and treatment through the domestic legal system. We saw that although the number and effectiveness of available avenues have increased in recent years they still fall some way short of a comprehensive mechanism for the definition and protection of prisoners' rights. Until relatively recently that would have been the end of the matter as regards available forms of redress. However, since the end of World War II prisoners have also been able to turn to a developing body of institutions and legal doctrine for the protection of human rights at an international level. The impact of these international human rights mechanisms in the United Kingdom has been considerable. Indeed, it is arguable that without the prodding of the European Convention on Human Rights (ECHR) neither the administration nor the judiciary in the United

Kingdom would have done very much to recognize any legal rights for prisoners, and that a book such as this would not have been possible. With the incorporation of that Convention into UK law through the Human Rights Act 1998 (HRA) it has now become possible for prisoners to invoke such rights in domestic courts. As we argue at various points in this book, the HRA has opened up a range of new possibilities for prison law, even if the courts have sometimes failed to show enthusiasm for using the Act to rethink the form and content of the legal regulation of prison life in the United Kingdom. However, it is important to remember that the coming into force of the HRA has not brought an end to the international supervision of prisons. If prisoners and their representatives continue to feel aggrieved, even after a decision of a domestic court which considers the HRA, they will still have the option of seeking redress from Strasbourg, an option not open to the State if it feels unhappy with interpretations of the HRA. In addition there remain a range of other international human rights provisions which have still not been incorporated into domestic law, but which continue to be significant for those interested in prison law in the United Kingdom.

3.02 That prisoners should be an object of concern of human rights treaties and institutions is hardly surprising, since it was the treatment of prisoners in the period immediately before and during World War II that was one of the main inspirations for the human rights law-making that came after it. Revelations of what had happened in the concentration camps of Nazi Germany and its occupied territories gave rise to a widespread feeling that it was no longer enough to leave each government to define the civil rights of its citizens and that some kind of international declaration of rights and supervision mechanism was necessary. The concrete expression of these views was the (non-binding) United Nations Universal Declaration of Human Rights in 1948. It was to be followed by a series of treaties which have subsequently become more content- and region-specific.[1] Although it was initially assumed in most of these agreements that government-to-government negotiation would be the mechanism by which the rights guaranteed would be ensured, human rights institutions have an increasing degree of autonomy from the governments which created them, and individuals have sought to assert their rights directly against sovereign States.

3.03 Just as the fate of prisoners was a strong motivating factor in the creation of international human rights treaties, so prisoners have featured strongly in the activities of the institutions set up to ensure the enforcement of those treaties. Applications from people in detention make up the majority of cases considered by both the

---

[1] Notably the European Convention on Human Rights (ECHR) (1950), International Covenant on Civil and Political Rights (ICCPR) (1966), Inter-American Convention on Human Rights (1969) and the African Charter of Human and Peoples Rights (1981). For an overview of these see T Buergenthal, *International Human Rights* (St Paul, Minn, 1988) or P Sieghart, *The International Law of Human Rights* (Oxford, 1983).

European Court of Human Rights (ECtHR) and the United Nations Human Rights Committee.[2] Although in some early applications to the European Commission it was argued that the rights guaranteed by the Convention should not apply fully to prisoners, that there were 'inherent limitations' on such rights imposed by the fact and significance of detention after a criminal conviction,[3] the Commission swiftly rejected this. While regularly acknowledging that the context of imprisonment may have an effect on the extent of the right guaranteed, especially that it must be borne in mind in the application of the limitation or 'clawback' clauses,[4] the European Commission and ECtHR have gone on to define and protect a wide range of rights in the prison context. These decisions have had a significant impact on the prison system of the United Kingdom in areas such as disciplinary procedures,[5] access to the courts and the outside world,[6] release procedures for life sentence prisoners and prisoners detained during Her Majesty's Pleasure,[7] the treatment of detainees,[8] prisoners' rights to marry,[9] and secrecy regarding prisons.[10]

Relevant International Conventions

The focus in this chapter is on matters of procedure rather than content. More **3.04** detailed consideration is given to how the content of international human rights norms comes to bear on prisoners' rights in the United Kingdom in the context of particular issues of discipline, transfer, segregation, etc, which are discussed in subsequent chapters. Most of this chapter is devoted to examination of the procedural mechanisms of perhaps the best known and most influential of the international human rights conventions, the ECHR. We go into some detail on this in the light of its importance and the fact that many lawyers in the United

---

[2] See J Fawcett, 'Applications to the European Convention on Human Rights' in M Maguire, J Vagg, and R Morgan, *Accountability and Prisons: Opening up a Closed World* (London, 1986) 63.

[3] See *Golder v UK* Series A No 18 (1975) 1 EHRR 524.

[4] The phrase 'clawback clauses' is that of Rosalyn Higgins in R Higgins, 'Derogation Under Human Rights Treaties' (1976–77) 48 British Yearbook of Intl L 281. It refers to provisions such as that in Art 8(2) of the ECHR which, after guaranteeing the right of privacy, goes on to add, '[t]here shall be no interference by a public authority with the exercise of this right except as is in accordance with the law and is necessary in a democratic society in the interests of national security, public safety or the economic well being of the country, for the prevention of disorder or crime, for the protection of health or morals, or for the protection of the rights and freedoms of others'.

[5] *Campbell and Fell v UK* Series A No 80 (1985) 7 EHRR 165; *Ezeh and Connors v UK* (2002) 35 EHRR 28.

[6] *Golder v UK* Series A No 18 (1975) 1 EHRR 524; *Silver v UK* Series A No 61 (1983) 5 EHRR 347.

[7] *Weeks v UK* Series A No 114 (1988) 10 EHRR 293; *Thynne, Wilson and Gunnell v UK* (1991) 13 EHRR 666; *Hussain v UK* (1996) 22 EHRR 1; *Stafford v UK* Application 46295/99, The Times, 31 May 2002.

[8] *Ireland v UK* Series A No 25 (1978) 2 EHRR 1.

[9] *Hamer v UK* (1982) 4 EHRR 139 (1979).

[10] *Harman v UK* 46 D & R 57 (1986).

Kingdom are still relatively unfamiliar with it. However, we also look at the procedures of other major human rights treaties relevant to this area, such as the
European Convention for the Prevention of Torture and Inhuman or Degrading
Treatment or Punishment (ECPT), the United Nations International Covenant
on Civil and Political Rights (ICCPR), and the United Nations Convention
against Torture and Other Cruel, Inhuman or Degrading Treatment or
Punishment (CAT). In addition we touch on other relevant international codes of
standards and on the work of UN agencies in relation to the treatment of those in
detention.

Status of International Conventions in UK Law

3.05 Before examining these various international law avenues it is worth making a
brief comment on their status in domestic law. As we indicated earlier, only the
ECHR has been incorporated into domestic law by the HRA. The main UN
human rights treaty, the ICCPR, although in many ways similar to the ECHR,
contains several provisions which go further than its Council of Europe equivalent. However, like any other treaty ratified by the United Kingdom the ICCPR
binds the United Kingdom at international level only and is not enforceable in the
domestic courts, since it has not been 'incorporated' by a statute of the UK
Parliament. Courts in the United Kingdom have indicated that where Parliament
has legislated and the words of the statute are clear then that statute must be given
effect, even if the statutory provision in question is in contravention of a human
rights treaty which the United Kingdom has ratified.[11] Since Parliament is presumed to act in accordance with the United Kingdom's international obligations,
however, a human rights treaty may be invoked to assist interpretation where the
statutory provision in question is ambiguous, even if the statute was not passed to
give effect to the treaty.[12] In the case of *R v Home Secretary, ex p Brind*[13] the applicants argued that Ministers and officials exercising discretionary powers granted
to them by statute were bound to exercise these in conformity with the ECHR,
that no reasonable Minister or official could do otherwise. This proposition is of
particular interest in the prison context, given the fact that the Prison Act 1952
does little more than confer power on the Secretary of State to make Prison Rules,
and these in turn confer considerable discretion on governors and prison officers.
It was not a proposition the House of Lords in *Brind* agreed with, however. Lord
Ackner, speaking for a unanimous House of Lords, indicated that in his view this
would be incorporating the Convention 'by the back door' and that it would go
beyond the judicial function. All the Lords seemed to acknowledge that the

[11] See *Salomon v Customs and Excise Commissioners* [1966] 3 All ER 871.
[12] See *R v Chief Immigration Officer Heathrow Airport, ex p Salamat Bibi* [1976] 3 All ER 843.
[13] [1991] 1 AC 696.

Secretary of State had to take the Convention into account in formulating rules where this was relevant, though it is not clear that this applies to lower officials exercising discretionary power conferred on them.[14]

With the coming into force of the HRA in October 2000 this question is no **3.06** longer relevant with regard to the ECHR. That, as we saw in the last chapter, has now given rise to new questions regarding the interpretation and application of the HRA. However, the effect of the ICCPR remains subject to the *Brind* test that the human rights instrument may only be resorted to when a pre-existing ambiguity can be discerned in the statute. This position has recently been subject to strong criticism,[15] and it may be that with the fear of unjustified judicial incorporation 'by the back door' now having been removed (as we now have legislative incorporation of the ECHR by the front door) the judiciary may be prepared to consider other human rights guarantees such as those in the ICCPR more sympathetically where they arguably go further than what is guaranteed by the HRA.

Even with incorporation the international realm remains relevant. Prisoners who **3.07** have exhausted their domestic remedies can still take their cases to Strasbourg, and there are a range of other international standards and mechanisms to which the United Kingdom is accountable in respect of its treatment of prisoners, at least at the level of international law.

B. The European Convention on Human Rights

Overview

The ECHR was signed on 4 November 1950 and came into force on 3 September **3.08** 1953. The United Kingdom was the first party to ratify it, in 1951. The Convention was the outcome of a resolution of the Consultative Assembly of the Council of Europe in August 1949 to produce a collective guarantee of human rights. Though the Convention's preamble states that it was framed 'to take the first steps for collective enforcement of certain rights stated in the Universal Declaration' it seems clear that one of the reasons for the drafting of a specifically European treaty was a perception that the 1948 Universal Declaration on Human Rights was too imprecise to be legally enforceable. Thus far the Convention has been ratified by 44 Member States, Bosnia and Herzegovina being the most recent to do so. The Convention is a text of 66 Articles, of which Articles 2 to 14 set out

---

[14] See on this *Fernandez v Home Secretary* [1981] Imm AR 1.
[15] Notably by Hunt in M Hunt, *Using Human Rights Law in English Courts* (Oxford, 1997) 37–41. For an exploration of the developing status of international law in domestic adjudication, see K Knop, 'Here and There: International Law in Domestic Courts' (2000) 32 New York U J of International L and Politics 501.

the rights that the parties undertake to guarantee to all within their jurisdiction.[16] In addition the Convention is now supplemented by 12 protocols, though not all of these have been ratified by all the contracting States.[17]

3.09　The responsibility for ensuring that the rights guaranteed under the Convention are protected lies first with the Member States. However, claims that they have failed to do so may also be raised with institutions established under the Convention in Strasbourg. With the ratification of Protocol 11 by sufficient States in October 1997, significant changes were made to the Convention enforcement mechanism.[18] These changes responded to the growing membership of the Council of Europe, the huge backlog of applications registered with the Commission, and the threat posed to the legitimacy of the Convention system by the inordinate delays in determining applications.

3.10　Under the old system, applicants first had to make an application to the European Commission of Human Rights, whose primary task was to determine the admissibility of applications, but which also supervised friendly settlements and gave a written opinion on the merits. Applications which the Commission found admissible and which were not resolved by way of friendly settlement might then be considered by the ECtHR (especially where the Commission was of the opinion that there was a violation). The court was empowered to give a judgment and order the payment of compensation in cases of a violation. Alternatively, admissible applications might be referred to the Committee of Ministers for resolution. With the ratification of Protocol 11 a new ECtHR came into force on 1 November 1998, with jurisdiction over both admissibility and merits. The Commission continued to sit until October 1999 to deal with cases declared admissible by it before November 1998. All cases registered but not declared admissible by that date, all cases which the Commission failed to deal with by October 1999, and of course all new cases, are referred to the court. Under the current system the Committee of Ministers has no role in deciding upon the merits of applications, but retains a role in supervising the enforcement of judgments of the court. In our discussion of the mechanics of making an application in this chapter, we deal exclusively with the new procedure before the single court. However, we will on occasions refer to the jurisprudence of the Commission on admissibility questions. The criteria for the admissibility of applications remains unchanged under the new system and it is likely that this jurisprudence will remain very relevant.

---

[16] See the text of the Convention in Appendix 5. For a detailed examination of the practice and procedure of the ECtHR, see J Simor and B Emmerson, eds, *Human Rights Practice* (London, 2001) ch 19; R Clayton and H Tomlinson, *The Law of Human Rights* (Oxford, 2000) ch 23, and L Clements, N Mole and A Simmons, *European Human Rights: Taking a Case under the Convention* (2nd edn, London, 1999).

[17] The UK has ratified Protocols 2, 3, 5, 8, 10, and 11.

[18] See 'Explanatory Report to the Eleventh Protocol, Council of Europe' (1995) 17 EHRR 514.

The ECHR provides for applications to be made to its institutions by both indi- **3.11**
viduals who are located in a Member State[19] and Member States against each
other. When the Convention was first drafted it was expected that international
human rights guarantees would be enforced primarily through Article 33, which
permits inter-state actions. This procedure has been invoked by States parties in a
number of cases, normally concerned with the treatment of those detained under
suspicion of criminal involvement.[20] However, the real development of the
Convention has been in the area of complaints by individuals of violations of the
Convention under Article 34. These outnumber applications by States by over
60,000 to under 20. The United Kingdom has accepted compulsory jurisdiction
of the court in respect of such applications since 1965.[21] Without the large volume
of individual applications and the generally robust approach that the Strasbourg
institutions have taken to the protection of human rights the ECHR might have
had a very limited impact indeed.

Making an Application

Initiating a Convention application is remarkably simple. The applicant need **3.12**
only send a letter to the Secretary of the Court in Strasbourg setting out the facts
of the case and a statement of the Articles which the applicant alleges have been
breached. He should also indicate why he considers the admissibility criteria
(which will be discussed in greater detail below) have been satisfied. Although an
applicant can conduct his case entirely on his own, applicants represented by
lawyers have a much higher success rate. Initially any application will be assigned
to a lawyer in the Court's Registry, who since 1 January 2002 is required to register it.[22] When this happens it will be given a case number (hence references in the
reports to application 27915/95, application 27915 which was registered in
1995, for example) and a member of the court will be appointed rapporteur in
respect of the application.[22a]

The court is composed of one member from each of the Member States. The mem- **3.13**
bers of the court are elected by the Parliamentary Assembly of the Council of Europe

---

[19]   They need not be citizens of that Member State or even of any Member State.

[20]   See, eg, *Ireland v UK* (1978) 2 EHRR 25; *Denmark, Sweden and Norway v Greece*, Yearbook
12 (1969); *France v Turkey*, Yearbook 28 (1985), 150.

[21]   With the entry into force of Protocol 11 the acceptance of the Court's compulsory jurisdiction in cases brought by individuals is no longer at the discretion of Member States, as it was in
1953–98. The background to the UK's acceptance of the right of individual petition is examined in
Lester, 'UK Acceptance of the Strasbourg Jurisdiction: What Really went on in Whitehall in 1965'
[1998] PL 237.

[22]   The practice of Court lawyers writing a warning letter to the applicant where a case appeared
inadmissible before registering it was discontinued at the start of 2002 in the interests of efficiency.

[22a]   See r 48 of the Court Rules of Procedure. For a discussion of those Rules, see L Clements,
'Striking the Right Balance: The New Rules of Procedure for the European Court of Human
Rights' [1999] European Human Rights L Rev 266.

and sit on the court in their individual capacities. They are independent of the government of the State from which they come. They are required to be people of high moral character who either possess the qualifications for high judicial office or are 'jurisconsults of recognised competence'.[23] Court members are elected for six-year terms and can be re-elected. However the Convention aims to renew the terms of office of half of the judges every three years, and to this effect provides that the terms of office of half the judges of the new court (chosen by lot) will expire after three years. Unlike the Commission and the old court the new ECtHR is a full time body. To support it in its work the court is assisted by a full-time Registry staffed by over 300 lawyers, translators and administrative staff from among the Member States.[24]

3.14 The first task of the court is to decide on the admissibility of the application under the Convention. The Rapporteur in each case will direct their efforts primarily to doing this and may seek further information from the applicant and/or the respondent State. Boyle has observed that ensuring that a case is formally communicated to the respondent government for observations 'ought to be the minimum goal of any application under the Convention prepared by a lawyer'.[25] Ultimately the Rapporteur makes his report to the court, either to one of the Chambers of the court or, more usually, to a committee of three members of it.[26] Where the case goes to a Committee of Three it may, if unanimous, declare an application inadmissible or strike it off its list. This decision is final and no appeal from it is available. However, under Article 45 the Committee is required to give reasons for its decision though these tend to be rather brief. Where the Committee takes no such decision or where the Rapporteur decides the case should be referred directly to a Chamber, then the application will be considered as regards both admissibility and merits by a Chamber of seven judges. All inter-state cases must be considered by a Chamber. At any time in its consideration of an application a Chamber is entitled to relinquish jurisdiction to a Grand Chamber of 17 judges, unless one of the parties objects. Article 30 indicates that the Chamber may relinquish jurisdiction where the case 'raises a serious question affecting the interpretation of the Convention or the protocols thereto, or where resolution of a question before the Chamber might have a result inconsistent with a judgment previously delivered by the Court'.

---

[23] Art 21(1).

[24] Members of the registry are recruited by the Secretary General of the Council of Europe. Its most senior members, the Registrar and Deputy Registrar, are appointed by the Court.

[25] See K Boyle, 'Practice and Procedure on Individual Applications in the European Convention on Human Rights' in H Hannum (ed), *Guide to International Human Rights Practice* (2nd edn, Philadelphia, Penn, 1994), and A Drzemczewski, 'The International Organisation of the European Court of Human Rights: The Composition of Chambers and the Grand Chamber' (2000) European Human Rights L Rev 233.

[26] Art 27(1).

Friendly Settlement

The court has power to hold a hearing in order to decide issues of both admissi- **3.15**
bility and merits. However as all hearings are now required to be in public,
whereas hearings of the Commission could take place in private, it seems unlikely
that the court will wish to hold hearings in those cases where a friendly settlement
is possible. The friendly settlement procedure, inherited from the old
Commission, is now governed by Article 38 and remains a confidential procedure. Any such settlement must be 'on the basis of regard for Human Rights as
defined in the Convention'.[27] The Commission practice was usually to invite the
parties to a meeting to discuss a settlement but largely to leave the question
whether there would be a settlement to the parties themselves. Where the parties
indicated that they were willing to settle the Commission then became involved
in assisting them to establish the terms of the settlement, sometimes shuttling
between the parties, who never met. On other occasions the defendant State and
the applicant reached an agreement without the involvement of the Commission.

Settlements are normally reached on the basis of the payment of money to the **3.16**
applicant and/or some change in the applicant's situation, for example reduction
of a prison sentence, or allowing the applicant to remain in the country. On some
occasions such settlements have been accompanied by government commitments
to administrative, or more rarely legislative, reforms. In the *McComb*[28] case, for
example, the UK Government agreed to institute a procedure whereby prisoners'
legal mail would only be examined in their presence. As the court's task is to ensure
that settlements are reached on the basis of respect for human rights it theoretically
has the power to veto settlements which allow the violation that gave rise to the
application to remain in existence. However the Commission never refused a settlement reached by the parties, a stance which has led to some criticism. In the
Northern Irish case of *Farrell v UK*,[29] for example, the Commission accepted an
agreement by the Government to pay the applicant, the widow of one of three men
shot dead by soldiers, £37,500 without any admission of liability or commitment
to review the law on lethal force.[30] Also, in the inter-state case of *France et al v
Turkey*[31] the settlement accepted largely consisted of an obligation on Turkey to
make a number of confidential reports regarding its progress towards eradicating

---

[27] Art 38(1)(b).
[28] 50 D & R 81 (1988).
[29] (1983) 5 EHRR 466.
[30] T Opsahl, 'Settlement based on respect for Human Rights under the European Convention
on Human Rights' in *Proceedings of the Sixth International Colloquy about the European Convention
on Human Rights* (Dordrecht, 1988), 970, comments about the *Farrell* case however that 'from the
Commission's point of view this was not a case of general interest, but one concerning a unique
incident'.
[31] Yearbook 28 (1985) 150.

some serious breaches of human rights, including torture and detention without trial, without any means of taking further action should these prove inadequate. The court does not appear to have been significantly more critical of the terms of friendly settlements than was the Commission. If a friendly settlement is reached the court will strike the case out of its list by way of a decision which is confined to a brief statement of the facts and solution reached.[32] Under Article 37(2)(b) the court may also strike a case out at any time if the parties have informally resolved the matter. However, many cases are now dealt with on paper only.

Hearing Before the Court

3.17 Where a case has not been declared inadmissible by a Committee of Three or resolved by way of friendly settlement it may proceed to a hearing before the court, normally in a Chamber of seven judges but sometimes—in cases of particular significance or complexity—before a Grand Chamber of 17. At any such hearing the applicant will be invited to make a submission either in person or by a representative. The State will also be invited to make representations. The court has a power to call witnesses itself and may also call witnesses at the request of the parties. It has no power, however, to compel witnesses to attend. With the coming into force of Protocol 11 the practice developed under the court's Rules of Procedure of allowing interventions by interested third parties has now been formalized. Article 36(2) now provides that the President of the court may 'in the interest of the proper administration of justice' invite any person concerned who is not the applicant to submit written comments or take part in hearings. Such third party interventions, mostly by non-governmental organizations, have proved increasingly significant in the court's decision-making.[33] Member States one of whose nationals is an applicant may also intervene in the case.[34]

Fact-finding

3.18 The court has taken over the fact-finding role once accorded to the Commission. In most cases the facts can be easily discerned from the judgments of the national courts below. However where no such record exists (for example in cases alleging violations of rights of access to the courts or to an adequate remedy) or it is argued that the record is inadequate to dispose of the case then the court may seek to ascertain the facts for itself. The Commission has conducted extensive fact-finding hearings in respect of cases from Turkey, where the applicants have alleged serious violations of human rights and the lack of adequate national remedies. To

---

[32] Art 39.
[33] See M Nowicki, 'NGOs before the Commission and Court of Human Rights' (1996) 14 Netherlands Q of Human Rights 289.
[34] As in the *Soering* case (*Soering v UK* Series A No 137 (1989) 11 EHRR 202) where the applicant was a German national although the UK was the defendant State.

do so, the Commission appointed delegates to conduct hearings from Turkey.[35] This sort of role now falls to the court, which has also, under Rule 41(2) of its Rules of Procedure, appointed one or more members of a Chamber to act as delegates for the whole Chamber when such a fact-finding inquiry is deemed necessary. Though the court may request documents and other information from States it appears to have no power to compel them to provide them. States failing to supply information may however be in breach of their obligation under Article 38(1)(a) of the Convention to 'furnish all necessary facilities' to the court.[35a]

The Decision of the Court

Once the hearing stage is complete the court may conclude that the application is **3.19** inadmissible, in which case it goes no further. No appeal is available against this decision. Article 29(3) indicates that the court should take its decision on admissibility separately from that on the merits unless, in exceptional cases, it decides otherwise. Where the court decides that an application is admissible it will then proceed to give its view on the merits of the application. The court reaches its decisions by majority and has provision for the publication of dissenting views and separate concurrences. However its decision does not become binding on the parties automatically. For three months after the date of the judgment either party may request that the decision be referred to the Grand Chamber.[36] Article 43(2) indicates that a panel of five judges will consider this request and may accede to it where the case raises a serious question affecting the interpretation of the Convention or a serious issue of general importance. Some human rights lawyers have expressed concern about this power to seek review of judgments, fearing it will primarily be used by States to delay decisions. However it appears that it was the minimum that States were prepared to accept in order to achieve a single-tier system.[37] So far the court has agreed to refer 16 decisions of Chambers to the Grand Chamber. In the first of these to be heard the Grand Chamber upheld the decision below.[37a]

---

[35] See, generally, A Reidy, F Hampson, and K Boyle, 'Dealing with Gross Violations of Human Rights: Turkey and the ECHR' (1997) 15 Netherlands Q of Human Rights 161.

[35a] The court made such a finding in *Tanrikulu v Turkey*, Decision of the Court 8 July 1999 (2000) 30 EHRR 950 where the Turkish authorities failed to respond to repeated requests for an investigation file relating to an alleged killing by the security forces and provided no reasons as to why two prosecutors failed to appear before the Court delegates.

[36] However the parties may indicate at any time within that period that they will not refer the case, whereupon the judgment becomes binding.

[37] See A Drzemczewski and J-M Ladewig, 'Principal Characteristics of the New ECHR Control Mechanism' (1994) 15 Human Rights LJ 81.

[37a] See *Metfah and others v France* Decision of the Court, 26 July 2002.

Compensation and Costs

3.20 The court has no power to order States to take any particular steps. However under Article 41, the court has jurisdiction to award 'just satisfaction' to a successful applicant. The court can make an order for the award of compensation where it finds a breach and concludes that the law of the State in question allows partial or no reparation for the violation in question. Applicants who seek compensation should ask for it in their memorials to the court; but awards of compensation are discretionary, and in a number of cases the court has held that the decision itself is adequate compensation for the violation. The general, aim of the Court is to restore the victim to the position which they would have been in without the breach of the Convention. Hence compensation is most appropriate where the applicant has suffered a loss which has not been put right in some other way, for example where property has already been restored to the applicant by the time of the hearing. Compensation is available for both pecuniary losses, such as loss of property, and non-pecuniary losses such as personal injury or mental distress.[38] However some observers have suggested that the court has shown a reluctance to order compensation for violations involving convicted prisoners, preferring to suggest a finding of violation is sufficient redress.[39] The applicants' costs have often been recovered under Article 41's predecessor, Article 50. As with claims for compensation, requests for costs should be included in memorials to the court. The court only gives remuneration for costs actually incurred, so where a lawyer has given his or her services free of charge or costs have been covered by domestic legal aid no award will be made.[40] As with awards of compensation, the court's approach to the award of costs has not been free from criticism as lacking in principle or consistency.[41]

Implementation of Judgments

3.21 The task of supervising the implementation of judgments of the court, which Member States have committed themselves to abide by in Article 46(1), falls to the Committee of Ministers. This is composed of the foreign ministers of Member States of the Council of Europe, or more usually their permanent representatives in

---

[38] For a table of 'just satisfaction' awards for the violation of each of the Convention articles, see J Simor and B Emmerson, n 16 above, Appendix A9.

[39] See A Mowbray, 'The European Court of Human Rights Approach to Just Satisfaction' [1997] PL 647, 652.

[40] While the costs must have been incurred, in the sense that the applicant has a liability to pay them, the applicant need not show that they have been, or will be, paid: in *Pakelli v Germany* (1983) 6 EHRR 1, the Court stated that costs could be awarded to an applicant even if, through lack of means, he would not have been able to pay them himself in any event.

[41] See C Gray, *Remedies in International Law* (Oxford, 1987) 158. Clements, Mole and Simmons observe that costs can include those of domestic proceedings taken to exhaust domestic remedies providing the applicant would otherwise have been responsible for those costs, eg where they were not legally aided: see L Clements, N Mole and A Simmons, *European Human Rights: Taking a Case under the Convention* (2nd edn, London, 1999).

Strasbourg. Generally it performs this function by seeking reports from defendant States on the steps they have taken to comply with the Convention. The Committee requires reports every two months as to what has been done in respect of the individual applicant and every six months as regards the Member State's actions to deal with the general issue raised by the finding of a violation. Cases have remained on the Committee's agenda for up to ten years before its issuing of a final resolution accepting that the Member State is in compliance. In this time it may have issued interim resolutions expressing concern or making suggestions on aspects of the State's report. However, beyond keeping the case on its agenda and exercising diplomatic pressure there is relatively little the Committee can do with a State which refuses to implement a judgment.[42] Ultimately the main sanction available for non-compliance lies in the statute of the Council of Europe, which, like the Committee, predated the Convention. This allows for the expulsion of a member from the Council. So far this has not occurred, the Committee coming closest to it over the *Greek* case.[43] In that case Greece's withdrawal from the Council rendered the issue moot.

The Admissibility Criteria

3.22 The admissibility criteria have proved to be a substantial hurdle for many applications. Less than 25 per cent of those applications registered have ultimately been found to be admissible by the Commission.[44] Hence lawyers making applications need to ensure that they meet these criteria. These are largely contained in Articles 34 to 35 of the Convention. The most significant are the following.

That the Applicant be a Victim

3.23 States invoking the Article 33 procedure against other Member States do not have to show that they, or any of their nationals, have been affected by an alleged breach of the Convention. They are granted a general right to complain of alleged breaches in order to enforce the Convention. As regards individual applications, however, Article 34 states that applications may be made by 'any person, non-governmental organisation and groups of individuals' who claim to be the victims of a breach of the Convention. Individuals or groups cannot bring an action as an *actio popularis*; they must show that they particularly are affected in some way by the breach of the Convention. The lack of an *actio popularis* is perhaps a defect in a Convention dedicated to ensuring the most effective protection of the human rights of all in the Member States, since obvious human rights violations may go unchallenged for lack of a victim prepared to pursue a case through the lengthy

---

[42] A particularly prominent current example being Turkey's continuing refusal to pay the compensation ordered by the court in *Loizidou v Turkey*, Decision of the Court 28 July 1998.

[43] Yearbook 12 (1969), 1.

[44] In the period 1 January 2000 to 31 December 2000 the Court declared 6,769 applications inadmissible, and found 1,082 admissible. This figure is, however, on the rise. In 1990 only about 7% of applications were declared admissible.

procedures that Strasbourg requires. Non-governmental organizations (NGOs) in particular could play a useful role in highlighting and challenging such violations. In the prison context this might be especially valuable in respect of conditions in remand prisons, where prisoners may not see the value of launching cases that may take five years to reach a decision. Under the Convention, NGOs may only bring a claim if they themselves have been a victim of an alleged violation or if they represent someone who has been.

3.24 The notion of 'victim' in Article 34 is not limited to direct victims. In a series of decisions the Commission has indicated that it also encompasses 'indirect victims', near relatives of the victim or a third party who is so closely connected with the victim that the violation concerned is also prejudicial to her, or in so far as she has a valid personal interest in the termination of the violation. The Commission has also recognized a right to petition for those who have not yet suffered from a breach of the Convention but run a significant risk of doing so in the future. This view has been developed in a number of cases, mainly involving the right to privacy and family life guaranteed by Article 8, where the significant factors appear to have been that the victim be a member of an identified class (such as gays in *Norris v Ireland*[45] or schoolchildren in a school where corporal punishment was practised, as in *Campbell v Cosans*[46]) and that the potential violation already have an effect on their lives (for example, in *Norris* a gay applicant's vulnerability to harassment and blackmail or in *Bruggemann and Scheuten v Federal Republic of Germany*[47] the limitation on a woman's sexual freedom raised by the prohibition of abortion). In addition those who suspect but cannot prove themselves to be victims may be entitled to bring claims where it is government secrecy which prevents them from ascertaining whether they are victims, as in the telephone-tapping case of *Klass v Federal Republic of Germany*.[48]

Exhaustion of Domestic Remedies

3.25 Article 35 of the Convention indicates that the general rule of international law, that international tribunals may not be seized of a case until all domestic remedies have been exhausted, applies to the Convention. Early in its case law the Commission made it clear that the applicant's obligation is to exhaust all domestic remedies that are 'effective and sufficient' to provide a remedy for the breach of the Convention alleged.[49] This reference to remedies that are effective and sufficient is especially important in the prison context, given the existence of internal remedies and the limited effectiveness of judicial review. It gives rise to a number of points.

---

[45] Series A No 142 (1991) 13 EHRR 186 (1988).
[46] Series A No 48 (1982) 4 EHRR 293.
[47] Yearbook 19 (1976), 382.
[48] Series A No 21 (1978) 2 EHRR 214.
[49] *De Becker* Series A No 4 (1962) 1 EHRR 43.

First it means that the applicant need not exhaust avenues of remedy that are dis- **3.26**
cretionary in character. Only remedies that are mandatory are deemed effective.
Thus applicants need not pursue applications for pardons or petitions of mercy or
appeals to bodies that are merely advisory in character. While effective remedies
are not confined to judicial remedies it would appear that to be effective administrative remedies must be capable of being binding on the authorities. Internal
Prison Service grievance procedures may amount to an effective remedy in these
terms, where the claim relates to the application, rather than the content, of
Prison Rules. The position is less clear as regards the Prisons Ombudsman. As the
Ombudsman is only empowered to make recommendations which can be
overruled by the Secretary of State there must remain doubts whether he can
provide an effective remedy which must be exhausted before a prisoner goes to
Strasbourg.

The second implication is that even those remedies which might be thought **3.27**
effective can be rendered otherwise by circumstances. In particular, judicial remedies may be rendered ineffective where it is clear by established case law of the
national courts in question that no remedy is available on the facts as alleged by
the applicant. Thus in the case of *Campbell and Fell v UK*,[50] where prisoners challenged the conduct of disciplinary proceedings in a prison, the Commission held
they did not have to seek judicial review in the English courts before bringing the
case to Strasbourg as the settled case law of the English courts at the time the application was brought was that judicial review of decisions made in the prison was
unavailable (this was a pre-*St Germain* application, though in the *Kavanagh*[51]
case, concerned with refusal to transfer an Irish prisoner back to Northern Ireland,
the Commission again found judicial review not to be in need of exhaustion). In
this situation, as with the issue of what forums are effective, the test the
Commission applied was whether the application has a 'reasonable likelihood
of success'; where there is a doubt the applicant ought to invoke the doubtful
remedy. The Commission made it clear that it would judge this for itself, and that
acting on advice given in good faith by a lawyer that a remedy would not be
sufficient and effective was not enough to exhaust domestic remedies where the
Commission decided that the remedy did have a reasonable chance of success.[52]
However, it is generally safe to assume that a lawyer's opinion of the chances of
success in domestic law will be accepted where it is not clearly unreasonable. With
the introduction of the HRA, which allows Convention arguments to be raised
directly in UK courts, it has become more difficult to plead the argument
in Strasbourg that domestic judicial proceedings do not constitute an adequate

---

[50] Series A No 80 (1985) 7 EHRR 165.
[51] Application 19085/91, Commission Decision, 9 December 1992.
[52] For one case where the Commission disagreed with counsel's estimate of the likelihood of success and therefore ruled the application inadmissible see *K, F and P v UK*, 40 D & R 298 (1984).

remedy.[53] The one area where this may remain true is where the applicant argues that his Convention rights have been infringed by primary legislation (for example by s 16A of the Prison Act 1952 with respect to mandatory drugs testing). As courts in the United Kingdom have no power to order a remedy in favour of the applicant, should they find a violation, it can be argued that no effective domestic judicial remedy exists.

3.28 The Commission has indicated that applicants must have raised all the issues that they wish to raise in the Convention proceedings before the domestic tribunal in order to show that they have exhausted domestic remedies. With the introduction of the HRA there is no excuse for applicants not having their Convention claims fully explored before national courts. Ignorance of a remedy or negligence in failing to raise it, for example through missing a time limit, will not be an excuse for failing to exhaust it. In *Castells v Spain*[54] the court stressed that it is sufficient that the Convention claims have been raised in substance, even if the applicant has referred to similar domestic constitutional provisions rather than the language of the Convention.

3.29 Applicants will be excused from exhausting a domestic remedy where they claim that they are victims of an administrative practice, a claim most usually made in cases concerning allegations of ill treatment. The Commission has indicated that an administrative practice will often render domestic remedies ineffective 'by the difficulty of securing probative evidence and administrative enquiries would either not be instituted or, if they were, would be likely to be half hearted and incomplete'.[55] The Commission saw an administrative practice as consisting in the repetition of acts which form a pattern and which are officially tolerated at 'the level of the direct superiors of those immediately responsible or that of a higher authority'. In the *Donnelly*[56] case, however, the Commission held that the authorities paying compensation to those injured by ill treatment, coupled with a willingness to investigate the incidents, was sufficient to displace the claim that there had been an administrative practice; paying of compensation coupled with official indifference would not have been sufficient.

The Six Months Rule

3.30 Under Article 35(1) of the Convention, in addition to exhausting all domestic remedies the applicant must submit his application to the court within six months of the 'final decision' in his case. The two would appear to be linked, in that the final decision would normally be that which exhausts all domestic remedies. The link has caused some problems in that an applicant may exhaust a remedy only to

---

[53] For a pre-HRA case in which judicial review was held not to be an effective remedy for the purposes of Art 13 of the Convention, see *Smith and Grady v UK* (1999) 29 EHRR 493.
[54] Series A No 236 (1992) 14 EHRR 445.
[55] *Greek* case, Yearbook 16 (1973), 212.
[56] Yearbook 16 (1973), 212.

be told by the court that this remedy was not an effective remedy and that the final decision was taken earlier. That earlier time may be in excess of six months previously and the applicant may then find himself out of time. On the other hand an applicant, fearing that he may fall foul of the six months rule, may submit an application earlier, only to be told that the application is inadmissible for failure to exhaust domestic remedies. However, since such applications, inadmissible by reason of failure to exhaust domestic remedies, may always be resubmitted once domestic remedies have been exhausted, an applicant who is doubtful about the effectiveness of the domestic remedy he is pursuing might at the same time lodge an application with Strasbourg. It is only required that domestic remedies be exhausted by the time the Commission comes to rule on admissibility, not when the application is submitted. For the purposes of the six month rule the initial letter to the court counts as notification rather than the date of registration. However where this is not followed up by further submissions within a reasonable time the court may deem the application out of time.

Where no effective domestic remedy exists the six months are taken to run from **3.31** the time of the action allegedly causing the violation. However in the *De Becker* case the Commission indicated that this did not apply to cases of a continuing violation. What the Commission appeared to have in mind here is a violation brought about by operation of legislation, where no effective remedy existed, rather than a judicial or executive decision.[57] Yet what exactly was contemplated by this was not entirely clear and the issue of what constitutes a continuing violation remains underdeveloped. It does however suggest that prisoners complaining of violations of human rights arising out of their conditions or regime need not be too concerned about the effect of the six months rule. In *McFeeley v UK*, the applicant complained about repeated punishments for refusals to obey the prison rules. The Commission considered that, for the purposes of time limits, time only began to run 'after this state of affairs had ceased to exist'.[58]

Manifestly Ill-founded

This provision, contained in Article 35(3), is the catch-all admissibility criterion. **3.32** A number of Commission and Court decisions indicate that the standard applied is whether the application discloses a prima facie breach of the Convention.[59] Applications ruled inadmissible on this ground may be so as a result of a finding that the facts are not as alleged by the applicant or that even if as alleged they do not disclose an arguable breach of the Convention. Since no appeal is available against this decision, and since a finding of inadmissibility on this ground is likely to discourage further applications on the point, many commentators are unhappy

---

[57] *De Becker* had been sentenced to permanent deprivation of civil rights by a Belgian court for collaboration in World War II.

[58] Application 8317/78, 20 DR 44, 76.

[59] See the *Pataki* case, Yearbook 3 (1960), 56.

with this ground of inadmissibility, or at least with the fact that the decision to dismiss an application on this ground can be reached by simple majority vote.[60] This unhappiness is compounded by the suggestion that the Court uses this ground to dispose of cases that appear close on other admissibility criteria.

3.33   A number of other criteria of admissibility can be dealt with relatively quickly. Article 35(1)(a) indicates that applications cannot be accepted if they are anonymous. However, Strasbourg officials have proved reasonably flexible regarding this and have admitted applications where from the documents they have been able to ascertain the identity of the applicant. Applicants' wishes for anonymity as regards the public are respected—hence the number of *X v UK* and similar cases. Applications may also be declared inadmissible on the ground that they raise 'substantially the same matter as has already been examined by the Court' (Article 35(1)(b)); but it seems clear that this is designed only to discourage identical applications rather than applications from different people which are based on similar facts. Even a second application by a person regarding the same issues as an application already dismissed may escape the sanction of this provision if it discloses new facts. Applications that are an 'abuse of petition' are also subject to being ruled inadmissible. This appears to refer to applications begun purely for propagandistic purposes or to escape the consequences of a legitimate decision.[61] This provision would not appear to endanger 'test case' litigation. However, it seems that breach of the Convention's rules about confidentiality during the consideration of an application may be seen as an abuse of the right of petition.

Interim Measures

3.34   When making an application to the court an applicant may also wish to consider whether to request that the court take any interim measures in his case. Such measures are especially important where someone faces deportation or expulsion from a Member State or where they are under the threat of torture or death, since the application may take several years to be resolved. The Convention does not make any provision for interim measures, unlike, for example, the American Convention on Human Rights, Article 63(2) of which empowers the Inter-American Court (acting alone or at the request of the Commission where a case has not yet been referred to it) to adopt such provisional measures as it deems

---

[60]   See P Van Dijk and G Van Hoof, *Theory and Practice of the European Convention on Human Rights* (2nd edn, Dewenter, 1990) 107. Harris, O'Boyle, and Warbrick display a similar unease, asking how it can be that a case which may have been the subject of extensive argument among Commission members can be dismissed as not being arguable: see D Harris, M O'Boyle, and C Warbrick, *Law of the European Convention on Human Rights* (London, 1995) 62–78.

[61]   See eg the *Ilse Koch* case, Yearbook 5 (1962), 126, where the wife of the former commandant of the Buchenwald concentration camp, who had been convicted of elementary human rights offences, submitted a petition claiming she was innocent without making reference to any aspect of the Convention.

pertinent 'in cases of extreme gravity and urgency'.[62] However, in rule 39 of its Rules of Procedure the ECtHR provides that, '[t]he Chamber or, where appropriate, its President may, at the request of a party or of any other person concerned, or of its own motion, indicate to the parties any interim measure which it considers should be adopted in the interests of the parties or of the proper conduct of the proceedings before it'. The reference to the court 'indicating' such measures to the parties shows that such a measure is not intended to be binding, and the court has in the past indicated that failing to comply with such a recommendation would not be a violation of Article 34.[63] It is disappointing that the opportunity was not taken in Protocol 11 to make compliance with interim measures a binding obligation on Member States.

Legal Aid

In the early days of the Convention most applications were made by non-lawyers.[64] However, by the late 1980s over 50 per cent of registered applications were made by lawyers. Now, following rule 36(3) of the court's Rules of Procedure, representation is obligatory in hearings before a Chamber unless the President of the Chamber decides otherwise. As cases involved increasingly complex legal points the need for legal aid, which was not available in domestic systems for Convention applications, was recognized. In the United Kingdom, for example, public funding is available only in respect of work on the Convention which is relevant to the domestic legal application. However, with the coming into force of the HRA this will often be more extensive work than has been true in the past. **3.35**

The Convention legal aid scheme is contained in rules 91–96 of the court's Rules of Procedure. Rule 92 indicates that legal aid will be available where the court is satisfied that it is necessary for the proper conduct of the case and that the applicant has insufficient means to meet all or part of the costs entailed. The applicant will be required to make a declaration regarding their financial circumstances. **3.36**

Legal aid will be available on application to the court to cover expenses from the time that the applicant is asked for written comments on the Government's observations at the admissibility stage. The fees available to the applicant's representatives are intended to be set at the rate of civil legal aid in the State from which the applicant comes and aid will be granted also to cover the lawyer's and applicant's travelling and subsistence expenses.[65] **3.37**

---

[62] See eg *Provisional Measures in the Case of Bustios and Rojas regarding Peru* (1990) 11 Human Rights LJ 257, where the Inter-American Court ordered Peru to safeguard the lives of two journalists about whom an application was pending.

[63] See *Cruz Varas v Sweden* Series A No 201 (1992) 14 EHRR 1.

[64] In 1955–70 applications introduced by lawyers always made up less than 20% of the total number of applications.

[65] For a fuller legal discussion of Convention legal aid see Clements, Mole and Simmons, n 41 above, 91–97.

The Future of the Convention System

3.38 The Convention is in many ways a victim of its own success. As its prestige and effectiveness have grown so ever more applications are made to it. The Court took over 30 years to decide its first 200 cases; it delivered 889 judgments between 1 January and 31 December 2001. The number of applications to the Court now exceeds 13,000 a year. Naturally this increase in workload has put great strain on the ability of the Court to deal with cases expeditiously although it can point to a significant increase in output over the past five years.

3.39 Protocol 11, which gives rise to the single and full-time court structure, was designed with this stress on resources very much in mind.[66] Whether it achieves a reduction in delays in considering applications remains to be seen. There are many who believe such changes were necessary simply in order for the system to stand still. The new court faces new challenges.[67] Whereas for much of its history the Convention system has been involved in essentially fine-tuning legal systems which do broadly respect human rights,[68] it has recently been dealing with cases from Turkey involving the type of human rights violations more familiar to the regional system of the Americas.[69] A rapidly rising number of cases from Central and Eastern Europe pose similar problems and require an engagement with legal systems with very different traditions from pre-1990 Convention Member States. As we shall see in Chapter 5 one aspect is that the Court is now beginning to rule on some particularly egregious conditions of imprisonment. Already after only a year of Protocol 11 being in operation, on the occasion of the Court's fiftieth birthday, it was calling on Member States to devote more resources to the Convention institutions lest the backlog of cases become impossible to deal with. The Committee of Ministers subsequently established an evaluation group which recommended a number of measures to reduce the Court's workload, none of which have yet been acted on by Member States.[69a]

---

[66] For the background to Protocol 11 see, eg, the symposium in (1988) 9 Human Rights LJ and two articles by H Schermers: 'The Eleventh Protocol to the European Convention on Human Rights' (1994) 20 ELR 367 and 'Adoption of the Eleventh Protocol to the European Convention on Human Rights' (1995) 20 ELR 559.

[67] For a summary of some of the challenges faced by the new Court see N Bratza and M O'Boyle, 'The Legacy of the Commission to the New Court Under the Eleventh Protocol' [1997] European Human Rights L Rev 211.

[68] The exceptions perhaps being in dealing with human rights during states of emergency.

[69] See n 35 above; for a comparison with the Inter-American system, see T Farer in D Harris and S Livingstone (eds), *The Inter-American System of Human Rights* (Oxford, 1998), ch 2.

[69a] However, Member States did agree to a 10% increase in the Court's budget when approving the establishment of the evaluation group.

C. The European Convention for the Prevention of Torture and Inhuman or Degrading Treatment or Punishment

Whereas the European Convention on Human Rights invokes a wide range of **3.40** concerns, the ECPT focuses on one of the most serious human rights violations, one that cannot be derogated from even in time of war or emergency. It is also a human right that is always of particular concern to people in detention. The Convention was signed in 1987 and entered into force on 1 January 1989. It has 44 members, including the United Kingdom.[70]

Overview

The Convention introduces a new enforcement mechanism into international **3.41** human rights law by providing for regular visits by an independent Committee for the Prevention of Torture (CPT) to 'places where persons are deprived of their liberty by a public authority' (Article 2) in any of the Member States. Unlike the ECHR there is no provision for individuals to bring their claims of torture or inhuman or degrading treatment before the Committee. As will be seen below, the UN Torture Convention provides for this to occur by way of an optional protocol. This does not mean however that individual prisoners or lawyers representing them have no input into the Committee's deliberations and reports. Again unlike the UN Torture Convention, the European equivalent provides no definition of torture or inhuman or degrading treatment or punishment. The jurisprudence of the Strasbourg institutions on Article 3 of the ECHR (which is discussed in greater detail in Chapter 5) obviously plays a part in their working definition, but in reports made by the Committee so far it has clearly taken the view that its remit goes much further than this and extends to general conditions of imprisonment in so far as they may give rise to at least a risk of degrading treatment.[71]

The Convention provides for the creation of a Committee with a number of mem- **3.42** bers equal to the States parties. The members are required by Article 4(2) of the Convention to be 'persons of high moral character, known for their competence in the field of human rights or having professional expertise in the areas

---

[70] See, generally, A Cassese, 'The New Approach to Human Rights: The European Convention for the Prevention of Torture' (1989) 83 AJIL 128 and R Morgan and M Evans, *Combating Torture in Europe—The work and standards of the European Committee for the Prevention of Torture* (Council of Europe, 2001). Protocol One of the Convention also permits non-Council of Europe states to accede to the Convention with the approval of Member States. Yugoslavia became the first state to do so in June 2002.

[71] The CPT's Second General Report in 1992 provides a good introduction to its view of its remit and approach: CPT/Inf (92) 3. For information on the CPT's more recent activities, see the Eleventh General Report: CPT/Inf (2000) 16.

covered by the Convention'.[72] Although nominated by the Member States each of these experts serves in an independent capacity. Although in the early years of the Convention's existence lawyers predominated among its membership there has more recently been an increase in the number of doctors and people with operational experience of prison management.[73] To protect their independence the Committee has taken the decision that members shall not take part in a visit to their own country. The remit of the Committee, set out in Article 1 of the Convention, is broad: '[t]he Committee shall, by means of visits, examine the treatment of persons deprived of their liberty with a view to strengthening, if necessary, the protection of such persons from torture and from inhuman or degrading treatment or punishment'. Reports of the Committee thus far indicate that this broad mandate will be fully utilized. The first report on the United Kingdom, for example, looked not just at prisoners' physical conditions and the disciplinary regime but also at such matters as medical care, reception procedures, staff–inmate relations, and the training of prison officers.[74] The CPT's 2000 report on the United Kingdom examines in detail the problem of prison overcrowding and its effects on health, privacy, and levels of violence in prison.[75] Its latest report, published in 2002, raises concerns about ill-treatment of prisoners, poor material conditions of detention, impoverished regimes in some establishments (including the Close Supervision Centre at HM Prison Woodhill), limited healthcare, the management of drug-related problems, and detention facilities for children.[76] The Committee's most recent visit to the United Kingdom, in February 2002, was to examine the treatment of prisoners

---

[72] For a discussion of the composition and operation of the Committee see M Evans and R Morgan, *Preventing Torture: A Study of the European Convention for the Prevention of Torture and Inhuman or Degrading Treatment or Punishment* (Oxford, 1998) ch 5.

[73] The CPT currently has 37 members. In its Tenth General Report (CPT/Inf (2000) 13), the CPT notes that 'the numbers of members with a medical background is no longer on a par with that of lawyers in the Committee. The CPT trusts that it will be possible gradually to rectify this situation in the course of future elections; in particular, it would be highly desirable to have more forensic doctors in the Committee. As regards other professional fields, there is now an adequate number of CPT members with specialised practical experience in penitentiary systems; however, the Committee would welcome more members with relevant experience of police work. It must also be added that the proportion of women among the CPT's membership is currently rather low (9 out of 36)' (para 18). By Assembly Resolution 1248 (2001), adopted on 23 May 2001, the Parliamentary Assembly proposed additional measures to ensure that the lists of candidates for membership meet the needs of the CPT.

[74] See *Report to the United Kingdom Government on the Visit to the United Kingdom Carried Out by the European Committee for the Prevention of Torture and Inhuman or Degrading Treatment or Punishment*, CPT/Inf (91) 15.

[75] *Report to the United Kingdom Government on the visit to the United Kingdom and the Isle of Man carried out by the European Committee for the Prevention of Torture and Inhuman and Degrading Treatment or Punishment*, CPT/Inf (2000) 1.

[76] *Report to the Government of the United Kingdom on the visit to the United Kingdom carried out by the European Committee for the Prevention of Torture and Inhuman and Degrading Treatment or Punishment from 4 to 16 February 2001*, CPT/Inf (2002) 6.

certified by the Home Secretary as suspected international terrorists and detained under the Anti-Terrorism, Crime and Security Act 2001. The delegation interviewed, in private, all prisoners currently detained under that legislation, and examined the conditions of detention in HM Prison Highdown and the high security unit at HM Prison Belmarsh. The report is awaited.

Convention Visits

The Committee's main mechanism for fulfilling its remit is the programme of visits. Under Article 7 it is required to carry out visits to places of detention (which has generally meant prisons and police stations, though mental hospitals and immigration detention centres have also be examined under this provision) in Convention countries. Under Article 17(3) it is indicated that the Committee shall not visit places which representatives of the International Committee of the Red Cross (ICRC) 'effectively visit on a regular basis by virtue of the Geneva Conventions of 12 August 1949 and the Additional Protocols of 18 June 1977 thereto'. This raises an interesting question in respect of prisons in Northern Ireland which the ICRC regularly visit. However since such visits take place on an ad hoc basis, the conflict in Northern Ireland not being seen by the ICRC as either an international or non-international armed conflict within the meaning of the Geneva Conventions, Northern Irish prisons which contain a high number of people convicted of terrorist offences have been accepted to be within the Committee's remit. In practice the Committee has divided Convention countries into 'large' and 'small' and has usually sought to visit two large and one small country in each year. It may also conduct ad hoc visits to particular countries or places of detention within a country. With the increasing number of Member States that visiting regime has come under strain and the Committee has now set itself a target of a periodic visit to a country every four years, with more frequent ad hoc visits to deal with matters of urgent concern or to follow up on concerns raised on previous visits.[77] Under Article 9 a State may make representations to the Committee against a visit, or against a visit to a particular place of detention, at that time. Such representations may only be based on specific grounds set out in Article 9(1) which include national defence, public safety, serious disorder at the place of detention, the medical condition of a person, or that an urgent interrogation relating to a serious crime is in progress. Where such representations are made the State is then required to enter into consultation with the Committee 'in order to clarify the situation and seek agreement on arrangements to enable the Committee to exercise its functions expeditiously'. The Committee is required to notify a country that a visit is taking place and thereafter Article 8(2) places a number of specific obligations on the Member State visited. These include giving

3.43

---

[77] In its Twelfth Annual Report the CPT again stressed the increasing significance of ad hoc visits and that it was seeking a 'better balance' between periodic and ad hoc visits, CPT/Inf (2002) 15.

the members of the Committee (at least two members of which make each visit) unrestricted access both to its territory and to places where people are deprived of their liberty and the right of unrestricted movement within both. Under Article 14 the Committee may ask certain experts (often medical or prison administration personnel) to accompany its visit. Again these will not be experts from the State visited. Although States cannot deny access to Committee members (subject to Article 9) they may declare that a particular expert will not be allowed to participate in a visit to their territory. In addition to access the Committee must also be furnished with full information on places where people are detained and any other information it needs to carry out its task. Other provisions of Article 8 guarantee the Committee the right to communicate freely with people it feels can provide relevant information and to interview in private people deprived of their liberty. The practice so far has been for the Committee to meet with both government and non-governmental groups (including prison reform and human rights groups) at the beginning of its visit, before it has visited any place of detention. Once the places of detention have been visited the Committee will then have another meeting with government officials, where it will outline its provisional findings and seek further information, before leaving the country.

Reports

3.44 After the completion of a visit the Committee draws up a report on the facts as it has found them during the visit and any recommendations it has regarding measures which might better ensure the objectives of Article 1. Such a report is sent to the Member State concerned and remains confidential unless the State requests that it be published. Such a request may also be accompanied by the Member State's comments on the report, which must also be published. As the CPT indicates in its Twelfth Annual Report, 89 of its 129 submitted reports have currently been made public, with governments having given undertakings that they will permit several more to be published.[77a] The reports have generally contained a request for governments to report back to the Committee within a year on the steps they have taken to comply with the Committee's recommendations. Where they fail to do so, or prove unco-operative in other ways, then under Article 10(2) the Committee may make a public statement if two-thirds of its members agree. To date only three public statements have been released, two relating to conditions in police detention in Turkey, and the most recent on the failure of the Russian authorities to co-operate with some aspects of an inquiry into detention conditions in the Chechen Republic.

3.45 After fifteen years in operation it is clear that the CPT has made a useful contribution to the strengthening of measures to protect prisoners' human rights. Its mem-

---

[77a] For example no reports have yet been published on the 7 visits the CPT has undertaken to Russia. The Ukraine has recently authorized the publication of 3 reports on visits undertaken there.

bership has grown and its mode of operation provides a model for the draft optional protocol to the UN Convention Against Torture which seeks to achieve the same thing on a global scale. While Evans and Morgan comment that it has 'so far exercised at best a marginal influence on the domestic policy of member states'[77b] they also observe that it has had significant success in forcing the closure of seriously substandard accommodation and that its reports are extensively utilized in the European political process, for example in discussions over Turkish accession to the EU. The detailed reports produced by the CPT have provided a valuable source of public information on conditions in places of detention in Member States and its recommendations provide a focus for those in those Member States seeking reform of law and practice in prisons. The cumulative impact of its comments on specific countries and the more general report it submits to the Committee of Ministers each year under Article 12 already provide a guide to European 'good practice' in relation to prison conditions and regimes and appear to have greater influence on the decisions of the ECtHR than the European Prison Rules (to be discussed below) appear to have enjoyed thus far.[78] Like many international institutions, however, the CPT has almost no enforcement powers beyond negotiation with the Member State and public disapproval of failure to comply with its recommendations. If those recommendations are complied with this should prove sufficient. If they are not, and a State consistently fails to meet the standards set by the CPT, it will be interesting to see whether the members of the CPT will be able to develop a more effective strategy for ensuring compliance within the boundaries of the powers they have at present. As with the ECtHR, problems posed by human rights abuses in detention in Turkey and parts of eastern Europe are likely to pose that question with particular intensity in the next few years.

D. United Nations International Covenant on Civil and Political Rights

Though the European Convention is, to most people in the United Kingdom, the **3.46** better-known and more influential human rights convention, arguably the UN International Covenant on Civil and Political Rights (ICCPR) is the more comprehensive and certainly is subscribed to by more countries around the world, 148 to the European Convention's 44. The ICCPR was one outcome of the attempts

---

[77b] See Evans and Morgan, above n 72, at 344.

[78] The standards provided by the Second Report, on general conditions of imprisonment, and the Third Report, on health care in prisons, are of particular value and are referred to more extensively in Chs 5 and 6 of this book. The Eleventh Report contains a discussion of CPT standards in respect of imprisonment, focusing on staff-prisoner relations, inter-prisoner violence, prison overcrowding, large capacity dormitories, access to natural light and fresh air, transmissible diseases, high security units, and life-sentenced and long-term prisoners. The Tenth Report addresses the issue of women deprived of their liberty, and the Ninth Report focuses on juveniles in detention.

of the UN Commission on Human Rights to produce an international Bill of Rights after 1945. Though the (non-binding) Declaration of Human Rights was adopted relatively swiftly by the UN General Assembly in 1948 it took another 18 years to produce a binding treaty. Indeed the Commission found it impossible, for political and legal reasons, to produce one treaty to incorporate all the rights to which it sought to give recognition. In the end two treaties were adopted by the General Assembly in 1966, the ICCPR and the Economic, Social and Cultural Rights Covenant (ESCRC). Both received the requisite number of ratifications to come into force in 1976. Although some of the rights contained in the ESCRC, such as rights to health or education, have relevance to the situation of prisoners, the more obviously relevant Covenant is the ICCPR.

Covenant Rights

3.47 Most of the rights contained in the ICCPR have equivalents in the ECHR, but the UN treaty is more expansive on a number of points. Most obviously of relevance to prisoners is Article 10, which provides that people deprived of their liberty 'shall be treated with humanity and with respect for the inherent dignity of the human person' and goes on to indicate in Article 10(3) that the 'penitentiary system shall comprise treatment of prisoners the essential aim of which shall be their reformation and social rehabilitation'. Article 10 also indicates that unconvicted prisoners shall be separated from the convicted and adult prisoners from juveniles.[79] A number of other rights in the ICCPR also find no equivalents in the ECHR, such as the right of citizens to take part in public affairs (Article 25), to equality before the law (Article 26), and the rights of ethnic, religious, or linguistic minorities to enjoy their own culture, profess and practise their own religion, or use their own language (Article 27). Considerations of whether the rights guaranteed under the ICCPR are being upheld in the United Kingdom's prisons will be considered at appropriate points in the course of this book.[80]

3.48 As a treaty ratified by the United Kingdom but not incorporated by an Act of Parliament, the ICCPR has the same status in domestic law as the ECHR had before the HRA came into force. The United Kingdom has not ratified the Optional Protocol to the Covenant, which entitles the Human Rights Committee established under the Covenant to receive complaints by individuals against that State party and which is now producing an important jurisprudence of relevance to prison conditions.[81] Therefore enforcement is primarily by way of the periodic

---

[79] For a general discussion of these articles see P Ghandi, 'The Human Rights Committee and Articles 7 and 10 of the International Covenant on Civil and Political Rights 1966' (1990) 13 Dalhousie LJ 758, also S Joseph, J Schultz and M Castan, *The International Covenant on Civil and Political Rights: Cases, Materials and Commentary* (Oxford, 2000) ch 9.

[80] For an overview, see S Livingstone, 'Prisoners' Rights' in D Harris and S Joseph (eds), *The International Covenant on Civil and Political Rights and United Kingdom Law* (Oxford, 1995), 269.

[81] We consider some of this in the chapters on Prison Conditions and Immigration Detention.

report that States party to the Covenant are required to submit to the Human Rights Committee under Article 40 of the ICCPR. The Committee is composed of 18 human rights experts, nominated by States, but who serve in an independent capacity for periods of four years. Members of the Committee are required by Article 28(2) to be 'persons of high moral character and recognized competence in the field of human rights, consideration being given to the usefulness of the participation of some persons having legal experience'.

State Reporting

States are required to report 'periodically' to the Committee; currently its practice is **3.49** to have them report every three years (the United Kingdom has submitted five reports, the last in 1999).[82] The Committee gives States guidance on what they must report and usually reports contain descriptions both of general legal measures to protect human rights in the reporting State and of measures addressed to particular Articles of the Covenant. These reports are then considered by the Committee at one of its hearings, usually devoting two or three days to each country report. Governments send delegations to these hearings to present the report orally and be questioned on it by the Committee members. In recent years Committee members have made increasing use of material submitted by both domestic and international human rights organizations as the basis for many of their questions, although the organization submitting the information will not be explicitly referred to. While Article 40(2) requires States to indicate to the Committee 'factors and difficulties, if any, affecting implementation of the Covenant' it is not surprising that State reports tend to present that State in the most favourable light possible. Alternative sources of information are therefore vital if the Committee is effectively to perform its role of thoroughly examining the extent to which the Covenant is being implemented.

The Covenant indicates in Article 40(4) that the Committee shall 'transmit its **3.50** reports, and such general comments as it may consider appropriate, to the States Parties'. General Comments play much more the same role as the enunciation of CPT standards in annual reports. General Comments 20 and 21, on Articles 7 and 10 respectively, are especially important in the prison context.[82a] Until 1992 the Committee refrained from publishing the comments it made on reports by States parties, but these are now published, together with recommendations for reform. In its fourth examination of a report from the United Kingdom the Committee expressed concern at the use of strip searching in UK prisons, in light of there being available alternative measures of discovering concealed weapons or drugs. In its

---

[82] For a summary of the UK's first four reports and their reception see F Klug, K Starmer, and S Weir, 'The British Way of Doing Things: The United Kingdom and the International Covenant on Civil and Political Rights 1976–94' [1995] PL 504. For a summary of the fifth report, see M Cunneen, 'UN Committee Reports on UK Human Rights', February 2002 *Legal Action* 6.
[82a] Both were issued in 1992.

examination of the United Kingdom's fifth Report, the Committee commented on, among other things, the problem of racist violence in prisons, the detention of asylum seekers, and the refusal to allow convicted prisoners the right to vote. The Committee was particularly forthright on the issue of voting, stating that:

> The Committee is concerned at the State party's maintenance of an old law that convicted prisoners may not exercise their right to vote. The Committee fails to discern the justification for such a practice in modern times, considering that it amounts to an additional punishment and that it does not contribute towards the prisoner's reformation and social rehabilitation, contrary to Article 10, paragraph 3, in conjunction with Article 25 of the Covenant. The State party should reconsider its law depriving convicted prisoners of the right to vote.[83]

E. The United Nations Convention against Torture and other Cruel, Inhuman or Degrading Treatment or Punishment

3.51 The extent to which torture is viewed as perhaps the most universally abhorred violation of human rights can be seen by the fact that the United Nations also has a Convention (the CAT) specifically devoted to it.[84] The UN Convention in this area preceded the European treaty, being adopted by the General Assembly in 1984 and coming into force in 1987. A total of 128 States had ratified it by the beginning of 2002. Though the CAT refers to 'other cruel, inhuman or degrading treatment or punishment' its main focus is on torture and it provides a definition for this in Article 1 as any act by which severe pain or suffering, whether physical or mental, is intentionally inflicted on a person for such purposes as obtaining from him or a third person information or a confession, punishing him for an act he or a third person has committed, or intimidating or coercing him or a third person, or for any reason based on any discrimination of any kind, when such pain or suffering is inflicted by or at the instigation of or with the consent or acquiescence of a public official or other person acting in an official capacity. It does not include pain or suffering arising only from, inherent in or incidental to lawful sanctions.

3.52 Most of the substantive obligations the Convention places on States parties relate purely to the prevention and punishment of torture. These include prohibiting extradition or expulsion where there are substantial grounds for believing the person would be in danger of being tortured if returned (Article 3), making torture a criminal offence in domestic law (Article 4), establishing the principle of universal jurisdiction over those suspected of torture (Articles 6 and 7), and deeming

---

[83] UNHRC, *Concluding Observations of the Human Rights Committee: United Kingdom of Great Britain and Northern Ireland*, 6 December 2001, CCPR/CO/73/UK, para 10. This is in direct conflict with the view of the Divisional Court in *R (Pearson) v Home Secretary* [2001] HRLR 39, discussed further in Ch 5.

[84] As has the Organization of American States, whose Convention to Prevent and Punish Torture was opened for signature in 1985 and entered into force in 1987.

torture–related offences to be extraditable offences in extradition treaties (Article 8). Some obligations overlap the categories of torture and the other forms of treatment prohibited in the Convention (which are more likely to be relevant to those detained in the United Kingdom). These include training of law enforcement personnel and of those medical personnel and public officials involved in the detention of people in the legal obligations under the Convention (Article 10), keeping under systematic review interrogation rules and practices as well as arrangements for custody and detention with a view to preventing torture etc (Article 11), and ensuring that individuals who allege such mistreatment will be able to have their complaint promptly and impartially examined (Articles 12 and 13).

Reporting Systems

Like the ICCPR the Torture Convention provides for a system of periodic report-   **3.53** ing to a Committee of experts. The Committee established under the Convention consists of ten members elected to serve in their independent capacity for terms of four years. They are required to be 'experts of high moral standing and recognized competence in the field of human rights' and Article 17(2) provides that States should bear in mind the usefulness of nominating people who also serve on the Human Rights Committee. This is a legacy from the original Swedish draft for the Torture Convention which provided for the Human Rights Committee to examine the reports. In addition to considering State reports, which are required to be submitted every four years, there is also provision for States to indicate that they are willing for the Committee to receive inter-state (Article 21) or individual (Article 22) complaints that they are failing to meet their obligations under the Convention. The United Kingdom has made a declaration only in respect of Article 21. Article 20 also entitles the Committee to undertake an inquiry where it receives 'reliable information which appears to it to contain well founded indications that torture is being systematically practised in the territory of a state party'. Such an inquiry would be confidential, though at the end of such proceedings the Committee could include a summary account of them in its annual report. Only two such inquiries, in relation to Egypt and Turkey have been undertaken to date. An Optional Protocol has also been drafted which would permit the CAT committee to make on-site visits much in the way that the CPT does, but although the Human Rights Commission has recommended its adoption, the General Assembly has yet to approve it and open it for signature.

The main mode of operation of the Torture Committee is therefore again the   **3.54** non-judgmental consideration of State reports, through in recent years the number of examinations of individual communications has risen. Like the Human Rights Committee, the Torture Committee has shown itself increasingly willing to receive information from non-official sources when formulating questions to put to State delegations during consideration of their reports. The Torture

Committee's remit in Article 19(3) requires it to make general comments on each report and to submit these to the State party concerned. It may also include these comments, together with any observations on these comments by the State party, in its annual report to the General Assembly. This is a public document and reports so far have disclosed some fairly strong criticism of the failure of some States to assure the Committee that they were meeting their obligations under the Convention.[85] However, commentators have observed that the Committee is seriously under-resourced and is struggling to deal effectively with the volume of reports it receives, many of which are insubstantial and require further investigation.[85a] The United Kingdom has so far made three periodic reports to this Committee, the most recent in 1998. The fourth report is due in 2002. In respect of prisons the Committee's strongest concerns in examining the second report in 1995 related to the use of strip searching.[86] In relation to the 1998 report, the Committee commented in particular on the human rights situation in Northern Ireland, the number of deaths in custody in the United Kingdom, prison overcrowding, and the use of prisons to detain asylum seekers.

F. Other International Mechanisms

3.55 A range of other international mechanisms exist which are of relevance to the treatment of those in detention. These can be divided into further standard-setting instruments, most of which are non-binding even at an international level, and further mechanisms of investigation.

Other International Standards

3.56 One further binding international standard worth mentioning is the UN Convention on the Rights of the Child (CRC). Perhaps the most generally accepted human rights convention, with 191 ratifications, the CRC obviously has a limited and specific relevance to imprisonment. However it sets important standards in relation to the treatment of young people in custody, which the United Kingdom appears to be in breach of by detaining young people in adult jails.[87] Like the ICCPR the enforcement of the CRC is supervised by reports to an independent committee.

---

[85] See the comments of Rapporteur Burns pronouncing himself 'not satisfied' by the reasons given by the UK for failing to introduce further safeguards in respect of treatment of terrorist suspects in police detention in Northern Ireland, CAT/C/SR.92.

[85a] See R Bank 'Country Orientated Procedures under the Convention Against Torture: Towards a New Dynamism' in P Alston and J Crawford (eds), *The Failure of UN Human Rights Treaty Monitoring* (Cambridge, 2000) 145–74.

[86] See H Gowan, 'The United Kingdom's Second Periodic Report under the UN Torture Convention' [1996] European Human Rights L Rev 34.

[87] See Art 37(c) and Howard League, *Lost Inside: The Imprisonment of Teenage Girls* (London, 1997).

European Prison Rules

At the level of non-binding international standards the most significant for the **3.57** treatment of people in prison are the standard minimum rules, the UN Standard Minimum Rules for the Treatment of Prisoners (1955) and the European Prison Rules (1987). The content of these is very similar and we concentrate here on the European Prison Rules. The Rules offer more detailed standards on many aspects of imprisonment than are provided by human rights conventions. The tradition of drawing up model prison rules on an international level goes back to 1935, when the League of Nations adopted the first set of Standard Minimum Rules.

Unlike some European countries the United Kingdom has not incorporated the **3.58** European Prison Rules into its domestic law and hence the obligations contained in the Rules are not enforceable in UK courts. Also the European Commission of Human Rights has indicated that breach of the European Rules will not amount to a violation of Article 3 of the Convention.[88] However, the Rules may be taken into account in interpreting the obligations of States under the Convention. Indeed the only enforcement mechanism that exists with respect to the European Rules is oversight by the European Committee for Co-operation in Prison Affairs, a five-member expert body established by the European Committee on Crime Problems. This considers State reports on the extent to which the Rules are being implemented every five years. The Committee has not however published any of the United Kingdom's reports since 1983.

Nevertheless the Rules are a valuable reference source for those campaigning for **3.59** changes in the UK Prison Rules and seeking the development of a code of standards. Their overall philosophy, largely set out in rules 1–6, is influenced by notions of respect for human dignity, ensuring that punishment is limited to deprivation of liberty, and a stress on treatment aimed at re-educating and re-socializing a prisoner, values which are prominent in many European prison systems. As will be pointed out on several occasions in this book, the Prison Rules and prison administration practices fall short of what is required by the European Rules, and it must be remembered that this is falling short of what is largely a minimum standard. As one commentator observed, the European Rules 'set standards which provide a threshold that satisfies basic considerations of humanity without imposing unacceptable burdens upon governments which are themselves constrained by resource considerations and political priorities'.[89]

UN Standard Minimum Rules and other UN Guidelines

The UN Standard Minimum Rules are now over 40 years old and arguably are in **3.60** need of revision to reflect changes in human rights law since the time of their

---

[88] Application 7341/76, discussed in A Reynaud, *Human Rights in Prisons* (Strasbourg, 1987) 34.
[89] See K Neale, 'The European Prison Rules: Contextual, Philosophical and Practical Aspects' in J Muncie and R Sparks, *Imprisonment: European Perspectives* (London, 1991) 203.

adoption. However, rather than revisit old standards the UN has tended to adopt a new series of guidelines with respect to the treatment of people in detention.[90] These include the Basic Principles for the Treatment of Prisoners (1990), the Standard Minimum Rules for Administration of Juvenile Justice (also known as the 'Beijing Rules') (1985) and the UN Rules for the Protection of Juveniles Deprived of their Liberty (1990).[91] Perhaps the most valuable is the Body of Principles for the Protection of All Persons Under any Form of Detention or Imprisonment (1988).[92] We refer to these in relation to a number of issues concerning detention in prison and in immigration detention.

Investigation Mechanisms

3.61 Certain other international mechanisms which are relevant to the treatment of prisoners can be mentioned briefly. The UN Sub-commission for the Prevention of Discrimination and the Protection of Minorities has, since 1973, included on its agenda every year an item on the human rights of people subjected to any form of detention. This report includes recommendations on how to improve the protection of human rights of those in detention. The Sub-commission's parent body, the Commission on Human Rights, established in 1985 a Special Rapporteur on Torture. The Special Rapporteur has the task primarily of responding to information that comes to him regarding acts of torture anywhere in the world. He carries out this mandate by requesting immediate information from the State in question and by making recommendations to those governments concerned. A summary of the Special Rapporteur's actions each year is published and includes reference to the countries from which information was sought and to which recommendations were made.[93]

[90] For a general discussion of these standards see N Rodley, 'The Treatment of Prisoners in International Law' (Oxford, 2nd edn, 1999), esp ch 5, 11–12.

[91] All of these standards can be found in R Wallace, *International Human Rights: Text and Materials* (London, 1997) 507–639.

[92] UN Doc A/43/49; for a summary see T Treves, 'The UN Body of Principles for the Protection of Detained or Imprisoned Persons' (1990) 84 AJIL 578.

[93] For a discussion of the Special Rapporteur's power and function see M Bossuyt, 'The Development of Special Procedures of the United Nations Commission on Human Rights' (1985) 6 Human Rights LJ 179.

4

SECURITY CATEGORIZATION
AND ALLOCATION

4.01

Imprisonment in the modern era has always been accompanied by a desire to separate and classify prisoners according to both the reason for their imprisonment and their perceived threat to the good order and discipline of the prison regime (the former frequently influencing the latter). The Prison Act 1865 required prisoners to be separated according to their sex, whether or not they were criminal prisoners or debtors, and whether or not they were undergoing punishment for a prison offence. Separate cells were required to be provided sufficient to accommodate prisoners in each category.[1] Previous legislation had been even more complex and exhaustive, reflecting the Victorian obsession with labelling and regulating the process of punishment, including punishment for debt.[2]

---

[1] Prison Act 1865, s 17(5) stated that '[i]n a prison where criminal prisoners are confined such prisoners shall be prevented from holding any communication with each other, either by every prisoner being kept in a separate cell by day and by night, except when he is at chapel or taking exercise, or by every prisoner being confined by night to his cell and being subjected to superintendence during the day as will, consistently with the provisions of this Act, prevent his communicating with any other prisoner'.

[2] See the seven-fold division of prisoners in Prison Act 1842, s 17, which included a requirement to prevent communication between the seven classes.

4.02 Since the 1960s the basis for the separation and differential treatment accorded to adult male prisoners has been security categorization. The Learmont Report concluded that 'categorization is fundamental to security. It is the key to ensuring the safe custody of prisoners and work on its improvement must be given proper priority.'[3] It went on to recommend a change in the system of security categorization from that in existence since the mid 1960s so that procedures would be introduced which were better attuned to the security profiles of individual prisoners. This aspect of his report has not been implemented although it is clear that a greater percentage of prisoners are now subject to higher security categories than used to be the case before the publication of the Woodcock and Learmont Reports.[4] The significance of the policy of security categorization is that it does not flow from a judicial finding or any formal administrative procedure, yet it has a major impact on both a prisoner's life within prison and, most importantly, his prospects of early release. Below we set out the criteria for the security categorization of adult male prisoners before looking in greater detail at the decision-making process in relation to categories B, C, and D, which represent the vast majority of such prisoners. We then examine the different procedures governing allocation to category A and describe the particular regime to which Exceptional Risk Category A prisoners are subject in Special Secure Units. Finally, we look at the principles governing the categorization and allocation of lifers, women prisoners, and young offenders. Security categorization has been a fertile source of challenges under the Human Rights Act, and this chapter also considers the approach of the courts in this area.

A. Categorization: The Criteria

4.03 The Prison Act 1952 vests the Secretary of State with a broad power to make rules 'for the regulation and management of prisons . . . and for the classification, treatment, employment, discipline and control of persons required to be detained therein'.[5] Rule 7 of the Prison Rules provides further guidance on the basis for classification:

---

[3] *Review of Prison Service Security in England and Wales and the Escape from Parkhurst Prison on 3 January 1995* (Cm 3020, 1995), para 5.8.

[4] The former Director-General of the Prison Service, Derek Lewis, made clear in his interesting account of his action-packed term of office (*Hidden Agendas: Politics, Law and Disorder*, (London, 1997)) that neither former Chief Constable Sir John Woodcock nor General Sir John Learmont was held in high regard by senior Prison Service personnel. The Woodcook inquiry team was described as insular and inflexible and the final report was said to have a 'literary style [which] appeared to owe much to Jeffrey Archer'. Learmont was described as 'an expert on billets and blankets' and 'a big man, with a bull neck, a propensity to bark orders and an attention span measured in seconds rather than minutes'. In view of this it is perhaps unsurprising that the Prison Service did not feel the need to implement his complicated views on security categorization.

[5] Prison Act 1952, s 47(1).

(1) Prisoners shall be classified, in accordance with any directions of the Secretary of State, having regard to their age, temperament and record and with a view to maintaining good order and facilitating training and, in the case of convicted prisoners, of furthering the purpose of their training and treatment as provided by Rule 3.

(2) Unconvicted prisoners:

   (a) shall be kept out of contact with convicted prisoners as far as the governor considers it can reasonably be done, unless and to the extent that they have consented to share residential accommodation or participate in any activity with convicted prisoners; and

   (b) shall under no circumstances be required to share a cell with a convicted prisoner.

(3) Prisoners committed or attached for contempt of court, or for failing to do or abstaining from doing anything required to be done or left undone:

   (a) shall be treated as a separate class for the purposes of this rule;

   (b) notwithstanding anything in this rule, may be permitted to associate with any other class of prisoners if they are willing to do so; and

   (c) shall have the same privileges as an unconvicted prisoner under rules 20(5), 23(1) and 35(1).

(4) Nothing in this rule shall require a prisoner to be deprived unduly of the society of other persons.[6]

In its pre-1964 form, rule 7 (then rule 3) expressly forbade the mixing of convicted and unconvicted prisoners in living accommodation under any circumstances. The current rule is designed to reduce the pressures in local prisons caused by overcrowding by expressly permitting remand and convicted prisoners to share residential accommodation where the remand prisoner consents. Plainly, the division of prisoners according to sex and whether or not they are convicted or on remand deserves no further comment. It is security categorization which gives rise to controversy and, in particular, the consequences of allocation to Category A. The published directions which the Secretary of State has issued to explain the basis on which categorization decisions are made are the so-called Mountbatten criteria, based as they are on the recommendations of Earl Mountbatten's Inquiry into prison escapes and security, established in the aftermath of the escape of George Blake from Wormwood Scrubs in 1966. The current criteria, most recently set out in PSO 0900, have remained almost unchanged since the Mountbatten Inquiry and are as follows:

* Category A: those prisoners whose escape would be highly dangerous to the public or to the police or to the security of the state, no matter how unlikely that escape might be; and for whom the aim must be to make escape impossible.[7]

---

[6] Subsection (2) was substituted by SI 1995/983, reg 2, Sch, para 1.

[7] The Category A definition, and in particular the phrase 'no matter how unlikely that escape might be', is in the process of redrafting by the Home Office in the light of the decision of Turner J in *R (Pate) v Home Secretary*, 17 May 2002. The claimant was a disabled Category A prisoner who had been convicted of serious sexual offences and was assessed as presenting a serious risk to the

* Category B: prisoners for whom the very highest conditions of security are not necessary but for whom escape must be made very difficult.
* Category C: prisoners who cannot be trusted in open conditions but who do not have the resources and will to make a determined escape attempt.
* Category D: prisoners who can be reasonably trusted in open prisons.[8]

B. Categories B, C, and D

Administrative Guidance

4.04 Administrative guidance on the classification and allocation of convicted adult male prisoners to Categories B, C, and D is contained in PSO 0900, which replaces Chapter 7 of the Prison Service's *Manual on Sentence Management and Planning*.[9] The general approach, as set out in para 1.2, is that:

> Prisoners must be categorized objectively according to the likelihood that they will seek to escape and the risk that they would pose should they do so. In the majority of cases, consideration of these two factors alone will be sufficient to determine the prisoner's security category. However, a small number of prisoners while presenting little risk of escape or risk to the public, and who would ordinarily be assigned to a low security category will, because of their custodial behaviour, require a higher category so that they may be sent to a prison with levels of supervision commensurate with the risk they pose to control. The categorisation forms therefore permit consideration of control to influence the final security category. *The security category must take account of these considerations alone* . . . Although consideration of control factors is permitted, factors such as ability to mix with other prisoners, educational, training or medical needs, and the availability of

---

public. He argued that, in taking into account only the risk on escape, and omitting any consideration of the fact that escape was extremely unlikely, the policy amounted to an unlawful fettering of discretion. Both the risk to the public on escape *and* the likelihood that that risk would materialize ought to be taken into account. Turner J held that, although the general aim of making escape near impossible for dangerous prisoners was legitimate, 'such part of the policy which does not differentiate between the escape potential of individual prisoners is illegal and must be quashed' (para 39).

[8] In addition to the four security categories may be added a further classification or security decision, namely 'escape risk'. *The Security Manual* indicates that a prisoner may be placed on an 'escape list' of prisoners when there has been a recent escape attempt from closed conditions or an escort or where there is reliable security intelligence that an escape is being contemplated. Where a prisoner is identified as at risk of escape, the governor must ensure his recategorization to Category B and give him written reasons for the decision. Escape list prisoners are subject to very strict security measures and wear yellow patches on their clothing.

[9] This discussion of PSO 0900 incorporates the amendments introduced by PSI 43/01, which introduces a new category of 'semi-open' for female prisoners and includes 'identified resettlement needs' as a factor to be taken into account when allocating male prisoners. The new emphasis on the latter may well be a result of the report of the Chief Inspectors of Prison and Probation, *Through the Prison Gate: A Joint Thematic Review by HM Inspectorates of Prisons and Probation* (London, 2001), which considered that not enough account was taken by the Prison Service of prisoners' needs on release.

vacancies at suitable establishments should not be taken into account at this stage. They are for consideration during allocation. . . . Every prisoner must be placed in the lowest security category consistent with the needs of security and control. A prisoner must be assigned to the correct security category even if it is clear that it will not be possible to allocate him to a particular establishment for prisoners in that category.

The inclusion of control as a factor in categorization was introduced for the first time by PSO 0900. The effect of its inclusion is to allow prisoners to be placed in a security category higher than needed for the protection of the public, purely to make it easier for prison staff to control them. It is highly questionable whether this development is consistent with the principles underpinning the categorization process, which is to take into account purely risk and not administrative convenience.

The criteria to be taken into account when making a categorization decision are set out in para 1.2.4. All prisoners must be regarded as probably suitable for Category D on first categorization unless they are:

(1) sentenced to over 12 months for any offence of violence; or
(2) convicted of any but the most minor sexual offence; or
(3) have a previous sentence of over 12 months for any violent or sexual offence and did not successfully serve part of that sentence in an open prison; or
(4) have current or previous convictions for arson or any drugs offence involving importation or dealing; or
(5) have a recent history of escapes or absconds.

Once these criteria have been applied, those prisoners who are not allocated to Category D should be regarded as probably suitable for Category C unless they:

(1) are sentenced to over seven years for any violent or sexual offence; or
(2) have a previous sentence of over seven years for any violent or sexual offence and did not successfully serve part of that sentence in a Category C prison; or
(3) have a current sentence exceeding ten years; or
(4) have a recent history of escape from closed conditions or have significant external resources which they might use to assist an escape attempt.

It follows that allocation to Category B takes place by a process of elimination against the above criteria. In practice it is (or should be) reserved for prisoners convicted either currently or in the past of a serious violent, sexual, or drug-related offence but who do not merit placement in the very highest security category—Category A. By the same token, those convicted of non-violent offences or serving short or medium sentences would not normally be categorized higher than Category C.

The Decision-making Process

4.05 Decisions about placement in Categories B–D are made by 'Observation, Classification and Allocation Units' (OCA) at Area level and depend largely on the content of current and previous custodial records, pre-trial reports and antecedents, the nature of the charge, and any remarks made by the sentencing judge.[10] The categorization process should take place in two stages—a provisional paper assessment using form ICA 1 (Initial Categorization and Allocation document), followed by consideration of any issues which might override the provisional category suggested. The OCA Unit officer completes the categorization section of form ICA 1 which is an algorithm using as its database details of the current offence, sentence, previous convictions and custodial sentences (especially for sexual offences and/or violence) together with previous escapes, escape attempts or absconds. Having recorded the base data the OCA Unit Officer completes the algorithm resulting in a provisional security category. The officer must then either indicate that the provisional security category applies or recommend that it be overridden with reasons cited, for example that a minor offender has a known tendency to violence or other factors which point to a need to depart from the algorithm. The OCA Unit must decide in each case if it requires internal reports from, for example, the prison medical officer, psychologist or chaplain. PSO 0900 states, rather vaguely, that the officer may recommend that the provisional security category be overridden 'as a result of control considerations or other factors': para 1.5.11. Some examples are given: matters not covered by the algorithm, like a previous sentence successfully served in an open prison (though it is surprising that this is not something automatically taken into account) or a known tendency to violence by an apparently minor offender, or an unusual combination of factors which produces an 'obviously unreasonable result' from the algorithm.

4.06 All remand prisoners or those convicted and awaiting sentence are (unless they have been provisionally placed in Category A) placed in Category U (Unclassified) and will normally be assumed to require accommodation suitable for Category B. But PSO 0900 makes clear that there is no reason in principle why an unconvicted or unsentenced prisoner could not be held in a Category C prison if suitable facilities exist. Such decisions should be made by governors and approved by Area Managers.

4.07 The allocation of prisoners to training prisons following conviction is a process distinct from categorization, though in practice the two procedures will be completed by the same OCA unit officer. PSO 0900 warns that in such cases the

---

[10] Officers in the OCAs exercise their powers as delegates of the Secretary of State under the *Carltona* principle.

officer responsible 'must be alert to the danger of allowing his or her conclusions on allocation to influence those on categorization'. The allocation of prisoners is influenced by four priorities which may sometimes conflict—the needs of security, the needs of control, the need to make maximum use of available spaces in training prisons, and the needs of the individual prisoners. PSO 0900 states that while the main factor influencing allocation to a particular prison should be the prisoner's security category, account must also be taken of:

(1) His suitability for particular types of accommodation (factors such as vulnerability, age etc).
(2) His medical and/or psychiatric needs that may require a particular type or level of care.
(3) The need for identified offence-related behavioural programmes to confront assessed risk.
(4) His home area or that of his likely visitors.
(5) His educational or training needs or potential.
(6) The published allocation criteria for individual establishments.
(7) Identified resettlement needs.

The decision must be recorded, along with reasons, on the prisoner's ICA 1. PSO 0900 emphasizes that '[i]t is not acceptable, under any circumstances, to modify the process or outcome of prisoners' security categorisation in order to achieve a better match between prisoners and available spaces'.

Having been given an initial security category following first reception into prison, Category B or C prisoners serving over 12 months but less than four years are recategorized every six months. Category B or C prisoners serving four years or more must be recategorized annually. Category D prisoners do not require regular recategorization reviews, but may be placed in a higher security category at any time if there is an increase in the risk they pose. The recategorization review is conducted by a categorization board or a single manager within the prison. The review involves a conventional risk assessment procedure. The basis for the recategorization review will be reports prepared as part of the prisoner's sentence plan review together with any other reports or comments by wing staff. In addition, reports on progress relating to the differential privilege system operating in the prison will be taken into account. Where recategorization is recommended, the prison security department is always consulted and the final decision rests with a governor grade. The prisoner must be informed of the reasons for the decision, and can appeal against the decision by submitting a Complaint form to the manager of the assessing officer, or the Chair of the Board of Visitors.

Denial of Guilt and Categorization Decisions

How does a denial of guilt of the index offence affect a prisoner's prospects of **4.08** being recategorized to a lower security category? This question was considered by

Laws J in *R v Home Secretary, ex p Fenton-Palmer* in which a number of prisoners challenged the refusal of the Prison Service to place them in Category D on the basis that the decision-maker improperly took account of the fact that they continued to deny their guilt, treating that circumstance as conclusive when it should have been regarded as no more than one factor to be considered.[11] All the applications failed on their individual merits but Laws J set out the principles which apply in this area (as well as in the field of parole decisions where prisoners deny their guilt). He said that the decision-maker must assume the prisoner's guilt of the offence(s) of which he has been convicted. The Prison Service cannot act as if it were the Court of Appeal. The decision-maker's first duty is to assess the risk to the public. It is unlawful for the decision-maker to refuse to recategorize a prisoner on the ground only that he continues to deny his guilt. But in some cases, particularly cases of serious persistent violent or sexual crime, a continued denial of guilt will almost inevitably mean that the risk posed by the prisoner to the public if he is de-categorized remains high, or at least cannot be objectively assessed. In such a case, it will be permissible to refuse to de-categorize the prisoner concerned.

Procedural Fairness and Categories B, C, and D

4.09 What are the procedural fairness requirements of the decision-making process which determines whether a prisoner is initially allocated to category B, C or D or his subsequent recategorization to a more restrictive category? In *R v Home Secretary, ex p Peries*[12] an attempt was made to equate a decision to recategorize a prisoner from D to B with a decision to allocate him to Category A, thereby triggering the procedural fairness requirements which the Divisional Court held in *R v Home Secretary, ex p Duggan*[13] to be appropriate to the latter decision-making process. It was argued that just as allocation to Category A has a direct effect on a prisoner's prospect of being released on licence, so too does recategorization from D to C or C to B or a refusal to consider de-categorization from B to C or from C to D. Accordingly, the *Duggan* principles should apply with equal force to such decisions thereby requiring the Prison Service to give all prisoners prior notice of a recategorization decision, disclosure of all material to be considered (subject to the requirements of public interest immunity), and an opportunity to make representations before the decision is taken. In a conservative judgment, Jowitt J rejected

---

[11] 24 March 1997, CO/2051/96. Laws J commented that CI 7/88 'much like the Secretary of State's directions in relation to parole, plainly puts the risk factor at the forefront of any decision as to re-categorization from C to D incline to accept (and it was not disputed) that the reasoning in *Zulfikar* and *Lillycrop* applies with equal force to such decisions'. The approach taken in these cases has been confirmed in *R v Parole Board and Home Secretary, ex p Oyston*, The Independent, 17 April 2000, CA; *R (Callaghan) v Home Secretary and Parole Board*, [2001] EWHC Admin 208; *R (Wilkes) v Home Secretary* [2001] EWHC Admin 210. For a full discussion of the *Zulfikar/Lillycrop/Oyston* principles in relation to parole decisions see paras 12.49–12.50.

[12] [1998] COD 150.

[13] [1994] 3 All ER 277.

this argument, holding that allocation to Category A was clearly distinguishable from placement in any other security category. Most extraordinarily, he accepted the submission on behalf of the Home Secretary that a Category D prisoner does not necessarily have a significantly better prospect of being released on licence than someone in Category C. He also accepted the submission on behalf of the Executive that the consequences of extending the *Duggan* principles to all categorization decisions would be too burdensome on the administration. The only obligation which was recognized was a duty to give reasons for adverse recategorization decisions—a duty which was conceded on behalf of the Home Secretary. It follows that unless and until *Peries* is overturned prisoners who are recategorized within Categories B–D are significantly worse off than prisoners allocated to category A in terms of the requirements of fairness imposed on the Prison Service. Some inroads have been made on *Peries* by the Court of Appeal in *R (Hirst) v Home Secretary*,[14] where the Court of Appeal considered the requirements of fairness when recategorizing a post-tariff discretionary life sentence prisoner. In the context of the discretionary life sentence, Lord Woolf CJ accepted that 'the recategorisation of a prisoner from Category C to Category B significantly affects the prospects of his being released on licence'.[15] This conclusion was reached after considering statistical evidence on the security category of released life sentence prisoners. Lord Woolf went on to say that, since the recategorization decision had such effects

> it seems to me that a decision of this nature as a matter of fairness should not be taken until Mr Hirst had been fully involved. He should have been given a reasonable period to make representations before the decision was taken. He should have been given that opportunity after he had been told the grounds upon which it was appropriate to recategorise him.[16]

It may be, therefore, that the courts are becoming more willing to accept that recategorization decisions have such an impact on prisoners as to require higher standards of procedural fairness. Although the life sentence (discussed further below) is a special case, much of the reasoning in *Hirst* should logically be of general application, and may eventually cast doubt on *Peries*.[17]

---

[14] [2001] EWCA Civ 378; The Times, 22 March 2001; discussed further below, in the context of lifers, at para 4.33.

[15] ibid, para 18.

[16] ibid, para 26.

[17] *Hirst* was considered by the High Court in *R (McLeod) v Prison Service* [2002] EWHC 390. Following recategorization from Category D to Category C, the claimant, a determinate sentenced prisoner, was told by the Parole Board that he was not suitable for early release. The claimant argued that there should have been disclosure of the material on which the recategorization was based, and an opportunity to make representations. Newman J noted that the adverse effect of recategorization is greater in the case of a discretionary life sentenced prisoner (such as Hirst) than a determinate sentenced prisoner. In dismissing the claim, he stressed that the Parole Board had refused release for a number of reasons, security category being only one of them. This leaves the issue very much alive in cases where release is refused solely or largely on the basis of categorization. Since an adverse recategorization decision reflects the Prison Service's assessment of risk, an assessment which the Parole

C. Category A

4.10   The highest security category is Category A and is reserved for those prisoners whose escape would be highly dangerous to the public or the police or the security of the state, no matter how unlikely that escape might be, and for whom the aim must be to make escape impossible.[18] It is of universal application in the sense that it is the only category which is capable of applying to all prisoners, whether convicted or remand, lifer or determinate sentence, male or female, adult or juvenile. When the Mountbatten Report was published in 1966 only about 120 prisoners were regarded as needing the very highest level of security. By the time of the Learmont Inquiry into Prison Security, there were some 750 Category A prisoners.

4.11   A decision to place a prisoner in Category A is made by the Category A committee, a permanent body comprised of senior Prison Service personnel which meets on a regular basis throughout the year. When prison establishments first receive prisoners charged with certain serious offences they are required to report their cases to the Category A Committee, which will consider whether they should be placed provisionally in Category A. If a prisoner is classified as provisionally Category A he is subject to broadly the same security conditions as a prisoner who is confirmed in Category A following conviction and sentence.

4.12   Upon conviction, the case of every provisional Category A prisoner is reviewed by the Category A Committee which considers his case with the benefit of a reception report from the governor of the prison (invariably a dispersal prison) to which he has been transferred. The report is required to be lodged with the Category A Review Team, which acts as the Secretariat to the Category A Committee, within ten days of the prisoner's reception and should append the Order for Imprisonment (Court form 5035), the Trial Record Sheet (Court form 5089), and a list of previous convictions together with any other available information considered to be of relevance to the determination of security category. This process of review is in accordance with the policy announced in Parliament in December 1992 by the then Minister of State responsible for prisons, Mr Peter Lloyd. He said that:

> In the light of the security audit undertaken last year . . . it has been decided to change the procedures for reviewing the security status for category A prisoners. Security status will continue to be reviewed on conviction and at least annually thereafter but referral to the category A Committee will be limited to new cases and to those cases where recommendations have been made for a change to the security

---

Board is clearly likely to take into account, both for lifers and determinate sentenced prisoners, it is submitted that the impact on prospects of release may in many cases be little different for the two categories of prisoner.

[18]   But see n 7 above.

category either by the holding prison or by Prison Service headquarters. The category A Committee comprises senior officials of the Prison Service including governors and staff of prisons normally holding category A prisoners; a senior medical officer; and a senior police adviser. Its role is:

1 to consider whether prisoners recently convicted of very serious offences should be retained in security category A, which is reserved for those whose escape from prison custody would be highly dangerous to the public or the police or the security of the State;

2 to consider all cases of category A prisoners where recommendations have been made for a change in security status; and to review cases where no such recommendations have been made for 5 years; and

3 to make recommendations to the Director General of the Prison Service. All other cases will be considered at least annually by officials of the directorate of custody. The new procedures are designed to improve efficiency in the administration of category A prisoners while ensuring that changes in security status are well founded and that no prisoner remains in category A any longer than is necessary.[19]

What this policy means in practice is that every provisional category A prisoner has his categorization reviewed by the Category A Committee immediately following conviction but, thereafter, the Committee only considers the case again where there is a recommendation from the relevant governor (based on all the reports received) that the security category can be downgraded because the assessment of dangerousness in the event of escape has diminished or where five years have elapsed since the Committee last considered the prisoner's case. Where no recommendation for downgrading is made, the annual review is conducted by the Category A Review Team without reference to the Committee, with the inevitable result that allocation to Category A is maintained for another year. Whereas the ministerial policy refers to a process of annual reviews, the Prison Service stated in *R v Home Secretary, ex p Duggan*[20] that 'security assessment remains a continuous responsibility of Prison Service staff both at establishments and at Headquarters . . . the Category A Section is in continuous receipt of security information about prisoners from establishments and from the police and other agencies'. It is implicit in this approach that where a good case can be made out for a review of categorization sooner than 12 months following the last decision, the Prison Service is obliged to consider such an exceptional review.

Escape Risk Classification within Category A

Those prisoners who are placed in Category A (both convicted and unconvicted) **4.13** are further assigned by the Category A Committee to one of three escape risk

---

[19] Parliamentary Answer, Hansard, December 1992. The current procedure, which reflects the Hansard Statement, is contained in PSO 1010, which consolidates and replaces all previous guidance on the Category A review procedure.

[20] [1994] 3 All ER 277.

classifications: Standard Escape Risk, High Escape Risk, and Exceptional Escape Risk. The criteria announced by the Category A Committee in relation to this form of classification are as follows:

Standard Escape Risk
Most category A prisoners are classified as Standard Escape Risk. They are not considered to have the determination or skill to overcome the range of security measures which apply to the custody and movement of category A prisoners. There is no current information to suggest that they have associates or resources which could be used to plan and carry out an assisted escape attempt. They have no history of escape or determined escape planning. Even so, the Prison Service must assume that they would take any opportunity to escape and that, if unlawfully at large, they would pose a very serious threat to the public, the police or the security of the State.

High Escape Risk
A small proportion of category A prisoners are classified as High Escape Risk. They have a history and background which suggests that they have both the ability to plan an escape and the determination to carry it out. There is usually current information to suggest that they have associates or resources which could be used to plan and carry out an assisted escape attempt. There is usually also information that the prisoner or associates have access to firearms or explosives and have been willing to use them in committing crime or in avoiding capture. Category A High Escape Risk prisoners are likely to be major criminals. Examples include terrorists belonging to substantial organizations and armed robbers and major drug dealers who operate in powerful and violent gangs.

Exceptional Escape Risk
A very small number of category A prisoners are classified as Exceptional Escape Risk. In addition to having the features applying to High Escape Risk, they are usually criminals who pose a particularly grave danger to the public and who are regarded as extremely valuable members of their organizations or groups. Such prisoners would be strongly motivated to attempt to escape from all but the most secure conditions.[21]

The policy announced by the Minister of State in 1992 concerning the circumstances in which a Category A prisoner's case is referred to the Category A Committee on annual review is limited to categorization and thus has no application to escape risk classification. It follows that in the absence of an overall recommendation for downgrading from Category A, a Category A prisoner will not have his case referred to the Category A Committee for consideration of a recommendation that his escape risk classification be reduced from Exceptional to High

---

[21] An analysis (albeit anecdotal) of those prisoners who end up being placed in Exceptional as opposed to High Risk reveals that the supposed distinction between an 'extremely valuable' member of a criminal organization (who will end up as an Exceptional Escape Risk) and a 'major criminal' who belongs to a criminal organization who will be 'High Escape Risk' is highly subjective and arbitrary. Thus many prisoners convicted of IRA offences found themselves spending many years in SSUs as Exceptional Risk prisoners in circumstances where it was hard to believe that they could be regarded as more highly valued by the IRA than many others who were not so allocated.

or from High to Standard. Rather, this decision will always be taken by the Category A Review Team alone. This is a somewhat baffling approach. There is such an obvious and clear link between the risk classification within Category A and the categorization decision itself that it seems surprising that a rigid line is drawn. But in *R v Home Secretary, ex p Arif,* Collins J rejected the submission that, properly construed, the Ministerial policy envisaged a reference to the Committee when there existed a recommendation either for downgrading of category or escape risk.[22]

Procedural Fairness and Category A

As previously stated, security categorization is a vital determinant of the kind of **4.14** regime which a prisoner is likely to enjoy. At one extreme, allocation to Category D leads to location in an open prison with a relaxed regime, relatively easy contact with the outside world, and home visit privileges. At the other end of the scale, Category A status leads to a relatively impoverished regime with great emphasis on observation, regulation, and security. Where the prisoner is classified as Exceptional Risk Category A, he is subject to the uniquely deprived regime of detention in a Special Secure Unit. In *Payne v Home Office* Cantley J listed six disadvantages to a prisoner flowing from allocation to Category A:

> 1. there are only a relatively small number of prisons suitable for his safe accommodation; this may result in his being detained in a prison which is more distant from persons from whom he wishes to have visits than some less secure prison would be; 2. he can have visits only from a solicitor, a probation officer, a prison visitor or a person who has been passed as suitable by the Home Office; 3. his cell is a specially secure one and it is liable to be searched more frequently than other cells; he is also under closer surveillance, and this may sometimes result in his sleep being disturbed when the officer who is looking into his cell cannot be sure in a dim light that there is more than a carefully arranged heap of bedclothes on his bed; 4. he cannot attend general vocational training classes or concerts, nor can he attend the ordinary church services, although he has regular visits from the chaplain and can take communion in his cell if he wishes; 5. he can attend only educational classes of not more than two students, and so he has less frequent opportunity to attend educational classes; 6. he is not likely, to say the least, to be put on parole while he is a category A prisoner.[23]

---

[22] [1997] COD 477. See also *R v Governor of HM Prison Dartmoor, ex p Brown,* 5 May 2000, CO/5010/1998, QB, in which the applicant unsuccessfully sought disclosure of the information which formed the basis of the decision to place him on the escape list and transfer him from Dartmoor to Parkhurst.

[23] 2 May 1977. The plaintiff, Roger Payne, appeared in person before the court. Four years later, and with legal representation, he challenged the Parole Board's refusal to give reasons for a rejection of an application for parole (see *Payne v Lord Harris of Greenwich* [1981] 1 WLR 754). Cantley J complimented Mr Payne on his 'well-sustained argument of admirable lucidity and learning which, both in manner and in matter, would have done credit to a professional lawyer and advocate'.

But despite the drastic consequences attendant upon allocation to Category A (in his case for seven years), Payne failed in his action for a declaration that such allocation was invalid by reason of breaches of the rules of natural justice—specifically the fact that he was not told of the material before the Category A Committee, nor given an opportunity to make representations, nor informed subsequently of the reasons for the decision.[24] The court accepted the existence of a general duty to act fairly in reaching categorization decisions (and was content to accept the Home Office's assurance that it did always act fairly) but held that 'the full panoply of the rules of natural justice is wholly inappropriate to the classification of prisoners'. In reasoning which exemplified the old 'hands off' approach towards prison affairs which was maintained until the early 1980s, Cantley J held that any application of the right to be heard would:

> as a matter of general principle . . . seriously hamper, and in some circumstances could frustrate, the efficient and proper government of prisons. . . . Very considerable difficulties would arise if the nature of the case to be considered by the classifying authorities were to be communicated to the prisoner in any detail sufficient to enable him to present relevant observations of his own.

He also held that Parliament had by s 47(2) of the 1952 Act expressly provided for procedural fairness requirements in the prison disciplinary process and must thereby have intended that such requirements were not applicable to the process of classification.

Ex p Duggan

4.15 Payne remained good law until it was finally overruled by the Divisional Court in *R v Home Secretary, ex p Duggan*,[25] a decision reached after the House of Lords had held in *R v Home Secretary, ex p Doody*[26] that mandatory life sentence prisoners were entitled to certain minimum procedural fairness safeguards in relation to the fixing of their tariffs. In *Duggan*, Rose LJ accepted the argument that allocation to Category A had a direct effect on a prisoner's prospects of release on licence and thus affected the liberty of the subject. In reality, no Category A prisoner would ever be considered suitable for immediate release either by the Parole Board or the Home Secretary. In the circumstances, fairness therefore demanded that the purely administrative process of allocating some prisoners to Category A be subject to a duty of prior disclosure of the gist of every matter of fact and/or

---

[24] It was by no means obvious why Payne had remained in Category A for so long. He had been convicted of murder in 1968 but the majority of convicted murderers avoid Category A status throughout their imprisonment. He had two previous convictions for relatively minor offences of assault; it was accepted by the Home Office that he had been a model prisoner, and he had never been the subject of psychiatric treatment. Accordingly the argument that 'although you haven't been told the reason it is plain enough' could not possibly apply to Payne's case, emphasizing the injustice of his apparently arbitrary allocation.

[25] [1994] 3 All ER 277.

[26] [1994] 1 AC 531.

opinion relevant to the proposed categorization decision so that the prisoner could make effective representations to the decision-making body. The Divisional Court also held that reasons had to be given for any decision to maintain a prisoner in Category A. Both the duty of prior disclosure and the duty to give reasons were expressed to be subject to the requirements of public interest immunity. Thus the Prison Service is not obliged to disclose any material which might imperil prison security or the safety of informers. The court also held that the initial decision to place a prisoner in Category A could be taken without affording the above procedural safeguards to the prisoner concerned. In recent times, the Prison Service has not applied a rigid policy of refusing to provide reasons or to consider representations in the cases of remand prisoners provisionally allocated to Category A following their first reception. This is sensible. The basis of Rose LJ's reasoning in *Duggan* was to ensure that the Prison Service should not be prevented from enforcing what it considered to be necessary security precautions in the case of every prisoner by rigid procedural fairness requirements. But so long as an initial, provisional allocation to Category A can lawfully be made there is no logic or justice in deliberately waiting for one year before providing reasons or considering representations with a view to changing the provisional decision. Administrative convenience should not be given much, if any, weight here, and indeed it would be extraordinary if unconvicted prisoners enjoyed lesser rights than those extended to the sentenced population. Thus, all remand prisoners unhappy with their allocation to Category A should seek disclosure of the reasons and make representations in respect of them where they wish to do so. Having said that, it will be a rare case indeed where a successful challenge can be mounted to a decision to place a remand prisoner in provisional Category A. Such a decision will invariably be based on, as yet, untested evidence supplied by the police, and the Prison Service will not be acting unlawfully by assuming that it is true before a jury has had an opportunity to consider its reliability.[27]

The Gist Document

In the years since the *Duggan* decision, the Category A Review Team has formulated a standard approach to the drafting of the gist document for disclosure to the prisoner concerned. The gist document tends to recite the prisoner's index offence, previous convictions, custodial behaviour, and work undertaken on offending behaviour before briefly summarizing what recommendations emerge from the (unidentified) reports submitted. The gist therefore makes it impossible

4.16

---

[27] See eg the reasoning of the Court of Appeal when refusing leave to move for judicial review in *R v Home Secretary, ex p Togher*, 1 February 1995. Ms Togher was a Category A remand prisoner charged with serious offences involving importation of Class A drugs. She was of good character and had recently given birth to a baby girl when she was arrested. As a result of her categorization she was separated from her baby because there are no mother and baby facilities for Category A prisoners anywhere in the penal system. She was acquitted at trial.

to know whether a negative recommendation emerges from someone in a good position to form a view on dangerousness or someone with either little relevant knowledge or a motive to damn the prisoner concerned. Sometimes it seems that the sole basis for a continuing concern about dangerousness is the index offence without reference to more recent, relevant information and events. Very often the gist only summarizes an opinion about dangerousness without any identification of the facts which lie behind it. In *R v Home Secretary, ex p Grove*,[28] Morrison J rejected a judicial review challenge to the Category A Review Team's decision to keep the applicant in Category A. The gist document wrongly recorded the applicant's offence (he had been convicted of manslaughter, not murder), and contained vague allegations of drug abuse and bullying. The judge considered that, although these errors were 'unfortunate', they did not taint the ultimate decision. He did stress that 'in future gist documents are to be more carefully prepared and those documents should be as full as is practicable, consistent with the constraints there are in relation to decisions of this sort'.

4.17 It is strongly arguable that this approach is not in accordance with the declarations granted in *Duggan* which referred to a duty to disclose every matter of fact and opinion which impinges on the categorization decision, and prisoners who are concerned at the paucity of their gist documents should press for further and better particulars of vague, generalized allegations or opinions. In *R v Home Secretary, ex p McAvoy*, a prisoner convicted of a notorious armed robbery and who had remained in Category A for 13 years sought to extend the *Duggan* principles by arguing that in all cases fairness demanded the disclosure, not merely of the gist of reports before the Category A Committee, but of the reports themselves, subject only to considerations of public interest immunity.[29] Without access to the full reports it was submitted that there would be an unacceptable risk of an erroneous decision because the prisoner's ability to make properly informed representation would be limited. It was also pointed out that the task of the Category A Committee and that of the Parole Board were similar. Each body was required to assess the current level of risk presented by a prisoner and it was anomalous that a prisoner should be entitled to enjoy full disclosure of reports before the Parole Board but only a gist of those before the Category A Committee. The Court of Appeal rejected the argument, holding that the House of Lords in *Doody* had (in the context of determining the tariff for mandatory lifers) endorsed the approach of providing the gist of material relied on rather than the original material itself. The court found that the procedure adopted by the Category A Review Team was 'perfectly satisfactory and perfectly fair'. Moreover, the case had shown

---

[28] 12 June 2000, CO/3551/1999, QB.
[29] [1998] 1 WLR 790. The applicant had been convicted as one of the Brinks Mat gold bullion robbers.

that those responsible for the review were prepared to reconsider in the circumstances of any particular case whether additional material should be made available. This was, in the court's view, a sufficient safeguard. *McAvoy* was upheld by the Court of Appeal in an extremely conservative judgment in *R (Manjit Singh Sunder) v Home Secretary*.[30] The court considered that *McAvoy* had not been affected by the Human Rights Act: Article 5 was not engaged by the refusal to recategorize the claimant from A to B, since the continued detention flowed from the original sentence of life imprisonment, and Article 6 is not engaged since categorization decisions do not determine a prisoner's civil rights or obligations.[31] The courts in *McAvoy* and *Sunder* placed great faith in the Review Team's willingness to order disclosure in appropriate cases. However, it must be said that experience suggests that the occasions on which the Review Team is willing to expand in a meaningful way upon the original gist are few and far between. In general, only an application for permission for judicial review will prompt an informed response which goes beyond the broad generalizations set out in the gist. Paragraph 4.1 of PSO 1010, 'Category A Prisoners: Reviews of Security Category' states that '[i]n the normal case a gist is all that will be required although there could be particular cases where fairness might require the disclosure of an actual report. *The Head of the Category A Review Team at Headquarters will decide whether, exceptionally, a particular case requires disclosure of an actual report.*' The Review Team's assessment of whether fairness requires disclosure may be challenged by judicial review in an appropriate case. In *R (Matthew Williams) v Home Secretary*[30a] the claimant, a post-tariff discretionary life sentence prisoner who had been involved in the Parkhurst prison escape, sought judicial review of the Category A Review Team's refusal to disclose the full report, and to allow him an oral hearing. His category A classification had a particularly serious effect on his prospects of release, since the Discretionary Lifer Panel of the Parole Board had decided that he remained a risk to the public, but had made as much progress as possible in category A conditions, and were therefore very unlikely to release him while he remained in Category A. The Court of Appeal held that the requirements of Article 5(4)—the right to a review of the legality of continued detention—are met by the Parole Board review process, and that therefore the Category A review does not engage that Article. Yet an adverse categorization decision can in effect preclude release by the Parole Board. Since both processes have a severe impact on the prospects of liberty, it is in principle illogical to confine the requirements of

---

[30] [2001] EWCA Civ 1157.

[30a] [2002] EWCA Civ 498.

[31] The refusal to extend Art 6 to categorization decisions, on the basis that they do not determine civil rights or obligations, is part of a general trend on the part of the courts to keep Art 6 out of the prison context. The fact that traditional public law principles of fairness, in cases such as *Duggan*, have imposed procedural safeguards in cases where Art 6 has been held not to apply, highlights the limitations of the 'civil rights and obligations' requirement in Art 6.

Article 5(4) to one half of the closely integrated process.[32] However, despite these conclusions Lord Phillips MR did voice some criticisms of the Category A review process. While not considering that Article 5(4) applied, he noted the obvious fact that a life sentenced prisoner is very unlikely to be released from Category A conditions. Lord Phillips was concerned at the quality of the material prepared for the Category A review, which differed greatly from that prepared for the Parole Board. He also noted that the Prison Service policy of disclosing further information than the standard gist had never been applied in any case. The court considered that in exceptional cases, such as that of the claimant, full disclosure and an oral hearing would be required. Lord Phillips stated that:

> On the basis of reports which had not been available to the DLP or been made available to the appellant or his legal advisers, the review team reached conclusions adverse to him which were seriously damaging to his prospects of release. In rejecting the application for an oral hearing the review team misdirected itself by evaluating the theory of the DLP's statutory jurisdiction disproportionately above the practical realities, and over-emphasising the differences between its own functions and those of the DLP without sufficiently recognising the link between them.

To that extent, the decision is a helpful one for prisoners: the challenge for prisoners now will be to convince the courts that their case is 'exceptional' and requires further disclosure and/or an oral hearing. The decision is also notable for its frank recognition of the impact that category reviews have on the prospects of liberty, and on the link between such reviews and the work of the Parole Board. This recognition may make the beginning of a domestic jurisprudence which goes beyond the European Court of Human Rights' restrictive interpretation of Article 5. *Williams* did not overrule *McAvoy*, but clearly shows more judicial concern about whether the safeguards in which the court put so much faith in *McAvoy* actually work in practice.

Spent Convictions

4.18 The extent to which the Category A Committee and the Review Team are entitled to take account of spent convictions when assessing a prisoner's risk to the public was considered by the High Court in *R v Home Secretary, ex p Purcell*.[33] Mr Purcell had convictions for violence dating back to the period 1973–76, all of which were spent under the Rehabilitation of Offenders Act 1974. He challenged the 1995 decision to allocate him to Category A on the basis that the Committee

---

[32] The illogicality of this position does flow from an orthodox application of the Strasbourg case law. The ECtHR's decision in *Ashingdane v UK* Series A No 93 (1985) 7 EHRR 528, in which the Court held that Art 5 relates only to the bare decision to detain, and not the quality, nature or restrictiveness of detention, currently provides a block to attempts to extend the protection of Art 5 to decisions in the prison context, such as categorization, which do not *directly* relate to loss of liberty, however great the knock-on effects of those decisions may be.

[33] *The Times*, 5 March 1998.

and the Review Team could not, when considering his security category in relation to his 1993 index offence of attempted murder, rely on his spent convictions as revealing a pattern of unaddressed violent behaviour. Forbes J rejected this argument holding (on the basis of a concession by Counsel for the prisoner) that the Category A Committee and Review Team are each a judicial authority within the meaning of the Rehabilitation of Offenders Act 1974 and, accordingly, could exercise a judicial discretion to take account of spent convictions in order to do justice, in all the circumstances, to the task allocated to them.[34]

D. Special Secure Units

A minority of Category A prisoners are categorized as Exceptional Risk according to the belief that, in addition to sharing the characteristics of High Risk prisoners, they are regarded as extremely valuable members of criminal organizations or groups with a strong motivation to escape. For such prisoners, this categorization means automatic removal from the 'normal' regime for Category A prisoners within the dispersal system and indefinite imprisonment within one of the three Special Secure Units (SSUs) within Whitemoor, Full Sutton, and Belmarsh prisons.[35] SSUs are not to be confused with Close Supervision Centres designed to contain persistently disruptive prisoners.[36] Allocation to an SSU bears no relationship to the prisoner's behaviour in prison. A prisoner may behave like a saint in custody but if the Prison Service concludes that he fulfills the criteria for Exceptional Risk he will be held in an SSU regardless.   **4.19**

The system of SSUs has its origins in the well publicized escapes of two of the   **4.20**
Great Train Robbers (Charles Wilson and Ronnie Biggs) and George Blake between 1964 and 1966. It became clear that there were no specially secure prisons anywhere in England and Wales, and the first response was to set up Special Security Wings at Durham and Leicester prisons. Later a third wing was adapted at Parkhurst. These proved to be expensive and highly oppressive regimes, and by the late 1970s it was agreed that with the growing number of prisoners convicted of IRA offences, and the consequent pressure on the existing secure facilities, the only option was to expand capacity with purpose-built units rather than adapting wings in existing prisons.

---

[34] A judicial authority is defined in s 4(6) of the 1974 Act as including 'proceedings before any tribunal, body or person having power (a) by virtue of any enactment, law, custom or practice . . . to determine any question affecting the rights, privileges, obligations or liabilities of any person . . .'. This almost certainly does embrace the Home Secretary's power to categorize prisoners under r 3 of the Prison Rules 1964.

[35] The Belmarsh SSU holds remand prisoners awaiting trial. There is a high security court building within 100 yards of Belmarsh prison and an underground tunnel which connects the two.

[36] See r 46. Close Supervision Centres are dealt with in more detail in Ch 10 at paras 10.39–10.45.

4.21   In 1988 the first purpose-built SSU was opened in Full Sutton dispersal prison, near York. In 1991 a second was opened in the newly built Whitemoor prison in Cambridgeshire, and there is now a third SSU in Belmarsh prison, south east London, which houses all remand prisoners categorized as Exceptional Risk.

The Regime

4.22   The regime in all SSUs is determined by the Operating Standards for Special Secure Units which were developed and published in the wake of the Woodcock and Learmont reports.[37] Woodcock's conclusions were devastating for the Prison Service. Appointed to investigate how it was that six Exceptional Risk prisoners were able to break out from supposedly the most secure conditions in the prison system in possession of loaded weapons, he said that there had been a 'yawning gap between the Prison Service's ideals and actual practice' and that 'the findings of the Enquiry describe an awful story where it appears that everything which could have gone wrong has in fact done so'.[38] The report identified two underlying themes and beliefs which had affected the regime at the Whitemoor SSU. First, a universal belief that the SSU was escape proof and, secondly, a deeply held inherent fear on the part of governor grades of another Strangeways-style riot. Woodcock concluded that '[t]he ethos of impregnability lulled staff into believing that no matter what happened the inmates could never get out. When added to the fear of riot, this set the scene for a regime of non-confrontation where the prisoners were able to push back the boundaries of acceptable practice at every opportunity.'[39]

4.23   In the face of such savage criticism and the immediate acceptance by Ministers of all of Woodcock's recommendations, the Prison Service set about redesigning the recently built SSUs and drafting a set of core operating standards with one pur-

---

[37] Derek Lewis describes in his memoirs of his term as Director-General how former Home Secretary Michael Howard was determined to be seen to act for political reasons when the damning judgment of the Woodcock Report was published: '[i]n order to protect himself, Howard was keen to accept all sixty-four recommendations in the Woodcock Report at once before anyone had a chance to assess whether they were affordable, let alone good value for money. It was clear that great expenditure would be involved. But there was no time for such considerations.' The result was massive expenditure on security measures, especially on SSUs all of which were redesigned and reconstructed according to the logic of total security.

[38] Former Director-General Derek Lewis described the Woodcock Report in highly critical terms: '[a] tabloid editor's dream, it would have made wonderful newspaper copy, written in an easy sensational style, punctuated by phrases that would have leapt straight into the headlines. It was highly critical of lax management at Whitemoor and of support from headquarters as well as of many individuals. Yet it managed to conceal the main failing of the inquiry; its inability to identify how the escape had been allowed to happen by tracing how the guns vital to its success had got into the prison': see *Hidden Agendas: Politics, Law and Disorder* (London, 1997) 158–159.

[39] A public, courtroom examination of how the Whitemoor escape had managed to take place was eventually prevented when the trial of the alleged escapers was halted as an abuse of the process of the court by reason of prejudicial press publicity contained in the Evening Standard.

pose in mind—'to ensure that prisoners held within them do not escape'.[40] And it is clear that when required to balance the needs of security against those of humanity, security is the decisive factor. In addition to the isolation and impoverishment inevitably caused by being held on an indefinite basis in a small, physically secure unit (literally a prison within a prison) with no more than eight to ten other prisoners to associate with, the Operating Standards demand intense, intrusive control and monitoring of every aspect of human activity.

Thus, every prisoner's cell is searched in detail at least once a fortnight on an arbitrary basis and the prisoner himself is strip searched. Each prisoner must change his cell at least once a month, preventing any sense of settlement or continuity of environment. No curtains, blinds or other obstructions are permitted on any internal observation window 'except to preserve decency in shower areas'. Cell furniture is strictly limited (as is the amount of personal property allowed). SSU prisoners are constantly subject to staff and camera supervision save when in their cells or the toilet/shower area. Most drastically, for a three-year period between 1995 and 1998, all visits, both legal and family/social, within SSUs were required to take place in closed conditions, ie with a glass partition between prisoner and visitor preventing any form of physical contact. This policy applied even though the closed visits policy required both visitor and prisoner to undergo rigorous searching procedures and the visit (including a legal visit) was required to take place in the sight of staff and a camera monitor. **4.24**

All telephone calls, including calls to lawyers, are simultaneously monitored and recorded and must be conducted in English. There are no opportunities for constructive work within the SSUs, the only option being cleaning the SSU itself. Education classes are available but not on the same basis and with the same variety as in the normal dispersal regime. The possibility of undergoing offending behaviour courses (an essential requirement for the attainment of parole) is very limited. Religious worship must take place within the SSU, thereby depriving the prisoner of taking in part in religious services with fellow prisoners in the main prison. **4.25**

The SSU regimes were created by the Prison Service without having first commissioned any research on the effects on health of long term incarceration within them. Faced with applications for judicial review brought by SSU prisoners who sought to challenge the legality of the regime, the Prison Service commissioned the former Chief Medical Officer, Sir Donald Acheson, in May 1996 to 'conduct a review into whether the regimes in the SSUs at Whitemoor, Full Sutton and Belmarsh prisons have a significant adverse effect on the health of prisoners held there and to report any findings to the Director of Security'. **4.26**

---

[40] Operating Standards for Special Secure Units, January 1997.

The Acheson Report

4.27   The Acheson Report was delivered in June 1996 after examining conditions in all three SSUs.[41] It commented that the post-Woodcock regimes had only been running for a short time at the time of the investigation and only 18 prisoners were affected by it. As a result 'evidence based on the views and present medical condition of the prisoners is insufficient on its own to allow definite conclusions to be drawn about the long term effects, if any, of the regime on health'. Nonetheless, Acheson concluded that the physical restrictions of the Belmarsh and Full Sutton SSUs carried potential risks to mental health because of their cramped design, the lack of natural light and the limited view from the cells. He also expressed concern about the average length of time that prisoners spent in SSUs (five years with a range between 11 months and ten years) and the fact that prisoners could not expedite their progress through the SSU system by good behaviour left them 'with a sense of helplessness without goals or indicators of progress'. Most significantly, Acheson criticized the regime of closed family visits, noting and agreeing with the Woodcock Report's view that depriving a prisoner for many years of any physical contact with family and children 'might not be deemed defensible' on humanitarian grounds, and concluding that 'the release of pressure provided in open visits with family members and their effect on maintaining a link with the outside world is highly desirable in the interests of health'. The Acheson Report expressly recommended that in the interests of health SSU prisoners should have access to open visits with their immediate family, but for more than a year after its publication the Prison Service steadfastly refused to accept this aspect of the report.[42] In March 1997, Amnesty International published a report based on its investigation into the conditions in which prisoners are held in SSUs. It concluded that they constitute 'cruel, inhuman or degrading treatment in breach of international law standards and, furthermore, that these conditions have seriously interfered with the exercise of remand prisoners' right to a fair trial'.[43] The Chief Inspector of Prisons visits the SSUs as a part of the general programme of visits. However, the

---

[41] *Review of the Effects on Health of the Regimes in the Special Secure Units at Full Sutton, Whitemoor and Belmarsh Prisons.* The report has never been made publicly available.

[42] The maintenance of the closed visits policy seemed especially arbitrary when prisoners convicted of IRA offences were transferred from the SSU system directly to prisons in Northern Ireland without a formal process of de-categorization but to very different prison regimes.

[43] *Special Security Units: Cruel, Inhuman or Degrading Treatment,* March 1997, AI Index EUR 45/06/97. The Amnesty report's findings received some support one year later in the UN Special Rapporteur's report on the independence of judges and lawyers in the UK (March 1998). He concluded in relation to closed legal visits that 'in the absence of evidence that solicitors are abusing their professional responsibilities, the closed visits with the SSUs constitute an undue interference with the lawyer/client relationship and create unnecessary impediments for adequate trial preparation. At a minimum, the burden should be upon the prison officials on a case by case basis to demonstrate that the closed visits are an exceptional measure necessary to maintain prison security.'

findings of the most recent visit to Whitemoor have not been made publicly available.[44] While this may be justified for security reasons, it deprives prisoners and their representatives of an important independent assessment of SSU conditions. In contrast, the results of a full inspection of Belmarsh SSU were made public, bringing to light worrying aspects of the deprived living conditions in the Unit, which was described as having an 'overriding oppressive atmosphere'.[45]

Challenging SSU Conditions

In *R v Home Secretary, ex p O'Dhuibhir and O'Brien*[46] two exceptional risk prisoners challenged the closed visits policy then in force, arguing, in relation to legal visits, that it interfered with the free flow of communication between prisoner and lawyer and was thus unlawful on the principles set out in *Ex p Leech (No 2)*.[47] On family visits it was argued that all prisoners retained the residual right to a degree of physical contact with their immediate families and that to deny such contact, potentially for years on end, was calculated to result in family break up and to increase the risk of mental illness in prisoners. Having identified the basic rights infringed by the closed visits policy (which had been introduced by a non-statutory Instruction to Governors) it was submitted that it failed the 'self-evident and pressing need/minimum interference necessary' test adopted in *Leech (No 2)* where interference with a fundamental right takes place without express Parliamentary approval. This was because the evidence tended to show that the laudable aims of security could be achieved by less intrusive, alternative methods such as proper screening and searching procedures and a case by case approach to any institution of closed visits.

4.28

Both the Divisional Court and the Court of Appeal rejected the prisoners' argument. In the Court of Appeal, Kennedy LJ held that the *Leech (No 2)* approach was not relevant because it turned on whether subordinate legislation (rule 33(3)) was too widely worded having regard to the enabling provision in the statute. Having concluded that the relevant rule in *Ex p O'Dhuibhir*, which gave the Home Secretary a general power to place restrictions on the communications between prisoners and others, was plainly intra vires the rule-making power, he held that the self-evident and pressing need test had no role to play. He concluded that:

4.29

---

[44] See HM Inspector of Prisons, *Report on a full announced inspection of HM Prison Whitemoor, 6–15 November 2000.*
[45] HM Inspector of Prisons, *Report on HM Prison Belmarsh*, 11–20 May 1998, para 6.28.
[46] [1997] COD 315.
[47] [1994] QB 198.

Once that it recognized all that remains is to decide whether the instruction to governors can be said to be unreasonable in a *Wednesbury* sense. I am not suggesting for a moment that the courts will not examine with care as to its rationality a measure which, at least in relation to family visits, has obviously got much to be said against it, but [the applicants'] approach, if correct, seems to me to create the impossible position that judges not prison service officials become the ultimate arbiters of what security demands. No discretion is left to the official. Any step taken in the interest of security which interferes, however slightly, with access to lawyers or family is liable to be set aside if in the opinion of the court it is not the minimum step necessary to meet a self-evident and pressing need. Neither common sense nor authority drives me to that conclusion.

It is perhaps understandable that the court should have expressed concern that it was being required to form an objective assessment of what the minimum demands of security should be in relation to a policy which only affects a small group of prisoners said to present the highest security risk. But so long as Parliament fails to pass any fresh primary legislation affecting the prison system and instead chooses to rely on a 46-year-old statute which does no more than create a series of enabling and deeming provisions designed to call on the Home Secretary to create and police an internal regime for prisons, it is inevitable that the courts will be required to adjudicate upon any interference with basic rights via the mechanism of necessary implication. *The Leech (No 2)* test ensures that in striking a balance between the fundamental rights of prisoners and the requirements of security, discipline, and control, the court is not powerless in the face of a decision which would otherwise escape *Wednesbury* review with ease. Prisoners are already disadvantaged in this regard because it has been held in a case concerning the right of access to the courts by free citizens that such a right could only be cut down by an express provision in primary legislation.[48]

4.30 Fortunately, the House of Lords has subsequently confirmed, in two important decisions, that the Court of Appeal in *Ex p O'Dhuibhir* erred in seeking to avoid the application of the *Leech (No 2)* approach on the basis that *Leech* simply concerned the vires of a particular Prison Rule. As discussed in Chapter 1, *Ex p Simms*

---

[48] In *R v Lord Chancellor, ex p Witham* [1998] QB 575 (the court fees case) Laws J held that 'if the concept of a constitutional right is to have any meaning it must surely sound in the protection which the law affords to it. . . . In the unwritten legal order of the British State at a time when the common law continues to accord a legislative supremacy to Parliament, the notion of a constitutional right can in my judgment inhere only in this proposition, that the right in question cannot be abrogated by the State save by specific provision in an Act of Parliament, or by regulations whose vires in main legislation specifically confers the power to abrogate. General words will not suffice.' The court accordingly decided that the Lord Chancellor had no power to make an Order under the Supreme Court Act 1981 which had the practical effect of denying access to the courts to people on low incomes, as Parliament had not expressly authorized him to do such a thing. In *Raymond v Honey* [1983] 1 AC 1 the House of Lords had accepted that a prisoner's right of access to the courts might be restricted by necessary implication based on a construction of the legislative framework regulating prisons and prisoners.

and O'Brien[49] and *Daly*[50] now make it perfectly clear that any policy which interferes with a prisoner's fundamental rights will have to satisfy the proportionality test. Not only must the policy fulfil legitimate aims—security, control, etc—but the policy must not go further than is strictly necessary to achieve those aims. *Ex p Simms and O'Brien* and *Daly* confirm, not only that proportionality is the test for all infringements of prisoners' rights, but that the courts will look closely at the Prison Service's assertions about what is really necessary to ensure security, control etc. In *Daly*, Lord Bingham felt free to disagree with the Prison Service's evidence—including evidence from Martin Narey, the Director-General—about the necessity of cell searching in the prisoner's absence. These decisions remove all doubt that any policy applied by the Prison Service will be lawful only to the extent that it is permitted by the Rules and the Act. And whether or not the Rules authorize the curtailment or abrogation of a fundamental right depends on the application of the proportionality test, as applied in *Leech (No 2), Ex p Simms and O'Brien* and *Daly*. This is an extremely welcome development, bringing some consistency to the whole area of prisoners' rights litigation. The point about *Leech (No 2)* was that it identified a particular test to be applied by the court once it was established that a fundamental right was being interfered with without express Parliamentary approval whatever the source of such interference. To seek, as in *Ex p O'Dhuibhir*, to avoid the consequences of applying the test in a hard case, where security concerns are at the forefront, was to undermine the very protection which the common law extends in order to give meaning to the concept of a fundamental or constitutional right.[51] Regardless of the source of authority for the deprived regimes in SSUs, those regimes are now open to full judicial scrutiny.[52]

E. Lifers

Adult male life sentence prisoners (other than those who are placed in Category A) are categorized and allocated on an entirely different basis from that applicable **4.31**

---

[49] [2000] 2 AC 115.

[50] [2001] 2 AC 532. Lord Steyn cited with approval the test proposed by Lord Clyde in the Privy Council in *de Freitas v Permanent Secretary of Ministry of Agriculture, Fisheries, Lands and Housing* [1999] 1 AC 69: in determining whether a limitation (by an act, rule or decision) is arbitrary or excessive the court should ask itself 'whether: (i) the legislative objective is sufficiently important to justify limiting a fundamental right; (ii) the measures designed to meet the legislative objective are rationally connected to it; and (iii) the means used to impair the right or freedom are no more than is necessary to accomplish the objective' (at 80).

[51] See also the speeches of Lord Steyn and Lord Browne-Wilkinson in a decision predating *Ex p Simms and O'Brien* and *Daly, R v Home Secretary, ex p Pierson* [1998] AC 539, in which their Lordships also endorsed the *Leech (No 2)* approach to statutory construction where fundamental rights are engaged.

[52] The possibility of challenging particular aspects of prison conditions is discussed in Ch 5.

to determinate sentence prisoners.[53] The relevant principles are to be found in chapter 3 of the *Lifer Manual,* which states that a typical lifer goes through the following stages of his sentence prior to release on licence:

Remand centre/local prison;
First Stage—High Security/Category B (also known as allocation to a Main Centre);
Second Stage—High Security/Category B/Category C;
Third Stage—Category D/Open/Semi-open/Resettlement.

The manual then explains that 'all life sentence prisoners (with the exception of category A) take the category of the prison in which they are held'. What this means in practice is that a lifer's progress through the system depends on an assessment by the Lifer Allocations Unit at Prison Service Headquarters of his suitability for gradually decreasing levels of security culminating in his eventual allocation to an open prison as the prospect of release on licence becomes ever closer.

Progressing Through the System

4.32 The stages of the lifer system are considered in more detail in Chapter 13. Immediately following conviction, the lifer is returned to a local prison where consideration is given to his allocation to one of the three First Stage prisons, or Main Centres, which hold lifers (Gartree, Wakefield, and Wormwood Scrubs). While he is being held in the local prison, an initial life sentence report must be prepared and, for mandatory lifers, the process of tariff-setting begins. The period spent in the Main Centre is usually three years but this may be reduced for those with low tariffs (less than ten years). During this time the initial Life Sentence Plan is prepared which will influence the lifer's likely progress through the system, and the first progress reports are called for by the Parole and Lifer Review Group.[54]

4.33 Having completed his stint in the First Stage prison, the next stage is allocation to a Second Stage prison. The prisoner remains so allocated until the Lifer Allocations Unit considers that he is suitable for a Third Stage prison. The *Lifer Manual* states that 'the lifer will be expected to show significant progress before transfer to a Category C prison'. This generally means progress in terms of addressing offending behaviour. A similar policy dictates the issue of transferring a lifer to open conditions, which is almost always a pre-requisite to release on life licence. *The Lifer Manual* explains that 'for all lifers transfer to an open prison is subject to Ministerial approval following a recommendation for such a move from the Parole Board'.

---

[53] At the end of March 2001, there were 4,700 lifers, an increase of almost 40% in five years: HM Prison Service, *Annual Report and Accounts 2000–2001* (HC 29, 2001).
[54] See the Prison Service's *Lifer Manual: A guide for members of the Prison and Probation Services.*

The effect of such a policy may be detrimental for the lifer who happens to have a **4.34** long tariff but who is in fact regarded as a low security risk (ie unlikely to try to escape) and who is assessed as no longer dangerous to the public after a relatively short time in custody. Policy would appear to dictate that such a prisoner must stay in Category B conditions until three years before his first review by the Parole Board. And a move to open conditions would be ruled out until the first Parole Board review (three years before the expiry of the tariff), at which time the necessary recommendation may be made to the Minister that he is suitable for open conditions, unless the Home Secretary made an exceptional reference of the prisoner's case to the Parole Board pursuant to the Criminal Justice Act 1991, s 32(2), solely to obtain their views on the issue of open conditions. It is strongly arguable that to refuse to consider such a reference or to refuse until a certain date to contemplate moving to conditions of less security a prisoner who satisfies the allocation criteria would amount to an unlawful fetter of the Home Secretary's discretion as contained in s 12 of the Prison Act 1952.[55]

F. Adult Female Prisoners

The majority of adult female prisoners are serving relatively short sentences, and **4.35** the principles governing their allocation are somewhat simpler than those which apply to adult males.[56] Unless a woman prisoner is placed in Category A (in which case she will be allocated to Holloway, while on remand, or to Durham H wing) she will be allocated to either open, closed or semi-closed conditions depending on the outcome of a risk assessment which focuses on the needs of security and control. Allocation thereafter depends on a number of factors—age, home area, current offence and sentence, medical requirements, whether time spent in local authority care, time left to serve, any outstanding appeal, whether the prisoner is likely to escape or abscond, and whether she is liable to be detained under the Immigration Act 1971. Categorization of female prisoners follows the procedure laid down in form ICA 3. PSO 0900 provides that a female prisoner should be placed in open conditions unless:

---

[55] The problems of moving lifers through the system were highlighted by the Chief Inspectors of Prisons and Probation in their report *Joint Thematic Review of Lifers*. They pointed out that the shortage of designated lifer places resulted in many newly sentenced lifers spending long periods in local prisons before moving to first stage lifer prisons. The shortage of lifer places also causes difficulties in ensuring that low risk lifers are released on the expiry of their tariff. The Prison Service has set up a Lifer Steering Group to oversee implementation of the report's recommendations. The priority is to increase the number of first stage lifer places in order to move lifers out of local prisons in a reasonable time.

[56] However, women make up a fast growing sector of the prison population, and an increasing number are serving life, or long determinate, sentences. In 2000–01, the female prison population rose 5% to 3,552: HM Prison Service, *Annual Report and Accounts 2000–2001* (HC 29, 2001).

(1) the current sentence is three years or more;

(2) the current offence is a serious offence of actual or threatened violence or harm, a sexual offence or relates to drug dealing or importation;

(3) the prisoner has previously received a sentence of three years or more within the past five years; has a previous conviction within the past five years for a serious offence of the types set out above, or the pattern of offending gives cause for concern;

(4) the nature of Schedule 1 status gives cause for concern;

(5) there are concerns about the prisoner's association with serious criminals;

(6) the prisoner is diagnosed or is suspected of suffering from any psychiatric or psychological problems;

(7) there are further charges outstanding or the prisoner is awaiting further sentencing;

(8) there is concern about any escape or abscond from any form of custody, breach of licence, community service order or community sentence during the past three years;

(9) the prisoner is subject to enforcement action under the Immigration Act 1971.

If only criteria 8 or 9 apply, the prisoner must be given an initial 'semi-open' classification. If any of the other criteria apply, the initial categorization will be 'closed'.

4.36 As with male offenders, the process of categorization is followed by the allocation decision. If a prisoner is given a 'closed' security category, she will automatically be allocated to closed conditions. However, prisoners initially categorized as 'semi-open' or 'open' must then be assessed to see whether they are suitable for allocation to semi-open or open conditions. It might be assumed that logically those who do not require closed conditions would be allocated to open (or semi-open) conditions, but in fact a number of extra criteria are taken into account at this stage, including whether:

(1) there are issues of control which warrant close levels of supervision;

(2) there is a genuine clinical need for the prisoner to have access to a health care centre staffed 24 hours;

(3) the prisoner is considered unlikely to be able to cope in semi-open or open conditions;

(4) there is an open F2052SH (form documenting the risk of self harm) and the case conference has decided that a transfer to open conditions would not be in the prisoner's best interest; or

(5) the prisoner is known or suspected of currently using drugs; is undergoing a detoxification programme or has recently completed a detoxification programme.

It is interesting to note that, when summarizing the reasons for allocation to a closed conditions, as well as having been assigned a closed security category or been assessed as unsuitable for open conditions, PSO 0900 includes a further head: that 'there were other significant issues which indicated that location in a closed establishment was in the prisoner's own interests'. There is no question of allocating male prisoners to a higher security category than risk requires because it is 'in their own interests'.

Once it has been finally decided whether the prisoner will be allocated to open or **4.37** closed conditions, a place must be found at a suitable establishment. There are currently only two semi-open prisons, at Morton Hall and Drake Hall. Unlike in the case of male prisoners, significant allocation issues include enabling childcare arrangements to be sorted out, and to facilitate visits from children or other family members. While these are important factors, it is difficult to see why they are not considered important in relation to male prisoners, particularly since the right to respect for private and family life, enshrined in Article 8 of the Convention, applies irrespective of gender.

Re-allocation between closed, semi-open and open conditions is based on a clear **4.38** change of risk and in all cases time left to serve is an important factor, as well as prison behaviour, position of trust, the existence of a recommendation for parole, and any successful release on temporary licence. The recategorization process takes place on form RC3, and takes into account the same type of information as the process for male prisoners. To move from closed to semi-open conditions, the prisoner must demonstrate a clear change in risk to the public, and that, although they are still at risk of absconding from an open prison, they would be unlikely to abscond from a semi-open prison. However, prisoners can also be recategorized straight from closed to open conditions: they do not have to spend a period in semi-open conditions if that level of security is not required.

The allocation and management of female lifers is dealt with by the Allocations **4.39** Unit of the Custody Group. As with determinate sentence prisoners, female lifers, other than those placed in Category A, are fitted either for open, semi-open or closed conditions. But in the first stage of their sentence, all lifers are placed in closed conditions. There are two Main Centres for female lifers (at Durham and Bullwood Hall) where the first stage of the life sentence is completed. Holloway prison holds women at any stage of a life sentence who require medical care. After a period of (usually) less than three years at the Main Centre, the second stage is allocation to one of four closed prisons—Cookham Wood, Holloway, New Hall, and Styal. While held in the second stage establishment, the emphasis is towards preparing for the first Parole Board review even though this may be some years away. The lifer will be mixing with other lifers about to move on to the final (open) stage of imprisonment as well as prisoners serving fixed term sentences. The final stage will be transfer to an open prison, a move which depends on risk assessment and the proximity of likely release on licence.

G. Young Offenders

Males

4.40 Detention in a Young Offenders Institution (YOI) can be imposed on offenders aged between 18 and 20 inclusive, under s 79 of the Powers of Criminal Courts (Sentencing) Act 2000.[57] The Secretary of State's power to depart from the general obligation to place a young offender in a designated YOI is limited to permission 'from time to time [to] direct than an offender . . . shall be detained in a prison or remand centre . . . for a temporary purpose' if under 18. In practice, a young offender may only lawfully be held in a prison or remand centre where exceptional circumstances apply, such as a temporary non-availability of a place in a designated YOI. This requirement reflects the provisions of Article 37 of the UN Convention of the Rights of the Child.[58]

4.41 Male young offenders are placed in one of four security categories: Category A, restricted status ('offenders sentenced to detention in a Young Offender Institution whose escape would present a serious risk to the public and who are required to be held in designated secure accommodation'), closed conditions and open conditions. Categorization of all male young offenders, other than those provisionally categorized A, Restricted Status, those sentenced to life imprisonment or those sentenced to be detained at Her Majesty's Pleasure, is carried out on form ICA 2. This contains an algorithm similar to that on ICA 1, which produces a provisional security categorization which may then be altered by the officer concerned, for similar reasons as in the case of adult prisoners. The usual factors

---

[57] When s 61 of the Criminal Justice and Court Services Act 2000 comes into force, the sentence of detention in a YOI will be abolished, and the sentence of imprisonment will be extended to cover not only adult offenders, but those aged 18–20 inclusive.

[58] Art 37 of the 1995 Convention on the Rights of the Child states that 'every child [ie person under 18] deprived of his liberty shall be separated from adults unless it is considered in the child's best interests not to do so'. The UK ratified the Convention with a reservation that Art 37 should not apply where there is a lack of suitable accommodation or adequate facilities for a particular individual in any institution. The Home Office does not consider that the Children Act 1989, with its duty to protect the welfare of children, applies to prisons. The Howard League for Penal Reform is currently challenging this position: see Press Release, 29 July 2002: '[a]s well as a general failure of prisons to meet the needs of teenagers, the Howard League believes they are at risk of significant harm from high levels of violence, impoverished regimes and excessive use of physical restraint by staff. Between April 2000 and January 2002 control and restraint was used 3,615 times on children . . . The Children Act brought into British law obligations enshrined in the UN Convention on the Rights of the Child . . . Whilst these standards apply to children anywhere in the country, including those serving sentences in local authority secure units, they are not provided for the 2,858 young people aged 15 to 17 currently in prison.'

relevant to risk assessment apply—current and past offence(s) being the most significant. Once categorized, young offenders must be allocated to a prison. PSO 0900 states that 'two, often conflicting, priorities must govern the allocation of Young Offenders: the needs of security and the needs of individual Young Offenders'. It goes on to state that:

[w]hile the main factor to be considered in determining a Young Offender's alloca-
tion must always be his security category, and a young prisoner who has been
assigned to a particular security category should be considered for allocation to a
Young Offender Institution of that category, account must also be taken of:
  His suitability for particular types of accommodation (factors such as vulnerabil-
  ity, immaturity, etc);
  His medical and/or psychiatric needs that may require a particular level of care;
  The need for identified offence related behavioural programmes to confront
  assessed risk;
  His home area, or that of his visitors; maintenance of family ties;
  His educational or training needs;
  Any restrictions on allocation criteria agreed with local authorities, governors,
  Area Managers or Estate Planning Section in Headquarters.

Further, all receiving YOIs must have a published list of acceptance criteria which is signed by the Governor and the Area Manager and reviewed at least every 12 months.

Young offenders will be assessed against these criteria, and the final allocation to **4.42** an open or closed institution will reflect the assessment of both their security risk and their needs. As with female offenders, the concept of need features in a way that it does not when adult males are being allocated.

Young offenders, both male and female, sentenced to be detained during Her **4.43** Majesty's Pleasure or detention for life will,[59] depending on their age and circum- stances, either be held in a secure children's home run by a local authority, in one of four long term YOIs (Aylesbury, Castington, Moorland, and Swinfen Hall), or in Glenthorne Youth Training Centre, run by the Department of Health. Allocation decisions are made by a dedicated Unit. Those who start their sen- tences in the child care system are usually transferred to the penal system at about the age of 18. Thereafter they must be transferred to an adult prison before their twenty-second birthday when they become subject to the categorization and allocation procedures applicable to adult lifers. Inevitably, the majority of young offenders serving indeterminate sentences will not be eligible for open prison conditions before they reach the adult system.

---

[59] Under ss 90 or 91 of the Powers of Criminal Courts (Sentencing) Act 2000, formerly s 53 of the Children and Young Persons Act 1933.

Females

4.44 At the date of writing there is no designated YOI anywhere in England and Wales for female young offenders. There are five women's prisons of which parts have been designated as YOIs and it is to these that all female young offenders are or should be allocated. Just as with adult females, the only distinction is between closed and open conditions. Notwithstanding the passage of the 1988 Criminal Justice Act, which introduced the principle that young offenders under 18 could only ever be placed in an adult prison or remand centre for temporary purposes, the Prison Service operated for many years an unlawful policy in relation to female offenders between 15–17 which was finally exposed and declared illegal in *R v Home Secretary, ex p Flood*.[60] The illegality stemmed from the terms of CI 2/91, which purported to authorize the allocation of all female young offenders to prisons according to criteria which bore no necessary relation to the individual offender but instead reflected the interests of prison management. One of the criteria said to justify a departure from the principle of exclusive allocation to a designated YOI was one which purported to permit young offenders following sentence to be held in a remand centre (ie a prison) for allocation purposes. As there was nowhere else within the prison system to which allocation of female young offenders could take place, the Circular left no discretion whatsoever in the allocation officers to whom the Secretary of State's discretion had been delegated. The Divisional Court held that as the 1988 Act made it plain that Parliament was authorizing the Secretary of State on occasion to place a particular offender under 18 temporarily in a prison or remand centre it was unlawful to authorize a general practice of so doing. Nor did it authorize a practice of keeping young offenders in a prison or remand centre for however long it takes (possibly the whole length of the sentence) to make a lawful placement in a designated YOI.

H. The Detention and Training Order

4.45 Section 73 of the Crime and Disorder Act 1998 established a new sentence, the Detention and Training Order (DTO), for offenders aged under 18. That sentence is now contained in ss 100–107 of the Powers of Criminal Courts (Sentencing) Act 2000. From 1 April 2000, the DTO is the main custodial sentence for those aged 12–17.[61] Allocation is carried out by the Youth Justice Board. Sentences can be carried out in a variety of establishments, but if the Board considers it necessary to allocate the juvenile to a Prison Service establishment,

---

[60] [1998] 1 WLR 156.
[61] Powers of Criminal Courts (Sentencing) Act 2000, s 100(2)(b) provides for the Secretary of State to extend the DTO to those aged 10 and 11. This has not so far been done.

PSO 0900, para 4.1.1, provides that they 'will inevitably be allocated initially to a closed Young Offender Institution'. Recategorization is then carried out as set out in ICA 2 (for male juveniles) and ICA 3 (for female juveniles). For male juveniles, there are now three juvenile-only establishments at Huntercombe, Werrington and Wetherby, and ten juvenile units in YOIs.

5

LIVING CONDITIONS IN PRISON

A. Introduction

The topic of prison conditions is a large and diverse one. Many of the issues men- **5.01**
tioned in other chapters in this book, notably matters of healthcare or of discipline
and powers to maintain good order, have a significant impact on the conditions in
which prisoners serve their sentences. In this chapter we will however concentrate on
prisoners' day to day living conditions, on matters which in the outside world people
can provide for themselves or through the help of State agencies but on the inside
must be provided by the prison authorities.[1] Thus issues of food, work, education,
and living space all pose difficult questions of entitlement and resource allocation.[2]

Prison conditions arguably reached their nadir in England and Wales in the late **5.02**
1980s. A combination of a rising prison population and decaying prison estate
produced conditions which were criticized from many quarters. Complaints

---

[1] The vulnerable situation of prisoners was cogently expressed by Lightman J in *R v Governor of Frankland Prison, ex p Russell* [2001] 1 WLR 2027, who referred to 'the overriding obligation of the governor to care for those in his custody who have no means to obtain food or clothing (the necessities of life) save from him' (para 9).

[2] Logan has described these as 'quality of confinement' issues: see C Logan, 'Well Kept: Comparing Quality of Confinement in Public and Private Prisons' (1992) 83 J of Criminal L and Criminology 577.

abounded of prisoners spending most of their time (up to 23 hours a day) in their cells, with little to do and not even adequate access to washing or toilet facilities. In the late 1980s Her Majesty's Chief Inspector of Prisons, Judge Stephen Tumim (as he then was), published a series of reports castigating the state of Britain's prisons. In his 1988 *Annual Report*, for example, he observed how in many 'establishments 'cell windows and outside walls are smeared with excrement and . . . parcels of faeces'—wrapped in newspaper or items of clothing—litter the ground outside'.[3] In 1991 the European Committee for the Prevention of Torture (CPT), making its first visit to the United Kingdom under the European Convention for the Prevention of Torture and Inhuman or Degrading Treatment or Punishment (ECPT), declared that the 'cumulative effect of overcrowding, lack of integral sanitation and inadequate regimes' at three British prisons amounted to inhuman and degrading treatment.[4]

5.03   To some extent prison conditions have improved in the past decade. An extensive programme of building new prisons and refurbishing old ones has removed some of the worst features of imprisonment that characterized the 1980s, especially for the remand prisoner. 'Slopping out' was ended in April 1996 and all prisoners now have 24-hour access to toilet facilities. Since 1994-95 no prisoners have been held three to a cell designed for one in England and Wales, although in 2000 an average of 17.2 per cent of prisoners were held two to a cell designed for one.[5] The average prisoner had 23.7 hours of purposeful activity per week.[6] However, such improvements are neither universal nor irreversible. In 1995 the Chief Inspector's team walked out of Holloway rather than complete its investigation in protest at the conditions it found there, and the Chief Inspector's reports still disclose many prisons to be disturbingly overcrowded, dirty, or dangerous places.[7] Moreover, those improvements in conditions which have been achieved remain vulnerable as the rise in the prison population continues to exceed expectations and the capa-

---

[3] See *Annual Report of the Chief Inspector of Prisons for England and Wales 1988–89* (HC 491, 1990).

[4] See *Report to the United Kingdom Government on the Visit to the United Kingdom carried out by the European Committee for the Prevention of Torture and Inhuman or Degrading Treatment or Punishment from 29 July 1990 to 10 August 1990*, CPT/Inf (91)15.

[5] Home Office, *Prison Statistics England and Wales 2000* (Cm 5250, 2001) 126.

[6] ibid, 123.

[7] See, eg, recent reports on Winson Green (March 2001), which the Chief Inspector described as 'filthy beyond compare'; Brixton (January 2001): health wing accommodation the worst the Chief Inspector had seen anywhere in England and Wales; Chelmsford (November 2000): a 'sick' institution, with one attempted hanging per month; Rochester (January 2000): 'a disgrace', 'institutionalised neglect', 'filthy, vandalised, infested with vermin, and subjected to an impoverished regime in which the only constant is unpredictability'. As well as continuing problems with the physical conditions of confinement, recent years have seen numerous prison officers, particularly from HM Prison Wormwood Scrubs, facing charges of violence against prisoners. See also *R v Fry*, 19 March 2002, where the Court of Appeal upheld substantial prison sentences imposed on prison officers for assault and fabricating disciplinary charges.

city of the Prison Service to build or refurbish prisons.[8] The only one of the Woolf Report's 12 main recommendations in his 1991 inquiry which the Government rejected out of hand was that of a legal ceiling on the number of prisoners in each prison which would require Parliamentary approval to be exceeded. It may come back to haunt and undermine the work done to achieve his other recommendations.

The extent to which the law has proved a guarantor of adequate living conditions **5.04** in prison is limited. The law intervenes in this area through two modes of operation. One is the policing of the application of particular rules and standards relating to matters such as heating, food, time out of cell, and exercise. The other is through examining whether conditions fall below minimum human rights standards of protection from torture, inhuman or degrading treatment, or punishment. However while many such standards exist to enable courts to perform the former task, for example in the Prison Rules, Operating Standards, Health Care Standards, or contracts negotiated with respect to private prisons, they turn out to be either too general or of such uncertain legal force as not to be of much value. When it comes to the second task the courts themselves have indicated that only the most unpleasant conditions, those which pose an imminent threat to life or health, will be seen as falling below minimum human rights standards. Courts in the United States, operating under the banner of the Eighth Amendment to the Constitution's prohibition on 'cruel and unusual punishment', have been prepared to scrutinize prison conditions more closely (arguably because such conditions were so much worse even than those of Britain in the 1980s), to the extent that most of the state prisons in the United States have operated under a court order at one time or another. However, even there changes in judicial philosophy and personnel, plus a significant input from the legislature, have led to a reduction of the judicial role in the past decade.

The history of judicial involvement in challenging prison conditions in the **5.05** United States is considered at the end of this chapter. We also examine the jurisprudence of international human rights tribunals with regard to challenges to prison conditions, a jurisprudence which has become more significant in the United Kingdom following the entry into force of the Human Rights Act 1998 (HRA). Before that we consider the law on specific aspects of prison conditions.

---

[8] In 2002 the average daily prison population in England and Wales reached 70,000, its highest ever figure. Current Home Office projections estimate it will reach 80,300 by 2007. See Home Office Statistical Bulletin 2/00.

B. Reception and Induction

5.06 The initial shock of imprisonment can be severe. The provision of information about regimes, procedures and sentence plans is vital in helping prisoners to come to terms with their environment and to assert their rights and entitlements. Prison Rule 10(1) provides that:

> (1) Every prisoner shall be provided, as soon as possible after his reception into prison, and in any case within 24 hours, with information in writing about those provisions of these Rules and other matters which it is necessary that he should know, including earnings and privileges, and the proper means of making requests and complaints.

Such information includes a copy of the Prison Rules, if requested. Unfortunately, information provision is often patchy, with prisoners often having only a vague idea of the details of the regime, how to get help, what rights they have and how to complain.[9] Access to complaints procedures was dealt with in Chapter 2. PSO 0550 deals with the more specific process of information provision on immediate entry into custody.[10] There are two stages to arrival in custody: reception and induction. Reception is fairly basic, aiming to 'confirm the legal basis of detention, establish effective control over the prisoner, ensure the immediate well-being of the prisoner, including healthcare screening, record/provide essential information, complete various formal processes, contribute to ensure provision and safety for the first night, and provide a smooth transition to induction'.[11] One essential aspect of ensuring a prisoner's immediate well-being is to screen for risk of suicide and self-harm, opening a form F2052SH if necessary. Suicide prevention is dealt with in more detail in Chapter 6.[12]

5.07 After the basic reception process comes induction. This process is to be adapted to the requirements of the individual prisoner, but aims to deal with the prisoner's emotional needs, outside circumstances, and integration into the prison. Outside circumstances are often the main cause of anxiety for those recently admitted to prison: family, housing and financial issues often require help and support,

---

[9] The Prisoners' Advice Service, in its 2000–01 Review, observes that '[a]lthough [the Prison Rules] are the basic guidance on how prisons are run, and all other Prison Service Orders and Instructions are subsidiary to them, many prisoners have never been shown a copy of the Rules, and do not know what is actually in them. They are therefore disadvantaged when attempting to contest breaches of the rules' (p 13).

[10] Reception and induction for prisoners under 18 years old, as well as other aspects of the regime for such prisoners, are governed by PSO 4950. The requirements are similar in structure to those for adult prisoners, but with particular emphasis on providing emotional support, education, role models, and involving the young prisoner's family. Special aspects of the regime for women prisoners are considered in Ch 11.

[11] PSO 0550.

[12] paras 6.33–6.40.

though the Chief Inspector of Prisons has recently expressed concern that these issues often go inadequately addressed, not just on entry into prison but for the entirety of the sentence.[13] Legal issues, such as legal aid and pending appeals, also need to be addressed. PSO 0550 makes the provision of certain information mandatory: all prisoners must be told of the availability of the Prisoners' Information Book,[14] the Prison Rules and any specific rules of the prison, information on prison life, opportunities in the prison, and formal procedures such as sentence calculation, categorization, and incentives and earned privileges.[15] Life sentenced prisoners have a special Prisoners' Information Book, and must be given additional relevant information about their sentence. The means by which information is supplied is critical: the Prisons Ombudsman notes that one unobtrusively displayed poster advising prisoners about how to complain may easily be overlooked, whereas more widespread distribution of leaflets contributes to prisoners' awareness of their entitlements.

C. Accommodation and Recreation

The current legal provisions regarding prison accommodation are somewhat thin, **5.08** although the introduction of PSO 1900, 'Certified Prisoner Accommodation', aims to set more clearly specified targets in order to 'contribute to achieving the Prison Service aim of providing decent living conditions for all prisoners'. Prison Act 1952, s 14 indicates that a cell may only be used if an official acting on behalf of the Secretary of State has issued a certificate in respect of it. This certificate may indicate the period for which a prisoner may be separately confined in the cell and place a limit on the number of prisoners that can be held in it.[16] Certificates now refer to 'Baseline' Certified Normal Accommodation (CNA), also known as 'uncrowded capacity'. This indicates the sum total of all certified accommodation in the establishment, 'the good, decent standard of accommodation that the Service aspires to provide to all prisoners', defined on the basis that the accommodation provides space for a single bed, storage for personal possessions, a chair and table area, circulation and movement, and the ability to use the toilet in private.[17]

---

[13] *Through the Prison Gate: A Joint Thematic Review by HM Inspectorates of Prisons and Probation* (London, 2001).

[14] See also PSO 0400, 'Prisoners' Information Book'.

[15] The Prison Service Standard on Regimes includes, as a Key Audit Baseline, requirements that information about regimes and means of accessing them is displayed in reception and on each wing/unit, presented in a way that all prisoners can understand, if necessary with assistance. It also requires that each prisoner has a personal or group officer and ready access to advice, guidance and help with personal problems.

[16] PSO 1900 on Certified Prisoner Accommodation. Prison Rule 26(1) provides that '[n]o room or cell shall be used as sleeping accommodation for a prisoner unless it has been certified in the manner required by section 14 of the Prison Act 1952 in the case of a cell used for the confinement of a prisoner'.

[17] See Prison Service Standard on Accommodation.

Certificates also refer to 'CNA in Use', which is baseline CNA minus cells not available for immediate use through damage or ongoing work, and 'Maximum Capacity', also known as 'crowded capacity'.[18] The latter is the total number of prisoners an establishment can hold on the basis that each cell provides adequate space for a bed, which may be two-tier, storage, a chair and table area, circulation and movement, and the ability to use the toilet with some privacy. This number of prisoners must be accommodated without serious risk to good order, security, and the proper running of the planned regime. Operational Capacity 'will normally be equal to, or greater than baseline CNA', though it is unlikely to be greater than the sum total of the maximum capacity of all cells or rooms.

5.09 PSO 1900 introduced measurable standards for cell certification, stressing that a cell may only legally be used if it has been certified in accordance with the Prison Act 1952 and the Prison Rules, and making Area Managers responsible for certification. They are responsible for ensuring that each certified cell has adequate heating, lighting and ventilation. Each cell must also have an alarm system to allow prisoners to summon help, and the system must be tested at least daily.[19] Governors, or controllers of private prisons, must have confinement conditions checked regularly. Any accommodation which does not meet the required standards must be reported to the Area Manager, and any accommodation that presents a serious risk to health must be taken out of use immediately. However, under Prison Rule 26(2) the number specified in a certificate may be exceeded with the leave of the Secretary of State.

5.10 The English position is therefore somewhat weaker, in both law and practice, than that required by the European Prison Rules. Rule 14(1) of these indicates that accommodation at night will normally be in individual cells 'except in cases where it is considered that there are advantages in sharing accommodation with other prisoners' (the English Circular Instruction indicates the wisdom of having some double cells for suicide prevention purposes). Some other European jurisdictions have been more exacting. In the Netherlands housing more than one prisoner in a cell was prohibited by statute for nearly 50 years.[20]

---

[18] The Chief Inspector of Prisons has noted the problem of '[h]ealth Care beds inappropriately included in an overcrowded Certified Normal Accommodation (CNA) figure, with the likelihood that this may result in new arrivals being placed beside severely mentally disordered prisoners': *Report on an Unannounced Follow-up Inspection of HMP Winchester, 26–28 March 2001*, 3.

[19] The poor condition of alarm systems in HM Prison Chelmsford was castigated by the ECtHR for contributing to the death of a prisoner at the hands of a mentally ill cellmate: *Edwards v UK* (2002) 35 EHRR 19, para 63.

[20] The removal of the prohibition on double-celling in 1994 was fiercely debated in the Netherlands and indicates that numbers throughout Europe are posing new threats to prisoners' rights. For a discussion see R van Swaaningen and G de Jonge, 'The Dutch Prison System and Penal Policy in the 1990s: From Humanitarian Paternalism to Penal Business Management' in V Ruggiero, M Ryan and J Sims (eds), *Western European Penal Systems* (London: Sage, 1995) 24.

There are similarly unspecific rules on space, lighting, heating, ventilation, sanitation, and bedding. Only the last is expressly referred to in the Prison Rules, and there all that rule 27 indicates is that prisoners should be given bedding that is 'adequate for warmth and health'. The Standing Orders, Prison Service Standards and Operating Standards provide some more detail but not always that much more and, as we have already observed, the latter two are of particularly weak legal force. Standing Order 14(4)(a) and Operating Standard I3 indicate that prisoners must be given access to baths or showers a minimum of three times a week; SO 14(25)(c) that cells should be scrubbed once a week; SO 14(27) that bedding should be laundered 'regularly'. Operating Standard I9 states that in the cases of sheets and pillowcovers this should be weekly. Operating Standard I2 now states that access should be provided for prisoners to toilets and hand washing facilities 24 hours a day. But Standing Orders do not indicate what the minimum cell size should be (although Operating Standard H2 indicates that refurbished single cell accommodation should be 5.5 square metres) or what quality of lighting it should have, though they do indicate that the temperature in cells should be kept at 68 degrees centigrade. Nor do they say anything about the level of noise, which is a major problem in prisons. Although Prison Rule 30 indicates that a prisoner is normally entitled to spend time in the open air each day, '[i]f the weather permits and subject to the need to maintain good order and discipline . . . for such period as may be reasonable in the circumstances', the Standing Orders do not elaborate on this by specifying how much time a prisoner should normally spend outside his cell.[21] Again one must look for guidance on this to an Operating Standard, U2, which indicates that prisoners should normally be unlocked and able to be out of their cells for 12 hours a day. Increased time out of cell is one of the seven key earnable privileges in the Incentives and Earned Privileges scheme, discussed below.

5.11

Other jurisdictions have been much more forthcoming on the issue of accommodation. In the American federal prison system minimum standards have been produced that, for example, indicate that prisoners should have at least 60 square feet of cell space and that if they have less than 80 square feet they should not spend more than ten hours a day in their cells. The CPT has also suggested in several reports that around seven metres square is adequate for one prisoner and that remand prisoners, in particular, should spend at least eight hours a day out of their cell.[22] That having standards is not a panacea is however indicated by the fact that around 60 per cent of American prisoners serve their sentences in less than the federal minimum.

5.12

---

[21] The European Committee for the Prevention of Torture (CPT) has stressed that '*all prisoners without exception* (including those undergoing cellular confinement as a punishment) should be offered the possibility to take outdoor exercise daily. It is also axiomatic that outdoor exercise facilities should be reasonably spacious and whenever possible offer shelter from inclement weather': *Second General Report,* CPT/Inf(92)3, para 48.

[22] See ibid, paras 43, 47.

5.13   When the CPT made its second visit to the United Kingdom in 1994 it observed
that there had been some improvement in conditions in Leeds and Wandsworth
but remained concerned that two prisoners were often being held in a cell barely
adequate for one. In its most recent report on the United Kingdom, the CPT
expressed concern at the continuing cramped prison conditions, in addition to
the dirty and unsanitary accommodation at Feltham and Pentonville.[23] The new
PSO concerning certification does not specify a minimum amount of space per
prisoner (although as we have seen the Operating Standards do make a recommendation in this area) but does state that decent conditions in each uncrowded
place must include enough personal space to sleep comfortably and dress and
undress, as well as adequate space to store those items a prisoner may have in possession. However, it may be doubted whether this goes far enough to guarantee
that all prisoners have adequate living accommodation, especially if they spend
most of their day in their cells. If the prison population continues its rapid rise
more prisoners are likely to find themselves detained two to a cell designed for one
and the Prison Service will struggle to maintain its target of not detaining three to
a cell designed for one. Even US courts, which have been prepared to examine
conditions more closely than most, have stopped short of finding overcrowding
per se to be unlawful. In *Rhodes v Chapman*[24] the Supreme Court indicated that
the practice of putting two prisoners in a cell designed for one did not in itself constitute a violation of the prohibition on 'cruel and unusual punishment' contained
in the Eighth Amendment to the Constitution. Later courts in the United States
interpreting this decision have however indicated that, when combined with
other factors, overcrowding may amount to a constitutional violation.[25]

5.14   In a heartening development, the English courts have begun to recognize that
overcrowding in itself is, if not necessarily unlawful, certainly undesirable, with
far-reaching effects on the quality of regimes. In his judgment in *R v Kefford*,[26]
Lord Woolf observed that:

---

[23]   *Report to the Government of the United Kingdom on the visit to the United Kingdom carried out
by the European Committee for the Prevention of Torture and Inhuman or Degrading Treatment or
Punishment*, CPT/Inf (2001) 6.
[24]   452 US 337 (1981). See also *Piche v Canada (Solicitor General)* (1989) 47 CCC (3d) 495—
double bunking of prisoners did not violate s 7 of the Canadian Charter.
[25]   See eg *Tyler v Black* 811 F 2d 424 (8th Cir 1987) where the court held that double celling in
small cells with solid 'boxcar' like doors was cruel and unusual punishment.
[26]   [2002] EWCA Crim 519, The Times, 7 March 2002, paras 3–4, writing jointly with Rose LJ
and Judge LJ. At the Modernizing Criminal Justice Conference on 20 June 2002, Lord Woolf CJ
said that conditions in some prisons were 'no longer tolerable, and that overcrowding could lead to
riots on a scale not seen since Strangeways'. 'We would be foolish if we did not recognise the danger
of repetition now that some of the causes of those disturbances have reappeared.' According to The
Times, 22 July 2002, Phil Wheatley, Deputy Head of the Prison Service, sent David Blunkett a
report warning of the threat of riots due to overcrowding, and listing HM Prisons Brixton,
Holloway, Dartmoor, Onley, Dovegate and Ashfield (two of which are privately run) as the most
overcrowded in England and Wales.

> The prison system should not have to operate so close to its overcrowded capacity. . . . The stage has now been reached when it would be highly undesirable if the prison population were to continue to rise. The overcrowding of the prison system is not only a matter for grave concern for the Prison Service, it is also a matter of grave concern for the criminal justice system as a whole. Prison sentences are imposed by the courts normally for three purposes: to punish the offender concerned, to deter other offenders and to stop the offender committing further offences in the future. The ability of the Prison Service to tackle a prisoner's offending behaviour and so reduce reoffending is adversely affected if a prison is overcrowded . . .

It is clear that Lord Woolf sees overcrowding as a threat to the other improvements which he helped to bring about. However, it is striking that the Court of Appeal did not refer at all to the impact that overcrowding has on the prisoners who have to live in such conditions. The next step for prisoners will be to persuade the domestic courts that severe overcrowding may contravene Article 3 of the European Convention on Human Rights (ECHR), the prohibition on inhuman and degrading treatment. The Strasbourg case law on this issue is discussed below. Arguments against overcrowding must, however, be carefully framed. Attacks on overcrowding can simply be countered by building more prisons, as has happened in the last decade. The real issue, it is suggested, is the soaring rate of imprisonment, which must be addressed by looking at sentencing practices and alternatives to prison, rather than by simply expanding the number of cells.[27] As the CPT observes, 'throwing increased amounts of money at the prison estate will not offer a solution'.[28]

D. Searches and Mandatory Drug Testing

Searches

Prison Rule 41(1) requires that every prisoner should be searched when taken into custody by an officer, on reception into a prison and 'subsequently as the governor thinks necessary or as the Secretary of State may direct'. This is obviously a very wide discretion and the rules make no distinction between the different types of   **5.15**

---

[27] This point was forcefully made by the Court of Appeal, ibid, paras 5–8. See also the Howard League for Penal Reform's '5 Point Action Plan' to ease the prison population crisis: 7 March 2002. The Howard League recommends that the Home Secretary (1) uses his executive powers to release all prisoners currently serving sentences of less than three months; (2) demands with immediate effect that women and children only be sentenced to prison if convicted of serious or violent offences; (3) urges judges to consider reducing sentence lengths for all but the most serious offenders; and in the longer term (4) considers placing a statutory limit on the prison population; (5) implements the proposal of the Prison Governor's Association and immediately removes the powers of magistrates to pass a custodial sentence.

[28] *Eleventh General Report*, CPT/Inf(2001) 16, para 28.

search involved, even between cell searches and personal searches] Some jurisdictions are more exacting. Section 46 of the Canadian Corrections and Conditional Release Act 1992, for example, divides searches into 'frisk searches', 'non intrusive searches', 'strip searches', and 'body cavity searches'. Only 'frisk' and 'non intrusive' searches can be carried out without reasonable suspicion. The only limitations imposed on the manner of the search contained in rule 41 are that it must be conducted in as 'seemly a manner as is consistent with anything being concealed', and that a prisoner should not be subject to a strip search in the sight of another prisoner or a person of a different sex. The *Security Manual* builds on this and indicates, in para 66.21, that strip searches should be carried out before and after a visit, during a cell search (in closed prisons), and otherwise as the governor directs. It also provides guidance on the manner of conducting such searches, namely where only one part of the body should be exposed at any one time. Intimate searches (of bodily orifices) should only be conducted by a medical practitioner and then with the consent of the prisoner.[29] Non-strip searches may be carried out by officers of a different sex but Home Office guidance indicates that while female prison officers may be involved in searches of male prisoners, male officers should not be involved in searching female prisoners.

5.16 Although the power is wide, like any discretionary power its exercise is subject to judicial review. Hence prison staff in deciding to search should direct their minds to the purposes for which the power is granted, essentially to look for items smuggled into the prison (notably drugs) or things which might assist an escape. Searches whose purpose was purely to harass a prisoner would undoubtedly be seen as an abuse of discretion. Similarly the power to search is subject to the requirement of reasonableness, as regards both the decision to search and the manner of its execution. Thus courts have suggested that while a random cell search might be upheld as furthering reasonable aims of institutional security, a decision to subject all prisoners to a strip search or body cavity search without any advance reason to suspect the need for this might be viewed as a decision no reasonable governor would reach.[30] However the policy of routine strip searches before and after visits has been upheld by the Divisional Court in *R v Home Secretary, ex p Mohammed Zulfikar*.[31]

---

[29] *Security Manual*, para 67.14 indicates such consent should only be overridden when the doctor feels this is necessary to prevent death or serious harm to the prisoner, and then only with the agreement of the governor and after obtaining a second medical opinion.

[30] See, eg, the Northern Irish case of *Re Baker and Others' Applications* (1992) 8 NIJB 86 where a strip search of all women prisoners in a jail was upheld, but only as there was evidence that something had been smuggled in and the Governor had no information about which particular prisoners were involved. In *Weatherall, Conway and Spearman v Disciplinary Tribunal of Collins Bay Penitentiary* (1987) 11 FTR 279 the Canadian Federal Court struck down random strip searches as contrary to ss 7 and 8 of the Charter.

[31] 21 July 1995.

Where an unlawful search is of a prisoner's person rather than his cell, the prisoner **5.17** may be able to obtain damages for assault. Following the Learmont Report, more regular random cell searches were introduced and prisoners were required to leave their cells while such searches took place. In *R v Home Secretary, ex p Main*[32] a prisoner challenged one aspect of this procedure, namely that where he had legal papers in his cell a search in his absence created a risk that his legal correspondence would be read by prison staff, contrary to rule 37A (now rule 39). In support he cited a 1996 ruling of the Prison Ombudsman which upheld a prisoner's complaint and recommended that he be present when any inspection of his legal correspondence occurred. However the Court of Appeal rejected the challenge. Kennedy LJ took the view that to do a thorough search, consistent with the needs of security, prison staff would have to look through legal papers to ensure that they were what they claimed to be. He further noted that Prison Service guidance was that staff should not read such material. As a result he concluded that any interference with confidential communication between a prisoner and his lawyer was the minimum necessary to ensure that security was maintained. The argument that the prisoner should be present when such examination took place, the normal post-*Leech* situation when a governor wishes to examine legal mail, was rejected after an argument that the prisoner's presence might intimidate or distract the searching officer.

The *Leech* principles of legality and close judicial scrutiny of interferences with **5.18** prisoners' rights were firmly reasserted by the House of Lords in *R (Daly) v Home Secretary*.[33] That decision, discussed more generally in Chapter 2, is of wide-ranging importance. For present purposes, the significance of the case lies in their Lordships' finding that the post-Woodcock policy of searching through a prisoner's legal correspondence in the absence of the prisoner was unlawful, since it could not be taken to be authorized by s 47(1) of the Prison Act 1952. The claimant did not argue that no searches of legal mail were lawful, merely that he had a right to be present during the search.

Lord Bingham, in a judgment with which the rest of the Committee agreed, con- **5.19** sidered that:

> Some rights, perhaps in an attenuated or qualified form, survive the making of the [custodial] order. And it may well be that the importance of such surviving rights is enhanced by the loss or partial loss of other rights. Among the rights which, in part at least, survive are three important rights, closely related but free standing, each of them calling for appropriate legal protection: the right of access to a court; the right of access to legal advice; and the right to communicate confidentially with a legal adviser under the seal of legal professional privilege. Such rights may be curtailed

---

[32] [1999] QB 349.
[33] [2001] 2 AC 532.

only by clear and express words, and then only to the extent reasonably necessary to meet the ends which justify their curtailment.[34]

Lord Bingham went on to find that the policy amounted to a significant infringement of Mr Daly's common law right to the confidentiality of his privileged legal correspondence. The question, then, was whether the policy could be justified 'as a necessary and proper response to the acknowledged need to maintain security, order and discipline in prisons and prevent crime'. The Home Office argued, relying on evidence from the Director-General of the Prison Service, that searching in the presence of prisoners created a risk of intimidation, a risk of staff becoming conditioned to relax security, and the danger of disclosing searching methods. Lord Bingham did not accept that these considerations, if they had any weight at all, outweighed the right at issue. His conclusions are worth quoting at length, as an example of close judicial scrutiny of infringements of prisoners' rights:

> In considering these justifications, based as they are on the extensive experience of the prison service, it must be recognised that the prison population includes a core of dangerous, disruptive and manipulative prisoners, hostile to authority and ready to exploit for their own advantage any concession granted to them. Any search policy must accommodate this inescapable fact. I cannot however accept that the reasons put forward justify the policy in its present blanket form. Any prisoner who attempts to intimidate or disrupt a search of his cell, or whose past conduct shows that he is likely to do so, may properly be excluded even while his privileged correspondence is examined so as to ensure the efficacy of the search, but no justification is shown for routinely excluding all prisoners, whether intimidatory or disruptive or not, while that part of the search is conducted. .... The policy cannot in my opinion be justified in its present blanket form. The infringement of prisoners' rights to maintain the confidentiality of their privileged legal correspondence is greater than is shown to be necessary to serve the legitimate public policy objectives already identified.[35]

In reaching this conclusion, Lord Bingham relied primarily on 'an orthodox application of common law principles derived from the authorities and an orthodox domestic approach to judicial review'.[36] However, he made it clear that an application of the right to respect for correspondence, under Article 8 of the Convention, would lead to the same result.

5.20 As well as potentially infringing privacy rights, excessive searches which might be said to degrade a prisoner (for example regular strip searching, especially if physical force is used to carry out such searches) might also constitute a breach of Article 3 of the ECHR. In *Valasinas v Lithuania*[37] the Third Section of the court found degrading treatment where a male prisoner was subjected to a strip search in front of female prison officers and in circumstances where the officers con-

---

[34] para 5.
[35] para 19.
[36] para 23.
[37] Application 44558/98, 12 BHRC 266.

ducting the search touched his sexual organs with their bare hands. The court stressed that 'while strip searches may be necessary on occasions to ensure prison security or prevent disorder or crime, they must be conducted in an appropriate manner'.

In the United States the Supreme Court has ruled that prisoners do not have any **5.21** privacy interest as regards their cells, and hence that the protections of the Fourth Amendment do not apply to cell searches.[38] The court has not ruled on whether the Fourth Amendment, which protects against unreasonable searches, applies to prisoners in respect of personal searches, but lower courts have ruled that blanket rules requiring body cavity searches of prisoners,[39] or visitors,[40] without any showing of probable cause (the American equivalent of reasonable suspicion) violate the Constitution. Searches of visitors to prisons in England and Wales are permitted by rule 71 of the Prison Rules, though scrutiny of the exercise of this discretion may be even more exacting than of the power to search prisoners. A county court indicated in 1992 that a strip search of a visitor to a prison gave rise to an action for damages because it was not conducted in as seemly a manner as possible and involved a violation of bodily integrity.[41]

Drug Testing

As a result of amendments which introduced s 16A into the Prison Act in 1994, **5.22** powers are now conferred on prison officers to conduct mandatory drug tests of prisoners by way of requiring a prisoner to provide a urine sample. Failure to supply a sample on request may lead to disciplinary proceedings being brought under rule 50(19). More detailed regulations on mandatory drug testing are set out in rule 50. These indicate that prisoners required to provide a sample may be kept apart from other prisoners for up to five hours where they are unable to do so.[42] The rules state that prisoners should be required to provide a sample in 'such degree of privacy for the purposes of providing the sample as may be compatible with the need to prevent or detect any adulteration or falsification of the sample'.[43]

---

[38] See *Hudson v Palmer*, 468 US 517 (1984).
[39] See *Weber v Dell*, 804 F 2d 796 (2nd Cir 1986).
[40] See *Blackburn v Snow*, 771 F 2d 556 (1st Cir 1985).
[41] *Bayliss and Barton v Home Secretary and Governor HM Prison Frankland*, February 1993 *Legal Action* 16. See also *Wainwright v Home Office* [2002] 3 WLR 405, discussed in detail below at Ch 7.
[42] Prison Rule 50(7). Further detail on the appropriate procedures is given in PSO 3601, 'Mandatory Drugs Testing', and PSO 3605, 'Procedures for the Independent Analysis of Mandatory Drug Test Samples'. Paragraph 2.1.1 of the latter states that 'Prisoners are entitled to have a sample which tests positive under the Mandatory Drug Testing (MDT) programme analysed by an independent laboratory before any disciplinary proceedings concerning that charge are completed. This practice is an important procedural safeguard and integral feature of the overall fairness of the MDT programme.' It is unclear whether there is widespread awareness of this entitlement among prisoners.
[43] Prison Rule 50(8).

In particular no one should be required to provide a sample in the presence of a person of the opposite sex. Since the passing of the Prisons (Alcohol Testing) Act 1997 similar provisions have been in force with regard to testing for alcohol.[44]

5.23   The provisions on mandatory drug testing were unsuccessfully challenged in *R v Home Secretary, ex p Tremayne*.[45] The Divisional Court rejected the claim that such provisions were in contravention of Article 6 or 8 of the ECHR as they neither violated the presumption of innocence nor amounted to an unnecessary interference with privacy. As we have seen, the introduction of the HRA has led to challenges based on the right to privacy with respect to powers to search in prison, although the courts have tended to prefer to decide cases on traditional common law principles. The rather more detailed Canadian provisions referred to earlier in this section were motivated by a fear that broad search powers contained in regulations were vulnerable to challenge under the Canadian Charter post-1982.[46] Courts in the United Kingdom may come to question whether such significant invasions of privacy as strip searches can really be said to be 'prescribed by law' when their justification can only be found in Prison Service Orders and Instructions.

E. Food

5.24   The Woolf Report observed that the quality of prison food featured in more complaints from prisoners than anything else.[47] Rule 24(2) of the Prison Rules indicates that food should be 'wholesome, nutritious, well prepared and served, reasonably varied and sufficient in quantity'. Until 1988 remand prisoners were entitled to receive food from friends or relatives. The rule change which prohibited this was held to be intra vires the Prison Act.[48]

---

[44] Now contained in s 16B of the Prison Act 1952.

[45] 2 May 1996, CO3550/95. The decision of the Divisional Court was upheld by the Court of Appeal in an unreported decision of 3 October 1996. See also *R v Home Secretary, ex p Russell*, The Times, 31 August 2000, QB. The claimant refused to submit to a 'random' mandatory drug test (MDT), since he considered that, given the frequency with which he was ordered to do so, the tests were not genuinely random. He was disciplined for refusing to provide the sample. Lightman J considered that whether or not an order to provide a sample for a random MDT is genuinely random is relevant to whether the order is lawful. Once the claimant had raised the issue, the Governor had to investigate. Failure to do so made the disciplinary finding of guilt unlawful. The Prison Service responded to this case by agreeing to routine disclosure of details of the computerized selection process to all prisoners ordered to give a sample for a random MDT.

[46] Especially when the courts found that mandatory urine testing based only on regs violated the Charter: see *Jackson v Disciplinary Tribunal Joyceville Penitentiary* (1990) 55 CCC (3d) 50. For a general background to these developments, see S Livingstone, 'Designing a New Legal Framework for Prison: The Experience of the Canadian Corrections and Conditional Release Act 1992' (1995) 24 Anglo-American L Rev 426.

[47] See *Prison Disturbances: April 1990* (Cm 1456, 1991), 397. However the situation may subsequently have improved. In his 1996 report the Prisons Ombudsman noted that only 1% of the complaints he received related to food: (Cm 3687, 1996), 10.

[48] See *R v Home Secretary, ex p Simmons* [1989] COD 332.

The requirements of rule 24 were considered by Lightman J in *R v Governor of* **5.25**
Frankland Prison, ex p Russell.[49] The applicants in that case had been placed in the
segregation unit as a result of disciplinary offences. They were required to wear
prison clothes, which they refused to do, remaining naked or wrapped only in a
blanket throughout their confinement. The Governor instituted a policy whereby
any prisoner in the segregation unit who refused to wear prison clothes to collect
his three meals a day from the servery was entitled to only one meal a day, which
would be brought to him in his cell. In holding this policy to be unlawful,
Lightman J set out a series of principles governing the provision of food in prison:

(1) The obligation of the governor to provide adequate food is an obligation to
make food immediately available to prisoners who want to eat it. Food is made
immediately available if the prisoners are allowed free access to the place where
it is to be collected or eaten. If the governor lays down conditions for obtaining
such access (e.g. wearing prison clothes), so long as the prisoners are not content
to comply with those conditions, and for that reason are excluded from access,
their free access to the food is withdrawn.
(2) The rights of a prisoner to the provision of adequate food cannot be withdrawn
or limited as a punishment or sanction or as a method of coercion.
(3) Subject to his overriding obligation to provide prisoners with adequate food,
the governor in the exercise of his powers of management is free to decide the
times and places where food is to be made available . . .
(4) The governor can lay down conditions which regulate access to the place where
food is to be made available. . . . But neither the imposition of such conditions
nor the failure of a prisoner to comply with them (or with an order requiring
compliance) can excuse the governor from performance of the obligation to
provide food to that prisoner or can detract from the fundamental right of the
prisoner to adequate food.[50]

While the Governor did not necessarily have to give the claimants meals at the
same time, or the same food, he had a duty to provide food which was not only
sufficient for survival, but adequate for nutritional needs, having taken professional dietary advice. That duty was breached by providing only one meal a day.[51]
This decision is particularly important in that it recognizes that deprivation of
food is never an acceptable disciplinary sanction.[52]

---

[49] [2000] 1 WLR 2027.
[50] para 17.
[51] Lightman J was not impressed with the Governor's condescending attitude to Mr Russell's
protest, which he 'somewhat cavalierly dismissed as his "childishness"' (para 18).
[52] This is consistent with the decision of the European Commission in *McFeeley v UK* (1981) 3
EHRR 161, in which it was held that placing the applicant on a restricted diet as a disciplinary award
was 'a stringent and wholly undesirable form of punishment'. However, the Commission surprisingly considered that such treatment did not breach Art 3. Although Art 3 was raised in *Russell*,
Lightman J decided the case solely on domestic law principles.

5.26 The *Directory and Guide on Religious Practices in HM Prison Service* indicates that prisoners are entitled to a diet which accords with the demands of their religion 'as agreed between a relevant religious body and Prison Service Headquarters'.[53] There is also a requirement that the food be inspected 'regularly' by the medical officer and 'at frequent intervals by the Board of Visitors'. PSO 5000 indicates the need for all food to be prepared in hygienic conditions and for those preparing food to be supervised by suitably qualified staff. It also indicates that where it cannot be served centrally it should be transported to cells at an appropriate temperature. However, a 1997 report by the National Audit Office indicated concern that too often meals had gone cold by the time they reached prisoners.[54] In some prisons facilities exist for prisoners to cook their own food, although the Learmont Report was sharply critical of extensive use of this for Category A prisoners and called for it to be available only as an earned privilege.[55]

5.27 PSO 5000, 'Prison Catering Services', provides for the inspection of catering facilities and arrangements for the transportation and serving of food by Home Office Health and Safety Officers according to standards laid down in the Food Safety (Temperature Control) Regulations 1995 and the Food Safety (General Food Hygiene) Regulations 1995.[56] The PSO also indicates that the catering area of each establishment should have at least one hygiene check a year and that the inspection system is itself subject to unannounced random independent validation checks by environmental health officers. Not until the 1990 Food Safety Act removed Crown Immunity in respect of prison kitchens could court proceedings be taken in respect of standards in prison establishments which fall below those required in the Food Act 1984.

5.28 Under Prison Rule 22 prisoners are prohibited from having any alcohol except with the permission of the medical officer and may have tobacco only as a privilege.

F. Clothing

5.29 Under Prison Rule 23 prisoners must be provided with clothing that is 'adequate for warmth and health'. This requirement does not apply to unconvicted prisoners and women prisoners, who may wear their own clothes, as may sentenced prisoners in Northern Ireland. An application by a prisoner serving a sentence in a UK prison that being required to wear prison clothing constituted a breach of

---

[53] PSO 5000, para 3.22, gives guidance to prison catering services as to the dietary requirements of the major religions.
[54] See The Guardian, 7 November 1997.
[55] See *Review of Prison Service Security in England and Wales* (Cm 3020, 1995), para 2.216.
[56] SI 1995/2200 and SI 1995/1763.

the right of privacy as protected by Article 8 of the ECHR was declared admissible. The Commission went on to hold though that the restriction was justifiable in the interests of public safety and for the prevention of crime.[57] However the Woolf Report, observing that there is a significant amount of freedom for long-term prisoners in dispersal prisons as to what they wear, recommended that all prisoners should eventually be entitled to wear their own clothes and that to begin this process prisoners should be entitled to wear their own clothes during visits.[58] Wearing one's own clothing has now become one of the seven key earnable privileges.[59]

The Rules also require the provision of suitable clothing for work. Operating **5.30** Standard M2 indicates that prisoners should be provided with sufficient clothing to have a daily change of shirt, socks, and underpants, with trousers and sweat-shirts being able to be changed once a week. Prisoners serving sentences of over three months should be provided with new prison issue footwear. Operating Standard M5 indicates that prisoners should be provided with laundry services which meet specified hygiene standards and should be advised of all local laundry arrangements.

G. Work

Prison Rule 31(1) states that all convicted prisoners are required to do a maximum **5.31** of ten hours' useful work a day. Unconvicted prisoners are not required to work but should be provided with work if they wish. Although Article 4 of the ECHR prohibits forced or compulsory labour it contains an exception in Article 4(3)(a) for ordinary work done in the course of detention. Many complaints in prisons concern the lack of work and its limited character. The average number of hours of 'purposeful activity' per week for prisoners is approximately 22, and in remand prisons it falls to around 20.[60] Prisoners also continue to be employed on repetitive and low-skilled tasks. In 1983 the Chief Inspector of Prisons, in a report on a riot at Albany Gaol, observed that one of its causes was that long term prisoners were still involved in sewing mailbags.[61] The CPT commented, 'much of the little work that was available in the three prisons [visited] was of a dull, repetitive nature and did not involve the acquiring of any skills that might be of some use to the

---

[57] See *X v UK* D & R 33 (1983) 5. In *McFeeley v UK* (1981) 3 EHRR 161, the Commission rejected the claim of Northern Irish prisoners that requiring them to wear prison uniform violated their freedom of expression as it denied their claim to be prisoners of war.
[58] See (Cm 1456, 1991), 397.
[59] PSO 4000, 'Incentives and Earned Privileges', para 1.5.2.
[60] See HM Prison Service, *Annual Report and Accounts 2000–01* (HC 29, 2001).
[61] See *Report of HM Chief Inspector of Prisons for England and Wales* 1983 (HC 618, 1984), para 1.03.

inmate outside prison'.[62] These conditions may well be in breach of the European Prison Rules. Rule 72(3) of these indicates that 'sufficient work of a useful nature shall be provided to keep prisoners actively involved for a normal working day', while rule 72(4) indicates that 'so far as possible the work provided shall be such as will maintain or increase the prisoners' ability to earn a normal living after release'.[63] Neither the Prison Rules in England and Wales nor the Standing Orders contain any reference to these issues.

5.32 As the Woolf Report notes, prisoners' pay has also been an issue of constant dispute. The Report noted that prisoners' average pay was £2.65 a week, well below that in many other European countries, and recommended an increase to £8. In response to this the Government introduced a new prisoners' pay scheme in late 1992. Disappointingly, prisoners were not included in the National Minimum Wage Act 1998. A long overdue update to pay structures, if barely any increase in the absurdly low rates of pay, was introduced by PSO 4460 in early 2002. PSO 4460 provides for a rate of £2.50 per week if a prisoner is unemployed due to an absence of work available in the prison, or is not working due to short-term sickness. Long-term sickness or retirement, maternity leave and caring full time for children entitles a prisoner to £3.25 per week. Prisoners doing any work must be paid an Employed Rate, which is currently set at a minimum of £4 per week. Prisoners who are employed in work, education, training or offending behaviour programmes must receive at least the minimum employed rate. Thereafter governors have the discretion, subject to agreement with Area Managers, to set pay rates for different jobs at their prison. These should produce an average wage of £6 per week for each prisoner, a target which limits the governor's budget. The Prison Service must be contacted where a prisoner's standard rate is set at more than £12. PSO 4460 indicates that prisoners will only be paid if their work achieves an acceptable standard and output, and it is still a disciplinary offence under rule 51(21) if a prisoner 'intentionally fails to work properly or, being required to work, refuses to do so'.

5.33 Prisoners are not, however, regarded as employees of the prison in the course of their work.[64] This has significant consequences, since it means that the Health and Safety at Work Act 1974 is largely inapplicable in prisons and cannot be invoked by prisoners who suffer through breaches of it, even though Standing Order

---

[62] See *Report to the United Kingdom Government on the Visit to the United Kingdom carried out by the European Committee for the Prevention of Torture and Inhuman or Degrading Treatment or Punishment from 29 July 1990 to 10 August 1990*, CPT/Inf (91)15, para 55.

[63] This rule represents one resolution of the debate that was particularly prominent in the 18th and 19th centuries as to whether prison work should be hard and repetitive, so as to punish better, or varied and useful, better to equip the prisoner for life after release. See D Garland, *Punishment and Welfare* (Aldershot, 1985), 12–16.

[64] See *Pullen v Prison Commissioners* [1957] 3 All ER 470.

6A(15) allows for inspections by the Health and Safety Executive and requires the giving of every assistance to them. The courts have also indicated that the Factories Acts are inapplicable to prison industries.[65] Prisoners injured at work are therefore thrown back on the common law duty to provide a safe system of work and have succeeded in negligence actions arising out of their injuries at work.[66] The Standing Orders also provide that where a prisoner's injury at work results in incapacity upon release the prisoner may be made an ex gratia payment at the same rate as disablement benefit under the Industrial Injuries Act 1975 following certification by a Department of Social Services Medical Board.

Race Discrimination

Prisoners may invoke legislation that protects people against race discrimination. **5.34**
However, until recently the legislation mainly covered discrimination in the field of employment and in the provision of goods, facilities and services. Prisoners do not count as employees, but it was possible to argue that certain types of discrimination suffered in prison related to the provision of goods, facilities or services. However, such discrimination claims were extremely rare. In *Alexander v Home Office*[67] Alexander, who was of Caribbean origin, successfully sued for damages after he was refused a higher-paying job in a prison kitchen on the basis of two assessment reports which contained racially discriminatory remarks. Alexander challenged his treatment, invoking s 20(1) of the Race Relations Act 1976, which prohibits discrimination in the provision of goods and services to the public or a section of the public, rather than s 4, which relates to discrimination in employment. The Home Office originally defended the case on the ground that prisoners were not a 'section of the public', but abandoned this point at trial. The availability of race discrimination legislation to prisoners is particularly significant given that black people form up to 25 per cent of the prison population at some prisons, and the Chief Inspector of Prisons has on several occasions drawn attention to racial tensions in prison.

Prisoners' protection from discrimination was strengthened by the Race Relations **5.35**
(Amendment) Act 2000, which prohibits race discrimination by public authorities in carrying out any of their public functions. This means that prisoners' redress will no longer be confined to cases of discrimination in the provision of 'goods, facilities and services', as in *Alexander*, but will extend, for example, to decisions on discipline, segregation and access to facilities and privileges. Claims for compensation can be brought in the county court, with the possible support of the Commission for Racial Equality. Prisoners who have been discriminated

---

[65] ibid.
[66] See *Ferguson v Home Office*, The Times, 8 October 1977.
[67] [1988] 2 All ER 118.

against on the ground of disability may also have a claim under Pt III of the Disability Discrimination Act 1995.[68]

H. Education and Offending Behaviour Programmes

5.36 Prison Rule 32 indicates that every prisoner able to profit from education should be encouraged to do so and that programmes of educational study should be arranged at every prison. It also indicates that prisoners should be afforded 'reasonable facilities' to engage in private study, for example by distance learning. Operating Standard U8 indicates that each prison should provide a programme, based on a needs assessment, for 50 weeks a year as regards morning and afternoon education and for 42 weeks a year as regards evening education.

5.37 The provision of education in prisons has undergone considerable change following the passing of the Further and Higher Education Act 1992 which permitted the contracting out of prison education and removed its provision from the hands of local education authorities. Although a number of factors, including legal action by lecturers in prison, delayed the contracting process, the bulk of new contracts were eventually introduced by late 1993. The impact that contracting out has had on the provision of prison education remains unclear. A National Association of Teachers in Further and Higher Education (NATFHE) report in 1994 was severely critical of its impact on the morale of prison education staff[69] but a Prison Reform Trust report the following year painted a more positive picture of staff anxious to work with the new regime.[70]

5.38 In 2001, the management of the contracted out services was transferred from the Prison Service to the Department for Education and Skills (DfES).[71] The Department now has a Prisoners' Learning and Skills Unit to oversee the running of the prison education system. A 2001 NATFHE report suggested that this transfer has helped to improve the situation in some respects. The introduction of a basic core curriculum has also had a positive effect. However, the report highlighted continuing problems such as insufficient attention paid to the type and variety of prison when developing policies, the vulnerability of education budgets, difficulty in recruiting and retaining qualified teaching staff, operational difficulties in getting students to classes, and a narrow and impoverished core

---

[68] For detailed discussion of the various anti-discrimination provisions, see A McColgan (ed), *Discrimination Law Handbook* (London, 2002).

[69] See NATFHE, *Prison Education After Competitive Tendering* (London, 1994).

[70] See N Flynn and D Price, *Education in Prisons: A National Survey* (London, 1995).

[71] See DfES, *Improving Prisoners' Learning and Skills* (London, 2001). The Report deplores the perception of education as a 'recreational' activity, and sets out a focus on basic numeracy, literacy and training for specific jobs (such as working in call centres). The emphasis appears to be on equipping prisoners for low-paid, low-skill work on release.

curriculum. The curriculum appeared to be based on the needs of a medium sized category C training prison for men, and to concentrate on very basic skills training, leaving many prisoners out of opportunities. The fact that education attracts a lower rate of pay than other types of prison work is also an unfair disincentive to attend classes, the report considered. What remains clear is that education resources are under stress and the amount of education provision available to prisoners has declined in recent years.[72] Prisoners also frequently complain about significant variations in the curriculum at different prisons, which means that they are not able to continue courses they have started after they are transferred.[73] The Prison Core Curriculum is now contained in PSO 4200. PSO 4205, the current Prison Service guidance on education in prisons, sets 'outcome targets' for prison education:

(1) All education and training, and where possible PE, undertaken during the core day will be aimed at reducing offending behaviour as part of a prisoners' sentence plan . . .

(2) The education programme must enable prisoners to achieve nationally accredited qualifications in key and basic skills up to level 2, which will enhance their employability on release. The Prison Core Curriculum (PSO 4200) must be in place to facilitate this.

(3) Opportunities for achieving key and basic skills in workshops, PE, catering and other vocational training will be provided by establishments, supported by the advice and guidance of the education department.

This allows a great deal of discretion to the individual prison, though scarce **5.39** resources mean that prisons struggle to meet even the basic targets. As well as classes provided in the prisons themselves, prisoners may also pursue correspondence courses and work for national qualifications, including Open University degrees, at the discretion of the governor. In order to do so they may obtain and retain, at their own expense, books and up to two periodicals. PSO 4201 provides that, if the prisoner cannot pay for the Open University course from private funds or from third parties such as relatives or charitable trusts, the prisoner may apply to the governor for funding from the prison materials budget.[74] In its response to the Woolf Report the Home Office indicated that it would extend access to National Vocational Qualifications.

Education is voluntary for all adult prisoners, but young offenders of compulsory **5.40** school age are required to attend education or vocational training courses for 15 hours a week. Prison Service Orders indicate that all courses should be devised in

---

[72] The average number of education and skills training per prisoner per week has risen from 4.08 in 1998 to 6.62 in 2000, although the statistics note, rather vaguely, that from April 2000, this figure 'includes any work activities containing an educational element': Home Office, *Prison Statistics: England and Wales 2000* (Cm 5250) 132.

[73] See Prison Reform Trust (1992) 19 Prison Report, 4.

[74] PSO 4201 also sets out in detail the operation of the Open University scheme in prisons.

accordance with a number of objectives, including the improvement of prospects for successful social resettlement, employment prospects on release, and the prisoner's morale, attitudes, and self-respect. Unlike in some European prison systems, however, achieving educational qualifications does not have any formal effect on improving a prisoner's prospect of release.[75]

5.41 Education is one area where the United Kingdom appears to be falling well short of its obligations under the European Prison Rules. These provide for a 'comprehensive education programme in every institution' (rule 77), for education to be regarded as a regime activity that attracts the same status and remuneration as work (rule 78), and for education programmes to be integrated as far as possible into the educational system of the country (rule 81). The last requirement was considered during the review that led to market testing but appears to have been rejected in favour of allowing free competition for education provision. With regard to education attracting the same remuneration as other activities it is worth noting that the Prison Reform Trust's 1995 survey of prison education found that in over half the prisons it surveyed prisoners on work or training activities were paid more than prisoners on education.[76] The 2001 NATFHE report also considered that this pay discrepancy discouraged prisoners from attending classes.

5.42 In recent years there has been a growth of specific offending behaviour programmes, notably the Sex Offenders Treatment Programme (SOTP), which have assumed increasing importance in release decisions (see Chapters 13 to 14). Most of these programmes are provided on a contract basis or by other departments within the prison.[77] A disturbing development is the tendency to make progress through the Incentives and Earned Privileges (IEP) levels dependent on participation in treatment programmes, even for prisoners who deny their guilt. To offer material rewards for participation in treatment surely robs it of its voluntary nature, showing a marked lack of respect for prisoners' autonomy and reducing the therapeutic value of such treatment.[78]

---

[75] In France, for example, under Art 721–1 of the Code of Criminal Procedure the *juge de l'application des peines* (judge who oversees the execution of the sentence) may reduce the sentence by up to a month for each year if a prisoner passes a school, university or professional examination.

[76] See N Flynn and D Price, *Education in Prisons: A National Survey* (London, 1995) 28.

[77] In 2000–01 5,986 prisoners completed some sort of offending behaviour programme, and 786 prisoners completed SOTP programmes. See *Prison Service, Annual Reports and Accounts 2000–2001* (HC 29, 2001).

[78] In *R (Potter) v Home Secretary* [2001] EWHC Admin 1041; [2002] ACD 27, Moses J held that there was nothing unfair about requiring Potter, who was serving a sentence for serious sexual offences, to attend an SOTP, even though he denied his guilt. It was held to be fair and rational to use the IEP system to create incentives for participation in such courses. One of the other claimants was even willing to attend less specific offending behaviour courses, but this was not considered sufficient. However, the court stressed that whether denial of guilt is a good reason or not to require attendance on an SOTP depends upon the individual circumstances of each prisoner, so this judgment should not be taken to be the last word on the subject.

I. Facilities and Privileges

As is discussed more extensively in Chapter 2 of this book, there has been an **5.43** important debate over whether prisoners have any rights, or simply privileges which are dependent on co-operative behaviour. As a result of litigation and political action it is now clear that prisoners have certain rights, for example to fair disciplinary hearings or to make applications to the courts, which cannot be removed at the discretion of the prison authorities. However, it also remains clear that such rights are limited and amount only to minimum standards. Beyond that the prison authorities retain substantial discretion as to prisoners' access to goods, facilities, and services. In response to concerns expressed in the Woodcock Report and by the then Home Secretary, Michael Howard, there developed the idea that while all prisoners are entitled to a basic level of goods and facilities, enjoyment of a higher level should only be obtained through evidence of good behaviour. As a result, in 1995 the national IEP Scheme was introduced. The scheme has five stated aims; to encourage responsible behaviour, to encourage hard work and other constructive activity, to encourage sentenced prisoners to progress through the prison system, to create a more disciplined, better controlled, and safer environment for prisoners and staff, and finally to establish the principle that privileges should be earned through good behaviour and performance and can be taken away where a prisoner's behaviour falls below acceptable standards. The scheme in practice ties in with the provision of prisoner compacts, recommended by the Woolf Report, whereby the prison sets out what it will offer at each level of privilege and what standards of behaviour it expects from the prisoner. Compacts are, as with so much of the paperwork of prison life, legally unenforceable.[79]

The details of the national framework of the scheme is set out in PSO 4000. This **5.44** requires each prison to devise a scheme in relation to seven 'key earnable privileges'. These are:

(1) access to private cash at a rate of £2.50 per week at basic, £10 at standard, and £15 at enhanced (for unconvicted prisoners the figures are £15 at basic and £30 at standard);

(2) extra and improved visits (see Chapter 7 for further discussion);

(3) eligibility to participate in higher rates of pay schemes;

(4) earned community visits, subject to sentence criteria and risk assessment, if the prisoner is a female prisoner, Category D prisoner, or a young offender suitable for outside activities;

(5) access to in-cell television;

---

[79] See PSO 4000, ch 5, for a model compact setting out the behavioural requirements for each privilege level.

(6) ability to wear own clothes;

(7) time out of cell for association between the establishment's minimum and 12 hours.

In addition a prison may include a range of other privileges in its scheme; such as cooking facilities, electronic games, or own bedding.[80] In-cell television—the source of much public disquiet—became a key earnable privilege for the first time with the introduction of PSO 4000. The privileges should normally be provided at three levels—basic, standard, and enhanced—although it is recognized that (6) and (7) above are best provided when all the prisoners in a prison are at the same level (or at least when a 'privilege wing' can be established). At basic level it is clear that prisoners should be entitled to established legal entitlements and should not be excluded from things like behaviour modification programmes. However, their general range of choice as to activities will be more circumscribed than other prisoners.

5.45 Prison Rule 8(4) requires governors to indicate at each prison what system of privileges is in operation, including the procedures for determining when a prisoner is entitled to a higher level of privileges and when a privilege previously granted may be removed. It also indicates that a prisoner should be given a statement of reasons why a privilege has been removed, and a statement of the means by which he may appeal against it. In *R v Home Secretary, ex p Hepworth*[81] the Divisional Court indicated that it would take an exceptionally strong case to justify review of the criteria on which earned privileges could be granted or removed, 'something in the nature of bad faith or crude irrationality'. The decision predated the introduction of the HRA. PSO 4000 does not explicitly address the requirements of the Act, but it is clear that any criteria adopted have to conform with it, and a prisoner could not be punished for acting in ways permitted by it, for example for exercising rights of free expression. Currently PSO 4000 makes it clear that privileges may be removed for a pattern of behaviour which, in the view of the privileges board at the prison, fails to comply with the prison's published criteria for the earning and retention of privileges. The reasons required need not be very lengthy but must be sufficient to enable the prisoner to understand (a) what criteria he has failed to meet and (b) on what grounds this is considered to be the case. As we discuss further in Chapter 9, the operation of the earned privileges scheme has obvious implications for the use of disciplinary powers, and threatens to undermine the guarantees against the arbitrary use of power that have been introduced into the formal adjudications system.

---

[80] Appendix 1 of PSO 4000 supplies a non-exhaustive list. In *R v Home Secretary, ex p Bowen*, 26 January 1998, FC397/7354/D, the Court of Appeal rejected an argument that allowing different privilege regimes at different prisons constituted unlawful delegation of the Secretary of State's Prison Act, s 47(1) powers.

[81] [1998] COD 146.

A thorough review of the functioning of the incentives and earned privileges **5.46** scheme was carried out for the Home Office in 1999.[82] The study found that the scheme was much more popular with staff than with prisoners. While the majority of prisoners felt that the principle behind the scheme was fair, they also felt that it operated unfairly in practice. Prison staff, on the other hand, felt that the scheme helped them to communicate with and motivate prisoners, and that it helped to reward quieter and better behaved prisoners. However, the study highlighted the lack of consistency between prisons, and the sense of unfairness when prisoners were transferred between prisons and lost their enhanced status. Most worryingly, the study found no significant overall improvements to prisoner behaviour in the establishments studied, and lower perceptions of staff fairness, regime fairness, consistency of treatment and progress in prison.[83] PSO 4000 aims to address the concerns raised by the study, as well as by the Chief Inspector of Prisons, the Prisons Ombudsman and Boards of Visitors, all of whom expressed concern that the system was being used in a haphazard and disciplinary manner. It remains to be seen whether the Order's added emphasis on consistency and co-ordination, quality of schemes, and fair and just processes will be translated into practice, with any effect on the perceived unfairness of the system.[84] Interestingly, PSO 4000 states that privileges devised by establishments should be 'likely to be acceptable to reasonable public opinion', creating a possible tension between legitimacy in the eyes of the public and in the eyes of those in prison.

More detailed information on all facilities available within prisons is set out in **5.47** Standing Order 4 and includes a range of things, of which the most significant are perhaps personal possessions, tobacco, books and newspapers, a radio, and association with other prisoners. Most facilities are available to all prisoners. A

---

[82] A Liebling, G Muir, G Rose and A Bottoms, 'Incentives and Earned Privileges for Prisoners – an Evaluation', Home Office Research, Development and Statistics Directorate Research Finding 87 (London, 1999).

[83] In *R (Cooper) v Governor HM Prison Littlehey* [2002] EWCA Civ 632, Sedley LJ assessed the 'carrot and stick' approach of the IEP scheme: '[t]he carrot is always legitimate; the stick is not always legitimate because, if the stick represents punishment, punishment will not be lawfully administered if it is not administered under the Prison Rules' (p 4). The claimant in that case challenged the prison's policy of denying access to education to prisoners on the basic regime, unless they successfully applied to the prison for such access to continue. While refusing the claimant an extension of time to pursue the claim, Sedley LJ said, 'I hope that, without the need of further litigation, this will be taken on board by those who have responsibility for these things, and that prisoners who find themselves in the future on the wrong end of an Incentives and Earned Privileges scheme will not find their education (which is of fundamental importance, even if it is not a legal right) has gone too.' (p 7)

[84] PSI 90/1999, which introduces PSO 4000, makes it clear that the previous IEP scheme had come in for heavy criticism, and that the new Order 'contains some modifications to earlier policy and stronger emphasis on certain issues which will help to ensure that local schemes are fair, consistent with national policy, and more resistant to successful legal challenge' (para 5). The inclusion of the last aim is revealing, showing the Prison Service's ever-present reluctance to submit to judicial scrutiny.

governor may, however, add to the list with the authorization of the Area Manager and include some of them within the list of privileges which are included in the earned privileges scheme.

The Right to Vote

5.48   We have seen that the conditions in which prisoners live, and the extent to which they are able to contact and engage with the outside world, are defined and limited by a mass of rules and regulations. Many things taken for granted outside are privileges which have to be fought for by prisoners. One such contested privilege is the right to vote. This is removed from prisoners by s 3(1) of the Representation of the People Act 1983. In *R (Pearson) v Home Secretary*[85] three prisoners argued that this restriction is incompatible with Article 3 of the First Protocol and Article 14 of the ECHR. While Article 3 on its face only requires states to hold free elections, the Strasbourg authorities have interpreted this to confer a right to vote and to stand for elections. However, successive governments have withdrawn that right from prisoners. Their reasons were summarized by the Home Secretary in the course of the litigation:

> By committing offences which by themselves or taken with any aggravating characteristics including the offender's character and previous criminal record require a custodial sentence, such prisoners have forfeited the right to have a say in the way the country is governed for that period. There is more than one element to punishment than forcible detention [sic]. Removal from society means removal from the privileges of society, amongst which is the right to vote.

5.49   However, this view is clearly too simple. As we have seen, a series of landmark prison cases—*Raymond v Honey, Simms, Daly*[86]—have emphasized that prisoners do *not* lose all of 'the privileges of society'. Rather, they retain all rights not lost expressly or by necessary implication, and it is far from clear that loss of voting rights is a necessary consequence of imprisonment (particularly since prisoners in many European jurisdictions are entitled to vote). However, the Divisional Court upheld the limitation. Kennedy LJ considered that:

> On the face of it there would seem to be no reason why Parliament should not, if so minded, in its dual role as legislator in relation to sentencing and as guardian of its institutions, order that certain consequences shall follow upon conviction or incarceration without transgressing in any way the philosophy expounded in Raymond v Honey and subsequent cases.

Kennedy LJ then drew on domestic authorities to emphasize that the courts should allow the legislature a discretionary area of judgment in considering controversial policy issues, and considered case law from Strasbourg, Canada and

---

[85]   [2001] HRLR 39.
[86]   [1983] 1 AC 1; [2000] 2 AC 115; [2001] 2 AC 532.

South Africa. He came to the conclusion that the disenfranchisement was permissible, while remaining vague about its precise justification:

> Of course as far as an individual prisoner is concerned disenfranchisement does impair the very essence of his right to vote, but that is too simplistic an approach, because what Article 3 of the First Protocol is really concerned with is the wider question of universal franchise, and 'the free expression of the opinion of the people in the choice of the legislature'. In the case of a convicted prisoner serving his sentence the aim may not be easy to articulate. Clearly there is an element of punishment, and also an element of electoral law. . . . Perhaps the best course is that suggested by Linden JA [of the Canadian Federal Court of Appeal], namely to leave to philosophers the true nature of this disenfranchisement whilst recognising that the legislation does different things.[87]

When considering proportionality, Kennedy LJ also gave a great deal of deference to Parliament's assessment:

> [T]here is a broad spectrum of approaches among democratic societies, and the United Kingdom falls into the middle of the spectrum. In course of time this position may move, either by way of further fine tuning, as was done recently in relation to remand prisoners and others, or more radically, but its position in the spectrum is plainly a matter for Parliament not the courts.[88]

This reasoning was held to apply even to post-tariff discretionary life sentence **5.50** prisoners, who have served the amount of time considered necessary for retributive purposes and are now held purely on the basis of risk. While one cannot criticize the court for according some respect to the view of Parliament on this issue, the reasoning in this case shows such a degree of deference that it is difficult to discern the justification for the disenfranchisement. If more European jurisdictions accord convicted prisoners the vote, the issue may well be revisited, either in the domestic courts or in Strasbourg.[89]

Personal Possessions

Perhaps the most important facilities relate to items of personal possession that **5.51** prisoners are entitled to retain in their cells. SO 4(7) indicates that prisoners are allowed to have 'sufficient property in possession to lead as normal and individual an existence as possible within the constraints of the prison environment and the limitations under this and other standing orders'. Items which come within this category are stated in SO 4(9). This indicates that, among other things, prisoners will be allowed to retain in their possession at least six newspapers and periodicals, at least three books, a sound system, smoking materials, up to 80 cigarettes (except

---

[87] para 40.
[88] para 41.
[89] Unconvicted prisoners and civil detainees do, of course, have the right to vote, and the appropriate arrangements are set out in PSO 4650, 'Prisoners' Voting Rights'.

where smoking is prohibited), a battery shaver, and a manual typewriter (but not an electronic typewriter or computer). Prison governors may add to what is already a very detailed list.

5.52 Prisoners increasingly require access to IT facilities, and such access is governed by PSI 02/01, which places a priority on access for work connected with a prisoner's legal proceedings. Facilities may be withdrawn either as a result of a disciplinary punishment or where the governor considers that the number of items in a cell hinders searching, prevents the cell from being tidy, presents a risk to health, safety, security, or discipline, or cannot be moved with a prisoner on transfer. Following the Woodcock Report in 1994 the Prison Service has introduced the notion of 'volumetric control' of prisoner's property whereby all of a prisoner's property should fit into two boxes plus a sound system or other outsize item and legal papers.[90] Removal of facilities as a result of a disciplinary hearing is obviously subject to judicial review of the procedures by which the disciplinary verdict was reached. However, removal by way of a governor's exercise of discretion could also be challenged by way of judicial review, notably by way of the *Wednesbury* 'unreasonableness' standard. Although *Hepworth*[91] suggests that the criteria by which privileges are granted or removed is largely immune from judicial review, once a set of criteria has been adopted a prisoner acting consistently with them can argue that he has a legitimate expectation that, at the very least, any privilege accorded to him should not be removed without a hearing.[92] Further, a prisoner would be able to argue, under Article 8 of the ECHR, that an arbitrary or unfair removal of possessions constituted an unlawful interference with his private life. Article 1 of Protocol 1, the right to property, also protects against the arbitrary deprivation of possessions.

5.53 SO 4 also governs the acquisition of further possessions. It indicates that prisoners may purchase further books, newspapers, or audio cassettes. Except for prisoners in Category C or D establishments, these must be ordered direct from publishers, booksellers, or registered record clubs.[93] Governors may waive this requirement in respect of books provided by friends or relatives. The Standing Order gives a governor power to withhold a book, newspaper, or audio cassette if he or she considers that the content presents a threat to good order or discipline or 'where the medical officer considers that possession of the material is likely to have

---

[90] See Prison Service Standard on Prisoners' Property.
[91] *R v Home Secretary, ex p Hepworth* [1998] COD 146.
[92] See *R v Home Secretary, ex p Hargreaves* [1997] 1 All ER 397, 413–414, on the need for any representation to be 'clear and unambiguous' if it was to have this effect.
[93] Prisoners are also entitled to access to the prison shop to purchase snacks and products with their earnings and private cash. The level of access and the amount of money which can be spent varies according to whether the prisoner is on the basic, standard or enhanced regime: see Prison Service Standard on the Prison Shop.

an adverse effect on the prisoner's physical or mental condition' (SO 4(35)).[94] The Standing Order also indicates that the governor may impose restrictions on material which he considers 'is likely to cause offence by reason of its indecent or violent or racist content or is racially or sexually discriminatory'. This may seem a welcome policy declaration against racism and sexism but it also indicates how attenuated a prisoner's right to privacy is, even in his own cell. In the outside world racial and sexual discrimination is generally permitted in the 'private' sphere (the household exemption from anti-discrimination statutes for example, or the different treatment of public display of pornography from its private possession). In prison, it seems, virtually no privacy rights remain.

A decision to prevent a particular book or newspaper coming into the prison **5.54** could also be challenged on judicial review grounds and might be subject to review for violation of the ECHR's Articles on the rights to privacy or to receive information. However the Commission has generally upheld official action in this area after fairly cursory review.[95]

J. Safety

As has been indicated earlier, the prison authorities have a duty towards the prisoner **5.55** to provide a safe system of work, a duty that may be enforced by common law actions for negligence.[96] A duty has also been recognized to exist in respect of attacks on prisoners by other prisoners.[97] However, since the actions are based on negligence the context is all-important, as the key question is whether the authorities have done all that could reasonably be asked of them to prevent the prisoner being injured. We have discussed this issue in greater detail in Chapter 2 but it is worth briefly summarizing its implications for issues of prisoner safety at this point.

---

[94] The Prisoners' Advice Service challenged the decision of the Governor of HM Prison Full Sutton to impose a blanket ban on materials from a publisher established to provide free educational literature to prisoners, on the ground of good order and discipline. PAS argued that the threat would have to be specifically defined in relation to particular books, and that the blanket ban was a disproportionate restriction on prisoners' rights under Art 10 of the ECHR (free expression). The Governor accepted that the ban was 'unreasonable' and withdrew it. See Prisoner's Legal Rights Group Bulletin No 17, December 2001.

[95] See R Clayton and H Tomlinson, *The Law of Human Rights* (Oxford, 2000), ch 15.

[96] Prison Service Standard 'Enterprise and Work' summarizes the prison's duties as an employer: an accident book must be kept, all accidents and near-misses are to be reported to headquarters, all staff must be aware of and trained in the applicable health and safety legislation, all relevant documents must be displayed in the workplace, risk assessments must be undertaken and health and safety audits carried out annually. PSO 4250, 'Physical Education', sets out the duties of the various prison staff to ensure safe equipment and practices for prisoners' PE.

[97] See *Ellis v Home Office* [1953] 2 QB 135. See also *H v Home Office,* The Independent, 6 May 1992, where a prisoner was awarded damages after negligent disclosure of his past convictions for sex offences led to him being assaulted by other prisoners. He was unable to recover anything in respect of his having to go on r 43 (now r 45) segregation subsequent to the assault.

5.56 Cases on sex offenders, who are generally accepted to be at a higher risk of attack than most prisoners, illustrate the difficulties that are experienced in arriving at an appropriate standard. In *Egerton v Home Office*[98] May J refused to find that the authorities had been negligent, despite the fact that the officers supervising Egerton were unaware of his offences or the fact that he had just come off rule 43 (now rule 45) following a similar attack, on the grounds that even an experienced officer could not have foreseen the actual attack that took place. However in *Steele v Northern Ireland Office*[99] a prisoner accused of sex offences recovered damages for an assault by other prisoners even though he had refused advice from the prison staff to be accommodated in a protective wing. Prisoners who are not seen as sex offenders or otherwise 'vulnerable' may have even greater difficulty in succeeding in such actions. In *Palmer v Home Office*,[100] for example, a prisoner was stabbed in a workshop by another prisoner who, despite the fact that he was regarded as dangerous, had been entrusted with a pair of scissors. The court took the view that it was impossible to segregate a dangerous prisoner indefinitely and that the governor had a legitimate concern to provide work where available.

5.57 In *Thompson v Home Office*,[101] a prisoner who had been attacked with a razor blade by another inmate in HM YOI Swinfen Hall sued for negligence. The Home Office argued that there had been no breach of duty, since the system for issuing razor blades in Swinfen Hall at the time was reasonable, and that the claimant had not proved causation. The Court of Appeal emphasized that 'prison governors, and especially those in charge of Young Offender Institutions, have to make balancing judgments between tight security and a regime aimed at rehabilitation in which the inmates are allowed to exercise responsibility'. The court did not consider that any deficiencies in the system would have caused the claimant's injuries. This meant that, in order to succeed, he would have to show that the system itself was negligently adopted. This high threshold had not been met by the claimant. These restrictive decisions make it very difficult for prisoners, who have to look to the prison for protection from attack, to obtain compensation for injuries inflicted by fellow inmates. Particularly in light of the fact that prisoners are not considered eligible for criminal injuries compensation, this leaves many prisoners without redress for serious assaults unless they can meet the demanding tests required by the courts. However, all the decisions discussed above made it clear that they turned on the facts of the particular cases, leaving it open for prisoners to argue that their own cases are serious enough to justify a finding of negligence.

5.58 PSO 1702 sets out a very welcome Prison Service anti-bullying strategy, recognizing the prison's responsibility to protect prisoners, and the severe effects that

---

[98] [1978] Crim LR 494.
[99] (1988) 12 NIJB 1.
[100] The Guardian, 31 March 1988.
[101] [2001] EWCA Civ 331; The Independent, 16 March 2001.

mistreatment by fellow prisoners can have. Although the document is not legally enforceable, a prisoner who suffered bullying which went undetected due to failures in the prison anti-bullying system would be able to rely on the Order as an indicator of the contents of any duty of care owed to him.

Prisoners may now also invoke the HRA in this area. The Strasbourg Court has made it clear that Article 2 of the ECHR contains positive obligations to take reasonable measures to protect people from harming themselves[102] or being harmed by others[103] where the authorities know or ought to know that there is a real and immediate risk of harm. Whether there has been a breach of Article 2 will depend on issues of fact, such as what the authorities knew at the relevant time, and questions of judgment as to what action they could reasonably be expected to take. It may turn out that this standard is not significantly different from that which currently prevails in negligence. **5.59**

The European Court of Human Rights (ECtHR) has also turned its attention to threats to detainees' safety from those responsible for detaining them. In the late 1990s it made its first findings of torture in cases involving people detained in police or military custody. The case of *Selmouni v France*[104] is especially significant. In that case the applicant was frequently beaten by police officers over a number of days in custody, and was subjected to frightening and humiliating acts, such as being threatened with a blowtorch and being urinated upon by officers. Lesser forms of violence against prisoners may amount to inhuman or degrading treatment.[105] The ECtHR has also indicated that Article 3 requires that all allegations of torture, inhuman or degrading treatment are investigated in a prompt and thorough manner.[106] The court has found violations of Article 3 where there was a substantial delay in conducting any investigation, or where the authorities failed to identify relevant witnesses or obtain relevant documents. In addition to conducting an investigation, the State must also ensure that its law provides adequate means to identify and punish whoever is responsible for the treatment in question. As we have already seen in discussing deaths in custody (where a similar obligation arises in respect of Article 2), this requirement has already given rise to significant legal developments in the domestic courts. **5.60**

---

[102] See *Keenan v UK* Application 27229/95 (2001) 33 EHRR 38.
[103] See *Osman v UK* [1999] 1 FLR 193.
[104] (2000) 29 EHRR 403.
[105] See *Ribitsch v Austria* Series A No 336 (1996) 21 EHRR 573.
[106] See, eg, *Labita v Italy*, 6 April 2000, ECtHR. Violation of Art 3 where delay of 14 months in conducting investigation and few steps taken to identify and question those alleged to be responsible for assaults on the applicant.

K. Challenging Conditions

Introduction

5.61 Thus far we have focused on specific aspects of prison conditions. However, prisoners do not experience these conditions in isolation from each other. Deterioration in one aspect of conditions is often combined with deteriorations in others. While taken individually the quality of prison food, cell size, opportunities for work and exercise, or hygiene conditions may not fall below minimum standards. However, where they are all experienced at the same time they may create an especially unpleasant living environment. Particularly in circumstances of significant overcrowding and a lack of financial resources, prisoners may experience a marked deterioration in their living conditions. Where prisons are overcrowded it becomes extremely difficult to provide prisoners with adequate accommodation and immediate access to facilities like work or healthcare. Food and hygiene come under greater pressure. With inadequate resources, deterioration in the physical plant of prisons is not addressed, and prisons may lack sufficient adequately trained staff, in turn leading either to fewer opportunities for association or less safe conditions where prisoners are allowed to associate.

5.62 In addition to seeking to invoke legal remedies to challenge specific aspects of their living conditions, prisoners have also sought to use more general constitutional or human rights provisions to challenge these more general conditions of imprisonment. The federal courts in the United States led the way on this in the 1960s and 1970s when they began to declare that conditions at individual prisons, or indeed entire state prison systems, amounted to 'cruel and unusual punishment' in violation of the Eighth Amendment to the Constitution. In *Holt v Sarver*[107] the District Court declared, 'if Arkansas is going to operate a Penitentiary System, it is going to have to be a system that is countenanced by the Constitution of the United States'.

Prisoners' applications regularly focused on a number of factors in order to convince courts that, taken as a whole, the 'totality of conditions' violated the Constitution.[108] These included overcrowding, inadequate physical facilities, lack of medical care, poor food, inadequate sanitation, lack of protection from violence, and a lack of rehabilitation systems. Many disclosed appalling conditions, including the maintenance of discipline by armed 'trusty' prisoners,[109] the

---

[107] 309 F Supp 362 (DC Ark 1970).
[108] I Robbins and M Buser, 'Punitive Conditions of Prison Confinement: An analysis of *Pugh v Locke* and Federal Court Supervision of State Penal Administration Under the Eighth Amendment' (1977) 29 Stanford L Rev 892, 906–915.
[109] See *Holt v Sarver* 309 F Supp 362 (DC Ark 1970).

holding of prisoners in punitive isolation with as many as six prisoners to a four foot by eight foot cell with no beds, lights, or running water,[110] and the keeping of prisoners with untreated contagious diseases in the general population.[111]

Initially the US courts did not spell out in too much detail the standard for a violation of the Eighth Amendment, and were content to order a remedy where they found that, taken as a whole, conditions 'shocked the conscience' when viewed in relation to 'evolving standards of decency'.[112] However, as more of these cases were appealed to the Supreme Court in the more conservative climate of the 1980s, a judicial retreat began, both in respect of the precise standard of conditions required to infringe the Eighth Amendment and the powers of the courts to order remedies once such a finding had been made. In *Rhodes v Chapman*[113] the Supreme Court stated that overcrowding in itself would not amount to cruel and unusual punishment, and some of the majority indicated that they would look closely at whether the authorities displayed 'wanton indifference' to the prisoners' living conditions. Subsequent decisions have made it clear that, in order to find a violation, the court now requires the plaintiffs to demonstrate the presence of both objective and subjective elements. The objective element is that the conditions must involve a deprivation of the 'minimal civilised measure of life's necessities'.[114] By this the court appears to mean basic human needs such as food, clothing, or shelter. The subjective element focuses on whether the deprivations in question have been inflicted with the knowledge or at least the 'deliberate indifference' of prison officials. This phrase first appeared in *Estelle v Gamble*[115] and has been further refined in cases such as *Wilson v Seiter*[116] and *Farmer v Brennan*.[117] In *Farmer* the court held that a fact finder could infer that the defendants had knowledge of a risk if circumstantial evidence suggested that this risk was obvious.[118] **5.63**

The consequence of these decisions was to make prison conditions cases more difficult and expensive to pursue. Whereas in the 1970s and most of the 1980s it was sufficient for plaintiffs to demonstrate the level of deprivation in a prison in order to succeed at trial or, more often, to secure a consent decree addressing broad ranging conditions issues, now a great deal more time and energy must be devoted **5.64**

---

[110] See *Pugh v Locke* 406 F Supp 318 (DC Ala 1976).
[111] See *Gates v Collier* 501 F 2d 1291 (5th Cir 1974).
[112] For a general analysis, see I Robbins and M Buser, 'Punitive Conditions of Prison Confinement: An analysis of *Pugh v Locke* and Federal Court Supervision of State Penal Administration Under the Eighth Amendment' (1977) 29 Stanford L Rev 892, 901–902.
[113] 452 US 337 (1981).
[114] Language taken from *Rhodes v Chapman*, ibid, 347 and approved in *Wilson v Seiter* 111 S Ct 2321 (1991).
[115] 429 US 97 (1976).
[116] 501 US 294 (1991).
[117] 511 US 825 (1994).
[118] 114 S Ct 1970, 1981 (1994).

to identifying specific violations related to more specific standards, and to demonstrating the culpability of prison officials. Although the courts have not explicitly revived the 'inability to pay' defence that was rejected in *Estelle*,[119] prison authorities can now raise this as part of an argument that they were not indifferent to a particular risk. Opportunities for challenging prison conditions have been further reduced by the enactment of the Prison Litigation Reform Act of 1995,[120] which has made it more difficult for prisoners to file suits and has imposed significant limits on lawyers' fees in prison conditions cases. However, its greatest impact is on the consent decrees agreed between state officials and prisoners' lawyers, which were perhaps the greatest engine for judicially sponsored reform of US prisons. The Act now prohibits a court from issuing a consent decree unless the defendants are willing to admit that they are violating federal law, and requires the termination of all consent decrees within two years of its passage unless the court holds a trial and finds an ongoing violation. Every decree issued thereafter will also have to come to an end after two years unless a continuing violation is established.

5.65 As a result of these judicial and legislative developments, litigation now has a much more limited impact on conditions in US prisons. However, a significant number of applications are still pursued, and the courts have continued to give significant decisions on aspects of prison conditions, for example the compatibility of security regimes in 'super maximum' prisons with constitutional provisions.[121] The American experience remains worth looking at, if only for the wide use of innovative remedies in such cases. These have included the closing of institutions or the release of prisoners, but more usually have taken the form of detailed plans to remedy overcrowding, inadequate staffing, lack of medical care, or poor sanitation. Frequently judges have appointed special committees or masters to oversee the implementation of such plans. Judges have also awarded damages to prisoner plaintiffs and contempt fines against recalcitrant prison authorities.[122]

5.66 Views remain divided as to whether this intervention has been beneficial. States with prisons under court orders still spend less per prisoner than those with no such prisons,[123] and there is evidence that the adversarial character of prison litigation has produced significant resistance to change.[124] Other observers have

---

[119] The Supreme Court refused to pronounce on this in *Wilson v Seiter*.

[120] HR 3019, Public Law No 104–34 (1986). For a discussion of the statute see S O'Bryan, 'Closing the Courthouse Door: The Impact of the Prison Litigation Reform Act's Physical Injury Requirement on the Constitutional Rights of Prisoners' (1997) 83 Virginia L Rev 1189.

[121] See, eg, *Madrid v Gomez* 889 F Supp 1146 (1995).

[122] See, generally, Note, '"Mastering" Intervention in Prisons' (1979) 88 Yale LJ 1062; also S Sturm, 'Resolving the Remedial Dilemma: Strategies of Judicial Intervention in Prisons' (1990) 138 U of Pennsylvania L Rev 805.

[123] See C Smith, 'Federal Judges Role in Prisoner Litigation: What's Necessary? What's Proper?' (1986) 70 Judicature 144, at 148–149.

[124] See S Ekland-Olson and S Martin, 'Organizational Compliance with Court-Ordered Reform' (1988) 22 L and Society Rev 359.

suggested that intervention by federal judges with a limited understanding of prison dynamics has produced a vacuum of power in prisons, which has been filled by prison gangs which a demoralized staff do little to restrain.[125] However, there have clearly been some success stories, where prison litigation has brought about a marked improvement in prisoners' living conditions,[126] and evidence that the pressure of litigation has assisted reformers within prison administrations to make the changes they want.[127] Yet at the beginning of the 21st century there were more people in American prisons than ever before and the pressure on space and resources continued to produce cramped, unhealthy, and frightening conditions for many prisoners.[128] One of the main lessons of the American experience is therefore that the improvement of conditions within prisons cannot be separated from issues about who should be sent to prison in the first place.

Prior to the introduction of the HRA the prospects of a successful American-style **5.67** challenge to conditions in the United Kingdom seemed remote, due to both procedural and substantive limitations. The procedural limitations, some of which have not disappeared, included the difficulty of bringing claims as a group, and the issue, which we explore in Chapter 2, of whether a claim should be brought in public or private law. The substantive limitation was the absence of an equivalent provision to the US Eighth Amendment. Some innovative efforts were made to get round this limitation, using the action for false imprisonment and the 1688 Bill of Rights. Although Ackner LJ raised some hopes in *Middleweek v Chief Constable of Merseyside*[129] that prison conditions could become so bad as to render the detention unlawful, this was rejected in *Hague v Deputy Governor of Parkhurst Prison*,[130] where Ackner LJ joined the rest of his brethren in rejecting this statement and in holding that s 12(1) of the Prison Act 1952 provided a complete defence to any claims that a prisoner's conditions rendered his or her detention unlawful. All their Lordships accepted, though, that a prisoner might still have an action in negligence in respect of his conditions. Lord Bridge indicated that such an action might lie without proof of physical injury or prejudice to health 'if

---

[125] See, eg, J DiIulio, 'The Old Regime and the Ruiz Revolution: The Impact of Federal Intervention on Texas Prisons' in J DiIulio (ed), *Courts, Corrections and the Constitution* (New York, 1991) 51.

[126] See L Yackle, *Reform and Regret: The Story of Federal Judicial Involvement in the Alabama Prison System* (New York, 1989).

[127] See J Jacobs, 'The Prisoners Rights Movement and its Impacts 1960–80' in N Morris and M Tonry (1980) 2 *Crime and Justice: An Annual Review of Research* 429, for discussion of the use made by reforming prison administrators of conditions suits. Sturm has also argued that prison litigation has been effective in producing desirable change where it has acted as a 'catalyst' for changes produced through the interaction of prison staff, prisoners, lawyers and courts: see S Sturm, 'The Legacy and Future of Corrections Litigation' (1994) 142 U of Pennsylvania L Rev 639.

[128] On 30 June 2001 the Justice Department estimated the total US prison and jail population to be 1,965,495.

[129] [1992] 1 AC 179 (the case was decided in 1985).

[130] [1992] 1 AC 58.

a person lawfully detained is kept in conditions which cause him for the time being physical pain or a degree of discomfort which can properly be described as intolerable'.[131] The rest of the Committee appeared somewhat more cautious and anxious to allow such actions, as Lord Goff put it, 'only in respect of the type or types of damages which, on accepted legal principles will give rise to an action'.[132] This approach would appear likely to limit claims to circumstances where prisoners have suffered some actual injury, and would be unlikely to provide a remedy for conditions which are dirty, overcrowded, or oppressive without causing tangible injury. Medical evidence of the impact which specific conditions have on prisoners is likely to be particularly important to the success or failure of any such claim.[133]

5.68 The Bill of Rights also proved of limited assistance. Its protection against 'cruell and unusuall punishment' was extensively explored by Tudor Evans J in *Williams v Home Office (No 2)*, a challenge to the 'control unit' system introduced to deal with difficult prisoners in the 1970s. Williams had spent 180 days in these units, which had no basis in the Prison Act or Rules, in either total or near total isolation from other prisoners. Tudor Evans J concluded that the words of the Bill of Rights had to be read disjunctively, so that the punishment to be unlawful had to be both cruel and unusual. Examining whether the conditions were cruel, he adopted a test which looked at whether they fell below an 'irreducible minimum, judged by contemporary standards of public morality'.[134] He also accepted that treatment which was disproportionate to the conduct or character of the prisoner in question could be cruel. Applying these tests, he found that the measures were not disproportionate, given that Williams was considered to be a dedicated troublemaker. Nor did he find them cruel; the unit was similar in design to that recommended by a report of the Advisory Council on the Penal System, the conditions in it were not that different from those experienced on rule 45 segregation, and prisoners spent much less time in the unit than in similar units in the United States and Canada which the courts there had held to be lawful. Despite the finding the Home Office had already closed the control units in 1975. Although the Court of Appeal was subsequently to look more favourably on a prisoner's invocation of the Bill of Rights in *R v Home Secretary, ex p Herbage (No 2)*,[135] this only arose as regards a discovery application where the prisoner, who was severely overweight, challenged his detention on the ground floor of the medical wing of

---

[131] ibid, 165.

[132] ibid, 167.

[133] Reports on the impact of Special Secure Units on the mental health of prisoners, eg Amnesty International, *United Kingdom: Special Secure Units: Cruel, Inhuman or Degrading Treatment* (AI Index: EUR 45/06/97), raise questions about whether the operation of such units breaches the duty of care owed to prisoners. See further the discussion in Ch 10.

[134] [1981] 1 All ER 1211, 1245.

[135] [1987] QB 1077.

Pentonville Prison. In dealing with the discovery application the court indicated that they felt that breaches of the Bill of Rights could not be justified by reference to the Prison Rules, as these were delegated legislation and the Bill of Rights took precedence over them. Purchas LJ also added, without ruling on the facts in the instant case, that holding a sane person in the psychiatric wing of a prison for purely administrative reasons might well be 'cruell and unusuall' punishment. However, Herbage's case never came to trial and so the point was not definitively tested.

Article 3 of the ECHR

These cases are now likely to be superseded by the provisions of the HRA, and in particular Article 3 of the ECHR, which provides protection against torture or other forms of inhuman or degrading treatment or punishment. This prohibition has already been the object of significant consideration by the European Commission and ECtHR.[136] These decisions have not settled on any very precise definition of the Article, but as regards the general approach to interpretation the Commission has indicated that the Convention is a 'living instrument which must be interpreted in the light of present day conditions'.[137] The first requirement is that the ill-treatment must attain a 'minimum level of severity'. The court has frequently indicated[138] that the assessment of this minimum is relative: 'it depends on all the circumstances of the case, such as the duration of the treatment, its physical and mental effects and, in some cases, the sex, age and state of health of the victim.' Once this is satisfied, the Strasbourg institutions have gone on to examine other factors and have indicated that treatment would be degrading to a person if it 'grossly humiliates him before others or drives him to act against his will or conscience'.[139] Inhuman treatment has been described as 'at least such treatment as deliberately causes severe suffering, mental or physical, which, in the particular situation is unjustifiable'.[140] A number of decisions have also indicated that the Article 3 elements are cumulative: what is torture will also be inhuman and degrading treatment. **5.69**

Recent years have seen significant development in the ECtHR's jurisprudence on prison conditions, especially as the court begins to engage with conditions in some of the overcrowded and antiquated prisons of southern and eastern Europe. An important starting point is that the court has moved beyond its regular statement that, in order to attain the requisite minimum, the suffering and humiliation **5.70**

---

[136] For a general discussion of this jurisprudence see J Simor and B Emmerson (eds), *Human Rights Practice* (London, 2000, and supplements); R Clayton and H Tomlinson, *The Law of Human Rights* (Oxford, 2000, and supplements).

[137] See *Tyrer v UK* Series A No 26 (1978) 2 EHRR 1.

[138] eg, in *Ireland v UK* (1978) 2 EHRR 25.

[139] *The Greek Case* (1969) 12 Yearbook 1.

[140] ibid, 186.

involved 'must go beyond that inevitable element of suffering or humiliation connected with a given form of legitimate treatment or punishment'. It has now also added that:

> Nevertheless, under this provision the State must ensure that a person is detained in conditions which are compatible with respect for his human dignity, that the manner and method of the execution of the measure do not subject him to distress or hardship of an intensity exceeding the level of suffering inherent in detention and that, given the practical demands of imprisonment, his health and well-being are adequately secured.[141]

5.71 In reaching a decision as to whether conditions of imprisonment breach Article 3, the court has examined the conditions as a whole, with a particular emphasis on the duration for which the prisoner experienced them. Issues of cell size, sanitation arrangements, heating, lighting, food and the opportunity for recreation and exercise have all been taken into account. The court has shown an increasing willingness to draw upon the general standards for imprisonment set out in the Second General Report of the CPT (to be discussed in more detail below).[142] While medical evidence of a deterioration in the prisoner's health is relevant to a decision on whether Article 3 has been infringed (and essential for cases on medical treatment, to be discussed in Chapter 6), the court has moved away from a focus on this issue, to rule that conditions have aroused feelings of anguish and inferiority capable of humiliating and debasing a prisoner without requiring medical reports indicating that this is the case.[143] In addition, while evidence of intention on the part of the prison authorities to humiliate is a factor to be taken into account in deciding whether treatment is degrading, the court has made it clear that 'the absence of such purpose cannot conclusively rule out a finding of violation of Article 3'.[144] What does appear to be especially influential is whether the authorities have taken any steps to alleviate the degrading conditions, with the need for an urgent response increasing in proportion to the impact of the conditions on the prisoner. Thus in *Price v UK*[145] the failure of the police to do anything to alleviate the suffering of a severely disabled prisoner detained overnight in a cell where she was unable to sleep properly or reach the bell to call for assistance with the toilet facilities, and where her requests for blankets went unanswered, contributed to a finding of a breach of Article 3 even though the prisoner was only detained for a short period.

5.72 Decisions on whether or not there has been a breach of Article 3 turn on a range of factors, and therefore only general guidance can be derived from examination

---

[141] See, eg, *Kudla v Poland* Application 30210/96 (2002) 35 EHRR 11.
[142] CPT/Inf (92) 3.
[143] See, eg, *Peers v Greece* Application 28524/95 (2001) 33 EHRR 51.
[144] See, eg, *Kalashnikov v Russia*, 15 July 2002, ECtHR.
[145] Application 33394/96 (2002) 34 EHRR 53.

of particular cases. Overcrowding has featured in nearly all of them, and while the court has rejected the idea that overcrowding per se is in breach of Article 3, it has indicated that significant overcrowding, combined with other factors, can amount to degrading treatment. Thus in *Kalashnikov v Russia* the court unanimously found a breach of Article 3 where the prisoner was detained in a dormitory cell measuring 21 square metres. Designed to hold eight people, it held at least 14 people during the four years the applicant was held there, and at times may even have reached 24. Prisoners had to take turns sleeping and were confined to these cells for all but two hours a day. The cells were infected with pests, and at times prisoners suffering from tuberculosis and syphilis were detained there. The toilet was filthy and prisoners lacked any privacy from their cellmates when using it. Though less severe, the conditions in *Peers v Greece* were also held to amount to a breach of Article 3. There the applicant was detained for two months in a 7 metre square cell designed for one person, but which he had to share with another prisoner. Ventilation was poor, the cell was windowless, and the applicant had to spend much of his time confined to his bed. Again the toilet facilities lacked privacy, there being no screen between the sunken toilet on which the prisoner had to squat and the rest of the cell.

In both of these cases the court drew on the CPT's general recommendations **5.73** regarding cell size, especially its recommendation that prisoners be detained in cells which afforded each prisoner 7 square metres. However, in *Valasinas v Lithuania*[146] it indicated that this factor alone was not determinative of whether Article 3 was complied with, and other factors would be taken into account. In *Valasinas* the applicant was again detained in a dormitory that offered him less than 3 square metres per prisoner. However, the court felt that this was compensated by the large size of the dormitories overall (ranging between 55 and 92 square metres), the opportunities for prisoners to move around them and to leave the cell for much of the day and participate in entertainment activities. Heating and ventilation were seen to be adequate, and although the toilet facilities were not ideal (including a lack of free toilet paper, although this could be bought in the prison shop) prisoners were screened from each other when using the toilet. In reaching its conclusion that there was no breach of Article 3, the court seemed to be influenced by the fact that, unlike in *Peers* or *Price*, the authorities were aware of the problems with conditions in the prison and had made some effort to improve the situation.

Although the ECtHR has, since the beginning of the 21st century, taken the step **5.74** of indicating that some prison conditions may amount to a breach of Article 3, it still appears to require a fairly significant deviation from what it regards as the normal conditions of imprisonment. Many in the United Kingdom might regard the

---

[146] Application 44558/98, 12 BHRC 266.

prison conditions which prevailed in the *Valasinas* case as being well below the acceptable minimum, but it must be recalled that the court is seeking to establish a standard which will apply throughout Europe, and may be concentrating its efforts on some of the worst conditions. It remains to be seen whether courts in the United Kingdom, applying Article 3 under the HRA, will stick rigidly to the Strasbourg standard or will seek to evolve a sense of 'minimum standards' which is more exacting. There are some examples of this occurring already. In the Scottish decision of *Napier v Scottish Ministers*,[147] the Outer House of the Court of Session granted an order transferring a remand prisoner to alternative conditions because he was detained in conditions which breached Article 3. He shared an extremely small cell with another prisoner for the majority of the day, there was inadequate light and ventilation, and the cell did not have a toilet.

Other Means of Challenging Prison Conditions in International Law

5.75 In addition to the ECHR, the United Kingdom is a signatory to several other international human rights treaties, notably the UN International Covenant on Civil and Political Rights (ICCPR), which contain prohibitions on torture and inhuman and degrading treatment or punishment.[148] With the advent of the HRA the provisions of Article 3 of the ECHR are now part of UK law. Those of the ICCPR remain binding on the United Kingdom only at the international level, and are not directly applicable in UK law. However, as the wording of the ICCPR provision is almost identical to that of the ECHR, it remains to be seen to what extent the judiciary in the United Kingdom will draw upon it when interpreting the relevant provisions of the HRA. In addition the United Kingdom is a signatory to both the UN and European Conventions against torture.[149] In the case of the European Convention this carries the obligation to allow inspections of Britain's prisons by the Committee established under the Convention.

---

[147] The Times, 15 November 2001. See also *Peers v Greece* Application 28524/95 (2001) 33 EHRR 51, where the court found that the appalling conditions in a Greek prison, including heat, overcrowding, lack of private access to toilet facilities and lack of ventilation amounted to inhuman and degrading treatment. There was no evidence that there was a positive intention of humiliating or debasing the applicant. However, the court stressed that this is not determinative: the prison conditions, looked at objectively, 'diminished the applicant's human dignity and arose in him feelings of anguish and inferiority capable of humiliating and debasing him and possibly breaking his physical or moral resistance', (para 75) and therefore violated Art 3.

[148] The European provision is in Art 3 of the ECHR, the ICCPR provision is Art 7. Both prohibit torture and cruel, inhuman, or degrading treatment or punishment. The UN provision also specifically prohibits the subjection of anyone without their consent to medical or scientific experimentation.

[149] These are the Convention against Torture and Other Cruel, Inhuman or Degrading Treatment or Punishment, UN Doc A/RES/39/46 (1984), and the European Convention for the Prevention of Torture and Inhuman or Degrading Treatment or Punishment (1987).

European Convention on the Prevention of Torture (ECPT)[150]

In Chapter 3 we explored the organization of the ECPT and its value as a form of **5.76** international redress for prisoners who feel that their rights have been infringed. In this section we look more specifically at what the European Committee for the Prevention of Torture (CPT) has said on prison conditions and also at its observations on conditions in UK prisons. The Committee has made five periodic and two ad hoc visits to places of detention in the United Kingdom since 1990, and on each occasion its reports have highlighted important concerns with aspects of prison conditions.

As noted in Chapter 3, the CPT produces two types of reports, reports on visits to **5.77** individual state parties and annual reports. In both of these, but especially in the latter, it has sought to provide guidance to Member States on how to reduce the risk of subjecting detainees to torture, inhuman or degrading treatment. In 2001 the Committee collected these standards.[151] The section on imprisonment draws extensively on, but also goes beyond, the important statement in the Second General Report, which has been especially influential both within the CPT's subsequent reports and in the jurisprudence of the ECtHR. Four issues feature particularly prominently in these standards. These are overcrowding, activities, hygiene and access to natural light and fresh air. In respect of overcrowding the CPT has stated that:

> all the services and activities within a prison will be adversely affected if it is required to cater for more prisoners than it was designed to accommodate. . . . Moreover the level of overcrowding in a prison, or in a particular part of it, might be such as to be in itself inhuman or degrading from a physical standpoint.[152]

The CPT has not offered any precise guidance on how many prisoners should be **5.78** detained in a prison but it has, in its Second General Report, suggested that prison cells designed for single occupancy should be at least 7 square metres. In its Eleventh General Report in 2001 it indicated an opposition in principle to the dormitory style accommodation found in many parts of central and eastern Europe. Noting that cultural and other factors may incline countries to provide accommodation in this form, the CPT observed that 'there is little to be said in favour of—and a lot to be said against—arrangements under which tens of prisoners live and sleep together in the same dormitory'.[153] The Committee has also expressed a strong view that building more prisons is not a viable long-term solution to the problems of overcrowding.

---

[150] For an overview on the CPT's standards on conditions of detention see M Evans and R Morgan, *Preventing Torture: A Study of the European Convention for the Prevention of Torture and Inhuman or Degrading Treatment or Punishment* (Oxford, 1998), ch 8.

[151] 'Substantive' Sections of the CPT's General Reports CPT/Inf (99) 1.

[152] Second General Report, para 46.

[153] Eleventh General Report CPT/Inf (2001) 16, para 29.

5.79 Turning to activities, the CPT has stated that a 'satisfactory programme of activities is of crucial importance for the well-being of prisoners',[154] and has expressed particular concern that remand prisoners are not left to languish in their cells for weeks or months. The CPT has indicated that even remand prisoners should be able to spend at least eight hours a day out of their cells, and sentenced prisoners significantly longer. The requirement that all prisoners should be offered the opportunity to take at least one hour of exercise in the open air each day is seen by the CPT as fundamental. This includes prisoners undergoing cellular confinement as a punishment. The CPT adds that it is 'axiomatic that outdoor exercise facilities should be reasonably spacious and whenever possible offer shelter from inclement weather'.[155] Its position on hygiene has hardened on a number of points over the years. For example in the Second General Report the Committee indicated that it 'did not like' the practice of 'slopping out' but has subsequently gone on in some country reports to describe it as 'degrading'.[156] The CPT favours locating a toilet facility in an annex to the cell, or providing prisoners with access to external toilets at all times without undue delay. It has further indicated that access to bathing facilities once a week is an 'absolute minimum' and that ideally prisoners should have access much more frequently than this, especially where they are working. Prisoners should also be presented with clean bedlinen on arrival and should be allowed to change this more regularly than once a fortnight. In respect of heating, lighting and ventilation the CPT has been reluctant to prescribe optimum temperatures but has on occasion commented when it has found conditions to be too hot or cold during its country visits. It has taken a strong line on the need for prisoners to have access to natural light and fresh air, criticizing in its Eleventh General report the practice, in some countries, of fitting metal shutters or plates to cell windows as security devices.

5.80 The CPT has stressed that the issue of conditions is cumulative, and the extent to which conditions in any particular prison amount to degrading treatment can be exacerbated or reduced by other factors in addition to the above, notably relationships between prisoners and staff and prisoners' access to the outside world. Certainly this has been the approach it has pursued in its visits to the United Kingdom.[157] In the first of these it found conditions at Leeds, Brixton and Wandsworth prisons to be degrading especially due to overcrowding, lack of integral sanitation and inadequate regime activities.[158] Although in its subsequent

---

[154] Second General Report, para 47.

[155] ibid, para 48.

[156] For a discussion of the evolution of this position see R Morgan and M Evans, 'CPT Standards: An Overview' in R Morgan and M Evans (eds), *Protecting Prisoners: The Standards of the European Committee for the Prevention of Torture in Context* (Oxford, 1999) 39.

[157] For an overview of these see S Shaw, 'The CPT's Visits to the United Kingdom' in Morgan and Evans, ibid, 265.

[158] CPT/Inf (91) 15.

reports the Committee observed that conditions in UK prisons had improved, it commented in its most recent report in 2001 that much still remained to be done to ensure that the Prison Service meets its own objective of holding all prisoners in a 'safe, decent and healthy environment'.[159] In particular the 2001 report expressed concern at overcrowding in parts of the UK prison system, noting that at Pentonville two prisoners were detained in cells measuring 8.5 square metres, and that the requirement that prisoners be offered an hour in the open air each day was not being honoured because of staff shortages or agreed working conditions.

Increasingly reports of the CPT are invoked by applicants to the ECtHR in claim-   **5.81**
ing breaches of Article 3 of the ECHR. The court has made it clear that findings by the CPT that detention conditions in a particular prison are 'degrading' will not ensure that an application brought by a prisoner detained in those conditions will succeed.[160] In *Aerts v Belgium* a majority of the court concluded that while the conditions in the psychiatric wing of Lantin Prison were found at the material time by the CPT to be 'below the minimum acceptable', the applicant had not demonstrated that he had suffered any serious ill effects as a result of them.[161] However, the court has paid regular attention to these reports and, in particular, has drawn upon the CPT's standards laid down in its general reports when assessing whether different aspects of prison conditions cumulatively amount to a breach of Article 3.[162]

UN Provisions: Articles 7 and 10 of the International Covenant on Civil and Political Rights and the Convention Against Torture

Like the ECHR, the ICCPR contains a prohibition on torture, inhuman or   **5.82**
degrading treatment or punishment (Article 7). In addition it also provides that '[a]ll persons deprived of their liberty shall be treated with humanity and with respect for the inherent dignity of the human person' (Article 10). The UN Human Rights Committee (HRC), which oversees enforcement of the ICCPR, has considered a significant number of cases arising out of prison conditions. Although in its early jurisprudence the HRC tended to conflate findings of violations of Article 7 with those of Article 10,[163] more recently it has sought to distinguish the two. As the authors of a leading casebook on the ICCPR observe,

---

[159] CPT/Inf (2002) 6.

[160] For an overview of decisions in this area see W Peukert, 'The European Convention for the Prevention of Torture and the European Convention on Human Rights' in Morgan and Evans, op cit, n 156 above, 85.

[161] (2000) 29 EHRR 50.

[162] See especially *Peers v Greece* Application 28524/95 (2001) 33 EHRR 51, where the court drew both on the general standards on overcrowding and on a CPT report of a visit to the prison where the applicant was detained.

[163] See, generally, P Ghandi, 'The Human Rights Committee and Articles 7 and 10 of the International Covenant on Civil and Political Rights 1966' (1990) 13 Dalhousie LJ 758; S Livingstone, 'Prisoners Rights' in D Harris and S Joseph (eds), *The International Covenant on Civil and Political Rights and United Kingdom Law* (Oxford, 1995) 270–285.

violations of Article 10 appear to be found in respect of general prison conditions, while those of Article 7 relate more to treatment meted out to a particular individual, though the distinction still lacks a certain clarity.[164]

5.83 In respect of both Articles the HRC's approach is to look at the conditions as a whole, including reference to the duration of the conditions and their impact on the applicant. However, even relatively brief actions can amount to breaches of Article 7 if sufficiently serious, for example in *Garcia v Ecuador* where the applicant was chained to a chair throughout a night without even being given a glass of water.[165] The HRC has expressed particular concern as regards isolation of prisoners and incommunicado detention. In *Shaw v Jamaica*[166] incommunicado detention for eight months was found to breach Article 7, and in *Mukong v Cameroon*[167] the HRC reached a similar conclusion where the applicant had been kept locked in his cell for several days, deprived of food and threatened with torture and death. Denial of medical treatment, especially where this results in a deterioration of the prisoner's mental or physical condition and mistreatment of prisoners by prison staff may also amount to breaches of Article 7. In *Edwards v Jamaica*[168] the HRC found a breach of Article 7 where the applicant had been detained for 10 years in a cell measuring 6 feet by 14 feet, was permitted out of the cell for only three and a half hours a day and was provided with no recreational facilities. The length of time in which the applicant was kept in these conditions appears to have been especially influential in leading the HRC to make a finding of a violation of Article 7 in this case, but most of such cases are decided under Article 10. Many result from the conditions on death row in Jamaica's St Catherine's District Prison. Although the HRC has rejected the approach of the Privy Council and ECtHR that the length of time on death row may in itself amount to inhuman or degrading treatment,[169] it has indicated that the conditions in which prisoners await execution may, when combined with the length of that period, result in a violation of Articles 7 and 10.

5.84 Most of the findings of violations of Article 10 concern overcrowded and unhygienic conditions, which have persisted for a significant period of time and from which the prisoner has little respite. A typical case is *McLeod v Jamaica*,[170] where the applicant was detained in a cell measuring 2 square metres for 23 hours a day, spending much of his waking day in darkness. Other decisions have concerned

---

[164] See S Joseph, J Schultz and M Castan (eds), *The International Covenant on Civil and Political Rights: Cases, Materials and Commentary* (Oxford, 2000) 197.
[165] Communication No 319/1988.
[166] No 704/1996.
[167] No 458/1991.
[168] No 529/1993.
[169] Notably in *Johnson v Jamaica* No 588/1994 (1997) 4 IHRR 21.
[170] No 734/1997 (1999) 6 IHRR 19.

the lack of adequate bedding,[171] natural light[172] and the preparation of food in unhygienic conditions.[173] Although some of these decisions have invoked the UN Standard Minimum Rules, which date from 1955, there has been surprisingly little reference to the more recent and exacting UN Body of Principles for the Protection of All Persons under Any Form of Detention or Imprisonment (1988).

As indicated in Chapter 3, the UN Convention Against Torture also provides for a mechanism whereby individual complaints of torture, inhuman or degrading treatment or punishment may be lodged with the Human Rights Committee. To date, however, most of its jurisprudence has concerned challenges to decisions to extradite or expel people to countries where they may face torture, rather than challenges to prison conditions. **5.85**

---

[171] *McTaggart v Jamaica* No 749/1997 (1999) 6 IHRR 24.
[172] *Yassen and Thomas v Guyana* No 676/1996 (1999) 6 IHRR 6, no opportunity to experience natural light except for one hour a day out of cell.
[173] *Matthews v Trinidad and Tobago* No 569/1993 (1999) 6 IHRR 15, food prepared and eaten less than 15 feet from an open sewer.

6

HEALTHCARE IN PRISONS

6.01 The provision of healthcare raises particular problems in the prison context. As with any large institution, the population of prisons contains within it a range of health problems. These problems may well be exacerbated in the prison environment through factors such as confinement, lack of exercise, violence, and drugs.[1] Attending to the mental and physical health needs of prisoners within the closed environment of prisons already poses significant problems for medical practitioners. However, the medical profession also has another role within the prison environment, one which relates to the operation of prisons as part of the criminal justice system. Doctors are involved in providing reports on prisoners for trial or parole purposes. They may also have to decide whether prisoners are fit for work or punishment. At times prison authorities have placed great faith in the ability of the medical profession to change the offending behaviour of those imprisoned or control their conduct while in prison. Whether the medical profession can reconcile these 'welfare' and 'discipline' roles, and to what standards they should be made accountable, are questions at the heart of the provision of healthcare in prison.

---

[1] The complex health needs of the prison population are summarized in British Medial Association, 'Prison Medicine: A crisis waiting to break' (London, 2001), available online at www.bma.org.uk.

A. International Standards on Healthcare in Prison

6.02   The provision of medical care in prisons has been a focus of concern for many international standard setting bodies, both within the field of medicine specifically and more widely. A good starting point is the recognition by both the UN Human Rights Committee and the European Commission on Human Rights that lack of medical treatment can violate international prohibitions on torture, inhuman or degrading treatment.[2] The conditions in which this has been found are, however, quite extreme, with the Human Rights Committee, in particular, appearing reluctant to find a breach where at least some medical treatment has been provided for serious illness or injuries. The European Court of Human Rights (ECtHR) has indicated that Article 3 of the European Convention on Human Rights (ECHR) requires that the conditions of a prisoner's detention 'do not subject him to distress or hardship of an intensity exceeding the unavoidable level of suffering inherent in detention and that, given the practical demands of imprisonment his health and well being are adequately secured by, among other things, providing him with the requisite medical attention'.[3] The guarantee in Article 7 of the Civil and Political Rights Covenant (ICCPR) that 'no one shall be subjected without his free consent to medical or scientific experimentation' was also clearly influenced by the experience of experiments being conducted on prisoners in the prisons and concentration camps of Nazi Germany. The standards devised by the United Nations and the Council of Europe with regard to the treatment of those imprisoned both include specific sections on medical services. Rule 26 of the European Prison Rules, for example, indicates that 'at every institution there shall be available the services of at least one qualified general practitioner' and that the services of a qualified dentist shall be available to every prisoner. It also indicates that where hospital facilities are provided in a prison 'their equipment, furnishings and pharmaceutical supplies shall be suitable for the medical care and treatment of sick prisoners, and there shall be a staff of suitably qualified officers'.[4]

6.03   Perhaps the most detailed set of standards is that contained in the set of principles of medical ethics for prison medical staff adopted by the UN General Assembly in

---

[2] See, eg, *Spence v Jamaica*, Communication 599/1994, (1997) 4 IHRR 359; *Douglas v Jamaica*, Communication 571/1994, (1997) 4 IHRR 387; *Hurtado v Switzerland*, Series A No 280–A; *D v UK* (1997)24 EHRR 423.

[3] See *Kudla v Poland* Application 30210/96 (2002) 35 EHRR 11. The court also indicated that Art 3 could not be interpreted as laying down a general obligation to release or transfer a detainee to a civilian hospital on health grounds. Despite the applicant's suicidal condition in this case it found no breach of Art 3 as he had undergone regular psychiatric examination and treatment.

[4] European Prison Rule 26(2).

1982.[5] While these principles have no binding legal force, they do represent an important code of conduct, and the concluding document of the Vienna World Conference on Human Rights in 1993 called again on States to give effect to them. Central to these principles are the ideas that the role of medical staff in prisons is purely that of looking after the medical needs of the prisoner and that there should be equality between healthcare offered to prisoners and that offered to the rest of the population. Principle 1, for example, states that health personnel must provide treatment to prisoners 'of the same quality and standard as is afforded to those who are not imprisoned or detained'. Principle 3 states that it is a contravention of medical ethics for health personnel to be involved in any professional relationship with prisoners 'which is not solely to evaluate, protect or improve their physical and mental health'. Although the Principles do envisage health personnel being involved in certifying prisoners as fit for treatment or punishment, this is stated to be a contravention of medical ethics where it 'may adversely affect their physical or mental health and . . . is not in accordance with the relevant international instruments'.[6] In view of recent controversies over the use of physical restraints of prisoners undergoing medical treatment in the United Kingdom, Principle 5 is worth quoting in full:

> It is a contravention of medical ethics for health personnel, especially physicians, to participate in any procedure for restraining a prisoner or detainee unless such a procedure is determined in accordance with purely medical criteria as being necessary for the protection of the physical or mental health or the safety of the prisoner or detainee himself, or of his fellow prisoners or detainees, or of his guardians, and presents no hazard to his physical or mental health.

The reports of the European Committee for the Prevention of Torture (CPT) have also been a useful source of international good practice in relation to health care in prisons. In its Third General Report the CPT offered some general observations on the provision of healthcare in prisons.[7] The CPT also stressed as a central principle that prisoners are entitled to the same level of medical care as persons living in the community at large. This is arguably a stronger requirement than that currently contained in European Prison Rule 26(2). The CPT offers guidance on such matters as access to a doctor, patient's consent and confidentiality, professional independence, and professional competence. We will return to what the CPT has had to say on some of these matters when we look at specific aspects of health care in prisons. At this point, however, it is worth highlighting the CPT's

---

[5] *The Principles of Medical Ethics Relevant to the Role of Health Personnel, Particularly Physicians, in the Protection of Prisoners and Detainees against Torture and Other Cruel, Inhuman or Degrading Treatment or Punishment*, UN Doc A/37/51 (1982). Para 24 of SO 13 on Healthcare indicates that medical officers should at all time have regard to these principles when carrying out their duties.

[6] Principle 4(b).

[7] CPT/Inf(93) 12, 13–23. For a more general discussion of the role of the CPT see Ch 3 of this book.

observations on professional independence. The CPT recognizes that the peculiar position of prison medical staff 'can give rise to difficult ethical choices and conflicts'. It suggests that, in order to guarantee independence, it is important that healthcare personnel in prison 'should be aligned as closely as possible with the mainstream of health care provision in the community at large'.[8] In the interests of safeguarding the doctor/patient relationship it recommends that:

> he should not be asked to certify that a prisoner is fit to undergo punishment. Nor should he carry out any body searches or examinations requested by an authority, except in an emergency when no other doctor can be called in.[9]

This is a particularly strong statement of the need to ensure that the doctor's primary responsibility is to the medical needs of the prisoner rather than the discipline needs of the prison. As we shall see, it is not clear that the legal framework of prison healthcare in the United Kingdom is adequate to ensure this.

B. The Organization of Healthcare in Prison

6.04 Healthcare in prisons in England and Wales is provided by the Health Care Service for Prisoners (HCSP). This is the latest title for a division of the Prison Service formerly known as the Prison Medical Service. The HCSP is headed by the Director of Prison Health, who is a member of the Prison Service Board and also heads the Prison Health Policy Unit. There has been frequent discussion as to whether healthcare services in prisons should be provided by the National Health Service. In 1979 the Royal College of Psychiatrists called for the integration of the prison medical service into the NHS, and although neither the House of Commons Social Services Select Committee[10] nor the Woolf Report was prepared to go that far, the then Chief Inspector of Prisons subsequently added his voice to those calling for this change.[11] Advocates of integration argue that it would end the isolation of prison healthcare staff from current developments in standards and training in the NHS, hence raising the standard of healthcare in prisons; that it would ensure greater continuity in healthcare for prisoners between the prison and the community they came from and may return to; that it would integrate prison healthcare staff into accountability procedures in the NHS; that it might reduce the cost of healthcare in prisons;[12] and, finally, that it might send a clearer

---

[8] As the complaints in *Silver v UK* Series A No 61 (1983) 5 EHRR 347 related to correspondence between 1972 and 1977 the Home Office had amended and published its Standing Orders by the time the case reached the court. See also Ch 7 for a detailed discussion of the case law on prisoners' correspondence.

[9] ibid, para 73.

[10] *Third Report from the Social Services Committee: Prison Medical Service*, Paper 72–1 (London, 1986).

[11] See *Prisoner or Patient?: A New Strategy for Health Care in Prisons* (London, 1996).

[12] ibid, 13, indicates that the HCSP spends £1,000 per prison place per year on healthcare as opposed to £415 per year spent by the NHS on age group 16–64.

signal to governors and medical officers themselves that they are healthcare professionals first and prison staff second. Opponents of such a change argue that it neglects the specific organizational problems of providing healthcare in prisons and suggest that NHS authorities may have difficulty with accommodating the specific statutory responsibilities of prison medical staff.[13]

To date these recommendations have not been acted upon, but it is clear that the HCSP has sought to move closer to NHS practices and standards in recent years. After a 1990 efficiency scrutiny a Health Advisory Committee for the HCSP was established and the HCSP published a series of Healthcare Standards for prison healthcare personnel, which were designed to approximate to current NHS standards. Although these standards have no legal force they are worth considering as guides to good practice in disputes over the required standard of healthcare in prison, and we will refer to them during the course of this chapter. The relationship between the HCSP and NHS is also strengthened by the fact that much medical care in prison, notably psychiatric care and substance abuse counselling, is provided by NHS staff on a contract basis. **6.05**

However, even these developments left much to be desired in terms of ensuring parity of treatment between prisoners and NHS patients. In 1999 the Department of Health, the National Assembly for Wales and the Home Office established two new national units—the Prison Health Policy Unit and the Prison Health Task Force—jointly run by the Prison Service and the NHS, with the aim of reviewing and improving standards of healthcare in prison. These two bodies came into being on 1 April 2000, recognizing that: **6.06**

> Although the greater part of most prisoners' health care is delivered by the Prison Service rather than the NHS, it has always been the aim to ensure that prisoners get decent health care to standards equivalent to that in the NHS. But it is generally recognised that this aim is not being met; in some places the gulf between NHS standards of care and prisoner care is very disturbing. In particular there are problems with inadequate provision for prisoners with mental health problems and with the recruitment and retention of properly trained healthcare staff.[14]

Under this new initiative, every prison has to carry out a Health Needs Assessment with a view to identifying problem areas. There is a detailed programme of work to improve healthcare in all medical areas, and to revise the Healthcare Standards, which had been found to be inadequate in many areas.[15] It is too early to know whether this development will produce tangible benefits for prisoners, but the

---

[13] This issue has been raised throughout Europe, but only Norway has fully integrated healthcare in prisons into its national health system. For a discussion see K Tomasevski, *Prison Health: International Standards and National Practices in Europe* (Helsinki, 1992) 12.

[14] Prison Health Policy Unit and Task Force, *Prison Health Handbook* (London, 2000), Introduction.

[15] See (2000) 1 Prison Health Newsletter 7. In particular, Healthcare Standards 1 and 5 (reception screening) and 8 (clinical management of substance misusers) are under review.

recognition of the serious problems faced by the prison medical service, and the commitment to changing them, is certainly to be welcomed. However, the British Medical Association has warned that the problems faced by healthcare services in prison are deep-rooted, stemming from an unsupportive culture in which prison governors interfere with doctors' clinical judgment, staff become demoralized and recruitment becomes difficult, and services are chronically underfunded. Only with proper funding and support, and a genuine recognition that medical staff should be given the freedom to treat prisoners as they think appropriate, rather than as the prison thinks expedient, will there be a long-term improvement in prison healthcare.[16]

C. The Legal Position of the Prison Medical Officer

6.07 Section 7(1) of the Prison Act 1952 indicates that every prison shall have a medical officer. At larger prisons the medical officer may be assisted by a number of junior medical officers, and at all prisons he will be assisted by a number of nursing staff. Some of these will be civilian nurses, and some will be prison officers with or without nursing qualifications. As the Chief Inspector of Prisons has observed, this can lead to considerable confusion for a prisoner.[17] At smaller prisons, especially, the medical officer may be a local GP who provides his or her services on a part time contract basis. However the HCSP continues to have difficulties in finding sufficient staff for medical officer posts. According to reports up to 20 per cent of medical officer posts are not filled.[18]

6.08 Apart from s 7, and the rather curious hangover of s 17, which indicates that a medical officer may not apply painful tests to detect whether a prisoner is malingering or for any other purpose *without the consent of the Secretary of State or the Board of Visitors* (one wonders whether it would be consistent with international obligations to do so even with their permission), the Prison Act has little to say on

---

[16] British Medical Association, 'Prison Medicine: A crisis waiting to break' (London, 2001), available online at www.bma.org.uk.

[17] 'At present, a patient, presenting him or herself for medical attention, is faced by nursing staff with a variety of uniforms, grades and qualifications within the same establishment': *Prisoner or Patient?: A New Strategy for Health Care in Prisons* (London, 1996) 2.

[18] See The Independent, 26 January 1995, and British Medical Association, n 1 above. However, the Department of Health, with the Prison Service, began to address recruitment issues with two reports, 'Nursing in Prisons' (October 2000) and 'Doctors working in Prisons' (December 2001). These reports made a number of recommendations for increasing recruitment, including improved pay and conditions, clinical independence and the introduction of specific qualifications in prison healthcare. A summary of recruitment strategies can be found at www.doh.gov.uk/prisonhealth/faq.htm.

medical personnel in a prison.[19] More detailed guidance must be sought from the Prison Rules and Standing Order 13 on Health Care. Prison Rule 20(1) indicates that the medical officer of the prison 'shall have the care of the health, mental and physical, of the prisoners in that prison'. Paragraph 1 of SO 13 indicates that the most senior of the medical officers by grade will be the Managing Medical Officer and he or she is accountable both to the Director of the HCSP for 'maintaining appropriate standards of medical and nursing care' and to the governor of the prison 'for the general performance, efficiency and cost effectiveness of the medical, nursing and pharmaceutical services and the conduct of the medical staff'.[20]

Duties of Examination

Standing Orders indicate that prisoners must be examined by a medical officer 'as soon as possible and no later than 24 hours' after their reception into prison and after temporary absences. The Healthcare Standards lay down guidelines on how such examinations should be conducted. It has been argued in the past that such examinations lack privacy and comprehensiveness.[21] Current Healthcare Standards indicate that initial screening should at least be conducted by an appropriately trained healthcare worker, who should see the prisoner for an average of ten minutes.[22] This should be followed up by a full examination by a doctor within 24 hours.[23] The medical officer must also conduct surgeries for all prisoners who wish to see a doctor and visit prisoners undergoing in-patient treatment or observation. Standing Orders indicate that prisoners placed in special accommodation or in any kind of mechanical restraint should be visited at least twice daily; those in disciplinary cellular confinement every day; and in Good Order and Disciplinary solitary confinement at least every three days, with every day being preferable. Those on 'own protection' rule 45 should be visited every seven days. It is perhaps surprising that less frequent visiting is required in relation to prisoners on GOAD than in disciplinary solitary confinement even though the former often lasts much longer than the latter. Indeed, the Prison Rules only require daily visiting in respect of prisoners undergoing disciplinary solitary confinement. However, Circular Instructions suggest that daily visits should also

6.09

---

[19] However s 22 (which gives the Secretary of State power to have a prisoner temporarily removed for medical treatment) and s 28 (which permits temporary release on the grounds of ill health) would obviously require the advice of the medical officer.

[20] The Managing Medical Officer is assisted in the performance of his duties by a Health Care Manager, defined by para 8 of SO 13 as the most senior nursing officer. The Chief Inspector of Prisons has argued that this division of managerial responsibilities has led to confusion and a lack of overall management of healthcare provision in prisons. See Chief Inspector of Prisons, *Annual Report for 1994–95* (London, 1996), para 5.07.

[21] Notably by the European Committee for the Prevention of Torture in its report on the 1990 visit to Leeds and Brixton, CPT/Inf (91) 15 at 47.

[22] Health Care Standard 1.1(e).

[23] Health Care Standard 1.2.

be made to those on GOAD rule 45. Prisoners should also be separately examined before discharge or transfer. It is for the medical officer to decide whether a prisoner who has fallen ill should be admitted to the prison hospital or requires treatment in an outside hospital. In the latter case, Standing Orders indicate that approval must be sought from headquarters, with separate approval required from the relevant unit when a Category A prisoner is involved. Only where 'the medical officer is of the opinion that any delay would endanger the prisoner's life will he or she personally authorise the prisoner's removal'.[24] A prisoner removed to an outside hospital remains in the legal custody of the prison and subject to security restraints which may include handcuffing while in hospital.[25] Prison Rule 21(1) indicates that a medical officer has a duty to report to the governor on the case of any prisoner whose health 'is likely to be injuriously affected by continued imprisonment or any conditions of imprisonment'. Where he does so, the governor is then under a duty to send this report to the Secretary of State.

6.10 In addition to a duty to provide medical care, the Prison Rules place the medical officer under a duty regularly to inspect prison food,[26] and Standing Orders indicate that he or she should inspect the prison twice a year with regard to general conditions for health and hygiene.[27]

Duties of Certification

6.11 The prison medical officer also has a number of obligations which involve him more closely in the disciplinary aspects of the prison. He must consider whether a prisoner is unfit for work,[28] whether he is fit for adjudication, and whether he is in a fit state of health for solitary confinement, either as a punishment[29] or on GOAD grounds.[30] The medical officer's approval is also necessary to place a prisoner under restraint, and Prison Rule 49(3) indicates that the governor shall give effect to any recommendations which the medical officer makes in relation to placing a prisoner under restraint. The extent of the medical officer's involvement in these decisions and the fact that, as a member of the prison staff, the medical

---

[24] SO 13, para 57.

[25] Guidance contained in the *Security Manual*, paras 60.20–60.21, indicates that restraints should be applied in the case of prisoners from closed prisons and must be removed at the request of senior healthcare staff only where immediate treatment is required, where the prisoner is in pain, or where these pose an immediate risk to health. Where these conditions are not met staff may keep the restraints in place if they are in any doubt whether a risk of escape remains.

[26] Prison Rule 24(3).

[27] SO 13, para 6. The inspection should cover 'heating, ventilation, light, sanitary conditions, water supply, food, clothing, bedding, the general state of cleanliness and other matters as he or she considers appropriate'. The report is to be submitted to the governor who should then send it to the Health Care Directorate at headquarters.

[28] r 31(2).

[29] r 58.

[30] r 45(3).

officer remains under the general rule 62 obligation of all officers to 'conform to these Rules and the rules and regulations of the prison, to assist and support the governor in their maintenance and obey his lawful instructions' has led some to question to what extent a prison medical officer can retain professional independence and ensure that his or her first obligation is to the patients. As one commentator has observed, the prison medical officer:

> is part and parcel of the prison hierarchy intimately involved in the maintenance of order and discipline. His consent is necessary before a prisoner can be kept under special restraint or before a prisoner can be subject to an award of cellular confinement. No individual, however skilled and compassionate a doctor, can maintain a normal prisoner-patient relationship with a man who the next day he may acquiesce in subjecting to solitary confinement.[31]

In addition to the legal structure, many prison medical staff observe that their dependence on the prison governor for resources and security further compromises their independence. As we have seen earlier, the CPT has recommended that prison medical staff should not be involved in certifying as fit for punishment prisoners for whom they may also be providing healthcare. Doctors have also been involved in urging their colleagues in prison medicine not to be too eager to acquiesce in security demands for restraints to be applied to prisoners.[32] Yet while the resources available for healthcare in prisons remain limited and the use of punishment does have adverse effects on people's health, the need for some involvement of the prison medical staff in these decisions seems inevitable.[33] Minimizing the effect of this involvement on their independence remains a constant struggle.

D. The Prisoner's Right to the Provision of Healthcare

In addition to setting out the duties of medical officers, Prison Rule 20 also con- **6.12** fers some rights on prisoners. Rule 20(2), for example, indicates that every request by a prisoner to see the medical officer shall be recorded by the prison officer to whom it is made and promptly passed on to the medical officer. The Rules do not indicate whether the medical officer then has an obligation to see the prisoner who has made the request, but as we have seen already, SO 13 indicates that the medical officer has a duty to arrange surgeries for all prisoners who have requested a doctor. Failure to respond to requests, especially if a serious illness or injury is involved, might well be a breach of human rights prohibitions against inhuman or degrading treatment.

---

[31] M Brazier, 'Prison Doctors and their Involuntary Patients' [1982] PL 283, 285.
[32] British Medical Association, *Guidance for Doctors Providing Medical Care and Treatment to those Detained in Prison* (London, 1996).
[33] Indeed this is required by international standards such as r 38(1) of the European Prison Rules.

6.13 Prison Rule 20(5) states that unconvicted prisoners have the right, providing they agree to pay any expense involved, to be treated by a registered doctor or dentist of their choice. Convicted prisoners have the right to an examination by a doctor of their choice only when this is necessary for the pursuit of legal proceedings which they have initiated.[34] Although Standing Orders make provision for a medical officer to seek a second opinion, and Prison Rule 20(4) suggests that he should do so if time permits before performing any serious operation, it does not appear that a convicted prisoner has any right to a second opinion.[35] Neither the Rules nor the Standing Orders contain any guidance on whether female prisoners are entitled to be treated by a female medical practitioner. It appears that within the Prison Service this right is recognized but a woman prisoner exercising it may find that she then faces a considerable wait for treatment.[36]

E. Confidentiality and Access to Records

6.14 General legal principles of doctor–patient confidentiality apply in prisons. Therefore it will normally be a breach of confidentiality for a doctor to reveal to a third party (who is not involved in the medical care of the prisoner) anything disclosed or discovered in his treatment of his prisoner-patient. However, there are exceptions to this principle where the information relates to matters which pose a real threat to the physical safety of third parties. The Court of Appeal recognized that confidentiality involved a balancing exercise and would not be breached in these circumstances in *W v Egdell*.[37] There a doctor was asked to prepare a report on W, who had killed five people, for the purpose of litigation regarding W's possible release from a secure hospital. After W withdrew his application for release,

---

[34] Prison Rule 38(1): this examination may be in the sight but out of the hearing of a prison officer.

[35] Principle 25 of the UN Body of Principles for the Protection of All Persons under Any Form of Detention or Imprisonment, UN Doc A/43/49 (1988), indicates that all imprisoned persons should have the right to 'request or petition a judicial or other authority' for a second medical opinion or examination. It is not clear that this principle is currently given effect to in the UK.

[36] See HM Chief Inspector of Prisons, *Women in Prison: A Thematic Review* (London, 1997), para 9.24; HM Inspector of Prisons, *Follow-up to Women in Prison: A Thematic Review* (London, 2001), para 2.102. The Chief Inspector also notes, at para 2.98, that 'we continue to have concerns that the health care needs of women might be swamped by those of the majority male prisoner population. Despite the fact that a specific health care standard for women is in preparation, we continue to favour the appointment of an Operational Head of Women's Health with overall responsibility for health care in prisons where women are held.' See also CPT, *Tenth General Report*, CPT/Inf (2000) 13, para 32, '[i]nsofar as women deprived of their liberty are concerned, ensuring that [the] principle of equivalence of care is respected will require that health care is provided by medical practitioners and nurses who have specific training in women's health issues, including in gynaecology'.

[37] [1990] Ch 359. A recent analysis of the correct approach to the confidentiality of medical records can be found in the decision of the Court of Appeal in *A Health Authority v X (No 1)* [2002] 2 All ER 780.

Dr Egdell discovered that the director of the hospital in which W was currently detained was unaware of some of the things he noted in his report, including W's longstanding interest in firearms and explosives. He therefore sent the director a copy of the report. In finding no breach of confidence the Court of Appeal accepted that these matters did raise threats to the physical security of the director and his staff and noted that Dr Egdell had made his disclosure only to a very limited number of people.[38] A doctor may therefore disclose information received during a consultation which indicates a clear threat to the safety of staff or other prisoners,[39] but not where it does not reach this level of threat.

The Managing Medical Officer is responsible for ensuring that proper medical **6.15** records are kept on prisoners.[40] An Inmate Medical Record (IMR) should be opened for each prisoner on reception and should be transferred with a prisoner if he moves on to another prison. Medical officers may request prisoners' medical records from the doctor with whom they are registered outside the prison, but these can only be made available with the prisoner's consent. Under the Access to Health Records Act 1990 prisoners can obtain all medical records created after 1 November 1991 which relate to them.[41] Access to earlier records must also be given where it would be necessary to make the subsequent records intelligible. However, a doctor may refuse to disclose information where he feels that it would be likely to cause serious harm to the mental or physical health of the patient or of any other individual, or where it is likely to identify any other individual.[42] Such a discretion is of particular importance with regard to psychiatric reports in the prison context. Prisoners may also seek the disclosure of health records during litigation where they are regarded as relevant to the conclusion of the litigation. Again, however, the courts have a power to deny access if this is regarded as not in the public interest, a ground which operates on much the same basis as the discretion to refuse in the Access to Health Records Act.

---

[38] Contrast *X v Y* [1988] 2 All ER 648 where disclosure to national newspapers of the fact that two doctors working in a hospital had AIDS (a fact discovered from reading their medical reports) was found to be a breach of confidence sufficient to warrant an injunction. The same result was reached by the Court of Appeal in a similar situation in *H (A Healthcare Worker) v Associated Newspapers Ltd* [2002] EMLR 23.

[39] Though he does not appear to be under a duty in general medical law to do so: see M Brazier, *Medicine, Patients and the Law* (2nd edn, London, 1992) 58.

[40] SO 13, para 5.

[41] Access to Health Records Act 1990, s 3(1). Access can be refused under s 5(1) if a doctor is of the opinion that disclosure is likely to cause serious harm to the physical or mental health of the patient or other person; or where it could identify another person (other than a medical practitioner) who provided the information.

[42] ibid, s 5(1). The Discretionary Lifer Panel Rules contain a similar provision.

F. Consent to Treatment

6.16 As with people in the outside community, prisoners, providing that they are of the requisite physical and mental competence, have a right to refuse treatment. Therefore a doctor may not impose treatment on a prisoner who refuses to accept it, even when such treatment is in the prisoner's best interests.[43] There is an exception where a prisoner has been rendered temporarily incompetent and emergency treatment is required.[44] Competence is defined in terms of whether someone has 'sufficient understanding to make an informed choice'.[45] In light of these parameters it must be doubtful whether the current guidance in para 25 of SO 13 is in conformity with the law. This indicates that in general prisoners are free to accept or decline any medical treatment offered to them, but that invasive medical procedures may be carried out without the patient's consent where without such procedures 'the patient's life would be endangered, serious harm to him or her or to others would be likely, or there would be an irreversible deterioration in the prisoner's condition'. In the leading medical case *of Re C (Adult: Refusal of Treatment)*[46] Thorpe J granted an injunction in respect of a paranoid schizophrenic who refused to allow doctors to amputate his foot after he contracted gangrene, despite the doctors involved testifying that there was an 85 per cent chance of death occurring if this was not done. Noting that, despite his delusions that he was an internationally recognized doctor in practice, C satisfied the threefold test of (1) comprehending and retaining treatment information; (2) retaining it; and (3) weighing it in the balance to arrive at a choice, Thorpe J concluded that his consent could not be overridden.[47]

---

[43] See *Re T (Adult: Refusal of Treatment)* [1993] Fam 95; *Re C (Adult: Refusal of Treatment)* [1994] 1 WLR 290. See also the discussion in Prisoners' Legal Rights Group Bulletin No 7, and R Harper, *Medical Treatment and the Law* (Family Law, 1999).

[44] See *Re F (Mental Patient: Sterilisation)* [1990] 2 AC 1.

[45] See *Re W (A Minor) (Medical Treatment: Court's Jurisdiction)* [1993] Fam 64.

[46] [1994] 1 WLR 290. *Re C* was applied in the prison context in *Re W (Adult: Refusal of medical treatment)*, The Independent, 17 June 2002. The applicant was a 30-year-old Category A prisoner in a Close Supervision Centre. He wounded his leg and was preventing it from healing, in an attempt to be transferred back to a secure hospital for treatment for his mental health problems. Three psychiatrists formed the view that, although he had a mental disorder, his mental capacity was commensurate with the decision to refuse treatment, even if the refusal of treatment was life threatening. He applied to the court for a declaration that he had the capacity to refuse medical treatment: the declaration was granted by Butler-Sloss P.

[47] A similar result was reached in *St George's Healthcare Trust v S* [1999] Fam 26, in which the court held that S, who was 36 weeks pregnant and suffering from pre-eclampsia, could not be forced to submit to treatment against her will, despite the serious risk posed by her condition to her life and that of the unborn child.

Food and Fluid Refusal

The issue of whether prisoners who go on hunger strike may be force fed has raised **6.17** particularly contentious issues with regard to consent. Despite a (much criticized) precedent from the suffragette period that prisoners on hunger strike should be force-fed,[48] the Prison Service appears to have taken the view in recent years that prisoners refusing food or fluids should not be forcibly fed while they remain capable of rational judgment. This approach was followed during the 1981 hunger strike at the Maze prison in Northern Ireland when ten prisoners starved themselves to death and artificial feeding was resorted to only in the case of prisoners who lost consciousness and whose families consented. It is also reflected in current Standing Orders and a Healthcare Service 'Dear Doctor Letter' of 1996 which indicate that a prisoner refusing food and/or fluids must be informed of the likely consequences of his actions and that he may only be given food or fluid without his consent if his capacity for rational action is impaired by illness. Only when that situation is reached does it lie in the clinical judgment of the medical officer (after full consultation with an outside consultant) to consider resorting to artificial feeding.[49] Instead, emphasis is placed on closely monitoring the prisoner's condition and providing him with information on his changing medical condition and prospects. The High Court has endorsed this policy in *R v Home Secretary, ex p Robb*,[50] in which it granted the Home Office a declaration that it had no obligation to resort to artificial feeding of a prisoner on hunger strike who retained the capacity for rational judgment. In that case, Thorpe J took the view that this situation was governed by the general law on capacity, and indicated that even if death resulted from hunger striking it would not amount to suicide.[51] He

---

[48] *Leigh v Gladstone* (1909) 26 TLR 139; for a critical review see G Zellick, 'The Forcible Feeding of Prisoners: An Examination of the Legality of Enforced Therapy' [1976] PL 153.

[49] SO 13, para 40–1. This position is also endorsed by the Tokyo Declaration of 10 October 1975 on Guidelines for Medical Doctors Concerning Torture and Other Cruel, Inhuman or Degrading Treatment or Punishment. In *R v Collins, ex p Brady* [2000] Lloyd's Rep Med 355, the claimant, a prisoner on hunger strike, applied for judicial review of the decision of his responsible medical officer to force feed him pursuant to s 63 of the Mental Health Act 1983, which provides that 'the consent of a patient shall not be required for any medical treatment given to him for the mental disorder from which he is suffering . . . if the treatment is given by or under the direction of the responsible medical officer'. Maurice Kay J refused the application. He considered that, since s 63 was a derogation from the rights of self determination and bodily integrity, the courts would review decisions under s 63 particularly closely (post-HRA, this would be expressed as the proportionality test). However, he found that, on the facts of the case, the claimant's decision to go on hunger strike was a feature or manifestation of his personality disorder, and accordingly his force feeding constituted necessary medical treatment for his mental disorder, within the meaning of s 63. Maurice Kay J accepted that the same decision made by somebody of sound mind would have to be respected, but decided that in this case the claimant's decision and his continued adherence to it resulted from his personality disorder. For commentary, see 'Ian Brady, force-feeding, UK law and human rights' (2000) Health Law 5, 1.

[50] [1995] 1 All ER 677.

[51] The decision in *Leigh v Gladstone* was expressly disapproved of.

also considered several US cases which suggested that the prisoner's individual autonomy could be overridden if justified by the needs of security or order in the prison, but observed that the Home Office had not raised any such issues in this particular case. Some commentators have considered whether, if such considerations were raised, for example if there were fears that prisoners would riot if a hunger striker died, intervention might be justified—in other words whether there remains a power to do so even if no duty is recognized.[52] However, feeding someone who remains of rational capacity to refuse against his or her will would seem to come close to degrading treatment, as prohibited by international standards.[53] Healthcare staff could also argue that codes of professional ethics prohibited their involvement.

Voluntary Consent in the Prison Context

6.18   While the cases above consider the extent to which general medical law on consent is attenuated by the prison environment, it has been argued that the coercive nature of prisons renders dubious the extent to which prisoners can ever be taken to have freely consented to treatment. This issue was raised in *Freeman v Home Office*.[54] There the plaintiff, a life sentence prisoner, alleged that he had been forcibly injected with drugs and that in any case he could not be said to be 'voluntarily' giving his consent since he was a prisoner in a coercive environment, and could certainly not be said to be giving it voluntarily where he was not fully informed of the potential consequences of the drug. The Court of Appeal upheld the trial judge's rejection of the plaintiff's factual allegations and concluded that a prisoner was as capable as anyone else of giving his consent to medical treatment. While in some ways this is a welcome decision, because otherwise prisoners may be deprived of any legal recognition of agency in the prison context, it may also underestimate the extent to which the coercive environment and lack of access to independent medical advice do impact on the reality of consent, and the extent to which prisoners need greater safeguards to ensure that consent is voluntary.

G. The Standard of Healthcare in Prisons

6.19   Healthcare workers in prisons owe a duty of care to those they treat. The general standard of medical care, quoted in many cases involving prisoners, is:

---

[52] See, eg, I Kennedy, 'Note' (1995) 3 Medical L Rev 189.

[53] In *X v Germany* (1984) 7 EHRR 152, however, the Commission considered that the State's duty to protect prisoners' right to life under Art 2 of the ECHR overrides any Art 3 claim that the prisoner might have in relation to enforced medical treatment to prevent injury or death.

[54] [1984] 1 All ER 1036.

that of the ordinary skilled man exercising and professing to have that special skill. A man need not possess the highest expert skill; it is well established law that it is sufficient if he exercises the ordinary skill of an ordinary competent man exercising that particular art . . . [a doctor] is not guilty of negligence if he has acted in accordance with a practice accepted as proper by a responsible body of medical men skilled in that particular art. [55]

However, some judicial observations have thrown doubt on the extent to which this test is appropriate in the prison setting. In *Knight v Home Office*[56] Pill J indicated that this standard of care will be assessed relative to the resources available to medical staff in the prison, and that while a failure to provide any medical services at a prison would clearly be a breach of duty it must be acknowledged that 'resources available for the public service are limited and that the allocation of resources is a matter for parliament'.[57] In this particular case, Pill J observed that a prison's failure to provide the same level of staff to observe a suicide risk who was subject to a hospital order as would be available in a psychiatric hospital was not a breach of duty.

Pill J's conclusion appeared to be that while a psychiatric hospital had a role of curing people, a prison had a duty only to detain people in custody (out of which a duty to prevent them injuring themselves arose), and hence should not be judged by the same medical standards. His decision not to specify by what standard a prison might be judged is an unsatisfactory one. It can be argued that a prison, while it continues to hold the physically or mentally ill rather than transferring them to a hospital, should be judged by the same standards that would apply in institutions to which people would have been admitted had they not been detained. To do otherwise harks back to ideas that prisoners lose more than their liberty when detained. One wonders whether Pill J would have come to the same conclusion in a case involving a remand prisoner.[58]   **6.20**

---

[55] See *Bolam v Friern Hospital Management Committee* [1957] 1 WLR 582. For a recent application of this principle, see *Zinzuwadia v Home Office*, 7 December 2000, QB. The claimant, the widow of a prisoner who had committed suicide by hanging himself in his cell, brought a claim in negligence against the prison psychiatrist, who had decided to put him on 15-minute observations rather than continuous observance. One witness, a professor of psychiatry, considered that this decision did not meet the *Bolam* standard, and one witness considered that the standard was satisfied. The court held that it could not, on the balance of probabilities, make a finding of negligence. It expressed the standard as follows: '[t]he defendant is not to be held negligent if he acted in accordance with a practice accepted as proper by a responsible body of practitioners skilled in his field. The standard is that of the reasonable average. Of course where there are different bodies of respectable opinion the court may prefer one body of opinion to another but that is no basis for a finding of negligence.'

[56] [1990] 3 All ER 237.

[57] ibid, 243.

[58] The High Court specifically refused to follow *Knight*—without overruling it—in the context of maternity care in *Brooks v Home Office* [1999] 2 FLR 33. The court rejected the claimant's case on the facts, but also rejected the Home Office argument that *Knight* was authority for the proposition that a pregnant woman in prison is not entitled to the same level of care as one at liberty. All pregnant women are entitled to the same high standard of care, regardless of whether or not they are serving a prison sentence.

6.21 In light of the developing law of Article 2 of the ECHR it must be doubted whether the approach adopted in *Knight* might be inconsistent with the Convention. The Article 2 case law, which is of great relevance to the issue of psychiatric care in prison, is discussed in detail in Chapter 2.[59]

H. Complaints in Respect of Healthcare

6.22 Complaints in respect of healthcare in prisons can be made in much the same way as any other complaints. Where the matter relates to clinical decisions it will be considered by the Managing Medical Officer and, if the prisoner is dissatisfied with the reply or where the complaint relates to the clinical decisions of the Managing Medical Officer, it can then be referred to the Governor.[60] Decisions concerning the exercise of clinical judgment of doctors are excluded from the remit of the Prisons Ombudsman, although about 3 per cent of the complaints he received in 1996 related to medical issues.[61]

6.23 Healthcare staff in prisons also remain subject to the complaints and discipline procedures of the professional bodies to which they belong. Therefore doctors working in prisons can be disciplined by the Professional Conduct Committee of the General Medical Council if they are found guilty of 'serious professional misconduct'.[62]

I. Specific Issues in Relation to Prisons

Treatment of HIV Positive Prisoners

6.24 The Prison Service in England and Wales first recorded receiving HIV positive prisoners in 1984. In its 1995 report on HIV and AIDS in prisons the Prison Service's AIDS Advisory Committee stated that 449 cases of HIV positive prisoners had been recorded in the 1984–95 period. In the same period, 30 prisoners were notified as having AIDS, of whom 12 died.[63] However, the accuracy of these statistics has been subject to criticism,[64] and the Prison Service itself acknowledges

---

[59] paras 2.108–2.119.
[60] See PSO 2510, 'Prisoners' Request and Complaints Procedures', and Ch 2, where the complaints system is discussed in greater detail.
[61] His current Report does not give a specific figure for complaints relating to medical issues, though it would be expected that the proportion would remain fairly consistent.
[62] Medical Act 1983, s 36(1)(c). The phrase 'serious professional misconduct' has been interpreted by the Privy Council in *Doughty v General Dental Council* [1988] AC 164 to mean a serious falling short of the standard expected among practitioners.
[63] AIDS Advisory Committee, *The Review of HIV and AIDS in Prison* (London, 1995), 7.
[64] See, eg, P Thomas, 'AIDS/HIV in Prisons' (1990) 29 Howard J 1.

the likelihood of significant under-reporting. As with the advent of AIDS in the general public in the early 1980s, its recognition in prisons produced high levels of anxiety among staff and prisoners. Given the high proportion of young people, the most sexually active section of the population in prison, plus a large number of intravenous drug users, there were initially great concerns that prisons would become 'breeding grounds' for HIV in the general population.[65] Although British prisons avoided the use of mandatory testing and did not resort to the extensive segregation of HIV positive prisoners that characterized some American prison systems,[66] some prisons did initially respond by allocating HIV prisoners to the prison hospital or special wings, a policy which (even when requested by prisoners) some commentators saw as making HIV positive prisoners lead 'an extremely deprived existence with little to distract them from the morbid contemplation of their situation'.[67] In its Third Report the CPT opposed this approach, stating that 'there is no medical justification for the segregation of an HIV positive prisoner who is well'.[68] As knowledge of HIV and AIDS has grown, both within the general population and more specifically in prison, the Prison Service has moved away from this sort of restrictive regime, and its policy is now to treat HIV/AIDS much like any other illness, especially with regard to confidentiality issues. Much emphasis has been placed on education and training, both for prisoners and prison staff.

Current policy advice, contained in Circular Instruction 30/1991 and Healthcare **6.25** Standard 7, is that any prisoner should be offered a test where his or her past medical history or an initial examination leads a doctor to recommend it. If a prisoner refuses to take a test this may be recorded on his or her IMR and he or she may be advised to have a further consultation but '[i]nmates who refuse a test should not be subject to pressure, direct or indirect, to change their mind'.[69] Prisoners

---

[65] Home Office commissioned research concludes that, '[i]n general, the bulk of HIV/AIDS risk-behaviours cease on coming into prison, although the residual behaviour tends to be more risky. Where drug risk behaviour is concerned, for example, the vast majority of injectors cease injecting when they come into prison and the remainder do so less frequently. However, those who continue to inject are more likely to share and are therefore more likely to be at risk of HIV/AIDS infection. Where sex risk behaviour is concerned, there was no evidence that same-sex activity was any higher in prison than outside': J Strang, J Heuston, M Gossop, J Green and T Maden, 'HIV/AIDS risk behaviour among adult male prisoners', Home Office Research, Development and Statistics Department, Research Findings No 82 (London, 1998). This suggests that, while the risks of HIV infection in prisons should not be exaggerated, there are some genuine risks which cannot be overlooked.
[66] Policies often found to be constitutional, as in *Harris v Thigpen*, 941 F 2d 1495 (11th Cir 1991). US courts have also upheld decisions by prison authorities not to segregate those who are HIV positive when this has been challenged by other prisoners. See, eg, *Cameron v Metcuz*, 705 F Supp 454 (ND Indiana 1989).
[67] See U Padel, *HIV, AIDS and Prisons* (London, 1988), 16.
[68] Third Report, 18 (1993), CPT/Inf (93) 12. This was also the policy of Council of Europe Recommendation 1080 (1988) on the treatment of HIV/AIDS in prison.
[69] CI 30/1991, para 17.

agreeing to take a test should be offered counselling before doing so and after the result is obtained, especially if the result is positive. If a positive result is obtained then this will also be recorded on the IMR but should remain confidential to the prisoner and his doctor. The relevant Circular Instruction provides that this information may be shared with other healthcare personnel, but only where the prisoner has been advised of this and his or her consent obtained.[70] At most prisons now, prisoners diagnosed as HIV positive will not be subject to any particular restrictions and information on their status should not be disclosed to other prisoners.

6.26 Aspects of the law have been regarded by some as playing an unnecessarily restrictive role when it comes to dealing with HIV/AIDS in prison. Needle exchanges, often utilized outside prison, run contrary to prohibitions on drug use in prison and are seen as contrary to Prison Service policy on discouraging drug use in prison. Similarly prison administrators have shied away from providing condoms in prison, arguing that as prison is not a 'private place' the Sexual Offences Act 1967 is inapplicable and even consensual homosexual activity in prison remains an offence. However the AIDS Advisory Committee has observed that there are no recorded instances of criminal prosecutions or disciplinary proceedings resulting from consensual sexual activity in prison. As a result they argued that condoms could be made available through health centres in prisons, a recommendation which has yet to be implemented.

6.27 The Prison Service policy of allowing prisoners access to condoms only when a medical officer considered that there was a known risk of HIV infection as a result of HIV risk sexual behaviour was challenged in *R v Home Secretary, ex p Fielding*.[71] The claimant, a gay prisoner who had sex with other inmates, argued that this policy constituted an unjustified interference with a gay prisoner's ability to obtain the means to ensure safe sex. He argued that it is extremely difficult to determine whether a sexual partner is HIV positive. If a gay prisoner presents himself to the prison authorities and requests condoms, the only inference that can properly be drawn is that he is intending to have penetrative sex, which will by definition carry the risk of HIV infection, and that therefore no question of the clinical judgment of a doctor arises. Latham J was not convinced:

> I consider that the Prison Service is entitled to take the view that it should not be seen to encourage homosexual activity in prison. That might be the message which would be given to the prison population, and the public at large, if condoms were available on demand. That is a matter of judgment for the Prison Service. Further, condoms have uses other than those for which they were designed; it seems to me to be reasonable for the Prison Service to consider it necessary for that reason that some

---

[70] CI 30/1991, para 28. In *TV v Finland* (1994) 18 EHRR CD 178, disclosure of HIV status to prison health workers was found to be a justified interference with private life.
[71] [1999] COD 525.

control should be exercised. . . . In these circumstances, it does not seem to me to be irrational to leave the decision to the prison medical officer. He is the one who can judge whether or not a request for a condom is made for genuine health reasons.

This judgment is regrettable in several respects. It places great emphasis on public **6.28** opinion. However, the case concerned lawful and consensual sex between adults, something which, whether approved of or not, public opinion cannot stop in society at large. The judgment graphically illustrates the extent to which prisoners' lives are subject to scrutiny which would be unimaginable on the outside. The requirement of approval by a medical officer makes prisoners dependent on medical consent for what is really an issue of personal choice, albeit with health implications, rather than of clinical judgment. It can only deter prisoners from trying to get condoms, leading to more unsafe sex and a greater risk of HIV infection.

Finally, it is worth noting that reluctance to involve prisoners in drug trials, a **6.29** reluctance which derives partly from international prohibitions on involving prisoners in medical experiments against their will, may have prevented prisoners from benefiting from the positive effects of trial drugs.[72] The creation of a Prison Service Research Ethics Committee in recent years has gone some way to dealing with some of these problems, but concerns remain.

Drug Misuse in Prisons

Although studies of drug use in prison are of recent origin and have produced no **6.30** definitive figure, there is a consensus that drug use in prison is high and on the increase.[73] Dealing with the misuse of drugs (and abuse of other substances) in prisons is a particularly complex and difficult issue. On the one hand, especially since the early 1990s, the issue has been seen as an essentially disciplinary one. In 1994 amendments to the Prison Act and Prison Rules created the legal framework for a regime of mandatory testing of prisoners for drugs by way of taking a urine sample.[74] The Prison Service indicated that it would not tolerate drug abuse in prison

---

[72] See J McHale and A Young, 'Policy, Rights and the HIV Positive Prisoner' in S McVeigh and S Wheeler (eds), *Law, Health and Medical Regulation* (London, 1992) 111. The extent to which prisoners can challenge compulsory HIV testing under Arts 3 and 8 of the ECHR is considered in D Valette, 'AIDS behind bars: prisoners' rights guillotined' (2002) 41(2) Howard J 107. See also H Arnott, 'HIV/AIDS, prisons and the Human Rights Act' [2001] European Human Rights L Rev 71.

[73] For one study, albeit in a small local prison, which found that 75% of those surveyed claimed that they used drugs in prison see J Keene, 'Drug Misuse in Prison: Views from Inside: A Qualitative Study of Prison Staff and Inmates' (1997) 36 Howard J 28. In a written answer on 18 May 1998 Joyce Quin MP indicated that of over 45,000 random drug tests in the first three quarters of 1997–98, 17% had tested positive for cannabis, 0.2% for amphetamines and 4.1% for opiates: Hansard, HC vol 1789, col 243.

[74] Prison Service policy on the use of mandatory drug testing is now contained in PSO 3601. The impact of mandatory drug testing on drug use in prisons is considered by K Edgar and I O'Donnell, 'Mandatory drug testing in prisons: the relationship between MDT and the level and nature of drug misuse', Home Office Research Study 189 (London, 1998).

and included reducing the level of drug use among its corporate objectives. Prison Rule 51(9) makes it a disciplinary offence for a prisoner either to administer a controlled drug to himself or to prevent someone else administering it to him. Under powers conferred by s 16A of the Prison Act and Prison Rule 50 prison officers can request prisoners to provide a urine sample to be tested for evidence of drug consumption. This may be done either on a random basis or where there is a reasonable suspicion that a prisoner has been taking drugs.[75] Prisons are directed to carry out a target number of random tests per month and to put those with disciplinary records of drug abuse on a regular programme of testing.[76] Refusal to provide a sample is a basis for charging a prisoner with the disciplinary offence of refusing to obey a lawful order, and prisoners testing positive for drugs may also face loss of privileges and downgrading to a more restrictive regime.

6.31 On the other hand, the Prison Service has acknowledged that drug and substance abuse pose major health problems in prison and has indicated its support for the treatment aspects of broader government policy initiatives on drugs.[77] Drugs policy in prison therefore also provides for prisoners to have entry to drug treatment programmes of varying length and intensity.[78] Prison Health Care Standard 8 sets out a regime for identifying and treating those involved in substance abuse in prison, including the prescribing of methadone to those dependent on opiates. PSO 3600 sets out a system called CARATs (counselling, assessment, referral, advice and throughcare services), which aims to identify prisoners with a drug problem and provide suitable, relatively short-term help, with a view to referral to longer-term programmes if needed, and if the prisoner's sentence is long enough. The system recognizes that:

> The majority of prisoners with a history of drug-related problems have not previously received assistance. It is recognised that there is a paucity of services which sufficiently address the needs of women, black drug users, poly drug users and primary stimulant users. Many may also have untreated health problems and undiagnosed mental health problems. CARAT services will be identifying those prisoners and pioneering brief approaches as well as trying to access other services on their behalf. This will require the input of the widest range of expertise and keeping up to date with developments in all specialisms.[79]

---

[75] Random testing has been upheld by the Divisional Court *in R v Home Secretary, ex p Tremayne*, 2 May 1996.

[76] See the Prison Service Policy Document, *Drug Misuse in Prison* (London, 1995), 7–8. Between April 2000 and March 2001, 7.5% of mandatory drug tests carried out tested positive for cannabis (a reduction from 10.2% in the previous year), 4.7% for opiates, 0.2% for cocaine, and 1.3% for benzodiazepines: see *Prison Statistics England and Wales 2000* (Cm 5250, 2001), 135.

[77] See, eg, the White Paper, *Tackling Drugs Together: A Strategy for England* 1995–98 (London, 1995).

[78] These include 1–2 day courses, 12–14 week courses in dedicated drug rehabilitation units, and long term therapeutic communities, as well as Voluntary Drug Testing Units.

[79] PSI 8/2001, para 2.4. A summary of the approach to drug use in prisons is set out in the 'Drug Strategy' Prison Service Standard. See also M Malloch, 'Caring for drug users? The experiences of women prisoners' (2000) 39 Howard J 354.

There is clearly a potential tension between these two approaches to drug misuse in prison. Prisoners interested in participating in substance abuse programmes may be concerned that they will face disciplinary penalties if they admit involvement in drug taking.[80] When the mandatory drug testing programme was introduced in 1995, there were concerns that it would lead to the replacement of cannabis by opiates such as heroin (which stays in the system for a shorter period) or increased alcohol abuse, contrary to the aim of reducing drug dependency. There is some evidence that this has been the case.[81] In its 1995 document *Drug Misuse in Prison* the Prison Service has sought to reconcile these two objectives by indicating, for example, that all those convicted of disciplinary offences involving drugs will be offered advice or counselling and that those voluntarily offering to enter compacts to be drug free should not necessarily be subjected to disciplinary penalties if they test positive. In addition, PSO 3620, which sets guidelines for the use of Voluntary Drug Testing Units, states that, if a prisoner who has agreed to take part in voluntary drug testing fails a test, this should not automatically lead to exclusion from the unit. Their presence in the unit should be reviewed, taking into account 'all facets of behaviour and standards of performance, taking into account any mitigating factors'.[82]

In the end, though, the relative levels of expenditure on drug testing and drug treatment programmes may indicate which policy is seen by the Prison Service as having greater prominence. It was estimated in 1997 that only £5 million per year was available for treatment programmes, as opposed to the £30 million annually spent on mandatory testing.[83] However, in early 1998 there were signs of a change in the policy towards drugs as the Prison Service announced that it would be substantially reducing the level of random mandatory drug tests and would be encouraging governors to discriminate between more and less harmful drug use in disciplinary decisions. The introduction of the CARATs scheme in 2000 was also supported by £76 million from the Government's Comprehensive Spending Review on Illegal Drugs, with the specific remit of enhancing the quality and availability of drug treatment services to prisoners.[84] This recognition that prison drug treatment services deserve funding in their own right is to be welcomed.

6.32

---

[80] Although para 6.96 of the *Prison Discipline Manual* (London, 1995) indicates that prisoners should not be charged on the basis of positive test results obtained by way of any voluntary testing arrangement.

[81] See, eg, J Teers, 'Testing for Drugs in an Open Prison' (1997) 40 Prison Report 12.

[82] para 3.12. PSO 3620 also stresses that '[p]otentially far-reaching decisions must not be based on an evidential standard lower than for [mandatory drug testing]. The defining point must therefore be removal from the drug testing programme and/or a failed screening test followed by a clear admission of drug use by the prisoner rather than a single unsupported failed drug screening test. Accordingly, prisons should not include in parole dossiers or otherwise inform the Parole Board of any unsubstantiated positive voluntary drug screening test results' (para 3.16).

[83] ibid.

[84] See PSO 3601, PSO 3620, and PSI 8/2001.

Suicides in Prison

6.33   Suicide remains the highest cause of death in prisons. The number of prisoners committing suicide rose sharply after 1987, and in 1996 reached 65, the highest figure in any one year.[85] The rate of suicides in prison is over four times that in the general population.[86] Given the high rate of such suicides and the fact that many appear to result from problems in coping with the experience of imprisonment,[87] one can argue that the Prison Service has a clear responsibility to take action to reduce this figure.[88]

6.34   In this section we consider the standard of care required by the courts, and the Prison Service's suicide prevention policies. Article 2 of the ECHR also has an impact on this area, since it imposes on all state agencies a positive duty to protect life. The Article 2 issues are considered in Chapter 2,[89] and should be read in conjunction with this section.

6.35   The existence of a duty of care in respect of known suicide risks was reaffirmed by the Court of Appeal and the House of Lords in *Reeves v Commissioner of Police for the Metropolis*.[90] Lord Hope expressed the duty as follows:

> In my opinion it is necessary at the outset to identify the duty which was owed to the deceased by the commissioner. There is no doubt that the commissioner was right to concede that he owed a duty of care to the deceased while he remained in police custody. The deceased had been identified as a suicide risk, having on two previous occasions attempted to strangle himself with a belt after being placed in a cell. It was the commissioner's duty to take reasonable care not to provide him with the opportunity of committing suicide by making use of defects in the cell door. The risk was not that he would injure himself accidentally if given that opportunity, but that he would do so deliberately. That is the nature of an act of suicide by a person who is of sound mind. It is a deliberate act of self-destruction by a person who intends to end

---

[85] *Prison Service Annual Report and Accounts 1996–97* (HC 274, 1997–98), 24.

[86] See, generally, A Liebling, *Suicides in Prison* (London, 1992).

[87] Liebling observes that whereas about 90% of those who attempt or succeed in committing suicide in the outside community have a history of psychiatric problems, this can be said of only about 40–50% of prisoners. The remainder, mostly prisoners under the age of 26, 'may be impulsive, situationally induced and preventable'. See A Liebling, 'Prison Suicide: What Progress Research?' in A Liebling (ed), *Deaths in Custody: Caring for People at Risk* (London, 1994), 44 and A Liebling, 'Risk and Prison Suicide' in H Kaushall and J Pritchard (eds), *Good Practice in Risk Assessment and Risk Management* (1997). See also A Liebling, 'Suicide in Prison: Ten Years On' (2001) 138 Prison Service J 35-41.

[88] For a strong statement of the view that prison suicides are preventable providing appropriate attitudes are fostered and procedures followed, see L Hayes, 'Custodial Suicide: Overcoming the Obstacles to Prevention' in A Liebling (ed), *Deaths in Custody: Caring for People at Risk* (London, 1994) 169.

[89] paras 2.108-2.119.

[90] [1999] QB 169; [2000] 1 AC 360. The Court of Appeal and the House of Lords rejected any argument that in respect of suicides where the deceased was accepted to be sane the defence of volenti non fit injuria was available.

his own life. So I think that the commissioner's duty can most accurately be described as a duty to take reasonable care to prevent the deceased, while in police custody, from taking his own life deliberately.[91]

However, the legal extent of this duty of care appears somewhat limited. We have already seen that in *Knight v Home Office*[92] the court held that prison authorities would not be required to reach the same standard of care in the prison hospital as might be required of a psychiatric hospital in dealing with someone at risk of committing suicide. Pill J also concluded that the prison medical staff had not been negligent in deciding not to place the prisoner on continuous watch in the hospital despite the fact that a noose had been found in his cell about a month before he committed suicide. Observing that 'suicide gestures were not uncommon in prison'[93] Pill J took the view that the prisoner was one of a number of suicide risks in Brixton at the time and that the medical staff's decision that he was not one of the most serious was a reasonable one. Inquest juries have been prepared to require a more pro-active approach by prison authorities in returning verdicts that suicides in prison were aggravated by lack of care.[94] The Court of Appeal circumscribed the scope for such verdicts in *R v North Humberside and Scunthorpe Coroner, ex p Jamieson*.[95] Rejecting the argument that it was open to an inquest jury to return a lack of care verdict in respect of a prisoner who was in the hospital ward after a suicide attempt but not under continuous watch, Sir Thomas Bingham MR indicated that the lack of care verdict was akin to neglect and should only be available in suicide cases where gross neglect was directly connected with the deceased's suicide, 'for example if a prison warder observes a prisoner in his cell preparing to hang a noose around his neck, but presses on without any attempt to intervene'.[96] However, the prospects of obtaining a neglect verdict have been improved by the decision of the Court of Appeal in *Amin*, discussed at paras 2. 117 and 2. 118 above.

Knight was a case where existing Prison Service suicide prevention policies were **6.36** followed, even if there was room for disagreement as to the efficacy of these policies and the judgments made by those implementing them. Where, however, there has been a significant failure to follow policy before the suicide of a prisoner

---

[91] ibid, 379.
[92] [1990] 3 All ER 237.
[93] ibid, 244.
[94] See, eg, *R v Coroner for Birmingham, ex p Secretary of State* (1990) 155 JP 107. However the jury's verdict was quashed by the Divisional Court.
[95] [1994] 3 All ER 972.
[96] ibid, 991. Depressingly, such cases seem to exist. In January 1997 an inquest jury brought in a verdict of lack of care in respect of a prisoner who died in the custody of Securicor staff who left him hanging for 10 minutes because they believed that he was feigning. See Prison Reform Trust (1997) 40 Prison Report 11. For recent case studies and up to date commentary and analysis, see www.inquest.org.uk, and M Branthwaite, 'Deaths in Custody—Causes and Legal Consequences' (2001) 69 Medico-Legal J 107. See also D Coles and H Shaw, 'Deaths in prison and their investigation: a critical overview' (2001) 138 Prison Service J 15–19.

liability may be incurred. This was the case in *Kirkham v Chief Constable of Greater Manchester*.[97] Here the prisoner was identified as a suicide risk by the arresting police officers but this information was not passed on to staff in the prison to which he was remanded. As a result he was placed in an ordinary cell rather than in the hospital wing for observation. Farquharson LJ defined the duty of care in question as a 'duty on the person having custody of another to take all reasonable steps to avoid acts or omissions which he could reasonably foresee would be likely to harm the person for which he is responsible'.[98]

6.37 The issue of duty of care was revisited by the Court of Appeal in *Orange v Chief Constable of West Yorkshire*.[99] The claimant's husband had been arrested during the night for being drunk and disorderly, and placed in a police cell. The door of the cell was a gate with vertical steel bars and a horizontal crossbar. He was allowed to keep all his clothing, including his belt, and was monitored by visits at 30 minute intervals and a closed circuit television (on which the door of the cell could not be seen). He was not considered to be a suicide risk. However, he hanged himself by his belt from the horizontal bar on the gate. On the claimant's behalf it was argued that the law should recognize that those who have been taken into custody, whether a police station or a prison, fall into a category in respect of which there is a significantly enhanced risk of suicide. It is difficult, if not impossible, to predict whether an individual, except in extreme circumstances, presents a significant suicide risk, and that those responsible for the custody of prisoners owe a duty of care to *all* prisoners to take some steps to reduce opportunities for suicide. The precise content of that duty could be worked out on a case by case basis. In this case, it was argued, while there was no specific reason to think that Mr Orange was a suicide risk, he was drunk, and there is material to suggest that a person who is drunk is less likely to think and act rationally. Further, he was allowed to keep his belt and was placed in a cell with a door which easily allowed him to hang himself. Latham LJ, writing for the court, considered *Kirkham* and *Reeves*. Since both those cases involved people who were known suicide risks, the duty of care had not been in issue. Although it was argued for the claimant that the House of Lords in *Reeves* had recognized a general proposition that those in custody are at enhanced risk of suicide and therefore in enhanced need of protection, Latham LJ concluded that:

> The consequence of [counsel for the claimant's] argument is that every person taken into custody, whether police custody or the custody of the Prison Service, is to be treated as a suicide risk. We do not consider that that is the appropriate response of the court to the material before us. There is no doubt that a custodian owes a duty of care to those taken into custody. As we have said, the duty is to take reasonable care for that person's health and safety. In determining the extent of that duty, it is

---

[97] [1990] 3 All ER 246.
[98] ibid, 253.
[99] [2002] QB 347.

clearly relevant to take into account the fact that there is an increased risk of suicide amongst such prisoners. But that does not mean that suicide is a foreseeable risk in relation to every prisoner. As Lord Hope said in *Reeves's* case [2000] 1 AC 360, 378, suicide can be both unforeseen and unforeseeable. Nor do we consider that it would be fair, just and reasonable to impose upon either the police or the prison authorities a general obligation to treat every prisoner as if he or she were a suicide risk. The consequence would be an unacceptable level of control and precaution, not only as an obligation placed upon the authorities, but also as an imposition on the individual prisoner. . . . In my judgment, the increased risk of suicide amongst prisoners can properly be said to give rise to an obligation, within the general duty of care the custodian has for the prisoner's health and safety, to take reasonable steps to identify whether or not a prisoner presents a suicide risk. The obligation to take reasonable care to prevent a prisoner from taking his own life deliberately only arises where the custodian knows or ought to know that the individual prisoner presents a suicide risk.[100]

Accordingly, the court held that the police had taken reasonable steps to assess whether Mr Orange was a suicide risk and had been justified in concluding that he was not. The duty of care to prevent him from taking his own life deliberately did not, therefore, arise, and the police had not been negligent. Given the vulnerability of those in custody, and the proven risk of suicide, both in those for whom it could be predicted and those for whom it could not, it is unfortunate that the Court of Appeal refused to impose a general duty to take reasonable steps to prevent prisoners from taking their own lives. Making the existence of that duty dependent on the assessment of a police officer or prison officer, in a situation where suicide risk is notoriously difficult to predict, offers a regrettably low level of protection. The Court of Appeal considered that a blanket duty of care would be too onerous. However, the contents of that duty would depend on the facts of the individual case, as in all other areas of negligence.

6.38 In 1999, the Chief Inspector of Prisons published *Suicide is Everyone's Concern: A Thematic Review*.[101] The Review is a broad-ranging study and a work of great humanity: as we see below, it has prompted the Prison Service to review its policies on suicide prevention. Drawing on recent research, the Review identifies three broad types of prisoner who are at particular risk of suicide: younger prisoners with a history of previous self-injury, whose distress is acute and who are particularly vulnerable to the impact of imprisonment; an older group of long sentenced prisoners who are often at the beginning of their sentences and who feel guilt and shame and a lack of hope about the future; and psychiatrically ill prisoners whose mental state is confused and who are socially isolated and poorly equipped to cope with imprisonment.[102] The Review notes that '[t]he dynamics

---

[100] paras 42–43.
[101] *Suicide is Everyone's Concern: A Thematic Review by HM Chief Inspector of Prisons for England and Wales* (London, May 1999).
[102] para 2.9.

of life in the total institution of a prison are not easy to convey to the general community, which has little comprehension of the pain of imprisonment',[103] and that '[w]hen people are committed to custody, they are removed from their normal environment. This separation also takes away their normal support network and ways of coping. It is therefore implicit that the Prison Service's duty of care should include adequate means to sustain prisoners in difficulty and enable them to cope as far as possible with the burden of custody.'[104] The Review contains serious criticisms of the way some deaths in custody are handled by prisons, though it also recognizes that many prison staff do act to support those at risk. It also contains a detailed analysis of current Prison Service policy and practice, identifying an inconsistent level of effectiveness of Suicide Awareness Teams, and stressing the need for different strategies for different groups in the prison population. The 'at risk' form F2052SH should not be seen as an end in itself. Risk assessment and overall quality of life in the prison must be tackled in a systematic fashion, the Review concludes.

6.39 The Prison Service has revised its guidance on suicide prevention several times in recent years.[105] The main themes of these policy revisions has been to encourage multi-disciplinary intervention, through the use of Suicide Awareness Teams and a Suicide Awareness Support Unit in Prison Service Headquarters, and reducing the perception within prisons that suicide risks are largely a medical problem which can be dealt with by sending someone to the prison hospital. The role of medical staff is still crucial, and Health Care Standard 1.1(g) indicates that healthcare workers carrying out initial assessment at reception should assess a prisoner's suicide risk and ensure members of staff responsible for carrying out preventive measures are fully informed if a prisoner is identified as being a suicide risk. Where someone is identified as a risk it is also for a doctor to assess within 24 hours whether a prisoner 'at risk' should be moved to the hospital or remain in the general population, usually subject to 15-minute watch. However, IG 1/94 also indicates that all staff have a role in identifying suicide risks and preventing suicides. In a very welcome development, the use of strip cells for those who are disturbed and suicidal was withdrawn by PSI 27/2000, which stated that '[t]he practice is widely recognised as degrading and contrary to the values and principles of the Prison Service. . . . Prisoners report that being in strip conditions does not in itself lessen suicidal feelings; often they feel worse for the experience, feeling degraded and punished. Fear of being placed in strip conditions is cited as a factor which discourages people from disclosing suicidal feelings. Evidence suggests that although placement in strip conditions may offer temporary respite, the measure

---

[103] para 3.2.
[104] para 3.14.
[105] For a summary of these developments see D Neal, 'Prison Suicides: What Progress Policy and Practice' in A Liebling (ed), *Deaths in Custody: Caring for People at Risk* (London, 1994) 54.

is unsuccessful in the long term. The use of strip cells, therefore, in any part of an establishment is wholly inappropriate for prisoners who have been identified at risk of suicide/self-injury.' The PSI suggests the following alternatives to the use of strip cells:

- continuous personal supervision by a member of staff on a one-to-one basis, possibly using a gated cell;
- refurbishing/enhancing unfurnished cells to a decent standard but removing obvious ligature points;
- installation of a gated cell which allows not only direct observation but also the potential for interaction;
- installation of a care/crisis suite/cell;
- increased use of listeners/buddies;
- increased access to Samaritans and other agencies, including dedicated phones (including mobile phones with pre-set number);
- maximizing the use of multi-occupancy accommodation in healthcare centres;
- reassessing staffing in healthcare centres to ensure that staff are trained in the management of suicidal prisoners.

While not legally binding in themselves, the extent to which this guidance is fulfilled in any particular case will be relevant to any negligence claim against the prison, assuming that a duty of care has been established.

As well as ending the use of strip cells, there has been a significant increase in the **6.40** use of listener and befriending schemes. All staff are encouraged to play a role in sharing information about suicide risks and assisting in suicide prevention, notably through forming positive relationships with prisoners. IG 79/94, which supplements the requirements of IG 1/94, stresses that when a Self Harm At Risk form (F2052SH) is opened on a prisoner, every effort must be made to place the prisoner in suitable shared and/or supervised accommodation. A monitoring procedure must be in place to ensure that the prisoner is not left alone. The 15-minute special watch is to be supplementary to 'other supportive, precautionary measures'. In its 1990 report on the United Kingdom the CPT observed that constructive relationships between staff and prisoners, as well as between prisoners, were a key element of suicide prevention. It also noted that 'the central plank' of a suicide prevention strategy must be to address problems of overcrowding and inadequate regimes. This task appears to be beyond suicide prevention strategies as currently formulated. As we discussed above, the work of the Chief Inspector of Prisons has prompted a more far-reaching review of the Prison Service's policies on suicidal prevention. The Chief Inspector explicitly linked suicide prevention to the provision of decent conditions and constructive, supportive regimes. The Prison Service is currently preparing a new PSO entitled 'Suicide and Self-Harm

Prevention'.[106] At the time of writing, this was due for release shortly. It is to be hoped that the Chief Inspector's recommendations will be put into practice.[107]

Mental Illness in Prison

6.41   Studies of the prison population have regularly indicated that a substantial number of prisoners have mental health problems. A 1991 Home Office commissioned study found that 37 per cent of sentenced prisoners were suffering from psychiatric disorders (for women prisoners the figure was 56 per cent).[108] A 1998 study commissioned by the Department of Health found that, out of a sample group of 3,200 prisoners, 78 per cent of male remand, 64 per cent of male sentenced, and 50 per cent of female prisoners suffered from some form of personality disorder. Compared to 0.4 per cent of the general population, 7 per cent of male sentenced, 10 per cent of male remand, and 14 per cent of female prisoners suffered from functional psychosis, including schizophrenia and delusional disorders. There was a marked prevalence of neurotic symptoms and sleep problems. The rates of suicidal thoughts were also worryingly high—46 per cent of male remand prisoners had thought of suicide in their lifetime, 35 per cent in the past year, and 12 per cent in the week prior to interview. Over a quarter of the female remand prisoners interviewed had tried to commit suicide in the year before interview.[109] As well as suffering from legally recognized mental illness, a substantial proportion of prisoners, notably those with drug or alcohol dependency, may be viewed as mentally ill by doctors but not by the law.[110]

6.42   Provision exists under the Mental Health Act 1983 to transfer either remand or sentenced prisoners to psychiatric hospitals on the direction of the Secretary of State. For such transfers to occur two doctors, one of them approved as having particular expertise in the treatment of mental illness, must indicate that

---

[106] PSO 2700. This will replace all current Prison Service guidance on the issue. It is supplemented by Prison Service Standard 60.

[107] Following the Chief Inspector's Thematic Review, the Prison Service carried out its own internal review on suicide prevention strategy, the results of which were accepted by the Director-General and by Ministers. The recommendations include 'an all-round pro-active approach . . . which encourages a supportive culture in prisons based on good staff-prisoner relationships, a constructive regime and a physically safe environment. There will be improved identification and case arrangements for high risk prisoners. The Review's recommendations will be developed and piloted in five establishments—Wandsworth, Feltham, Eastwood Park, Leeds and Winchester—evaluated, and rolled out to other prisons' (Prison Service press release, 5 February 2001). It is to be hoped that these initiatives will be translated into official Prison Service policy in the near future.

[108] J Gunn, T Madden, and M Swinton, *Mentally Disordered Offenders* (London, 1992).

[109] *Psychiatric Morbidity among prisoners in England and Wales* (London, 1998). See also D Melzer, 'Prisoners with psychosis in England and Wales: a one-year national follow-up study' (2002) 41 Howard J 1.

[110] Mental Health Act 1983, s 1(3) excludes drug and alcohol dependency from its definition of 'mental disorder'.

the prisoner is suffering from one of the prescribed conditions in s 1 of the 1983 Act.[111] Transfer of a remand prisoner may only take place if the prisoner is stated to be suffering from mental illness or severe mental impairment of a nature or degree which makes it appropriate for him to be detained in hospital for medical treatment, and that he is in urgent need of such treatment.[112] Transfers of sentenced prisoners are normally made with restrictions if the sentence has any further time to run. As a result, should the hospital or a Mental Health Review Tribunal subsequently indicate to the Secretary of State that the prisoner is no longer suffering from mental disorder or that no effective treatment can be given to him in hospital then the Secretary of State has a range of options at his disposal, including returning the offender to prison or releasing him on licence.[113]

The aim of these provisions is to ensure that those who are mentally ill receive **6.43** therapeutic care in hospital rather than remaining in prison. However, the Act requires that where a direction is made a bed must be available in a hospital within 14 days. Difficulties in complying with this requirement have tended to undermine the objectives of the Act. NHS psychiatrists have often been reluctant to provide hospital accommodation, either because of doubts that mentally disordered offenders are treatable or as a result of concerns about the risk they pose.[114] Three Special Hospitals, at Ashworth, Broadmoor, and Rampton, exist to provide secure accommodation for those seen as especially dangerous (whether offenders or not), but places in these hospitals are also in short supply and many mentally disordered offenders do not qualify.

Although there has been a recent increase in those transferred from prison to hos- **6.44** pital,[115] it seems inevitable that many mentally disordered people will continue to be accommodated in prisons.[116] With regard to the standard of care they can expect, *Knight* stands for the proposition that this does not have to equate to that available in a psychiatric hospital, but that it must still be a reasonable standard relative to the available resources. The Chief Inspector of Prisons has indicated

---

[111] These are mental illness, psychopathic disorder, mental impairment, or severe mental impairment.

[112] Mental Health Act 1983, s 48(1). For an examination of how s 48 works in practice, see R Mackay and D Machin, 'The operation of section 48 of the Mental Health Act 1983: an empirical study of the transfer of remand prisoners to hospital' (2000) 40 British J of Criminology 727.

[113] Mental Health Act 1983, s 50(1).

[114] Such reluctance has a long history. See A Grounds, 'Mentally Disordered Prisoners' in E Player and M Jenkins (eds), *Prisons After Woolf: Reform through Riot* (London, 1994) 178, 180, on opposition expressed by asylum superintendents in the late 19th century to admitting criminal patients.

[115] In 1996 a total of 746 offenders were transferred from prison to hospital. This represents a threefold rise since 1989. See *Statistics of Mentally Disordered Offenders* 1996, Home Office Statistical Bulletin 20/97 (London, 1997).

[116] For a critique and alternative proposals see Penal Affairs Consortium, *An Unsuitable Place for Treatment: Diverting Mentally Disordered Offenders from Custody* (London, 1998).

concern that current levels of provision may not even reach this.[117] Healthcare Standard 2 sets out the standards to be attained by local prisons and remand centres with regard to mental health services. It provides that a doctor who is psychiatrically qualified will have clinical responsibility for the services, that other healthcare workers should have received training in this field, and that an analysis of the mental health needs of the prison population should be undertaken every three years.[118]

6.45 All prisoners admitted to the healthcare centre should be examined within four hours and a present mental state assessment made.[119] The standards indicate that in respect of prisoners exhibiting challenging behaviour, seclusion should be used only as a last resort, and that medication should be prescribed only for clinical reasons and should be administered with the informed consent of the patient.[120] The one exception to the requirement of the need for consent is where two doctors certify that it is necessary to save life or prevent serious harm to the patient or others, or to prevent irreversible deterioration in the patient's condition. This exception is not limited to those prisoners diagnosed as suffering from one of the forms of mental disorder set out in the Mental Health Act, and it may be wondered whether the common law exception to the requirement for a prisoner's consent to treatment stretches so far as to justify treatment designed to prevent an irreversible decline in the patient rather than a threat of injury to himself or others.[121]

[117] 'Given that all establishments will have a number of mentally disordered inmates they must be enabled to provide proper psychiatric consultant supervision. At present this is not systematically provided': *Prisoner or Patient?: A New Strategy for Health Care in Prisons* (London, 1996) 3.

[118] Healthcare Standard 2. Mental health services for prisoners are currently under review: the Department of Health states that, '[a]t the end of July 2000, the Department of Health published *The NHS Plan* setting out a programme of investment and reform to deliver a health service fit for the 21st century. Prison health is given a specific mention as part of the commitment to better mental health services. Within the new partnerships between the NHS and local prisons, some 300 additional mental health staff will be employed by 2004 through the new NHS workforce strategy. And also by 2004, 5000 prisoners at any time should be receiving more comprehensive mental health services in prison. All people with severe mental illness will be in receipt of treatment, and no prisoner with serious mental illness will leave prison without a care plan and a care co-ordinator.' Department of Health, at www.doh.gov.uk/prisonhealth/faq.htm.

[119] Standard 2.5(d).
[120] Standard 2.4.
[121] Standard 2.4(f).

7

whole chapter

ACCESS TO THE OUTSIDE WORLD AND MAINTENANCE OF FAMILY CONTACTS

A. Introduction

Maintaining links between prisoners and the outside world, especially with their **7.01** families, is seen as a vital aspect of their rehabilitation and preparation for release. Prison Rule 4 indicates that 'special attention' shall be paid to maintaining contacts between prisoners and their families, and that a prisoner should be 'encouraged' to develop contacts with the outside world which 'best promote the interests of his family and his own social rehabilitation'. In its response to the Woolf Report the Home Office observed that visits and home leave were 'key elements in meeting the Prison Service's obligations to those in its care'.[1] The European Prison Rules also place great stress on the importance of maintaining contact with the outside world. Rule 65(c) for example, which is part of the rule setting out the main objectives of the prison regime, indicates that the regime should be designed and managed so as 'to sustain and strengthen those links with relatives and the outside community that will promote the best interests of prisoners and their families'. Indeed, with the decline of faith in the rehabilitative capacity of prison itself, contact with the outside world as a means of reducing the debilitating effects of

---

[1] See Home Office, *Custody, Care and Justice* (Cm 1647, 1991), para 7.35.

institutionalization has come to be seen as perhaps the most important rehabilita-tive strategy in the prison context. It is also of course important for the prisoner's family, who, while unconvicted of anything, also effectively serve a sentence in terms of restrictions on their lives for the time that a close relative is in prison. Location of prisons plays a large part in determining how substantial this contact will be, as the further away a prisoner is detained from his family the more difficult it will be to maintain contact. In this respect it is interesting to note the recom-mendation in the Woolf Report that, where possible, prisoners should be detained in 'community prisons', close to the community with which they have the great-est links.[2] However, even if most prisoners were to be located close to their fam-ilies the character of the prison regime is likely to play the most important role in determining the nature of contact with the outside world.

7.02 Prison policy in this area has in fact almost come full circle. In the 17th and 18th centuries the dividing line between prison and the outside world was a flexible one. Traders and prostitutes came in to work within the prison walls. Prisoners with sufficient money could entertain visitors in their cells. This changed in the late 18th and early 19th centuries, when reformers urged isolation from the plea-sures and corruptions of the outside world as the best means of producing changes in the disposition of criminals.[3] It was this era that witnessed the development of a rule of silence in prisons and which greatly limited contact between prisoners and those on the outside. Although the reform justification for limitations on contact has largely gone, in the early 21st-century prison security has been given as the reason for maintaining restrictions, though institutional habits and conser-vatism may play a greater role. Nevertheless, the last two decades have witnessed an overall relaxation in the rules governing such matters as letters, visits, and home leave, even if this progress has been marked by steps backward as well as forward. The European Commission and Court of Human Rights have played an espe-cially prominent role in prompting these changes. Domestic courts have been less to the fore in this area, though they have given several important decisions on pris-oners' access to the courts, and are tentatively beginning to develop domestic law in the light of the Human Rights Act 1998 (HRA). Yet although the United Kingdom has made progress in this field, it still lags behind many European sys-tems in its approach to matters like home leave and conjugal visits. It is on such matters that a significant amount of energy is likely to be expended in the next few years.

---

² See *Prison Disturbances: April 1990* (Cm 1456, 1991), para 11.69. For further discussion of the idea of community prisons, see Prison Reform Trust (1991) 19, *Prison Report*.
³ See, generally, C Harding, B Hines, R Ireland, and P Rawlings, *Imprisonment in England and Wales: A Concise History* (London, 1985), ch 4.

B. Legal Contacts

Read to end of Chapter.

The Evolving Right to Privileged Legal Correspondence

In the early 1970s prisoners' letters were still routinely read and stopped. The **7.03**
Prison Rules indicated that letters could be read at any time and stopped when
deemed to be 'objectionable', a broad category on which no further clarification
was available.

The breakthrough in the move away from this restrictive regime came in the area of **7.04**
prisoners' letters to lawyers. In *Golder v UK*[4] the European Court of Human Rights
(ECtHR) ruled that the prison authorities could not refuse to forward a letter to a
prisoner's lawyer on the ground that it referred to a matter which had not been
raised or decided upon within the prison. Golder had actually written to the Home
Secretary seeking permission to contact a solicitor regarding a potential libel claim
against a prison officer and had been refused. In Strasbourg the ECtHR indicated
that this refusal violated his right under Article 6 of the European Convention on
Human Rights (ECHR) to a fair hearing in a case involving a potential civil right.
Although Article 6 did not expressly guarantee a right of access to the courts the
majority of the ECtHR were of the opinion that the right to a fair hearing established in that Article would be meaningless if a Member State could deny access to
the courts in the first place. The court also indicated that stopping Sidney Golder
from corresponding with his solicitor violated his right to respect for his correspondence guaranteed by Article 8. This aspect of the decision arguably turned out to be
even more significant as, in doing so, the court rejected the Government's arguments that there were inherent limitations on the exercise of rights established in
the Convention when it came to prisoners. Instead the court took the view that any
lawful restrictions on prisoners' exercise of their Article 8 rights had to be found in
the limitation clauses of Article 8(2). In this case they did not see how any of these
could justify preventing a prisoner from corresponding with a solicitor.

The *Golder* case was a major development, in the context both of correspondence **7.05**
and of the potential of the ECHR to respond to prisoners' claims.[5] As regards the
issue of legal correspondence it was to be endorsed by the Commission and court
in *Silver v UK*.[6] Though this case had a greater impact on non-legal correspondence and will be discussed in greater detail below, it did indicate that stopping a
letter to a solicitor on the ground that the complaints it contained had not previously been raised in the internal complaints mechanism—the 'prior ventilation

---

[4] Series A No 18 (1975) 1 EHRR 524.
[5] See G Zellick, 'The Rights of Prisoners and the European Convention on Human Rights'
(1975) 38 MLR 683.
[6] Series A No 61 (1983) 5 EHRR 347; the Commission's decision is available at (1981) 3 EHRR
475.

rule'—did violate Article 8 and was not necessary in a democratic society to satisfy any of the legitimate aims set out in Article 8(2).

7.06 In response to these decisions the Home Office, by Standing Orders and Circular Instructions rather than amendments to the Prison Rules, replaced the prior ventilation rule with a 'simultaneous ventilation' rule, whereby complaints could be sent to solicitors providing that they were at the same time being raised in the internal complaints mechanism. This was to fare no better than the prior ventilation rule. Though the ECtHR in *Silver* appeared prepared to wear this solution,[7] this time it was the domestic courts which found it unacceptable.

7.07 The case was *R v Home Secretary, ex p Anderson*.[8] In that case a prison Governor had prevented a prisoner from having an interview with his lawyer to discuss a potential civil claim relating to his treatment in prison because the prisoner had not simultaneously submitted this claim to the internal disciplinary procedure. The Governor invoked Standing Orders issued by the Secretary of State under the then rule 33(1), which required all complaints to be simultaneously examined through the internal procedure. In the Divisional Court, Robert Goff LJ concluded that this provision was an impediment to a prisoner's right of access to the courts. Goff LJ took the view that the right of access to a court was a 'constitutional right'[9] and that this could be removed only by primary legislation. The relevant piece of primary legislation in question, s 47(1) of the Prison Act 1952, said nothing explicitly about restricting access to the courts. Hence Goff LJ took the view that any Prison Rule or Standing Order which purported to do this would be ultra vires the Prison Act. Moreover, access to legal advice was regarded as effectively part of this right of access to the courts. Goff LJ noted that prisoners, especially those who lacked knowledge or confidence, would be unlikely to pursue their cases through the courts without the assistance of a lawyer. In addition he observed that requiring prisoners first to submit their claim to an internal procedure might discourage justified claims being brought through the fear of being subject to a rule 47(12) disciplinary charge of making false and malicious allegations against an officer (an offence since dispensed with). With this decision the simultaneous ventilation rule also bit the dust.

7.08 In reaching his decision Goff LJ drew on the authority of *Raymond v Honey*,[10] which had been decided a year earlier. In that case the House of Lords had concluded that a governor could not prevent a prisoner sending documents to the

---

[7] As the complaints in *Silver* related to correspondence between 1972 and 1977 the Home Office had amended and published its Standing Orders by the time the case reached the court.
[8] [1984] QB 778.
[9] Drawing on *Chester v Bateson* [1920] 1 KB 829.
[10] [1983] 1 AC 1.

High Court to pursue a claim for contempt. The claim arose out of the Governor stopping the prisoner's original letter to his solicitor which contained an allegation of theft against an assistant governor. Again the authorities had relied on Standing Orders interpreting the then rules 33 and 37. However, the House of Lords indicated that such an interpretation could not interfere with a prisoner's right of access to the courts for much the same reasons as Goff would advance in *Anderson*. Lord Wilberforce indicated that 'a prisoner retains all civil rights and obligations which are not taken away expressly or by necessary implication', words which have been regularly quoted by every prisoners' rights advocate ever since.

As a result of these decisions the Prison Rule and Standing Orders governing legal **7.09** correspondence were modified to indicate that such correspondence could not be read or stopped where the prisoner was a 'party to legal proceedings'. This phrase was interpreted by the Court of Appeal in *Guilfoyle v Home Office*[11] to mean that once a writ had been issued, correspondence acquired such a privileged status.[12] However this still left a substantial amount of correspondence between prisoners and their lawyers, notably that relating to *contemplated* litigation, vulnerable to being read and stopped. The Prison Service remained of the view that it was entitled to examine such correspondence well into the 1990s. Again the combined effect of decisions in Strasbourg and the domestic courts was to produce a reconsideration and revision.[13]

The European case was *Campbell v UK*.[14] Here a Scottish prisoner complained **7.10** that routine reading of legal correspondence concerning contemplated legal proceedings amounted to a breach of Article 8. Following a number of earlier decisions which indicated that monitoring of prisoners' communications with their lawyers breached Convention provisions[15] the ECtHR found the United Kingdom to be in violation of the Convention by eight votes to one. The court took the view that only in 'exceptional circumstances', for example where the authorities have reason to believe that legal privilege was being abused to send out material endangering prison security, could legal correspondence be read or

---

[11] [1981] 1 QB 309.

[12] The case itself concerned an application to the European Commission of Human Rights, and Lord Denning MR reached the rather surprising conclusion that, as the Commission could not reach a binding decision, a prisoner sending it an application could never be seen as a 'party to legal proceedings'. Fortunately this interpretation was not followed by the Prison Service which granted all correspondence relating to Strasbourg applications privileged status.

[13] For a general discussion of these cases see I Cram, 'Interfering with Gaol Mail: Prisoners' Legal Letters and the Courts' [1993] LS 356.

[14] Series A No 233–A (1993) 15 EHRR 137.

[15] Notably *S v Switzerland* Series A No 227 (1992) 14 EHRR 670 where the court found monitoring of a prisoner's conversations with his defence lawyer to be in breach of Art 6(3) of the ECHR and *Schoenberger and Durmaz v Switzerland* Series A No 137 (1989) 11 EHRR 202, where interception of a letter from a lawyer to a prisoner was found in breach of Art 8.

stopped.[16] The following year the Court of Appeal gave an even more emphatic endorsement of this principle in its judgment in *R v Home Secretary, ex p Leech*.[17] Overturning a decision of Webster J which suggested the risk of something being smuggled in or out of prison in legal mail justified a rule permitting the reading of all legal correspondence, Steyn LJ stressed again the idea that restricting a prisoner's confidential communication with his lawyer placed a hindrance on his fundamental right of access to the courts. Given the fundamental character of this right, both in domestic and international law, Steyn LJ took the view that any restrictions on it must be justified by a self evident and pressing need. Moreover any such interference must be the minimum necessary to ensure that the need was met. It was thus left to the Secretary of State to demonstrate that such a need existed and that restrictions imposed to satisfy it were the minimum necessary to satisfy that end. In other words the burden lay on the Secretary of State to demonstrate that such security interests as he had could not be satisfied in any other way. As the main security consideration turned out to be that something unconnected with the legal issues on which advice was sought might be included with the papers (including drugs or money), and as this could be assuaged by examining the contents in front of the prisoner, the Court of Appeal had little difficulty in indicating that the Prison Rules were ultra vires the Prison Act on this matter. *Leech* appeared to have established that legal correspondence was entitled to near absolute privilege and that only in the most exceptional circumstances would this be subject to restriction. However in *Ex p Main* the Court of Appeal indicated a retreat from the *Leech* position.[18] All the judges there accepted the idea that prisoners' legal correspondence could be examined without the prisoner being present during a cell search and only Kennedy LJ explicitly accepted the idea that the 'minimum interference' test was appropriate when dealing with legal correspondence. Judge LJ appeared to feel the appropriate question was whether the measures adopted were a 'disproportionate or irrational response' to established security concerns. Chadwick LJ did not pronounce on this issue.

7.11 This restrictive approach to prisoners' correspondence rights was comprehensively demolished by the House of Lords in *R (Daly) v Home Secretary*.[19] Daly's

---

[16] The court has further endorsed this view in *Diana v Italy* and *Domenichini v Italy*, both decided on 15 November 1996, where it found breaches of Art 8 where prisoners' letters to lawyers were stopped. Italy argued that as the decisions to stop the letters were made by a judge any such interference was 'prescribed by law' but the court unanimously took the view that since the relevant law specified no grounds on which correspondence might be interfered with and no time limits in respect of this that there was a breach of Art 8(1), without even having to consider whether such interference was 'necessary in a democratic society'. See also *Faulkner v UK* Application 37471/97 (2002) 35 EHRR 27, where the court found a violation of Art 8 in respect of a prisoner in Scotland: the prison had failed, without justification, to send a letter of the applicant's to the Scottish Minister of State.
[17] [1994] 4 QB 198.
[18] *R v Home Secretary, ex p Main* [1998] 2 All ER 491.
[19] [2001] 2 AC 532.

cell, in which he stored correspondence with his solicitor about his security cate-gorization reviews and parole, was searched in his absence pursuant to the stand-ard cell searching policy set out in paras 17.69–17.74 of the *Security Manual*. He complained that the blanket policy was unlawful and constituted a dispropor-tionate interference with his Article 8 rights. Giving the leading speech, Lord Bingham drew on the line of authorities from *Anderson* to *Campbell* and *Leech*, reiterating the fundamental importance of access to the courts in the following terms:

> Any custodial order inevitably curtails the enjoyment, by the person confined, of rights enjoyed by other citizens. He cannot move freely and choose his associates as they are entitled to do. It is indeed an important objective of such an order to curtail such rights, whether to punish him or to protect other members of the public or both. But the order does not wholly deprive the person confined of all rights enjoyed by other citizens. Some rights, perhaps in an attenuated or qualified form, survive the making of the order. And it may well be that the importance of such surviving rights is enhanced by the loss or partial loss of other rights. Among the rights which, in part at least, survive are three important rights, closely related but free standing, each of them calling for appropriate legal protection: the right of access to a court; the right of access to legal advice; and the right to communicate confidentially with a legal adviser under the seal of legal professional privilege. Such rights may be cur-tailed only by clear and express words, and then only to the extent reasonably neces-sary to meet the ends which justify the curtailment.[20]

Lord Bingham went on to say that, since the policy clearly infringed prisoners' rights to confidential communication with legal advisers, the test was whether the extent of this infringement can be 'justified as a necessary and proper response to the acknowledged need to maintain security, order and discipline in prisons and to prevent crime'.[21] He considered that it was not justified, since less restrictive alternatives were available to fulfil the Prison Service's legitimate aims. This test of proportionality is to be applied in both the common law and Convention context:

> I have reached the conclusions so far expressed on an orthodox application of com-mon law principles derived from the authorities and an orthodox domestic approach to judicial review. But the same result is achieved by reliance on the European Convention. Article 8(1) gives Mr Daly a right to respect for his corres-pondence. While interference with that right by a public authority may be per-mitted if in accordance with the law and necessary in a democratic society in the interests of national security, public safety, the prevention of disorder or crime or for the protection of the rights and freedoms of others, the policy interferes with Mr Daly's exercise of his right under article 8(1) to an extent much greater than necessity requires.[22]

---

[20] para 5.
[21] para 18.
[22] para 23.

Lord Cooke emphasized, in a statement of wide-ranging importance, that the bare rationality test is an inappropriate tool for analysing infringements of rights: '[i]t may well be . . . that the law can never be satisfied in any administrative field by a finding that the decision under review is not capricious or absurd'.[23] However, contrary to the Court of Appeal in *Main*, the House of Lords in *Daly* made it quite clear that the blanket policy at issue satisfied neither the bare rationality test nor the more searching standard of proportionality.[24]

Legal Correspondence: The Present Law

7.12 The pre-*Daly* decisions resulted in a number of changes in the rules governing prisoners' correspondence and visits from lawyers. Prisoners' written, but not physical, access to the courts has also been altered substantially. The rules are now contained in Prison Rule 38 and 39 and in Standing Order 5, which was published in order to comply with the ruling of the ECtHR in the *Silver* case.[25] Rule 39 now provides that 'any correspondence' between a prisoner and his lawyer may only be opened, read, or stopped in two circumstances. First, rule 39(2) indicates that such correspondence may be opened if the governor has reasonable cause to believe that it contains an 'illicit enclosure'. This is defined by rule 39(6) as including 'any article possession of which has not been authorised in accordance with the Rules' and any correspondence to or from anyone but the prisoner, his or her legal adviser, and the courts. Secondly, rule 39(3) provides that such correspondence may be opened, read, or stopped where the governor has reasonable cause to believe that 'its contents endanger prison security or the safety of others or are otherwise of a criminal nature'. All such mail should be marked 'Prison Rule 39' but even if not marked in such a way should be treated as legal correspondence where it is clearly addressed to a legal adviser. Where staff have reasonable cause to believe that legal correspondence does contain an illicit enclosure they should notify the prisoner, and Prison Rule 39(4) states that such mail should only be opened in the presence of the prisoner (unless he or she has refused and signed a waiver). IG 113/95 indicates that any decision to read a letter must be taken by the governor personally and that the correspondence officer, when he is of the view that the governor should consider the matter, must seal the correspondence

---

[23] para 32.
[24] This landmark decision has been of little comfort to many prisoners, since at the time of writing the Prison Service has not produced guidance to implement the judgment. Relying on this failure, some governors continue to allow cell searching—including the searching of privileged correspondence—in prisoners' absence, despite the fact that the House of Lords clearly ruled this to be unlawful, Prison Service guidance or not, unless there are clear and specific security reasons relating to the individual prisoner.
[25] In *Silver v UK* Series A No 61 (1983) 5 EHRR 347 the court indicated that to comply with the Art 8(2) requirement that all restrictions be 'prescribed by law' the content of such restrictions should be available in the public domain if prisoners are to know them and adapt their conduct to them.

in the presence of the prisoner for forwarding to the governor. Where illicit enclosures are discovered or letters read which turn out to contain material contrary to rule 39(3), they will be separated from the legal correspondence which will then be sent on to its addressee. However, the prisoner may face subsequent disciplinary charges. As a result of Prison Rule 39(6) and Standing Order 5A(35) privilege attaches to all letters to lawyers, courts (including the European Commission and Court of Human Rights and the European Court of Justice), and the Criminal Cases Review Commission.[26]

The precise scope of privilege has been slowly expanded by the courts. Until *Daly,* **7.13** it appeared that this level of privilege only attached to legal correspondence at the point of sending and receipt. Following recommendations in the Woodcock Report that all cell searches should occur in the absence of prisoners, the Prison Service took the view that this must apply also to legal papers. In *R v Home Secretary, ex p Main*[27] a prisoner challenged the operation of this policy at Whitemoor prison as inconsistent with the *Leech* position on privileged legal correspondence. The challenge was strengthened by the fact that the Prison Ombudsman had upheld a complaint on the same issue, ruling that Prison Service policy should be amended to allow the prisoner to remain in his cell during the search of legal papers, after which they would be sealed or placed in a bag. The Court of Appeal was unpersuaded. Both Kennedy and Judge LJJ seemed much impressed by Prison Service arguments that non-legal material, including plans or drugs, could be hidden in legal papers. They felt that instructions to officers not to read such material during an examination constituted a sufficient safeguard. Yet much the same arguments were advanced by the Prison Service in *Leech* and *Campbell.* If a prisoner does identify material as including legal correspondence it should not be beyond the resources of prison staff to separate this from other documents and search it alone in the presence of the prisoner.

Reason reasserted itself in *Daly,* discussed in more detail in the previous section. **7.14** For present purposes it is important to note that the House of Lords completely rejected the Prison Service's arguments about the practical necessity of searching cells in the prisoner's absence. Lord Bingham took particular account of the fact that cell searching in Scotland is generally done in the prisoner's presence, apparently with no threat to security. He also refused to believe that 'prison officers when examining legal correspondence employ any sophisticated technique which would be revealed to the prisoner if he were present, although he might no doubt be encouraged to secrete illicit materials among his legal papers if the examination

---

[26] The requirements in the Prison Rules, Standing Orders and Instructions to Governors are summarized in PSO 1000, *The Security Manual,* ch 36. This version of ch 36 was introduced by PSI 57/2001.

[27] [1998] 2 All ER 491.

were obviously very cursory'.[28] Further, he was not persuaded that prison officers could be conditioned by manipulative prisoners into searching less thoroughly. Any prisoners who did prove disruptive or intimidating during cell searches could, of course, be dealt with by excluding them from such searches without subjecting all prisoners to the blanket policy.

Lawyers' Visits

7.15 Though Prison Rule 38(1) allows legal visits in sight but out of hearing of a prison officer only where the prisoner is a party to legal proceedings, SO 5A(34) widens this entitlement to cover nearly all legal visits. Apart from visits to discuss legal proceedings to which the prisoner is a party, pending adjudications and applications to Strasbourg, prisoners may also have in sight, but out of hearing, visits from legal advisers in two other circumstances. The first is where the prisoner wishes to consult about possible legal proceedings, the second where he wishes to consult about other legal business (for example about selling a house or making a will) that does not involve possible proceedings. For the former SO 5A(34)(b) requires that the prisoner indicate in advance that the visit is to discuss possible legal proceedings but not what such contemplated proceedings are about. For the latter the prisoner must disclose in advance the purpose of the visit. Where such legal visits take place the legal adviser will be entitled to take notes and use a cassette recorder (providing the legal adviser gives an undertaking that the recording will be used purely in connection with the legal business that the visit related to) as an exception to the normal prohibition contained in SOs 5A(26) and 5A(29).

7.16 Following the Whitemoor escape of September 1994, closed visits were introduced for all Exceptional Risk Category A prisoners, including visits with legal advisers. In a closed visit prisoners are separated from visitors by a glass partition and communication must take place through a telephone or grill. No physical contact is possible and documents must be passed between the prisoner and a visitor through a slot at the bottom of the partition. Two prisoners challenged this on the ground that, as per *Leech*, it constituted a hindrance of their communication with their lawyers and hence of their access to the courts.[29] The applicants noted, for example, that the passing of documents and ensuring that communications took place out of the hearing of prison officers were rendered difficult by such circumstances, especially where the prisoner was represented by several lawyers. In a clear retreat from *Leech* the Court of Appeal rejected such contentions. In *R v Governor of Whitemoor Prison, ex p O'Dhuibhir*[30] Kennedy LJ took the view that

---

[28] [2001] 2 AC 532, para 19.
[29] The UN Special Rapporteur on the Independence of Judges and Lawyers indicated concern in his 1996 Annual Report that the closed visits policy hampered unfettered access of prisoners to legal advice: E/CN 4/1996/37.
[30] [1997] COD 315.

the *Leech* test applied only where the vires of a Prison Rule was at stake and not merely, as here, the lawfulness of an Instruction to Governors. In this sort of case he felt the *Wednesbury* reasonableness test was appropriate and had little difficulty in finding that, in view of the fact that these were IRA prisoners and that the Prison Service had shown itself willing to make exceptions where the lawyer in question could demonstrate that they could not obtain proper instructions in closed conditions, this test was satisfied. It is perhaps surprising to see the more exacting *Leech* test invoked when dealing with a Prison Rule, which has at least been considered by Parliament, but not in respect of an administrative instruction. The applicants strongly argued that once it had been established that the restrictions constituted a hindrance to effective lawyer–client communications then the 'minimum necessary interference' test of *Leech* was applicable. The court however saw this order as merely regulating the manner of communications between the lawyer and the prisoner, not as amounting to an interference with the right.

This approach is clearly unsustainable in light of the decision of the House of **7.17** Lords in *Daly*, discussed above, and *O'Dhuibhir* can no longer be considered a correct statement of the law. In any event, the particular policy at issue in *O'Dhuibhir* was discontinued in July 1997, from which date legal visits were allowed to take place in open conditions. The issue may, however, become live again as prisoners, particularly terrorist suspects on remand in maximum security conditions, again become subject to highly restrictive visiting regimes.

Access to Legal Resources

As public funding is available for most of the claims that prisoners are likely to **7.18** want to make, including civil actions and judicial review, there has been little discussion whether prisoners are denied access to law. The ECHR establishes that prisoners have a right of access to the courts, and through this a right of access to lawyers.[31] It also indicates that any restrictions on access must be 'proportionate to the aim sought' (for example preventing vexatious litigation) and should not be such that 'the very essence of the right is impaired'.[32] As the right is required to be an effective one the ECtHR has indicated that in some circumstances the provision of legal aid may be required.[33] This will generally be where the applicant is asserting a 'civil right' as defined by the Convention,[34] where the matter is

---

[31] See *Golder v UK* Series A No 18 (1975) 1 EHRR 524 and also *Campbell v UK* Series A No 233–A (1992) 15 EHRR 137.
[32] See *Ashingdane v UK* Series A No 93 (1985) 7 EHRR 528.
[33] See *Airey v Ireland* Series A No 32 (1979) 2 EHRR 305.
[34] Largely confined to what would be seen as 'private law' rights in the UK. For a discussion of this complex issue see R Clayton and H Tomlinson, *The Law of Human Rights* (Oxford, 2000 and supplements) 11.60.

complex, where the applicant cannot effectively represent him or herself, and where there is a reasonable chance of success. Any restrictions on prisoners' rights of access to law would therefore face a number of significant obstacles.

7.19 This is a matter which has much exercised courts in the United States following the Supreme Court's 1977 decision in *Bounds v Smith*.[35] In that case the court indicated that the Fourteenth Amendment to the Constitution guaranteed prisoners a right of 'meaningful access' to the courts. The state was under an obligation to ensure this and the court indicated that there was a number of ways that this could be done, either by providing free legal assistance to prisoners or by ensuring that there was an adequate law library in each prison which jailhouse lawyers and individual inmates could then use. However, in line with the more restrictive trend of prisons cases in the United States in the 1990s, the Supreme Court has later narrowed this by indicating that the duty on prison authorities is simply to ensure access to the courts. The court added that prisoners need to show 'actual injury' to a legal claim they are pursuing, for example that it caused a complaint they were pursuing to be dismissed because they were unable to research pleadings requirements, in order to succeed in a claim of a constitutional violation.[36] In England and Wales PSO 6710 specifies that prison libraries must keep certain legal materials (including this text!) relevant to the filing of appeals or challenges to aspects of imprisonment.

7.20 An issue which has arisen more recently is the extent to which prisoners are entitled to access to computers, as well as printed materials, in order to have effective access to justice. PSI 02/01 provides that '[a]ny prisoner who requests access to IT facilities for legal work and demonstrates a real need for this (ie refusing the request would raise a real risk of prejudicing the legal proceedings) must be granted access to the IT provided for this purpose for the periods specified. Whether such access must be in possession or not will depend on the completion of a risk assessment.'[37] Lack of in-cell electricity is not a valid reason for refusing

---

[35] 430 US 817 (1977).

[36] See *Lewis v Casey*, 116 S Ct 2174 (1996).

[37] In *R (Ponting) v Governor of HMP Whitemoor* [2002] EWCA Civ 224, the Court of Appeal considered the application of a prisoner who complained that the conditions on which he was granted access to IT for legal purposes infringed his rights under Arts 6 and 8. The applicant, who was dyslexic, wished to use his own computer, printer and software to prepare his case and communicate with his solicitors. The prison refused, but allowed him access to another computer, on condition that he only used it in his cell at limited times and stored the disks and computer in possession of the prison. There were also conditions as to supervision and inspection. The court recognized the increasing importance of IT to prisoners. However, it held that this particular regime did not deprive the applicant of effective access to a court, and that any interference with his privacy rights was required by legitimate policy considerations and was not disproportionate (Clarke LJ dissenting on the issue of whether it was disproportionate to prevent the claimant from using the computer in the daytime: he thought that it was). Despite the fact that the court applied the *Daly* test and required that the infringement of Art 6 be justified and disproportionate, the case differs from *Daly* since the court was very unwilling to subject the Prison Service's assertions about the needs of

in-cell IT access. Despite this entitlement to IT, in practice prisoners who have been granted such access in principle often find that they are on a long waiting list: if their legal proceedings are imminent and the computer is really essential, it is surely arguable that such practical restrictions infringe Article 6.

Production at Court

Where prisoners wish to appear themselves before courts the judiciary have been **7.21** less willing to facilitate them. In *Becker v Home Office*[38] it was held that the Governor was entitled to recover from the prisoner the costs of producing a prisoner at court to pursue a civil claim. In *Ex p Greenwood*[39] this was extended to allow the Home Secretary to refuse to direct the Prison Governor to produce a prisoner to the court to pursue a private prosecution unless the prisoner gave an undertaking in advance that he would pay the costs of production. The situation was more fully considered in *Ex p Wynne*.[40] There the applicant had obtained leave for judicial review actions against the Governor and Home Secretary but had subsequently been refused legal aid. He sought to be allowed to appear in person but when given an application to do so tore it up, possibly because appearance would be conditional on his agreeing to pay the costs of production. His subsequent judicial review action failed on the grounds that without filling in the application he could not claim that the Governor had unlawfully refused his application. However in the Court of Appeal Lord Donaldson MR suggested that in some circumstances requiring an applicant to agree to pay would constitute an unlawful interference with his right of access to the courts.

Lord Donaldson MR observed that the then relevant provision, s 29(1) of the **7.22** Criminal Justice Act 1961,[41] empowered the Home Secretary to order production where he felt it was 'desirable in the interests of justice'. Even where it was desirable, and Lord Donaldson felt it nearly always would be, that still left the Home Secretary a discretion. In exercising it he could look at a range of factors, in particular whether the nature of the case and its procedures required the applicant's presence. Where the procedure was entirely written, for example, it probably would not. Where the Home Secretary found such presence to be necessary, if the procedure was oral and the applicant had no counsel for example, a decision not to allow production would be subject to review and the prisoner's inability to pay production costs would not be a good reason for refusal. To do so would be to put

---

security to searching scrutiny. A similar view was taken in *R v Governor HM Prison Risley, ex p Cooper* [2002] EWHC 125, where denial of access to the internet to research legal materials was upheld on the grounds that the prisoner already had sufficient access to legal materials.

[38] [1972] 2 QB 407.
[39] *R v Home Secretary, ex p Greenwood*, The Times, 2 August 1986.
[40] *R v Home Secretary, ex p Wynne* [1993] 1 All ER 574.
[41] Repealed and re-enacted by the Crime (Sentences) Act 1997, Sch 1, para 3(1).

prisoners who could afford to pay in a better position than those who could not and in any case Lord Donaldson MR felt that as a prisoner should not have to pay for his own imprisonment and had no control over where he was detained such costs should be limited to those of transport from the prison closest to the court. Where an action was against the Prison Service itself there was a danger that the Home Secretary, in exercising this discretion, might appear a judge in his own cause. Therefore Lord Donaldson suggested he might seek the guidance of the court on this matter.

7.23 The other Court of Appeal judges were less willing to endorse the view that conditioning production on payment of costs was unreasonable, Staughton LJ indicating that prisoners were not entitled to equal access to the courts with other people and McCowan LJ suggesting that the right to go to court was one of those forfeited by necessary implication of imprisonment. Nevertheless they also felt it would be wise for the Home Secretary to seek the view of the court, a view supported by a unanimous House of Lords which did not reach the payment issue. All the judges involved in the case appeared to agree that *R v Governor of Brixton Prison, ex p Walsh*[42] remained good law. There the House of Lords upheld the Governor's refusal to produce a prisoner for a remand hearing because of a lack of adequate staff resources. Despite what Lord Fraser referred to as a 'scandalous' situation of delay of the applicant appearing on charges the court unanimously concluded that the Governor had not acted unreasonably in refusing production. Unlike *Wynne* the prisoner in *Walsh* was not being prevented from appearing at the trial of the matter in which he was concerned and so the ultimate outcome was not being prejudiced. However the court could perhaps have sent a clearer signal that justice delayed is justice denied.[43]

7.24 Guidance on the production of prisoners, in the light of Article 6 of the ECHR, is set out in PSO 4625.[44] It leaves the legal test for production unchanged—under the Crime (Sentences) Act 1997, the Secretary of State, usually through powers

---

[42] [1984] 2 All ER 609.

[43] In *R v Home Secretary, ex p Harding*, 15 December 2000, Kennedy LJ held that it was not necessary for the interests of justice to produce a prisoner litigant in person at his application for permission to appeal against a refusal of leave to seek judicial review, since he could express himself very clearly on paper. Kennedy LJ was also very mindful of the fact that 'as a serving Category A prisoner, in a prison situated 200 miles from this building, it would involve a substantial amount of expenditure of public funds in order to bring him to this building in order to make such representations as he might wish to make. In my judgment, those are powerful factors' (para 3).

[44] Brief guidance on the production of prisoners at the request of the police is contained in PSO 1801. In an attempt to reduce the necessity for moving prisoners to criminal courts, PSO 1030, pursuant to s 57 of the Crime and Disorder Act 1998, enables defendants in local prisons to attend preliminary hearings at magistrates' courts by video conferencing link with the prison, and also in some circumstances to have video conferences with their legal representatives. All local prisons, and other prisons containing inmates on remand, must construct sufficient video booths. In the light of widespread problems with getting prisoners to court on time for minor appearances, this scheme would be welcome if it functioned efficiently.

delegated to the governor, must decide whether production of the prisoner is 'desirable in the interests of justice'. The PSO aims to provide guidance for the exercise of this discretion, and is clearly based on the line of cases discussed above. Chapter 1 lists the types of proceedings where production may be requested: these include family and housing matters as well as criminal and civil actions. Quasi-judicial matters such as medical examinations for civil damages claims, and Criminal Injuries Compensation Authority hearings are also covered. Chapter 2 sets out the Article 6 considerations which must be taken into account. The prison must consider whether it is necessary for the prisoner to attend 'personally at court at the relevant stage' in order for the proceedings to be fair. This involves considering such factors as whether the case is arguable (a matter not usually within the knowledge of the prison service, it might be thought) and whether the prisoner is legally represented. Chapter 3 sets out the criteria which help to decide whether production is in the interests of justice or not, and Chapter 4 deals with practical and security issues. Interestingly, Chapter 5 states that the ability and willingness of the prisoner to contribute to the cost of production must not be taken into account when considering whether to allow him or her to be produced at court: the decision must be made purely on the basis of justice and security considerations. The PSO is a step forward from the common law approach, though it remains to be seen how generously it will be implemented in practice, and whether justice is really given priority over resource issues.

C. General Correspondence

Development of a Right to Correspond

The present rules on general prisoners' correspondence are a direct outcome of the **7.25** *Silver* case, decided by the European Commission of Human Rights in 1980 and affirmed by the ECtHR in 1983. The case arose out of numerous complaints from prisoners of censorship of their correspondence after the *Golder* case in 1975.[45] The Commission eventually selected the complaints of six prisoners and one relative, relating to 62 letters which had been stopped between 1972 and 1976. These included letters to MPs, lawyers, journalists, and relatives, among others. The letters had been stopped on a number of grounds, some because they raised complaints about treatment that had not been dealt with internally (the 'prior ventilation rule' referred to earlier), some because the prisoner had not asked to correspond with people who were not friends or relatives, and some because they contained matter which was seen as 'objectionable' and would therefore be prohibited under Prison Rule 33(3) (now 37(3)).

34

---

[45] *Golder v UK* Series A No 18 (1975) 1 EHRR 524.

7.26   The Commission held for the applicants that stopping the letters constituted a breach of Article 8 as regards nearly all of the complaints. In particular the Commission took the view that, since any stopping of a letter was prima facie a violation of Article 8's protection of the right of correspondence, to be valid such interference had to come within the justified limitations of Article 8(2). The first requirement to do so was that the restrictions be 'prescribed by law', which, the court had indicated in the *Sunday Times* case,[46] meant that the norm must be 'formulated with sufficient precision to enable the citizen to regulate his conduct: he must be able—if need be with appropriate advice—to foresee, to a degree that is reasonable in the circumstances, the consequences which a given action may entail'.[47] Most of the restrictions invoked to justify stopping the letters fell at this stage. The Commission held that they could not be reasonably foreseen from the simple declaration that correspondence would be interfered with if found to be objectionable. Though Standing Orders and Circular Instructions did spell out more precisely the criteria for deciding what sort of correspondence was regarded as objectionable, these were not available to prisoners or their relatives. Only restrictions based on material which attempted to stimulate public agitation, circumvent prison regulations, or which contained threats of violence or discussed the crimes of others were held to be foreseeable from the language of rule 33(3).

7.27   In addition to failing to meet the criterion of being prescribed by law, the Commission took the view that many of the restrictions failed to justify a violation of Article 8 because they were over-broad and were not necessary in a democratic society to meet the legitimate grounds for restriction set out in Article 8(2). This finding applied notably to the prior ventilation rule, the restriction on corresponding with those other than friends and relatives without obtaining permission, and a number of the content-based restrictions on correspondence. These included prohibiting letters containing material intended for publication, representations concerning the prisoner's trial conviction and sentence, complaints about prison treatment, the stimulation of public petitions, and material which contained grossly improper language. Those grounds which had been held to be foreseeable and hence 'in accordance with law' were also regarded as being justified as necessary to prevent disorder or ensure the protection of the freedoms of others.[48]

7.28   In response to the *Silver* decision the Home Office undertook to publish SO 5, relating to communications, so that prisoners would have a much better idea of

---

[46]   *Sunday Times v UK* Series A No 30 (1979) 2 EHRR 245.
[47]   ibid, para 49.
[48]   *Silver v UK* (1983) 5 EHRR 347 imposed rather more stringent restrictions on prison censorship than the US Supreme Court in *Turner v Safely*, 482 US 78 (1987), where it held that any restrictions were constitutional providing they were 'reasonably related' to legitimate penological justifications and upheld a broad based restriction on prisoners corresponding with other prisoners who were not family members.

inclusion of what sort of material might lead to a letter being stopped.[49] They also reviewed the criteria on which censorship can take place and SO 5B(2) now expressly states that '[t]he provisions affecting correspondence set out in this Order are necessary to meet the operational needs summarised above, while complying with Articles 8 and 10 of the European Convention on Human Rights'.

Correspondence: The Present Law

In order to comply with the HRA, the new rule 34, entitled 'Communications **7.29** generally', was introduced. This provides that any restrictions imposed on prisoner communications by the Secretary of State (or a governor acting on his behalf) must either be shown not to interfere with the Convention rights of any person, or must be necessary on the grounds specified in Article 8(2) and proportionate. Chapter 36 of the *Security Manual*, a revised version of which was introduced by PSI 57/2001, also emphasizes the requirements of the Convention. The current SO 5B(34) sets out restrictions on 'general correspondence', which SO 5B(33)(1) defines as correspondence with family, friends, and other organizations. Correspondence which does not come within this categorization is that with legal advisers, the Parliamentary Commissioner for Administration, the Criminal Cases Review Commission, and the courts. The restrictions remain fairly extensive but those ruled in violation of Article 8 by the *Silver* court have been removed or modified. In the case of indecent or offensive language, for example, this can only be grounds for stopping a letter if it appears that the intention of the writer is to cause distress or anxiety to the recipient or any other person. Material intended for publication can be stopped only if it is intended in return for payment, if it is for an organization which the governor has decided that the prisoner should not correspond with on security and good order grounds under SO 5B (26),[50] if it concerns the prisoner's own crime or the crime of others, except where this consists of serious representations or forms part of a serious comment about the criminal justice system, or where it refers to individual members of staff in such a way that they might be identified. Most of the other restrictions concern material which might threaten prison or national security (including coded messages), which take the form of threats to others outside the prison, or which involves business transactions outside a number of business exceptions outlined in SO 5B(34)(10).

---

[49] Other states took similar measures to deal with *Silver*. In France, eg, the Décrets in the Code de Procédure Pénale, Art D 413–20, were altered by decree of 26 January 1983 to bring them into line with the *Silver* requirements.

[50] To take this action the governor must have reason to believe that the person or organization concerned 'is planning or engaged in activities which present a genuine and serious threat to the security or good order of the establishment or of any other Prison Department establishment'. Governors are required to consult with headquarters before coming to this decision.

7.30   Most of these restrictions would now appear to satisfy the ECtHR's application of Article 8 in *Silver*. The Commission and Court there indicated that the main problem lay in the blanket or over-broad nature of the restrictions. The court did however acknowledge the legitimacy of the type of interests the Government claimed it was seeking to protect by the restrictions. These included the security of the prison, the safety of people inside and outside it, and the maintenance of good order in the prison. This suggested that more narrowly drawn restrictions would be upheld. However, the court would continue to apply a balancing test to these restrictions, examining them to discover whether they 'correspond to a pressing social need' and are 'proportionate to the legitimate end pursued'. Those on indecent language and material intended for publication might still fall on the wrong side of the line.[51] Letters to MPs, restrictions on which were found to be unlawful in *Silver*,[52] are now the subject of their own Standing Order—SO 5D. This indicates that letters to UK MPs may be read but may be stopped only if they contain material which it would be an offence to send (ie obscene material). Letters to MEPs, however, are essentially treated in the same way as general correspondence and hence may be stopped on a much broader range of grounds. Correspondence with the Parliamentary Commissioner for Administration is treated in the same way as letters to UK MPs.

7.31   Prisoners are no longer limited to a particular list of correspondents, with the need to get approval to write to anyone not on that list. The presumption now in SO 5B(19) is that a prisoner can correspond with whomever he wishes. However Standing Orders still place some restrictions on whom a prisoner may correspond with. These include minors (where the person with parental responsibility for the minor requests that the prisoner not be allowed to write to the minor), convicted prisoners in other institutions or ex-offenders (where the governor feels this is undesirable on rehabilitation or security and good order grounds), victims of the offence, and organizations which the governor has reason to believe pose a threat to security or good order at that or any other prison. The restrictions on writing to victims do not apply where the victim is a close relative or the prisoner is unconvicted, although such letters may be censored where their content breaches SO 5B(34). Prisoners are generally not allowed to write to box numbers or receive anonymous letters.

---

[51]   In the Commission's judgment in *Silver v UK* (1981) 3 EHRR 475 it stressed with regard to restrictions on material intended for publication the importance of access to the media in a democratic society. With respect to restrictions on indecent language it stressed the democratic right of everyone to freedom of expression, even if this involves the use of terms which others might find vulgar and shocking and added, at para 406, '[t]he freedom may be particularly important for persons, such as prisoners, subject to the daily frustrations of a closed community life'.

[52]   See also *McCallum v UK* Series A No 183 (1991) 13 EHRR 597, where the letters were stopped under the requirements of Scottish Standing Orders that any allegations of ill treatment should first have been submitted to internal complaints review.

Where a letter is stopped the prisoner will be informed and, in the case of letters **7.32** containing prohibited material, invited to rewrite the letter. Following recommendations in the Woolf Report the routine reading of prisoners' letters has decreased greatly. SO 5B(32)(1) now provides that routine reading should take place only in a limited number of categories; namely all prisoners (of whatever security category) held at maximum security establishments or who are from such establishments but temporarily accommodated elsewhere, all prisoners categorized Category A or being considered for Category A (wherever detained), all prisoners (of whatever category) detained in separate units designed to hold Category A prisoners and all prisoners on the Escape List. For all other prisoners routine reading should only occur 'as an exceptional measure'[53] where there is reason to believe that: it will assist in preventing or detecting criminal activities or threats to the security or good order of the prison; that a prisoner or his or her correspondent may attempt to infringe the established restrictions; or where it may be in a prisoner's own interests (for example where a severely depressed prisoner is expecting to receive bad news). These provisions would appear to be in conformity with human rights norms. Indeed the ECtHR has regularly upheld the practice of reading prisoners' mail.[54] All mail may be opened and inspected for illicit enclosures but SO 5B(31)(2) indicates that at open prisons this should only be done if there is reason to suspect that it contains an illicit enclosure. Chapter 36 of the *Security Manual* provides that where routine reading is in place, prisoners must be informed of the fact. Reading may continue only for as long as is necessary and proportionate, and each case must be reviewed at least every six months.

Ending routine reading also has an effect on the number and length of letters that **7.33** prisoners may send and receive, as staff resources for censorship purposes are the main factor in placing limits on this. Where there is no routine reading there may still be random reading, in accordance with Chapter 36 of the *Security Manual*, which indicates that no more than 5 per cent of mail should be randomly read. In those prisons where routine censorship has been ended no limits are placed on the length of prisoners' letters or how many they may send or receive. Such absence of limitations is considerably more generous than the Prison Rules, as rule 35(2)(a) entitles a convicted prisoner only to send and receive one letter a week, although

---

[53] SO 5B(32)(2).

[54] See, eg, *Boyle and Rice v UK* Series A No 131 (1988) 10 EHRR 425. The US Supreme Court has also held that prison authorities can read prisoners' correspondence in *Procunier v Martinez*, 416 US 396 (1974). In *Thornburgh v Abbott*, 490 US 401 (1989) the Supreme Court indicated that it would subject restrictions on incoming mail to less scrutiny than those on outgoing mail. However, in *Puzinas v Lithuania* Application 44800/98, 14 March 2002, the ECtHR did find a breach of Art 8. The claimant's ingoing and outgoing mail—including a letter to his wife and a letter from the European Commission on Human Rights—had been opened in the applicant's absence and censored by the prison authorities. No reasons were given to justify the interference, which the court therefore found to be unnecessary in a democratic society.

under rule 35(1) unconvicted prisoners are not subject to any limits in the number of letters they send or receive.[55]

7.34 The rule 35(2)(a) letter is referred to by Standing Orders as the 'statutory letter', postage costs of which are to be met out of public expense and which may not be stopped as or during punishment. In addition SO 5B(6A)(2) indicates that even at prisons where routine reading is in force convicted prisoners should normally be allowed to send at least one 'privilege' letter per week and as many more as are compatible with available staff resources for censorship purposes. Such letters may be paid for out of prison earnings or private cash. As a privilege the right to send such letters can be removed as part of a disciplinary award. In prisons where routine censorship prevails letters are normally limited to four sides of A4. A third class of letters also exists, known as 'special letters'. These are permitted to deal with a number of specific circumstances, such as to deal with family or personal business affairs, transfer to another prison, or to contact a probation officer regarding employment on release.[56] Letters on transfer should be sent at the public expense and the governor has a discretion to charge other special letters at the public expense. Despite rule 35(1), SO 5B(8) limits unconvicted prisoners to two statutory letters a week and as many further privilege letters as they wish.

D. Visits

7.35 Under Prison Rule 35(2)(b) a convicted prisoner is entitled to two visits every four weeks (although this can be reduced to one by a direction of the Secretary of State). Like the letter allowed every week under rule 35(2)(a) this is referred to by Standing Orders as the 'statutory visit' and it should normally last at least one hour (unless the number of visits taking place and staff resources make this impossible, in which case they may be reduced to 30 minutes). Statutory visits by relatives qualify for funding under the assisted visits scheme.[57] Like the statutory letter the statutory visit cannot be withdrawn as part of punishment, unlike the 'privilege visits' which may be made available at an institution in addition to the statutory

---

[55] The European Commission has in one case upheld restrictions on the number of letters a prisoner may send on the ground that this was justified for the prevention of disorder: see *Chester v UK*, 68 D & R 65 (1990).

[56] The full list is given in SO 5B(7). Prisoners who are non-UK nationals may also write to their consulate or High Commission on the same basis.

[57] Details of the scheme are set out in PSO 4405, including eligibility, type of travel which will be subsidized, and subsistence payments. Applications are now made to the Assisted Prison Visits Unit of the Prison Service. Despite accepting that, for low-income families, inadequate financial assistance for prison visits constitutes an interference with family life, the Court of Appeal in *R (McManus) v Head of Assisted Prison Visits* [2001] EWCA Civ 966 was reluctant to consider in depth how much state assistance such families are entitled to. However, the court did not rule such an inquiry out, if sufficient evidence were to be presented.

visit. However, under SO 5A(9) a governor may defer a visit while a prisoner is in cellular confinement where the governor believes that, because of the prisoner's behaviour or attitudes, removal from cellular confinement for the purposes of a visit would be clearly impracticable or undesirable. It follows therefore that a prisoner in cellular confinement should not have a visit deferred as a form of punishment or pressure to modify behaviour. If a visit is deferred the prisoner can be given the opportunity of writing an extra statutory letter instead of accumulating visits.

7.36 Standing Orders do not indicate a minimum number of privilege visits that may be allowed. This appears to be left up to the governor of each prison depending on available resources. As a result, disparities are likely to arise between prisons which may adversely affect prisoners on transfer from one prison to another.[58] Standing Orders also make provision for 'special visits', to deal with family or personal business, or where the prisoner is seriously ill. Such 'special visits', like legal visits or those by probation officers, MPs, priests or ministers, consular officers, the Parliamentary Commissioner for Administration, or police officers, do not count against a prisoner's allocation of visits. Prisoners may choose to accumulate visits over a period of time and then seek temporary transfer to a prison closer to home in order to take these visits (normally over a period of a month). Category A prisoners, who are often detained a considerable distance from their homes and families, are especially encouraged to make use of this facility. SO 5A(11) indicates that a minimum of three and a maximum of 26 visits may be accumulated. The same Standing Order indicates that temporary transfer for accumulated visits should take place no more than once a year.

7.37 Unconvicted prisoners are entitled by rule 35(1) to as many visits as they wish, which should normally be for up to 15 minutes a day, Monday to Saturday. However, SO 5A(4) indicates that where available staff resources make compliance with this rule impracticable the Area Manager can authorize a reduction in the frequency of visits as long as the aggregate of 90 minutes of visiting a week is maintained. Despite the apparently mandatory language of rule 35(1) one judicial review challenge to the denial of visits to unconvicted prisoners failed where the court took the view that in the circumstances the governor was not acting unreasonably.[59]

7.38 As regards who can visit a prisoner, SO 5A(30) and SO 5A(31) give particular prominence to the visits of close relatives. These are defined as spouses or persons

---

[58] It is worth noting that in *Boyle and Rice v UK* Series A No 131 (1988) 10 EHRR 425, the Commission took the view that a reduction in the number and quality of visits as a result of a transfer did not amount to a breach of Art 8 or 14.

[59] See the Northern Irish case of *Mulvenna v Governor HM Prison Belfast*, 23 December 1985, where the court upheld restriction of visits for remand prisoners to one and a half visits a week on the ground that this was not a clearly unreasonable response to staffing limitations.

with whom the prisoner was living as man or wife before imprisonment,[60] parents, or those in loco parentis, children, or children to whom the inmate is in loco parentis, brothers, sisters, and fiancés or fiancées (providing the governor is satisfied that a genuine intention to marry exists). While the governor may refuse visits from such people on security and good order grounds, SO 5A(31) indicates that this should be done only in exceptional cases. Where a prisoner's close relative is in another prison establishment then, subject to requirements of security and the availability of transport and accommodation, visits may take place at three monthly intervals. MPs may also visit prisoners as of right on production of a special visiting order issued by the governor.

7.39 Other visitors are also allowed but the governor may refuse these on security or good order grounds. He may also refuse them, according to SO 5A(32), where he has good reason to believe that the visit would seriously impede the rehabilitation of the prisoner. Decisions by governors to refuse visits are subject to judicial review as they potentially infringe the rights of both the prisoner and the visitor. In a Northern Irish case, *McCartney v Governor HM Prison, Maze*,[61] the decision of the Secretary of State to deny a convicted IRA prisoner visits from a Sinn Fein local councillor (on the ground that Sinn Fein was a political party which supported the IRA) was upheld as reasonable despite the absence of any claims that this specific councillor's visit posed a threat to the security of the prison. Limitations on who may visit could also be reviewed under Articles 8 and 14 of the ECHR. Decisions of the Commission in this area show a greater reluctance to scrutinize official restrictions than is apparent with restrictions on correspondence, at least where they do not involve close family members or amount substantially to prohibiting the prisoner contact with the outside world.[62] The court and Commission have given the national authorities a margin of appreciation in regulating prisoners'

---

[60] No reference is made in the SOs to gay or lesbian partners. In one American case visiting restrictions on gay and lesbian partners were held to be unconstitutional under the due process clause as the institution could not demonstrate any legitimate aims to be served by such restrictions: *Doe v Sparks*, 733 F Supp 227 (1990). Canadian prisons allow visits by same sex partners, after settlement of a case involving a challenge to denying access to the family visits to same sex partners under the equality provisions of the Canadian Charter.

[61] (1987) 11 NIJB 94.

[62] Visits, unlike correspondence, are not expressly referred to in Art 8 and therefore are raised under the more general respect for family life provisions. It is well established that a prisoner retains the right to respect for his family life, and that prisoners are therefore entitled to the assistance of the prison in maintaining contact with their families: *X v UK* Application 9054/80, 30 DR 113. In considering the precise requirements of Art 8 in a particular case, the court will take account of the 'ordinary and reasonable requirements of imprisonment' and the measure of discretion accorded to the authorities to regulate contact: *Campbell and Fell v UK* (1984) 7 EHRR 165. The relationship between mother and child is subject to particular protection: see Ch 11. In the case of *Kavanagh v UK* Application 19085/91, the Commission indicated, although finding no violation in the instant case, that significant limitations on visits from family members may well raise Art 8 issues. A prisoner's detention far from home may in some circumstances violate Art 8: *McCotter v UK* Application 18632/91, Commission Decision, 9 December 1992.

visits. However, the Court of Appeal has indicated that the margin of appreciation has no place in the domestic application of Article 8, suggesting that the courts will scrutinize such restrictions particularly closely.[63] While visits from legal advisers and priests or ministers will generally be allowed (and may take place out of the hearing of an officer and without restrictions on the use of notes or tape recording) those from journalists in a professional capacity will generally be prohibited, although the governor has a discretion to allow them. SO 5A(37A) provides that when journalists are permitted to visit in a professional capacity they may be required to sign an undertaking that no material obtained during the interview may be used for professional purposes except as permitted by the governor. This provision was upheld by the Court of Appeal in *R v Home Secretary, ex p Simms*.[64] In that case two prisoners sought judicial review of decisions to deny visits by journalists who refused to sign such undertakings. While the Divisional Court held such a requirement to be an unnecessary interference with the prisoner's freedom of expression, Kennedy LJ in the Court of Appeal took the view that a convicted prisoner lost any 'right' to communicate orally with journalists as part and parcel of imprisonment. He was of the opinion that once incarcerated a prisoner had no right to receive visits from anyone but relatives and lawyers. Since the court rejected any argument that the right to communicate with journalists was analogous to the right to communicate with lawyers in *Leech*,[65] the restriction was analysed under reasonableness standards. Here both Kennedy and Judge LJ seemed to have little difficulty in deciding that the restrictions were not unreasonable, though neither expanded on this in any great detail beyond noting that prisoners were still free to communicate with journalists via letters.

A different approach was taken by the House of Lords. Lord Steyn analysed the free speech rights at stake, emphasizing that the prisoners in question wished to communicate with journalists in order to overturn what they said were their wrongful convictions: **7.40**

---

[63] *R (P) v Home Secretary* [2001] 1 WLR 2002, CA. The court drew the following conclusions from a review of the Strasbourg authorities: '(i) the right to respect for family life is not a right which a prisoner necessarily loses by reason of his/her incarceration; (ii) on the other hand, when a court considers whether the state's reasons for interfering with that right are relevant and sufficient, it is entitled to take into account (a) the reasonable requirements of prison organisation and security and (b) the desirability of maintaining a uniform regime in prison which avoids any appearance of arbitrariness or discrimination; (iii) whatever the justification for a general rule, Convention law requires the court to consider the application of that rule to the particular case, and to determine whether in that case the interference is proportionate to the particular legitimate aim being pursued; (iv) the more serious the intervention in any given case (and interventions cannot come very much more serious than the act of separating a mother from a very young child), the more compelling must be the justification.' (para 78).
[64] [1999] QB 349.
[65] [1994] QB 198.

The value of free speech in a particular case must be measured in specifics. Not all types of speech have an equal value. For example, no prisoner would ever be permitted to have interviews with a journalist to publish pornographic material or to give vent to so-called hate speech. Given the purpose of a sentence of imprisonment, a prisoner can also not claim to join in a debate on the economy or on political issues by way of interviews with journalists. In these respects the prisoner's right to free speech is outweighed by deprivation of liberty by the sentence of a court, and the need for discipline and control in prisons. But the free speech at stake in the present cases is qualitatively of a very different order. The prisoners are in prison because they are presumed to have been properly convicted. They wish to challenge the safety of their convictions. In principle it is not easy to conceive of a more important function which free speech might fulfil.[66]

While their Lordships did not consider that paras 37 and 37A were unlawful in themselves, they did not justify the blanket ban imposed, which was accordingly unlawful. Such a ban went far beyond what was justified in the interests of security or control. This was succinctly expressed by Lord Hoffmann:

> What this case decides is that the principle of legality applies to subordinate legislation as much as to Acts of Parliament. Prison regulations expressed in general language are also presumed to be subject to fundamental human rights. The presumption enables them to be valid. But it also means that properly construed, they do not authorise a blanket restriction which would curtail not merely the prisoner's right of free expression, but its use in a way which could provide him with access to justice.[67]

7.41 The extent of prisoners' rights to communicate with journalists was further considered by the High Court in *R (Hirst) v Home Secretary*.[68] Mr Hirst was the General Secretary of the Association of Prisoners, a body set up by prisoners to promote their interests. After the Association was founded, he gave several radio interviews. The Governor warned him not to conduct any further interviews. The day after the warning, he gave a further radio interview by telephone, about judicial review proceedings in which he was involved. The claimant was disciplined for disobeying the lawful order of the Governor, contrary to rule 51(22). He was subsequently transferred, and sought an undertaking from the Governor of the new prison that he would be allowed to give pre-recorded interviews on matters of legitimate public interest. He offered several conditions, including allowing the content of the interview to be checked by the Governor before broadcast. The request was rejected, and this refusal was challenged by way of judicial review. The claimant argued that his Article 10 rights were engaged, and that although the Home Office decision pursued a legitimate aim, namely security, it was dispro-

---

[66] [2000] 2 AC 115, 127.
[67] ibid, 132.
[68] [2002] EWHC 602; [2002] UKHRR 758.

portionately restrictive. In a detailed judgment, Elias J analysed the application of the proportionality test in the prison context:

> In general, as the analysis of Lord Clyde in the *de Freitas* case makes clear, the onus is on the party seeking to interfere with an Article 10 right to show that the interference is designed to meet a legitimate objective recognised in Article 10(2); that the means adopted are rationally connected to the objective; and that the Convention right is not impaired more than is necessary to achieve the objective. However, where the right is removed as the deliberate and considered response to the need to provide an effective penal policy, there is in truth no room for the court to apply the principle of minimum response. Once it is determined that the appropriate sentence requires the denial of the right to exercise freedom of speech in certain contexts, then there is no other step which can secure that particular objective. If that element of the sentence were not imposed, the sanction would be a different and lesser one. In these circumstances the issue is not whether restricting freedom of speech as part of the penalty is the minimum required to achieve the particular objective sought; that is inherent in what is considered to be the necessary objective. Rather it is whether even if it is the minimum compatible with achieving the desired and legitimate objective, it nevertheless impacts disproportionately on the Convention rights.[69]

Elias J went on to state that:

> [W]here the state has deliberately chosen to deprive prisoners of their rights as part of their punishment, the courts will not readily interfere with that decision, particularly where it reflects the democratic will, but even then they may do so where the denial of the right is disproportionate to the penal objective. Whether this is so will depend largely upon the significance of the particular right interfered with.
>
> By contrast, for those aspects of freedom of speech which the prisoner is entitled to retain notwithstanding the sentence, it seems to me that in practice the proportionality principle applies in a different way, even though the theoretical framework remains the same. There may still be legitimate reasons for interfering with that freedom, in the sense that they fall within the terms of Article 10(2). But where the law permits such interference to occur, the government must show that the means used to impair the right go no further than is necessary to accomplish those legitimate objectives. The aim of the relevant policy here [para 6.10 of PSO 4400, which prohibits calls to the media other than in 'exceptional circumstances'] is not deliberately to deprive the prisoner of his Convention right; it is to recognise that right and only to interfere with it so far as is necessary to achieve a specific objective or objectives. The courts can with more confidence exercise a tighter review of the restriction to ensure that it does not unnecessarily interfere with Convention rights.[70]

Elias J considered that rules restricting access to the telephone for dealing with the media could not be considered part of the sentence of imprisonment. On behalf of the Home Office, it was argued that such media contact falls within Lord

---

[69] [33].
[70] [39]–[40].

Steyn's category, in *Simms*, of 'debate on the economy or on political issues', and is thus denied as part of the sentence of imprisonment. Elias J disagreed, considering that access to the media in order to express concerns about matters affecting the rights or interests of prisoners as a group did not fall into Lord Steyn's category, and that there was no other basis for saying that restrictions on such access constitute an integral part of the sentence of imprisonment. Accordingly, the policy had to meet the proportionality test. While Elias J 'would certainly not be willing to say that a prisoner should be entitled as a matter of course to have access to the media by telephone whenever the conditions proposed by the claimant are satisfied',[71] and considered that 'the prison authorities are justified in making the right to contact the media by telephone one that can be exercised only exceptionally',[72] he considered that the Home Office's arguments about security and control do not justify a blanket ban on such interviews. In particular, he did not accept that writing to the media would always be an acceptable substitute for a telephone interview. While PSO 4400 was not, therefore, unlawful on its face, Elias J granted a declaration that 'the policy which in all circumstances denies the claimant the right to contact the media by telephone whenever his purpose is to comment on matters of legitimate public interest relating to prisons and prisoners is unlawful'.[73] As in *Simms*, the principle of legality operated to read a policy which potentially infringed Convention rights in such a way as to ensure the protection of those rights.

Conditions for Visits

7.42 Visits by police officers in connection with an offence are required to be conducted in accordance with PACE and Code C of its Codes of Practice. Such visits should be in the sight and may be in the hearing of a prison officer and SO 5A(39)(4) indicates that a prisoner is not required to remain in an interview beyond the time necessary for the police to explain the purpose of the interview.

7.43 Standing Orders indicate that visits should take place 'under the most humane conditions possible'.[74] In practice the quality of visiting conditions varies widely.[75] Unless special security considerations are thought to dictate otherwise they should normally take place in an open visiting area where the prisoner and visitors

---

[71] [77]. These conditions were that the journalist indicate in advance the scope of the interview, that the call be monitored by the prison, and comments made, that the journalist be vetted in advance, and that the prisoner and the journalist give an assurance about the contents of the interview (see [83]).

[72] ibid.

[73] [88].

[74] SO 5A(24)(1).

[75] See V Stern, *Bricks of Shame: Britain's Prisons* (London, 1987) 1046. For a view that conditions have become increasingly restrictive in the wake of the Learmont Report see U Padel, 'It's Not Just a Visit' (1998) 43 Prison Report 18.

may sit at a table and may embrace. Up to three people will normally be permitted on a visit, with children under 10 years old not counting towards this total.[76] Except where the visit is a legal visit or one by an MP, priest, or minister, visits will normally be in the sight and hearing of prison officers. This usually means that prison officers will be in the room where visits take place, but the governor may direct closer oversight of a visit where he feels security or good order considerations require this. Notes may not be taken or made in an interview without the permission of the governor although SO 5A(26) indicates that 'in general the degree of control should be commensurate with the level of censorship in force at the establishment'. Nor are tape recordings permitted in visits, though this is subject to exceptions for visits by legal advisers, MPs, consular officials, priests, and ministers, or members of the European Committee for the Prevention of Torture.

SO 5A(24)(2) provides for closed visits 'where security or control considerations **7.44** so require'. In practice these seem to occur in two circumstances: first where the prisoner is classified Exceptional Risk, though even this is not done routinely now, and secondly where he or she has been found to have smuggled drugs into the prison or tested positive for drugs. In the *O'Dhuibhir*[77] case the Court of Appeal showed greater sympathy for the applicant's complaints in respect of closed family visits than closed legal visits. It noted that the family visits policy prohibited any physical contact between prisoners and their children, who might not be old enough to benefit significantly from purely verbal communication. However the court concluded that such restrictions could not be shown to be unreasonable. Gibson LJ noted that this policy had been approved by the Learmont Report as it applied to Exceptional Risk prisoners and cited American cases such as *Block v Rutherford*[78] which endorsed prohibitions on contact family visits for prisoners awaiting trial.

As has been indicated elsewhere in this book both prisoners and their visitors are **7.45** liable to be searched. This includes children and even babies.[79] Search of a visitor

---

[76] In 1998, a child protection policy was introduced in PSO 4400. It provided that prison governors had to identify all visitors who presented a potential risk to children: such prisoners are only to be allowed to receive visits from their own children or siblings, other than in exceptional circumstances. In *R (Banks) v Governor of Wakefield Prison*, 24 September 2001, this policy was challenged. The claimant was serving a discretionary life sentence for, inter alia, gross indecency on an eight year old boy. He also had a previous conviction for indecent assault on a boy while in a detention centre. The prison refused permission for him to be visited by his young nephew, and the claimant argued that the policy was ultra vires Prison Rule 4 and that the decision breached his right to family life under Art 8. Harrison J held that the policy was lawful, since it was not rigid, and that on the facts the relationship between claimant and nephew was not close enough to engage Art 8.

[77] [1997] COD 315.

[78] 468 US 576 (1984).

[79] The Prison Service acknowledged doing this in 1996 after it stated that drugs had been found in babies' nappies at some prisons: see The Guardian, 14 September 1996.

probably requires a greater level of suspicion that he or she is taking an unauthorized article into the prison than the search of a prisoner, though it seems that routine rub-down searches of visitors are becoming an increasingly common occurrence.[80] If an unauthorized article—for the specific provisions on drug smuggling, see below—is found during a search or an officer observes a visitor passing or receiving an unauthorized article then the visit may be stopped; similarly if a visitor is seen to be tape-recording the visit. Violation of the prohibition on passing unauthorized articles may be a ground for refusing future visits by the person involved. Where however that person is a close relative a total ban, or a ban for a substantial period of time, as a result of an incident of passing an unauthorized article would appear to go beyond the scope of exceptional circumstances referred to in SO 5A(31) and might violate Article 8 of the ECHR. The validity of any such ban would be especially questionable if the article in question was trivial and was unrelated to escape or to bringing drugs into the prison.

7.46 The question of drug smuggling through visits is one of particular concern to the Prison Service, which has issued PSO 3620, 'Measures to deal with visitors and prisoners who smuggle drugs through visits'. The rules are similar to the provisions for visitors found passing other unauthorized articles, but more stringent: social visitors, including family members, who are found to be smuggling controlled drugs through visits 'will normally be banned under Prison Rule 73 or YOI Rule 71A from the prison for a period of at least 3 months, unless on the facts of the case there are exceptional reasons for not doing so'. The PSO further provides that, where such a ban is not imposed, '[g]overnors must, save in exceptional circumstances, require visits by that visitor (to any prisoner) to be held in closed

---

[80] In *Wainwright v Home Office* [2002] 3 WLR 405, the appellants, a mother and her son (who suffered from cerebral palsy) argued that they had been unlawfully strip searched when visiting at Armley prison. The search was carried out under r 86(1), as refined by a more detailed policy set out by the prison. The Court of Appeal judgment turns mainly on whether the appellants were entitled to damages for the tort of breach of privacy: the court concluded that they were not, since there is no such tort at common law (for discussion of the privacy aspect of the case, see Matrix Media and Information Group, *Privacy and the Media: The Developing Law* (London, 2002), ch 1). However, one of the appellants was still entitled to damages for assault and battery. The Home Office sought, by comparing r 86(1) (which does not say that searches of visitors must be 'seemly') to r 39(2) (which says that searches of prisoners must be as seemly as consistent with discovering anything concealed), to argue that this means that searches of a visitor do not in fact have to be seemly. Buxton LJ said that 'I regret that this point was ever taken. A rule as broad as rule 86, giving power over persons who have committed no crime, and who attend as part of the accepted social policy that prisoners' families are entitled to contact with them, cannot have been intended by Parliament, and cannot be justified, in terms that give largely unlimited powers to the prison authorities' (para 121). Further, despite the fact that the appellants had signed a consent form, the fact that it had not been explained to them meant that the Home Office could not avail itself of the defence of consent (see paras 116–119). Buxton LJ specifically rejected the idea that, even if a visitor's consent is real, they have consented to a generalized strip search. Their consent, if any, extends only to a seemly search which is limited to what is strictly necessary.

or non contact conditions for at least 6 months'.[81] Bans of longer than three months must be reviewed at three-monthly intervals. A finding that a visitor has been smuggling drugs to a prisoner can also lead to that prisoner being subject to mandatory drug testing and disciplinary charges. Such a finding is also to be taken into account when reviewing the prisoner's status on the Incentives and Earned Privileges scheme, allocation, and suitability for Home Detention Curfew. If the finding is taken to have a bearing on risk to the public or escape risk, it can also have a bearing on the prisoner's security categorization.

Conjugal Visits

The issue of whether prisoners are entitled to conjugal visits has been raised before **7.47** the European Commission on Human Rights, which found that a ban on such visits did not violate Article 8 of the Convention.[82] Several European jurisdictions do, however, provide for such visits, or for more extensive family visits, on the prison premises. The Dutch prison system, for example, allows for one such 'private' visit a month.[83] Although the Home Office carried out a review of its policy in 1992 it was decided not to make any changes. This has remained the policy despite the greater restrictions on home leave introduced in 1994 which are discussed later in this chapter.

In *R (Mellor) v Home Secretary*[84] the Court of Appeal considered a related issue, **7.48** namely whether the claimant, a serving prisoner, was entitled, in the absence of conjugal visits, to facilities in order to have a child with his wife by artificial insemination. He gave evidence that, by the time he was released, his wife may well be too old to have a child safely. The Prison Service contended in evidence that it is an explicit consequence of imprisonment that prisoners should not have the opportunity to have conceive children while serving their sentences, until they come to a stage to be entitled to temporary release. The Prison Service also relied on the public concern which would allegedly arise if such facilities were allowed to prisoners, and to the undesirability of allowing children to be born into single

---

[81] In *R (Stewart) v Governor of HMP Ranby and Home Secretary*, CO/2595/2001, the claimant had been charged on three occasions for failing mandatory drug tests. On each occasion he was placed on closed visits for 12 visits; the three sentences were to run consecutively, amounting to 36 closed visits. The claimant argued that the use of closed visits was an additional punishment outside those permitted by the Prison Rules, that a standard tariff had been applied without any consideration of his individual circumstances, and that he had not been allowed to make representations and had been given no reasons. After permission was granted by Scott Baker J, the Home Secretary agreed to review the use of cumulative awards of closed visits, and quashed the imposition of closed visits in the applicant's case.
[82] See *X v UK* Application 6564/74 2 D & R 105 (1975) and *X and Y v Switzerland* Application 8166/78 13 D & R 241 (1978).
[83] See D Downes, *Contrasts in Tolerance: Post War Penal Policy in the Netherlands and in England and Wales* (Oxford, 1988) 176.
[84] [2002] QB 13.

parent families. Lord Phillips MR, after reviewing the Strasbourg case law on Articles 8 and 12, concluded that

> It is not obvious that the signatories to the Convention would have agreed that a man who had, by imprisonment, been justifiably deprived of the enjoyment of family life and the exercise of conjugal rights, should be entitled to inseminate his wife artificially in order to produce a child in whose development and support he could play no part.[85]

The moralistic reasoning of both the Prison Service and the court in this case demonstrates again the extent to which prisoners' lives come under scrutiny in a way in which the lives of others do not. However, Lord Phillips MR did consider that, while a refusal to allow artificial insemination will not *generally* be a disproportionate interference with a prisoner's right to found a family under Article 12 of the Convention, it may be disproportionate where the refusal does not merely delay, but actually *prevents* the founding of a family. This is an extremely high threshold. Both on the issue of conjugal visits and artificial insemination, the British attitude to the level of deprivation which is legitimized by a sentence of imprisonment is considerably harsher than other countries in Europe.

7.49 Interestingly, in view of the refusal of conjugal visits, the Home Office at one time refused to allow prisoners to marry (or leave to marry outside the prison), partly on the ground that a prisoner would be unable to cohabit with his or her wife or husband. In *Hamer v UK*[86] the European Commission on Human Rights rejected this argument, on the ground that marriage was primarily a legal status which did not require cohabitation, as well as others based on security and public interest. It found that refusal to allow a prisoner to marry while detained was a breach of Article 12. The position has been changed by the Marriage Act 1983 and marriages may now take place in places of detention.

E. Telephones

7.50 Prisoners have always been entitled to make a request to the prison governor to use a telephone. Such calls have generally only been allowed to legal advisers or to close relatives to deal with a family problem. However, in 1988 the Home Office began the introduction of cardphones into prisons, a development which Woolf observed could lead to less emphasis on letters and the censorship thereof. Woolf encouraged further extension of the cardphone scheme as a good way of enabling prisoners to maintain more regular and meaningful contact with their families

---

[85] [43].

[86] (1982) 4 EHRR 139. In the US the Supreme Court indicated that restrictions on prisoner marriage could only be justified for reasons of 'compelling necessity': see *Turner v Safely* 482 US 78 (1987).

and to provide a better outlet for emotions that build up in the conditions of prison life. Young prisoners in particular have found telephone contact with their families to be an important way of lessening the isolation of prison life. In response the Home Office decided in late 1991 to extend the provision of card-phones to all parts of the prison estate, with the exception of special security units. In 1994, after the Woodcock Report criticized abuse of official telephones in Whitemoor SSU, their availability was extended to the entire system.

Operating Standard Q21 indicates that designated telephones should be available **7.51** for use by prisoners on reception, during association periods, and at other specified times. Governors are directed to bear in mind the need for foreign nationals to make calls abroad at specified times. The use of cardphones is governed currently by PSO 4400. This indicates that prisoners may obtain as many as they wish of the special cards—which do not operate on the public cardphone system—but should not normally retain more than two with unused units on them at one time. Cards are to be paid for out of private cash and therefore the operation of the incentives scheme at any prison may affect a prisoner's access to phonecards.

All calls using the cardphones can be monitored and may be stopped if they breach **7.52** the conditions of use set out in PSO 4400. In addition, calls to chatline services or Directory Inquiries are electronically barred, as are incoming calls. The PSO prohibits any calls to the media where it is intended that the call itself or the information communicated in it will be used for publication or broadcast. This limitation (which goes further than SO 5B(34)(9) on correspondence) was introduced after it emerged that prisoners had been contacting radio phone-in programmes. One such prisoner challenged the restriction in *R v Home Secretary, ex p Bamber*[87] but the Court of Appeal, on an appeal against refusal of leave, upheld this blanket ban on communication with the media. In so deciding the court seemed impressed with the idea that (unlike communications by letter) the authorities had no means of examining whether a prisoner's statement on the telephone would be in conformity with the rules until it was made. Rose LJ also observed that it remained open to prisoners to request permission in advance to telephone the media on a matter they would be required to disclose. As with *Simms* the *Bamber* case raises the question to what extent prisoners' rights of access to the outside world extends to participation in public debate as opposed to the maintenance of family contacts. The European Commission on Human Rights has found an application by Bamber to be 'manifestly ill founded', largely on the grounds that the authorities could not otherwise exercise effective control over communications.[88] However it

[87] 15 February 1996.
[88] *Bamber v UK* Application 33742/96, Commission Decision, 11 September 1997.

did acknowledge, contrary to *Simms*, that convicted prisoners retain a right to freedom of expression.[89]

7.53 Prisoners are barred from access to STD code information and to the telephone directory. The PSO provides that where a prisoner needs to know a particular number, he must make an application to an officer, explaining why he needs to know the number. If he needs to know an area code, he must get staff to look it up. Calls to mobile phone numbers are prohibited. Category A prisoners are restricted to making calls to people on a pre-approved list. As with correspondence, calls may only be made to victims in very limited circumstances and where a member of the public informs the Prison Service that he or she does not wish to receive calls from a particular prisoner then such calls should be prevented. The PSO indicates that monitoring of most calls will be done in accordance with Chapter 15 of the *Security Manual*. This should be done randomly, and a notice should be prominently displayed near the designated telephones indicating that calls are liable to be monitored and recorded. With Category A prisoners, those on the vulnerable or escape list and those who have been convicted of or remanded in custody for offences involving obscene calls or letters, all calls must be continuously monitored and tape-recorded and such tape recordings may be admissible in legal or disciplinary proceedings. Calls to legal advisers or the Samaritans should not be monitored and should be made in conditions which afford some privacy. However *in R v Home Secretary, ex p Kaniogulari*[90] the Divisional Court accepted that it would not always be possible to locate telephones in places where prisoners could not be overheard. It was satisfied that the prisoner always had the alternative of using the post or requesting use of the official telephone. The same court also rejected the argument that the recording of conversations breached principles of legal confidentiality, on the grounds that it was technically impossible to ensure that only selected calls were recorded and that there were sufficient internal safeguards to ensure that calls were not unnecessarily listened to.

7.54 The prison service is moving away from the cardphone system, especially as a result of concerns over the use of cardphones as a form of currency within prisons. A system has been trialled at dispersal prisons whereby prisoners are given individual PIN numbers and calls can only be made to pre-approved numbers. This scheme has still not been extended to all prisons, and in many the cardphone system continues to apply.

7.55 As access to telephones is such a recent phenomenon, the legal principles governing it remain unclear, though they are generally considered to be analogous to

---

[89] The extent to which various aspects of the right to freedom of expression survive a sentence of imprisonment was analysed in detail by Elias J in *R (Hirst) v Home Secretary* [2002] EWHC 602, discussed at para 7.41 above.
[90] [1994] COD 562.

those relating to correspondence. In cases on telephone tapping the ECtHR has treated telephone conversations as correspondence, and so it seems likely that restrictions on the use of telephones by prisoners would be liable to scrutiny for potential breaches of Articles 8 and 10 of the Convention in the same way as mail censorship.

F. Temporary Release

While frequent contact by letter, telephone, and visit can reduce the isolating and **7.56** debilitating effect of prison on both prisoners and their families, it remains contact within the prison environment. It is therefore limited, takes place under prison authority scrutiny, and is removed from the pleasures and strains of outside living to which prisoners will have to return. More meaningful contact with families and the outside world in general can be provided by home leave during sentence.[91] Home leave provides greater time for family problems to be worked through (though it can also increase them) and for long-term prisoners in particular can reduce that sense of shock at changes in the world when a prisoner is released after a long time inside. Most prison systems in Continental Europe have recognized this and provided for regular home leave from an early stage in the prisoner's sentence. In the United Kingdom, Woolf was critical of the limited home leave arrangements. However, far from becoming more generous after his report these have actually become more restrictive since 1994, when the Home Secretary targeted home leave as being given too easily and explicitly sought to reduce the number of prisoners eligible for temporary release.

Qualifying Criteria for Temporary Release

The present arrangements for the grant of temporary release, or temporary **7.57** licence as it is referred to, are set out in Prison Rule 9 and Instruction to Governors 36/1995.[92] These have limited available temporary release from prison to three types; *compassionate* licence, *facility* licence, and *resettlement* licence. The character of each of these temporary release powers and specific eligibility criteria for them will be discussed in turn. However it is worth first noting that certain types of prisoner are ineligible for any form of temporary release.

---

[91] In Germany, eg, home leave is available for up to 21 days a year after six months of the sentence have been served: see R Vogler, *Germany: A Guide to the Criminal Justice System* (London, 1989) 70.
[92] As amended by PSI 46/1998 (to allow temporary release for young offenders in a wider range of situations) and PSI 53/2000 (to extend these situations to adult female prisoners, and adult males in open conditions). This allows prisoners to be considered for temporary release for employment and accommodation interviews and to resolve urgent problems with issues such as housing. At the time of writing, the Prison Service was in the process of preparing a PSO to replace IG 36/1995.

This includes Category A prisoners or those on the escape list, unconvicted or unsentenced prisoners, prisoners who have been convicted or sentenced on some charges but await resolution of others, and prisoners subject to extradition proceedings.[93] Life sentence prisoners are eligible for all types of release (providing they are not excluded as falling into the above criteria) only after they have received a provisional release date or have moved to open conditions.[94] Special rules also apply to them in relation to each type of licence which will also be referred to. Before any release on licence can be granted a risk assessment must be undertaken of a prisoner, which looks at factors such as whether the prisoner presents an unacceptable risk of further offending, or to public safety, or of failing to comply with licence conditions. The input of the police and probation services may be sought in making this risk assessment, especially in cases involving offences of violence. The views of the victim of a crime may also be sought, especially where the prisoner may be released into an area where the victim lives. Prison Rule 9(5) also indicates that release will not be granted if, taking into account the proportion of the sentence served and frequency of releases granted he is of the opinion that release of the prisoner would be likely to undermine public confidence in the administration of justice.

7.58 While decisions on temporary release are for the Home Secretary, they are normally delegated to the governor in the prison where the applicant is detained, although headquarters units will be involved in decisions relating to life sentence prisoners. In prisons where mandatory drug testing is in force prisoners may be required to undergo drug tests before release, with release being cancelled if the test proves positive unless compelling reasons exist for allowing it to go ahead. Prisoners released on temporary licence are subject to conditions specified in their licence and to recall at any time should they be believed to be in breach of them. Failure to return from a period of temporary licence renders them liable to disciplinary or criminal proceedings. Where a prisoner is convicted of a further offence while on licence Prison Rule 9(6) indicates that he or she should not subsequently be granted temporary licence unless in the opinion of the Secretary of State this would not be likely to undermine public confidence in the administration of justice.

---

[93] These exclusions are not contained in the Prison Rules, and there must at least be an argument that a complete exclusion of these categories from any consideration of temporary release, regardless of considerations of risk or need, constitutes an unlawful fettering of discretion.

[94] Category C life sentence prisoners are also eligible for 'escorted absences' if they have had good institutional behaviour and have made good progress in tackling their offending behaviour. Such absences, also known as 'town visits', allow a prisoner to visit the local area under supervision. This is an important part of the rehabilitation process: see PSI 63/2000.

Compassionate Licence

This can be granted where the prisoner has exceptional personal reasons falling **7.59** within one of four categories. First, visits to dying close relatives, funerals, or other tragic personal circumstances. 'Close relatives' is limited to spouses (including partners lived with immediately before reception), parents, and children but IG 36/1995 indicates that 'it may be appropriate, in the light of different family relationships that exist within some communities' to extend it further than this. Visits for funerals are generally limited to sufficient time to attend the burial service and one hour of family mourning thereafter. Secondly, primary carers, who have responsibility for children or elderly relatives on release. The maximum duration for such visits is likely to be five days. Thirdly, release for marriage or other religious ceremonies. This will be available only where it has been decided that such ceremonies should or cannot take place in the prison and release will only be for the period of the ceremony. The final form of release on compassionate licence is that for medical appointments. This is an unescorted form of release. However where an appointment is urgent and so a full risk assessment cannot be undertaken or where the case involves a lifer who has not served six months in open conditions it may be possible to arrange for an escorted visit under s 22(2)(b) of the Prison Act. Lifers who have received a provisional release date can apply for compassionate licence four months after receiving this date or after a minimum of four months in open conditions. If they do not have a provisional release date they must have spent six months in open conditions.

Facility Licence

This is stated to have the twofold purpose of (1) enabling prisoners to particip- **7.60** ate in regime related courses, like work or educational programmes, and restorative activities such as restoring individual property; (2) enabling them to attend official proceedings or exceptionally visit legal advisers. Governors are directed to consider whether the activity is constructive, whether it can only be achieved outside prison, and also that they should not authorize release where it would 'attract reasonable public concern, particularly in relation to the nature of the offence or the nature of the activity'. In addition to the generally ineligible groups Category B prisoners may not apply for facility licence. Determinate sentence prisoners are only eligible to apply after they have served at least a quarter of their sentence. Lifers can apply on much the same grounds as apply to compassionate licence.

Facility licences are normally granted for no more than five consecutive days and **7.61** on a day release basis. However back to back consecutive licences may be granted for working out schemes or educational programmes and exceptionally prisoners may be released for shift work overnight. Initial grants of facility licence for lifers are likely to be only for one day at a time and releases for more than three days require headquarters approval.

Resettlement Licence

7.62 The third type of licence is seen as most appropriate towards the end of a prisoner's sentence and is for the purposes of (1) enabling a prisoner to maintain family ties and links with the community; (2) making suitable arrangements for accommodation, work, and training on release. For determinate sentence prisoners the point at which they become eligible depends on the length of their sentence and the date when it began. If a prisoner is serving less than four years he or she may apply for resettlement licence after one third of the single term or four months after sentence, whichever is earlier (although adult prisoners sentenced to less than one year may not apply). If he or she is sentenced to more than four years after 1 October 1992 (when the Criminal Justice Act 1991 came into force) they may apply after reaching half of the single term, but if refused parole on that date will have to wait six months after a first refusal and two months after any subsequent refusal to apply for resettlement licence. Where a prisoner is granted parole he or she may apply for resettlement licence to be taken not earlier than four weeks before release. If sentenced to more than four years before 1 October 1992 eligibility to apply for resettlement licence arises after completing one third of the single term and after having received a parole decision. Rejections of parole delay eligibility in the same way as for those sentenced under the 1991 Act. In either case the point at which eligibility arises may be put back by disciplinary punishments of added days. Lifers who do not have a provisional release date may apply for resettlement licence after nine months in open conditions. Otherwise their position is the same as with regard to compassionate and facility licence.

7.63 Paragraph 5.11 of IG 36/1995 indicates that 'the frequency and duration of resettlement licence should be determined by the purpose and need for the release, with more stress on quality rather than quantity'. It goes on to indicate though that the duration of each release should be for between one and five days, with at least eight week intervals between each licence. In the case of lifers it is recommended that licence should only be granted during the working week, when the supervising probation officer will be available, at least for the first few grants of leave.

Decisions on Temporary Release

7.64 Where temporary release is refused the governor should indicate to the prisoner why this decision has been taken. In doing so all information which has been taken into account in making the risk assessment should be disclosed to the prisoner unless the governor takes the view that such information should be withheld in the interests of national security, to prevent disorder or crime (including within the prison), where disclosure may put a third party at risk, or where its disclosure might affect the mental or physical health of the prisoner.

The post 1994 policy has clearly led to a reduction in temporary release, which the   **7.65**
Home Secretary aimed to reduce by 40 per cent. Although this appears to have been met by strong prisoner opposition it is worth noting that the Prison Ombudsman noted a significant decline in the number of complaints relating to temporary release in 1996. In *Ex p Hargreaves*[95] the Court of Appeal rejected a prisoner's challenge, based on legitimate expectation grounds, to the changes in home leave arrangements introduced in 1994. However, while this decision indicates that prisoners have no legitimate expectation that any particular home leave scheme will remain in force it remains open for them to challenge any failure to apply the existing criteria for temporary licence to their case.

G. Home Detention Curfew

The Home Detention Curfew (HDC) is a form of early, monitored release, and is   **7.66**
an important new link between prisoners and the outside world. This section should be read in conjunction with Chapter 12, which explains the system of release from prison for fixed term prisoners. The HDC scheme came into force on 28 January 1999. Under s 34A of the Criminal Justice Act 1991, as amended by ss 99 and 100 of the Crime and Disorder Act 1998, most prisoners serving sentences of more than three months and less than four years may be released on an electronically monitored curfew (popularly known as 'tagging') for a period before their automatic or conditional release date (halfway through their prison sentence). The tagging is administered by private companies, and stops at the halfway point of the sentence. The system is set out in PSO 6700, as amended,[96] and is not entirely straightforward. This section summarizes the eligibility criteria, the operation of the scheme, and the options for challenging decisions in relation to eligibility or recall.

In the spring of 2002, the prison population reached 70,000 for the first time,   **7.67**
leading to serious fears about overcrowding. Research also suggested that the HDC scheme was being underused. The Home Secretary, David Blunkett, responded to these concerns by introducing what he called 'Presumptive HDC'. This was given effect to by the Prison Service in PSI 19/2002. Since 1 May 2002, there are therefore two types of prisoner for these purposes: those eligible for 'presumptive' HDC and those eligible for the standard scheme. We consider presumptive HDC first.

---

[95] *R v Home Secretary, ex p Hargreaves* [1997] 1 WLR 906.
[96] Amended by PSI 9/2001 and PSI 19/2002.

7.68   The criteria for presumptive HDC are that the prisoner is serving a sentence of more than three months and less than 12 months, that he is not serving a sentence listed at Annex A of PSI 19/2002,[97] that he has not been convicted of any of the offences in Annex A within three years of the date of sentence for the current offence, and that he has no history of sexual offending. In addition, the statutory exclusions for the general HDC scheme apply, discussed below. If a prisoner fails to meet any of these criteria, he is referred to the standard scheme, discussed below. The PSI states that prisoners being assessed under the standard scheme must not be disadvantaged by the existence of the new scheme.

7.69   If, when a prisoner fills out his HDC2 form (a form used in all HDC cases, discussed further below), it appears that he will be eligible for presumptive HDC, a streamlined presumptive HDC assessment is carried out. This involves confirmation of the suitability of the proposed accommodation, confirmation that the other people at the address understand the impact of the curfew and have raised any issues they wish to be considered, and that there are no concerns relating to the victims. If the assessment is satisfactory, governors must release the prisoner on HDC unless there are 'exceptional and compelling reasons to refuse release'.[98] After this streamlined procedure, the presumptive scheme functions identically to the standard scheme.

7.70   The standard scheme is rather complicated. All prisoners serving sentences of between three months and four years are eligible for HDC, with the following exceptions:

(1)   violent and sex offenders serving an extended sentence under s 58 of the Crime and Disorder Act 1998;

(2)   prisoners serving a sentence under s 1 of the Prisoners (Return to Custody) Act 1995, for failure to return to custody following a period of temporary release;

(3)   prisoners subject to a hospital order, hospital direction or transfer direction under ss 37, 45A, or 47 of the Mental Health Act 1983;

---

[97] These are: ABH, AOABH, aggravated burglary, arson, assaulting a court/prison officer, assaulting a police officer, assault with intent to cause ABH/GBH/to resist arrest/to rob, attempted murder, common assault, conspiracy to aid/abet/incite murder, conspiracy to riot, causing death by reckless driving, inflicting GBH, infanticide, manslaughter, murder, possession of a firearm with intent to endanger life, rioting, robbery, threatening or disorderly behaviour, violent disorder, wounding, cruelty to or neglect of children, conspiracy to cause an explosion, conspiracy to hijack, causing an explosion, hijacking, kidnapping, administering poison, 'prevention of terrorism' (it is unclear to which specific offences this refers), treason, any drugs offence, any sexual offence, and all other violent offences. This extensive list somewhat reduces the applicability of the presumptive scheme.

[98] These include clear evidence that the prisoner is planning further crime while in custody, evidence of violence or threats of violence in prison on a number of occasions (what this number might be is not specified), dealing in class A drugs in custody, and other matters of similar gravity relating to public safety.

(4) prisoners serving a sentence imposed under paras 3(1)(d) or 4(1)(d) of Sch 2 to the Criminal Justice Act 1991 in a case where the prisoner had failed to comply with a requirement of a curfew order;

(5) prisoners who have at any time been recalled to prison from HDC, under s 38(1)(a) of the 1991 Act, unless they successfully appealed against the recall;

(6) prisoners currently liable to removal from the United Kingdom under s 46 of the Criminal Justice Act 1991;

(7) prisoners who have, during their current sentence, been released on HDC or been given early compassionate release under s 36 of the 1991 Act and have been recalled to prison under s 39(1) or (2) of the Act;

(8) prisoners who have at any time been returned to prison under s 40 of the 1991 Act;

(9) prisoners who have not served the requisite period of their sentence until there are fewer than 14 days remaining until the halfway point of sentence;

(10) prisoners who have not yet reached the age of 18;

(11) fine defaulters and civil or criminal contemnors, since they are not serving a sentence of imprisonment;

(12) prisoners who are required on release to register with the police under Pt I of the Sex Offenders Act 1997.[99]

Category A prisoners may, exceptionally, be serving a sentence of less than four years, in which case they are not excluded from HDC. However, PSO 6700 states that, since such prisoners have already been assessed as presenting a serious risk to the public, establishments will only consider such prisoners for HDC if the prisoner requests it, and only if 'there are exceptional circumstances to merit initiating the [HDC] risk assessment'.[100]

If a prisoner does not fall into any of these statutory exceptions, their HDC eligibility date must be calculated and notified to them along with their conditional or automatic release date.[101] The minimum length of HDC is usually 14 days. The HDC eligibility date depends on the sentence length: **7.71**

- three months or more but less than four months: after 30 days have been served;
- four months or more, but less than eight months: after one quarter of the sentence has been served;

---

[99] These prisoners were previously eligible for HDC, although individual authorization from the Director-General was required, and applications would be scrutinized extremely closely. However, s 65 of the Criminal Justice and Court Services Act 2000 removed all eligibility, and PSI 9/2001 amended PSO 6700 accordingly.

[100] para 2.5.1.

[101] For an explanation of the calculation of release dates, see Ch 12.

- eight months or more, but less than four years: 60 days less than the halfway point of the sentence.

If there are any changes in circumstances which affect the release date, for example the imposition of additional days as a result of disciplinary offences, the eligibility date for HDC is recalculated along with the other release dates.

7.72   Once the HDC date is calculated, the risk assessment process must begin at least ten weeks in advance. That process will build on the risk information gathered during the sentence, in particular the Initial Categorisation Form.[102] During sentence, prisoners must also be encouraged to work towards gaining HDC, for example by ensuring that suitable accommodation is available. There are two types of risk assessment: the suitability assessment and the enhanced assessment. The suitability assessment is completed on form HDC1, by a member of the seconded probation team or a suitable member of prison staff, if authorized by the Governor. It contains the following steps:

(1) The prisoner fills in form HDC2, giving details on proposed release address etc, or stating that he or she does not wish to be considered for HDC (in which case the process ends).

(2) A member of staff who has regular contact with the prisoner fills in part 2 of HDC2, commenting on suitability for the scheme.

(3) The probation officer or other officer considers the forms and the available papers, including mental health evidence if required.

(4) If it is apparent on the initial scrutiny that the prisoner is not suitable for HDC, the application can be considered without input from the home probation service, though the enhanced assessment must still be completed (see below).

(5) If the prisoner is not considered unsuitable on initial scrutiny, form HDC3 is sent for completion by the probation service for the area where the prisoner wishes to be released. They seek the views of victims and residents of the area, where appropriate.

(6) The prisoner's probation officer, or other authorized officer, completes form HDC1 by summarizing the prisoner's suitability for HDC, including a review of the core documents, risk prediction scores[103] and suitability

---

[102] This is used to assign prisoners to a security category: see Ch 4.

[103] PSO 6700, s 5.12 gives general guidance on the risk assessment. It states that the 'assessment of risk for HDC must . . . balance any risk to the public presented by the bringing forward of the release date against the potential benefits of incorporating a period of Home Detention Curfew within the prisoner's sentence. Assessment of risk must be on objective evidence of the prisoner's past record and current behaviour, and must be conducted in a way that is consistent with Prison Service values, rigorously and fairly and free from discrimination. It must be remembered that conduct in the establishment may bear no relation to the risk that the prisoner might present to the family or general public.'

for release. They must refer the case for enhanced assessment only if (a) the core documents, member of staff's report and Probation Service comments suggest that there is a prima facie case for not granting HDC, or (b) the risk prediction score indicates that the prisoner is in the statistically high risk category for reconviction for sex offences, violent offences, or reimprisonment, or (c) the offender is serving over one year and does not have a successful record or release on temporary licence or earned community visits, ie any prisoner serving over 12 months who has not both been granted and successfully completed release on temporary licence.

(7) Unless there are clear grounds to require the enhanced assessment, the HDC1 is then forwarded to the governor to confirm the assessment and authorize release.

7.73 If an enhanced assessment is required, this is completed on form HDC4 by a body comprising at least a governor grade, a seconded probation officer or member of the throughcare team, and if possible a member of staff with regular contact with the prisoner. The board considers the HDC1 form and core documents, and in particular the previous criminal history, offending behaviour work in prison, behaviour in prison (including disciplinary offences), any known external factors which may affect the likelihood of re-offending, home circumstances and the stability of close relationships.

7.74 If release is authorized by the governor after either of these assessment procedures, the prisoner must be released on licence under s 34A of the 1991 Act.[104] Form HDC7 must be faxed 14 days in advance to the tagging contractor, the Probation Service, the National Identification Service at Scotland Yard, and the home probation service. The governor authorizing release sets the curfew conditions, which must not be less than nine hours home detention per day, apart from the day of release. The curfew will normally be for 12 hours a day. Different conditions may be set for different days, and the governor must take into account any recommendation from the home probation service, including reasonable working hours, childcare arrangements, religious observance, regular hospital appointments, appointments at benefit offices and with the Probation Service. The prisoner must not be released until he or she has given written consent to the conditions. Given that PSO 6700 says that '[i]f the prisoner does not consent to the conditions, he or she must not be released until the conditional or automatic release date', there is a considerable amount of pressure to give consent. After release, a person on HDC can apply to the governor to have the conditions varied.

---

[104] There are two types of licence, depending on whether the prisoner is sentenced to more or less than 12 months. For the former, the only conditions relate to the curfew and the commission of new offences. For the latter, the licence will also contain the appropriate 'automatic conditional release' conditions (see Ch 12), which subsist until the three quarter point of sentence, minus the period spent on curfew. Sample licences are set out at Annex E of PSO 6700.

7.75 Prisoners are given form HDC5 to inform them that they have been assessed as suitable for HDC. They are also told that the decision is provisional, and may be reversed in the light of subsequent behaviour in prison or new information. If considered unsuitable, prisoners are notified on form HDC6.[105] They must be given reasons for the refusal, and told of their right to appeal through the request/complaint procedures. Forms HDC1 and HDC4 must be made available if requested, either before or after the decision on HDC. Where these are requested before the HDC decision, the prisoner must be given the chance to make oral or written representations before the board's decision. The views of victims or local residents may be kept confidential, in accordance with Chapter 9 of PSO 2200 on Sentence Management and Planning. The legitimacy of refusing HDC on the basis of information which the prisoner cannot see is questionable, and PSO 6700 attempts to deal with this problem in the following terms:

> Decisions on suitability for HDC cannot normally be made on the basis of a third party's concerns being disclosed to the prisoner, so that he or she has the opportunity to challenge them. However, if the home probation service is provided with information by the victim or a resident at the proposed curfew address which that person wishes to remain confidential, the member of probation staff compiling the report may choose to incorporate the necessary information in a disclosable form unattributably within their own analysis, or to express the information in broad terms.[106]

If the Probation Service wishes to keep information completely confidential, this must be authorized by the governing governor. The PSO states that the general rule is that all information, from whatever source, which has been taken into account during the risk assessment must be disclosed if requested, except where non-disclosure is *necessary* on the basis of:

---

[105] Notification, appeals and disclosure are dealt with in PSO 6700, ch 7, amended in light of the decision of the High Court in *R v Home Secretary, ex p Allen* [2000] COD 179, in which Hidden J ruled that fairness requires that an applicant for release on HDC be given the information on which the assessment is to be made, before the decision is taken, and the opportunity to make written or oral representations. This decision was appealed by the Secretary of State. The Court of Appeal (judgment of Laws LJ) considered that, although the revised version of PSO 6700 does appear to give prisoners the right to see all documentation during the initial assessment process and not just on appeal, this is not required by law: 'I would hold that prisoner's rights of fairness are fulfilled as a matter of law if they are accorded at the appeal stage. They include the right to know the gist of matters that may be held against him, the right to see what are called discloseable documents if he requests them, and of course the right to make representations written or oral at his option. The fact that the revised document PSO 6700 appears to give bigger rights, in so far as it contemplates that the prison might request and receive documents during the currency of its first assessment stage, in this process is no doubt to be commended. I by no means would seek to discourage the Secretary of State from taking a position that may be larger than the law requires. But upon my view of the matter the legal position is as I have stated it.' (Judgment of 10 March 2000; The Times, 21 March 2000).

[106] para 7.5.

- national security;
- the prevention of crime or disorder, including information relevant to prison security;
- the protection of information which may put a third party at risk;
- medical or psychiatric risk to the prisoner if the information is disclosed.

Decisions about HDC can be raised first through the prison and complaints pro- **7.76**
cedure.[107] Complaints are dealt with first in the prison, preferably by a governor of a higher grade than the governor involved in the original decision. The prisoner must be allowed to make oral or written representations if he or she wishes, and the governor must look at the decision afresh and address all points raised by the prisoner. The governor may seek further information. If upholding the original decision, he or she must give written reasons, and if those reasons are the same as for the original refusal, he or she must seek to expand on those reasons and clarify why they apply. If prisoners wish to appeal further, they can take their complaint to the Area Manager. Complaints about curfew conditions can also be raised through the complaints procedure, though signing the release licence is taken to be a withdrawal of any appeal against the curfew conditions. If prisoners are initially considered suitable for HDC and this assessment is changed, they are entitled to appeal in the same way as if they had had an initial refusal.

As well as the powers to recall in respect of breaches of standard licence conditions, **7.77**
s 38A(1) of the 1991 Act provides that people on HDC may be recalled to prison if:

(1) they fail to comply with the curfew conditions of their licence;
(2) it is no longer possible to monitor the curfew at the specified address; or
(3) the person is considered to represent a threat to public safety.

Recall decisions are made by the Parole Unit at Prison Service Headquarters. The prisoner will be arrested by the police and returned by the escort contractors to the nearest establishment categorized for prisoners of that type. There is a right of appeal against recall: within 24 hours of being notified by the receiving prison, the Parole Unit faxes to the prison a 'revocation dossier', including a letter to the prisoner setting out the reasons for recall and explaining the appeal process. The dossier must be disclosed to the prisoner within one working day of receipt. The prisoner then completes an attached form, and the prison must return the form to the Parole Unit Appeals Section, again within one working day. The prisoner may submit written representations to the Appeals Section or to a member of staff, who should forward them to the Appeals Section within one working day. If the

---

[107] Information on the right of appeal, the right to see documents, and the right to make oral or written representations to the governor dealing with the appeal is included on form HDC6.

recall was because of unsuitability of the address, the prisoner may be released if a new suitable address is found. Recalled prisoners who do not appeal successfully are released at their conditional or automatic release date at the halfway point of the sentence.

8

INTER-PRISON TRANSFERS
AND THE REPATRIATION OF
PRISONERS FROM ABROAD

The issue of inter-prison transfer for reasons of good order and discipline will be **8.01** discussed in Chapter 10 below and will not be raised here. In this chapter we consider the issue of transfer in three different situations where no formal or informal disciplinary motivation is involved. First, we look at transfers within the prison system of England and Wales. Secondly, we look at the possibility of transfer between the different penal systems of the United Kingdom, Northern Ireland, and the Channel Islands. Finally, we consider the question of the repatriation of prisoners from abroad to complete their sentences in England and Wales.

A. Transfer within England and Wales

The basic statutory provision governing the transfer of prisoners within England **8.02** and Wales is a simple enabling one. Section 12(2) of the Prison Act 1952 entitles the Secretary of State to determine the prison to which a prisoner is committed and to direct the removal of a prisoner from the prison in which he is held to any other prison. More detail is provided in Standing Order 1H. This indicates that prisoners may be transferred to relieve overcrowding, among other reasons, but that in selecting prisoners to transfer for this reason appellants and those whose domestic circumstances would be gravely prejudiced should not be chosen. Before a transfer takes place the prison medical officer should certify that the prisoner is fit to travel and should give any special information about the prisoner's health to the medical officer of the receiving institution 24 hours in advance of the transfer.[1]

8.03 Relatives of prisoners often claim that they are given insufficient notice of transfers and may even arrive for a visit only to find that the prisoner has been moved. Unfortunately this appears more likely to happen to those with furthest to travel, namely the relatives of Category A prisoners held in dispersal prisons. The Standing Order indicates that advance notification of moves should not be given to Category A prisoners or their potential visitors. The governor also has the discretion to refuse advance notification to the relatives of any other prisoners where he feels this might pose a threat to security or good order. Should such visitors arrive without being notified of a move the prison is directed to consider their claim for reimbursement of travelling expenses. In respect of other prisoners where the governor does not perceive such a threat prisoners are normally allowed to notify their intending visitors by a first-class letter (not counted against their usual allowance) or, if there is insufficient time, a telephone call.

8.04 The reference to the undesirability of moving prisoners where this may severely prejudice their domestic circumstances may have been influenced by the one significant challenge in the courts to transfer decisions. This occurred *in R v Home Secretary, ex p McAvoy.*[2] Mr McAvoy, a Category A remand prisoner on a robbery charge, was transferred from Brixton to Winchester—over 60 miles away—without warning. He claimed that this prejudiced his right to a fair trial as Winchester had poorer consultation facilities and it would be difficult for his chosen counsel in London to visit him there. He also asserted that it would be difficult for his parents to visit him in Winchester because of their ill health. Webster J accepted that these were relevant considerations to any transfer decision and that the Home Secretary would have erred in law if he failed to take account of them. Indeed, he acknowledged that the move might lead to the applicant requiring a new counsel. However, in the end he refused to interfere with the Home Secretary's decision as it was taken for 'operational and security reasons' (primarily it appeared that Brixton was not deemed to be secure enough for the prisoner and London's other high-security prison at Wormwood Scrubs was felt to be inappropriate). As Webster J observed:

> The Secretary of State's powers under section 12 are, in my view, reviewable in exercise but they are also very wide. In my view it is undesirable—if not impossible—for this court to examine operational reasons for a decision made under that section; and to examine security reasons for a decision made under that section could, in my view, be dangerous and contrary to the policy of that statutory provision, which is

---

[1] The operational details of inter-prison transfers are dealt with in PSO 6200.
[2] [1984] 1 WLR 1408.

to confer an absolute discretion, within the law, on the Secretary of State to make such executive decisions as he thinks fit for operational and security reasons.[3]

This decision was in marked contrast to the same judge's more interventionist rhetoric in *Tarrant*,[4] delivered the same year, and displays a traditional judicial reluctance to interfere with discretionary powers of the governor or Secretary of State. Although in theory it does leave some scope for challenges to transfer decisions where the administration has stated an irrelevant reason, only a very naïve governor or Secretary of State would fail to invoke 'operational and security' reasons after this decision in the knowledge that these are unlikely to be probed too deeply by the High Court.[5] Indeed in the (pro-HRA) *Kavanagh* case (which will be discussed in greater detail below) the European Commission on Human Rights indicated that after *McAvoy*, prisoners seeking to challenge transfer decisions under Article 8 of the European Convention on Human Rights (ECHR) did not have to take judicial review to exhaust their domestic remedies.

B. Transfers between the UK Penal Systems

If moving a prisoner from one part of England and Wales to another may impair **8.05** his contact with family and friends, how much more is this likely to be impaired when the prisoner is detained in another jurisdiction? Given the existence of three separate jurisdictions within the United Kingdom, people from one may find themselves detained in another as a result of being charged or convicted of a crime committed in that other jurisdiction. A comprehensive code governing transfer between the three jurisdictions in the United Kingdom and the Channel Islands now exists in Sch 1 (Pt I) to the Crime (Sentences) Act 1997. The new provisions

---

[3] ibid, 1417B. See the judgment, in similar terms, of Moses J in *R v Featherstone Prison, ex p Bowen* [1999] CLY 4106. The exercise of, or refusal to exercise, the transfer power will be ultra vires if it infringes a prisoner's right to a fair trial: see *R v Home Secretary, ex p Quinn* [2000] UKHRR 386. In that case the claimant, who was on charges of prison mutiny, argued that the failure to transfer him left him open to the risk of retribution from prison officers and therefore prejudiced his right to a fair trial. Richards J accepted the argument in principle, though he found that on the facts there was no real danger of retaliation.

[4] *R v Home Secretary, ex p Tarrant* [1985] QB 251.

[5] Courts in the US have reached similar conclusions. In *Meachum v Fano*, 427 US 215 (1976) the Supreme Court held that there were no constitutionally required due process safeguards where a prisoner was transferred within the Massachusetts prison system, even where the move involved going to more onerous conditions, as a prisoner had no right or expectation created by state or federal law that he would serve his sentence in one prison. The court affirmed this even when dealing with inter-state transfers in *Olim v Wakinekona*, 461 US 238 (1983), a case involving a Hawaii–California transfer of over 2,500 miles. This was despite an extensive Federal Bureau of Prisons procedure whereby the prisoner could put his view to a hearing and be represented by counsel. However, in *Vitek v Jones*, 445 US 480 (1980) transfer from an ordinary prison to a state mental hospital was held to require due process safeguards.

give the Secretary of State wide powers to arrange for the transfer of prisoners between the various UK penal jurisdictions in the following circumstances:

(1) Where a person who is either remanded in custody or serving a prison sentence in any part of the United Kingdom applies for transfer to another UK jurisdiction pending his trial or to serve the remainder of his sentence the Home Secretary may make an order for transfer to an 'appropriate institution'.

(2) If it appears to the Secretary of State that a person remanded in custody or serving a sentence in any part of the United Kingdom should be transferred to another part of the United Kingdom or to any of the Channel Islands for the purpose of attending criminal proceedings against him there, the Secretary of State may make an order securing such transfer.

(3) Finally, the Schedule provides in general terms for the transfer of a prisoner to *any place* within the United Kingdom or Channel Islands 'for other judicial purposes' where he or she is either remanded in custody in any part of the United Kingdom, serving a prison sentence or otherwise detained in a prison.[6]

In addition to the power to transfer a prisoner in the above circumstances, there is also now a power to transfer the supervision of a person undergoing or about to undergo supervision in any part of the United Kingdom to another part of the United Kingdom or to any of the Channel Islands. Any such order will mean in effect that supervision is continued by an appropriate person in the new jurisdiction.

8.06 Schedule 1, Pt II deals with the effect of transfers conducted under Pt I. The Criminal Justice Act 1961 had provided for inter-jurisdictional transfers of prisoners to be made on a permanent or a temporary basis. However, permanent transfers were generally refused where, as a consequence of differing early release provisions applying in the different jurisdictions, a reduction in time to serve would have been likely to result. A 1992 inter-departmental working group in the Home Office recognized the particular problems posed in relation to the permanent transfer of long term prisoners to Northern Ireland because of the different

---

[6] The criterion governing such transfer is that the Secretary of State is satisfied that the attendance of the prisoner at that other place is 'desirable in the interests of justice or for the purposes of any public inquiry'. This provision replaces Criminal Justice Act 1961, s 29, and covers the transfer of prisoners from prison to police stations to answer another charge, to appear as a prosecution witness, to help recover stolen property or other items, to be interviewed in connection with serious arrestable offences, or to take part in an identification parade. Under the previous legislation, the power to order transfer pursuant to s 29 of the 1961 Act was (save in the case of Category A prisoners) delegated to individual governors who were advised that each request for production must be individually considered on its merits to see if the 'interests of justice' test was met and that governors were not obliged automatically to meet police requests. Where a prisoner is transferred to a police station he is then in the custody of the police and accordingly the Prison Rules no longer apply.

early release provisions and recommended that consideration be given to amend-ing the legislation to overcome the problem. It was the acceptance of this recom-mendation which led to the new provisions in the 1997 Act which enable prisoners to be transferred to another jurisdiction on either an unrestricted or a restricted basis.[7]

The Home Secretary's policy in relation to inter-jurisdictional transfers under the 1997 Act was set out in a lengthy Parliamentary Answer on 28 October 1997. In the case of an unrestricted transfer, the administration of the prisoner's sentence will become a matter entirely for the receiving jurisdiction. The prisoner may therefore be free to benefit from more liberal early release provisions than exist in England and Wales. A restricted transfer will be subject to conditions whereby the sending jurisdiction will continue to administer certain specified aspects of the sentence. All transfers will continue to require the consent of the Home Secretary of both the sending and the receiving jurisdictions. Normally, transfer requests will be approved only where the prisoner has at least six months left to serve in the receiving jurisdiction before his or her release date at the time of making the request and where the prisoner has no outstanding appeal against conviction or sentence, is not charged with further criminal proceedings, and is not liable to any further period of imprisonment in lieu of payment of any outstanding monetary orders made by a court. **8.07**

Criteria for Transfer: Unrestricted and Restricted Transfers

Home Office policy asserts that each application for transfer will be considered on its individual merits, taking into consideration: **8.08**

(1) the purpose for which the transfer is requested;
(2) whether the prisoner was ordinarily resident in the jurisdiction to which transfer is sought prior to the imposition of the current sentence, or whether members of the prisoner's close family are resident in that juris-diction and there are reasonable grounds for believing that the prisoner will receive regular visits from them; or whether the prisoner has demonstrated through preparations that he has made for his life following release from

---

[7] The law and politics of the transfer issue were thrown into sharp relief by requests by prisoners from Northern Ireland, convicted of offences in England, to be transferred back to Northern Ireland to serve their sentences. A significant number of these prisoners had been convicted of IRA-related offences and had received very lengthy sentences. Requests for transfer from many of these prisoners, whose families live in Northern Ireland, had in the past frequently been turned down (particularly by Michael Howard) despite the availability of space in high-security prisons in Northern Ireland. Relatives' groups and prison reform groups were frequent critics of such refusals on the grounds that they impose unnecessary burdens on relatives who have to travel long distances to visit prisoners, that they make rehabilitation more difficult, and that transfer appears to be denied not on administrative or security grounds but out of a desire to punish the prisoners for their involvement in terrorism.

prison that he intends to reside in the receiving jurisdiction upon release and he is in the latter stages of his sentence.

8.09 When considering whether to make an unrestricted or a restricted transfer, the Parliamentary Statement says that the Secretary of State of the sending jurisdiction will take into account the period and terms of transfer requested by the prisoner and whether, as a consequence of an unrestricted transfer, there would be likely to be any effect on the length of time which the prisoner would be required to serve or on any post-release supervision requirement. Where an unrestricted transfer is granted, the prisoner will be required to serve the remainder of his or her sentence in the receiving jurisdiction as if that sentence had been passed there and will be subject for all purposes to the statutory and other provisions applying to prisoners within the receiving jurisdiction. A prisoner granted a restricted transfer will automatically remain, for the duration of his or her transfer, subject to the law governing release on licence, automatic release, post-release supervision, and recall applicable in the sending jurisdiction. In addition any other condition relating to the terms of a prisoner's detention as the Secretary of State of the sending jurisdiction may deem appropriate in any particular case or class of case may be attached to the transfer.

8.10 A prisoner transferred on a restricted basis will normally become subject for all purposes, other than those specified in any conditions attached to the transfer, to the statutory and other provisions applying to prisoners in the receiving jurisdiction (including, for example, such matters as categorization). The Parliamentary Statement goes on to say that applications for temporary release for compassionate or other purposes of facilitating family ties will normally become the responsibility of the jurisdiction to which the prisoner is transferred. Prisoners will be able to apply for a period of temporary release under the provisions existing in the receiving jurisdiction. Each application will be considered by the 'appropriate authority' in the receiving jurisdiction on its own merits and in accordance with the relevant criteria applying in that jurisdiction. Prisoners will normally therefore no longer be eligible to apply for temporary release under the provisions applying in the sending jurisdiction.

8.11 Where however a restricted transfer is time limited (for example to enable the prisoner to enjoy accumulated visits) or for a purpose other than to facilitate family ties (to attend judicial proceedings or to receive medical treatment), and the prisoner is expected to return to the sending jurisdiction, decisions on temporary release will continue to be made by the sending jurisdiction.

8.12 The effect of any conditions attached to a transfer should be explained to the prisoner concerned prior to transfer and any conditions imposed may be reviewed at the request of the prisoner or either of the Secretaries of State at any time during the duration of the transfer. A restricted transfer will not be made unrestricted without the consent of the prisoner concerned.

A prisoner granted a restricted transfer may be returned to the sending jurisdic- **8.13**
tion at any time if this proves necessary, for example, if the purpose for which
transfer was granted is, in the opinion of the Secretary of State, no longer being
fulfilled or at the request of the receiving jurisdiction (in the case of disruptive
behaviour) or in the interests of the administration of the sentence (such as consideration by the Parole Board or to undergo post-release supervision).

Transfer requests by a remand prisoner will receive consideration but in view of **8.14**
the need to ensure that the prisoner is available for court hearings as necessary,
normally such requests are only granted where there are compelling or compassionate reasons for doing so. The Parliamentary Statement makes clear that when
a transfer is agreed, the timing of the move will be subject to operational and
security considerations in the sending and receiving jurisdictions.

Challenging Transfer Decisions

Legal challenges to the operation of the discretion to transfer have not in the past **8.15**
proved to be particularly successful. In *McComb*[8] Taylor LJ observed that s 26(1)
of the Criminal Justice Act 1961 (the predecessor to the current provisions in the
1997 Act) gave the Home Secretary an unfettered discretion in respect of decisions whether to transfer or not. McComb had been sentenced to 17 years for conspiracy to cause explosions. His request for transfer was refused on the basis of a
policy adopted by the Home Secretary in 1989 that transfer might be refused
where a prisoner's crimes were thought to be so serious as to make it inappropriate that he should benefit from a substantial reduction in the time served if
that were the outcome of transfer.[9] Since at the time McComb was sentenced
remission was available for half of one's sentence in Northern Ireland as opposed
to one-third in England it was argued that transfer would mean he would serve
nearly three years less than if he had stayed in England, as under s 26(4) of
the 1961 Act transferred prisoners were treated as having been sentenced in the
jurisdiction to which they were transferred.[10] Taylor LJ concluded that this was a

---

[8] *R v Home Secretary, ex p McComb* [1991] COD 415.
[9] The full criteria were: (1) that the prisoner had six months of his sentence to serve; (2) that the
prisoner was ordinarily resident in the receiving jurisdiction prior to imprisonment or that his close
family currently resided there and that there were reasonable grounds for believing that it was his
firm intention to take up residence on release; (3) that both sentencing and receiving authorities
were reasonably satisfied that the inmate would not be disruptive or pose an unacceptable risk to
security. Even if these criteria were satisfied transfer could still be refused if there were grounds that
the inmate was seeking transfer primarily to get a reduction in sentence or where 'the inmate's
crimes were so serious as to render him or her undeserving of any degree of public sympathy or to
make it inappropriate that the inmate should benefit from a substantial reduction in time left to
serve, if that would be a consequence of transfer'.
[10] As a result of the Prevention of Terrorism Act 1989 prisoners in Northern Ireland convicted
of 'scheduled' offences after 1 March 1989 were entitled to only one-third remission on their sentence. There is no parole scheme in Northern Ireland.

legitimate factor for the Home Secretary to take into account in reaching his decision whether to transfer or not and that while family unity was important it was not the overriding criterion. He noted that if the prisoner had a co-accused who had also received 17 years but whose family were in England he would end up serving significantly less than that co-accused. Nor did Taylor LJ find the decision unreasonable on *Wednesbury* principles.

8.16 Another ground of challenge in *McComb* was that refusal of transfer violated the guarantee of a right to family life protected by Article 8 of the ECHR. This was disposed of on the grounds that the Convention was not enforceable in English law and that, in any case, the limitations on the right to family life contained in Article 8(2) were applicable here. The European Commission appears to agree with this view. In *Kavanagh v UK*[11] it ruled inadmissible an application by a Northern Irish prisoner sentenced to life with a recommended term of 35 years for murder and causing explosions. Observing that nothing in Article 8 gave a prisoner a right to choose where he was detained and that separation of a detained person and his family is one of the inevitable consequences of imprisonment the Commission indicated that only in 'exceptional circumstances' would detention of a prisoner a long way from his family violate the Convention. Noting the security risk presented in transferring the applicant, who was a Category A prisoner, the fact that his mother was entitled to 13 state-assisted visits a year, and that he had been permitted to marry another prisoner, and have a number of visits from her, the Commission concluded that there were no exceptional circumstances in this case.

8.17 These decisions would appear to make any legal challenge to the operation of inter-jurisdiction transfer decisions very difficult, at least in the absence of very extreme facts. It may be however that the new policy towards transfers and the long term prospect of peace in Northern Ireland will make inter-jurisdictional transfer a less controversial subject.

C. The Repatriation of Prisoners from Abroad

8.18 If imprisonment in a different jurisdiction within the United Kingdom can be a distressing and isolating experience for prisoners and relatives alike, how much more distressing is it to be detained outside the United Kingdom?[12] Prisoners detained abroad may be unfamiliar with the language and culture of the country in which they are imprisoned and visits from relatives will probably be very infre-

---

[11] Application 19085/91, Commission Decision, 9 December 1992. Kavanagh's mother and sister were also applicants.
[12] In summer 2002, the charity Prisoners Abroad had 1,492 clients held in foreign prisons.

quent. Similar observations apply in respect of foreign prisoners imprisoned in the United Kingdom. Since 1983 however an international treaty, the Convention on the Transfer of Sentenced Persons,[13] has existed to facilitate the transfer of prisoners between countries which are parties to this Convention. The Preamble to the Convention makes clear that its fundamental purpose is to further the end of justice and the social rehabilitation of sentenced persons by ensuring that 'foreigners who are deprived of their liberty as a result of the commission of a criminal offence should be given the opportunity to serve their sentences within their own society'. In the United Kingdom this Convention was incorporated into domestic law by the Repatriation of Prisoners Act 1984.[14]

Criteria for Repatriation

Between Convention members transfer can take place providing a number of criteria are met. These are: **8.19**

(1) that the prisoner be a national of the receiving or 'administering' State;
(2) that the judgment is final and enforceable (because all available remedies have been exhausted);
(3) that at the time of the request for transfer the prisoner still has at least six months of his sentence to serve or that the sentence is indeterminate;
(4) that the prisoner agrees to the transfer (the sentencing State has the obligation to ensure that this is done voluntarily and in compliance with the law governing consent in that State);
(5) that both of the State parties agree;
(6) that the acts or omissions which form the basis of the prisoner's criminal conviction in the sentencing State would constitute a criminal offence if done in the administering State. For this final condition of dual criminal liability to be satisfied it is not necessary that the criminal offence be precisely the same under both the law of the administering and receiving States. The basic idea is that the essential constituent elements of the offence be comparable under the law of both States.

---

[13] 22 ILM 530.

[14] The 1984 Act was subsequently amended by the Criminal Justice Act 1991, Sch 11, para 35, and by the Prisoners and Criminal Proceedings (Scotland) Act 1993, Sch 5, para 3, and then finally by the Crime Sentences Act 1997, Sch 2, paras 1–3, 5–7, and 9–11. As only part of the Crime (Sentences) Act 1997 was enacted some further consequential amendments were required which were introduced in the Crime and Disorder Act 1998. The effect of all this is that tracing and then understanding the statutory history of what should be a reasonably simple area of law is a nightmare for lawyers and probably completely incomprehensible to the non-lawyer. One further complication, though of limited relevance for the time being, was introduced by ss 42–48 of the International Criminal Court Act 2001. Under that Act, neither Sch 1 to the Crime (Sentences) Act 1997 nor the Repatriation of Prisoners Act 1984 apply to those serving a sentence in the UK pursuant to a sentence of the ICC. Sections 43 and 44 of the Act make provision for transfers in certain circumstances.

Continued Enforcement

8.20 While either State can amnesty or pardon a transferred prisoner, decisions on any review of the original conviction are purely for the courts of the sentencing State.

8.21 Where a prisoner is transferred the Convention envisages two radically different procedures which affect the nature of the sentence to be served by a prisoner after his transfer to the administering State. These are known as 'continued enforcement' (Article 10) and 'conversion' (Article 9). The United Kingdom has chosen the former option, set out in Article 10 of the Convention. The continued enforcement procedure involves acceptance of the principle that the administering State is bound by the legal nature and duration of the sentence determined by the sentencing State (Article 10(1)). But Article 10(2) goes on to add that if the sentence is, by its nature or duration, incompatible with the law of the administering State then that State may, by a court or administrative order, adapt the sanction to the punishment or measure prescribed by its own law for a similar offence. As to its nature, the punishment or measure shall, as far as possible, correspond with that imposed by the sentence to be enforced. It shall not aggravate, by its nature or duration, the sanction imposed in the sentencing State, nor exceed the maximum prescribed by the law of the administering State.[15]

8.22 Whichever scheme is adopted under the Convention, Article 9(3) makes clear that:

> The enforcement of the sentence shall be governed by the law of the administering state and that state alone shall be competent to take all appropriate decisions.

It follows that the Convention requires the administering State to accept the legal nature and duration of 'the sentence' under the continued enforcement procedure, but in enforcing 'the sentence' the administering State applies its own laws including laws which regulate the timing of release on licence.

The *Read* Decision

8.23 To give effect to these provisions Parliament chose the somewhat inelegant language of s 3(3) of the 1984 Act which directs the Secretary of State, in continuing the sentence, to have regard to the 'inappropriateness' of the transfer warrant containing provisions which:

> (a) are equivalent to more than the maximum penalties (if any) that may be imposed on a person who, in the part of the United Kingdom in which the prisoner is to be detained, commits an offence corresponding to that in respect of which the prisoner is required to be detained in the country or territory from which he is transferred or

---

[15] This is the principle of the non-aggravation of penalties recognized by Lords Steyn and Hope in their speeches in *R v Home Secretary, ex p Pierson* [1998] AC 539.

(b) are framed without reference to the length—
    (i) of the period during which the prisoner is, but for the transfer, required to be detained in that country or territory; and
    (ii) of so much of that period as will have been, or treated as having been, served by the prisoner when the said provisions take effect.

The impact of this section was considered by the House of Lords in *Read v Home Secretary*.[16] Read had been convicted of importing counterfeit currency into Spain. In view of the fact that the amount involved was not regarded as large he was given the minimum sentence available for this offence, which was 12 years and one day. The sentencing judges regarded even this as excessive and under an available procedure petitioned the Government to reduce this to six years. In the meantime Read sought and obtained transfer. The Home Secretary took the view that, as the maximum sentence under English law for an equivalent offence was ten years, he could not reduce Read's sentence to any less than ten years if he was to 'adapt' the sentence under Article 10 rather than 'convert' it under Article 11. It was accepted, however, that ten years was reserved for the most serious offences and Read's did not fall into that category. If he had committed the same offence in the United Kingdom he would have received no more than four years. His lawyers sought a declaration that the Home Secretary was entitled to reduce the sentence he would serve in England to this.

This view proved successful in the Divisional Court[17] where Parker LJ took the **8.24** view that Parliament had authorized the Secretary of State to do no more than implement the United Kingdom's international obligations and that to do so he had to find a sentence that was equivalent to that 'prescribed by law' for a similar offence. In the opinion of Parker LJ to discover what was 'prescribed by law' with respect to sentencing in the United Kingdom one looked to the decisions of the courts and not merely to the maximum terms indicated in statutes. Hence to comply with international obligations the Home Secretary could consider a term lower than the English maximum.

Lord Bridge (whose speech was agreed with by the other members of the House of **8.25** Lords) allowed the Secretary of State's appeal. He noted that the statute was framed to operate any international agreement for the transfer of prisoners that the United Kingdom might enter into. It would even allow the transfer to and detention of prisoners in the United Kingdom for acts done abroad which did not constitute offences in the United Kingdom. It seems unlikely, however, that this would extend to crimes (such as imprisonment for anti-State activities) whose content involves the violation of international human rights treaties to which the United Kingdom is a party. Acknowledging that in this case the Home Secretary

---

[16] [1989] 1 AC 1014.
[17] ibid, 1021.

had to act in accordance with the Transfer Convention Lord Bridge concluded that 'similar offence' referred to the category of the offence rather than its particular circumstances. This simply meant importing counterfeit money. In deciding what term to award for the offence he felt the Home Secretary was correct in drawing a distinction between continuing the sentence of the sentencing State and converting it. The former involved coming as close as possible to the duration awarded in the sentencing State without exceeding the administering State's maximum. The latter amounted to a resentencing process which would more closely have looked at what was appropriate in the administering State. In reaching his decision he was especially influenced by the explanatory memorandum to Article 10 which indicated that 'the administering state may adapt the sanction to the nearest equivalent available under its own law' and that the 'duration . . . corresponds to the amount of the original sentence'. Hence in a situation, such as here, where the sentencing State imposes a sentence in excess of the English maximum for an offence the Home Secretary can do no more than reduce it to the English maximum.

8.26 Disappointing as it is for prisoners such as Mr Read, and although the Convention provision is not free from ambiguity, there is much to be said for Lord Bridge's position. Article 10 indicates that the administering State is bound by the duration of sentence but goes on to add that this is not so where that exceeds the receiving State's maximum. Article 11 (which deals with the conversion approach) however does not indicate that the administering State is bound by the duration of the sentence imposed by the sentencing State but only that in converting the sentence it is not bound by the minimum for the offence provided by the law of the administering State. This would appear to give the administering State greater freedom to reduce the duration of a sentence while the reference to the minimum for that offence would appear to indicate that the term 'offence' refers to the broad category rather than the precise circumstances referred to by Parker LJ.[18]

---

[18] Further problems can arise when the sentence passed in the foreign state has no equivalent in the UK. In *R (Dillon) v Home Secretary* [2002] EWHC 732, the claimant, a British national, was convicted of serious sexual offences in Denmark and sentenced to 'safe custody', a sentence allowing for psychiatric treatment and detention in a normal prison. He applied for transfer to the UK. The Home Office accepted this, but stated that the sentence would have to be adapted. Initially, they took the view that the sentence should be treated as a hospital order under ss 37 and 41 of the Mental Health Act 1983. After taking advice from Lord Bingham, they changed their view, stating that the sentence would instead be treated as a discretionary life sentence with a minimum custodial period of seven years. The claimant initially consented, but then sought to challenge the warrant, arguing that the hospital order was more appropriate. After examining the nature of safe custody, Grigson J considered that it was punitive in nature and was used in place of a determinate custodial sentence. It was used in Denmark in circumstances where an offender had committed a serious offence and there were good grounds to believe that he would be a danger to the public. He considered that Lord Bingham's view was correct, and that it was open to the Home Secretary to conclude that a discretionary life sentence was appropriate.

Calculating the Release Date

A vital, but regrettably complex, issue for any prisoner considering transfer to the   **8.27**
United Kingdom is: what is the basis for calculating his release date on being
repatriated to the United Kingdom? Will he be better off in terms of his earliest
release date by staying put or in being repatriated to the United Kingdom? The
answer to this question lies not in the Convention but rather in the provisions of
the 1984 Act as amended by the Criminal Justice Act 1991 and subsequently by
the Crime (Sentences) Act 1997. Section 1(1) provides for the issuing of a warrant
by the Secretary of State to authorize the transfer of a prisoner from abroad to the
United Kingdom. Section 1(4) creates a duty on the Secretary of State to notify
the prisoner of the effect of the warrant and s 1(5) demands that the prisoner's
consent to transfer is obtained.[19] The effect of the issuing of the transfer warrant
is to authorize detention in the United Kingdom in accordance with such provisions as may be contained in the warrant. Consequently, after repatriation to the
United Kingdom, the prisoner is held under the authority of the warrant and not
under the terms of the original, foreign sentence.

The Act gives the Secretary of State a discretion as to the type of provisions that   **8.28**
may be contained in the transfer warrant, namely those which 'appear to him to
be appropriate for giving effect to the international arrangements in accordance
with which the prisoner is transferred'. But the discretion is not entirely open-
ended. In framing the warrant, the Home Secretary is required by the 1984 Act to
have regard to:

(1) the length of the sentence originally imposed; and
(2) the period that has been or will be treated as having been served by the pris-
     oner when the warrant takes effect.

The vexed question of the eligibility of a repatriated prisoner for release on licence
was contained in the seemingly benign Sch 2, para 2(1), to the 1984 Act (as
amended by the Criminal Justice Act 1991) which states that the prisoner's 'sentence' shall be deemed to begin on the day on which the relevant provisions take
effect (ie when the prisoner is delivered to the prison specified in the warrant[20]).
However Sch 2, para 2(2) provided the Home Secretary with a discretionary
power to specify in the warrant a period to be taken into account in determining
the question of a prisoner's eligibility for release on licence. Under the 1984 Act

---

[19] Art 6(2) states that the sentencing State shall provide the administering State with a certified
copy of the judgment and the law on which it was based, a statement indicating how much of the
sentence has already been served, including information on any pre-trial detention, remission, and
other factors relevant to the enforcement of the sentence, and a declaration containing the consent
to transfer.
[20] Repatriation of Prisoners Act 1984, s 3(5).

the period specified would then be deemed to have increased the prisoner's sentence and the amount of time he had served only in relation to the question whether he was eligible for release on licence. When the 1984 Act was amended by the Criminal Justice Act 1991 two unforeseen problems emerged which were identified in *R v Home Secretary, ex p Ellaway and Cheeseman*.[21] The first problem was highlighted by the case of Mr Cheeseman which demonstrated that because of the inclusion by amendment of the automatic release provisions for long and short term prisoners in the 1991 Act as relevant under Sch 2, para 2(2), to the 1984 Act, repatriated long term prisoners were in fact in a more favourable position than those who served their entire sentence in this country. This was because the remission that the prisoner was entitled to in the foreign jurisdiction was included (and was therefore deemed to have been served) in the amount which the Home Secretary specified should be taken into account when calculating a prisoner's eligibility for release on licence under the 1991 Act. Thus it was being counted twice over.[22] The Home Office conceded that Mr Cheeseman was entitled to this extra benefit as the law stood but removed the anomaly by further amending the 1984 Act in the Crime Sentences Act 1997. Schedule 2 to the 1997 Act saved the existing law for those who were repatriated before 26 October 1996[23] but altered it for those who were sentenced after the commencement of the Schedule by deleting certain sections of the 1991 Act as relevant when the Home Secretary specified a period to be taken into account.[24]

8.29 It follows that the only remaining sections of the 1991 Act relevant to the period specified by the Home Secretary in the warrant are ss 34(3) and (5), and 35(1) which concern eligibility for release of a discretionary life prisoner (where he has served the punitive period of his tariff and the Parole Board has recommended release) and eligibility for release on licence for a long term prisoner when he or she has served half of his or her sentence. The net effect of these amendments is that the period specified in the warrant (namely the time already served) has effect only in relation to eligibility for release on parole and not in relation to the automatic release provisions. The policy behind the amendments is to ensure that a period is not specified in a transfer warrant which would result in the prisoner

---

[21] [1996] COD 328, DC.

[22] In *R v Home Secretary, ex p Milhench*, 20 March 1997, DC, CO/4094/96, Simon Brown LJ commented that 'rather surprisingly, to my mind, the untoward consequences of specifying a period under para 2(2), of the Schedule to the Repatriation of Prisoners Act 1984 was only properly appreciated by the Prison Service in early 1996, some four or five years after the amendments were made. Less surprising, as it seems to me, once the problem was appreciated, it was taken into account in deciding whether or not to specify a period. The power is of course a discretionary one.'

[23] Apparently the date on which the Bill was presented to Parliament.

[24] The deleted sub-sections are s 33(1)(b) (automatic release on licence for those serving sentences of over 12 months and under four years when they have served half their sentence) and s 33(2) (automatic release on licence for those sentenced to for or more years after they have served two thirds of their sentence).

receiving what would be regarded as an unjustified benefit in comparison with domestic prisoners.[25]

The second anomaly arising from the pre-1997 Act position was revealed in *Ex p Ellaway*. Mr Ellaway was a short term prisoner who challenged the fact that his automatic release date was calculated as the half-way point of the balance of the sentence that he had to serve when he was repatriated rather than the half-way point of the original sentence that was imposed in the foreign jurisdiction. The approach of the Home Secretary demonstrated that he was drawing a distinction in this respect between long and short term prisoners. The Divisional Court held that the Home Secretary was entitled to draw such a distinction as para 2(2) provided him with a wide discretion and Parliament too had made such a distinction between long and short term prisoners. The amendment to the 1984 Act made by the Crime (Sentences) Act 1997 discussed above removes any potential for the period specified in the warrant to count towards the calculation of the automatic release date in the case of a short (or long) term prisoner. For the avoidance of doubt (and according with common sense) Sch 2, para 3(3), to the 1997 Act states that the question whether a prisoner is a long term or short term prisoner (when he or she returns to this jurisdiction) for the purposes of the Criminal Justice Act 1991 will be determined according to the sentence which was originally imposed.[26] **8.30**

---

[25] This can, of course, leave repatriated prisoners worse off than if they had been sentenced in the UK. This discrepancy was challenged in *R v Home Secretary, ex p Oshin* [2000] 1 WLR 2311. The High Court considered that it was not unlawful that the total time eventually served in prison may depend on the date of repatriation. The Convention and the domestic provisions were designed to ameliorate the hardship of having been convicted and sentenced abroad, rather than to equate the position of those sentenced abroad with those sentenced in the UK.

[26] As at mid-2002 the UK had signed bilateral Prisoner Transfer Agreements with the following countries: Brazil, Egypt, Hong Kong, Morocco, Barbados, Thailand, Cuba, Guyana, Venezuela and Suriname. The UK is also a member of the Scheme for the Transfer of Convicted Offenders within the Commonwealth: other members of the Scheme are Canada, Grenada, Malawi, Nigeria, Trinidad and Tobago, Zimbabwe and Mauritius. The UK has also acceded to the Council of Europe Convention on the Transfer of Sentenced Prisoners, to which, as of 31 May 2002, 50 countries had acceded. A copy of the Convention, together with an up to date list of signatories, can be found at http://conventions.coe.int/treaty/en/Treaties/Html/112.htm.

9

PRISON DISCIPLINE

A. Introduction

In this chapter we examine the prison system's formal disciplinary order. We look **9.01** at the nature of disciplinary offences, the procedures followed in adjudicating on them, and the punishments imposed on those who fall foul of them. This is an area where prisoners and prison authorities have often had very different perceptions. As Justice commented in 1983, '[i]t is in the context of discipline that the sharpest conflicts between prisoner and prison staff are apt to occur'.[1] There can be little doubt about the need for the maintenance of order in prisons; without it prisoners and staff may face the climate of fear and violence that has been at the heart of many prison conditions cases in the United States. A code of disciplinary offences and punishments is clearly one way of maintaining that order though, as other chapters in this book make clear, it is not the only one.

However, the operation of the discipline system in prisons has its own potential **9.02** for disorder, growing out of inmates' perception that the rules they are charged with breaking are highly arbitrary and the procedures employed to convict them

---

[1] See Justice, *Justice in Prisons* (London, 1983).

significantly unfair. The Woolf Report observed that how discipline is administered can have a very significant impact on how prisoners view the fairness of the prison system as a whole. A strong perception of unfairness can be an important factor in the creation of disturbances.[2]

9.03   In the UK prison system, two factors in particular raise concerns about the system's appearance of fairness. First, while breaches of prison rules may have adverse disciplinary consequences for prisoners, we have already seen that breaches by prison officers or administrators do not have any clear legal consequences for them. Secondly, until very recently, the enforcement of prison discipline remained primarily in the hands of prison officials themselves. Until August 2002 all disciplinary charges were adjudicated on by prison governors, whose ability to manage their prisons is heavily dependent on retaining the support of the prison officers who bring the charges.

9.04   To preserve the appearance and reality of fairness such a situation cries out for independent scrutiny of the exercise of disciplinary powers, the type of scrutiny which the judiciary, with its training and expertise in matters of procedure and fact-finding, is ideally placed to provide. Yet for most of the 20th century judges in the United Kingdom refused to examine the fairness of prison discipline proceedings. When called upon to do so they invoked analogies with military discipline, arguing that '[i]t is of the first importance that the cases be decided quickly'.[3] Judicial review, and the procedural standards it protects, were seen as only likely to cause delay and thus undercut the main purpose of disciplinary proceedings, the swift restoration of order. This military analogy was not without foundation. As Edward Fitzgerald has observed, the model for prison discipline devised at the end of the 19th century was taken from the army and the understanding of those who devised this model was that it would be a purely internal affair, with the administration deciding on its own procedure and no interference from outside bodies.[4] The factor which, however, clearly distinguished prison discipline from that in the army was that prisoners and prison staff often had radically opposed interests and perceptions, unlike soldiers and their commanders. Even more significantly, the scale of punishments handed out by prison disciplinary tribunals, notably the loss of remission for periods that ran into years, was far more severe than the analogy of parade ground discipline.

---

[2] See *Prison Disturbances: April 1990* (Cm 1456, 1991), para 14.437.
[3] The view is that of Lord Denning in *Fraser v Mudge* [1975] 3 All ER 78.
[4] E Fitzgerald, 'Prison Discipline and the Courts' in M Maguire, J Vagg, and R Morgan (eds), *Accountability and Prisons: Opening Up a Closed World* (London, 1986) 29.

The Development of Judicial Review of Discipline Hearings

What seems to have changed judicial attitudes was the scale of the disciplinary **9.05** punishments resulting from the Hull Prison Riots of 1976. These came before the courts in the *St Germain* litigation.[5] The punishments in those cases, some amounting to up to two years' loss of remission, were clearly much more severe than those of the parade ground variety. The judges in *St Germain* appear to have been prompted by this severity to investigate the quality of procedures followed before such punishments were imposed. Even then the military metaphor was not entirely given up. Rather, disciplinary proceedings for more serious offences were considered analogous to court martial proceedings, where more formal proced-ures were envisaged, while those on less serious charges continued to be referred to in parade ground terms. Hence for a number of years hearings by Boards of Visitors were subject to judicial review as to the quality of their procedures but governors' hearings, the vast majority, remained immune, a view confirmed in 1985 by the English Court of Appeal decision *of R v Deputy Governor Camp Hill Prison, ex p King*.[6] A year after the *King* decision the Northern Irish Court of Appeal reached a different conclusion in *In re McKiernan's Application*,[7] thus creating a period of uncertainty which was only resolved by the House of Lords decision in *Leech v Deputy Governor, Parkhurst Prison*,[8] which upheld the Northern Irish view.

The outcome of *St Germain* was that the courts began to conduct an examination **9.06** of the procedures followed in Board of Visitors hearings. Often they were not impressed by what they found there and a string of decisions followed on the call-ing of witnesses, cross-examination, the interpretation of offences, the burden of proof, and the circumstances in which a prisoner should have legal representation, which will be examined in more detail below. By 1988 the House of Lords felt able to comment that 'there seems no reason to doubt that . . . the courts' infrequent interventions have improved the quality of justice administered by boards of visi-tors'.[9] As regards governors' hearings such review has taken longer to get going and judges have always indicated that the standards required will be less strict, reflect-ing the less severe punishments available to governors and the closer relationship such proceedings have to general prison order. However in Northern Ireland in particular a significant jurisprudence has evolved regarding the procedural requirements of governors' disciplinary offences.

---

[5] *R v Board of Visitors of Hull Prison, ex p St Germain (No 1)* [1979] QB 425; *R v Board of Visitors of Hull Prison, ex p St Germain (No 2)* [1979] 1 WLR 1401.
[6] [1985] QB 735.
[7] See *McKiernan v Governor, HM Prison Maze* (1985) 6 NIJB 6.
[8] [1988] 1 AC 533.
[9] ibid.

9.07 Despite the procedural changes influenced by judicial review and effected by changes to Standing Orders, Home Office Circulars, and training for adjudicators, many critics remained unsatisfied. A particular target of their criticisms was the fact that Boards of Visitors continued to perform the dual role of watchdog to ensure standards for the treatment of prisoners were met and adjudicating tribunal for the most serious disciplinary offences. Although the Government rejected a proposal from a committee of inquiry which it established in 1986 that Boards lose their disciplinary functions,[10] in the wake of the Strangeways riot it accepted the same proposal when made in the Woolf Report. At the start of 1992, therefore, the prison disciplinary system entered a very new and uncertain phase.

B. Prison Discipline Hearings: The Retreat from a Dual System

9.08 Section 47 of the Prison Act 1952 gives the Home Secretary power to make rules relating to discipline. The disciplinary offences and basic structure for adjudicating them are set out in rules 51–61. The Prison Rules relating to discipline have been frequently amended. Until 1989 they provided for a distinction between 'disciplinary offences', adjudicated upon by governors, and 'grave' (escape attempts or gross personal violence against other inmates) or 'especially grave' offences (gross personal violence against prison officers and mutiny), which were referred to Boards of Visitors.[11] The main distinction lay in the punishments these two tribunals could order. While governors were limited to the forfeiture of 28 days' remission and three days' solitary confinement, Boards could order forfeiture of up to 180 days' remission and 56 days' solitary confinement for conviction on a 'graver offence', and on conviction of an 'especially grave' offence, unlimited loss of remission. Boards could also order more substantial periods of exclusion from associated work, stoppage of earnings, and exclusion from privilege than could governors.

9.09 The power to order loss of substantial periods of remission proved especially significant when it came to judicial review challenges. Although the Prison Rules only indicated that prisoners 'may' be granted remission, it was clear from after World War II that they would always be granted remission in accordance with the prevailing scheme. As a result the courts came to reject prison authority arguments that remission was only a privilege and that prisoners who lost remission as a result of disciplinary hearings did not lose anything they were entitled to.[12] Even

---

[10] *Committee on the Prison Disciplinary System* (The Prior Report) (Cmnd 9641, 1985).

[11] Technically the Prison Rules until 1989 required the governor first to refer the case to the Secretary of State who could then delegate the power to hear the case to the Board. In practice this is always what occurred.

[12] See *R v Board of Visitors of Highpoint Prison, ex p McConkey,* The Times, 23 September 1982.

if remission could not be said, under the prevailing statutory framework, to be a right it was clearly at least a 'legitimate expectation', in that prisoners could expect their release date to be automatically brought forward by the remission to which they were entitled. The effect of removing remission for a disciplinary conviction was to make a prisoner spend more days in prison than he would otherwise have done. Once courts accepted this, they were open to the argument that had prisoners been facing another sentence in a criminal court they would at least have had a certain level of procedural protections.[13] Though the courts have been reluctant fully to analogize prison disciplinary hearings to criminal proceedings, and especially reluctant in the case of governors' hearings, they have focused on cases involving substantial losses of remission, such as the 720 days in the *St Germain* litigation, as particularly in need of procedural safeguards. Similarly the European Court of Human Rights (ECtHR), in its decision in *Campbell and Fell v UK*,[14] observed that a loss of remission of 570 days was a particularly important factor in its conclusion that the applicants were facing 'criminal charges' and hence were entitled to be legally represented under Article 6(3) of the Convention.

Partly in response to these decisions, the Rules were amended in 1983 to remove **9.10** the power to order unlimited loss of remission. However, concerns remained over whether it was a good idea to have Boards perform the dual functions of being a watchdog as regards the prison administration but also the adjudicator of more serious charges, a position in which they would often have to uphold the administration against the prisoner. Board members often defended their adjudicatory function on the grounds that their knowledge of the circumstances at the prison put them in a better position to understand the events and personalities involved in discipline hearings and that their disciplinary function gave them greater respect among prison staff and hence influence when it came to their supervisory function. Critics, though, argued that prisoners are unlikely to put their trust in Board members who may the next day be ordering stiff disciplinary punishments against them, and that in order to maintain their influence with the prison administration Board members may feel under pressure to provide disciplinary convictions. Moreover, they argued that in view of the significant punishments which Boards could hand out, some legal training or judicial experience should be required.[15] The European Commission in the *Campbell and Fell* case took the view that the Board could not be seen as an 'independent tribunal' as required by Article 6(1) of the Convention in light of the fact that its members were only appointed for short periods by the Home Secretary and could be removed by him. This view was not upheld by the court.

---

[13] It is worth noting that the US Supreme Court has refused to see loss of good time credits as in any way analogous to a criminal conviction: see *Superintendent Massachusetts Correctional Institution, Walpole v Hill*, 472 US 445 (1985).

[14] Series A No 80 (1985) 7 EHRR 165.

[15] For a discussion of these criteria see Justice, *Justice in Prisons* (London, 1983) 55–56.

The Prior and Woolf Reports and Prison Discipline

9.11 Concerned by these criticisms, and perhaps even more by the possibility that many prisoners would be legally represented at Board hearings in the wake of the *Campbell and Fell* and *Tarrant* decisions, the Government established a committee under the chairmanship of Mr Peter Prior to examine the prison disciplinary system. Among the Prior recommendations was that the Boards lose their adjudicatory function. This would go to specially created Prison Disciplinary Tribunals, each of which would have a legally qualified chair. Initially this view found some favour with the Home Office but the Government finally decided against it, strongly influenced, it seems, by a view that legal representation was not being granted as often as expected before Boards and proved less of a problem than feared when granted.[16] Hence although further revisions to the Prison Rules in 1989 abolished the distinctions between offences, grave offences, and especially grave offences and reduced the maximum loss of remission on any one charge to 120 days, they still permitted governors to refer charges to boards where they felt the punishments they could give on conviction would, 'having regard to the nature and circumstances of the offence, be inadequate'.[17]

9.12 The issue would not go away and after the 1990 riots the Woolf Committee was charged with looking at the structure of disciplinary hearings again. It endorsed the recommendation of Prior, which it referred to as 'the most authoritative source on the prison discipline system', that Board members lose their disciplinary function, drawing on materials which questioned not just whether Boards could preserve the appearance of fairness but whether their practice had been satisfactory. In particular Woolf referred to a study of attitudes among prisoners which showed a clear feeling that Boards were the least satisfactory tribunal to appear before,[18] and the Committee's own conclusions after talking with some Board members that the latter felt they would be letting the governor down if they did not return a conviction. It also referred to the conclusions of justices' clerks involved in a pilot scheme to give legal advice to Board members: '[t]hose who were ready to state a point of view indicated by a considerable majority that the Board of Visitors did not use the same care in approaching LOR [loss of remission] as justices would have approached imprisonment'.[19] However, Woolf differed from Prior as regards what should replace Boards. Concluding that the Prior proposals had been 'on the table for some time without being taken up', it decided a return to first principles

---

[16] For a discussion of post-Prior developments see R Light and K Mattfield, 'Prison Disciplinary Hearings: The Failure of Reform' (1988) 27 Howard J 266.
[17] See r 51(1), as amended by the Prison (Amendment) Rules 1989, SI 1989/30.
[18] See J Ditchfield and D Duncan, 'The Prison Disciplinary System: Perceptions of its Fairness and Adequacy by Inmates, Staff and Members of Boards of Visitors' (1987) 26 Howard J 122.
[19] *Prison Disturbances: April 1990* (Cm 1456, 1991) para 14.394.

was appropriate and that a clearer distinction should be drawn between disciplinary and criminal penalties. The former could continue to be adjudicated upon by governors, the latter should be adjudicated upon by the criminal courts, where the penalties could be greater but so would be the procedural safeguards.

Woolf's proposals were largely adopted and the Board's disciplinary functions **9.13** abolished in 1992. From then on governors were responsible for hearing all internal discipline charges, though there was also a greater emphasis on referring more serious criminal charges to the police for prosecution through outside courts. However there always remained a concern, which increased with the advent of the Human Rights Act 1998 (HRA), that such a system was in breach of Article 6(1) of the European Convention on Human Rights (ECHR) in that at least some discipline charges amounted to 'criminal charges' under the Convention definition and that if so governors could not satisfy the requirement of being an 'independent and impartial tribunal' in hearing them. Though previous decisions of the Commission suggested that the UK system was Convention compliant and though it survived an early HRA challenge in *R (Greenfield) v Home Secretary*,[20] the ECtHR was eventually to conclude in *Ezeh and Connors v UK*[21] that governors could not hear disciplinary charges consistently with Article 6, at least where they had power to add extra days to the prisoner's sentence as a punishment upon conviction. The reasoning in *Ezeh and Connors* will be discussed further below in relation to the conduct of the hearing, and the case has been taken by the UK Government to the Grand Chamber of the ECtHR. However, at this point it has produced a change in the Prison Rules regarding prison discipline, and it is on these Rules that the following discussion is based.[22]

C. Decision-making on Disciplinary Charges: The Present System

Governors are now instructed to lay a disciplinary charge within 48 hours, in **9.14** compliance with rule 53(1), but to refer the facts of any suspected criminal offence to the police (more detailed guidelines refer especially to assault, escape, possession of weapons or class A drugs, criminal damage of an amount exceeding £2,000, arson, robbery with violence, mutiny, and any mass disturbance). Guidance in the Standing Orders then indicates that the governor should open the disciplinary hearing and satisfy himself or herself that there is a case to answer before adjourning it pending the police and Crown Prosecution Service (CPS) inquiry. If a decision to prosecute is taken then the case will go to an outside court

---

[20] [2002] 1 WLR 545.
[21] Applications 39665/98 and 40086/98 (2002) 35 EHRR 28.
[22] Prison (Amendment) Rules 2002, SI 2002/2116, which came into force on 15 August 2002.

and the disciplinary charge will not be proceeded with.[23] If it is decided not to prosecute then the governor may reactivate the disciplinary hearing; however, the *Discipline Manual* states that if it is clear that the police or CPS have decided that a prosecution cannot be brought because the available evidence is insufficient, and the disciplinary charge is similar to and relies on the same evidence as the potential charge, the governor should dismiss the disciplinary charge. In addition, where the resumption of internal proceedings is likely to create an appearance of unfairness out of proportion to the seriousness of the alleged disciplinary offence, the governor should consider whether the charge should be dismissed. In other cases it is open to the governor to proceed with the charge.[24]

9.15 Thus if the CPS has decided that a prosecution would not be in the public interest, the option remains open for the governor to prefer disciplinary charges. The range of criminal offences to which prisoners can be subject has been expanded by the creation of the offence of mutiny in the Prison Security Act 1992. Mutiny was one disciplinary charge which because of its complexity and potentially severe penalties gave rise to a right to legal representation for prisoners charged with it. Dropped as a disciplinary offence in 1989, its conversion into a criminal offence was recommended by the Prior Committee. Section 1(2) of the Act defines mutiny as 'where two or more prisoners, while on the premises of any prison, engage in conduct which is intended to further a common purpose of overthrowing lawful authority in that prison'. Where a mutiny is in progress prisoners who refuse to submit to lawful authority, having been given a reasonable opportunity to do so, without lawful excuse, are defined as participating in it. Mutiny carries a maximum ten-year sentence and prosecutions can only be brought with the consent of the Director of Public Prosecutions.

9.16 Where governors decide not to refer the events to the police they then must make a further decision as to whether to deal with the charge themselves or refer it to an adjudicator. The adjudicator (in many ways a throwback to Prior's rejected ideas of a Prison Disciplinary Tribunal) has been introduced following the *Ezeh and Connors* decision. If the governor decides that the offence is so serious that additional days should be awarded if the prisoner is found guilty, then the charge should be referred to an adjudicator.[25] Some guidance on when this is appropriate may be gleaned from the current PSI 61/2000 on the use of additional days as a

---

[23] Doing so could be in violation of r 36(1) of the European Prison Rules, which state that a prisoner should not be punished twice for the same act. However, in *R v Hogan* [1960] 3 All ER 149 the court found that a disciplinary conviction on an escape offence was no bar to subsequent criminal proceedings.

[24] *Prison Discipline Manual* (London, 1995), para 11.6.

[25] The governor should also refer any other charges arising out of the same incident to the adjudicator. Even if the governor concludes initially that the charge is insufficiently serious to refer this view may be revised after the hearing has begun and the governor may then transfer it to an adjudicator.

punishment. If the governor decides the offence is not sufficiently serious then he or she can then deal with the case himself or herself. In larger prisons governors will often delegate the hearing of charges to deputy governors.

In the discipline sphere, as elsewhere, the advent of private prisons as a result of the **9.17** Criminal Justice Act 1991 poses new questions. The Act indicates that responsibility for discipline is to rest with the Home Office-appointed controller rather than the privately appointed director, and Prison Rule 82 indicates that in contracted-out prisons references in the prison rules to the disciplinary powers of governors are to be read as references to the controller.

D. Prison Discipline Offences

The disciplinary offences a prisoner may be charged with are set out in rule 51. **9.18** There are 25 of these. Some of these are general offences which might be found in any disciplinary code, such as assault[26] or destroying property belonging to another,[27] while others more clearly relate to the prison[28] environment, such as denying an officer access to any part of the prison or intentionally obstructing an officer in the execution of his duty.[29] New offences of racially aggravated assault, racially aggravated damage to property, using threatening, abusive or insulting racist words or behaviour and displaying or drawing racist words, drawings or symbols appear for the first time in the 1999 Rules.[30] When the Prior Committee examined the code of discipline offences in 1985 it recommended revisions to produce a code which:

(1) is in clear, simple terms for staff to operate (bearing in mind that it is prison officers, not lawyers, who are responsible for identifying and laying the correct charge);

(2) makes clear to prisoners what constitutes an offence, and states clearly the degree of fault, knowledge etc which needs to be proved;

(3) identifies and sets out separately important or common offences for which no separate charge exists at present; and thereby;

(4) reduces the need and scope for the controversial catch-all 'good order and discipline' offence.[31]

---

[26] r 51(1).
[27] r 51(17). Guidance on the application and interpretation of these offences is contained in PSI 51/2000.
[28] r 51(3) and (6).
[29] r 47(6).
[30] r 51(1A), (17A), (20A), and (24A).
[31] *Committee on the Prison Disciplinary System* (The Prior Report) (Cmnd 9641, 1985), para 7.16.

The revised disciplinary code which emerged after this inquiry in 1989 goes a long way towards meeting these requirements. It abolished two of the most notorious offences, that of 'making a false and malicious allegation against an officer' and that of 'repeatedly making groundless complaints'. These had long been criticized by prison reform groups as discouraging legitimate complaints, although the Prior Committee itself, mindful of the fact that libel actions are not a practical option for prison officers unfairly accused, had actually recommended their retention in a modified form. The new code also tightens up the mental element requirements of most offences. For example the old offence of being 'idle, careless or negligent at work or, being required to work, refuses to do so'[32] has been replaced by one which finds a prisoner guilty of an offence against discipline if he 'intentionally fails to work properly or, being required to work, refuses to do so'.[33] The old rule against having an unauthorized article in one's cell has been replaced by a more simple rule which prohibits having an unauthorized article in one's possession.[34]

9.19 In addition to Prior, the judiciary had begun to indicate in a number of cases that it would interpret prison discipline offences strictly and that, as with the criminal law, it would construe ambiguities in favour of the defendant. Thus in *R v Board of Visitors, Highpoint Prison, ex p McConkey*[35] McCullough J quashed a disciplinary conviction of 'offending against good order and discipline' in respect of a prisoner against whom nothing had been established but that he had remained in a cell while others were smoking cannabis. It was neither alleged nor proven that he had actively encouraged others to smoke cannabis. McCullough J indicated that an element of mens rea had to be part of the definition of this offence. Similarly in *Ex p King* the Court of Appeal concluded that a governor had misconstrued a prison rule prohibiting having an unauthorized article (a hypodermic needle) in one's cell where he had found the prisoner guilty after concluding that the prisoner knew the article to be in the cell. The governor had failed to inquire whether the prisoner had control over it, the court noting that prisoners were often required to share cells with people they were afraid of crossing.[36] However, the proposal of Justice that the prison rules include a general defences article[37] (relating for example to self-defence, mistake, or lawful excuse) has not been adopted although Prison Rule 52 does set out specific defences (based on authorization and lack of knowledge or consent) to the rule 51(9) offence of administer-

---

[32] Old r 47(17).
[33] r 51(21).
[34] r 51(12).
[35] The Times, 23 September 1982.
[36] *R v Deputy Governor, Camphill Prison, ex p King* [1985] QB 735. For further support for the view that disciplinary offences ought to be construed in line with the criminal law see *R v Board of Visitors, Thorpe Arch Prison, ex p De Houghton*, The Times, 22 October 1987.
[37] Justice, *Justice in Prisons* (London, 1983) 48–49.

ing a controlled drug. Moreover, to continue the criminal law analogy of *McConkey*, failure of a governor to consider such pleas should be susceptible to judicial review.[38]

One offence which Prior ultimately did not recommend be removed was the **9.20** catch-all offence of 'in any way offends against good order and discipline'.[39] This was finally abolished by the 1999 Rules, although the similar offence of 'disobeys any lawful order'[40] lives on in the 1999 Rules. The former offence had been heavily criticized as maintaining a highly discretionary discipline regime and one that may be in contravention of the United Kingdom's obligations under rule 35(a) of the European Prison Rules. This requires that conduct constituting a disciplinary offence shall be 'provided for and determined by the law or by the regulation of the competent authority'. Examples of the sort of conduct which had bizarrely been punished under this rule are numerous and include 'making cat like noises in the presence of the prison dog' or 'playing the piano in the education block'.

The abolition of this offence is a major step forward. It is unlikely to be missed, even for the purposes of maintaining good order and discipline, since commentators examining the recent use of rule 43(21) found that normally activity charged under it could be dealt with by laying a charge under another, existing, disciplinary offence.[41]

E. The Conduct of Prison Discipline Hearings

Prison Rule 54(2) indicates that at any inquiry into a charge a prisoner is to be **9.21** given a full opportunity of hearing what is alleged against him and a full opportunity to present his own case. Courts have indicated that this rule is essentially declarative of the principles of natural justice, which apply to the hearing of disciplinary charges. While the principles of natural justice, or its modern equivalent, fairness, are applicable to all administrative decisions with the capacity to affect citizens adversely, their content varies with the significance of the decision and the character of the issues to be considered.[42] At one end stands the need simply for a decision maker who has no personal or pecuniary interest in the outcome, at the other the full procedural protections of a criminal trial.

---

[38] Such a defence is especially important where the charge is 'fighting with any person', eg r 47(4). The Ombudsman in his *1996 Annual Report* (Cm 3487, 1997), para.7.6 has indicated that in some of the cases sent to him governors have failed to explore all possible defences.

[39] r 47(21).

[40] r 51(22).

[41] P Quinn, 'Reflexivity Run Riot': The Survival of the Prison Catch-all' (1995) 34 Howard J 354 found that all of the 61 charges he examined could have been laid under other rules while N Loucks, *Anything Goes: The Use of the 'Catch-all' Disciplinary Rule in Prison Service Establishments* (London, 1995) found this to be true of 97.5% of the 1,707 offences she surveyed.

[42] See, generally P Craig, *Administrative Law* (4th edn, London, 1999).

9.22 Although the courts recognized Board of Visitors hearings, particularly where they could involve unlimited loss of remission if the prisoner were convicted, as coming close to criminal trials, they fell short of applying the analogy fully. Hearsay evidence, for example, has always been accepted as permissible in all forms of prison discipline hearings. Since governors' hearings have only more recently become the object of judicial scrutiny, at least in England and Wales, the procedural standards required in them are less fully developed. Cases in Northern Ireland, however, suggest that a less rigorous approach will be required and that the courts will be more prepared to consider whether on an examination of the proceedings as a whole the prisoner was given a fair hearing as opposed to focusing on particular aspects of the hearing and signalling what is required by way of procedural fairness in respect of each. Courts have spoken of the need for governors' hearings to be conducted in a 'firm, fair and crisp manner' and have said that they will not be reviewed simply for technical breaches which cause no injustice.[43]

9.23 Under Article 6(1) of the ECHR, '[i]n the determination of his civil rights and obligations or of any criminal charge against him, everyone is entitled to a fair and public hearing within a reasonable time by an independent and impartial tribunal established by law'. Although people in the common law world are used to associating the phrase 'civil rights' with rights against the State the Convention takes its meaning more from the civil law world, where civil rights connotes civil or private law rights. While the boundary between public and private rights is often blurred (especially when it comes to semi-contractual rights against the State)[44] it seems clear that prison disciplinary hearings fall outside the first half of Article 6(1). However, in *Campbell and Fell v UK*[45] the ECtHR indicated that prison discipline hearings *could* amount to 'criminal proceedings' within the meaning of Article 6. Such a determination is particularly significant as criminal charges attract further explicit procedural requirements under Article 6, including the right to legal representation. Rejecting the Government's claim that there was a clear division between disciplinary and criminal offences, the court indicated that it would take three factors into account in deciding whether or not a charge would fall into the criminal category. These were the domestic classification as criminal or disciplinary, the nature of the offence itself and whether it would normally appear in a criminal code, and the nature and severity of the penalty faced. In *Campbell and Fell*, where the prisoners faced mutiny charges and risked unlimited loss of remission (one of them actually losing 570 days' remission), the court concluded these criteria were satisfied.

---

[43] See *In re McEvoy and Others' Application* (1991) 8 NIJB 89.
[44] For a discussion of the meaning of the phrase 'civil rights' see J Simor and B Emmerson, *Human Rights Practice* (London, 2000), paras 6.002–6.021.
[45] Series A No 80 (1985) 7 EHRR 165.

The *Campbell and Fell* case left open the question of whether all forms of loss of **9.24** remission would amount to the imposition of criminal charges. In a previous decision the court appeared to accept that any punishment involving the deprivation of liberty implicated a criminal charge.[46] In *Campbell and Fell* it appeared to reject the argument that loss of remission, being a privilege, did not involve any loss of liberty and hence might arguably be indicating that any loss of remission would constitute a deprivation of liberty.[47] However, the court's language initially suggested a more cautious approach. It indicated that 'by causing detention to continue for substantially longer than would otherwise have been the case, the sanction came close to, even if it did not technically constitute, deprivation of liberty'. This gave the impression that not all losses of remission will amount to deprivation of liberty and in a number of cases the Commission indicated that some punishments which added additional days to the prisoner's effective date of release might fall short of being criminal charges.[48]

This view was clearly influential when domestic courts came to grapple with the **9.25** Strasbourg case law in the context of disciplinary proceedings following the advent of the HRA. In *R (Carroll, Greenfield and Al Hasan) v Home Secretary*[49] the Court of Appeal held that such proceedings were not criminal, within the meaning of Article 6, and did not therefore attract Article 6 safeguards. Carroll and Al-Hasan had refused to squat during a search. They were charged with disobeying a lawful order, and both were found guilty. Mr Carroll was punished with the imposition of two additional days, 10 days' cellular confinement and the stoppage of earnings for 19 days. Al-Hasan was punished with stoppage of earnings for 15 days and loss of privileges. Greenfield was given 21 additional days for administering a controlled drug. The applicants argued that the ability to impose up to 42 additional days' imprisonment, which would keep them in prison for up to 42 days longer than envisaged by the original sentence of the court, inevitably meant that the proceedings were criminal in character. The court considered that, in the context of s 42(2) of the Criminal Justice Act 1991, when additional days are awarded they are aggregated to the period that the prisoner would otherwise have to serve before release on licence. In a piece of hair-splitting reasoning, Lord Woolf CJ considered that the additional days do not have the effect of adding to a prisoner's sentence. Rather, they simply postpone a prisoner's release on licence. This might seem to amount to exactly the same thing: an additional loss of liberty

---

[46] See *Engel v Netherlands* Series A No 22 (1976) 1 EHRR 647.
[47] (1985) 7 EHRR 165, 197.
[48] See V Treacey, 'Prisoners Rights Lost in Semantics' (1989) 28 Howard J 27, for the view that Art 6 is applicable to all losses of remission. However in *Pelle v France*, 50 D & R 263 (1986) the Commission suggested that a possible 18 days' loss of remission was not sufficient. Generally see C Kidd, 'Disciplinary Proceedings and the Right to a Fair Criminal Trial Under the European Convention on Human Rights' (1987) 36 ICLQ 856.
[49] [2002] 1 WLR 545.

flowing directly from the finding of guilt. Taking into account the criteria for a criminal charge set out in *Engel v Netherlands*,[50] the court was influenced by the fact that none of the offences precisely replicated a criminal offence, would not result in a criminal record, and could be remitted.

Ezeh and Connors v UK

9.26 However, the Court of Appeal's decision offered only brief reassurance for the Prison Service. Within a few months the Third Section of the ECtHR came to a very different conclusion in *Ezeh and Connors v UK*.[51] Ezeh was found guilty at an adjudication of using threatening words, and Connors was found guilty of assault. The former received a punishment which included 42 added days, and the latter one which included seven added days. Both made requests for legal representation, which were refused by the governor hearing the case. The ECtHR took the view that although the charges could not clearly be described as being of a 'criminal' character in themselves (the assault concerned a relatively minor incident) they did have 'a certain colouring which does not coincide with that of a purely disciplinary matter'. More significant, though, was the issue of the penalty. The court rejected the idea that the move in the 1991 Criminal Justice Act from a penalty of loss of remission to that of added days had any material significance, noting that 'the fact remains the applicants were detained in prison beyond the date on which they would otherwise have been released as a consequence of separate disciplinary proceedings unrelated to the original conviction'. It then turned to consider the severity of the potential penalty and actual penalty imposed, observing that deprivations of liberty imposed as a punishment normally belong to the sphere of criminal charges 'except those which by their nature, duration or manner of execution cannot be appreciably detrimental'. Noting that even the seven additional days in Connors's case was equivalent to a two week sentence imposed by an outside court, it concluded that no such exception was met in this case. Although the applicants did not raise the point, the Government conceded that if the disciplinary charges at issue did amount to 'criminal charges' within the meaning of Article 6(1) then governors could not be said to afford an independent and impartial tribunal. Hence the need for fresh Prison Rules and the rapid creation of an adjudicator to hear more serious disciplinary charges. The case also raises the potential for significant compensation claims by prisoners detained beyond their anticipated release date as a result of added days awarded in governor's adjudications.

---

[50] [1976] 1 EHRR 647.
[51] Applications 39665/98 and 40086/98 (2002) 35 EHRR 28.

Laying a Charge and Notice of the Hearing

Under Prison Rule 53(1) a charge must be laid as soon as possible and, except in **9.27** exceptional circumstances, no longer than 48 hours after the incident.[52] Paragraph 2.1 of the *Discipline Manual* indicates that the charge should normally be laid by the officer who witnessed the incident or against whom the alleged offence is committed. Officers are advised to consult a senior member of staff to ensure that the correct charge is laid. Prisoners charged are required to be given a Notice of Report (Form 1127) which sets out the notice of the offence charged and, according to the *Discipline Manual*, should be 'sufficiently detailed to leave prisoners in no doubt as to what is alleged against them'. Failure to inform a prisoner of the charge in advance is clearly a ground for judicial review,[53] and the courts have indicated that simply repeating the words of the alleged offence is insufficient to give the prisoner notice of what is alleged against him.[54] Paragraph 2.9 of the *Discipline Manual* indicates that Form 1127 should be served on the prisoner at least two hours before the hearing. In some cases this may be too short, especially where complex factual or legal issues are involved. In the *Tarrant*[55] case dicta suggest that on a complex charge like mutiny 24 hours' notice might be necessary.

Laying the correct charge is especially important, as the Court of Appeal indicated **9.28** in *R v Board of Visitors, Dartmoor Prison, ex p Smith*[56] that the requirements of rule 53(1) are mandatory. There the court quashed a Board decision to convict a prisoner of assault after having acquitted him of causing gross personal violence on the ground that the lesser offence must be contained in the greater. The court took the view that nothing in the Prison Rules entitled the Board to substitute a different charge for the one laid. One effect of proceeding on the assault charge which had not specifically been laid was that the prisoner had no opportunity to prepare a defence to it. In a Northern Irish case the High Court indicated that prisoners could not be convicted of two separate offences arising out of the same incident.[57] Once the charges have been laid the tribunal should normally hear them in the order in which they have been laid.[58]

---

[52] *Prison Discipline Manual*, para 2.3, notes that this requirement is strict and applies irrespective of whether those 48 hours include a weekend or holiday.

[53] See *R v Board of Visitors, Long Lartin Prison, ex p Cunningham*, 17 May 1988.

[54] *R v Board of Visitors, Swansea Prison, ex p Scales*, The Times, 21 February 1985.

[55] *R v Home Secretary, ex p Tarrant* [1985] QB 251.

[56] [1987] QB 106. See also *R v Board of Visitors, Gartree Prison, ex p Sears*, The Times, 20 March 1985.

[57] eg in *In re Murphy's Application* (1988) 8 NIJB 94, the prisoner was convicted of both using abusive language and offending against good order and discipline by the governor out of a single incident of swearing at a prison officer.

[58] A recommendation of Hodgson J in *R v Board of Visitors, Gartree Prison, ex p Mealey*, The Times, 14 November 1981. The *Discipline Manual* recommends that where several charges are laid against a prisoner in respect of a single incident it may be best to hear all the evidence before reaching a finding on any one of the charges.

The Danger of Bias

9.29 The problem of actual or apparent bias has been a particularly difficult one for the prison discipline system. Given that the governors involved in hearing charges have a fairly close relationship with the prison officers bringing the charges, it must be asked whether the appearance of impartiality can ever fully be achieved. The courts rejected a fairly direct attempt to raise this question in *R v Board of Visitors, Frankland Prison, ex p Lewis*,[59] where the applicant argued that a member of a Board hearing a disciplinary charge of possessing drugs in his cell could not be impartial as only a few weeks previously the Board member had been on the Local Review Committee that turned down his parole application. As a member of that committee the Board member would be aware of the applicant's previous convictions for drugs offences. Woolf J concluded that the appropriate test was whether a reasonable and fair-minded bystander, knowing all the facts, would have a reasonable suspicion that a fair trial for the applicant was not possible.[60] Among the facts that such a hypothetical bystander would have to take into account was the dual role of Board members. Woolf J noted that where a Board member was aware of a possible appearance of unfairness (which the member here apparently was not, as he did not remember the parole hearing) he or she would have to exercise his or her discretion whether or not to sit. This approach has also been taken with respect to governors' adjudications in *Ex p Hibbert*.[61] If anything these pose even greater problems than Board adjudications did. However the Divisional Court took the view that there would need to be 'something outside the normal situation' to justify intervention in response to a bias accusation. In this case the governor conducting the adjudication was a security governor with a general knowledge of what was happening in the prison. Not enough, in the eyes of the Divisional Court, to give rise to an appearance of bias. Interestingly, in light of the views that Woolf subsequently expressed in his Report on the role of Board members in disciplinary proceedings, in the *Lewis* case he urged Board members not to be too eager to disqualify themselves as:

> they are offences which are primarily against discipline and in order to deal with those kind of offences, it is important that those who adjudicate upon them should have knowledge of the workings of prisons in general and the particular prison of which the prisoner concerned is an inmate.[62]

---

[59] [1986] 1 WLR 130.

[60] The test is derived from the judgment of Ackner LJ in *R v Liverpool City Justices, ex p Topping* [1983] 1 All ER 490. The test for bias was restated by the House of Lords in *Magill v Porter; Magill v Weeks* [2002] 2 WLR 37. Lord Hope, after considering the Strasbourg and domestic case law, affirmed that: '[t]he question is whether the fair-minded and informed observer, having considered the facts, would conclude that there was a real possibility that the tribunal was biased' (para 103).

[61] *R v HM Prison Service, ex p Hibbert*, 16 January 1997.

[62] [1986] 2 All ER 272.

However, while the courts have shown themselves unwilling to consider possibil- **9.30**
ities of structural bias in the discipline system they have been prepared to review
more obvious deviations from established practice. In *R v Governor, Pentonville
Prison, ex p Watkins*[63] Judge J indicated that if the prison officer preferring charges
was in the room where the adjudication took place before the prisoner entered or
remained behind after the prisoner left this would offend the appearance of
fairness.[64] Governors are also required to consider whether hearing evidence in
relation to other charges, either against this prisoner or other prisoners, might
prejudice their decisions. Therefore the *Discipline Manual* recommends that
where several prisoners are charged with offences arising out of a single incident
the governor may consider separate hearings, perhaps conducted by different governors. Likewise where one prisoner is charged with several offences arising out of
different incidents. Either way a governor must be careful not to reach a finding
based on evidence heard at another adjudication.[65] In his 1996 report, however,
the Prisons Ombudsman indicated that governors had not always followed guidance in this area and that he had quashed findings as a result.[66]

Segregation Prior to the Hearing

The laying of a disciplinary charge may not end the conflict which gave rise to it. **9.31**
Mainly to prevent the continuation of conflict, governors are given powers to segregate prisoners prior to adjudication. However, criticism of the use of these powers
is frequent. Critics argue that rather than being a discretionary last resort to prevent
a difficult situation becoming worse they have been used automatically to segregate
all prisoners pending adjudications. They have noted that under the old rule 48(2)
segregation pending a hearing did not require the approval of the Board or Secretary
of State, unlike what is now rule 45 segregation. In addition such prisoners have
often been segregated in punishment cells, hence depriving them of facilities and
heightening the sense that the prisoner is already regarded as guilty.[67] On a practical
level segregation also hampers a prisoner's ability to prepare his defence at adjudication, especially as regards discovering and interviewing potential witnesses.

One consequence of granting legal representation for some Board hearings was **9.32**
that prisoners could spend more time in pre-hearing segregation as both sides

---

[63] [1992] COD 329.
[64] In *In re Grogan's Application* (1988) 8 NIJB 87 Carswell J reached a similar conclusion and
quashed a Board's award where a governor remained behind with the Board after the prisoner and
everyone else left, even though the judge accepted that the governor did not take any part in the
Board's deliberations.
[65] *Prison Discipline Manual*, para. 4.6; see also *R v Board of Visitors, Walton Prison, ex p Weldon*
[1985] Crim LR 514, where an adjudication was quashed for failure to exercise a discretion where a
Board refused a prisoner's request for separate charges to be heard by separate adjudicators.
[66] *Annual Report* 1996 (Cm 3487, 1997), paras 7.10–7.17.
[67] See the criticisms in Justice, *Justice in Prisons* (London, 1983) 59.

took greater care over the preparation of their case. With the abolition of Board hearings the risk of this occurring was diminished as governors' hearings normally occurred fairly quickly after the charge was laid. However, the problem may reappear post August 2002 as adjudicators have up to 28 days to first inquire into charges referred to them.[68]

9.33 The *Manual on Adjudications* indicates that governors should segregate only when necessary, for example where there is a risk of collusion, or threats to witnesses or to alleged victims. Rule 53(4) permits pre-hearing segregation only before the governor's first inquiry. Thereafter all segregation, including that pending the hearing of criminal offences, must be on the basis of rule 45. As has been indicated elsewhere in this text, such decisions are susceptible to judicial review. The adjudications manual also indicates that reasons should be given for any decision to segregate prior to a hearing, that prisoners on pre-hearing segregation should not be housed in punishment cells 'unless there is no other suitable cell available elsewhere' (a frequent problem in older prisons), and that they should not be deprived of any privileges that they are normally entitled to 'except those that are incompatible with segregation'.[69]

Fitness for Adjudication

9.34 Prison Rule 58 requires that no punishment of cellular confinement may be imposed unless the medical officer has certified that the prisoner is in a fit state of health to be dealt with in this way. It is also established practice that before an adjudication takes place a medical officer should certify whether the prisoner is fit for adjudication. In the past medical officers may have tended to run these two separate questions together, but form F256 now clearly requires a medical officer to offer opinions on each issue separately. Examinations should normally take place on the morning of the hearing. Where this is not possible because the prison does not have a full time medical officer, the Adjudications Manual recommends that it take place as soon as possible after the adjudication and that in such circumstances the adjudicator cannot impose a sentence of cellular confinement. If a medical officer decides that a prisoner is not fit for adjudication he should indicate for how long this is likely to remain true. Ultimately the decision as to fitness is for the governor or adjudicator but he or she may wish to hear independent medical evidence where the prisoner or his representative expresses concern at a finding of fitness.[70] Even if a governor decides initially that a prisoner is fit for adjudication he or she may reconsider this at any time during the proceedings.

---

[68] r 53(3).
[69] *Prison Discipline Manual*, para 4.18.
[70] See *R v Home Secretary, ex p Lee*, 19 February 1987.

Legal Representation at Adjudications

No area of the requirements of natural justice in the context of Board of Visitors **9.35** hearings was more fiercely fought than that of legal representation. As one of the authors of this text has argued, it was not without good reason that prisoners' advocates saw this as a particularly significant procedural guarantee to enshrine.[71] The presence of lawyers not only offered prisoners the skills of those with greater experience of arguing before tribunals, but also brought a genuinely external element into the closed world of prison discipline and put Board members on notice that the quality of their adjudications was under scrutiny. In addition it changed the character of discipline proceedings. Rather than convicted prisoners, whose veracity and motivation the Board might suspect, arguing against the word of prison officers, one would have professional lawyers defending their clients. Boards were always likely to listen to their arguments with greater respect.

Early attempts to secure legal representation in discipline hearings fared no better **9.36** than most prisoners' claims. In 1975 Lord Denning MR, in an unreserved judgment, invoked the military model and concerns about delay in hearings being inimical to discipline to dismiss brusquely an application on this point.[72] An early European application also proved fruitless, the Commission in *Kiss v UK*[73] becoming stuck on the point that loss of remission could not constitute a deprivation of liberty within the meaning of Article 5 as the prisoner was lawfully sentenced to prison and remission was not a matter of right.

With the demise of the military model in the first *St Germain* case[74] it was always **9.37** likely that the issue of legal representation would arise again. The first real breakthrough, however, came in the European Commission of Human Rights decision in *Campbell and Fell v UK*.[75] There the Commission indicated that the classification of offences as disciplinary under domestic law would not render them immune from being regarded as 'criminal' offences under the Convention if certain conditions were met. The Commission indicated that it would look at the initial classification under domestic law, whether the content of the disciplinary offence also normally appeared in criminal codes, and the seriousness of the penalties prescribed for the offence. Applying these criteria to prisoners who faced possible unlimited loss of remission and actually received up to 570 days' loss of

---

[71] See, generally, S Livingstone, 'Prisoners and Board of Visitors Hearings: A Right to Legal Representation After All?' (1987) 38 Northern Ireland LQ 144. For a similar view regarding Canada see M Jackson, 'The Right to Counsel in Prison Disciplinary Proceedings' (1986) 20 U of British Columbia L Rev 221.

[72] *Fraser v Mudge* [1975] 3 All ER 78.

[73] *Kiss v UK* 7 D & R 55 (1976).

[74] *R v Board of Visitors of Hull Prison, ex p St Germain (No 1)* [1979] QB 425.

[75] (1983) 5 EHRR 207.

remission for mutiny and assault offences it concluded they had been charged with 'criminal offences'. Under Article 6(3) of the Convention all those charged with criminal offences are entitled to be legally represented.

The Tarrant Criteria

9.38 The ECtHR was to affirm the decision of the Commission on the Article 6(3) point in *Campbell and Fell* within two years. Before it did so the Divisional Court in England also recognized that at least in limited circumstances natural justice could require a right to legal representation in Board of Visitors discipline hearings. Like *Campbell and Fell* the case of *R v Home Secretary, ex p Tarrant*[76] arose out of mutiny hearings following disturbances, this time at Wormwood Scrubs and Albany. Webster J quashed the convictions handed down by the Board on the ground that they had failed even to consider whether they had a discretion to grant representation. If they had considered it he indicated that they would have had to take a number of factors into account. These were:

(1) the seriousness of the charge and the potential penalty;
(2) the likelihood that difficult points of law would arise;
(3) the capacity of a prisoner to present his own case;
(4) procedural difficulties, such as the inability of prisoners to trace and interview witnesses in advance;
(5) the need for reasonable speed in deciding cases;
(6) the need for fairness between prisoners and between prisoners and prison officers.

Moreover Webster J indicated that as regards some offences, such as mutiny, where the penalties were severe and points of law complex, no reasonable Board exercising its discretion could decline to grant representation.[77]

9.39 The *Tarrant* case sparked a significant rethink in the Home Office regarding the whole prison disciplinary system and led directly to the establishment of the Prior Committee. That Committee eventually came down against a right of representation in all disciplinary cases. Prior concluded that having a legally qualified chair, as it recommended for its proposed Prison Disciplinary Tribunal, would protect prisoners against procedural carelessness while the costs and potential delays resulting from having representation in all cases were too much to bear.[78] The Government did not disagree with this view and so essentially the position on representation remained unchanged.

---

[76] [1985] QB 251.
[77] Fitzgerald, n 4 above, at 37, praises this decision as a 'tribute to the resources of the common law that the court was able to find a way round the seeming impasse of *Fraser v Mudge* [[1975] 1 WLR 1132]'.
[78] See *Committee on the Prison Disciplinary System* (The Prior Report) (Cmnd 9641, 1985), paras 10.9–10.23, for the Committee's views on the issue of legal representation.

However, even before Prior reported the pendulum was swinging against repre- **9.40**
sentation. In *R v Board of Visitors, Blundeston Prison, ex p Norley*[79] Webster J
returned to the issue and indicated that where the prisoner was articulate, his
defence essentially factually based, and the charge not among the most serious, a
Board would not as a rule be held to have gone wrong in exercising their discretion to refuse to permit representation. Boards generally became more prepared to
refuse representation, and few were adversely reviewed as a result.[80] There was also
a lack of lawyers with knowledge of or interest in the area.[81] After the Prior Report
the trend against representation moved even more swiftly. In *R v Board of Visitors,
Risley Remand Centre, ex p Draper*[82] the Court of Appeal upheld the view of the
Divisional Court that a potential 180 days' loss of remission was not sufficiently
serious to require legal representation if none of the other *Tarrant* factors were present. It also indicated that a fairly narrow view would be taken of what constituted
a point of law requiring representation.

The death knell for attempts to establish a right of representation, at least in the **9.41**
UK context, came with the House of Lords decision in *Hone and McCartan v
Board of Visitors, Maze Prison.*[83] In a case brought by prisoners in Northern Ireland
to raise the issue of whether a right to representation existed, Lord Goff, for a
unanimous House, indicated that he could not find a right to representation in
either natural justice or the ECHR and was much concerned by the problem of
delays if representation were granted as of right. At the time his position found
some support in Strasbourg jurisprudence, but this has now been overturned by
the ECtHR's decision in *Ezeh and Connors*, which clearly establishes that prisoners have such a right under Article 6(3)(c) of the Convention, at least where they
face a potential penalty of added days.

Current Procedure for Requests of Legal Representation

The 2002 amendments to the Prison Rules now create two different regimes with **9.42**
respect to legal representation. Where a case is referred to an adjudicator Prison
Rule 54(3) makes it clear that the prisoner shall automatically be given the right
to be legally represented. Where, on the other hand, jurisdiction is retained by the
governor then he or she must look at the *Tarrant* criteria to decide if representation is appropriate. The Prior Committee and the Woolf Report recommended
against allowing representation before governors, and in *Hone and McCartan*
Lord Goff indicated that he found it difficult to imagine when the rules of natural

---

[79] 4 July 1984. See also *R v Board of Visitors, Swansea Prison, ex p McGrath*, The Times,
21 November 1984.
[80] See R Morgan, 'More Prisoners Denied Lawyers' Help' (1987) 91 New Society 1283.
[81] See R Light and K Mattfield, 'Prison Disciplinary Hearings: The Failure of Reform' (1988) 27
Howard J 266, 270.
[82] The Times, 24 May 1988.
[83] [1988] 1 All ER 381.

justice would ever require representation before a governor. However, in Northern Ireland, governors' adjudications have been quashed because they failed even to consider a request for representation. Yet further decisions have indicated that where governors do give their minds to the issue only very rarely will they be vulnerable to judicial review if they decide not to grant representation.[84] In *In re Reynolds Application*[85] Higgins J indicated that only where a prisoner was clearly unable to conduct his or her defence, for example where a prisoner was mentally subnormal, would a governor be under an obligation to grant representation. Cases in England since the 1992 changes have also demonstrated a reluctance to intervene where governors refuse representation.[86] As governors will no longer be hearing cases involving deprivation of added days this reluctance may be only likely to grow, although an increase in governors' powers to order 21 days' cellular confinement (previously 14) may give some judges pause for thought.

9.43 The *Discipline Manual* does however indicate that prisoners appearing before governors on disciplinary charges should be asked if they wish to be legally represented, normally at the start of the hearing. A prisoner should always be entitled to consult a lawyer in advance of an adjudication and the hearing should be adjourned if he has not had time to do this. In one case concerning a Board of Visitors hearing the prisoner sought judicial review because his application had only been considered, and rejected, on the day of the hearing. He argued that once the Board had been gathered for a hearing it would be very reluctant to adjourn to allow a prisoner's legal representative to prepare his or her defence. Rejecting the application the High Court indicated that this was a fairly straightforward case involving an articulate prisoner, where the prisoner would have been unlikely to get legal representation anyway.[87] This case would now be looked at differently in light of *Ezeh and Connors* and this European decision may have a very significant impact on the conduct of prison discipline proceedings. Figures produced for the court hearing showed that legal representation was sought in only 250 cases and granted in less than 200 in the approximately 600,000 adjudications which took place in the period 1994–98. Given that additional days has been the most popular punishment it is likely that governors will be referring a substantial proportion of cases to adjudicators in the future. Prisoners will be entitled to be legally represented at all these hearings, though it remains to be seen whether they will normally exercise this right.

9.44 As an alternative to being legally represented a prisoner may request that a friend or adviser be allowed to attend and, at the discretion of the adjudicator, address

---

[84]   *In re Carroll's Application* (1987) 10 NIJB 23.
[85]   (1987) 8 NIJB 82.
[86]   See *R v HM Prison Service, ex p Hibbert*, 16 January 1997. Governor's decision to refuse representation was upheld as this was a 'simple case' of alleged assault.
[87]   *R v Board of Visitors, Parkhurst Prison, ex p Norney* [1990] COD 133.

the tribunal on his behalf. The criteria for allowing the appearance of such an adviser, often known as a *McKenzie* friend,[88] are the same as those relating to legal representation, with the additional issue of whether the friend is available and a suitable person to assist.[89]

Procedure and Evidence at a Disciplinary Hearing

The *Discipline Manual* indicates that '[a]djudicators [which would include gov- **9.45** ernors hearing discipline charges] should ensure that the general atmosphere is as relaxed as possible while maintaining sufficient formality to emphasise the importance of the proceedings'.[90] The manual specifically states that 'eyeballing' (the practice of prisoners having to stand throughout the hearing with two officers facing them) is not permitted and that prisoners must be allowed to sit at a table and be provided with writing material throughout the adjudication. Prisoners should also be given a copy of form 1145 (Explanation of Procedure at Disciplinary Charge Hearings) and should have access to the *Prison Discipline Manual*. However, it has been held that refusal to allow a prisoner a copy of the manual will not invalidate the adjudication if the court feels that the prisoner is well aware of its contents.[91]

When the hearing begins the prosecution will produce its evidence first. This nor- **9.46** mally consists of the report of the prison officer laying the charge. Attempts by prisoners to gain access to the statements made before the hearing by prison officers or prosecution witnesses have not proved wholly successful, courts generally ruling that prisoners are well aware of the nature of the allegations.[92] However, some decisions indicate that where the prisoner claims that there is a discrepancy between what the witness claims now and what he claimed at a previous hearing or in his original report it would be unfair not to allow the prisoner access to that previous report.[93] In *R v Board of Visitors, Wandsworth Prison, ex p Raymond*[94] Webster J indicated that in the interests of fairness prisoners should be allowed access even to welfare reports prepared upon them. Even then he held that failure to do so would not make the hearing unfair and that the Board still had a discretion not to make them available, for example if they were likely to distress the prisoner unduly by revealing serious family problems previously unknown to the prisoner. This advice is now reflected in para 2.20 of the *Discipline Manual* which

---

[88] Following *McKenzie v McKenzie* [1970] 3 All ER 1034, where it was first recognized.
[89] *Prison Discipline Manual*, para 3.9, makes it clear that other prisoners are not excluded from being McKenzie friends.
[90] para 4.7.
[91] See *R v Governor, Pentonville Prison, ex p Watkins* [1992] COD 329.
[92] See, eg, *R v Board of Visitors, Albany Prison, ex p Mayo*, 18 March 1985 and *In re Crockard's Application* (1986) 7 BNIL 65.
[93] *R v Board of Visitors, Gartree Prison, ex p Mealey*, The Times, 14 November 1981.
[94] The Times, 17 June 1985.

indicates that disclosure should be refused only where doing so would constitute a real risk to the author or it comes under one of the exceptions to the Access to Health Records Act 1990. In cases heard before adjudicators and involving the potential loss of additional days, the adjudicator should also have regard to the idea of 'equality of arms' which has been developed by the ECtHR in its jurisprudence on fair trial issues.[95]

Hearsay Evidence and Cross-examination

9.47 In the second *St Germain*[96] case Geoffrey Lane LJ indicated that prison tribunals were not to be treated as equivalent to courts of law as regards the rules of evidence. Therefore hearsay evidence was admissible. However, he went on to add that 'it is clear that the entitlement of the Board of Visitors to admit hearsay evidence is subject to the overriding obligation to provide the accused with a fair hearing'.[97] In particular, in circumstances where hearsay evidence formed a substantial part of the case against the prisoner, he or she should be given the opportunity of questioning those who gave such evidence.

9.48 Again, depending on the nature of that evidence and the particular circumstances of the case, a sufficient opportunity to deal with the hearsay evidence may well involve the cross examination of the witness whose evidence is initially before the board in the form of hearsay.[98]

9.49 One recent dispute relating to hearsay evidence has concerned the refusal of the Prison Service to allow questioning of experts who prepared urine test reports in cases arising out of mandatory drug testing. This was examined by the Divisional Court in *R v Governor, Swaleside Prison, ex p Wynter*.[99] In that case the court upheld the policy contained in para 6.99 of the *Prison Discipline Manual* that a governor was not obliged to call the relevant laboratory scientist as a witness where the prisoner challenged the scientific validity of a confirmation certificate.[100] Although Blofeld J indicated that prisoners should be provided with more information relating to how the test was conducted, he concluded that a conviction based on test certificates alone was not necessarily unsafe.[101]

---

[95] For an example of the application of this to disclosure issues see *Rowe and Davis v UK* (2000) 30 EHRR 1.

[96] *R v Hull Board of Visitors, ex p St Germain (No 2)* [1979] 3 All ER 545.

[97] ibid, 552.

[98] ibid, 553. *Prison Discipline Manual*, para 5.7, indicates that a conviction based solely on hearsay would clearly be unsafe.

[99] (1998) 10 Admin LR 597.

[100] para 6.99 indicates that where a prisoner pleads not guilty the hearing should be adjourned and the sample sent for a second, confirmation test. The prisoner also has the right to arrange for an independent analysis. The Prison Service indicated in this case that independent analysis had been sought in 165 of the 16,324 adjudications arising out of mandatory drug testing in 1997.

[101] Guidance issued before this judgment in PSI 20/1998 suggests requests for the laboratory scientist to appear as a witness should be granted only where the prisoner has queries about the test

Calling Witnesses

The right to cross-examination was also established in *St Germain (No 2)*. In one **9.50** decision it has been indicated that the governor may allow cross-examination to be made only through him.[102] The *Discipline Manual* suggests that this should be done only where the prisoner is abusing the right of cross-examination; even then the governor or adjudicator is under an obligation to ensure the prisoner's right to present his defence is complied with.[103] Another right established by *St Germain (No 2)* was the right to call witnesses. Indeed it is arguable that no procedural right has become more clearly established. In *St Germain (No 2)* Geoffrey Lane LJ indicated that tribunals had a discretion to allow prisoners to call witnesses, and they should be reluctant to exercise it against the prisoner except in the case where he or she was simply calling witnesses in an attempt to prolong or disrupt the hearing. Mere arguments of administrative convenience would not suffice. He added:

> It would clearly be wrong if, as has been alleged in one instance before us, the basis for the refusal to allow a prisoner to call a witness was that the chairman considered there was ample evidence against the accused. It would equally be an improper exercise of the discretion if the refusal was based on an erroneous understanding of the prisoner's defence, for example, that an alibi did not cover the material time or day, whereas in truth and in fact, it did.[104]

In a subsequent decision Glidewell J went so far as to say that refusal to allow a **9.51** prisoner to call a witness would be prima facie unfair.[105] Arguably the high-water mark of this strong line on the calling of witnesses came *in R v Board of Visitors, Blundeston Prison, ex p Fox-Taylor*,[106] where Phillips J indicated that failure of the prison authorities to inform the prisoner of a witness material to the prisoner's defence that they, but not the prisoner, were aware of could render the adjudication unfair. The decision shows a strong commitment to making available to the prisoner all material which is relevant to his defence. This contrasts with the rather more ambiguous judicial pronouncements concerning prisoners' access to previous statements made by officers, witnesses, or probation officers. However, where the prisoner is aware of but does not call the witness the tribunal will not act unfairly if they decide not to call the witness.[107] Nor has the tribunal any power to compel a witness to attend who does not want to do so.

---

which go beyond general matters (such as the effects of passive smoking) which can be answered by reference to the mandatory drug testing manual.

[102] See *Ex p Mayo*, 18 March 1985.

[103] It is worth noting that the US Supreme Court refused to recognize any right to cross-examination in *Wolff v McDonnell*, 418 US 539 (1974), although ABA Standards and many state prison rules provide for cross-examination.

[104] [1979] 3 All ER 545, 550.

[105] *R v Board of Visitors, Nottingham Prison, ex p Mosely*, The Times, 23 January 1981.

[106] [1982] 1 All ER 646.

[107] See *R v Board of Visitors, Liverpool Prison, ex p Davies*, The Times, 16 October 1982.

9.52 Northern Irish decisions on governors' hearings indicate that the right to call witnesses is likely to remain fundamental, even given the lesser degree of procedural formality required in these hearings.[108] Decisions refusing to allow prisoners to call witnesses are likely to be upheld only where the witness could not assist the prisoner's case, for example where the tribunal has already decided for the prisoner on the point he or she wants to call the witness on.[109]

The Burden of Proof

9.53 Despite court rulings, in the context of legal representation and admissibility of evidence, that prison discipline hearings cannot be analogized to criminal trials, the Divisional Court in *Tarrant* indicated that the criminal standard of proof, that of proof beyond a reasonable doubt, applies in prison discipline hearings. The Woolf Report refers to this as supporting its view that transferring cases to outside courts will not result in prisoners escaping punishment for disciplinary offences because sufficient evidence is difficult to obtain in the prison context. The approach of the UK courts on this issue compares very favourably with those in the United States, the Supreme Court having declared in *Superintendent, Massachusetts Correctional Institution, Walpole v Hill*,[110] that it was sufficient that the conviction was supported by 'some evidence on the record'. However, while the criminal standard applies courts do seem willing to allow prison tribunals to draw rather wide inferences from the facts. This may need to be revisited given that the ECHR Article 6(2) provision on the presumption of innocence now clearly applies to prison disciplinary proceedings, at least those involving the potential loss of additional days.

F. Disciplinary Punishments

9.54 Where a prisoner has been found guilty of a disciplinary punishment the governor may impose one or more of a number of punishments. These are set out in rule 55 of the Prison Rules as:

(1) caution;
(2) forfeiture of privileges for up to 42 days;
(3) exclusion from associated work for up to 21 days;
(4) stoppage of earnings for up to 84 days;
(5) cellular confinement for up to 21 days;
(6) loss of property a prisoner is entitled to have under rule 43(1) for any period;
(7) removal from his wing or living unit for up to 28 days.

---

[108] See *In re Quinn's Application* (1988) 2 NIJB 10; *In re Rowntree's Application* (1991) 11 NIJB 67.
[109] See, eg, *Ex p Watkins* [1992] COD 329.
[110] 472 US 445 (1985).

The latter two punishments were introduced in 2002 in the wake of *Ezeh and Connors*. Where a case is referred to an adjudicator he or she may impose any of these punishments and in addition may make an award of not more than 42 additional days.

If a prisoner is found guilty on more than one charge arising out of an incident the **9.55** punishments imposed may be ordered to run consecutively, but in the case of a punishment of additional days made by an adjudicator the total period should not exceed 42 days, and in the case of a punishment of cellular confinement the total period should not exceed 21 days.

The most frequently utilized punishment, at least in male prisons, has remained **9.56** forfeiture of remission (prior to 1992) or additional days.[111] This fact disappointed both the Prior Committee and Woolf LJ. Both suggested that this may have had a lot to do with a lack of alternatives, especially as regards loss of privileges, since in many prisons prisoners had few privileges to lose. They suggested that as conditions improved and prisoners had greater access to privileges this might become a more frequently used penalty, and one more likely to have a deterrent effect, especially for long term prisoners. As noted in Chapter 5, these recommendations have been given effect, but not through the formal discipline system. The Prior Committee noted that many prison reform groups argued that loss of remission, since it prolonged loss of liberty, should only be imposed by courts or similarly constituted tribunals. Governors, however, argued that retention of the power to remove remission was essential to deal quickly with disciplinary situations which need to be cooled or 'where an offence at risk of becoming fashionable needs to be stamped out quickly'.[112] They were successful until the *Ezeh and Connors* decision and indeed were able to get the Government to increase the maximum number of additional days from 28 in 1992 to 42 in 1994. Now it is clear that governors will face the choice of exploring again the value of other forms of punishment or relinquishing control over most adjudications.

The *Discipline Manual* indicates that there is no central tariff of punishments **9.57** but that governors (and presumably now adjudicators) should take into account factors such as the seriousness of the offence, the prisoner's behaviour during sentence, the effect of the offence on the regime, and the need to deter the prisoner and others from committing similar offences. They should also strive for consistency within the institution. PSI 61/2000 stresses that the imposition of

---

[111] In 2000 there was an average of 99 awards of additional days per 100 population, thus making additional days the most frequently awarded punishment (the next two were forfeiture of privileges—72 awards per 100—and stoppage or reduction of earnings—68 per 100). This average figure breaks down to 98 per 100 for male prisoners and 124 per 100 for females: see Home Office, *Prison Statistics England and Wales 2000* (Cm 5250, 2001) 148. Guidance on the use of additional days, and the related ECHR requirements, are set out in PSI 61/2000.

[112] *Committee on the Prison Disciplinary System* (The Prior Report) (Cmnd 9641, 1985), para 8.50.

additional days, and the number of days imposed, must be proportionate to the aim of securing good order and discipline in the prison, and that alternative punishments must have been considered. Particular difficulties attend unconvicted prisoners and life sentence prisoners. As the additional days provision only applies to short and long term determinate sentence prisoners, both of these groups are excluded. As regards unconvicted prisoners, rule 59(1) indicates that they may be given a prospective award of additional days, to take effect only if they are subsequently convicted and imprisoned. As for life sentence prisoners, the *Discipline Manual* indicates that where at the time of the adjudication the prisoner has been given a prospective date of release a recommendation may be given to the Home Secretary or Parole Board that this date be postponed. The additional days awarded will also be recorded on the prisoner's record, which will be available to the review committee considering whether a life sentence prisoner can be recommended for release. The tariff set for discretionary life sentence prisoners in accordance with s 28 of the Crime (Sentences) Act 1997 appears to be unaffected by any award of additional days.

9.58 After award of additional days, cellular confinement is perhaps the most severe punishment. It is certainly the most severe form of punishment available to governors where they have retained jurisdiction. Standing Orders indicate that this should be reserved for serious offences of an anti-social kind and that no such punishment shall be imposed if the medical officer does not certify that the prisoner is fit to undergo such punishment. In addition prisoners undergoing such punishments should be observed by an officer at least once an hour and visited daily by the chaplain and by the medical officer when necessary. The maximum period of cellular confinement that can be awarded is 21 days and consecutive punishments of cellular confinement for different offences which would take the time served beyond 21 days should not be ordered. Prisoners who are sent to cellular confinement should be detained in an ordinary cell with only a table, stool, and chamber pot (the bed being removed except at night) and should be entitled to all facilities not inconsistent with being in solitary confinement unless they have received a separate punishment of loss of facilities.

9.59 Loss of facilities refers to those facilities available under SO 4. Even where this punishment is given the *Discipline Manual* indicates that, unless specifically indicated, prisoners should not be deprived of educational notebooks, attendance at classes, and correspondence courses. They should also be allowed to have radios, general notebooks, and to buy postage stamps. Governors are directed that exclusion from associated work may be looked upon as an alternative to solitary confinement, although the two may be combined. In general where more than one punishment is awarded for separate offences it is for the governor to order whether they will run consecutively or concurrently. Whichever is chosen must be clearly indicated to the prisoner.

Many disciplinary punishments are suspended under rule 60(1) for up to six **9.60** months. They then may be, but do not have to be, activated if the prisoner is convicted of another offence against discipline.

G. Appeals Against Disciplinary Conviction or Punishments and Remitting of Punishments

Where a prisoner feels that a disciplinary conviction is wrongful or a punishment **9.61** excessive he may petition the Secretary of State under rule 61(1) to seek the remission or mitigation of the punishment. The new rule changes in 1992 also gave the Secretary of State power to quash an award, the lack of which power had been commented on unfavourably in *Leech*.[113] These complaints will be dealt with by Area Managers. Area Managers do not conduct a rehearing but instead will examine the record of the adjudication. In conducting such a review the crucial consideration is whether the proceedings were conducted in accordance with legal requirements of fairness. However, Area Managers can also look at the merits of the decision.

Prior to August 2002 where additional days were imposed adult prisoners could **9.62** apply within six months (four months for young offenders) of the disciplinary decision to have this remitted, provided that in that period the prisoner had not had a suspended award activated or been given a further punishment of additional days for a subsequent offence. An application to remit additional days was not an appeal against the decision or the severity of the punishment. The application was made to the governor, who was instructed to consider whether remission was appropriate to reward prisoners who had taken a constructive approach towards imprisonment (for example through making the most of work or education activities) or to acknowledge a genuine change of attitude on the prisoner's behalf. However, this had to be balanced against the need to preserve the deterrent effect of the original offence, and was unlikely to exceed 50 per cent.[114] Interestingly the changes in the Prison Rules which created the office of the adjudicator to hear those offences where awards of additional days are appropriate do not say anything expressly about who is to deal with applications to remit such awards. One must presume that the same system remains in place, with initial applications now being made to the adjudicator rather than the prison governor.

In view of the fact that such applications to quash or mitigate a disciplinary **9.63** decision remain within the prison administration many prisoners have expressed dissatisfaction with this procedure. Such dissatisfaction is hardly assuaged by the

---

[113] [1988] AC 533.
[114] para 8.15.

fact that less than 10 per cent of such applications result in any change to the decision or punishment. The Prior Committee shared such concerns and argued that '[t]he availability of an effective appeal process where any substantial issue or right of liberty is at stake is an important element of the perceived fairness of a disciplinary system. Procedures need to be open, accessible, prompt and decisive.'[115] It also stressed the need for this appeal procedure to be independent of the original decision maker, and therefore recommended that in respect of governors' decisions involving loss of remission in excess of seven days this should be to the Prison Disciplinary Tribunal. In respect of appeals from that body it recommended the creation of a Prison Disciplinary Appeal Tribunal. In addition to providing an adequate avenue for grievances about decisions it felt an appeal structure could assist the development of consistency in decisions about punishments.

9.64 The Government originally accepted Prior's notion of a right of appeal from governors' decisions (but not the creation of an Appeal Tribunal from the Prison Disciplinary Tribunal) but the idea was lost with the decision not to put most of the Prior recommendations into effect. Instead petitions against adjudications were brought under the jurisdiction of Area Managers. However, the Woolf Report was to revive concerns about the place of appeals in the disciplinary system. Focusing purely on governors' adjudications, Woolf argued that there was still a need for some system of independent review. He argued that this function could be performed by the proposed Complaints Adjudicator. Whereas Prior argued that appeals against convictions should be by way of rehearing, Woolf was content to allow the Complaints Adjudicator to review the record of the proceedings and conduct a rehearing only if he or she deemed it necessary. On the other hand, Woolf envisaged this appeal mechanism applying to all decisions of the governor, whereas Prior limited it to decisions resulting in loss of remission exceeding seven days.

9.65 The Government eventually accepted these recommendations and included the exercise of disciplinary powers within the jurisdiction of the Prison Ombudsman (since 2001 the Prisons and Probation Ombudsman). As we have seen when examining the Ombudsman's powers in Chapter 2, he does not have power to rehear disciplinary procedures but can review both the procedure and the merits of the hearing via an examination of the documentary record. The Ombudsman can also visit a prison to take evidence from a prisoner or prison officer. In his 2002 report the Ombudsman observed that disciplinary adjudications made up 17 per cent of the total number of complaints submitted to him, the highest single item.[116] About 40 per cent of complaints regarding adjudications meet the eligi-

---

[115] *Committee on the Prison Disciplinary System* (The Prior Report) (Cmnd 9641, 1985), para 12.7.
[116] *Annual Report 2001–02* (Cm 5530, 2002) 8.

bility criteria but only about 34 per cent of complaints overall were upheld or locally resolved in 2001. However, this rate remains significantly above that of a purely internal system and suggests that the Ombudsman may have gone some way towards providing the safeguard of an independent check on the fairness of proceedings sought by Prior and Woolf. However in light of the 2002 changes post *Ezeh and Connors,* which do create an independent adjudicator somewhat along the lines Prior suggested, it may be that the idea of an independent appeal tribunal will be revisited again.

As has been seen earlier in this chapter, prisoners may always challenge disciplin- **9.66** ary hearings by way of judicial review. They will also now be able to rely on the full range of protections appropriate to defendants in a criminal trial, developed by the ECtHR in the context of its Article 6 jurisprudence. However the decline in the number of disciplinary adjudications producing judicial reviews in the 1990s suggests that at least some of prisoners' concerns regarding the fairness of such hearings may have been met by a combination of a reduction in the scale of punishments available, more detailed guidance to governors and better appeal mechanisms.

H. Conclusion

There have clearly been very significant changes in prison discipline procedures **9.67** over the past 20 years. Even before the alterations prompted by the Woolf Report a combination of judicial review and modifications in the Prison Rules had reduced maximum penalties appreciably and ensured that prisoners would have the opportunity to put their side of the case. No longer could governors or Boards dismiss them out of hand. However, examination of the prison discipline statistics raises questions about how much has changed in substance as opposed to form. Throughout the 1980s both the total number of offences punished in prisons and the number per prisoner steadily rose, at least for male prisoners.[117] Although figures for charges dismissed are not so readily available it does not seem that they have wavered much from the 6 per cent that prevailed in 1991.[118] In other words,

---

[117] The total number of offences punished rose from 63,391 in 1980 to 105,200 in 2000. This breaks down into an average of 163 offences punished per 100 population: 159 for males and 256 for females. Breaking those figures down by race is striking: for white males, there were 152 offences punished per 100 population, whereas for black males the figure was 213, South Asian 119, and Chinese and other ethnic groups 125. For white females the average was 254; black females 174, South Asian females 33, Chinese and other ethnic groups 284: Home Office, *Prison Statistics England and Wales 2000* (Cm 5250, 2001) 141, 145, 150, 151.

[118] The Home Office *Prison Statistics England and Wales 2000* (Cm 5250, 2001) record only proven offences. They specifically exclude charges not proven, dismissed, quashed, pending and not completed (a total of 15,700 in 2000): p 142.

the development of greater procedural guarantees does not seem to have had any effect on the scale of disciplinary punishment occurring in the United Kingdom's prisons. If prisoners thought in 1980 that too many wrongful disciplinary punishments were being handed out there seems to be little reason why they should think otherwise in 2002. It remains to be seen whether the use of adjudicators for the more serious disciplinary offences will bring about a change in the pattern of punishment in prisons.

9.68 Some will argue that the history of perceived illegitimacy was the result of the courts' failure fully to apply the criminal law model to prison discipline proceedings. They would claim that if access to statements, the right to cross-examination, the right to legal representation, and the provision of an adjudicator seen to be independent had been provided this would have produced a significant change in the outcome of hearings. There was, however, little chance of the domestic courts ever going this far; the very existence of a separate discipline system suggested that different procedures were considered appropriate.[119] Now that the criminal model is in place—for the more serious offences, at least—it will be fascinating to see whether the system functions more fairly or transparently. While the extension of criminal law safeguards to prisoners is a very welcome development, there are reasons for questioning whether this will have a dramatic effect on prison life. These reasons lie in the role which disciplinary offences and punishments play within a prison. Whereas the intervention of the criminal law in outside society is an infrequent and somewhat distant form of social control, disciplinary law in prisons reinforces a constant and pervasive regulation of prisoners' lives. Most disciplinary charges relate to behaviour which amounts, in effect, to refusing to comply with the social order designed by the prison administration. The relationship of disciplinary punishments to social control is particularly clear in women's prisons, where prisoners are much more likely to be put on report for swearing, talking back, or even self-mutilation, than in male prisons.[120] Such conduct was seen as at variance with the images of reformed 'normal' women the prison regime sought to achieve. When combined with the structural inequalities of prison hearings, where prison staff are always more likely to be believed when it comes to disputed issues of fact, it seems clear that prison justice will continue to be of a fairly rough kind. The justice dispensed by adjudicators in the more serious cases may turn out to be less rough, but as Michel Foucault has

---

[119] The Supreme Court of Canada rejected the argument that prison discipline hearings should be regarded as criminal trials and hence subject to detailed Charter guarantees for the protection of the rights of criminal defendants in *R v Shubley* [1990] 1 SCR 3. In his 1996 report the Prisons Ombudsman indicated a concern that governors were in some ways treating adjudications *too much like* criminal trials in that they were neglecting a duty to conduct an investigation into the facts and possible explanations of conduct. See Cm 3487, para. 7.3.
[120] See the discussion in R Dobash, R Dobash and S Gutteridge, *The Imprisonment of Women* (Oxford, 1986) 146.

argued, attempts to appeal to legal rights (or sovereignty as he refers to it here) against disciplinary power are likely to prove ultimately fruitless 'because sovereignty and disciplinary mechanisms are two absolutely integral constituents of the general mechanism of power in our society'.[121]

9.69 Now that governors can no longer award additional days, there is a search for other forms of punishment. As well as the new punishment of removal from the prisoner's cell, this role may now be taken by the Incentives and Privileges scheme. PSO 4000 indicates that each establishment operating a scheme must publish the criteria by which privileges may be lost and the process which will be followed in reaching such decisions. This should include the opportunity for a prisoner to make representations and the need to give prisoners reasons for decisions. Given the lower levels of deprivation involved and the fact that this scheme is designed to operate through giving incentives as well as removing privileges, carrot as well as stick, it might be argued that a lower level of procedural safeguards is appropriate. However there is always the risk that it will turn out to be more stick than carrot, and that the sort of arbitrary abuse of power that once was found in disciplinary proceedings will now reappear in the operation of this scheme. Research into the functioning of the system certainly suggests that it is widely seen as unfair, inconsistent and disciplinary.[122]

9.70 We have seen in this chapter that perceptions of injustice have the capacity to produce substantial disturbances in prison, and that such disturbances in turn may lead to judicial intervention which re-examines the forms of justice in prison. One such intervention, clearly the most significant of recent years, is the *Ezeh and Connors* judgment. Interestingly, it has taken the Strasbourg court to re-think the nature of discipline in prisons, finding the criminal model appropriate soon after that model had been rejected by the domestic courts. The extent to which this will give prisoners a greater sense of justice remains to be seen.

---

[121] M Foucault, 'Two Lectures' in *Power/Knowledge: Selected Interviews and Other Writings 1972–77* (New York, 1980) 108. Hugh Collins describes a similar process in labour law whereby the formal equality of the employment contract is undermined by a web of disciplinary rules in the workplace. When these rules become a source of conflict legal intervention, premised always ultimately on the legitimate authority of management, does little more than curb the greatest excesses of management power but leaves untouched, and therefore legitimizes, 'normal' forms of arbitrary power. See H Collins, 'Capitalist Discipline and Corporatist Law' (1982) 11 ILJ 78, 170.

[122] A Liebling, G Muir, G Rose and A Bottoms, 'Incentives and Earned Privileges for Prisoners—an Evaluation', Home Office Research, Development and Statistics Directorate Research Finding 87 (London, 1999), discussed in greater detail at para 5.45 above.

10

MAINTAINING GOOD ORDER
AND DISCIPLINE

10.01   Good order and discipline (GOAD) is maintained in prisons by a combination of disciplinary and non-disciplinary powers. In Chapter 9 we described how the disciplinary powers of the governor operate. In this chapter we analyze the array of non-disciplinary powers available to the prison authorities which exist to regulate and enforce what is perceived to be in the interests of the good order and discipline of the prison regime.

10.02   By non-disciplinary we mean those powers whose exercise does not depend upon proof of the commission of a specific disciplinary or criminal offence by the prisoner affected. They may not therefore be imposed as a punishment. They derive their authority from s 47(1) of the Prison Act which authorizes the making of rules for the 'discipline and control' of prisoners. Precisely because they are broader and can be invoked independently of the 'official' disciplinary system, these non-disciplinary powers are a major source of discontent amongst prisoners. This is largely because they can achieve as drastic a change in the quality of a prisoner's life as a disciplinary punishment yet their use is unaccompanied by the statutory procedural safeguards which prisoners enjoy under the disciplinary system. From the point of view of the prison authorities, there is the obvious attraction that because the very purpose of the powers is to assist in maintaining security, discipline, and control the courts have displayed a great reluctance at the prospect of 'second guessing' managerial decisions in sensitive areas of prison administration. Even though the House of Lords held in *R v Deputy Governor of Parkhurst Prison, ex p Hague*[1] that the supervisory jurisdiction of the High Court does extend to include all decisions taken in pursuance of the prison rules, this remains an area where the existing legislative framework in practice gives governors and Area officials an almost unfettered discretion to regulate prisoners' lives.[2]

10.03 In the light of such judicial circumspection it is perhaps hardly surprising that many prisoners regard the Prison Service claim that these powers are never used as a means of bypassing the official disciplinary system with a degree of suspicion. Conscious or malicious abuse of public law powers is always remediable but in prison proof of such abuse is hard to achieve, thus making it difficult for the courts effectively to scrutinize an unlawful resort to non-disciplinary measures.[3] As we seek to demonstrate in the final section of this chapter, this is not an area in which the jurisprudence of the European Convention on Human Rights (ECHR) has led to major changes since the Human Rights Act 1998 (HRA) has come into force.

10.04 When a prisoner is believed to be a threat to GOAD, he may be dealt with in one of four ways by the prison authorities. First, he may be segregated under rule 45 of the Prison Rules in the prison where he is perceived to be a threat. Secondly, he may be temporarily transferred under IG 28/1993 to a different prison with the expectation of immediate rule 45 segregation on arrival. Thirdly, there is the possibility of allocation to a Close Supervision Centre (CSC) for prisoners believed to present special problems of control and security.[4] Finally, a disruptive, violent prisoner may be subjected to an approved method of restraint and/or confined in a special cell in whichever prison he may be.

10.05 The first two options give rise to a number of overlapping considerations many of which received detailed consideration in the important case *of R v Deputy*

---

[1] [1992] 1 AC 58.

[2] In *Hague* the Home Office argued before the Divisional Court that the High Court had no jurisdiction to quash a r 43 (now r 45) segregation decision. It lost and during the course of argument before the Court of Appeal conceded that jurisdiction did exist, but only after a rejection of a complaint to the Board of Visitors or of a petition to the Secretary of State, and then only by way of review of such rejection. The Court of Appeal rejected this 'second stage' approach but accepted that the court should employ great caution before exercising its discretion in issues affecting prison management. No appeal was pursued by the Home Office to the House of Lords on this point.

[3] Absent proof of a deliberate or malicious abuse of power by prison staff—which would give rise to a private law claim for misfeasance in a public office—an application for judicial review will be the only way in which a prisoner may be able to challenge the use of non-disciplinary powers. But judicial review is generally conducted on affidavit evidence and is not regarded as an effective way of resolving disputed issues of fact, although in exceptional circumstances the court may order discovery, cross-examination, and interrogatories: see Fordham's *Judicial Review Handbook* (3rd edn, Oxford, 2001). For a useful academic account of the difficulties which arise in maintaining good order or discipline within prisons, see Sparks, Bottoms, and Hay, *Prisons and the Problem of Order* (Oxford, 1996).

[4] The transfer of a prisoner to a CSC is governed by r 46.

Governor of Parkhurst Prison, ex p Hague.[5] Below we examine each area in turn before looking at the approach of the European Court of Human Rights (ECtHR) in claims brought under Article 3 of the Convention, which forbids the infliction of inhuman or degrading treatment or punishment.

A. Segregation Under Rule 45

Under rule 45(1) of the Prison Rules (rule 46 of the Young Offender Institution **10.06** Rules) a prison governor has the power to remove a prisoner from normal association 'where it appears desirable for the maintenance of good order or discipline or in his own interests'. In this chapter we are solely concerned with segregation in the interests of GOAD, 'own interests' segregation giving rise to different considerations.[6]

The full text of rule 45 is as follows: **10.07**

(1) Where it appears desirable, for the maintenance of good order or discipline or in his own interests, that a prisoner should not associate with other prisoners, either generally or for particular purposes, the governor may arrange for the prisoner's removal from association accordingly.

(2) A prisoner shall not be removed under this Rule for a period of more than 3 days without the authority of a member of the board of visitors or of the Secretary of State. An authority given under this paragraph shall be for a period not exceeding one month, but may be renewed from month to month except that, in the case of a person aged less than 21 years who is detained in prison, such an authority shall be for a period not exceeding 14 days, but may be renewed from time to time for a like period.

(3) The governor may arrange at his discretion for such a prisoner as aforesaid to resume association with other prisoners, and shall do so if in any case the medical officer or a medical practitioner such as is mentioned in rule 20(3) so advises on medical grounds.[7]

(4) This rule shall not apply to a prisoner the subject of a direction given under rule 46(1).

---

[5] The judgments delivered in both the Divisional Court and the Court of Appeal are included in the report at [1992] 1 AC 58.

[6] The Woolf Report (Cm 1456, 1991) criticized the fact that r 43 (now r 45) covers both GOAD and 'own protection' segregation, commenting at para 12.196 that '[i]t is unhelpful that the Rule should be applied to two very different categories of prisoners. What the establishment should be seeking to achieve in relation to the two categories is quite different. In the case of the prisoner separated for reasons of good order or discipline, the removal from association needs to be fairly strictly imposed if the object of the exercise is to be achieved. In the case of the vulnerable prisoner, on the other hand, it is accepted that any more separation than is necessary to protect the prisoner is undesirable. The object from the start should be to return the prisoner to association if this is possible.'

[7] r 20(3) provides that: '[t]he medical officer may consult a medical practitioner who is a fully registered person within the meaning of the Medical Act 1983. Such a practitioner may work within the prison under the general supervision of the medical officer.'

The governor's power to segregate is therefore limited to a period of three days, but this can be extended for up to a month with the authority of either a member of the Board of Visitors or a representative of the Secretary of State (in reality, a senior Prison Service official). In practice prisoners can be segregated for unlimited lengths of time throughout their sentence with the periodically (monthly) renewed agreement of these authorities. The former Chief Inspector of Prisons, Sir James Hennessy, commented in his 1985 special report on the use of segregation that it 'can entail living under an impoverished and monotonous regime which may even be psychologically harmful'.[8] Though the Home Office prefers the term 'segregation', the description 'solitary confinement' more accurately describes the reality of what is involved.

10.08 Prisoners on GOAD segregation are held in virtual isolation, shut in their cells in the punishment block for 23 hours per day, and are deprived of most opportunities for work, education, and recreation. The Woolf Report confirmed this unhappy state of affairs, commenting that 'while segregation under Rule [45] is not intended to be a punishment the use of the Rule will invariably adversely affect the inmate who is made subject to it. In most establishments, anyone segregated under Rule [45] will be subjected to regime restrictions very similar to those undergoing punishment'.[9]

Rule 45 Analysed

10.09 Rule 45 has three material limbs. The initial provision in sub-paragraph (1) makes clear that it is the governor of the prison in which the prisoner is for the time being (ie in whose custody he is under s 13 of the Prison Act 1952) who alone may arrange for his removal from association within that prison.[10] Paragraph (2) requires reasoned consideration to be given by the Board of Visitors member or the Secretary of State to the question whether and for how long the initial three-day period of segregation is to be extended.[11] In other words, neither the Board of

---

[8] *A Review of the Segregation of Prisoners Under Rule 43*, Report by HM Chief Inspector of Prisons (London, 1985) (Hennessy Report); see also para 2.29 of the Report.

[9] See the Woolf Report (Cm 1456, 1991), para 12.267.

[10] *Ex p Hague* [1992] 1 AC 58, 105–108, *per* Taylor LJ.

[11] ibid. CI 6/1993 alerts Boards of Visitors to the fact that before a Board member authorizes continued segregation he must make a personal visit to the prisoner concerned. It states that '[t]he Coordinating Committee of Boards of Visitors have told us that some Board members authorize continued segregation by telephone without seeing the inmate. This is contrary to the training they receive. Also it is in the interests of justice that a Board member should see the inmate in person before authorizing continued segregation. . . . An initial telephone authorization should be given only in exceptional circumstances—such as freak weather conditions—which prevent a Board member attending the establishment within 3 days.' The Circular is a welcome example of the Prison Service's willingness to extend its policy requirements beyond the meagre procedural fairness requirements of *Ex p Hague*. PSO 1700 states that '[d]uring rota visits, members of the Board of Visitors must speak to all prisoners in the segregation unit, including those awaiting adjudication, and record personally in the occurrence book that they have done so' (para 1.1.7).

Visitors member nor the Secretary of State should act as a rubber stamp of the governor's initial decision. Paragraph (3) makes clear that governors must keep the need for segregation under constant review despite the grant of authority for an extension by up to one month and must permit the resumption of association on receipt of medical advice.

The second and third of these provisions have no purpose other than to protect **10.10** the individual prisoner's interests. The first provision operates both in the interests of sound prison administration by permitting non-disciplinary segregation and in the prisoner's interest by confining that power to the governor in whose custody he is. Paragraph (4) makes it clear that the rule 45 safeguards which do not appear in rule 46—the requirement of authorization by the Board of Visitors after three days—cannot be applied to those placed in CSCs, rendering their situation even more powerless.

The terms of rule 45 make it clear that association with other prisoners is not a **10.11** privilege under the Rules but the norm (otherwise there would be no need for rule 45). Being on rule 45 is neither a status nor a classification which a prisoner carries from prison to prison. Rather it is the fact of being subjected to a temporary regime by prescribed means and for ascertainable statutory purposes within a particular prison.

Comprehensive guidance both to governors and to Boards of Visitors on the oper- **10.12** ation of rule 45 is to be found in Circular Instruction 26/1990.[12] Originally drafted in the wake of the *Report of the Prison Department Working Group on the Management of Vulnerable Prisoners* (May 1989), CI 26/1990 was amended in 1991 in the light of recommendations contained in the Woolf Report and represents a significant shift in attitude in terms of both the occasions when segregation may be justified and the safeguards which should accompany its use. PSO 1700 now gives further guidance on the correct use of rule 45, and lays down basic requirements for the regime in Segregation Units. The Order sets out the following aim: '[u]se of segregation will achieve the correct balance between the requirement to maintain order and discipline and the respect for human dignity'. The Introduction sets out the principles which should guide the operation of the Segregation Unit. It should:

1. Hold all prisoners segregated from normal location safely and securely;
2. Treat all prisoners fairly and with dignity;
3. Help those prisoners removed from association for reasons of good order and discipline to address the negative aspects of their behaviour and return positively to normal location; and

---

[12] This is still in force as guidance on the use of r 45, even after PSO 1700 has come into force: see the Service Standard on Segregation Units.

> 4. Ensure the safety of prisoners who may have been removed from association in their own interests and plan for their safe return to a normal regime.

10.13 Like the previous policy document, PSO 1700 accepts the Woolf Report's conclusion that segregation should not be used unless it is absolutely necessary, and must not be regarded as the instant remedy for control problems in the prison. It states that GOAD segregation under rule 45 must only take place where there are reasonable grounds for believing that a prisoner's behaviour is likely to be so disruptive that maintaining the prisoner on normal location becomes impossible. Examples of such situations include: where there is evidence of a planned or imminent breach of security, incitement to others to breach security or prison discipline, a risk to the safety of staff or prisoners or risk of damage to prison property, consistent failure to co-operate with anti-bullying strategies, dirty protests, or where the prisoner is subject to police or internal investigations into serious offences committed while in prison. This list of examples is a welcome step, showing that segregation should really only be used in very serious situations.

10.14 Annex C of CI 26/1990 indicates that where the governor wishes to extend segregation beyond three days neither he nor the Board of Visitors member who is required to authorize such extension ought routinely to assume that the maximum permitted period of one month is the appropriate period to authorize. Indeed it points out that in GOAD cases authorization for the maximum period should rarely be necessary and that 'the Board member will decide, in the light of the governor's advice, for how long a period to authorize continued segregation and will not automatically give authority for the maximum of one month. The member may decide to give authority for only a few days initially, pending the opportunity to interview the inmate, or for any period less than the maximum which may seem sufficient in the circumstances of the case.' PSO 1700 is less detailed, stating simply that if the Board member gives authority for continued segregation 'it need not be for the maximum period. The member may decide to give authority for only a few days initially, or for any period less than the maximum which they consider appropriate in the circumstances of the case.'[13]

10.15 The Woolf Report was critical of the role of the Board of Visitors in authorizing extensions to segregation and called for this aspect of their functions to be ended, pointing out that 'whatever is the true position, when a Board member gives such authority, prisoners do not see him as acting to safeguard their interests but as the arm of management . . . this is not consistent with or helpful to the Board's watchdog role' (para 12.270). The Report went on to recommend that in future it should be the responsibility of the Area Manager to authorize any extension to segregation and that any more than one extension beyond 28 days should only be

---

[13] para 3.1.1.

justified in exceptional circumstances. Boards of Visitors should carefully supervise and monitor the exercise of the power to segregate. But these recommendations were not accepted by the Prison Service.[14]

The use of rule 45 segregation as a punishment is an improper and unlawful abuse   **10.16**
of power even though, as has been said, the regime to which rule 45 prisoners are
subjected is frequently indistinguishable from that endured by prisoners undergoing the punishment of cellular confinement. PSO 1701, which gives further
guidance on the correct use of rule 45, states that '[s]egregation under Rule 45
may only be used where there is no other reasonable way to maintain the good
order or discipline within an establishment. Under no circumstances must it be
used with the intention of inflicting a punishment on a prisoner.'[15] Paragraph 6 of
CI 26/1990 informs governors of the broad pre-emptive purpose behind their
rule 45 power:

> Segregation under rule [45] is designed to assist governors to prevent trouble and
> governors may use it for this purpose in respect of known subversive inmates . . .
> either on reception or at any subsequent stage of their time in custody. It is not nec-
> essary to wait until a prisoner has actually jeopardized control. It is sufficient that he
> should have shown that it is his intention to do so; and it is right to take into account
> a history of disruptive behaviour, either inside or outside the institutional setting.

Such advice immediately reveals the dangers inherent in a power which requires
only past reputation to trigger its use. According to the Prison Service, it is not
necessary for a prisoner actually to have done anything which threatens good
order and discipline in the prison to which he has recently been transferred. On
reception the governor can take account of what it is alleged he did at his previous
prison (where he may have been discontented for numerous reasons no longer
relevant once he was moved) or even his behaviour outside prison and decide on
that basis to order segregation. Of course the very act of segregating before anything has happened may well then trigger behaviour which will be seen retrospectively to justify the decision to use rule 45 and so the merry-go-round may
continue.

Rule 45 as an Alternative to Disciplinary Charges

From the prisoner's point of view the blurred division between supposedly non-   **10.17**
punitive rule 45 segregation and punitive cellular confinement is reinforced by
the knowledge that the courts have held that it is not an abuse of power for a governor to segregate a prisoner instead of requiring a disciplinary charge to be laid,

---

[14] PSO 1700 provides that '[t]he Area Manager for the establishment is nominated to exercise
the Secretary of State's power to authorise a continuation of segregation in exceptional circumstances' (para 3.2.1). However, the primary role of authorizing continued segregation remains with
the Board of Visitors.
[15] para 1.1.3.

even where the reason for not laying a charge is dubious. Christopher Hague's case[16] clearly demonstrated the injustice of this approach. He was placed on rule 45 and transferred from Parkhurst to Wormwood Scrubs because it was alleged that he was stirring up trouble amongst other Category A inmates at Parkhurst over the decision occasionally to withdraw exercise facilities from all Category A prisoners for security reasons. There was no dispute that Mr Hague and others had complained about this through legitimate channels but the decision to transfer him pursuant to CI 10/74 (one of the predecessors to IG 28/1993 and PSO 1700) was based on specific allegations, which Mr Hague disputed, that he had deliberately gone on exercise at a time when he knew he should not have and that he subsequently told the deputy governor of his intention to continue his defiance. On any view Mr Hague's alleged conduct both in substance and in law amounted to an offence contrary to then rule 47(21) ('in any way offends against good order and discipline'). Yet the governor admitted that a decision was deliberately taken not to charge him because this might embarrass those prison officers who, as Mr Hague had claimed, had seen him on exercise but chose not to give him a direct order to return to his wing. In the Divisional Court, Ralph Gibson LJ held that avoiding embarrassment to prison staff, whose function it was to maintain discipline, could be a legitimate reason for not preferring a charge. He went on to state that:

> There is also . . . no obligation in a prison governor to prefer a disciplinary charge as a precondition of acting upon information which demonstrates commission by a prisoner of an offence against discipline before he may act upon that information as a ground for placing the prisoner on rule [45] for transfer under CI 10/74. Such a precondition would impose on the exercise of the governor's discretion, in his task of maintaining discipline, a fetter which is not expressly imposed by the prison rules and which, in our judgment, is not only not implicitly required by those rules, upon their proper construction, but seems to us to be contrary to the fullness of discretion which in such matters those rules intend a prison governor to have.

This aspect of Mr Hague's attack upon his segregation was not pursued in the Court of Appeal and thus represents the current law.

10.18 It is submitted that it represents an extremely unfortunate bias in favour of administrative discretion in an area where the courts ought to be alert to protect prisoners from potential abuses of power. The avoidance of embarrassment to officers may be a good enough reason for exercising the discretion not to lay a disciplinary charge but it is surely an impermissible reason for resorting instead to segregation under rule 45. This objection is not met if rule 45 required prisoners to be granted a fair hearing because segregation can continue indefinitely whereas disciplinary awards need not involve segregation at all and cellular confinement cannot exceed 14 days if awarded by a governor.

---

[16] *R v Home Secretary, ex p Hague* [1992] 1 AC 58.

The Rule 45 Regime

So far as the regime to which rule 45 prisoners are subjected is concerned, PSO   **10.19**
1701 ('Removal from Association: Good Order or Discipline'), which gives further guidance on the use of rule 45, seeks to emphasize that '[t]he regime for each
prisoner segregated for the purpose of good order or discipline must be no less
than the level of privileges provided under the Prison Rules. . . . Governor grades
are required to make a judgment on the balance between the needs of the individual and the maintenance of order or the safety of staff and prisoners.' But it is hard
not to see this, along with the statement that 'use of segregation will achieve the
correct balance between the requirement to maintain order and discipline and the
respect for human dignity' as pious aspirations in the face of overwhelming evidence that segregation under rule 45 does involve the conscious infliction of a comparatively deprived regime with little or no opportunity to earn the privileges
available to other prisoners under the terms of PSO 4000.[17]

A prisoner who is placed on rule 45 in conditions indistinguishable from those   **10.20**
imposed on a prisoner undergoing punishment, possibly in an adjacent cell, could
however legitimately seek to challenge a refusal to grant him ordinary facilities
and privileges save in so far as these can be shown to be wholly incompatible with
his segregation. The wording of rule 45(1) ('should not associate with other prisoners, *either generally or for particular purposes*') makes it clear that not every decision to segregate can justify total isolation from fellow prisoners. Each case
requires separate reasoning and justification.

B. Instruction to Governors 28/1993

Transfer of Disruptive Prisoners

If an allegedly disruptive prisoner cannot effectively be segregated in the prison   **10.21**
where he is confined, a second option available to prison management is a (short
term) transfer pursuant to IG 28/1993.[18] The practice of short term transfers in

---

[17] In July 1995 IG 74/95 introduced the National Framework for Incentives and Earned
Privileges for prisoners which is intended to ensure that prisoners earn privileges by their 'responsible behaviour and participation in hard work and other constructive activity'. The system is now
governed by PSO 4000. All governors are asked to operate local incentive schemes and produce a list
of key earnable privileges and r 8 was amended to reflect this change. As a result prisoners on r 45
GOAD segregation in some prisons find themselves unable to earn certain privileges.
[18] On the face of it, this PSI expired in November 1998. However, PSI 38/2000 on the
Management of Disruptive Prisoners confirmed that PSI 28/93 is still in force. The Prisoners'
Advice Service has likened the annual Prison Service statement that PSI 28/93 is still in force to the
annual government renewal of the Prevention of Terrorism Act: *Prisoners' Legal Rights Group
Bulletin No 11,* June 2000.

the interests of good order and discipline (known to prisoners as 'ghosting') has given rise to considerable controversy. Such transfers will normally be from a dispersal prison to certain designated local prisons where a small number of cells are kept permanently available for such use. It is applied to those prisoners who are regarded as seriously disruptive or subversive and for whom location in the dispersal prison's segregation unit is not considered appropriate or practical either because of their capacity to exercise a disruptive influence from the unit or because their very location there might provide a focal point for unrest in the general prison population.

10.22 The procedure to be followed in the event of such a short term GOAD transfer is set out in IG 28/1993 ('Management Strategy for Disruptive Inmates').[19] It was a predecessor of this document, CI 10/74, which gave rise to the decision in *Hague*. The *Hague* case is central to this area of law, involving as it does a consideration both of the procedural fairness requirements attendant upon segregation/transfer and of the issue of private law remedies arising from its use.

10.23 The result of the *Hague* litigation was that the Court of Appeal held that CI 10/74 was unlawful in that it breached two of the protective provisions contained in rule 43 (now rule 45). In the first place, it sanctioned the practice of dispersal prison governors launching a prisoner on to what was frequently a succession of transfers in segregation with no subsequent decision ever taken by governors in the receiving prisons. As the prisoner arrived at the receiving prison he was immediately and automatically placed in segregation without any decision being taken by the receiving governor solely on the basis that he was a '10/74' man. The Circular led to the rule 45 label attaching to a prisoner as he moved from prison to prison instead of requiring an assessment by each governor as he acquired custody of the individual concerned.

10.24 Secondly, it contemplated that authority to segregate for the full 28 day period would routinely be granted by the Secretary of State whenever a dispersal governor opted to use CI 10/74, wholly bypassing the role of the Board of Visitors and the requirement inherent in rule 45(2) that a reasoned decision had to be made not only as to whether authority for continued segregation should be granted but for how long it should be granted.

10.25 In the wake of the *Hague* litigation, the Prison Service replaced CI 10/174 with a new circular, CI 37/90, which remedied the unlawful advice in CI 10/74. In particular it emphasized that a decision to segregate a transferred prisoner must be taken by the receiving governor and not be determined by the sending governor or Prison Service Headquarters. It also created an obligation to give reasons after

---

[19] PSI 38/2000 states that the Prison Service (Security Group and Directorate of High Security Prisons) will be producing a thoroughly revised version of IG 28/1993 and, indeed, this may have occurred by the date of publication of this edition.

any disciplinary transfer decision. But by 1993 the Prison Service had formed the view that the arrangements in CI 37/1990 were inadequate to deal with the problem of subversive prisoners. The new strategy, set out in IG 28/1993, involves a five–stage management programme for disruptive prisoners which extends beyond the dispersal prisons to all prisoners in Category B training prisons as well as sentenced prisoners in local prisons. The scheme also provides for a greater degree of control by Prison Service Headquarters in imposing a transfer on a potentially reluctant governor together with a right of appeal in the aggrieved governor to challenge such a decision.

The Five-fold Strategy

IG 28/1993 envisages the first stage in relation to a prisoner who becomes disruptive or subversive as a consideration of disciplinary action together with counselling the prisoner with the aim of persuading him to change his behaviour. If this fails, the governor should then consider whether segregation within the parent prison under rule 45 is appropriate. Only if these options are unsuccessful should a governor move to stage 2, which involves a temporary transfer from a Category B or dispersal prison of a disruptive prisoner to a designated 'primary' cell in a local prison. When a governor is considering such a transfer he is obliged to consult with the Control, Population, and Incident Management Section (itself a sub-section of the Security Group) who will advise on the availability of primary cells within the prison estate. A stage 2 temporary transfer must not exceed one calendar month and the expectation is that at the end of that period the prisoner will be returned to the sending prison. IG 28/1993 states that 'staff in both prisons should be working with the inmate to a common goal of returning him to the parent establishment on normal location' (para 17) and thus it assumes that upon arrival at the receiving prison, the prisoner will be segregated by the governor under rule 45. In fairness, the Instruction makes clear that such a decision is exclusively within the discretion of the receiving governor who cannot be dictated to by Headquarters, but in reality the chances of the local prison governor deciding not to order segregation upon receiving a prisoner transferred under IG 28/1993 must be slim. The degree of overcrowding in most local prisons makes it highly likely that rule 45 segregation will frequently be the easier option for the harassed local prison governor faced with a prisoner already regarded as a control problem by the transferring governor with whom he will invariably have spoken. **10.26**

If the parent prison governor does not wish the prisoner to be returned to his prison after one month he is required to submit a reasoned case to Headquarters which will consider whether to insist on the prisoner's return or whether it will arrange an appropriate re-allocation. This involves a move to stage 3 under which all re-allocations will be to other dispersal prisons, Category B training prisons, or another local prison. This stage will be centrally managed by the Control, **10.27**

Population, and Incident Management Section and once again receiving governors can be compelled to accept a prisoner subject to the right of internal appeal.

10.28 Stage 4 involves the transfer of a disruptive prisoner to one of the CSCs within the prison system pursuant to rule 46 of the Prison Rules (these are located at Woodhill and Durham prisons). These units are to be distinguished from Special Secure Units which exist to hold Exceptional Risk Category A prisoners in the very highest conditions of security. The criteria for admission to a CSC are considered below.

10.29 The final stage in the strategy contained in IG 28/1993 is not so much a discrete management option but instead a scheme for continuous assessment of those very few prisoners who, because of their persistently disruptive behaviour, are regarded as unsuitable even for containment in a CSC. Under this scheme of assessment, the prisoner concerned will be allocated to a different prison (potentially of any type) where there will be a six-weekly review of his behaviour. Though IG 28/1993 does not say so, it seems inevitable that such a transfer will involve a return to rule 45 segregation. Any further disruptive behaviour in the receiving prison will result in further transfer 'to relieve the pressure on the holding establishments'. It seems clear that once a prisoner has reached stage 5, he faces a future of indefinite segregation and transfer until his behaviour has changed for the better.

10.30 It was the possibility of persistent short-term transfers accompanied by rule 45 segregation which gave rise to much criticism over the past 15 years. The Woolf Report accepted the need for some kind of transfer option as a means of dealing with a specially difficult situation which the governor cannot resolve within his own prison, but warned that the provisions of CI 37/90 (the predecessor to IG 28/1993) needed to be closely monitored by the Prison Service to ensure that particular prisoners are not placed on a permanent 'carousel' within the prison system (para 12.253).

10.31 For the avoidance of doubt IG 28/1993 does emphasize a number of common standards applicable to all stages of the five-fold strategy for dealing with disruptive prisoners, as follows:

- no inmate should be transferred as a form of punishment;
- the reasoned grounds for transfer must be recorded and noted on the inmate's record;
- inmates must be advised in writing of the reasons for their transfer or segregation within 24 hours of such actions;
- requests/complaints about a transfer must be replied to within seven days by the governor of the establishment where the transfer decision was taken;
- intending visitors should be notified of an inmate's transfer, including, where appropriate, by the inmate himself;
- decisions on segregating inmates under rule 45 are matters for the governor, and subsequently the Board of Visitors, in the establishment in which the inmate is then being held.

C. Procedural Fairness and Rule 45 Segregation

There is a significant difference between what the law requires and what Prison **10.32**
Service policy promises in terms of the procedural fairness requirements attendant upon a decision to segregate a prisoner, whether or not such a decision arises
following a transfer initiated for reasons of good order or discipline under IG
28/1993. As a matter of law, a prisoner has no right to be heard either before he is
initially segregated by the governor under rule 45(1) or before authority to extend
segregation beyond three days is sanctioned by a member of the Board of Visitors
or the Secretary of State under rule 45(2).

In *Hague* both the Divisional Court and the Court of Appeal rejected the argu- **10.33**
ment that the draconian effect of segregation against a prisoner's will justified a
legal right to a hearing in order to respond to the proposed reasons for his segregation. At the time of Hague's appeal to the Court of Appeal, a governor's power
to segregate was limited to an initial period of 24 hours, and it was therefore conceded that this limitation, combined with the fact that segregation decisions
would usually be urgent, made it impractical to argue for a full-blown hearing
before the governor's initial decision. At the stage of seeking authority for continued segregation however no such 'emergency' rationale was applicable and thus, it
was submitted, an informal hearing before the Board of Visitors member was both
practicable and necessary.

The Court of Appeal was unimpressed by this argument. Relying on dicta in **10.34**
Payne v Lord Harris of Greenwich (a parole case), Taylor LJ said:

> [A]part from the urgency of decisions under rule 43 [now rule 45], there may well
> be other public policy grounds for not giving reasons in advance to the prisoner so
> as to enable him to make representations. Giving reasons would often require
> unwise disclosure of information. Such disclosure could reveal to prisoners the
> extent of the governor's knowledge about their activities. It could reveal the source
> of such information, thereby putting informants at risk. It could cause an immedi-
> ate escalation of trouble.[20]

The court held further that the specific inclusion of natural justice requirements
in rule 49 (now rule 54) of the Prison Rules and their absence from rule 43 (now
rule 45) gave powerful support to the Home Office argument that the 'full
panoply' of the rules of natural justice was not intended to apply to segregation
decisions in contrast with disciplinary proceedings which may result in punitive

---

[20] [1981] 1 WLR 754. By contrast in *R v Parole Board and Home Secretary, ex p Wilson* [1992]
QB 740 Taylor LJ referred to *Payne* as a case 'decided in 1981 when established views on prisoners
rights were very different from those of today' and ruled that it would be unjust to apply it in 1992
to deny a discretionary lifer access to reports and other material before the Parole Board when considering the question of releasing him on licence.

action. Of course the 1990 amendment to rule 43, reproduced in the current rule 45, (giving a governor the power to segregate a prisoner for up to three days without the need for authority from the Board of Visitors or the Secretary of State) made it that much harder to argue that at the stage of seeking authority for a continuation of segregation there could ever be any question of an urgent decision having to be taken which would be obstructed by a legal requirement to provide a hearing (however informally) to the prisoner concerned. While *Hague* remains authority for the proposition that prisoners have no right in law to be heard by either the governor or the Board of Visitors before it is decided to initiate or continue rule 45 segregation, subsequent decisions tend to indicate that the Court of Appeal's reasoning is no longer good law.[21]

10.35 As with the right to be heard, so too with the requirement to give reasons after a segregation decision has been made. The Divisional Court had held in *Hague* that the general duty upon a governor to act fairly when making a decision to segregate required, by necessary implication, adequate notice to the prisoner concerned within a reasonable time of the reasons for the decision. Without such an obligation it was pointed out that the prisoner's right to complain to the Board of Visitors against his segregation under rule 95(1) (now rule 78(1)) would be rendered ineffective.

10.36 The Court of Appeal reversed this favourable finding. Pointing out that there was no general rule in public law that reasons be given for administrative decisions, it held that the same policy reasons which made it inappropriate to give reasons before a segregation decision was made applied with equal force after the event. Once again, later decisions suggest that a different outcome would now be reached were the matter to be re-litigated.[22]

10.37 There was no appeal to the House of Lords on any of the procedural fairness issues because, soon after judgment was delivered by the Court of Appeal, the Prison Service replaced CI 10/1974 with CI 37/1990. The new Instruction provided clear and emphatic guidance to governors about the need to give reasons for both a transfer and a segregation decision, guidance which is repeated in IG 28/1993. Paragraph 9 of IG 28/1993 makes clear that prisoners who are segregated or transferred must be told in writing of the reasons for the decision within 24 hours of such action. The significance of this obligation is that by the time a decision has to be taken by the Board of Visitors member (or exceptionally the Secretary of State) about continuing segregation beyond three days, the prisoner concerned

---

[21] See now *R v Home Secretary, ex p Doody* [1994] 1 AC 531 and *R v Home Secretary, ex p Duggan* [1994] 3 All ER 277.
[22] While it remains the case that there is no general duty to give reasons for administrative decisions, the general trend post-*Hague* has been towards greater openness or 'transparency' in decision-making as Lord Mustill commented in his seminal speech in *Doody* [1994] 1 AC 531, 561E–566E.

must be in possession of written reasons for his segregation. This, coupled with the obligation in CI 6/1993 upon a Board of Visitors personally to visit a prisoner before extending his segregation, at least ensures that meaningful representations can be made to whoever is considering an extension of segregation. CI 26/1990 falls short of requiring the Board of Visitors member to provide a hearing to a prisoner before authorizing continued segregation but comes close to it. In the 1991 addendum the Prison Department states that:

> a member of the Board of Visitors whose authority is being sought for continued segregation should be encouraged to see and speak with the inmate, if necessary at some length, before deciding whether to give such authority. In addition Board members should be invited to see and speak with any inmates under segregation in the course of regular rota visits . . . even when cases are not due for formal review.

The language of 'encourage' and 'invite' properly reflects the fact that Board members are not subject to Prison Service instructions but the intention is clear. Similar safeguards are reproduced in PSO 1700.

10.38 The effect of the administrative guidance contained in IG 28/1993, CI 26/1990 and PSOs 1700 and 1701 is that prisoners may rely on the doctrine of legitimate expectation in support of a claim to an entitlement to be given reasons for a transfer or segregation decision and a right to be heard before segregation is extended beyond three days. It follows that a failure to give reasons for a transfer/segregation decision after 24 hours or a failure to provide some kind of hearing to a prisoner before authorizing continued segregation beyond three days could leave the prison authorities vulnerable to a successful application for judicial review.[23]

D. Transfer to a Close Supervision Centre Under Rule 46

10.39 As indicated above, stage 4 of the management strategy for dealing with persistently disruptive prisoners is to transfer them to one of the five CSCs contained in Woodhill (where there are three CSCs) and Durham prisons.[24] The CSC system—which came into operation in February 1998—has replaced the previous system of Special Units described in IG 28/1993. The idea of developing Special Units had come from the 1984 Report of the Control Review Committee

---

[23] But note that in *R v Home Secretary, ex p Ross*, The Times, 9 June 1994, the Court of Appeal, in rejecting a renewed application for leave to move for judicial review, held that in discharging his duty to give reasons for the transfer of an allegedly disruptive prisoner, a governor was not required to give 'chapter and verse'. A general explanation that the prisoner was being transferred because he was a 'disruptive prisoner who is doing his best to destabilize the wing' was held to be a sufficient statement of the governor's reasons. It was also said that a governor could make a transfer decision if he thought a prisoner's behaviour might in any way threaten the smooth running of the prison.

[24] There was originally a third CSC at HM Prison Hull, but this was closed in March 1999 and moved to Durham. As well as the special CSC units, two specified cells in the segregation unit of each high security prison have been designated as CSC cells pursuant to r 46(1).

(Managing the Long Term Prison System), which addressed the question of how to deal with the minority of prisoners whose control problems could not be dealt with in normal conditions. While in the Unit, prisoners were not subject to rule 45, although security was intense.

10.40 The Woolf Report described the Units as attempting 'to provide a generous regime to counterbalance their claustrophobic environment' with a consequent need for intensive staffing, and commented that 'there is more than a philosophical difficulty about apparently providing the best conditions and facilities for those who behave the worst'. While the case for some form of Special Unit was accepted, Woolf recommended that the aim should be to return the prisoners concerned to 'normal' prison life before release.

Eligibility

10.41 Eligibility for a place in the former Control Review Committee Special Units was likely, according to IG 28/1993, to involve a prisoner with a history of disruptive and aggressive behaviour and who:

- has been violent to staff and/or inmates;
- has regularly incurred disciplinary reports;
- has caused serious damage to property in prison;
- has shown dangerous behaviour, such as rooftop protests, hostage taking;
- has a history of mental abnormality;
- has failed to respond to the earlier strategy measures to improve control (ie has failed stages 1–3 of IG 28/1993).

It was not considered necessary to amend the Prison Rules to authorize the transfer of a disruptive prisoner to a Special Unit, presumably because it was not suggested that such prisoners were being segregated from other prisoners. They 'enjoyed' the right to normal association with the limited number of other prisoners located in the Units.

10.42 Having spent a year reviewing the operation of the Special Unit system during 1997–98, the Prison Service decided that it was no longer the most appropriate method for managing the most difficult and disruptive prisoners in the system. Accordingly, the CSC system was designed and a new rule 43A introduced. This was largely reproduced by rule 46 of the 1999 Prison Rules, which states:

(1) Where it appears desirable, for the maintenance of good order or discipline or to ensure the safety of officers, prisoners or any other person, that a prisoner should not associate with other prisoners, either generally or for particular purposes, the Secretary of State may direct the prisoner's removal from association accordingly and his placement in a close supervision centre of a prison.

(2) A direction given under paragraph 1 of this rule shall be for a period not exceeding one month but may be renewed from time to time for a like period, and shall continue to apply notwithstanding any transfer of a prisoner from one prison to another.

(3) The Secretary of State may direct that such a prisoner as aforesaid shall resume association with other prisoners either within a close supervision centre or elsewhere.

(4) In exercising any discretion under this rule, the Secretary of State shall take account of any relevant medical considerations which are known to him.

A number of points arise from the terms of rule 46 (which received no public debate prior to its introduction). First, it seems clear that on initial allocation to a CSC a prisoner will be segregated from other prisoners within the CSC. Secondly, such allocation and segregation may only be initiated by the Home Secretary (in reality one of his officers in the Directorate of high security prisons at Prison Service headquarters). Thirdly, an initial rule 46 allocation/segregation decision lasts for one month and there is no need to obtain the approval of any 'independent' person or body such as the Board of Visitors or the medical officer. Fourthly, a rule 46 segregation decision may be renewed from month to month without any need for an independent review by any person or body. Finally, rule 46 contains no express procedural fairness safeguards such as a duty to give reasons for the proposed decision (or any extension of it) and the right to be heard thereafter.[25]

An early explanation of how the CSC system is supposed to operate was given in a letter to the Prison Reform Trust journal, Prison Report, from the Director of Dispersal prisons.[26] Describing CSCs as part of a national management strategy which aims to secure the return of disruptive prisoners to a settled and acceptable pattern of behaviour, the Director claimed that prisoners will not be transferred to the CSC system to be punished. The emphasis is supposed to be therapeutic rather than punitive, with prisoners having the opportunity to progress from a very structured regime through to more open regimes in preparation for a return to normal prison location. On entry to a CSC, an individual programme is drawn up and (in theory) agreed by the prisoner, his personal officer, and the Centre manager. A prisoner's time in the CSC will be determined by individual assessment against targets, personalized compacts, and general regime compliance. **10.43**

The extent to which standards of procedural fairness apply to the decision to allocate a prisoner to a CSC was considered by the High Court in *R v Home Secretary,* **10.44**

---

[25] There is a further difficulty with the terms of r 46. It would seem that a CSC may be 'created' wherever the Prison Service decides—they are not separate establishments but simply wings or areas within a prison. Rule 45(4) makes it clear that the potential exists for the Home Secretary to circumvent the procedural requirements of r 45—which requires the approval of a Board of Visitors' member for segregation beyond three days—by using r 46 instead.

[26] Spring 1998 edn at 26; now the Director of high security prisons.

ex p Mehmet.[27] On behalf of Mehmet it was argued that the decision to allocate to a CSC is one which affects a prisoner adversely, and which therefore triggers the requirements of procedural fairness, as developed in the cases of *Wilson, Doody* and *Duggan*. It was argued that the allocation to a CSC has a knock-on effect on a prisoner's categorization, and therefore on his prospects for release. Against this, it was argued that allocation to a CSC does not affect legal rights, and that any effect on categorization is caused by the prisoner's pre-CSC behaviour, allocation to a CSC being a beneficial step aimed at getting the prisoner's behaviour under control to allow him to return to the regular prison system. Turner J rejected the arguments in favour of procedural fairness, stating that:

> It was, in my judgment, correctly submitted that the mere fact of allocation does not adversely impact on the prospects of parole. In truth, as the respondent submitted, it was the prisoner's conduct before and not as the result of allocation which was likely to be a factor which would affect the prospect of release on parole. It was pointed out that if the effect of allocation to a CSC was beneficial, in accordance with one of its stated purposes, then prospects of release were enhanced rather than damaged as the result of allocation. . . . In conclusion, I hold that allocation of a prisoner to a CSC does not so affect his personal rights that the common law will intervene by requiring that he should have been given by standards of procedural fairness the opportunity to make representations against his allocation.

The issue was subsequently resolved by the introduction of a right to make representations into the Operating Standards, making CSC prisoners no longer dependent on the common law for procedural protection. Of more lasting interest are Turner J's serious criticisms of the setting up and running of the CSC system. He said that:

> I would not wish to leave this case without observing that, to some extent at least, the department has brought these proceedings on itself. It was slow in devising and disseminating operating standards. It was, moreover, dilatory in the extreme about disclosing their very existence. Although the department has succeeded on the issue raised in these proceedings, it is apparent that it soon came to be recognised that due to the unimaginative manner in which the CSC regime was introduced, prisoners failed properly to understand the reasons why the scheme was introduced and became deeply disillusioned about it.

10.45 The system of CSCs was subject to wide-ranging criticism by the then Chief Inspector of Prisons in the report *Inspection of Close Supervision Centres: A Thematic Inspection*, published in March 2000. This report was the product of an extensive programme of inspections, covering all parts of the CSC estate, and interviews with prisoners and staff. The Chief Inspector was highly critical of many aspects of the CSC regime. He was particularly concerned that there was a lack of accountability in the system for referring prisoners to a CSC. Unlike the previous system, which involved members of the Board of Visitors, the current

---

[27] (1999) 11 Admin LR 529.

CSC Selection Committee consists purely of Prison Service staff, chaired by the Director of High Security. The Chief Inspector noted that, '[i]t was never specified that this group would fulfil a watchdog function. . . . Without this the Prison Service leaves itself open to severe and justifiable criticism in this particularly sensitive area of its practice.'[28] The Chief Inspector was also extremely critical of the regimes, particularly in Woodhill, which he described as 'sterile and void of stimulation',[29] noting the crippling sense of boredom which pervaded the units. He noted the socially isolating and dehumanizing effect of the fact that prisoners in some of the Woodhill units were only ever unlocked by officers in full riot gear, inevitably causing some prisoners to act up to the brutal image that was expected of them. Most importantly, the interviews with inmates show the deep sense of frustration caused by the apparent impossibility of ever leaving the CSC system. Far from enabling a structured return to the normal system, CSCs appeared in many cases to make mentally vulnerable prisoners worse, and to hold out no hope of progress.

> Most of the responses referred to the sterility of the regime and the impasse that resulted when trust broke down. Prisoners referred to the restrictions in units A and D [the more restrictive units at Woodhill] as creating 'angry individuals' and 'monsters'. One prisoner said 'It's making me worse. I used to have violent thoughts and impulses but had got rid of them. Now they are coming back. I don't want to be like this. Now I'm back to square one.' Others referred to a sense of hopelessness: 'despite receiving good written reports I'm not making progress', and 'I cannot see any way to end it'.[30]

All this was summarized as 'the unhealthy and dysfunctional nature of the CSC system, which in its current form was unable to support the mental health of either the prisoners or the staff within it'.[31] As well as being an example of fearless reporting on the part of the Prisons Inspectorate, the report paints a very worrying picture of the lives of some of the most isolated and controlled people in the prison system. The CSC system emerges from the report as both unaccountable and counterproductive.

E. Special Cells and Approved Restraints

In addition to powers to segregate and transfer prisoners in the interests of good order or discipline, the Prison Rules contain two emergency provisions (rules 48   **10.46**

---

[28] para 1.42. The Committee for the Prevention of Torture (CPT) has also asked for clarification about the selection procedures for CSCs: see *Report to the Government to the United Kingdom on the visit to the United Kingdom carried out by the European Committee for the Prevention of Torture and Inhuman or Degrading Treatment or Punishment from 4 to 16 February 2001*, para 63.
[29] para 2.2.
[30] para 4.17.
[31] para 2.73.

and 49) which enable prison management to deal with an allegedly violent, disruptive prisoner by confining him temporarily in special accommodation or subjecting him to an approved method of restraint. The two powers can be—and frequently are—used in tandem.

10.47 Their use must be seen in the context of the general principle governing the use of force against prisoners by prison staff to be found in rule 47:

> (1) An officer in dealing with a prisoner shall not use force unnecessarily and, when the application of force to a prisoner is necessary, no more force than is necessary shall be used.
>
> (2) No officer shall act deliberately in a manner calculated to provoke a prisoner.

It is to be noted that nothing in the Prison Act or the Rules stipulates *when* force is necessary. Prison officers have the powers of constables (who may use reasonable force when acting in the execution of their duties) and, though prison officers enjoy no special power authorizing the use of force, it must be assumed that they may use force against prisoners in so far as it can be shown to be reasonably necessary to enforce lawful orders or regulations pursuant to the Act and the Rules.[32] It has been said that a lawful order 'is presumably one which can derive support from the Prison Rules or any rule or regulation of the prison or is necessary to the discharge of the proper functions of the prison authorities in keeping the prisoners in custody in a safe, orderly and efficient manner'.[33]

10.48 Accordingly such guidance as is given to staff in Prison Service Instructions and Orders about dealing with violent or refractory prisoners is merely illustrative of the general principle that only such force as is reasonably necessary to effect a lawful purpose (including, of course, self-defence) may be used at any time. Force may never however be used to punish a prisoner, corporal punishment for disciplinary infractions having been abolished.[34]

Special Cells

10.49 Section 13(6) of the Prison Act provides that '[i]n every prison special cells shall be provided for the temporary confinement of refractory or violent prisoners'. (It was presumably thought that the use of special cells for this purpose required express

---

[32] Prison Act 1952, s 8.

[33] *Halsbury's Laws* (4th edn, London, 1982), vol 37, para 1163.

[34] PSO 1600 states that '[a]ll reasonable efforts must be made to manage violent, refractory or disturbed behaviour by persuasion or other means which do not entail the use of force. The use of force must always be regarded as a matter of last resort.' The Order requires prison officers who resort to force when dealing with a prisoner to complete a Use of Force Report on form F2326. Reports should always be submitted if it is believed that the inmate has been or could have been injured or if any of the officers present has been injured. Use of Force Reports are intended to be in addition to filling out an F213 (Report of Injury to an Inmate).

Parliamentary sanction over and above the general power in s 47(2) to make rule for the 'discipline and control' of prisoners.) Accordingly, rule 48 states that:

(1) The governor may order a refractory or violent prisoner to be confined temporarily in a special cell, but a prisoner shall not be so confined as a punishment, or after he has ceased to be refractory or violent.

(2) A prisoner shall not be confined in a special cell for longer than 24 hours without a direction in writing given by a member of a board of visitors or by an officer of the Secretary of State (not being an officer of the prison). Such direction shall state the grounds for the confinement and the time during which it may continue.

As with rule 45 it is immediately clear that a prisoner may be placed in a special cell under this provision without any disciplinary proceedings being instituted against him. Indeed, the accommodation may never be imposed as a punishment following conviction for a disciplinary offence precisely because it is regarded as fit only for temporary use to deal with an emergency situation. However, unlike rule 45, rule 48 may not be used pre-emptively. Before a prisoner can lawfully be placed in a special cell he must actually be behaving in a 'refractory or violent' manner. It is not enough that a prison officer anticipates such behaviour. And so if prison staff choose to act under this power before such behaviour has been exhibited, their actions are unlawful and any force used to move the prisoner concerned to the cell renders them vulnerable to an action for assault.

PSO 1600

Guidance on the use of rule 48 is to be found in PSO 1600 ('Use of Force'). The **10.50** Order states at para 4.2.2 that '[a] prisoner must not be confined in special accommodation as a punishment and, as soon as the original justification for the use of the special accommodation has ceased, the prisoner must be moved from that accommodation'. Confusingly the Order refers in general terms to 'special accommodation' rather than the term used in the rule ('special cell') and then proceeds to describe 'special accommodation' as including two types of cell—a cell which has been designated as a special cell and an unfurnished cell.

In practice a special cell is usually equipped with a double door, has no access to **10.51** natural light, is virtually sound-proof, and is much smaller than a normal cell. Instead of a bed, there is a raised wooden platform. Prisoners refer to it as 'the strong box' or 'the box', a description which more accurately describes the degree of sensory deprivation involved.

An unfurnished cell is stated in PSO 1600 to be: **10.52**

[A] cell which is designated and usually used for ordinary accommodation purposes but from which the usual furniture has been removed and which is either totally unfurnished or does not contain basic items of furniture such as a table and a chair.

This, somewhat verbose, definition appears to suggest that any cell can temporarily be used to confine a prisoner under rule 48 simply by removing a table and chair even if it is the prisoner's normal cell. This is surely not the purpose of the rule 48 power, and in practice most prisoners who are believed to be so 'refractory or violent' as to justify the use of rule 48 are placed in a special cell on the punishment block.

10.53 A special cell has no medical justification and requires no medical authorization in order to justify its use. It is clearly a measure based on pure control considerations. However, the Order gives no guidance as to when use of such cells is appropriate, beyond stating that they are to be used to confine 'violent or refractory' prisoners. The Order's predecessor, SO 3E, stated that such a cell may only be used 'if it is necessary in order to prevent the prisoner causing self-injury, injuring another prisoner or staff, or damaging property, or creating a serious disturbance'. These criteria are almost identical to those contained in rule 49(1) which governs the use of restraints (see para 10.56 below). Although rule 48 speaks of the governor ordering confinement in a special cell, the emergency nature of the power necessarily means that the initial decision will almost always be taken by prison officers. PSO 1600 states that where the governor in charge cannot be contacted the decision can be taken by the officer for the time being in charge of the prison, who must refer his decision at the earliest opportunity to the governor. The Order also sets out detailed requirements for the recording of all decisions under rule 48, for notifying the medical officer to enable an early examination of the prisoner, and also for informing the Board of Visitors so that a member may visit and inquire.[35]

10.54 Rule 48 expressly forbids the use of special cell accommodation after the prisoner has ceased to be refractory or violent, but PSO 1600 states that if it is sought to continue its use beyond 24 hours, the written authority of the Board of Visitors must be obtained. The temporary, emergency nature of the power makes it hard to see how detention beyond 24 hours could ever be justified, particularly in the light of medical evidence suggesting that whatever calming effect the special cell may initially produce it tends to exacerbate aggressive feelings when used for too long. As with the authorization of rule 48 segregation beyond three days, a Board of Visitors member who is approached to extend rule 48 beyond 24 hours should never act as a rubber stamp but should instead require clear justification from the governor for its continuance. PSO 1600 also demands that a written record must be kept on form F2325 of the reasons for extending rule 48 incarceration in a special cell.

---

[35] The decision to place in special accommodation or to use a mechanical restraint must be recorded on form F2323. A copy of each such form must be put before the Board of Visitors.

Removal of Clothing

Whenever a prisoner is placed in a special cell, it seems to be common practice in **10.55**
most prisons for him to be stripped as a matter of routine of all his clothing (or at
least to his underpants) and given paper 'protective clothing'. It is hard to see that
this practice can ever be justified save in circumstances where there is a risk of the
prisoner injuring himself or committing suicide by hanging with the clothing, in
which case it hardly seems suitable to use the special cell at all. SO 3E states that
'where a prisoner is placed in special accommodation or a mechanical restraint is
used and, as part of the protective arrangements, it is necessary to deprive the prisoner of normal clothes, the prisoner must be provided with protective clothing so
that he/she can be decently dressed'. The important word here is 'necessary'. This
is not the same as 'convenient' or 'desirable'. A prisoner who is forcibly stripped
for no reason other than the fact that he is being placed in a special cell could legitimately sue for assault unless it can be shown that removing his ordinary clothing
is clearly necessary to prevent him harming himself. Forcing a prisoner to wear
paper clothing invariably increases the sense of humiliation and degradation
brought about by location in a special cell and, where it is not necessary, invariably
gives substance to the charge that the purpose is to punish.[36]

Approved Restraints

The use of mechanical methods of restraint is expressly sanctioned by rule 49 **10.56**
though, unlike the issue of special cells, the Prison Act is silent on the subject, leaving it as a matter within the general rule-making power to maintain discipline and
control. It is appropriate to set out rule 49 in full:

(1) The governor may order a prisoner to be put under restraint where this is
necessary to prevent the prisoner from injuring himself or others, damaging property or creating a disturbance.

(2) Notice of such an order shall be given without delay to a member of the
board of visitors, and to the medical officer or to a medical practitioner
such as is mentioned in rule 20(3).

(3) On receipt of the notice the medical officer, or the medical practitioner
referred to in paragraph (2), shall inform the governor whether there are
any medical reasons why the prisoner should not be put under restraint.
The governor shall give effect to any recommendation which may be made
under this paragraph.

---

[36] The use of special cells for non-medical reasons has grown significantly between 1986 and
2000. In 1986 special cells/unfurnished cells were used on 1,466 male prisoners. By 2000 this had
risen to 2,132. For female prisoners the number in 2000 was only 83: Home Office, *Prison Statistics
England and Wales 2000* (Cm 5250, 2001) 138.

(4) A prisoner shall not be kept under restraint longer than necessary, nor shall he be so kept for longer than 24 hours without a direction in writing given by a member of the board of visitors or by an officer of the Secretary of State (not being an officer of a prison). Such a direction shall state the grounds for the restraint and the time during which it may continue.

(5) Particulars of every case of restraint under the foregoing provisions of this Rule shall be forthwith recorded.

(6) Except as provided by this rule no prisoner shall be put under restraint otherwise than for safe custody during removal, or on medical grounds by direction of the medical officer or of a medical practitioner such as is mentioned in rule 20(3). No prisoner shall be put under restraint as a punishment.

(7) Any means of restraint shall be of a pattern authorized by the Secretary of State, and shall be used in such manner and under such conditions as the Secretary of State may direct.

10.57 As with special cells, administrative policy on the use of approved restraints is contained in PSO 1600. It stresses that there is only one approved method of mechanical restraint, namely a body belt (with metal cuffs for both male and female prisoners). No other method of restraint may lawfully be used against a prisoner. The PSO adds that '[i]n particular, for the purpose of this order, ratchet handcuffs are not a mechanical restraint'. This is a significant advance on the previous policy document, SO 3E, which allowed the use of wrist and ankle straps. Lest there be any doubt about the exceptional nature of this power, PSO 1600 states that:

> A mechanical restraint may be used only in order to prevent a prisoner causing self-injury, injuring another prisoner or member of staff, or damaging property, when its use is absolutely necessary to achieve the required objective and has been approved in accordance with this Order. Every effort must be made to avoid the use of mechanical restraints. The option to use special accommodation instead of a mechanical restraint must be considered first. This does not preclude the use of mechanical restraints in addition to special accommodation, where the circumstances of the case so demand, and where a prisoner cannot safely be left unrestrained in special unfurnished accommodation.

10.58 In fact it is by no means unusual for a restraint to be applied to a prisoner inside a special cell and in many cases it is hard to see how this can be justified. For example, a disgruntled prisoner emerges from his cell in the segregation unit and in a fury empties the contents of his chamber pot over a member of staff but then shows no further aggressive intent and moves to return to his cell. He has certainly committed a disciplinary offence and may properly be charged with assaulting the officer concerned. But would staff be justified in grabbing him and then dragging him to a special cell before unceremoniously incarcerating him inside a body belt? The answer must be 'No'. However enraged they may be, they are not entitled to mete out summary justice in advance of the governor's adjudication. In any event neither the special cell nor the body belt can be used to punish. Since the prisoner has ceased to behave in a 'violent or refractory' manner and indicated his desire to return to his cell, any force applied to him would be unlawful and certainly an effort forcibly to drag him to a special cell and place him in a body belt would be incapable of justification. Yet there are many recorded examples of just this kind of behaviour by a prisoner prompting a show of force on the part of staff, who no doubt feel that a single act of violence against them may justify immediate reloca- tion to a special cell and, if their efforts meet with resistance, the application of a body belt to protect them on leaving the cell.

The Rodrigues Case

The case of *Rodrigues v Home Office*[37] is a good illustration of the need for strict **10.59** justification of the use of powers contained in rules 48 and 49 and indeed it was the first recorded example of a prisoner successfully suing the Home Office for damages for assault arising from the use of an approved method of restraint. The plaintiff (R) was a 23-year-old prisoner serving a five-year prison sentence at Wandsworth Prison for a variety of offences of dishonesty and violence. He was regarded by the authorities as a control problem and had spent a number of weeks in segregation when an incident occurred which led to him being taken to a spe- cial cell. When he was unlocked for exercise he became annoyed about a request to search him and slammed his cell door on a prison officer, slightly injuring the officer's hand. Notwithstanding that R was not offering any further violence and indeed was now inside his cell, the senior officer on duty ordered that he be restrained and taken to the special cell, where he was stripped to his underpants. Later the same day, the deputy governor and medical officer visited R in the spe- cial cell and when the door was opened he lunged towards the senior officer and threw a piece of broken floor tile. A struggle ensued and R was restrained on the floor before he was put in a body belt. He remained in the belt for approximately 24 hours. The opinion of psychiatrists on behalf of both R and the Home Office was that the average time for detaining any person in a body belt was two to three hours and that its use was justified only as a last resort when it was immediately necessary to prevent a prisoner from behaving violently. Her Honour Judge Norrie held, giving judgment for R, that although the initial decision to place R in the body belt was reasonable because of his violent behaviour, staff were under a duty to remove it as soon as possible. She stated that use of a body belt was a wholly exceptional measure and that mere threats and abuse by a prisoner were not enough to justify its application. The decision taken by the deputy governor to order restraint overnight for a 12-hour period without review was unlawful. On

---

[37] A decision of a County Court judge (Her Honour Judge Norrie), 16 December 1988, Croydon County Court. There is a brief case report at February 1989 *LAG Bulletin* 14.

the evidence of prison staff, R's behaviour thereafter did not justify the use of the body belt. It was particularly significant that on three separate occasions staff removed a single arm from the belt in order to let R feed himself while still detained in the special cell and no violence took place but still staff restored the restraint. They claimed that R remained a threat to staff but could only point to abusive language as evidence of this. R was awarded £750 in damages for assault based on a period of approximately 20 hours' wrongful detention in the body belt.[38]

10.60 The case shows that prison management must provide an effective procedure for the constant monitoring of any prisoner detained in a body belt and must persist in efforts to remove it right from the outset. There is no standard, reasonable period which may be imposed to give 'a taste of restraint' and identical reasoning applies to location in a special cell.

10.61 The use of mechanical and non-mechanical restraints (special cells, protective rooms, and body belts, etc) has grown over the past decade and a half. In 1986 a total of 1,235 male prisoners were subject to some form of restraint on non-medical grounds whereas by 2000 this had increased to 1,632.[39] These figures indicate either a greater willingness by staff to resort to extreme methods of control or an increase in violent, disruptive incidents involving prisoners. The former Chief Inspector of Prisons, Judge Tumim, frequently expressed concern that staff did resort to control and restraint techniques, as well as the use of body belts, too often and that 'use of force' reports are not correctly filled out by staff, thus making it difficult properly to assess if staff have acted reasonably.

10.62 It is normal to find that officers involved in a control and restraint incident do no more than describe the part of the body which they restrained and then parrot the claim that 'no more force than was necessary was used'. This simply does not begin to comply with the requirement to justify the use of force.

---

[38] In the course of the case Judge Norrie accepted the invitation of counsel for the plaintiff to visit Wandsworth Prison and actually see the special cell. On arrival at the prison she asked to be placed inside a body belt and then to be locked inside the cell for a few minutes to gain some appreciation of what the experience entailed. The facts and reasoning behind the *Rodrigues* judgment are set out in Annex 3 to CI 55/1990 and para 21 of the Circular states that two general principles emerge from the case—(a) systematic arrangements must be made for the regular review of cases while they are running, especially those involving the use of mechanical restraint and the arrangements must have regard to the circumstances and not to mere administrative convenience; and (b) a prisoner must not be kept under restraint when the prisoner has ceased acting violently and there is no other demonstrable reason to believe that the restraint could not be safely removed.
[39] *Prison Statistics 2000* (Cm 5250, 2001), 138.

Article 3 of the ECHR

Article 3 of the ECHR, which prohibits the infliction of torture or inhuman or   **10.63**
degrading treatment or punishment, has not hitherto proved to be an effective
protection against the use of non-disciplinary sanctions such as long-term segregation. Since the ECtHR has defined torture as 'deliberate inhuman treatment
causing very serious and cruel suffering', those cases which have reached the
Commission or the ECtHR arising from the use of solitary confinement (whether
punitive or non-punitive) have focused on what constitutes inhuman or degrading treatment or punishment.

There is no absolute standard for the kinds of treatment and punishment prohib-   **10.64**
ited by Article 3. In its ruling in *Ireland v UK*, the court said that:

> [I]ll treatment must attain a minimum level of severity if it is to fall within the scope
> of Article 3. The assessment of this minimum is, in the nature of things, relative; it
> depends on all the circumstances of the case, such as the duration of the treatment,
> its physical or mental effects and, in some cases, the sex, age and state of health of the
> victim.[40]

More specifically the Commission has defined inhuman treatment or punishment as any treatment which 'deliberately causes severe suffering, mental or physical, which in the particular situation is unjustifiable'.[41] Degrading treatment or
punishment is caused 'if it grossly humiliates a person before others or drives him
to act against his will or his conscience'[42] or if it 'constitutes an insult to the applicant's human dignity'[43] or if it is 'designed to arouse in victims feelings of fear,
anguish and inferiority capable of humiliating and debasing them and possibly
breaking their physical or moral resistance'.[44]

Article 3 and Solitary Confinement

The Strasbourg authorities have generally taken the view that solitary   **10.65**
confinement is in principle undesirable, particularly where the prisoner
was detained on remand, and requires exceptional reasons for its imposition.
But the segregation of a prisoner from the prison community for security, disciplinary, or protective reasons does not in itself constitute inhuman treatment or

---

[40] Series A No 25 (1979–80) 2 EHRR 25.
[41] *Greek case*, Yearbook 12 (1969) 186.
[42] ibid.
[43] *X, Y & C v Belgium*, Application 8930/80.
[44] *Ireland v UK* Series A No 25 (1979–80) 2 EHRR 25, para 167. See also *Soering v UK* (1989)
11 EHRR 429, para 100.

punishment.[45] In assessing the compatibility of solitary confinement with Article 3, regard must be had to the stringency of the measure, its duration, the objective pursued, and the effects on the person concerned. Also relevant is the extent to which a basic minimum possibility of human contact has been left to the detainee.[46] In *Krocher and Moller v Switzerland* the Commission stated: '[t]he question that arises is whether the balance between the requirements of security and basic individual rights was not disrupted to the detriment of the latter'.[47] In that case the prison conditions included isolation, constant artificial lighting, permanent surveillance by closed-circuit television, denial of access to newspapers and radio, and the lack of physical exercise. While expressing serious concern about the compatibility of such a combination of measures with the terms of Article 3, the Commission concluded that they did not amount to inhuman or degrading treatment and accepted the argument that such conditions were necessary to ensure security inside and outside the prison. The applicants were considered to be dangerous terrorists who were liable to escape if given the chance. In other cases the Commission has accepted that stringent security measures within a prison may be justified where a prisoner was 'extremely dangerous',[48] 'able to manipulate situations and encourage other prisoners to acts of indiscipline',[49] or where he had used firearms at the time of his arrest. It is also clear that a relevant factor taken into account by the Commission is whether the measures imposed on

---

[45] See *Koskinen v Finland* (1994) 18 EHRR CD 146; *Bouajila v Switzerland*, Comm Rep July 1993, paras 102–104; *Dhoest v Belgium* Application 10448/83 55 D & R 5 (1987), 20–21.

[46] *X v Federal Republic of Germany* Application 6038/73 Coll 44 (1973) 115; *Baader, Meins, Meinhof and Grundmann v Federal Republic of Germany* Application 6166/73, Yearbook 18 (1975) 132, paras 144–146; *Ensslin, Baader and Raspe v Federal Republic of Germany* Applications 7572/76, 7586/76 and 7587/76, Yearbook 21 (1978) 418, paras 454–460; *Kröcher and Möller v Switzerland*, D & R 34 (1983) 24, paras 51–55.

[47] D & R 34 (1983) 24, paras 51–55. In *Hilton v UK* (1981) 3 EHRR 104 the applicant complained of being segregated on r 43 (now r 45) resulting in 23 hours' solitary confinement. The Commission noted the conditions of overcrowding, under-staffing, the rigorous, impersonal application of disciplinary measures (on occasions to the point of absurdity) but found no violation. A minority dissented stating that they found it inadmissible that a prison system should reduce a prisoner to an 'animal like state' whatever his difficulties. A different outcome might be achieved today. In *Treholt v Norway* Application 14610/89 71 D & R 168 (1991) the applicant had been sentenced to 20 years' imprisonment for espionage and his detention included periods of solitary confinement with sensory isolation. The Commission found no violation. See also *R v Denmark* Application 10263/83 (1986) 8 EHRR 60 which concerned a prisoner held for 20 months on remand in solitary confinement. He was allowed to listen to the radio and watch TV; to exercise in the open air for one hour per day; to borrow books from the library. He also had daily contact with prison staff in connection with food and exercise. He also had contact with others at court and at police interviews(!). He received controlled visits from his family. The Commission found that the charges he faced (homicide and drug trafficking) were grave and justified solitary confinement. It noted that a balance must be struck between the requirements of the investigation and the effect solitary confinement will have.

[48] *M v UK* Application 9907/82, D & R 35 (1984) 13, para 34.

[49] *X v UK* Application 8324/78.

a prisoner are the result of a deliberately unco-operative attitude on the part of the applicant.

It is clear that any Article 3 claim will require cogent medical evidence to establish **10.66** not merely a direct causal link between the prison conditions complained of and the injured or deteriorating health of the applicant but also that the conditions were such as to 'destroy the personality and cause severe mental and physical suffering'.[50] Of course it may be difficult for a doctor or psychiatrist who has no knowledge of a prisoner's mental or physical health when he was at liberty to assess the precise impact of solitary confinement upon him as opposed to, say, the general effects of long term imprisonment. In the case of *Ensslin, Baader and Raspe*, all members of the German terrorist group, the Red Army Faction, who were held in high security conditions in Stammheim Prison, the Commission said that medical reports did not 'make it possible to establish accurately the specific effect of this isolation in relation to their mental and physical health, as compared with other factors'.[51]

The Commission has ruled that complete absolute sensory isolation combined **10.67** with complete social isolation does constitute inhuman treatment for which no security considerations can be prayed in aid by way of justification. In making this clear however a series of decisions has distinguished this form of treatment from 'removal from association with other prisoners for security, disciplinary and protective reasons', which does not by itself constitute conduct in breach of Article 3.[52] The opportunity on rule 45, for example, to meet prison officers, medical officers, lawyers, and relatives and to have contact with the outside world via newspapers and radios prevents it from amounting to complete social or sensory isolation. A depressing feature of the Commission's approach to Article 3 cases has been its reluctance to require strict compliance with modern penological views as set out in the Minimum Rules for the Treatment of Prisoners (1973) and, more recently, the European Prison Rules.[53] In *Eggs v Switzerland*, for example, the Commission took the position that 'the conditions of detention which in certain

---

[50] *Ensslin, Baader and Raspe v Federal Republic of Germany* Applications 7572/76, 7586/76 and 7587/76, Yearbook 21 (1978) 418, para 454.

[51] ibid.

[52] Report of 25 January 1976 in *Ireland v UK* Series B 23/I, 379; *McFeeley v UK* Application 8317/78, D & R 20 (1980) 44, para 82; report of 16 December 1982, *Krocher and Moller*, D & R 34 (1983) 24, para 53; and *R v Denmark* Application 10263/83, D & R 41 (1985) 149.

[53] The European Prison Rules were adopted by the Committee of Ministers on 12 February 1987. In *Koskinen v Finland* (1994) 18 EHRR CD 146 the Commission rejected as manifestly ill-founded an application by a Finnish prisoner who alleged that the lengthy periods of isolation to which he had been subjected and the conditions of his detention violated Art 3. The Commission noted that the CPT had inspected conditions for prisoners in solitary confinement in the Helsinki Central prison and made a number of serious criticisms of them but declined to find that these amounted a breach of Art 3.

aspects did not come up to the standard of the "Minimum Rules" did not thereby alone amount to inhuman or degrading treatment'.[54] The lesson both from domestic jurisprudence and that of the ECtHR is that too frequently the balance between the perceived requirements of security and basic individual rights will be determined in favour of the former.[55]

---

[54] Application 7341/76, Yearbook 20 (1977) 448, para 460.

[55] A striking contrast to the more conservative approach of the domestic courts and the ECtHR can be seen in the decision of the Supreme Court of South Africa in *Whittaker & Morant v Roos*, 1912 AD 92. The plaintiffs were charged with conspiring to cause explosions in Johannesburg during the course of a bitter strike on the tramway system and were placed in solitary confinement cells for some two weeks while awaiting trial. Under prison regulations, the cells were exclusively reserved to punish convicted prisoners and the plaintiffs were awarded damages for their unlawful confinement in actions in delict (the equivalent in Dutch-Roman law of a tort). In an extraordinary judgment Lord de Villiers, the Chief Justice, said that '[i]t surely cannot be the policy of the law that wealth or position should give . . . advantage to an accused person. It often acts harshly enough that a man without money or friends is kept imprisoned until he can be tried, while the man of position is free until tried with every opportunity of preparing his defence. That harshness would become absolutely intolerable if directors of prisons or governors of gaols had it within their power to add to the misfortune of imprisonment the disgrace and torture of confinement in a small punishment cell of four feet by nine without sufficient light, with no bed to sleep upon, with insufficient means of exercise, without books to read, without the companionship of a single soul and without even the consolation afforded by a smoke. The object of the imprisonment before trial is to obtain the appearance of the accused at the trial, and not to punish him.' It is a sobering thought that a South African court in 1912 was willing to award a remedy in damages to prisoners for an experience which today would almost certainly not result in similar compensation from either the domestic courts or the ECtHR.

11

WOMEN PRISONERS

Around 5 per cent of the current prison population are women.[1] The Prison **11.01** Rules require that men and women be held in separate accommodation[2] and hence separate institutions exist for the detention of female prisoners. There are currently 17 of these institutions, very few of which were specifically designed for that purpose.[3] The rest were either small units in male prisons or were facilities converted from other uses, such as male prisons, psychiatric units, or stately homes.[4] The small number of women's prisons means that some of the difficulties of imprisonment become exacerbated for women. They are often held further away from their families than male prisoners, especially while on remand,[5] although women prisoners are more likely to have sole childcare responsibility

---

[1] *Prison Statistics: England and Wales* 2000 (Cm 5250, 2001), put the female population at 3,350 out of a total average daily population of 64,600.

[2] r 12(1) states that women prisoners 'shall normally be kept separate from male prisoners'.

[3] See NACRO, *Women Prisoners: Towards a New Millennium* (London, 1996) 9, and HM Chief Inspector of Prisons, *Follow-up to Women in Prison: A Thematic Review*, (London, 2001), ch 1. Two more female prisons are due to open: Ashford in Middlesex, a dedicated female establishment, and Peterborough, a shared male/female site. For many years young women offenders, including juveniles, were accommodated with adult female prisoners. The current Prison Service policy is to accommodate all women prisoners under the age of 21 separately, 18–20 year olds in designated Young Offender Units in female prisons, and, in conjunction with the Youth Justice Board, 15–17 year olds in secure local authority accommodation.

[4] The presence of a number of former stately homes in the female prisoner estate is one reason why there is significantly more dormitory prison accommodation for women than men.

[5] Women remand prisoners from the Midlands, eg, tend to be detained either in Holloway in the south or Styal in the north. See E Player, 'Women's Prisons After Woolf' in Player (ed), *Prisons After Woolf: Reform through Riot* (London, 1994) 203, 215. Styal replaced Risley as the local women's prison in the North West.

than men in prison.[6] The limited facilities available for women who are classified as a high security risk or are sentenced to lengthy periods of imprisonment mean they will spend more of their sentence in a single prison than most male prisoners. The choice of work and education facilities is often more limited than that available to male prisoners.[7]

11.02 The situation of women in prison has become a matter of increasing public concern as their numbers have risen significantly in recent years.[8] Moreover, whereas the proportion of men imprisoned for acts of violence and sex offences has been increasing, women still tend to be imprisoned primarily for property and drugs offences.[9] In addition to the rising population the conditions of women prisoners have come to public notice as a result of high profile incidents such as an outcry over the shackling of women prisoners while giving birth[10] and the Chief Inspector of Prisons' decision to walk out of Holloway prison rather than continue his visit in December 1995. In early 1997 the Chief Inspector of Prisons produced a highly critical report on the situation of women prisoners.[11] The main theme of this report, which contained 160 recommendations, was the failure of the Prison Service to identify and respond to the particular needs of women prisoners. The Chief Inspector argued that too often the Prison Service treated women prisoners exactly the same as men and failed to consider the specific situation of women when designing regimes and policies. The report quoted one correspondent saying:

---

[6] The 1991 Prison Survey estimated that 47% of female prisoners, as opposed to 32% of male prisoners, were responsible for dependent children at the time of imprisonment. See R Walmsley, L Howard, and S White, *The National Prison Survey 1991: Main Findings*, Home Office Research Study 128 (London, 1992) 13. The same survey found that whereas 90% of male prisoners said their children were being looked after by wives or partners this was true of only 23% of female prisoners, with 52% saying other relatives were looking after their children, and 12% stating that children were in local authority care. A 1994 Howard League survey found that 12% of female prisoners' children ended up in local authority care while only 17% were being cared for by the child's father, *The Voice of a Child: The Impact of Children of their Mother's Imprisonment* (London, 1994). A 1997 study found that 55% of women prisoners had at least one child under 16: Home Office Research Study 162, *Imprisoned women and mothers* (London, 1997).

[7] It may also vary significantly between women's prisons: see NACRO, n 3 above, 10.

[8] The average number of women prisoners has more than doubled in the last decade, rising from 1,559 in 1991 to 3,350 in 2000: *Prison Statistics: England and Wales 2000* (Cm 5250, 2001) 3.

[9] *Prison Statistics: England and Wales* 2000 (Cm 5250, 2001) 87, notes that around 60% of receptions of women prisoners are for theft, handling, and drugs offences as opposed to around 27% for male prisoners. In *R v Mills* [2002] EWCA Crim 519, The Times, 7 March 2002, Lord Woolf CJ urged sentencing judges to consider non-custodial options for women convicted of non-violent offences, particularly where they have childcare responsibilities.

[10] Especially as highlighted in a Channel Four news programme on the shackling of a woman at Whittington Hospital in January 1996. The ECtHR has declared inadmissible an application relating to the use of handcuffs while attending a prenatal clinic: *Kleuver v Norway* Application 45837/99. However, the court has not ruled on the use of handcuffs while giving birth, which obviously raises more serious issues under Arts 3 and 8 of the Convention.

[11] *Women in Prison: A Thematic Review* (London, 1997).

It is not merely a question of women receiving equal treatment to men: in the prison system equality is everywhere conflated with uniformity; women are treated as if they are men.[12]

It goes on to add '[w]e heard the description "cons in skirts" at one establishment'. The Chief Inspector called for an assessment of women's needs to be made and for policies to be revised in the light of this. Its chief recommendation was for the appointment of a Director of Women's Prisons, replacing the situation where female prisons are managed on a geographical basis by Area Managers who report to one of two Operational Directors.[13]

This Report led to some positive changes in the operation of women's prisons. A **11.03** Women's Policy Group was set up in the Directorate of Regimes, along with an Operational Manager of Women's Prisons. The Chief Inspector, in a follow-up review in 2000,[14] noted that there has been a number of improvements in the running of women's prisons, in the quality of the regimes, and the treatment of prisoners. However, key problems remained: in particular, the relatively small number of women's prisons still leads to the majority of female prisoners being incarcerated far from home, and the desperate shortage of places in mother and baby units is a continuing problem. Many prisoners still do not receive enough help in preparing them for release, ensuring that they have a home to go to and that they have maintained adequate contact with their families. One of the issues which most disappointed the Chief Inspector is the total failure to implement his 1997 recommendation that levels of security should be reduced for the majority of women prisoners, since the level of risk to the public and the likelihood of absconding are very low. The Chief Inspector noted that since 1997, the number of women prisoners in the three open prisons had reduced, and that the creation of a new category of semi-open prisons decreases the availability of open places even further, causing those suitable for open conditions to be located even further from their homes.[15]

A. The Legal Regime Governing Women's Imprisonment

The legal structure governing prisons reflects the notion that it is mostly men who **11.04** are imprisoned. Despite the fact that women prisoners are detained in separate

---

[12] ibid, para 3.46.
[13] ibid, para 3.50.
[14] *Follow-up to Women in Prison: A Thematic Review* (London, 2000).
[15] See para 2.06. In his introduction to the Home Office Consultation Paper *The Government's Strategy for Women Offenders* (London, 2000), the then Home Secretary Jack Straw said, 'I . . . reject any call for preferential treatment for women offenders'. Given what is known about the treatment of women prisoners, there seems to be little current risk that the Prison Service will be accused of preferential treatment.

institutions from men, there is no specific set of Prison Rules for female prisoners, as exists for young offenders who are also held in separate prisons from adults.[16] The lack of a specific set of Rules arguably operates to the detriment of women prisoners. For example, when the Rules on temporary release were made more restrictive in 1996 this applied equally to female prisoners, even though there was little concern as to increased risk of women prisoners absconding or committing offences on temporary release. Instead of a separate set of rules the language of the Prison Rules refers to a prisoner as 'he' and the presence of a specific Prison Rule, rule 12, on 'women prisoners' shows that female prisoners are regarded as the exception to the generality. Therefore most Prison Rules and Prison Service Orders/Instructions apply equally to men and women. However, several Prison Rules do explicitly spell out a different legal regime for women prisoners. The most significant, that relating to pregnant prisoners, will be discussed in greater detail later in this chapter. The other relates to the procedures governing searches of female prisoners.

Searches

11.05 Prison Rule 41(3) indicates that no prisoner shall be stripped and searched in the sight or presence of an officer not of the same sex. This applies to both male and female prisoners. However the relevant Instructions go further, indicating that whereas female officers may conduct rub down searches of male prisoners such searches of female prisoners should only be carried out by female officers. The Chief Inspector's report on women's prisons expressed concern that there was an excessive use of strip searching in women's prisons, without sound security reasons always being evident and that officers involved in strip searching had not been fully trained to comprehend the sensitivities this involved. Noting that nearly half the prisoners in a survey it conducted reported having been abused the Report recommended that 'staff should approach strip searching on the assumption that any individual might have a history of being abused' and that decisions to strip search women in closed conditions should only be taken on the authority of a governor of grade 4 or above.[17] The follow-up Review notes that 'despite the lack of training, the majority of staff were evidently sensitive to the issues around the strip searching of women. In recent inspections and during our visits we have found no evidence of the use of

---

[16] It is worth noting that the ICCPR, Art 10(3) indicates that juvenile offenders should be separated from adult prisoners but is silent on the issue of segregation of male and female prisoners. European Prison Rules, r 11(2) states that '[m]ales and Females shall in principle be detained separately, although they may participate together in organized activities as part of an established treatment program'. Although some have expressed support for mixed sex prisons, see P O'hAdhmaill, 'Sexual Apartheid in the Prison System' (1994) 28 Prison Report 26, others have argued strongly against this on the ground that it endangers women who may already have been the victims of male violence: see C Tchaikovsky, 'Mixed Prisons: Misogynistic and Misguided' (1991) 16 Prison Report 12.

[17] *Women in Prison: A Thematic Review* (London, 1997), paras 5.28–5.29.

intimidation and control during strip searching.'[18] However, the Chief Inspector was concerned at the continuing lack of staff training in strip searching female prisoners, and at the lack of any plans to adapt the instructions on the use of handcuffs to state that they should only be used in exceptional circumstances.[19]

Differences in Rule Application

While the same Prison Rules apply to men and women, they are not necessarily applied in the same way. The area of prison discipline is a good example of this. Women prisoners have traditionally been subject to more frequent disciplinary punishment than men. In 2000 male prisoners were subject to 163 disciplinary punishments per 100 population while for female prisoners the number was 256.[20] Studies have suggested that women prisoners are more likely to be put on report for swearing, talking back, or even self-mutilation than in men's prisons.[21] This in turn may reflect a different orientation to the use of formal disciplinary powers in women's prisons, more towards reinforcing images of 'proper women' than maintaining internal order. Similarly women prisoners appear more likely to be placed on rule 45 than male prisoners, though less likely to be on 'own protection' rule 45.[22] **11.06**

Education and work facilities are another area where the same rules may not produce the same results. Women prisoners have often argued that facilities available to them in these areas are inferior to those provided in mens' prisons.[23] **11.07**

B. Differences and Discrimination

Where differences are made however, either in the content of the rules or their application, then the question arises whether such differences amount to discrimination. In the *Alexander* case[24] the Home Office accepted that s 20(1) of the Race Relations Act 1976, relating to the provision of 'goods, facilities and services', **11.08**

---

[18] *Follow-up to Women in Prison: A Thematic Review* (London, 2000), para 2.33.

[19] ibid, paras 2.29 and 2.32.

[20] See *Prison Statistics: England and Wales 2000* (Cm 5250, 2001) 145. In 1994 the figures were 207 and 262 respectively. A similar disparity exists between male and female young offenders centres, the 2000 figures being 357 and 383 respectively.

[21] See R Dobash, R Dobash and S Gutteridge, *The Imprisonment of Women* (Oxford, 1986) 146; also A Manderaka-Sheppard, *The Dynamics of Aggression in Women's Prisons in England* (Aldershot, 1986), ch 3.

[22] According to the *Prison Statistics 1995* (Cm 3355, 1996) female prisoners were on 'governor's decision' r 43 (now r 45) at a rate of 1.06/100 and male 0.66/100 (21 to 351), while for 'own protection' r 43 (now r 45) the rates were 0.55/100 for women and 1.70 for men (11 to 894). More recent statistics are not currently available.

[23] Although the Chief Inspector's report does not comment on this issue, it does recommend a better assessment of the specific education and training needs of women prisoners: *Women in Prison: A Thematic Review* (London, 1997), para 10.07.

[24] *Alexander v Home Office* [1988] 2 All ER 118.

applied to prisons and the provision of a job in prison came within this statutory definition. It appears therefore that the similar section of the Sex Discrimination Act 1975[25] would equally apply to prisons such that women provided with goods, facilities, and services on a basis that is 'less favourable' than that provided to men (or vice versa)[26] would be entitled to claim discrimination. However whereas claims of racial discrimination usually arise from alleged differential treatment *within* a single prison the separation of male from female prisoners means that claims of sex discrimination can only arise as *between* prisons. Prisons can argue that they are providing services only to men or women and therefore cannot be accused of providing them on a less favourable basis to one sex. Although some American women prisoners have successfully challenged differential access to work and education programmes[27] there do not appear to have been similar challenges in the United Kingdom. Establishing that a computer course is available at a male prison five miles away does not mean that there is discrimination where the authorities fail to provide a similar course at a women's prison, since there may be a significant level of difference in the facilities available at comparable men's prisons. The issue may be more interestingly posed at the small number of prisons (currently four) where the women's prison is located on the same site as a male prison. Even here any claim against the governor of the women's prison would fail as that prison could not be accused of discriminating against women. Whether a claim against the Prison Service would have more success remains uncertain, as the Prison Service could still argue that comparisons across rather than within facilities cannot be made. At this point the issue arises whether women prisoners could have access to the course or work activity offered to men. Rule 11(2) of the European Prison Rules clearly envisages this possibility and the Committee for the Prevention of Torture (CPT) has welcomed some degree of mixed gender association in prison[28] but although some experimental 'mixing' of men and women for education and recreation activities occurred at Risley prison[29] the

---

[25] Sex Discrimination Act 1975, s 29(1). Section 29(2)(d) of this Act gives education as one of the examples of the sorts of facilities and services covered by the statute.

[26] See Sex Discrimination Act 1975, ss 1(1), 2.

[27] See B Bershad, 'Discriminatory Treatment of the Female Offender in the Criminal Justice System' (1985) 26 Boston College L Rev 389. However recently US courts have been unsure as to what level of scrutiny should be applied in respect of equality claims by women prisoners. In *Klinger v Nebraska Department of Correctional Services*, 31 F 3d 727 (8th Cir 1994) the Court of Appeals took the view that women prisoners were not 'similarly situated' to male prisoners so that equality claims were inappropriate. However in *Women Prisoners of the District of Columbia Department of Corrections v District of Columbia*, 877 F Supp 634 (DDC 1994) the court found that given similar custody levels and sentence structures, female prisoners in the District of Columbia could be compared with male equivalents and went on to find equal protection violations in respect of work and education programmes.

[28] '[P]rovided that the prisoners agree to participate and are adequately supervised' 10th Annual Report, para 24 CPT/Inf (2000) 13.

[29] Though Home Secretary Michael Howard recommended the ending of this when it came to public notice: see The Guardian, 5 April 1995.

Prison Service appear to take the view that it is ruled out, or at least strongly discouraged, by Prison Rule 12(1).

Differences in rule application could also be susceptible of challenge by way of **11.09** judicial review on the ground that such different treatment was 'unreasonable'. Thus far, however, the judiciary has not shown much interest in facilitating this approach. In the Northern Irish case of *In re Spence*[30] the prisoner challenged a practice of the Northern Ireland Prison Service whereby female prisoners serving 12 years and more were considered eligible for pre-release home leave 24 months before their earliest date for release as opposed to 12 months for male prisoners. The case is particularly interesting in that although most of the formally declared aspects of 'different treatment' in the Prison Service favour women, few discrimination claims have been brought by men. McCollum J appeared to have little difficulty in holding that the authorities did act reasonably on the grounds that women were recognized as having greater family responsibilities but adding that he would have found the decision reasonable even if made for purely administrative reasons. In an interesting dictum however he added that he was of the opinion that some aspects of failure to recognize differences between male and female prisoners in applying the rules, such as in relation to security measures,[31] might be unfair.

The European Convention on Human Rights (ECHR), and its incorporation **11.10** into UK law, might offer a further avenue for raising equality claims. However, the Convention's equality guarantee, Article 14, is limited to the avoidance of discrimination as this relates to other rights guaranteed by the Convention. Nevertheless women could argue that blanket restrictions on visits or home leave (which implicate Article 8's guarantees of family life) are discriminatory if applied to them but based on assumptions (regarding security and the risk of escape) which only apply to male prisoners. The European Court of Human Rights (ECtHR) has been prepared to find discrimination where men and women are treated differently based on unjustified assumptions about women,[32] but it is not clear whether it would be prepared to find likewise where unjustified assumptions result in men and women being treated the same.[33] The domestic case law on this issue has yet to develop.

---

[30] [1993] NILR 97.
[31] ibid, 101.
[32] *Schuler and Zgraggen v Switzerland* Series A No 263 (1994) 16 EHRR 405.
[33] For a discussion see S Livingstone, 'Article 14 and the Prevention of Discrimination in the European Convention on Human Rights' [1997] 1 European Human Rights L Rev 25 and R Clayton and H Tomlinson, *The Law of Human Rights* (Oxford, 2000 and supplements).

C. Medical Care, Pregnancy, and Children in Prison

11.11   Medicine has always played a particularly prominent role in the lives of women in prison. The 'medical model' of prison regimes, whereby prisoners are seen as ill and in need of treatment, was even more readily accepted in relation to women prisoners in the 1960s and 1970s, leading notably to the reconstruction of Holloway prison as a psychiatric facility.[34] However, despite the accepted failure of that model as a means of dealing with all or most women prisoners there does not appear to have been any attempt by the Prison Service to examine the specific health needs of women prisoners. While the National Health Service in recent years has moved towards the recognition that women have specific health needs and towards the principle of allowing women the choice of access to a female medical practitioner, the Chief Inspector's report found that this was not fully implemented in the Prison Service.[35] In general the Chief Inspector's report noted a failure in the Prison Service to confront specific health issues relating to women and urged that there should be a specific healthcare standard on women's health. Such a standard has still not been produced. However, in his follow-up review the Chief Inspector did notice some improvements in healthcare for women prisoners, with the introduction of well woman clinics and an improvement in the access of women prisoners to female doctors. Mental health issues remained a major concern.

11.12   One area where the specific health needs of women are given recognition within the prison system is in relation to pregnancy and initial childcare. Where a prisoner who is pregnant is likely to give birth shortly before release, then Standing Orders indicate that arrangements should be made for her early release or transfer to a local hospital to give birth. They also suggest that particular care should be taken when reporting the birth to the Register of Births that the place of birth is not given as a prison establishment. The conditions under which pregnant women are taken to hospital gave rise to considerable public controversy when it emerged that post-Woodcock and Learmont recommendations were being applied to pregnant prisoners so that they attended hospital shackled to a prison officer.[36] Revised instructions have now been issued, in amendments to the security manual, which indicate that all restraints should be removed when a pregnant woman prisoner arrives at the hospital for an ante-natal clinic unless there is

---

[34] For a general discussion see J Sim, *Medical Power in Prisons* (Buckingham, 1990), ch 6.

[35] *Women in Prison: A Thematic Review* (London, 1997), para 9.24, where it is observed that women will often face significant delays if they insist on being seen by a female doctor or nurse. In its 10th Annual Report the CPT also indicated a need to ensure that healthcare for women is supplied by medical practitioners and nurses with specific training in women's health issues.

[36] 'The Shame I felt in Chains', The Guardian, 11 January 1996.

recognized to be a particularly high risk of escape.[37] The prisoner should normally be escorted to hospital by two female officers but they should not be present in the delivery room or where an intimate examination is taking place unless requested to be so by the prisoner. The Order also indicates that the birthing partner should be permitted to attend the birth where the governor feels this poses no risk to security or safety. As with medical care in outside hospitals generally the whole issue of the conditions in which pregnant prisoners are treated raises questions as to the legitimate sphere of the prison's authority and that of the doctor. While the prisoner remains in the custody of the prison authorities even while in an outside hospital they would arguably be failing in their duty of care to the prisoner if they allowed considerations of security to override a doctor's recommendations as to the conditions in which she or he needed to treat a pregnant patient.

Mother and Baby Units

Following the birth of a baby to a prisoner (or where a woman with a very young child is detained in prison) she may apply to keep the baby in a Mother and Baby Unit.[38] Prison Rule 12(2) entitles the Secretary of State to permit a female offender to have her baby in prison with her 'subject to any conditions he thinks fit'. Currently four mother and baby units exist, with a total capacity of 68 children. The units in Holloway and New Hall accommodate children up to nine months while those in Styal and Askham Grange can accommodate children up to 18 months old. PSO 4801[39] indicates that a range of factors should be taken into account in deciding whether to admit a mother and child to the unit.[40] These include whether it is in the best interest of the child to be placed in a mother and baby unit, whether the mother is able to demonstrate behaviour and attitude which is not detrimental to the safety and well-being of other Unit residents, or the good order and discipline of the unit, whether the mother has provided a urine sample which tests negative for drugs, and whether the mother's ability and eligibility to care for a child is not impaired by health or legal reasons. The PSO stresses that each case must be considered on an individual basis. In order to secure admission to the unit a mother must sign an agreement to accept the conditions of admission to the unit. These include a commitment to be drug free and to permit

11.13

---

[37] PSI 05/97, amending *Security Manual*, para 60.25. US courts have indicated that shackling pregnant prisoners during and immediately after labour would violate the Eighth Amendment: see *Women Prisoners of the District of Columbia Department of Corrections v District of Columbia*, 877 F Supp 634 (DDC 1994), 668–669b.

[38] For a detailed history of the system of mother and baby units, and an analysis of the ways in which the system, as it stood in 1999, needed improvement, see HM Prison Service, *Report of a Review of Principles, Policies and Procedures on Mothers and Babies/Children in Prison* (London, 1999). This was followed by HM Prison Service, *Response and Action Plan* (December 1999).

[39] PSO 4801, 'The Management of Mother and Baby Units and the Application Process.' See also the Prison Service Standard on Mother and Baby Units.

[40] PSO 4801, para 3.5.

her baby to be searched where the governor considers that this is necessary. The prisoner's security classification is also relevant. Under the previous guidance, prisoners classified Category A were normally refused admission to a unit.[41] In *R v Home Secretary, ex p Togher*[42] the Court of Appeal refused leave for a judicial review challenge by a prisoner with a two-month-old child who had been classified 'provisional Category A' in relation to a drugs importing charge and refused access to the mother and baby unit while on remand at Holloway. Despite medical advice, given at the time of the prisoner's arrest, that it would be inappropriate to separate the mother from a child she was still breast feeding, Hirst LJ took the view that the Secretary of State had not acted unreasonably after evidence was given that the prisoner was suspected of being part of a drugs smuggling organization with sufficient contacts to mount an escape attempt in which violence might be used. PSO 4801 does not specifically mention security category, though it is highly likely that that will continue to be a relevant factor in allocating prisoners to mother and baby units.

11.14   Once a mother and baby have been admitted to a unit a multi-disciplinary team including the prison medical officer and a child psychologist should draw up a plan for both mother and child. The mother retains parental responsibility for the child under s 3(1) of the Children Act 1989 while it is in the unit and she should hold the child's personal health record card. Any medical treatment of the child should only take place with the mother's consent.

11.15   Prison Service guidance indicates that a mother should only be removed from a mother and baby unit where the governor feels that because of a disciplinary offence or blatant or persistent misconduct it is no longer possible for the mother to remain in the unit.[43] It appears also that a positive drug test or failure to allow the baby to be searched may also be grounds for removal from the unit. In *R v Home Secretary, ex p Hickling*[44] a mother challenged her removal from a mother and baby unit at Askham Grange to Bullwood Hall, which did not have a unit and which resulted in her child being taken into care. The governor of Askham Grange had taken this action on the ground that the mother had committed several disciplinary offences, and he took the view that her conduct was having a detrimental effect on both her baby and the others in the unit. In rejecting a challenge based on procedural unfairness and unreasonableness grounds the Divisional Court noted that the governor had consulted a paediatrician and given the prisoner several opportunities to modify her conduct. Even though the paedi-

---

[41]   One exception was made to this in respect of Roisin McAliskey, who was remanded pending extradition proceedings in relation to an alleged IRA attack in Germany. However Ms McAliskey did not return to prison following the birth of her child.

[42]   1 February 1995, LEXIS Transcript.

[43]   PSO 4801.

[44]   [1986] 1 FLR 543.

atrician had felt ideally that the child should remain with the mother, the governor's decision in the light of other considerations as to security and the operation of the unit was felt sufficient to dismiss any claims that he had acted unreasonably.

The *Hickling* case predates the United Kingdom's ratification of the UN **11.16** Convention on the Rights of the Child. Article 3(1) of this indicates that in all actions by state authorities the 'best interests of the child shall be a primary consideration'. This suggests that a decision by a governor to remove a mother and child from a unit purely on the basis of the mother's disciplinary record might violate the Convention (as well as raising improper purpose issues under judicial review). Current guidance indicates that a mother can be removed from the unit if she tests positive for drugs.[45] However to do this where a governor has not thought whether this poses any threat to the welfare of the child or to other children in the unit could be subject to challenge.[46] Similarly legal questions may arise over the power to search children, including strip searches. As discussed elsewhere Prison Rules clearly give a power to search prisoners, officers, and those entering or leaving a prison whenever they feel this to be necessary. Beyond this however they must fall back on common law search powers. These would suggest that a search of a child could only be justified when reasonable suspicion existed that something was concealed about the child. As with a commitment to a drug free environment a mother must give her consent to the child being searched as a condition of entering the unit. However given the coercive circumstances in which this consent is sought it must be wondered what weight it carries.

Even if a mother keeps to all the terms of the agreement with the unit, PSO 4801 **11.17** envisages that she will be separated from her baby at the age of 18 months, at the latest. The rigid nature of this policy was challenged by two female prisoners with babies in the case of *R (P and Q) v Home Secretary*.[47] Both were due to be separated from their babies at 18 months: P had a long sentence to serve and Q was serving a shorter sentence and had no realistic childcare alternatives. The Divisional Court refused their application for judicial review: it considered that the Prison Service was entitled to have a general policy, and that it has a wide discretion as to the facilities and services which it is prepared to provide for female prisoners and their babies. In an important judgment, the Court of Appeal allowed Q's appeal and made a number of observations on the operation of the policy. Giving the judgment of the court, Lord Phillips MR set out in detail the history and policy of MBUs and the research into the damaging effects of separating a mother and her young child. In a statement which shows that the Human Rights Act has made a

---

[45] PSO 4801, paras 6.2 and 6.3.

[46] It is worth noting that the maximum penalty for testing positive for drugs is 42 added days. To remove a mother who might have over a year to serve from the unit purely as a result of a disciplinary punishment might be seen as disproportionate.

[47] [2001] 1 WLR 2002, CA.

difference to the outcome of at least one prisoners' rights case, and that it may yet mark a cultural and legal shift, Lord Phillips said that:

> Before the introduction of a rights-based culture into English public law these appli-
> cations for judicial review would have been quite unarguable. A body charged with
> public law responsibilities has always been entitled to form a policy, and, so long as
> it is always alert to the possibility that the policy should be relaxed in any given case,
> it will be doing nothing unlawful if it applies the policy generally in the performance
> of its public law functions.[48]

However, Lord Phillips MR continued, cases such as *Daly*[49] show that interferences with a fundamental right must now be scrutinized closely by the court to see whether they are necessary and proportionate to the attainment of a legitimate aim. He then considered the Strasbourg case law on Article 8, noting in particular[50] that English courts may not come to the same results as the ECtHR and Commission since the margin of appreciation, which has saved a number of Article 8 infringements in Strasbourg, does not apply at the domestic level.[51] In reaching his conclusions, Lord Phillips MR agreed with the Divisional Court to the extent that the Prison Service is entitled to have a policy. He went on:

> The only question we have to decide is whether the Prison Service is entitled to oper-
> ate its policy in a rigid fashion, insisting that all children leave by the age of 18
> months at the latest (give or take a few weeks if their mother is about to be released),
> however catastrophic the separation may be in the case of a particular mother and
> child, however unsatisfactory the alternative placement available for the child, and
> however attractive the solution of combining day care outside prison with remain-
> ing in prison with the mother.
>   In our view the policy must admit of greater flexibility than that. We say so for
> two interrelated reasons. The first is that the policy's own declared aim, both in gen-
> eral and in individual cases, is to promote the welfare of the child. . . . We accept that
> this aim has to be set in the context of what prison and the Prison Service is all about.
> It cannot therefore . . . be the only aim. But, if the effect of the policy upon an indi-
> vidual child's welfare will be catastrophic, the policy is not fulfilling its own objec-
> tives. The policy documents themselves contemplate the need for individual
> consideration.
>   The second reason is that the interference with the child's family life which the
> Prison Service has allowed and encouraged to develop must be justified under
> Article 8(2).[52]

---

[48] [56].

[49] [2001] 2 AC 532.

[50] In relation to *Ouinas v France* (1990) 65 DR 265, a case in which the applicant was serving a long sentence in a prison too far away for his daughter to visit him. The Commission expressed serious concern as to the lack of effort made by the prison authorities to move him closer to his daughter's home, but, taking into account the margin of appreciation, concluded that the measure was not disproportionate (277–278).

[51] [75].

[52] [100]–[102].

In the case of P, who had a long sentence yet to serve and would, therefore, inevitably be separated from her child at some point, the separation at 18 months was held not to be disproportionate. In the case of Q, however, since she had a short time left to serve and since the child, if separated, would suffer from a lack of stable childcare, the separation was held not to be justified.

As well as being an important indication of the domestic courts' approach to **11.18** Article 8 issues in prison, the case is of practical importance to mothers facing separation from their babies. Their cases must now be considered on a much more individualized basis, and the 18 month limit cannot be considered absolute. In practice, those with long sentences are still likely to be separated from their child at around 18 months, but for mothers with shorter sentences, the Prison Service may now have to find more flexible ways to keep them and their child together.

12

RELEASE FROM PRISON: FIXED TERM PRISONERS

For all prisoners the fundamental concern is when liberty will be regained. Most **12.01** prison systems have some mechanism whereby release can be achieved earlier than the sentence of the court would appear to demand, either by a scheme of automatic remission of sentence, or by selective release on parole, or both in combination.[1] In

---

[1] In almost every European jurisdiction there is a single early release mechanism rather than a parole and remission system working in tandem. In the US the parole system has been under attack for the past 15 years but no state has abolished parole altogether since 1984. Despite recent reforms, Canada retains a parole/remission scheme which most closely mirrors the pre-1991 system in England and Wales. In addition to the regular parole scheme in England and Wales, the Home Secretary, as part of the prerogative of mercy, has a discretion to recommend special remission of part of a prisoner's sentence, for example in recognition of outstanding bravery or assistance to the authorities. The exercise of this prerogative is subject to review by the courts, but should not be seen as a sentencing exercise: see *R (B) v Home Secretary* [2002] EWHC Admin 587.

this chapter we examine the law and practice which determines the early release of prisoners serving fixed term (determinate) sentences in England and Wales. Despite the passage of the Crime (Sentences) Act 1997 and the Crime and Disorder Act 1998, this area of law continues to be largely governed by the Criminal Justice Act 1991. In Chapters 13 and 14 we turn to examine the law and practice governing the release of mandatory and discretionary life sentence prisoners (including persons sentenced to be detained during Her Majesty's Pleasure). Before analyzing the provisions which affect determinate sentenced prisoners however we will examine how remission, and eventually parole, came to be standard features of a sentence of imprisonment. This exercise is not merely of historical interest. Many of the principles articulated by the courts in relation particularly to parole remain relevant as the courts continue to grapple with new laws affecting the administration of early release schemes. Finally, we consider current proposals for reform of the sentencing and parole framework, which may well bring about fundamental changes in the next few years.

A. The 19th Century Reforms[2]

12.02 The system of transporting English criminals to America before the Revolutionary War of Independence, and later to Australia in the 19th century, demonstrated the potential benefits of the early release of prisoners from a sentence served entirely in prison. Transportation involved a staged process of detention abroad in the colonies during which discipline was gradually eased. It culminated in the grant of a 'ticket of leave', an 'indulgence' dependent on good behaviour which enabled a convict to attain a large degree of freedom within the colony, though he could not leave until his sentence had ended. The success of the system convinced prison legislators that such a release scheme was not only practical but also cheaper than continued imprisonment to the end of the sentence.[3]

12.03 The phased abandonment of transportation, which began during the 1840s, and the introduction of the sentence of penal servitude in 1853, meant that new measures had to be designed to deal with the release in the home country of convicts

---

[2] Sean McConville's fascinating study of the development of the English prison system from 1750 to 1948, *A History of English Prison Administration* (London, 1981), is the basis for this summary of the gestation period of parole and remission. For a more recent analysis of the history of parole, the operation of the current system and the current proposals for reform, see R Hood and S Shute, 'The Changing Face of Parole in England and Wales—A Story of Well-intentioned Reforms and Some Unintended Consequences' in C Prittwitz et al (eds), *Festschrift für Klaus Lüderssen* (Baden-Baden, 2002).

[3] The 1779 Gaols Act had helped to establish imprisonment with hard labour as a standard punishment for felony. The 'discovery' of Australia by Cook led to the use of transportation to Australia, which began in 1787 and continued to be the mainstay of penal treatment for long term prisoners ('convicts') up until 1857.

who were previously subject to transportation. The issue of allowing convicts to be released at home was politically highly sensitive.[4] Prior to the 1850s a small number of convicts had been released directly from the Hulks either as a result of pardons or, in the case of those serving short sentences, upon the expiry of their sentences.[5] These convicts were those who were unfit for transportation, and a practice developed whereby they were recommended for pardons after serving half their sentences. But the idea of releasing at home large numbers of convicts before their sentences had ended was something which shocked and alarmed wide sections of the public, who were largely unaware that such a scheme had operated in the colonies under transportation.

During the early 1850s the guiding philosophy of the recently formed Directorate **12.04** of Convict Prisons under its Director, Sir Joshua Jebb, was to structure the sentence of penal servitude so as to keep alive 'an invigorating hope and a salutary dread at every stage of the progress of the prisoner'.[6] Jebb favoured a system of remission of sentence as the best means of sustaining the 'invigorating hope' in the heart of every convict but until 1857 his advice went unheeded by the Home Office. The passage of the 1857 Penal Servitude Act finally led to the establishment of a formal scheme whereby sentences of three years were subject to one sixth remission for good behaviour, the proportion gradually increasing so that sentences of 15 years or more were subject to one-third remission. Eligibility for remission depended on a system of good marks and conduct badges which gave

---

[4] In 1847 the Home Secretary, Sir James Graham, had warned reformers of the danger to public security if transportation was abandoned and replaced by releasing convicts at home: 'I fear that the British public, which has the expense, will lose all the benefit of annual relief to Society from the Transportation or Exile of Criminals, if yearly . . . the Ranks of the Thieves and Cutthroats are to be recruited by public servants from our Hulks and Gaols. The new System may be less expensive; but I doubt whether the Community will gain, if the value of Life and Property is to be considered' (quoted in Sean McConville, *A History of English Prison Administration* (London, 1981) vol i, 387).

[5] The American War of Independence brought an end to transportation in 1776 and so the Government invented the Hulks as an alternative. They were phased out in 1857. In the 1980s the Government resorted to using a former cross-channel ferry to house asylum seekers who were being detained pending a decision on their claims, an unfortunate reminder of Victorian values. Criminal Justice and Public Order Act 1994, s 100 provided for the Home Secretary to declare to be a prison a 'floating structure or part of such a structure'. This was designed to enable the Prison Service to use 'floating structures' as a contingency measure to relieve overcrowding. The first such 'prison ship' opened in Portland harbour in 1996.

[6] In 1842 Lord Stanley, the Colonial Secretary, had issued policy instructions in respect of the organization of the system of transportation indicating that he did not 'contemplate a state of things in which the convict, suffering under the sentence of the law, should ever be excluded from the hope of amending his condition by blameless or meritorious behaviour, or from the fear of enhancing the hardships of it by misconduct. On the contrary, to keep alive an invigorating hope and a salutary dread at every stage of the progress of the prisoner . . . appears to us to be an indispensable part of the discipline to which he should be subjected. Further, we contemplate the necessity of subjecting every convict to successive stages of punishment, decreasing rigour at each successive step, until he reaches that ultimate stage . . . of a pardon, either absolute or conditional, though not ever entitled to demand the indulgence of right' (quoted in Sean McConville, *A History of English Prison Administration* (London, 1981) vol i, 400).

public recognition of a prisoner's progress towards eventual early release on a ticket of leave.

12.05 Despite a moral panic in the late 1850s caused by an outbreak of garroting, which increased public alarm at the idea of unreformed convicts roaming the streets, the principle of early release survived the 1863 Royal Commission on Penal Servitude. But the Commission's recommendation that remission should be dependent not merely on good conduct but rather on the quantity of productive work achieved was accepted.[7] The remission scheme was amended several times during the last quarter of the 19th century. In 1891 it was fixed that male convicts would be eligible for one-quarter remission and female convicts for one-third. And in 1898 the anomaly that remission was only available to convicts and not to ordinary prisoners (who had been convicted of less serious offences) was ended.[8] There was, however, a difference between the terms of remission granted to prisoners and convicts. While ordinary prisoners were completely free from the day of their early release, convicts remained vulnerable to recall to prison until the end of their sentence if they were guilty of 'misconduct', even if this fell short of the commission of a criminal offence. In this sense, remission of a convict's sentence bore some resemblance to the later system of parole with its concept of a licence liable to be revoked in the event of any breach of its conditions.

B. Movement Towards a Parole System

12.06 For the next 40 years the early release of prisoners remained largely unaltered in its structure. In 1940 the pressure on prison places brought about by detention under wartime regulations led to an increase in remission for both prisoners and convicts to one-third. In 1948 penal servitude was abolished and with it went the convict licence.[9] From then on, apart from lifers or recidivists undergoing corrective training or preventive detention, all adult prisoners became eligible for release at their remission dates without being subject to any form of licence. In 1973 new rules provided that time spent on remand would attract remission as well as counting towards the length of sentence. Remission remained at one-third until in 1987 another period of intense pressure on prison places led to an announcement by the

---

[7] McConville comments that the marks system was primarily concerned with ensuring obedience and productivity and that reformation was viewed as an incidental benefit. He cites the remarks of the Directorate of Convict Prisons in 1867 to the effect that '[i]t is difficult, and indeed impossible, to express any decided opinion upon the real amount of good conduct effected upon the minds of the convicts by the efforts made for their reformation; secluded as they are from the world, they are more parts of a machine than free agents' (ibid, vol i, 403).

[8] The Gladstone Committee recommended that remission and the marks system should be extended to ordinary prisoners partly on the grounds of equity and partly for rehabilitative reasons.

[9] After the passage of the Criminal Justice Act 1948, under-21-year-olds and Borstal trainees remained subject to supervision under licence.

Home Secretary that for those serving sentences of 12 months or less, remission would be increased to 50 per cent.

While remission had been a consistent feature of imprisonment since the mid-19th century, a parole system is of relatively recent origin.[10] Unlike the United States, where a parole scheme was first introduced at New York's Elmira Reformatory in the 1870s, it was not until the passage of the Criminal Justice Act 1967 that prisoners became entitled to consideration for release on parole.[11] And whereas the American scheme was developed against a background of largely indeterminate sentencing, the scheme which was applied in England and Wales was implanted into a structure of almost exclusively fixed sentences with the 'parolable' portion precisely specified.[12] Prior to the introduction of parole, prisoners were able to be released for short periods for certain express purposes. This included visits to seriously ill relatives, funerals, work in outside jobs as discharge approached, or attending classes not provided by the prison system. In addition some prisoners could take home leave shortly before they were released as a means of re-establishing contact with families. But only a small proportion of the population qualified for these privileges. Parole, by contrast, was potentially available to all-comers.

12.07

C. The Criminal Justice Act 1967

The idea of a system based on the selection of prisoners suitable for early release on licence was of course not entirely new, as we have seen. The novelty was to extend it to all determinate sentenced prisoners. In the 1965 White Paper, *The Adult Offender* (which followed closely the passage of the Murder (Abolition of Death Penalty) Act 1965), it was proposed that a 'prisoner who has shown promise or determination to reform . . . should be able to earn a further period of freedom on parole [eg over and above the one-third remission] of up to one third of his sentence'. It went on to express the rehabilitative ideal that:

12.08

---

[10] The word 'parole' is derived from the French expression for 'word of honour'.

[11] 'In the initial American parole plan, youthful reformatory inmates were sentenced to indeterminate terms. Elmira's Board of Managers was authorized to parole anyone at any time after 1 year's confinement. An elaborate review process preceded the decision to approve or deny release on parole. Inmates were required to earn a specified number of marks in order to be eligible for parole. If released, individual offenders were expected to obey certain rules and to submit willingly to supervision by selected persons in the outside community. Failure of a parolee to obey the rules could result in return to Elmira' (quoted in Henry Burns, *Correctional Reform: Britain and the USA Compared and Contrasted* (1978)).

[12] The American system of indeterminate sentencing caused a substantial decline in the judiciary's sentencing role since parole boards were empowered to release an inmate at any time between the fixed minimum and maximum terms. In the absence of appeals against sentence, parole in the US has always had an explicit resentencing purpose.

prisoners who do not of necessity have to be detained for the protection of the public are in some cases more likely to be made into decent citizens if, before completing the whole of their sentence, they are released under supervision with a liability to recall if they do not behave. . . . What is proposed is that a prisoner's date of release should be largely dependent upon his response to training and his likely behaviour on release. A considerable number of long term prisoners reach a recognizable peak in their training at which they may respond to generous treatment but after which, if kept in prison, they may go downhill. . . . These arrangements would afford the strongest incentive to reform and greatly assist the task of prison administration.

The White Paper's proposals found expression in the Criminal Justice Act 1967, and the basic features of the scheme remained in place for the next 25 years. The Act provided for the appointment by the Home Secretary of a Parole Board and beneath it a network of Local Review Committees (LRCs).[13] Save in one respect, the function of the Board was advisory. The Board's duty was to advise the Home Secretary about the release on licence of determinate and life sentence prisoners, the conditions to be attached to such licences, and the recall to prison of prisoners whose cases were referred to the Board for consideration. It was assisted in its task by the LRCs, whose job it was to commence the process of reviewing the suitability for release on parole of every prisoner who had become eligible for it.[14] The only direct contact which a prisoner had with the reviewing process was a personal interview with a single member of the LRC to whom any representations had to be made. The LRC's report and recommendation would then be forwarded to the Parole Board for it to consider and make a recommendation. Finally the case would be referred to the Home Office Parole Unit where the ultimate decision would be taken, usually by civil servants but sometimes by the appropriate Minister, or even, in rare cases, by the Home Secretary personally. No reasons were given for a decision to refuse parole nor did a prisoner have any right of access to material before the various bodies considering his suitability for release on licence.[15]

12.09 The tripartite structure of Home Secretary, Parole Board, and LRC did not disguise the fact that in each case the ultimate responsibility for release remained with the Home Secretary under what was described as a 'dual key' system of responsibility. As the 1987 Carlisle Report observed, 'the Home Secretary could not grant parole without a positive recommendation from the Parole Board but

---

[13] See the Criminal Justice Act 1967, ss 59–62.

[14] The size and composition of LRCs varied from place to place but every panel considering cases had to include one of the prison governors, a probation officer from outside the prison, a member of the Board of Visitors, and two independent members chosen by the governor.

[15] See *Payne v Lord Harris of Greenwich* [1981] 1 WLR 754 and the Local Review Committee Rules 1967 (SI 1967/1462), which set out a comprehensive code governing the procedures for considering suitability for release on licence. The Court of Appeal in *Payne* held that the rules of natural justice did not require the code to be supplemented by any further implied duties or rights.

could deny parole even where a positive recommendation had been made'.[16] The one exception to the Board's purely advisory role was in the case of a prisoner recalled to prison following the revocation of his licence. If in such a case the Board recommended that person's immediate re-release, the Home Secretary was obliged to give effect to that recommendation.[17]

The parole system came into operation on 1 April 1968. Every prisoner serving a **12.10** determinate sentence became eligible for release on licence after he had served one-third of his sentence (including time spent on remand) or at least 12 months after sentence, whichever was the longer. The licence lasted until the day the prisoner would ordinarily have been released, that is, after serving two-thirds of his sentence. It followed that the minimum qualifying period (MQP) which the prisoner had to serve was 12 months before he could be released on parole even if he was eligible for parole after serving one-third (the remand time did not count towards the MQP).

D. The Scheme in Practice

From 1968 until 1983 the parole system operated without any significant alter- **12.11** ation to its fundamental principles. But, as the Carlisle Committee commented, it was not without its critics. The publication of the May Committee Report in October 1979 marked an important change away from the belief that prison could ever truly be rehabilitative.[18] The parole scheme had been conceived at a time when optimism was high that prison could change people for the better and that 'experts' could identify and select those prisoners best suited for early release. If prison could not reform people, what was the justification for a selective system of early release? A second factor was the twin assault from different wings of the political spectrum which attacked parole as either being 'soft on criminals' at a time when the crime rate continued to rise or, alternatively, too arbitrary and lacking in basic procedural fairness safeguards necessary to ensure that all prisoners were considered equally and on the basis of reliable, relevant information. As more and more prisoners were released on licence it became harder to resist the argument that parole could not be considered as a mere privilege, undeserving of

---

[16] *The Parole System in England and Wales*, Report of the Review Committee Chaired by Lord Carlisle of Bucklow QC (Cm 532, 1988).

[17] In *R v Chairman of the Parole Board, ex p Gunnell* (1985) Crim LR 105, the Court of Appeal held that anything short of a recommendation for immediate release meant that release remained a matter for the Secretary of State's discretion. Accordingly a recommendation for release subject to a satisfactory release plan did not bind the Home Secretary to order immediate release. Similarly, a recommendation for release after a prisoner has served a sentence imposed subsequent to his release on licence is not a binding recommendation for immediate release pursuant to s 39(5)(b); see *R v Home Secretary, ex p de Lara*, 22 March 1995, CO 748/95, Owen J.

[18] *Report of the Committee of Inquiry into the United Kingdom Prison Services* (Cmnd 7673, 1980).

the full panoply of the rules of natural justice.[19] Finally, the existence of the MQP for release on licence led to the anomaly that the great majority of prisoners serving less than two years had to stay in prison until they had served two-thirds of their sentence whereas those serving three or four years (or even longer) were gaining freedom after serving a third of their sentence. Why should prisoners sentenced for more serious crimes be eligible for release at an earlier stage than those sentenced for relatively minor ones?

12.12 This latter criticism was met by the passage of s 33 of the Criminal Justice Act 1982 which enabled the Home Secretary to reduce by order the 12 months minimum qualifying period for parole. The Act also gave the Home Secretary a power to order the release of certain categories of prisoners up to six months early where the consent of both Houses of Parliament was obtained. This 'executive release' power was a measure of last resort designed to avert any potential breakdown in the prison system threatened by overcrowding in local prisons. Section 33 was subsequently repealed by Criminal Justice Act 1991, s 101(2), Sch 13.

E. 1983: The Brittan Policy

12.13 In 1983 major changes to the parole system were announced by the new Home Secretary, Leon Brittan, in the course of his first speech to the Conservative Party Conference in Blackpool. Responding to what he described as 'growing public criticism about the gap between the length of sentence passed and the length of the sentence actually served' and a feeling that the public 'do want to know with certainty what will actually happen to the most serious offenders and . . . [that] what happens will reflect the gravity of the offences that have been committed', he indicated that he would in due course make a statement to Parliament setting out the new policy. This was done on 30 November 1983 when Mr Brittan announced three changes to the existing policy.[20] The first of these measures affected all prisoners serving more than five years for sexual offences or those involving drug trafficking, arson, or violence. In future, the Home Secretary said that he would use his discretion to ensure that such prisoners would be granted parole 'only when release under supervision for a few months before the end of a sentence is likely to reduce the long-term risk to the public, or in circumstances which are genuinely exceptional'. Only compelling reasons would lead to release on licence in the future, he said. The second change affected lifers convicted of the murder of police or prison officers, terrorist murderers, sexual or sadistic murderers of children, and murderers by firearm in the course of robbery. Such persons

---

[19] For further argument in favour of the extension of natural justice principles, see the evidence called in support of the applicant in *Payne v Lord Harris of Greenwich* [1981] 1 WLR 754.
[20] *Hansard* (series 6), vol xlix, Written Answers, cols 505–508 (1983).

would now expect to serve at least 20 years in custody, and other murderers, outside these categories, might merit equal treatment to mark the seriousness of the offence. The Home Secretary's statement made it clear that, although he would consult with the Parole Board about how these new policy objectives would be achieved in practice so that the Board's role was maintained, he had not consulted the Board in advance of the announcement. It was also made clear that the policy would be retrospective, and thus prisoners with release dates already identified were suddenly faced with the devastating destruction of their expectation of freedom. The policy changes were promptly challenged in the courts by four prisoners (two lifers and two serving fixed sentences) affected in this way, but the Home Secretary's right to alter his policy was upheld, finally, in the House of Lords.[21]

The third and final change announced by Mr Brittan was a liberalizing one. Using **12.14** the new power contained in s 33 of the Criminal Justice Act 1982, the Home Secretary reduced the minimum qualifying period for parole from 12 to six months with effect from 1 June 1984.[22] The effect of this was that whereas before only those serving a minimum of 19 and a half months could in practice attract parole, now those serving as little as ten and a half months were able to benefit. It meant that 2,500 more prisoners were out on parole at any one time.

F. The Carlisle Committee and the 1990 White Paper

Though it was the least controversial aspect of the Brittan policy changes at the **12.15** time of their announcement, it was the extension of parole to those serving six months which ultimately produced the greatest pressure for yet more reform and led to the setting up of a Review Committee under Lord Carlisle QC in July 1987. Only a year after the more liberal policy had come into force, the judiciary had begun to express its disquiet about the way in which parole was operating for those serving less than two years' imprisonment.[23] There were four main concerns. First, too many prisoners serving less than two years were being paroled. A rate of 75–80 per cent had turned parole into an entitlement rather than a privilege to be earned.

---

[21] *Re Findlay* [1985] 1 AC 318. The case reached the House of Lords after both the Divisional Court and the Court of Appeal had been divided over the lawfulness of the policy and its mode of implementation. See also the Court of Appeal's decision in *R v Home Secretary, ex p Hargreaves* [1997] 1 WLR 906 and K Markus and M Westgate, 'Unilever and Hargreaves: A Cross-Analysis' [1997] JR 220.

[22] Eligibility for Release on Licence Order 1983, SI 1983/1959.

[23] In the autumn of 1985 the Lord Chief Justice drew the attention of the Home Secretary to mounting concern among members of the judiciary about the way in which parole was operating for those sentenced to less than two years' imprisonment. A working group proposed a number of administrative changes to ensure that more information was available to LRCs when considering cases. It also proposed that the presumption in favour of parole which the Home Office and the Parole Board had asked LRCs to apply in under two-year cases should be withdrawn and all cases, irrespective of sentence length, be considered on the basis of relative risks and benefits.

Secondly, the lower six-month minimum qualifying period meant that prisoners serving anything between nine and 18 months came out in practice on the same day, just as before those serving between 18 months and three years were freed at the same time. Since there were far more prisoners serving between nine and 18 months and far more were granted parole, the anomaly was simply exacerbated. Thirdly, the expansion of parole had undermined the partly suspended sentence introduced by the Criminal Justice Act 1982 in that prisoners who had received an unsuspended sentence frequently emerged earlier from prison than those subject to partial suspension. Finally, the rule that time spent on remand counted towards both the total sentence and the one-third to be served for parole eligibility but not towards the MQP created anomalies which were made the greater by the reduction in 1983 of the MQP. There were also significant practical consequences for the work of the Parole Board and the LRCs, whose case-load increased dramatically.[24] It was widely felt that a system of selective release on licence for short-term prisoners had become unworkable.

12.16 It was against this background of judicial concern and administrative strain that the Carlisle Committee was appointed with a remit 'to examine the operation of the parole scheme in England and Wales, its relationship with the current arrangements for remission, time spent in custody on remand, and partly and fully suspended sentences and their effect on the time which offenders sentenced to imprisonment spend in custody'. With the announcement in July 1987 that remission was to be increased to 50 per cent for those serving 12 months or less, there was an ever increasing discrepancy between the prospects of early release for prisoners serving relatively short sentences and those long-term prisoners subject to the strictures of the 1983 Brittan policy. The Carlisle Committee identified the problem as one which had gone to the heart of the parole system as a whole, pointing out that 'there has in some quarters been the feeling that parole for those serving 2 years or more (something loosely referred to as "section 60 parole") is the real thing and parole for those serving less than 2 years ("section 33 parole") something different'.[25] It concluded that the introduction of 50 per cent remission for those serving 12 months or less and the lowering of the minimum qualifying period for parole had created an unacceptable disparity between what sentences say and what they mean. The effect of parole and remission, taken together, had over the years

---

[24] In 1983 only 265 prisoners serving less than two years were considered for parole whereas in 1986 it was 10,603. By 1991 the Board and LRCs were considering 33,000 cases in all and, though parole was more sparingly granted to long term prisoners as a result of the Brittan policy, the entitlement to be reviewed after a third of the sentence remained unchanged. As a result many prisoners stayed in prison for longer and had more reviews than before.

[25] 'Section 60' was a reference to s 60 of the Criminal Justice Act 1967, which provided the power for prisoners serving determinate sentences to be released on licence by the Home Secretary. Strictly all parole cases were s 60 cases but the term was used loosely to describe those cases which were not handled under the streamlined s 33 procedure introduced by the Criminal Justice Act 1982, which was applicable to all sentences below two years.

'created an increasing unreality in the criminal justice system and handed to the executive too much control over the length of custodial sentences served'.[26]

Quite apart from the anomalies resulting from the different way in which parole **12.17** and remission affected sentences of different length, there was an increasing volume of criticism from a wide range of opinion which questioned the obsessive secrecy surrounding the process of parole decision-making, its arbitrariness and lack of fairness. There was also fierce criticism of the effect of the Brittan policy on long-term and life sentence prisoners. The Carlisle Committee summed this up in the following terms:

> [B]y making the change administratively, rather than by inviting Parliament to amend the law, the Home Secretary had modified the criteria for parole without being able to adjust the actual eligibility rules. Thus everyone still had to be reviewed after only a third of the sentence and to preserve the legality of the policy the Home Secretary had to make it clear that parole would still be granted in exceptional cases. This meant that prisoners, prison staff, probation staff, the Parole Board, the LRCs and indeed the Home Office itself were all required to go through a process which in the vast majority of cases was entirely nugatory. Not only was this wasteful of everyone's time but for the prisoner and his family it was positively harmful. The prisoner, though knowing his chances were slim, normally felt unable to get out of the process for fear of prompting his family to conclude that he did not really want to come home. His family were inevitably encouraged by the mere fact of a visit from the home probation officer to think that release was a real possibility. As a result, when parole was refused, as it almost invariably was, the relationship between inmates and their families was frequently damaged.[27]

Against this background the Carlisle Committee made a number of wide-ranging recommendations, the most important of which were that:

(1) The MQP should be abolished and replaced with a minimum qualifying sentence for parole. Parole should be available only to those sentenced to more than four years with the parole eligibility date fixed at one-half of sentence rather than one-third. Misconduct in prison should delay both the parole eligibility date and the release date if parole is not granted. Those not granted parole should continue to be released after two-thirds of sentence, subject to any disciplinary awards for misconduct.

(2) All prisoners sentenced to more than four years should be subject to a period of supervision on release until the three-quarters point of their sentence.

(3) All prisoners sentenced to four years' imprisonment or less should be required to serve half of the sentence in custody, plus any additional days for misconduct in prison, and half in the community.

---

[26] *The Parole System in England and Wales*, Report of the Review Committee Chaired by Lord Carlisle of Bucklow QC (Cm 532, 1988), para 194.
[27] ibid, para 172.

(4) Remission should be abolished.

(5) All released prisoners, whatever the length of their sentences, should be liable, if convicted of another offence punishable with imprisonment committed before the end of the original sentence, to be ordered by the court to serve part or all of the portion of that sentence outstanding in addition to any new custodial sentence imposed.

(6) The parole decision should be based on a more specific test with the criteria for parole prescribed by statute. The decision-making process should be more open, with disclosure of reports to prisoners (save in highly exceptional cases) and the giving of meaningful reasons for a refusal to grant parole.

(7) The Home Secretary's responsibility for releasing determinate sentence prisoners on licence should cease and the decision to release prisoners on parole should be taken by the Parole Board alone. With the greatly reduced work-load of the Parole Board, LRCs should be abolished.[28]

12.18 The 1990 White Paper, *Crime, Justice and Protecting the Public*, had at its core the aim of ensuring that convicted criminals are punished according to the seriousness of the offence so that 'they get their just deserts'.[29] It generally accepted the recommendations of the Carlisle Report, save in two important respects.[30] It did not agree that the Home Secretary should withdraw completely from the responsibility for decisions to release all determinate sentenced prisoners, but instead expressed the view that he should continue to consider the release of those serving very long determinate sentences of seven years or more, who will necessarily have committed very serious crimes. It also rejected the proposal that reports before the Parole Board should be disclosed to prisoners. It did so on the somewhat dubious grounds that 'the likely benefits of greater openness outweigh its disadvantages' since 'there is a risk that openness could lead to less full and telling reports and so to less well informed decisions'.[31]

---

[28] The work of the Parole Board, and the extent to which it is achieving the results expected by the Carlisle Committee, was considered by R Hood (who was on the Carlisle Committee) and S Shute in 'Parole Decision-making: Weighing the Risk to the Public', Home Office Research, Development and Statistics Directorate Research Findings No 114. After detailed research, they concluded that the Carlisle Committee 'expected that, by moving the eligibility date forward from one-third to a half of the sentence, and by providing supervision for all prisoners whether paroled or not, a higher, not a lower, proportion of prisoners would be granted parole. This has not happened. While the findings of this research show that parole decisions are in line with the Home Secretary's Directions, these Directions, together with the Board's interpretation of them, have undoubtedly created a more risk-averse approach than originally expected by the Carlisle Committee. It will always be necessary to strike a balance between the risk to the public and the liberty that might be accorded to the individual prisoner. These findings question whether the right balance has been found.'

[29] Cm 965, 1990.

[30] ibid, para 6.11.

[31] ibid, para 6.26.

Neither the Carlisle Committee nor the White Paper dealt specifically with the **12.19** position of life sentence prisoners. But two important decisions by the European Court of Human Rights (ECtHR) ensured that the procedure for dealing with the release and subsequent recall of those prisoners given a discretionary life sentence would have to be amended in the light of a finding that English law was in breach of Article 5(4) of the European Convention on Human Rights (ECHR).[32] (We deal with these changes in Chapter 14, which examines in detail the release procedures governing discretionary lifers and persons detained during Her Majesty's Pleasure.) The pressure for widespread reform of the system governing the early release of prisoners culminated in the passage of the Criminal Justice Act 1991, an Act which remains in force to a significant extent despite the passage of the Crime (Sentences) Act 1997 ('the 1997 Act'), the Crime and Disorder Act 1998 ('the 1998 Act') and the Powers of Criminal Courts (Sentencing) Act 2000 ('the 2000 Act').

The 1997 Act was one of the final legislative initiatives of the Conservative **12.20** Government. As such, it sought to implement the provisions of the 1996 White Paper, *Protecting the Public—the Government's Strategy on Crime in England and Wales*.[33] The Act contained several highly controversial provisions, including those designed to introduce mandatory minimum sentences for certain offences (these were compared to the notorious American 'three-strikes' provisions).[34] Of particular note in the context of early release from prison, however, was the Act's attempt to introduce 'honesty in sentencing'. The White Paper stated that:

> The Government believes that the sentence passed by the court should mean what it says. Accordingly, the Government proposes that the present early release provisions should be abolished . . . prisoners will have to earn early release by co-operation and positive good behaviour. No part of this will be granted as of right.[35]

---

[32] *Weeks v UK* (1988) 10 EHRR 293, and *Thynne, Wilson and Gunnell v UK* (1991) 13 EHRR 666. The release and recall of prisoners subject to a mandatory life sentence will, of course, also have to be amended in light of the decision of the ECtHR in *Stafford v UK* Application 46295/99 (2002) 35 EHRR 32.

[33] Cm 3190, 1996.

[34] Now contained in the Powers of Criminal Courts (Sentencing) Act 2000. However, the extent to which these sentences are 'mandatory' has been greatly reduced by the decision of the Court of Appeal in *R v Offen* [2001] 1 WLR 253. Under the Crime (Sentences) Act 1997, mandatory sentences were to be imposed for the second 'serious offence' other than in 'exceptional circumstances'. However, taking into account Arts 3 and 5 of the ECHR, and the prohibition on arbitrary detention, the court held that, in every case where a defendant did not pose an unacceptable risk to the public, the position was to be considered 'exceptional'. This example of creative judicial use of the Human Rights Act (HRA) can hardly be what the Conservative Government expected when enacting those provisions, but is, it is submitted, essential to prevent the mandatory sentences from violating the Convention.

[35] (Cm 3190, 1996), 44. The relevant provisions can be found in ss 10–28 of the 1997 Act but the Labour Government has indicated it does not intend to implement them—see SI 1997/2200.

The terms of the 1997 Act were heavily criticized by both members of the judiciary and the academic community. Speaking during the Second Reading of the Bill in the House of Lords, Lord Bingham of Cornhill stated that 'if, as the century and the millennium slide to a close, our penal thinking is to be judged by the thinking which animates this Bill, then I for one will shrink from the judgment of history'. DA Thomas further characterized the Act as representing 'a low point in the development of English sentencing legislation'.[36] Almost certainly with these criticisms in mind, the Labour Government has, to date, implemented only a fraction of the 1997 Act's provisions.[37] In a written answer delivered on 30 July 1997, the Home Secretary explained his decision not to activate the 1997 Act's provisions in relation to early release stating that:

> [T]he same effect can be achieved in a far more clear and straightforward way by ensuring that judges and magistrates spell out in open court what the sentence they have imposed really means in practice.[38]

The consequence is that the law continues to be governed primarily by the 1991 Act, although, as noted, the Crime and Disorder Act has resulted in some changes to the 1991 position. The relevant provisions of the 1991 Act are considered below, before turning to current proposals for reform of the system.

G. The Criminal Justice Act 1991: A Summary

12.21 The 1991 Act, as amended, impacts in different ways on determinate sentence prisoners depending on whether they are serving less than four years or four years or more.[39] Transitional provisions apply to deal with the position of prisoners sentenced prior to 1 October 1992, when the Act came into force.

Short Term Prisoners (Less than Four Years)

(1) They must be released after serving half their sentence unconditionally if the sentence is for less than 12 months (s 33(1)(a)) and on licence if the sentence is for 12 months or more (s 33(1)(b)).

---

[36] See DA Thomas, 'The Crime (Sentences) Act 1997' (1998) Crim LR 83. Clarkson further described the terms of the 1997 Act as 'vote-catching provisions' which should be 'left to rot on the shelf and never brought into operation'. See CMV Clarkson, 'Beyond Just Deserts: Sentencing Violent and Sexual Offenders' (1997) 36 Howard J 284 at 292.

[37] See SI 1997/2200.

[38] *Hansard*, HC col 262 (30 July 1997).

[39] It is interesting to note that in *Roy Ensley* [1996] 1 Cr App R (S) 294, the Court of Appeal held that where a sentencer decides, in light of the gravity of an offence committed by two offenders and their respective antecedents, that the proper sentence for one offender is less than four years and for the other four years or more, the fact that one offender will be a 'short term prisoner' and the other a 'long term prisoner' (and therefore required to serve a greater proportion of the sentence) does not give rise to unjustified disparity of sentence.

(2) The Secretary of State has the power to release on licence short term prisoners serving more than three months but less than 12 months provided such prisoners have served a requisite period. Thus, where a prisoner is sentenced for a term of three months or more but less than four months, he may be released on licence after serving 30 days. Where the sentence imposed is for four months or more but less than eight months, the prisoner may be released after serving a period equivalent to one-quarter of the term. And, finally, where a prisoner is sentenced to a term of eight months or more (but less than 12 months) a period that is 60 days less than one-half of the term is to be served before the prisoner may be released on licence. Such release licences are to include 'curfew conditions' which essentially require that any person released on licence remains, for periods of time to be specified in the licence, at a set location. Curfew conditions remain in force until the date when the released person would (but for his release) have served one-half of his sentence, and breach of a curfew condition may lead to the Secretary of State revoking the prisoner's licence and the prisoner being recalled to prison (ss 34A and 37A, inserted by the Crime and Disorder Act 1998).[40]

(3) A short term prisoner may be returned to prison by a court if he commits any offence punishable with imprisonment before the date on which he would (but for his release) have served his sentence in full (Powers of Criminal Courts (Sentencing) Act 2000, s 116, which reproduces s 40 of the 1991 Act). He may be ordered to return for the whole or any part of the period which (a) begins with the date of the order, and (b) is equal in length to the period between the date on which the new offence was committed and the date on which he would (but for his release) have served the original sentence of imprisonment in full. A magistrates' court does not have the power to order such a person to be returned to prison for a period of more than six months, but may commit him on bail or in custody to the Crown Court, which may return him to prison for up to the periods set out in (a) and (b).

(4) A person returned to prison under s 116 is to be released on licence from prison after serving one-half of the sentence imposed so long as that sentence is for 12 months or less. Where the person is so released the licence is to remain in force for a period of three months, during which time breach of the licence conditions can result in either (a) the imposition of a fine or (b) a sentence of imprisonment (made up of the time between the breach of the licence condition and the expiry date of the licence) (s 34A, as added by the Crime and Disorder Act 1998).

---

[40] The operation of the HDC system is set out in more detail in Ch 7, paras 7.66–7.77.

(5) A short term prisoner's licence shall (unless revoked or suspended) remain in force until the date on which he would (but for his release) have served three-quarters of his sentence (s 37(1)).

(6) A short term prisoner sentenced for an offence committed after 1 January 1999, or a long term prisoner who has been released on licence may have his licence revoked by the Secretary of State and be returned to prison, either on the recommendation of the Parole Board, or without such a recommendation if it appears to the Secretary of State that it is expedient in the public interest to recall that person before such a recommendation is practicable. A person who is recalled may make representations in writing, and must, on his return to prison, be informed of the reasons for his recall and of his right to make representations (s 39).[41] The Home Secretary must refer to the Parole Board the case of a prisoner who is either recalled under s 39(2) or who is recalled under s 39(1) and who makes representations about it (s 39(4)) and where the Board recommends his immediate release on licence the Home Secretary must give effect to the recommendation.[42]

(7) A short term prisoner may be released on licence on compassionate grounds at any time and the Parole Board need not be consulted by the Secretary of State (s 36(1) and (2)).

---

[41] Before the Crime and Disorder Act 1998, s 39 applied only to long term prisoners, with the recall of short term prisoners covered by s 38 of the 1991 Act. Section 38 still applies to short term prisoners sentenced for an offence committed before 1 January 1999. The decision to apply the same system to the recall of both long and short term determinate sentence prisoners brings some welcome consistency into this complex area of the law.

[42] In *R (Banks) v Home Secretary* [2002] EWHC Admin 381, the claimant, who had been recalled and whose release the Parole Board refused to recommend, argued that the entire s 39 recall process was incompatible with Arts 5(4) and 6 of the ECHR. The Divisional Court (Simon Brown LJ and Goldring J) dismissed the application. They considered that, where detention followed conviction and a determinate sentence and where the sentence was based on the seriousness of the offence, Art 5(4) was satisfied by the trial process and any appeal. Moreover, Art 6 had no application to the case. The process of revocation of a licence was one of administrative recall and did not involve the determination of civil rights and obligations, or of a criminal charge, within the meaning of Art 6(1). This case, clearly a justifiable interpretation of the Strasbourg case law, highlights the limitations of the Convention in providing procedural protections in the realm of administrative decision-making. It will be interesting to see whether the ECtHR's judgment in *Ezeh and Connors* leads to an extension of the role of Art 6 in this context. *Banks* was applied by Turner J in *R (West) v Parole Board* [2002] EWHC Admin 769, to similar effect. See also *R (Akhtar) v Home Secretary* [2001] EWHC Admin 38. The same result was reached in Scotland: see *Varey v Scottish Ministers* (2001) SC 162. Nor will domestic administrative law usually intervene in the s 39 process: in *R (Biggs) v Home Secretary* [2002] EWHC Admin 1012, Richards J took the view that it will generally be inappropriate to challenge the Secretary of State's decision to recall a prisoner under s 39(2) by way of judicial review on the ground of reasonableness. He stressed that s 39(2) is an emergency procedure, involving the exercise of an extremely broad discretion by the Home Secretary, and therefore a reasonableness or rationality challenge was very unlikely to succeed. However, Richards J also stressed the importance of the Parole Board's review of the recall decision, 'which enables the merits of recall, and in particular the balance of hardship and risk, to be properly assessed by an expert body with the benefit of full information' (para 24).

(8) A short term prisoner who is guilty of a disciplinary offence under the Prison Rules may be awarded additional days in prison as a punishment (s 42).[43]

(9) Special provisions apply to young offenders (s 43) and fine defaulters/contemnors (s 45).

Long Term Prisoners (Four Years or More)

(1) A long term prisoner must be released on licence after he has served two-thirds of his sentence (s 33(2)). **12.22**

(2) A long term prisoner serving between four and under 15 years imposed after 1 October 1992 shall, if recommended by the Parole Board, be released on licence when he has served one-half of his sentence (s 35(1), s 50(2), and Parole Board (Transfer of Functions) Order 1998[44]) and any conditions attached to or inserted in his licence must be in accordance with the recommendation(s) of the Parole Board (s 37(5), s 50(3) and the Parole Board (Transfer of Functions) Order 1998).

(3) A long term prisoner serving more than 15 years may be released on licence by the Secretary of State, if so recommended by the Parole Board, after serving half his sentence (s 35(1)).

(4) Any long term prisoner released on licence shall remain subject to the conditions of the licence until the date on which he would (but for his release) have served three-quarters of his sentence (s 37(1)).

(5) A long term prisoner serving 15 years or more, or between four and 15 years, may be recalled by the Secretary of State either upon the recommendation of the Parole Board (s 39(1)) or without its recommendation if the conditions of s 39(2) are fulfilled, and has the right to be given reasons for, and to make representations against, recall (see (6) above).

(6) A long term prisoner who is recalled under s 39(1) must, in any event, be released on licence after he would have served three-quarters of his sentence (but for his release) (s 33(3)), with the terms of the licence remaining in force until expiry of the whole sentence, unless the offence is a sexual one and s 44 applies, in which case he may be recalled until the expiry of his original sentence.

(7) The Home Secretary must refer to the Parole Board the case of a long term prisoner who is either recalled under s 39(2) or who is recalled under

---

[43] At the time of writing, s 42 was still on the statute book, though the Government has made it clear that, in light of the decision of the ECtHR in *Ezeh and Connors v UK* that the imposition by governors of additional days for a wide range of prison offences does not comply with Art 6 of the ECHR, it will carry out extensive reforms of the prison disciplinary system. As we saw in Ch 9, the UK is seeking to have the ECtHR's decision reviewed by the Grand Chamber, but in any event, has introduced the Prison (Amendment) Rules 2002, SI 2002/2116 to reform the disciplinary system.
[44] SI 1998/3218.

s 39(1) and who makes representations about it (s 39(4)) and where the Board recommends his immediate release on licence the Home Secretary must give effect to the recommendation.

(8) A long term prisoner may be released at any time by the Secretary of State on compassionate grounds after consultation with the Parole Board (s 36).

(9) A long term prisoner may be returned to prison if he commits an offence punishable with imprisonment before the date on which he would have served his sentence in full (Powers of Criminal Courts (Sentencing) Act 2000, s 116(1)).

(10) Additional days in prison may be awarded to any long term prisoner who commits a disciplinary offence during the course of his imprisonment (s 42).[45]

Determinate Sentence Prisoners: Three Release Schemes

12.23 The 1991 Act introduced radically new arrangements for the early release of prisoners sentenced on or after 1 October 1992, wholly replacing the previous scheme of automatic remission and selective release on parole. These arrangements apply to all prisoners, although the Act makes special provisions to deal with those sentenced before 1 October 1992, defined as 'existing prisoners'.[46]

12.24 The 1991 Act creates three different routes to freedom for determinate sentence prisoners based on the length of their sentence, as follows:

---

[45] See n 43 above.

[46] For a useful summary of the various release schemes provided for by the 1991 Act, see Prison Service Order 6000 'Parole, Early Release and Recall Manual'. Schedule 12 to the 1991 Act contained important provisions governing the application of the release schemes introduced by the Act to prisoners sentenced before 1 October 1992 but who remain in custody beyond that date. These prisoners are referred to as 'existing prisoners'. Schedule 12, para 8(1) also defines an 'existing licensee' as someone who at commencement has already been released on licence under s 60 of the Criminal Justice Act 1967 and whose licence remains in force at commencement. The aim of the transitional arrangements is to ensure that existing prisoners/licensees are treated, at worst, no less favourably than they would have been under the old parole scheme. Existing prisoners are not subject to the supervision or 'at risk' provisions of the 1991 Act and will continue to be treated as 'existing prisoners' throughout the currency of their sentence even if they subsequently receive a concurrent or consecutive sentence or a revised sentence on appeal after 1 October 1992. It follows that an existing prisoner who is released on parole and subsequently has his licence revoked will be treated as an existing prisoner on return to prison. An existing prisoner at commencement who has been released and fulfilled all the liabilities of the sentence but who is subsequently returned to prison on a fresh sentence will obviously be liable to the 1991 Act's provisions in full. An existing prisoner or licensee who received a sentence of more than 12 months but less than four years would ordinarily be treated as a short term prisoner but is in fact treated as a long term prisoner. This ensures that such prisoners fall to be dealt with under the discretionary release scheme and Sch 12, para 8(6) makes provision to adjust the normal points for eligibility for release on licence and unconditional release so that they reproduce the old system of release on licence at one-third and entitlement to unconditional release after two-thirds.

Automatic Unconditional Release

This covers short term prisoners (including young offenders) serving sentences of up to 12 months, who are released automatically at the half-way stage of their sentence without statutory supervision (the 'automatic release date' or ARD). Released prisoners are 'at risk' of being returned to custody until the expiry of their full sentence if they commit a further imprisonable offence during this time.[47] The court dealing with the new offence may add all or part of the outstanding period of the original sentence (at the time the further offence was committed) to any new sentence it may impose.

Automatic Conditional Release Scheme

This covers short term prisoners (including young offenders aged 18 and over) serving sentences of 12 months to under four years who will be released automatically at the half-way point of the sentence under licence (the 'conditional release date' or CRD). There is no selection process and release may be delayed only if additional days have been awarded as a result of disciplinary adjudication(s). Released prisoners are then subject to supervision by the probation service to the three-quarter stage of the sentence (the 'licence expiry date'). Prisoners who breach their licence conditions are 'at risk' of being returned to custody by the magistrates' court or Crown Court if they commit a further imprisonable offence before the expiry of their sentence.

12.25

Discretionary Release Scheme

This covers long term prisoners serving sentences of four years or more who will be eligible for discretionary release on licence by the Parole Board (in the case of those serving under 15 years) or the Home Secretary (in the case of those serving 15 years or more) from the half-way point of sentence (the 'parole eligibility date' or PED). Those not released before the two-thirds point of their sentence will be released automatically at that stage under licence (the 'non-parole release date' or NPD). They are subject to supervision by the probation service to the three-quarters point (the 'licence expiry date' or LED). The 'at risk' provisions apply from the date of release until the expiry of the full sentence (the 'sentence expiry date' or SED). Additional days awarded as a result of disciplinary adjudication(s) automatically put back the PED, the NPD and the LED. The SED is not altered however. Conversely, dates must be advanced by any additional days remitted under rule 59. Time spent unlawfully at large (UAL) will affect all sentence dates including the SED.

12.26

---

[47] And, with regard to short term prisoners serving between three and 12 months, see para 12.21(2) above.

The Single Term

12.27 Before a prisoner's release date is calculated it is essential to identify the release scheme applicable to his case. For this purpose the 1991 Act, as amended, provides for all terms of imprisonment to be considered as a 'single term'.[48] A single term can be made up of a single sentence, consecutive sentences, or a combination of multiple concurrent and overlapping sentences. The single term runs from the date of the prisoner's first entry into custody following sentence for the full term of the sentence(s) imposed by the court, and it is the length of the single term that determines the applicable release scheme. For the purpose of determining the single term, sentence length should not be reduced by time on remand or police custody time. Thus in *R v Home Secretary, ex p Probyn*,[49] the Divisional Court rejected the argument that the time the applicant had spent in custody on remand (261 days of a four-year sentence) should be deducted from his sentence. Had the court accepted the applicant's argument, the result would have been for him to be classified as a 'short term', rather than 'long term', prisoner. The court held, however, that a prisoner's status as a long term or short term prisoner is to be determined by the sentence or sentences of the court, not by the amount of time which a prisoner happened to have spent on remand prior to sentence.[50]

12.28 Calculation of release dates can only take place after the SED of each sentence within the term has been adjusted to take account of remand and police custody time. In practice, the calculation of release dates in the light of time spent in custody has caused difficulties, particularly where a prisoner has been sentenced to

---

[48] Criminal Justice Act 1991, s 51(2): '[f]or the purposes of any reference in this Part, however, expressed, to the term of imprisonment to which a person has been sentenced or which, or part of which, he has served, consecutive terms and terms which are wholly or partly concurrent shall be treated as a single term if – (a) the sentences were passed on the same occasion; or (b) where they were passed on different occasions, the person has not been released under this Part at any time during the period beginning with the first and ending with the last of those occasions'. Under s 51(2A), '[w]here a suspended sentence of imprisonment is ordered to take effect, with or without any variation of the original term, the occasion on which that order is made shall be treated for the purposes of subsection (2) above as the occasion on which the sentence is passed'.

[49] [1998] 1 WLR 809.

[50] In *Probyn*, the court considered a previous ruling of the Divisional Court in *R v Home Secretary, ex p François* [1997] 2 Cr App R (S) 359 (which was subsequently upheld by the House of Lords—see [1999] 1 AC 43). In *François*, it was held that where consecutive sentences are imposed on different occasions, they are to be treated as a single term by virtue of s 51(2) of the 1991 Act for purposes of determining whether the prisoner was a short term or long term prisoner. Accordingly if a term of imprisonment is added to an existing term of imprisonment (the existing term of imprisonment being less than four years) so that the prisoner becomes subject to an aggregate of four years or more, the prisoner becomes a long term prisoner in respect of the whole. In *R (Akhtar) v Governor of HM Prison New Hall and Home Secretary* [2001] EWHC Admin 175, the High Court considered whether 17 days spent on bail from the High Court in judicial review proceedings should count towards the claimant's sentence. They considered that the claimant was not 'serving her sentence' during those 17 days, since she was not under the control of the prison authorities, and that those days did not therefore count for sentence calculation purposes.

one or more concurrent sentences. Difficulties in this regard were already apparent before the passage of the 1991 Act, and in some ways the passage of that Act only added to the confusion as to the correct statutory position.[51] As the law stands, s 67 of the Criminal Justice Act 1967 continues to govern the effect of time spent on remand in custody.[52] However, new arrangements will come into place if ss 87 and 88 of the Powers of Criminal Courts (Sentencing) Act 2000 are brought into force (see para 12.36 below).

The first case which illustrated the difficulties in calculating time on remand **12.29** against the duration of a sentence was *R v Governor of Blundeston Prison, ex p Gaffney*.[53] In *Gaffney* the applicant was convicted of a series of offences in May 1979 and committed to the Crown Court for sentence. He was detained in custody pending sentence (the first custody period) only to be released when the Crown Court deferred sentence. During the deferment period, the applicant was convicted by another magistrates' court of a further series of offences and was again detained in custody pending sentence (the second custody period). The applicant was finally sentenced to 37 months in prison for the first series of offences and three years concurrent therewith for the second series of offences. Consequently the applicant was required to serve the longer sentence of 37 months reduced, under s 67(1) of the Criminal Justice Act 1967, 'by any period during which he was in custody . . . in connection with [the] sentence or the offence'.

When his term of imprisonment (less *both* periods of custody) expired, the appli- **12.30** cant applied for a writ of habeas corpus addressed to the governor of the prison to show cause why he should not be released immediately. The court held, however, that as the three year sentence imposed for the second set of offences had been incorporated into the longer sentence of 37 months, the applicant was only entitled to have the time spent in custody in relation to the first set of offences credited against his sentence—that was the only period in which he had been in custody 'in connection with' his sentence of 37 months. Stated alternatively, the court determined that the 1967 Act did not allow remand time to be aggregated and that individual sentences could only attract credit for remand time directly attributable to the offences for which a sentence is imposed. This same logic was subsequently applied in *R v Home Secretary, ex p Read*[54] despite the fact that

---

[51] See DA Thomas, 'Sentencing Legislation—The Case for Consolidation' [1997] Crim LR 406.

[52] s 67(1), so far as material, provides: '[t]he length of any sentence of imprisonment imposed on an offender by a court shall be treated as reduced by any period during which he was in custody by reason only of having been committed to custody by an order of a court made in connection with any proceedings relating to that sentence or the offence for which it was passed or any proceedings from which those proceedings arose . . .'.

[53] [1982] 1 WLR 697.

[54] (1987) 9 Cr App R (S) 206.

s 104(2) of the 1967 Act suggested otherwise.[55] The result was that defendants stood to lose full and effective credit for time spent on remand.

12.31 In *R v Governor of H M Prison Styal, ex p Mooney,*[56] the Divisional Court was invited to reconsider *Gaffney* and *Read* in light of the passage of the 1991 Act. The 1991 Act, as noted, provides in s 51(2) that all terms of imprisonment should be considered to constitute a single term. In *Mooney* it was argued that s 67 of the 1967 Act should be interpreted in conformity with s 51(2) of the 1991 Act, ie that each of the different periods of time spent in custody should be deducted from the aggregate sentence passed for all offences. The court rejected this suggestion, finding that 'section 51(2) simply does not address the question of deduction of time spent on remand'.[57] Accordingly, it was determined that the facts of Ms Mooney's case were to be governed by the 1967 Act as interpreted in *Gaffney* and *Read*.

12.32 In *R v Governor of Brockhill Prison, ex p Evans*, however, the Divisional Court finally rejected the line of reasoning applied in *Gaffney* and *Mooney*.[58] Essentially the position established by Evans is that all relevant remand time should be aggregated and deducted from a prisoner's sentence (subject always to the rule that time could never be counted more than once). In the case of consecutive sentences, the consecutive terms should be treated as the single term and the aggregate time spent in custody deducted accordingly. Where concurrent terms were imposed on the same occasion, the single term would be the longest of the concurrent terms, and the aggregate time in custody deducted accordingly; where concurrent sentences imposed on different occasions, the terminal date would be the date on which the last of the sentences would expire.

12.33 The Court of Appeal in *Evans* was highly critical of the difficulties which had been caused by the existence of so many overlapping pieces of legislation and called for the enactment of a comprehensive statutory consolidation of sentencing provisions. Lord Bingham commented that:

---

[55] s 104(2) of the 1967 Act provides that 'for the purpose of any reference in this Act, however expressed, to the term of imprisonment or other detention to which a person has been sentenced or which, or part of which, he has served, consecutive terms and terms which are wholly or partly concurrent, shall be treated as a single term'.
[56] [1996] 1 Cr App R (S) 74.
[57] *per* Simon Brown LJ, ibid, 77.
[58] [1997] 2 WLR 236. It should be noted that *Gaffney* and *Mooney* had already been doubted by the Divisional Court in *R v Home Secretary, ex p Naughton* [1997] 1 WLR 118. In this case, the applicant had been given several sentences to be served consecutively. The applicant argued on the basis of *Gaffney* that the relevant period of time spent in custody vis-à-vis each of the sentences imposed should be deducted accordingly. The respondent argued that such an approach would lead to absurd results The court recognized the difficulties caused by the logic in *Gaffney* and suggested that it might be appropriate for the *Gaffney* approach to be looked at again or for the matter to be addressed in legislation. However, because the court was able to dismiss the instant application on its facts, it avoided having to reject explicitly the *Gaffney* line of reasoning.

The principle that a prisoner's release date should be beyond dispute, and that the provisions governing it should be easy to apply, is of great importance, for reasons both of fairness and good administration. It is not, on any showing, a test which the present provisions meet. They are not clear to the courts, or the legal profession, or prisoners, or (it would seem) the prison authorities. They are certainly not simple. It appears that defendants are remaining in prison when the sentencing court did not intend that they should.[59]

As noted above, the Powers of Criminal Courts (Sentencing) Act 2000 contains provisions which seek to address the difficulties referred to in taking account of time spent on remand. Sections 87 and 88 of the 2000 Act, when brought into force, will require a court, when passing sentence, to direct that the number of days spent on remand in custody in respect of the offence, or a related offence, shall count as time served as part of the sentence. 'Remanded in custody' is defined in s 88 as being held in police detention, remanded in or committed to custody by an order of the court, remanded or committed to local authority accommodation under s 23 of the Children and Young Persons Act 1969, or remanded, admitted or removed to hospital under ss 35, 36, 38 or 48 of the Mental Health Act 1983. It is to be hoped that these sections, when in force, will bring some clarity to this area of the law.[60]

---

[59] *per* Lord Bingham of Cornhill, [1997] 2 WLR 236 at 252. Indeed, on the point that 'defendants are remaining in prison when the sentencing court did not intend that they should', Thomas has noted that '[t]he result of the confusion over the statutory position in the earlier cases is that over a period of 15 years, an unknown number of prisoners have probably served more time in prison than they should, and the Home Office is bracing itself for claims for damages for false imprisonment': see DA Thomas, 'Sentencing Legislation—The Case for Consolidation' [1997] Crim LR 406, 407. As for the possibility of a welter of false imprisonment claims, see the decision of the House of Lords in Ms Evans' subsequent claim for compensation: *R v Governor of Brockhill Prison, ex p Evans (No 2)* [2001] 2 AC 19, in which their Lordships upheld the Court of Appeal's award (by a majority) of damages for 59 days of false imprisonment caused by the miscalculation of Ms Evans' release date. Their Lordships considered that, in detaining her after her lawful release date, the prison Governor had acted in excess of the powers conferred on him by Parliament. The fact that he had complied with the law as the court had at that time declared it to be was not sufficient justification for false imprisonment, which is a tort of strict liability. They raised the amount of compensation to £5,000.

[60] In *R v Home Secretary, ex p A* [2000] 2 AC 276, the House of Lords considered whether remand in non-secure local authority accommodation (with added conditions) under s 23 of the Children and Young Persons Act 1969 counted as a 'relevant period' for the purposes of s 67. They considered that, to come within s 67, remand must be to a place where liberty was so restricted as to amount to a form of custody. Remand in a non-secure home, even with a curfew condition, was not sufficiently restrictive to come within s 67. In *Burgess v Home Office*, 22 February 2000, Maidstone County Court, the court accepted that periods of remand in custody during the claimant's trial counted as a 'relevant period' under s 67 and were therefore to be deducted from his eventual sentence. This decision was reversed by the Court of Appeal: see [2001] 1 WLR 93.

H. Decision-making and Procedural Fairness under the Discretionary Release Scheme

12.34   As we have seen, the discretionary release scheme (DRS) applies to two categories of determinate sentence prisoners—those serving between four years and under 15 years and those serving 15 years or more.[61] The discretionary release of the former is decided exclusively by the Parole Board, while the release of the latter is still governed by a 'dual key' system of responsibility. The Home Secretary may release if the Parole Board so recommends but he is not obliged to release upon its recommendation.[62]

12.35   What is the structure for decision-making under the DRS? The 1990 White Paper stated that the arrangements for making the parole decision should be 'equitable and fair and be seen to be so; they should be simple and easy to understand for all parties; delays should be avoided'. Under the old parole system the main criticisms were that prisoners had no right to a hearing before the Parole Board deciding their case, there was no right to have access to the written material before the Board, the criteria for release were unclear (and unpublished), and reasons were not given for a decision to refuse parole. In what ways, if any, do the current provisions meet these criticisms?[63]

---

[61] The original scheme applied to those serving between four and seven years, but the Parole Board's jurisdiction was extended to those serving up to 15 years by the Parole Board (Transfer of Functions) Order 1998, SI 1998/3218.

[62] Sch 12, para 8(7). The extent to which it is ever appropriate to allow a member of the Executive to depart from a release recommendation of the Parole Board must be seriously in doubt in light of the decision of the ECtHR in *Stafford v UK* Application 46295/99 (2002) 35 EHRR 32. Although that decision related only to mandatory life sentence prisoners, it raised important issues of the separation of powers and the problematic nature of executive involvement in release decisions. It was estimated that the 1991 Act would reduce the Parole Board's caseload from 24,000 to 4,000 cases per year. In 2000–01 the Board considered 5,576 determinate sentence cases (of which 46% were granted parole, 3.8% of whom were recalled to custody during 2000–01 as a result of committing a further offence while on licence): *Annual Report and Accounts of the Parole Board 2001/01* (HC 235, 2001) 50.

[63] The next section draws heavily on Prison Service policy towards the decision-making process as set out in Prison Service Order 6000. The functioning of the Parole Board was considered in detail in the Government's *Comprehensive Review of Parole and Lifer Processes* (London, 2001). The Review makes almost 120 recommendations over a wide range of issues relating to parole for determinate sentenced prisoners and mandatory and discretionary lifers. Particular criticisms were made about delays in the provision of information and the completion of parole dossiers, and about the effectiveness of hearings. The Review contains many recommendations intended to 'streamline' the parole process, which in most cases appear to mean cutting costs by involving fewer Parole Board members in each case, by employing volunteers to do certain tasks, such as interviewing prisoners, and by making more sparing use of psychiatrists. Reducing delays in the process would be welcome, particularly given widespread concerns that current review times for discretionary lifers are not meeting the standards in Art 5(4) of the ECHR. However, reducing the amount of expertise and the breadth of input into each case surely risks compromising the quality of decision-making.

Timing of Reviews

Under the DRS a prisoner's first parole review must commence in the prison **12.36** where he is located 26 weeks before his PED. If additional days are awarded once the first review has started but before his parole dossier has been sent to the Parole Board, the review continues as normal and the details of the adjudication(s) are included in the dossier.[64] The Board must be notified if additional days are awarded after the dossier has been sent to the Board or if the prisoner escapes (and is therefore unlawfully at large). Second and subsequent reviews must commence 26 weeks before the anniversary of the PED and will not be delayed by additional days awarded in the interim period. Review dates are however put back by any days spent unlawfully at large.

To initiate the review process for the first time or subsequently on the anniversary **12.37** of the PED, each prisoner is provided with a copy of an application form for release on licence. This gives an opportunity to apply for or to opt out of consideration for parole. A prisoner who initially decides to opt out may change his mind but may do so only once and provided that there are at least nine months to his non-parole release date.

Right of Access to Material before the Board

The Carlisle Committee was strongly in favour of the view that a system of open **12.38** reporting should be introduced into the parole system, giving prisoners a right to have access to all material/reports before the Parole Board save in exceptional cases where the Board is satisfied that disclosure would cause 'specific harm' to a third party or the prisoner himself.[65] It stressed that one of the vices of the old system was that:

> [s]ecrecy breeds rumour and suspicion. Inmates suspect that a prison officer or probation officer has spoiled their chances of parole even when in fact he has submitted a fair and favourable report. Sometimes an officer may write something which is unintentionally misleading or inaccurate but the prisoner will have no opportunity to correct it or put his side of the story.

---

[64] The position on the award of additional days has been substantially revised following the decision of the ECtHR in *Ezeh and Connors v UK* Applications 39665/98 and 40086/98 (2002) 35 EHRR 28. The decision is discussed in greater detail in Ch 9. For present purposes, it appears that the Government intends to remit any additional days imposed after the coming into force of the HRA for offences which are criminal, rather than disciplinary, in nature (a difficult distinction to apply in practice). These additional days will no longer count to postpone the PED. All references to additional days in this section must therefore be read in light of this qualification. The Prison (Amendment) Rules 2002, SI 2002/2116 have set up a dual system of disciplinary hearings, with less serious cases being heard by the governor, who cannot award additional days, and more serious cases being heard by an independent adjudicator.

[65] *The Parole System in England and Wales*, Report of the Review Committee Chaired by Lord Carlisle of Bucklow QC (Cm 532, 1988), para 336.

The idea that open reporting might somehow inhibit the production of reliable, honest reports had also received short shrift from the Divisional Court in *R v Home Secretary, ex p Benson*.[66] Mr Benson was a discretionary lifer who, having been granted leave to apply for judicial review of the Home Secretary's decision not to release him despite three favourable recommendations from the Parole Board, sought discovery of certain medical reports which had been available to both the Parole Board and the Home Secretary. The Home Secretary resisted the application and relied on the 'candour' argument to the effect that those who pre-pare medical reports for parole decisions might feel unable to give as full and can-did an assessment of a prisoner as they would wish if they knew the report might not remain confidential. Lloyd LJ was unimpressed with this reasoning, saying:

> I find myself unconvinced by that argument. I cannot believe that a professional man, such as a doctor, would trim his views or be less than candid just because he thought that his report might one day see the light of day. If that is true of medical men in general, then I cannot follow why it should not be true of a prison medical officer just because he is working in a prison context.

Lloyd LJ went on to hold that he was not deciding that a prisoner is entitled to have his medical reports produced in every case where the Parole Board declines to recommend his release on parole. The reason Mr Benson was entitled to see the reports was that he had succeeded in obtaining leave to apply for judicial review and he had established that the medical reports were not only relevant but indeed central to his application. Nevertheless the reasoning of the court was an import-ant rejection of the most commonly cited argument against a duty of general dis-closure of adverse material to prisoners. And in a subsequent case under the old parole scheme (albeit decided after the passage of the 1991 Act) it was held that a determinate sentence prisoner who had been released in 1976 on a licence due to expire in 1977, but whose licence was revoked in 1976 when he left the country without permission, was entitled to be told of any adverse material before the Parole Board which was considering whether to release him after he was finally arrested in 1992![67]

12.39 Despite the weight of opinion in favour of disclosing reports to prisoners, the White Paper rejected the creation of a general duty of disclosure. Having stated that 'the Government will give further consideration to the detailed arrangements for making the parole decisions in the future, with the aim of moving towards dis-closing reports made to the Board', it concluded that 'there is a risk that openness could lead to less full and telling reports and so to less well informed decisions'.[68]

---

[66] The original hearing was an interlocutory application for discovery before the Divisional Court [1989] COD 329. The substantive hearing of Mr Benson's application for judicial review was reported in The Times, 21 November 1988. See also *R v Lancashire CC, ex p Huddleston* [1986] 2 All ER 941.

[67] *R v Parole Board, ex p Georghiades* (1993) 5 Admin LR 457.

[68] White Paper, para 6.26.

This concern was finally set aside however, and in 1992 a new policy of 'open reporting' and full disclosure in relation to the parole process was implemented. In essence, it ensures that prisoners are given access to their parole dossier and then provided with an opportunity to make representations to the Parole Board and the Home Secretary (where relevant). **12.40**

Under the current policy, the responsibility for compiling a prisoner's parole dossier rests with the Parole Clerk in the prison where the prisoner concerned is located. The Clerk is required to request reports and compile a complete dossier in time so that it reaches the Parole Board member who will interview the prisoner between 15 and 16 weeks before the PED. The Clerk must then ensure that the final dossier (including the external probation officer's report and the assessment of the interviewing Board member) reaches the Parole Board Secretariat no later than 11 weeks before the PED. **12.41**

The dossier should be structured chronologically and contain reports from a wide range of sources.[69] All reporters are told that reports must be written with a view to open reporting. When he is handed his copy of the dossier (17 weeks before his PED), the prisoner is also given a disclosure and prisoner's representations form. This form, containing all that the prisoner wishes to say on the content of his dossier, must then be sent to the Parole Board Secretariat 11 weeks before the PED (thereby coinciding with the arrival of the dossier itself). If a prisoner is concerned or unhappy about any aspect of the dossier he may make a complaint or seek legal advice. The Board should defer any consideration of the prisoner's case while a case is pending.[70] **12.42**

Withholding Information from the Prisoner

Prison Service policy presumes that all parole reports are disclosed to the prisoner concerned. However it provides for the withholding of certain information in exceptional circumstances. Thus, information will be withheld: **12.43**

---

[69] PSO 6000 states that a final parole dossier must include (where applicable) (1) front cover sheet, (2) summary of offence from police or pre-sentence report or pre-sentence psychiatric report, (3) court papers, (4) court transcription of sentencing remarks, (5) list of previous convictions, (6) pre-sentence medical or psychiatric report, (7) copy of previous parole dossiers, (8) copy of previous parole refusal notice, (9) adjudications and additional days awarded, (10) prison parole report, (11) seconded probation officer's report, (12) report(s) on offence-related work, (13) prison medical/psychiatric/psychological reports, (14) Parole Board member interview report, (15) prisoner's disclosure form/representations, (16) parole assessment report. For more detailed explanation of what the individual documents should contain, see PSO 6000, Appendix J, 29.

[70] The contents of the dossier must be accurate. In *R v Parole Board and Home Secretary, ex p Higgins*, 22 September 1998, QB, the claimant's dossier contained a police report which wrongly described the offence for which he was imprisoned. He challenged the refusal of parole on the basis that irrelevant considerations had been taken into account, namely the inaccurate statement of fact. The High Court granted the application and quashed the refusal of parole. Since no accurate statement of the offence had been included in the dossier, it could not be said that the Parole Board had been able to consider the 'nature and circumstances' of the offence, as required by the Home Secretary's directions.

(1) In the interests of national security.

(2) For the prevention of disorder or crime. This includes information relevant to prison security.

(3) For the protection of information received in confidence from a third party or other information which may put a third party at risk.

(4) If, on medical and/or psychiatric grounds, it is felt necessary to withhold information where the mental and/or physical health of the prisoner could be impaired.

It is for the governor to decide on any request to withhold information, although he or she is encouraged to seek advice from the Parole Unit of the Prison Service before upholding any request. In reaching a decision, the governor is enjoined to consider whether the document is material to the parole application and, if so, whether it could be rewritten to exclude information which is not disclosable without reducing its impact. If not, the governor must consider whether a redacted version may be prepared for disclosure to the prisoner with the full version disclosed to the Board. Where this occurs, the Board must receive both versions of the report so it can appreciate what has been withheld from the prisoner. Whenever it is decided to withhold or redact a report, the prisoner must be given written notice of what has occurred although obviously not provided with information about the document(s) concerned.

The Interview with the Parole Board Member

12.44 Neither the 1991 Act nor the 1997 Act provides a right to an oral hearing before the Parole Board to a fixed term prisoner. Indeed, it was one of the disappointments of the Carlisle Committee that the majority did not favour such a right in cases where the Board did not feel able to grant parole after considering any written material before it. Instead, as the majority of the Carlisle Committee recommended, the 1991 Act gives the Board a discretion to arrange for one of its members to interview the prisoner before it reaches a decision.[71] During the passage of the 1991 Act through the House of Lords, Earl Ferrers expressed the Government's view that:

> it is important for an inmate to have an interview with someone involved in the decision-making process. We intend, by virtue of [s 32(5)] to issue rules which would ensure that all inmates receive such an interview. The advantage of this approach is that it allows for flexibility and changes to the system in the light of experience . . . the interview should be an administrative arrangement designed to assist the Board and not a legal right from which other rights could be inferred.[72]

---

[71] Criminal Justice Act 1991, s 32(3).
[72] *Hansard*, HL vol 529, col 115 (21 May 1991).

Existing policy ensures that all prisoners who are considered for parole are given an interview by a single member of the Parole Board (but not necessarily a member of the panel which considers the case).[73] It is the responsibility of the Parole Clerk to send a request for such an interview to the Parole Board Secretariat 23 weeks before the prisoner's PED. The Secretariat then sets the interview date, which is generally 15 to 17 weeks before the PED. By the date of the interview, the Parole Board member will have received the prisoner's dossier (although PSO 6000 states that 'the interview need not be postponed if one or two reports are missing'). The interview must be conducted in private (subject to security considerations). The interviewing member has a checklist of points to be covered and following the interview he or she writes a report for the panel of the Board which will consider the case. The prisoner is entitled to have a copy of his dossier present with him for the interview. A copy of the typed report of the interview will be disclosed to the prisoner for him to comment upon as part of his representations to the Board. This whole process must be completed within two weeks.

The Parole Decision: Who Decides?

12.45 The Parole Board has delegated authority from the Home Secretary to make decisions on the parole applications of those prisoners sentenced after 1 October 1992 to four years' or more but less than 15 years' imprisonment. For those serving 15 years or more, the Parole Board makes recommendations to the Home Secretary. For those serving under 15 years, the Board Secretariat will send the notification of the decision to the prison. For those serving 15 years or more, the Secretariat sends its recommendations to the Parole Unit at Prison Service Headquarters.

The Home Secretary's Directions to the Parole Board

12.46 The Carlisle Committee recommended statutory criteria for parole, and that the parole decision should not be a form of resentencing. The White Paper endorsed the view that clear and published criteria for parole should become the lynchpin of an integrated parole system 'linking the decision to release, arrangements for taking that decision, the conditions of the licence and the arrangements for supervision in the community'. Section 32(6) of the 1991 Act gives the Home Secretary

---

[73] The Prison Service *Comprehensive Review of Parole and Lifer Processes* (March 2001) suggested that once the Offender Assessment System (OASys) being developed jointly by the Prison and Probation Services becomes available in parole dossiers, it will no longer be necessary for Parole Board members to conduct interviews with prisoners to explore areas of risk. The Parole Board resists this proposal: see *Annual Report and Accounts of the Parole Board 2000/01* (HC 235, 2001) 15. However, in the Parole Board Inaugural Lecture, delivered on 30 April 2002, Home Office Minister Beverley Hughes stated that, while some more research is being done on the issue, she considered that 'the evidence does suggest that the interviews add little value to the Board's core task of risk assessment'. This ignores the extent to which the legitimacy of the parole process may be undermined in the eyes of prisoners if decisions are taken by a body whose representatives they never have a chance to meet.

a discretion to give directions to the Parole Board as to matters to be taken into account in discharging any of its functions under the Act.[74] The most recent directions for the Parole Board to take into account when considering the release and recall of prisoners were published in 2002. So far as the release of determinate sentence prisoners is concerned, the Directions have as their emphasis the need to prepare for safe release, the major consideration being the risk to the public of a further offence being committed at a time when the offender would otherwise be in prison. Accordingly, the Directions state:

1. In deciding whether or not to recommend release on licence, the Parole Board shall consider primarily the risk to the public of a further offence being committed at a time when the prisoner would otherwise be in prison and whether any such risk is acceptable. This must be balanced against the benefits, both to the public and the offender, of early release back into the community under a degree of supervision which might help rehabilitation and so lessen the risk of re-offending in the future. The Board shall take into account that safeguarding the public may often outweigh the benefits to the offender of early release.

2. Before recommending early release on licence, the Parole Board shall consider whether:

   i. The safety of the public will be placed unacceptably at risk. In assessing such risk the Board shall take into account: the nature and circumstances of the original offence; whether the prisoner has shown by his attitude and behaviour in custody that he is willing to address his offending behaviour by understanding its causes and its consequences for the victims concerned, and has made positive effort and progress in doing so;

      in the case of a violent or sexual offender, whether the prisoner has committed other offences of sex or violence, in which case the risk to the public of release on licence may be unacceptable;

      that a risk of violent or sexual offending is more serious than a risk of other types of offending.

   ii. the longer period of supervision that parole would provide is likely to reduce the risk of further offences being committed.

   iii. the prisoner is likely to comply with the conditions of his licence.

   iv. the prisoner has failed to meet the requirements of licence supervision, temporary release or bail on any previous occasion and, if so, whether this makes the risk of releasing him on licence unacceptable.

   v. the resettlement plan will help secure the offender's rehabilitation.

   vi. the supervising officer has prepared a program of supervision and has recommended specific licence conditions.[75]

12.47 The Home Secretary's training guidance (which does not form part of the Directions issued under Criminal Justice Act 1991, s 32(6)) requires 12 factors to

---

[74] In *R v Home Secretary, ex p Fenton-Palmer*, March 1997, CO/2051/96, Laws J emphasized the use of the word 'directions' in s 32(6) of the 1991 Act, stating that 'the power is not merely to issue guidance, such as one sometimes finds in statutes conferring a supervisory role within a particular regime upon the Secretary of State'.

[75] Both the Home Secretary's Directions and the Training Guidance covering all aspects of the Board's functions are to be found in Appendix 9.

be taken into account by the Parole Board when making a recommendation about parole. Plainly, any prisoner making representations to the Board (either in writing or orally during the interview with the Board member) should seek to address each factor as it applies to his individual case:

a the offender's background, including any previous convictions and their pattern, and responses to any previous periods of supervision;

b the nature and circumstances of the original offence;

c where available, the sentencing judge's comments and probation and medical reports prepared for the court;

d any risk to the victim or possibility of retaliation by the victim, victim's family, or local community;

e any risk to other persons, including persons outside the jurisdiction;

f any available statistical indicators as to the likelihood of re-offending;

g attitude and behaviour in custody including offences against prison discipline;

h attitude to other inmates and positive contributions made to prison life;

i remorse, insight into offending behaviour, attitude to the victim and steps taken, within available resources, to achieve any treatment or training objectives set out in a sentence plan;

j realism of the release plan and resettlement prospects, including home circumstances and the likelihood of co-operation with supervision, relationship with the home probation officer, attitude of the victim and local community, extent to which the release plan continues rehabilitative work started in the prison, and the extent to which it lessens or removes the occurrence of circumstances which led to the original offence;

k any medical or psychiatric considerations;

l any other information, including representations by or on behalf of the offender, which may have a bearing on risk assessment.

The way in which assessment of risk is made by the Parole Board was the subject **12.48** of a detailed study in 2000.[76] The authors, one of whom served on the Carlisle Committee, considered that:

> The proportion of prisoners granted parole at some point of their sentence has fallen from around 70 per cent under the old system to less than a half now. Why has this happened? There is no doubt that the emphasis placed on risk in successive versions of the Secretary of State's directions (and consequently in training for Parole Board members) has created a generally cautious approach. But it is also true, as this research has shown, that Parole Board members often believe that the risk of reconviction during the parole licence period is substantially higher than that indicated by the actuarially-based risk of reconviction score (ROR) which is based on a reliable follow-up study.[77]

---

[76] R Hood and S Shute, 'The Parole System at work: a study of risk based decision-making', Home Office Research Study 202 (London, 2000).

[77] ibid, 77.

This highly risk-averse approach, encouraged by the Secretary of State, appears to keep many prisoners inside for far longer than is really necessary to protect the public.[78]

Prisoners who Deny their Guilt

12.49   A frequent problem arises in the parole process where a prisoner maintains his innocence of his index offence (or possibly a previous conviction).[79] Such a prisoner will, understandably, not consider that he needs to address his offending behaviour and thus will not be eligible for attendance at courses designed to deal with this issue (such as the Sex Offenders' Treatment Programme or SOTP). Equally, he may find it difficult to achieve recategorization to a lesser security category, which will also affect his prospects of release on licence. How is such a person to be dealt with by the Parole Board? This issue has been considered by the High Court and the Court of Appeal in a number of decisions.[80] In *R v Home Secretary, ex p Lillycrop*, Butterfield J summarized the principles which must guide the Board when faced with a 'denier' in the following terms:

> We consider that the Parole Board must approach its consideration of any application for parole on the basis that the applicant has committed the offences of which he has been convicted. It is not the function of the Parole Board to investigate possible miscarriages of justice or to give effect in their considerations to any personal misgivings they may have about the correctness of any particular conviction.
>
> That being so, where the pattern of offending behaviour is such that there is a significant risk of a further offence being committed, particularly an offence of a violent or sexual nature, and an applicant has not demonstrated by his conduct in prison that such risk has been reduced to an acceptable level, then a recommendation for parole is unlikely to be made. Part of that conduct in prison to which a panel of the Parole Board will inevitably and rightly look will be the extent to which an applicant has examined the behaviour which has led to his imprisonment. Where

---

[78] Hood and Shute argue that 'if the Board were to release those prisoners who are not only low risk but are recommended by both their prison-based and their home probation officer, the parole rate would increase by more than a quarter – but without any increase in the average reconviction rate of parolees as a whole. The effect over a year would be to release approximately 550 more prisoners on parole, 96 per cent of whom would not be predicted to commit a serious offence while on parole licence.' Ibid, 78.

[79] The Parole Board carried out a study of cases considered by it between 17 April and 27 July 2001, in which a prisoner who denied his or her guilt sought parole. Overall, 31% of those prisoners were awarded parole, compared to 46% of all prisoners in the 2000–01 period. The percentages of the prisoners who denied their offences and were granted parole varied greatly as between offence types, from 19% for sexual offences to 78% for drugs offences: *Annual Report and Accounts of the Parole Board 2000/01* (HC 235, 2001).

[80] The decisions include *R v Home Secretary, ex p Zulfikar* [1996] COD 256; *R v Home Secretary, ex p Zulfikar (No 2)*, May 1996, DC; *R v Home Secretary, ex p Lillycrop*, The Times, 13 December 1996; *R v Home Secretary, ex p Fenton-Palmer*, 24 March 1997, CO/2051/97, DC; *R v Parole Board and the Home Secretary, ex p Oyston*, The Independent, 17 April 2000; *R (Callaghan) v Home Secretary and Parole Board* [2001] EWHC Admin 208; *R (Wilkes) v Home Secretary* [2001] EWHC Admin 210.

because of denial that the offence has been committed no such examination has taken place it will be more difficult for an applicant to satisfy the Board that the risk he posed when he was sentenced to a term of imprisonment has been reduced to an acceptable level. We repeat and emphasize that each case must turn on its own particular facts.

Statistically there will always be a risk of a further offence being committed at a time when the prisoner would otherwise be in prison. The task of the Parole Board is to assess the extent of the risk and to determine in the light of that assessment whether the risk is small enough to contemplate early release. It should be noted that the Directions. . . . place emphasis on the violent or sexual offender and in particular the fact that the risk of further violent or sexual offending is more serious than other types of offending . . .

For the reasons clearly set out in Zulfikar (No 1) with which we respectfully agree it is an impermissible approach for the Parole Board to say in respect of an applicant: '[t]his man denies his guilt; therefore, without considering the circumstances further, we will not recommend parole'. However, a denial of guilt coupled with an unwillingness to address offending behaviour is a factor to which the Board must have regard in assessing the risk to the public of further offending. It will be for the Parole Board to determine the extent to which, if at all, this factor should influence their determination.'

It would be hard to improve on this summary and indeed in a subsequent application Laws J made clear that he considered that no further elaboration was necessary of the principles which must guide the Board in its approach.[81] However, prisoners who consider that the Parole Board or the Home Secretary have not dealt correctly with their denial of guilt are, of course, still entitled to take their case to court. The *Lillycrop* and *Zulfikar* approach was approved by the Court of Appeal in *Oyston*, where Lord Bingham CJ stated that: **12.50**

Convicted prisoners who persistently deny commission of the offence or offences of which they have been convicted present the Parole Board with potentially very difficult decisions. Such prisoners will probably not express contrition or remorse or sympathy for any victim. They will probably not engage in programmes designed to address the causes of their offending behaviour. Since they do not admit having offended they will only undertake not to do in the future what they do not accept having done in the past. Where there is no admission of guilt, it may be feared that a prisoner will lack any motivation to obey the law in future. Even in such cases, however, the task of the Parole Board is the same as in any other case: to assess the risk that the particular prisoner, if released on parole, will offend again. In making this assessment the Parole Board must assume the correctness of any conviction. It

---

[81] In *Ex p Fenton-Palmer*, 24 March 1997, CO/2051/97, DC, Laws J made it clear that he did not regard repeat litigation in this area as appropriate in the light of the guidance issued by the Divisional Court in *Ex p Lillycrop*. On the issue of the Board's inability to examine and question whether a prisoner was actually guilty, he accepted that there might, perhaps, be rare circumstances where it would be right for the Board to inquire into a prisoner's reasons for denying his guilt though he found it hard to envisage sensible examples. What the Board could never do however was embark on the question of whether in fact a particular prisoner was guilty.

can give no credence to the prisoner's denial. Such denial will always be a factor and may be a very significant factor in the Board's assessment of risk, but it will only be one factor and must be considered in the light of all other relevant factors. In almost any case the Board would be quite wrong to treat the prisoner's denial as irrelevant, but also quite wrong to treat a prisoner's denial as necessarily conclusive against the grant of parole.

Further problems can arise for those who deny their guilt when they are eventually released on licence. They will naturally be unwilling to comply with licence conditions requiring them to carry out offending behaviour work when they assert that they have not offended in the first place. In *R (Wilkes) v Home Secretary*,[82] the claimant, who had been in prison for a sexual offence but denied his guilt, challenged the imposition of a licence condition requiring him to 'comply with any requirements reasonably imposed by your supervising officer for the purposes of ensuring that you address your sexual offending behaviour'. He argued that this condition was unreasonable, since he could not attend a SOTP while denying his guilt, and was therefore faced with a choice between admitting his guilt and being recalled to prison. The court held that, on the facts of the case, the requirements were 'broad and flexible' and did not require the claimant to admit guilt. Rather, he would simply be assessed by a psychologist to see what, if any, options were available. Any unreasonable requirements could be challenged in due course. It is important to note that the court relied on the fact that, on examination, the claimant was not faced with a choice between admitting guilt and being recalled. In cases where the licence requirements are more onerous, a released prisoner may well have grounds to challenge those conditions.

Giving Reasons for a Parole 'Knock-back'

12.51 Nothing caused more bitterness and frustration under the old parole system than the refusal to give any reasons for a 'knock-back'—a decision to refuse parole. The decision of the Court of Appeal in *Payne v Lord Harris of Greenwich* to the effect that the general duty of fairness imposed on the Parole Board did not include a duty to disclose to a mandatory life sentence prisoner the reasons for a refusal to release him on licence was, until recently, a road-block in the path of any attempt to enhance the procedural rights of all prisoners under the parole system.[83] The Court of Appeal refused to follow *Payne* in the later case of *R v Parole Board, ex p Wilson*,[84] a case concerning a discretionary lifer, and in *R v Parole Board, ex p Creamer and Scholey* Rose J (as he then was) indicated his personal view that *Payne* was no longer good law even for mandatory lifers.[85] Nonetheless, *Payne*

---

[82] 15 March 2001.
[83] [1981] 1 WLR 754. But see now *R v Home Secretary, ex p Doody* [1994] 1 AC 531 in which the House of Lords finally overruled *Payne*.
[84] [1992] QB 740.
[85] [1993] COD 162.

remained the law so far as determinate sentence prisoners were concerned until the Prison Service changed its policy in 1992 and issued Circular Instruction 85/1992. This provided for the issuing to prisoners of a note setting out the detailed reasons of the Board for a parole knock-back. As Butterfield J remarked in *Ex p Lillycrop*, although the instruction does not have the force of law, 'with increasing emphasis on the importance of openness in the conduct of the decision making process with reference to the granting of parole it is now the universal practice to give reasons to the prisoner affected. The demands of natural justice and fairness require disclosure.'[86]

As for the content of the duty to give reasons, Butterfield J went on to state: **12.52**

> [The] decision letter should contain a succinct and accurate summary of the reasons leading to the decision reached. When formulating their reasons the members of a panel are not required to create some elaborate formal exegesis or a detailed analysis of the facts they have considered and the application of those facts to the relevant law. The purpose of the reasons is to tell the prisoner in broad terms why parole has not been recommended, bearing in mind that in most cases the prisoner will himself have been provided with the documentation available to the Board.[87]

There is no right of appeal against a refusal to grant parole. Where a decision is the **12.53** subject of a challenge by way of judicial review, the Divisional Court has made clear that though it will receive evidence on affidavit from the Parole Board 'to elucidate or, exceptionally, correct or add to the reasons' originally communicated to the prisoner, it will be cautious in its approach to such evidence. In particular, 'a Court should not substitute the reasons contained in proffered evidence for the

---

[86] Transcript, 9.

[87] R Hood and S Shute, 'The Parole System at work: a study of risk based decision-making', Home Office Research Study 202 (London, 2000) 78, found widespread dissatisfaction with the reasons given for refusal of parole: 'the majority of prisoners who were refused parole thought that the reasons they were given were unfair. Very few regarded them as a spur to a more positive approach to their remaining period in prison and many resented the fact that although they had been denied parole they still faced stringent licence conditions when they came to be released after serving two-thirds of their sentence.' In the context of mandatory and discretionary lifers, the High Court has arguably been more demanding in relation to the standard of reason-giving. See eg *R v Home Secretary, ex p Evans*, 2 November 1994, CO 2454/94, DC, in which Simon Brown LJ strongly criticized the Parole Board's failure to explain why it was disagreeing, in the face of unanimous evidence from report writers, with the recommendation of the LRC that a recalled mandatory lifer could gain nothing by further testing in open conditions—'where as here the Board find themselves unable to follow what I have already described as the clear, emphatic and unanimous view of the LRC and those reporting to them, they should explain why, in language sufficiently clear and terms sufficiently full to ensure that the LRC properly understand the basis of the difference between them. Of course, such reasons may not, are perhaps unlikely to, convince the LRC of the rightness of the Board's decisions. But they must at least indicate the Board's essential thinking.' It is hard to see why less stringent standards should apply as between a refusal to grant parole to a fixed term prisoner and a mandatory lifer. See also *R v Home Secretary, ex p Pegg* [1995] COD 84 and *R v Parole Board, ex p Lodomez* [1994] COD 525. The latter case concerned the standard of reasoning to be expected from a Discretionary Lifer Panel under r 15(2) of the Parole Board Rules 1992.

reasons advanced in a decision letter' as 'to do so would unquestionably raise the perception, if not the reality, of subsequent rationalization of a decision that had not been properly considered at the time'.[88]

Order to Return to Prison for Offence Committed during Currency of Original Sentence

12.54   The Carlisle Committee recommended that all released prisoners should be liable, if convicted of another offence punishable with imprisonment committed before the end of the original sentence, to be ordered by the court to serve part or all of that portion of the sentence outstanding at the time the fresh offence was committed. This would be in addition to any new custodial sentence that might be imposed concurrently or consecutively. Thus a prisoner may spend up to half his sentence in the community, but he will still be under sentence for the whole period of that sentence and 'at risk' of being returned to prison if he offends again. The Carlisle Committee was concerned to ensure that early release should no longer mean that the sentence ends prematurely (as happened under the old scheme of remission), thereby restoring some meaning to the full sentence originally imposed by the court.

12.55   This aim is achieved by s 116 of the Powers of Criminal Courts (Sentencing) Act 2000, which replaced (in identical terms) s 40 of the 1991 Act. It applies to a short or long term prisoner (but not a lifer) who is released on licence and who, before the date on which he would (but for his release) have served his sentence in full, commits an offence punishable with imprisonment. Where a court convicts the prisoner of the fresh offence it may order him to be returned to prison for the whole or part of the period which remained between the date of the fresh offence and the expiry of the full original sentence (s 116(1)(a) and (b)). It does not matter if the prisoner is not convicted of the fresh offence until after the expiry of the full term of his original sentence—the key issue is whether the fresh offence was committed before the original sentence came to an end. A magistrates' court has the power to order a prisoner to return to prison under s 116 for a maximum of six months but may commit any prisoner in custody or on bail to the Crown Court for sentence pursuant to s 42 of the Powers of Criminal Courts Act 1973. The order to return to prison is to be regarded as a sentence of imprisonment. When exercising its powers under s 116, a court must order the period for which the offender is returned under s 116 to be served either before the sentence imposed

[88] *Ex p Lillycrop*, The Times, 13 December 1996. See also *R v Parole Board, ex p Gittens* [1994] COD 351. In *Ex p Lillycrop*, the Divisional Court made clear that any statement which is advanced to explain or elucidate the reasoning of the Board (or the Home Secretary) set out in the decision notice must clearly set out the source of the maker's knowledge and belief.

for the new offence, or concurrently with that sentence.[89] Further, the sentence for the fresh offence shall not be influenced by the fact of the order to return to prison. These provisions may have implications for whether, upon return to prison, the prisoner is treated as a short or long term prisoner. For example, a court may decide that the fresh offence merits a three-year sentence and, if so, must impose that irrespective of the fact that it may also be ordering a return to prison for 12 months. It then goes on to decide whether the order to return to prison should be made to run before the fresh sentence or concurrently with that sentence. If it decides to make it run consecutively, the prisoner's single term becomes four years and he is liable to be dealt with under the DRS.

In *R v Lowe; R v Leask*[90] the appellants argued that an order to return under s 40 **12.56** of the 1991 Act (now s 116 of the 2000 Act) should be seen as a re-activation of the old sentence, and that s 102 of the 1998 Act therefore precluded the imposition of a term of imprisonment consecutive to the re-activated period. The Court of Appeal rejected this argument. Lord Bingham CJ, giving the judgment of the court, stated that:

> The defendants argue that when an offender is ordered under section 40 of the Act of 1991 to serve an unexpired part of an earlier sentence, the court which so orders is not imposing a new sentence of imprisonment but re-activating an old sentence of imprisonment, from which the offender has been released under Part II of the Act of 1991: therefore, it is said, the imposition of a sentence consecutively to such a term is specifically precluded by section 102. The short answer to that submission is that by virtue of section 40(4)(a) of the Act of 1991, the period for which a person is ordered under that section to be returned to prison is to be taken to be a sentence of imprisonment for the purposes of Part II of the Act of 1991, and there is nothing in section 102 to preclude the imposition of a term consecutive to that sentence at any time before the offender has been released from that sentence.[91]

The relationship between the court's powers under s 116 of the 2000 Act and the **12.57** Secretary of State's powers under s 39 of the 1991 Act is a complex one, and was

---

[89] See *R v Clerkenwell Magistrates' Court, ex p Feely* [1996] 2 Cr App R (S) 309. *R v Harrow Justices, ex p Jordan* [1997] 1 WLR 84 is of interest in this context. In this case the applicant, while on release on licence, was convicted of assault, an offence triable only summarily. The justices imposed a custodial sentence of three months from which, by virtue of time spent on remand, he was almost immediately released. The justices also committed him in custody to the Crown Court for consideration of the question whether his licence should be revoked and he should be returned to prison. The applicant sought to challenge the committal order on the ground that any period of return imposed by the Crown Court could not be served before or concurrently with the sentence imposed for the new offence. The court granted the application, finding that on a proper construction of s 40 the justices should deal with the questions of return and sentence for the new offence together, or where they felt that the matter could be dealt with more appropriately by the Crown Court, they should commit both questions. Accordingly, the procedure adopted by the justices had been erroneous and the order for committal would be quashed.
[90] [2000] 1 WLR 153.
[91] ibid, 158.

considered in *R (Akhtar) v Home Secretary*.[92] In that case, the claimant had been released on licence from a short term sentence of 18 months. She committed, and was sentenced for, a further offence, and was ordered by the magistrates' court to return to prison for a month under s 116. The Home Secretary then decided to recall her under s 39 for breaching her licence. She argued that, once the magistrates' court has acted under s 116, it is not open to the Home Secretary to recall under s 39 on the basis of the same facts. The court distinguished the two functions—the magistrates' court power under s 116 is essentially a sentencing function triggered by commission of a further offence, and the Home Secretary's recall power is based on a risk assessment. The Home Secretary was therefore entitled to order recall, though the court recognized that the two powers overlap to some extent, and that therefore sentencing courts and the Home Secretary should take account of each other's decisions when exercising their functions. This is arguably too weak a recommendation to protect those on licence from serving disproportionate punishments for breach of their licence conditions.

12.58 Section 116 (and before it s 40) represents a major change from the pre-1991 Act position because it applies even where the fresh offence is committed after the expiry of the licence period and where release is 'unconditional' (for example, in the last quarter of the sentence). Under the Criminal Justice Act 1967 the sanction of revocation of a licence only applied during the unexpired part of the licence, not the original sentence, and was limited to offences punishable on indictment with imprisonment.[93]

Breach of Licence Conditions and Recall to Prison

12.59 Quite separately from the power to order a return to prison under s 40, the 1991 Act created a summary offence applicable to short term prisoners of failing to comply with the conditions of a licence (s 38(1)). The convicting court was able, in addition to a fine, to suspend the licence and recall the prisoner to prison for a period not exceeding six months but not, of course, if this exceeded the remaining period of the licence (s 38(2)). On the suspension of the licence the prisoner was deemed to be detained pursuant to the original sentence (s 38(3)). Section 38 of the 1991 Act was, however, repealed by the 1998 Act in order to harmonize the regime for recall of long and short term prisoners.

12.60 Since 1999, both long and short term prisoners fall to be dealt with under s 39, which gives the Home Secretary the power to revoke a short term or long term prisoner's licence, whether or not there is a technical breach of the licence condi-

---

[92] [2001] EWHC Admin 38, QB.

[93] s 116 has the potential greatly to increase the prison population. Estimates have been made that with a return to prison rate of 20%, the overall prison population may increase by as much as 2,000.

tions, and recall him to prison either on the recommendation of the Parole Board (s 39(1)) or without such a recommendation where it appears expedient in the public interest to recall before it is practicable to consult the Board (s 39(2)). In relation to the revocation and recall decision, the Home Secretary has issued Directions to the Board under s 32(6) of the 1991 Act which identify the criteria to be applied.[94] The Parole Board must consider whether:

a. The prisoner's continued liberty would present an unacceptable risk of a further offence being committed. The type of re-offending involved does not need to involve a risk to public safety;[95] or
b. The prisoner has failed to comply with one or more of his licence conditions, and that failure suggests that the objectives of probation supervision have been undermined; or
c. The prisoner has breached the trust placed in him or her by the Secretary of State in releasing him or her on licence, whether through failure to comply with one or more of the licence conditions, or any other means.[96]

Any prisoner recalled under either s 39(1) or (2) must be given the reasons for **12.61** recall, any documents relevant to the recall decision, and must be informed of his right to make written representations to the Parole Board, which has an absolute power to order immediate release at the first review following the recall to prison.[97] There is no entitlement to an oral hearing before the Board, although any request for such a hearing must be considered on its merits, as the Board does have a discretion to hold an oral hearing where fairness dictates it to be necessary.[98] The Secretary of State's directions relating to representations against recall, issued in 2002, direct the Parole Board to take into account the three recall criteria, set out

---

[94] The Directions appear in full at Appendix 8. In 2000–01 there were 1,336 requests for the recall of short term prisoners. The request was upheld by the Parole Board in 301 cases. For long term prisoners the figures were 533 and 287 respectively: *Annual Report and Accounts of the Parole Board 2000/01* (HC 235, 2001) 20. The Report states that '[t]he Board has a number of concerns about the way these provisions work. The Secretary of State's Directions under which the Board considers these cases require it to make an assessment of risk to the public. However, for short-term prisoners, who will never have been through a parole board review, there is often inadequate information available to the Board on which to base a risk assessment. . . . Of equal concern is that where the Board accepts a prisoner's representations, it has no alternative under the current legislation but to direct his immediate release. This causes difficulties for the Prison and National Probation Services since elements of the original release plan, such as accommodation, may no longer be in place and new arrangements have to be made very quickly' (ibid).
[95] The lack of any need to show a risk to public safety is a feature of the Secretary of State's most recent direction, issued in 2002. This dramatically widens the scope for recall to prison, and it must be asked whether recall for a possible future offence involving no risk to the public is a justifiable deprivation of liberty.
[96] This condition is particularly nebulous, giving little help either to the Parole Board or to released prisoners about what behaviour will result in a return to prison.
[97] The recommendation must be one which not only appears to be on its face but is capable in practice of being one for immediate release from prison (see n 17 above).
[98] *R v Parole Board, ex p Davies*, 25 November 1996, Collins J. The case concerned the Board's refusal to hold an oral hearing in the case of a recalled mandatory lifer but the principle that the Board has a discretion to hold an oral hearing is of general application.

in the previous paragraph, in addition to whether 'the prisoner is likely to comply with licence conditions in the future, taking into account in particular the effect of the further period of imprisonment since recall'.

I. Extended and Longer than Commensurate Sentences

12.62 A sentencing court has at its disposal two forms of determinate sentence which specifically aim to protect the public from violent or sexual offenders. The first sentence is a *longer than commensurate custodial term*, imposed under s 80(2)(b) of the Powers of Criminal Courts (Sentencing) Act 2000. This can be imposed only if an additional custodial term to that which is commensurate to the gravity of the offence is necessary to protect the public from serious harm. The second measure is the *extended sentence*, under s 85 of the 2000 Act. Here, the preventative measure is not custodial, but is designed to keep the prisoner on licence beyond the expiry of the commensurate sentence, with power to recall if that is necessary for the protection of the public. The sentencing court can impose an extension period (extended licence) where it considers that the normal licence period which follows release from a commensurate sentence would not be adequate for the purpose of preventing the commission by him or her of further offences, and for his or her rehabilitation. The harm from which the public is being protected here is of a much lesser degree than under s 80(2)(b). However, although the section speaks merely of 'further offences', there is no doubt that the offences in question must be imprisonable.[99] To be able to resort to detention (by the power of recall) as a means of protecting the public from offences which do not themselves warrant incarceration would clearly be disproportionate, and thus contrary to Articles 3 and 5 of the ECHR.[100] Further, there is a built-in assumption in the extended sentence (in fundamental contrast to the discretionary life sentence) that when the prisoner is released from the commensurate term, the risk of re-offending will continue to be more than minimal. It is precisely because the risk will continue at an unacceptable level that the extended sentence is passed in the first place. However, one fundamental aspect of the extended sentence is that the element of public protection from the ongoing risk after the expiry of the commensurate sentence is to be provided by way of a period of longer than normal supervision in the community, *not* by way of ongoing detention.

12.63 The question whether a prisoner subject to an extended sentence is a long term or short term prisoner for the purposes of the release schemes in the 1991 Act is to be determined by reference to the full extended term, meaning that the vast majority of such prisoners will count as long term, rather than short term prisoners. These

---

[99] See *R v Home Secretary, ex p Stafford* [1999] 2 AC 38.
[100] See *R v Offen* [2000] 1 WLR 253.

provisions are clearly aimed at protecting the public, although there is a definite punitive sting to the provisions by which such prisoners, uniquely, may be made to serve their full sentence if they re-offend on licence (see below). Extended sentence prisoners are, however, entitled to periodic reviews of the extended part of their detention. In *R (Giles) v Parole Board*,[101] Elias J held that, where the criteria which justified an offender's detention depended on personal characteristics which were capable of change, then review of the continued lawfulness of the detention was required under Article 5(4) of the ECHR. Although the seriousness aspect and the protective aspect of an extended sentence need not bear any relationship to each other, once a court had identified part of a sentence as having a protective nature, that part of the sentence attracted the right in Article 5(4) and the continued detention had to be subject to proper periodic review. This adds an important safeguard to this extremely punitive measure.

Where any prisoner subject to an extended sentence is released on licence, the **12.64** licence remains in force (subject to any revocation under s 39 of the 1991 Act) until the end of the extension period of the sentence. Sections 33(3) and 33A(1) of the 1991 Act do not apply to such prisoners, meaning that if they are released and then recalled to prison, they have no right to release at the three-quarter point of the sentence but can be kept in prison for the full duration of the sentence. However, recalled extended sentence prisoners are entitled to seek discretionary release by having their cases referred to the Parole Board, which is empowered to direct their release under ss 39(5A) and 44A of the 1991 Act, added by the 1998 Act. The power to recall in s 39, and the power of re-release in s 44A, must be exercised so as to give effect to the objectives of the extended sentence, discussed above. The release power in s 44A mirrors the language of s 28 governing the release of discretionary life sentence prisoners and detainees at Her Majesty's Pleasure: the Board is to direct the prisoner's release 'if it is satisfied that it is no longer necessary for the protection of the public that [the prisoner] should be confined (but not otherwise)'.

Neither s 28 nor s 44A lay down the test the Board must apply in determining **12.65** whether or not it is satisfied that continued detention is or is not necessary to protect the public. As we have seen, it is necessary in both cases to look to the purpose of the sentence to ascertain the proper test. In the case of the extended sentence, the purpose is, as stated, to protect the public from the commission of further imprisonable offences, and to rehabilitate the prisoner. However, in contrast to the discretionary life sentence, it is the intention of the extended sentence to achieve those aims by a longer than normal period of *supervision on licence in the community*. The Panel is not concerned, in the case of an extended sentence prisoner, to ask itself whether the risk of re-offending is now no more than minimal,

---

[101] [2002] 1 WLR 654. Leave to appeal to the House of Lords has been granted.

because it is not a condition of the prisoner's release in the first place that the risk should be no more than minimal. The Panel is concerned to ask itself whether the object of the sentence in so far as it relates to the protection of the public from the commission of imprisonable offences can be achieved, as was intended, by supervision in the community. Accordingly, it must be the case that, only where, during the period on licence, the prisoner has committed a further imprisonable offence, or behaved in a manner which demonstrates that the risk of his committing such an offence cannot be managed by supervision, does the recall power arise. If the test for release from an extended sentence were to be treated as identical to the discretionary life sentence, ie no more than minimal risk of re-offending, then the difference between the custodial longer than commensurate sentence (s 80(2)(b)) and the non-custodial extended sentence (s 85) would disappear. Any prisoner who upon release from the commensurate sentence was believed to present more than a minimal risk of re-offending could be recalled to prison as soon as he left the prison gate and detained under the extended sentence until the Board was satisfied that the risk he posed of committing further imprisonable offences was no more than minimal. This is plainly an absurd result, not intended by Parliament, which intended one preventative measure to be custodial and the other, concerned with the management of a lesser degree of risk, to be non-custodial.[102]

J. Young Offenders (Under 21)

12.66 There are special arrangements governing the release and supervision of young offenders sentenced to detention in a young offenders institution (YOI)[103] and to those given determinate sentences under s 91 of the Powers of Criminal Courts (Sentencing) Act 2000 (formerly s 53 of the Children and Young Persons Act 1933). Under s 65 of the 1991 Act, anyone aged under 22 at the time of release from one of these sentences will be subject to young offender supervision for a minimum of three months or until their 22nd birthday if that is a shorter period even if this goes beyond the end of the sentence. Supervision may be by a probation officer or a social worker.

12.67 Young offenders aged under 18 serving sentences of exactly 12 months or less must be released on a notice of supervision issued by the governor on behalf of the

---

[102] At the time of writing, the correct approach to extended sentences, and in particular the role of the Parole Board, was due to be considered by the Administrative Court in *R (Sims) v Home Secretary*.

[103] Pursuant to ss 79, 96 and 97 of the Powers of Criminal Courts (Sentencing) Act 2000. Since the introduction of the Detention and Training Order in the Crime and Disorder Act 1998, the DTO has become the principal sentence of detention for offenders aged 12–17, with detention in a YOI reserved for those aged 18, 19 and 20.

Home Secretary. Young offenders aged 18–22 serving sentences of under 12 months must also be released on a notice of supervision.

Young offenders serving more than 12 months are released on a standard adult **12.68** licence depending on the length of the sentence. But if the licence period is less than three months due to remand time, supervision must continue for three months from release and a notice of supervision must be issued to make up the difference.

Breach by a young offender of a licence issued under s 65 of the 1991 Act is pur- **12.69** sued in the magistrates' court. The court may impose a fine or a custodial sentence of up to 30 days.

Young offenders sentenced before 1 October 1992 to a determinate sentence **12.70** under s 91 of the 2000 Act are eligible for early release at the same stage in their sentence as other prisoners but they have no entitlement to release at the two thirds point of their sentence. If the Board recommends release and this is agreed by the Secretary of State, a young offender in this category must be released on licence until the sentence expiry date.

K. Early Release on Compassionate Grounds

A prisoner—whether fixed term or one serving an indeterminate sentence—may **12.71** be released permanently on compassionate grounds. This power is conferred upon the Home Secretary by s 36 of the 1991 Act in relation to fixed term prisoners and by s 30 of the 1997 Act in relation to lifers. It arises where the Home Secretary is satisfied that exceptional circumstances exist which justify the prisoner's release on compassionate grounds. All prisoners, including fixed term prisoners who have not reached their PED, are eligible for release on compassionate grounds.

Prison Service policy states that early release may be considered on the basis of a **12.72** prisoner's medical condition or as a result of tragic family circumstances. The basic principles are that the release of the prisoner will not put the safety of the public at risk and that there is some specific purpose to be served by early release. Release will not normally be made on the basis of facts of which the sentencing court or the Court of Appeal were aware. The detailed criteria governing early release on compassionate grounds are set out at Appendix 8.[104]

---

[104] See Appendix 8.

12.73 Early release on medical grounds may be considered where a prisoner is suffering from a terminal illness and death is likely to occur soon.[105] Three months is considered an appropriate period by the Prison Service and so a clear medical opinion on life expectancy must be obtained. Early release may also be considered where the prisoner is bedridden or severely incapacitated (for example, those confined to wheelchairs, paralyzed, or severe stroke victims). Applications will also be considered if further imprisonment would endanger the prisoner's life or reduce his/her life expectancy. Conditions which are self-induced (such as by hunger strike) will not normally qualify a prisoner for release.

12.74 Early release due to tragic family circumstances is less common than on medical grounds. In many cases, a temporary release will be regarded as more appropriate. The death of a relative would not usually be sufficient to justify early release under current policy. Consideration will be given where a spouse has died or is seriously ill and there is no one to care for the children. Much will depend on what alternative resources exist in the community. All applications for early release on compassionate grounds must be lodged with the Parole Unit. The final decision rests with Ministers but senior officials have delegated authority to refuse applications.

12.75 If early release is approved, the Parole Unit issues a standard parole licence which runs until the prisoner's original licence expiry date (in the case of fixed term prisoners). As with any offender, a prisoner released must comply with the licence conditions. However there is no question of recalling a prisoner simply because of a change in his or her compassionate circumstances. If a prisoner makes an unexpected recovery from a terminal illness, he or she would remain on licence in the community.

L. The Halliday Report

12.76 The structure of sentencing and parole may well change in the lifetime of this edition, perhaps dramatically, in light of *Making Punishments Work: Report of a Review of the Sentencing Framework for England and Wales* ('the Halliday Report').[106] This review, chaired by John Halliday, contains numerous proposals for fundamental reform, from the philosophy underpinning sentencing to the time at which prisoners should be released and the contents of their licences. As one pair of commentators puts it, 'the signs are that the Halliday Report will not

---

[105] For an application of these criteria, see *R v Home Secretary, ex p Smith*, 8 May 2000, where the High Court considered—somewhat harshly—that although the claimant was severely ill from a terminal disease, since it was uncertain when he would actually die, he did not qualify for compassionate release.

[106] The Report is available online at www.homeoffice.gov.uk/cpg/halliday.htm.

sit on the shelf gathering dust, but that its recommendations will prove highly salient in terms of the immediate political agenda'.[107]

The Halliday Report contains many recommendations which are not directly relevant to the present chapter, but which are likely to shape the background against which prisoners are released. It begins by identifying what are perceived to be the current problems with the sentencing framework—a 'narrow sense of purpose', a muddled approach to the relevance of previous convictions, the fact that short prison sentences do not achieve much, the fact that even for longer sentences, the licence conditions only bite up to the three-quarter point, the fact that the current framework does not encourage 'continuous review' of an offender's progress while under sentence, the confused philosophical underpinnings of the 1991, 1997 and 1998 Acts, and the lack of transparency in the sentencing process. The Report goes on to review the principles which should underpin the sentencing framework. Of particular relevance for our purposes, the Report stresses that imprisonment should only be used when no other sentence would be adequate, and that courts should have a clear discretion to pass a non-custodial sentence, even when a short prison sentence would also be justified. **12.77**

The Report examines parole in two different categories: prison sentences of less than 12 months, and sentences longer than 12 months. With regard to the first category, the Report is extremely critical of the current position: despite amounting to six months or less in custody, sentences of under 12 months are: **12.78**

> nevertheless used for large numbers of persistent offenders, with multiple problems and high risks of reoffending, whose offences (and record) are serious enough to justify a custodial sentence, but not so serious that longer prison sentences would be justified. A more effective recipe for failure could hardly be conceived.[108]

The Report recommends that all such sentences should normally consist of a period in prison, up to a maximum of three months, and a period of compulsory supervision in the community, subject to conditions and requirements whose breach may lead to return to prison. The period of supervision would be a minimum of six months, and a maximum amount which would take the sentence as a whole to 12 months. In cases where a court considered that there was no need for a supervisory period, it should be able to order a period in custody, without post release supervision, of up to three months. These proposals, if implemented, would be a significant change to the Automatic Unconditional Release scheme, making the post-release part of the sentence more onerous.

---

[107] E Baker and CMV Clarkson, 'Making Punishments Work? An Evaluation of the Halliday Report on Sentencing in England and Wales' [2002] Crim LR 81.
[108] para 3.2.

12.79   On sentences of more than 12 months, the Report states that:

> It continues to make sense that prison sentences should be served partly in prison
> and partly in the community, so that resettlement and behaviour after release can be
> steered and monitored under conditions whose breach may necessitate return to
> prison. But to make prison sentences more meaningful and effective, they should be
> served in full. The first half should always be in prison. Whether any part of the
> second half need be in prison should depend on the offender's compliance with con-
> ditions imposed on release. Those conditions should be based on up to date assess-
> ments of risks, and of needs for continuing work to prevent re-offending and protect
> the public.[109]

The Report also recommends that the sentencing court should carry out a pre-
release review to determine, on advice from the prison and probation services, the
content of the second half of the sentence. It is very critical of release schemes
which depend on discretion, such as the Home Detention Curfew (HDC), arguing that these are expensive and reduce public confidence. The Report argues for
the removal of HDC before the half-way point of the sentence, though it could
still be used as one means of control in the second half of the sentence. This would
have significant effects on the prison population, particularly since increased use
of HDC before the half-way point is one of the current means of reducing prison
overcrowding. The Report recommends, in effect, that discretion be reserved for
keeping prisoners in prison for longer, rather than letting them out earlier.
Discretionary release should be reserved for violent and sexual offenders who
need, in the view of the courts, to be detained for longer to avoid risks of serious
harm to the public. Offenders who present such a risk should, it is recommended,
be eligible for a new sentence, the effect of which would be to make their release
during the second half of the sentence dependent on a decision by the Parole
Board. Courts would also have the power to extend the supervisory part of the
sentence.

12.80   The Report supports the idea of 'intermittent custody', various versions of which
are used in other European countries. However, it recognizes that it is not currently
clear where or how 'intermittent' prisoners would be accommodated. It requires the
Home Office to establish a review of the existing 'intermediate estate' for accommodating and managing offenders partly in the community and partly in custody.
The review should be carried out in the next year, after which fresh recommendations may emerge. Such a form of custody would be welcome if it mitigated the
isolating and disruptive effects of a prison sentence. The critical issue is who would
be subject to such a sentence. If it would be used only for those who would go to
prison in any event, it would clearly be a progressive step. However, such sentences
should be treated with caution if they were to be used to bring into the prison system those who would formerly have served purely community sentences.

---

[109] para 4.14.

In relation to recall to prison, the Report recommends that breach of conditions **12.81** imposed on release from prison should be enforceable administratively, through recall to prison, subject to a review hearing by a court (generally a district judge). Such hearings would generally be by TV link, with a right to appear in person in cases of serious dispute. The reviewing court would not have the power to vary the length of the recall, but only to overturn the decision to recall. If the court authorized the recall, the prisoner would be eligible for further review hearings. In cases of serious dispute, it is proposed that legal aid would be available. If the breach of conditions occurred during the community part of prison sentences of under 12 months, re-release would be possible after recall only if there were four months or more of the sentence left to serve. Re-release from sentences of 12 months or more would be possible, subject to a review hearing 12 months after the date of recall. Courts would also have a new 'sentence review' capacity, which would deal with breaches of community sentences, hear appeals against recall to prison, authorize pre-release plans for offenders on release from custody and review progress during the community element of custodial sentences.

It is not clear from the Report, and from the Government's response, whether all **12.82** of its recommendations will be implemented, and exactly how they would work in practice. What is clear is that the Report envisages a move away from the current system. The half-way point is still significant, but the second half of a custodial sentence is made much more uncertain, with much heavier supervision and a greater onus on the prisoner to earn his or her freedom by compliance with a potentially onerous list of obligations. Genuine continuity of care and supervision, crossing the gap from prison to release, would be welcome. However, it has been observed that:

> [d]espite its emphasis on rehabilitation and reparation, nobody should be under any illusion: the package of measures contained in the Report are already heavily punitive. In the light of the 'populist punitiveness' that has pervaded much criminal justice policy development in recent years there must be a real danger that increased political input will facilitate an even greater escalation of punishment levels.[110]

---

[110] E Baker and CMV Clarkson, 'Making Punishments Work? An Evaluation of the Halliday Report on Sentencing in England and Wales' [2002] Crim LR 81, 97.

13

MANDATORY LIFERS

A. Introduction

The mandatory life sentence is in a state of uncertainty. The decision of the   **13.01** European Court of Human Rights (ECtHR) in *Stafford v UK*,[1] discussed in greater detail below, has removed the involvement of the Home Secretary in the release of those serving mandatory life sentences, and has extended the safeguards of Article 5 of the European Convention on Human Rights (ECHR) to such prisoners. The House of Lords is due to consider, in the autumn of 2002, challenges to the mandatory nature of the sentence itself, and to the power of the Home Secretary to set the tariff. *Stafford*, and any judgment of the House of Lords requiring reform of the current system, will need to be implemented by primary legislation. At the time of writing, no such legislation has yet been proposed. In this

---

[1] Application 46295/99 (2002) 35 EHRR 32.

chapter, therefore, we examine the legislative history of the mandatory life sentence. We then consider the current role and effect of executive policy and the decisions of the courts on the actual administration of the sentence by the Home Secretary and the Parole Board. Having attempted an historical overview, we seek to state the current (pre-*Stafford*) law and practice affecting mandatory lifers at the different stages of the sentence in more practical terms, indicating the likely areas of reform.

13.02 By s 1(1) of the Murder (Abolition of the Death Penalty) Act 1965, Parliament established a mandatory life sentence for all persons convicted of murder, irrespective of the circumstances surrounding the individual crime.[2] In so doing, it also abolished the death penalty for all categories of murder.[3] What was obviously viewed in 1965 as a liberalizing measure is now generally regarded by lawyers, judges, politicians, and academic observers as an unjust, irrational anachronism.[4] Notwithstanding the introduction of 'automatic' life sentences in the Crime (Sentences) Act 1997, the sentence for murder remains unique as the one offence where the sentencing judge has no discretion whatsoever.[5] As Lord Mustill stated in his important speech in *R v Home Secretary, ex p Doody*:

> The sentencing of a convicted murderer according to English law is a unique formality. Although it is a very grave occasion it is a formality in this sense, that the task

---

[2] If the defendant is aged 18 but under 21 years, the sentence is custody for life (s 93 of the Powers of Criminal Courts (Sentencing) Act 2000) or, if the defendant is under 18, detention during Her Majesty's pleasure (s 90 of the Powers of Criminal Courts (Sentencing) Act 2000). When s 61 of the Criminal Justice and Court Services Act 2000 is brought into force, custody for life will be abolished, and those aged 18, 19 or 20 and convicted of murder will be sentenced to life imprisonment. The position of HMP detainees, as they are commonly described, is dealt with in Ch 14.

[3] Abolition was initially for an experimental period of five years but was confirmed by affirmative resolution of both Houses of Parliament in 1969.

[4] The former LCJ, Lord Bingham, and his two predecessors, Lord Taylor and Lord Lane, have all spoken in strong terms of the unfairness and distortion to basic sentencing principles which the mandatory life sentence has created. Yet successive Home Secretaries who publicly favour greater 'honesty' in sentencing fail to carry this principle through to its logical conclusion in relation to the crime of murder. For an interesting series of essays on the arguments for reform of the mandatory life sentence, and other related issues, see A Ashworth and B Mitchell, *Rethinking English Homicide Law* (Oxford, 2000).

[5] Powers of Criminal Courts (Sentencing) Act 2000, s 109 (formerly Crime (Sentences) Act 1997, s 2) requires a judge to pass an automatic/mandatory life sentence on a defendant convicted of a second serious offence committed after commencement (October 1997) unless the court is persuaded that exceptional circumstances relating to either of the offences or to the offender justify a different course. However, the extent to which these sentences are 'mandatory' has been greatly reduced by the decision of the Court of Appeal in *R v Offen* [2001] 1 WLR 253. Under the Crime (Sentences) Act 1997, mandatory sentences were to be imposed for the second 'serious offence' other than in 'exceptional circumstances'. However, taking into account Arts 3 and 5 of the ECHR, and the prohibition on arbitrary detention, the court held that, in every case where a defendant did not pose an unacceptable risk to the public, the position was to be considered 'exceptional'. This example of creative judicial use of the HRA can hardly be what the Government expected when enacting those provisions, but is, it is submitted, essential to prevent the mandatory sentences from violating the Convention.

of the judge is entirely mechanical. Once a verdict of guilty is returned the outcome is preordained. No matter what the opinion of the judge on the moral quality of the act, no matter what circumstances there may be of mitigation or aggravation, there is only one course for him to take, namely to pass a sentence of life imprisonment.[6]

The mandatory life sentence is also unique in that it remains the only prison sen- **13.03** tence in which a politician, the Home Secretary, rather than a judicial body, determines the length of an offender's detention.[7] The current statutory provision which governs this state of affairs is s 29 of the Crime (Sentences) Act 1997. It states:

> (1) If recommended to do so by the Parole Board, the Secretary of State may, after consultation with the Lord Chief Justice together with the trial judge if available, release on licence a life prisoner who is not one to whom section 28 above applies.
> (2) The Parole Board shall not make a recommendation under subsection (1) above unless the Secretary of State has referred the particular case, or the class of case to which that case belongs, to the Board for its advice.[8]

It may be argued that separating any consideration of mandatory lifers from the **13.04** development of law and practice in relation to discretionary lifers (including persons detained during Her Majesty's Pleasure) is an artificial exercise. In order fully to appreciate the dynamic relationship between legal theory and *realpolitik*, as it has affected mandatory and discretionary lifers, it is better to view this area of prison law as a whole rather than as discrete entities. Nevertheless, we have ultimately taken the view that in the interests of simplicity and clarity it is better to divide our analysis in a way which accords both with the view Parliament and the Home Secretary have taken of the mandatory and discretionary life sentence and (perhaps more importantly in view of the Human Rights Act 1998 (HRA)) the view which the ECtHR has, historically, taken of the two sentences. Having analysed the nature of the mandatory life sentence in its different phases, according to the requirements of law and administrative policy, we consider the more practical issues of how a lifer progresses through the life sentence system, the role of the Parole Board and the law which regulates the recall to prison of mandatory lifers. It may well be that the next edition of this book considers both mandatory and discretionary life sentences together, but at present it is too soon to tell how

---

[6] [1994] 1 AC 531, 549E.

[7] The position is, of course, set to change in the light of *Stafford v UK*, but here we describe the system as it stands. In this chapter, and indeed throughout this book, we include in the definition 'mandatory life sentence' and 'mandatory lifer' persons between 18 and 21 who are convicted of murder and are sentenced to custody for life under s 93 of the Powers of Criminal Courts (Sentencing) Act 2000. The term 'discretionary lifer' includes persons under 18 who are convicted of murder and are sentenced to detention during Her Majesty's pleasure under s 90 of the Powers of Criminal Courts (Sentencing) Act 2000 as well as persons who receive an 'automatic' life sentence for a second serious offence under s 109 of the Powers of Criminal Courts (Sentencing) Act 2000.

[8] The section repeats in identical language the wording in the previous statutory provision, s 35(2) and (3) of the Criminal Justice Act 1991.

the administration of the two sentences will converge in response to recent judicial decisions. In advance of legislative change, the Home Office has begun to refer mandatory life sentence cases for oral hearing, with priority given to lifers in open prisons approaching tariff expiry.

B. The Legislative History of the Mandatory Life Sentence[9]

13.05 The abolition of the death penalty by the Murder (Abolition of Death Penalty) Act 1965 was not the first occasion on which a mandatory life sentence had been introduced. The Homicide Act 1957 imposed a mandatory life sentence for certain categories of murder while maintaining the death penalty for others.[10] And it had never been the case that all convicted murderers actually suffered death by hanging as the punishment for their crime. Just as the Royal Prerogative of mercy had been used during the 19th century to commute the death sentence to one of life imprisonment in respect of the wide range of felonies for which capital punishment remained the sentence fixed by law, so too after s 1 of the Offences Against the Person Act 1861 provided that the mandatory penalty for murder was sentence of death the prerogative of mercy was used to mitigate the harshness of an apparently inflexible law.

13.06 Accordingly, there had always been a pool of life sentence prisoners within the prison system—some convicted of murder, others of lesser crimes—whose release date from custody was determined by the Executive. The Criminal Justice Act 1948 put the Home Secretary's power to release lifers on licence and to recall them on a statutory basis. Section 57 provided as follows:

> (1) The Secretary of State may, at any time if he thinks fit, release on licence a person serving a term of imprisonment for life subject to such conditions as may be specified in the licence, and the Secretary of State may, at any time, modify or cancel any such condition.
>
> (2) The Secretary of State may, at any time by order, recall to prison a person released on licence under this section, but without prejudice to the power of the Secretary of State to release him on licence again; and when any person is so recalled his licence shall cease to have effect and he shall, if at large, be deemed unlawfully at large.[11]

---

[9] For a more detailed account of this subject, see the *Report of the Committee on the Penalty for Homicide* (Chairman, Lord Lane of St Ippollitts) published by the Prison Reform Trust (London, 1993). See also the *Report of the House of Lords Select Committee on Murder and Life Imprisonment* (HL Paper 78–I).

[10] Until the 1957 Act English law had never admitted the idea that there were different degrees of murder but stuck to the division of criminal homicide into murder, for which the death sentence was mandatory, and manslaughter, for which only a maximum sentence of imprisonment for life was prescribed. The 1957 Act broke with this approach and reserved the death penalty for five categories of capital murder. For a fascinating account of this aspect of English legal history, see HLA Hart, *Punishment and Responsibility: Essays in the Philosophy of Law* (Oxford, 1957).

[11] Prison Act 1952, s 27 re-enacted identical provisions. The current release power is to be found in Crime (Sentences) Act 1997, s 29.

And so well before the passage of the 1965 Act there was in place a statutory system for release on licence and recall, and a developing practice that life sentence prisoners should generally be released on licence after serving a finite term of years. As Professor Hart stated in his essay on 'Murder and the Principles of Punishment' (written in 1957),[12] 'under the practice prior to the Homicide Act 1957, a murderer whose death sentence had been commuted to one of life imprisonment very rarely served a period of more than 15 years and the usual period was very much less'.

Thus, it was clearly understood that a sentence to life imprisonment for murder **13.07** did not, in fact, mean a sentence to lifelong detention as the term merited by way of punishment for the individual offence of murder. When in 1965 it was decided to make life imprisonment the mandatory punishment for murder, Parliament explicitly recognized that 'life did not mean life' despite what the judge was required to say when passing sentence.[13] In the course of debates prior to the passage of the 1965 Act there was much discussion about what the life sentence did in fact mean. Viscount Dilhorne remarked that 'I know perfectly well that the sentence passed is a sentence of life imprisonment. There has been controversy about what that means. It does not mean life.' He went on to say that the average term was in the region of nine years.

And so Parliament legislated against the background of a clear awareness that the **13.08** life sentence they were introducing as the uniform sentence for all murders did not order lifelong detention as punishment for the individual offence any particular murderer had committed. This was made clear in the words of the statute itself by the fact that Parliament provided by s 1(2) of the 1965 Act for the judge to declare in open court the minimum period that he thought should elapse before release on licence was authorized. That would have been meaningless if 'life' meant lifelong detention in custody.[14]

---

[12] HLA Hart, *Punishment and Responsibility: Essays in the Philosophy of Law* (Oxford, 1957).
[13] Earlier, the Report of the *Royal Commission on Capital Punishment* (London, 1953) proposed that the sentence of life imprisonment which was then mandatory for those convicted of murder but reprieved from hanging should be replaced by a sentence 'during Her Majesty's Pleasure' to bring the sentence more in line with reality. They argued that since everyone knew that such a prisoner would not be kept in prison until he died, the term 'life imprisonment' was an empty formula. The Royal Commission included Sir Alexander Maxwell, formerly Permanent Under Secretary at the Home Office, as a member and Sir Frank Newsam, his successor and long term colleague, gave evidence. At this time it was accepted in the Home Office that adult reprieved murderers whose sentence was commuted to life would never actually be made to serve a life sentence—the only exceptions would be persons who were dangerous by reason of insanity.
[14] The reason Parliament provided that the period anticipated at the time of sentence as an appropriate minimum time was not to be *predetermined* from the outset but merely *recommended* was that Parliament recognized that the actual release date must depend on the prisoner's future progress in custody, which could not be predicted at the time of sentence (*Hansard*, HC, cols 887–888 (21 December 1964)). It was this legislative intention not to permit predetermination of the release date, rather than any distrust of the judiciary's views as to what punishment required, which led to the judiciary having a consultative role only as to the minimum term to be served. It

13.09 As we shall see below, the argument that the mandatory life sentence is fundamentally different from the discretionary life sentence (because the former is essentially punitive in nature, whereas the latter is imposed for protective purposes) is one which has been consistently maintained by the Home Secretary both before the domestic courts and the ECtHR.[15] Yet the legislative history of the mandatory sentence shows the distinction to be highly dubious. The dubious nature of the distinction was finally recognized by the ECtHR in *Stafford*,[16] discussed further below.

C. The Introduction of Parole and the Development of Executive Policy and Practice

13.10 As a concession to those who feared excessive leniency by the Executive in relation to the release of convicted murderers (who would no longer hang), the 1965 Act obliged the Home Secretary to consult the Lord Chief Justice and the trial judge (if available) before releasing any mandatory lifer on licence.[17] This requirement to consult was extended two years later in two respects. First, the Criminal Justice Act 1967 required the Home Secretary to consult the judges in relation to discretionary as well as mandatory lifers. Secondly, the 1967 Act, which created the Parole Board as the statutory body designed to implement the new arrangements for release on licence introduced by the Act, also imposed a duty on the Board to advise the Home Secretary on the exercise of his discretion to release life sentence prisoners on licence.[18] At the same time, the Home Secretary was required to consult the Board before releasing a life sentence prisoner.[19] According to the new 'dual-key' statutory scheme, the Home Secretary could not release a lifer without a favourable recommendation from the Parole Board, but he was not obliged to follow the Board's advice. When he was minded to accept the Board's recommendation, he had first to consult the Lord Chief Justice and the trial judge (if available) before actually authorizing release.

---

was because the judiciary could not see into the future, not because the Home Secretary was considered a better judge of what punishment required. And for the same reason that the judiciary was given only a consultative role at the time of actual release, namely because it was not considered necessarily to be the best judge of what progress the prisoner had made in custody.

[15] See *Wynne v UK* (1994) 19 EHRR 333 where the ECtHR rejected the argument that the mandatory life sentence should attract Art 5(4) safeguards in the same way as the discretionary life sentence because both sentences contain a punitive and a protective element.

[16] *Stafford v UK* Application 46295/99 (2002) 35 EHRR 32.

[17] Murder (Abolition of Death Penalty) Act 1965, s 2.

[18] See Criminal Justice Act 1967, s 59(3).

[19] Criminal Justice Act 1967, s 61(1). For a detailed account of the development of law and practice from 1967 onwards, see the speech of Lord Mustill in *Ex p Doody* [1994] 1 AC 531, 551H–556B.

In practice the advice of the Parole Board was not obtained (absent exceptional **13.11** circumstances) until the Board conducted its first review of a prisoner's progress after seven years in custody. And the views of the judges were not at this stage sought unless a positive release recommendation by the Board was seriously in prospect. In 1972 the practice altered when a Joint Committee of the Home Office and the Parole Board was set up with the aim of creating a more discriminating procedure for reviewing lifers.[20] It was a feature of both the pre-1972 system and the Joint Committee's role that the involvement of the Parole Board began at an earlier stage than it does today. And an inevitable feature of this involvement was that the Board became involved in considering not just when it would be safe to release a lifer but also how much punishment was merited by the individual offence of murder.[21] Against this background, the 1993 Report of the Committee on the Penalty for Homicide commented that:

> It seems clear that, from the start, there were two factors that determined release—first, considerations of punishment (or 'tariff') characterised by the Parole Board in its 1970 Report as 'whether the time served is appropriate to the crime' and, secondly, considerations of the risk to the public of further offences if the offender is released. Indeed one might ask whether any other fact could rationally be taken into account.[22]

The 1983 and 1987 Policy Statements

It was not, however, until 1983 that any public statement of the policy which lay **13.12** behind the practical administration of the life sentence was made by a Home Secretary, and when it was, it was in the context of a significant change in the consultation procedures. Following his speech to the Conservative Party Conference in 1983, Leon Brittan announced a series of radical changes in existing policies relating to the release of prisoners on parole and licence.[23] These included what

---

[20] The Joint Committee made an initial assessment of all life sentence cases after four years (later reduced to three) in custody. The Committee would then fix a date for the first review by the Parole Board or, where this was not considered appropriate at such an early stage, fix a date for further consideration by the Joint Committee in some years' time. As Lord Mustill commented in *Ex p Doody* [1994] 1 AC 531, 552F–H, '[w]e see here the origins of the crucial practical distinction between setting a date for release and setting a date of the first consideration of release'.

[21] In its 1970 report the Parole Board acknowledged that its function had a 'sentencing character' in relation to lifers: '[w]ith life sentence cases, however, the sentence is indeterminate and our functions assume a sentencing character because there is no fixed term. The question is not simply whether the conditions, bearing in mind the nature of the offence, are held to justify granting parole. The primary question is whether the time served is appropriate to the crime.'

[22] The Committee, which was chaired by former LCJ, Lord Lane, comprised a number of highly respected experts in the field of criminal justice policy including David Faulkner CB, Professor Terence Morris, Lord Windlesham, Sir Patrick Russell, Sir Louis Blom-Cooper QC, and Edward Fitzgerald QC.

[23] *Hansard*, HC, cols 505–508 (30 November 1983). The entire policy statement is reproduced at Appendix 9. The Brittan policy was (unsuccessfully) challenged in *Re Findlay* [1985] AC 318 by both fixed and life sentence prisoners on the basis that the policy frustrated their legitimate expectations and because the Home Secretary had implemented the changes without consulting the Parole Board.

Lord Mustill was to call in *Ex p Doody* 'the creation of a completely new philosophy and practice for the release of life prisoners on licence'. He listed those features as follows:

(1) The Joint Home Office/Parole Board committee which had been established to recommend the date for the first review by the Parole Board was disbanded.

(2) Instead the Home Secretary would himself, after consulting the judges 'on the requirements of retribution and deterrence', fix the date for the first review.

(3) The review would normally take place three years before the expiry of the 'period necessary to meet the requirements of retribution and deterrence'. This would give sufficient time for preparation for release, if the Parole Board were to recommend it.

(4) Subject to exceptional circumstances the first review would, in fact, take place on the date so fixed.

(5) Meanwhile progress of the prisoner would be kept under regular review by the Home Office.

(6) The consultation with the judges required by s 61 of the Criminal Justice Act 1967 would take place when release was an actual possibility. This would, therefore, be a second such consultation.

(7) In the case of certain types of murder, the prisoner would not normally be released until 20 years, or even longer, had been served.

(8) Mr Brittan's announcement contained the following important passage:[24]

> These new procedures will separate consideration of the requirements of retribution and deterrence from consideration of risk to the public, which has always been and will continue to be, the pre-eminent factor determining release. They will enable the prisoner and other staff responsible for considering and reporting on life sentence cases, the Local Review Committee and the Parole Board, to concentrate on risk. The judiciary will properly advise on retribution and deterrence. But the ultimate discretion whether to release will remain with me.

13.13 As we have indicated above, long before Mr Brittan's 1983 statement, the Parole Board had recognized that, in reviewing the cases of mandatory lifers, they were, in reality, engaged in a quasi-sentencing exercise to determine how much of their sentence prisoners should serve *in custody* for their offence. The 1983 statement to Parliament was in effect an express acknowledgment of what had been implicit throughout—namely that the mandatory life sentence does not order lifelong punitive detention but authorizes detention for purposes that are partly punitive and partly preventative.[25]

---

24 [1994] 1 AC 531, 553B–D.
25 In his judgment in the Court of Appeal in *Ex p Doody* [1993] QB 157, Glidewell LJ explained it thus: '[s]o far as I am aware this [the 1983 policy statement] was the first occasion on which it was made clear that the period which elapses before a prisoner serving a life sentence is released is

What was *new*, then, about the statement and the policy it introduced was the **13.14** clear division of the sentence into two parts—the first exclusively punitive and the second preventive. Under this new procedure the Home Secretary, after consultation with the judiciary, fixed in the case of every life sentence prisoner a term of years as '*the* period necessary to meet the requirements of retribution and deterrence'. This became known as the tariff. Thus the prisoner's first review by the local review committee (as a preliminary stage to review by the Parole Board) was normally fixed to take place 'three years before the expiration of the period necessary to satisfy the requirements of retribution and deterrence'. This was the beginning of the second phase in which the 'pre-eminent factor determining release' was risk. A life prisoner who had completed his tariff could, on the face of it, expect to be released unless he was still considered to be a risk to the public. The 1983 policy statement applied to mandatory and discretionary lifers alike.[26]

As a result of the decision of the Divisional Court *in R v Home Secretary, ex p* **13.15** *Handscomb*[27] the procedures introduced by the 1983 statement were refined somewhat in 1987. Thus, in his 1987 statement, the Home Secretary announced two changes:

(1) That the tariff period for all lifers would be determined at an early stage of their imprisonment. The factors to be taken into account were the factors known at the time of sentence on the basis of the material before the court and the criteria to be applied (retribution and deterrence) were the same as those applied in an orthodox sentencing exercise.

(2) That, in the case of discretionary lifers, the punitive phase would be calculated by reference to the fixed term that they would have served but for the mental element which led to the imposition of the life sentence; and that the Home Secretary would consider himself bound by the judicial view on the tariff.[28]

---

determined by consideration of two factors, namely: the period necessary to satisfy retribution and deterrence, which has come to be called "the tariff"; and a possible further period if it is thought by the Parole Board and/or the Secretary of State that the prisoner would pose an unacceptable risk of danger to the public were he to be released at the end of the tariff period'.

[26] The Brittan statement did reflect the logic of the position that the determination of the tariff was closely akin to a sentencing decision to this extent. The principle of non-aggravation of a penal term, once fixed, was implicitly recognized by the express undertaking that 'except where a prisoner has committed an offence for which he has received a further custodial sentence, the first formal review date will not be put back'. Thus whilst the policy did allow for a reduction of the tariff and advancement of the first review date in the light of subsequent progress in prison, it did not permit an increase of the tariff and further putting back of the first review date. This analysis was accepted by the majority in *R v Home Secretary, ex p Pierson* [1998] AC 539.

[27] (1988) 86 Cr App R 59.

[28] The only distinction introduced by the 1987 statement between discretionary and mandatory lifers was that the Home Secretary reserved the right in the case of mandatory lifers to fix a punitive term that was different from that recommended by the judiciary and, if necessary, longer. But the 1987 statement retained the basic two-stage division for all lifers.

The 1991 Rumbold Statement

13.16   The result of the 1983 and 1987 statements was that detention under the mandatory life sentence was shown to have a clear two-phase rationale that was both
accessible to prisoners and understandable by them. And the courts (in such cases
as *Ex p Bradley*,[29] *Ex p Cox*,[30] and *Ex p Creamer and Scholey*[31]) expressly acknowledged the basic similarity between the two-phase detention under a mandatory
life sentence and the similar two-phase detention under a discretionary life sentence. This led to the demand that both sentences should be accorded a similar
right to a judicial determination of the length of each phase (as had been recognized by the ECtHR in the case of discretionary lifers[32]). It was not to be. On 16
July 1991, in the course of a Parliamentary debate on the Criminal Justice Bill, the
Minister of State, Mrs Angela Rumbold, drew a distinction between the mandatory and discretionary life sentence which had not previously been spelled out in
earlier policy statements. Almost certainly unaware of the litigious consequences
she was triggering, she said that:

> Mandatory life sentence cases, however, raise quite different issues [from those
> raised by discretionary life sentences] . . . In a discretionary case, the decision on
> release is based purely on whether the offender continues to be a risk to the public.
> The presumption is that once the period that is appropriate to punishment has
> passed, the prisoner should be released if it is safe to do so. The nature of the manda-
> tory life sentence is different. The element of risk is not the decisive factor in hand-
> ing down a life sentence. *According to the judicial process, the offender has committed
> a crime of such gravity that he forfeits his liberty to the State for the rest of his life—if
> necessary, he can be detained for life without the necessity for subsequent judicial inter-
> vention.* The presumption is, therefore, that the offender should remain in custody
> until and unless the Home Secretary concludes that the public interest would be bet-
> ter served by the prisoner's release than by his continued detention. In exercising his
> continued discretion in that respect, the Home Secretary must take account, not
> just of questions of risk, but of how society would view the prisoner's release at that
> juncture. The Home Secretary takes account of the judicial recommendation, but
> the final decision is his.[33]

The suggestion that a mandatory lifer has 'committed a crime of such gravity that
he forfeits his liberty for the rest of his days' involved an appeal to the theory of the
mandatory life sentence which was (and remains) wholly inconsistent with the
practice of the Executive in relation to mandatory lifers. And in *Ex p Doody* Lord
Mustill commented in strong terms that when analyzing what the requirements
of fairness demanded in relation to the tariff-fixing exercise, the inconsistent

---

[29]   [1991] 1 WLR 134, 149C–D.
[30]   (1991) 5 Admin LR 17.
[31]   [1993] COD 162.
[32]   *Thynne, Wilson and Gunnell v UK* (1991) 13 EHRR 666.
[33]   *Hansard*, HC, col 309 (16 July 1991) emphasis added.

theory enunciated by Mrs Rumbold had to be left 'entirely out of account' because it was impossible to reconcile with the regime in place since 1983.[34]

The July 1993 Howard Statement

One might have expected that with the *Doody* decision the 'Rumbold theory' of   **13.17** the mandatory life sentence would have bitten the dust once and for all on the basis that it might be desirable to bring theory and practice into line following a compelling analysis by the House of Lords. It was not to be. In his Parliamentary statement in response to *Ex p Doody* (which had introduced a number of procedural fairness safeguards into the exercise of tariff fixing for mandatory lifers[35]) former Home Secretary Michael Howard merely noted Lord Mustill's comments on the inconsistency between theory and practice raised by the Minister of State's 1991 Parliamentary statement.[36] He then proceeded baldly to reassert the Rumbold philosophy (which had been criticized but not actually declared unlawful in Doody) as the way in which he intended to exercise his discretion in the future.[37]

---

[34] [1994] 1 AC 531. It seems certain that the primary purpose of Mrs Rumbold's statement was to explain and justify the Government's decision to deny to mandatory lifers the procedural safeguards which it was extending to discretionary lifers in the 1991 Bill following the decision of the ECtHR in *Thynne, Wilson and Gunnell v UK* (1991) 13 EHRR 666, namely a judicial determination on the tariff and a right to a post-tariff review of detention by the Parole Board of a kind which would satisfy the requirements of Art 5(4) of the ECHR.

[35] Having completed his summary of the history of the mandatory life sentence, Lord Mustill said at 556B–E that he believed it 'has shown how, in contrast with the position as regards discretionary life sentences, the theory and the practice for convicted murderers are out of tune. The theory—and it is the only theory which can justify the retention of the mandatory life sentence— was restated by Mrs Rumbold less than two years ago. It posits that murder is an offence so grave that the proper "tariff" sentence is invariably detention for life although as a measure of leniency it may be mitigated by release on licence. Yet the practice established by Mr Brittan in 1983 and still in force founds on the proposition that there is concealed within the life term a fixed period of years, apt to reflect not only the requirements of deterrence but also the moral quality of the individual act ("retribution"). These two philosophies of sentencing are inconsistent. Either may be defensible, but they cannot both be applied at the same time.' Lord Mustill's approach was to derive a mandatory lifer's procedural rights primarily from administrative practice and not from the rationale of the sentence. He declined to go the whole way and recognize that the Rumbold theory of the mandatory life sentence was no longer sustainable even as a theory. And he recognized that the difference in philosophy between the mandatory and discretionary sentences meant that the courts were not entitled to 'judicialize' the tariff phase via the medium of judicial review.

[36] *Hansard*, HC, WA cols 863–865 (27 July 1993). Mr Howard's statement is set out in full in Appendix 9.

[37] Michael Howard's defiance reflected the aggressive, populist tone which characterized his term of office and his relationship with the judges but in truth Lord Mustill's speech left the Home Secretary with ample scope to return to the 'discredited' Rumbold philosophy. The House of Lords in *Doody* did not hold that the Rumbold theory was incorrect or unlawful, and indeed it maintained the Home Secretary's right to determine the tariff because the task was that of fixing a tariff penal element when the 'true tariff sentence is life imprisonment' (558H). Finally, Lord Mustill reasserted the Home Secretary's right to have regard to 'broader considerations of a public character than those which apply to an ordinary sentencing function' when carrying out his task of tarifffixing.

13.18 Howard's statement contained two further controversial changes to existing policy. First, he made it clear that he reserved the right 'exceptionally' to increase a tariff already fixed and communicated to a mandatory lifer whenever he 'or a successor in my office conclude that, putting aside questions of risk, the minimum requirements of retribution and deterrence will not have been satisfied at the expiry of the period which had previously been determined'. In other words, a new Home Secretary (possibly one determined to make his mark as tough on violent criminals) could re-visit tariffs fixed by his predecessors and increase them on the basis that they were too 'soft'. The lawfulness of this assertion was challenged in *R v Home Secretary, ex p Pierson* but not authoritatively determined because no clear ratio emerged from the five speeches delivered in the House of Lords.[38]

13.19 Secondly, the Howard statement purported to reserve the right to detain mandatory lifers who had completed their tariffs and were no longer a danger to the public on the basis that their 'early release' (ie release before the prisoner's death) would not be 'acceptable to the public'. The legality of what has become known as 'phase three detention' has not yet been tested because no Home Secretary has ever (to date) sought to justify the continued detention of a mandatory lifer by reference to this third criterion.[39] Should it ever be resorted to, the prospects of a successful challenge (whether by judicial review or under the HRA) must be good. The 'public interest' may be a relevant factor for the Home Secretary (and the judges) to take into account in determining how long the tariff should be and how great a risk to the public is acceptable. But if a mandatory lifer deserves no further punishment and is no risk to the public, then any *legitimate* interest in continuing to detain him or her evaporates.

---

[38] *Hansard*, HC, WA cols 863–865 (27 July 1993). Mr Howard's statement is set out in full in Appendix 9. By a curious quirk of legal history, *Ex p Pierson* did not truly involve a conscious increase of a lifer's tariff by a Home Secretary as contemplated by the July 1993 Howard statement. It was only when the case reached the courts that it became clear that the Home Secretary thought he was simply confirming a previously communicated tariff (of 20 years) and had never believed he needed to rely on a claimed power to aggravate a tariff previously fixed and communicated. The case of Myra Hindley was different in that her case and that of her co-defendant, Ian Brady, remain the only examples of any Home Secretary actually deciding to increase a tariff previously determined by a predecessor, albeit 'provisionally' so determined. In his judgment in *Ex p Hindley* Lord Bingham CJ closely analysed the five speeches delivered in *Pierson* and concluded that a different majority comprising Lords Goff, Browne-Wilkinson, and Lloyd had accepted the lawfulness of a general power to increase tariffs subject to any argument capable of being founded on legitimate expectation. But this was an obiter remark bearing in mind his conclusion that the principle of non-aggravation of penalties only applied in relation to tariffs which had been fixed and communicated to the prisoner. In Ms Hindley's case, the Divisional Court found that her 'provisional' 30-year tariff had been neither fixed nor communicated to her.

[39] As we shall see below, the continued detention of Myra Hindley was not justified by reference to the 'public acceptability' criterion although her case was almost certainly the inspiration for its invention.

The November 1997 Policy Statement

The final twist in the history of policy towards the administration of the manda- **13.20**
tory life sentence came with the policy statement issued by Home Secretary Jack
Straw on 10 November 1997. Formally intended to be an authoritative response
to the House of Lords' ruling in *Ex p Pierson*, the statement was made after argument had concluded (but before judgment was delivered) in the important case of
R v Home Secretary, ex p Stafford[40] and before argument began in the Divisional
Court in *R v Home Secretary, ex p Hindley*.[41] It constituted a bold assertion
by Mr Straw that anything Michael Howard could do he could slavishly follow.
Straw's statement began by declaring that the majority of the House of Lords in *Ex
p Pierson* had found that it was lawful for a Home Secretary to increase a tariff
previously fixed and communicated, as Howard's 1993 statement had claimed.[42]
He also made clear (in order to deal with Lord Goff's particular concern in
Pierson) that this power would have retrospective effect. He then proceeded to
reassert the Rumbold philosophy towards the mandatory life sentence while at the
same time modifying policy in relation to 'whole life' tariff prisoners by claiming
that he was open to the possibility that exceptional progress by such prisoners
might result in a reduction in tariff.[43] Finally, the statement made an important
clarification to previous policy concerning the release of post-tariff mandatory lifers. While re-asserting the possibility of 'phase three detention', Straw explained
that in considering the issue of risk in the post-tariff phase he would no longer be
confining himself to the widely held understanding that the 'risk' to be considered
in the post-tariff phase was of the released lifer committing a further violent

---

[40] [1998] 1 WLR 503. We consider this case in more detail below when we examine the post-
tariff phase of the mandatory life sentence.

[41] [1998] 2 WLR 505.

[42] The statement (and argument later advanced on the Home Secretary's behalf in the Court
of Appeal in *Ex p Stafford*) explained this conclusion on the basis that Lord Goff's decision to
allow the appeal of Mr Pierson was solely based on the retrospectivity argument, thereby implying
that Lord Goff must have *accepted* the principle that in future tariffs fixed under the 1993 policy
were capable of being increased or 'aggravated'. Having so analysed Lord Goff's speech, the
speeches of Lord Steyn and Lord Hope were categorized as minority opinions on the key issue of
whether the claimed power to aggravate a tariff was an unlawful exercise of the Home Secretary's
broad release discretion.

[43] This modification to the Howard policy cut away an important ground in Myra Hindley's
application for judicial review. She had intended to argue that the previous policy was unlawful
because it failed to allow for the possibility of release before death on the ground of a lifer's exceptional progress in prison. It was only the possibility of such flexibility which had saved the Home
Secretary's policy of 20-year tariffs for certain categories of murderer in *Re Findlay* [1985] AC 318
from being quashed as an improper fetter on the broad release discretion. This attack on the illegality of Howard's policy was accepted by the Divisional Court, but Jack Straw's amended policy cured
the problem.

offence.[44] Rather, for the future, the word 'risk' meant a risk that the lifer might commit a further imprisonable offence. In fact, the Court of Appeal's ruling in *Ex p Stafford* (delivered two weeks after the Straw policy statement) held that in refusing to release Mr Stafford because of a fear that he might commit a non-violent, imprisonable offence, the Home Secretary had not departed from his stated policy and had not acted unlawfully.[45] We consider the full implications of this decision below when we examine the post-tariff phase of a mandatory lifer in more detail.

D. The ECHR and Mandatory Lifers

13.21 What this analysis of the development of policy and practice has shown is that, historically, there has been a substantial gap between the mandatory and discretionary life sentences, both in terms of the philosophy which is said to underpin them and the statutory procedures for administering them. This gap was most recently supported by the ECtHR in *Wynne v UK*.[46] In that case, the ECtHR rejected the argument that mandatory lifers should be accorded the same rights as discretionary lifers to an Article 5(4) parole review in the post-tariff phase of

---

[44] Mr Straw's carefully drafted statement sought to present this aspect of his policy as a confirmation of existing policy rather than a fundamental change to it. The statement was issued after argument had concluded in *Ex p Stafford* [1998] 1 WLR 503 in which a central issue was whether the Home Secretary's previous policy statements and argument to both the domestic courts and the ECtHR had used the word 'risk' in the post-tariff phase to mean a risk to the life or limb of the public. Counsel for the Home Secretary had argued that previous policy was crystal clear and that the Home Secretary had never publicly confined his release power in the way contended for by the applicant. Yet until Mr Straw's statement, no Home Secretary had stated in any policy statement concerned with the release of mandatory lifers that release would depend on proof that there was no longer an unacceptable risk of the commission of any imprisonable offence—which, of course, includes a wide range of petty offences wholly unrelated to the reason for the mandatory lifer being in the arms of the State in the first place. For a detailed analysis of this issue, see the judgment of Buxton LJ in *Ex p Stafford* at 520E–531A.

[45] It had been submitted on Mr Stafford's behalf that the use of the word 'risk' in successive policy statements in the context of the release of post-tariff mandatory lifers had become a term of art and meant danger to the public in the sense of a risk to life or limb. It was also pointed out that in numerous cases before the courts (including the ECtHR in *Hussain v UK* (1996) 22 EHRR 1) over many years, the Home Secretary had accepted that in the post-tariff phase the same test of dangerousness would apply to mandatory and discretionary lifers as well as HMP detainees. The only arguable departure from this consistent approach lay in the Directions to the Parole Board issued by the Home Secretary under s 32(6) of the 1991 Act in which it was stated that the Board should consider before making a release recommendation whether the risk that the lifer will commit a further imprisonable offence is minimal. It was this fact which persuaded Morritt and Buxton LJJ that the Home Secretary had sufficiently stated his policy to indicate that risk, in the context of mandatory lifers, meant a risk of the released lifer committing any imprisonable offence. But Buxton LJ reached this conclusion with some reluctance, commenting that the matter could have been put more clearly before life sentence prisoners and the public. The reservations expressed by the domestic courts helped to persuade the ECtHR to revisit the issue in *Stafford v UK*, discussed in detail below.

[46] (1994) 19 EHRR 333.

detention. It did so on the basis that the mandatory life sentence is imposed automatically as the punishment for the offence of murder irrespective of the dangerousness of the offender.[47] It also relied on the fact that the release of a mandatory
lifer is entirely a matter within the discretion of the Home Secretary, who is not
bound by the judicial recommendation as to the length of tariff 'and who is free
under English law to have regard to other criteria than "dangerousness" following
the expiry of the tariff period in deciding whether the prisoner should be released'.

However, ever since the House of Lords made it clear in *R v Home Secretary, ex p V*   **13.22**
& T[48] and in *Ex p Pierson*[49] that the exercise of tariff-fixing is a sentencing exercise, it was strongly arguable that the setting of a mandatory lifer's tariff should
attract Article 6 safeguards, ie that it should be done by judges in open court, not
by the Home Secretary. This also has implications in the post-tariff phase as, logically, it is no longer possible to characterize the formal pronouncement of a life
sentence as ordering lifelong punitive detention—the analysis which underlay the
decision in *Wynne*.

At the time of writing the previous edition of this book, there seemed little   **13.23**
prospect of Parliament reconsidering of its own motion either the retention of the
mandatory life sentence for murder or the release procedure which regulates its
operation. However, a series of domestic and European decisions forced the issue.
The following section examines those domestic decisions, and how they paved the
way for the ECtHR's decision in *Stafford*.

Anderson and Taylor[50]

The judgment of the Divisional Court

The claimants were both convicted murderers who challenged the power of the   **13.24**
Home Secretary to fix the tariff (or punitive) element of their mandatory life sentences. In each case the Home Secretary had determined their tariffs at a level
higher than that recommended by the judiciary (ie the trial judge and the Lord
Chief Justice). The issue in each case was whether the Home Secretary had acted
compatibly with the claimant's Convention right under Article 6(1) to have the
tariff period of his life sentence determined by 'an independent and impartial tribunal established by law'. All three judges rejected the claimants' application, but
their reasoning is different in important respects.

---

[47] The mandatory life sentence was first analysed as ordering lifelong punitive detention for an
adult convicted of murder in the Myra Hindley case (*X v UK*) before the European Commission in
1975. It was upheld in *Thynne, Wilson and Gunnell v UK* (1991) 13 EHRR 666. However, see now
Stafford, discussed below.
[48] [1997] 3 WLR 23.
[49] [1998] AC 539.
[50] [2001] HRLR 33, QB; [2002] 2 WLR 1143, CA.

13.25 Most significantly, the majority (Sullivan and Penry-Davey JJ) expressed the view that, but for domestic and ECtHR authority, they would have held that the exercise of tariff setting *did* attract Article 6 protection. They considered that the reasoning of the ECtHR in *Wynne*[51] was flawed, in that it proceeded on a formalistic rather than a substantive analysis of the reality of the mandatory life sentence. In dismissing the claimants' submissions and holding that Article 6 had no application to the tariff-fixing exercise conducted by the Home Secretary in a mandatory life sentence case, Rose LJ concluded that:

> A proper distinction between discretionary and mandatory sentences has been at the heart of recent House of Lords and Privy Council decisions. That distinction has been accepted in Strasbourg and it is pertinent to alleged breaches of Article 6 as well as Article 5 (4).[52]

The judgment of Sullivan J, however, was radically different in its approach to the applicability of Article 6. In the first paragraph of his judgment he said that:

> If the question raised in these applications was free from authority, I would have had no hesitation in concluding that for the purpose of deciding whether the claimants' rights under Article 6 had been infringed the Court should look at substance rather than form. . . . The undeniable fact is that in fixing a tariff in an individual case, the Home Secretary is making a decision about the punishment of the convicted man. (see per Lord Steyn in Pierson at p.585D).[53]

But Sullivan J agreed with Rose LJ that the matter was not free from authority, and he proceeded critically to analyze the state of the domestic and Strasbourg authority which compelled him, reluctantly, to dismiss the claimants' challenge. His reasoning is worth setting out at length:

> Is it possible to say that the distinction so clearly established in domestic law is no longer sustainable in the light of Article 6.1? On the authorities as they stand at present, the answer to that question has to be 'no'. In *Thynne, Wilson and Gunnell* the European Court of Human Rights ('the Court') drew a distinction between the objectives of the discretionary life sentence and 'the punitive purposes' of the mandatory life sentence.
>
> In *Wynne v United Kingdom* the Applicant challenged the validity of that distinction. The Applicant's submissions were rejected, the Court in paragraph 36 of its judgment saw 'no cogent reasons to depart from the finding in the *Thynne, Wilson and Gunnell* case', having stated in paragraph 35, that the mandatory life sentence belonged to a 'different category'. The Court's reasons for reaching that conclusion have been set out in full in the judgment of Rose LJ.
>
> I confess that I do not find the Court's reasoning in paragraph 35 of its judgment convincing. Once it is recognised that the sentence of life imprisonment for murder authorises, but does not require lifelong punitive detention, and is imposed regardless of the facts of the particular case and the circumstances of the individual offender, it follows that there will be a need for a further, tariff fixing stage.

---

[51] (1994) 19 EHRR 333.
[52] [40].
[53] [42].

If one looks at substance rather than form, the punishment is made to fit the crime (and the criminal) at the latter stage. The purely formal pronouncement of sentence of life imprisonment by the trial judge is merely the start of the sentencing process not the end. That this is the reality is well understood by Parliament, the public and prisoners.

However, it has to be acknowledged that the Court's decision in *Wynne* has been followed by the Commission in the cases of *Ryan, Bromfield* and *Raja* and, most recently, in *Venables v United Kingdom* the Court, referring to *Wynne*, drew a distinction between 'the mandatory life sentence imposed on adults for murder which constitutes punishment for life' and the sentence of detention during Her Majesty's pleasure which, 'is open-ended' (see paragraph 110 of the court's judgment).

The Court was concerned with Article 5.4 in *Wynne*, but it seems to me that the court's reasoning, if it is accepted, applies with equal force to Article 6.1. That was certainly the view of the Commission in *Ryan, Bromfield* and *Raja* and of the Court itself in *Venables v United Kingdom*.

Whilst this Court is not bound by the judgments of the European Court of Human Rights and the decisions of the Commission referred to above, it must take them into account in deciding whether there has been a breach of Article 6.1 (see section 2(1) of the Human Rights Act 1998). Notwithstanding the reservations expressed above, I would be slow to depart from such a consistent line of authority from the Court and the Commission. Moreover, *Wynne* was referred to with approval by Lord Steyn at page 49H of his speech, (with which the remainder of their Lordships agreed) in *Stafford*. Rejecting what was, 'in reality an appeal for a more rational system', Lord Steyn referred to both *Doody* and *Wynne* and concluded:

> As matters stand at present the duality is embedded into our law by primary legislation.

Since that duality has been endorsed by *Wynne* in the context of the Convention, I am driven to the conclusion that these applications must be dismissed.[54]

Penry-Davey J delivered a brief judgment agreeing with the reasoning of Sullivan J, adding that this was 'a position that I accept with considerable reluctance'.[55]

The judgment of the Court of Appeal

13.26 In the Court of Appeal, as in the Divisional Court, all three judges ultimately dismissed the claimants' challenges on the basis that domestic and Strasbourg case law compelled such an outcome. But once again, a majority (Simon Brown and Buxton LJJ) expressed the clear view that, free from authority, they would have held that Article 6 (and Article 5(4)) applied to the mandatory life sentence as it applies to the discretionary life sentence and the sentence of detention during Her Majesty's Pleasure. In expressing these views the majority gave detailed explanations of why they considered the reasoning of the ECtHR in *Wynne*[56] to be seriously flawed and ripe for review by the European Court.

---

[54] [46]–[53].
[55] [54].
[56] (1994) 19 EHRR 333.

13.27 Lord Woolf CJ summarized the legislative and administrative framework which surrounds the tariff system, as well as the state of the domestic and Strasbourg case law. Like Rose LJ in the Divisional Court, Lord Woolf expressed no view as to the correctness of the reasoning process in *Wynne*, but considered that domestic and ECHR authority compelled the rejection of the claimants' arguments.

> The law is not always logical and it has been the approach of both Parliament and the courts in this jurisdiction and so far of the ECtHR to give a particular status to the life sentence for murder. From an historical perspective, connected with the abolition of capital punishment, the attitude of Parliament is understandable. It could also well be the case that this is an area where the ECtHR considered it right to show deference to the attitude so clearly adopted by Parliament. If this was the position of the ECtHR, it is an approach with which we should not differ.

13.28 At the outset Simon Brown LJ made the (plainly correct) point that although the claimants' challenge was to the Home Secretary's power to set tariffs for mandatory lifers, and therefore focused on the requirements of Article 6, their case necessarily involved a consideration of the applicability of Article 5(4). He then proceeded at paragraphs 34–45 to summarize the relevant Strasbourg case law in relation to the three different types of indeterminate sentence in UK domestic law before outlining the essence of the claimants' case. They placed particular reliance, he observed, on:

> the way the Crown put its case to the Court of Appeal Criminal Division (sitting also as a Divisional Court) in *R (Lichniak) v Secretary of State for the Home Department* [2001] 3 WLR 933 in which two mandatory life prisoners challenged their sentences as incompatible with Articles 3 and 5 of the Convention. To escape the complaint under Article 3 that the applicants were being subjected to 'inhuman or degrading . . . punishment', [Counsel for the Home Secretary] contended that the punishment is not that the offender must stay in prison for the rest of his life but rather that he will be detained until, having taken account of tariff and risk, he is released on life licence.

13.29 The claimants argued that the Crown's position was irreconcilable with the notion of a lifelong punitive sentence, such as has formed the essential basis for distinguishing mandatory life sentences throughout the ECtHR's jurisprudence. Simon Brown LJ then proceeded to summarize the arguments advanced in response on behalf of the Home Secretary and his conclusion in relation to each of them:

> I accept, of course, that the mandatory life sentence is unique. But not all the offences for which it is imposed can be regarded as uniquely grave. Rather the spectrum is a wide one with multiple sadistic murders at one end and mercy killings at the other. Lifelong punitive detention will be appropriate only exceptionally. As for 'broader considerations of a public character', it is difficult to understand quite what these are. Regard must not be had to 'public clamour'—see *Venables*. There is, of course, 'the need to maintain public confidence in the system of criminal justice' (see the Home Secretary's statement to Parliament on 10 November 1997). To my

mind, however, this can and should be catered to in the fixing of the tariff. The retributive element of the tariff should reflect the public's moral outrage at an offence. Surely the maintenance of public confidence in the system cannot require longer incarceration than that which properly reflects society's entitlement to vengeance. Sometimes, I recognise, that will require a whole life tariff. But why should not the judges determine that? The third and last point, as to retrospectively increasing the tariff, is a narrow one. The same problem could presumably arise in a discretionary life sentence case. In truth, however, it begs rather than answers the question whether the initial fixing of the tariff is properly to be regarded as an exercise in sentencing.

In short, I find none of [Counsel for the Home Secretary's] arguments convincing. Neither singly nor cumulatively do they seem to me to provide a principled basis for treating tariff-fixing in mandatory life cases differently from the similar exercise required for discretionary life prisoners and Her Majesty's pleasure detainees. In all three cases the exercise is in substance the fixing of a sentence, determining the length of the first stage of an indeterminate sentence—that part of it which (subject only to the need for continuing review in Her Majesty's pleasure cases) must be served in custody before any question of release can arise.[57]

Having thus explained his 'deep misgivings . . . about the cogency of the reasoning by which mandatory life sentences are singled out for exclusion from protection under Articles 5 (4) and 6 . . .',[58] Simon Brown LJ acknowledged that these misgivings had not been reflected in the pre-HRA decisions of the House of Lords. Notwithstanding his 'clear view . . . that the existing mandatory life sentence regime breaches Article 6 (1) (and for that matter Article 5 (4)). . .' he concluded that the right approach now that the HRA was in force was to treat the Strasbourg case law as determinative: **13.30**

> In the end there are two factors which have persuaded me to regard the Strasbourg case law as for the present determinative. First, that whatever advantage we might enjoy through our domestic knowledge and experience of the mandatory life sentence regime could perhaps be thought balanced (or even conceivably outweighed) by the ECtHR's deeper appreciation of the true ambit and reach of Articles 5(4) and 6(1) of the Convention. It is, after all, not the characterisation of the mandatory life sentence in abstract, but rather its characterisation in the context of the application of these two Articles, which lies at the heart of this case.
>
> The second factor which weighs with me is that of comity. True, this court is not bound by ECtHR judgments, any more than that court is bound by them. Where, however, as here, the ECtHR itself is proposing to re-examine a particular line of cases, it would seem somewhat presumptuous for us, in effect, to pre-empt its decision. For my part, I shall be surprised if the present regime for implementing mandatory life sentences survives the ECtHR's re-examination of the issue in *Stafford*. The final decision, however, I am persuaded should be theirs. I would accordingly dismiss these appeals.[59]

---

[57] [52]–[53].
[58] [58].
[59] [65]–[66].

13.31 Buxton LJ's explanation of his reasoning process was similar to that of Simon Brown LJ. Like Simon Brown LJ, Buxton LJ ultimately concluded that domestic and Strasbourg authority constrained the Court of Appeal to dismiss the claimants' challenge not least because of the question of 'comity to which adherence to an international system such as that of the Convention gives rise'.[60]

13.32 As this summary shows, four of the six judges who heard argument in *Anderson and Taylor* reached the clear and emphatic conclusion that Article 6 applies to the exercise of tariff fixing in the case of mandatory life sentence prisoners and that the reasoning which underpins the ECtHR's decision in *Wynne* was critically flawed in that, as Buxton LJ pointed out, it is 'based on factual or analytical premises as to the nature of the law of the contracting state concerned that have been rejected by the highest court of that state'.[61] It was therefore clear that, but for the constraining effect of pre-HRA domestic authority and the decision in *Wynne* (as well as later Strasbourg Court and Commission decisions which have followed it) the domestic courts would have ruled that Article 6 does indeed apply to mandatory life sentence prisoners as it applies to the other categories of indeterminate sentence. And for the reasons given by Simon Brown LJ, it necessarily followed that Article 5(4) would be held to apply to the post-tariff stage of the mandatory life sentence.

Ex p Lichniak and Pyrah[62]

13.33 In this case two prisoners challenged their mandatory life sentences on the grounds that the imposition of such a sentence upon them was arbitrary and disproportionate and therefore incompatible with Articles 3 and 5 of the ECHR. The Court of Appeal rejected both arguments. The relevance of this ruling lies in the means by which the Home Secretary sought (successfully) to resist the claimants' argument that the mandatory life sentence was capable of producing arbitrary and disproportionate punishment in breach of Article 3. This was set out in paras 21 and 47 of the judgment of the court:

> [Counsel for the Home Secretary] goes on to submit that there was a very good reason by the European Court decided the *V and T* cases as it did—namely because an indeterminate sentence (whether it be mandatory life imprisonment or detention during Her Majesty's pleasure) allows for and involves in practice an individualized assessment of tariff, risk and recall so that it is neither degrading nor arbitrary. It may be that an assessment should not be made by the Executive but that is not something for consideration in this case.
>
> [Counsel for the Home Secretary] submits that if a sentence of detention during Her Majesty's pleasure which has to be imposed without regard to the circumstances of the offence or the offender is not arbitrary, bearing in mind the

---

[60] [88].

[61] [82].

[62] [2002] QB 296.

Convention's concern for the young, how can it be said that in the case of an adult a mandatory life sentence of life imprisonment is arbitrary? Its purpose, he submits, is to punish the offender by subjecting him to an indeterminate sentence under which he will only be released when he has served the tariff part of his sentence and when it is considered safe to release him and even then for the rest of his life he will be recalled. That is not merely the effect of the sentence, it is the sentence.

The Court of Appeal accepted this analysis, holding that: **13.34**

We accept that a sentence cannot be arbitrary for an adult when an equivalent sentence has been found not to be so in the case of a young offender and when in each case the application of the sentence is individualized and everyone knows that it will be individualized from the moment it is imposed.[63]

However, this approach on the part of the Home Secretary was fundamentally inconsistent with the notion that a mandatory life sentence involves the imposition of a lifelong punitive sentence, ie the very notion which underlies the reasoning in paras 33–35 in *Wynne*, and the essential basis for distinguishing the mandatory life sentence from other indeterminate sentences in the ECtHR jurisprudence. The Government characterized the mandatory life sentence as an indeterminate sentence which allows for and involves in practice 'an individualized assessment of tariff, risk and recall', and the acceptance of that characterization underlies the Court of Appeal's judgment in *R (Lichniak and Pyrah)*. However, once it was accepted that it is an indeterminate sentence of this nature, no legitimate distinction can be drawn between the mandatory life sentence on the one hand and the other forms of indeterminate sentence on the other (discretionary life and detention during Her Majesty's Pleasure (HMP)). The very factors that led the ECtHR to accord special rights to persons sentenced to detention during HMP must apply equally to mandatory life sentence prisoners. Both are subject to a mandatory, indeterminate sentence and in both cases the purpose of the sentence is partly punitive and partly preventative. Accordingly, the mandatory life sentence is analytically indistinguishable from the sentence of detention during HMP, as analysed by the ECtHR in *Singh*[64] and *V and T*[65] before the introduction of the current statutory regime.

Stafford v UK[66]

The applicant was convicted of murder in 1967 and received a mandatory life sentence, from which he was released on licence in 1979. One of his licence conditions was that he remain in the United Kingdom unless his probation officer   **13.35**

---

[63] [48].
[64] *Singh and Hussain v UK* (1996) 22 EHRR 1.
[65] *T and V v UK* (2000) 30 EHRR 121.
[66] Application 46295/99 (2002) 35 EHRR 32.

agreed to his travelling abroad. Soon after release, he left the United Kingdom, in breach of his licence, and went to live in South Africa. In September 1980, his licence was revoked and thereafter he was considered to be unlawfully at large. In April 1989, he was arrested in the United Kingdom, having returned from South Africa with a false passport. His licence was revoked and he remained in prison. He made representations to the Parole Board against the decision to return him to prison, but the Board rejected those recommendations and recommended a further review in 1990, at which point they recommended his release and the Home Secretary accepted the recommendation. In 1994 he was convicted of counterfeiting offences and sentenced to six years' imprisonment. The Home Secretary revoked his licence on the advice of the Parole Board. The Parole Board recommended his release in 1996, but this recommendation was rejected by the Home Secretary. Mr Stafford sought judicial review of this decision: the litigation in the English courts went all the way to the House of Lords, and is discussed below at paras 13.63–13.66.

13.36 Before the court, Mr Stafford argued that it was obsolete under domestic law to regard a mandatory life prisoner as having forfeited his liberty for life. He argued that cases such as *Doody*,[67] *V and T*[68] and *Pierson*[69] showed the courts' recognition of the similarity between the tariff-fixing exercise and a conventional sentencing exercise. He also argued that to detain a post-tariff mandatory life sentence prisoner by reference to concerns about non-violent offences which bore no relation to the index offence amounted to arbitrary detention within the meaning of Article 5(1) of the ECHR, since it had insufficient connection with the object of the legislature and the original sentence of the court. The Government argued that the purpose of the mandatory life sentence was to confer power on the Home Secretary to decide when, if at all, it was in the public interest to allow the prisoner to return to society on life licence, and to empower the Home Secretary to recall the prisoner if he considered it to be in the public interest. It argued that, in deciding whether it was in the public interest to release the applicant, the Home Secretary must be entitled to have regard to the risk of non-violent, as well as violent, offending. The Government relied heavily on *Wynne*,[70] and argued that there had been no relevant developments in domestic or Convention case law which would justify the court departing from its previous decisions.

13.37 The latter argument did not impress the court. It accepted that it should not depart from its previous decisions 'without cogent reason'.[71] However, it also stressed that, since 'the Convention is first and foremost a system for the protec-

---

[67] [1994] 1 AC 531.
[68] [1997] 3 WLR 23.
[69] [1998] AC 539.
[70] (1994) 19 EHRR 333.
[71] para 68.

tion of human rights, the Court must . . . have regard to the changing conditions in Contracting States and respond, for example, to any emerging consensus as to the standards to be achieved'.[72] In light of the 'significant developments in the domestic sphere', it considered it appropriate to reassess the position.[73]

The court reviewed the history of, and the philosophy underpinning, the manda-   **13.38**
tory life sentence. It considered the development of its own case law on discretionary life sentence prisoners and HMP detainees, as well as mandatory lifers, and the decisions in *Anderson and Taylor*[74] and *Lichniak and Pyrah*.[75] It concluded that:

> [W]ith the wider recognition of the need to develop and apply, in relation to mandatory life prisoners, judicial procedures reflecting standards of independence, fairness and openness, the continuing role of the Secretary of State in fixing the tariff and in deciding on a prisoner's release following its expiry, has become increasingly difficult to reconcile with the notion of separation of powers between the executive and the judiciary.[76]

The court went on to say that:

> [I]t may now be regarded as established in domestic law that there is no distinction between mandatory life prisoners, discretionary life prisoners and juvenile murderers as regards the nature of tariff-fixing. It is a sentencing exercise. The mandatory life sentence does not impose imprisonment for life as a punishment. The tariff, which reflects the individual circumstances of the offence and the offender, represents the element of punishment. The Court concludes that the finding in *Wynne* that the mandatory life sentence constituted punishment for life can no longer be regarded as reflecting the real position in the domestic criminal justice system of the mandatory life prisoner.[77]

Applying this to the facts of Mr Stafford's case, the court concluded that he must   **13.39**
be regarded as having exhausted the punishment element for his offence of murder, otherwise he would not have been released in 1979. His continued detention, after the expiry of the sentence for the counterfeiting offences, was therefore not justified as punishment for the original offence. Nor—in contrast to the applicant in *Weeks*—was continued detention justified on the basis of mental instability and risk of violent offending. Accordingly, there had been a breach of Article 5(1).

On Article 5(4), Mr Stafford argued that, since the only legitimate basis for his   **13.40**
continued detention was risk to the public, a factor subject to change, he was entitled to review of his continued detention by a body satisfying the requirements of Article 5(4). He argued that these safeguards cannot be said to be incorporated

---

[72] para 68.
[73] para 69.
[74] [2002] 2 WLR 1143.
[75] [2002] QB 296.
[76] para 78.
[77] para 79.

into the sentence by the original trial process. Further, the fact that the Parole Board had power to direct his release on his initial recall was not enough. Article 5(4) applied to his post-tariff detention as a whole and, when it did later recommend his release, this was not binding on the Home Secretary.

13.41 The Government argued simply that the requirements of Article 5(4) were met by the original trial and appeal procedures, and that no new issues of lawfulness concerning his detention arose requiring the possibility of recourse to a court or similar body with power to order release. It tried to maintain the argument that mandatory adult lifers are in a unique position, and that the sentence was imposed because of the inherent gravity of the offence and not because of the presence of factors susceptible to change over time. Further, the Parole Board's power to direct release was a sufficient safeguard.

13.42 The court's conclusion was as follows:

> After the expiry of the tariff, continued detention depends on elements of dangerousness and risk associated with the objectives of the original sentence of murder. These elements may change with the course of time, and thus new issues of lawfulness arise requiring determination by a body satisfying the requirements of Article 5(4). It can no longer be maintained that the original trial and appeal proceedings satisfied, once and for all, issues of compatibility of subsequent detention of mandatory life prisoners with the provisions of Article 5(1) of the Convention.

The court also considered that, for the purposes of Article 5(4), the fact that the Parole Board could order the applicant's release was insufficient, since the power of decision still lay with the Home Secretary. Article 5(4) had therefore been violated.

13.43 This decision is of immense significance to all post-tariff mandatory life sentence prisoners. It means that any mandatory lifers who have served the tariff part of their sentence, or who are due to have a Parole Board review at the end of their tariff, are entitled to an oral hearing before the Parole Board. Further, if the Parole Board recommended release, the Home Secretary would not be entitled to depart from that recommendation: in effect, the 'dual-key' scheme can no longer be operated, and mandatory lifers, like discretionary lifers, are entitled to release if the Parole Board so recommends. The full range of Article 5 rights will apply to the review process, just as they apply to discretionary lifers. The likely response to *Stafford* is to extend to mandatory lifers the procedures applied to those serving discretionary life sentences, including the system of Parole Board hearings. A detailed guide to the system of Parole Board reviews for discretionary lifers is contained in Chapter 14, and should now be referred to as a guide until clear policies on the management of mandatory lifers are produced by the Government.

13.44 It should be noted that the ECtHR's decision does not remove all Home Office involvement in the management of life sentence prisoners—if the Parole Board recommends a programme of action short of release, the Home Office still retains a discretion as to how to put that into practice. One question left unresolved by *Stafford* is whether the Home Secretary is entitled to ignore a Parole Board direction that a mandatory lifer be transferred to open conditions. That issue is currently before the ECtHR, and it may be that the eventual decision constrains the Home Office yet further in this area.[78]

The decision in *Stafford* does not, of course, remove the Home Secretary's power **13.45** to set the tariff in mandatory life sentence cases. However, at the time of writing both *Anderson and Taylor* and *Lichniak and Pyrah* were pending in the House of Lords. It may well be, therefore, that the reforms of the mandatory life sentence did not finish with *Stafford*. The two appeals raise the fundamental issue of whether *any* sentencing involvement by the executive, rather than the judiciary, can be justified, and the extent to which the mandatory nature of the sentence is lawful. It will be interesting to see whether the House of Lords sees *Stafford* as reforming the mandatory life sentence sufficiently, or whether it sees the ECtHR's decision as a mandate to carry out further reforms.[78a]

E. The Tariff Phase of the Mandatory Life Sentence

Setting the Tariff

In this section we examine in practical terms how a mandatory lifer's tariff is cur- **13.46** rently determined. As we have seen, the Home Secretary's power to set the tariff in mandatory life sentence cases has not been affected by the ECtHR's decision in *Stafford*. However, it may be that the House of Lords will decide, in *Anderson and Taylor*, that this aspect of the Home Secretary's powers is no longer compatible with the Convention. It is important to understand the development of the law in this area, since what appears as an unfettered power of tariff-setting has in fact become increasingly judicialized. Ironically, it is the growing judicialization of

---

[78] In *R v Home Secretary, ex p Draper*, The Independent, 20 March 2000, the claimant, a mandatory lifer who had received a Parole Board recommendation that he be transferred to open conditions, argued that procedural fairness required the Home Secretary, if he wanted to reject the recommendation, to disclose the Parole Board's reasons and issue a 'minded to refuse' letter in order to allow further recommendations to be made before taking a final decision. Sullivan J rejected this argument. He accepted that there may be cases in which fairness requires that the prisoner be given some indication of the matters which are of concern to the Home Secretary, in order to address those, particularly where fresh material has emerged that was not before the Parole Board. The Home Secretary in evidence made it clear that he would disclose the full text of the Parole Board's advice in such cases, but not cases where all issues had been fully explored before the Board. Since the applicant's case did not involve any fresh issues which had not been before the Parole Board, the application failed. The case is important, though, in committing the Home Office to disclosing the Parole Board recommendation and allowing comments from the lifer in cases where new material *has* emerged since the Parole Board considered the issue.

[78a] See Preface for a summary of the House of Lords' ruling on the appeals.

tariff-setting—now recognized as a sentencing exercise—which may save the Home Secretary's position before the House of Lords.

13.47 As we have seen, the tariff is the term used to describe the period which a mandatory lifer must serve in prison to satisfy the requirements of retribution and deterrence.[79] The tariff is set by the Home Secretary[80] (either personally or by a Home Office Minister) as soon after conviction as possible and following consideration of the views of the trial judge, the Lord Chief Justice, and any representations which the prisoner wishes to make. Until the decision of the House of Lords in *Ex p Doody*[81] mandatory lifers did not have the right to know what the judicial view on tariff was or whether or not the Home Secretary had departed from the judicial recommendation when determining it in secret. The procedures now in place reflect the ruling of the House of Lords in *Ex p Doody* and may be summarized as follows.[82] After the trial, the trial judge prepares a standard form report which identifies the significant aspects of the case and the judge's opinion on what the tariff should be.[83] Such a report is made even when the trial judge has made a min-

---

[79] 'Tariff' is also sometimes used to describe the 'relevant part' of the sentence determined by the trial judge for discretionary lifers to reflect the seriousness of the offence. The most recent judicial Practice Statement on the life sentence, given by Lord Woolf CJ on 31 May 2002 ([2002] 1 WLR 1789), says about the word 'tariff': '[t]his term, in accordance with the advice of the [Sentencing Advisory Panel], will no longer be used because it has commonly been misunderstood. The present Statement refers instead to "minimum term" to make it clearer that, even when released, the offender has not served his sentence, which continues for the remainder of his life' (para 2). We continue to use the term 'tariff', simply because it is widely used and understood, but without seeking to minimize the potential significance of the post-tariff and post-release parts of the life sentence.

[80] As we have seen, this aspect of the Home Secretary's powers is under challenge in the House of Lords in *Anderson and Taylor*.

[81] [1994] 1 AC 531.

[82] For several years after the *Doody* decision, a major administrative procedure involving disclosure to all mandatory lifers of the tariffs set in their case took place. This process involved disclosure not just of the initial judicial views on tariff but also, where applicable, their further recommendations when they were reconsulted after the new procedures were put in place in 1983. The post-*Doody* disclosure letter also informed the prisoner of the Home Secretary of the day's secret and undisclosed decision on tariff and his reasons (if any) for departing from the judicial recommendation. The prisoner was then invited to make representations prior to a new post-*Doody* tariff decision being made. In many of the older cases, it became clear that record keeping was poor and the Tariff Unit was unable to do more than speculate about the information which was before the Home Secretary of the day when he fixed the tariff. In many cases where the judicial view was departed from, no reasons were recorded.

[83] Until relatively recently, trial judges simply wrote in confidence direct to the Home Secretary with no particular format to structure the expression of their views on tariff. *Practice Statement (Crime: Life Sentences)* [2002] 1 WLR 1789 states that the normal starting point for setting a tariff for an adult offender convicted of murder is 12 years in normal cases and 16 years in aggravated cases (replacing the previous single normal tariff of 14 years). The Practice Statement sets out guidelines in relation to the normal starting point, mitigating and aggravating factors, and very serious cases. It also stresses that 'an offender is most unlikely to be released on the expiry of the minimum term and for the purpose of calculating the earliest date of normal release on licence the minimum term is approximately the equivalent of a determinate sentence of twice its length. So a minimum term of 14 years is equivalent to a determinate sentence of approximately 28 years (See *Re Thompson (tariff recommendations)* [2001] 1 All ER 737,)' (para 3).

imum recommendation under s 1(2) of the 1965 Act. The report is then submitted to the Lord Chief Justice who gives his views on the appropriate tariff, specifying either a specific number of years or a range. The views of the trial judge and the Lord Chief Justice are then communicated to the Home Secretary (in practice, the Tariff Unit of the Parole and Lifer Review Group based at Prison Service Headquarters).

The next stage involves disclosure to the prisoner of the views of the trial judge and **13.48** the Lord Chief Justice. Since 1994 the level of disclosure has improved, and prisoners who indicate that they do wish to make representations are sent copies of the documentation which will be placed before the Home Secretary when the tariff representations are considered. These should include letters and reports from the trial judge and the verbatim views of the Lord Chief Justice. The prisoner is informed that he should make any representations within two months of the date of the notification letter but this is not a rigid time limit. A lifer may approach a solicitor to make representations on his behalf. The final stage involves the setting of the tariff, giving reasons for any departure from the judicial recommendations.[84] The decision, with reasons (where appropriate) is communicated in writing to the prisoner concerned. The Home Secretary is *not* obliged to accept the judicial view on tariff. The justification for this was explained by Lord Mustill in *Doody* in the following terms:

> Parliament has not by statute conferred on the judges any role, even as advisers, at the time when the penal element of a mandatory sentence is fixed. But for the fact that the Home Secretary decided when formulating the new scheme, to retain in a modified shape the existing practice of inviting the opinions of the judges, they would never enter the picture at all. *The Secretary of State is compelled, or at least entitled, to have regard to broader considerations of a public character than those which apply to an ordinary sentencing function.* It is he and not the judges who is entrusted with the task of deciding upon the prisoner's release, and it is he who has decided, within the general powers conferred upon him by statute, to divide his task into two stages.[85]

Departing From the Judicial View on Tariff

In considering what scope exists for challenging the Home Secretary's decision to **13.49** fix a tariff at odds with the judicial recommendation, it is important to recall the words of Lord Bingham CJ (as he then was) in *R v Home Secretary, ex p Hindley* to

---

[84] Where there is a difference between the views of the trial judge and the LCJ, it is the latter's opinion which amounts to the judicial recommendation, any departure from which requires justification by the Home Secretary.

[85] Emphasis added. The italicized words were relied on by the ECtHR in *Wynne v UK* (1994) 19 EHRR 333 to deny mandatory lifers the Art 5(4) safeguards which had been extended to discretionary lifers in *Thynne, Wilson and Gunnell v UK* (1991) 13 EHRR 666. See now the judgment of the ECtHR in *Stafford v UK* Application 46295/99 (2002) 35 EHRR 32.

the effect that 'this is a highly judgmental matter on which reasonable minds may differ' and that the 'threshold of irrationality for purposes of judicial review is a high one. This is because responsibility for making the relevant decision rests with another party and not with the court.'[86] In the light of these remarks (and the outcome of Ms Hindley's application before the Divisional Court and the House of Lords) it is hard to see that a bare rationality challenge of a tariff decision would ever stand a good prospect of success. On the other hand, a challenge which asserts irrationality, coupled with an attack on the inadequacy of the Home Secretary's reasons for departing from the judicial recommendation, will be better placed to succeed even though the most that can be gained will be a second chance for the Home Secretary to improve upon his reasoning. Because tariff fixing has now been recognized as having the character of a sentencing exercise, it is strongly arguable that the Home Secretary must give effect to the sentencing principle that requires a sentencing judge to explain the factual basis upon which he sentences and which requires him to give reasons for rejecting any major mitigating factor.[87] In *Ex p Hindley* Lord Bingham CJ commented that in giving his reasons for departing from the judicial view on tariff, the Home Secretary is not obliged to reply 'as if in a pleading' to all the points made by a prisoner but it is implicit in the Divisional Court's decision that major points must be addressed and answered.[88]

Departing From the Jury's Verdict When Setting the Tariff

13.50   In fixing the tariff, the Home Secretary is not entitled to act inconsistently with the verdict of the jury in the (very rare) cases where the jury's verdict is capable of conveying a particular factual basis for the finding of guilt.[89] This limited principle was established in *R v Home Secretary, ex p Causabon-Vincent*[90] in which a lifer challenged the Home Secretary's decision to fix his tariff on the basis that he

---

[86] [1998] 2 WLR 505, 526A. In Ms Hindley's case the objection was that Michael Howard and, later, Jack Straw had increased her tariff from the 25-year minimum term recommended by Lord Lane to whole life. See also the decision *in R v Home Secretary, ex p Raja and Riaz*, 16 December 1994, DC, where the court declined to quash as irrational ministerial tariffs which exceeded by 10 years the judicial recommendations, although criticism was made of the inadequate disclosure of the judicial views on tariff and the Home Secretary's reasons for departing from them.

[87] See *R v Solomon and Triumph* (1984) 6 Cr App R (S) 120 and the approach of the Court of Appeal (Criminal Division) towards Newton hearings designed to establish the factual basis for sentence.

[88] In Ms Hindley's case, it was argued that the Home Secretary had not made clear whether he accepted her claim that she had assisted Ian Brady to murder children under fear, threat, and coercion which, in effect, amounted to duress, and she relied on compelling contemporaneous evidence which supported her account. In giving reasons for imposing a whole life tariff, the Home Secretary merely indicated that he had 'taken into account' Ms Hindley's claims without expressly stating that he accepted them or rejected them. Lord Bingham was satisfied that this meant the Home Secretary had accepted Ms Hindley's version of events but Astill J criticized the Home Secretary's reasons as barely adequate in all the circumstances.

[89] English juries almost never give special verdicts which convey a particular factual basis for a finding of guilt and in most cases the sentencing judge is entitled to formulate his own findings from the available evidence to determine the factual basis for sentence.

[90] [1997] COD 245.

had committed a contract killing notwithstanding the Home Secretary's acceptance of the fact that the jury's verdict on his co-defendant (who was convicted
only of manslaughter) meant that the jury must have taken the view that the
killing was not a premeditated contract killing. In the event, the Court of Appeal
dismissed the application on the basis that the Home Secretary had misinter-
preted the meaning of the jury's verdicts.[91] Its reasoning made clear that it would
be difficult, if not impossible, for there to be a conflict between the function of the
jury and the Home Secretary in this area. Lord Woolf MR said that:

> [T]he Secretary of State is not entitled to act arbitrarily. He must respect the proper
> function of the jury. . . . However when coming to assess the facts which are relevant
> for determining tariff he is entitled to make his own judgment of the relevant cir-
> cumstances and here he will normally pay close attention to any views expressed by
> the judge since the judge having been present at the trial is usually in the best posi-
> tion to assess these in a way which will assist the Secretary of State.

The Principle of Non-aggravation of Penalties

As we have seen, *Ex p Pierson*[92] concerned a challenge to the assertion, first made   **13.51**
by Michael Howard in his July 1993 policy statement, that the Home Secretary
enjoyed a general power to increase the tariffs of mandatory lifers. The applicant
had argued that once it was recognized that the exercise of tariff-setting was
sufficiently akin to a sentencing exercise to attract the basic principles applicable
to the imposition of any punishment, the remaining question was whether there
was a principle that a punishment, once fixed, should not be increased.[93] Lord

---

[91] The Court of Appeal reached this conclusion having analysed the reasoning of the Court of
Appeal (Criminal Division) when quashing the co-defendant's conviction for manslaughter on the
basis of a misdirection by the trial judge. The Crown's case at trial had been that a woman called
Dunbar had hired Causabon-Vincent and a man called Parsons to murder her lesbian lover as part of
a premeditated contract-killing. The jury convicted Causabon-Vincent and Parsons of murder but
convicted Dunbar only of manslaughter on the basis, one assumes, that Dunbar may have only asked
the men to frighten her lover but not to kill her or cause her really serious bodily harm. Logically, this
would have meant that the killers had not committed a premeditated murder but that one or other
had gone beyond the scope of what had been agreed and thereby committed an unpremeditated
killing. However Lord Woolf disagreed both with the trial judge and the Home Secretary that it
could be inferred from the jury's verdicts that they had taken a particular view of Causabon-Vincent's
role in the murder. He pointed out that juries have to consider the position of each accused separately
and there may be many reasons why a jury reaches different verdicts against different defendants on
the same evidence. He concluded that it was not implicit in the verdict of the jury in this case that
Causabon-Vincent was not a party to a contract or otherwise premeditated killing.
[92] [1998] AC 539.
[93] Reliance was placed on the limited allowance made by the common law (see *R v Menocal*
[1980] AC 598 and *R v Nodjoumi* (1985) 7 Cr App R (S) 183) and by s 47(2) of the Supreme Court
Act 1981 for alterations of a sentence by way of an increase by the sentencer; the courts' approach to
the legitimate expectations of offenders in deferred sentences; the recognition of the principle of
non-retrospectivity by the courts in other cases concerned with lifers' tariffs such as *McCartney*
[1994] COD 528 and the strict insistence in the European Convention on the Transfer of Prisoners
that a principle of non-aggravation of the original sentence be applied once a prisoner is transferred
to serve his sentence in another jurisdiction.

Steyn and Lord Hope held that there was such a principle, the latter characterizing it as a rule of 'substantive fairness', and they concluded that the Howard statement was unlawful in so far as it purported to assert a general power to revisit tariffs. Lord Browne-Wilkinson held that 'while the law leans against any increase in penalty once imposed, there is no general principle that such an increase is contrary to law'. Lord Lloyd rejected the argument that there was a rule of 'universal justice' that in the interests of certainty and finality, a penalty once imposed should not be increased. Lord Goff's speech did not rule on this issue in clear terms since he based his decision on a close construction of the July 1993 statement and concluded that Mr Howard had not even purported to confer on himself a power to increase his predecessor's tariffs.

13.52   However Mr Straw's November 1997 policy statement, issued in response to *Pierson*, boldly asserted that a majority of the House of Lords had indeed accepted as lawful the claimed general power to increase tariffs, even those fixed and communicated to a prisoner. And Lord Bingham CJ (as he then was) in *Ex p Hindley* certainly appeared to accept this analysis. But his remarks were obiter in the light of his finding that the principle of non-aggravation identified by Lords Steyn and Hope in *Pierson* depended on a strict view of the words 'fixed' and 'communicated'. In the circumstances, it will require the House of Lords in a different case to establish once and for all whether the Home Secretary is indeed constrained in his task of tariff-fixing by a sentencing principle of non-aggravation of penalties.

Legitimate Expectation

13.53   In *Re Findlay* a number of prisoners, including two lifers, challenged the policy contained in Leon Brittan's 1983 statement which had the effect of frustrating the very real hopes of imminent release on licence which they each held.[94] In the case of the life sentence prisoners, they were in open prisons looking forward to release in the foreseeable future. The sudden announcement of a tariff policy which retrospectively affected certain categories of convicted murderers such as them meant that they were removed overnight to closed conditions, destined to spend several more years in custody before release could be contemplated. They challenged the Brittan policy as unlawful on a number of grounds, including that it frustrated their legitimate expectations. The House of Lords rejected the argument. Lord Scarman dealt with the complaint raised by asking:

> [W]hat was their legitimate expectation? Given the substance and purpose of the legislative provisions governing parole, the most that a convicted prisoner can legitimately expect is that his case will be examined individually in the light of whatever policy the Secretary of State sees fit to *adopt provided always that the adopted policy is a lawful exercise of the discretion conferred upon him by the statute.* Any other view

---

[94]   [1985] 1 AC 318.

would entail the conclusion that the unfettered discretion conferred by the statute upon the minister can in some cases be restricted so as to hamper, or even to prevent, changes of policy. Bearing in mind the complexity of the issues which the Secretary of State has to consider and the importance of the public interest in the administration of parole I cannot think that Parliament intended the discretion to be restricted in this way.[95]

The italicized words are of some importance. *Findlay* concerned the legality of introducing a policy of minimum 20-year tariffs for the first time. It was not concerned with the legality of a policy of increasing tariffs once they had been fixed (because none had been fixed in the past). In the light of the speeches delivered in the House of Lords in *Ex p V and T* and in *Pierson* (which have undoubtedly recognized that the Home Secretary is not free to act entirely as he pleases when he fixes a tariff) it is important to understand that in his speech in *Findlay* Lord Scarman was not stating that the Home Secretary is free to adopt any policy he likes in the field of tariff setting or, for that matter, when deciding whether to release a mandatory lifer. As Lord Browne-Wilkinson pointed out in *Ex p V and T* what saved the Brittan tariff policy from being held unlawful in *Re Findlay* was that it contained within it flexibility, in exceptional circumstances, to have regard to circumstances not limited to the gravity of the offence but including 'other relevant factors such as prison record, personal or family circumstances'.[96] But the principle enunciated by Lord Scarman in *Findlay* does mean that the Home Secretary is free to change his policy towards the release of mandatory lifers in a way which frustrates substantive expectations of release so long as the new policy does not offend against basic principles of common law and justice. Of course, in the light of *Stafford*, any tariff-setting discretion does not extend to a discretion whether or not to release, since such a decision must now be that of the Parole Board.

The Ministerial Ten-year Review

In his 1983 policy statement, Leon Brittan undertook to review every case where **13.54** a life sentence prisoner has been detained for ten years. That policy was confirmed by Michael Howard and, initially, Jack Straw. However, in a statement on 9 July 1998, Jack Straw announced that such reviews would no longer take place. He stated that '[t]hose convicted of murder are now fully informed about the tariff-setting process and may make representations at any time about the length of their

---

[95] Emphasis added. It is important to recognize that *Findlay* [1985] AC 318 was decided on the basis of a characterization of the function of granting parole as granting 'early release' which is, arguably, inconsistent with the theory of the life sentence as analysed by the House of Lords in *Doody* [1994] 1 AC 531, *Pierson* [1998] AC 539, and by Buxton LJ in *Ex p Stafford* [1998] 1 WLR 503.

[96] [1997] 3 WLR 23, 48B. However, the ECtHR eventually found against the Government when *V and T* reached Strasbourg: see (2000) 30 EHRR 121, discussed further in Ch 14 in the context of discretionary lifers and HMP detainees.

tariff. In addition, they may at any time make representations for their tariff to be reduced to take account of exceptional circumstances, including exceptional progress in prison. . . . In these circumstances, the ten year review is now redundant.'[97]

Whole Life Tariffs

13.55 A small number of mandatory lifers have been given 'whole life' tariffs, meaning that they should spend the rest of their lives in prison as punishment for their individual crime(s).[98] In *R v Home Secretary, ex p Hindley*,[99] one of the bases for Ms Hindley's attack on her whole life tariff was that it was unlawful for a whole life tariff to be set in *any* case. It was argued on her behalf that a person sentenced to life imprisonment is sentenced to life imprisonment with the possibility of release on licence and not to 'life imprisonment without parole'. Furthermore, it was argued that even Mr Straw's modified policy (which acknowledges that in exceptional circumstances a whole life tariff might be reduced by reason of the prisoner's exceptional progress in custody) frustrates the intention of Parliament and amounts to an unlawful fetter of the Home Secretary's release discretion because it creates a category of life sentence prisoners who are all but excluded from any possibility of parole. The Divisional Court rejected these arguments, holding that there was no reason in principle why a crime or crimes, if sufficiently heinous, should not be regarded as deserving lifelong incarceration for purposes of pure punishment. Moreover, so long as the whole life tariff policy allowed for the possibility of a reduction in exceptional circumstances, as Mr Straw's policy plainly does on its face, it did not amount to an unlawful fettering of discretion.[100] The same conclusions were reached by the Court of Appeal. The court considered that the policy was not unlawful, since the Home Secretary was entitled to conclude that an offence was so heinous that either, as Lord Woolf MR expressed it, he could not fix a period after which punishment and deterrence would not require the prisoner to be incarcerated, or as Hutchison LJ and Judge LJ put it, the requirements of retribution and deterrence could not be met except by lifelong incarceration. However, the Court of Appeal, like the Divisional Court, stressed that the Home Secretary still had to review the position from time to time. As long as he undertook to do so, the policy did not amount to an unlawful fettering of discretion.

---

[97] *Hansard*, HC, cols 587–588 (9 July 1998).

[98] In *Ex p Hindley* it was revealed that there were 26 such lifers in December 1997.

[99] [2001] 1 AC 410.

[100] The Divisional Court did find that Michael Howard's July 1993 policy had been unlawful because, as Lord Bingham CJ said, it 'expressly said that the purpose of periodical reviews would be solely to consider whether the whole life tariff should be converted to a tariff of a determinate period and should be confined to the considerations of retribution and deterrence. By that [Mr Howard] must be taken to have meant that no consideration would be given to factors such as exceptional progress in prison.'

The case went on appeal to the House of Lords, where the Committee upheld the **13.56** decision of the lower court. Lord Steyn, with whom their Lordships agreed, began by rejecting the appellant's argument that s 1(1) of the Murder (Abolition of the Death Penalty) Act 1965, read in light of s 27 of the Prison Act 1952[101] precluded a life sentence which actually extended to the natural life of the prisoner. Lord Steyn went on to note that:

> On instructions counsel for the Secretary of State volunteered and gave assurances to the House that [the 1997 policy statement] means that the Secretary of State is prepared to reconsider and review any whole life tariff decision from time to time even in the absence of exceptional progress. In these circumstances counsel for the Secretary of State submitted that the policy of imposing a whole life tariff merely involves the expression of the current view of the Secretary of State that the requirements of retribution and deterrence make it inappropriate ever to release such a prisoner. It does not rule out reconsideration. The Secretary of State envisages the possibility of release in the event of exceptional progress in prison; and, even in absence of such progress, the Secretary of State is prepared to reconsider any whole life tariff decision from time to time. Given this clarification on behalf of the Secretary of State I would hold that it is impossible to say that the Secretary of State has unlawfully fettered his discretion.[102]

Lord Steyn also rejected the argument that the Secretary of State is required to refer such cases to the Parole Board, since the Board's task is to advise on risk, not on tariff. Like the lower courts, he went on to conclude that 'there is nothing logically inconsistent with the concept of a tariff by saying that there are cases where the crimes are so wicked that even if the prisoner is detained until he or she dies it will not exhaust the requirements of retribution and deterrence'.[103]

The conclusions of the domestic courts on this issue are, of course, thrown into **13.57** severe doubt by the decision in *Stafford*.[104] The Home Secretary is no longer entitled to decide on whether *post-tariff* mandatory lifers are to be released or not. Myra Hindley's case was slightly different, in that her tariff was a whole life one. However, the power of the Home Secretary, a member of the Executive, to decide unilaterally on a whole life tariff, precluding the involvement of the Parole Board, and then to retain sole discretion to consider release, is clearly untenable. Reform of the system as it was set out in the 1997 policy statement is inevitable. This section considers practice as it stands at the time of writing. It is clear, however, that greatly increased Parole Board involvement is inevitable.

---

[101] Which provided that release of a life sentence prisoner could take place only if and when the Secretary of State so directed in the exercise of his discretion.

[102] [2001] 1 AC 410, 417.

[103] ibid.

[104] In fact, the national press was quick to point out that Myra Hindley could have been one of the most high-profile beneficiaries of the ruling in *Stafford*.

13.58   All prisoners who are given whole life tariffs currently have their tariffs reviewed after 25 years in custody. This is a ministerial review and not a review by the Parole Board. Under Michael Howard's policy (revealed in his 7 December 1994 statement) this review was limited to considerations of retribution and deterrence (ie has anything emerged which shows that the crime was not as heinous as once thought). Recognizing that the Divisional Court would almost certainly find this to be unlawful in Myra Hindley's imminent application for judicial review of her whole life tariff, Home Secretary Jack Straw issued his modified policy which makes clear that the 25-year review will take into account whether the prisoner has made exceptional progress in custody, just as applies to the ten-year reviews for lifers with determinate tariffs.

F. The Post-tariff Phase of the Mandatory Life Sentence

13.59   The first review of a mandatory lifer's case by the Parole Board normally takes place three or three and a half years before the expiry of his or her tariff.[105] In his statement of 9 July 1998, Jack Straw stated that, 'the first Parole Board review for mandatory and discretionary life sentenced prisoners will be brought forward by six months to start three and a half years before tariff expiry, but normally only when the prisoner has been in Category C prison conditions for 12 months or more at that point. Cases falling just outside the 12 month criterion, and cases where exceptional circumstances exist, will be considered for early review on their merits. In addition, reviews for all mandatory life sentenced prisoners who are in open conditions will commence 18 months after arrival rather than after two years as is now the practice.' Below (under the heading 'Progressing through the lifer system') we consider how preparations for the first and subsequent Parole Board reviews are structured. In this section we focus on the Home Secretary's policy towards mandatory lifers in the post-tariff phase. As with the other parts of this chapter, we have decided still to include a discussion of the system as it stood pre-*Stafford*, since no concrete proposals for reform are available at the time of writing, and it is important to understand the system as a whole. As mentioned above, the reformed system is likely to be very similar to that applied to discretionary life sentence prisoners, a guide to which can be found in Chapter 14. That chapter is likely to be of use to both types of life sentenced prisoner during the transitional period. However, the structure of the Parole Board's deliberations, the type of evidence they are likely to consider, and the factors which they will take into account will

---

[105] The date will be deferred if the prisoner escapes or absconds because the first review date is based on time in custody. The first review date can also be altered if a lifer receives a further prison sentence. When a mandatory lifer's parole date for the additional sentence is after the tariff expiry date, the Parole Board review date will be deferred to the date of the extra sentence. When the Parole Board review date is before tariff expiry, the date will not change.

remain the same after the system is reformed, the key distinction being simply that the Home Secretary is not entitled to override any release direction they may give.

As we have seen, s 29 of the Crime (Sentences) Act 1997 preserved the dual-key **13.60** mechanism for the release of mandatory lifers which has been in place since the parole system was created by the Criminal Justice Act 1967. Under that section, the Home Secretary was not entitled to release a mandatory lifer without a favourable recommendation from the Parole Board (and after consulting the trial judge, if available, and the Lord Chief Justice) but he was not obliged to follow the Parole Board's advice. The broad release discretion was vested in the Home Secretary, not a judicial body.

The Parole Board becomes seised of a mandatory lifer's case only when the case is **13.61** referred to the Board by the Home Secretary under s 29(2) of the 1997 Act. As already stated, it is the Home Secretary's policy to make a first reference to the Board three years before the tariff expiry date and every two years thereafter. In considering a lifer's case, the Board can make one of three recommendations—no further progress (known as a 'knockback'); a move to open conditions; release.[106]

The Directions to the Parole Board

In conducting its review of a mandatory lifer's case, the Board is required to follow **13.62** the Directions issued to it by the Home Secretary pursuant to s 32(6) of the Criminal Justice Act 1991.[107] The Directions which deal with the release decision are as follows:

(1) The Home Secretary takes the final decision on the release of mandatory life sentence prisoners ('lifers') and that decision might be taken on grounds that go beyond the risk posed by the prisoner. The Home Secretary is also concerned with the wider political implications, including the effect on public confidence in the life sentence system which release may have, ie how the public would be likely to respond to the lifer being released at that juncture. (This part of the Direction is clearly no longer valid in the light of *Stafford*.)

(2) The Parole Board's responsibilities in the release consideration are whether, having regard to the degree of risk involved of the lifer committing further imprisonable offences after release, it remains necessary for the protection of the public for the lifer to be confined.

---

[106] We consider the criteria which affect the possibility of a move to open conditions in the section 'Progressing through the lifer system' at paras 13.68–13.77.

[107] s 32(6) states that '[t]he Secretary of State may also give to the Board directions as to the matters to be taken into account by it in discharging any functions under this Part; and in giving any such directions the Secretary of State shall in particular have regard to (a) the need to protect the public from serious harm from offenders and (b) the desirability of preventing the commission by them of further offences and of securing their rehabilitation'.

(3) Each case should be considered on its individual merits.

(4) Before recommending release, the Parole Board should consider whether:

   (a) the lifer has shown by his performance in prison that he has made positive efforts to address his attitudes and behavioural problems and the extent to which progress has been made in doing so such that the risk that he will commit a further imprisonable offence after release is minimal;

   (b) the lifer is likely to comply with the conditions of the life licence and the requirements of supervision.

(5) Before deciding whether or not to recommend release, the Parole Board must take into account all of the papers submitted to it.

The Board is given further assistance on how to approach its task in the Training Guidance on the Release of Mandatory Lifers issued by the Home Secretary. But this guidance does not form part of the Directions issued under s 32(6).[108]

The Test to be Applied in the Post-tariff Phase: *Ex p Stafford*[109]

13.63 It can be seen that the Directions refer specifically to the risk of the lifer committing 'further imprisonable offences after release', not a risk that he might commit a further offence presenting a danger to the life or limb of the public. Though the original Directions issued by the Home Secretary in 1993 had also referred to further imprisonable offences, not violent ones, it was widely believed by prisoners, lawyers and, indeed, the Parole Board that in fact the Home Secretary would not seek to detain a post-tariff mandatory lifer solely on the ground that there was a fear that he might commit a non-violent imprisonable offence on release. This belief was however dispelled in early 1997 when the Home Secretary informed a recalled mandatory lifer, Dennis Stafford, that he would not be released because it was believed he might commit further non-violent offences.[110] His case, of course, eventually became *Stafford v UK*, the judgment which we have already discussed. In this section we look at the domestic decisions which preceded the ECtHR's decision. Even though it was accepted that there was no significant risk that Mr Stafford might commit an offence involving violence, he was required to spend a further two years in open conditions before his case could next be reviewed by the Parole Board.[111] Mr Stafford applied for judicial review of both the release

---

[108] The full text of the Training Guidance is to be found at Appendix 9.

[109] *R v Home Secretary, ex p Stafford*: [1999] 2 AC 38, HL; [1998] 1 WLR 503, CA; (1997) 147 NLJ 1494, QB.

[110] It was accepted in argument before the Court of Appeal in Mr Stafford's case that his was the only example to date in which the Home Secretary had decided to prolong a lifer's detention solely on the basis that there was an unacceptable risk of him committing further non-violent imprisonable offences. Quite why the decision was taken in his case of all cases was never explained.

[111] Since his conviction for the index offence of murder in 1967, Mr Stafford had not committed a single further offence involving violence either inside or outside prison. He had been recalled to prison on two occasions however, the first time for being unlawfully at large (in South Africa) for some nine years and the second following his conviction for fraud in July 1994 for which he received

decision and the requirement that he spend two years in open conditions. Before the Divisional Court, the decision not to release was challenged on two grounds. First, it was submitted that a policy of detaining a post-tariff mandatory lifer who is no longer considered to be dangerous was ultra vires the Home Secretary's broad release discretion. Secondly, it was submitted that the Home Secretary's own policy statements and previous decisions of the courts had established that the true test for the release of mandatory lifers, as well as discretionary lifers and HMP detainees, was one of dangerousness. It was submitted that the use of the word 'risk' in policy statements issued by successive Home Secretaries between 1983 and 1993 had become a term of art meaning a risk of danger to the life or limb of the public.

13.64 Collins J held that in exercising his release discretion with regard to mandatory lifers, the Home Secretary is not entitled to extend the detention of a mandatory lifer beyond the point where he has completed his tariff and is no longer dangerous in the sense of presenting a more than minimal risk to life or limb. It was clear that Collins J took the view that the Home Secretary had always approached the release of post-tariff mandatory lifers in the same way as he considered the release of discretionary lifers and young persons convicted of murder. He could not see in the light of the adoption of the tariff system (which divided the life sentence into punitive and protective phases) that it was rational to distinguish between the different categories of person who end up with a life sentence since in each case they were subject to indeterminate imprisonment because of the nature of the offences they had originally committed.

13.65 The Court of Appeal disagreed with this analysis.[112] Lord Bingham held that Parliament had done nothing to circumscribe or control the exercise of the Home Secretary's broad release discretion (by now contained in s 29 of the Crime (Sentences) Act 1997) in the way that Collins J had held it was constrained. In other words, it was legitimate for the Home Secretary to draw a distinction between a mandatory and a discretionary lifer/HMP detainee and to apply a policy to the former which involves prolonging their detention merely because of a belief that they might commit a further imprisonable offence, albeit a non-violent one, if released on licence. Lord Bingham also held that the Home Secretary had made it clear both in his policy statements and in the Directions to the Parole Board issued pursuant to s 32(6) of the Criminal Justice Act 1991 that in deciding whether to release a mandatory lifer he would have regard to considerations of a broader character than danger to the public. Accordingly, the decision not to

---

a six-year sentence. By the time the Home Secretary refused to release him on licence in early 1997, his fixed term sentence had expired and his continued detention was attributable solely to the revocation of his licence.

[112] [1998] 1 WLR 503. In July 1998 the House of Lords dismissed Mr Stafford's appeal, largely for the same reasons advanced by Lord Bingham: [1999] 2 AC 38.

release the applicant was not a departure from the Home Secretary's announced policy but in conformity with it.[113]

13.66 Buxton LJ agreed with the Lord Chief Justice and Morrit LJ in his final conclusion but his reasoning was different in a number of significant respects. He agreed that Parliament has consistently drawn a distinction between the mandatory lifer and discretionary lifers/HMP detainees. He therefore concluded that it must be wrong to argue that it is irrational for the Home Secretary to apply a different policy towards the former than to the latter. Nevertheless he then proceeded to state a number of principles which logically point to a conclusion that it is in fact unlawful to detain a mandatory lifer on the basis of a fear of commission of any imprisonable offence. Specifically he stated that:

> It is no longer realistic to regard a mandatory life prisoner simply as someone who has forfeited his life to the State or who is in mercy unless there is an exercise in his favour of an inscrutable executive discretion. I refer in particular to what was said by Lord Mustill in *Doody* [1994] 1 AC 557B.

This is a highly significant starting point for any analysis of the true nature of the mandatory life sentence because it is the theory that a convicted murderer has, uniquely in comparison with other lifers, forfeited his liberty forever to the State which underpins the entire basis of the distinction drawn by the Home Secretary between mandatory lifers and discretionary lifers/HMP detainees.[114] Buxton LJ proceeded to analyze the various policy statements and court rulings which dealt with the Home Secretary's policy towards his release discretion, including the Directions to the Parole Board issued in 1993 pursuant to s 32(6) of the Criminal Justice Act 1991, and made clear his dissatisfaction with the lack of clarity in the Home Secretary's explanation of his policy. Finally, he considered the implication of a policy which envisaged indefinite detention based on a risk of committing any imprisonable offence, as follows:

> The category of imprisonable offence is extremely wide and can encompass many matters that are *wholly unrelated, both in nature and in seriousness, to the reasons for the life sentence prisoner being within the power of the State in the first place.* I also find it uncomfortable that that criterion should be used as the justification for continued imprisonment. We were told in argument that the test of imprisonable offence, rather than of fault of a purely moral or social nature, was used because faults of the latter nature would be unconnected with the original reasons for the subject's incarceration, but in reality that lack of connection exists, or at least is strongly threatened, by the imprisonable offence criterion also.[115]

---

[113] It was clear however that Lord Bingham was troubled by the facts of Mr Stafford's case. When judgment was handed down, he commented that all members of the court had found it to be an anxious and difficult case. The concluding remarks of his judgment reflect this concern. He stated that 'the imposition of what is in effect a substantial term of imprisonment by the exercise of executive discretion, without trial, lies uneasily with ordinary concepts of the rule of law'.

[114] See, most recently, the Home Secretary's policy statement of 10 November 1997.

[115] Emphasis added.

This analysis comes very close to accepting that it is indeed contrary to a fundamental principle of the common law to detain a mandatory lifer beyond the point where he is dangerous as such detention is unrelated to the original purpose of the sentence. In other words, the Home Secretary's policy results in the creation of a form of arbitrary executive detention without trial.[116] The ECtHR did, in effect, accept that this was the case in holding that the United Kingdom had violated Article 5(4) of the ECHR.

The 10 November 1997 Policy Statement

In argument before the Court of Appeal and before Collins J in *Ex p Stafford*, the   **13.67** Home Secretary had submitted that his policy governing the release of mandatory lifers had been clearly and unambiguously set out in successive policy statements issued between 1983 and 1993 to the effect that dangerousness was *not* the decisive test in the post-tariff phase of the mandatory life sentence. However after argument had concluded in the Court of Appeal, but before judgment was handed down, the Home Secretary issued a new policy statement on 10 November 1997 which was principally intended to respond to the decision of the House of Lords in *Ex p Pierson*.[117] As well as explaining how the Home Secretary would approach tariff fixing and reconsideration of tariffs fixed by his predecessors, the statement contained the following passage:

> I take the opportunity to confirm that my approach on the release of adults convicted of murder once tariff has expired will reflect the policy set out in the answer given on 27 th July 1993. In particular, the release of such a person will continue to depend not only on the expiry of tariff and on my being satisfied that the level of risk of his committing further imprisonable offences presented by his release is acceptably low but also on the need to maintain public confidence in the system of criminal justice. The position of a prisoner subject to a mandatory life sentence continues to be distinct from that of a prisoner serving a discretionary life sentence a decision on whose final release is a matter for the Parole Board alone.[118]

The reference to continuing the Michael Howard approach towards the release of mandatory lifers once tariff has expired (as set out in Howard's 27 July 1993

---

[116] It is to be noted that the Home Secretary's decision to continue to detain Mr Stafford was *not* sought to be justified by reference to what has become known as the 'third phase' of detention under the mandatory life sentence which first appeared in the Home Secretary's statement of 27 July 1993 (issued in response to *Doody*), ie the 'public acceptability of early release'. Rather, it was claimed that the question whether it was 'safe' to release the applicant involved consideration of whether he might commit offences of dishonesty upon release on licence, not merely offences creating risk to life or limb.

[117] [1998] AC 539.

[118] The statement was clearly drafted to take account of the possibility that the Court of Appeal might rule in *Stafford* that the Home Secretary's previous policy statements had indicated that the release and recall of mandatory lifers was governed by a dangerousness test rather than an 'imprisonable offences' criterion. The reference to 'imprisonable' offences in Mr Straw's statement was the first time the test had been spelled out in a policy statement as opposed to the Directions to the Parole Board and was clearly designed to make clear that which had not been clear before.

statement) indicated that the new Home Secretary did not intend to abandon Mr Howard's claim that he was entitled to detain a lifer who no longer presented a risk to the public purely by reference to 'the public acceptability of early release'. As previously stated, no Home Secretary has ever in fact refused to release a lifer on this ground. Post-*Stafford*, of course, no Home Secretary will have the opportunity to put this policy into practice. However, the Parole Board may have to grapple with the consequences of releasing some very controversial mandatory lifers.

G. Progressing Through the Lifer System

13.68   The progress of all lifers (discretionary and mandatory) through their sentence is governed by a formal policy set out in the *Lifer Manual* published by the Parole and Lifer Review Group of the Prison Service.[119] The manual states that the management of life sentence prisoners is based upon the principle that they have a planned and structured career through the prison system and, where appropriate, progress to conditions of lower security. Further, they are treated as a group whose special needs are recognized within the prison system, though not necessarily by separation or special privileges.

13.69   The life sentence is structured by reference to the different prisons to which a lifer will be allocated depending on how long he has been in prison and what 'progress' he has made during the sentence. Thus a typical lifer will go through the following stages of the sentence prior to release on licence:

(1) remand centre/local prison;[120]

(2) First Stage—High Security/Category B (also known as allocation to a Main Centre);[121]

(3) Second Stage—High Security/Category B[122]/Category C;[123]

---

[119] PSO 4700.

[120] After conviction the lifer returns to a local prison. During this period he must be allotted to a Main Centre by the Lifer Allocation Unit of the Custody Group. An initial LSP must be prepared in accordance with the *Life Manual*, ch 8 and the tariff-setting process begins.

[121] There are three Main Centres for adult male lifers—Gartree, Wakefield, and Wormwood Scrubs. The period spent in a Main Centre is usually three years but this may be reduced (eg prisoners with tariffs of less than ten years and who are making exceptionally good progress). During this period the initial assessment must be completed, the initial LSP must be developed, and any special needs identified. The first progress reports under the LSP will be called for by the Parole and Lifer Review Group.

[122] The lifer will be held in a Category B training or dispersal prison until he is considered suitable by the Lifer Allocation Unit for a transfer to a Category C prison. It is during the period in Category B/dispersal prison that much of the work necessary to address offending behaviour (as identified by the LSP) is expected to be carried out.

[123] Once considered suitable for conditions of lower security, the lifer will be moved to a Category C prison. During this period, the *Lifer Manual* states that offence-related work continues but the focus changes towards preparation for release on licence. Local outside visits may be allowed at this stage subject to appropriate risk assessments.

(4) Third Stage—Category D/open[124]/semi-open/resettlement.[125]

Each life sentence prisoner has a Life Sentence Plan (LSP), a revised version of **13.70** which was introduced in 2001–2. The former LSP F2181 has been replaced by the revised LSP F2181R, which aims to provide 'a new structure for sentence planning running from remand to release; an integrated reporting system which replaces the F75; a single sentence planning framework which integrates the contributions of different staff in establishments to the decision making process about risk, decategorisation and transfer'.[126] The new LSP has the following sections:

- LSP 0: Opened in local prisons and remand centres to identify potential life sentence prisoners.
- LSP 1: Opened in local prisons and remand centres, to record information on newly convicted lifers (this consists of a post conviction immediate needs assessment; initial allocation to First Stage prison; post conviction induction report; local prison lifer profile; multi-agency lifer risk assessment panel report; pre-transfer report to First Stage prison).
- LSP 2: Opened at First Stage prisons, to initiate a sentence management plan (consists of an offence analysis; risk factor summary; psychiatric evaluation; psychological evaluation; educational evaluation; sentence planning objectives).
- LSP 3: Used in First, Second and Third Stage prisons to record annual reviews, achievement of sentence planning targets, progress and pre-transfer reports (consists of a record of sentence planning and review boards and progress reports; sentence planning and review board report; record of achievements in offence-related targets; record of achievements in non offence-related targets; progress reports; pre-transfer report).
- LSP 4: Opened in Second Stage Category C and Third Stage prisons, to record progress through escorted absences, release on temporary licence, final pre-release offending behaviour programmes, progress in open conditions,

---

[124] The *Lifer Manual* states that for most (ie not necessarily *all*) mandatory and discretionary lifers, transfer to open conditions following satisfactory progression through Category B and C closed prisons is a prerequisite to release on life licence. For all lifers, transfer to open conditions is subject to ministerial approval following a recommendation from the Parole Board. (Whether or not ministerial involvement in the transfer decision is compatible with the Convention is currently being considered by the ECtHR.) The purpose of the period in open prison conditions is to test lifers in 'more challenging conditions' before being considered for transfer to a pre-release employment scheme (PRES) or resettlement prison prior to release on licence and to provide facilities for supervised outside activities and temporary release in preparation for release.

[125] The release of a lifer is usually subject to the satisfactory completion of a period of six to nine months in a PRES hostel or at Latchmere House or Kirklevington resettlement prisons. During this period the lifer will undergo final testing on conditions as near as possible to those he or she will encounter on release and will be encouraged to gain work experience.

[126] *Lifer Manual*, para 8.1.

and preparation for release (consists of a record of escorted absences and release on temporary licence; escorted absence reports; open conditions progress review; open conditions failure report).

- LSP 5: Opened in local prisons to record details of recalled lifers, including reasons for recall, information about the lifer and recommendations for allocation to a lifer prison (consists of recalled lifer immediate needs assessment; recommended allocation for a recalled lifer; post recall induction report; local prison recalled lifer profile; recalled lifer transfer report).

13.71   The *Lifer Manual* states that 'the LSP has been designed to allow as much of its contents as possible to be disclosable'.[127] The only material which is not considered disclosable is: any sections quoting specific evidence from the Confidential Summary Dossier; material covered by the Victim's Charter; medical information that healthcare staff have decided should not be disclosed to the lifer; security sensitive information; any section containing a diagonal red or black stripe. All the rest of the LSP is to be disclosed to the lifer. The importance of involving lifers is stressed in the *Lifer Manual*, which emphasizes that lifers should be required to attend at least part of all sentence planning and annual review boards, that they must be given a clear indication of how progress to date has been measured, and what further sentence planning targets need to be met. Given the widespread feeling among lifers that they are being assessed against goals which are never clearly explained, this is a welcome commitment, if the promised involvement can be put into practice.

The Review Process

13.72   There are five different types of review of lifers within the life sentence system: the annual internal review by the Lifer Review Board at the prison, the review of Category A prisoners, the interim progress reports (formerly called the F75 review, but reformed early in 2002) requested by the Parole and Lifer Review Group every five years (or sooner if progress has been made), the Parole Board review and the Ministerial review at the 25-year point of whole life tariff prisoners. We have already dealt above with the ten- and 25-year Ministerial reviews, and the Category A review process is covered separately in Chapter 4. In this section we focus on the internal review process, the interim progress report and the role of the Parole Board in reviewing mandatory lifers.

Lifer Review Board

13.73   Every designated lifer prison is required to have a Lifer Review Board which comprises representatives of all departments within the prison which have something to contribute to the lifer's progress, physical and mental health, training, and

---

[127]   para 8.5.

assessment. The Board is required, according to the *Lifer Manual*, to undertake a thorough review of all life sentence cases at regular intervals of not more than 12 months. It is also instructed to 'invite the lifer to attend whenever possible'. The reports of the Lifer Review Board proceedings are retained locally and whenever a change of regime or transfer is recommended, a copy must be sent to the Allocations Unit of the Custody Group. The Lifer Review Board is responsible for overseeing the preparation of the LSP.

Progress Reports

Up to the time of a lifer's first Parole Board review the Parole and Lifer Review Group at Prison Service Headquarters calls for progress reports on each lifer at regular intervals (at least every five years). Such reports used to be called F75 reviews. The system of reporting was changed with effect from 1 January 2002, after which date all reviews take place on form LSP3E, and are to be called progress reports.[128] This change is part of the overhaul of the LSP, carried out in response to widespread criticisms of the management of life sentence prisoners, including from the Chief Inspectors of Prisons and Probation.[129] The most significant difference is that, under the new system, the Lifer Unit can call for a progress report 'whenever a lifer establishment recommends that significant change or progress has been made. If no such recommendation is made after a period of five years has elapsed Lifer Unit will automatically call for an LSP3E Progress Report.'[130] Instead of an automatic review every three years, therefore, prisoners may now wait five years between reviews. **13.74**

These reviews are required to enable the prisoner's progress and life sentence plan to be monitored and to provide staff with a chance to comment on progress and other factors which might justify a transfer or change in the prisoner's security category. The chapter of the *Lifer Manual* which dealt with F75 reviews recognized that an interim review 'may affect the rights of a prisoner in a material way by, for example, recommending a change of regime'. Accordingly, it stated that lifers should normally be permitted the same degree of access to completed F75 reports as that provided for Parole Board dossiers. The revised version of Chapter 8 does **13.75**

---

[128] *Lifer Manual*, ch 4 sets out transitional provisions: 'In order not to disadvantage lifers who may previously have been informed of an interim F75 date that falls after 1 January 2001 a one-off supplementary review will be offered. This single review will only apply to current lifers. They may then accept or decline the review at the appropriate time. Lifers may of course decide to accept a supplementary review even if there have been no positive recommendations from staff in the intervening annual reviews. Once the supplementary review has been completed the lifers concerned will be subject to the revised reporting system' (para 4.3). All supplementary reviews for current lifers are to be completed by 31 December 2005.

[129] Their report, *Lifers: A Joint Thematic Review* (London, 1999) contains a detailed examination of all aspects of the lifer system, and has been influential in shaping the current system.

[130] para 4.1.

not deal with these issues, but the previous guidance would appear to apply, suitably adapted.

Parole Board Review

13.76   As stated above, a mandatory lifer will normally have his/her first Parole Board review three years before the expiry of the tariff. In cases where a tariff of three years or less has been set, the first review will begin as soon as the necessary arrangements can be made. As with fixed term prisoners, neither the 1991 nor the 1997 Act provides a mandatory lifer with a legal right to an oral hearing before the Parole Board, and so the review process proceeds by way of the compilation of a parole dossier and an opportunity for the lifer to make written representations to the Board. The Board does however have a discretion to hold an oral hearing and it will be acting illegally if it refuses to consider a request by a lifer for such a hearing.[131]

13.77   The panel of the Board which considers a mandatory lifer's case may make one of three possible recommendations—no further progress, a move to open conditions, or release. The principles which apply to the Board's consideration of lifers who deny their guilt of the index offence are the same as those which apply to fixed term prisoners.[132] In considering whether to recommend a move to open conditions, the Board is required to comply with the Directions issued by the Home Secretary under s 32(6) of the 1991 Act.[133] These make clear that the Home Secretary regards a period in open conditions as essential for most lifers and that in considering whether to make such a recommendation the Board must balance the risks against the benefits to be gained from such a move. The Directions state that such consideration is 'somewhat different from the judgement to be made when deciding if a lifer should be released: in those cases the Parole Board is asked only to consider risk'. In *Ex p Stafford*, Lord Bingham made clear that as a matter of common sense as much as anything else, the need for a lifer to spend as long as two years in open conditions will vary depending on whether he is being considered for initial release on licence as opposed to release following a recall to prison.[134]

---

[131]   See the decision of Collins J in *R v Parole Board, ex p Gerald Davies*, 25 November 1996, CO/1007/96. The case concerned the Board's refusal to hold an oral hearing in the case of a recalled lifer where the arguments in favour of such a hearing are obviously stronger. But the principle that the Board must consider in each case whether justice demands an oral hearing is of general application. It is understood that the Board has never in fact granted a request for an oral hearing in the case of a fixed term prisoner or mandatory lifer.

[132]   See paras 12.52 to 12.53 above for a detailed discussion of the relevant principles.

[133]   'Transfer of Life Sentence Prisoners to Open Conditions'. The full text of the Directions together with the Training Guidance are at Appendix 9.

[134]   Mr Stafford had spent many years at liberty (albeit unlawfully at large for the most part) before his recall to prison. He challenged as irrational the Home Secretary's decision that he should spend a further two years in prison before his next Board review. The Court of Appeal rejected the

Until the ECtHR's judgment in *Stafford*, the ultimate decision, whether in rela- **13.78** tion to a move to open conditions or release on licence, rested with the Home Secretary. The courts have held that, where he rejects the Board's views, he is obliged to give written reasons for his decision, and they have frequently criticized the quality of the Home Secretary's reasoning in this area.[135] Successful irrationality challenges to the merits of the Home Secretary's decision-making are however very rare indeed. As discussed above, the release decision is no longer that of the Home Secretary, though it may be that he still retains some powers over transfers to open conditions, in which case the case law on reasons will still be relevant.

Revocation of Licence and Recall to Prison

Whether or not a mandatory lifer can be said to have forfeited his life to the State, **13.79** it is true to say that he remains accountable to the State for the remainder of his life. This is because he is required to comply with the conditions of his life licence once he is released from custody.[136] The sanction in relation to a lifer who either

---

irrationality challenge but Lord Bingham commented that '[w]hile a powerful case can be made for testing in open conditions a mandatory life sentence prisoner who has been institutionalized by long years of incarceration in closed conditions, such a case loses much of its force in the case of a man who has, since serving the punitive term of his life sentence, demonstrated his capacity for living an independent and apparently lawful life by doing so for a number of years. The imposition of what is in effect a substantial term of imprisonment by the exercise of executive discretion without trial lies uneasily with ordinary concepts of the rule of law. I hope that the Secretary of State may, even now, think it right to give further consideration to this case.' The Home Secretary did review the decision and Mr Stafford was told he would only have to do six months in open conditions before his next review.

[135] See eg *R v Home Secretary, ex p Cox* (1991) 5 Admin LR 17; *R v Home Secretary, ex p Follen* [1996] COD 169; *R v Home Secretary, ex p Evans*, 2 November 1994, DC; *R v Home Secretary, ex p Pegg* [1995] COD 84; and *R v Home Secretary, ex p Freeman*, 5 June 1998, CO 451/98, Turner J, a decision in which the Home Secretary's refusal to release a mandatory lifer was quashed for want of adequate reasons and on the ground that it was irrational.

[136] The standard conditions on a life licence are that the licensee shall place himself under the supervision of a probation officer; that he shall report to and keep in touch with that officer in accordance with the officer's instructions; that he shall, if required, receive visits from the officer where the licence holder is living; that he shall reside only where approved by his probation officer; that he shall work only where approved by his probation officer and inform the probation officer at once if he loses his job; and that he shall not travel outside the UK without the prior permission of his probation officer. There is, somewhat surprisingly, no standard condition that a prisoner shall not commit any imprisonable offence. The precise contents of the licence, particularly now that victim's rights are given increasing prominence, have been the subject of several legal challenges. In *R (Craven) v Home Secretary and Parole Board* [2001] EWHC Admin 850, the claimant challenged the lawfulness of a condition that he not enter a specified area without the prior permission of his probation officer as a disproportionate interference with his rights under Art 8 of the ECHR. The court recognized that the claimant's Art 8 rights were engaged. It considered that the restriction, since it was imposed to minimize the distress caused to the victim's family by encountering their daughter's murderer, was in accordance with law and pursued a legitimate aim under Art 8(2), namely the protection of the rights and freedoms of others. However, the court considered that the original exclusion zone—Newcastle and North Tyneside—was too large, and therefore a disproportionate interference with the claimant's rights. The size of the zone was reduced to an acceptable size before the hearing.

breaches his licence conditions or whose behaviour 'gives cause for concern' is the revocation of his licence and his recall to prison. The statutory basis for revocation in the case of both mandatory and discretionary lifers is to be found in s 32 of the Crime (Sentences) Act 1997.

13.80 The Act makes clear that revocation and recall will normally occur after the Parole Board has considered the facts of a particular case and recommended to the Home Secretary that this is an appropriate course of action pursuant to s 32(1) of the 1997 Act. Section 32(2) however gives the Home Secretary a power to recall a lifer without any recommendation from the Board 'where it appears to him that it is expedient in the public interest to recall that person before such a recommendation is practicable'. The normal route for recall will be a recommendation from either the police or the probation service that a lifer is giving cause for concern and for the Parole and Lifer Review Group to refer the matter to the Parole Board for it to consider. It should only be in cases of genuine emergency that the Board is by-passed before a recall decision is made. This will usually be because of a fear of imminent violent re-offending (or disappearance, possibly abroad).[137]

13.81 Whenever a lifer is recalled to prison (whether under s 32(1) or (2)), the Act gives him/her a right to know the reasons for his recall and a right to make written representations in relation to it. Section 32(4) of the 1997 Act imposes a duty on the Home Secretary to refer to the Board the case of any lifer who makes representations against his recall following a recommendation to that effect by the Parole Board as well as the case of a lifer who is recalled pursuant to the 'emergency' power contained in s 32(2). Following such a reference the Parole Board possesses

---

[137] It is clear that in order to justify a recall decision, the Home Secretary does not have to wait for the police to arrest the licensee, still less for there to have been a criminal trial in relation to specific charges—see *R v Home Secretary, ex p Macneill*, The Times, 26 May 1994. The Directions to the Parole Board make clear that recall will be appropriate if the licensee's continued liberty would present an unacceptable risk to the public or the licensee is likely to commit further imprisonable offences. See also *Ex p Stafford* [1998] 1 WLR 503. In terms of procedural protection, there is a critical difference between prisoners recalled under the emergency procedures in s 32(2) and those recalled in the normal manner under s 32(1). Following emergency recall, the Home Secretary can refer the matter to the Parole Board, but is not bound to follow the Board's advice, unlike in formal referrals to the Board under s 32(4). In *In the matter of Peter C*, 22 January 2001, the appellant was a recalled mandatory lifer who was recalled under s 32(2). The Home Secretary referred to the Board for advice, but rejected their release recommendation. Refusing the appeal, Lord Phillips MR said that '[i]t is plain, when one considers the 1991 Act, that the overall statutory scheme places no requirement on the Secretary of State to comply with the advice of the Parole Board simply because he has exercised the statutory power to refer a question to the Parole Board for their advice. It seems to me that that is precisely the position that pertains where he exercises that power, sensibly, because of the delay that is going to occur before the full review, as a check to see whether, on the information then available, the Parole Board shares his view that an emergency recall is justified. If he does not, he then reconsiders the position, but he is not bound as a matter of law to follow the advice of the Parole Board.' Of course, those recalled under the emergency provisions will still have a Parole Board review under s 32(4) in due course, the result of which will be binding on the Home Secretary.

a unique power within the statutory framework regulating the mandatory lifer. Although a mandatory lifer has as yet no statutory entitlement to an oral hearing before a panel of the Parole Board,[138] the Board does have a power to make a binding direction for the prisoner's immediate re-release on licence if it considers that this is the appropriate course to take in the light of all the facts.[139] In other words, so long as the Board directs the 'immediate' release on licence of the recalled mandatory lifer, the Home Secretary is obliged to 'give effect to the direction'. The word 'immediate' means what it says. A direction which is subject to any condition not capable of immediate fulfillment will not bind the Home Secretary and the prisoner will then fall to be dealt with under the normal release power in s 29 of the 1997 Act.[140]

Because the Board becomes functus officio once it has dealt with a case referred to it by the Home Secretary it is absolutely vital that the Board makes clear precisely what it intends to achieve when considering a recall case under s 32(5) of the 1997 Act.[141] Thus, if the Board wishes to await developments (for example the outcome of a pending criminal trial) before deciding whether or not to direct immediate release on licence, it must make clear that it is adjourning consideration of the case and that no recommendation or direction is being made in the interim. A direction which states that the prisoner should be released if he is acquitted at a pending criminal trial and following further consideration by the Board, cannot be construed as a direction for 'immediate release on licence' to which the Home Secretary must give effect. Accordingly, when the case next returns to the Board, it will not have a binding power to direct release and the Home Secretary will enjoy an absolute discretion in the release decision.[142] **13.82**

---

[138] Although, following *Stafford*, the Home Office is in the process of introducing such hearings, priority being given to mandatory lifers in open conditions who are approaching tariff expiry.

[139] See s 32(5) of the 1997 Act. In considering the recall decision, the Board is once again required to comply with the Directions issued by the Home Secretary governing the recall of mandatory lifers. There is also separate Training Guidance. Both the Directions and the Guidance are to be found at Appendix 8.

[140] See *R v Home Secretary, ex p Gunnell* [1984] Crim LR 170 and *R v Home Secretary, ex p De Lara*, 22 March 1995, DC.

[141] In *R v Home Secretary, ex p Evans*, 2 November 1994, DC, Simon Brown LJ compared the function of the Parole Board to the decision-making under the Parliamentary Commissioner Act 1967. In *R v Parliamentary Commissioner for Administration, ex p Dyer* [1994] 1 WLR 521 the DC held that the Commissioner is functus once he has sent his report to the Minister concerned and he may not re-open his investigation without a further referral by the Minister.

[142] This is exactly what happened in *R v Home Secretary, ex p De Lara*, 22 March 1995, DC, and the result was that even though the Board did recommend immediate release following his acquittal on the criminal charge which prompted his recall, the Home Secretary declined to accept the Board's 'recommendation' (for that is all it was capable of being). It was far from clear that the Board actually appreciated that its initial disposal of the case would have this effect.

14

DISCRETIONARY LIFERS AND HMP DETAINEES

A. Introduction

In the previous chapter we examined the law, policy, and practice which govern **14.01** the progress of mandatory life sentence prisoners through their sentence and their release from prison on licence.[1] In terms of the former, there is no significant

---

[1] The term mandatory lifer covers two types of sentence—the mandatory sentence of life imprisonment imposed on persons over 21 found guilty of murder and the sentence of custody for life imposed on a person aged over 18 but under 21 at the time of the offence who is convicted of murder. The latter sentence arises from the terms of the Powers of Criminal Courts (Sentencing) Act 2000, s 93, whereas the former arises under s 1(1) of the Murder (Abolition of Death Penalty) Act 1965. When s 61 of the Criminal Justice and Court Services Act 2000 is brought into force, custody

difference between the policy which determines the progress of mandatory lifers through the life sentence system and that which applies to discretionary lifers and persons detained during Her Majesty's Pleasure ('HMP detainees').[2] Until recently, however, there were major differences in terms of the release procedures as between the two different types of indeterminate sentence. In a nutshell, until the decision of the European Court of Human Rights (ECtHR) in *Stafford v UK*, which we looked at in the previous chapter, the release of mandatory lifers remained within the discretion of the Home Secretary. By contrast, the release of discretionary lifers and HMP detainees has for some years been determined by the Parole Board. In this chapter we examine how the current situation came about and what the law and administrative practice have to say about the release of discretionary lifers[3] (including those persons who receive an 'automatic' life sentence under s 109 of the Powers of Criminal Courts (Sentencing) Act 2000[4] and HMP detainees.[5] Once legislation is introduced to implement the decision of the ECtHR in *Stafford*, the procedures in this chapter will also apply to mandatory lifers.

B. The Rationale for the Discretionary Life Sentence

14.02 While murder is the only offence which attracts a mandatory life sentence, there are several others where it may be imposed in the discretion of the sentencing judge. The use of a discretionary life sentence dates from the 1950s, when it was developed as a form of preventive detention for unstable, dangerous offenders.[6] It tends to be imposed for manslaughter, rape, buggery, or arson. The rationale for

---

for life wsill be abolished, and those aged 18, 19 or 20 and convicted of murder will be sentenced to life imprisonment.

[2] Accordingly, paras 13.68–13.77 above, which deal with 'Progressing through the lifer system' apply to all lifers save in relation to the powers and procedures of the Parole Board.

[3] We use the term 'discretionary lifer' to mean persons who have received a life sentence for a violent or sexual offence, the sentence for which is not fixed by law (eg rape, manslaughter, buggery, or arson). In the case of persons aged under 18, the equivalent sentence is known as detention for life (Powers of Criminal Courts (Sentencing) Act 2000, s 91). Where a person aged 18 or over but under 21 at the time of the offence is convicted of any offence for which a discretionary life sentence would have been considered appropriate had he been 21 or over, the court imposes a sentence of custody for life pursuant to the Powers of Criminal Courts (Sentencing) Act 2000; but see n 1 above.

[4] s 109, formerly s 2 of the Crime (Sentences) Act 1997, requires a court to sentence a defendant to life imprisonment upon his conviction for a second 'serious' offence unless the judge considers that there are exceptional circumstances relating to either of the offences which justify passing a determinate sentence.

[5] The sentence of detention during Her Majesty's Pleasure pursuant to the Powers of Criminal Courts (Sentencing) Act 2000, s 91 is the only sentence available to the courts for a person convicted of murder who was aged under 18 at the time of the offence. While it is therefore a mandatory sentence, the statutory regime which governs tariff-setting and release is now almost identical to that which affects discretionary lifers, as we explain below.

[6] See David Thomas, *Current Sentencing Practice* (London, 1982).

passing such a sentence is a desire to protect the public from an offender who, at the date of sentencing, has some quality of instability which makes it unsafe, in the opinion of the judge, to pass a determinate sentence. At the same time, the fact that release is discretionary gives rise to the possibility that an offender who progresses rapidly, so that he ceases to be regarded as a danger, may achieve freedom earlier than he would if a lengthy determinate sentence were imposed.[7]

Criteria for Imposing a Discretionary Life Sentence

The provisions in s 80 of the Powers of Criminal Courts (Sentencing) Act 2000 **14.03** for determining whether imprisonment is justified, and if so the length of imprisonment, apply to discretionary life sentences in the same way as determinate sentences. Section 80(2)(b) allows a discretionary life sentence, as with other indeterminate custodial sentences, to be imposed if it is 'necessary to protect the public from serious harm from the offender'. Since s 161 of the 2000 Act states that sentences can only be imposed under s 80(2)(b) for violent or sexual offences, the discretionary life sentence is therefore restricted to those situations. As long as the restriction to violent or sexual offences is borne in mind, the previous guidance from the courts remains valid.[8] The Court of Appeal identified the criteria which had to be met before a judge could pass a discretionary life sentence in the criminal appeal of *R v Hodgson*.[9] They are:

(1) When the offence or offences in themselves are grave enough to require a very long sentence.[10]

(2) When it appears from the nature of the offences or from the defendant's history that he is a person of unstable character likely to commit such offences in the future.

(3) When, if the offences are committed, the consequences to others may be specially injurious, as in the case of sexual offenders or cases of violence.

In a later appeal, Lord Lane CJ emphasized that most exceptional circumstances must exist before a discretionary life sentence may be imposed, saying that:

> [I]t is reserved broadly speaking for offenders who for one reason or another cannot be dealt with under the provisions of the Mental Health Act yet who are in a mental state which makes them dangerous to the life or limb of the public. It is sometimes impossible to say when the danger will subside, therefore an indeterminate sentence is required so that the prisoner's progress may be monitored and so that he will be

---

[7] The discretionary life sentence involves a departure from the basic principle of proportionality in sentencing since, of necessity, judges are imposing a more draconian sentence than the individual offence otherwise merited.

[8] See M Wasik, *Emmins on Sentencing* (London, 2001) 4.3.7.

[9] (1968) 53 Cr App R 13.

[10] The Court of Appeal was envisaging that only where the fixed sentence would otherwise have been 15 years or more would a discretionary life sentence be imposed. Offences warranting far lesser sentences now attract the imposition of a discretionary life sentence.

kept in custody only so long as public safety may be jeopardised by his being let loose at large.[11]

Lord Lane's reference to the need to monitor the prisoner and release him once public safety no longer demands his incarceration is of course a vital consideration, since it makes clear that punishment is not the purpose of a resort to the life sentence. Indeed frequently (though almost certainly wrongly according to the *Hodgson* criteria) judges passed discretionary life sentences in circumstances where only a relatively short sentence of three or four years would have been imposed had a purely punitive, determinate sentence been passed. This fact was of great significance when the domestic courts and the ECtHR came to review the practice whereby prisoners serving discretionary life sentences were considered for release on licence on exactly the same basis as those serving mandatory life sentences for murder.

C. The Development of the Domestic Case Law

14.04   In four cases decided between 1987 and 1992, the English courts acknowledged the special position of discretionary lifers and identified a number of rights which could be derived from the discrete rationale applicable to their sentences. The decision of the Divisional Court in *R v Home Secretary, ex p Handscomb* was the first breakthrough.[12] At the centre of the applications for judicial review brought by four discretionary lifers was the Home Secretary's policy of delaying for as long as three or four years the first reference of every lifer's case to the Local Review Committee and the Parole Board for the initial review of his suitability for release to be conducted. A similar period elapsed before the Home Secretary consulted the relevant judge (if available) and the Lord Chief Justice about the 'tariff' applicable to a lifer, that is, that period of time necessary to satisfy the requirements of punishment and deterrence. Since the process of review leading to eventual release on parole lasted, on average, some three years it followed that the effect of the policy was inevitably that all lifers were detained for a minimum of six to seven years. The court held this policy to be *Wednesbury* unreasonable in so far as it applied to discretionary lifers, because it ignored the rationale of their sentence, which demanded that they should not be detained as punishment for any longer than they would have been detained under a fixed-term sentence (with full remission) had a life sentence not been imposed in order to protect the public. At the point where his tariff expired, a discretionary lifer was entitled to be released if, upon review, it was decided that he was no longer dangerous. Accordingly, the court said

---

[11]   *R v Wilkinson* (1983) 5 Cr App R (S) 105.
[12]   (1988) 86 Cr App R 59. In the earlier case of *Ex p Gunnell* (1985) Crim LR 105, no argument had been advanced about the special rationale applicable to the discretionary life sentence.

it was essential to consult the trial judge and the Lord Chief Justice immediately after a life sentence was passed so that, at the outset of custody, the Home Secretary could fix the date of first review by the Parole Board and efforts could be made to monitor the prisoner's progress with that date in mind. The court also held that, in determining how long a discretionary lifer ought to be detained for punitive purposes, the Home Secretary should fix the first review date strictly in accordance with the judicial view on the appropriate tariff. In other words, the Home Secretary had no discretion to create his own tariff by a form of executive resentencing. This latter point was eventually overruled by the Court of Appeal[13] but *Handscomb* was important in that, for the first time, a distinction was clearly made between discretionary and mandatory lifers, requiring different procedures to be adopted to ensure that the process of consideration for release on parole did not frustrate the purpose of the sentence.

The following year, in *R v Home Secretary, ex p Benson*, the Divisional Court exam-   **14.05**
ined the test which the Parole Board and the Home Secretary had to apply when considering whether further detention was justified after the expiry of a discretionary lifer's tariff.[14] Mr Benson had been sentenced to life imprisonment in 1972 for attempted grievous bodily harm because he was considered to have a dangerous, psychopathic personality. By 1988, however, the Parole Board had recommended his release on three occasions and a 1985 medical report (obtained on discovery) described him as 'a manipulative and immature fantasiser with a damaged personality [but] he is not dangerous'. The Home Secretary's refusal to order his release was accordingly challenged on the basis that he must have misdirected himself as to the purpose of the discretionary life sentence or taken into account irrelevant matters when addressing the dangerousness issue. Lloyd LJ, commenting that dangerousness is an 'elusive quality and difficult to forecast', went on to identify what kind of risk had to be addressed by the Home Secretary:

> If risk to the public is the test, risk must mean risk of dangerousness. Nothing less will suffice. It must mean there is a risk of Mr Benson repeating the sort of offence for which the life sentence was originally imposed; in other words risk to life or limb.

On the facts, the court declined to find that the Home Secretary's refusal to accept the Parole Board's recommendation was perverse and pointed out that a decision whether or not to release on parole a discretionary lifer was a grave responsibility which the courts should be slow to characterize as irrational. Nevertheless it did find that two matters which the Home Secretary had relied on as counting against release were irrelevant to the dangerousness test, and accordingly quashed the decision to refuse parole. It was the first time a lifer had successfully challenged the

---

[13] See *R v Home Secretary, ex p Doody* [1992] 3 WLR 956, but see subsequently *R v Home Secretary, ex p McCartney* [1994] COD 528, CA, for the procedure for determining the tariff of a pre-1991 Act discretionary lifer pursuant to the Transitional Provisions in the 1991 Act.
[14] [1989] COD 329.

Home Secretary's exercise of his discretion to refuse to accept a Parole Board recommendation for release.

14.06 In *R v Parole Board, ex p Bradley*, the *Benson* test was approved, and this time the Divisional Court explored the degree of risk which must exist to justify the continued detention of a discretionary lifer in the post-tariff period.[15] It was submitted that, because a discretionary lifer is effectively serving 'extra time' after his tariff date has been passed, the test for release should be no lower than that which had to be satisfied in the first place when the life sentence was passed. In other words, the Parole Board had to be satisfied that there was a 'likelihood' of the prisoner committing offences dangerous to life or limb in the future. The Divisional Court rejected this argument and distinguished the test which the sentencing judge had to apply, before taking the drastic step of imposing a sentence which may well cause a defendant to serve longer in prison than his 'just deserts', from that which the Parole Board applies, often years later, which would have the effect of endangering public safety to an extent by enabling the prisoner's release back into society. In the circumstances, it was perfectly appropriate for the Board to formulate a lower test of dangerousness—one less favourable to the prisoner—and the court held that it was sufficient if the risk was 'substantial', which meant 'no more than that it is not merely perceptible or minimal'.

14.07 It was also argued on Mr Benson's behalf that the Court of Appeal decision in *Payne v Lord Harris of Greenwich*[16] did not bind the court to rule that reasons need not be given for a decision to refuse parole, nor to hold that he should be denied access to the reports before the Parole Board. Both these submissions were rejected by the court, but two years later, in *R v Parole Board and Home Secretary, ex p Wilson*[17] the Court of Appeal finally did overrule *Payne* (and the later decision of the Court of Appeal in *R v Parole Board and Home Secretary, ex p Gunnell*[18]) in so far as it applied to deny a discretionary lifer a right of access to any reports before the Parole Board considering his release on licence. Taylor LJ characterized *Payne* as having been decided in 1981 'when established views on prisoners' rights were very different from those of today' and listed six factors which had arisen since then which, in combination with the facts of Mr Wilson's case, 'constitute a formidable case for disclosure'.[19] Not least among these factors were the impending

---

[15] [1991] 1 WLR 134.
[16] [1981] 1 WLR 754.
[17] [1992] 1 QB 740.
[18] [1985] Crim LR 105.
[19] The six factors were: (1) the existence since 1983 of a parallel system of Mental Health Review Tribunals under s 72 of the Mental Health Act 1983, in which disclosure of medical reports takes place; (2) the publication of the Carlisle Report unanimously affirming the advantages of open reporting and the giving of reasons for parole refusals; (3) the publication of the House of Lords Select Committee Report on Murder and Life Imprisonment (a Committee including three former Chairmen of the Parole Board), which made similar recommendations; (4) the Government's

changes in the law brought about by the Criminal Justice Act 1991 and the decision of the ECtHR in the case pursued by Mr Wilson himself, *Thynne, Wilson and Gunnell*,[20] to which we turn next.

D. The Jurisprudence of the ECtHR

The two cases to reach the ECtHR, and which together transformed the rights of discretionary lifers, centred on Article 5(1) and (4) of the European Convention on Human Rights (ECHR). These state that: **14.08**

(1) Everyone has the right to liberty and security of person. No one shall be deprived of his liberty save in the following cases and in accordance with a procedure prescribed by law:

   (a) the lawful detention of a person after conviction by a competent court (. . .)

(4) Everyone who is deprived of his liberty by arrest or detention shall be entitled to take proceedings by which the lawfulness of his detention shall be decided speedily by a court and his release ordered if the detention is not lawful.

In *Weeks* it was argued that both these provisions had been breached.[21] Robert Weeks had been sentenced to life imprisonment in December 1966 at the age of 17, when he pleaded guilty to a bungled armed robbery during which no one was injured.[22] He was released on licence for the first time in 1976, but recalled to prison the following year. Between 1977 and 1986 he was released and re-detained several times and spent a further six years in custody. In his application to the ECtHR Mr Weeks argued, first, that his recalls to prison from 1977 onwards and consequent detention were in breach of Article 5(1)(a) of the ECHR because there was not a sufficient causal connection between the original conviction and sentence in 1966 and the later deprivations of liberty from 1977 onwards to satisfy the requirements of Article 5(1). In other words, it could not be said that his re-detention following his original release in 1976 was in accordance with 'a procedure prescribed by law' and undergone 'after conviction by a competent court'. The court rejected this argument. After analyzing the nature of a discretionary life sentence and the specific remarks made by the sentencing

---

White Paper generally accepting the Carlisle Report (Cm 532, 1988); (5) the decision of the ECtHR in *Thynne, Wilson and Gunnell v UK* and the consequent enactment of the 1991 Act.

[20] (1991) 13 EHRR 666.

[21] (1988) 10 EHRR 293.

[22] The facts of Mr Weeks' original case were startling in the light of subsequent events. He had entered a pet shop in Gosport, Hampshire, with a starting pistol loaded with blanks, pointed it at the owner, and told her to hand over the till. He stole 35 pence which were later found on the shop floor. Later he phoned the police and said he would give himself up. He was apprehended later by two police officers and, when he took out his starting pistol, it went off. Two blanks were fired causing no injury. It emerged that Weeks had committed the offence to pay back his mother the sum of £3 and she told him that morning that he would have to find lodgings elsewhere.

judge in Mr Weeks' case which placed it in a special category,[23] the court found that it was inherent in the life sentence that, whether Mr Weeks was inside or outside prison, his liberty was at the discretion of the Executive for the rest of his life, subject to the controls introduced by the Criminal Justice Act 1967. It was not for the court to review the appropriateness of the imposition of the life sentence in the first place and, on the special facts of the case, the court found there was a sufficient causal connection for the purposes of Article 5(1)(a) between the 1966 conviction and the 1977 recall to prison. The court inferred, however, that if a decision not to release a discretionary lifer or to re-detain him was based on grounds which were inconsistent with the objectives of the sentencing court, then the causal link might be broken and a detention which was lawful at the outset would be transformed into an arbitrary deprivation of liberty incompatible with Article 5.

14.09 The second and alternative argument advanced by Mr Weeks was that on his recall to prison in 1977, or at reasonable intervals throughout his detention, he had not been able to take proceedings to challenge his imprisonment which complied with the requirements of Article 5(4). The court held that the stated purpose of social protection and rehabilitation which underlay the imposition of the discretionary life sentence and the grounds relied upon by the sentencing judge in Mr Weeks' case were, by their very nature, susceptible of change with the passage of time. Accordingly, Mr Weeks was entitled to apply to a 'court' having jurisdiction to decide speedily whether or not his deprivation of liberty had become unlawful at the moment of his recall to prison and also at reasonable intervals during the course of his imprisonment. The Parole Board did not satisfy this requirement because to be a 'court' the body in question must not have merely advisory functions but must be competent to decide the lawfulness of detention and order release if the detention has become unlawful. Save in a recall case the Board had no power to order release. Furthermore, the lack of any right of access to the reports and other material before the Parole Board meant that the prisoner affected was not able properly to participate in the decision-making process, which was one of the principal guarantees of a judicial procedure for the purposes of the Convention. In these two important respects it followed that, in relation to both his original recall to prison and the periodic examination of his detention,

---

[23] The trial judge, Thesiger J, said that 'an indeterminate sentence is the right sentence for somebody of this age, of this character and disposition, who is attracted to this form of conduct. That leaves the matter with the Secretary of State who can release him if and when those who have been watching him believe that with the passage of years he has become responsible. It may not take long. Or the change may not occur for a long time—I do not know how it will work out. So far as the first count on the indictment is concerned, I think the right conclusion, terrible though it may seem, is that I pass the sentence which the law authorises me to pass for robbery and for assault with intent to rob with arms, that is life imprisonment. The Secretary of State can act if and when he thinks it is safe to act.'

the Parole Board could not be regarded as having satisfied the requirements of Article 5(4) in Mr Weeks' case.

The *Weeks* judgment did not lead to a change in the procedures for reviewing the **14.10** detention of all discretionary lifers. That came about as a result of the next case to reach the ECtHR, *Thynne, Wilson and Gunnell*.[24] Whereas Mr Weeks' case was highly unusual in that the original offence which led to the life sentence was not a particularly serious one on its facts, the three applicants in *Thynne* had all been convicted of very grave offences of rape and buggery. In response to the submission that their detention was also in breach of Article 5(4), the British Government sought to argue that *Weeks* had been decided on its own very special facts and that its reasoning could not apply to all discretionary lifers, especially those where punishment was a significant aspect of the original life sentence.[25] In short, it was submitted that it was impossible to disentangle the punitive and security components in the vast majority of discretionary life sentences.

The court rejected this argument and pointed out that the discretionary life sen- **14.11** tence had a clear lineage and purpose. It had developed as a measure to deal with mentally unstable and dangerous offenders and:

> although the dividing line may be difficult to draw in particular cases it seems clear that the principles underlying such sentences, unlike mandatory life sentences, have developed in the sense that they are composed of a punitive element and subsequently a security element designed to confer on the Home Secretary the responsibility for determining when the public interest permits the prisoner's release. This view is confirmed by the judicial description of the 'tariff' as denoting the period of detention considered necessary to meet the requirements of retribution and deterrence.[26]

In the case of all three applicants, though they had committed grave offences deserving long sentences, they had remained in prison beyond their tariff dates and accordingly, so the court found, they were in exactly the same position as Mr Weeks. The factors of mental instability and dangerousness which had led to the imposition of the life sentence were susceptible to change over time and new issues of lawfulness could thus arise in the course of their detention. It followed that they too were entitled to have their detention reviewed by a 'court' which satisfied the requirements of Article 5(4) in ways which the Parole Board and the machinery of the Criminal Justice Act 1967 did not.

---

[24] (1991) 13 EHRR 666.
[25] When sentencing Gunnell, Roskill J had said '[t]hese must be among the worst cases of rape or attempted rape ever to come before a court in this country . . . Punishment must be an element in this case and that punishment can only be achieved by imprisonment.'
[26] (1991) 13 EHRR 693, para 73.

14.12   The significance of the *Thynne* decision was clear. The process of reviewing the detention of discretionary lifers once they had completed the tariff portion of their sentences and on any recall to prison had to be changed in order to comply with the ECHR. The 1991 Act sought to achieve that change, though the Government was strict in its interpretation that a clear distinction had been drawn between discretionary and mandatory lifers. Since its introduction, the decisions of the ECtHR on the applicability of Article 5(4) to the sentence of detention during Her Majesty's Pleasure have forced further legislative change.[27] The special function of the Parole Board in relation to both discretionary lifers and HMP detainees is now governed by s 28 of the Crime (Sentences) Act 1997. As we saw in Chapter 13, these statutory provisions are likely to be extended to mandatory lifers in the near future. Below we will examine the rights conferred under the 1997 Act in relation to the release of discretionary lifers (including 'automatic' lifers under s 109 of the 2000 Act) and HMP detainees.

E. 'Automatic' Lifers: Section 109 of the Powers of Criminal Courts (Sentencing) Act 2000

14.13   Section 2 of the 1997 Act, a provision of great controversy, required a court to sentence a defendant to life imprisonment upon his conviction for a serious offence where he had a previous conviction (in any part of the United Kingdom) for a serious offence.[28] That provision was re-enacted as s 109 of the 2000 Act. The

---

[27] *Singh and Hussain v UK* (1996) 22 EHRR 1; *T and V v UK* (2000) 30 EHRR 121.

[28] A serious offence is defined, if committed in England, by subs 5 as (a) an attempt to commit murder, a conspiracy or an incitement to murder; (b) an offence under s 4 of the Offences Against the Person Act 1861 (soliciting murder); (c) manslaughter; (d) an offence under s 18 of the 1861 Act (wounding or causing GBH with intent); (e) rape or attempted rape; (f) an offence under s 5 of the Sexual Offences Act 1956 (sexual intercourse with a girl under 13); (g) an offence under s 16 (possession of a firearm with intent to injure), s 17 (use of a firearm to resist arrest), and s 18 (carrying a firearm with criminal intent) of the Firearms Act 1968; and (h) robbery where, at some time during the commission of the offence, the offender had in his possession a firearm or imitation firearm within the meaning of the 1968 Act. In relation to an offence committed in Scotland a serious offence is defined in subs 6 as (a) culpable homicide; (b) attempted murder, incitement or conspiracy to commit murder; (c) rape or attempted rape; (d) clandestine injury to women or an attempt to cause such injury; (e) sodomy, or an attempt to commit sodomy, where the complainer, that is to say, the person against whom the offence was committed, did not consent; (f) assault where the assault—(i) was aggravated because it was carried out to the victim's severe injury or the danger of the victim's life; or (ii) was carried out with an intention to rape or to ravish the victim; (g) robbery where, at some time during the commission of the offence, the offender had in his possession a firearm or imitation firearm within the meaning of the Firearms Act 1968; (h) an offence under ss 16, 17, or 18 of the 1968 Act; (i) lewd, libidinous, or indecent behaviour or practices; and (j) an offence under s 5(1) of the Criminal Law (Consolidation) (Scotland) Act 1995 (unlawful intercourse with a girl under 13). In relation to an offence committed in Northern Ireland serious offence is defined by subs (7) as: (a) an offence falling within paras (a) to (e) of subs (5); (b) an offence under s 4 of the Criminal Law Amendment Act 1885 (intercourse with a girl under 14); (c) an offence under Art 17 (possession of a firearm with intent to injure), Art 18(1) (use of a firearm to resist

sentence is mandatory unless the judge is satisfied that there are exceptional circumstances relating to either of the offences or to the offender which justify passing a determinate sentence. Despite the mandatory nature of the sentence, it is not to be equated with the mandatory life sentence imposed for murder. The underlying rationale for its imposition is preventive, in that the sentence proceeds on the basis of presumed dangerousness (hence eligibility for indeterminate, preventative detention).[29] Accordingly, the Act treats s 109 life sentences as discretionary life sentences to which the rights of s 28 attach.[30]

14.14 The courts at first interpreted the 'exceptional circumstances' clause very narrowly.[31] However, the applicability of s 109, and the extent to which the sentence can really be called 'automatic', was greatly reduced by the Court of Appeal in *R v Offen*.[32] The appellants argued that, in light of the very narrow interpretation given to the 'exceptional circumstances' clause, the automatic sentence amounted to an arbitrary deprivation of liberty, contrary to Article 5 of the ECHR. Lord Woolf CJ considered that the statute could be read, with the assistance of s 3 of the Human Rights Act 1998 (HRA), in order to comply with Article 5. However, that reading involved giving 'exceptional circumstances' a meaning which Parliament clearly did not intend it to bear. In one of the first notable examples of judicial creativity under the HRA, Lord Woolf considered that:

> Section 2 [now s 109] establishes a norm. The norm is that those who commit two serious offences are a danger or risk to the public. If in fact, taking into account all the circumstances relating to a particular offender, he does not create an unacceptable risk to the public, he is an exception to this norm. If the offences are of a different kind, or if there is a long period which elapses between the offences during which the offender has not committed other offences, that may be a very relevant indicator as to the degree of risk to the public that he constitutes. . . . In our judgment, section

---

arrest) or Art 19 (carrying a firearm with criminal intent) of the Firearms (Northern Ireland) Order 1981, SI 1981/155; and (d) robbery, where at some time during the commission of that offence, the offender had in his possession a firearm or imitation firearm within the meaning of that Order.

[29] As Edward Fitzgerald QC remarked ('Sentencing and the European Convention of Human Rights', paper delivered to Criminal Bar Association, April 1998), the new automatic life sentence raises issues under the ECHR. 'If Judges treat as exceptional circumstances relating to the offender the fact that he is not likely to re-offend (or rather has not been shown to be likely to re-offend) then the imposition of an automatic life sentence (with a modest initial tariff period) will not necessarily offend against the Convention. But the imposition of a measure of potentially life long preventative detention on someone who is not in fact likely to be dangerous in the future would violate Article 5 and be arbitrary. So judges should be invited to exercise their discretion to find exceptional circumstances under s 2(2) of the 1997 Act in such a way as to ensure that only those who are dangerous actually receive automatic life sentences.' Such a result was, in fact, achieved by the decision of the Court of Appeal in *R v Offen* [2001] 1 WLR 253.

[30] Subs (4) provides that an offence the sentence for which is imposed under subs (2), shall not be regarded as an offence the sentence for which is fixed by law. Section 28(1) and (2) defines a life prisoner to whom the section applies as, inter alia, one whose sentence was imposed for an offence the sentence for which is not fixed by law.

[31] See *Kelly* [2000] QB 198; *Buckland* [2000] 1 WLR 1262; *Williams* [2000] Crim LR 597.

[32] [2001] 1 WLR 253.

2 of the 1997 Act will not contravene Convention rights if courts apply the section so that it does not result in offenders being sentenced to life imprisonment when they do not constitute a significant risk to the public. Whether there is significant risk will depend upon the evidence which is before the court. If the offender is a significant risk, the court can impose a life sentence under section 2 without contravening the Convention. Either there will be no exceptional circumstances, or despite the exceptional circumstances the facts will justify imposing a life sentence.[33]

This interpretation means that s109 no longer achieves the purpose meant for it by the Conservative Government, namely imprisoning second sexual or violent offenders for life in all but the most extraordinary circumstances. Rather, risk is the key, bringing the s 109 sentence into line with the discretionary life sentence.

F. Tariff-setting in the Case of Discretionary Lifers

14.15 The introduction of the 1991 Act brought an end to the role of the Secretary of State in setting the period necessary to mark the requirements of retribution and deterrence. Though the decision in *Thynne*[34] was concerned only with the post-tariff period, a necessary implication of the ECtHR's analysis of the rationale of the discretionary life sentence is that the determination of the appropriate punitive period is a classic sentencing exercise which attracts Article 6(1) safeguards requiring the exercise to be conducted by a court. Reflecting this analysis, s 34(1) of the 1991 Act took away the Secretary of State's power to fix the tariff and passed it to the sentencing court. Section 34(1) was subsequently re-enacted as s 82A of the 2000 Act, which governs the position today.

14.16 The scheme requires the sentencing judge to consider first whether the later provisions of the section, governing the Parole Board's power to direct release, should apply to the defendant at all. The purpose of this discretion is for the court to determine whether the offence is so serious as to call for lifelong punishment.[35] A sentence imposed on punitive grounds alone is not governed by the *Hodgson* criteria. Rather its object is identical to the theoretical basis for the mandatory life sentence, being exclusively punitive. A discretionary life sentence imposed on punitive grounds does not encompass a preventive phase, and so the basis for the special function of the Parole Board is absent. Like mandatory lifers, their release was, until the ECtHR's decision in *Stafford*,[36] a matter for the Home Secretary to

---

[33] [97].

[34] *Thynne, Wilson and Gunnell v UK* (1991) 13 EHRR 666.

[35] There is only one known case in which a full life tariff has been imposed in the case of a discretionary lifer either by a court or by the Secretary of State acting under the transitional provisions contained in Sch 12, para 9 of the 1991 Act. In that case, the sentence was subsequently rescinded after legal proceedings were commenced.

[36] *Stafford v UK* Application 46295/99 (2002) 35 EHRR 32.

decide. Since that decision, of course, the release decision for those serving a purely punitive discretionary life sentence, as well as those serving mandatory life sentences, is purely in the hands of the Parole Board. There is therefore no practical distinction, for release purposes, between the two types of discretionary sentence, although the basis for the court's imposition of a discretionary life sentence will of course be relevant to the Parole Board's deliberations.

The scheme requires the court to express its conclusion that the indeterminate **14.17** sentence is called for on preventive grounds by specifying a period after which the special release provisions of the section will apply. The period specified marks the court's decision as to the appropriate tariff. Before the 1991 Act came into force it had been established in the line of cases including *Handscomb* that discretionary life sentence prisoners should not be punished more by reason of the indeterminate nature of the sentence than their fixed term counterparts. They should have the same opportunities to gain their release. It followed that the tariff period should not simply equate with the notional equivalent fixed term sentence that the offence would have attracted had it not been necessary to pass an indeterminate sentence to protect the public. From that notional equivalent a period should be subtracted to reflect the opportunities that a fixed term prisoner would have had to gain early release.

Section 82A of the 2000 Act enshrines the common law principle in statute, tak- **14.18** ing account of the new scheme for early release which the Act introduced for fixed term prisoners.[37] By s 82A the period is to be specified taking into account (a) the seriousness of the offence, or the combination of the offence and other offences associated with it; and (b) the provisions of s 34 as compared to those of ss 33(2) and 35(1) of the 1991 Act. Section 33(2) of the 1991 Act imposes a duty on the Secretary of State to release a long term prisoner (one serving a sentence of four years or more) after he has served two thirds of his sentence. Section 35(1) entitles a long term prisoner to be considered for discretionary release on licence as soon as he has served one half of his sentence. The scheme, therefore, requires the court to identify, according to ordinary sentencing principles, the notional equivalent fixed term sentence and then to specify a period which would secure a review by the Parole Board at some point within the period during which the offender, if sentenced to a fixed term, would have been eligible for parole but not subject to mandatory release.[38]

---

[37] This provision reproduces s 28 of the 1997 Act, and was inserted by the Criminal Justice (Court Services) Act 2000. An order under s 82A can be appealed like other sentences: *D* (1995) 16 Cr App R (S) 564. Under s 60 of the Criminal Justice and Court Services Act 2000, a court imposing a sentence of detention at Her Majesty's Pleasure must normally specify the tariff period in open court, in accordance with s 82A. Section 60 follows the decision of the ECtHR in *T and V v UK* (2000) 30 EHRR 121, discussed further below in the context of HMP detainees.
[38] See *Practice Direction (Crime: Life Sentences)* [1993] 1 WLR 223.

The Proper Approach to Tariff-setting by the Sentencing Court

14.19 The courts took some time to address how the discretion to specify a period between the halfway and two thirds point should be approached. An unsettled pattern has emerged from reported cases in which, though never made explicit by the sentencing judge, the period must have been specified at the two thirds point of the notional equivalent determinate sentence. Even then the sentences were unusually harsh when compared to fixed term equivalents. The long awaited judicial analysis arising from two cases has done something to turn the tide and to bring a reduction in specified periods.

14.20 The first case concerned a young woman, Donna Furber, who was sentenced to detention for life under s 53(2) of the Children and Young Persons Act 1933.[39] Having been convicted prior to the commencement of the 1991 Act, the Secretary of State set her tariff. Ms Furber had pleaded guilty to manslaughter on grounds of diminished responsibility. The Secretary of State certified a tariff of seven years. The notional equivalent determinate sentence lay between ten and a half and 14 years. In deciding where along the half way to two thirds point the judge should usually specify the tariff, the court took into account the duty imposed by s 44(1) of the 1933 Act:

> Every court in dealing with a child or young person who is brought before it, either as ... an offender or otherwise, shall have regard to the welfare of the child or young person and shall in a proper case take steps for removing him from undesirable surroundings, and for securing that proper provision is made for his education and training.

It also applied the reasoning of Lord Browne-Wilkinson in his judgment in *R v Home Secretary, ex p Thompson and Venables*,[40] where he analysed the sentencing judge's function under what was then s 34(2) of the 1991 Act when dealing with a young person. In his view, the provisions of s 44(1) required the sentencing court to take account of the need for flexibility in the treatment of the child, such that he will set the minimum tariff so as to ensure that at the earliest possible moment the matter comes under the consideration of the Parole Board, which will be able to balance the relevant factors including the progress of the child.[41] In Ms Furber's application, the Divisional Court held that these principles meant that in general the judge should specify a period at the earliest possible moment, namely the halfway point. By the time her case was heard she had served six years. The court declared that this exceeded any period that could have been selected had the proper approach been adopted. That approach has now been endorsed by the

---

[39] *R v Home Secretary, ex p Furber* [1998] 1 All ER 23.
[40] [1997] 3 WLR 23.
[41] *per* Lord Browne-Wilkinson at [1997] 3 WLR 52.

Court of Appeal in *R v M and L*[42] where, in addition, the proper approach to adult offenders was also the subject of comment. Even with an adult the judge should start by taking the half way point as this may well be appropriate in many cases. However, he can increase the period in the light of the circumstances or particular facts of the case.

Tariff-setting

Ex p Furber[43] is an example of the operation of the transitional provisions con- **14.21** tained in Sch 12, para 9 to the 1991 Act. As Ms Furber was convicted before the 1991 Act came into force, the power to fix the tariff was vested in the Home Secretary. The transitional provisions established new arrangements which required the Home Secretary to revisit all cases where convictions preceded October 1992 and to certify a period equivalent to that which the trial judge would have awarded had s 34 of the 1991 Act been in force at the time of sentence. This provision has been interpreted to mean that the Home Secretary cannot certify the period he thinks appropriate, but must adopt an identical approach to the sentencing court and so be guided by established sentencing practice and authorities.[44] If the period certified is so manifestly excessive as to be irrational when tested against those criteria the courts will quash the decision in judicial review proceedings even if the Home Secretary certified a period in accordance with the judicial recommendation.[45] In the light of the decisions in *Ex p Furber* and *Ex p M and L* it may be that there are a number of prisoners whose certified period can now be shown to be manifestly excessive. For many, however, it will be too late as they will have served their tariffs. Of course, since the ECtHR's decision in *T and V v UK*,[46] discussed in detail below, the Home Secretary no longer has the power to set the tariff of HMP detainees: like other discretionary lifers, their tariff is set by the sentencing court.

G. Persons Detained During Her Majesty's Pleasure

The sentence of detention during Her Majesty's Pleasure is mandatorily imposed **14.22** in cases of murder committed by children or young people who are aged 17 or under on the date of the commission of the offence.[47] The effect of the sentence is to authorize detention for as long as is considered necessary and, if necessary, for

---

[42] [1999] 1 WLR 485.
[43] [1998] 1 All ER 23.
[44] *R v Home Secretary, ex p McCartney* [1994] COD 528.
[45] *R v Home Secretary, ex p Chapman*, The Times, 25 October 1994; *R v Home Secretary, ex p Dowd*, 24 November 1994.
[46] (2000) 30 EHRR 121.
[47] Powers of Criminal Courts (Sentencing) Act 2000, s 90.

life, and to provide for lifelong liability to recall, when and if the HMP detainee is released on licence. The nature of the sentence and the procedural rights that it attracts have been subject to much recent litigation resulting, as with discretionary lifers, in decisions about release being vested in the Parole Board rather than the Executive, culminating in the changes required by the decision of the ECtHR in *T and V v UK*, which mean that the tariff for such sentences is now set in open court in the same way as other discretionary life sentences.

History of the Sentence of Detention at Her Majesty's Pleasure

14.23   Section 90 of the Powers of Criminal Courts (Sentencing) Act 2000, based on s 53(1) of the Children and Young Persons Act 1933, provides:

> Where a person convicted of murder [or any other offence the sentence for which is fixed by law as life imprisonment][48] appears to the court to have been aged under 18 at the time the offence was committed, the court shall (notwithstanding anything in this or any other Act) sentence him to be detained during Her Majesty's pleasure.

The notion of detention during Her Majesty's Pleasure originated in the Trial of Lunatics Act 1800 and was intended for the safe custody of insane persons charged with offences. The Act provided for the detention 'until his Majesty's Pleasure shall be known' of defendants acquitted of a charge of murder, treason, or felony on grounds of insanity at the time of the offence. In 1908 this form of detention was introduced in respect of offenders aged between 10 and 16 and eventually was amended to the currently worded s 90. The purpose of the original sentence was clearly preventive, it being inappropriate to punish those who are insane and so not responsible for their acts. The adoption of this same rationale in relation to children who murder is readily comprehensible. First, their youth has clear implications for the degree of responsibility which they can bear for their actions: it is misconceived to treat them the same as their adult counterparts by punishing them for life. Secondly, because of their youth, there is much room for change and development. By providing flexibility to determine the conditions of detention, the most suitable circumstances in which to secure their rehabilitation can be achieved.

14.24   Despite the partly preventive rationale of the sentence, no distinction was ever drawn by Parliament between the procedures applicable to release and recall in relation to HMP detainees and mandatory lifers. A series of Acts conferred a broad discretion on the Home Secretary to direct their release on licence,[49] culminating in s 35(2) of the Criminal Justice Act 1991. This provision empowered the Secretary of State to release on licence a mandatory life sentence prisoner

---

[48]   The words in square brackets were inserted by Criminal Justice and Court Services Act 2000, s 62(3), in relation to sentences passed after 30 November 2000.
[49]   eg Criminal Justice Act 1967, s 61(1).

(which included HMP detainees) if recommended to do so by the Parole Board and after consultation with the Lord Chief Justice and trial judge.

The administrative procedures introduced for the review of the continuing deten-   **14.25**
tion of HMP detainees changed over time. Originally, they gave effect to the primarily preventive and rehabilitative rationale, and provided for periodic review at regular intervals. However, when the Home Secretary introduced a new policy in relation to life sentence prisoners in 1983, the position of HMP detainees was equated with mandatory life sentence prisoners. The two sentences were assimilated in their entirety and, like their adult counterparts, HMP detainees were treated as having been sentenced to lifelong punishment. Under successive policies the Home Secretary set tariffs for HMP detainees in precisely the same way in which he did for adult murderers. The only concession made to the unique nature of the sentence was in taking account of the youth of an HMP detainee as a factor making him less culpable than his adult counterpart. Once a tariff had been set it was never revisited and until it had been served the prisoner's case for release would not be considered.

The Development of Case Law: The Post-tariff Stage

In contrast with the discretionary life sentence, the sentence of detention at Her   **14.26**
Majesty's Pleasure was subject to little scrutiny by the domestic courts before the issue of how the sentence fell to be treated under the ECHR was first considered by the ECtHR. In *R v Home Secretary, ex p Prem Singh*[50] the Divisional Court held that although the sentence was the statutory equivalent of the mandatory life sentence for murder, it was closer in substance to the discretionary life sentence, of which part is punitive and the balance justified only in the interests of public safety when the dangerousness test is satisfied. It was not a sentence imposed for the purpose of lifelong punishment. The issue before the court was whether HMP detainees should be afforded the same rights of disclosure as discretionary lifers in Parole Board reviews or whether, like mandatory lifers, they should have no right to see the documents upon which the Board would make its recommendation. Having equated the rationale of the sentence with that of discretionary lifers, and thereby distinguished it from the mandatory life sentence, the court followed *Ex p Wilson*[51] rather than *Payne*[52] and declared that the applicant was entitled to disclosure. Despite the decision in *Singh*, Home Secretary Michael Howard issued a Parliamentary statement on 27 July 1993 reiterating that he included in the category of 'mandatory life sentence prisoners' HMP detainees.

---

[50] [1993] COD 501.
[51] [1992] 1 QB 740.
[52] [1981] 1 WLR 754.

14.27   Mr Singh, together with another HMP detainee, took his case to Europe, arguing that, as with like discretionary lifers, the rationale of the sentence of detention during Her Majesty's Pleasure was not such as to authorize detention for life on grounds of punishment, but contained a preventive component which attracted the protections of Article 5(4) of the ECHR.[53] The court noted the mandatory nature of the sentence and the assimilation, both in statute and administrative practice, of the HMP sentence to the mandatory life sentence. It looked also at the preventive purpose to which the original use of the term 'during Her Majesty's Pleasure' was put. Ultimately the court was persuaded by none of these factors arising from the domestic context. Instead it took a principled approach, holding that the only possible justification for the imposition of an indeterminate term of detention on a convicted young person was a preventive rationale based on the need to protect the public. The court specifically raised the issue of whether life-long punishment imposed on a young person would violate the right under Article 3 not to be subjected to inhuman or degrading punishment. As a sentence with a preventive component, the court found that its ongoing implementation gave rise to considerations which centre on an assessment of the young offender's character and mental state. These necessarily required account to be taken of any developments in the HMP detainee's personality and attitude as he grew older. The court held that when an HMP detainee enters the post-tariff stage, the sentence more closely resembles a discretionary life sentence and attracts Article 5(4) guarantees, entitling him to have his detention reviewed by a 'court'.

14.28   As in *Thynne, Wilson and Gunnell*,[54] the court held that the old statutory scheme, in which the Parole Board's function was only advisory, did not satisfy the requirements of Article 5(4). The court also addressed the question of what form the Article 5(4) review should take and was influenced by two factors. First, it noted that a substantial term of imprisonment may be at stake, a factor calling for relatively greater procedural safeguards. Secondly, it highlighted the issues with which the Board must grapple in the post-tariff stage when assessing dangerousness, namely characteristics pertaining to the HMP detainee's personality and level of maturity. Together, these considerations persuaded the court that the applicants were entitled to an adversarial procedure involving an oral hearing, legal representation and the possibility of calling and questioning witnesses.[55]

---

[53]   *Hussain and Singh v UK* (1996) 22 EHRR 1.
[54]   (1991) 13 EHRR 666.
[55]   Following the decision of the ECtHR, the Home Secretary announced that pending legislation giving effect to the judgment he would institute oral hearings for all HMP detainees whose cases were referred after 1 August 1996. In *R v Parole Board, ex p Downing* [1997] COD 149, an HMP detainee whose case had been referred to the Parole Board before that date challenged the Board's refusal to grant him an oral hearing arguing that natural justice required such a procedural safeguard. Reliance was placed upon the rationale of the sentence and the inadequacy of a paper review as a mechanism to explore and test the issues relevant to his ongoing dangerousness. The Divisional Court was unpersuaded and the case is illustrative of how common law concepts of

The Crime (Sentences) Act 1997 assimilated the position of HMP detainees and **14.29** discretionary lifers in the post-tariff stage, and s 60 of the Criminal Justice and Court Services Act 2000 equated the provisions for tariff-setting. Below we examine the rights of both categories of prisoner under the Act.

The Tariff Stage

The 1997 Act did not affect the procedure governing the HMP sentence in the **14.30** tariff stage. Under those provisions, an HMP detainee's case would be referred to the Parole Board under s 28 as soon as he had served the period directed by the Secretary of State. The statute did not impinge, therefore, upon the policy of successive Home Secretaries to fix the tariff of HMP detainees. Following the decision of the ECtHR in *T and V v UK*,[56] however, the law has been changed in order to bring HMP detainees in line with other discretionary lifers at the tariff-setting, as well as post-tariff, stage. Before examining the ECtHR's decision in *T and V*, and the legislative response, we look at the domestic decisions which preceded it. The House of Lords did not fight shy of structuring the discretion at common law. Its opportunity to do so arose out of the convictions at the age of 10 of Robert Thompson and John Venables, eventually the applicants in *T and V*, for the notorious murder of two-year-old Jamie Bulger. In *R v Home Secretary, ex p Thompson and Venables*[57] the two boys, who were sentenced to detention at Her Majesty's Pleasure, sought to challenge the decision of the Home Secretary to fix their tariffs at 15 years. The case brought into sharp focus the need for a dispassionate approach to punishment, and provided the opportunity for the House of Lords to determine authoritatively the nature of the sentence and to draw out its implications for the tariff setting exercise.

The Secretary of State fixed the boys' tariffs in the face of and influenced by an **14.31** extraordinary public reaction to the killing. Though the boys were barely over the age of criminal responsibility, a substantial body of public opinion made no concessions to their age and lack of maturity and called for the most extreme punitive measures. After their convictions, the Secretary of State received the advice of the trial judge and Lord Chief Justice on the appropriate tariffs. The trial judge recommended a period of eight years and the Lord Chief Justice ten. The judicial recommendations were then disclosed to the public and a flurry of petitions made their way to the Home Office. One petition signed by 278,300 members of the

---

fairness can and do fail to deliver the full panoply of protections that are guaranteed by the ECHR. The interim arrangements were successfully challenged before the ECtHR in *Curley v UK* (2001) 31 EHRR 14. The applicant argued that HMP detainees were entitled, after the expiry of the tariff term, to a review of the lawfulness of their continued detention by a court with the power to hold adversarial proceedings and to direct release, and that since the interim arrangements did not provide this, they violated Article 5(4). The court agreed, finding a violation of Article 5(4).

[56] (2000) 30 EHRR 121.
[57] [1997] 3 WLR 23.

public called for the Home Secretary to set whole life tariffs. Another, signed by 6,000 people demanded a minimum period of 25 years. In addition, as a result of a campaign by the Sun newspaper, 20,000 coupons were signed demanding a whole life tariff. The Home Secretary set a tariff of 15 years. In doing so he expressly stated that he had taken the expressions of public concern, as evidenced by the petitions and other correspondence, into account. He considered that had the offences been committed by adults a tariff of 25 years would have been appropriate. To reflect the age of the two boys he fixed a tariff of two thirds of the appropriate period for an adult murderer.

14.32 The decision was challenged on a number of grounds. First it was argued that the whole concept of a tariff fixed by reference to the requirements of retribution and deterrence was inapplicable to HMP detainees in general and, in particular to children as young as ten. The sole criteria that should govern the detention of such a young offender are those of rehabilitation and the protection of the public. Secondly, it was argued that the notion of a pre-determined minimum punitive period was inconsistent with the rationale of the sentence of detention during Her Majesty's Pleasure. The existing policy failed to reflect the distinct rationale of an HMP detainee's sentence.[58]

14.33 The House of Lords rejected the first argument, unanimously holding that the sentence of detention during Her Majesty's Pleasure contains a substantial punitive element, entitling the Home Secretary to have regard to the requirements of retribution and deterrence even where the offender is a child as young as ten. As to the second argument, a majority of three to two held that there was an important distinction between the nature of the sentences imposed on young offenders and adults who are convicted of murder. Like the ECtHR the House of Lords held that the sentence of detention during Her Majesty's Pleasure did not order lifelong punitive detention. Persuaded by an analysis of the legislative history of the sentence, the majority concluded that the factors which had brought about its indeterminacy were different in nature and purpose from those pertaining to the adult sentence.[59] On the question whether it was lawful for the Home Secretary to set a provisional tariff, Lords Browne-Wilkinson and Hope concluded that it was, provided that it was subject to review and downward revision in the light of an HMP detainee's progress in custody. The same two judges also held that in fixing the tariff the Home Secretary was bound to take a very different course from that applicable to adult mandatory lifers. He must balance the requirements of retri-

---

[58] *per* Lord Browne-Wilkinson at 49C–E; Lord Steyn at 69C–73D; and Lord Hope at 77H–82E.

[59] In the Court of Appeal, Lord Woolf and Hobhouse LJ had also characterized the tariff fixing exercise as a sentencing function. This characterization did not, however, persuade the House of Lords that before setting a tariff the Home Secretary should obtain psychiatric and social inquiry reports.

bution against the welfare of the young offender in accordance with s 44(1) of the 1933 Act. Finally, the House of Lords held (by a majority) that the Home Secretary had been wrong to have regard to the public petitions. They viewed the tariff fixing exercise as comparable to a judicial sentencing exercise, requiring the Secretary of State to act in accordance with the principles which a sentencing judge would apply.[60] A judge, and hence the Secretary of State, would be bound to ignore such one sided petitions.

On 10 November 1997, Home Secretary Jack Straw responded to the judgment   **14.34** with the issue of a fresh policy statement in which he expressed his intention to continue to administer the sentence as one in which punishment forms a necessary component. Tariffs were still to be fixed at the outset, although they would be subject to review at the half-way point. As in the case of mandatory lifers, the Home Secretary continued to assert a power to set a tariff higher than the judicial recommendation, by reference to his perception of the need to 'maintain public confidence'. Though he allowed for the possibility of reducing the tariff on review in the light of an offender's progress, this was expressed as an exception to the general rule that the tariff should not be curtailed lightly. The more serious the circumstances of the offence, the higher the justification required to reduce it in the light of progress. The policy statement represented the narrowest possible interpretation that the Home Secretary could have placed upon the House of Lords' injunction that the tariff must be subject to review.

The decision in *Ex p Thompson and Venables* was far from the last judicial pro-   **14.35** nouncement moulding the sentence of detention at Her Majesty's Pleasure. In March 1998 the European Commission on Human Rights admitted Venables' and Thompson's applications to the court. In its judgment, the court held that, although 'it cannot be excluded, particularly in relation to a child as young as the applicant at the time of his conviction, that an unjustifiable and persistent failure to fix a tariff, leaving the detainee in uncertainty over many years as to his future, might . . . give rise to an issue under Article 3', there had been no violation in the present case, in view of the relatively short time in which no tariff had been in force after the decision of the domestic courts.[61] Nor did the court consider that the applicants' treatment violated Article 5(1) of the ECHR, since the sentence flowed from the finding of a competent court.

However, the court did find violations of Articles 6(1) and 5(4). On Article 6(1),   **14.36** despite the Government's arguments that the Secretary of State followed a fair procedure in fixing the tariff, the court considered that the fixing of the tariff amounted to a sentencing exercise, since the tariff period represents the period of imprisonment necessary for retribution and deterrence, with detention thereafter

---

[60] *per* Lord Goff at 41D–G; Lord Steyn at 73D–75C; Lord Hope at 85A–H.
[61] (2000) 30 EHRR 121, para 99.

justified only on the basis of risk. The Secretary of State was clearly not independent of the Executive, as required by Article 6, and therefore his power to set the tariff violated Article 6(1). On Article 5(4), the Government argued that there had been review by a court of the lawfulness of the detention, in that the sentence of detention during Her Majesty's Pleasure was imposed by the trial court following the conviction for murder. However, the court held that, 'given that the sentence of detention during Her Majesty's Pleasure is indeterminate and the tariff was initially set by the Home Secretary rather than the sentencing judge, it cannot be said that the supervision required by Article 5(4) was incorporated in the trial court's sentence'.[62] Accordingly, there had also been a violation of that Article.

14.37 This judgment, with its emphasis on the illegitimacy of executive sentencing, was relied upon several years later in *Stafford.* Its more immediate effect was to force the Government to change the law in order to give the trial judge responsibility for setting the minimum term for all offenders sentenced to be detained at Her Majesty's Pleasure after 30 November 2000. Under s 60 of the Criminal Justice and Court Services Act 2000, the court must specify the tariff period when it passes a sentence of detention at Her Majesty's Pleasure. The court does so in accordance with the principles set out in s 82A of the Powers of Criminal Courts (Sentencing) Act 2000.

14.38 A transitional mechanism was required to deal with HMP detainees who were still serving a minimum term set by the Home Secretary, but whose term could no longer be reviewed by the Home Secretary. On 13 March 2000 the Home Secretary issued a new policy statement which replaces the tariff-setting and review arrangements set out in the 10 November 1997 policy statement. The policy revises the practice of administering the sentence of HMP detention for existing detainees and for those sentenced before the new legislation came into force. Under the new policy, the tariff will be fixed once and for all by the Lord Chief Justice. For existing cases, where the tariff has already been fixed, the Home Secretary has undertaken to review the tariffs afresh in line with the principles in the *T and V* judgment, and has invited representations from those whose tariffs have not yet expired. Where no new representations are made he will fix the tariff in accordance with the original recommendation of the Lord Chief Justice, unless it is higher than that fixed by the Secretary of State. Where an existing detainee wishes to make recommendations, these will be put before the LCJ and the Home Secretary will adopt his recommendation.

14.39 In bringing into force the new policy, the Home Secretary abolished the periodic reviews for which provision was made in the 1997 policy. However, s 44(1) of the Children and Young Persons Act 1933 still applies, and requires that the sentencing court have regard to the welfare of the child. The Home Secretary's statement

---

[62] para 119.

of 13 March 2000 made it clear that the Lord Chief Justice was to take account of the detainee's welfare, when setting the tariff, by fixing a lower tariff than would otherwise be the case if periodic reviews had been maintained. On 27 July 2000 the Lord Chief Justice issued a Practice Statement setting out his approach to this exercise, but making no mention of the need to take into account the fact that HMP tariffs will no longer be open to automatic, periodic review.[63] However, it is plain that the Lord Chief Justice considers that the judgment of the House of Lords in *Ex p Thompson and Venables* as to the nature and rationale of the sentence, including the welfare component, does require there to be a mechanism to take into account exceptional progress and its impact on the HMP detainee, throughout the sentence. However, he does not consider that this is a role which the sentencing judge should perform, but rather that it should fall to the Secretary of State to provide for a review of tariff at some point before it has expired.[64] This is a sensible position, since the Lord Chief Justice cannot predict at the outset how the detainee may progress in custody, and how his or her welfare might be harmed by future detention. However, the Home Secretary will not now conduct a subsequent review. Currently, therefore, there is a clear tension between the judicial process of fixing the tariff 'once and for all', in line with Article 6 of the Convention, and the need for ongoing review identified by the House of Lords in *Ex p Thompson and Venables*. As the House of Lords explained, an essential component of that sentence is the welfare principle. A proper regard for that component requires that any tariff must be provisional and subject to downward review in the light of a detainee's progress. The need for ongoing review identified by the House of Lords did not turn upon the question of which authority, executive or judicial, was responsible for fixing the tariff. It turned on the nature of the sentence. This position is not affected by the decision of the ECtHR in *T and V*. The

---

[63] *Practice Statement (Juveniles: Murder tariffs)* [2000] 1 WLR 1655.

[64] This is made clear by the Lord Chief Justice in the recent *Statement (review of minimum terms set for young offenders detained at Her Majesty's pleasure)*, 26 July 2002. He considers the House of Lords' emphasis, in *Ex p Thompson and Venables*, on the Home Secretary's duty periodically to review the tariff in line with the welfare principle, and states that '[t]he Home Secretary does not consider that this statement as to his responsibility is relevant now that the minimum term is set by the trial judge ... It has been suggested that in these circumstances s44(1) of the 1993 Act requires judges to fix the lowest possible minimum term so as to ensure the Parole Board will consider the case at the correct time if a child happens to make exceptional progress. It is recommended that this suggestion is not followed although it is appreciated that the Home Secretary's view means that apparently exceptional progress by a child while in detention will not influence the date his case is considered by the Parole Board.' At the time of the Statement, he had reviewed 79 cases, with 30 further cases awaiting review. He states that, 'I will not reduce the minimum term unless, on the evidence placed before me by the prison service, I am satisfied that there has been a significant change in the offender's attitude and behaviour. I also look for evidence that the offender has expressed real regret about the crime committed and shown what is considered by the experienced writers of the reports that I see to be genuine concern for the unusually terrible consequences for the victim's family . . . Where such progress has been made, it is important to encourage further improvement by way of a modest reduction in the minimum term that has to be served before release can be considered by the Parole Board.'

only issue for the court was whether the tariff fixing exercise should be conducted by an independent and impartial tribunal and not the Executive. It does not follow from that decision that the tariff, when fixed by a judge, should be fixed once and for all. There is therefore a strong argument that the Home Secretary's policy statement of 13 March 2000 is unlawful, in so far as it leaves HMP detainees without periodic reviews of their tariff.[65]

H. Oral Hearings Before the Parole Board Under Section 28 of the 1997 Act

14.40   Section 28(7) of the Crime (Sentences) Act 1997 entitles a discretionary lifer (including an automatic lifer under s 109 of the 2000 Act) or HMP detainee to have his case referred to the Parole Board by the Secretary of State as soon as he has served the period specified by the court. It confers a right to further Parole Board reviews every two years thereafter so long as detention continues.[66] In the case of a prisoner who, in addition to the indeterminate term, is also serving a fixed term which expires after his tariff, he is entitled to have his case referred by the Secretary of State as soon as, but for the indeterminate sentence, he would have been entitled to be released under the fixed term.

14.41   It is an integral part of the decision in *Thynne* that once the penal element of the sentence has been completed its lawfulness falls immediately to be determined in accordance with the preventive rationale, whereby the justification for detention depends only on the question of ongoing dangerousness. Following the implementation of the 1991 Act, discretionary lifers found themselves waiting for a hearing for at least six months after their tariff expiry because the Home Office did not even commence the review process until their tariffs had expired. This practice was successfully challenged by a number of persons convicted of IRA offences whose tariffs expired during the ceasefire of 1995. The judgment of the Divisional Court represents one of the rare pre-HRA instances when the ECHR has been used as an aid to statutory construction, the relevant provisions of the 1991 Act having been introduced to give effect to the requirements of Article 5(4).[67] The policy has been amended in the light of the decision, and currently the cases of both discretionary lifers and HMP detainees are first referred to the Parole Board six months in advance of the expiry of their tariffs.[68]

---

[65] A challenge to the 13 March 2000 policy, on these grounds, is pending before the Administrative Court: *R (Smith) v Home Secretary*.

[66] On the frequency of reviews, see paras 14.78–14.81 below.

[67] *R v Home Secretary and Parole Board, ex p Norney* (1995) 7 ALR 861, and given effect to in IG 103/95.

[68] IG 103/1995. The same principle applies in the case of HMP detainees.

Ex p Noorkoiv

However, the system of arranging hearings is in the process of drastic reorganiza- **14.42** tion in light of the decision of the Court of Appeal in *R (Noorkoiv) v Home Secretary and Parole Board*.[69] Mr Noorkoiv was serving an automatic life sentence. His tariff expired on 21 April 2001. In accordance with policy, his case was referred to the Parole Board six months before tariff expiry, to be listed for hearing 'some time after 21 April 2001'. Due to organizational issues, cases from each prison were referred to the Parole Board in batches, for hearing once a quarter. Accordingly, Mr Noorkoiv did not receive a hearing until two months after the expiry of his tariff. He argued that this period violated Article 5(4) of the ECHR. After the expiry of his tariff, the only rationale for continued detention was risk, which had to be assessed 'promptly'. He argued that the two month delay was not 'prompt'.

The Court of Appeal agreed. In response to the Government's argument that the scheme was necessary because of resource issues, Buxton LJ (with whom Lord Woolf CJ and Simon Brown LJ agreed) commented that '[t]o the extent that the present scheme is seen as imposed on the Parole Board by constraints of resources, that factor cannot offset what is objectively a breach on the part of the state'.[70] With regard to the practice of setting hearing dates after tariff expiry, Buxton LJ considered that 'review of the lawfulness of detention after the tariff period means review of whether the prisoner should be detained after that period, and not that the review itself can only take place once that period has expired'.[71] The two month delay did not constitute a prompt review of detention. As Simon Brown LJ put it:

> Given the imperative need to release from prison any post-tariff prisoner who no longer remains a danger, (not least in these days of acute prison overcrowding), any system tending to delay such release (as the Parole Board's system does) requires the most compelling justification. Although by no means unsympathetic to the Parole Board's difficulties, at the end of the day I am not persuaded that any such compelling justification exists, or at any rate that it need continue to exist. Further resources must be found. No less importantly, the Parole Board must devise a new system for pre-tariff expiry hearings, which among other things will ensure, consistently with their statutory duty under section 28(5)(b), that they do not direct the release of a tariff-expired prisoner unless indeed at the date of that direction they are satisfied, as required by section 28(6)(b), that it is safe to do so. It can be done. As soon as reasonably practicable it now should be done.[72]

---

[69] [2002] EWCA Civ 770.
[70] [36].
[71] [40].
[72] [58].

What this means in practice is that such prisoners must have a Parole Board review which will allow their *release* on or very shortly after the tariff expiry date. In practical terms, this means that the review will have to take place before tariff expiry. This will require a reorganization on the part of the Parole Board: precise arrangements have not, at the time of writing, been put into place, but it is to be expected that the whole system will simply be started earlier, with dossiers being prepared, say, nine months in advance of tariff expiry instead of six.

Procedural Rules for Discretionary Lifer Panels

14.43 Section 32(5) of the 1991 Act empowers the Home Secretary to make rules 'with respect to the proceedings of the [Parole] Board, including provisions authorising cases to be dealt with by a prescribed number of its members or requiring cases to be dealt with at prescribed times'. The Parole Board Rules 1992, issued pursuant to s 32(5), provide a comprehensive code for the conduct of Discretionary Lifer Panel (DLP) hearings before the Parole Board. In 1997 they were reissued so as to extend their application to oral hearings for HMP detainees, and they govern all hearings conducted under ss 28 and 32 (recall cases) of the 1997 Act.[73] The reviews are conducted by three-person panels of the Parole Board, known as DLPs or HMP Panels. The Rules set out strict procedural timetables, but due to the late preparation of reports, it is often impossible for these to be met. The Parole Board is, in practice, fairly flexible about the deadlines set out below, if there are good reasons for delay.

The Appointment of the Panel

14.44 The chairman of the Parole Board appoints the Panels, each one of which must be chaired by a judge (rule 3). The constitution of Panels is not set out in the Rules but has been the subject of correspondence between the chairman of the Board and the Home Secretary. A High Court judge will chair each hearing which involves a prisoner convicted of terrorist offences, attempted murder/wounding of a police or prison officer, the sexual assault/mutilation and killing of a child, serial rape, manslaughter following release on a previous manslaughter sentence, and offences involving multiple life sentences. A Circuit judge will preside in other cases. The second member of the panel is usually a psychiatrist but, if there is clear evidence that no real concern exists about the prisoner's state of mind, a psychologist or probation officer may be appointed. The third member will be a lay member, criminologist, or psychologist/probation officer.

---

[73] See Appendix 7. The Parole Board Rules do not have the status of a Statutory Instrument and do not require parliamentary approval. Following the Government's *Comprehensive Review of Parole and Lifer Processes* (London, 2001), new Parole Board Rules are in preparation.

Representation

Each 'party' to the hearing may be represented (rule 6). 'Parties' means the pris-   **14.45**
oner and the Secretary of State. A prisoner may not be represented by a person
liable to detention under the Mental Health Act 1983, a serving prisoner, a prisoner currently on release on licence, or any person with an unspent conviction.
The Parole Board may appoint a representative where the prisoner does not
authorize someone to act on his behalf. Legal aid is available for legal representation before a DLP or HMP panel under the Criminal Defence Service contracts
(Advocacy Assistance) scheme.

Submission of Evidence

Within eight weeks of the listing of a case before a DLP or HMP Panel, the Home   **14.46**
Secretary must provide the Parole Board with certain specified information set out
in Sch 1 to the Rules. This is vital material since it covers not only the background
to the original offence and the sentencing judge's remarks but pre-trial reports
together with current reports on the prisoner's performance and behaviour in
prison. Most importantly it includes assessments of his suitability for release on
licence and an up-to-date home circumstances report prepared by a probation
officer. There will frequently be as many as eight to ten individual reports prepared by a wide range of people who have had contact with the prisoner during his
sentence. All these reports must be served on the prisoner or his representative at
the same time as they are served on the Parole Board (rule 5(1)). There is a discretion to withhold information from the prisoner where the Home Secretary
believes disclosure might adversely affect the health or welfare of the prisoner or
others (rule 5(2)). Information falling into this category will be kept separately
and disclosed to the Board, but not the prisoner, with reasons for the decision to
withhold. The chairman of the DLP or HMP Panel will then consider the matter
and make a ruling on whether to uphold the decision to withhold (rule 9(1)(d)).
Where information is withheld, it will nevertheless be disclosed by the Home
Secretary to the prisoner's representative if he is a barrister or solicitor, a registered
medical practitioner, or, in the view of the chairman, a suitably experienced or
qualified person (rule 5(3)). Plainly this can give rise to difficulties for a representative who may be privy to vital information of crucial or even decisive relevance
to the issue of dangerousness but upon which no instructions can be taken from
the prisoner. Indeed when the information is dealt with by the DLP or HMP
Panel, the prisoner will be excluded from that part of the hearing. In practice,
when such material is received, the Panel almost always authorizes disclosure to
the prisoner eventually.

The prisoner's initial representations about his case must be served on the Board   **14.47**
and the Home Secretary within 15 weeks of the case being listed for hearing (rule

8(1)). Any other documentary evidence which he wishes to adduce must then be served at least 14 days before the date of the hearing. By this time the prisoner will have had access to the material disclosed by the Home Secretary.[74]

14.48 Each party must apply in writing to the Board for permission to call witnesses before the DLP or HMP Panel within 12 weeks of the case being listed. The identity of the witness and the substance of the evidence must be disclosed. The chairman will then decide if the witness may be called and give reasons in writing for any refusal (rule 7). If a prisoner wishes any other person, such as a relative, to attend the hearing as an observer/supporter, this too must be agreed to by the Board, which will consult the governor of the prison where the hearing will take place (rule 6(5)).

Preliminary Hearing

14.49 The chairman will give preliminary consideration to the case papers and give directions on any request for attendance of witnesses, withholding of information, the timetable of proceedings, and the service of documents (rule 9(1)). Where necessary he may conduct an oral hearing in private and the prisoner will not attend unless he is unrepresented. Within 14 days of being notified of any direction given by the chairman, an aggrieved party may appeal to the chairman of the Board whose decision shall be final (subject to a challenge by way of judicial review).

The Hearing

14.50 An oral hearing will be held unless all parties agree otherwise (rule 10(1)). At least 21 days' notice of the date, time, and location of the hearing will be given (rule 11(2)). Hearings take place in the prison where the prisoner is detained and shall be held in private (rule 12). Save in so far as the chairman of the panel directs, information about the proceedings and the names of any persons concerned shall not be made public.[75] There is accordingly a presumption in favour of confidentiality unless an express direction to the contrary is given. There is a discretion to admit persons to the hearing on appropriate terms (rule 12(3)). The rules for the conduct of the hearing are intended to be flexible and to provide for informality (rule 13). Parties are entitled to appear before the Panel and be heard, hear and

---

[74] The timetable is rarely complied with by the Home Office. It is often the case that crucial reports are not submitted until days before the hearing. The Parole Board will entertain applications for deferrals where further preparation is required upon the receipt of late reports.

[75] In *P v Liverpool Daily Post Plc* [1991] 2 AC 370 the House of Lords held that a mental health review tribunal (MHRT) was a court to which the law of contempt applied but that a newspaper which published the date, time, and place of a hearing and the fact that a patient had been discharged was not guilty of contempt. It would however be a contempt to publish evidence and other material on which the tribunal's decision was based in breach of r 21(5) of the MHRT Rules 1983, SI 1983/942.

question each other's evidence (unless it involves withheld information), and put questions to witnesses called before the Panel. Hearsay evidence is admissible (rule 13(5)). At the conclusion of the evidence, the prisoner or his representative has a right to address the Panel (rule 13(7)). There is a general discretion to adjourn (rule 14).

The Secretary of State is always represented at hearings, usually by the Lifer **14.51** Liaison Officer, who is normally a grade 5 governor. Being unversed in advocacy, these representatives rarely participate beyond reading out the Secretary of State's written view of the prisoner's progress, the current risk he poses, and his suitability for release or a move to open conditions. In recall cases, however, the Secretary of State is usually represented by civil servants from Prison Service Headquarters. Increasingly, where the case is extremely complex (involving substantial factual disputes) or the outcome greatly in dispute, the Secretary of State will be represented by counsel.

Evidential Matters

Many oral hearings are relatively straightforward proceedings where facts are **14.52** agreed but opinions are in dispute. Here, the issues for determination by the panel are clear and revolve around how the evidence should be interpreted and judged against the criterion of ongoing dangerousness. It is invariably the case that a psychiatric report will be commissioned on behalf of the Home Office.[76] These are generally very poor reports consisting of little more than a recitation of the prisoner's history. Where conclusions about current risk are set out reasons in support do not usually accompany them. In the face of these reports it is often helpful for the prisoner's representative to commission an independent report from a consultant forensic psychiatrist and to apply to the Panel for a direction that the expert attend as a witness.

Where the prisoner is seeking a direction for release representatives must ensure **14.53** that a suitable release package has been established which can be presented to the Panel at the hearing. Prisoners who have spent many years in custody may find that they have lost contact with friends and family and do not have a suitable place

---

[76] Further difficulties arise when the Home Office commissions further reports *after* the DLP, on which the prisoner will have no chance to comment. In *R (Burgess) v Home Secretary*, Daily Telegraph, December 5, 2000, the claimant argued that the Home Secretary had acted procedurally unfairly in relying on a subsequent report from a psychologist from the Offending Behaviour Programmes Unit, commenting on the evidence before the DLP, in reaching a final decision, without disclosing the report or allowing the claimant to make representations. The Divisional Court dismissed the application, holding that the Secretary of State was not under a duty to disclose the report since it was not new evidence, but rather an 'in house' assessment of the existing material. This distinction appears to be a tenuous one: regardless of whether such a report is produced 'in house' or by an external expert, it contains further views and expert judgments upon which the prisoner should surely be allowed to comment.

to live. To be satisfied that it is safe to release, Panels often wish to see that there is a stable and structured environment available for the prisoner to move into on his release. More often than not the first post-release address is a hostel either run by the Probation Service or a charitable organization. To establish a release package requires the assistance of the home probation officer, on whom the responsibility for supervising the licence will fall. Not infrequently a prisoner may have a viable case for release which is not supported by the home probation officer. Even if that is the case the probation officer is obliged to assist the prisoner in establishing a release package by, for example, ascertaining which hostels are suitable and assist-ing in securing a place for the prisoner. In some cases it may also be sensible to set up psychiatric supervision in the community. Where prisoners are met with hos-tile probation officers who, because they consider that the prisoner should not be released, do not believe that they are obliged to assist in securing a suitable release package, representatives need to emphasize that the decision whether to direct release rests with the Parole Board alone and that by refusing to discharge their duties they are effectively usurping that function.[77] This follows because the Board will not be satisfied according to the statutory test unless an acceptable release package is in place. Where the prisoner is seeking a direction for release, representatives should apply for a witness order in respect of the home probation officer as the Panel will wish to hear directly about the release package and ascer-tain the degree of confidence that the probation officer feels about the prospect of release.[78]

---

[77] Such a situation arose in *R v Parole Board, ex p Robinson*, The Independent, 8 November 1999, DC. At the first DLP hearing, the Panel concluded that the applicant was a suitable risk for release. However, his home probation service opposed release, and no release plan was in place. The Chief Probation Officer wrote to the Lifer Review Unit stating that the applicant was not suitable for any of the available hostels, and that therefore no release plan could be drawn up. In light of that letter, the Panel held a further oral hearing, at which the issue of risk was reopened. The second Panel refused to direct release. The applicant challenged this decision. Simon Brown LJ concluded that '[j]ustice to discretionary life prisoners in the post-tariff period in my judgment requires that once a prisoner succeeds in the face of opposition in satisfying a panel that he can safely be released, that decision must be regarded as final and conclusive, subject only to the Secretary of State demonstrat-ing that it was fundamentally flawed or pointing to a supervening material change of circumstances. All that then remains is the making of detailed arrangements for the implementation of the decision within a comparatively short time. It is not for the Secretary of State or others opposing release . . . to question or seek to reopen the issue when the decision on risk is made against them. Nor are they to obstruct the implementation of the decision by reiterating their concerns or seeking to impose impossible conditions.' However, in *R (McFaddyn) v Home Secretary*, 4 March 2002, Roderick Evans J held that the Prison Service had not acted irrationally in failing to provide the claimant with a place on a sexual offending course, even though he had been recalled to prison and his re-release was unlikely without taking part in such courses, which he was willing to do.

[78] While the Panel has a power to adjourn under r 14 'for the purpose of obtaining further information or for such other purposes as it may think appropriate', such an adjournment cannot be ordered simply in order to reconsider risk, rather than to facilitate release. In *R v Parole Board, ex p Robinson*, The Independent, 8 November 1999, the applicant appeared before a DLP, which con-sidered that his risk level made him suitable for release. It adjourned in order to allow an appropri-ate release plan to be formulated. The matter came back before a different panel, which decided that

Where a prisoner disputes important evidence, experience has shown that the sys- **14.54**
tem is far from efficacious. Such disputes most commonly arise where a prisoner
has been recalled to prison and the hearing is taking place under s 32 of the 1997
Act. Recalls occur where the prisoner is alleged to have conducted himself on
licence in a way that manifests an unacceptable level of ongoing dangerousness. In
some cases this may be because he is failing to comply with his life licence to the
satisfaction of the probation service. In others, there may be a specific allegation,
such as a sexual assault in the case of a sex offender, which gives rise to the decision
to recall. In such cases it is clear that if the allegation is true, it is appropriate to
recall the prisoner. However, if the allegation is false, and in all other respects the
prisoner's behaviour on licence does not evince ongoing dangerousness, the Panel
should direct his release. The hearing itself will turn on establishing the truth or
falsity of the allegation.

Allegations which are central to questions of ongoing dangerousness not only **14.55**
arise in relation to recall cases, but can do so in s 28 hearings. For example, a prisoner may have absconded and an allegation is made in respect of his conduct while
at large. Or it may be alleged that a prisoner, whose index offence was drug related,
has been taking drugs while on home leave, or while on temporary release.

Whereas the expectation in an adversarial setting is that the party relying on an **14.56**
allegation will adduce evidence in support, the Secretary of State does not take this
approach. When made, the allegations tend to appear in written reports of probation officers (in recall cases) or prison officers. Without fail the Secretary of State
will then rely upon the allegation, accepting its truth, in forming his initial view
about whether the prisoner should be released, or moved to open conditions, or
progressed in some other way. Though there is provision in the Rules for the
Secretary of State to apply to the Board for a witness to attend, such an application
is never made in practice.

This means that the prisoner is very often left in the dark as to the precise particu- **14.57**
lars of the allegation—where and when the alleged conduct was said to have taken
place, what precisely it consisted of, and what evidence there is to support it.
Needless to say this places him in an extremely difficult position when it comes to
establishing whether he has an alibi or whether there is any other evidence he can
call to show that the allegations are false.

The provisions of s 32(3) of the Criminal Justice Act 1991 have a potentially **14.58**
important role to play here which is not currently being recognized by the Parole
Board. This empowers the Board to gather its own evidence, whether oral or

---

the risk was too great to allow release. The Divisional Court held that once the first panel had discharged its function to determine the risk, provided that there was nothing preliminary or provisional about that decision, it was to that extent functus officio. Furthermore, the first panel was
incorrect in thinking that it could not direct release until a release plan was in place.

written. This power, in conjunction with the power under the Rules to issue directions, arms the Board with some mechanism, albeit not a fully effective one, for ensuring that the best evidence is obtained. Usually that evidence will be the oral evidence of the maker of the allegations. There is nothing to prevent the Board, when faced with an unsubstantiated, though clearly relevant, allegation from taking measures itself to secure evidence in support of it,[79] or from directing the Secretary of State who is relying on the allegation to secure the attendance of witnesses or other evidence to support it.

14.59 One of the failings in the procedure governing oral hearings is that Panels do not have the power to subpoena witnesses.[80] However, it is possible to obtain a witness summons from the High Court under rule 34.4 of the Civil Procedure Rules. There is no reason why the Home Office cannot make use of this power in the way that prisoners' representatives have been forced to in order to secure the attendance of complainants.

14.60 The consequences for a prisoner faced with allegations of this kind are uninviting. He cannot safely let matters stand and submit that, as there is no direct evidence to support the allegation, the Parole Board should reject it. The Board is permitted to take account of hearsay evidence and can only direct release if it is positively satisfied that it is safe to do so. The Board may feel bound to take into account an allegation, even if based on hearsay evidence, and if it is one which manifests ongoing dangerousness, it will prevent the Board from being satisfied in accordance with the statutory test.

14.61 As a matter of law it would seem that evidence must reach a certain threshold of cogency and weight before it can safely be relied upon. So, if the Parole Board placed reliance upon a fifth hand hearsay account, there is every reason to believe that its decision would be susceptible to challenge by way of judicial review on the ground of procedural impropriety. But it is highly unsatisfactory to let matters be resolved after the event as this will inevitably take a long time and prolong the prisoner's detention. Furthermore, even if the Board accepts that the evidence is too weak safely to place reliance upon, the untested allegation may nonetheless contaminate the Board's approach to other evidence relating to the prisoner's risk and tip the balance against a decision to direct release.

---

[79] Indeed the efficacy of this power has already been tested in relation to a mandatory life sentence prisoner (*R v Parole Board, ex p Davies*, 25 November 1996, Collins J). Mr Davies succeeded in his application for judicial review of the decision of the Parole Board to recall him to prison under s 39 of the 1991 Act. The recall arose out of allegations that he had mistreated a disabled woman for whom he carried out voluntary work. The Board had no direct evidence before it from the alleged victim, but relied entirely on hearsay accounts contained in Probation Service reports. The court quashed the decision on the ground that the Board had failed to consider whether it should call for better evidence pursuant to its powers under s 32(3).

[80] The Parole Board is not a tribunal within the meaning of the Tribunals and Inquiries Act 1992 which empowers such bodies to subpoena witnesses.

In practice, therefore, prisoners' representatives often apply to the Panel for a **14.62** direction that the maker of the allegations attend as a witness. This is obviously unsatisfactory. The witness is not attending to support the prisoner's case. Yet, the witness is appearing on behalf of the prisoner. Fortunately Panels recognize that the witness is not a supporting one and do not prevent cross-examination. However, it is obviously improper for the prisoner's legal adviser to take a proof from the witness. They really can do not more than ensure that legal aid is available to pay for the witness' attendance. But, unless particulars of the allegation have been supplied by the Home Office, it is not until the cross-examination commences that the nature of the allegation becomes known. This is again highly unsatisfactory and can lead to adjournments of hearings in order that evidence to rebut the allegations can be obtained.

The best practice for representatives faced with such difficulties is to apply to the **14.63** Chair of a Panel for a direction that the Secretary of State call the maker of the allegation (and summon him/her if necessary); supply the prisoner with a statement setting out with sufficient particularity the nature of the allegations; and take measures to secure the disclosure of all relevant documentation (again by way of summon if necessary).

There are probably two factors which have contributed to the problem. The first, **14.64** a failure to apply public funds for the specific purpose of investigation and evidence gathering, affects both the Home Office and the Board. It is obvious that without such resources these bodies will be reluctant to discharge their investigative duties.

The second factor concerns the Board alone. It seems likely that most Board **14.65** members understand oral hearings to be adversarial proceedings and assume that they do not have any power themselves to gather evidence. But the power under s 32(3) adds an inquisitorial quality to Parole Board proceedings which has yet to be appreciated by the Board. The exclusively adversarial tradition from which the judges who chair Panels come may well blind them to the availability of this power.

The Board is further hampered by the absence of a power to subpoena witnesses. **14.66** Even if there is an improvement in the role played both by the Home Office and the Board, it is doubtful that a satisfactory position will be achieved without this power being incorporated into the procedural machinery. The Parole Board is exercising a judicial function. To do so effectively it must have the powers which courts possess to compel the attendance of witnesses and the production of documents. It will sometimes be the case that relevant documents are not in the possession of the Home Office, but are held by the Probation Service or some other body or person. Without a power to compel their production the process is weakened and the attainment of fairness compromised.

14.67 Until such changes are brought about, representatives of prisoners will be forced to undertake the role which properly rests with the Board and Home Office, of using the power to seek directions and to summons witnesses and documents in the High Court as a means of ensuring that sufficient particulars of allegations are given in advance of hearings and that the best evidence of those allegations is given at the hearings. It is to be hoped that the new Parole Board Rules, currently in preparation, will strengthen the procedural protection afforded to those appearing before the Parole Board. The interests of the prisoner in knowing and being able to respond to the allegations against him or her should not be seen as opposed to those of the Parole Board, since the Board's function is to gain as complete and accurate a picture as possible, based on full and reliable evidence. However, proceeding thoroughly, calling witnesses and making full documentation available takes time and money, which may be a powerful reason why reform will be slow in coming.

The Test to be Applied by the DLP

14.68 The test which Panels must apply is set out in s 28(6)(b) of the 1997 Act. Panels must be 'satisfied that it is no longer necessary for the protection of the public that the prisoner should be confined'. The 1997 Act does not place the burden of proof on the Home Secretary to establish that further detention is necessary, nor does it identify the level of risk applicable. The previous case law set out in *Benson/Bradley*[81] required there to be at least a substantial risk of further offences dangerous to life or limb (including serious sexual offences) and this is still relevant to s 28. The Board must be positively satisfied that the prisoner does not present a substantial risk of re-offending before it can direct release.[82] Accordingly the Panel cannot authorize further detention simply to prevent a prisoner from being a social nuisance or from committing further non-violent offences or sexual offences which are not serious. If it did so, it would be frustrating the purpose of the Act. It remains to be seen whether the *Benson/Bradley* test and the effective imposition of the burden of proof on the prisoner, are themselves contrary to Article 5(4).[83]

---

[81] [1991] 1 WLR 134.

[82] In *R v Parole Board, ex p Lodomez* [1994] COD 525, the Divisional Court confirmed that the statutory test requires that it be shown that the risk is low enough to release the prisoner, not that it is high enough to keep him in. The *Benson/Bradley* test was endorsed. In *R v Home Secretary, ex p Watson* [1996] 2 All ER 641 the Court of Appeal held that the test applicable under ss 34 and 39 of the 1991 Act (now ss 28 and 32 of the 1997 Act) requires that the Board is *positively* satisfied that further detention is no longer necessary for the protection of the public. This effectively places the burden on the prisoner to show that he can safely be released.

[83] Mr Watson (ibid) is taking his case to the European Commission to argue that the test applicable to his recall contravenes Art 5: Application 21387/93, declared admissible on 21 October 1996. The compatibility of the test in s 28(6)(b) with Art 5(1) and (4) of the ECHR was raised in *R (Hirst) v Parole Board* [2002] EWHC 1592. Mr Hirst, who was the applicant in *Hirst v UK* Application 40787/98 [2001] Crim LR 919, was due for a further Parole Board review, and argued

The test is easily stated but far from simple to apply. Risk assessment is a notori-   **14.69**
ously difficult and subjective exercise. There is no doubt that with the transparency brought about by the oral hearing procedure, risk assessment exercises
have become more sophisticated. When the first oral hearings took place in late
1992 full disclosure meant that for the first time it was possible to see just what
had been happening to prisoners during their sentence. In most cases prisoners
had been afforded little if any opportunity to engage in work aimed at tackling the
causes of the danger they presented. Progress through prison appeared not to be a
function of objective evidence of risk reduction, but more one of the time a prisoner had spent in prison. Panels often had very little evidence upon which to make
assessments of current dangerousness. The system has improved substantially in
recent years. Many more programmes are available to prisoners aimed at tackling
offending behaviour. While some are extremely crude, others are long and intensive and can provide both a mechanism for identifying the nature of the risk and
a means for its reduction. In the first category are courses such as anger management and alcohol awareness which often consist of only a few hours of group
work. Where a prisoner has a deep seated problematic response to anger or alcohol it is very doubtful that such courses provide an effective means of change. At
the other end of the spectrum is the Sex Offender Treatment Programme (SOTP).
This was first introduced in 1992. It is a group programme, lasting up to nine
months, which adopts a cognitive behavioural approach whose aim is to challenge
prisoners to confront the distorted thought patterns which they adopt to persuade
themselves of the acceptability of their criminal conduct. It seeks to provide prisoners with the tools to recognize their own dangerous thoughts and feelings, and
strategies to avoid risk-laden situations.

Though risk assessment is an inherently uncertain task, there are no conditions   **14.70**
precedent which a prisoner must meet before the Panel can direct his release. The
Secretary of State is extremely reluctant to support the release of any prisoner who
has not first spent a period in open conditions. For offenders who have spent
many years in prison this may be a sensible course as it affords an opportunity to
adjust to the changes that have taken place in the outside world. It also presents an
opportunity to test the prisoner in conditions which more closely resemble those
which prevailed at the time of the offence. However, the question is always
whether such a measure can be shown to be necessary in the particular prisoner's
case. The need to test a prisoner in open conditions will generally be stronger in

---

that the test that the Board was bound to apply was incompatible with the ECHR. Moses J declined
to give a final ruling on the compatibility of s 28(6)(b) with the ECHR, since he considered that,
without knowing the factual context of the decision, it was impossible to see what effect such a declaration would have on Mr Hirst's case. He considered that it was certainly arguable that settled law
indicated that the presumption of danger persisted until the panel ruled that there was no risk, but
that it was not possible to make a final ruling without knowing what effect the section had on the
particular review.

the case of discretionary lifers. For them the preventive sentence is imposed because of a specifically identified danger the continuance of which may call for testing. This is not so with HMP detainees for whom the sentence is mandatory, irrespective of whether they present any danger of further serious re-offending, and for many short-tariff automatic lifers. There will be many cases where the circumstances of the offence demonstrate that the murder was a wholly exceptional event, unlikely ever to be repeated. Such an HMP detainee should be released irrespective of whether he has reached open conditions as there is no purpose to be served by testing him there. However, the Parole Board has had difficulty coming to terms with the logic of this approach, and the number of lifers released from closed conditions is usually no more than one each year. This situation is not helped by directions to report writers, which assume that a move to open conditions is the norm.

Prisoners Who Deny Their Offences

14.71   How should a representative and the Panel treat a prisoner who maintains his innocence of the original offence? Of course as a matter of law this has no relevance to the requirements of s 28, but in practice it inevitably presents problems. Those assessing the prisoner for reports to be submitted to the Panel will often state that the refusal to accept guilt makes it hard (or sometimes impossible) to assess future dangerousness. In such circumstances the evidential basis will not exist for the Panel to conclude that release can properly be ordered. It is impossible to make a hard and fast rule for such cases.[84] Representatives must make clear to the prisoner what the consequences are of maintaining innocence and seek to direct the Panel to the objective material which exists both before and after sentence. The Panel is not the Court of Appeal and will inevitably assume that the

---

[84]   There has been a flood of cases in which the Parole Board's reasons for refusing to recommend the release of determinate sentence prisoners who were denying their offences have been subject to scrutiny (eg *R v Parole Board, ex p Zulfikar (No 1)* [1996] COD 256; *Ex p Zulfikar (No 2)* 1 May 1996, CA; *R v Parole Board, ex p Lillycrop*, The Times, 13 December 1996; *R v Home Secretary, ex p Fenton-Palmer*, 24 March 1997, DC, CO/2051/96; *R v Parole Board and Home Secretary, ex p Oyston*, The Independent, 17 April 2000; *R (Callaghan) v Home Secretary and Parole Board* [2001] EWHC Admin 208; *R (Wilkes) v Home Secretary* [2001] EWHC Admin 210. In *Ex p Zulfikar (No 1)*, the Divisional Court made it clear that denial cannot constitute an automatic bar to release. The Board must consider each case according to its own circumstances and the weight to be attached to denial will vary accordingly. At one end of the scale the court identified the first time offender, where the motivation for the offence is clear and does not point to a likelihood of re-offending. In such a case the weight to be attached to denial is limited. At the other end is the persistent offender who refuses to accept his guilt in the face of clear evidence and is unable to accept his propensity for such conduct which needs to be tackled if he is not to offend again. The court pointed out that denial in such circumstances may be determinative. Discretionary lifers have by definition committed serious offences and at the time of sentence were considered to have a propensity for such conduct. They clearly fall at the extreme end of the scale where denial will present a very significant obstacle in the path of their progress towards release. This approach was confirmed by the Court of Appeal in *Oyston*. For a full discussion of this issue see paras 12.49 and 12.50 above.

prisoner was properly convicted, but this need not prevent it from concluding that release presents an acceptable risk.

The Panel's Decision

The decision of the Panel shall be communicated in writing to the prisoner not more than seven days after the end of the hearing (rule 15). This is a welcome obligation since the tension of awaiting decisions concerning release can be a source of extreme anxiety. Under s 28(5) it is only a direction to release which binds the Home Secretary. Panels may sometimes find that they would be satisfied that it is no longer necessary for the protection of the public for a prisoner to be detained if release took place under certain conditions which do not obtain at the time of the hearing. The Panel may, for instance, consider that psychiatric supervision should be available or that the prisoner should reside in a probation hostel. In such cases, the Panel should be invited to consider the case in principle, and then to adjourn its decision in order that the requisite release package can be put together. Once this is done the Panel can reconvene in the absence of the parties to assess the suitability of the release package. If the Panel does not adjourn the decision, so retaining jurisdiction, its deliberations will be treated as a final determination that the prisoner is not suitable for release. Strictly speaking the prisoner will have to wait another two years before he can compel a further consideration of his case. The Secretary of State can, of course, refer the case earlier but it can never be assumed that he will do so. Any refusal can only be challenged by the limited mechanism of judicial review. **14.72**

The 1997 Act places the responsibility for taking the decision on the Parole Board. It is not obliged to adopt the opinions expressed in the reports it considers, whether they are expressed by expert psychiatrists or psychologists or reflect the unanimous views of all the report writers. If the Panel departs from recommendations contained in the reports, but does so on a rational basis, namely one that is supported by some of the material before it, the decision is not susceptible to judicial review.[85] **14.73**

---

[85] *R v Parole Board, ex p Telling* [1993] COD 500, DC; *R v Parole Board, ex p Lodomez* [1994] COD 525, and *R v Home Secretary and Parole Board, ex p Evans*, 2 November 1994, DC. This case concerned, inter alia, the Parole Board's refusal to adopt a unanimous recommendation for the release of a mandatory lifer made by report writers and the Local Review Committee. Though Mr Evans was a mandatory lifer the principles applicable are identical. In upholding the autonomy of the Parole Board the court did, however, criticize it for failing to have explained why it departed from the clear, emphatic, and unanimous views expressed. The strength and unanimity of opinion called for an explanation in language sufficiently clear and terms sufficiently full to ensure that the LRC could properly understand the basis of the difference between them.

The Panel's Reasons

14.74 Pursuant to rule 15(2), the Panel must give reasons for its decision. In *R v Parole Board, ex p Gittens* the Divisional Court held that the duty to give reasons required that the reasons given be intelligible and deal with the substantial points that have been raised.[86] When considering a subsequent application for judicial review in *Ex p Lodomez*, the Divisional Court applied these principles in quashing a refusal to direct release in the face of unanimously favourable reports. The Panel's reasons extended to a single sentence and were found to be 'grossly deficient'. The court was particularly influenced by the inability of the judge who chaired the panel and swore an affidavit in the judicial review proceedings to recall from a perusal of the reasons what precisely had persuaded the Panel to take the course it did. The court emphasized the importance of providing an adequately reasoned decision so that the prisoner can gauge whether the reasons afford support in law for the decision reached. The reasons must enable the prisoner and any reviewing court to see what views the Panel took about the points on which the prisoner relied.

14.75 Where the Panel does not direct release, then the Secretary of State has no power to order release. The Panel may indicate that release should only take place after a period of further testing in, say, open prison conditions or after a period in a pre-release employment scheme hostel (PRES). Alternatively, the Panel may recommend a further hearing in, say, 12 months so that progress can be closely monitored. In the first few years following the introduction of DLPs the Secretary of State did not restrict the matters about which the Panel might make recommendations. He has done so since, and now invites advice only on whether a prisoner should be moved to open conditions or a PRES. This power to recommend an early review in advance of the statutory biennial review was ended in 2002.

14.76 Despite these constraints Panels continue to make comments and proffer advice about the future management of prisoners falling outside the ambit of the Secretary of State's invitation.[87] In relation to all advice given, the Secretary of

---

[86] [1994] COD 351. See also *R (Gordon) v Parole Board* [2001] ACD 47, in which Smith J stated that 'I acknowledge of course that it is not incumbent upon the Board to set out its thought processes in detail or to mention every factor they have taken into account. However, in my judgment the balancing exercise they are required to carry out is so fundamental to the decision making process that they should make it plain that this has been done and to state broadly which factors they have taken into account.'

[87] In making recommendations about a prisoner's future management, the DLP has a relationship, not only with the Home Secretary in his reviewing function, but also with other branches of the Prison Service, eg the Category A Review Committee. In *R (Williams) v Home Secretary* [2002] EWCA Civ 498; [2002] 1 WLR 2264, the DLP considered that the claimant, who was a high risk Category A prisoner, had made as much progress as he could in addressing his offending behaviour while in that security category. The claimant argued that the Committee's continuing refusal to recategorize him was incompatible with his right under Art 5(4) to a fair hearing at the next DLP hearing. The Court of Appeal held that the two bodies had related but distinct roles. While they addressed the same issue, public safety, the Committee looked at escape risk and the DLP looked at

State is free to take a different course, though any unreasonable failure to follow a Panel's recommendation will be susceptible to judicial review.[88] In rejecting a recommendation of the Panel the Secretary of State must, in compliance with his duty of fairness, address the reasons given by the Panel for taking the view with which he is disagreeing.[89]

Despite the judgments in *Gittens* and *Lodomez*, panels have persistently failed to **14.77** give adequate reasons for their decisions. They tend to be formulaic and rarely address in detail the particular features of the case. Cogent and adequately

---

likely risk to the public on release. The Committee did not have to act in accordance with the DLP's views. Moreover, Art 5(4) did not preclude the Committee and the DLP from coming to different conclusions. The court did acknowledge, however, that this conclusion had to accept the risk of circularity in decision-making, with the recommendations of one body effectively thwarting the aims of the other. However, given the *Ashingdane* problem—that Art 5 deals only with liberty, not with conditions of detention (*Ashingdane v UK* (1985) 7 EHRR 528)—this unfortunate result is probably a correct application of the Convention case law.

[88] See *R v Home Secretary, ex p Douglas*, 15 June 1994, DC, where the Secretary of State's refusal to follow a DLP's recommendation that Mr Douglas should be transferred to open conditions was upheld on the ground that it had not been shown to be *Wednesbury* unreasonable. Mr Douglas was an arsonist whose offending had, on the evidence, been connected to an inability to deal with stress. Despite firm recommendations for a move to open conditions in the reports before the DLP, the Secretary of State relied upon references in some of those reports to the further work that was required in relation to stress management. Though others may have taken a less cautious approach the decision was clearly rational. See also *R v Home Secretary, ex p Bushell*, 14 December 1994, where the court again dismissed a challenge to the Home Secretary's refusal to follow a DLP recommendation for a transfer to open conditions. It was further argued that where the Home Secretary was minded to take a different course from that recommended by the Panel, he should inform the prisoner and afford him an opportunity to make representations. This argument was rejected on the ground that the Panel's decision itself provided sufficient support for the prisoner's case.

[89] *R v Home Secretary, ex p Murphy* [1997] COD 478. The extent to which the Secretary of State is entitled to depart from recommendations of the Board has been a subject of frequent litigation. In *R (Burgess) v Home Secretary* [2001] 1 WLR 93, the claimant, a discretionary life sentence prisoner, challenged the Home Secretary's refusal to accept the DLP's recommendation of a move to open conditions. He argued that the Home Secretary's decision was, in effect, a decision that release will be postponed further than the Parole Board envisaged, since the Board will rarely direct release from closed conditions. He argued that, in effect, the Home Secretary's veto undermines the effectiveness of the DLP's supervision, contrary to Art 5(4) of the ECHR. The Divisional Court rejected this argument, relying on the ECtHR's judgment in *Ashingdane v UK* (1985) 7 EHRR 528. In light of the Strasbourg case law, Art 5(4) did not apply to decisions about the conditions of detention, including whether or not a prisoner is held in open or closed conditions, despite the fact that that decision has an effect on the eventual length of detention. The courts have also shown hostility to rationality challenges to the Home Secretary's refusal to follow the Board's recommendation for a transfer to open conditions: see *R (Baxter) v Home Secretary* [2002] EWHC 779, Turner J. The combined effect of the Convention and domestic positions is that the Home Secretary retains, in effect, a power of impeding a prisoner's progress towards release, against the wishes of the Parole Board. In light of the growing recognition of the Home Secretary's lack of legitimacy to make decisions about the liberty of the individual, this is a regrettable lacuna. It does not sit easily with the courts' increasing willingness to intervene in related areas, such as tariff-setting. This aspect of the Home Secretary's powers is currently being reconsidered by the ECtHR in the case of a discretionary lifer whose Parole Board recommendation for open conditions and an early review was rejected by the Home Secretary.

particularized reasons are not important to a prisoner merely so that he can ascertain whether an unfavourable decision is lawful. They are as significant where the Panel is making recommendations to the Secretary of State. In many cases it will be clear from the outset that the prisoner is not ready to be released and no such direction will be sought by the prisoner. Rather, the hearing provides a means of persuading the Secretary of State to take measures to move the prisoner forward in the system. Where the reasons relied upon by the Panel in making a recommendation relate to matters which only emerged at the hearing, it is vital that they are comprehensively set out in the written decision. Decisions following Parole Board hearings are taken by Ministers and civil servants at Prison Service Headquarters. Though the Secretary of State is represented at the hearing, he and his civil servants cannot be taken to know what evidence emerged. The only means by which he can become informed is through the Parole Board's reasons. If the Board does not make explicit the grounds for its decision the Secretary of State cannot be criticized for failing to take those grounds into account.

Timing of Reviews

14.78 Under s 28(7) of the 1997 Act, as we have seen, discretionary lifers and HMP detainees are entitled to a Parole Board review every two years after the tariff has passed. However, this does not mean that in every case a two year gap between reviews will be justified or lawful. In several important cases, the ECtHR has considered the timing of reviews in light of Article 5(4) of the Convention.

14.79 In *Oldham v UK*,[90] the applicant was a discretionary lifer released on licence. He was recalled three years later, and his recall was confirmed following a hearing before the DLP, which considered that he needed to do further work on 'alcohol, anger and relationships'. The next review was set for two years later, at which point he was released. He argued that this two-year delay breached Article 5(4) of the ECHR, arguing that he had addressed the areas of concern raised by the DLP within eight months of recall.[91] He also argued that there was no need for a gradual reintroduction to society, since he had spent three years at liberty before his recall. Several reports had recommended his release sooner than the two-year period, but these had been ignored. The Government argued that the two-year period was necessary for him to undertake the courses and be suitably assessed. The court considered that, in the circumstances, the two-year delay was unreasonable. The applicant's detention had not been reviewed 'speedily' within the meaning of Article 5(4).

---

[90] (2001) 31 EHRR 813.
[91] In those eight months he had attended courses on Anger Management, Relationships, Alcohol Awareness and Men and Violence.

In *Hirst v UK*,[92] the applicant was also serving a discretionary life sentence. In **14.80** October 1996, his case came up for a two-yearly review before the DLP, which recommended transfer to open conditions so that the applicant could be further tested and prepared for release. The Home Secretary rejected this recommendation, but directed an early review of the case, after 18 months. In July 1998, the DLP again considered the applicant's case. It declined to order release, but again recommended transfer to open conditions. The Home Secretary again rejected that recommendation. Before the ECtHR, Mr Hirst argued that since his tariff expired in 1994, his continued detention was justified only on the basis of risk, and that Article 5(4) accordingly required that risk be reviewed promptly. He argued that an automatic review every two years was unreasonably long, particularly since there was no mechanism for him to apply to the DLP during the intervening period, and no provision for any judicial control over the length of the period between reviews, the decision to hold earlier reviews being at the discretion of the Home Secretary. He argued that where there was a realistic prospect of release or real progress towards release, as shown in his case, the appropriate intervals between periodic reviews ought to be no longer than one year, as was the case with patients held under mental health provisions. The court found a violation of Article 5(4):

> It is evident therefore that the applicant was a prisoner who had developed considerably during the course of his sentence and could not be considered as a person in respect of whom no further change of circumstance could be envisaged. Against this background, the Court is not satisfied that the periods of twenty one months and two years which elapsed were justified by considerations of rehabilitation and monitoring.
>
> It was in any event open to the Secretary of State, the Government asserted, to bring forward the date of the review where a prisoner showed unexpectedly rapid progress in addressing problems. The Court has already noted the flexibility in the system as mitigating the application of an automatic two-year review system. However, while the DLP could recommend earlier review and the Secretary of State direct and earlier date, there was no possibility for an applicant himself to apply for a review within the two year period. The applicant in the present case was therefore unable to bring his case back before the Parole Board in the absence of the Secretary of State's exercising his discretion in his favour exceptionally.[93]

What these cases mean is that the two-year period must be treated as a maximum, **14.81** not as the standard time between reviews in every case. Particularly for prisoners who are making marked improvements in prison, or have been recalled and need only to address very specific issues, two years between reviews will often be too

---

[92] Application 40787/98 [2001] Crim LR 919.
[93] paras 42–43.

long, and the Parole Board and Secretary of State are under a clear duty to keep matters under frequent review.[94]

Recall Cases

14.82 A discretionary lifer or HMP detainee who is recalled to prison under s 32 of the 1991 Act has identical rights to an oral hearing, save that the rules are more flexible and designed to ensure an early hearing following recall. The test to be applied is the same[95] and the Panel has a power to direct release following a hearing. As discussed, s 32 hearings will often require the Panel to determine issues of fact (such as whether the conduct which gave rise to the recall actually occurred) and representatives should be aware of the evidential problems to which such issues can give rise. Naturally, where a lengthy period has elapsed before recall, the evidence will have to be all the more cogent before it can justify continued detention. Where a recall case arises because the prisoner has been charged with further offences, the recall hearing should be deferred until the outcome of the prosecution is known. Even if the prisoner is acquitted the Panel will be entitled to consider the allegations itself, though the fact of the acquittal is obviously relevant. If the prisoner is convicted and sentenced to a term of imprisonment in respect of the offence, the recall hearing should be deferred until the point at which but for his recall he would have been released in respect of that sentence. One practical problem is the length of time taken to convene recall hearings. In many cases, this can take over a year. These delays raise troubling issues of the 'speediness' of reviews under Article 5(4) of the Convention. The ECtHR has declared admissible one such complaint from a recalled HMP detainee[96] and a number of domestic damages claims under Article 5(5) are pending.

---

[94] See also *R (Dodson) v Parole Board and Home Secretary*, 3 October 2000, in which Gibbs J stressed that applying the two year norm without giving proper reasons would be unlawful. In directing a further review in two years, the Parole Board has to give adequate reasons as to why the two-year period is necessary. Whether the two-year period is justified depends on the facts of the particular case, and cases such as *Hirst* and *Oldham* should not be relied on in a blanket fashion: see *R (Macneil) v HMP Lifer Panel* [2001] EWCA Civ 448; The Times, 18 April 2001. In *R (Kelly) v Home Secretary* [2001] EWHC Admin 331, the High Court held that, once a case has been referred to the Board, the Home Secretary has no legal power to determine when the Board's hearing should take place. The proper course, rather than asking the Home Office to require the Board to expedite the case, is to wait until the review commences and then to make an application to the Board for expedition. However, this will clearly not help if the start of the Board's review has been delayed. Under Art 5(4) of the ECHR, the State as a whole has an obligation to ensure prompt reviews of detention, and in cases of delay an application to the court would be appropriate to enforce that obligation.

[95] *R v Parole Board, ex p Watson* (1996) 1 WLR 906.

[96] Application 53236/99.

15

DETENTION UNDER THE
IMMIGRATION ACT

The experience of imprisonment is not limited to those who are charged with or **15.01** convicted of a criminal offence. At the end of 2001 an average of around 1,800 people were in detention under powers contained in the Immigration Act 1971, including around 250 at the controversial Oakington Reception Centre, and the numbers continue to rise.[1] Many of these are held in Immigration Detention Centres rather than prisons. However, an increasing number will find themselves accommodated in prison service establishments. The highest proportion of these detainees are asylum seekers, and over 700 asylum seekers are currently detained in criminal prisons,[2] a situation which has led to substantial domestic and international criticism.[3]

---

[1] See I Macdonald and F Webber, *Macdonald's Immigration Law and Practice* (5th edn, London, 2001) ch 17 for a detailed discussion of immigration detention. An analysis of the situation in the late 1990s can be found in HM Chief Inspector of Prisons, *Report of an Unannounced Short Inspection of Campsfield House Detention Centre on 13–15 October 1997* (London, 1998). Up to date statistics can be found in Home Office Research and Statistics Directorate, *Asylum Statistics United Kingdom 2000* (Home Office, September 2001). The statistics do not always differentiate between those held under the Immigration Act in general, and asylum seekers in particular, so it can be difficult to know how many Immigration Act detainees at any one time have applied for asylum.

[2] The Home Office *Asylum Statistics 2000* (ibid) state that, at the time of compilation, 741 detainees currently held under the Immigration Act had, at some point, sought asylum.

[3] See, eg, Amnesty International, *Summary of Concerns raised with the Human Rights Committee*, November 2001, AI Index EUR 45/024/2001, submitted in the context of the UN HRC's examination of the fifth periodic report of the UK in October 2001.

A. Immigration Act Power of Detention

15.02 The main powers to detain immigrants are contained in Sch 2 to the 1971 Immigration Act. Important changes to the system of immigration detention were also made by the Immigration and Asylum Act 1999. It is important to note that, both under domestic law and under Article 5 of the European Convention on Human Rights (ECHR), the power to detain is purely ancillary. It exists solely to facilitate the exercise of other immigration functions, and only for as long as strictly necessary. This means that excessively long detention, or, for example, detention for the purpose of removal where there is no prospect of removing the person to the designated country, is unlawful.[4] Detention may occur either on arrival or after the person has spent a period of time in the United Kingdom. On arrival an immigration officer may decide to detain a person to decide whether they are subject to immigration control, whether they should be given or refused leave to enter, or whether leave to enter previously granted should be suspended or cancelled.[5] Such detention will normally be to check visas, letters of invitation, passports etc. More than 10,000 people a year are subject to such detention, but most for only a few hours.[6] However, where the immigration officer then decides that a person does not have the right of entry, the person will be told this and the officer may then decide whether to detain pending removal from the United Kingdom or grant temporary admission.[7] Temporary admission is usually conditional on residing at a fixed address[8] and reporting regularly to a police station or immigration office. The lack of contacts in the United Kingdom renders asylum seekers especially vulnerable to decisions to detain, although only about 5–10 per cent of asylum seekers appear to be detained.[9] Restrictions on employment are also commonly imposed, creating additional economic hardship for many vulnerable individuals and families.

---

[4] See *Re Wasfi Suleiman Mahmood* [1995] Imm AR 311, QB. Laws J stressed the limited nature of the power to detain: '[w]hile of course Parliament is entitled to confer power of administrative detention without trial, the courts will see to it that . . . the statute that confers it will be strictly and narrowly construed and its operation and effect will be supervised by the court according to high standards'.

[5] Immigration Act 1971, Sch 2, para 16, as amended by the Immigration and Asylum Act 1999. This states that persons may be detained anywhere the Secretary of State directs.

[6] The CPT found average detention periods in the mid 1990s to be two to nine hours. See *Report to the United Kingdom Government on the visit to the United Kingdom carried out by the European Committee for the Prevention of Torture and Inhuman or Degrading Treatment or Punishment* (CPT) from 15 May to 31 May 1994, CPT/Inf (96) 11, para 178.

[7] Sch 2, para 21(1).

[8] This could be accommodation provided under s 4 of the Immigration and Asylum Act 1999.

[9] See Amnesty International, *Prisoners Without a Voice: Asylum Seekers in the United Kingdom* (London, 1995) 10. The current political climate suggests that these percentages may rise: see Amnesty International, *Summary of Concerns raised with the Human Rights Committee*, November 2001, AI Index EUR 45/024/2001 27, citing the Government's commitment to increasing the number of detention centre places to 2,790 by autumn 2001.

Alternatively, people may be detained after spending a period of time in the **15.03** United Kingdom. These tend to be 'overstayers' (who originally had a right of entry for a period of time which has now expired), 'illegal entry cases' (who are believed to have entered the country in some illegal manner), people subject to deportation orders following a conviction for a criminal offence and people whose deportation is deemed necessary for the public good (such as on national security grounds).[10] Any of these groups may include people who prior to or at the time of their detention make applications for asylum.

The broad nature of these detention powers was confirmed in the 1995 case of **15.04** *R v Home Secretary, ex p Khan*.[11] In that case the Court of Appeal overturned a Divisional Court decision holding that immigration officers had no power to detain asylum seekers, since their powers to detain were ancillary to powers to remove and the Asylum and Immigration Appeals Act 1993 had indicated that asylum seekers could not be removed while their applications were pending. The Court of Appeal saw no reason to believe that the provisions of the 1993 Act were in any way intended to reduce the powers of immigration officers under the Immigration Act 1971. Further, errors in the decision-making process which result in someone being unnecessarily detained do not give rise to a cause of action.[12]

The policy of the Home Office is that detention should only be used as a last resort **15.05** and where there are grounds for believing that the person will not comply with any grounds stated for temporary admission.[13] The likelihood of such a failure to

---

[10] For a summary of the Immigration Act powers in respect of such groups see I Macdonald and F Webber, *Macdonald's Immigration Law and Practice* (5th edn, London, 2001) ch 17.

[11] [1995] Imm AR 348. Para 16(2) of the 1971 Act was amended, in light of this decision, by s 15 of the Immigration and Asylum Act 1999, which confirms that the prohibition on removal while asylum claims are pending does not preclude the power to detain.

[12] See *W v Home Office* [1997] Imm AR 302, where the Court of Appeal found no duty of care existing where the applicant was detained after a questionnaire filled in by another applicant was mistakenly put on his file, leading immigration officers to doubt his Liberian nationality, an important factor in the decision to detain.

[13] Letter from Home Office Minister Charles Wardle MP to Amnesty International, cited in Amnesty International, *Prisoners Without a Voice: Asylum Seekers in the United Kingdom* (London, 1995) 10. This policy is set out in Immigration Service Instructions of 3 December 1991 and 20 September 1994, which indicate that factors such as whether someone has a previous history of absconding or has otherwise abused immigration laws (eg using false documents to gain entry) will be regarded as relevant to the exercise of the discretion. These guidelines were subsequently disclosed in *R v Home Secretary, ex p Brezinski and Glowacka*, 19 July 1996. These guidelines must now be read in light of the principles set out in the 1998 White Paper, *Fairer Faster and Firmer—A Modern Approach to Immigration and Asylum* (Cm 4018, 1998), which confirms the presumption in favour of temporary admission and release, and the *Operational Enforcement Manual* (21 December 2000). In a welcome development, the White Paper stresses that evidence of torture should strongly suggest temporary admission rather than detention, and that careful regard should be paid to the mental and physical health of those who may be detained. However, Macdonald and Webber report that '[a] number of reputable organizations including the Medical Foundation for the Care of Victims of Torture and Bail for Immigration Detainees report that torture victims are still being

comply is to be assessed in light of any available evidence as to, inter alia, previous absconding or failure to comply with conditions, the likelihood and imminence of removal, the extent of ties with the United Kingdom, and other compassionate factors. It has been argued that the failure to spell out in law that detention should only take place where there is a *substantial risk* of a detainee absconding creates a risk of arbitrary detention incompatible with the ECHR.[14] Moreover, organizations such as Amnesty International have argued that often judgments as to who does or does not constitute a significant risk of absconding are highly impressionistic and subjective.[15] With particular regard to asylum seekers, some have expressed the view that there is a clear but different rationale for detention, namely to deter asylum seekers from a number of selected countries.[16]

15.06   Since the Human Rights Act 1998 (HRA) came into force, Article 5 of the ECHR has played a greater role in the debate about immigration detention. Article 5 states that deprivations of liberty are only legitimate in six specified situations, and then only in accordance with a procedure prescribed by law. One of those specified cases, Article 5(1)(f), is:

> the lawful arrest or detention of a person to prevent his effecting an unauthorised entry into the country or of a person against whom action is being taken with a view to deportation or extradition.

This means that, as well as being in accordance with the domestic rules, immigration detention must be for a legitimate purpose and must be necessary and proportionate. The precise requirements of Article 5(1)(f) were considered at length by the High Court and the Court of Appeal in *R (Saadi) v Home Secretary*.[17] That case related to the Oakington 'reception centre', designed to hold those who had entered the United Kingdom, both legally and illegally, while their cases were determined. The centre was to hold those whose cases were considered by the immigration authorities to be 'simple'. The Home Office accepted that people detained in Oakington were not at risk of absconding: indeed, lack of such risk

---

detained too frequently' (*Macdonald's Immigration Law and Practice* (5th edn, London, 2001), para 17.8, n 6). See also Alison Harvey, *The detention of asylum seekers*, a conference paper given at the University of Cambridge Institute of Criminology, 20 March 2001. The UN High Commissioner for Refugees has also issued guidelines on the detention of asylum seekers: *Guidelines on applicable Criteria and Standards relating to the Detention of Asylum Seekers* (February 1999).

[14]   Expressed in an opinion for Justice by Nick Blake QC on the detention of asylum seekers in the UK.

[15]   For an analysis of the decision-making process, see the study by L Weber, *Deciding to Detain* (University of Cambridge Institute of Criminology, 2000).

[16]   The deputy representative of the UN High Commission for Refugees in London indicated a similar view when he stated '[w]hat we object to is that detention is being used to deter asylum seekers', The Economist, 14 February 1998. If such a policy is being pursued it would appear to contravene domestic law, since it would amount to using the Immigration Act powers for an improper purpose: see *R v Governor of Ashford Remand Centre, ex p Asgar* [1971] 1 WLR 129, as well as international obligations.

[17]   [2001] EWHC Admin 670; [2002] 1 WLR 356.

was one criterion for admission, since the centre did not have particularly tight security. The detention was purely to make sure that the detainees were available at all times so that their applications could be processed quickly. The Government argued that the detention was with a view to removal, and was therefore justified under the second limb of Article 5(1)(f). In a forceful and persuasive judgment, Collins J rejected that argument. He considered that 'a person who arrives and seeks leave to enter cannot properly be regarded as someone "against whom action is being taken with a view to deportation" . . . it is not compatible with asylum seekers' rights under the Refugee Convention to regard the investigation of claims for asylum in all cases as being action with a view to deportation.'[18] Nor was Collins J impressed with the Government's alternative argument, namely that the detention was justified under the first limb of Article 5(1)(f). He accepted that the detention of asylum seekers may be lawful in some circumstances, but considered that the detention of those who are at no risk of absconding, simply for reasons of administrative convenience, was disproportionate and a clear breach of Article 5(1)(f).

In a narrow and restrictive decision clearly influenced by political considerations, relying on regressive conceptions of national sovereignty and taking the narrowest possible view of Article 5, the Court of Appeal reversed the decision of Collins J. The court considered that detention pending consideration of a claim for asylum falls within the scope of Article 5(1)(f)—although it is nowhere mentioned in that Article—and that 'in the current situation of increased immigration', such detention is justified, provided that it is for a limited period. They rejected the idea that detention is only justified if there is some risk of absconding or other risk to the public. The requirement of proportionality, they considered, relates only to the *length* of the detention and not to whether it is necessary in the first place. **15.07**

> The inroad that we believe that the European Court has made into the right of immigration authorities to detain aliens pending consideration of the applications for leave to enter, or their deportation, is that these processes must not be unduly prolonged. It is in relation to the duration of detention that the question of proportionality arises. . . . The Secretary of State has determined that, in the absence of special circumstances, it is not reasonable to detain an asylum seeker for longer than about a week, but that a short period of detention can be justified where this will enable speedy determination of his or her application for leave to enter.

The Oakington arrangement was therefore lawful. The Court of Appeal's judgment shows an astonishing hostility to the Convention rights, which are seen as 'inroads' on some pre-existing national sovereignty. This is a far cry from cases such as *Daly*,[19] where the courts have stressed that all interferences with fundamental rights must be carefully scrutinized and that the courts are entitled to

---

[18] ibid at [30]–[31].
[19] [2001] 2 AC 532.

require detailed evidence from the authorities as to why the interference is really necessary. There is a strong argument that the Oakington regime constitutes arbitrary detention, since the decision to detain is taken not on the basis of risk but rather on pure considerations of administrative convenience.[20] Article 5(1) provides an exhaustive list of the situations in which detention is lawful, and administrative convenience is not one of them. However, the Oakington centre seems set to function for the foreseeable future.

15.08 Concerns as to arbitrariness have been increased by the fact that detainees are not given full written reasons for detention.[21] There is no requirement in the Immigration Acts that reasons be given for detention, but since October 1999, immigration officers have completed a checklist to explain the reasons for detention. The use of a checklist, while an improvement on the old situation where no reasons need be given at all, still falls short of the sort of individualized reasons required by Article 5 of the ECHR, and leads to detainees being given very little, if any, basis on which to challenge their detention. Consequently any efforts to assess the justifications for such detentions are at a disadvantage. This lack of reasons may well constitute a breach of Article 5(2) of the ECHR, as the court has on several occasions indicated that this Article requires that a detainee be given sufficient reasons, whether at the time of their arrest or 'promptly' afterwards, to enable them to consider whether they should seek to challenge their continued detention.[22]

---

[20] The UN HRC has stated that it 'is concerned that asylum-seekers have been detained in various facilities on grounds other than those legitimate under the Covenant, including reasons of administrative convenience'. It also raised other concerns: '[t]he Committee notes, moreover, that asylum-seekers, after final refusal of their request, may also be held in detention for an extended period when deportation might be impossible for legal or other considerations. The Committee is also concerned that the practice of dispersing asylum-seekers may have adverse effects on their ability to obtain legal advice, and upon the quality of that advice. Dispersal, as well as the voucher system of support, have on occasion led to risks for the physical security of asylum-seekers.' *Concluding Observations of the Human Rights Committee: United Kingdom of Great Britain and Northern Ireland*, 6 December 2001, CCPR/CO/73/UK, para 16.

[21] The CPT, *Report to the United Kingdom Government on the visit to the United Kingdom carried out by the European Committee for the Prevention of Torture and Inhuman or Degrading Treatment or Punishment* from 15 May to 31 May 1994, CPT/Inf (96) 11, para 231, noted frequent complaints from detainees at Campsfield House and Pentonville Prison that they had not been told why they were detained or what was happening in their case. HM Chief Inspector of Prisons has also called for detainees to be given a written statement of reasons, *Report of an Unannounced Short Inspection of Campsfield House Detention Centre on 13–15 October 1997* (London, 1998), para 1–21. The 1999 White Paper *Fairer, Faster and Firmer* introduced a commitment to written reasons being given on initial detention and every month after that. The Detention Centre Rules 2001, SI 2001/238 require, for the first time, written reasons to be given for detention, on first detention and then monthly.

[22] See eg *Fox, Campbell and Hartley v UK* Series A No 182 (1991) 13 EHRR 157.

Length of Detention

The Immigration Act does not place any time limits on detention, but some guid-   **15.09**
ance was offered by the High Court in *R v Governor of Durham Prison, ex p Hardial
Singh*.[23] In that case Woolf J (as he then was) stated that the period of detention is
impliedly limited to the period which is reasonably necessary for the purpose for
which it is given (whether this be completing an examination or making necessary
arrangements for removal). He went on to indicate that the Home Secretary was
under a duty to exercise all reasonable expedition to ensure that the necessary steps
were taken within a reasonable time. Failure to do so could entitle the detainee to
a successful habeas corpus application in respect of unlawful detention.[24] In examining the lawfulness of detentions under Article 5(1)(f) of the ECHR the
Strasbourg authorities have indicated that prolonged detention with respect to
deportation proceedings may bring into question the lawfulness of the detention.
The Commission has indicated that such proceedings must be conducted with
'requisite diligence'.[25] However, it will examine the conduct both of the applicant
and of the state. There will be no violation if the applicant's conduct has prolonged the proceedings. In *Chahal v UK*,[26] for example, the court ruled that a
period of four years in detention pending deportation did not violate Article
5(1)(f), since the applicant had been partly responsible for delaying proceedings
for this time as he pursued an asylum application. The UN Human Rights
Committee, however, appeared to take a more robust approach when it decided
in 1997 that four years' detention of an asylum seeker in Australia violated Article
9(1) of the International Covenant on Civil and Political Rights (ICCPR).[27]
Currently over 30 per cent of detained asylum seekers in the United Kingdom
spend over six months in detention and detentions in excess of one year are not
unknown.[28] It is worth noting that in this respect immigration detainees are

---

[23] [1984] 1 WLR 704.

[24] In *Hardial Singh* Woolf J (as he then was) was disposed to grant such an application but
adjourned it for three days after the Home Office offered information that the necessary steps for a
deportation order in this case would very shortly be taken. In *In re Wasfi Mohamood* [1995] Imm
AR 311, the High Court applied *Hardial Singh* and held that ten months' detention to obtain travel
documents to effect removal was excessive. *Hardial Singh* was also applied by the Privy Council
when considering the situation of Vietnamese asylum seekers in Hong Kong, many of whom had
been detained for very long periods: *Tan Te Lam v Superintendent of Tai A Chau Detention Centre*
[1997] AC 97, PC.

[25] See eg *X v UK* (1977) 12 D & R 207.

[26] (1997) 23 EHRR 413. However, it must be remembered that this was an exceptional case due
to the security issues involved.

[27] *A v Australia* Communication 560/1993.

[28] See Amnesty International, *Cell Culture: The Detention and Imprisonment of Asylum Seekers in
the United Kingdom* (London, 1996) 11, finding that 32% of detained asylum seekers had been
detained for six months or more and that 6% had been detained in excess of a year. However the
Home Office, *Asylum Statistics United Kingdom 2000*, table 9.1, claimed in 2000 that only 10%
were detained in excess of six months.

clearly worse off than those accused of criminal offences, where time limits for periods on remand have now been set.

Review of Detention

15.10 Unusually among western democracies, the United Kingdom does not provide for automatic independent review of immigration detention decisions. In Canada, for example, detainees must be brought before an adjudicator within seven days.[29] There is an internal review of detentions within the Immigration Service within seven days and thereafter at monthly reviews by more senior levels within the Immigration Service, so that after six months a detainee's case should be reviewed by a Director of the Service. However, many groups have expressed doubts as to the value of such reviews.[30]

15.11 Instead, to seek their liberty detainees must find their way round a complex legal maze of available remedies. Detainees often suffer from a lack of information about these remedies, although at least in the case of asylum seekers it is now government policy to inform the Refugee Legal Centre when decisions to remove are being considered. The power to detain has as its corollary the power to release on bail. Those detained under the Immigration Act 1971 can in almost all cases seek bail under Sch 2, para 22 to the Act.[31] Asylum and Immigration Act 1999, Pt III also contained provisions extending the right to apply for bail, but the Government has stated that these provisions will not be brought into force. Applicants detained at a port may seek bail from the Immigration Appeals Authority after seven days if no decision has been reached on their case. Applicants with pending appeals or judicial review proceedings can seek bail from the immigration appellate authority or the High Court as appropriate. The Chief Adjudicator, in guidance notes issued in 2000, stresses that there is a common law presumption in favour of bail, and that therefore the burden of proof rests on the Secretary of State (through the immigration authorities) to prove that detention is necessary.[32] However, in practice the grant of bail will normally require evidence of somewhere the detainee can reside and a number of sureties. The provision of sureties is not essential,[33] but in practice it is quite clear that a lack of sureties is

---

[29] For international comparisons see Justice, *Providing Protection: Towards Fair and Effective Asylum Procedures* (London, 1997) 63.

[30] Amnesty International, *Prisoners Without a Voice: Asylum Seekers in the United Kingdom* (London, 1995) 34, commented that 'given the vacuity of so many of the "reasons" for detention cited by Immigration Officers in response to enquiries from detainees' legal representatives, it is highly questionable whether these internal reviews amount to more than a "rubber stamping" of the original decision to detain'.

[31] The current version of this paragraph incorporates amendments made by the Asylum and Immigration Act 1996 and the Asylum and Immigration Act 1999.

[32] 'Bail: Guidance notes for Adjudicators from the Chief Adjudicator', 22 September 2000.

[33] See the decision of the Court of Appeal in *R v Home Secretary, ex p Lamin Minteh*, 8 March 1996, where the court stressed that a practice of requiring sureties in every case regardless of the risk of absconding was unlawful.

likely to be highly prejudicial to a bail application. Asylum seekers may find this especially difficult to provide. Where someone has been detained after entry she will not even be able to apply for bail until it has been decided not to allow her to remain in the United Kingdom and she has lodged an appeal against this decision. As a result, such detainees may spend a considerable time in detention before even being able to seek bail.[34] Where instead a detainee seeks to challenge the lawfulness of her detention she has several legal alternatives. Habeas corpus and judicial review of the decision to detain are to a certain extent overlapping remedies. The former tends to be used more where the 'jurisdictional facts', such as whether the person had a valid passport or came within the criteria of those liable to be detained, is at issue, the latter where these facts are accepted but the challenge focuses on the exercise of an immigration officer's discretion, and with the compatibility of the decision with the ECHR, in particular Article 5.[35] Before the HRA came into force, the court was only empowered to decide on whether immigration officers had lawful grounds for their decision to detain and not as to the appropriateness of the detention in this case. Now, of course, it can also examine whether the detention complies with the requirements of Article 5. Bail is available where an applicant seeks either judicial review or habeas corpus, but the power to grant bail is subsidiary to the substantive application, so that if, for example, permission to apply for judicial review is refused, the High Court no longer has jurisdiction to grant bail.[36] Detainees can also pursue rights of appeal under the Immigration Act, but unless bail is granted by the Adjudicator (as discussed above) they will remain in detention for the duration of this appeal. As we have seen earlier, a detainee may also seek habeas corpus where they feel that their detention has continued for an excessive length of time, but again the courts have not shown a willingness to accede to such applications.

In the previous edition of this book, we doubted whether the provisions enabling immigration detainees to challenge their detention complied with Article 5(4) of the ECHR and its requirement that everyone deprived of his liberty can take proceedings by which the lawfulness of his detention is reviewed 'speedily' by a court. **15.12**

---

[34] Amnesty International, *Prisoners Without a Voice: Asylum Seekers in the United Kingdom* (London, 1995) 39, found in a survey of asylum seekers detained as illegal entrants that they spent an average of 63 days in detention before becoming eligible to apply for bail. For a much fuller explanation of procedures regarding bail see I Macdonald and F Webber, *Macdonald's Immigration Law and Practice* (5th edn, London, 2001), ch 17.

[35] For a discussion of the appropriate avenue see *R v Home Secretary, ex p Khawaja* [1984] AC 74 and *R v Home Secretary, exp Muboyayi* [1992] QB 244. See also Macdonald and Webber, ibid, para 17.27.

[36] The High Court's power to grant bail was considered in detail by Collins J in *R v Home Secretary, ex p Kelso* [1998] INLR 603, QB. The effect of this decision is that, in almost all cases, the High Court has the power to consider the application for bail on its merits, rather than simply reviewing the reasonableness of the refusal of bail. This approach was approved by the Court of Appeal in *R (Doku) v Home Secretary*, 30 November 2000, CA.

While habeas corpus and judicial review proceedings are available throughout the period of detention, we doubted whether the courts were empowered to examine, as the Convention requires, whether detention is in conformity not just with domestic law but also with Convention guarantees.[37] The right to apply for bail does provide a means of examining whether detention is justified as well as lawful, but it cannot be said that this is a 'speedy' form of redress when a detainee cannot apply for bail until he has spent seven days in detention and when adjudicators take an average of three months to consider bail applications.[38] In the *Chahal* case the ECtHR did find a breach of Article 5(4) where national security considerations had been invoked to limit the scope of the court's inquiry when considering the detainee's habeas corpus application.[39] The Strasbourg Court indicated that Article 5(4) did not require that a reviewing court be able to substitute its view for that of the administration on all questions relating to the detention but took the view that it must be able to examine matters which are 'essential' for deciding whether detention was lawful under Article 5(1)(f). This includes the issue of whether the detention was in keeping with the purpose of Article 5 and hence whether or not it can be described as 'arbitrary'. The Human Rights Committee has indicated that detention of an asylum seeker, for example, will be arbitrary where it is 'not necessary in all the circumstances of the case to prevent flight or interference with evidence'.[40]

15.13 As the current provisions for reviewing immigration detention are not established in the statute, they are open to challenge under the HRA. In *Amuur v France*[41] the lack of detailed guidance on how long detainees could be held and the procedures by which detainees could access legal or humanitarian assistance proved fatal for the state's defence of the Article 5 claim. The court stressed that the reviewing court or tribunal must be able to review the *conditions* under which individuals are being held, to impose a limit on the length of detention, and to consider whether detention is necessary and proportionate. It is not clear whether the High Court on a habeas corpus or judicial review application would review the legality of detention by reference to the conditions of detention in anything other than the

---

[37] In *Amuur v France* (1996) 22 EHRR 533 the ECtHR indicated that immigration detention beyond a few hours amounts to a deprivation of liberty under Art 5(1). Such a deprivation must be 'in accordance with the law' and the court made it clear that such a requirement extends beyond compliance with national law to embrace the requirements of legality set down in the Convention. See Amnesty International, *Prisoners Without a Voice: Asylum Seekers in the United Kingdom* (London, 1995) 43.

[38] See Amnesty International, ibid, 43. These delays caused great concern to the UN Working Group on Arbitrary Detention: see UN Commission on Human Rights, 55th Session, 18 December 1998, E/CN.4/1999/Add.3, para 18.

[39] *Chahal v UK* (1997) 23 EHRR 413. Parliament has subsequently responded to this decision by passing the Special Immigration Appeals Commission Act 1997, which provides a new mechanism for dealing with appeals in national security related cases.

[40] *A v Australia* Communication 560/1993, para 9.2.

[41] (1996) 22 EHRR 533.

most exceptional circumstances. Further, the 'necessary and proportionate' inquiry goes beyond *Wednesbury* review, leaving it unclear whether the traditional domestic approach to reviewing the legality of detention complies with the ECHR. However, the situation may be improved following the coming into force of the HRA. Under the Act, proportionality has become an integral part of domestic law when the courts are considering the legality of infringements of fundamental rights, including the right to liberty under Article 5 of the ECHR. While this makes domestic law theoretically compatible with the Convention, it remains to be seen whether the legality of detention will in fact be searchingly reviewed, particularly in cases with a political or security dimension. The judgment of the Court of Appeal in *Saadi*[42] certainly does not suggest that the courts will be fearless in protecting immigration detainees' right to liberty.

B. Places of Detention

Immigration Act 1971, Sch 2, para 18(1) indicates that those detained under the provisions of the Act may be held in 'such places as the Secretary of State may direct'.[43] Currently, Immigration Act detainees are held in one of eight specialist Immigration Detention Centres or in one of a number of prisons throughout the country. Two of the Immigration Detention Centres, Yarl's Wood[44] and Campsfield, as well as Oakington Reception Centre, are operated on a day to day basis by Group 4 Falck. Tinsley House removal/detention centre at Gatwick Airport is managed by Wackenhut,[45] and Harmondsworth is managed by UK Detention Services. There are further detention centres at Heathrow Airport, Manchester Airport, Dover Harbour and Longport. Ultimate management responsibility for these centres remains with the Immigration Service. They each have a Board of Visitors, and the Chief Inspector of Prisons has asserted that they come within his jurisdiction. There are dedicated immigrations wings in HM Prison Haslar, HM Prison Lindholme and HM Prison Rochester, managed by the Prison Service for the Immigration Service and staffed by prison officers (with a small group of sentenced prisoners to provide cleaning and catering services, as immigration detainees cannot be required to work in order to provide these and generally have not wanted to work for prison wages).

15.14

---

[42] [2002] 1 WLR 356.

[43] This has included police cells, airports, and even a ship, The Earl William, which was used for a time in 1987.

[44] Currently closed after being partially destroyed by fire in February 2002.

[45] In May 2002, Wackenhut was taken over by Group 4 Falck, raising serious concerns both about the company's dominance of the 'market' in immigration detention and about standards of treatment: Wackenhut owns Australasian Correctional Management, which runs all Australian detention centres, including the notorious centre at Woomera.

15.15 The total number of places available in these detention centres and dedicated prison wings is around 1,800. This is well below the total number of people detained under the Immigration Act every year and is even well below the total number in detention at any one time. Hence a significant number of detainees are held in Prison Service establishments. At the time of writing, 48 prisons contained immigration detainees, some with over 100 and some with only two or three. In the past it has not been entirely unusual for only one detainee to be held in a prison. The Chief Inspector of Prisons has expressed concern that some prisons are unsuitable for holding Immigration Act detainees, especially asylum seekers, as have a number of Boards of Visitors.[46] During its 1994 visit to the United Kingdom the European Committee for the Prevention of Torture (CPT) went further, arguing that while conditions in Pentonville were adequate, prison was simply an inappropriate place to detain those who are neither charged with nor convicted of a criminal offence.[47] In its response to the United Kingdom's fifth periodic report, the UN Human Rights Committee stated quite clearly that it 'considers unacceptable any detention of asylum-seekers in prisons'.[48] Detainees themselves have drawn attention to problematic conditions, notably through hunger strikes at Rochester Prison and the fire and escape at Yarl's Wood detention centre.

C. Conditions of Immigration Act Detainees

15.16 Different rules apply to those detained in Immigration Detention Centres as opposed to criminal prisons. In the Detention Centres there is a set of 'house rules' but no formal means of enforcing these. This leads to problems for both prisoners and staff, for example regarding the powers of staff to use control and restraint techniques.[49] The detention regime is fairly relaxed with detainees having free association during the day and sleeping in unlocked dormitories at night. Those held in criminal prisons (and in the Haslar Holding Centre which is managed by the Prison Service) are subject to the Prison Rules, and Standing Orders make it clear that they should be treated like remand prisoners with regard to matters such as work, visits, and correspondence.[50] As a result Immigration Act detainees held

---

[46] eg in respect of Pentonville Prison where both the Chief Inspector and the Board expressed such concerns in reports in March 1994.

[47] CPT, *Report to the United Kingdom Government on the visit to the United Kingdom carried out by the European Committee for the Prevention of Torture and Inhuman or Degrading Treatment or Punishment* from 15 May to 31 May 1994, CPT/Inf (96) 11, para 230.

[48] *Concluding Observations of the Human Rights Committee: United Kingdom of Great Britain and Northern Ireland*, 6 December 2001, CCPR/CO/73/UK, para 16.

[49] The legal position of staff would appear to be that they have no more legal authority to use force than any other citizen.

[50] Current Prison Service policy is set out in PSO 4630, 'Management of Immigration Act Detainees'.

in Prison Service establishments may be subject to disciplinary charges or the use of rule 45. Given that many will lack adequate English, issues concerning a need for representation to ensure the fairness of any disciplinary proceedings come to the fore.

As observed earlier, a number of commentators have expressed concern over the conditions of Immigration Act detainees, especially asylum seekers, in criminal prisons. Often a number of detainees will be held together with unconvicted prisoners in one wing of a prison. However, the situation of a single detainee held in a criminal prison is only one cause for concern. Problems have also arisen regarding the access of Immigration Act detainees to legal advice. Current guidance indicates to governors that asylum applicants who have lodged an appeal against refusal of asylum under the 1993 Asylum and Immigration Appeals Act will invariably require a meeting with a representative from the Refugee Legal Centre or some other legal representative to pursue this appeal and that, in view of the time limits set down in the Act, such requests for visits must be dealt with as a matter of urgency. **15.17**

Immigration Detention Centres have also been subject to criticism as regards their conditions. Although the more relaxed regime generally means that there are fewer difficulties with gaining access to legal representation, there have been concerns about whether detainees have been given sufficient information to know of and be able to exercise their rights. Detainees complain of boredom and of a regime which offers them little to do except think about their case. Amnesty has also drawn attention to the limited healthcare facilities at Campsfield House.[51] The lack of such facilities, in particular facilities for diagnosing and treating mental health problems, may have contributed to the suicide of a number of asylum applicants in the past decade. Detention centres have on occasion transferred detainees to better equipped prison hospitals for treatment. They have also, it appears, been prepared to transfer detainees to criminal prisons where a prisoner is being 'disruptive' (a definition which includes those who have gone on hunger strikes or led protests). Such transfers occur without the prisoner having the opportunity to be given reasons or put his case. While prison transfer cases such as *McAvoy*[52] and *Hargreaves*[53] would appear to suggest that someone in lawful custody[54] has no legitimate expectation of the continuation of any particular regime of custody, such disciplinary transfers without due process would seem to be inconsistent with the UN Body of Principles for the Protection of All Persons **15.18**

---

[51] *Prisoners Without a Voice: Asylum Seekers in the United Kingdom* (London, 1995) 61. The CPT has expressed similar concerns, especially with regard to psychiatric and psychological services, as did the Chief Inspector of Prisons' 1997 inspection.

[52] [1984] 1 WLR 1408.

[53] [1997] 1 All ER 397.

[54] Which immigration detainees are by virtue of Immigration Act 1971, Sch 2, para 18(2).

under Any Form of Detention or Imprisonment.[55] At Harmondsworth the CPT also found that two prisoners (who again were participating in food refusal) were kept in isolation rooms, but were unable to discern the rules under which decisions to place people in isolation were taken. In its response the Government stressed that such decisions were never taken for disciplinary reasons and avoided the issue of what rules governed their use.[56] The Chief Inspector of Prisons did, however, return to this issue in his report on Campsfield, where he called for a clear set of rules to indicate the rights and responsibilities of detainees and suggested these should make it clear that their status is closely analogous to that of unconvicted prisoners.[57]

D. Conclusions and Critique

15.19 The legal regime governing the detention of people seeking asylum or other lawful entry into the United Kingdom is deficient in several areas. Although the percentage of detainees to the total number of claimants remains low, too many people are being detained unnecessarily and for too long, especially for a system which claims only to use detention as a last resort in situations where the detainee would otherwise abscond and become unavailable for a decision to be reached. The United Kingdom is unusual in that it detains people seeking asylum, and especially unusual in that it detains them for long periods and in criminal prisons. The ECtHR has recognized that, when an asylum seeker is detained, this relates 'not to those who have committed criminal offences but to aliens who, often fearing for their lives, have fled from their own country'.[58] Despite some much-needed reforms, this statement finds little recognition in domestic law. Decisions on who should or should not be detained appear to be based on vague, arbitrary, and largely unreviewable criteria.[59] The failure to give detainees full written reasons for their detention and the inadequacy of reasons once given may violate international human rights standards,[60] as may the lack of adequate mechanisms

---

[55] Principle 30 indicates that 'detained persons should have the right to be heard before any disciplinary action is taken'.

[56] This is despite the fact that the terms of the contract with Group 4 indicate that people may be placed in isolation 'for their safety, the safety of staff or of other detainees and visitors'. See *Final Response of the United Kingdom Government to the report of the European Committee for the Prevention of Torture and Inhuman or Degrading Treatment or Punishment (CPT) on its visit to the United Kingdom from 15 to 31 May 1994*, CPT/Inf (96) 12, 48.

[57] *Report of an Unannounced Short Inspection of Campsfield House Detention Centre on 13–15 October 1997* (London, 1998), paras 1–38.

[58] *Amuur v France* (1996) 22 EHRR 533, para 43.

[59] Contrary to international human rights standards set out in *Amuur v France* (1996) 22 EHRR 533 and *A v Australia* Communication 560/1993.

[60] In addition to the points made above regarding Art 5(2) of the ECHR it is also worth noting that such flaws may also be in contravention of Principles 11 and 13 of the UN Body of Principles for the Protection of All Persons under any Form of Detention or Imprisonment.

for reviewing detention and securing release. Conditions of detention, both in the Immigration Detention Centres and criminal prisons, also leave something to be desired. Ultimately there must be significant doubt whether the United Kingdom is doing all it can to comply with Conclusion 44 of the intergovernmental Executive Committee of the Programme of the UN High Commissioner for Refugees that:

> the conditions of detention of refugees and asylum seekers shall be humane. In particular, refugees and asylum seekers shall, whenever possible, not be accommodated with persons detained as common criminals.

16

CONCLUSIONS: PRISONS AND THE LAW

A. Introduction

In this final chapter we attempt an assessment of the relationship between law and **16.01** prisons that has developed since the demise of the judicial 'hands off' approach, both in the United Kingdom and in Strasbourg, in the 1970s. We will consider two issues in particular. The first is the extent to which a coherent approach by the legal system and in particular the judiciary towards prisons and prisoners' rights has developed in that period. The second is what actual impact the courts' willingness to extend the rule of law to prisons has made on conditions and relationships within prisons. Neither of these matters, especially the second, has as yet been the object of much study in the United Kingdom. Legal writing has tended to emphasize the development of the law in relation to particular aspects of prison administration, whether it be discipline, access, or release. Sociologists of the prison have not paid much attention to the impact of law on prison regimes. Therefore our conclusions must be tentative. Both lawyers and sociologists in the United States have examined these issues in greater detail and we will be examining some aspects of their work to provide possible models for study of the experience in the United Kingdom.

Despite the tentative nature of our conclusions we have included this chapter as **16.02** we believe it is the next stage for prison law in the United Kingdom. There is a need now to consider in a more systematic way how legal regulation of prisons has developed, and whether we can now speak of a distinct subject of prison law as opposed to a series of decisions and regulations on particular areas of prison life. There is also a need to consider what impact legal intervention has had on the lives of prisoners and prison staff, whether it has produced change, and what form this change has taken. Without asking, let alone answering, these questions, the future legal regulation of prisons may fail to respond adequately to the problems of all who live and work in prisons. This is not to say that law can provide all the answers to the problems of prisons, just that we need to consider what answers it currently provides and what problems it could address. Before examining these two issues however it is necessary to appraise the relationship that existed between prisons and the law before the beginnings of judicial intervention in the 1970s if we are to see how judicial oversight of the prison may have led to changes.

B. The Paradox of Prisons and the Law

16.03 In one sense there is no more legal institution than the prison. Liberal political theory posits an opposition of the public (the State) and the private (variously seen as the individual, family, or company). Whereas the various forms of the private are seen as somehow 'natural' the State is seen as 'artificial' and any intervention of the public into the private realm is seen as in need of justification.[1] The normal form of such justification is the existence of a public interest that outweighs the private interest subject to regulation, a public interest whose genuineness and legitimacy, in the democratic version of liberal theory, can ultimately be traced back to the expression of public will in elections and the delegation of that will to elected representatives. The expression of that public interest takes the form of law and in this sense the State is the law (hence the German term of Rechtsstaat often used by political theorists); if officials detain someone or remove his property without legal authority they are no longer acting as officials of the State. That many political theorists would argue that the State precedes the law, in the sense that a monopoly on force in a society creates the right to make law, rather than the other way round, need not concern us here. We are interested in the claims to legitimate authority the State makes.

16.04 There can be few more significant interventions by the public into the private than imprisoning someone; only the imposition of the death penalty comes to mind. The decision to imprison a person, to take away her capacity to act in private society and to subject her constantly and totally to the supervision of the State, stands therefore in need of particularly clear justification by law. It is no accident then that decisions about what grounds justify imprisoning people are

---

[1] For a general discussion of the relation of public and private in liberal political theory see R Unger, *Knowledge and Politics* (New York, 1975), ch 2.

amongst the most fiercely contested in political debate and that the legal system has developed its most extensive procedural safeguards in the area of criminal law. Such safeguards can be seen as driven by the need to ensure that only people who do actually come within the scope of the grounds specified as justifying imprisonment actually find themselves subject to it.[2] Prisons therefore are entirely the creation of law. Without law they cannot be justified (hence the tort of false imprisonment) nor arguably would they be necessary. When the American radical, George Jackson, commented, 'the ultimate expression of law is not order, it's prison'[3] there was at least one sense in which he was clearly correct.

However, while much public and legal discussion is occupied by the question of who is to be sent to prison it is often almost assumed that the State's coercive involvement ends with the decision to imprison. This is untrue. The State does not at present (nor has it ever really) simply lock people up and throw away the key. Instead people in prison are usually required to work (if convicted), are required to take baths and submit to medical examinations, and find that they cannot take exercise, eat meals, or even go to the toilet whenever they want. Prison is therefore a continuing experience of coercion, of having nearly every aspect of one's life regulated by the State and of being dependent on the State for nearly every necessity of life. To some extent this experience of near total coercion/dependency is the inevitable outcome of imprisonment and exclusion from the outside world. To a greater extent though it is a consequence of the particular regime operating in prisons. As we observed in Chapter 7, the separation between prisons and the outside world was much less before the late 18th century than it is today, goods and services flowed into and out of the prison at the behest of prisoners (at least those who had money) more freely than they do now. Even in the late 20th century the experience of the 'compound system' in Northern Irish prisons shows that prisons can exist with a much lesser degree of daily regulation of inmates' lives than is normally seen as necessary.[4] In the compounds, which were open to all prisoners convicted of terrorist-related offences between 1973 and 1976, prisoners were not required to get up or go to sleep at particular times, were not required to do prison work, and had no set times for association. In most 21st-century prisons, however, the commitment to ensuring security, order, and rehabilitation of prisoners means that there is significant regulation of inmates' daily lives (often more so in medium than in maximum security environments).

16.05

---

[2] Public trial and fair hearing rights can also be seen as fulfilling other functions in addition to the avoidance of mistakes as to who has committed an offence, such as participation in law enforcement and the legitimization of punishment.

[3] G Jackson, *Blood in my Eye* (London, 1972) 119.

[4] For a discussion of the compound regime see C Crawford, 'Long Kesh: An Alternative Perspective', MSc thesis, Cranfield Institute of Technology (1979).

16.06 We do not intend to imply that 18th-century gaols or the Northern Irish compounds were 'better' prison environments than that which prevails in most contemporary prisons in England and Wales. More extensive regulation may well be justified in the interests of the public, staff, and prisoners themselves. It must be said, however, that such regulation stands in need of justification; that the State cannot regulate people's lives without justification for each element of regulation (that is, at least if it is accepted that prisoners remain legal subjects and human beings, a position which was not unequivocally held when a prisoner was subject to 'civil death' by the fact of imprisonment).[5]

The Prison as a Lawless Agency

16.07 It can be argued though that this extensive intervention is constantly justified through the myriad of Prison Rules, Prison Service Orders and Prison Service Instructions. Prison is an extensively rule-bound institution where the prison authorities can almost always point to a rule at some level of the hierarchy as the basis for any action that they take. Indeed prisoners frequently list as one of their main complaints about their experience of prison that 'there are too many silly rules'.[6] Many prison officers take a pride in doing things 'by the book' and look with disfavour on decisions to ignore breaches of the rules or reach informal arrangements with prisoners. Given this density of rules in prison, this extensive literature of legal justification for intervention in prisoners' lives, why is it that some commentators have referred to prison as a 'lawless agency'?[7]

16.08 The commentators who made this judgment have argued that prisons formed islands of lawless discretion in a society guided by the values and often the practice of the rule of law. They claimed that in prisons the authorities, especially those at the lowest level,[8] exercised arbitrary power over prisoners' lives. One must make allowances for the fact that these comments have been made in respect of State prison systems in the United States, whose rule-making structures have always been more informal and decentralized than in the United Kingdom, and that they were made before extensive federal judicial oversight of prison regimes became the norm. Nevertheless such comments do strike a chord in the British prison system, certainly in its pre-*St Germain* days, and point towards the paradox of prisons, the creatures of law and highly rule-bound institutions, being places where often the rule of law is absent.[9]

---

[5] Until the Forfeiture Act 1870 convicted felons forfeited all their land and chattels.

[6] eg in the *National Prison Survey* 1991 (London, 1992).

[7] See D Greenberg and F Stender, 'The Prison as a Lawless Agency' (1972) 21 Buffalo L Rev 799.

[8] See B Hirschkop and D Milleman, 'The Unconstitutionality of Prison Life' (1969) 55 Virginia L Rev 795.

[9] See the discussion of prison discipline in M Fitzgerald and J Sim, *British Prisons* (2nd edn, Oxford, 1982) 74–82, after which the authors conclude '[a]s in the other aspects of imprisonment we have discussed discretion, arbitrariness, expediency and unfairness are the hallmarks of discipline in British prisons'.

The Limitation of the Prison Rules

When prisoners claim that there are too many silly rules they are obviously **16.09** expressing a view that too many of these rules work against them. There is no necessary reason why this should always be the case. Even the most coercive system of rules is capable of being a double-edged sword, offering rights as well as burdens, constraining as well as legitimizing the exercise of power.[10] A reading of the Prison Rules shows them hardly to be the most coercive set of rules ever devised: many of their provisions offer protection to prisoners against excessive action by the authorities.[11] Indeed they compare favourably with many consumer contracts or housing agreements. Yet many prisoners clearly do not perceive them in this way and feel that the authorities have unlicensed power to do what they want. In terms of everyday life in prisons this view may well be exaggerated but arguably it has more than a grain of truth because of three related factors.

First, as has been pointed out several times in this book, the Prison Rules them- **16.10** selves are mostly vague and confer discretionary powers on the authorities. They do not set out a clear and comprehensive scheme of rights and duties on behalf of prisoners, with the result that it is often difficult to say exactly whether a particular act by the prison authorities or direction given to a prisoner is within the scope of the Rules or not. Indeed the survival of the disciplinary offence of 'disobeying any lawful order' indicates that there remains a scope of legitimate power for the authorities which is not clearly captured by the content of the Rules.[12] Prison Service Orders and Instructions do narrow down the extent of this discretion somewhat but invocation of them by prisoners is inhibited by the second factor, the lack of information about the Rules. Despite the requirement of Prison Rule 10 that a copy of the Prison Rules be displayed and made available to any prisoner who wishes to see them (though there is no positive duty to acquaint prisoners with them), researchers have frequently found that prisoners experience difficulty in informing themselves of the content of the Rules. So much greater then is the difficulty in becoming acquainted with the content of Prison Service Orders and Instructions, where no obligation to publish exists. Prodded originally by some European Court of Human Rights (ECtHR) decisions the Government has now undertaken to make the Orders available but has made no similar commitment in

---

[10] For an exposition of this view see EP Thompson, *Whigs and Hunters* (London, 1977) 258–269.

[11] See, eg r 47 (limiting the use of force to what is reasonably necessary), r 24 (on food quality), and r 31 (limiting work to a maximum of ten hours a day).

[12] See, eg, the discussion in N Loucks (ed), *Prison Rules: A Working Guide* (London, 1993) 15–20. Researchers found the prisoners were still not given copies of the Prison Rules on reception at prison and that prison officers still frequently denied requests to see Standing Orders and Circular Instructions. Operating Standard A2 still only provides that '[r]elevant Information should be provided to the prisoner at the appropriate time'.

respect of Instructions. This is despite the latter's importance to decisions such as rule 45 segregation, transfer between prisons, and dealing with prisoners diagnosed HIV positive. Without knowledge of the contents of these secondary documents prisoners are in a fairly weak position to challenge claims that there is pre-existing authority for decisions taken by officers and the prison administration.

16.11 Yet even when prisoners did challenge decisions and did have good grounds for believing that such decisions were not authorized by the Rules they found, at least in pre-*St Germain* days, that such challenges fell on deaf ears. Breaches by the authorities, even of their own rules and directions, generally attracted no sanction within the prison system and until *St Germain* met no reproach in the courts. The combination of these three factors, lack of specificity in the Rules, lack of information as to their content, and lack of impartial applicability of them to prisoner and prison officer alike, deprived the extensive code of rules in prison of the character of being an expression of the rule of law.[13] Instead they became the rather threadbare cloak of a highly discretionary and frequently arbitrary regime.

Prison Regimes and Prison Law

16.12 Yet it was also a regime that sociologists of prison life have observed was well suited to (or indeed developed into) a particular style of control system within prisons. In his review of the literature on management regimes in prisons Ditchfield outlines a typology of four basic management models. The first of these is the 'authoritarian' model. In this all power is vested in either the prison governor or prison officers. Prisoners have no rights, although privileges (such as the more attractive prison jobs or a blind eye turned to rule infractions) may be extended to prisoners perceived by both prisoners and prison officers as leaders of the inmate population. The selective granting of privileges is aimed at ensuring the conformity of prisoners who might otherwise prove troublesome. Control, in this model, is maintained by 'a combination of terror, often brutal corporal punishment, some rudimentary incentives and favouritism'. The second model he terms 'bureaucratic-lawful'. In this model formal rules and standards exist to reduce discretion and make those who exercise power accountable, at least to the level above them in the official hierarchy. In this regime control is maintained less by coercion than by providing clear and consistent treatment of prisoners, by assuring them that they are not subject to arbitrary power. Prison officers often react to this loss of total power by becoming increasingly bureaucratized themselves, through the for-

---

[13] This type of requirement is often seen as essential by what might be described as 'procedural' approaches to the rule of law, approaches which do not include any substantive rights in their definition. See, eg, J Raz, 'The Rule of Law and Its Virtue' (1977) 93 LQR 195.

mation of unions, and lobby for clearer job assignments and higher staffing levels. The third he describes as 'shared powers'. This he sees as arising with the increasing emphasis on 'rehabilitation' and 'treatment' of prisoners (often of a medical or psychological character) in the prison systems of the 1950s and 1960s. This model provided for a greater involvement of civilian professional staff (such as teachers or psychologists) in prisons which in turn led to conflicts in approaches and objectives between 'treatment' and 'custody' staff. Inmate pressure groups evolved to play their part in this dispute and the prison administration found itself needing to respond to such groups to maintain control. However inmate influence is greatest in the fourth model, that of 'inmate control'. This is the view some writers take of gang influence in several American prisons. These gangs have effectively gained control of the prison and it is only through negotiation with gang leaders, and indeed between gang leaders, that control is tentatively maintained.[14]

As observed earlier most of the examples around which such theories are constructed come from the United States. Not since the late 19th century does it seem that anything like a pure form of the authoritarian model has operated in British prisons. Nor has anything like the inmate control model ever prevailed in prisons in England and Wales. Yet for most of the last century, despite the rehabilitative rhetoric of the Prison Commissioners,[15] the regime in most English prisons seems to have been closer to the authoritarian than the bureaucratic lawful model. The metaphor of prison as a military regime is often employed in early prison discipline cases and like an army the authoritarian model needs rules but not law. Breaches of rules are a matter of censure from the next level above, not of rights for the level below.   **16.13**

The adoption of more formal discipline and complaints procedures, tribunals in release decisions, and the move towards giving reasons for decisions show the prison system in the United Kingdom moving more towards a bureaucratic model in the last third of the 20th century. Making the prison service an agency and introducing contracted-out prisons and prisoners' compacts all accelerate this trend, given their emphasis on targets, performance indicators, and auditing of results. The extent to which legal intervention is responsible for the moves in this direction is difficult to ascertain. The growth in the inmate population, a perceived rise in the number of difficult and dangerous prisoners, rising staff costs, and the change in the culture of public services have probably played a greater role   **16.14**

---

[14] J Ditchfield, *Control in Prisons: A Review of the Literature* (London, 1990) 9.
[15] In the inter-war years especially the English Prison Commissioners stressed the reformative potential of prison. Such an approach, which aimed to 'treat' prisoners, also emphasizes the notion of prisoners as objects rather than the subjects of rights: see W Forsythe, *Penal Discipline, Reformatory Projects and the English Prison Commissioners 1895–1939* (Exeter, 1990).

in the feeling that there was a need for change.[16] The authoritarian model emphasized 'getting by' or 'doing your time' with the minimum of friction, but lacked the capacity to develop priorities and objectives that are needed when 'getting by' is clearly no longer enough. It is also important not to over-emphasize the move from one model to another. Most studies of prison regimes have noted how even the change in a governor can have an enormous impact on a prison; it is probably safe to assume that, even if the ideology of prison management is moving towards the bureaucratic, aspects of a more authoritarian regime continue to prevail in many prisons.

16.15 Nevertheless the courts have clearly had an impact and the next two sections examine what this has been. Before doing so it is worth returning to the notions of liberal political theory and the notion of government under law that we considered at the beginning of this section. To many commentators the idea that these notions describe the British constitution has always been something of a joke.[17] Pointing to the extensive survival of prerogative powers, the power of Parliament to pass any legislation it chooses unrestrained by any constitutional norms, the ability of the governing party (which often represents a minority of the electorate) to control Parliament, the vague power-conferring nature of many of the statutes passed, extensive government secrecy, and the weakness of other Parliamentary checks such as the committee system, they have suggested the rule of law has a rather weak grip on British politics. Despite the constitutional battles of the 17th and 18th centuries they see the British constitution as remaining a 'top down' affair where the sovereign has the fact of power but delegates some limitations on it to citizens, rather than a 'bottom up' arrangement where the sovereign's power is granted, conditionally and on limited terms, entirely by the will of the populace. That the person of sovereign has changed from the monarch to the governing political party and civil service does not in the end alter the character of the fundamental relationship.

16.16 This critical vision suggests that the legal position of prisoners is not an aberration, but rather a heightening of the normal relation of the State and citizen in the United Kingdom. However with the introduction of the Human Rights Act 1998 (HRA), devolved administrations in Northern Ireland, Scotland, and Wales and freedom of information legislation, the constitution of the United Kingdom may be moving more in the direction of its rule of law claims than the critics' vision. The extent to which such notions of rights permeate to prisons

---

[16] Some criminologists have argued that the whole criminal justice system is moving in the direction of emphasizing 'managerialism' as its dominant ideology now that the authoritarian model has largely proved unworkable and the reform model unsuccessful. See, eg, M Feeley and J Simon, 'The New Penology: Notes on the Emerging Strategy of Corrections and its Implications' (1992) 30 Criminology 449.

[17] See, eg, M Loughlin, *Public Law and Political Theory* (Oxford, 1992), esp 184–230.

may be one vital test of the extent to which these formal constitutional developments produce actual constitutional relations more in line with the liberal
vision.

C. Judicial Intervention in Prison Life

In the 1970s the judiciary, at both the domestic and European level, moved away   **16.17**
from the 'hands off' approach to legal claims by prisoners. The *St Germain* case in
England and the *Golder* case in Strasbourg were major breakthroughs in the
willingness of courts to apply ordinary legal principles to the exercise of power in
prisons. In the 1980s prisoners' cases began to feature ever more frequently in the
judicial review and European Convention caseloads. Courts also began to appear
more comfortable with the role of reviewing rules and practices in prisons.
Whereas in the early 1970s judges had commented that it was 'intolerable' that
prison officers should have to go about their work with the threat of judicial
review hanging over them,[18] by the late 1980s predictions that 'the tentacles of the
law' would reach into every aspect of prison life were not enough to discourage the
House of Lords from holding that it had power to review the decisions of governors.[19] The judicial approach to prisons in the 1980s has often been referred to by
commentators as an example of the judiciary at its most progressive, as one casebook observed: '[g]enerally, and as part of a process that is not yet complete, the
courts have displayed a remarkable and quite unexpected willingness to involve
themselves in the control of prison administration'.[20]

Yet the view that the courts have proved themselves to be firm guardians of pris-   **16.18**
oners' rights has not gone unchallenged. Other writers have argued that judicial
intervention has been limited and that its impact on prisoners' lives has been far
less significant than many lawyers assume.[21] This more critical view is one that we
largely share. We believe that judicial intervention, while very welcome and
important, has been partial and that its focus has primarily been on establishing
the authority of courts over the actions of prison administrators rather than on
defining and protecting the rights of prisoners. It has been at its most extensive
when dealing with matters which lawyers are generally most comfortable with:
issues of jurisdiction, access to courts, and trial procedures. It has been much less

---

[18] See Lord Denning MR in *Becker v Home Office* [1972] 2 QB 407.
[19] See the speech of Lord Bridge in *Leech v Deputy Governor, Parkhurst Prison* [1988] AC 533.
[20] See S Bailey, D Harris, and B Jones, *Civil Liberties: Cases and Materials* (3rd edn, London, 1991), 684.
[21] See, eg, the views of G Richardson, 'Prisoners and the Law: Beyond Rights' in C McCrudden and G Chambers (eds), *Individual Rights and the Law in the United Kingdom* (Oxford, 1993), ch 6; C Gearty, 'The Prisons and the Courts' in J Muncie and R Sparks (eds), *Imprisonment: European Perspectives* (London, 1991) 219; S Livingstone, 'Prisoners Have Rights, But What Rights' (1988) 51 MLR 525.

extensive when dealing with matters that involve the control and management of prisoners, such as transfer, segregation, safety, and living conditions. Yet decisions relating to these matters arguably have at least as great an impact on prisoners' lives and are in just as great a need of minimum standards and process values. In the words of one experienced American prison litigator, while courts have ensured that prisoners are no longer treated as slaves of the State, they have yet to recognize them as citizens behind bars.[22]

16.19 To support our argument it is worth looking again at the record of the courts in dealing with a variety of prisoners' claims. We believe that this record shows that the willingness of the judiciary to intervene varies with the type of issue posed. It also demonstrates that generally the European Commission and ECtHR have proved more protective of prisoners' rights than those in England, perhaps because the legal standards they apply explicitly require them to conceptualize questions in terms of rights and legitimate restrictions on them.

Establishing Jurisdiction over Prison Administration

16.20 Clearly the issue on which judges have been most activist is in establishing their own jurisdiction over actions of the prison administration. The initial steps regarding this in domestic law were taken in the first *St Germain* case, where the Court of Appeal rejected the idea that any judicial oversight of the actions of prison officers and administrators would rapidly render the prisons unmanageable. However, this was still intervention on a fairly narrow front. Shaw LJ stressed the idea that 'the courts are in general the ultimate custodians of the rights and liberties of the subject whatever his status and however attenuated those rights and liberties may be as a result of some punitive or other process',[23] but his brethren based their decisions more on the quasi-judicial powers of a Board of Visitors hearing disciplinary charges. This gave the impression that the hearing of serious disciplinary charges could in some way be hived off from the general running of the prison and that judicial intervention would not affect the day-to-day actions of prison officers and governors. If this was the impression that the majority of the Court of Appeal wanted to give it was not entirely successful, as in the next nine years courts did show themselves willing at least to consider complaints by prisoners which did not relate purely to the exercise of disciplinary powers by Boards of Visitors.[24] Whether they had authority to do so remained unclear, and indeed the Court of Appeal decision in *Ex p King*[25] suggested that judicial control did not

---

[22] A Bronstein, 'Criminal Justice: Prisons and Penology' in N Dorsen (ed), *Our Endangered Rights* (New York, 1984) 221.

[23] [1979] 1 All ER 701, 716.

[24] See, eg, *R v Home Secretary, ex p McAvoy* [1984] 1 WLR 1408 (transfer); *R v Home Secretary, ex p Hickling* [1986] 1 FLR 543 (separation of mother and baby); *R v Home Secretary, ex p Herbage (No 2)* [1987] QB 872 (prison conditions).

[25] *R v Deputy Governor Camphill Prison, ex p King* [1985] QB 375.

even extend to the exercise of disciplinary powers by governors. This view was of course to be rejected by the House of Lords in the *Leech* case.[26]

The decision in *Leech* not only clearly established that governors exercising disciplinary powers were subject to judicial review, it also hinted that judicial supervision of governors' powers might extend beyond the discipline sphere. In rhetoric that echoed Shaw LJ in *St Germain* Lord Bridge observed that historically development of the courts' jurisdiction had been impeded 'by the court's fear that unless an arbitrary boundary is drawn it will be inundated by a flood of unmeritorious claims'.[27] Disciplinary powers of governors were always exercised more frequently than those of Boards. They were much more clearly seen by prison administrators as one of the governor's resources to maintain order in a prison, resources which included the power to segregate or transfer. Hence it was always likely to be more difficult to claim that opening their exercise to judicial review still left the 'administration' of a prison outside judicial scrutiny. Any lingering doubts about the courts' willingness to extend jurisdiction to prison administration were removed by the House of Lords decision in *Hague*.[28] This decision unequivocally brought the exercise of discretionary powers in prisons within the ambit of judicial review. When combined with the courts' recognition of prisons owing prisoners a duty of care to ensure that they are not injured during the course of their imprisonment[29] it marks a clear victory for the views of Shaw LJ in *St Germain* and a declaration that the rule of law applies to prisons. The courts have indicated that the prison authorities must act within their legal powers, that indeed their power to make decisions affecting prisoners' lives comes entirely from the law, and that the courts stand ready to police breaches of those legal powers. They do not however give any real endorsement to a notion of prisoners having any rights which they might assert against the authorities, or rights which might shape or constrain the exercise of official power. Indeed in *Hague* the House of Lords rejected the idea that even some of the Prison Rules might confer rights on a prisoner to seek compensation in respect of breaches of the Rules, even though such breaches might have had a very adverse effect on a prisoner's life. **16.21**

The impression the courts give is primarily of a desire to ensure that the bureaucracy functions correctly according to its defined goals. There is less concern with shaping what those goals might be, something which goes some way towards explaining the greater degree of caution courts have displayed when it comes to ruling on the content of the prison authorities' powers. Nevertheless decisions establishing jurisdiction also play a valuable role by ensuring that the public light **16.22**

[26] *Leech v Deputy Governor, Parkhurst Prison* [1988] AC 533.
[27] ibid.
[28] *Hague v Deputy Governor, Parkhurst Prison* [1992] 1 AC 58.
[29] See *Pullen v Prison Commissioners* [1957] 3 All ER 470.

of litigation will be shone on what is often a closed world in prisons. Even if prisoners' cases prove unsuccessful, public hearings and often media coverage of them can lead to debate and reappraisal of a particular policy pursued in prisons.

16.23 At the European level the Commission and ECtHR cast off any ideas that prisons might be beyond the scope of the Convention in the *Golder* case.[30] In that case the court rejected any notion that prisoners were subject to 'inherent limitations' on their rights by the fact of their imprisonment. Instead the court indicated that the application of the qualifying clauses contained in many Articles of the ECHR would have to take account of the fact that the applicant was imprisoned and that a particular regime obtained in prisons which justified some restrictions which would not be acceptable in the outside world. This approach subjects prison administrations to the obligation to protect prisoners' human rights and enables prisoners to assert those rights. Moreover it justifies restrictions on rights by reference to the need to maintain security and safety in prison establishments as opposed to a moral judgment that prisoners should forfeit certain rights as part of their punishment, a view that was always hard to sustain when it came to restrictions on the rights of remand prisoners. As we shall see later, this basis has not prevented the European institutions from often giving a fairly limited reading to the content of prisoners' rights, but it may have encouraged a more serious examination of the interests to be considered in explaining that content than has always been evident in the English courts.

Access to Lawyers and the Courts

16.24 A second area of extensive judicial activity has been that of prisoners' access to legal advice and judicial proceedings. In many ways this follows as a natural consequence of the assertion of jurisdiction. If prisoners are unable to bring their claims before the courts then it is unlikely that the courts will have the opportunity to ensure that the prison administrators are acting within their powers. Hence courts in England have effectively dismantled barriers to prisoners petitioning the courts and even have gone so far as to speak in terms of such restrictions being 'unconstitutional', something rarely alluded to in British case law.[31] As a result of the decisions in *Raymond v Honey* and *Ex p Anderson* the prison authorities may not stop correspondence which is sent directly to the courts. In order to ensure effective access to the courts it has increasingly been recognized that prisoners should have unimpeded access to legal advice with respect to claims or potential claims. Here the European bodies were initially more to the fore than the domestic judiciary with the decisions in *Golder, Boyle and Rice, McComb*, and *Campbell*

---

[30] *Golder v UK* Series A No 18 (1975) 1 EHRR 524; an earlier Commission decision to the same effect can be seen in (1961) 5 Yearbook 126.
[31] See the observations of Lord Bridge in *Raymond v Honey* [1983] 1 AC 1.

effectively establishing that prison authorities may not stop or even read any correspondence between prisoners and their lawyers regarding ongoing or even potential litigation. However courts in the United Kingdom subsequently caught up with these European developments, notably in the second *Leech* case.[32] The views of Steyn LJ in this case, that a Prison Rule which interfered with civil rights could be upheld only if it constituted 'the minimum interference necessary' to achieve the statutory objectives, has good claim to be regarded as the high water mark of prisoners' rights case law thus far. The case forcefully asserted that prisoners had a right to privileged correspondence with their lawyers as an adjunct to their right of access to the courts. Although the courts retreated from this position in the *O'Dhuibir* case, with the coming of the HRA the decision in *Daly* has restored a strong emphasis on access to the judicial system as being one of the prisoner's most strongly guarded rights.

Disciplinary Hearings

As we pointed out in Chapter 9 of this book, prison discipline is arguably the area **16.25** where the courts were busiest in the 1980s. After jurisdiction over Board hearings was established in the first *St Germain* case the courts spent much of that decade developing the scope of procedural requirements to ensure a fair hearing of disciplinary charges by Boards. Guidance on calling witnesses, cross-examination, availability of statements, the burden of proof, interpretation of charges, and legal representation has all been forthcoming from the English courts. Though the Prison Rules remained unchanged by this litigation much of the guidance given by it was incorporated into Circular Instructions and the adjudications manual. The ECtHR played a less prominent role here than in the issue of access to lawyers and the courts. However its one major intervention, in the *Campbell and Fell* case,[33] was arguably a particularly influential one as without this decision (or at least without the Commission's decision) the *Tarrant*[34] court in England might not have reached its conclusion that legal representation was required in at least some circumstances in discipline hearings.

Questions of what is required to ensure a fair hearing when someone is facing a **16.26** charge that might lead to punishment on conviction are of course questions that most lawyers are very comfortable with, even if they may disagree sharply on answers. They are matters which lawyers who are involved in criminal trials deal with every day.[35] Indeed when Boards of Visitors had powers to order unlimited

---

[32] *R v Home Secretary, ex p Leech* [1994] QB 198.
[33] Series A No 80 (1985) 7 EHRR 165.
[34] *R v Home Secretary, ex p Tarrant* [1985] QB 251.
[35] By this we mean that lawyers constantly work within the framework of these concepts, not that they are necessarily raising issues of the legal definition of fair trial every day. See, generally, J Morison and P Leith, *The Barrister's World* (London, 1991).

loss of remission on conviction for certain disciplinary offences they had powers considerably in excess of most criminal courts (at least where a prisoner's length of sentence resulted in him being entitled to over six months' remission).[36] It may not be entirely fanciful to suggest that at least in the early discipline cases judicial willingness to intervene resulted from a feeling that a non-judicial body (or at least non-explicitly judicial) should not be entitled to hand out more severe punishments and with fewer constraints than a judicial body. As those punishment powers were reduced the courts showed a decreasing willingness to intervene in the conduct of discipline hearings and stopped short of applying the full procedural protections of the criminal law to Board hearings by refusing to recognize a right to legal representation in the *Hone* case.[37]

16.27 As we have argued in Chapter 9, in the end the courts appeared happy to allow Board hearings to continue with what was effectively a medium level of process requirements. However political and administrative pressures led to their demise, with the criticisms in the Woolf Report being their death-knell. The removal of more serious offences to outside courts leaves only governors with limited powers to convict and order punishment within the prison system. Such powers are much less extensive than those of courts and much more clearly integrated into issues of prisoner management and control. While domestic courts, notably in *Greenfield*, appeared prepared to tolerate governors making use of such powers, albeit under a limited level of judicial supervision, the ECtHR has reiterated the principle that only a judicial body should be involved in the deprivation of liberty in *Ezeh and Connors*. It now may fall again to the legislature to decide whether this area of the regulation may become more fully judicialized, including the introduction of an appeal mechanism and the availability of some form of legal representation in all discipline hearings.

Release Procedures

16.28 The fastest growing area of judicial intervention in recent years has been in reviewing the procedures governing the release of life sentence prisoners. Again the ECtHR took the lead by indicating in the *Weeks* case[38] that decisions to recall discretionary life sentence prisoners released on licence should be subject to some sort of judicial procedure, and subsequently in *Thynne, Wilson and Gunnell*[39] that decisions not to release discretionary lifers purely on the grounds of their continuing dangerousness also required a judicial hearing. The decision in *Hussain*[40] on

---

[36] Magistrates' Courts Act 1980, s 31(1); magistrates may not impose a sentence of imprisonment in excess of six months.

[37] *Hone v Board of Visitors, Maze Prison* [1988] 1 All ER 321.

[38] *Weeks v UK* Series A No 143–A (1988) 10 EHRR 293.

[39] *Thynne, Wilson and Gunnell v UK* Series A No 190 (1991) 13 EHRR 666.

[40] *Hussain v UK* (1996) 22 EHRR 1.

HMP prisoners continued this trend of injecting greater judicial control over the release of indeterminate sentence prisoners. While the ECtHR stopped short of extending this approach to mandatory lifers in the Wynne case,[41] it eventually came to recognize in *Stafford* that the differences between the discretionary and mandatory regime were not so great as to justify a different approach as to the role of politicians in decision-making and the scope of judicial supervision.

Even before the ECtHR's decision in *Stafford* the domestic courts had made **16.29** significant advances in asserting a prisoner's right to a fair procedure. As is discussed in Chapter 13 of this book the courts narrowed the scope of the Home Secretary's discretion in respect of the release of mandatory life sentence prisoners, notably as regards the tariff element. Decisions such as *Doody*,[42] *Pierson*,[43] and *Thompson and Venables*[44] indicated both that the Home Secretary would be constrained by strict procedural obligations in tariff setting and that the courts are prepared to exercise control over the substantive exercise of that discretion. Until *Stafford* removed the obstacle of *Wynne* the courts stopped short of applying the full logic of their decisions. However, with the decision in *Anderson* the House of Lords has endorsed the view that the Home Secretary does not have a role in deciding a lifer's tariff.

The life sentence cases have been one of the most significant aspects of judicial **16.30** intervention in respect of prisons and have resulted in substantial changes in law and practice. In doing so the domestic and European courts have subjected what was previously a highly discretionary, secretive, and frequently arbitrary aspect of decision-making within the prison system to a significant level of regulation. This regulation emphasizes the values of a fair process and hence has given prisoners an element of participation in decision-making that affects their lives which is, formally at least, generally absent in the rest of the prison system. Yet there is also a way in which judicial activity in this area can be seen as another facet of the struggle between the administration and the courts and of the courts taking back a function, control of sentencing, which they see as naturally belonging to them rather than to the administration. The speeches of Lords Steyn and Hope in the *Pierson* case strongly articulate a view that this is a function which belongs properly in the judicial rather than the executive sphere. Judicial evidence to the House of Lords Select Committee on the sentence for murder was largely in favour of determinate sentencing and subsequently leading members of the judiciary have lent their support to this view in other fora.[45] With faith waning in the

---

[41] *Wynne v UK* Series A No 294–A (1994).
[42] *R v Home Secretary, ex p Doody* [1993] 1 All ER 151.
[43] *R v Home Secretary, ex p Pierson* [1997] 3 All ER 577.
[44] *R v Home Secretary, ex p Thompson and Venables* [1998] AC 407.
[45] See *Report of the Select Committee on Murder and Life Imprisonment* [1988–99] HL Paper 781–III; also the Prison Reform Trust's *Report of the Committee on the Penalty for Homicide* (London, 1993), chaired by former Lord Chief Justice, Lord Lane.

rehabilitative ideals that inspired the use of indeterminate sentences (though arguably this has been replaced by protecting the public from 'dangerous' people as the guiding principle), those who argue for non-judicial control of sentencing appear to be on weaker ground. Yet because life sentence release decisions can be seen as an aspect of sentencing rather than prison administration the judiciary may be more comfortable with exercising a substantial degree of control over how such decisions are reached.

Discretionary Powers of Prison Administration

16.31 When it comes to the discretionary powers that prison administrators are granted over prisoners' everyday lives, powers to segregate, classify, or transfer, we witness a much more limited level of judicial intervention.

16.32 As was noted earlier the courts have shown a willingness to extend their jurisdiction over such powers, notably in the *Hague* case. However, when it comes to defining the legitimate scope of such powers, and by extension the legitimate scope of prisoners' rights to challenge their exercise, there has been a reluctance to import any procedural requirements, let alone any substantive guidelines. Thus it has been indicated that prisoners have no right to any form of hearing in respect of decisions to transfer either between prisons[46] or between jurisdictions,[47] segregate,[48] or remove their babies from the prison.[49] All of these decisions may have a major impact on the lives of prisoners and often also on the lives of their families. Yet the courts seem to have accepted the view that there is a need for swift, decisive, and sometimes secret action to maintain security and order within the prison and that a greater level of process would unduly inhibit this. Only in respect of security classifications has there been a break with the idea that such internal discretionary powers can be exercised free from the opportunity for the prisoner to make an input. However there, as the decision in *Ex p Duggan*[50] makes clear, it is the impact that classification has on release which has triggered a heightened level of judicial scrutiny. This brings the exercise of this power within the same ambit as disciplinary hearings and lifer release procedures as impacting on the prisoner's interest in not being arbitrarily detained longer than the sentencing court ordered. This is an interest the courts have shown themselves willing to protect.

16.33 That prisoners may not have a hearing in respect of what are seen as purely 'internal' matters does not mean that the administration may act arbitrarily in making

---

[46] See *R v Home Secretary, ex p McAvoy* [1984] 1 WLR 1408.
[47] See *R v Home Secretary, ex p McComb*, The Times, 15 April 1991.
[48] See *Williams v Home Secretary (No 2)* [1982] 1 All ER 1811.
[49] *R v Home Secretary, ex p Hickling* [1986] 1 FLR 543; *R v Home Secretary, ex p Togher*, 1 February 1995.
[50] *R v Home Secretary, ex p Duggan* [1994] 3 All ER 277.

them. The courts have indicated that they will strike down exercises of discretionary power where they go beyond the scope of the powers granted or result in a decision which is clearly unreasonable. However a decision such as that in *R v Home Secretary, ex p McAvoy*[51] indicates how unlikely it is that such a conclusion will ever be reached. There the Divisional Court indicated that it could look at the Home Secretary's decision to transfer a prisoner to another prison and decide whether it was one no reasonable Secretary of State would have made. Once the Home Secretary indicated that the decision was made for 'operational and security' reasons the court swiftly ended its inquiry in his favour. Yet, as one commentator has noted, 'given the nature of the subject matter, it will not be difficult for the Home Office, quite fairly, to characterize all movement of prisoners as being for either operational or security reasons. Indeed, so broad are these criteria that it is hard to visualize such a move being made on any other basis.'[52]

These decisions suggest a strong reluctance to interfere with the exercise of discretionary administrative powers in the prison context. As we have seen throughout this book the statutory framework currently confers broad discretion on prison administrators. Until the passing of the HRA there has been no countervailing code of constitutional or statutory rights of prisoners which judges might invoke to limit the exercise of such discretion. Although the doctrine of legitimate expectation might have offered a promising avenue to constrain the making and execution of policy in respect of such discretionary powers, this has been left in a state of some uncertainty after the *Hargreaves* case.[53] That the courts have failed to give strong effect to notions of legitimate expectations in the prison context is particularly disappointing given that there is significant evidence that prisoners see disregard of declared rules or their sudden change as key to undermining the legitimacy of prison administration.[54]   **16.34**

Prisoners' Living Conditions

While the cases in the categories discussed above refer to situations where the State makes decisions which affect prisoners' lives, those in this category reflect situations where the State has failed to act. Complaints relating to overcrowding or insanitary conditions, inadequate medical treatment, or a lack of safety often allege neglect and lack of action by the State. Perhaps because of a traditional   **16.35**

---

[51] [1984] 1 WLR 1408.
[52] See C Gearty, 'The Prisons and the Courts' in J Muncie and R Sparks (eds), *Imprisonment: European Perspectives* (London, 1991) 228.
[53] *R v Home Secretary, ex p Hargreaves* [1997] 1 All ER 397.
[54] This is one of the themes of the Woolf Report and also of R Sparks, A Bottoms, and W Hay, *Prisons and the Problem of Order* (Oxford, 1996), esp 335.

reluctance to impose affirmative duties on the State, prisoners' claims in this area have met with little success. Hence claims relating to medical treatment in *Freeman* and *Knight*[55] were unsuccessful and suggest a lack of willingness in the courts to concern themselves with issues of medical treatment in prison, which have been the subject of extensive discussion among doctors and prison reform groups. The negligence cases relating to prisoner assaults[56] largely demonstrate that the courts' sympathies lie initially with the difficult task of the authorities. Only where clear warning signs have been ignored or where the authorities have been grossly neglectful have prisoners been able to recover in respect of assaults committed by other prisoners. The courts do not appear to see themselves as having a role of encouraging prison administrators to review their approach to ensuring prisoner safety.[57]

16.36 Perhaps most disturbing in this area has been judicial reluctance to respond to prisoner claims of inhuman and degrading living conditions. We observed in Chapters 2 and 5 that there are significant procedural hurdles to bringing a conditions case before the British courts. Nevertheless ways have been found to present conditions issues to the judiciary, which have effectively discouraged further efforts. Perhaps the worst example of such judicial passivity occurred in the *Williams* case[58] and exhibited deference to actions of the authorities which even they came to understand as indefensible. The narrow, possibly very narrow, scope for judicial intervention in respect of 'intolerable' conditions that was sketched out by the House of Lords in the *Hague* case does not hold out too much hope for those seeking to change inhuman and degrading prison conditions by way of court action. If the views of Lord Goff in that decision prevail then conditions suits will probably only be available where the treatment of the prisoner is such as to justify a finding of negligence, an approach which will require some evidence of physical injury. Lord Bridge suggested a broader basis for claims of intolerable conditions but in seeming to permit negligence claims without proof of injury it lacks much support in precedent. Only in the *Herbage* case[59] has there been clear judicial endorsement for the idea that inhuman conditions, however they have occurred, are a matter of judicial concern. Even then this was in a case primarily concerned with discovery and the court had no need to give any indication of what steps it would be prepared to take to remedy a set of conditions that amounted to cruel and unusual punishment.

---

[55] See *Freeman v Home Office* [1984] 1 All ER 1036 and *Knight v Home Office* [1990] 3 All ER 237.

[56] See, eg, *Ellis v Home Office* [1953] 2 QB 135; *Egerton v Home Office* [1978] Crim LR 494; and *Palmer v Home Office*, The Guardian, 31 March 1988.

[57] Courts in the US, by including issues of safety and staffing levels in injunctions relating to Eighth Amendment prison conditions claims, have addressed these issues. Arguably they have also been faced by considerably higher levels of violence in American prisons.

[58] [1981] 1 All ER 1211.

[59] [1987] QB 1077.

Given the existence of an Article 3 prohibition on torture and inhuman or degrad-   **16.37**
ing treatment and punishment, one might expect the Strasbourg institutions to be
rather more forthright in tackling unsatisfactory living conditions in prisons.
Until recently however they had shown little enthusiasm for tackling prison
conditions, frequently repeating the mantra that certain conditions were the
inevitable consequence of imprisonment. With decisions such as those in *Peers*
and *Kalashnikov*, albeit dealing with appalling overcrowding or neglect, there is an
indication that the ECtHR is becoming prepared to be more prescriptive about
minimum conditions of imprisonment in Europe.

However, although the judiciary can claim little credit for it, conditions in   **16.38**
Britain's prisons have improved in the course of the 1990s. The ending of slopping
out in 1996 was a major breakthrough and the spectacle of prisoners being held
three to a cell designed for one has also been banished, though perhaps only temporarily given the rising prison population. Clearly the steady and well publicized
stream of reports from the Chief Inspector of Prisons condemning living conditions in prisons has had an impact on this, as has the damning observations of the
European Committee for the Prevention of Torture (CPT) in its first UK report
in 1990. The exact extent to which these influences played a role in the
Government's decision to embark upon an extensive programme of prison building and refurbishment in the 1990s will perhaps never be known, but it does offer
some support for the argument that non-judicial mechanisms may have an even
more significant role to play in relation to prison conditions.

The Human Rights Act and the Future of Judicial Intervention

Judges therefore have not intervened in a uniform way in prison life. Rather, the   **16.39**
more the issue relates in some way to deprivation of liberty the more willing they
have been to lay down procedures and standards. The more it looks like an issue
of prison management the more they have exhibited deference to the administration and a reluctance to uphold prisoners' claims. Such caution about reaching
too deeply into the internal administration of prisons is very understandable.
Judges may claim that they lack the expertise and information to set standards and
monitor performance as regards prison administration. Freed from the context of
litigation, though, members of the judiciary, such as Judge Tumim and Lord
Woolf, have made significant contributions to the debate on how prisons should
be treating prisoners.

Judges in the United Kingdom might also argue that the experience of the United   **16.40**
States, where the judiciary has intervened on a more extensive scale, has not been
a universally happy one. The federal judiciary in the United States has played a
prominent role in establishing procedures and standards to govern broad areas of
prison life. At its most extensive such intervention has placed individual prisons
or entire State prison systems under judicial supervision in the name of protecting

prisoners' constitutional rights. However, a fierce debate now rages whether such intervention has crossed the boundary that separates judicial from legislative action and whether the legitimacy of judicial action has thereby been undermined. Commentators also debate whether such intervention has produced more humane prison conditions or whether it has led to a breakdown in authority in prisons and an increase in violence perpetrated against both prison officers and other prisoners.

16.41 We have always argued in this book that there are good reasons for a significant level of judicial supervision of what happens in prisons. These lie in the fact that prisoners are, in the words of Chief Justice Stone of the US Supreme Court, a 'discrete and insular minority'.[60] Prisoners are not a popular political cause and it is therefore unlikely that their interests will receive much of a hearing in the political sphere. Politicians, in the United Kingdom as elsewhere, spend a fair amount of time discussing who should go to prison and for what, but much less time on what happens once they get there. The one time that prisons do force their way on to the political agenda is when a major disturbance occurs, a fact not lost on some prisoners. This suggests that leaving everything to the accountability of the Home Secretary to Parliament is a particularly weak safeguard of prisoners' interests. Courts are well placed to correct this deficit in accountability. They can do this without taking over the running of prisons, but instead by assisting the development of clearer standards and procedures within the prison that allow for effective prison management without sacrificing the principle that deprivation of liberty is sufficient punishment for an offender. An American writer, Susan Sturm, reviewing the American experience of judicial intervention, argues that judges who take on the function of being a 'catalyst' for change which enlists the participation of staff and prisoners in making changes are more likely to produce healthy and lasting changes than those who seek to 'direct' all changes themselves.[61]

16.42 The introduction of the HRA appeared to offer such an opportunity for an enhanced judicial role, especially as most of the 'law' governing prisons is not contained in primary legislation and hence can be overturned by the courts if it is not in conformity with the ECHR. The Act offered the opportunity of giving more detail to the 'rights' which Lord Wilberforce suggested were not lost upon conviction in a more concrete way than seemed available in the common law. Moreover some of the most significant developments in prisoners' rights law, notably as regards access and life sentence release procedures, had come about as regards Strasbourg decisions on the interpretation of the ECHR. However it was also arguable that the broad Convention standards were capable of being interpreted in a way that allowed authorities significantly to restrict the rights of those

---

[60] See n 4 to *US v Carolene Products* 304 US 144 (1938), 152–153.
[61] S Sturm, 'Resolving the Remedial Dilemma: Strategies of Judicial Intervention in Prisons' (1990) 138 U of Pennsylvania L Rev 805.

in prisons and that, in any case, the high water mark of the application of the Convention to the circumstances of prisoners had already been reached.

This was certainly the view the Prison Service took. There was no move for a new **16.43** Prison Act, few changes to the Prison Rules and the Prison Service undertook less training in the HRA than did the police and other parts of the public sector.[62] Initially their views would appear to have been vindicated. There has not been a 'flood' of prison cases coming before the courts under the HRA. Those cases where prisoners have prevailed invoking the new Act, such as *Daly*, are in areas such as legal correspondence where the courts have shown vigilance for the past 20 years when it comes to prisoners' rights. The areas where prisoners have been unsuccessful, such as in respect of artificial insemination, have related to discretionary powers with which the courts have always been reluctant to interfere, especially if countervailing security considerations have been raised. At the very least the introduction of the HRA has checked what some feared as a regressive trend in prisoners' rights litigation,[63] but perhaps most interesting is the fact that the ECtHR still remains more progressive on issues of prisoners' rights than its domestic equivalents. Probably the two most significant prisoners' cases of the past five years, *Stafford* and *Ezeh and Connors,* overturn decisions reached in the English courts after the HRA was introduced.

However it is unlikely that this will always be the case. Experience from other juris- **16.44** dictions, notably Canada, is that lawyers and courts may take a few years to become used to a new set of fundamental rights but will thereafter begin to explore their potential in new and creative ways. They are likely then to focus on finding a legal response to what is the most pressing issue of the time. In UK prisons this looks set for the next few years to be significant overcrowding and the consequent problems it brings, such as lack of opportunities for prisoners and increasing threats to prisoner safety. We may therefore see greater interest in the use of the Article 3 obligation to prevent torture, inhuman or degrading treatment or punishment. In recent years the ECtHR has begun to give more precise content to this obligation, particularly as regards prison conditions. In doing so it has drawn on the standards established by the CPT. Such standards are especially valuable as, whereas deriving rights for prisoners from general human rights law is often a matter of determining to what extent the right survives restrictions in the prison context, these are designed specifically for that context. They thus offer positive rights for prisoners which, as Genevra Richardson has argued,[64] may be the best way to take forward rights in the prison environment. Standards such as those of the CPT or the

---

[62] See Prison Reform Trust, *Prison Report* (September 2000) 2.

[63] See JM Schone 'The Short Life and Painful Death of Prisoners' Rights' (2001) 40 Howard J of Criminal Justice 70.

[64] See G Richardson, 'Prisoners and the Law: Beyond Rights' in C McCrudden and G Chambers (eds), *Individual Rights and the Law in the United Kingdom* (Oxford, 1993), ch 6; also D Van Zyl Smit, *South African Prison Law and Practice* (Durban, 1992) 65–67.

UN Body of Principles on all Persons Subject to Detention are not binding law in themselves but lawyers and courts may draw upon them to give content to more vague and general provisions such as the right to protection from degrading treatment or the right to free expression. As they are standards drawn up over a period of years by international bodies with wide experience of the challenges faced by prison authorities they may be less vulnerable to the backlash that judicial activism in the prison context experienced in the United States. However even success in this area may not alter the fact that prisons remain overcrowded and leave the United Kingdom with the same question which has faced policy makers in the United States over recent years, whether to comply with human rights standards by reducing the prison population or by building more new prisons.

D. The Impact of Judicial Intervention on Prison Life

16.45 At a formal level it is clear that the willingness of the courts to examine the lawfulness of actions by the prison authorities has had a significant impact. Earlier chapters of this book detail the legal changes that have come about since the courts renounced their 'hands off' policy with respect to prisons. There has been a complete overhaul of the prison disciplinary system. The procedures for deciding on the release of discretionary life sentence prisoners were comprehensively altered by the Criminal Justice Act 1991 and those for the release of mandatory life sentence prisoners have subsequently been subject to substantial change. Both the Prison Rules and Prison Service Orders regarding correspondence and, in particular, communications with lawyers have been rewritten on several occasions. The procedures regarding security classification, inter prison transfers and removal from association have all been significantly modified. Prisoners are now allowed to marry.

16.46 Not all of these changes have been reflected in primary or even secondary legislation. The Prison Act remains substantially the same as it was in 1952 and while there have been many detailed changes to the Prison Rules the basic format remains that of the 1964 Rules.[65] Most have found expression in changes to the Orders, Instructions, and Manuals which play such a central role in the daily life of prison administration. However it is less clear to what extent judicial intervention has altered the informal culture of prison life, to what extent the law plays an important role as opposed to government policy, staffing disputes, or prisoner disturbances, to name but three other factors. This is something that lawyers have generally paid less attention to in the United Kingdom.[66] What anecdotal evid-

---

[65] Northern Ireland adopted a new set of Rules in 1995.

[66] For an exception see G Richardson and M Sunkin, 'Judicial Review: Questions of Impact' [1996] PL 79. In the US such research is better developed. For a flavour of this debate see the books reviewed in S Rhodes, 'Prison Reform and Prison Life: Four Books on the Process of Court Ordered Change' (1992) 26 L and Society Rev 189.

ence there is suggests that prison staff and officials are more aware of the risk of legal challenge to their actions.[67] There is much talk of 'The Judge Over Your Shoulder'[68] and, following criticism of the early release of prisoners on erroneous legal advice in 1996, the Prison Service has undertaken a review of its needs with respect to legal services. Prisoners are also clearly more aware of the possibility of resorting to law and may see even unsuccessful legal actions as an empowering experience, one that puts them on a more equal plane with the prison authorities.[69] However a recent study of the use of powers to maintain order in prison, powers which have been the subject of significant legal scrutiny, suggests that compliance with legal requirements remains a fairly marginal concern in the minds of decision makers.[70]

Managerialism and Law

Nevertheless there are reasons for believing that law and the culture of legalism may become increasingly significant factors in prison administration in years to come. These lie in the changing character of prisons and prison regimes themselves. Of the four styles of prison regime outlined by Ditchfield the authoritarian is largely regarded as having had its day. It is seen as out of touch with a more avowedly egalitarian society, often brutalizing of both prisoners and staff, and frequently unworkable in practice. Prisons can only be run with some degree of co-operation from prisoners. The shared powers or reformative model has also substantially been discredited, its main failing being that there was little evidence that it produced any greater reduction in recidivism rates than was found in respect of prisoners emerging from more authoritarian regimes.[71] As the inmate control model remains largely the preserve of science fiction writers and the nightmare of prison administrators attention is increasingly focused on the bureaucratic-lawful or, in more recent vocabulary, 'managerialist', approach to prison regimes. This is a more modest approach which concerns itself with setting clear targets and objectives for the organization, identifying means to achieve these and instituting mechanisms for assessing whether they have been achieved.[72] Often, as this approach is concerned with setting aggregate targets and assessing the degree to which they are reached, it can seem that there is little concern with the fate of

16.47

---

[67] Former Director-General Derek Lewis observed that much of the time of deputy secretaries' meetings in the Home Office was taken up with discussion of the Home Secretary's prospects in forthcoming legal actions. D Lewis, *Hidden Agendas: Politics, Law and Disorder* (London, 1997) 35.
[68] Following a Cabinet Office publication of this name in 1987.
[69] See L Taylor, 'Bringing Power to Particular Account: Peter Rajah and the Hull Board of Visitors' in P Carlen and R Collinson (eds), *Radical Issues in Criminology* (London, 1980) 28.
[70] See R Sparks, A Bottoms and W Hay, *Prisons and the Problem of Order* (Oxford, 1996) 270.
[71] See the discussion in R Martinson, 'What Works? Questions and Answers About Prison Reform' (1974) 35 Public Interest 22.
[72] eg the Prison Service's Key Performance Indicators on *average* time out of cell or hours spent in useful activity *per* prisoner.

the individual, something the law generally takes great interest in. However managerialism, perhaps reflecting its origins in the private sector, also has a side which stresses the importance of delivering services to the consumer, including the prisoner.[73] As Bottoms observes, there is no reason why respect for rights may not be built into the objectives which the Prison Service seeks to achieve, even if the predominantly instrumentalist character of managerialism may naturally incline to a disregard of rights with respect to the means adopted to achieve objectives.[74]

16.48 At the very least, though, managerialism is much less likely to be hostile to legal intervention and a culture of legalism than other approaches to prison management. Whereas authoritarian and reform styles may view notions of compliance with externally imposed standards to uphold prisoners' rights with some hostility, managerialism has much less difficulty in accommodating this. Operating in accordance with pre-established standards and respecting the rights of those on the receiving end to see those standards met is not alien to this approach to prison administration.[75] This does not mean that the increasing prevalence of managerialism will dissolve tensions between the prisons and the courts. There will remain conflicts over what rights or objectives the prison should give effect to and to what extent. Moreover, as with all approaches to prison management, there will be times when theory and practice diverge and someone will need to provide a remedy for prisoners when the authorities fail to respect declared commitments.[76] Nor does it mean that managerialism is enshrined for all time. It remains vulnerable to gusts of populist opinion demanding a vaguely defined return to 'austere prisons' and to the more deeply rooted problem that it does not provide much by way of an explanation of why punishment occurs or what it hopes to achieve.[77] In the immediate future however this approach to imprisonment seems secure, and with the strengthening of legal values achieved by the HRA the stage is set for a more fruitful relationship of law and the prison than has prevailed for much of the last century.

---

[73] These different aspects of managerialist philosophy in criminal justice are developed in A Bottoms, 'The Philosophy and Politics of Punishment and Sentencing' in C Clarkson and R Morgan (eds), *The Politics of Sentencing Reform* (Oxford, 1995) 24–34.

[74] ibid, 33.

[75] In his study of prison administration over 50 years in one American prison Jacobs concludes that the managerialist regime adopted towards the end of his study 'might succeed where traditional and reform administrations had failed because it was capable of handling the greatly increased demands for rationality and accountability coming from the courts and the political system': J Jacobs, *Stateville: The Penitentiary in Mass Society* (Chicago, Ill, 1977) 209.

[76] Although this will often be someone like the Prison Ombudsman rather than the courts.

[77] A problem discussed further by J Simon and M Feeley, 'True Crime: The New Penology and Public Discourse on Crime' in T Blomberg and S Cohen (eds), *Punishment and Social Control: Essays in Honor of Sheldon L Messinger* (New York, 1995) 147, 171–172.

APPENDICES

APPENDIX 1

Prison Act 1952

(15 & 16 Geo 6 and 1 Eliz 2 c 52)

An Act to consolidate certain enactments relating to prisons and other institutions for offenders and relates matters with corrections and improvements made under the Consolidation of Enactments (Procedure) Act 1949

[1 August 1952]

Central administration

General control over prisons

1. All powers and jurisdiction in relation to prisons and prisoners which before the commencement of the Prison Act 1877 were exercisable by any other authority shall, subject to the provisions of this Act, be exercisable by the Secretary of State.

2. (*Repealed by the Prison Commissioners Dissolution Order 1963, SI 1963/597.*)

Officers and servants of Prison Commissioners

3.—(1) The Secretary of State [may, for the purposes of this Act, appoint such officers and [employ such other persons] as he] may, with the sanction of the Treasury as to number, determine.

(2) There shall be paid out of moneys provided by Parliament to [the officers and servants appointment under this section] such salaries as the Secretary of State may with the consent of the Treasury determine.

General duties of Prison Commissioners

4.—(1) [The Secretary of State] shall have the general superintendence of prisons and shall make the contracts and do the other acts necessary for the maintenance of prisons and the maintenance of prisoners.

(2) [Officers of the Secretary of State duly authorised in that behalf] shall visit all prisons and examine the state of buildings, the conduct of officers, the treatment and conduct of prisoners and all other matters concerning the management of prisons and shall ensure that the provisions of this Act and of any rules made under this Act are duly complied with.

(3) [The Secretary of State and his officers] may exercise all powers and jurisdiction exercisable at common law, by Act of Parliament, or by charter by visiting justices of a prison.

Annual report of Prison Commissioners

5.—[(1) The Secretary of State shall issue an annual report on every prison and shall lay every such report before Parliament.]

(2) The report shall contain—
  (a) a statement of the accommodation of each prison and the daily average and highest number of prisoners confined therein;
  (b) such particulars of the work done by prisoners in each prison, including the kind and quantities of articles produced and the number of prisoners employed, as may in the opinion of the Secretary of State give the best information to Parliament;
  (c) a statement of the punishment inflicted in each prison and of the offences for which they were inflicted . . .

Appointment and functions of her Majesty's Chief Inspector of Prisons

[5A.—(1) Her Majesty may appoint a person to be Chief Inspector of Prisons.

(2) It shall be the duty of the Chief Inspector to inspect or arrange for the inspection of prisons in England and Wales and to report to the Secretary of State on them.

(3) The Chief Inspector shall in particular report to the Secretary of State on the treatment of prisoners and conditions in prisons.

(4) The Secretary of State may refer specific matters connected with prisons in England and Wales and prisoners in them to the Chief Inspector and direct him to report on them.

(5) The Chief Inspector shall in each year submit to the Secretary of State a report in such form as the Secretary of State may direct, and the Secretary of State shall lay a copy of that report before Parliament.

(6) The Chief Inspector shall be paid such salary and allowances as the Secretary of State may with the consent of the Treasury determine.]

Visiting committees and boards of visitors

Visiting committees and boards of visitors

6.—(1) . . .

(2) The Secretary of State shall appoint for every prison . . . a board of visitors of whom not less than two shall be justices of the peace.

(3) Rules made as aforesaid shall prescribe the functions of . . . boards of visitors and shall among other things require members to pay frequent visits to the prison and hear any complaints which may be made by the prisoners and report to the Secretary of State any matter which they consider it expedient to report; and any member of a . . . board of visitors may at any time enter the prison and shall have free access to every part of it and to every prisoner,

(4) . . .

Prison officers

Prison Officers

7.—(1) Every prison shall have a governor, a chaplain and a medical officer and such other officers as may be necessary.

(2) Every prison in which women are received shall have a sufficient number of women officers; . . .

(3) A prison which in the opinion of the Secretary of State is large enough to require it may have a deputy governor or an assistant chaplain or both.

(4) The chaplain and any assistant chaplain shall be a clergyman of the Church of England and the medical officer shall be duly registered under the Medical Acts.

(5) . . .

Powers of prison officers

8. Every prison officer while acting as such shall have all the powers, authority, protection and privileges of a constable.

Powers of search by authorised employees

[8A.—(1) An authorised employee at a prison shall have the power to search any prisoner for the purpose of ascertaining whether he has any authorised property on his person.

(2) An authorised employee searching a prisoner by virtue of this section—
  (a) shall not be entitled to require the prisoner to remove any of his clothing other than an outer coat, jacket, headgear, gloves and footwear;
  (b) may use reasonable force where necessary; and
  (c) may seize and detain any unauthorised property found on the prisoner in the course of the search.

(3) In this section 'authorised employee' means an employee of a description for the time being authorised by the governor to exercise the powers conferred by this section.

(4) The governor of a prison shall take such steps as he considers appropriate to notify to prisoners the descriptions of persons who are for the time being authorised to exercise the powers conferred by this section.

(5) In this section 'unauthorised property', in relation to a prisoner, means property which the prisoner is not authorised by prison rules or by the governor to have in his possession, or as the case may be, in his possession in a particular part of the prison.]

Exercise of office of chaplain

9.—(1) A person shall not officiate as chaplain of two prisons unless the prisons are within convenient distance of each other and are together designed to receive not more than one hundred prisoners.

(2) Notice of the nomination of a chaplain or assistant chaplain to a prison shall, within one month after it is made, be given to the bishop of the diocese in which the prison

is situate; and the chaplain or assistant chaplain shall not officiate in the prison except under the authority of a licence from the bishop.

Appointment of prison ministers

10.—(1) Where in any prison the number of prisoners who belong to a religious denomination other than the Church of England is such as in the opinion of the Secretary of State to require the appointment of a minister of that denomination, the Secretary of State may appoint such a minister to that prison.

(2) The Secretary of State may pay a minister appointed under the preceding subsection such remuneration as he thinks reasonable.

(3) [The Secretary of State] may allow a minister of any denomination other than the Church of England to visit prisoners of his denomination in a prison to which no minister of that denomination has been appointed under this section.

(4) No prisoner shall be visited against his will by such a minister as is mentioned in the last preceding subsection; but every prisoner not belonging to the Church of England shall be allowed, in accordance with the arrangements in force in the prison in which he is confined, to attend chapel or to be visited by the chaplain.

(5) The governor of a prison shall on the reception of each prisoner record the religious denomination to which the prisoner declares himself to belong, and shall give to any minister who under this section is appointed to the prison or permitted to visit prisoners therein a list of the prisoners who have declared themselves to belong to his denomination; and the minister shall not be permitted to visit any other prisoners.

Ejectment of prison officers and their families refusing to quit

11.—(1) Where any living accommodation is provided for a prison officer or his family by virtue of his office, then, if he ceased to be a prison officer or is suspended from office or dies, he, or, as the case may be, his family, shall quit the accommodation when required to do so by notice of [the Secretary of State].

(2) Where a prison officer or the family of a prison officer refuses or neglects to quit the accommodation forty-eight hours after the giving of such a notice as aforesaid, any two justices of the peace, on proof made to them of the facts authorising the giving of the notice and of the service of the notice and of the neglect or refusal to comply therewith, may, by warrant under their hands and seals, direct any constable, within a period specific in the warrant, to enter by force, if necessary, into the accommodation and deliver possession of it to [a person acting on behalf of the Secretary of State].

Confinement and treatment of prisoners

Place of confinement of prisoners

12.—(1) A prisoner, whether sentenced to imprisonment or committed to prison on remand or pending trial or otherwise, may be lawfully confined in any prison.

(2) Prisoners shall be committed to such prisons as the Secretary of State may from time to time direct; and may by direction of the Secretary of State be removed during the term of their imprisonment from the prison in which they are confined to any other prison.

(3) A writ, warrant or other legal instrument addressed to the governor of a prison and identifying that prison by its situation or by any other sufficient description shall not be invalidated by reason only that the prison is usually known by a different description.

Legal custody of prisoner

13.—(1) Every prisoner shall be deemed to be in the legal custody of the governor of the prison.

(2) A prisoner shall be deemed to be in legal custody while he is confined in, or is being taken to or from, any prison and while he is working, or is for any other reason, outside the prison in the custody or under the control of an officer of the prison [and while he is being taken to any place to which he is required or authorised by or under this Act [or the Criminal Justice Act 1982] to be taken or is kept in custody in pursuance of any such requirement or authorisation.]

Cells

14.—(1) The Secretary of State shall satisfy himself from time to time that in every prison sufficient accommodation is provided for all prisoners.

(2) No cell shall be used for the confinement of a prisoner unless it is certified by an inspector that its size, lighting, heating, ventilation and fittings are adequate for health and that it allows the prisoner to communicate at any time with a prison officer.

(3) A certificate given under this section in respect of any cell may limit the period for which a prisoner may be separately confined in the cell and the number of hours a day during which a prisoner may be employed therein.

(4) The certificate shall identify the cell to which it relates by a number or mark and the cell shall be marked by that number or mark placed in a conspicuous position; and if the number or mark is changed without the consent of an inspector the certificate shall cease to have effect.

(5) An inspector may withdraw a certificate given under this section in respect of any cell if in his opinion the conditions of the cell are no longer as stated in the certificate.

(6) In every prison special cells shall be provided for the temporary confinement of refractory or violent prisoners.

15. (*Repealed by the Criminal Justice Act 1967, ss 66(2), 103(2), Sch 7, Pt I.*)

Photographing and measuring of prisoners

16. The Secretary of State may make regulations as to the measuring the photographing of prisoners and such regulations may prescribe the time or times at which and the manner and dress in which prisoners shall be measured and photographed and the number of copies of the measurements and photographs of each prisoner which shall be made and the persons to whom they shall be sent.

Testing prisoners for drugs

[**16A.**—(1) If an authorisation is in force for the prison, any prison officer may, at the prison, in accordance with prison rules, require any prisoner who is confined in the prison to provide a sample of urine for the purpose of ascertaining whether he has any drug in his body.

(2) If the authorisation so provides, the power conferred by subsection (1) above shall include power to require the prisoner to provide a sample of any other description specified in the authorisation, not being an intimate sample, whether instead of or in addition to a sample of urine.

(3) In this section—
    'authorisation' means an authorisation by the governor;
    'drug' means any drug which is a controlled drug for the purposes of the Misuse of Drugs Act 1971;

'intimate sample' has the same meaning as in Part V of the Police and Criminal Evidence Act 1984;
'prison officer' includes a prisoner custody officer within the meaning of Part IV of the Criminal Justice Act 1991; and
'prison rules' means rules under section 47 of this Act.]

Power to test prisoners for alcohol

[**16B.**—(1) If an authorisation is in force for the prison, any prison officer may, at the prison, in accordance with prison rules, require any prisoner who is confined in the prison to provide a sample of breath for the purpose of ascertaining whether he has alcohol in his body.

(2) If the authorisation so provides, the power conferred by subsection (1) above shall include power—

(a) to require a prisoner to provide a sample of urine, whether instead of or in addition to a sample of breath, and

(b) to require a prisoner to provide a sample of any other description specified in the authorisation, not being an intimate sample, whether instead of or in addition to a sample of breath, a sample of urine or both.

(3) In this section—
'authorisation' means an authorisation by the governor;
'intimate sample' has the same meaning as in Part V of the Police and Criminal Evidence Act 1984;
'prison officer' includes a prisoner custody officer within the meaning of part IV of the Criminal Justice Act 1991;
'prison rules' means rules under section 47 of this Act.]

Painful tests

17. The medical officer of a prison shall not apply any painful tests to a prisoner for the purpose of detecting malingering or for any other purpose except with the permission of [the Secretary of State] or the visiting committee or, as the case may be, board of visitors.

18. (*Repealed by the Criminal Justice Act 1967, ss 65, 103(2), Sch 7, Pt I.*)

Right of justice to visit prison

19.—(1) A justice of the peace for any county . . . may at any time visit any prison in that county . . . and any prison in which a prisoner is confined in respect of an offence committed in that county . . . , and may examine the condition of the prison and of the prisoners and enter in the visitors' book, to be kept by the governor of the prison, any observations on the condition of the prison or any abuses.

(2) Nothing in the preceding subsection shall authorise a justice of the peace to communicate with any prisoner on the subject of his treatment in the prison, or to visit any prisoner under sentence of death.

(3) The governor of every prison shall bring any entry in the visitors' book to the attention of the visiting committee or the board of visitors at their next visit.

20. (*Repealed by the Courts Act 1971, s 56, Sch 11, Pt IV.*)

Expenses of conveyance to prison

21. A prisoner shall not in any case be liable to pay the cost of his conveyance to prison.

Removal of prisoners for judicial and other purposes

22.—(1) Rules made under section forty-seven of this Act may provide in what manner an appellant within the meaning of [Part I of the Criminal Appeal Act 1968], when in custody, is to be taken to, kept in custody at, or brought back from, any place which he is entitled to be present for the purposes of that Act, or any place to which the Court of Criminal Appeal or any judge thereof may order him to be taken for the purpose of any proceedings of that court.

(2) The Secretary of State may—

(a) ...

(b) if he is satisfied that a person so detained requires [medical investigation or observation or] medical or surgical treatment of any description, direct him to be taken to a hospital or other suitable place for the purpose of the [investigation, observation or] treatment;

and where any person is directed under this subsection to be taken to any place he shall, unless the Secretary of State otherwise directs, be kept in custody while being so taken, while at that place, and while being taken back to the prison in which he is required in accordance with the law to be detained.

Power of constable etc to act outside his jurisdiction

23. For the purpose of taking a person to or from any prison under the order of any authority competent to give the order a constable or other officer may act outside the area of his jurisdiction and shall notwithstanding that he is so acting have all the powers, authority, protection and privileges of his office.

Length of sentence, release on licence and temporary discharge

Calculation of term of sentence

24.—(1) In any sentence of imprisonment the word 'month' shall, unless the contrary is expressed, be construed as meaning calendar month.

(2) ...

25–27. (*S 25(1), (7) repealed by the Criminal Justice Act 1991, s 101(2), Sch 13. Ss 25(2)–(6) repealed by the Criminal Justice Act 1967, s 103(2), Sch 7, Pt 1. Ss 26, 27 repealed by the Criminal Justice Act 1967, s 103(2), Sch 7, Pt I.*)

Power of Secretary of State to discharge prisoners temporarily on account of ill health

28.—(1) If the Secretary of State is satisfied that by reason of the condition of a prisoner's health it is undesirable to detain him in prison, but that, such condition of health being due in whole or in part of the prisoner's own conduct in prison, it is desirable that his release should be temporary and conditional only, the Secretary of State may, if he thinks fit, having regard to all the circumstances of the case, by order authorise the temporary discharge of the prisoner for such period and subject to such conditions as may be stated in the order.

(2) Where an order of temporary discharge is made in the case of a prisoner not under sentence, the order shall contain conditions requiring the attendance of the prisoner at any further proceedings on his case at which his presence may be required.

(3) Any prisoner discharged under this section shall comply with any condition stated in the order of temporary discharge, and shall return to prison at the expiration of the period stated in the order, or of such extended period as may be fixed by any subsequent order of the Secretary of State, and if the prisoner fails so to comply or return, he may be arrested without warrant and taken back to prison.

(4) Where a prisoner under sentence is discharged in pursuance of an order of temporary discharge, the currency of the sentence shall be suspended from the day on which he is discharged from prison under the order of the day on which he is received back into

prison, so that the former day shall be reckoned and the latter shall not be reckoned as part of the sentence.

(5) Nothing in this section shall affect the duties of the medical officer of a prison in respect of a prisoner whom the Secretary of State does not think fit to discharge under this section.

Discharged prisoners

29. (*Repealed by the Criminal Justice Act 1961, ss 21, 41(2), Sch 5.*)

Payments for discharged prisoners

[**30.** The Secretary of State may make such payments to or in respect of persons released or about to be released from prison as he may with the consent of the Treasury determine.]

Provision, maintenance and closing of prisons

Power to provide prisons, etc

33.—(1) The Secretary of State may with the approval of the Treasury alter, enlarge or rebuild any prison and build new prisons.

[(2) The Secretary of State may provide new prisons by declaring to be a prison—
   (a) any building or part of a building built for the purpose or vested in him or under his control; or
   (b) any floating structure or part of such a structure constructed for the purpose or vested in him or under his control.]

(3) A declaration under this section may with respect to the building of part of a building declared to be a prison make the same provisions as an order under the next following section may make with respect to an existing prison.

(4) A declaration under this section may at any time be revoked by the Secretary of State.

(5) A declaration under this section shall not be sufficient to vest the legal estate of any building in the [Secretary of State].

Jurisdiction of sheriff, etc

34.—(1) The transfer under the Prison Act 1877 of prisons and of the powers and jurisdiction of prison authorities and of justices in sessions assembled and visiting justices shall not be deemed to have affected the jurisdiction of any sheriff or coroner or, except to the extent of that transfer, of any justice of the peace or other officer.

(2) The Secretary of State may by order direct that, for the purposes of any enactment, rule of law or custom dependent on a prison being the prison of any county or place, any prison situated in that county or in the county in which that place is situated, or any prison provided by him in pursuance of this Act, shall be deemed to be the prison of that county or place.

[Prison property]

35.—[(1) Every prison and all real and personal property belonging to a prison shall be vested in the Secretary of State and may be disposed of in such manner as the Secretary of State, with the consent of the Treasury, may determine.

(2) For the purposes of this section the Secretary of State shall be deemed to be a corporation sole.

(3) Any instrument in connection with the acquisition, management or disposal of any property to which this section applies may be executed on behalf of the Secretary of

State by an Under-Secretary of State or any other person authorised by the Secretary of State in that behalf; and any instrument purporting to have been so executed on behalf of the Secretary of State shall be deemed, until the contrary is proved, to have been so executed on his behalf.

(4) The last foregoing subsection shall be without prejudice to the execution of any such instrument as aforesaid, or of any other instrument, on behalf of the Secretary of State in any other manner authorised by law.]

Acquisition of land for prisons

36.—(1) [The Secretary of State may purchase by agreement or] compulsorily, any land required for the alteration, enlargement or rebuilding of a prison or for establishing a new prison or for any other purpose connected with the management of a prison (including the provision of accommodation for officers or servants employed in a prison).

[(2) The [Acquisition of Land Act 1981] shall apply to the compulsory purchase of land by the Secretary of State under this section . . .]

(3) In relation to the purchase of land by agreement under this section, [the provisions of Part I of the Compulsory Purchase Act 1965 (so far as applicable) other than sections 4 to 8, section 10, and section 31, shall apply].

Closing of prisons

37.—(1) Subject to the next following subsection, the Secretary of State may by order close any prison.

(2) Where a prison is the only prison in the county, the Secretary of State shall not make an order under this section in respect of it except for special reasons, which shall be stated in the order.

(3) In this section the expression 'county' means a county at large.

(4) For the purposes of this and the next following section a prison shall not be deemed to be closed by reason only of its appropriation for use as a remand centre, detention centre or [youth custody centre] [or secure training centre].

38. (*Repealed by the Criminal Justice Act 1972, ss 59, 64(2), Sch 65, Pt II.*)

Offences

Assisting prisoner to escape

39. Any person who aids any prisoner in escaping or attempting to escape from a prison or who, with intent to facilitate the escape of any prisoner, conveys any thing into a prison or to a prisoner [sends any thing (by post or otherwise) into a prison or to a prisoner] or places any thing anywhere outside a prison with a view to its coming into possession of a prisoner, shall be guilty of felony and liable to imprisonment for a term not exceeding [ten years].

Unlawful conveyance of spirits or tobacco into prison, etc

40. Any person who contrary to the regulations of a prison brings or attempts to bring into the prison or to a prisoner any spirituous or fermented liquor or tobacco, or places any such liquor or any tobacco anywhere outside the prison with intent that it shall come into the possession of a prisoner, and any officer who contrary to those regulations allows any such liquor or any tobacco to be sold or used in the prison, shall be liable on summary conviction to imprisonment for a term not exceeding six months or a fine not exceeding [level 3 on the standard scale] or both.

Unlawful introduction of other articles

41. Any person who contrary to the regulations of a prison conveys or attempts to convey any letter or any other thing into or out of the prison or to a prisoner or places it anywhere outside the prison with intent that it shall come into the possession of a prisoner shall, where he is not thereby guilty of an offence under either of the two last preceding sections, be liable on summary conviction to a fine not exceeding [level 3 on the standard scale].

Display of notice of penalties

42. The Prison Commissioners shall cause to be affixed in a conspicuous place outside every prison a notice of the penalties to which persons committing offences under the three last preceding sections are liable.

Remand centres, detention centres and Borstal institutions

Remand centres, detention centres and youth custody centres

[**43.**—(1) The Secretary of State may provide—
- (a) remand centres, that is to say places for the detention of persons not less than 145 but under 21 years of age who are remanded or committed in custody for trial or sentence;
- [(aa) young offenders institutions, that is to say places for the detention of offenders sentenced to detention in a young offender institution [or to custody for life];]
- (b) ... *and*
- (c) ... [and]
- [(d) secure training centres, that is to say places in which offenders not less than 12 but under 17 years of age in respect of whom secure training orders have been made under section 1 of the Criminal Justice and Public Order Act 1994 may be detained and given training and education and prepared for their release.]

(2) The Secretary of State may from time to time direct—
- (a) that a woman aged 21 years or over who is serving a sentence of imprisonment or who has been committed to prison for default shall be detained in a remand centre or a youth custody centre instead of a prison;
- (b) that a woman aged 21 years or over who is remanded in custody or committed in custody for trial or sentence shall be detained in a remand centre of a prison;
- (c) that a person under 21 but not less than 17 years of age who is remanded in custody or committed in custody for trial or sentence shall be detained in a prison instead of a remand centre or a remand centre instead of a prison, notwithstanding anything in section 27 of the Criminal Justice Act 1948 or section 23(3) of the Children and Young Persons Act 1969.

(3) Notwithstanding subsection (1) above, any person required to be detained in an institution to which this Act applies may be detained in a remand centre for any temporary purpose [and a person [aged 18 years] or over may be detained in such a centre] for the purpose of providing maintenance and domestic services for that centre.

(4) Sections 5A, 6(2) and (3), 16, 22, 25 and 36 of this Act shall apply to remand centres, detention centres and youth custody centres and to persons detained in them as they apply to prisons and prisoners.

[(4A) Sections 16, 22 and 36 of this Act shall apply to secure training centres and to persons detained in them as they apply to prisons and prisoners.]

(5) The other provisions of this Act preceding this section, except sections 28 and 37(2) above, shall apply to [centres of the descriptions specified in subsection (4) above] and to persons detained in them as they apply to prisons and prisoners, but subject to such adaptations and modifications as may be specified in rules made by the Secretary of State.

[(5A) The other provisions of this Act preceding this section, except sections 5, 5A, 6(2) and (3), 12, 14, 19, 25, 28 and 37(2) and (3) above, shall apply to secure training centres and to persons detained in them as they apply to prisons and prisoners, but subject to such adaptations and modifications as may be specified in rules made by the Secretary of State.]

(6) References in the preceding provisions of this Act to imprisonment shall, so far as those provisions apply to institutions provided under this section, be construed as including references to detention in those institutions.

(7) Nothing in this section shall be taken to prejudice the operation of section 12 of the Criminal Justice Act 1982.]

44–46. (*Repealed by the Criminal Justice Act 1982, s 78, Sch 16.*)

Rules for the management of prisons and other institutions

Rules for the management of prisons, remand centres, detention centres and Borstal institutions

47.—(1) The Secretary of State may make rules for the regulation and management of prisons, remand centres[, young offender institutions or secure training centres] respectively, and for the classification, treatment, employment, discipline and control of persons required to be detained therein.

(2) Rules made under this section shall make provision for ensuring that a person who is charged with any offence under the rules shall be given a proper opportunity of presenting his case.

(3) Rules made under this section may provide for the training of particular classes of persons and their allocation for that purpose to any prison or other institution in which they may lawfully be detained.

(4) Rules made under this section shall provide for the special treatment of the following persons whilst required to be detained in a prison, that is to say—

> (a)–(c) . . .
>
> (b) any . . . person detained in a prison, not being a person serving a sentence or a person imprisoned in default of payment of a sum adjudged to be paid by him on his conviction [or a person committed to custody on his conviction].

[(4A) Rules made under this section shall provide for the inspection of secure training centres and the appointment of independent persons to visit secure training centres and to whom representations may be made by offenders detained in secure training centres.]

(5) Rules made under this section may provide for the temporary release of persons [detained in a prison, [remand centre] [, young offender institution or secure training centre], not being persons committed in custody for trial [before the Crown Court] or committed to be sentenced or otherwise dealt with by [the Crown Court] or remanded in custody by any court].

Miscellaneous

48. (*Repealed by the Criminal Justice Act 1961, s 41(2), (3), Sch 5.*)

Persons unlawfully at large

49.—(1) Any person who, having been sentenced to imprisonment, . . . [custody for life or youth custody] or ordered to be detained in a detention centre [or a young offenders institution], or having been committed to a prison or remand centre, is unlawfully at large, may be arrested by a constable without warrant and taken to the place in which he is required in accordance with law to be detained.

(2) Where any person sentenced to imprisonment, . . . or [youth custody], or ordered to be detained in a . . . *detention centre*, is unlawfully at large at any time during the period for which he is liable to be detained in pursuance of the sentence or order, then, unless the Secretary of State otherwise directs, no account shall be taken, in calculating the period for which he is liable to be so detained, of any time during which he is absent from the [place in which he is required in accordance with law to be detained]:

Provided that—

    (a) this subsection shall not apply to any period during which any such person as aforesaid is detained in pursuance of the sentence or order or in pursuance of any other sentence of any court [in the United Kingdom] in a prison, *youth custody centre, remand centre or detention centre*;

    (b), (c) . . .

(3) The provisions of the last preceding subsection shall apply to a person who is detained in custody in default of payment of any sum of money as if he were sentenced to imprisonment.

(4) For the purposes of this section a person who, after being temporarily released in pursuance of rules made under subsection (5) of section forty-seven of this Act, is at large at any time during the period for which he is liable to be detained in pursuance of his sentence shall be deemed to be unlawfully at large if the period for which he was temporarily released has expired or if an order recalling him has been made by the [Secretary of State] in pursuance of the rules.

50. (*Repealed in part by the Children and Young Persons Act 1969, s 72(4), Sch 6; remainder spend upon the repeal of s 18 of this Act by the Criminal Justice Act 1967, ss 65, 103(2), Sch 7, Pt I.*)

Supplemental

Payment of expenses out of moneys provided by Parliament

51. All expenses incurred in the maintenance of prisons and in the maintenance of prisoners and all other expenses of the Secretary of State . . . incurred under this Act shall be defrayed out of moneys provided by Parliament.

Exercise of power to make orders, rules and regulations

52.—(1) Any power of the Secretary of State to make rules or regulations under this Act and the power of the Secretary of State to make an order under section thirty-four or section thirty-seven of this Act shall be exercisable by statutory instrument.

(2) Any statutory instrument containing regulations made under section sixteen or an order made under section thirty-seven of this Act, . . . shall be laid before Parliament.

(3) The power of the Secretary of State to make an order under section six or section thirty-four of this Act shall include power to revoke or vary such an order.

Interpretation

53.—(1) In this Act the following expressions have the following meanings:—

'Attendance centre' means a centre provided by the Secretary of State under [section 16 of the Criminal Justice Act 1982];

'Prison' does not include a naval, military or air force prison; . . .

(2) For the purposes of this Act the maintenance of a prisoner shall include all necessary expenses incurred in respect of the prisoner for food, clothing, custody and removal from one place to another, from the period of his committal to prison until his death or discharge from prison.

(3) References in this Act to the Church of England shall be construed as including references to the Church in Wales.

(4) References in this Act to any enactment shall be construed as references to that enactment as amended by any other enactment.

Consequential amendments, repeals and savings

54.—(1), (2) . . .

(3) Nothing in this repeal shall affect any rule, order, regulation or declaration made, direction or certificate given or thing done under any enactment repealed by this Act and every such rule, order, regulation, direction, certificate or thing shall, if in force at the commencement of this Act, continue in force and be deemed to have been made, given or done under the corresponding provision of this Act.

(4) Any document referring to any Act or enactment repealed by this Act shall be construed as referring to this Act or to the corresponding enactment in this Act.

(5) The mention of particular matters in this section shall not be taken to affect the general application to this Act of section thirty-eight of the Interpretation Act 1889 (which relates to the effect of repeals).

Short title, commencement and extent

55.—(1) This Act may be cited as the Prison Act 1952.

(2) This Act shall come into operation on the first day of October, nineteen hundred and fifty-two.

(3) . . .

(4) Except as provided in . . . [the Criminal Justice Act 1961], this Act shall not extend to Scotland.

(5) This Act shall not extend to Northern Ireland.

(*Schs 1–4 are repealed or spent.*)

APPENDIX 2

The Prison Rules 1999 (SI 1999/728)

as amended by the Prison (Amendment) Rules 2000
(SI 2000/1794), the Prison (Amendment) (No 2) Rules 2000
(SI 2000/2641), and the Prison (Amendment) Rules 2002
(SI 2002/2116)

ARRANGEMENT OF RULES

PART I
INTERPRETATION

General

PART II
PRISONERS

General

Women prisoners

Religion

Medical attention

20. Medical attendance
21. Special illnesses and conditions
22. Notification of illness or death

Physical welfare and work

23. Clothing
24. Food
25. Alcohol and tobacco
26. Sleeping accommodation
27. Beds and bedding
28. Hygiene
29. Physical education
30. Time in the open air
31. Work

Education and library

32. Education
33. Library

Communications

34. Communications generally
35. Personal letters and visits
35A. Interception of communications
35B. Permanent log of communications
35C. Disclosure of material
35D. Retention of material
36. Police interviews
37. Securing release
38. Legal advisers
39. Correspondence with legal advisers and courts

Removal, search, record and property

40. Custody outside prison
41. Search
42. Record and photograph
43. Prisoners' property
44. Money and articles received by post

Control, supervision, restraint and drug testing

45. Removal from association
46. Close supervision centres
47. Use of force
48. Temporary confinement
49. Restraints
50. Compulsory testing for controlled drugs
50A. Observation of prisoners by means of an overt closed circuit television system

Offences against discipline

51. Offences against discipline
51A. Interpretation of rule 51

Part III

Officers of prisons

Part IV

Persons having access to a prison

Part V

Boards of visitors

Part VI

Supplemental

84. Contracted out functions at directly managed prisons
85. Revocations and savings

PART I

Citation and commencement

1. These Rules may be cited as the Prison Rules 1999 and shall come into force on 1st April 1999.

Interpretation

2.—(1) In these Rules, where the context so admits, the expression—

'adjudicator' means a person approved by the Secretary of State for the purpose of inquiring into a charge which has been referred to him;

'communication' includes any written or drawn communication from a prisoner to any other person, whether intended to be transmitted by means of a postal service or not, and any communication from a prisoner to any other person transmitted by means of a telecommunications system;

'controlled drug' means any drug which is a controlled drug for the purposes of the Misuse of Drugs Act 1971;

'convicted prisoner' means, subject to the provisions of rule 7(3), a prisoner who has been convicted or found guilty of an offence or committed or attached for contempt of court or for failing to do or abstain from doing anything required to be done or left undone, and the expression 'unconvicted prisoner' shall be construed accordingly;

'governor' includes an officer for the time being in charge of a prison;

'intercepted material' means the contents of any communication intercepted pursuant to these Rules;

'legal adviser' means, in relation to a prisoner, his counsel or solicitor, and includes a clerk acting on behalf of his solicitor;

'officer' means an officer of a prison and, for the purposes of rule 40(2), includes a prisoner custody officer who is authorised to perform escort functions in accordance with section 89 of the Criminal Justice Act 1991;

'prison minister' means, in relation to a prison, a minister appointed to that prison under section 10 of the Prison Act 1952;

'short-term prisoner' and 'long-term prisoner' have the meanings assigned to them by section 33(5) of the Criminal Justice Act 1991, as extended by sections 43(1) and 45(1) of that Act.

'telecommunications system' means any system (including the apparatus comprised in it) which exists for the purpose of facilitating the transmission of communications by any means involving the use of electrical or electro-magnetic energy.'

(2) In these Rules—

(a) a reference to an award of additional days means additional days awarded under these Rules by virtue of section 42 of the Criminal Justice Act 1991;

(b) a reference to the Church of England includes a reference to the Church in Wales; and

(c) a reference to a numbered rule is, unless otherwise stated, a reference to the rule of that number in these Rules and a reference in a rule to a numbered paragraph is, unless otherwise stated, a reference to the paragraph of that number in that rule.

PART II
PRISONERS

General

Purpose of prison training and treatment

3. The purpose of the training and treatment of convicted prisoners shall be to encourage and assist them to lead a good and useful life.

Outside contacts

4.—(1) Special attention shall be paid to the maintenance of such relationships between a prisoner and his family as are desirable in the best interests of both.

(2) A prisoner shall be encouraged and assisted to establish and maintain such relations with persons and agencies outside prison as may, in the opinion of the governor, best promote the interests of his family and his own social rehabilitation.

After care

5. From the beginning of a prisoner's sentence, consideration shall be given, in consultation with the appropriate after-care organisation, to the prisoner's future and the assistance to be given him on and after his release.

Maintenance of order and discipline

6.—(1) Order and discipline shall be maintained with firmness, but with no more restriction than is required for safe custody and well ordered community life.

(2) In the control of prisoners, officers shall seek to influence them through their own example and leadership, and to enlist their willing co-operation.

(3) At all times the treatment of prisoners shall be such as to encourage their self-respect and a sense of personal responsibility, but a prisoner shall not be employed in any disciplinary capacity.

Classification of prisoners

7.—(1) Prisoners shall be classified, in accordance with any directions of the Secretary of State, having regard to their age, temperament and record and with a view to maintaining good order and facilitating training and, in the case of convicted prisoners, of furthering the purpose of their training and treatment as provided by rule 3.

(2) Unconvicted prisoners:
   (a) shall be kept out of contact with convicted prisoners as far as the governor considers it can reasonably be done, unless and to the extent that they have consented to share residential accommodation or participate in any activity with convicted prisoners; and
   (b) shall under no circumstances be required to share a cell with a convicted prisoner.

(3) Prisoners committed or attached for contempt of court, or for failing to do or abstain from doing anything required to be done or left undone:
   (a) shall be treated as a separate class for the purposes of this rule;
   (b) notwithstanding anything in this rule, may be permitted to associate with any other class of prisoners if they are willing to do so; and
   (c) shall have the same privileges as an unconvicted prisoner under rules 20(5), 23(1) and 35(1).

(4) Nothing in this rule shall require a prisoner to be deprived unduly of the society of other persons.

Privileges

8.—(1) There shall be established at every prison systems of privileges approved by the Secretary of State and appropriate to the classes of prisoners there, which shall include arrangements under which money earned by prisoners in prison may be spent by them within the prison.

(2) Systems of privileges approved under paragraph (1) may include arrangements under which prisoners may be allowed time outside their cells and in association with one another, in excess of the minimum time which, subject to the other provisions of these Rules apart from this rule, is otherwise allowed to prisoners at the prison for this purpose.

(3) Systems of privileges approved under paragraph (1) may include arrangements under which privileges may be granted to prisoners only in so far as they have met, and for so long as they continue to meet, specified standards in their behaviour and their performance in work or other activities.

(4) Systems of privileges which include arrangements of the kind referred to in paragraph (3) shall include procedures to be followed in determining whether or not any of the privileges concerned shall be granted, or shall continue to be granted, to a prisoner; such procedures shall include a requirement that the prisoner be given reasons for any decision adverse to him together with a statement of the means by which he may appeal against it.

(5) Nothing in this rule shall be taken to confer on a prisoner any entitlement to any privilege or to affect any provision in these Rules other than this rule as a result of which any privilege may be forfeited or otherwise lost or a prisoner deprived of association with other prisoners.

Temporary release

9.—(1) The Secretary of State may, in accordance with the other provisions of this rule, release temporarily a prisoner to whom this rule applies.

(2) A prisoner may be released under this rule for any period or periods and subject to any conditions.

(3) A prisoner may only be released under this rule:
- (a) on compassionate grounds or for the purpose of receiving medical treatment;
- (b) to engage in employment or voluntary work;
- (c) to receive instruction or training which cannot reasonably be provided in the prison;
- (d) to enable him to participate in any proceedings before any court, tribunal or inquiry;
- (e) to enable him to consult with his legal adviser in circumstances where it is not reasonably practicable for the consultation to take place in the prison;
- (f) to assist any police officer in any enquiries;
- (g) to facilitate the prisoner's transfer between prisons;
- (h) to assist him in maintaining family ties or in his transition from prison life to freedom; or
- (i) to enable him to make a visit in the locality of the prison, as a privilege under rule 8.

(4) A prisoner shall not be released under this rule unless the Secretary of State is satisfied that there would not be an unacceptable risk of his committing offences whilst released or otherwise failing to comply with any condition upon which he is released.

(5) The Secretary of State shall not release under this rule a prisoner serving a sentence of imprisonment if, having regard to:

(a) the period or proportion of his sentence which the prisoner has served or, in a case where paragraph (10) does not apply to require all the sentences he is serving to be treated as a single term, the period or proportion of any such sentence he has served; and

(b) the frequency with which the prisoner has been granted temporary release under this rule,

the Secretary of State is of the opinion that the release of the prisoner would be likely to undermine public confidence in the administration of justice.

(6) If a prisoner has been temporarily released under this rule during the relevant period and has been sentenced to imprisonment for a criminal offence committed whilst at large following that release, he shall not be released under this rule unless his release, having regard to the circumstances of this conviction, would not, in the opinion of the Secretary of State, be likely to undermine public confidence in the administration of justice.

(7) For the purposes of paragraph (6), 'the relevant period':

(a) in the case of a prisoner serving a determinate sentence of imprisonment, is the period he has served in respect of that sentence, unless, notwithstanding paragraph (10), the sentences he is serving do not fall to be treated as a single term, in which case it is the period since he was last released in relation to one of those sentences under Part II of the Criminal Justice Act 1991 ('the 1991 Act');

(b) in the case of a prisoner serving an indeterminate sentence of imprisonment, is, if the prisoner has previously been released on licence under Part II of the Crime (Sentences) Act 1997 or Part II of the 1991 Act, the period since the date of his last recall to prison in respect of that sentence or, where the prisoner has not been so released, the period he has served in respect of that sentence; or

(c) in the case of a prisoner detained in prison for any other reason, is the period for which the prisoner has been detained for that reason;

save that where a prisoner falls within two or more of sub-paragraphs (a) to (c), the 'relevant period', in the case of that prisoner, shall be determined by whichever of the applicable sub-paragraphs produces the longer period.

(8) A prisoner released under this rule may be recalled to prison at any time whether the conditions of his release have been broken or not.

(9) This rule applies to prisoners other than persons committed in custody for trial or to be sentenced or otherwise dealt with before or by any Crown Court or remanded in custody by any court.

(10) For the purposes of any reference in this rule to a prisoner's sentence, consecutive terms and terms which are wholly or partly concurrent shall be treated as a single term if they would fall to be treated as a single term for the purposes of any reference to the term of imprisonment to which a person has been sentenced in Part II of the 1991 Act.

(11) In this rule:

(a) any reference to a sentence of imprisonment shall be construed as including any sentence to detention or custody; and

(b) any reference to release on licence or otherwise under Part II of the 1991 Act includes any release on licence under any legislation providing for early release on licence.

Information to prisoners

10.—(1) Every prisoner shall be provided, as soon as possible after his reception into prison, and in any case within 24 hours, with information in writing about those provisions of these Rules and other matters which it is necessary that he should know, including earnings and privileges, and the proper means of making requests and complaints.

(2) In the case of a prisoner aged less than 18, or a prisoner aged 18 or over who cannot read or appears to have difficulty in understanding the information so provided, the governor, or an officer deputed by him, shall so explain it to him that he can understand his rights and obligations.

(3) A copy of these Rules shall be made available to any prisoner who requests it.

Requests and complaints

11.—(1) A request or complaint to the governor or board of visitors relating to a prisoner's imprisonment shall be made orally or in writing by the prisoner.

(2) On every day the governor shall hear any requests and complaints that are made to him under paragraph (1).

(3) A written request or complaint under paragraph (1) may be made in confidence.

Women prisoners

Women prisoners

12.—(1) Women prisoners shall normally be kept separate from male prisoners.

(2) The Secretary of State may, subject to any conditions he thinks fit, permit a woman prisoner to have her baby with her in prison, and everything necessary for the baby's maintenance and care may be provided there.

Religion

Religious denomination

13. A prisoner shall be treated as being of the religious denomination stated in the record made in pursuance of section 10(5) of the Prison Act 1952 but the governor may, in a proper case and after due enquiry, direct that record to be amended.

Special duties of chaplains and prison ministers

14.—(1) The chaplain or a prison minister of a prison shall—
   (a) interview every prisoner of his denomination individually soon after the prisoner's reception into that prison and shortly before his release; and
   (b) if no other arrangements are made, read the burial service at the funeral of any prisoner of his denomination who dies in that prison.

(2) The chaplain shall visit daily all prisoners belonging to the Church of England who are sick, under restraint or undergoing cellular confinement; and a prison minister shall do the same, as far as he reasonably can, for prisoners of his denomination.

(3) The chaplain shall visit any prisoner not of the Church of England who is sick, under restraint or undergoing cellular confinement, and is not regularly visited by a minister of his denomination, if the prisoner is willing.

Regular visits by ministers of religion

15.—(1) The chaplain shall visit the prisoners belonging to the Church of England.

(2) A prison minister shall visit the prisoners of his denomination as regularly as he reasonably can.

(3) Where a prisoner belongs to a denomination for which no prison minister has been appointed, the governor shall do what he reasonably can, if so requested by the prisoner, to arrange for him to be visited regularly by a minister of that denomination.

Religious services

16.—(1) The chaplain shall conduct Divine Service for prisoners belonging to the Church of England at least once every Sunday, Christmas Day and Good Friday, and such celebrations of Holy Communion and weekday services as may be arranged.

(2) Prison ministers shall conduct Divine Service for prisoners of their denominations at such times as may be arranged.

Substitute for chaplain or prison minister

17.—(1) A person approved by the Secretary of State may act for the chaplain in his absence.

(2) A prison minister may, with the leave of the Secretary of State, appoint a substitute to act for him in his absence.

Sunday work

18. Arrangements shall be made so as not to require prisoners of the Christian religion to do any unnecessary work on Sunday, Christmas Day or Good Friday, or prisoners of other religions to do any such work on their recognised days of religious observance.

Religious books

19. There shall, so far as reasonably practicable, be available for the personal use of every prisoner such religious books recognised by his denomination as are approved by the Secretary of State for use in prisons.

Medical attention

Medical attendance

20.—(1) The medical officer of a prison shall have the care of the health, mental and physical, of the prisoners in that prison.

(2) Every request by a prisoner to see the medical officer shall be recorded by the officer to whom it is made and promptly passed on to the medical officer.

(3) The medical officer may consult a medical practitioner who is a fully registered person within the meaning of the Medical Act 1983. Such a practitioner may work within the prison under the general supervision of the medical officer.

(4) The medical officer shall consult another medical practitioner, if time permits, before performing any serious operation.

(5) If an unconvicted prisoner desires the attendance of a registered medical practitioner or dentist, and will pay any expense incurred, the governor shall, if he is satisfied that there are reasonable grounds for the request and unless the Secretary of State otherwise directs, allow him to be visited and treated by that practitioner or dentist in consultation with the medical officer.

(6) Subject to any directions given in the particular case by the Secretary of State, a registered medical practitioner selected by or on behalf of a prisoner who is a party to any legal proceedings shall be afforded reasonable facilities for examining him in connection with the proceedings, and may do so out of hearing but in the sight of an officer.

Special illnesses and conditions

21.—(1) The medical officer or a medical practitioner such as is mentioned in rule 20(3) shall report to the governor on the case of any prisoner whose health is likely to be injuriously affected by continued imprisonment or any conditions of imprisonment. The governor shall send the report to the Secretary of State without delay, together with his own recommendations.

(2) The medical officer or a medical practitioner such as is mentioned in rule 20(3) shall pay special attention to any prisoner whose mental condition appears to require it, and make any special arrangements which appear necessary for his supervision or care.

Notification of illness or death

22.—(1) If a prisoner dies, becomes seriously ill, sustains any severe injury or is removed to hospital on account of mental disorder, the governor shall, if he knows his or her address, at once inform the prisoner's spouse or next of kin, and also any person who the prisoner may reasonably have asked should be informed.

(2) If a prisoner dies, the governor shall give notice immediately to the coroner having jurisdiction, to the board of visitors and to the Secretary of State.

Physical welfare and work

Clothing

23.—(1) An unconvicted prisoner may wear clothing of his own if and in so far as it is suitable, tidy and clean, and shall be permitted to arrange for the supply to him from outside prison of sufficient clean clothing:

Provided that, subject to rule 40(3):

    (a) he may be required, if and for so long as there are reasonable grounds to believe that there is a serious risk of his attempting to escape, to wear items of clothing which are distinctive by virtue of being specially marked or coloured or both; and

    (b) he may be required, if and for so long as the Secretary of State is of the opinion that he would, if he escaped, be highly dangerous to the public or the police or the security of the State, to wear clothing provided under this rule.

(2) Subject to paragraph (1) above, the provisions of this rule shall apply to an unconvicted prisoner as to a convicted prisoner.

(3) A convicted prisoner shall be provided with clothing adequate for warmth and health in accordance with a scale approved by the Secretary of State.

(4) The clothing provided under this rule shall include suitable protective clothing for use at work, where this is needed.

(5) Subject to rule 40(3), a convicted prisoner shall wear clothing provided under this rule and no other, except on the directions of the Secretary of State or as a privilege under rule 8.

(6) A prisoner may be provided, where necessary, with suitable and adequate clothing on his release.

Food

24.—(1) Subject to any directions of the Secretary of State, no prisoner shall be allowed, except as authorised by the medical officer or a medical practitioner such as is mentioned in rule 20(3), to have any food other than that ordinarily provided.

(2) The food provided shall be wholesome, nutritious, well prepared and served, reasonably varied and sufficient in quantity.

(3) The medical officer, a medical practitioner such as is mentioned in rule 20(3) or any person deemed by the governor to be competent, shall from time to time inspect the food both before and after it is cooked and shall report any deficiency or defect to the governor.

(4) In this rule 'food' includes drink.

Alcohol and tobacco

25.—(1) No prisoner shall be allowed to have any intoxicating liquor except under a written order of the medical officer or a medical practitioner such as is mentioned in rule 20(3) specifying the quantity and the name of the prisoner.

(2) No prisoner shall be allowed to smoke or to have any tobacco except as a privilege under rule 8 and in accordance with any orders of the governor.

Sleeping accommodation

26.—(1) No room or cell shall be used as sleeping accommodation for a prisoner unless it has been certified in the manner required by section 14 of the Prison Act 1952 in the case of a cell used for the confinement of a prisoner.

(2) A certificate given under that section or this rule shall specify the maximum number of prisoners who may sleep or be confined at one time in the room or cell to which it relates, and the number so specified shall not be exceeded without the leave of the Secretary of State.

Beds and bedding

27. Each prisoner shall be provided with a separate bed and with separate bedding adequate for warmth and health.

Hygiene

28.—(1) Every prisoner shall be provided with toilet articles necessary for his health and cleanliness, which shall be replaced as necessary.

(2) Every prisoner shall be required to wash at proper times, have a hot bath or shower on reception and thereafter at least once a week.

(3) A prisoner's hair shall not be cut without his consent.

Physical education

29.—(1) If circumstances reasonably permit, a prisoner aged 21 years or over shall be given the opportunity to participate in physical education for at least one hour a week.

(2) The following provisions shall apply to the extent circumstances reasonably permit to a prisoner who is under 21 years of age—
  (a) provision shall be made for the physical education of such a prisoner within the normal working week, as well as evening and weekend physical recreation; the physical education activities will be such as foster personal responsibility and the prisoner's interests and skills and encourage him to make good use of his leisure on release; and
  (b) arrangements shall be made for each such prisoner who is a convicted prisoner to participate in physical education for two hours a week on average.

(3) In the case of a prisoner with a need for remedial physical activity, appropriate facilities will be provided.

(4) The medical officer or a medical practitioner such as is mentioned in rule 20(3) shall decide upon the fitness of every prisoner for physical education and remedial physical activity and may excuse a prisoner from, or modify, any such education or activity on medical grounds.

Time in the open air

30. If the weather permits and subject to the need to maintain good order and discipline, a prisoner shall be given the opportunity to spend time in the open air at least once every day, for such period as may be reasonable in the circumstances.

Work

31.—(1) A convicted prisoner shall be required to do useful work for not more than 10 hours a day, and arrangements shall be made to allow prisoners to work, where possible, outside the cells and in association with one another.

(2) The medical officer or a medical practitioner such as is mentioned in rule 20(3) may excuse a prisoner from work on medical grounds, and no prisoner shall be set to do work which is not of a class for which he has been passed by the medical officer or by a medical practitioner such as is mentioned in rule 20(3) as being fit.

(3) No prisoner shall be set to do work of a kind not authorised by the Secretary of State.

(4) No prisoner shall work in the service of another prisoner or an officer, or for the private benefit of any person, without the authority of the Secretary of State.

(5) An unconvicted prisoner shall be permitted, if he wishes, to work as if he were a convicted prisoner.

(6) Prisoners may be paid for their work at rates approved by the Secretary of State, either generally or in relation to particular cases.

Education and library

Education

32.—(1) Every prisoner able to profit from the education facilities provided at a prison shall be encouraged to do so.

(2) Educational classes shall be arranged at every prison and, subject to any directions of the Secretary of State, reasonable facilities shall be afforded to prisoners who wish to do so to improve their education by training by distance learning, private study and recreational classes, in their spare time.

(3) Special attention shall be paid to the education and training of prisoners with special educational needs, and if necessary they shall be taught within the hours normally allotted to work.

(4) In the case of a prisoner of compulsory school age as defined in section 8 of the Education Act 1996, arrangements shall be made for his participation in education or training courses for at least 15 hours a week within the normal working week.

Library

33. A library shall be provided in every prison and, subject to any directions of the Secretary of State, every prisoner shall be allowed to have library books and to exchange them.

Communications

Communications generally

34.—(1) Without prejudice to sections 6 and 19 of the Prison Act 1952 and except as provided by these Rules, a prisoner shall not be permitted to communicate with any person outside the prison, or such person with him, except with the leave of the Secretary of State or as a privilege under rule 8.

(2) Notwithstanding paragraph (1) above, and except as otherwise provided in these Rules, the Secretary of State may impose any restriction or condition, either generally or in a particular case, upon the communications to be permitted between a prisoner and other persons if he considers that the restriction or condition to be imposed—

(a) does not interfere with the convention rights of any person; or

(b)
    (i) is necessary on grounds specified in paragraph (3) below;
    (ii) reliance on the grounds is compatible with the convention right to be interfered with; and
    (iii) the restriction or condition is proportionate to what is sought to be achieved.

(3) The grounds referred to in paragraph (2) above are—
(a) the interests of national security;
(b) the prevention, detection, investigation or prosecution of crime;
(c) the interests of public safety;
(d) securing or maintaining prison security or good order and discipline in prison;
(e) the protection of health or morals;
(f) the protection of the reputation of others;
(g) maintaining the authority and impartiality of the judiciary; or
(h) the protection of the rights and freedoms of any person.

(4) Subject to paragraph (2) above, the Secretary of State may require that any visit, or class of visits, shall be held in facilities which include special features restricting or preventing physical contact between a prisoner and a visitor.

(5) Every visit to a prisoner shall take place within the sight of an officer or employee of the prison authorised for the purposes of this rule by the governor (in this rule referred to as an 'authorised employee'), unless the Secretary of State otherwise directs, and for the purposes of this paragraph a visit to a prisoner shall be taken to take place within the sight of an officer or authorised employee if it can be seen by an officer or authorised employee by means of an overt closed circuit television system.

(6) Subject to rule 38, every visit to a prisoner shall take place within the hearing of an officer or authorised employee, unless the Secretary of State otherwise directs.

(7) The Secretary of State may give directions, either generally or in relation to any visit or class of visits, concerning the day and times when prisoners may be visited.

(8) In this rule—
(a) references to communications include references to communications during visits;
(b) references to restrictions and conditions upon communications include references to restrictions and conditions in relation to the length, duration and frequency of communications; and
(c) references to convention rights are to the convention rights within the meaning of the Human Rights Act 1998.

Personal letters and visits

35.—(1) Subject to paragraph (8), an unconvicted prisoner may send and receive as many letters and may receive as many visits as he wishes within such limits and subject to such conditions as the Secretary of State may direct, either generally or in a particular case.

(2) Subject to paragraph (8), a convicted prisoner shall be entitled—
(a) to send and to receive a letter on his reception into a prison and thereafter once a week; and
(b) to receive a visit twice in every period of four weeks, but only once in every such period if the Secretary of State so directs.

(3) The governor may allow a prisoner an additional letter or visit as a privilege under rule 8 or where necessary for his welfare or that of his family.

(4) The governor may allow a prisoner entitled to a visit to send and to receive a letter instead.

(5) The governor may defer the right of a prisoner to a visit until the expiration of any period of cellular confinement.

(6) The board of visitors may allow a prisoner an additional letter or visit in special circumstances, and may direct that a visit may extend beyond the normal duration.

(7) The Secretary of State may allow additional letters and visits in relation to any prisoner or class of prisoners.

(8) A prisoner shall not be entitled under this rule to receive a visit from:
    (a) any person, whether or not a relative or friend, during any period of time that person is the subject of a prohibition imposed under rule 73; or
    (b) any other person, other than a relative or friend, except with the leave of the Secretary of State.

(9) Any letter or visit under the succeeding provisions of these Rules shall not be counted as a letter or visit for the purposes of this rule.

Interception of communications

35A.—(1) The Secretary of State may give directions to any governor concerning the interception in a prison of any communication by any prisoner or class of prisoners if the Secretary of State considers that the directions are—
    (a) necessary on grounds specified in paragraph (4) below; and
    (b) proportionate to what is sought to be achieved.

(2) Subject to any directions given by the Secretary of State, the governor may make arrangements for any communication by a prisoner or class of prisoners to be intercepted in a prison by an officer or an employee of the prison authorised by the governor for the purposes of this rule (referred to in this rule as an 'authorised employee') if he considers that the arrangements are—
    (a) necessary on grounds specified in paragraph (4) below; and
    (b) proportionate to what is sought to be achieved.

(3) Any communication by a prisoner may, during the course of its transmission in a prison, be terminated by an officer or an authorised employee if he considers that to terminate the communication is—
    (a) necessary on grounds specified in paragraph (4) below; and
    (b) proportionate to what is sought to be achieved by the termination.

(4) The grounds referred to in paragraphs (1)(a), (2)(a) and (3)(a) above are—
    (a) the interests of national security;
    (b) the prevention, detection, investigation or prosecution of crime;
    (c) the interests of public safety;
    (d) securing or maintaining prison security or good order and discipline in prison;
    (e) the protection of health or morals; or
    (f) the protection of the rights and freedoms of any person.

(5) Any reference to the grounds specified in paragraph (4) above in relation to the interception of a communication by means of a telecommunications system in a prison, or the disclosure or retention of intercepted material from such a communication, shall be taken to be a reference to those grounds with the omission of sub-paragraph (f).

(6) For the purposes of this rule 'interception'—
    (a) in relation to a communication by means of a telecommunications system, means any action taken in relation to the system or its operation so as to make

some or all of the contents of the communications available, while being transmitted, to a person other than the sender or intended recipient of the communication; and the contents of a communication are to be taken to be made available to a person while being transmitted where the contents of the communication, while being transmitted, are diverted or recorded so as to be available to a person subsequently; and

(b) in relation to any written or drawn communication, includes opening, reading, examining and copying the communication.

Permanent log of communications

35B.—(1) The governor may arrange for a permanent log to be kept of all communications by or to a prisoner.

(2) The log referred to in paragraph (1) above may include, in relation to a communication by means of a telecommunications system in a prison, a record of the destination, duration and cost of the communication and, in relation to any written or drawn communication, a record of the sender and addressee of the communication.

Disclosure of material

35C. The governor may not disclose to any person who is not an officer of a prison or of the Secretary of State or an employee of the prison authorised by the governor for the purposes of this rule any intercepted material, information retained pursuant to rule 35B or material obtained by means of an overt closed circuit television system used during a visit unless—

(a) he considers that such disclosure is—
  (i) necessary on grounds specified in rule 35A(4); and
  (ii) proportionate to what is sought to be achieved by the disclosure; or
(b)
  (i) in the case of intercepted material or material obtained by means of an overt closed circuit television system used during a visit, all parties to the communication or visit consent to the disclosure; or
  (ii) in the case of information retained pursuant to rule 35B, the prisoner to whose communication the information relates, consents to the disclosure.

Retention of material

35D.—(1) The governor shall not retain any intercepted material or material obtained by means of an overt closed circuit television system used during a visit for a period longer than 3 months beginning with the day on which the material was intercepted or obtained unless he is satisfied that continued retention of it is—

(a) necessary on grounds specified in rule 35A(4); and
(b) proportionate to what is sought to be achieved by the continued retention.

(2) Where such material is retained for longer than 3 months pursuant to paragraph (1) above the governor shall review its continued retention at periodic intervals until such time as it is no longer held by the governor.

(3) The first review referred to in paragraph (2) above shall take place not more than 3 months after the decision to retain the material taken pursuant to paragraph (1) above, and subsequent reviews shall take place not more than 3 months apart thereafter.

(4) If the governor, on a review conducted pursuant to paragraph (2) above or at any other time, is not satisfied that the continued retention of the material satisfies the requirements set out in paragraph (1) above, he shall arrange for the material to be destroyed.

Police interviews

36. A police officer may, on production of an order issued by or on behalf of a chief officer of police, interview any prisoner willing to see him.

Securing release

37. A person detained in prison in default of finding a surety, or of payment of a sum of
money, may communicate with and be visited at any reasonable time on a weekday by any
relative or friend to arrange for a surety or payment in order to secure his release from
prison.

Legal advisers

38.—(1) The legal adviser of a prisoner in any legal proceedings, civil or criminal, to which
the prisoner is a party shall be afforded reasonable facilities for interviewing him in connection with those proceedings, and may do so out of hearing but in the sight of an officer.

(2) A prisoner's legal adviser may, subject to any directions given by the Secretary of
State, interview the prisoner in connection with any other legal business out of hearing but
in the sight of an officer.

Correspondence with legal advisers and courts

39.—(1) A prisoner may correspond with his legal adviser and any court and such correspondence may only be opened, read or stopped by the governor in accordance with the
provisions of this rule.

(2) Correspondence to which this rule applies may be opened if the governor has reasonable cause to believe that it contains an illicit enclosure and any such enclosures
shall be dealt with in accordance with the other provision of these Rules.

(3) Correspondence to which this rule applies may be opened, read and stopped if the
governor has reasonable cause to believe its contents endanger prison security or the
safety of others or are otherwise of a criminal nature.

(4) A prisoner shall be given the opportunity to be present when any correspondence
to which this rule applies is opened and shall be informed if it or any enclosure is to be
read or stopped.

(5) A prisoner shall on request be provided with any writing materials necessary for
the purposes of paragraph (1).

(6) In this rule, 'court' includes the European Commission of Human Rights, the
European Court of Human Rights and the European Court of Justice; and 'illicit
enclosure' includes any article possession of which has not been authorised in accordance with the other provisions of these Rules and any correspondence to or from a
person other than the prisoner concerned, his legal adviser or a court.

Removal, search, record and property

Custody outside prison

40.—(1) A person being taken to or from a prison in custody shall be exposed as little as
possible to public observation, and proper care shall be taken to protect him from curiosity and insult.

(2) A prisoner required to be taken in custody anywhere outside a prison shall be kept
in the custody of an officer appointed or a police officer.

(3) A prisoner required to be taken in custody to any court shall, when he appears before
the court, wear his own clothing or ordinary civilian clothing provided by the governor.

Search

41.—(1) Every prisoner shall be searched when taken into custody by an officer, on his reception into a prison and subsequently as the governor thinks necessary or as the Secretary of State may direct.

(2) A prisoner shall be searched in as seemly a manner as is consistent with discovering anything concealed.

(3) No prisoner shall be stripped and searched in the sight of another prisoner, or in the sight of a person of the opposite sex.

Record and photograph

42.—(1) A personal record of each prisoner shall be prepared and maintained in such manner as the Secretary of State may direct.

(2) Every prisoner may be photographed on reception and subsequently, but no copy of the photograph shall be given to any person not authorised to receive it.

Prisoners' property

43.—(1) Subject to any directions of the Secretary of State, an unconvicted prisoner may have supplied to him at his expense and retain for his own use books, newspapers, writing materials and other means of occupation, except any that appears objectionable to the board of visitors or, pending consideration by them, to the governor.

(2) Anything, other than cash, which a prisoner has at a prison and which he is not allowed to retain for his own use shall be taken into the governor's custody. An inventory of a prisoner's property shall be kept, and he shall be required to sign it, after having a proper opportunity to see that it is correct.

(3) Any cash which a prisoner has at a prison shall be paid into an account under the control of the governor and the prisoner shall be credited with the amount in the books of the prison.

(4) Any article belonging to a prisoner which remains unclaimed for a period of more than 3 years after he leaves prison, or dies, may be sold or otherwise disposed of; and the net proceeds of any sale shall be paid to the National Association for the Care and Resettlement of Offenders, for its general purposes.

(5) The governor may confiscate any unauthorised article found in the possession of a prisoner after his reception into prison, or concealed or deposited anywhere within a prison.

Money and articles received by post

44.—(1) Any money or other article (other than a letter or other communication) sent to a convicted prisoner through the post office shall be dealt with in accordance with the provisions of this rule, and the prisoner shall be informed of the manner in which it is dealt with.

(2) Any cash shall, at the discretion of the governor, be—
  (a) dealt with in accordance with rule 43(3);
  (b) returned to the sender; or
  (c) in a case where the sender's name and address are not known, paid to the National Association for the Care and Resettlement of Offenders, for its general purposes:

Provided that in relation to a prisoner committed to prison in default of payment of any sum of money, the prisoner shall be informed of the receipt of the cash and, unless he objects to its being so applied, it shall be applied in or towards the satisfaction of the amount due from him.

(3) Any security for money shall, at the discretion of the governor, be—

(a) delivered to the prisoner or placed with his property at the prison;

(b) returned to the sender; or

(c) encashed and the cash dealt with in accordance with paragraph (2).

(4) Any other article to which this rule applies shall, at the discretion of the governor, be—

(a) delivered to the prisoner or placed with his property at the prison;

(b) returned to the sender; or

(c) in a case where the sender's name and address are not known or the article is of such a nature that it would be unreasonable to return it, sold or otherwise disposed of, and the net proceeds of any sale applied in accordance with paragraph (2).

Special control, supervision and restraint and drug testing

Removal from association

45.—(1) Where it appears desirable, for the maintenance of good order or discipline or in his own interests, that a prisoner should not associate with other prisoners, either generally or for particular purposes, the governor may arrange for the prisoner's removal from association accordingly.

(2) A prisoner shall not be removed under this rule for a period of more than 3 days without the authority of a member of the board of visitors or of the Secretary of State. An authority given under this paragraph shall be for a period not exceeding one month, but may be renewed from month to month except that, in the case of a person aged less than 21 years who is detained in prison such an authority shall be for a period not exceeding 14 days, but may be renewed from time to time for a like period.

(3) The governor may arrange at his discretion for such a prisoner as aforesaid to resume association with other prisoners, and shall do so if in any case the medical officer or a medical practitioner such as is mentioned in rule 20(3) so advises on medical grounds.

(4) This rule shall not apply to a prisoner the subject of a direction given under rule 46(1).

Close supervision centres

46.—(1) Where it appears desirable, for the maintenance of good order or discipline or to ensure the safety of officers, prisoners or any other person, that a prisoner should not associate with other prisoners, either generally or for particular purposes, the Secretary of State may direct the prisoner's removal from association accordingly and his placement in a close supervision centre of a prison.

(2) A direction given under paragraph (1) shall be for a period not exceeding one month, but may be renewed from time to time for a like period, and shall continue to apply notwithstanding any transfer of a prisoner from one prison to another.

(3) The Secretary of State may direct that such a prisoner as aforesaid shall resume association with other prisoners, either within a close supervision centre or elsewhere.

(4) In exercising any discretion under this rule, the Secretary of State shall take account of any relevant medical considerations which are known to him.

(5) A close supervision centre is any cell or other part of a prison designated by the Secretary of State for holding prisoners who are subject to a direction given under paragraph (1).

Use of force

47.—(1) An officer in dealing with a prisoner shall not use force unnecessarily and, when the application of force to a prisoner is necessary, no more force than is necessary shall be used.

(2) No officer shall act deliberately in a manner calculated to provoke a prisoner.

Temporary confinement

48.—(1) The governor may order a refractory or violent prisoner to be confined temporarily in a special cell, but a prisoner shall not be so confined as a punishment, or after he has ceased to be refractory or violent.

(2) A prisoner shall not be confined in a special cell for longer than 24 hours without a direction in writing given by a member of a board of visitors or by an officer of the Secretary of State (not being an officer of a prison). Such a direction shall state the grounds for the confinement and the time during which it may continue.

Restraints

49.—(1) The governor may order a prisoner to be put under restraint where this is necessary to prevent the prisoner from injuring himself or others, damaging property or creating a disturbance.

(2) Notice of such an order shall be given without delay to a member of the board of visitors, and to the medical officer or to a medical practitioner such as is mentioned in rule 20(3).

(3) On receipt of the notice, the medical officer, or the medical practitioner referred to in paragraph (2), shall inform the governor whether there are any medical reasons why the prisoner should not be put under restraint. The governor shall give effect to any recommendation which may be made under this paragraph.

(4) A prisoner shall not be kept under restraint longer than necessary, nor shall he be so kept for longer than 24 hours without a direction in writing given by a member of the board of visitors or by an officer of the Secretary of State (not being an officer of a prison). Such a direction shall state the grounds for the restraint and the time during which it may continue.

(5) Particulars of every case of restraint under the foregoing provisions of this rule shall be forthwith recorded.

(6) Except as provided by this rule no prisoner shall be put under restraint otherwise than for safe custody during removal, or on medical grounds by direction of the medical officer or of a medical practitioner such as is mentioned in rule 20(3). No prisoner shall be put under restraint as a punishment.

(7) Any means of restraint shall be of a pattern authorised by the Secretary of State, and shall be used in such manner and under such conditions as the Secretary of State may direct.

Compulsory testing for controlled drugs

50.—(1) This rule applies where an officer, acting under the powers conferred by section 16A of the Prison Act 1952 (power to test prisoners for drugs), requires a prisoner to provide a sample for the purpose of ascertaining whether he has any controlled drug in his body.

(2) In this rule 'sample' means a sample of urine or any other description of sample specified in the authorisation by the governor for the purposes of section 16A of the Prison Act 1952.

(3) When requiring a prisoner to provide a sample, an officer shall, so far as is reasonably practicable, inform the prisoner:

(a) that he is being required to provide a sample in accordance with section 16A of the Prison Act 1952; and

(b) that a refusal to provide a sample may lead to disciplinary proceedings being brought against him.

(4) An officer shall require a prisoner to provide a fresh sample, free from any adulteration.

(5) An officer requiring a sample shall make such arrangements and give the prisoner such instructions for its provision as may be reasonably necessary in order to prevent or detect its adulteration or falsification.

(6) A prisoner who is required to provide a sample may be kept apart from other prisoners for a period not exceeding one hour to enable arrangements to be made for the provision of the sample.

(7) A prisoner who is unable to provide a sample of urine when required to do so may be kept apart from other prisoners until he has provided the required sample, save that a prisoner may not be kept apart under this paragraph for a period of more than 5 hours.

(8) A prisoner required to provide a sample of urine shall be afforded such degree of privacy for the purposes of providing the sample as may be compatible with the need to prevent or detect any adulteration or falsification of the sample; in particular a prisoner shall not be required to provide such a sample in the sight of a person of the opposite sex.

Observation of prisoners by means of an overt closed circuit television system

50A.—(1) Without prejudice to his other powers to supervise the prison, prisoners and other persons in the prison, whether by use of an overt closed circuit television system or otherwise, the governor may make arrangements for any prisoner to be placed under constant observation by means of an overt closed circuit television system while the prisoner is in a cell or other place in the prison if he considers that—

(a) such supervision is necessary for—

   (i) the health and safety of the prisoner or any other person;

   (ii) the prevention, detection, investigation or prosecution of crime; or

   (iii) securing or maintaining prison security or good order and discipline in the prison; and

(b) it is proportionate to what is sought to be achieved.

(2) If an overt closed circuit television system is used for the purposes of this rule, the provisions of rules 35C and 35D shall apply to any material obtained.

Offences against discipline

Offences against discipline

51. A prisoner is guilty of an offence against discipline if he—

(1) commits any assault;

(1A) commits any racially aggravated assault;

(2) detains any person against his will;

(3) denies access to any part of the prison to any officer or any person (other than a prisoner) who is at the prison for the purpose of working there;

(4) fights with any person;

(5) intentionally endangers the health or personal safety of others or, by his conduct, is reckless whether such health or personal safety is endangered;

(6) intentionally obstructs an officer in the execution of his duty, or any person (other than a prisoner) who is at the prison for the purpose of working there, in the performance of his work;

(7) escapes or absconds from prison or from legal custody;

(8) fails to comply with any condition upon which he is temporarily released under rule 9;

(9) administers a controlled drug to himself or fails to prevent the administration of a controlled drug to him by another person (but subject to rule 52);

(10) is intoxicated as a consequence of knowingly consuming any alcoholic beverage;

(11) knowingly consumes any alcoholic beverage other than that provided to him pursuant to a written order under rule 25(1);

(12) has in his possession—
    (a) any unauthorised article, or
    (b) a greater quantity of any article than he is authorised to have;

(13) sells or delivers to any person any unauthorised article;

(14) sells or, without permission, delivers to any person any article which he is allowed to have only for his own use;

(15) takes improperly any article belonging to another person or to a prison;

(16) intentionally or recklessly sets fire to any part of a prison or any other property, whether or not his own;

(17) destroys or damages any part of a prison or any other property, other than his own;

(17A) causes racially aggravated damage to, or destruction of, any part of a prison or any other property, other than his own;

(18) absents himself from any place he is required to be or is present at any place where he is not authorised to be;

(19) is disrespectful to any officer, or any person (other than a prisoner) who is at the prison for the purpose of working there, or any person visiting a prison;

(20) uses threatening, abusive or insulting words or behaviour;

(20A) uses threatening, abusive or insulting racist words or behaviour;

(21) intentionally fails to work properly or, being required to work, refuses to do so;

(22) disobeys any lawful order;

(23) disobeys or fails to comply with any rule or regulation applying to him;

(24) receives any controlled drug, or, without the consent of an officer, any other article, during the course of a visit (not being an interview such as is mentioned in rule 38);

(24A) displays, attaches or draws on any part of a prison, or on any other property, threatening, abusive or insulting racist words, drawings, symbols or other material;

(25)
    (a) attempts to commit,
    (b) incites another prisoner to commit, or
    (c) assists another prisoner to commit or to attempt to commit, any of the foregoing offences.

51A. Interpretation of rule 51

(2) For the purposes of rule 51 words, behaviour or material are racist if they demonstrate, or are motivated (wholly or partly) by, hostility to members of a racial group (whether identifiable or not) based on their membership (or presumed membership) of a racial group, and 'membership', 'presumed', 'racial group' and 'racially aggravated' shall have the meanings assigned to them by section 28 of the Crime and Disorder Act 1998(a).

Defences to rule 51(9)

52. It shall be a defence for a prisoner charged with an offence under rule 51(9) to show that:

    (a) the controlled drug had been, prior to its administration, lawfully in his possession for his use or was administered to him in the course of a lawful supply of the drug to him by another person;

    (b) the controlled drug was administered by or to him in circumstances in which he did not know and had no reason to suspect that such a drug was being administered; or

    (c) the controlled drug was administered by or to him under duress or to him without his consent in circumstances where it was not reasonable for him to have resisted.

Disciplinary charges

53.—(1) Where a prisoner is to be charged with an offence against discipline, the charge shall be laid as soon as possible and, save in exceptional circumstances, within 48 hours of the discovery of the offence.

(2) Every charge shall be inquired into by the governor or as the case may be, the adjudicator.

(3) Every charge shall be first inquired into not later, save in exceptional circumstances or in accordance with rule 55A(5), than:

    (a) where it is inquired into by the governor, the next day, not being a Sunday or public holiday, after it is laid;

    (b) where it is referred to the adjudicator under rule 53A(2), 28 days after it is so referred.

(4) A prisoner who is to be charged with an offence against discipline may be kept apart from other prisoners pending the governor's first inquiry or determination under rule 53A.

Determination of mode of inquiry

53A.—(1) Before inquiring into a charge the governor shall determine whether it is so serious that additional days should be awarded for the offence, if the prisoner is found guilty.

(2) Where the governor determines:

    (a) that it is so serious, he shall:

        (i) refer the charge to the adjudicator forthwith for him to inquire into it;

        (ii) refer any other charge arising out of the same incident to the adjudicator forthwith for him to inquire into it; and

        (iii) inform the prisoner who has been charged that he has done so;

    (b) that it is not so serious, he shall proceed to inquire into the charge.

(3) If:
- (a) at any time during an inquiry into a charge by the governor; or
- (b) following such an inquiry, after the governor has found the prisoner guilty of an offence but before he has imposed a punishment for that offence,

it appears to the governor that the charge is so serious that additional days should be awarded for the offence if (where sub-paragraph (a) applies) the prisoner is found guilty, the governor shall act in accordance with paragraph (2)(a)(i) to (iii) and the adjudicator shall first inquire into any charge referred to him under this paragraph not later than, save in exceptional circumstances, 28 days after the charge was referred.

Rights of prisoners charged

54.—(1) Where a prisoner is charged with an offence against discipline, he shall be informed of the charge as soon as possible and, in any case, before the time when it is inquired into by the governor or as the case may be the adjudicator.

(2) At an inquiry into a charge against a prisoner he shall be given a full opportunity of hearing what is alleged against him and of presenting his own case.

(3) At an inquiry into a charge which has been referred to the adjudicator, the prisoner who has been charged shall be given the opportunity to be legally represented.

Governor's punishments

55.—(1) If he finds a prisoner guilty of an offence against discipline the governor may, subject to paragraph (2) and to rule 57, impose one or more of the following punishments:
- (a) caution;
- (b) forfeiture for a period not exceeding 42 days of any of the privileges under rule 8;
- (c) exclusion from associated work for a period not exceeding 21 days;
- (d) stoppage of or deduction from earnings for a period not exceeding 84 days;
- (e) cellular confinement for a period not exceeding 21 days;
- (f) [omitted];
- (g) in the case of a prisoner otherwise entitled to them, forfeiture for any period of the right, under rule 43(1), to have the articles there mentioned;
- (h) removal from his wing or living unit for a period of 28 days.

(2) A caution shall not be combined with any other punishment for the same charge.

(3) If a prisoner is found guilty of more than one charge arising out of an incident, punishments under this rule may be ordered to run consecutively but, in the case of a punishment of cellular confinement, the total period shall not exceed 21 days.

(4) In imposing a punishment under this rule, the governor shall take into account any guidelines that the Secretary of State may from time to time issue as to the level of punishment that should normally be imposed for a particular offence against discipline.

Adjudicator's punishments

55A.—(1) If he finds a prisoner guilty of an offence against discipline the adjudicator may, subject to paragraph (2) and to rule 57, impose one or more of the following punishments:
- (a) any of the punishments mentioned in rule 55(1);
- (b) in the case of a short-term prisoner or long-term prisoner, an award of additional days not exceeding 42 days.

(2) A caution shall not be combined with any other punishment for the same charge.

(3) If a prisoner is found guilty of more than one charge arising out of an incident, punishments under this rule may be ordered to run consecutively but, in the case of an award of additional days, the total period added shall not exceed 42 days and, in the case of a punishment of cellular confinement, the total period shall not exceed 21 days.

(4) This rule applies to a prisoner who has been charged with having committed an offence against discipline before the date on which the rule came into force, in the same way as it applies to a prisoner who has been charged with having committed an offence against discipline on or after that date, provided the charge is referred to the adjudicator no later than 60 days after that date.

(5) Rule 53(3) shall not apply to a charge where, by virtue of paragraph (4), this rule applies to the prisoner who has been charged.

Forfeiture of remission to be treated as an award of additional days

56.—(1) In this rule, 'existing prisoner' and 'existing licensee' have the meanings assigned to them by paragraph 8(1) of Schedule 12 to the Criminal Justice Act 1991.

(2) In relation to any existing prisoner or existing licensee who has forfeited any remission of his sentence, the provisions of Part II of the Criminal Justice Act 1991 shall apply as if he had been awarded such number of additional days as equals the numbers of days of remission which he has forfeited.

Offences committed by young persons

57.—(1) In the case of an offence against discipline committed by an inmate who was under the age of 21 when the offence was committed (other than an offender in relation to whom the Secretary of State has given a direction under section 13(1) of the Criminal Justice Act 1982 that he shall be treated as if he had been sentenced to imprisonment) rule 55 or as the case may be, rule 55A shall have effect, but—
  (a) the maximum period of forfeiture of privileges under rule 8 shall be 21 days;
  (b) the maximum period of stoppage of or deduction from earnings shall be 42 days;
  (c) the maximum period of cellular confinement shall be ten days;
  (d) the maximum period of removal from his cell or living unit shall be 21 days.

(2) In the case of an inmate who has been sentenced to a term of youth custody or detention in a young offender institution, and by virtue of a direction of the Secretary of State under section 99 of the Powers of Criminal Courts (Sentencing) Act 2000, is treated as if he had been sentenced to imprisonment for that term, any punishment imposed on him for an offence against discipline before the said direction was given shall, if it has not been exhausted or remitted, continue to have effect:
  (a) if imposed by a governor, as if made pursuant to rule 55;
  (b) if imposed by an adjudicator, as if made pursuant to rule 55A.

Cellular confinement

58. When it is proposed to impose a punishment of cellular confinement, the medical officer, or a medical practitioner such as is mentioned in rule 20(3), shall inform the governor whether there are any medical reasons why the prisoner should not be so dealt with. The governor shall give effect to any recommendation which may be made under this rule.

Prospective award of additional days

59.—(1) Subject to paragraph (2), where an offence against discipline is committed by a prisoner who is detained only on remand, additional days may be awarded by the adjudicator notwithstanding that the prisoner has not (or had not at the time of the offence) been sentenced.

(2) An award of additional days under paragraph (1) shall have effect only if the prisoner in question subsequently becomes a short-term or long-term prisoner whose sentence is reduced, under section 67 of the Criminal Justice Act 1967, by a period which includes the time when the offence against discipline was committed.

Removal from a cell or living unit

59A. Following the imposition of a punishment of removal from his cell or living unit, a prisoner shall be accommodated in a separate part of the prison under such restrictions of earnings and activities as the Secretary of State may direct.

Suspended punishments

60.—(1) Subject to any directions given by the Secretary of State, the power to impose a disciplinary punishment (other than a caution) shall include power to direct that the punishment is not to take effect unless, during a period specified in the direction (not being more than six months from the date of the direction), the prisoner commits another offence against discipline and a direction is given under paragraph (2).

(2) Where a prisoner commits an offence against discipline during the period specified in a direction given under paragraph (1) the person dealing with that offence may—

    (a) direct that the suspended punishment shall take effect;

    (b) reduce the period or amount of the suspended punishment and direct that it shall take effect as so reduced;

    (c) vary the original direction by substituting for the period specified a period expiring not later than six months from the date of variation; or

    (d) give no direction with respect to the suspended punishment.

(3) Where an award of additional days has been suspended under paragraph (1) and a prisoner is charged with committing an offence against discipline during the period specified in a direction given under that paragraph, the governor shall either:

    (a) inquire into the charge and give no direction with respect to the suspended award; or

    (b) refer the charge to the adjudicator for him to inquire into it.

Remission and mitigation of punishments and quashing of findings of guilt

61.—(1) The Secretary of State may quash any finding of guilt and may remit any punishment or mitigate it either by reducing it or by substituting another award which is, in his opinion, less severe.

(2) Subject to any directions given by the Secretary of State, the governor may remit or mitigate any punishment imposed by a governor or the board of visitors.

PART III

Officers of prisons

General duty of officers

62.—(1) It shall be the duty of every officer to conform to these Rules and the rules and regulations of the prison, to assist and support the governor in their maintenance and to obey his lawful instructions.

(2) An officer shall inform the governor promptly of any abuse or impropriety which comes to his knowledge.

Gratuities forbidden

63. No officer shall receive any unauthorised fee, gratuity or other consideration in connection with his office.

Search of officers

64. An officer shall submit himself to be searched in the prison if the governor so directs. Any such search shall be conducted in as seemly a manner as is consistent with discovering anything concealed.

Transactions with prisoners

65.—(1) No officer shall take part in any business or pecuniary transaction with or on behalf of a prisoner without the leave of the Secretary of State.

(2) No officer shall without authority bring in or take out, or attempt to bring in or take out, or knowingly allow to be brought in or taken out, to or for a prisoner, or deposit in any place with intent that it shall come into the possession of a prisoner, any article whatsoever.

Contact with former prisoners

66. No officer shall, without the knowledge of the governor, communicate with any person whom he knows to be a former prisoner or a relative or friend of a prisoner or former prisoner.

Communications to the press

67.—(1) No officer shall make, directly or indirectly, any unauthorised communication to a representative of the press or any other person concerning matters which have become known to him in the course of his duty.

(2) No officer shall, without authority, publish any matter or make any public pronouncement relating to the administration of any institution to which the Prison Act 1952 applies or to any of its inmates.

Code of discipline

68. The Secretary of State may approve a code of discipline to have effect in relation to officers, or such classes of officers as it may specify, setting out the offences against discipline, the awards which may be made in respect of them and the procedure for dealing with charges.

Emergencies

69. Where any constable or member of the armed forces of the Crown is employed by reason of any emergency to assist the governor of a prison by performing duties ordinarily performed by an officer of a prison, any reference in Part II of these Rules to such an officer (other than a governor) shall be construed as including a reference to a constable or a member of the armed forces of the Crown so employed.

PART IV

Persons having access to a prison

Prohibited articles

70. No person shall, without authority, convey into or throw into or deposit in a prison, or convey or throw out of a prison, or convey to a prisoner, or deposit in any place with intent that it shall come into the possession of a prisoner, any money, clothing, food, drink, tobacco, letter, paper, book, tool, controlled drug, firearm, explosive, weapon or other article whatever. Anything so conveyed, thrown or deposited may be confiscated by the governor.

Control of persons and vehicles

71.—(1) Any person or vehicle entering or leaving a prison may be stopped, examined and searched. Any such search of a person shall be carried out in as seemly a manner as is consistent with discovering anything concealed.

(2) The governor may direct the removal from a prison of any person who does not leave on being required to do so.

Viewing of prisons

72.—(1) No outside person shall be permitted to view a prison unless authorised by statute or the Secretary of State.

(2) No person viewing the prison shall be permitted to take a photograph, make a sketch or communicate with a prisoner unless authorised by statute or the Secretary of State.

Visitors

73.—(1) Without prejudice to any other powers to prohibit or restrict entry to prisons, or his powers under rules 34 and 35, the Secretary of State may prohibit visits by a person to a prison or to a prisoner in a prison for such periods of time as he considers necessary if the Secretary of State considers that such a prohibition is—

    (a) necessary on grounds specified in rule 35A(4); and

    (b) is proportionate to what is sought to be achieved by the prohibition.

(2) Paragraph (1) shall not apply in relation to any visit to a prison or prisoner by a member of the board of visitors of the prison, or justice of the peace, or to prevent any visit by a legal adviser for the purposes of an interview under rule 38 or visit allowed by the board of visitors under rule 35(6).

PART V

Boards of visitors

Disqualification for membership

74. Any person, directly or indirectly interested in any contract for the supply of goods or services to a prison, shall not be a member of the board of visitors for that prison and any member who becomes so interested in such a contract shall vacate office as a member.

Board of visitors

75.—(1) A member of the board of visitors for a prison appointed by the Secretary of State under section 6(2) of the Prison Act 1952 shall subject to paragraphs (3) and (4) hold office for three years, or such lesser period as the Secretary of State may appoint.

(2) A member—

    (a) appointed for the first time to the board of visitors for a particular prison; or

    (b) reappointed to the board following a gap of a year or more in his membership of it,

shall, during the period of 12 months following the date on which he is so appointed or (as the case may be) reappointed, undertake such training as may reasonably be required by the Secretary of State.

(3) The Secretary of State may terminate the appointment of a member if he is satisfied that—

    (a) he has failed satisfactorily to perform his duties;

    (b) he has failed to undertake training he has been required to undertake under paragraph (2), by the end of the period specified in that paragraph;

(c) he is by reason of physical or mental illness, or for any other reason, incapable of carrying out his duties;

(d) he has been convicted of such a criminal offence, or his conduct has been such, that it is not in the Secretary of State's opinion fitting that he should remain a member; or

(e) there is, or appears to be or could appear to be, any conflict of interest between the member performing his duties as a member and any interest of that member, whether personal, financial or otherwise.

(4) Where the Secretary of State:

(a) has reason to suspect that a member of the board of visitors for a prison may have so conducted himself that his appointment may be liable to be terminated under paragraph (3)(a) or (d); and

(b) is of the opinion that the suspected conduct is of such a serious nature that the member cannot be permitted to continue to perform his functions as a member of the board pending the completion of the Secretary of State's investigations into the matter and any decision as to whether the member's appointment should be terminated,

he may suspend the member from office for such period or periods as he may reasonably require in order to complete his investigations and determine whether or not the appointment of the member should be so terminated; and a member so suspended shall not, during the period of his suspension, be regarded as being a member of the board, other than for the purposes of this paragraph and paragraphs (1) and (3).

(5) A board shall have a chairman and a vice chairman who shall be members of the board.

(6) The Secretary of State shall—

(a) upon the constitution of a board for the first time, appoint a chairman and a vice chairman to hold office for a period not exceeding twelve months;

(b) thereafter appoint, before the date of the first meeting of the board in any year of office of the board, a chairman and vice chairman for that year, having first consulted the board; and

(c) promptly fill, after first having consulted the board, any casual vacancy in the office of chairman or vice chairman.

(7) The Secretary of State may terminate the appointment of a member as chairman or vice chairman of the board if he is satisfied that the member has—

(a) failed satisfactorily to perform his functions as chairman (or as the case may be) vice chairman;

(b) has grossly misconducted himself while performing those functions.

Proceedings of boards

76.—(1) The board of visitors for a prison shall meet at the prison once a month or, if they resolve for reasons specified in the resolution that less frequent meetings are sufficient, not fewer than eight times in twelve months.

(2) The board may fix a quorum of not fewer than three members for proceedings.

(3) The board shall keep minutes of their proceedings.

(4) The proceedings of the board shall not be invalidated by any vacancy in the membership or any defect in the appointment of a member.

General duties of boards

77.—(1) The board of visitors for a prison shall satisfy themselves as to the state of the prison premises, the administration of the prison and the treatment of the prisoners.

(2) The board shall inquire into and report upon any matter into which the Secretary of State asks them to inquire.

(3) The board shall direct the attention of the governor to any matter which calls for his attention, and shall report to the Secretary of State any matter which they consider it expedient to report.

(4) The board shall inform the Secretary of State immediately of any abuse which comes to their knowledge.

(5) Before exercising any power under these Rules the board and any member of the board shall consult the governor in relation to any matter which may affect discipline.

Particular duties

78.—(1) The board of visitors for a prison and any member of the board shall hear any complaint or request which a prisoner wishes to make to them or him.

(2) The board shall arrange for the food of the prisoners to be inspected by a member of the board at frequent intervals.

(3) The board shall inquire into any report made to them, whether or not by a member of the board, that a prisoner's health, mental or physical, is likely to be injuriously affected by any conditions of his imprisonment.

Members visiting prisons

79.—(1) The members of the board of visitors for a prison shall visit the prison frequently, and the board shall arrange a rota whereby at least one of its members visits the prison between meetings of the board.

(2) A member of the board shall have access at any time to every part of the prison and to every prisoner, and he may interview any prisoner out of the sight and hearing of officers.

(3) A member of the board shall have access to the records of the prison.

Annual report

80.—(1) The board of visitors for a prison shall, in accordance with paragraphs (2) and (3) below, from time to time make a report to the Secretary of State concerning the state of the prison and its administration, including in it any advice and suggestions they consider appropriate.

(2) The board shall comply with any directions given to them from time to time by the Secretary of State as to the following matters:
- (a) the period to be covered by a report under paragraph (1);
- (b) the frequency with which such a report is to be made; and
- (c) the length of time from the end of the period covered by such a report within which it is to be made;

either in respect of a particular report or generally; providing that no directions may be issued under this paragraph if they would have the effect of requiring a board to make or deliver a report less frequently than once in every 12 months.

(3) Subject to any directions given to them under paragraph (2), the board shall, under paragraph (1), make an annual report to the Secretary of State as soon as reasonably possible after 31st December each year, which shall cover the period of 12 months ending on that date or, in the case of a board constituted for the first time during that period, such part of that period during which the board has been in existence.

Part VI

Supplemental

Delegation by governor

81. The governor of a prison may, with the leave of the Secretary of State, delegate any of his powers and duties under these Rules to another officer of that prison.

Contracted out prisons

82.—(1) Where the Secretary of State has entered into a contract for the running of a prison under section 84 of the Criminal Justice Act 1991 ('the 1991 Act') these Rules shall have effect in relation to that prison with the following modifications—

    (a) references to an officer in the Rules shall include references to a prisoner custody officer certified as such under section 89(1) of the 1991 Act and performing custodial duties;

    (b) references to a governor in the Rules shall include references to a director approved by the Secretary of State for the purposes of section 85(1)(a) of the 1991 Act except—

        (i) in rules 45, 48, 49, 53, 53A, 54, 55, 57, 60, 61 and 81 where references to a governor shall include references to a controller appointed by the Secretary of State under section 85(1)(b) of the 1991 Act, and

        (ii) in rules 62(1), 66 and 77 where references to a governor shall include references to the director and the controller;

    (c) rule 68 shall not apply in relation to a prisoner custody officer certified as such under section 89(1) of the 1991 Act and performing custodial duties.

(2) Where a director exercises the powers set out in section 85(3)(b) of the 1991 Act (removal from association, temporary confinement and restraints) in cases of urgency, he shall notify the controller of that fact forthwith.

Contracted out parts of prisons

83. Where the Secretary of State has entered into a contract for the running of part of a prison under section 84(1) of the Criminal Justice Act 1991, that part and the remaining part shall each be treated for the purposes of Parts II to IV and Part VI of these Rules as if they were separate prisons.

Contracted out functions at directly managed prisons

84.—(1) Where the Secretary of State has entered into a contract under section 88A(1) of the Criminal Justice Act 1991 ('the 1991 Act') for any functions at a directly managed prison to be performed by prisoner custody officers who are authorised to perform custodial duties under section 89(1) of the 1991 Act, references to an officer in these Rules shall, subject to paragraph (2), include references to a prisoner custody officer who is so authorised and who is performing contracted out functions for the purposes of, or for purposes connected with, the prison.

(2) Paragraph (1) shall not apply to references to an officer in rule 68.

(3) In this rule, 'directly managed prison' has the meaning assigned to it by section 88A(5) of the 1991 Act.

Revocations and savings

85.—(1) Subject to paragraphs (2) and (3) below, the Rules specified in the Schedule to these Rules are hereby revoked.

(2) Without prejudice to the Interpretation Act 1978, where a prisoner committed an offence against discipline contrary to rule 47 of the Prison Rules 1964 prior to the coming into force of these Rules, those rules shall continue to have effect to permit the prisoner to be charged with such an offence, disciplinary proceedings in relation to such an offence to be continued, and the governor to impose punishment for such an offence.

(3) Without prejudice to the Interpretation Act 1978, any award of additional days or other punishment or suspended punishment for an offence against discipline awarded or imposed under any provision of the rules revoked by this rule, or those rules as saved by paragraph (2), or treated by any such provision as having been awarded or imposed under the rules revoked by this rule, shall have effect as if awarded or imposed under the corresponding provision of these Rules.

APPENDIX 3

The Young Offender Institution Rules 2000 (SI 2000/3371)

as amended by the Young Offender Institution (Amendment) Rules 2002 (SI 2002/2117)

ARRANGEMENT OF RULES

PART I
PRELIMINARY

PART II
INMATES

General

Release

Conditions

Part III
Officers of Young Offender Institutions

Part IV
Persons Having Access to a Young Offender Institution

Part V
Boards of Visitors

Part VI
Supplemental

Part I
Preliminary

Citation and commencement

1.— (a)   These Rules may be cited as the Young Offender Institution Rules 2000 and
            shall come into force on 1st April 2001.
     (b)   The Rules set out in the Schedule to this Order are hereby revoked.

Interpretation

2.—(1) In these Rules, where the context so admits, the expression—

'adjudicator' means a person approved by the Secretary of State for the purpose of inquiring into a charge which has been referred to him;

'communication' includes any written or drawn communication from an inmate to any other person, whether intended to be transmitted by means of a postal service or not, and any communication from an inmate to any other person transmitted by means of a telecommunications system;

'compulsory school age' has the same meaning as in the Education Act 1996;

'controlled drug' means any drug which is a controlled drug for the purposes of the Misuse of Drugs Act 1971;

'governor' includes an officer for the time being in charge of a young offender institution;

'inmate' means a person who is required to be detained in a young offender institution;

'intercepted material' means the contents of any communication intercepted pursuant to these Rules;

'legal adviser' means, in relation to an inmate, his counsel or solicitor, and includes a clerk acting on behalf of his solicitor;

'minister appointed to a young offender institution' means a minister so appointed under section 10 of the Prison Act 1952;

'officer' means an officer of a young offender institution;

'short-term prisoner' and 'long-term prisoner' have the meanings assigned to them by section 33(5) of the Criminal Justice Act 1991, as extended by sections 43(1) and 45(1) of that Act;

'telecommunications system' means any system (including the apparatus comprised in it) which exists for the purpose of facilitating the transmission of communications by any means involving the use of electrical or electro-magnetic energy.

(2) In these Rules a reference to—

(a) an award of additional days means additional days awarded under these Rules by virtue of section 42 of the Criminal Justice Act 1991;

(b) the Church of England includes a reference to the Church of Wales; and

(c) a reference to a numbered rule is, unless otherwise stated, a reference to the rule of that number in these Rules and a reference to a numbered paragraph is in a rule, unless otherwise stated, a reference to the paragraph of that number in that rule.

PART II

INMATES

General

Aims and general principles of young offender institutions

3.—(1) The aim of a young offender institution shall be to help offenders to prepare for their return to the outside community.

(2) The aim mentioned in paragraph (1) shall be achieved, in particular, by—

(a) providing a programme of activities, including education, training and work designed to assist offenders to acquire or develop personal responsibility, self-discipline, physical fitness, interests and skills and to obtain suitable employment after release;

   (b) fostering links between the offender and the outside community; and
   (c) co-operating with the services responsible for the offender's supervision after release.

Classification of inmates

4. Inmates may be classified, in accordance with any directions of the Secretary of State, taking into account their ages, characters and circumstances.

Release

Temporary release

5.—(1) The Secretary of State may, in accordance with the other provisions of this rule, release temporarily an inmate to whom this rule applies.

(2) An inmate may be released under this rule for any period or periods and subject to any conditions.

(3) An inmate may only be released under this rule:
   (a) on compassionate grounds or for the purpose of receiving medical treatment;
   (b) to engage in employment or voluntary work;
   (c) to receive instruction or training which cannot reasonably be provided in the young offender institution;
   (d) to enable him to participate in any proceedings before any court, tribunal or inquiry;
   (e) to enable him to consult with his legal adviser in circumstances where it is not reasonably practicable for the consultation to take place in the young offender institution;
   (f) to assist any police officer in any enquiries;
   (g) to facilitate the inmate's transfer between the young offender institution and another penal establishment;
   (h) to assist him in maintaining family ties or in his transition from life in the young offender institution to freedom; or
   (i) to enable him to make a visit in the locality of the young offender institution, as a privilege under rule 6.

(4) An inmate shall not be released under this rule unless the Secretary of State is satisfied that there would not be an unacceptable risk of his committing offences whilst released or otherwise of his failing to comply with any condition upon which he is released.

(5) Where at any time an offender is subject concurrently:
   (a) to a detention and training order; and
   (b) to a sentence of detention in a young offender institution,
he shall be treated for the purposes of paragraphs (6) and (7) as if he were subject only to the one of them that was imposed on the later occasion.

(6) The Secretary of State shall not release under this rule an inmate if, having regard to:
   (a) the period or proportion of his sentence which the inmate has served or, in a case where paragraph (10) does not apply to require all the sentences he is serving to be treated as a single term, the period or proportion of any such sentence he has served; and
   (b) the frequency with which the inmate has been granted temporary release under this rule,
the Secretary of State is of the opinion that the release of the inmate would be likely to undermine public confidence in the administration of justice.

(7) If an inmate has been temporarily released under this rule during the relevant period and has been sentenced to any period of detention, custody or imprisonment for a criminal offence committed whilst at large following that release, he shall not be released under this rule unless his release, having regard to the circumstances of his conviction, would not, in the opinion of the Secretary of State, be likely to undermine public confidence in the administration of justice; and for this purpose 'the relevant period':

    (a) in the case of an inmate serving a determinate sentence of imprisonment, detention or custody, is the period he has served in respect of that sentence, unless, notwithstanding paragraph (10), the sentences he is serving do not fall to be treated as a single term, in which case it is the period since he was last released in relation to one of those sentences under Part II of the Criminal Justice Act 1991 ('the 1991 Act') or section 100 of the Powers of the Criminal Courts (Sentencing) Act 2000 ('the 2000 Act'); or

    (b) in the case of an inmate serving an indeterminate sentence of imprisonment, detention or custody, is, if the inmate has previously been released on licence under Part II of the 1991 Act or Part II of the Crime (Sentences) Act 1997, the period since the date of his last recall to a penal establishment in respect of that sentence or, where the inmate has not been so released, the period he has served in respect of that sentence,

save that where an inmate falls within both of sub-paragraphs (a) and (b) above, the 'relevant period', in the case of that inmate, shall be determined by whichever of the applicable sub-paragraphs that produces the longer period.

(8) An inmate released under this rule may be recalled at any time whether the conditions of his release have been broken or not.

(9) This rule applies to inmates other than persons committed in custody for trial or to be sentenced or otherwise dealt with before or by the Crown Court or remanded in custody by any court.

(10) For the purposes of any reference in this rule to an inmate's sentence, consecutive terms and terms which are wholly or partly concurrent shall be treated as a single term if they would fall to be treated as a single term for the purposes of any reference to the term of imprisonment, detention or custody to which a person has been sentenced in Part II of the 1991 Act or to the term of a detention and training order in sections 100 to 103 of the 2000 Act.

(11) In this rule, any reference to release on licence under Part II of the 1991 Act includes any release on licence under any earlier legislation providing for early release on licence.

Conditions

Privileges

6.—(1) There shall be established at every young offender institution systems of privileges approved by the Secretary of State and appropriate to the classes of inmates thereof and their ages, characters and circumstances, which shall include arrangements under which money earned by inmates may be spent by them within the young offender institution.

(2) Systems of privileges approved under paragraph (1) may include arrangements under which inmates may be allowed time outside the cells and in association with one another, in excess of the minimum time which, subject to the other provisions of these Rules apart from this rule, is otherwise allowed to inmates at the young offender institution for this purpose.

(3) Systems of privileges approved under paragraph (1) may include arrangements under which privileges may be granted to inmates only in so far as they have met, and for so long as they continue to meet, specified standards in their behaviour and their performance in work or other activities.

(4) Systems of privileges which include arrangements of the kind referred to in paragraph (3) shall include procedures to be followed in determining whether or not any of the privileges concerned shall be granted, or shall continue to be granted, to an inmate; such procedures shall include a requirement that the inmate be given reasons for any decision adverse to him together with a statement of the means by which he may appeal against it.

(5) Nothing in this rule shall be taken to confer on an inmate any entitlement to any privilege or to affect any provision in these Rules other than this rule as a result of which any privilege may be forfeited or otherwise lost or an inmate deprived of association with other inmates.

Information to inmates

7.—(1) Every inmate shall be provided, as soon as possible after his reception into the young offender institution, and in any case within 24 hours, with information in writing about those provisions of these Rules and other matters which it is necessary that he should know, including earnings and privileges, and the proper method of making requests and complaints.

(2) In the case of an inmate aged under 18, or an inmate aged 18 or over who cannot read or appears to have difficulty in understanding the information so provided, the governor, or an officer deputed by him, shall so explain it to him that he can understand his rights and obligations.

(3) A copy of these Rules shall be made available to any inmate who requests it.

Requests and complaints

8.—(1) A request or complaint to the governor or Board of Visitors relating to an inmate's detention shall be made orally or in writing by that inmate.

(2) On every day the governor shall hear any oral requests and complaints that are made to him under paragraph (1).

(3) A written request or complaint under paragraph (1) may be made in confidence.

Communications generally

9.—(1) Without prejudice to sections 6 and 19 of the Prison Act 1952 and except as provided by these Rules, an inmate shall not be permitted to communicate with any person outside the young offender institution, or such person with him, except with the leave of the Secretary of State or as a privilege under rule 7.

(2) Notwithstanding paragraph (1), and except as otherwise provided in these Rules, the Secretary of State may impose any restriction or condition, either generally or in a particular case, upon the communications to be permitted between an inmate and other persons if he considers that the restriction or condition to be imposed—
    (a) does not interfere with the Convention rights of any person; or
    (b) is necessary on grounds specified in paragraph (3) below, provided that:
        (i) reliance on the grounds is compatible with the Convention right to be interfered with; and
        (ii) the restriction or condition is proportionate to what is sought to be achieved.

(3) The grounds referred to in paragraph (2) are—
  (a) the interests of national security;
  (b) the prevention, detection, investigation or prosecution of crime;
  (c) the interests of public safety;
  (d) securing or maintaining security or good order and discipline in the young offender institution;
  (e) the protection of health or morals;
  (f) the protection of the reputation of others;
  (g) maintaining the authority and impartiality of the judiciary; or
  (h) the protection of the rights and freedoms of any person.

(4) Subject to paragraph (2), the Secretary of State may require that any visit, or class of visits, shall be held in facilities which include special features restricting or preventing physical contact between an inmate and a visitor.

(5) Every visit to an inmate shall take place within the sight of an officer or employee of the young offender institution authorised for the purposes of this rule by the governor (in this rule referred to as an 'authorised employee'), unless the Secretary of State otherwise directs, and for the purposes of this paragraph a visit to an inmate shall be taken to take place within the sight of an officer or authorised employee if it can be seen by an officer or authorised employee by means of an overt closed circuit television system.

(6) Subject to rule 13, every visit to an inmate shall take place within the hearing of an officer or authorised employee, unless the Secretary of State otherwise directs.

(7) The Secretary of State may give directions, either generally or in relation to any visit or class of visits, concerning the day and times when inmates may be visited.

(8) In this rule—
  (a) references to communications include references to communications during visits;
  (b) references to restrictions and conditions upon communications include references to restrictions and conditions in relation to the length, duration and frequency of communications; and
  (c) references to Convention rights are to the Convention rights within the meaning of the Human Rights Act 1998.

Personal letters and visits

10.—(1) Subject to paragraph (7) an inmate shall be entitled—
  (a) to send and to receive a letter on his reception into a young offender institution and thereafter once a week; and
  (b) to receive a visit twice in every period of four weeks, but only once in every such period if the Secretary of State so directs.

(2) The governor may allow an inmate an additional letter or visit as a privilege under rule 6 or when necessary for his welfare or that of his family.

(3) The governor may allow an inmate entitled to a visit to send and to receive a letter instead.

(4) The governor may defer the right of an inmate to a visit until the expiration of any period of confinement to a cell or room.

(5) The board of visitors may allow an inmate an additional letter or visit in special circumstances, and may direct that a visit may extend beyond the normal duration.

(6) The Secretary of State may allow additional letters and visits in relation to any inmate or class of inmates.

(7) An inmate shall not be entitled under this rule to receive a visit from—

    (a) any person, whether or not a relative or friend, during any period of time that person is the subject of a prohibition imposed under rule 77; or

    (b) any other person, other than a relative or friend, except with the leave of the Secretary of State.

(8) Any letter or visit under the succeeding provisions of these Rules shall not be counted as a letter or visit for the purposes of this rule.

Interception of communications

11.—(1) The Secretary of State may give directions to any governor concerning the interception in a young offender institution of any communication by any inmate or class of inmates if the Secretary of State considers that the directions are—

    (a) necessary on grounds specified in paragraph (4); and

    (b) proportionate to what is sought to be achieved.

(2) Subject to any directions given by the Secretary of State, the governor may make arrangements for any communication by an inmate or class of inmates to be intercepted in a young offender institution by an officer or an employee of the young offender institution authorised by the governor for the purposes of this rule (referred to in this rule as an 'authorised employee') if he considers that the arrangements are—

    (a) necessary on grounds specified in paragraph (4); and

    (b) proportionate to what is sought to be achieved.

(3) Any communication by an inmate may, during the course of its transmission in a young offender institution, be terminated by an officer or an authorised employee if he considers that to terminate the communication is—

    (a) necessary on grounds specified in paragraph (4); and

    (b) proportionate to what is sought to be achieved by the termination.

(4) The grounds referred to in paragraphs (1)(a), (2)(a) and (3)(a) are—

    (a) the interests of national security;

    (b) the prevention, detection, investigation or prosecution of crime;

    (c) the interests of public safety;

    (d) securing or maintaining security or good order and discipline in the young offender institution;

    (e) the protection of health or morals; or

    (f) the protection of the rights and freedoms of any person.

(5) Any reference to the grounds specified in paragraph (4) in relation to the interception of a communication by means of a telecommunications system in a young offender institution, or the disclosure or retention of intercepted material from such a communication, shall be taken to be a reference to those grounds with the omission of sub-paragraph (f).

(6) For the purposes of this rule 'interception'—

    (a) in relation to a communication by means of a telecommunications system, means any action taken in relation to the system or its operation so as to make some or all of the contents of the communications available, while being transmitted, to a person other than the sender or intended recipient of the communication; and the contents of a communication are to be taken to be made available to a person while being transmitted where the contents of the communication, while being transmitted, are diverted or recorded so as to be available to a person subsequently; and

    (b) in relation to any written or drawn communication, includes opening, reading, examining and copying the communication.

Permanent log of communications

12.—(1) The governor may arrange for a permanent log to be kept of all communications by or to an inmate.

(2) The log referred to in paragraph (1) may include, in relation to a communication by means of a telecommunications system in a young offender institution, a record of the destination, duration and cost of the communication and, in relation to any written or drawn communication, a record of the sender and addressee of the communication.

Disclosure of material

13.—(1) The governor may not disclose to any person who is not an officer of a young offender institution or of the Secretary of State or an employee of the young offender institution authorised by the governor for the purposes of this rule any intercepted material, information retained pursuant to rule 12 or material obtained by means of an overt closed circuit television system used during a visit unless—

    (a) he considers that such disclosure is—
        (i) necessary on grounds specified in rule 11(4); and
        (ii) proportionate to what is sought to be achieved by the disclosure;
    (b) in the case of intercepted material or material obtained by means of an overt closed circuit television system used during a visit, all parties to the communication or visit consent to the disclosure; or
    (c) in the case of information retained pursuant to rule 12, the inmate to whose communication the information relates, consents to the disclosure.

Retention of material

14.—(1) The governor shall not retain any intercepted material or material obtained by means of an overt closed circuit television system used during a visit for a period longer than 3 months beginning with the day on which the material was intercepted or obtained unless he is satisfied that continued retention of it is—

    (a) necessary on grounds specified in rule 11(4); and
    (b) proportionate to what is sought to be achieved by the continued retention.

(2) Where such material is retained for longer than three months pursuant to paragraph (1) the governor shall review its continued retention at periodic intervals until such time as it is no longer held by the governor.

(3) The first review referred to in paragraph (2) shall take place not more than three months after the decision to retain the material taken pursuant to paragraph (1) and subsequent reviews shall take place not more than three months apart thereafter.

(4) If the governor, on a review conducted pursuant to paragraph (2) or at any other time, is not satisfied that the continued retention of the material satisfies the requirements set out in paragraph (1), he shall arrange for the material to be destroyed.

Police interviews

15. A police officer may, on production of an order issued by or on behalf of a chief officer of police, interview any inmate willing to see him.

Legal advisers

16.—(1) The legal adviser of an inmate in any legal proceedings, civil or criminal, to which the inmate is a party shall be afforded reasonable facilities for interviewing him in connection with those proceedings, and may do so out of hearing of an officer.

(2) An inmate's legal adviser may, with the leave of the Secretary of State, interview the inmate in connection with any other legal business.

Correspondence with legal advisers and courts

17.—(1) An inmate may correspond with his legal adviser and any court and such correspondence may only be opened, read or stopped by the governor in accordance with the provisions of this rule.

(2) Correspondence to which this rule applies may be opened if the governor has reasonable cause to believe that it contains an illicit enclosure and any such enclosure shall be dealt with in accordance with the other provisions of these Rules.

(3) Correspondence to which this rule applies may be opened, read and stopped if the governor has reasonable cause to believe its contents endanger prison or young offender institution security or the safety of others or are otherwise of a criminal nature.

(4) An inmate shall be given the opportunity to be present when any correspondence to which this rule applies is opened and shall be informed if it or any enclosure is to be read or stopped.

(5) An inmate shall on request be provided with any writing materials necessary for the purposes of paragraph (1).

(6) In this rule, 'court' includes the European Court of Human Rights and the European Court of Justice; and 'illicit enclosure' includes any article possession of which has not been authorised in accordance with the other provisions of these Rules and any correspondence to or from a person other than the inmate concerned, his legal adviser or a court.

Securing release of defaulters

18. An inmate detained in a young offender institution in default of payment of a fine or any other sum of money may communicate with, and be visited at any reasonable time on a weekday by, any relative or friend for payment in order to secure his release.

Clothing

19.—(1) An inmate shall be provided with clothing adequate for warmth and health in accordance with a scale approved by the Secretary of State.

(2) The clothing provided under this rule shall include suitable protective clothing for use at work, where this is needed.

(3) Subject to the provisions of rule 45(3), an inmate shall wear clothing provided under this rule and no other, except on the directions of the Secretary of State or as a privilege under rule 6.

(4) An inmate shall where necessary be provided with suitable and adequate clothing on his release.

Food

20.—(1) Subject to any directions of the Secretary of State, no inmate shall be allowed, except as authorised by the medical officer or medical practitioner as is mentioned in rule 27(3), to have any food other than that ordinarily provided.

(2) The food provided shall be wholesome, nutritious, well prepared and served, reasonably varied and sufficient in quantity.

(3) The medical officer, a medical practitioner such as is mentioned in rule 27(3) or any person deemed by the governor to be competent, shall from time to time inspect the food both before and after it is cooked, and shall report any deficiency or defect to the governor.

(4) In this rule, 'food' includes drink.

Alcohol and tobacco

21.—(1) No inmate shall be allowed to have any intoxicating liquor except under a written order of the medical officer or a medical practitioner such as is mentioned in rule 27(3) specifying the quantity and the name of the inmate.

(2) No inmate shall be allowed to smoke or to have any tobacco except in accordance with any directions of the Secretary of State.

Sleeping accommodation

22.—(1) No room or cell shall be used as sleeping accommodation for an inmate unless it has been certified by an officer of the Secretary of State (not being an officer of a young offender institution) that its size, lighting, heating, ventilation and fittings are adequate for health, and that it allows the inmate to communicate at any time with an officer.

(2) A certificate given under this rule shall specify the maximum number of inmates who may sleep in the room or cell at one time, and the number so specified shall not be exceeded without the leave of the Secretary of State.

Beds and bedding

23. Each inmate shall be provided with a separate bed and with separate bedding adequate for warmth and health.

Hygiene

24.—(1) Every inmate shall be provided with toilet articles necessary for his health and cleanliness, which shall be replaced as necessary.

(2) Every inmate shall be required to wash at proper times, have a hot bath or shower on reception and thereafter at least once a week.

(3) An inmate's hair shall not be cut without his consent.

Female inmates

25. The Secretary of State may, subject to any conditions he thinks fit, permit a female inmate to have her baby with her in a young offender institution, and everything necessary for the baby's maintenance and care may be provided there.

Library books

26. A library shall be provided in every young offender institution and, subject to any directions of the Secretary of State, every inmate shall be allowed to have library books and to exchange them.

Medical attention

Medical attendance

27.—(1) The medical officer of a young offender institution shall have the care of the health, mental and physical, of the inmates of that institution.

(2) Every request by an inmate to see the medical officer shall be recorded by the officer to whom it is made and promptly passed on to the medical officer.

(3) The medical officer may consult a medical practitioner who is a fully registered person within the meaning of the Medical Act 1983. Such a practitioner may work within the prison under the general supervision of the medical officer.

(4) The medical officer shall consult another medical practitioner, if time permits, before performing any serious operation.

(5) Subject to any directions given in the particular case by the Secretary of State, a registered medical practitioner selected by or on behalf of an inmate who is a party to any legal proceedings shall be afforded reasonable facilities for examining him in connection with the proceedings, and may do so out of hearing but in the sight of an officer.

Special illnesses and conditions

28.—(1) The medical officer or a medical practitioner such as is mentioned in rule 27(3) shall report to the governor on the case of any inmate whose health is likely to be injuriously affected by continued detention or any conditions of detention. The governor shall send the report to the Secretary of State without delay, together with his own recommendations.

(2) The medical officer or a medical practitioner such as is mentioned in rule 27(3) shall pay special attention to any inmate whose mental condition appears to require it, and make any special arrangements which appear necessary for his supervision or care.

Notification of illness or death

29.—(1) If an inmate dies, or becomes seriously ill, sustains any severe injury or is removed to hospital on account of mental disorder, the governor shall, if he knows his or her address, at once inform the inmate's spouse or next of kin, and also any person who the inmate may reasonably have asked should be informed.

(2) If an inmate dies, the governor shall give notice immediately to the coroner having jurisdiction, to the board of visitors and to the Secretary of State.

Religion

Religious denomination

30. An inmate shall be treated as being of the religious denomination stated in the record made in pursuance of section 10(5) of the Prison Act 1952, but the governor may, in a proper case after due inquiry, direct that record to be amended.

Special duties of chaplains and appointed ministers

31.—(1) The chaplain or a minister appointed to a young offender institution shall—
  (a) interview every inmate of his denomination individually as soon as he reasonably can after the inmate's reception into that institution and shortly before his release; and
  (b) if no other arrangements are made, read the burial service at the funeral of any inmate of his denomination who dies in that institution.

(2) The chaplain shall visit daily all inmates belonging to the Church of England who are sick, under restraint or confined to a room or cell; and a minister appointed to a young offender institution shall do the same, as far as he reasonably can, for inmates of his own denomination.

(3) If the inmate is willing, the chaplain shall visit any inmate not of the Church of England who is sick, under restraint or confined to a room or cell, and is not regularly visited by a minister of his own denomination.

Regular visits by ministers of religion, etc

32.—(1) The chaplain shall visit regularly the inmates belonging to the Church of England.

(2) A minister appointed to a young offender institution shall visit the inmates of his denomination as regularly as he reasonably can.

(3) The governor shall, if so requested by an inmate belonging to a denomination for which no minister has been appointed to a young offender institution do what he reasonably can to arrange for that inmate to be visited regularly by a minister of that denomination.

(4) Every request by an inmate to see the chaplain or a minister appointed to a young offender institution shall be promptly passed on to the chaplain or minister.

Religious services

33.—(1) The chaplain shall conduct Divine Service for inmates belonging to the Church of England at least once every Sunday, Christmas Day and Good Friday, and such celebrations of Holy Communion and weekday services as may be arranged.

(2) A minister appointed to a young offender institution shall conduct Divine Service for inmates of his denomination at such times as may be arranged.

Substitute for chaplain or appointed minister

34.—(1) A person approved by the Secretary of State may act for the chaplain in his absence.

(2) A minister appointed to a young offender institution may, with the leave of the Secretary of State, appoint a substitute to act for him in his absence.

Sunday work

35. Arrangements shall be made so as not to require inmates to do any unnecessary work on Sunday, Christmas Day or Good Friday nor inmates of religions other than the Christian religion to do any unnecessary work on their recognised days of religious observance (as in alternative, but not in addition, to those days).

Religious books

36. There shall, so far as reasonably practicable, be available for the personal use of every inmate such religious books recognised by his denomination as are approved by the Secretary of State for use in young offender institutions.

Occupation and links with the community

Regime activities

37.—(1) An inmate shall be occupied in a programme of activities provided in accordance with rule 3 which shall include education, training courses, work and physical education.

(2) In all such activities regard shall be paid in individual assessment and personal development.

(3) The medical officer or a medical practitioner such as is mentioned in rule 27(3) may excuse an inmate from work or any other activity on medical grounds; and no inmate shall be set to participate in work or any other activity of a kind for which he is considered by the medical officer or a medical practitioner such as is mentioned in rule 27(3) to be unfit.

(4) An inmate may be required to participate in regime activities for no longer than the relevant period in a day, 'the relevant period' for this purpose being—

    (a) on a day in which an hour or more of physical education is provided for the inmate, 11 hours;

    (b) on a day in which no such education is provided for the inmate, ten hours; or

    (c) on a day in which a period of less than an hour of such education is provided for the inmate, the sum of ten hours and the period of such education provided,

provided that he may not be required to participate in any one regime activity for more than eight hours in a day.

(5) Inmates may be paid for their work or participation in other activities at rates approved by the Secretary of State, either generally or in relation to particular cases.

Education

38.—(1) Provision shall be made at a young offender institution for the education of inmates by means of programmes of class teaching or private study within the normal working week and, so far as practicable, programmes of evening and weekend educational classes or private study. The educational activities shall, so far as practicable, be such as will foster personal responsibility and an inmate's interests and skills and help him to prepare for his return to the community.

(2) In the case of an inmate of compulsory school age, arrangements shall be made for his participation in education or training courses for at least 15 hours a week within the normal working week.

(3) In the case of an inmate aged 17 or over who has special educational needs, arrangements shall be made for education appropriate to his needs, if necessary within the normal working week.

(4) In the case of a female inmate aged 21 or over who is serving a sentence of imprisonment or who has been committed to prison for default and who is detained in a young offender institution instead of a prison, reasonable facilities shall be afforded if she wishes to improve her education, by class teaching or private study.

Training courses

39.—(1) Provision shall be made at a young offender institution for the training of inmates by means of training courses, in accordance with directions of the Secretary of State.

(2) Training courses shall be such as will foster personal responsibility and an inmate's interests and skills and improve his prospects of finding suitable employment after release.

(3) Training courses shall, so far as practicable, be such as to enable inmates to acquire suitable qualifications.

Work

40.—(1) Work shall, so far as practicable, be such as will foster personal responsibility and an inmate's interests and skills and help him to prepare for his return to the community.

(2) No inmate shall be set to do work of a kind not authorised by the Secretary of State.

Physical education

41.—(1) Provision shall be made at a young offender institution for the physical education of inmates within the normal working week, as well as evening and weekend physical recreation. The physical education activities shall be such as will foster personal responsibility and an inmate's interests and skills and encourage him to make good use of his leisure on release.

(2) Arrangements shall be made for each inmate, other than one to whom paragraph (3) and (5) applies, to participate in physical education for at least two hours a week on average or, in the case of inmates detained in such institutions or parts of institutions as the Secretary of State may direct, for at least 1 hour each weekday on average, but outside

the hours allotted to education under rule 38(2) in the case of an inmate of compulsory school age.

(3) If circumstances reasonably permit, a female inmate aged 21 years or over shall be given the opportunity to participate in physical education for at least one hour a week.

(4) In the case of an inmate with a need for remedial physical activity, appropriate facilities shall be provided.

(5) If the weather permits and subject to the need to maintain good order and discipline, a female inmate aged 21 years or over shall be given the opportunity to spend time in the open air at least once every day, for such period as may be reasonable in the circumstances.

Outside contacts

42.—(1) The governor shall encourage links between the young offender institution and the community by taking steps to establish and maintain relations with suitable persons and agencies outside the institution.

(2) The governor shall ensure that special attention is paid to the maintenance of such relations between an inmate and his family as seem desirable in the best interests of both.

(3) Subject to any directions of the Secretary of State, an inmate shall be encouraged, as far as practicable, to participate in activities outside the young offender institution which will be of benefit to the community or of benefit to the inmate in helping him to prepare for his return to the community.

After-care

43.—(1) From the beginning of his sentence, consideration shall be given, in consultation with the appropriate supervising service, to an inmate's future and the help to be given to him in preparation for and after his return to the community.

(2) Every inmate who is liable to supervision after release shall be given a careful explanation of his liability and the requirements to which he will be subject while under supervision.

Discipline and control

Maintenance of order and discipline

44.—(1) Order and discipline shall be maintained, but with no more restriction than is required in the interests of security and well-ordered community life.

(2) Notwithstanding paragraph (1), regimes may be established at young offender institutions under which stricter order and discipline are maintained and which emphasise strict standards of dress, appearance and conduct; provided that no inmate shall be required to participate in such a regime unless he has been first assessed as being suitable for it and no inmate shall be required to continue with such a regime if at any time it appears that he is no longer suitable for it.

(3) For the purposes of paragraph (2), whether an inmate is suitable for a stricter regime is to be assessed by reference to whether he is sufficiently fit in mind and body to undertake it and whether, in the opinion of the Secretary of State, experience of the regime will further his rehabilitation.

(4) In the control of inmates, officers shall seek to influence them through their own example and leadership, and to enlist their willing co-operation.

Custody outside a young offender institution

45.—(1) A person being taken to or from a young offender institution in custody shall be exposed as little as possible to public observation and proper care shall be taken to protect him from curiosity and insult.

(2) An inmate required to be taken in custody anywhere outside a young offender institution shall be kept in the custody of an officer appointed under section 3 of the Prison Act 1952 or of a police officer.

(3) An inmate required to be taken in custody to any court shall, when he appears before the court, wear his own clothing or ordinary civilian clothing provided by the governor.

Search

46.—(1) Every inmate shall be searched when taken into custody by an officer, on his reception into a young offender institution and subsequently as the governor thinks necessary or as the Secretary of State may direct.

(2) An inmate shall be searched in as seemly a manner as is consistent with discovering anything concealed.

(3) No inmate shall be stripped and searched in the sight of another inmate or in the sight of a person of the opposite sex.

Record and photograph

47.—(1) A personal record of each inmate shall be prepared and maintained in such manner as the Secretary of State may direct, but no part of the record shall be disclosed to any person not authorised to receive it.

(2) Every inmate may be photographed on reception and subsequently, but no copy of the photograph shall be given to any person not authorised to receive it.

Inmates' property

48.—(1) Anything, other than cash, which an inmate has at a young offender institution and which he is not allowed to retain for his own use shall be taken into the governor's custody.

(2) Any case which an inmate has at a young offender institution shall be paid into an account under the control of the governor and the inmate shall be credited with the amount in the books of the institution.

(3) Any article belonging to an inmate which remains unclaimed for a period of more than three years after he is released, or dies, may be sold or otherwise disposed of; and the net proceeds of any sale shall be paid to the National Association for the Care and Resettlement of Offenders, for its general purposes.

(4) The governor may confiscate any unauthorised article found in the possession of an inmate after his reception into a young offender institution, or concealed or deposited within a young offender institution.

Removal from association

49.—(1) Where it appears desirable, for the maintenance of good order or discipline or in his own interests, that an inmate should not associate with other inmates, either generally or for particular purposes, the governor may arrange for the inmate's removal from association accordingly.

(2) An inmate shall not be removed under this rule for a period of more than three days without the authority of a member of the board of visitors or of the Secretary of State.

An authority given under this paragraph shall in the case of a female inmate aged 21 years or over, be for a period not exceeding one month and, in the case of any other inmate, be for a period not exceeding 14 days, but may be renewed from time to time for a like period.

(3) The governor may arrange at his discretion for such an inmate to resume association with other inmates, and shall do so if in any case the medical officer or a medical practitioner such as is mentioned in rule 27(3) so advises on medical grounds.

Use of force

50.—(1) An officer in dealing with an inmate shall not use force unnecessarily and, when the application of force to an inmate is necessary, no more force than is necessary shall be used.

(2) No officer shall act deliberately in a manner calculated to provoke an inmate.

Temporary confinement

51.—(1) The governor may order an inmate who is refractory or violent to be confined temporarily in a special cell or room, but an inmate shall not be so confined as a punishment, or after he has ceased to be refractory or violent.

(2) A cell or room shall not be used for the purpose of this rule unless it has been certified by an officer of the Secretary of State (not being an officer of a young offender institution) that it is suitable for the purpose, that its size, lighting, heating, ventilation and fittings are adequate for health, and that it allows the inmate to communicate at any time with an officer.

(3) In relation to any young offender institution, section 14(6) of the Prison Act 1952 shall have effect so as to enable the provision of special rooms instead of special cells for the temporary confinement of refractory or violent inmates.

(4) An inmate shall not be confined under this rule for longer than 24 hours without a direction in writing given by a member of a board of visitors or by an officer of the Secretary of State not being an officer of the young offender institution.

Restraints

52.—(1) The governor may order an inmate to be put under restraint where this is necessary to prevent the inmate from injuring himself or others, damaging property or creating a disturbance.

(2) The governor may not order an inmate aged under 17 to be put under restraint, except that he may order such an inmate be placed in handcuffs where this is necessary to prevent the inmate from injuring himself or others, damaging property or creating a disturbance.

(3) Notice of such an order shall be given without delay to a member of the board of visitors and to the medical officer or a medical practitioner such as is mentioned in rule 27(3).

(4) On receipt of the notice, the medical officer, or the medical practitioner referred to in paragraph (3), shall inform the governor whether there are any reasons why the inmate should not be put under restraint. The governor shall give effect to any recommendation which may be made under this paragraph.

(5) An inmate shall not be kept under restraint longer than necessary, nor shall he be so kept for longer than 24 hours without a direction in writing given by a member of the board of visitors or by an officer of the Secretary of State (not being an officer of a young offender institution). Such a direction shall state the grounds for the restraint and the time during which it may continue.

(6) Particulars of every case of restraint under the foregoing provisions of this rule shall be forthwith recorded.

(7) Except as provided by this rule no inmate shall be put under restraint otherwise than for safe custody during removal, or on medical grounds by direction of the medical officer or a medical practitioner such as is mentioned in rule 27(3). No inmate shall be put under restraint as a punishment.

(8) Any means of restraint shall be of a pattern authorised by the Secretary of State, and shall be used in such manner and under such conditions as the Secretary of State may direct.

Compulsory testing for controlled drugs

53.—(1) This rule applies where an officer, acting under the powers conferred by section 16A of the Prison Act 1952 (power to test inmates for drugs), requires an inmate to provide a sample for the purposes of ascertaining whether he has any controlled drug in his body.

(2) In this rule 'sample' means a sample of urine or any other description of sample specified in the authorisation by the governor for the purposes of section 16A.

(3) When requiring an inmate to provide a sample, an officer shall, so far as is reasonably practicable, inform the inmate:
  (a) that he is being required to provide a sample in accordance with section 16A of the Prison Act 1952; and
  (b) that a refusal to provide a sample may lead to disciplinary proceedings being brought against him.

(4) An officer shall require an inmate to provide a fresh sample, free from any adulteration.

(5) An officer requiring a sample shall make such arrangements and give the inmate such instructions for its provision as may be reasonably necessary in order to prevent or detect its adulteration or falsification.

(6) An inmate who is required to provide a sample may be kept apart from other inmates for a period not exceeding one hour to enable arrangements to be made for the provision of the sample.

(7) An inmate who is unable to provide a sample of urine when required to do so may be kept apart from other inmates until he has provided the required sample, save that an inmate may not be kept apart under this paragraph for a period of more than five hours.

(8) An inmate required to provide a sample of urine shall be afforded such degree of privacy for the purposes of providing the sample as may be compatible with the need to prevent or detect any adulteration or falsification of the sample; in particular an inmate shall not be required to provide such a sample in the sight of a person of the opposite sex.

Supervision of inmates by means of an overt closed circuit television system

54.—(1) Without prejudice to his powers to make arrangements for the supervision of inmates in his custody, the governor may make arrangements for any inmate to be placed under constant supervision by means of an overt closed circuit television system placed in a cell, dormitory or other place in the young offender institution if he considers that—
  (a) such supervision is necessary for—
    (i) the health and safety of the inmate or any other person;
    (ii) the prevention, detection or prosecution of crime; or
    (iii) securing or maintaining security or good order and discipline in the young offender institution; and
  (b) it is proportionate to what is sought to be achieved.

(2) If an overt closed circuit television system is used for the purposes of this rule, the provisions of rules 13 and 14 shall apply to any material obtained.

Offences against discipline

55. An inmate is guilty of an offence against discipline if he—

(1) commits any assault;

(2) commits any racially aggravated assault;

(3) detains any person against his will;

(4) denies access to any part of the young offender institution to any officer or any person (other than an inmate) who is at the young offender institution for the purpose of working there;

(5) fights with any person;

(6) intentionally endangers the health or personal safety of others or, by his conduct, is reckless whether such health or personal safety is endangered;

(7) intentionally obstructs an officer in the execution of his duty, or any person (other than an inmate) who is at the young offender institution for the purpose of working there, in the performance of his work;

(8) escapes or absconds from a young offender institution or from legal custody;

(9) fails to comply with any condition upon which he was temporarily released under rule 5 of these rules;

(10) administers a controlled drug to himself or fails to prevent the administration of a controlled drug to him by another person (but subject to rule 56 below);

(11) is intoxicated as a consequence of knowingly consuming any alcoholic beverage;

(12) knowingly consumes any alcoholic beverage, other than any provided to him pursuant to a written order of the medical officer under rule 21(1);

(13) has in his possession—
(a) any unauthorised article, or
(b) a greater quantity of any article than he is authorised to have;

(14) sells or delivers to any person any unauthorised article;

(15) sells or, without permission, delivers to any person any article which he is allowed to have only for his own use;

(16) takes improperly any article belonging to another person or to a young offender institution;

(17) intentionally or recklessly sets fire to any part of a young offender institution or any other property, whether or not his own;

(18) destroys or damages any part of a young offender institution or any other property other than his own;

(19) causes racially aggravated damage to, or destruction of, any part of a young offender institution or any other property, other than his own;

(20) absents himself from any place where he is required to be or is present at any place where he is not authorised to be;

(21) is disrespectful to any officer, or any person (other than an inmate) who is at the young offender institution for the purpose of working there, or any person visiting a young offender institution;

(22) uses threatening, abusive or insulting words or behaviour;

(23) uses threatening, abusive or insulting racist words or behaviour;

(24) intentionally fails to work properly or, being required to work, refuses to do so;

(25) disobeys any lawful order;

(26) disobeys or fails to comply with any rule or regulation applying to him;

(27) receives any controlled drug or, without the consent of an officer, any other art-icle, during the course of a visit (not being an interview such as is mentioned in rule 16);

(28) displays, attaches or draws on any part of a young offender institution, or on any other property, threatening, abusive, or insulting racist words, drawings, symbols or other material;

(29)

(a) attempts to commit,

(b) incites another inmate to commit, or

(c) assists another inmate to commit or to attempt to commit,

any of the foregoing offences.

Defences to rule 55(10)

56. It shall be a defence for an inmate charged with an offence under rule 55(10) to show that—

(a) the controlled drug had been, prior to its administration, lawfully in his pos-session for his use or was administered to him in the course of a lawful supply of the drug to him by another person;

(b) the controlled drug was administered by or to him in circumstances in which he did not know and had no reason to suspect that such a drug was being administered; or

(c) the controlled drug was administered by or to him under duress or to him with-out his consent in circumstances where it was not reasonable for him to have resisted.

Interpretation of rule 55

57. For the purposes of rule 55 words, behaviour or material shall be racist if they demon-strate or are motivated (wholly or partly) by hostility to members of a racial group (whether identifiable or not) based on their membership (or presumed membership) of a racial group, and 'membership', 'presumed', 'racial group' and 'racially aggravated', shall have the meanings assigned to them by section 28 of the Crime and Disorder Act 1998.

Disciplinary charges

58.—(1) Where an inmate is to be charged with an offence against discipline, the charge shall be laid as soon as possible and, save in exceptional circumstances, within 48 hours of the discovery of the offence.

(2) Every charge shall be inquired into by the governor or, as the case may be, the adju-dicator.

(3) Every charge shall be first inquired into not later, save in exceptional circumstances or in accordance with rule 60A(5) or rule 65(4), than:

(a) where it is inquired into by the governor, the next day, not being a Sunday or a public holiday, after it is laid;

(b) where it is referred to the adjudicator under rule 58A(2), 28 days after it is so referred.

(4) An inmate who is to be charged with an offence against discipline may be kept apart from other inmates pending the governor's first inquiry.

Determination of mode of inquiry

58A.—(1) Before inquiring into a charge the governor shall determine whether it is so serious that additional days should be awarded for the offence, if the inmate is found guilty.

(2) Where the governor determines:
  (a) that it is so serious, he shall:
      (i)   refer the charge to the adjudicator forthwith for him to inquire into it;
      (ii) refer any other charge arising out of the same incident to the adjudicator forthwith for him to inquire into it; and
      (iii) inform the inmate who has been charged that he has done so;
  (b) that it is not so serious, he shall proceed to inquire into the charge.

(3) If:
  (a) at any time during an inquiry into a charge by the governor; or
  (b) following such an inquiry, after the governor has found the inmate guilty of an offence but before he has imposed a punishment for that offence,
it appears to the governor that the charge is so serious that additional days should be awarded for the offence if (where sub-paragraph (a) applies) the inmate is found guilty, the governor shall act in accordance with paragraph (2)(a)(i) to (iii) and the adjudicator shall first inquire into any charge referred to him under this paragraph not later than, save in exceptional circumstances, 28 days after the charge was referred.

Rights of inmates charged

59.—(1) Where an inmate is charged with an offence against discipline, he shall be informed of the charge as soon as possible and, in any case, before the time when it is inquired into by the governor or, as the case may be, the adjudicator.

(2) At an inquiry into charge against an inmate he shall be given an opportunity of hearing what is alleged against him and of presenting his own case.

(3) At an inquiry into a charge which has been referred to the adjudicator, the inmate who has been charged shall be given the opportunity to be legally represented.

Governor's punishments

60.—(1) If he finds an inmate guilty of an offence against discipline the governor may, subject to paragraph (3) and rule 65, impose one or more of the following punishments:
  (a) caution;
  (b) forfeiture for a period not exceeding 21 days of any of the privileges under rule 6;
  (c) removal for a period not exceeding 21 days from any particular activity or activities of the young offender institution, other than education, training courses, work and physical education in accordance with rules 37, 38, 39, 40 and 41;
  (d) extra work outside the normal working week for a period not exceeding 21 days and for not more than two hours on any day;
  (e) stoppage of or deduction from earnings for a period not exceeding 42 days;
  (f) in the case of an offence against discipline committed by an inmate who was aged 18 or over at the time of commission of the offence, other than an inmate who is serving the period of detention and training under a detention and training order pursuant to section 100 of the Powers of Criminal Courts (Sentencing) Act 2000, confinement to a cell or room for a period not exceeding seven days;
  (g) removal from his wing or living unit for a period not exceeding 21 days;
  (h) [omitted].

(2) If an inmate is found guilty of more than one charge arising out of an incident punishments under this rule may be ordered to run consecutively, but, in the case of a punishment of cellular confinement the total period shall not exceed ten days.

(3) A caution shall not be combined with any other punishment for the same charge.

(4) In imposing a punishment under this rule, the governor shall take into account any guidelines that the Secretary of State may from time to time issue as to the level of punishment that should normally be imposed for a particular offence against discipline.

Adjudicator's punishments

60A.—(1) If he finds an inmate guilty of an offence against discipline the adjudicator may, subject to paragraph (2) and to rule 65, impose one or more of the following punishments:

    (a) any of the punishments mentioned in rule 60(1);

    (b) in the case of an inmate who is a short-term prisoner or long-term prisoner, an award of additional days not exceeding 42 days.

(2) A caution shall not be combined with any other punishment for the same charge.

(3) If an inmate is found guilty of more than one charge arising out of an incident, punishments under this rule may be ordered to run consecutively but, in the case of an award of additional days, the total period added shall not exceed 42 days and, in the case of a punishment of cellular confinement, the total period shall not exceed ten days.

(4) This rule applies to an inmate who has been charged with having committed an offence against discipline before the date on which the rule came into force, in the same way as it applies to an inmate who has been charged with having committed an offence against discipline on or after that date, provided the charge is referred to the adjudicator no later than 60 days after that date.

(5) Rule 58(3) shall not apply to a charge where, by virtue of paragraph (4), this rule applies to the inmate who has been charged.

Confinement to a cell or room

61.—(1) When it is proposed to impose a punishment of confinement in a cell or room, the medical officer, or a medical practitioner such as is mentioned in rule 27(3), shall inform the governor whether there are any medical reasons why the inmate should not be so dealt with. The governor shall give effect to any recommendation which may be made under this paragraph.

(2) No cell or room shall be used as a detention cell or room for the purpose of a punishment of confinement to a cell or room unless it has been certified by an officer of the Secretary of State (not being an officer of a young offender institution) that it is suitable for the purpose; that its size, lighting, heating, ventilation and fittings are adequate for health; and that it allows the inmate to communicate at any time with an officer.

Removal from wing or living unit

62. Following the imposition of a punishment of removal from his wing or living unit, an inmate shall be accommodated in a separate part of the young offender institution under such restrictions of earnings and activities as the Secretary of State may direct.

Suspended punishments

63.—(1) Subject to any directions of the Secretary of State, the power to impose a disciplinary punishment (other than a caution) shall include a power to direct that the punishment is not to take effect unless, during a period specified in the direction (not being more than six months from the date of the direction), the inmate commits another offence against discipline and a direction is given under paragraph (2).

(2) Where an inmate commits an offence against discipline during the period specified in a direction given under paragraph (1), the person dealing with that offence may—

    (a) direct that the suspended punishment shall take effect; or

    (b) reduce the period or amount of the suspended punishment and direct that it shall take effect as so reduced; or

    (c) vary the original direction by substituting for the period specified therein a period expiring not later than six months from the date of variation; or

    (d) give no direction with respect to the suspended punishment.

(3) Where an award of additional days has been suspended under paragraph (1) and an inmate is charged with committing an offence against discipline during the period specified in a direction given under that paragraph, the governor shall either:

    (a) inquire into the charge and give no direction with respect to the suspended award; or

    (b) refer the charge to the adjudicator for him to inquire into it.

Remission and mitigation of punishments and quashing of findings of guilt

64.—(1) The Secretary of State may quash any findings of guilt and may remit a disciplinary punishment or mitigate it either by reducing it or by substituting a punishment which is, in his opinion, less severe.

(2) Subject to any directions of the Secretary of State, the governor may remit or mitigate any punishment imposed by a governor.

Adult female inmates: disciplinary punishments

65.—(1) In the case of a female inmate aged 21 years or over, rule 60 shall not apply, but the governor may, if he finds the inmate guilty of an offence against discipline, impose one or more of the following punishments:

    (a) caution;

    (b) forfeiture for a period not exceeding 42 days of any of the privileges under rule 6;

    (c) removal for a period not exceeding 21 days from any particular activity or activities of the young offender institution, other than education, training courses, work and physical education in accordance with rules 37, 38, 39, 40 and 41;

    (d) stoppage of or deduction from earnings for a period not exceeding 84 days;

    (e) confinement to a cell or room for a period not exceeding 21 days;

    (f) [omitted].

(1A) In the case of a female inmate aged 21 years or over, where a charge has been referred to the adjudicator, rule 60A shall not apply, but the adjudicator may if he finds the inmate guilty of an offence against discipline, impose one or more of the following punishments:

    (a) any of the punishments mentioned in paragraph (1);

    (b) in the case of an inmate who is a short-term or long-term prisoner, an award of additional days not exceeding 42 days.

(2) If an inmate is found guilty of more than one charge arising out of an incident, punishments under this rule may be ordered to run consecutively, but in the case of an award of additional days, the total period added shall not exceed 42 days.

(3) Paragraph (1A) applies to an inmate who has been charged with having committed an offence against discipline before the date on which that paragraph came into force, in the same was as it applies to an inmate who has been charged with having committed an offence against discipline on or after that date, provided the charge is referred to the adjudicator no later than 60 days after that date.

(4) Rule 58(3) shall not apply to a charge where, by virtue of paragraph (3), paragraph (1A) applies to the inmate who has been charged.

Forfeiture of remission to be treated as an award of additional days

66.—(1) In this rule, 'existing prisoner' and 'existing licensee' have the meanings assigned to them by paragraph 8(1) of Schedule 12 to the Criminal Justice Act 1991.

(2) In relation to any existing prisoner or existing licensee who has forfeited any remission of his sentence, the provisions of Part II of the Criminal Justice Act 1991 shall apply as if he had been awarded such number of additional days as equals the number of days of remission which he has forfeited.

PART III
OFFICERS OF YOUNG OFFENDER INSTITUTIONS

General duty of officers

67.—(1) It shall be the duty of every officer to conform to these Rules and the rules and regulations of the young offender institution, to assist and support the governor in their maintenance and to obey his lawful instructions.

(2) An officer shall inform the governor promptly of any abuse or impropriety which comes to his knowledge.

Gratuities forbidden

68. No officer shall receive any unauthorised fee, gratuity or other consideration in connection with his office.

Search of officers

69. An officer shall submit himself to be searched in a young offender institution if the governor so directs. Any such search shall be conducted in as seemly a manner as is consistent with discovering anything concealed.

Transactions with inmates

70.—(1) No officer shall take part in any business or pecuniary transaction with or on behalf of an inmate without the leave of the Secretary of State.

(2) No officer shall, without authority, bring in or take out, or attempt to bring in or take out, or knowingly allow to be brought in or taken out, to or for an inmate, or deposit in any place with intent that it shall come into the possession of an inmate, any article whatsoever.

Contact with former inmates, etc

71. No officer shall, without the knowledge of the governor, communicate with any person who he knows to be a former inmate or a relative or friend of an inmate or former inmate.

Communications to the press, etc

72.—(1) No officer shall make, directly or indirectly, any unauthorised communication to a representative of the press or any other person concerning matters which have become known to him in the course of his duty.

(2) No officer shall, without authority, publish any matter or make any public pronouncement relating to the administration of any institution to which the Prison Act 1952 applies or to any of its inmates.

639

Code of discipline

73. The Secretary of State may approve a code of discipline to have effect in relation to officers, or such classes of officers as it may specify, setting out the offences against discipline, the awards which may be made in respect of them and the procedure for dealing with charges.

PART IV
Persons Having Access to a YOUNG OFFENDER INSTITUTION

Prohibited articles

74. No person shall, without authority, convey into or throw into or deposit in a young offender institution, or convey to an inmate, or deposit in any place with intent that it shall come into the possession of an inmate, any article whatsoever. Anything so conveyed, thrown or deposited may be confiscated by the governor.

Control of persons and vehicles

75.—(1) Any person or vehicle entering or leaving a young offender institution may be stopped, examined and searched. Any such search of a person shall be carried out in as seemly a manner as is consistent with discovering anything concealed.

(2) The governor may direct the removal from a young offender institution of any person who does not leave on being required to do so.

Viewing of young offender institutions

76.—(1) No outside person shall be permitted to view a young offender institution unless authorised by statute or the Secretary of State.

(2) No person viewing a young offender institution shall be permitted to take a photograph, make a sketch or communicate with an inmate unless authorised by statute or the Secretary of State.

Visitors

77.—(1) Without prejudice to any other powers to prohibit or restrict entry to young offender institutions, or his powers under rules 9 and 10, the Secretary of State may prohibit visits by a person to a young offender institution or to an inmate in a young offender institution for such periods of time as he considers necessary if the governor considers that such a prohibition is—

    (a) necessary on grounds specified in rule 11(4); and
    (b) is proportionate to what is sought to be achieved by the prohibition.

(2) Paragraph (1) shall not apply in relation to any visit to a young offender institution or inmate by a member of the board of visitors of the young offender institution, or justice of the peace, or to prevent any visit by a legal adviser for the purposes of an interview under rule 16 or visit allowed by the board of visitors under rule 10(5).

PART V
BOARDS OF VISITORS

Disqualification for membership

78. Any person directly or indirectly interested in any contract for the supply of goods or services to a young offender institution shall not be a member of the board of visitors for that institution and any member who becomes so interested in such a contract shall vacate office as a member.

Appointment

79.—(1) A member of the board of visitors for a young offender institution appointed by the Secretary of State under section 6(2) of the Prison Act 1952 shall subject to paragraphs (3) and (4) hold office for three years or such shorter period as the Secretary of State may appoint.

(2) A member—

    (a) appointed for the first time to the board of visitors for a particular young offender institution; or

    (b) re-appointed to the board following a gap of a year or more in his membership of it,

shall, during the period of 12 months following the date on which he is so appointed or (as the case may be) re-appointed, undertake such training as may reasonably be required by the Secretary of State.

(3) The Secretary of State may terminate the appointment of a member if satisfied that—

    (a) he has failed satisfactorily to perform his duties;

    (b) he has failed to undertake training he has been required to undertake under paragraph (2), by the end of the period specified in that paragraph;

    (c) he is by reason of physical or mental illness, or for any other reason, incapable of carrying out his duties;

    (d) he has been convicted of such a criminal offence, or his conduct has been such, that it is not in the Secretary of State's opinion fitting that he should remain a member; or

    (e) there is, or appears to be, or could appear to be, any conflict of interest between the member performing his duties as a member and any interest of that member, whether personal, financial or otherwise.

(4) Where the Secretary of State:

    (a) has reason to suspect that a member of the board of visitors for a young offender institution may have so conducted himself that his appointment may be liable to be terminated under paragraph (3)(a) or (d); and

    (b) is of the opinion that the suspected conduct is of such a serious nature that the member cannot be permitted to continue to perform his functions as a member of the board pending the completion of the Secretary of State's investigations into the matter and any decision as to whether the member's appointment should be terminated,

he may suspend the member from office for such period or periods as he may reasonably require in order to complete his investigations and determine whether or not the appointment of the member should be so terminated; and a member so suspended shall not, during the period of the suspension, be regarded as being a member of the board, other than for the purposes of this paragraph and paragraphs (1) and (2).

(5) A board shall have a chairman and a vice chairman, who shall be members of the board.

(6) The Secretary of State shall—

    (a) upon the constitution of a board for the first time, appoint a chairman and a vice chairman to hold office for a period not exceeding 12 months;

    (b) thereafter appoint, before the date of the first meeting of the board in any year of office of the board, a chairman and a vice chairman for that year, having first consulted the board; and

   (c) promptly fill, after having first consulted the board, any casual vacancy in the office of chairman or vice chairman.

(7) The Secretary of State may terminate the appointment of a member as chairman or vice chairman of the board if he is satisfied that the member has—

   (a) failed satisfactorily to perform his functions as chairman or (as the case may be) vice chairman; or

   (b) has grossly misconducted himself whilst performing those functions.

Proceedings of boards

80.—(1) The board of visitors for a young offender institution shall meet at the institution at least once a month.

(2) The board may fix a quorum of not fewer than three members for proceedings.

(3) The board shall keep minutes of their proceedings.

(4) The proceedings of the board shall not be invalidated by any vacancy in the membership or any defect in the appointment of a member.

General duties of boards

81.—(1) The board of visitors for a young offender institution shall satisfy themselves as to the state of the premises, the administration of the institution and the treatment of the inmates.

(2) The board shall inquire into and report upon any matter into which the Secretary of State asks them to inquire.

(3) The board shall direct the attention of the governor to any matter which calls for his attention, and shall report to the Secretary of State any matters which they consider it expedient to report.

(4) The board shall inform the Secretary of State immediately of any abuse which comes to their knowledge.

(5) Before exercising any power under these Rules, the board and any member of the board shall consult the governor in relation to any matter which may affect discipline.

Particular duties

82.—(1) The board of visitors for a young offender institution and any member of the board shall hear any complaint or request which an inmate wishes to make to them or him.

(2) The board shall arrange for the food of the inmates to be inspected by a member of the board at frequent intervals.

(3) The board shall inquire into any report made to them, whether or not by a member of the board, that an inmate's health, mental or physical, is likely to be injuriously affected by any conditions of his detention.

Members visiting young offender institutions

83.—(1) The members of the board of visitors for a young offender institution shall visit the institution frequently, and the board shall arrange a rota for the purpose.

(2) A member of the board shall have access at any time to every part of the institution and to every inmate, and he may interview any inmate out of the sight and hearing of officers.

(3) A member of the board shall have access to the records of the young offender institution.

Annual report

84.—(1) The board of visitors for a young offender institution shall, in accordance with paragraphs (2) and (3), from time to time make a report to the Secretary of State concerning the state of the institution and its administration, including in it any advice and suggestions they consider appropriate.

(2) The board shall comply with any directions given to them from time to time by the Secretary of State as to the following matters—

(a) the period to be covered by a report under paragraph (1);

(b) the frequency with which such a report is to be made; and

(c) the length of time from the end of the period covered by such a report within which it is to be made,

either in respect of a particular report or generally; provided that no directions may be issued under this paragraph if they would have the effect of requiring a board to make or deliver a report less frequently than once in every 12 months.

(3) Subject to any directions given to them under paragraph (2), the board shall, under paragraph (1), make an annual report to the Secretary of State as soon as reasonably possible after 31st December each year, which shall cover the period of 12 months ending on that date or, in the case of a board constituted for the first time during that period, such part of that period during which the board has been in existence.

PART VI
SUPPLEMENTAL

Delegation by governor

85. The governor of a young offender institution may, with the leave of the Secretary of State, delegate any of his powers and duties under these Rules to another officer of that institution.

Contracted out young offender institutions

86.—(1) Where the Secretary of State has entered into a contract for the running of a young offender institution under section 84 of the Criminal Justice Act 1991 (in this rule 'the 1991 Act') these Rules shall have effect in relation to that young offender institution with the following modifications—

(a) references to an officer shall include references to a prisoner custody officer certified as such under section 89(1) of the 1991 Act;

(b) references to a governor shall include references to a director approved by the Secretary of State for the purposes of section 85(1)(a) of the 1991 Act except—

(i) in rules 49, 51, 52, 58, 58A, 60, 63, 64, 65 and 85 where references to a governor shall include references to a controller appointed by the Secretary of State under section 85(1)(b) of the 1991 Act; and

(ii) in rules 67(1), 71 and 81 where references to a governor shall include references to a director and a controller;

(c) rule 73 shall not apply in relation to a prisoner custody officer certified as such under section 89(1) of the 1991 Act and performing custodial duties.

(2) Where a director exercises the powers set out in section 85(3)(b) of the 1991 Act

(removal from association, temporary confinement and restraints) in cases of urgency, he shall notify the controller of that fact forthwith.

Contracted out parts of young offender institutions

87. Where the Secretary of State has entered into a contract for the running of part of a young offender institution under section 84(1) of the Criminal Justice Act 1991, that part and the remaining part shall each be treated for the purposes of Parts I to IV and Part VI of these Rules as if they were separate young offender institutions.

Contracted out functions at directly managed young offender institutions

88.—(1) Where the Secretary of State has entered into a contract under section 88A(1) of the Criminal Justice Act 1991 for any functions at a directly managed young offender institution to be performed by prisoner custody officers who are authorised to perform custodial duties under section 89(1) of that Act, references to an officer in these Rules shall, subject to paragraph (2), include references to a prisoner custody officer who is so authorised and who is performing contracted out functions for the purposes of, or for purposes connected with, the young offender institution.

(2) Paragraph (1) shall not apply to references to an officer in rule 73.

(3) In this rule 'directly managed young offender institution' means a young offender institution which is not a contracted out young offender institution.

Revocations and savings

89.—(1) Subject to paragraphs (2) and (3), the Rules specified in the Schedule to these Rules are hereby revoked.

(2) Without prejudice to the Interpretation Act 1978 ('the 1978 Act'), where an inmate committed an offence against discipline contrary to rule 50 of the Young Offender Institution Rules 1988 ('the 1988 Rules') prior to the coming into force of these Rules, the 1988 Rules shall continue to have effect to permit the prisoner to be charged with such an offence, disciplinary proceedings in relation to such an offence to be continued, and the governor to impose punishment for such an offence.

(3) Without prejudice to the 1978 Act, any award of additional days or other punishment or suspended punishment for an offence against discipline awarded or imposed under any provision of the Rules revoked by this rule, or the 1988 Rules as saved by paragraph (2), or treated by any such provision as having been awarded or imposed under the Rules revoked by this rule, shall have effect as if awarded or imposed under the corresponding provision of these Rules.

APPENDIX 4

Human Rights Act 1998
1998 Chapter 42

ARRANGEMENT OF SECTIONS

Introduction

21. Interpretation, etc
22. Short title, commencement, application and extent

Introduction

The Convention rights

1.—(1) In this Act 'the Convention rights' means the rights and fundamental freedoms set out in—
      (a) Articles 2 to 12 and 14 of the Convention,
      (b) Articles 1 to 3 of the First Protocol, and
      (c) Articles 1 and 2 of the Sixth Protocol,
as read with Articles 16 to 18 of the Convention.

(2) Those Articles are to have effect for the purposes of this Act subject to any designated derogation or reservation (as to which see sections 14 and 15).

(3) The Articles are set out in Schedule 1.

(4) The Secretary of State may by order make such amendments to this Act as he considers appropriate to reflect the effect, in relation to the United Kingdom, of a protocol.

(5) In subsection (4) 'protocol' means a protocol to the Convention—
      (a) which the United Kingdom has ratified; or
      (b) which the United Kingdom has signed with a view to ratification.

(6) No amendment may be made by an order under subsection (4) so as to come into force before the protocol concerned is in force in relation to the United Kingdom.

Interpretation of Convention rights

2.—(1) A court or tribunal determining a question which has arisen in connection with a Convention right must take into account any—
      (a) judgment, decision, declaration or advisory opinion of the European Court of Human Rights,
      (b) opinion of the Commission given in a report adopted under Article 31 of the Convention,
      (c) decision of the Commission in connection with Article 26 or 27(2) of the Convention, or
      (d) decision of the Committee of Ministers taken under Article 46 of the Convention,
whenever made or given, so far as, in the opinion of the court or tribunal, it is relevant to the proceedings in which that question has arisen.

(2) Evidence of any judgment, decision, declaration or opinion of which account may have to be taken under this section is to be given in proceedings before any court or tribunal in such manner as may be provided by rules.

(3) In this section 'rules' means rules of court or, in the case of proceedings before a tribunal, rules made for the purposes of this section—

(a) by the Lord Chancellor or the Secretary of State, in relation to any proceedings outside Scotland;

(b) by the Secretary of State, in relation to proceedings in Scotland; or

(c) by a Northern Ireland department, in relation to proceedings before a tribunal in Northern Ireland—

    (i)   which deals with transferred matters; and

    (ii) for which no rules made under paragraph (a) are in force.

Legislation

Interpretation of legislation

3.—(1) So far as it is possible to do so, primary legislation and subordinate legislation must be read and given effect in a way which is compatible with the Convention rights.

(2) This section—

(a) applies to primary legislation and subordinate legislation whenever enacted;

(b) does not affect the validity, continuing operation or enforcement of any incompatible primary legislation; and

(c) does not affect the validity, continuing operation or enforcement of any incompatible subordinate legislation if (disregarding any possibility of revocation) primary legislation prevents removal of the incompatibility.

Declaration of incompatibility

4.—(1) Subsection (2) applies in any proceedings in which a court determines whether a provision of primary legislation is compatible with a Convention right.

(2) If the court is satisfied that the provision is incompatible with a Convention right, it may make a declaration of that incompatibility.

(3) Subsection (4) applies in any proceedings in which a court determines whether a provision of subordinate legislation, made in the exercise of a power conferred by primary legislation, is compatible with a Convention right.

(4) If the court is satisfied—

(a) that the provision is incompatible with a Convention right, and

(b) that (disregarding any possibility of revocation) the primary legislation concerned prevents removal of the incompatibility,

it may make a declaration of that incompatibility.

(5) In this section 'court' means—

(a) the House of Lords;

(b) the Judicial Committee of the Privy Council;

(c) the Courts-Martial Appeal Court;

(d) in Scotland, the High Court of Justiciary sitting otherwise than as a trial court or the Court of Session;

(e) in England and Wales or Northern Ireland, the High Court or the Court of Appeal.

(6) A declaration under this section ('a declaration of incompatibility')—

(a) does not affect the validity, continuing operation or enforcement of the provision in respect of which it is given; and

(b) is not binding on the parties to the proceedings in which it is made.

Right of Crown to intervene

5.—(1) Where a court is considering whether to make a declaration of incompatibility, the Crown is entitled to notice in accordance with rules of court.

(2) In any case to which subsection (1) applies—

    (a) a Minister of the Crown (or a person nominated by him),

    (b) a member of the Scottish Executive,

    (c) a Northern Ireland Minister,

    (d) a Northern Ireland department,

is entitled, on giving notice in accordance with rules of court, to be joined as a party to the proceedings.

(3) Notice under subsection (2) may be given at any time during the proceedings.

(4) A person who has been made a party to criminal proceedings (other than in Scotland) as the result of a notice under subsection (2) may, with leave, appeal to the House of Lords against any declaration of incompatibility made in the proceedings.

(5) In subsection (4)—

    'criminal proceedings' includes all proceedings before the Courts-Martial Appeal Court; and

    'leave' means leave granted by the court making the declaration of incompatibility or by the House of Lords.

Public authorities

Acts of public authorities

6.—(1) It is unlawful for a public authority to act in a way which is incompatible with a Convention right.

(2) Subsection (1) does not apply to an act if—

    (a) as the result of one or more provisions of primary legislation, the authority could not have acted differently; or

    (b) in the case of one or more provisions of, or made under, primary legislation which cannot be read or given effect in a way which is compatible with the Convention rights, the authority was acting so as to give effect to or enforce those provisions.

(3) In this section 'public authority' includes—

    (a) a court or tribunal, and

    (b) any person certain of whose functions are functions of a public nature,

but does not include either House of Parliament or a person exercising functions in connection with proceedings in Parliament.

(4) In subsection (3) 'Parliament' does not include the House of Lords in its judicial capacity.

(5) In relation to a particular act, a person is not a public authority by virtue only of subsection (3)(b) if the nature of the act is private.

(6) 'An act' includes a failure to act but does not include a failure to—

    (a) introduce in, or lay before, Parliament a proposal for legislation; or

    (b) make any primary legislation or remedial order.

Proceedings

7.—(1) A person who claims that a public authority has acted (or proposes to act) in a way which is made unlawful by section 6(1) may—

(a) bring proceedings against the authority under this Act in the appropriate court or tribunal, or

(b) rely on the Convention right or rights concerned in any legal proceedings, but only if he is (or would be) a victim of the unlawful act.

(2) In subsection (1)(a) 'appropriate court or tribunal' means such court or tribunal as may be determined in accordance with rules; and proceedings against an authority include a counterclaim or similar proceeding.

(3) If the proceedings are brought on an application for judicial review, the applicant is to be taken to have a sufficient interest in relation to the unlawful act only if he is, or would be, a victim of that act.

(4) If the proceedings are made by way of a petition for judicial review in Scotland, the applicant shall be taken to have title and interest to sue in relation to the unlawful act only if he is, or would be, a victim of that act.

(5) Proceedings under subsection (1)(a) must be brought before the end of—

(a) the period of one year beginning with the date on which the act complained of took place; or

(b) such longer period as the court or tribunal considers equitable having regard to all the circumstances,

but that is subject to any rule imposing a stricter time limit in relation to the procedure in question.

(6) In subsection (1)(b) 'legal proceedings' includes—

(a) proceedings brought by or at the instigation of a public authority; and

(b) an appeal against the decision of a court or tribunal.

(7) For the purposes of this section, a person is a victim of an unlawful act only if he would be a victim for the purposes of Article 34 of the Convention if proceedings were brought in the European Court of Human Rights in respect of that act.

(8) Nothing in this Act creates a criminal offence.

(9) In this section 'rules' means—

(a) in relation to proceedings before a court or tribunal outside Scotland, rules made by the Lord Chancellor or the Secretary of State for the purposes of this section or rules of court,

(b) in relation to proceedings before a court or tribunal in Scotland, rules made by the Secretary of State for those purposes,

(c) in relation to proceedings before a tribunal in Northern Ireland—

(i) which deals with transferred matters; and

(ii) for which no rules made under paragraph (a) are in force, rules made by a Northern Ireland department for those purposes,

and includes provision made by order under section 1 of the Courts and Legal Services Act 1990.

(10) In making rules, regard must be had to section 9.

(11) The Minister who has power to make rules in relation to a particular tribunal may, to the extent he considers it necessary to ensure that the tribunal can provide an appropriate remedy in relation to an act (or proposed act) of a public authority which is (or would be) unlawful as a result of section 6(1), by order add to—

(a) the relief or remedies which the tribunal may grant; or

(b) the grounds on which it may grant any of them.

(12) An order made under subsection (11) may contain such incidental, supplemental, consequential or transitional provision as the Minister making it considers appropriate.

(13) 'The Minister' includes the Northern Ireland department concerned.

Judicial remedies

8.—(1) In relation to any act (or proposed act) of a public authority which the court finds is (or would be) unlawful, it may grant such relief or remedy, or make such order, within its powers as it considers just and appropriate.

(2) But damages may be awarded only by a court which has power to award damages, or to order the payment of compensation, in civil proceedings.

(3) No award of damages is to be made unless, taking account of all the circumstances of the case, including—

    (a) any other relief or remedy granted, or order made, in relation to the act in question (by that or any other court), and

    (b) the consequences of any decision (of that or any other court) in respect of that act,

the court is satisfied that the award is necessary to afford just satisfaction to the person in whose favour it is made.

(4) In determining—

    (a) whether to award damages, or

    (b) the amount of an award,

the court must take into account the principles applied by the European Court of Human Rights in relation to the award of compensation under Article 41 of the Convention.

(5) A public authority against which damages are awarded is to be treated—

    (a) in Scotland, for the purposes of section 3 of the Law Reform (Miscellaneous Provisions) (Scotland) Act 1940 as if the award were made in an action of damages in which the authority has been found liable in respect of loss or damage to the person to whom the award is made;

    (b) for the purposes of the Civil Liability (Contribution) Act 1978 as liable in respect of damage suffered by the person to whom the award is made.

(6) In this section—

    'court' includes a tribunal;

    'damages' means damages for an unlawful act of a public authority; and

    'unlawful' means unlawful under section 6(1).

Judicial acts

9.—(1) Proceedings under section 7(1)(a) in respect of a judicial act may be brought only—

    (a) by exercising a right of appeal;

    (b) on an application (in Scotland a petition) for judicial review; or

    (c) in such other forum as may be prescribed by rules.

(2) That does not affect any rule of law which prevents a court from being the subject of judicial review.

(3) In proceedings under this Act in respect of a judicial act done in good faith, damages may not be awarded otherwise than to compensate a person to the extent required by Article 5(5) of the Convention.

(4) An award of damages permitted by subsection (3) is to be made against the Crown; but no award may be made unless the appropriate person, if not a party to the proceedings, is joined.

(5) In this section—

'appropriate person' means the Minister responsible for the court concerned, or a person or government department nominated by him;

'court' includes a tribunal;

'judge' includes a member of a tribunal, a justice of the peace and a clerk or other officer entitled to exercise the jurisdiction of a court;

'judicial act' means a judicial act of a court and includes an act done on the instructions, or on behalf, of a judge; and

'rules' has the same meaning as in section 7(9).

Remedial action

Power to take remedial action

10.—(1) This section applies if—

    (a) a provision of legislation has been declared under section 4 to be incompatible with a Convention right and, if an appeal lies—

        (i) all persons who may appeal have stated in writing that they do not intend to do so;

        (ii) the time for bringing an appeal has expired and no appeal has been brought within that time; or

        (iii) an appeal brought within that time has been determined or abandoned; or

    (b) it appears to a Minister of the Crown or Her Majesty in Council that, having regard to a finding of the European Court of Human Rights made after the coming into force of this section in proceedings against the United Kingdom, a provision of legislation is incompatible with an obligation of the United Kingdom arising from the Convention.

(2) If a Minister of the Crown considers that there are compelling reasons for proceeding under this section, he may by order make such amendments to the legislation as he considers necessary to remove the incompatibility.

(3) If, in the case of subordinate legislation, a Minister of the Crown considers—

    (a) that it is necessary to amend the primary legislation under which the subordinate legislation in question was made, in order to enable the incompatibility to be removed, and

    (b) that there are compelling reasons for proceeding under this section,

he may by order make such amendments to the primary legislation as he considers necessary.

(4) This section also applies where the provision in question is in subordinate legislation and has been quashed, or declared invalid, by reason of incompatibility with a Convention right and the Minister proposes to proceed under paragraph 2(b) of Schedule 2.

(5) If the legislation is an Order in Council, the power conferred by subsection (2) or (3) is exercisable by Her Majesty in Council.

(6) In this section 'legislation' does not include a Measure of the Church Assembly or of the General Synod of the Church of England.

(7) Schedule 2 makes further provision about remedial orders.

Other rights and proceedings

Safeguard for existing human rights

11. A person's reliance on a Convention right does not restrict—

    (a) any other right or freedom conferred on him by or under any law having effect in any part of the United Kingdom; or

(b) his right to make any claim or bring any proceedings which he could make or bring apart from sections 7 to 9.

Freedom of expression

12.—(1) This section applies if a court is considering whether to grant any relief which, if granted, might affect the exercise of the Convention right to freedom of expression.

(2) If the person against whom the application for relief is made ('the respondent') is neither present nor represented, no such relief is to be granted unless the court is satisfied—

(a) that the applicant has taken all practicable steps to notify the respondent; or
(b) that there are compelling reasons why the respondent should not be notified.

(3) No such relief is to be granted so as to restrain publication before trial unless the court is satisfied that the applicant is likely to establish that publication should not be allowed.

(4) The court must have particular regard to the importance of the Convention right to freedom of expression and, where the proceedings relate to material which the respondent claims, or which appears to the court, to be journalistic, literary or artistic material (or to conduct connected with such material), to—

(a) the extent to which—
   (i) the material has, or is about to, become available to the public; or
   (ii) it is, or would be, in the public interest for the material to be published;
(b) any relevant privacy code.

(5) In this section—
'court' includes a tribunal; and
'relief' includes any remedy or order (other than in criminal proceedings).

Freedom of thought, conscience and religion

13.—(1) If a court's determination of any question arising under this Act might affect the exercise by a religious organisation (itself or its members collectively) of the Convention right to freedom of thought, conscience and religion, it must have particular regard to the importance of that right.

(2) In this section 'court' includes a tribunal.

Derogations and reservations

Derogations

14.—(1) In this Act 'designated derogation' means—

(a) the United Kingdom's derogation from Article 5(3) of the Convention; and
(b) any derogation by the United Kingdom from an Article of the Convention, or of any protocol to the Convention, which is designated for the purposes of this Act in an order made by the Secretary of State.

(2) The derogation referred to in subsection (1)(a) is set out in Part I of Schedule 3.

(3) If a designated derogation is amended or replaced it ceases to be a designated derogation.

(4) But subsection (3) does not prevent the Secretary of State from exercising his power under subsection (1)(b) to make a fresh designation order in respect of the Article concerned.

(5) The Secretary of State must by order make such amendments to Schedule 3 as he considers appropriate to reflect—

(a) any designation order; or

(b) the effect of subsection (3).

(6) A designation order may be made in anticipation of the making by the United Kingdom of a proposed derogation.

Reservations

15.—(1) In this Act 'designated reservation' means—

(a) the United Kingdom's reservation to Article 2 of the First Protocol to the Convention; and

(b) any other reservation by the United Kingdom to an Article of the Convention, or of any protocol to the Convention, which is designated for the purposes of this Act in an order made by the Secretary of State.

(2) The text of the reservation referred to in subsection (1)(a) is set out in Part II of Schedule 3.

(3) If a designated reservation is withdrawn wholly or in part it ceases to be a designated reservation.

(4) But subsection (3) does not prevent the Secretary of State from exercising his power under subsection (1)(b) to make a fresh designation order in respect of the Article concerned.

(5) The Secretary of State must by order make such amendments to this Act as he considers appropriate to reflect—

(a) any designation order; or

(b) the effect of subsection (3).

Period for which designated derogations have effect

16.—(1) If it has not already been withdrawn by the United Kingdom, a designated derogation ceases to have effect for the purposes of this Act—

(a) in the case of the derogation referred to in section 14(1)(a), at the end of the period of five years beginning with the date on which section 1(2) came into force;

(b) in the case of any other derogation, at the end of the period of five years beginning with the date on which the order designating it was made.

(2) At any time before the period—

(a) fixed by subsection (1)(a) or (b), or

(b) extended by an order under this subsection,

comes to an end, the Secretary of State may by order extend it by a further period of five years.

(3) An order under section 14(1)(b) ceases to have effect at the end of the period for consideration, unless a resolution has been passed by each House approving the order.

(4) Subsection (3) does not affect—

(a) anything done in reliance on the order; or

(b) the power to make a fresh order under section 14(1)(b).

(5) In subsection (3) 'period for consideration' means the period of forty days beginning with the day on which the order was made.

(6) In calculating the period for consideration, no account is to be taken of any time during which—

(a) Parliament is dissolved or prorogued; or

(b) both Houses are adjourned for more than four days.

(7) If a designated derogation is withdrawn by the United Kingdom, the Secretary of State must by order make such amendments to this Act as he considers are required to reflect that withdrawal.

Periodic review of designated reservations

17.—(1) The appropriate Minister must review the designated reservation referred to in section 15(1)(a)—

    (a) before the end of the period of five years beginning with the date on which section 1(2) came into force; and

    (b) if that designation is still in force, before the end of the period of five years beginning with the date on which the last report relating to it was laid under subsection (3).

(2) The appropriate Minister must review each of the other designated reservations (if any)—

    (a) before the end of the period of five years beginning with the date on which the order designating the reservation first came into force; and

    (b) if the designation is still in force, before the end of the period of five years beginning with the date on which the last report relating to it was laid under subsection (3).

(3) The Minister conducting a review under this section must prepare a report on the result of the review and lay a copy of it before each House of Parliament.

Judges of the European Court of Human Rights

Appointment to European Court of Human Rights

18.—(1) In this section 'judicial office' means the office of—

    (a) Lord Justice of Appeal, Justice of the High Court or Circuit judge, in England and Wales;

    (b) judge of the Court of Session or sheriff, in Scotland;

    (c) Lord Justice of Appeal, judge of the High Court or county court judge, in Northern Ireland.

(2) The holder of a judicial office may become a judge of the European Court of Human Rights ('the Court') without being required to relinquish his office.

(3) But he is not required to perform the duties of his judicial office while he is a judge of the Court.

(4) In respect of any period during which he is a judge of the Court—

    (a) a Lord Justice of Appeal or Justice of the High Court is not to count as a judge of the relevant court for the purposes of section 2(1) or 4(1) of the Supreme Court Act 1981 (maximum number of judges) nor as a judge of the Supreme Court for the purposes of section 12(1) to (6) of that Act (salaries etc.);

    (b) a judge of the Court of Session is not to count as a judge of that court for the purposes of section 1(1) of the Court of Session Act 1988 (maximum number of judges) or of section 9(1)(c) of the Administration of Justice Act 1973 ('the 1973 Act') (salaries etc.);

    (c) a Lord Justice of Appeal or judge of the High Court in Northern Ireland is not to count as a judge of the relevant court for the purposes of section 2(1) or 3(1) of the Judicature (Northern Ireland) Act 1978 (maximum number of judges) nor as a judge of the Supreme Court of Northern Ireland for the purposes of section 9(1)(d) of the 1973 Act (salaries etc.);

    (d) a Circuit judge is not to count as such for the purposes of section 18 of the Courts Act 1971 (salaries etc.);

(e) a sheriff is not to count as such for the purposes of section 14 of the Sheriff Courts (Scotland) Act 1907 (salaries etc.);

(f) a county court judge of Northern Ireland is not to count as such for the purposes of section 106 of the County Courts Act Northern Ireland 1959 (salaries etc.).

(5) If a sheriff principal is appointed a judge of the Court, section 11(1) of the Sheriff Courts (Scotland) Act 1971 (temporary appointment of sheriff principal) applies, while he holds that appointment, as if his office is vacant.

(6) Schedule 4 makes provision about judicial pensions in relation to the holder of a judicial office who serves as a judge of the Court.

(7) The Lord Chancellor or the Secretary of State may by order make such transitional provision (including, in particular, provision for a temporary increase in the maximum number of judges) as he considers appropriate in relation to any holder of a judicial office who has completed his service as a judge of the Court.

Parliamentary procedure

Statements of compatibility

19.—(1) A Minister of the Crown in charge of a Bill in either House of Parliament must, before Second Reading of the Bill—

(a) make a statement to the effect that in his view the provisions of the Bill are compatible with the Convention rights ('a statement of compatibility'); or

(b) make a statement to the effect that although he is unable to make a statement of compatibility the government nevertheless wishes the House to proceed with the Bill.

(2) The statement must be in writing and be published in such manner as the Minister making it considers appropriate.

Supplemental

Orders etc. under this Act

20.—(1) Any power of a Minister of the Crown to make an order under this Act is exercisable by statutory instrument.

(2) The power of the Lord Chancellor or the Secretary of State to make rules (other than rules of court) under section 2(3) or 7(9) is exercisable by statutory instrument.

(3) Any statutory instrument made under section 14, 15 or 16(7) must be laid before Parliament.

(4) No order may be made by the Lord Chancellor or the Secretary of State under section 1(4), 7(11) or 16(2) unless a draft of the order has been laid before, and approved by, each House of Parliament.

(5) Any statutory instrument made under section 18(7) or Schedule 4, or to which subsection (2) applies, shall be subject to annulment in pursuance of a resolution of either House of Parliament.

(6) The power of a Northern Ireland department to make—

(a) rules under section 2(3)(c) or 7(9)(c), or

(b) an order under section 7(11),

is exercisable by statutory rule for the purposes of the Statutory Rules (Northern Ireland) Order 1979.

(7) Any rules made under section 2(3)(c) or 7(9)(c) shall be subject to negative resolution; and section 41(6) of the Interpretation Act Northern Ireland) 1954 (meaning of

'subject to negative resolution') shall apply as if the power to make the rules were conferred by an Act of the Northern Ireland Assembly.

(8) No order may be made by a Northern Ireland department under section 7(11) unless a draft of the order has been laid before, and approved by, the Northern Ireland Assembly.

Interpretation, etc

21.—(1) In this Act—

'amend' includes repeal and apply (with or without modifications);

'the appropriate Minister' means the Minister of the Crown having charge of the appropriate authorised government department (within the meaning of the Crown Proceedings Act 1947);

'the Commission' means the European Commission of Human Rights;

'the Convention' means the Convention for the Protection of Human Rights and Fundamental Freedoms, agreed by the Council of Europe at Rome on 4th November 1950 as it has effect for the time being in relation to the United Kingdom;

'declaration of incompatibility' means a declaration under section 4;

'Minister of the Crown' has the same meaning as in the Ministers of the Crown Act 1975;

'Northern Ireland Minister' includes the First Minister and the deputy First Minister in Northern Ireland;

'primary legislation' means any—

    (a) public general Act;

    (b) local and personal Act;

    (c) private Act;

    (d) Measure of the Church Assembly;

    (e) Measure of the General Synod of the Church of England;

    (f) Order in Council—

        (i) made in exercise of Her Majesty's Royal Prerogative;

        (ii) made under section 38(1)(a) of the Northern Ireland Constitution Act 1973 or the corresponding provision of the Northern Ireland Act 1998;

        or

        (iii) amending an Act of a kind mentioned in paragraph (a), (b) or (c);

and includes an order or other instrument made under primary legislation (otherwise than by the National Assembly for Wales, a member of the Scottish Executive, a Northern Ireland Minister or a Northern Ireland department) to the extent to which it operates to bring one or more provisions of that legislation into force or amends any primary legislation;

'the First Protocol' means the protocol to the Convention agreed at Paris on 20th March 1952;

'the Sixth Protocol' means the protocol to the Convention agreed at Strasbourg on 28th April 1983;

'the Eleventh Protocol' means the protocol to the Convention (restructuring the control machinery established by the Convention) agreed at Strasbourg on 11th May 1994;

'remedial order' means an order under section 10;

'subordinate legislation' means any—

    (a) Order in Council other than one—

        (i) made in exercise of Her Majesty's Royal Prerogative;

        (ii) made under section 38(1)(a) of the Northern Ireland Constitution Act 1973 or the corresponding provision of the Northern Ireland Act 1998;

        or

    (iii) amending an Act of a kind mentioned in the definition of primary legislation;

(b) Act of the Scottish Parliament;

(c) Act of the Parliament of Northern Ireland;

(d) Measure of the Assembly established under section 1 of the Northern Ireland Assembly Act 1973;

(e) Act of the Northern Ireland Assembly;

(f) order, rules, regulations, scheme, warrant, byelaw or other instrument made under primary legislation (except to the extent to which it operates to bring one or more provisions of that legislation into force or amends any primary legislation);

(g) order, rules, regulations, scheme, warrant, byelaw or other instrument made under legislation mentioned in paragraph (b), (c), (d) or (e) or made under an Order in Council applying only to Northern Ireland;

(h) order, rules, regulations, scheme, warrant, byelaw or other instrument made by a member of the Scottish Executive, a Northern Ireland Minister or a Northern Ireland department in exercise of prerogative or other executive functions of Her Majesty which are exercisable by such a person on behalf of Her Majesty;

'transferred matters' has the same meaning as in the Northern Ireland Act 1998; and

'tribunal' means any tribunal in which legal proceedings may be brought.

(2) The references in paragraphs (b) and (c) of section 2(1) to Articles are to Articles of the Convention as they had effect immediately before the coming into force of the Eleventh Protocol.

(3) The reference in paragraph (d) of section 2(1) to Article 46 includes a reference to Articles 32 and 54 of the Convention as they had effect immediately before the coming into force of the Eleventh Protocol.

(4) The references in section 2(1) to a report or decision of the Commission or a decision of the Committee of Ministers include references to a report or decision made as provided by paragraphs 3, 4 and 6 of Article 5 of the Eleventh Protocol (transitional provisions).

(5) Any liability under the Army Act 1955, the Air Force Act 1955 or the Naval Discipline Act 1957 to suffer death for an offence is replaced by a liability to imprisonment for life or any less punishment authorised by those Acts; and those Acts shall accordingly have effect with the necessary modifications.

Short title, commencement, application and extent

22.—(1) This Act may be cited as the Human Rights Act 1998.

(2) Sections 18, 20 and 21(5) and this section come into force on the passing of this Act.

(3) The other provisions of this Act come into force on such day as the Secretary of State may by order appoint; and different days may be appointed for different purposes.

(4) Paragraph (b) of subsection (1) of section 7 applies to proceedings brought by or at the instigation of a public authority whenever the act in question took place; but otherwise that subsection does not apply to an act taking place before the coming into force of that section.

(5) This Act binds the Crown.

(6) This Act extends to Northern Ireland.

(7) Section 21(5), so far as it relates to any provision contained in the Army Act 1955, the Air Force Act 1955 or the Naval Discipline Act 1957, extends to any place to which that provision extends.

SCHEDULES

SCHEDULE 1
THE ARTICLES

PART I
THE CONVENTION

RIGHTS AND FREEDOMS

ARTICLE 2
RIGHT TO LIFE

1. Everyone's right to life shall be protected by law. No one shall be deprived of his life intentionally save in the execution of a sentence of a court following his conviction of a crime for which this penalty is provided by law.

2. Deprivation of life shall not be regarded as inflicted in contravention of this Article when it results from the use of force which is no more than absolutely necessary:
    (a) in defence of any person from unlawful violence;
    (b) in order to effect a lawful arrest or to prevent the escape of a person lawfully detained;
    (c) in action lawfully taken for the purpose of quelling a riot or insurrection.

ARTICLE 3
PROHIBITION OF TORTURE

No one shall be subjected to torture or to inhuman or degrading treatment or punishment.

ARTICLE 4
PROHIBITION OF SLAVERY AND FORCED LABOUR

1. No one shall be held in slavery or servitude.

2. No one shall be required to perform forced or compulsory labour.

3. For the purpose of this Article the term 'forced or compulsory labour' shall not include:
    (a) any work required to be done in the ordinary course of detention imposed according to the provisions of Article 5 of this Convention or during conditional release from such detention;
    (b) any service of a military character or, in case of conscientious objectors in countries where they are recognised, service exacted instead of compulsory military service;
    (c) any service exacted in case of an emergency or calamity threatening the life or well-being of the community;
    (d) any work or service which forms part of normal civic obligations.

ARTICLE 5
RIGHT TO LIBERTY AND SECURITY

1. Everyone has the right to liberty and security of person. No one shall be deprived of his liberty save in the following cases and in accordance with a procedure prescribed by law:

    (a) the lawful detention of a person after conviction by a competent court;

    (b) the lawful arrest or detention of a person for non-compliance with the lawful order of a court or in order to secure the fulfilment of any obligation prescribed by law;

    (c) the lawful arrest or detention of a person effected for the purpose of bringing him before the competent legal authority on reasonable suspicion of having committed an offence or when it is reasonably considered necessary to prevent his committing an offence or fleeing after having done so;

    (d) the detention of a minor by lawful order for the purpose of educational supervision or his lawful detention for the purpose of bringing him before the competent legal authority;

    (e) the lawful detention of persons for the prevention of the spreading of infectious diseases, of persons of unsound mind, alcoholics or drug addicts or vagrants;

    (f) the lawful arrest or detention of a person to prevent his effecting an unauthorised entry into the country or of a person against whom action is being taken with a view to deportation or extradition.

2. Everyone who is arrested shall be informed promptly, in a language which he understands, of the reasons for his arrest and of any charge against him.

3. Everyone arrested or detained in accordance with the provisions of paragraph 1(c) of this Article shall be brought promptly before a judge or other officer authorised by law to exercise judicial power and shall be entitled to trial within a reasonable time or to release pending trial. Release may be conditioned by guarantees to appear for trial.

4. Everyone who is deprived of his liberty by arrest or detention shall be entitled to take proceedings by which the lawfulness of his detention shall be decided speedily by a court and his release ordered if the detention is not lawful.

5. Everyone who has been the victim of arrest or detention in contravention of the provisions of this Article shall have an enforceable right to compensation.

ARTICLE 6
RIGHT TO A FAIR TRIAL

1. In the determination of his civil rights and obligations or of any criminal charge against him, everyone is entitled to a fair and public hearing within a reasonable time by an independent and impartial tribunal established by law. Judgment shall be pronounced publicly but the press and public may be excluded from all or part of the trial in the interest of morals, public order or national security in a democratic society, where the interests of juveniles or the protection of the private life of the parties so require, or to the extent strictly necessary in the opinion of the court in special circumstances where publicity would prejudice the interests of justice.

2. Everyone charged with a criminal offence shall be presumed innocent until proved guilty according to law.

3. Everyone charged with a criminal offence has the following minimum rights:

    (a) to be informed promptly, in a language which he understands and in detail, of the nature and cause of the accusation against him;

(b) to have adequate time and facilities for the preparation of his defence;

(c) to defend himself in person or through legal assistance of his own choosing or, if he has not sufficient means to pay for legal assistance, to be given it free when the interests of justice so require;

(d) to examine or have examined witnesses against him and to obtain the attendance and examination of witnesses on his behalf under the same conditions as witnesses against him;

(e) to have the free assistance of an interpreter if he cannot understand or speak the language used in court.

ARTICLE 7
NO PUNISHMENT WITHOUT LAW

1. No one shall be held guilty of any criminal offence on account of any act or omission which did not constitute a criminal offence under national or international law at the time when it was committed. Nor shall a heavier penalty be imposed than the one that was applicable at the time the criminal offence was committed.

2. This Article shall not prejudice the trial and punishment of any person for any act or omission which, at the time when it was committed, was criminal according to the general principles of law recognised by civilised nations.

ARTICLE 8
RIGHT TO RESPECT FOR PRIVATE AND FAMILY LIFE

1. Everyone has the right to respect for his private and family life, his home and his correspondence.

2. There shall be no interference by a public authority with the exercise of this right except such as is in accordance with the law and is necessary in a democratic society in the interests of national security, public safety or the economic well-being of the country, for the prevention of disorder or crime, for the protection of health or morals, or for the protection of the rights and freedoms of others.

ARTICLE 9
FREEDOM OF THOUGHT, CONSCIENCE AND RELIGION

1. Everyone has the right to freedom of thought, conscience and religion; this right includes freedom to change his religion or belief and freedom, either alone or in community with others and in public or private, to manifest his religion or belief, in worship, teaching, practice and observance.

2. Freedom to manifest one's religion or beliefs shall be subject only to such limitations as are prescribed by law and are necessary in a democratic society in the interests of public safety, for the protection of public order, health or morals, or for the protection of the rights and freedoms of others.

ARTICLE 10
FREEDOM OF EXPRESSION

1. Everyone has the right to freedom of expression. This right shall include freedom to hold opinions and to receive and impart information and ideas without interference by public authority and regardless of frontiers. This Article shall not prevent States from requiring the licensing of broadcasting, television or cinema enterprises.

2. The exercise of these freedoms, since it carries with it duties and responsibilities, may be subject to such formalities, conditions, restrictions or penalties as are prescribed by law and are necessary in a democratic society, in the interests of national security, territorial integrity or public safety, for the prevention of disorder or crime, for the protection of health or morals, for the protection of the reputation or rights of others, for preventing the disclosure of information received in confidence, or for maintaining the authority and impartiality of the judiciary.

ARTICLE 11
FREEDOM OF ASSEMBLY AND ASSOCIATION

1. Everyone has the right to freedom of peaceful assembly and to freedom of association with others, including the right to form and to join trade unions for the protection of his interests.

2. No restrictions shall be placed on the exercise of these rights other than such as are prescribed by law and are necessary in a democratic society in the interests of national security or public safety, for the prevention of disorder or crime, for the protection of health or morals or for the protection of the rights and freedoms of others. This Article shall not prevent the imposition of lawful restrictions on the exercise of these rights by members of the armed forces, of the police or of the administration of the State.

ARTICLE 12
RIGHT TO MARRY

Men and women of marriageable age have the right to marry and to found a family, according to the national laws governing the exercise of this right.

ARTICLE 14
PROHIBITION OF DISCRIMINATION

The enjoyment of the rights and freedoms set forth in this Convention shall be secured without discrimination on any ground such as sex, race, colour, language, religion, political or other opinion, national or social origin, association with a national minority, property, birth or other status.

ARTICLE 16
RESTRICTIONS ON POLITICAL ACTIVITY OF ALIENS

Nothing in Articles 10, 11 and 14 shall be regarded as preventing the High Contracting Parties from imposing restrictions on the political activity of aliens.

ARTICLE 17
PROHIBITION OF ABUSE OF RIGHTS

Nothing in this Convention may be interpreted as implying for any State, group or person any right to engage in any activity or perform any act aimed at the destruction of any of the rights and freedoms set forth herein or at their limitation to a greater extent than is provided for in the Convention.

ARTICLE 18
LIMITATION ON USE OF RESTRICTIONS ON RIGHTS

The restrictions permitted under this Convention to the said rights and freedoms shall not be applied for any purpose other than those for which they have been prescribed.

PART II
THE FIRST PROTOCOL

ARTICLE 1
PROTECTION OF PROPERTY

Every natural or legal person is entitled to the peaceful enjoyment of his possessions. No one shall be deprived of his possessions except in the public interest and subject to the conditions provided for by law and by the general principles of international law.

The preceding provisions shall not, however, in any way impair the right of a State to enforce such laws as it deems necessary to control the use of property in accordance with the general interest or to secure the payment of taxes or other contributions or penalties.

ARTICLE 2
RIGHT TO EDUCATION

No person shall be denied the right to education. In the exercise of any functions which it assumes in relation to education and to teaching, the State shall respect the right of parents to ensure such education and teaching in conformity with their own religious and philosophical convictions.

ARTICLE 3
RIGHT TO FREE ELECTIONS

The High Contracting Parties undertake to hold free elections at reasonable intervals by secret ballot, under conditions which will ensure the free expression of the opinion of the people in the choice of the legislature.

PART III
THE SIXTH PROTOCOL

ARTICLE 1
ABOLITION OF THE DEATH PENALTY

The death penalty shall be abolished. No one shall be condemned to such penalty or executed.

ARTICLE 2
DEATH PENALTY IN TIME OF WAR

A State may make provision in its law for the death penalty in respect of acts committed in time of war or of imminent threat of war; such penalty shall be applied only in the instances laid down in the law and in accordance with its provisions. The State shall communicate to the Secretary General of the Council of Europe the relevant provisions of that law.

SCHEDULE 2
REMEDIAL ORDERS

Orders

1.—(1) A remedial order may—
    (a) contain such incidental, supplemental, consequential or transitional provision as the person making it considers appropriate;

    (b) be made so as to have effect from a date earlier than that on which it is made;

    (c) make provision for the delegation of specific functions;

    (d) make different provision for different cases.

(2) The power conferred by sub-paragraph (1)(a) includes—

    (a) power to amend primary legislation (including primary legislation other than that which contains the incompatible provision); and

    (b) power to amend or revoke subordinate legislation (including subordinate legislation other than that which contains the incompatible provision).

(3) A remedial order may be made so as to have the same extent as the legislation which it affects.

(4) No person is to be guilty of an offence solely as a result of the retrospective effect of a remedial order.

Procedure

2. No remedial order may be made unless—

    (a) a draft of the order has been approved by a resolution of each House of Parliament made after the end of the period of 60 days beginning with the day on which the draft was laid; or

    (b) it is declared in the order that it appears to the person making it that, because of the urgency of the matter, it is necessary to make the order without a draft being so approved.

Orders laid in draft

3.—(1) No draft may be laid under paragraph 2(a) unless—

    (a) the person proposing to make the order has laid before Parliament a document which contains a draft of the proposed order and the required information; and

    (b) the period of 60 days, beginning with the day on which the document required by this sub-paragraph was laid, has ended.

(2) If representations have been made during that period, the draft laid under paragraph 2(a) must be accompanied by a statement containing—

    (a) a summary of the representations; and

    (b) if, as a result of the representations, the proposed order has been changed, details of the changes.

Urgent cases

4.—(1) If a remedial order ('the original order') is made without being approved in draft, the person making it must lay it before Parliament, accompanied by the required information, after it is made.

(2) If representations have been made during the period of 60 days beginning with the day on which the original order was made, the person making it must (after the end of that period) lay before Parliament a statement containing—

    (a) a summary of the representations; and

    (b) if, as a result of the representations, he considers it appropriate to make changes to the original order, details of the changes.

(3) If sub-paragraph (2)(b) applies, the person making the statement must—

    (a) make a further remedial order replacing the original order; and

    (b) lay the replacement order before Parliament.

(4) If, at the end of the period of 120 days beginning with the day on which the original order was made, a resolution has not been passed by each House approving the

original or replacement order, the order ceases to have effect (but without that affecting anything previously done under either order or the power to make a fresh remedial order).

Definitions

5. In this Schedule—
'representations' means representations about a remedial order (or proposed remedial order) made to the person making (or proposing to make) it and includes any relevant Parliamentary report or resolution; and
'required information' means—
    (a) an explanation of the incompatibility which the order (or proposed order) seeks to remove, including particulars of the relevant declaration, finding or order; and
    (b) a statement of the reasons for proceeding under section 10 and for making an order in those terms.

Calculating periods

6. In calculating any period for the purposes of this Schedule, no account is to be taken of any time during which—
    (a) Parliament is dissolved or prorogued; or
    (b) both Houses are adjourned for more than four days.

SCHEDULE 3
DEROGATION AND RESERVATION

PART I
DEROGATION

The 1988 notification

The United Kingdom Permanent Representative to the Council of Europe presents his compliments to the Secretary General of the Council, and has the honour to convey the following information in order to ensure compliance with the obligations of Her Majesty's Government in the United Kingdom under Article 15(3) of the Convention for the Protection of Human Rights and Fundamental Freedoms signed at Rome on 4 November 1950.

There have been in the United Kingdom in recent years campaigns of organised terrorism connected with the affairs of Northern Ireland which have manifested themselves in activities which have included repeated murder, attempted murder, maiming, intimidation and violent civil disturbance and in bombing and fire raising which have resulted in death, injury and widespread destruction of property. As a result, a public emergency within the meaning of Article 15(1) of the Convention exists in the United Kingdom.

The Government found it necessary in 1974 to introduce and since then, in cases concerning persons reasonably suspected of involvement in terrorism connected with the affairs of Northern Ireland, or of certain offences under the legislation, who have been detained for 48 hours, to exercise powers enabling further detention without charge, for periods of up to five days, on the authority of the Secretary of State. These powers are at present to be found in Section 12 of the Prevention of Terrorism (Temporary Provisions) Act 1984, Article 9 of the Prevention of Terrorism (Supplemental Temporary Provisions) Order 1984 and Article 10 of the Prevention of Terrorism (Supplemental Temporary Provisions) (Northern Ireland) Order 1984.

Section 12 of the Prevention of Terrorism (Temporary Provisions) Act 1984 provides for a person whom a constable has arrested on reasonable grounds of suspecting him to be guilty of an offence under Section 1, 9 or 10 of the Act, or to be or to have been involved in terrorism connected with the affairs of Northern Ireland, to be detained in right of the arrest for up to 48 hours and thereafter, where the Secretary of State extends the detention period, for up to a further five days. Section 12 substantially re-enacted Section 12 of the Prevention of Terrorism (Temporary Provisions) Act 1976 which, in turn, substantially re-enacted Section 7 of the Prevention of Terrorism (Temporary Provisions) Act 1974.

Article 10 of the Prevention of Terrorism (Supplemental Temporary Provisions) (Northern Ireland) Order 1984 (SI 1984/417) and Article 9 of the Prevention of Terrorism (Supplemental Temporary Provisions) Order 1984 (SI 1984/418) were both made under Sections 13 and 14 of and Schedule 3 to the 1984 Act and substantially re-enacted powers of detention in Orders made under the 1974 and 1976 Acts. A person who is being examined under Article 4 of either Order on his arrival in, or on seeking to leave, Northern Ireland or Great Britain for the purpose of determining whether he is or has been involved in terrorism connected with the affairs of Northern Ireland, or whether there are grounds for suspecting that he has committed an offence under Section 9 of the 1984 Act, may be detained under Article 9 or 10, as appropriate, pending the conclusion of his examination. The period of this examination may exceed 12 hours if an examining officer has reasonable grounds for suspecting him to be or to have been involved in acts of terrorism connected with the affairs of Northern Ireland.

Where such a person is detained under the said Article 9 or 10 he may be detained for up to 48 hours on the authority of an examining officer and thereafter, where the Secretary of State extends the detention period, for up to a further five days.

In its judgment of 29 November 1988 in the Case of *Brogan and Others*, the European Court of Human Rights held that there had been a violation of Article 5(3) in respect of each of the applicants, all of whom had been detained under Section 12 of the 1984 Act. The Court held that even the shortest of the four periods of detention concerned, namely four days and six hours, fell outside the constraints as to time permitted by the first part of Article 5(3). In addition, the Court held that there had been a violation of Article 5(5) in the case of each applicant.

Following this judgment, the Secretary of State for the Home Department informed Parliament on 6 December 1988 that, against the background of the terrorist campaign, and the over-riding need to bring terrorists to justice, the Government did not believe that the maximum period of detention should be reduced. He informed Parliament that the Government were examining the matter with a view to responding to the judgment. On 22 December 1988, the Secretary of State further informed Parliament that it remained the Government's wish, if it could be achieved, to find a judicial process under which extended detention might be reviewed and where appropriate authorised by a judge or other judicial officer. But a further period of reflection and consultation was necessary before the Government could bring forward a firm and final view.

Since the judgment of 29 November 1988 as well as previously, the Government have found it necessary to continue to exercise, in relation to terrorism connected with the affairs of Northern Ireland, the powers described above enabling further detention without charge for periods of up to 5 days, on the authority of the Secretary of State, to the extent strictly required by the exigencies of the situation to enable necessary enquiries and investigations properly to be completed in order to decide whether criminal proceedings should be instituted. To the extent that the exercise of these powers may be inconsistent with the obligations imposed by the Convention the Government has availed itself of the right of derogation conferred by Article 15(1) of the Convention and will continue to do so until further notice.

Dated 23 December 1988

The 1989 notification

The United Kingdom Permanent Representative to the Council of Europe presents his compliments to the Secretary General of the Council, and has the honour to convey the following information.

In his communication to the Secretary General of 23 December 1988, reference was made to the introduction and exercise of certain powers under section 12 of the Prevention of Terrorism (Temporary Provisions) Act 1984, Article 9 of the Prevention of Terrorism (Supplemental Temporary Provisions) Order 1984 and Article 10 of the Prevention of Terrorism (Supplemental Temporary Provisions) (Northern Ireland) Order 1984.

These provisions have been replaced by section 14 of and paragraph 6 of Schedule 5 to the Prevention of Terrorism (Temporary Provisions) Act 1989, which make comparable provision. They came into force on 22 March 1989. A copy of these provisions is enclosed.

The United Kingdom Permanent Representative avails himself of this opportunity to renew to the Secretary General the assurance of his highest consideration.

Dated 23 March 1989

PART II
RESERVATION

At the time of signing the present (First) Protocol, I declare that, in view of certain provisions of the Education Acts in the United Kingdom, the principle affirmed in the second sentence of Article 2 is accepted by the United Kingdom only so far as it is compatible with the provision of efficient instruction and training, and the avoidance of unreasonable public expenditure.

Dated 20 March 1952

Made by the United Kingdom Permanent Representative to the Council of Europe.

SCHEDULE 4
JUDICIAL PENSIONS

Duty to make orders about pensions

1.—(1) The appropriate Minister must by order make provision with respect to pensions payable to or in respect of any holder of a judicial office who serves as an ECHR judge.

(2) A pensions order must include such provision as the Minister making it considers is necessary to secure that—

(a) an ECHR judge who was, immediately before his appointment as an ECHR judge, a member of a judicial pension scheme is entitled to remain as a member of that scheme;

(b) the terms on which he remains a member of the scheme are those which would have been applicable had he not been appointed as an ECHR judge; and

(c) entitlement to benefits payable in accordance with the scheme continues to be determined as if, while serving as an ECHR judge, his salary was that which would (but for section 18(4)) have been payable to him in respect of his continuing service as the holder of his judicial office.

Contributions

2. A pensions order may, in particular, make provision—

    (a) for any contributions which are payable by a person who remains a member of a scheme as a result of the order, and which would otherwise be payable by deduction from his salary, to be made otherwise than by deduction from his salary as an ECHR judge; and

    (b) for such contributions to be collected in such manner as may be determined by the administrators of the scheme.

Amendments of other enactments

3. A pensions order may amend any provision of, or made under, a pensions Act in such manner and to such extent as the Minister making the order considers necessary or expedient to ensure the proper administration of any scheme to which it relates.

Definitions

4. In this Schedule—

    'appropriate Minister' means—

        (a) in relation to any judicial office whose jurisdiction is exercisable exclusively in relation to Scotland, the Secretary of State; and

        (b) otherwise, the Lord Chancellor;

    'ECHR judge' means the holder of a judicial office who is serving as a judge of the Court;

    'judicial pension scheme' means a scheme established by and in accordance with a pensions Act;

    'pensions Act' means—

        (a) the County Courts Act Northern Ireland 1959;

        (b) the Sheriffs' Pensions (Scotland) Act 1961;

        (c) the Judicial Pensions Act 1981; or

        (d) the Judicial Pensions and Retirement Act 1993; and

    'pensions order' means an order made under paragraph 1.

APPENDIX 5

The European Convention on Human Rights

as amended by Protocol no 11

The Governments signatory hereto, being Members of the Council of Europe,

Considering the Universal Declaration of Human Rights proclaimed by the General assembly of the United Nations on 10 December 1948;

Considering that this Declaration aims at securing the universal and effective recognition and observance of the Rights therein declared;

Considering that the aim of the Council of Europe is the achievement of greater unity between its Members and that one of the methods by which the aim is to be pursued is the maintenance and further realisation of Human Rights and Fundamental Freedoms;

Reaffirming their profound belief in those Fundamental Freedoms which are the foundation of justice and peace in the world and are best maintained on the one hand by an effective political democracy and on the other by a common understanding and observance of the Human Rights upon which they depend;

Being resolved, as the Governments of European countries which are like-minded and have a common heritage of political traditions, ideals, freedom and the rule of law, to take the first steps for the collective enforcement of certain of the Rights stated in the Universal Declaration;

Have agreed as follows:

Article 1

The High Contracting Parties shall secure to everyone within their jurisdiction the rights and freedoms defined in Section 1 of this Convention.

SECTION I

Article 2

1. Everyone's right to life shall be protected by law. No one shall be deprived of his live intentionally save in the execution of a sentence of a court following his conviction of a crime for which this penalty is provided by law.

2. Deprivation of life shall not be regarded as inflicted in contravention of this Article when it results from the use of force which is no more than absolutely necessary:

    (a) in defence of any person from unlawful violence;

    (b) in order to effect a lawful arrest or to prevent the escape of a person lawfully detained;

    (c) in action lawfully taken for the purpose of quelling a riot or insurrection.

Article 3

No one shall be subjected to torture or inhuman or degrading treatment or punishment.

Article 4

1. No one shall be held in slavery or servitude.

2. No one shall be required to perform forced or compulsory labour.

3. For the purpose of this Article the term 'forced or compulsory labour' shall not include:

    (a) any work required to be done in the ordinary course of detention imposed according to the provisions of Article 5 of this Convention or during conditional release from such detention;

    (b) any service of a military character or, in the case of conscientious objectors in countries where they are recognized, service exacted instead of compulsory military service;

    (c) any service exacted in case of an emergency or calamity threatening the life or well-being of the community;

    (d) any work of service which forms part of normal civic obligations.

Article 5

1. Everyone has the right to liberty and security of person. No one shall be deprived of his liberty save in the following cases and in accordance with a procedure prescribed by law:

    (a) the lawful detention of a person after conviction by a competent court;

    (b) the lawful arrest or detention of a person for non-compliance with the lawful order of a court or in order to secure the fulfilment of any obligation prescribed by law;

    (c) the lawful arrest or detention of a person effected for the purpose of bringing him before the competent legal authority on reasonable suspicion of having committed an offence or when it is reasonably considered necessary to prevent his committing an offence or fleeing after having done so;

    (d) the detention of a minor by lawful order for the purpose of educational supervision or his lawful detention for the purpose of bringing him before the competent legal authority;

    (e) the lawful detention of persons for the prevention of the spreading of infectious disease, of persons of unsound mind, alcoholics or drug addicts, or vagrants;

    (f) the lawful arrest or detention of a person to prevent his effecting an unauthorized entry into the country or of a person against whom action is being taken with a view to deportation or extradition.

2. Everyone who is arrested shall be informed promptly, in a language which he understands, of the reasons for his arrest and of any charge against him.

3. Everyone arrested or detained in accordance with the provision of paragraph 1(c) of this Article shall be brought promptly before a judge or other officer authorised by law to exercise judicial power and shall be entitled to trial within a reasonable time or to release pending trial. Release may be conditioned by guarantees to appear for trial.

4. Everyone who is deprived of his liberty by arrest or detention shall be entitled to take proceedings by which the lawfulness of his detention shall be decided speedily by a court and his release ordered if the detention is not lawful.

5. Everyone who has been the victim of arrest or detention in contravention of the provisions of this article shall have an enforceable right to compensation.

Article 6

1. In the determination of his civil rights and obligations or of any criminal charge against him, everyone is entitled to a fair and public hearing within a reasonable time by an independent and impartial tribunal established by law. Judgment shall be pronounced publicly but the press and public may be excluded from all or part of the trial in the interest of morals, public order or national security in a democratic society, where the interests of juveniles or the protection of the private life of the parties so require, or to the extent strictly necessary in the opinion of the court in special circumstances where publicity would prejudice the interests of justice.

2. Everyone charged with a criminal offence shall be presumed innocent until proved guilty according to law.

3. Everyone charged with a criminal offence has the following minimum rights:

   (a)   to be informed promptly, in a language which he understands and in detail, of the nature and cause of the accusation against him;
   (b)   to have adequate time and facilities for the preparation of his defence;
   (c)   to defend himself in person or through legal assistance of his own choosing or, if he has not sufficient means to pay for legal assistance, to be given it free when the interests of justice so require;
   (d)   to examine or have examined witnesses against him and to obtain the attendance and examination of witnesses on his behalf under the same conditions as witnesses against him;
   (e)   to have the free assistance of an interpreter if he cannot understand or speak the language used in court.

Article 7

1. No one shall be held guilty of any criminal offence on account of any act or omission which did not constitute a criminal offence under national or international law at the time when it was committee. Nor shall a heavier penalty be imposed than the one that was applicable at the time the criminal offence was committee.

2. This article shall not prejudice the trial and punishment of any person for any act or omission which, at the time when it was committed, was criminal according to the general principles of law recognized by civilized nations.

Article 8

1. Everyone has the right to respect for his private and family life, his home and his correspondence.

2. There shall be no interference by a public authority with the exercise of this right except such as in accordance with the law and is necessary in a democratic society in the interests of national security, public safety or the economic well-being of the country, for the prevention of disorder or crime, for the protection of health or morals, or for the protection of the rights and freedoms of others.

Article 9

1. Everyone has the right to freedom of thought, conscience and religion; this right includes freedom to change his religion or belief, and freedom, either alone or in community with others and in public or private, to manifest his religion or belief, in worship, teaching, practice and observance.

2. Freedom to manifest one's religion or beliefs shall be subject only to such limitations as are prescribed by law and are necessary in a democratic society in the interests of public safety, for the protection of public order, health or morals, or for the protection of the rights and freedoms of others.

Article 10

1. Everyone has the right to freedom of expression. This right shall include freedom to hold opinions and to receive and impart information and ideas without interference by public authority and regardless of frontiers. This article shall not prevent States from requiring the licensing of broadcasting, television or cinema enterprises.

2. The exercise of these freedoms, since it carries with it duties and responsibilities, may be subject to such formalities, conditions, restrictions or penalties as are prescribed by law and are necessary in a democratic society, in the interests of national security, territorial integrity or public safety, for the prevention of disorder or crime, for the protection of health or morals, for the protection of the reputation or rights of others, for preventing the disclosure of information received in confidence, or for maintaining the authority and impartiality of the judiciary.

Article 11

1. Everyone has the right to freedom of peaceful assembly and to freedom of association with others, including the right to form and to join trade unions for the protection of his interests.

2. No restrictions shall be placed on the exercise of these rights other than such as are prescribed by law and are necessary in a democratic society in the interests of national security or public safety, for the prevention of disorder or crime, for the protection of health or morals or for the protection of the rights and freedoms of others. This Article shall not prevent the imposition of lawful restrictions on the exercise of these rights by members of the armed forces, of the police or of the administration of the State.

Article 12

Men and women of marriageable age have the right to marry and to found a family, according to the national laws governing the exercise of this right.

Article 13

Everyone whose rights and freedoms as set forth in this Convention are violated shall have an effective remedy before a national authority notwithstanding that the violation has been committed by persons acting in an official capacity.

Article 14

The enjoyment of the rights and freedoms set forth in this Convention shall be secured without discrimination on any ground such as sex, race, colour, language, religion, political or other opinions, national or social origin, association with a national minority, property, birth or other status.

Article 15

1. In time or war or other public emergency threatening the life of the nation any High Contracting Party may take measures derogating from its obligations under this Convention to the extent strictly required by the exigencies of the situation, provided that such measures are not inconsistent with its other obligations under international law.

2. No derogation from Article 2, except in respect of deaths resulting from lawful acts of war, or from Articles 3, 4 (paragraph 1) and 7 shall be made under this provision.

3. Any High Contracting Party availing itself of this right of derogation shall keep the Secretary-General of the Council of Europe fully informed of the measures which it has taken and the reasons therefor. It shall also inform the Secretary-General of the Council of Europe when such measures have ceased to operate and the provisions of the Convention are again being fully executed.

Article 16

Nothing in Articles 10, 11 and 14 shall be regarded as preventing the High Contracting Parties from imposing restrictions on the political activity of aliens.

Article 17

Nothing in this Convention may be interpreted as implying for any State, group or person the right to engage in any activity or perform any act aimed at the destruction of any of the rights and freedoms set forth herein or at their limitation to a greater extent than is provided for in the Convention.

Article 18

The restrictions permitted under this Convention to the said rights and freedoms shall not be applied for any purpose other than those for which they have been prescribed.

Section II

Article 19

To ensure the observance of the engagements undertaken by the High Contracting Parties in the Convention and the Protocols thereto, there shall be set up a European Court of Human Rights, hereinafter referred to as 'the Court'. It shall function on a permanent basis.

Article 20

The Court shall consist of a number of judges equal to that of the High Contracting Parties.

Article 21

1. The judges shall be of high moral character and must either possess the qualifications required for appointment to high judicial office or be jurisconsults of recognised competence.

2. The judges shall sit on the Court in their individual capacity.

3. During their term of office the judges shall not engage in any activity which is incompatible with their independence, impartiality or with the demands of a full-time office; all questions arising from the application of this paragraph shall be decided by the Court.

Article 22

1. The judges shall be elected by the Parliamentary Assembly with respect to each High Contracting Party by a majority of votes cast from a list of three candidates nominated by the High Contracting Party.

2. The same procedure shall be followed to complete the Court in the event of the accession of new High Contracting Parties and in filling casual vacancies.

Article 23

1. The judges shall be elected for a period of six years. They may be re-elected. However, the terms of office of one-half of the judges elected at the first election shall expire at the end of three years.

2. The judges whose terms of office are to expire at the end of the initial period of three years shall be chosen by lot by the Secretary General of the Council of Europe immediately after their election.

3. In order to ensure that, as far as possible, the terms of office of one-half of the judges are renewed every three years, the Parliamentary Assembly may decide, before proceeding to any subsequent election, that the term or terms of office of one or more judges to be elected shall be for a period other than six years but not more than nine and not less than three years.

4. In cases where more than one term of office is involved and where the Parliamentary Assembly applies the preceding paragraph, the allocation of the terms of office shall be effected by a drawing of lots by the Secretary General of the Council of Europe immediately after the election.

5. A judge elected to replace a judge whose term of office has not expired shall hold office for the remainder of his predecessor's term.

6. The terms of office of judges shall expire when they reach the age of 70.

7. The judges shall hold office until replaced. They shall, however, continue to deal with such cases as they already have under consideration.

Article 24

No judge may be dismissed from his office unless the other judges decide by a majority of two-thirds that he has ceased to fulfil the required conditions.

Article 25

The Court shall have a registry, the functions and organisation of which shall be laid down in the rules of the Court. The Court shall be assisted by legal secretaries.

Article 26

The plenary Court shall
      (a) elect its president and one or two Vice-Presidents for a period of three years; they may be re-elected;
      (b) set up Chambers, constituted for a fixed period of time;
      (c) elect the Presidents of the Chambers of the Court; they may be re-elected;
      (d) adopt the rules of the Court, and
      (e) elect the Registrar and one or more Deputy Registrars.

Article 27

1. To consider cases brought before it, the Court shall sit in committees of three judges, in Chambers of seven judges and in a Grand Chamber of seventeen judges. The Court's Chambers shall set up committees for a fixed period of time.

2. There shall sit as an *ex officio* member of the Chamber and the Grand Chamber the judge elected in respect of the State Party concerned or, if there is none or if he is unable to sit, a person of its choice who shall sit in the capacity of judge.

3. The Grand Chamber shall also include the President of the Court, the Vice-Presidents, the Presidents of the Chambers and other judges chosen in accordance with the rules of the Court. When a case is referred to the Grand Chamber under Article 43, no judge from the Chamber which rendered the judgment shall sit in the Grand Chamber, with the exception of the President of the Chamber and the judge who sat in respect of the State Party concerned.

Article 28

A committee may, by a unanimous vote, declare inadmissible or strike out of its list of cases an application submitted under Article 34 where such a decision can be taken without further examination. The decision shall be final.

Article 29

1. If no decision is taken under Article 28, a Chamber shall decide on the admissibility and merits of individual applications submitted under Article 34.

2. A Chamber shall decide on the admissibility and merits of inter-State applications submitted under Article 33.

3. The decision on admissibility shall be taken separately unless the Court, in exceptional cases, decides otherwise.

Article 30

Where a case pending before a Chamber raises a serious question affecting the interpretation of the Convention or the protocols thereto, or where the resolution of a question before the Chamber might have a result inconsistent with a judgment previously delivered by the Court, the Chamber may, at any time before it has rendered its judgment, relinquish jurisdiction in favour of the Grand Chamber, unless one of the parties to the case objects.

Article 31

The Grand Chamber shall

    (a) determine applications submitted either under Article 33 or Article 34 when a Chamber has relinquished jurisdiction under Article 30 or when the case has been referred to it under Article 43; and

    (b) consider requests for advisory opinions submitted under Article 47.

Article 32

1. The jurisdiction of the Court shall extend to all matters concerning the interpretation and application of the Convention and the protocols thereto which are referred to it as provided in Articles 33, 34, and 47.

2. In the event of dispute as to whether the court has jurisdiction, the Court shall decide.

Article 33

Any High Contracting Party may refer to the Court any alleged breach of the provisions of the Convention and the protocols thereto by another High Contracting Party.

Article 34

The Court may receive applications from any person, non-governmental organisation or group of individuals claiming to be the victim of a violation by one of the High Contracting Parties of the rights set forth in the Convention or the protocols thereto. The High Contracting Parties undertake not to hinder in any way the effective exercise of this right.

Article 35

1. The Court may only deal with the matter after all domestic remedies have been exhausted, according to the generally recognised rules of international law, and within a period of six months from the date on which the final decision was taken.

2. The Court shall not deal with any application submitted under Article 34 that
    (a) is anonymous; or
    (b) is substantially the same as a matter that has already been examined by the Court or has already been submitted to another procedure of international investigation or settlement and contains no relevant new information.

3. The Court shall declare inadmissible any individual application submitted under Article 34 which it considers incompatible with the provisions of the Convention or the protocols thereto, manifestly ill-founded, or an abuse of the right of application.

4. The Court shall reject any application which it considers inadmissible under this Article. It may do so at any stage of the proceedings.

Article 36

1. In all cases before a Chamber of the Grand Chamber, a High Contracting Party one of whose nationals is an applicant shall have the right to submit written comments and to take part in hearings.

2. The President of the Court may, in the interest of the proper administration of justice, invite any High Contracting Party which is not a party to the proceedings or any person concerned who is not the applicant to submit written comments or take part in hearings.

Article 37

1. The Court may at any stage of the proceedings decide to strike an application out of its list of cases where the circumstances lead to the conclusion that
    (a) the applicant does not intend to pursue his application; or
    (b) the matter has been resolved; or
    (c) for any other reason established by the Court, it is no longer justified to continue the examination of the application.
However, the Court shall continue the examination of the application if respect for human rights as defined in the Convention and the protocols thereto so requires.

2. The Court may decide to restore an application to its list of cases if it considers that the circumstances justify such a course.

Article 38

1. If the Court declares the application admissible, it shall
    (a) pursue the examination of the case, together with the representatives of the parties, and if need be, undertake an investigation, for the effective conduct of which the States concerned shall furnish all necessary facilities;
    (b) place itself at the disposal of the parties concerned with a view to securing a friendly settlement of the matter on the basis of respect for human rights as defined in the Convention and the protocols thereto.

2. Proceedings conducted under paragraph 1 (b) shall be confidential.

Article 39

If a friendly settlement is effected, the Court shall strike the case out of its list by means of a decision which shall be confined to a brief statement of the facts and of the solution reached.

Article 40

1. Hearings shall be in public unless the Court in exceptional circumstances decides otherwise.

2. Documents deposited with the Registrar shall be accessible to the public unless the President of the Court decides otherwise.

Article 41

If the Court finds that there has been a violation of the Convention or the protocols thereto, and if the internal law of the High Contracting Party concerned allows only partial reparation to be made, the Court shall, if necessary, afford just satisfaction to the injured party.

Article 42

Judgments of Chambers shall become final in accordance with the provisions of Article 44, paragraph 2.

Article 43

1. Within a period of three months from the date of the judgment of the Chamber, any party to the case may, in exceptional cases, request that the case be referred to the Grand Chamber.

2. A panel of five judges of the Grand Chamber shall accept the request if the case raises a serious question affecting the interpretation or application of the Convention or the protocols thereto, or a serious issue of general importance.

3. If the panel accepts the request, the Grand Chamber shall decide the case by means of a judgment.

Article 44

1. The judgment of the Grand Chamber shall be final.

2. The judgment of a Chamber shall become final
>   (a) when the parties declare that they will not request that the case be referred to the Grand Chamber; or
>   (b) three months after the date of the judgment, if reference of the case to the Grand Chamber has not been requested; or
>   (c) when the panel of the Grand Chamber rejects the request to refer under Article 43.

3. The final judgment shall be published.

Article 45

1. Reasons shall be given for judgments as well as for decisions declaring applications admissible or inadmissible.

2. If a judgment does not represent, in whole or in part, the unanimous opinion of the judges, any judge shall be entitled to deliver a separate opinion.

Article 46

1. The High Contracting Parties undertake to abide by the final judgment of the Court in any case to which they are parties.

2. The final judgment of the Court shall be transmitted to the Committee of Ministers, which shall supervise its execution.

Article 47

1. The Court may, at the request of the Committee of Ministers, give advisory opinions on legal questions concerning the interpretation of the Convention and the protocols thereto.

2. Such opinions shall not deal with any question relating to the content or scope of the rights or freedoms defined in Section I of the Convention and the protocols thereto, or with any other question which the Court or the Committee of Ministers might have to consider in consequence of any such proceedings as could be instituted in accordance with the Convention.

3. Decisions of the Committee of Ministers to request an advisory opinion of the Court shall require a majority vote of the representatives entitled to sit on the Committee.

Article 48

The Court shall decide whether a request for an advisory opinion submitted by the Committee of Ministers is within its competence as defined in Article 47.

Article 49

1. Reasons shall be given for advisory opinions of the Court.

2. If the advisory opinion does not represent, in whole or in part, the unanimous opinion of the judges, any judge shall be entitled to deliver a separate opinion.

3. Advisory opinions of the Court shall be communicated to the Committee of Ministers.

Article 50

The expenditure on the Court shall be borne by the Council of Europe.

Article 51

The judges shall be entitled, during the exercise of their functions, to the privileges and immunities provided for in Article 40 of the Statute of the Council of Europe and in the agreements made thereunder.

SECTION III

Article 52

On receipt of a request from the Secretary General of the Council of Europe any High Contracting Party shall furnish an explanation of the manner in which its internal law ensures the effective implementation of any of the provisions of the Convention.

Article 53

Nothing in this Convention shall be construed as limiting or derogating from any of the human rights and fundamental freedoms which may be ensured under the laws of any High Contracting Party or under any other agreement to which it is a Party.

Article 54

Nothing in this Convention shall prejudice the powers conferred on the Committee of Ministers by the Statute of the Council of Europe.

Article 55

The High Contracting Parties agree that, except by special agreement, they will not avail themselves of treaties, conventions or declarations in force between them for the purpose of submitting, by way of petition, a dispute arising out of the interpretation or application of this Convention to a means of settlement other than those provided for in this Convention.

Article 56

1. Any State may at the time of its ratification or at any time thereafter declare by notification addressed to the Secretary General of the Council of Europe that the present

Convention shall, subject to paragraph 4 of this Article, extend to all or any of the territories for whose international relations it is responsible.

2. The Convention shall extend to the territory or territories named in the notification as from the thirtieth day after the receipt of this notification by the Secretary General of the Council of Europe.

3. The provisions of this Convention shall be applied in such territories with due regard, however, to local requirements.

4. Any State which has made a declaration in accordance with paragraph 1 of this article may at any time thereafter declare on behalf of one or more of the territories to which the declaration relates that it accepts the competence of the Court to receive applications from individuals, non-governmental organisations or groups of individuals as provided by Article 34 of the Convention.

Article 57

1. Any State may, when signing this Convention or when depositing its instrument of ratification, make a reservation in respect of any particular provision of the Convention to the extent that any law then in force in its territory is not in conformity with the provision. Reservations of a general character shall not be permitted under this article.

2. Any reservation made under this article shall contain a brief statement of the law concerned.

Article 58

1. A High Contracting Party may denounce the present Convention only after the expiry of five years from the date on which it became a party to it and after six months' notice contained in a notification addressed to the Secretary General of the Council of Europe, who shall inform the other High Contracting Parties.

2. Such a denunciation shall have the effect of releasing the High Contracting Party concerned from its obligations under this Convention in respect of any act which, being capable of constituting a violation of such obligations, may have been performed by it before the date at which the denunciation became effective.

3. Any High Contracting Party which shall cease to be a member of the Council of Europe shall cease to be a Party to this Convention under the same conditions.

4. The Convention may be denounced in accordance with the provisions of the preceding paragraphs in respect of any territory to which it has been declared to extend under the terms of Article 56.

Article 59

1. This Convention shall be open to the signature of the members of the Council of Europe. It shall be ratified. Ratifications shall be deposited with the Secretary General of the Council of Europe.

2. The present Convention shall come into force after the deposit of ten instruments of ratification.

3. As regards any signatory ratifying subsequently, the Convention shall come into force at the date of the deposit of its instrument of ratification.

4. The Secretary General of the Council of Europe shall notify all the members of the Council of Europe of the entry into force of the Convention, the names of the High Contracting Parties who have ratified it, and the deposit of all instruments of ratification which may be effected subsequently.

Done at Rome this 4th day of November 1950, in English and French, both texts being equally authentic, in a single copy which shall remain deposited in the archives of the Council of Europe. The Secretary General shall transmit certified copies to each of the signatories.

APPENDIX 6

The European Prison Rules 1987

Revised European Version of the Standard Minimum Rules for the Treatment of Prisoners

Preamble

The purposes of these rules are:

    (a) to establish a range of minimum standards for all those aspects of prison administration that are essential to humane conditions and positive treatment in modern and progressive systems;

    (b) to serve as a stimulus to prison administrations to develop policies and management style and practice based on good contemporary principles of purpose and equity;

    (c) to encourage in prison staffs progressional attitudes that reflect the important social and moral qualities of their work and to create conditions in which they can optimise their own performance to the benefit of society in general, the prisoners in their care and their own vocational satisfaction;

    (d) to provide realistic basic criteria against which prison administrations and those responsible for inspecting the conditions and management of prisons can make valid judgments of performance and measure progress towards higher standards.

It is emphasised that the rules do not constitute a model system and that, in practice, many European prison services are already operating well above many of the standards set out in the rules and that others are striving, and will continue to strive, to do so. Wherever there are difficulties or practical problems to be overcome in the application of the rules, the Council of Europe has the machinery and the expertise available to assist with advice and the fruits of the experience of the various prison administrations within its sphere.

In these rules, renewed emphasis has been placed on the precepts of human dignity, the commitment of prison administrations to humane and positive treatment, the importance of staff roles and effective modern management approaches. They are set out to provide ready reference, encouragement and guidance to those who are working at all levels of prison administration. The explanatory memorandum that accompanies the rules is intended to ensure the understanding, acceptance and flexibility that are necessary to achieve the highest realistic level of implementation beyond the basic standards.

Part I
The Basic Principles

1. The deprivation of liberty shall be effected in material and moral conditions which ensure respect for human dignity and are in conformity with these rules.

2. The rules shall be applied impartially. There shall be no discrimination on grounds of race, colour, sex, language, religion, political or other opinion, national or social origin, birth, economic or other status. The religious beliefs and moral precepts of the group to which a prisoner belongs shall be respected.

3. The purposes of the treatment of persons in custody shall be such as to sustain their health and self-respect and, so far as the length of sentence permits, to develop their sense of responsibility and encourage those attitudes and skills that will assist them to return to society with the best chance of leading law-abiding and self-supporting lives after their release.

4. There shall be regular inspections of penal institutions and services by qualified and experienced inspectors appointed by a competent authority. Their task shall be, in particular, to monitor whether and to what extent these institutions are administered in accordance with existing laws and regulations, the objectives of the prison services and the requirements of these rules.

5. The protection of the individual rights of prisoners with special regard to the legality of the execution of detention measures shall be secured by means of a control carried out, according to national rules, by a judicial authority or other duly constituted prison administration.

6.   (1) These rules shall be made readily available to staff in the national languages.
    (2) They shall also be available to prisoners in the same languages and in other languages so far as is reasonable and practicable.

PART II

THE MANAGEMENT OF PRISON SYSTEMS

Reception and registration

7.   (1) No person shall be received in an institution without a valid commitment order.
    (2) The essential details of the commitment and reception shall immediately be recorded.

8. In every place where persons are imprisoned a complete and secure record of the following information shall be kept concerning each prisoner received:
    (a) information concerning the identity of the prisoner;
    (b) the reasons for commitment and the authority therefor;
    (c) the day and hour of admission and release.

9. Reception arrangements shall conform with the basic principles of the rules and shall assist prisoners to resolve their urgent personal problems.

10.   (1) As soon as possible after reception, full reports and relevant information about the personal situation and training programme of each prisoner with a sentence of suitable length in preparation for ultimate release shall be drawn up and submitted to the director for information or approval as appropriate.
    (2) Such reports shall always include reports by a medical officer and the personnel in direct charge of the prisoner concerned.
    (3) The reports and information concerning prisoners shall be maintained with due regard to confidentiality on an individual basis, regularly kept up to date and only accessible to authorised persons.

The allocation and classification of prisoners

11.   (1) In allocating prisoners to different institutions or régimes, due account shall be taken of their judicial and legal situation (untried or convicted prisoner, first offender or habitual offender, short sentence or long sentence), of the special requirements of their treatment, of their medical needs, their sex and age.

(2) Males and females shall in principle be detained separately, although they may participate together in organised activities as part of an established treatment programme.

(3) In principle, untried prisoners shall be detained separately from convicted prisoners unless they consent to being accommodated or involved together in organised activities beneficial to them.

(4) Young prisoners shall be detained under conditions which as far as possible protect them from harmful influences and which take account of the needs peculiar to their age.

12. The purposes of classification or re-classification of prisoners shall be:

(a) to separate from others those prisoners who, by reasons of their criminal records or their personality, are likely to benefit from that or who may exercise a bad influence; and

(b) to assist in allocating prisoners to facilitate their treatment and social resettlement taking into account the management and security requirements.

13. So far as possible separate institutions or separate sections of an institution shall be used to facilitate the management of different treatment régimes or the allocation of specific categories of prisoners.

Accommodation

14. (1) Prisoners shall normally be lodged during the night in individual cells except in cases where it is considered that there are advantages in sharing accommodation with other prisoners.

(2) Where accommodation is shared it shall be occupied by prisoners suitable to associate with others in those conditions. There shall be supervision by night, in keeping with the nature of the institution.

15. The accommodation provided for prisoners, and in particular all sleeping accommodation, shall meet the requirements of health and hygiene, due regard being paid to climatic conditions and especially the cubic content of air, a reasonable amount of space, lighting, heating and ventilation.

16. In all places where prisoners are required to live or work:

(a) the windows shall be large enough to enable the prisoners, *inter alia*, to read or work by natural light in normal conditions. They shall be so constructed that they can allow the entrance of fresh air except where there is an adequate air conditioning system. Moreover, the windows shall, with due regard to security requirements, present in their size, location and construction as normal an appearance as possible;

(b) artificial light shall satisfy recognised technical standards.

17. The sanitary installations and arrangements for access shall be adequate to enable every prisoner to comply with the needs of nature when necessary and in clean and decent conditions.

18. Adequate bathing and showering installations shall be provided so that every prisoner may be enabled and required to have a bath or shower, at a temperature suitable to the climate, as frequently as necessary for general hygiene according to season and geographical region, but at least once a week. Wherever possible there should be free access at all reasonable times.

19. All parts of an institution shall be properly maintained and kept clean at all times.

Personal hygiene

20. Prisoners shall be required to keep their persons clean, and to this end they shall be provided with water and with such toilet articles as are necessary for health and cleanliness.

21. For reasons of health and in order that prisoners may maintain a good appearance and preserve their self-respect, facilities shall be provided for the proper care of the hair and beard, and men shall be enabled to shave regularly.

Clothing and bedding

22.   (1) Prisoners who are not allowed to wear their own clothing shall be provided with an outfit of clothing suitable for the climate and adequate to keep them in good health. Such clothing shall in no manner be degrading or humiliating.

      (2) All clothing shall be clean and kept in proper condition. Underclothing shall be changed and washed as often as necessary for the maintenance of hygiene.

      (3) Whenever prisoners obtain permission to go outside the institution, they shall be allowed to wear their own clothing or other inconspicuous clothing.

23. On the admission of prisoners to an institution, adequate arrangements shall be made to ensure that their personal clothing is kept in good condition and fit for use.

24. Every prisoner shall be provided with a separate bed and separate and appropriate bedding which shall be kept in good order and changed often enough to ensure its cleanliness.

Food

25.   (1) In accordance with the standards laid down by the health authorities, the administration shall provide the prisoners at the normal times with food which is suitably prepared and presented, and which satisfies in quality and quantity the standards of dietetics and modern hygiene and takes into account their age, health, the nature of their work, and so far as possible, religious or cultural requirements.

      (2) Drinking water shall be available to every prisoner.

Medical services

26.   (1) At every institution there shall be available the services of at least one qualified general practitioner. The medical services should be organised in close relation with the general health administration of the community or nation. They shall include a psychiatric service for the diagnosis and, in proper cases, the treatment of states of mental abnormality.

      (2) Sick prisoners who require specialist treatment shall be transferred to specialised institutions or to civil hospitals. Where hospital facilities are provided in an institution, their equipment, furnishings and pharmaceutical supplies shall be suitable for the medical care and treatment of sick prisoners, and there shall be a staff of suitably trained officers.

      (3) The services of a qualified dental officer shall be available to every prisoner.

27. Prisoners may not be submitted to any experiments which may result in physical or moral injury.

28.   (1) Arrangements shall be made wherever practicable for children to be born in a hospital outside the institution. However, unless special arrangements are made, there shall in penal institutions be the necessary staff and accommodation for the confinement and postnatal care of pregnant women. If a child is born in prison, this fact shall not be mentioned in the birth certificate.

(2) Where infants are allowed to remain in the institution with their mothers, special provision shall be made for a nursery staffed by qualified persons, where the infants shall be placed when they are not in the care of their mothers.

29. The medical officer shall see and examine every prisoner as soon as possible after admission and thereafter as necessary, with a view particularly to the discovery of physical or mental illness and the taking of all measures necessary for medical treatment; the segregation of prisoners suspected of infectious or contagious conditions; the noting or physical or mental defects which might impede resettlement after release; and the determination of the fitness of every prisoner to work.

30. (1) The medical officer shall have the care of the physical and mental health of the prisoners and shall see, under the conditions and with a frequency consistent with hospital standards, all sick prisoners, all who report illness or injury and any prisoner to whom attention is specially directed.

(2) The medical officer shall report to the director whenever it is considered that a prisoner's physical or mental health has been or will be adversely affected by continued imprisonment or by any condition of imprisonment.

31. (1) The medical officer or a competent authority shall regularly inspect and advise the director upon:

(a) the quantity, quality, preparation and serving of food and water;
(b) the hygiene and cleanliness or the institution and prisoners;
(c) the sanitation, heating, lighting and ventilation of the institution;
(d) the suitability and cleanliness of the prisoners' clothing and bedding.

(2) The director shall consider the reports and advice that the medical officer submits according to Rules 30, paragraph 3, and 31, paragraph 1, and, when in concurrence with the recommendations made, shall take immediate steps to give effect to those recommendations; if they are not within the director's competence or if the director does not concur with them, the director shall immediately submit a personal report and the advice of the medical officer to higher authority.

32. The medical services of the institution shall seek to detect and shall treat any physical or mental illness or defects which may impede a prisoner's resettlement after release. All necessary medical, surgical and psychiatric services including those available in the community shall be provided to the prisoner to that end.

Discipline and punishment

33. Discipline and order shall be maintained in the interests of safe custody, ordered community life and the treatment objectives of the institution.

34. (1) No prisoner shall be employed, in the service of the institution, in any disciplinary capacity.

(2) This rule shall not, however, impede the proper functioning of arrangements under which specified social, educational or sports activities or responsibilities are entrusted under supervision to prisoners who are formed into groups for the purposes of their participation in régime programmes.

35. The following shall be provided for and determined by the law or by the regulation of the competent authority:

(a) conduct constituting a disciplinary offence;
(b) the types and duration of punishment which may be imposed;
(c) the authority competent to impose such punishment;
(d) access to, and the authority of, the appellate process.

36. (1) No prisoner shall be punished except in accordance with the terms of such law or regulation, and never twice for the same act.

(2) Reports of misconduct shall be presented promptly to the competent authority who shall decide on them without undue delay.

(3) No prisoner shall be punished unless informed of the alleged offence and given a proper opportunity of presenting a defence.

(4) Where necessary and practicable prisoners shall be allowed to make their defence through an interpreter.

37. Collective punishments, corporal punishment, punishment by placing in a dark cell, and all cruel, inhuman or degrading punishment shall be completely prohibited as punishments for disciplinary offences.

38. (1) Punishment by disciplinary confinement and any other punishment which might have an adverse effect on the physical or mental health of the prisoner shall only be imposed if the medical officer, after examination, certifies in writing that the prisoner is fit to sustain it.

(2) In no case may such punishment be contrary to, or depart from, the principles stated in Rule 37.

(3) The medical officer shall visit daily prisoners undergoing such punishment and shall advise the director if the termination or alteration of the punishment is considered necessary on grounds of physical or mental health.

Instruments of restraint

39. The use of chains and irons shall be prohibited. Handcuffs, restraint-jackets and other body restraints shall never be applied as a punishment. They shall not be used except in the following circumstances:

(a) if necessary, as a precaution against escape during a transfer, provided that they shall be removed when the prisoner appears before a judicial or administrative authority unless that authority decides otherwise;

(b) on medical grounds by direction and under the supervision of the medical officer;

(c) by order of the director, if other methods of control fail, in order to protect a prisoner from self-injury, injury to others or to prevent serious damage to property; in such instances the director shall at once consult the medical officer and report to the higher administrative authority.

40. The patterns and manner of use of the instruments of restraint authorised in the preceding paragraph shall be decided by law or regulation. Such instruments must not be applied for any longer time than is strictly necessary.

Information to, and complaints by, prisoners

41. (1) Every prisoner shall on admission be provided with written information about the regulations governing the treatment of prisoners of the relevant category, the disciplinary requirements of the institution, the authorised methods of seeking information and making complaints, and all such other matters as are necessary to understand the rights and obligations of prisoners and to adapt to the life of the institution.

(2) If a prisoner cannot understand the written information provided, this information shall be explained orally.

42. (1) Every prisoner shall have the opportunity every day of making requests or complaints to the director of the institution or the officer authorised to act in that capacity.

(2) A prisoner shall have the opportunity to take to, or to make requests or complaints to, an inspector of prisons or to any other duly constituted authority entitled to visit the prison without the director or other members of the staff being present. However, appeals against formal decisions may be restricted to the authorised procedures.

(3) Every prisoner shall be allowed to make a request or complaint, under confidential cover, to the central prison administration, the judicial authority or other proper authorities.

(4) Every request or complaint addressed or referred to a prison authority shall be promptly dealt with and replied to by this authority without undue delay.

Contact with the outside world

43. (1) Prisoners shall be allowed to communicate with their families and, subject to the needs of treatment, security and good order, persons or representatives of outside organisations and to receive visits from these persons as often as possible.

(2) To encourage contact with the outside world there shall be a system of prison leave consistent with the treatment objectives in Part IV of these rules.

44. (1) Prisoners who are foreign nationals should be informed, without delay, of their right to request contact and be allowed reasonable facilities to communicate with the diplomatic or consular representative of the state to which they belong. The prison administration should co-operate fully with such representatives in the interests of foreign nationals in prison who may have special needs.

(2) Prisoners who are nationals of states without diplomatic or consular representation in the country and refugees or stateless persons shall be allowed similar facilities to communicate with the diplomatic representative of the state which takes charge of their interests or national or international authority whose task it is to serve the interests of such persons.

45. Prisoners shall be allowed to keep themselves informed regularly of the news by reading newspapers, periodicals and other publications, by radio or television transmissions, by lectures or by any similar means as authorised or controlled by the administration. Special arrangements should be made to meet the needs of foreign nationals with linguistic difficulties.

Religious and moral assistance

46. So far as practicable, every prisoner shall be allowed to satisfy the needs of his religious, spiritual and moral life by attending the services or meetings provided in the institution and having in his possession any necessary books or literature.

47. (1) If the institution contains a sufficient number of prisoners of the same religion, a qualified representative of that religion shall be appointed and approved. If the number of prisoners justifies it and conditions permit, the arrangement should be on a full-time basis.

(2) A qualified representative appointed or approved under paragraph 1 shall be allowed to hold regular services and activities and to pay pastoral visits in private to prisoners of his religion at proper times.

(3) Access to a qualified representative of any religion shall not be refused to any prisoner. If any prisoner should object to a visit of any religious representative, the prisoner shall be allowed to refuse it.

Retention of prisoners' property

48. (1) All money, valuables, and other effects belonging to prisoners which under the regulations of the institution they are not allowed to retain shall on admission to the institution be placed in safe custody. An inventory thereof shall be signed by the prisoner. Steps shall be taken to keep them in good condition. If it has been found necessary to destroy any article, this shall be recorded and the prisoner informed.

(2) On the release of the prisoner, all such articles and money shall be returned except insofar as there have been authorised withdrawals of money or the authorised sending of any such property out of the institution, or it has been found necessary on hygienic grounds to destroy any article. The prisoner shall sign a receipt for the articles and money returned.

(3) As far as practicable, any money or effects received for a prisoner from outside shall be treated in the same way unless they are intended for and permitted for use during imprisonment.

(4) If a prisoner brings in any medicines, the medical officer shall decide what use shall be made of them.

Notification of death, illness, transfer, etc

49. (1) Upon the death or serious illness of or serious injury to a prisoner, or removal to an institution for the treatment of mental illness or abnormalities, the director shall at once inform the spouse, if the prisoner is married, or the nearest relative and shall in any event inform any other person previously designated by the prisoner.

(2) A prisoner shall be informed at once of the death or serious illness of any near relative. In these cases and wherever circumstances allow, the prisoner should be authorised to visit this sick relative or see the deceased either under escort or alone.

(3) All prisoners shall have the right to inform at once their families of imprisonment or transfer to another institution.

Removal of prisoners

50. (1) When prisoners are being removed to or from an institution, they shall be exposed to public view as little as possible, and proper safeguards shall be adopted to protect them from insult, curiosity and publicity in any form.

(2) The transport of prisoners in conveyances with inadequate ventilation or light, or in any way which would subject them to unnecessary physical hardship or indignity shall be prohibited.

(3) The transport of prisoners shall be carried out at the expense of the administration and in accordance with duly authorised regulations.

PART III

PERSONNEL

51. In view of the fundamental importance of the prison staff to the proper management of the institutions and the pursuit of their organisational and treatment objectives, prison administrations shall give high priority to the fulfilment of the rules concerning personnel.

52. Prison staff shall be continually encouraged through training, consultative procedures and a positive management style to aspire to humane standards, higher efficiency and a committed approach to their duties.

53. The prison administration shall regard it as an important task continually to inform public opinion of the roles of the prison system and the work of the staff, so as to encourage public understanding of the importance of their contribution to society.

54.   (1) The prison administration shall provide for the careful selection on recruitment or in subsequent appointments of all personnel. Special emphasis shall be given to their integrity, humanity, professional capacity and personal suitability for the work.

   (2) Personnel shall normally be appointed on a permanent basis as professional prison staff and have civil service status with security of tenure subject only to good conduct, efficiency, good physical and mental health and an adequate standard of education. Salaries shall be adequate to attract and retain suitable men and women; employment benefits and conditions of service shall be favourable in view of the exacting nature of the work.

   (3) Whenever it is necessary to employ part-time staff, these criteria should apply to them as far as that it is appropriate.

55.   (1) On recruitment or after an appropriate period of practical experience, the personnel shall be given a course of training in their general and specific duties and be required to pass theoretical and practical tests unless their professional qualifications make that unnecessary.

   (2) During their career, all personnel shall maintain and improve their knowledge and professional capacity by attending courses of in-service training to be organised by the administration at suitable intervals.

   (3) Arrangements should be made for wider experience and training for personnel whose professional capacity would be improved by this.

   (4) The training of all personnel should include instruction in the requirements and application of the European Prison Rules and the European Convention on Human Rights.

56. All members of the personnel shall be expected at all times so to conduct themselves and perform their duties as to influence the prisoners for good by their example and to command their respect.

57.   (1) So far as possible the personnel shall include a sufficient number of specialists such as psychiatrists, psychologists, social workers, teachers, trade, physical education and sports instructors.

   (2) These and other specialist staff shall normally be employed on a permanent basis. This shall not preclude part-time or voluntary workers when that is appropriate and beneficial to the level of support and training they can provide.

58.   (1) The prison administration shall ensure that every institution is at all times in the full charge of the director, the deputy director or other authorised official.

   (2) The director of an institution should be adequately qualified for that post by character, administrative ability, suitable professional training and experience.

   (3) The director shall be appointed on a full-time basis and be available or accessible as required by the prison administration in its management instructions.

   (4) When two or more institutions are under the authority of one director, each shall be visited at frequent intervals. A responsible official shall be in charge of each of these institutions.

59. The administration shall introduce forms of organisation and management systems to facilitate communication between the different categories of staff in an institution with a view to ensuring co-operation between the various services, in particular, with respect to the treatment and re-socialisation of prisoners.

60. (1) The director, deputy, and the majority of the other personnel of the institution shall be able to speak the language of the greatest number of prisoners, or a language understood by the greatest number of them.

    (2) Whenever necessary and practicable the services of an interpreter shall be used.

61. (1) Arrangements shall be made to ensure at all times that a qualified and approved medical practitioner is able to attend without delay in cases of urgency.

    (2) In institutions not staffed by one or more full-time medical officers, a part-time medical officer or authorised staff of a health service shall visit regularly.

62. The appointment of staff in institutions or parts of institutions housing prisoners of the opposite sex is to be encouraged.

63. (1) Staff of the institutions shall not use force against prisoners except in self-defence or in cases of attempted escape or active or passive physical resistance to an order based on law or regulations. Staff who have recourse to force must use no more than is strictly necessary and must report the incident immediately to the director of the institution.

    (2) Staff shall as appropriate be given special technical training to enable them to restrain aggressive prisoners.

    (3) Except in special circumstances, staff performing duties which bring them into direct contact with prisoners should not be armed. Furthermore, staff should in no circumstances be provided with arms unless they have been fully trained in their use.

Part IV
Treatment Objectives and Régime

64. Imprisonment is by the deprivation of liberty a punishment in itself. The conditions of imprisonment and the prison and the prison régimes shall not, therefore, except as incidental to justifiable segregation or the maintenance of discipline, aggravate the suffering inherent in this.

65. Every effort shall be made to ensure that the régimes of the institutions are designed and managed so as:

    (a) to ensure that the conditions of life are compatible with human dignity and acceptable standards in the community;

    (b) to minimise the detrimental effects of imprisonment and the differences between prison life and life at liberty which tend to diminish the self-respect or sense of personal responsibility of prisoners;

    (c) to sustain and strengthen those links with relatives and the outside community that will promote the best interests of prisoners and their families;

    (d) to provide opportunities for prisoners to develop skills and aptitudes that will improve their prospects of successful resettlement after release.

66. To these ends all the remedial, educational, moral, spiritual and other resources that are appropriate should be made available and utilised in accordance with the individual treatment needs of prisoners. Thus the régimes should include:

    (a) spiritual support and guidance and opportunities for relevant work, vocational guidance and training, education, physical education, the development of social skills, counselling, group and recreational activities;

    (b) arrangements to ensure that these activities are organised, so far as possible, to increase contacts with and opportunities within the outside community so as to enhance the prospects for social resettlement after release;

(c) procedures for establishing and reviewing individual treatment and training programmes for prisoners after full consultations among the relevant staff and with individual prisoners who should be involved in these as far as practicable;

(d) communications systems and a management style that will encourage appropriate and positive relationships between staff and prisoners that will improve the prospects for effective and supportive régimes and treatment programmes.

67. (1) Since the fulfilment of these objectives requires individualisation of treatment and, for this purpose, a flexible system of allocation, prisoners should be placed in separate institutions or units where each can receive the appropriate treatment and training.

(2) The type, size, organisation and capacity of these institutions or units should be determined essentially by the nature of the treatment to be provided.

(3) It is necessary to ensure that prisoners are located with due regard to security and control but such measures should be the minimum comparable with safety and comprehend the special needs of the prisoner. Every effort should be made to place prisoners in institutions that are open in character or provide ample opportunities for contacts with the outside community. In the case of foreign nationals, links with people of their own nationality in the outside community are to be regarded as especially important.

68. As soon as possible after admission and after a study of the personality of each prisoner with a sentence of a suitable length, a programme of treatment in a suitable institution shall be prepared in the light of the knowledge obtained about individual needs, capacities and dispositions, especially proximity to relatives.

69. (1) Within the régimes, prisoners shall be given the opportunity to participate in activities of the institution likely to develop their sense of responsibility, self-reliance and to stimulate interest in their own treatment.

(2) Efforts should be made to develop methods of encouraging co-operation with and the participation of the prisoners in their treatment. To this end prisoners shall be encouraged to assume, within the limits specified in Rule 34, responsibilities in certain sectors of the institution's activity.

70. (1) The preparation of prisoners for release should begin as soon as possible after reception in a penal institution. Thus, the treatment of prisoners should emphasise not their exclusion from the community but their continuing part in it. Community agencies and social workers should, therefore, be enlisted wherever possible to assist the staff of the institution in the task of social rehabilitation of the prisoners particularly maintaining and improving the relationships with their families, with other persons and with the social agencies. Steps should be taken to safeguard, to the maximum extent compatible with the law and the sentence, the rights and other social benefits of prisoners.

(2) Treatment programmes should include provision for prison leave which should also be granted to the greatest extent possible on medical, educational, occupational, family and other social grounds.

(3) Foreign nationals should not be excluded from arrangements for prison leave solely on account of their nationality. Furthermore, every effort should be made to enable them to participate in régime activities together so as to alleviate their feelings of isolation.

Work

71. (1) Prison work should be seen as a positive element in treatment, training and institutional management.
    (2) Prisoners under sentence may be required to work, subject to their physical and mental fitness as determined by the medical officer.
    (3) Sufficient work of a useful nature, or if appropriate other purposeful activities shall be provided to keep prisoners actively employed for a normal working day.
    (4) So far as possible the work provided shall be such as will maintain or increase the prisoner's ability to earn a normal living after release.
    (5) Vocational training in useful trades shall be provided for prisoners able to profit thereby and especially for young prisoners.
    (6) Within the limits compatible with proper vocational selection and with the requirements of institutional administration and discipline, the prisoners shall be able to choose the type of employment in which they wish to participate.

72. (1) The organisation and methods of work in the institutions shall resemble as closely as possible those of similar work in the community so as to prepare prisoners for the conditions of normal occupational life. It should thus be relevant to contemporary working standards and techniques and organised to function within modern management systems and production processes.
    (2) Although the pursuit of financial profit from industries in the institutions can be valuable in raising standards and improving the quality and relevance of training, the interests of the prisoners and of their treatment must not be subordinary to that purpose.

73. Work for prisoners shall be assured by the prison administration:
    (a) either on its own premises, workshops and farms; or
    (b) in co-operation with private contractors inside or outside the institution in which case the full normal wages for such shall be paid by the persons to whom the labour is supplied, account being taken of the output of the prisoners.

74. (1) Safety and health precautions for prisoners shall be similar to those that apply to workers outside.
    (2) Provision shall be made to indemnify prisoners against industrial injury, including occupational disease, on terms not less favourable than those extended by law to workers outside.

75. (1) The maximum daily and weekly working hours of the prisoners shall be fixed in conformity with local rules or custom in regard to the employment of free workmen.
    (2) Prisoners should have at least one rest-day a week and sufficient time for education and other activities required as part of their treatment and training for social resettlement.

76. (1) There shall be a system of equitable remuneration of the work of prisoners.
    (2) Under the system prisoners shall be allowed to spend at least a part of their earnings on approved articles for their own use and to allocate a part of their earnings to their family or for other approved purposes.
    (3) The system may also provide that a part of the earnings be set aside by the administration so as to constitute a savings fund to be handed over to the prisoner on release.

Education

77. A comprehensive education programme shall be arranged in every institution to provide opportunities for all prisoners to pursue at least some of their individual needs and aspirations. Such programmes should have as their objectives the improvement of the prospects for successful social resettlement, the morale and attitudes of prisoners and their self-respect.

78. Education should be regarded as a régime activity that attracts the same status and basic remuneration within the régime as work, provided that it takes place in normal working hours and is part of an authorised individual treatment programme.

79. Special attention should be given by prison administrations to the education of young prisoners, those of foreign origins or with particular cultural or ethnic needs.

80. Specific programmes of remedial education should be arranged for prisoners with special problems such as illiteracy or innumeracy.

81. So far as practicable, the education of prisoners shall:
    (a) be integrated with the educational system of the country so that after their release they may continue their education without difficulty.
    (b) take place in outside educational institutions.

82. Every institution shall have a library for the use of all categories of prisoners, adequately stocked with a wide range of both recreational and instructional books, and prisoners shall be encouraged to make full use of it. Wherever possible the prison library should be organised in co-operation with community library services.

Physical education, exercise, sport and recreation

83. The prison régime shall recognise the importance to physical and mental health of properly organised activities to ensure physical fitness, adequate exercise and recreational opportunities.

84. Thus a properly organised programme of physical education, sport and other recreational activity should be arranged within the framework and objectives of the treatment and training régime. To this end space, installations and equipment should be provided.

85. Prison administrations should ensure that prisoners who participate in these programmes are physically fit to do so. Special arrangements should be made, under medical direction, for remedial physical education and therapy for those prisoners who need it.

86. Every prisoner who is not employed in outdoor work, or located in an open institution, shall be allowed, if the weather permits, at least one hour of walking or suitable exercise in the open air daily, as far as possible, sheltered from inclement weather.

Pre-release preparation

87. All prisoners should have the benefit of arrangements designed to assist them in returning to society, family life and employment after release. Procedures and special courses should be devised to this end.

88. In the case of those prisoners with longer sentences, steps should be taken to ensure a gradual return to life in society. This aim may be achieved, in particular, by a pre-release régime organised in the same institution or in another appropriate institution, or by conditional release under some kind of supervision combined with effective social support.

89.   (1) Prison administration should work closely with the social services and agencies that assist released prisoners to re-establish themselves in society, in particular with regard to family life and employment.

(2) Steps must be taken to ensure that on release prisoners are provided, as necessary, with appropriate documents and identification papers and assisted in finding suitable homes and work to go to. They should also be provided with immediate means of subsistence, be suitably and adequately clothed having regard to the climate and season, and have sufficient means to reach their destination.

(3) The approved representatives of the social agencies or services should be afforded all necessary access to the institution and to prisoners with a view to making a full contribution to the preparation for release and after-care programme of the prisoner.

PART V
ADDITIONAL RULES FOR SPECIAL CATEGORIES

90. Prison administration should be guided by the provisions of the rules as a whole so far as they can appropriately and in practice be applied for the benefit of those special categories of prisoners for which additional rules are provided hereafter.

Untried prisoners

91. Without prejudice to legal rules for the protection of individual liberty or prescribing the procedure to be observed in respect of untried prisoners, these prisoners, who are presumed to be innocent until they are found guilty, shall be afforded the benefits that may derive from Rule 90 and treated without restrictions other than those necessary for the penal procedure and the security of the institution.

92. (1) Untried prisoners should be allowed to inform their families of their detention immediately and given all reasonable facilities for communication with family and friends and persons with whom it is in their legitimate interest to enter into contact.

(2) They shall also be allowed to receive visits from them under humane conditions subject only to such restrictions and supervision as are necessary in the administration of justice and of the security and good order of the institution.

(3) If an untried prisoner does not wish to inform any of these persons, the prison administration should not do so on its own initiative unless their are good overriding reasons as, for instance, the age, state of mind or any other incapacity of the prisoner.

93. Untried prisoners shall be entitled, as soon as imprisoned, to choose a legal representative, or shall be allowed to apply for free legal aid where such aid is available and to receive visits from that legal adviser with a view to their defence and to prepare and hand to the legal adviser, and to receive, confidential instructions. On request they shall be given the free assistance of an interpreter for all essential contacts with the administration and for their defence. Interviews between prisoners and their legal advisers may be within sight but not within hearing, either direct or indirect, of the police or institution staff. The allocation of untried prisoners shall be in conformity with the provisions of Rule 11, paragraph 3.

94. Except when there are circumstances that make it undesirable, untried prisoners shall be given the opportunity of having separate rooms.

95. (1) Untried prisoners shall be given the opportunity of wearing their own clothing if it is clean and suitable.

(2) Prisoners who do not avail themselves of this opportunity, shall be supplied with suitable dress.

694

(3) If they have no suitable clothing of their own, untried prisoners shall be provided with civilian clothing in good condition in which to appear in court or on authorised outings.

96. Untried prisoners shall, whenever possible, be offered the opportunity to work but shall not be required to work. Those who choose to work shall be paid as other prisoners. If educational or trade training is available, untried prisoners shall be encouraged to avail themselves of these opportunities.

97. Untried prisoners shall be allowed to procure at their own expense or at the expense of a third party such books, newspapers, writing materials and other means of occupation as are compatible with the interests of the administration of justice and the security and good order of the institution.

98. Untried prisoners shall be given the opportunity of being visited and treated by their own doctor or dentist if there is reasonable ground for the application. Reasons should be given if the application is refused. Such costs as are incurred shall not be the responsibility of the prison administration.

Civil prisoners

99. In countries where the law permits imprisonment by order of a court under any non-criminal process, persons so imprisoned shall not be subjected to any greater restriction or severity than is necessary to ensure safe custody and good order. Their treatment shall not be less favourable than that of untried prisoners, with the reservation, however, that they may be required to work.

Insane and mentally abnormal prisoners

100. (1) Persons who are found to be insane should not be detained in prisons and arrangements shall be made to remove them to appropriate establishments for the mentally ill as soon as possible.
(2) Specialised institutions or sections under medical management should be available for the observation and treatment of prisoners suffering gravely from other mental disease or abnormality.
(3) The medical or psychiatric service of the penal institutions shall provide for the psychiatric treatment of all prisoners who are in need of such treatment.
(4) Action should be taken, by arrangement with the appropriate community agencies, to ensure where necessary the continuation of psychiatric treatment after release and the provision of social psychiatric after-care.

APPENDIX 7

European Convention for the Prevention of Torture and Inhuman or Degrading Treatment or Punishment

The member States of the Council of Europe, signatory hereto,

Having regard to the provisions of the Convention for the Protection of Human Rights and Fundamental Freedoms;

Recalling that, under Article 3 of the same Convention, 'no one shall be subjected to inhuman or degrading treatment or punishment';

Noting that the machinery provided for in that Convention operates in relation to persons who alleged that they are victims of violations of Article 3;

Convinced that the protection of persons deprived of their liberty against torture and inhuman or degrading treatment or punishment could be strengthened by non-judicial means of a preventive character based on visits;

Have agreed as follows:

CHAPTER I

Article 1

There shall be established a European Committee for the Prevention of Torture and Inhuman or Degrading Treatment or Punishment (hereinafter referred to as 'the Committee'). The Committee shall, by means of visits, examine the treatment of persons deprived of their liberty with a view to strengthening, if necessary, the protection of such persons from torture and from inhuman or degrading treatment or punishment.

Article 2

Each Party shall permit visits, in accordance with this Convention, to any place within its jurisdiction where persons are deprived of their liberty by a public authority.

Article 3

In the application of this Convention, the Committee and the competent national authorities of the Party concerned shall co-operate with each other.

CHAPTER II

Article 4

1. The Committee shall consist of a number of members equal to that of the Parties.

2. The members of the Committee shall be chosen from among persons of high moral character, known for their competence in the field of human rights or having professional experience in the areas covered by this Convention.

3. No two members of the Committee may be nationals of the same State.

4. The members shall serve in their individual capacity, shall be independent and impartial, and shall be available to serve the Committee effectively.

Article 5

1. The members of the Committee shall be elected by the Committee of Ministers of the Council of Europe by an absolute majority of votes, from a list of names drawn up by the Bureau of the Consultative Assembly of the Council of Europe; each national delegation of the Parties in the Consultative Assembly shall put forward three candidates, of whom two at least shall be its nationals.

2. The same procedure shall be followed in filling casual vacancies.

3. The members of the Committee shall be elected for a period of four years. They may be re-elected once. However, among the members elected at the first election, the terms of three members shall expire at the end of two years. The members whose terms are to expire at the end of the initial period of two years shall be chosen by lot by the Secretary General of the Council of Europe immediately after the first election has been completed.

Article 6

1. The Committee shall meet in camera. A quorum shall be equal to the majority of its members. The decisions of the Committee shall be taken by a majority of the members present, subject to the provisions of Article 10, paragraph 2.

2. The Committee shall draw up its own rules of procedure.

3. The Secretariat of the Committee shall be provided by the Secretary General of the Council of Europe.

Chapter III

Article 7

1. The Committee shall organise visits to places referred to in Article 2. Apart from periodic visits, the Committee may organise such other visits as appear to it to be required in the circumstances.

2. As a general rule, the visits shall be carried out by at least two members of the Committee. The Committee may, if it considers it necessary, be assisted by experts and interpreters.

Article 8

1. The Committee shall notify the Government of the Party concerned of its intention to carry out a visit. After such notification, it may at any time visit any place referred to in Article 2.

2. A Party shall provide the Committee with the following facilities to carry out its task:
- (a) access to its territory and the right to travel without restriction;
- (b) full information on the places where persons deprived of their liberty are being held;
- (c) unlimited access to any place where persons are deprived of their liberty, including the right to move inside such places without restriction;
- (d) other information available to the Party which is necessary for the Committee to carry out its task. In seeking such information, the Committee shall have regard to applicable rules of national law and professional ethics.

3. The Committee may interview in private persons deprived of their liberty.

4. The Committee may communicate freely with any person whom it believes can supply relevant information.

5. If necessary, the Committee may immediately communicate observations to the competent authorities of the Party concerned.

Article 9

1. In exceptional circumstances, the competent authorities of the Party concerned may make representations to the Committee against a visit at the time or to the particular place proposed by the Committee. Such representations may only be made on grounds of national defence, public safety, serious disorder in places where persons are deprived of their liberty, the medical condition of a person or that an urgent interrogation relating to a serious crime is in progress.

2. Following such representations, the Committee and the Party shall immediately enter into consultations in order to clarify the situation and seek agreement on arrangements to enable the Committee to exercise its functions expeditiously. Such arrangements may include the transfer to another place of any person whom the Committee proposed to visit. Until the visit takes place, the Party shall provide information to the Committee about any person concerned.

Article 10

1. After each visit, the Committee shall draw up a report on the facts found during the visit, taking account of any observations which may have been submitted by the Party concerned. It shall transmit to the latter its report containing any recommendations it considers necessary. The Committee may consult with the Party with a view to suggesting, if necessary, improvements in the protection of persons deprived of their liberty.

2. If the Party fails to co-operate or refuses to improve the situation in the light of the Committee's recommendations, the Committee may decide, after the Party has had an opportunity to make known its views, by a majority of two-thirds of its members to make a public statement on the matter.

Article 11

1. The information gathered by the Committee in relation to a visit, its report and its consultations with the Party concerned shall be confidential.

2. The Committee shall publish its report, together with any comments of the Party concerned, whenever requested to do so by that Party.

3. However, no personal data shall be published without the express consent of the person concerned.

Article 12

Subject to the rules of confidentiality in Article 11, the Committee shall every year submit to the Committee of Ministers a general report on its activities which shall be transmitted to the Consultative Assembly and made public.

Article 13

The members of the Committee, experts and other persons assisting the Committee are required, during and after their terms of office, to maintain the confidentiality of the facts or information of which they have become aware during the discharge of their functions.

Article 14

1. The names of persons assisting the Committee shall be specified in the notification under Article 8, paragraph 1.

2. Experts shall act on the instructions and under the authority of the Committee. They shall have particular knowledge and experience in the areas covered by this Convention and shall be bound by the same duties of independence, impartiality and availability as the members of the Committee.

3. A Party may exceptionally declare that an expert or other person assisting the Committee may not be allowed to take part in a visit to a place within its jurisdiction.

CHAPTER IV

Article 15

Each Party shall inform the Committee of the name and address of the authority competent to receive notifications to its Government, and of any liaison officer it may appoint.

Article 16

The Committee, its members and experts referred to in Article 7, paragraph 2 shall enjoy the privileges and immunities set out in the Annex to this Convention.

Article 17

1. This Convention shall not prejudice the provisions of domestic law or any international agreement which provide greater protection for persons deprived of their liberty.

2. Nothing in this Convention shall be construed as limiting or derogating from the competence of the organs of the European Convention on Human Rights or from the obligations assumed by the Parties under that Convention.

3. The Committee shall not visit places which representatives or delegates of Protecting Powers or the International Committee of the Red Cross effectively visit on a regular basis by virtue of the Geneva Conventions of 12 August 1949 and the Additional Protocols of 8 June 1977 thereto.

CHAPTER V

Article 18

The Convention shall be open for signature by the member States of the Council of Europe. It is subject to ratification, acceptance or approval. Instruments of ratification, acceptance or approval shall be deposited with the Secretary General of the Council of Europe.

Article 19

1. This convention shall enter into force on the first day of the month following the expiration of a period of three months after the date on which seven member States of the Council of Europe have expressed their consent to be bound by the Convention in accordance with the provisions of Article 18.

2. In respect of any member State which subsequently expresses its consent to be bound by it, the Convention shall enter into force on the first day of the month following the expiration of a period of three months after the date of the deposit of the instrument of ratification, acceptance or approval.

Article 20

1. Any State may at the time of signature or when depositing its instrument of ratification, acceptance or approval, specify the territory or territories to which this Convention shall apply.

2. Any State may at any later date, by a declaration addressed to the Secretary General of the Council of Europe, extend the application of this Convention to any other territory specified in the declaration. In respect of such territory the Convention shall enter into force on the first day of the month following the expiration of a period of three months after the date of receipt of such declaration by the Secretary General.

3. Any declaration made under the two preceding paragraphs may, in respect of any territory specified in such declaration, be withdrawn by a notification addressed to the Secretary General. The withdrawal shall become effective on the first day of the month following the expiration of a period of three months after the date of receipt of such notification by the Secretary General.

Article 21

No reservation may be made in respect of the provisions of this Convention.

Article 22

1. Any Party may, at any time, denounce this Convention by means of a notification addressed to the Secretary General of the Council of Europe.

2. Such denunciation shall become effective on the first day of the month following the expiration of a period of twelve months after the date of receipt of the notification by the Secretary General.

Article 23

The Secretary General of the Council of Europe shall notify the member States of the Council of Europe of:

    (a) any signature;

    (b) the deposit of any instrument of ratification, acceptance or approval;

    (c) any date of entry into force of this Convention in accordance with Articles 19 and 20;

    (d) any other act, notification or communication relating to this Convention, except for action taken in pursuance of Articles 8 and 10.

ANNEX
PRIVILEGES AND IMMUNITIES

Article 16

1. For the purpose of this annex, references to members of the Committee shall be deemed to include references to experts mentioned in Article 7, paragraph 2.

2. The members of the Committee shall, while exercising their functions and during journeys made in the exercise of their functions, enjoy the following privileges and immunities:

    (a) immunity from personal arrest or detention and from seizure of their personal baggage and, in respect of words spoken or written and all acts done by them in their official capacity, immunity from legal process of every kind;

    (b) exemption from any restrictions on their freedom of movement on exit from and return to their country of residence, and entry into and exit from the country in which they exercise their functions, and from alien registration in the country which they are visiting or through which they are passing in the exercise of their functions.

3. In the course of journeys undertaken in the exercise of their functions, the members of the Committee shall, in the matter of customs and exchange control, be accorded:

    (a) by their own Government, the same facilities as those accorded to senior officials travelling abroad on temporary official duty;

    (b) by the Governments of other Parties, the same facilities as those accorded to representatives of foreign Governments on temporary official duty.

4. Documents and papers of the Committee, in so far as they relate to the business of the Committee, shall be inviolable. The official correspondence and other official communications of the Committee may not be held up or subjected to censorship.

701

5. In order to secure for the members of the Committee complete freedom of speech and complete independence on the discharge of their duties, the immunity from legal process in respect of words spoken or written and all acts done by them in discharging their duties shall continue to be accorded, notwithstanding that the persons concerned are no longer engaged in the discharge of such duties.

6. Privileges and immunities are accorded to the members of the Committee, not for the personal benefit of the individuals themselves but in order to safeguard the independent exercise of their functions. The Committee alone shall be competent to waive the immunity of its members; it has not only the right, but is under a duty, to waive the immunity of one of its members in any case where, in its opinion, the immunity would impede the course of justice, and where it can be waived without prejudice to the purpose for which the immunity is accorded.

APPENDIX 8

Criminal Justice Act 1991

as amended

1991 Chapter 53

Part II
Early Release of Prisoners

Preliminary

The Parole Board

32.—(1) The Parole Board shall be, by that name, a body corporate and as such shall

    (a) be constituted in accordance with this Part; and

    (b) have the functions conferred by this Part in respect of long-term and short-term prisoners and by Chapter II of Part II of the Crime (Sentences) Act 1997 ('Chapter II') in respect of life prisoners within the meaning of that Chapter.

(2) It shall be the duty of the Board to advise the Secretary of State with respect to any matter referred to it by him which is connected with the early release or recall of prisoners.

(3) The Board shall deal with cases as respects which it makes recommendations under this Part or Chapter II on consideration of—

    (a) any documents given to it by the Secretary of State; and

    (b) any other oral or written information obtained by it,

and if in any particular case the Board thinks it necessary to interview the person to whom the case relates before reaching a decision, the Board may authorise one of its members to interview him and shall consider the report of the interview made by that member.

(4) The Board shall deal with cases as respects which it gives directions under this Part or Chapter II on consideration of all such evidence as may be adduced before it.

(5) Without prejudice to subsections (3) and (4) above, the Secretary of State may make rules with respect to the proceedings of the Board, including provision authorising cases to be dealt with by a prescribed number of its members or requiring cases to be dealt with at prescribed times.

(6) The Secretary of State may also give to the Board directions as to the matters to be taken into account by it in discharging any functions under this Part or Chapter II; and in giving any such directions the Secretary of State shall in particular have regard to—

    (a) the need to protect the public from serious harm from offenders; and

    (b) the desirability of preventing the commission by them of further offences and of securing their rehabilitation.

(7) Schedule 5 to this Act shall have effect with respect to the Board.

New arrangements for early release

Duty to release short-term and long-term prisoners

33.—(1) As soon as a short-term prisoner has served one-half of his sentence, it shall be the duty of the Secretary of State—

    (a) to release him unconditionally if that sentence is for a term of less than twelve months; and

    (b) to release him on licence if that sentence is for a term of twelve months or more.

(2) As soon as a long-term prisoner has served two-thirds of his sentence, it shall be the duty of the Secretary of State to release him on licence.

(3) As soon as a short-term or long-term prisoner who—

    (a) has been released on licence under this Part; and

    (b) has been recalled to prison under section 39(1) or (2) below,

would (but for his release) have served three-quarters of his sentence, it shall be the duty of the Secretary of State to release him on licence.

(3A) In the case of a prisoner to whom section 44A below applies, it shall be the duty of the Secretary of State to release him on licence at the end of the extension period (within the meaning of section 85 of the Powers of Criminal Courts (Sentencing) Act 2000).

(4) ...

(5) In this Part—

    'long-term prisoner' means a person serving a sentence of imprisonment for a term of four years or more;

    'short-term prisoner' means a person serving a sentence of imprisonment for a term of less than four years.

Duty to release prisoners: special cases

33A.—(1) As soon as a prisoner—

    (a) whose sentence is for a term of less than twelve months; and

    (b) who has been released on licence under section 34A(3) or 36(1) below and recalled to prison under section 38A(1) or 39(1) or (2) below,

would (but for his release) have served one-half of his sentence, it shall be the duty of the Secretary of State to release him unconditionally.

(2) As soon as a prisoner—

    (a) whose sentence is for a term of twelve months or more; and

    (b) who has been released on licence under section 34A(3) below and recalled to prison under section 38A(1) below,

would (but for his release) have served one-half of his sentence, it shall be the duty of the Secretary of State to release him on licence.

(3) In the case of a prisoner who—

    (a) has been released on licence under this Part and recalled to prison under section 39(1) or (2) below; and

    (b) has been subsequently released on licence under section 33(3) or (3A) above and recalled to prison under section 39(1) or (2) below,

section 33(3) above shall have effect as if for the words 'three-quarters' there were substituted the words 'the whole' and the words 'on licence' were omitted.

34. ...

Power to release short-term prisoners on licence

34A.—(1) Subject to subsection (2) below, subsection (3) below applies where a short-term prisoner aged 18 or over is serving a sentence of imprisonment for a term of three months or more.

(2) Subsection (3) below does not apply where—

(a) the sentence is an extended sentence within the meaning of section 85 of the Powers of Criminal Courts (Sentencing) Act 2000;

(b) the sentence is for an offence under section 1 of the Prisoners (Return to Custody) Act 1995;

(c) the sentence was imposed under paragraph *4(1)(d) or 5(1)(d)* 4(1C)(d) or 5(1C)(d) of Schedule 3 to the Powers of Criminal Courts (Sentencing) Act 2000 in a case where the prisoner had failed to comply with a requirement of a curfew order;

(d) the prisoner is subject to a hospital order, hospital direction or transfer direction under section 37, 45A or 47 of the Mental Health Act 1983;

(da) the prisoner is subject to the notification requirements of Part I of the Sex Offenders Act 1997;

(e) the prisoner is liable to removal from the United Kingdom for the purposes of section 46 below;

(f) the prisoner has been released on licence under this section at any time and has been recalled to prison under section 38A(1)(a) below;

(g) the prisoner has been released on licence under this section or section 36 below during the currency of the sentence, and has been recalled to prison under section 39(1) or (2) below;

(h) the prisoner has been returned to prison under section 116 of the Powers of Criminal Courts (Sentencing) Act 2000 at any time; or

(j) the interval between—

(i) the date on which the prisoner will have served the requisite period for the term of the sentence; and

(ii) the date on which he will have served one-half of the sentence,

is less than 14 days.

(3) After the prisoner has served the requisite period for the term of his sentence, the Secretary of State may, subject to section 37A below, release him on licence.

(4) In this section 'the requisite period' means—

(a) for a term of three months or more but less than four months, a period of 30 days;

(b) for a term of four months or more but less than eight months, a period equal to one-quarter of the term;

(c) for a term of eight months or more, a period that is 60 days less than one-half of the term.

(5) The Secretary of State may by order made by statutory instrument—

(a) repeal the words 'aged 18 or over' in subsection (1) above;

(b) amend the definition of 'the requisite period' in subsection (4) above; and

(c) make such transitional provision as appears to him necessary or expedient in connection with the repeal or amendment.

(6) No order shall be made under subsection (5) above unless a draft of the order has been laid before and approved by a resolution of each House of Parliament.

Power to release long-term and life prisoners

35.—(1) After a long-term prisoner has served one-half of his sentence, the Secretary of State may, if recommended to do so by the Board, release him on licence.

(2) ...

(3) ...

Power to release prisoners on compassionate grounds

36.—(1) The Secretary of State may at any time release a [short-term or long-term prisoner] on licence if he is satisfied that exceptional circumstances exist which justify the prisoner's release on compassionate grounds.

(2) Before releasing a long-term prisoner under subsection (1) above, the Secretary of State shall consult the Board, unless the circumstances are such as to render such consultation impracticable.

Duration and conditions of licences

37.—(1) Subject to [subsections (1A), (1B) and (2)] below, where a short-term or long-term prisoner is released on licence, the licence shall, subject to . . . any revocation under section 39(1) or (2) below, remain in force until the date on which he would (but for his release) have served three-quarters of his sentence.

[(1A) Where a prisoner is released on licence under section 33(3) or (3A) above, subsection (1) above shall have effect as if for the reference to three-quarters of his sentence there were substituted a reference to the whole of that sentence.]

[(1B) Where a prisoner whose sentence is for a term of twelve months or more is released on licence under section 33A(2) or 34A(3) above, subsection (1) above shall have effect as if for the reference to three-quarters of his sentence there were substituted a reference to the difference between—

(a) that proportion of his sentence; and
(b) the duration of the curfew condition to which he is or was subject.]

(2) Where a prisoner whose sentence is for a term of less than twelve months is released on licence under [section 34A(3) or 36(1) above], subsection (1) above shall have effect as if for the reference to three-quarters of his sentence there were substituted a reference to one-half of that sentence.

(3) ...

(4) A person subject to a licence [under this Part] shall comply with such conditions . . . as may for the time being be specified in the licence; and the Secretary of State may make rules for regulating the supervision of any description of such persons.

[(4A) The conditions so specified may in the case of a person released on licence under section 34A above whose sentence is for a term of less than twelve months, and shall in any other case, include on the person's release conditions as to his supervision by—

(a) an officer of a local probation board appointed for or assigned to the petty sessions area within which the person resides for the time being; or
(b) where the person is under the age of 18 years, a member of a youth offending team established by the local authority within whose area the person resides for the time being.]

[(5) The Secretary of State shall not include on release, or subsequently insert, a condition in the licence of a long-term prisoner, or vary or cancel any such condition, except after consultation with the Board.]

(6) For the purposes of subsection (5) above, the Secretary of State shall be treated as having consulted the Board about a proposal to include, insert, vary or cancel a condition in any case if he has consulted the Board about the implementation of proposals of that description generally or in that class of case.

(7) The power to make rules under this section shall be exercisable by statutory instrument which shall be subject to annulment in pursuance of a resolution of either House of Parliament.

Curfew condition to be included in licence under section 34A

37A.—(1) A person shall not be released under section 34A(3) above unless the licence includes a condition ('the curfew condition') which—

 (a) requires the released person to remain, for periods for the time being specified in the condition, at a place for the time being so specified (which may be an approved probation hostel); and
 (b) includes requirements for securing the electronic monitoring of his whereabouts during the periods for the time being so specified.

(2) The curfew condition may specify different places or different periods for different days, but shall not specify periods which amount to less than 9 hours in any one day (excluding for this purpose the first and last days of the period for which the condition is in force).

(3) The curfew condition shall remain in force until the date when the released person would (but for his release) have served one-half of his sentence.

(4) The curfew condition shall include provision for making a person responsible for monitoring the released person's whereabouts during the periods for the time being specified in the condition; and a person who is made so responsible shall be of a description specified in an order made by the Secretary of State.

(5) The power conferred by subsection (4) above—

 (a) shall be exercisable by statutory instrument; and
 (b) shall include power to make different provision for different cases or classes of case or for different areas.

(6) Nothing in this section shall be taken to require the Secretary of State to ensure that arrangements are made for the electronic monitoring of released persons' whereabouts in any particular part of England and Wales.

(7) ...

Misbehaviour after release

38. ...

Breach of curfew condition

38A.—[(1) If it appears to the Secretary of State, as regards a person released on licence under section 34A(3) above—

 (a) that he has failed to comply with the curfew condition;
 (b) that his whereabouts can no longer be electronically monitored at the place for the time being specified in that condition; or
 (c) that it is necessary to do so in order to protect the public from serious harm from him,

the Secretary of State may, if the curfew condition is still in force, revoke the licence and recall the person to prison.

(2) A person whose licence under section 34A(3) above is revoked under this section—

(a) may make representations in writing with respect to the revocation;

(b) on his return to prison, shall be informed of the reasons for the revocation and of his right to make representations.

(3) The Secretary of State, after considering any representations made under subsection (2)(b) above or any other matters, may cancel a revocation under this section.

(4) Where the revocation of a person's licence is cancelled under subsection (3) above, the person shall be treated for the purposes of sections 34A(2)(f) and 37(1B) above as if he had not been recalled to prison under this section.

(5) On the revocation under this section of a person's licence under section 34A(3) above, he shall be liable to be detained in pursuance of his sentence and, if at large, shall be deemed to be unlawfully at large.

(6) In this section 'the curfew condition' has the same meaning as in section 37A above.]

Recall of long-term prisoners while on licence

39.—(1) If recommended to do so by the Board in the case of a short-term or long-term prisoner who has been released on licence under this Part, the Secretary of State may revoke his licence and recall him to prison.

(2) The Secretary of State may revoke the licence of any such person and recall him to prison without a recommendation by the Board, where it appears to him that it is expedient in the public interest to recall that person before such a recommendation is practicable.

(3) A person recalled to prison under subsection (1) or (2) above—

(a) may make representations in writing with respect to his recall; and

(b) on his return to prison, shall be informed of the reasons for his recall and of his right to make representations.

(4) The Secretary of State shall refer to the Board—

(a) the case of a person recalled under subsection (1) above who makes representations under subsection (3) above; and

(b) the case of a person recalled under subsection (2) above.

(5) Where on a reference under subsection (4) above the Board—

(a) ...

(b) recommends in the case of any person,

his immediate release on licence under this section, the Secretary of State shall give effect to the recommendation.

[(5A) In the case of a prisoner to whom section 44A below applies, subsections (4)(b) and (5) of that section apply in place of subsection (5) above.]

(6) On the revocation of the licence of any person under this section, he shall be liable to be detained in pursuance of his sentence and, if at large, shall be deemed to be unlawfully at large.

40. ...

Release on licence following return to prison

40A.—(1) This section applies (in place of sections 33, 33A, 37(1) and 39 above) where a court passes on a person a sentence of imprisonment which—

(a) includes, or consists of, an order under section 116 of the Powers of Criminal Courts (Sentencing) Act 2000; and

(b) is for a term of twelve months or less.

(2) As soon as the person has served one-half of the sentence, it shall be the duty of the Secretary of State to release him on licence.

(3) Where the person is so released, the licence shall remain in force for a period of three months.

(4) If the person fails to comply with such conditions as may for the time being be specified in the licence, he shall be liable on summary conviction—

    (a) to a fine not exceeding level 3 on the standard scale; or

    (b) to a sentence of imprisonment for a term not exceeding the relevant period, but not liable to be dealt with in any other way.

(5) In subsection (4) above 'the relevant period' means a period which is equal in length to the period between the date on which the failure occurred or began and the date of the expiry of the licence.

(6) As soon as a person has served one-half of a sentence passed under subsection (4) above, it shall be the duty of the Secretary of State to release him, subject to the licence if it is still subsisting.

Remand time and additional days

Remand time to count towards time served

41.—*(1) This section applies to any person whose sentence falls to be reduced under section 67 of the Criminal Justice Act 1967 ('the 1967 Act') by any relevant period within the meaning of that section ('the relevant period').*

    (2) For the purpose of determining for the purposes of this Part—

        (a) whether a person to whom this section applies has served one-half or two-thirds of his sentence; or

        (b) whether such a person would (but for his release) have served three-quarters of that sentence,

the relevant period shall, subject to subsection (3) below, be treated as having been served by him as part of that sentence.

[(1) Where a person is sentenced to imprisonment for a term in respect of an offence, this section applies to him if the court directs under section 9 of the Crime (Sentences) Act 1997 that the number of days for which he was remanded in custody in connection with—

    (a) the offence; or

    (b) any other offence the charge for which was founded on the same facts or evidence;

shall count as time served by him as part of the sentence.

(2) For the purpose of determining for the purposes of this Part whether a person to whom this section applies—

    (a) has served, or would (but for his release) have served, a particular proportion of his sentence; or

    (b) has served a particular period,

the number of days specified in the direction shall, subject to subsections (3) and (4) below, be treated as having been served by him as part of that sentence or period.]

(3) Nothing in subsection (2) above shall have the effect of reducing the period for which a licence granted under this Part to a short-term or long-term prisoner remains in force to a period which is less than—

    (a) one-quarter of his sentence in the case of a short-term prisoner; or

    (b) one-twelfth of his sentence in the case of a long-term prisoner.

709

[(4) Where the period for which a licence granted under section 33A(2), 34A(3) or 36(1) above to a short-term prisoner remains in force cannot exceed one-quarter of his sentence, nothing in subsection (2) above shall have the effect of reducing that period.]

Additional days for disciplinary offences

42.—(1) Prison rules, that is to say, rules made under section 47 of the 1952 Act, may include provision for the award of additional days—

    (a) to short-term or long-term prisoners; or

    (b) conditionally on their subsequently becoming such prisoners, to persons on remand,

who (in either case) are guilty of disciplinary offences.

(2) Where additional days are awarded to a short-term or long-term prisoner, or to a person on remand who subsequently becomes such a prisoner, and are not remitted in accordance with prison rules—

    (a) any period which he must serve before becoming entitled to or eligible for release under this Part; and

    (b) any period for which a licence granted to him under this Part remains in force,

shall be extended by the aggregate of those additional days.

Special cases

Young offenders

43.—(1) Subject to subsections (4) and (5) below, this Part applies to persons serving sentences of detention in a young offender institution, or determinate sentences of detention under [section 91 of the Powers of Criminal Courts (Sentencing) Act 2000], as it applies to persons serving equivalent sentences of imprisonment.

(2) . . .

(3) References in this Part to prisoners, or to prison or imprisonment, shall be construed in accordance with [subsection (1)] above.

(4) In relation to a short-term prisoner under the age of 18 years to whom subsection (1) of section 33 above applies, that subsection shall have effect as if it required the Secretary of State—

    (a) to release him unconditionally if his sentence is for a term of twelve months or less; and

    (b) to release him on licence if that sentence is for a term of more than twelve months.

(5) In relation to a person under the age of 22 years who is released on licence under this Part, [section 37(4A)] above shall have effect as if the reference to supervision by [an officer of a local probation board] included a reference to supervision by a social worker of a local authority social services department.

Extended sentences for sexual or violent offenders

44.—[(1) This section applies to a prisoner serving an extended sentence within the meaning of [section 85 of the Powers of Criminal Courts (Sentencing) Act 2000].

(2) Subject to the provisions of this section and section 51(2D) below, this Part, except [section] 40A, shall have effect as if the term of the extended sentence did not include the extension period.

(3) Where the prisoner is released on licence under this Part, the licence shall, subject to any revocation under section 39(1) or (2) above, remain in force until the end of the extension period.

(4) Where, apart from this subsection, the prisoner would be released uncondition-ally—

    (a) he shall be released on licence; and

    (b) the licence shall, subject to any revocation under section 39(1) or (2) above, remain in force until the end of the extension period.

(5) The extension period shall be taken to begin as follows—

    (a) for the purposes of subsection (3) above, on the date given by section 37(1) above;

    (b) for the purposes of subsection (4) above, on the date on which, apart from that subsection, the prisoner would have been released unconditionally.

(6) Sections 33(3) and 33A(1) above and section 46 below shall not apply in relation to the prisoner.

(7) For the purposes of sections 37(5) and 39(1) and (2) above the question whether the prisoner is a long-term or short-term prisoner shall be determined by reference to the term of the extended sentence.

(8) In this section 'extension period' has the same meaning as in [section 85 of the Powers of Criminal Courts (Sentencing) Act 2000].]

Re-release of prisoners serving extended sentences

44A.—[(1) This section applies to a prisoner serving an extended sentence within the meaning of [section 85 of the Powers of Criminal Courts (Sentencing) Act 2000] who is recalled to prison under section 39(1) or (2) above.

(2) Subject to subsection (3) below, the prisoner may require the Secretary of State to refer his case to the Board at any time.

(3) Where there has been a previous reference of the prisoner's case to the Board (whether under this section or section 39(4) above), the Secretary of State shall not be required to refer the case until after the end of the period of one year beginning with the disposal of that reference.

(4) On a reference—

    (a) under this section; or

    (b) under section 39(4) above,

the Board shall direct the prisoner's release if satisfied that it is no longer necessary for the protection of the public that he should be confined (but not otherwise).

(5) If the Board gives a direction under subsection (4) above it shall be the duty of the Secretary of State to release the prisoner on licence.]

Fine defaulters and contemnors

45.—(1) Subject to subsection (2) below, this Part ([except sections 33A, 34A [and 35]] above) applies to persons committed to prison *or to be detained under section 108 of the Powers of Criminal Courts (Sentencing) Act 2000*—

    (a) in default of payment of a sum adjudged to be paid by a conviction; or

    (b) for contempt of court or any kindred offence,

as it applies to persons serving equivalent sentences of imprisonment; and references in this Part to short-term or long-term prisoners, or to prison or imprisonment, shall be construed accordingly.

(2) In relation to persons committed as mentioned in subsection (1) above, the provisions specified in subsections (3) and (4) below shall have effect subject to the modifications so specified.

711

(3) In section 33 above, for [subsections (1) to (3)] there shall be substituted the following subsections—

'(1) As soon as a person committed as mentioned in section 45(1) below has served the appropriate proportion of his term, that is to say—
  (a) one-half, in the case of a person committed for a term of less than twelve months;
  (b) two-thirds, in the case of a person committed for a term of twelve months or more,
it shall be the duty of the Secretary of State to release him unconditionally.

(2) As soon as a person so committed who—
  (a) has been released on licence under section 36(1) below; and
  (b) has been recalled under [section 39(1) or (2)] below,
would (but for his release) have served the appropriate proportion of his term, it shall be the duty of the Secretary of State to release him unconditionally.'

(4) In section 37 above, for subsections (1) to (3) there shall be substituted the following subsection—

'(1) Where a person committed as mentioned in section 45(1) below is released on licence under section 36(1) above, the licence shall, subject to—
  (a) ...
  (b) any revocation under section 39(1) or (2) below,
continue in force until the date on which he would (but for his release) have served the appropriate proportion of his term; and in this subsection "appropriate proportion" has the meaning given by section 33(1) above.'

Persons liable to removal from the United Kingdom

46.—(1) In relation to a long-term prisoner who is liable to removal from the United Kingdom, section 35 above shall have effect as if the words 'if recommended to do so by the Board' were omitted.

(2) In relation to a person who is liable to removal from the United Kingdom, [section 37 above shall have effect as if subsection (4A) were omitted].

(3) A person is liable to removal from the United Kingdom for the purposes of this section if—
  (a) he is liable to deportation under section 3(5) of the Immigration Act 1971 and has been notified of a decision to make a deportation order against him;
  (b) he is liable to deportation under section 3(6) of that Act;
  (c) he has been notified of a decision to refuse him leave to enter the United Kingdom; or
  (d) he is an illegal entrant within the meaning of section 33(1) of that Act.

Persons extradited to the United Kingdom

47.—(1) A short-term or long-term prisoner is an extradited prisoner for the purposes of this section if—
  (a) he was tried for the offence in respect of which his sentence was imposed—
    (i) after having been extradited to the United Kingdom; and
    (ii) without having first been restored or had an opportunity of leaving the United Kingdom; and
  (b) he was for any period kept in custody while awaiting his extradition to the United Kingdom as mentioned in paragraph (a) above.

(2) *If, in the case of an extradited prisoner, the court by which he was sentenced so ordered, section 67 of the 1967 Act (computation of sentences of imprisonment) shall have effect in relation to him as if a period specified in the order were a relevant period for the purposes of that section.*

[(2) In the case of an extradited prisoner, section 9 of the Crime (Sentences) Act 1997 (crediting of periods of remand in custody) shall have effect as if the days for which he was kept in custody while awaiting extradition were days for which he was remanded in custody in connection with the offence, or any other offence the charge for which was founded on the same facts or evidence.]

(3) The period that may be so specified is such period as in the opinion of the court is just in all the circumstances and does not exceed the period of custody mentioned in subsection (1)(b) above.

(4) In this section—

'extradited to the United Kingdom' means returned to the United Kingdom—

   (i)   in pursuance of extradition arrangements;

   (ii) under any law of a designated Commonwealth country corresponding to the Extradition Act 1989;

   (iii) under that Act as extended to a colony or under any corresponding law of a colony; or

   (iv) in pursuance of a warrant of arrest endorsed in the Republic of Ireland under the law of that country corresponding to the Backing of Warrants (Republic of Ireland) Act 1965, [or]

   [(v) in pursuance of arrangements with a foreign state in respect of which an Order in Council under section 2 of the Extradition Act 1870 is in force;]

'extradition arrangements' has the meaning given by section 3 of the Extradition Act 1989;

'designated Commonwealth country' has the meaning given by section 5(1) of that Act.

48. . . .

Supplemental

Alteration by order of relevant proportions of sentences

49.—(1) The Secretary of State may by order made by statutory instrument provide—

   (a) that the references in section 33(5) above to four years shall be construed as references to such other period as may be specified in the order;

   (b) that any reference in this Part to a particular proportion of a prisoner's sentence shall be construed as a reference to such other proportion of a prisoner's sentence as may be so specified.

(2) An order under this section may make such transitional provisions as appear to the Secretary of State necessary or expedient in connection with any provision made by the order.

(3) No order shall be made under this section unless a draft of the order has been laid before and approved by resolution of each House of Parliament.

Transfer by order of certain functions to Board

50.—(1) The Secretary of State, after consultation with the Board, may by order made by statutory instrument provide that, in relation to such class of case as may be specified in the order, the provisions of this Part specified in subsections [(2) or (3)] below shall have effect subject to the modifications so specified.

(2) In section 35 above, in subsection (1) for the word 'may' there shall be substituted the word 'shall'; but nothing in this subsection shall affect the operation of that subsection as it has effect in relation to a long-term prisoner who is liable to removal from the United Kingdom (within the meaning of section 46 above).

[(3) In section 37 above, in subsection (5) for the words 'after consultation with the Board' there shall be substituted the words 'in accordance with recommendations of the Board', and subsection (6) shall be omitted.]

(4) . . .

(5) No order shall be made under this section unless a draft of the order has been laid before and approved by resolution of each House of Parliament.

Interpretation of Part II

51.—(1) In this Part—
'the Board' means the Parole Board;

. . .

'long-term prisoner' and 'short-term prisoner' have the meanings given by section 33(5) above (as extended by sections 43(1) and 45(1) above);
'sentence of imprisonment' does not include a committal in default of payment of any sum of money, or for want of sufficient distress to satisfy any sum of money, or for failure to do or abstain from doing anything required to be done or left undone.
'sexual offence' and 'violent offence' have the same meanings as in [the Powers of Criminal Courts (Sentencing) Act 2000].

[(2) For the purposes of any reference in this Part, however expressed, to the term of imprisonment to which a person has been sentenced or which, or part of which, he has served, consecutive terms and terms which are wholly or partly concurrent shall be treated as a single term if—

(a) the sentences were passed on the same occasion; or
(b) where they were passed on different occasions, the person has not been released under this Part at any time during the period beginning with the first and ending with the last of those occasions.

(2A) Where a suspended sentence of imprisonment is ordered to take effect, with or without any variation of the original term, the occasion on which that order is made shall be treated for the purposes of subsection (2) above as the occasion on which the sentence is passed.

(2B) Where a person has been sentenced to two or more terms of imprisonment which are wholly or partly concurrent and do not fall to be treated as a single term—

(a) nothing in this Part shall require the Secretary of State to release him in respect of any of the terms unless and until the Secretary of State is required to release him in respect of each of the others;
(b) nothing in this Part shall require the Secretary of State or the Board to consider his release in respect of any of the terms unless and until the Secretary of State or the Board is required to consider his release, or the Secretary of State is required to release him, in respect of each of the others;
(c) on and after his release under this Part he shall be on licence for so long, and subject to such conditions, as is required by this Part in respect of any of the sentences; . . .

(d) . . .

(2C) Where a person has been sentenced to one or more terms of imprisonment and to one or more life sentences (within the meaning of section 34 of the Crime (Sentences) Act 1997), nothing in this Part shall—

(a) require the Secretary of State to release the person in respect of any of the terms unless and until the Secretary of State is required to release him in respect of each of the life sentences; or

(b) require the Secretary of State or the Board to consider the person's release in respect of any of the terms unless and until the Secretary of State or the Board is required to consider his release in respect of each of the life sentences.

(2D) Subsections (2B) and (2C) above shall have effect as if the term of an extended sentence (within the meaning of [section 85 of the Powers of Criminal Courts (Sentencing) Act 2000]) included the extension period (within the meaning of that section).]

(3) ...

[(4) Section 161(4) of the Powers of Criminal Courts (Sentencing) Act 2000 (meaning of 'protecting the public from serious harm') shall apply for the purposes of this Part as it applies for the purposes of that Act.]

The Crime (Sentences) Act 1997,
Part II
Effect of Custodial Sentences
Chapter II
Life Sentences

Release on licence

Duty to release certain life prisoners

28.—(1) A life prisoner is one to whom this section applies if—

    (a) the conditions mentioned in subsection (2) below are fulfilled; or

    (b) he was under 18 at the time when he committed the *offence* for which his sentence was imposed.

(2) The conditions referred to in subsection (l)(a) above are—

    (a) that the prisoner's sentence was imposed for an offence the sentence for which is not fixed by law; and

    (b) that the court by which he was sentenced for that offence ordered that this section should apply to him as soon as he had served a part of his sentence specified in the order.

(3) A part of a sentence specified in an order under subsection (2)(b) above shall be such part as the court considers appropriate taking into account—

    (a) the seriousness of the offence, or the combination of the offence and other offences associated with it; and

    (b) the effect of any direction which it would have given under section 9 above if it had sentenced him to a term of imprisonment.

(4) Where in the case of a life prisoner to whom this section applies the conditions mentioned in subsection (2) above are not fulfilled, the Secretary of State shall direct that this section shall apply to him as soon as he has served a part of his sentence specified in the direction

(5) As soon as, in the case of a life prisoner to whom this section applies—

    (a) he has served the part of his sentence specified in the order or direction ('the relevant part'); and

    (b) the Parole Board has directed his release under this section,

it shall be the duty of the Secretary of State to release him on licence.

(6) The Parole Board shall not give a direction under subsection (5) above with respect to a life prisoner to whom this section applies unless—

    (a) the Secretary of State has referred the prisoner's case to the Board; and

    (b) the Board is satisfied that it is no longer necessary for the protection of the public that the prisoner should be confined.

(7) A life prisoner to whom this section applies may require the Secretary of State to refer his case to the Parole Board at any time—

    (a) after he has served the relevant part of his sentence; and

    (b) where there has been a previous reference of his case to the Board, after the end of the period of two years beginning with the disposal of that reference; and

    (c) where he is also serving a sentence of imprisonment or detention for a term, after the time when, but for his life sentence, he would be entitled to be released;

and in this subsection 'previous reference' means a reference under subsection (6) above or section 32(4) below.

(8) In determining for the purpose of subsection (5) or (7) above whether a life prisoner to whom this section applies has served the relevant part of his sentence, no account shall be taken of any time during which he was unlawfully at large within the meaning of section 49 of the Prison Act 1952.

(9) An offence is associated with another for the purposes of this section if it is so associated for the purposes of Part I of the 1991 Act.

Power to release other life prisoners

29.—(1) If recommended to do so by the Parole Board, the Secretary of State may, after consultation with the Lord Chief Justice together with the trial judge if available, release on licence a life prisoner who is not one to whom section 28 above applies.

(2) The Parole Board shall not make a recommendation under subsection (1) above unless the Secretary of State has referred the particular case, or the class of case to which that case belongs, to the Board for its advice.

Power to release life prisoners on compassionate grounds

30.—(1) The Secretary of State may at any time release a life prisoner on licence if he is satisfied that exceptional circumstances exist which justify the prisoner's release on compassionate grounds.

(2) Before releasing a life prisoner under subsection (1) above, the Secretary of State shall consult the Parole Board, unless the circumstances are such as to render such consultation impracticable.

Licences and recall

Duration and conditions of licences

31.—(1) Where a life prisoner is released on licence, the licence shall, unless previously revoked under section 32(1) or (2) below, remain in force until his death.

(2) A life prisoner subject to a licence shall comply with such conditions (which shall include on his release conditions as to his supervision by a probation officer) as may for the time being be specified in the licence; and the Secretary of State may make rules for regulating the supervision of any description of such persons.

(3) The Secretary of State shall not include on release, or subsequently insert, a condition in the licence of a life prisoner, or vary or cancel any such condition, except—

   (a) in the case of the inclusion of a condition in the licence of a life prisoner to whom section 28 above applies, in accordance with recommendations of the Parole Board; and

   (b) in any other case, after consultation with the Board.

(4) For the purposes of subsection (3) above, the Secretary of State shall be treated as having consulted the Parole Board about a proposal to include, insert, vary or cancel a condition in any case if he has consulted the Board about the implementation of proposals of that description generally or in that class of case.

(5) The power to make rules under this section shall be exercisable by statutory instrument which shall be subject to annulment in pursuance of a resolution of either House of Parliament.

(6) In relation to a life prisoner who is liable to removal from the United Kingdom (within the meaning given by section 24(2) above), subsection (2) above shall have effect as if the words in parentheses were omitted.

Recall of life prisoners while on licence

32.—(1) If recommended to do so by the Parole Board in the case of a life prisoner who has been released on licence under this Chapter, the Secretary of State may revoke his licence and recall him to prison.

(2) The Secretary of State may revoke the licence of any life prisoner and recall him to prison without a recommendation by the Parole Board, where it appears to him that it is expedient in the public interest to recall that person before such a recommendation is practicable.

(3) A life prisoner recalled to prison under subsection (1) or (2) above—
   (a) may make representations in writing with respect to his recall; and
   (b) on his return to prison, shall be informed of the reasons for his recall and of his right to make representations.

(4) The Secretary of State shall refer to the Parole Board—
   (a) the case of a life prisoner recalled under subsection (1) above who makes representations under subsection (3) above; and
   (b) the case of a life prisoner recalled under subsection (2) above.

(5) Where on a reference under subsection (4) above the Parole Board—
   (a) directs in the case of a life prisoner to whom section 28 above applies;
      or
   (b) recommends in the case of any other life prisoner,
his immediate release on licence under this section, the Secretary of State shall give effect to the direction or recommendation.

(6) On the revocation of the licence of any life prisoner under this section, he shall be liable to be detained in pursuance of his sentence and, if at large, shall be deemed to be unlawfully at large.

Miscellaneous and supplemental

Life prisoners transferred to England and Wales

33.—(1) This section applies where, in the case of a transferred life prisoner, the Secretary of State, after consultation with the Lord Chief Justice, certifies his opinion that, if—
   (a) the prisoner's offence had been committed after the commencement of this Chapter; and
   (b) he had been sentenced for it in England and Wales,
the court by which he was so sentenced would have ordered that section 28 above should apply to him as soon as he had served a part of his sentence specified in the certificate.

(2) This section also applies where, in the case of a transferred life prisoner, the Secretary of State certifies his opinion that, if—
   (a) the prisoner's offence had been committed after the commencement of this Chapter; and
   (b) he had been sentenced for it in England and Wales,
the Secretary of State would have directed that section 28 above should apply to him as soon as he had served a part of his sentence specified in the certificate.

(3) In a case to which this section applies, this Chapter except section 29(1) above shall apply as if—

    (a) the transferred life prisoner were a life prisoner to whom section 28 above applies; and

    (b) the relevant part of his sentence within the meaning of section 28 above were the part specified in the certificate.

(4) In this section 'transferred life prisoner' means a person—

    (a) on whom a court in a country or territory outside England and Wales has imposed one or more sentences of imprisonment or detention for an indeterminate period; and

    (b) who has been transferred to England and Wales, in pursuance of—

        (i) an order made by the Secretary of State under paragraph 1 of Schedule 1 to this Act or section 2 of the Colonial Prisoners Removal Act 1884; or

        (ii) a warrant issued by the Secretary of State under the Repatriation of Prisoners Act 1984,

    there to serve his sentence or sentences or the remainder of his sentence or sentences.

(5) A person who is required so to serve the whole or part of two or more such sentences shall not be treated as a life prisoner to whom section 28 above applies unless the requirements of subsection (1) or (2) above are satisfied as respects each of those sentences; and subsections (5) and (7) of section 28 above shall not apply in relation to such a person until after he has served the relevant part of each of those sentences.

Interpretation of Chapter II

34.—(1) In this Chapter 'life prisoner' means a person serving one or more life sentences; but—

    (a) a person serving two or more such sentences shall not be treated as a life prisoner to whom section 28 above applies unless the requirements of section 28(1) above are satisfied as respects each of those sentences; and

    (b) subsections (5) and (7) of that section shall not apply in relation to such a person until after he has served the relevant part of each of those sentences.

(2) In this section 'life sentence' means any of the following imposed for an offence, whether committed before or after the commencement of this chapter, namely—

    (a) a sentence of imprisonment for life;

    (b) a sentence of detention during Her Majesty's pleasure or for life under section 53 of the 1933 Act; and

    (c) a sentence of custody for life under section 8 of the 1982 Act.

(3) In this Chapter 'court' includes a court-martial and 'trial judge' includes a trial judge advocate; and in subsection (2) above—

    (a) the reference to section 53 of the 1933 Act includes a reference to subsections (3) and (4) of section 71A of the Army Act 1955 and the Air Force Act 1955 and section 43A of the Naval Discipline Act 1957; and

    (b) the reference to section 8 of the 1982 Act includes a reference to subsections (1A) and (1B) of those sections.

The Parole Board Rules 1997

Made 6 October 1997
Coming into force 6 October 1997

PART I
INTRODUCTORY

PART II
GENERAL

PART III
HEARING

PART IV
MISCELLANEOUS

SCHEDULES

PART I
INTRODUCTORY

Title and commencement and revocation

1. (1) These Rules may be cited as the Parole Board Rules 1997 and shall come into force on 6th October 1997.

(2) The Parole Board Rules 1992 are hereby revoked.

Application and interpretation

2. (1) Subject to rule 19, these Rules apply where a prisoner's case is referred to the Board by the Secretary of State under section 28(6)(a), section 28(7) or section 32(4) of the Act.

(2) In these Rules, unless a contrary intention appears—

'Board' means the Parole Board, continued by section 32(1) of the Criminal Justice Act 1991,

'Chairman' means the chairman of the Board appointed under paragraph 2 of Schedule 5 to the Criminal Justice Act, 1991,

'governor' includes a director of a contracted out prison,

'panel' means those members of the Board constituted in accordance with rule 3,

'parties' means the prisoner and the Secretary of State,

'prisoner' means a person to whom section 28 of the Act applies,

'the Act' means the Crime (Sentences) Act 1997.

PART II
GENERAL

Appointment of panel

3. (1) The Chairman shall appoint three members of the Board to form a panel for the purpose of conducting proceedings in relation to a prisoner's case.

(2) The members of the panel appointed under paragraph (1) shall include a person who holds or who has held judicial office and who shall act as chairman of the panel.

Listing the case for hearing

4. The Board shall list the case for hearing and, as soon as practicable thereafter, notify the parties of the date when the case was so listed.

Information and reports by the Secretary of State

5. (1) Within eight weeks of the case being listed, the Secretary of State shall serve on the Board and, subject to paragraph (2), the prisoner or his representative—

(*a*) the information specified in Part A of Schedule 1 to these Rules,

(*b*) the reports specified in Part B of that Schedule, and

(*c*) such further information that the Secretary of State considers to be relevant to the case.

(2) Any part of the information or reports referred to in paragraph (1) which, in the opinion of the Secretary of State, should be withheld from the prisoner on the ground that its disclosure would adversely affect the health or welfare of the prisoner or others, shall be recorded in a separate document and served only on the Board together with the reasons for believing that its disclosure would have that effect.

(3) Where a document is withheld from the prisoner in accordance with paragraph (2), it shall nevertheless be served as soon as practicable on the prisoner's representative if he is—

(*a*) a barrister or solicitor,

(*b*) a registered medical practitioner, or

(*c*) a person whom the chairman of the panel directs is suitable by virtue of his experience of professional qualification;

provided that no information disclosed in accordance with this paragraph shall be disclosed either directly or indirectly to the prisoner or to any other person without the authority of the chairman of the panel.

Representation, etc.

6. (1) Subject to paragraph (2), a party may be represented by any person who he has authorised for that purpose.

(2) The following are ineligible to act as a representative before the Board—

    (*a*) any person liable to be detained under the Mental Health Act 1983,

    (*b*) any person serving a sentence of imprisonment;

    (*c*) any person who is on licence having been released under Part III of the Criminal Justice Act 1967 or under Part II of the Criminal Justice Act 1991 or under Part II of the Act,

    (*d*) any person with a previous conviction for an imprisonable offence which remains unspent under the Rehabilitation of Offenders Act 1974.

(3) Within three weeks of the case being listed, a party shall notify the Board and the other party of the name, address and occupation of any person authorised in accordance with paragraph (1).

(4) Where a prisoner does not authorise a person to act as his representative, the Board may, with his agreement, appoint someone to act on his behalf.

(5) A party may apply, in accordance with the procedure set out in rule 7 (1) and (2), to be accompanied at the hearing by such other person or persons as he wishes, in addition to any representative he may have authorised; but before granting any such application the Board shall obtain the agreement of—

    (*a*) in the case where the hearing is to be held at a prison, the governor, and

    (*b*) in any other case, the person in whom is vested the authority to agree.

Witnesses

7. (1) Where a party wishes to call witnesses at the hearing, he shall make a written application to the Board, a copy of which he shall serve on the other party, within 12 weeks of the case being listed, giving the name, address and occupation of the witness he wishes to call and the substance of the evidence he proposes to adduce.

(2) The chairman of the panel may grant or refuse an application under paragraph (1) and shall communicate his decision to both parties, giving reasons in writing, in the case of a refusal, for his decision.

Evidence of the prisoner

8. (1) Where the prisoner wishes to make representations about his case, he shall serve them on the Board and the Secretary of State within 15 weeks of the case being listed.

(2) Any other documentary evidence that the prisoner wishes to adduce shall be served on the Board and the Secretary of State at least 14 days before the date of the hearing.

Directions

9. (1) Subject to paragraph (3), the chairman of the panel may give, vary or revoke directions for the conduct of the case, including directions in respect of—

    (*a*) the timetable for the proceedings,

    (*b*) the varying of the time within which or by which an act is required, by these Rules, to be done,

    (*c*) the service of documents,

    (*d*) as regards any documents which have been received by the Board but which have been withheld from the prisoner in accordance with rule 5(2), whether the disclosure of such documents would adversely affect the health or welfare of the prisoner or others, and

    (*e*) the submission of evidence;

and following his appointment under rule 3, the chairman of the panel shall consider whether such directions need to be given at any time.

(2) Within 14 days of being notified of a direction under paragraph (1)(d), either party may appeal against it to the Chairman, who shall notify the other party of the appeal; the other party may make representations on the appeal to the Chairman whose decision shall be final.

(3) Directions under paragraph (1) may be given, varied or revoked either

    (*a*) of the chairman of the panel's own motion, or

    (*b*) on the written application of a party to the Board which has been served on the other party and which specifies the direction which is sought;

but in either case both parties shall be given an opportunity to make written representations or, where the chairman of the panel thinks it necessary, and subject to paragraph (6)(b), to make oral submissions at a preliminary hearing fixed in accordance with paragraph (4).

(4) Where the chairman of the panel decides to hold a preliminary hearing, he shall give the parties at least 14 days' notice of the date, time and place which has been fixed in respect thereof.

(5) A preliminary hearing shall be held in private and information about the proceedings and the names of any persons concerned in the proceedings shall not be made public.

(6) Except in so far as the chairman of the panel otherwise directs, at a preliminary hearing—

    (*a*) the chairman of the panel shall sit alone, and

    (*b*) the prisoner shall not attend save where he is unrepresented.

(7) The chairman of the panel shall take a note of the giving, variation or revocation of a direction under this rule and serve a copy on the parties as soon as practicable thereafter.

PART III
THE HEARING

Oral hearing

10. (1) Except in so far as both parties and the chairman of the panel agree otherwise, there shall be an oral hearing of the prisoner's case.

(2) The prisoner shall, within five weeks of the case being listed, notify the Board and the Secretary of State whether he wishes to attend the hearing.

Notice of hearing

11. (1) When fixing the date of the hearing the Board shall consult the parties.

(2) The Board shall give the parties at least three weeks notice of the date, time and place scheduled for the hearing or such shorter notice to which the parties may consent.

Location, privacy of proceedings

12. (1) The hearing shall be held at the prison or other institution where the prisoner is detained.

(2) The hearing shall be held in private and, except in so far as the chairman of the panel otherwise directs, information about the proceedings and the names of any persons concerned in the proceedings shall not be made public.

(3) The chairman of the panel may admit to the hearing such terms and conditions as he considers appropriate.

Hearing procedure

13. (1) At the beginning of the hearing the chairman of the panel shall explain the order of proceeding which the panel proposes to adopt.

(2) Subject to this rule, the panel shall conduct the hearing in such manner as it considers most suitable to the clarification of the issues before it and generally to the just handling of the proceedings; it shall so far as appears to it appropriate, seek to avoid formality in the proceedings.

(3) The parties shall be entitled to appear and be heard at the hearing and take such part in the proceedings as the panel thinks proper; and the parties may hear each others' evidence, put questions to each other, call any witnesses who the Board has authorised to give evidence in accordance with rule 7, and put questions to any witness or other person appearing before the panel.

(4) The chairman of the panel may require any person present at the hearing who is, in his opinion, behaving in a disruptive manner to leave and may permit him to return, if at all, only on such conditions as he may specify.

(5) The panel may receive in evidence any document or information notwithstanding that such document or information would be inadmissible in a court of law but no person shall be compelled to give any evidence or produce any document which he could not be compelled to give or produce on the trial of an action.

(6) The chairman of the panel may require the prisoner, or any witness appearing for the prisoner to leave the hearing where evidence is being examined which the chairman of the panel, in accordance wirh rule 9(1)(d) (subject to any successful appeal under rule 9(2)), previously directed should be withheld from the prisoner as being injurious to the health or welfare of the prisoner or another person.

(7) After all the evidence has been given, the prisoner shall be given a further opportunity to address the panel.

Adjournment

14. (1) The panel may at any time adjourn a hearing for the purpose of obtaining further information or for such other purposes as it may think appropriate.

(2) Before adjourning any hearing, the panel may give such directions as it thinks fit for ensuring the prompt consideration of the application at a resumed hearing.

(3) Before the panel resumes any hearing which was adjourned without a further hearing date being fixed it shall give the parties not less than 14 days' notice, or such shorter notice to which all parties may consent, of the date, time and place of the resumed hearing.

The decision

15. (1) Any decision of the majority of the members of the panel shall be the decision of the panel.

(2) The decision by which the panel determines a case shall be recorded in writing with reasons, signed by the chairman of the panel, and communicated in writing to the parties not more than seven days after the end of the hearing.

PART IV
MISCELLANEOUS

Time

16. Where the time prescribed by or under these Rules for doing any act expires on a Saturday, Sunday or public holiday, the act shall be in time if done on the next working day.

Transmission of documents etc.

17. Any document required or authorised by these Rules to be served or otherwise transmitted to any person may be sent by pre-paid post or delivered,

(*a*) in the case of a document directed to the Board or the chairman of the panel, to the office of the Board;

(*b*) in any other case, to the last known address of the person to whom the document is directed.

Irregularities

18. Any irregularity resulting from failure to comply with these Rules before the panel has determined a case shall not of itself render the proceedings void, but the panel may, and shall, if it considers that the person may have been prejudiced, take such steps as it thinks fit, before determining the case, to cure the irregularity, whether by the amendment of any document, the giving of any notice, the taking of any step or otherwise.

References to the Board following recall

19. Where the Secretary of State refers a prisoner's case to the Board under section 32(4) of the Act, and the prisoner has made representations under section 32(3) of the Act, these Rules shall apply subject to the following modifications—

(*a*) rules 5(1), 6(3), 7(1), 8(1) and (2), 9(2) and (4), 10(2), 11(2), 14(3) and 15(2) shall apply as if for references to the periods of time specified therein there were substituted a reference to such period of time as the chairman of the panel shall in each case determine, taking account of both the desirability of the Board reaching an early decision in the prisoners' case and the need to ensure fairness to the prisoner;

(b) rule 5 shall apply as if for the references in paragraph (l)(a) and (b) of that rule to the information and reports specified in Schedule 1 there were substituted a reference to the information and reports specified in Schedule 2.

SCHEDULE 1   Rule 5(1)

INFORMATION AND REPORTS FOR SUBMISSION TO THE
BOARD BY THE SECRETARY OF STATE ON A
REFERENCE TO THE BOARD UNDER
SECTION 28(6)(a) OR 28(7) OF THE ACT

PART A
INFORMATION RELATING TO THE PRISONER.

1. The full name of the prisoner.

2. The age of the prisoner.

726

3. The prison in which the prisoner is detained and details of other prisons in which the prisoner has been detained, the date and reasons for any transfer.

4. The date the prisoner was sentenced and the details of the offence.

5. The previous convictions and parole history, if any, of the prisoner.

6. The comments, if available, of the trial judge in passing sentence.

7. Where applicable, the conclusions of the Court of Appeal in respect of any appeal by the prisoner against conviction or sentence.

8. The details of any life sentence plan prepared for the prisoner which have previously been disclosed to him.

PART B
REPORTS RELATING TO THE PRISONER

1. Any pre-trial and pre-sentence reports examined by the sentencing court and any post-trial police report on the circumstances of the offence(s).

2. Any report on a prisoner while he was subject to a transfer direction under section 47 of the Mental Health Act 1983.

3. Any current reports on the prisoner's performance and behaviour in prison and, where relevant, on his health including any opinions on his suitability for release on licence (reports previously examined by the Board need only be summarised) as well as his compliance with any sentence plan.

4. An up-to-date home circumstances report prepared for the Board by a Probation Officer, including reports on the following:
    (a) details of the home address, family circumstances, and family attitudes towards the prisoner;
    (b) alternative options if the offender cannot return home;
    (c) the opportunity for employment on release;
    (d) the local community's attitude towards the prisoner (if known), including the attitudes and concerns of the victim(s) of the offence(s);
    (e) the prisoner's response to previous periods of supervision;
    (f) the prisoner's behaviour during any temporary leave during the current sentence;
    (g) the prisoner's response to discussions of the objectives of supervision where applicable;
    (h) an assessment of the risk of re-offending;
    (i) a programme of supervision;
    (j) a recommendation for release; and
    (k) recommendations regarding any special licence conditions.

SCHEDULE 2   Rule 5(1) and 19(b)

INFORMATION AND REPORTS FOR SUBMISSION TO THE
BOARD BY THE SECRETARY OF STATE ON A
REFERENCE TO THE BOARD UNDER
SECTION 32(4) OF THE ACT

PART A
INFORMATION RELATING TO THE PRISONER.

1. The full name of the prisoner.

2. The age of the prisoner.

3. The prison in which the prisoner is detained and details of other prisons in which the prisoner has been detained, the date and reasons for any transfer.

4. The date the prisoner was sentenced and the details of the offence.

5. The previous convictions and parole history, if any, of the prisoner.

6. The details of any life sentence plan prepared for the prisoner which have previously been disclosed to him.

7. The details of any previous recalls of the prisoner including the reasons for such recalls and subsequent re-release on licence.

8. The statement of reasons for the most recent recall which was given to the prisoner under section 32(3)(6) of the Act.

9. The details of any memorandum which the Board considered prior to making its recommendation for recall under section 39(1) of the Act or confirming the Secretary of State's decision to recall under section 32(2) of the Act, including the reasons why the Secretary of State considered it expedient in the public interest to recall that person before it was practicable to obtain a recommendation from the Board.

PART B
Reports relating to the prisoner

1. The reports considered by the Board prior to making its recommendation for recall under section 32(1) of the Act or its confirmation of the Secretary of State's decision to recall under section 32(2) of the Act.

2. Any other relevant reports.

APPENDIX 9

Directions to the Parole Board under the Criminal Justice Act 1991, section 32(6) and Accompanying Training Guidance

SECRETARY OF STATE'S DIRECTIONS TO THE PAROLE BOARD—RELEASE OF DETERMINATE SENTENCE PRISONERS

1. In deciding whether or not to recommend release on licence, the Parole Board shall consider *primarily* the risk to the public of a further offence being committee at a time when the prisoner would otherwise be in prison and whether any such risk is acceptable. This must be balanced against the benefit, both to the public and the offender, of early release back into the community under a degree of supervision which might help rehabilitation and so lessen the risk of re-offending in the future. The Board shall take into account that safeguarding the public may often outweigh the benefits to the offender of early release.

2. Before recommending early release on licence, the Parole Board shall consider whether:—

(1) The safety of the public will be placed unacceptably at risk. In assessing such risk, the Board shall take into account:
- (a) the nature and circumstances of the original offence;
- (b) whether the prisoner has shown by his attitude and behaviour in custody that he is willing to address his offending behaviour by understanding its causes and its consequences for the victims concerned, and has made positive effort and progress in doing so;
- (c) in the case of a violent or sexual offender, whether the prisoner has committed other offences of sex or violence, in which case the risk to the public of release on licence may be unacceptable;
- (d) that a risk of violent or sexual offending is more serious than a risk of other types of offending.

(2) The longer period of supervision that parole would provide is likely to reduce the risk of further offences being committed.

(3) The prisoner is likely to comply with the conditions of his licence.

(4) The prisoner has failed to meet the requirements of licensed supervision, temporary release or bail on any previous occasion and, if so, whether this makes the risk of releasing him on licence unacceptable.

(5) The resettlement plan will help secure the offender's rehabilitation.

(6) The supervising officer has prepared a programme of supervision and has recommended specific licence conditions.

SECRETARY OF STATE'S DIRECTIONS TO THE PAROLE BOARD— DIRECTIONS RELATING TO THE RECALL OF DETERMINATE SENTENCE PRISONERS SUBJECT TO LICENCE (ISSUED 2002)

Where an offender is subject to a custodial sentence, the licence period is an integral part of the sentence, and compliance with licence conditions is required. In most cases, the licences are combined with supervision by a probation officer, social worker or member of a youth offending team. (The exception to this is the use of Home Detention Curfew licenses for adult prisoners serving a sentence of less than 12 months.)

The objectives of supervision are:

- to protect the public
- to prevent re-offending
- to ensure the prisoner's successful reintegration into the community

Initial recommendation for a recall

In determining whether or not to recommend to the Secretary of State (under Section 39(1) of the Criminal Justice Act 1991) the recall of a prisoner who is subject to licence, the Parole Board shall consider whether:

(a) the prisoner's continued liberty would present an unacceptable risk of a further offence being committed. The type of re-offending involved does not need to involve a risk to public safety;

or

(b) the prisoner has failed to comply with one or more of his or her license conditions, and that failure suggests that the objectives of probation supervision have been undermined;

or

(c) the prisoner has breached the trust placed in him or her by the Secretary of State in releasing him or her on licence, whether through failure to comply with one or more of the licence conditions, or any other means.

Where a prisoner has been charged for an offence committed whilst subject to Home Detention Curfew licence, the Board shall additionally take into account that it is desirable for such a prisoner to be recalled to custody, unless it is clearly apparent that the conduct that has led to the prisoner being charged does not merit recall.

Each individual case shall be considered on its merits, without discrimination on any grounds.

DIRECTIONS RELATING TO REPRESENTATIONS AGAINST RECALL (ISSUED 2002)

1. When a prisoner's license has been revoked and the person has been returned to custody, he or she will be served with the papers on which the decision to recall was taken and informed of the rights to make representations under Section 39(3) of the Criminal Justice Act 1991.

2. When considering a prisoner's representations, the Parole Board shall determine whether:

(a) the prisoner's liberty would present unacceptable risk of a further offence being committee. The type of re-offending involved does not need to involve a risk to public safety.

(b) whilst on licence, the prisoner failed to comply with one or more of his or her licence conditions and that failure suggested that the objects of probation supervision had been undermined;

or
  (c) the prisoner had breached the trust placed in him or her by the Secretary of State either by failing to comply with one or more of his licence conditions, or any other means;

and
  (d) the prisoner is likely to comply with licence conditions in the future, taking into account in particular the effect of the further period of imprisonment since recall.

Each individual case should be decided on its merits, without discrimination on any grounds.

DIRECTIONS TO THE PAROLE BOARD UNDER SECTION 32(6) OF THE CRIMINAL JUSTICE ACT 1991—RELEASE OF MANDATORY LIFE SENTENCE PRISONERS

1. The Home Secretary takes the final decision on the release of mandatory life sentence prisoners ('lifers') and that decision might be taken on grounds that go beyond the risk posed by the prisoner. The Home Secretary is also concerned with the wider political implications, including the effect on public confidence in the life sentence system which release may have, i.e. how the public would be likely to respond to the lifer being released at that juncture.

2. The Parole Board's responsibilities in the release consideration are whether, having regard to the degree of risk involved of the lifer committing further imprisonable offences after release, it remains necessary for the protection of the public for the lifer to be confined.

3. Each case should be considered on its individual merits.

4. Before recommending release, the Parole Board should consider whether:
  (a) the lifer has shown by his performance in prison that he has made positive efforts to address his attitudes and behavioural problems and the extent to which progress has been made in doing so such that the risk that he will commit a further imprisonable offence after release is minimal.
  (b) the lifer is likely to comply with the conditions of the life licence and the requirements of supervision.

5. Before deciding whether or not to recommend release, the Parole Board must take into account all of the papers submitted to it.

TRAINING GUIDANCE ON THE RELEASE OF MANDATORY LIFE SENTENCE PRISONERS

(*These do not form part of the Directions to the Parole Board issued under section 32(6) of the Criminal Justice Act 1991.*)

1. The Directions to the Parole Board refer to the matters which the Board should take into account when reviewing the release of mandatory life sentence prisoners. The Board will wish to be aware that in considering a Board recommendation for release the Secretary of State will look at each individual recommendation on its merits, but will generally wish to be satisfied on items 4(1) and 4(b) of the Directions.

2. The following factors should generally be taken into account when recommending release on life licence. The weight and relevance attached to each factor differs and may vary according to the circumstances of the case:
  (a) the offender's background, including any previous convictions and their pattern;

(b) the nature and circumstances of the original offence and the reasons for it;

(c) where available, the sentencing judge's comments and probation and medical reports prepared for the court;

(d) attitude and behaviour in custody, including offences against prison discipline;

(e) behaviour during any home leave or other outside activities undertaken while in open conditions;

(f) attitude to other inmates and staff and positive contributions to prison life;

(g) insight into attitudes and behavioural problems, attitude to the offence and degree of remorse and steps taken to achieve the treatment and training objectives set out in the life sentence plan;

(h)

   (i) realism of the release plan and resettlement prospects, including home circumstances and the likelihood of co-operation with supervision, relationship with the home Probation Officer, attitude of the local community,

   (ii) extent to which the release plan continues rehabilitative work started in prison and the extent to which it lessens or removes the occurrence of circumstances which led to the original offence;

(i) any risk to other persons, including the victim's family and friends or possibility of retaliation by the victim's family or local community;

(j) possible need for special licence conditions to cover concerns which might otherwise militate against release;

(k) any medical, psychiatric or psychological considerations (particularly where there is a history of mental instability).

3. The reasons for a recommendation to release or not to release a lifer should be given and will be disclosed to the prisoner by the Home Office.

4. If release is not recommended, guidance on the timing of the next review should be given. This will normally be in a *minimum of two years'* time although earlier or later reviews may be appropriate in certain circumstances. In such cases, the Parole Board should explain its recommendations.

DIRECTIONS TO THE PAROLE BOARD UNDER SECTION 32(6) OF THE CRIMINAL JUSTICE ACT 1991—TRANSFER OF LIFE SENTENCE PRISONERS TO OPEN CONDITIONS

1. A period in open conditions is essential for most life sentence prisoners ('lifers'). It allows the testing of areas of concern in conditions which are nearer to those in the community than can be found in closed prisons. Lifers have the opportunity to take home leave from open prisons and, more generally, open conditions require them to take more responsibility for their actions.

2. In considering whether a lifer should be transferred to open conditions, the Parole Board should balance the risks against the benefits to be gained from such a move. Such consideration is, thus, somewhat different from the judgement to be made when deciding if a lifer should be released: in those cases, the Parole Board is asked only to consider risk.

3. The principal factors which the Parole Board should take into account when evaluating the risks of transfer against the benefits are:

   (a) whether the lifer has made *sufficient* progress towards tackling offending behaviour to minimise the risk and gravity of re-offending and whether the benefits suggest that a transfer to open conditions is worthwhile at that stage; and

   (b) whether the lifer is trustworthy enough not to abscond or to commit further offences (either inside or outside the prison).

4. Each case should be considered on its individual merits.

5. Before recommending transfer to open conditions, the Parole Board should consider whether:

(a) the extent to which the risk that the lifer will abscond or commit further offences while in an open prison is minimal;

(b) the lifer has shown by his performance in closed conditions that he has made positive efforts to address his attitudes and behavioural problems and the extent to which significant progress has been made in doing so;

(c) the lifer is likely to derive benefit from being able to continue to address areas of concern in an open prison and to be tested in a more realistic environment.

6. Before deciding whether or not to recommend transfer to open conditions, the Parole Board must take into account all of the papers submitted to it.

TRAINING GUIDANCE ON THE TRANSFER OF LIFE SENTENCE PRISONERS TO OPEN CONDITIONS

(These do not form part of the Directions to the Parole Board issued under section 32(6) of the Criminal Justice Act 1991.)

1. The Directions to the Parole Board refer to the matters which the Board should take into account when considering the transfer to open conditions of mandatory life sentence prisoners. The Board will wish to be aware that in considering a Board recommendation for transfer to open conditions the Secretary of State will look at each individual recommendation on its merits, but will generally wish to be satisfied on items 3(a) and 3(b) of the Directions.

2. The following factors should generally be taken into account when recommending transfer to open conditions. The weight and relevance attached to each factor differs and may vary according to the circumstances of the case.

(a) the lifer's background, including any previous convictions and their pattern;

(b) the nature and circumstances of the original offence and the reasons for it;

(c) where available, the sentencing judge's comments and probation and medical reports prepared for the court;

(d) attitude and behaviour in custody, including offences against prison discipline;

(e) attitude to other inmates and staff and positive contributions to prison life;

(f) areas of concern in the lifer's offending behaviour;

(g) insight into attitudes and behavioural problems, attitude to the offence and degree of remorse and steps taken to achieve the treatment and training objectives set out in the Life Sentence Plan;

(h) the extent to which the lifer has social skills and the ability to relate to others;

(i) any medical, psychiatric or psychological considerations (particularly where there is a history of mental instability);

(j) response to outside activities;

(k) the lifer's relationship with the Probation service and other outside support such as family and friends;

(l) the benefit that the lifer will derive from a transfer to open conditions.

3. Although a move to open conditions should be based on an assessment of risk and benefits, the emphasis should be on the risk aspect and, in particular, on the need to have made significant progress in changing attitudes and tackling behavioural problems without which a move to open conditions will not generally be considered.

4. The reasons for a recommendation to transfer or not to transfer a lifer should be given and will be disclosed to the prisoner by the Home Office.

5. Guidance on the timing of the next review should be given. This will normally be in *a minimum of two years'* time, although earlier or later reviews may be appropriate in certain circumstances. In such cases the Parole Board should explain its recommendation.

Directions to the Parole Board under Section 32(6) of the Criminal Justice Act 1991—Recall of Mandatory Life Sentence Prisoners

1. When a life sentence prisoner ('lifer') is released from custody he becomes subject to a life licence for the rest of his life and may be recalled to prison if his behaviour gives cause for concern. The Secretary of State may revoke a lifer's licence and recall him to prison on the recommendation of the Parole Board or without such a recommendation if it appears to him that it is expedient in the public interest to recall a lifer before such a recommendation is practicable.

2. In deciding whether to recommend the recall of a mandatory lifer release on life licence, the Parole Board should consider:

    (a) whether the licensee's continued liberty would present a risk to the safety of other persons or the licensee is likely to commit further imprisonable offences;

    (b) the extent to which the licensee has failed to comply with the conditions of the licence or otherwise failed to co-operate with the supervising officer;

    (c) whether the licensee is likely to comply with the conditions of the licence and agree to supervision if allowed to remain in the community.

3. Before deciding to recall a life sentence prisoner released on licence, the Parole Board must take into account the supervising officer's recommendation as to whether the licensee should remain on licence.

4. Each case should be considered on its individual merits.

5. Before recommending recall, the Parole Board must take into account all of the papers submitted to it.

Training Guidance on the Recall of Mandatory Life Sentence Prisoners

(*These do not form part of the Directions to the Parole Board issued under section 32(6) of the Criminal Justice Act 1991.*)

1. The Directions to the Parole Board refer to the matters which the Board should take into account when considering the recall of mandatory life sentence prisoners. The Board will wish to be aware that in considering a Board recommendation for recall the Secretary of State will look at each individual recommendation on its merits, but will generally wish to be satisfied on items 2(a), (b) and (c) of the Directions.

2. The following factors should generally be taken into account when considering the recall of a mandatory life sentence prisoner. The weight and relevance attached to each factor differs and may vary according to the circumstances of the case.

    (a) the offender's background, including any previous convictions and their pattern;

    (b) the nature and circumstances of the original offence and the reasons for it;

    (c) the areas of concern arising from the original offence;

    (d) the extent to which the original areas of concern have reappeared or others have arisen while on life licence;

    (e) general behaviour on life licence; including response to supervision, compliance with licence requirements and co-operation with the supervising officer;

    (f) the extent and seriousness of any further offences committed while on licence and/or charges which have been laid in connection with such offences;

(g) home circumstances, including the licensee's relationship with his family and friends and the suitability of his accommodation;

(h) work record including relationships with colleagues and employers;

(i) where applicable, performance during previous periods on licence;

(j) the recommendation of the supervising authority;

(k) any other information (e.g. from police, social services, psychiatrist) which may have a bearing on whether the licensee should be permitted to remain on life licence.

3. The reasons for the Board's recommendations should be given and will be disclosed to the prisoner by the Home Office.

Compassionate Release Criteria

(*These are not issued under any statutory authority.*)

The criteria applied in medical and tragic family circumstances cases are as follows:

(i) *Medical*

—the prisoner is suffering from a terminal illness and death is likely to occur soon; or the prisoner is bedridden or similarly incapacitated; *and*

—the risk of re-offending is past; *and*

—there are adequate arrangements for the prisoner's care and treatment outside prison; *and*

—early release will bring some significant benefit to the prisoner or his/her family.

(ii) *Tragic family circumstances*

—the circumstances of the prisoner or the family have changed to the extent that if he/she served the sentence imposed, the hardship suffered would be of exceptional severity greater than the court could have foreseen; *and*

—the risk of re-offending is past; *and*

—it can be demonstrated beyond doubt that there is a real and urgent need for the prisoner's permanent presence with his/her family; *and*

—early release will bring some significant benefit to the prisoner or his/her family.

(iii) *General*

The following factors need also to be considered:

—whether *temporary release* under the Prison Rules could significantly reduce the prisoner's and/or family's suffering;

—the length of the sentence still outstanding; the effect on the overall sentence passed by the court if early release is granted; and any remarks which the trial judge made on sentencing which may have a bearing on the question of release;

—the wishes of the prisoner and his/her family and the level of benefit which would derive to the prisoner and/or the family from permanent release;

—in medical cases, the diagnosis and prognosis; in particular whether there is a specific estimate of life expectancy; and the degree of incapacitation.

In addition the Secretary of State may release a prisoner if he is satisfied that other exceptional circumstances exist.

APPENDIX 10

Ministerial Statements on the Life Sentence

Wednesday, 30 November 1983

QUESTION: To ask the Secretary of State for the Home Department, if he will make a further statement on his proposals to restrict the release on parole of violent offenders and drug traffickers and on the release of life sentence prisoners.

REPLY: From the Home Secretary, Leon Brittan.

Parole. On 4 August 1975, the Rt Hon Member for Glasgow, Hillhead, as Home Secretary, made a statement about the ways in which he proposed to exercise the discretion given him in the Criminal Justice Act 1967 with regard to the release of prisoners on parole. That statement was made after consulting the Parole Board and agreeing with them new guidelines for parole selection.

Since then the numbers of prisoners released on parole licence have steadily increased, and in 1982 of all prisoners released from sentences which qualified them for parole consideration 66.3 per cent had been granted parole. I do not propose to exercise my discretion in ways which will significantly affect this trend since it accords with my broad strategy for dealing with crime and offenders.

I must, however, take account of the general public concern about the increase in violent crime and the growing criticism of the gap between the length of sentence passed and the length of sentence actually served in certain cases. I have therefore decided to use my discretion to ensure that prisoners serving sentences of over five years for offences of violence or drug trafficking will be granted parole only when release under supervision for a few months before the end of a sentence is likely to reduce the long-term risk to the public, or in circumstances which are genuinely exceptional. The offences concerned are those where the Secretary of State may not order the early release of prisoners under section 32 of the Criminal Justice Act 1982 and are set out in Schedule 1 of that Act. In 1982 about 240 prisoners sentenced for these offences were recommended for parole before their final review: in future, there will have to be the most compelling reasons before I would agree to parole being granted in such cases.

I have consulted the Parole Board about how this objective might best be achieved in a way that ensures that the crucial role of the Board in the parole scheme is maintained. The Parole Board expressed a wish to continue to see all of the cases that are currently scrutinised by the Board, following the initial review by the Local Review Committees, in order to give full consideration to the circumstances of each individual prisoner. Accordingly, I have agreed that the present practice should continue on the understanding that the reviews will take account of the policy contained in this statement. Under the statute the acceptance or rejection of a Parole Board recommendation is, of course, a matter for me.

I am asking the Parole Board to implement this new policy with immediate effect. This statement will be issued to Local Review Committees for their guidance. The Board intends to publish the text in its next Annual Report as an addition to the detailed 'Criteria for Selection for Parole', in which there will also be some minor consequential amendments.

Life sentence prisoners. The release of life sentence prisoners is at the discretion of the Home Secretary, subject to a favourable recommendation by the Parole Board and to consultation with the Lord Chief Justice and, if he is available, the trial judge. Taking account again of the public concern about violent crime, in future I intend to exercise my discretion so that murders of police or prison officers, terrorist murders, sexual or sadistic murders of children and murders by firearm in the course of robbery can normally expect to serve at least 20 years in custody; and there will be cases where the gravity of the offence requires a still longer period. Other murders, outside these categories, may merit no less punishment to mark the seriousness of the offence.

At present I look to the judiciary for advice on the time to be served to satisfy the requirements of retribution and deterrence and to the Parole Board for advice on risk. I shall continue to do so.

The Joint Parole Board/Home Office Committee was established in 1973 to give initial consideration, usually after a life sentence prisoner had been detained for about three years in custody, to the date for the first formal consideration of the case by the Parole Board machinery. The Lord Chief Justice has agreed with me that this is the appropriate time to obtain an initial judicial view on the requirements of retribution and deterrence. In future, therefore, I will decide the date of the first reference of a case to a Local Review Committee following the initial consultation with the judiciary. The Joint Committee has therefore been disbanded.

The first Local Review Committee review will normally take place three years before the expiry of the period necessary to meet the requirements of retribution and deterrence. This would give sufficient time for preparation for release if the parole Board recommended it, having considered risk. The judiciary will also be consulted when release is an actual possibility to meet fully the requirements of section 61 of the Criminal Justice Act 1967.

These new procedures will separate consideration of the requirements of retribution and deterrence from consideration of risk to the public, which always has been, and will continue to be, the pre-eminent factor determining release. They will enable the prison and other staff responsible for considering and reporting on life sentence cases, the Local Review Committees and the Parole Board, to concentrate on risk. The judiciary will properly advise on retribution and deterrence. But the ultimate discretion whether to release will remain with me.

Life sentence prisoners who already have a provisional date of release are unaffected by these new arrangements. Those who have reached the stage of being held in an open prison are similarly unaffected, because the four prisoners whose release in the relatively near future would not have accorded with my view of the gravity of their offences have already been returned to closed prisons. Life sentence prisoners whose cases the Joint Committee has asked to consider again will, at the time fixed for that consideration, have a date fixed for their first Local Review Committee review after consultation with the judiciary as I have outlined above. Those who have a date for review by the Local Review Committee already fixed will be reviewed as arranged, but the judiciary will be consulted on retribution and deterrence before the case is referred to the Parole Board.

When a date for a first, or subsequent, formal review is set for several years ahead, the Home Office will review the case on the basis of reports of the kind now prepared for formal reviews, at regular, and in any event not longer than three year, intervals. Moreover, Governors will be told to report at once any exceptional development requiring action. These procedures will ensure that I can consider any special circumstances or exceptional progress which might justify changing the review date. But except where a prisoner has committed an offence for which he has received a further custodial sentence, the first formal review date will not be put back. Ministers will review every case when a life sentence prisoner has been detained for ten years.

Friday, 1 March 1985

QUESTION: To ask the Secretary of State for the Home Department, if he will make a statement on his policy of referring to the Parole Board the cases of life sentence prisoners who have already spent long periods in custody.

REPLY: From the Home Secretary, Leon Brittan.

On 30 November 1983 I informed the House of my policy on life sentence prisoners. The first stage in the formal review by the Parole Board machinery is the reference of the case to the Local Review Committee (LRC) at the prison at which the life sentence prisoner is held. The date of this first formal review is normally set for three years before the expiry of the period thought necessary to meet the requirements of retribution and deterrence which I decide after consultation with the judiciary. When this period is longer than twenty years, however, I have decided that the date of the first formal review should nonetheless still be set after seventeen years in custody at, or close to, the date when the case would again have been considered by the now disbanded joint Parole Board/Home Office Committee. Both the prison staff and the prisoner are, however, informed that reviews set in these special circumstances do not in any way imply that twenty years has been set as the period necessary to meet the requirements of retribution and deterrence.

In accordance with this policy, I am asking the LRCs at the prisons in which Ian Brady and Myra Hindley are detained to consider their cases as soon as possible and for the Parole Board subsequently to make their recommendations to me. The review of these cases does not mean either that the periods of detention necessary to meet the requirements of retribution and deterrence have been completed or are near completion; or that the Parole Board will recommend the release of either prisoner; or that I would necessarily accept such a recommendation if it were made.

Thursday, 23 July 1987

QUESTION: To ask the Secretary of State for the Home Department whether he will make a further statement about the Government's response to the Divisional Court Judgment in the case of *Handscomb and others.*

REPLY: From the Home Secretary, Douglas Hurd.

As I indicated in reply to a Question from the Rt Hon Member for Glasgow, Govan (Mr Bruce Millan) on 29 April, the Divisional Court judgment in the case of *Handscomb and others* upheld the lawfulness of the policy for the release of life sentence prisoners announced in reply to a Question from the Hon Member for Hampshire East (Mr Michael Mates) on 30 November 1983 at Cols 505–7. One feature of that policy was the change made in the arrangements for fixing the date on the first formal consideration of the case of a life sentence prisoner by the Parole Board machinery. Since 1973 that date had been fixed on the advice of the Joint Parole Board/Home Office Committee. Under the revised arrangements, however, this review normally takes place three years before the expiry of the time thought necessary to satisfy the requirements of retribution and deterrence and is fixed following consultation with the judiciary on what in their view that time should be. The Divisional Court were critical of two aspects of the way in which that policy has been applied in those cases where a life sentence is awarded at the discretion of the trial judge, that is for offences other than murder (for which the life sentence is mandatory). They concluded that in such cases the consultation with the judiciary on the question of the period necessary to meet the requirements of retribution and deterrence in an individual case should take place as soon as practicable after the imposition of the sentence and should not be delayed for around three to four years as is the case at present; and that, to accord with the stated policy, the first review date in such cases should always be set in accordance with the judicial view on the requirements of retribution and deterrence and account should not be taken of other factors in setting that date.

Under the previous arrangements the Joint Committee gave initial consideration to the timing of the first formal review of a case by the Parole Board machinery after the prisoner had been detained for about three years. Over the years this arrangement had become less and less effective, with the result that the Committee was recommending a date for a first formal review in only about half the cases referred to it. One of the reasons for adopting the new procedure announced in 1983 was that this element of uncertainty in the system was removed. The decision to consult the judiciary about the requirements of retribution and deterrence for the purpose of fixing the date of the first formal review of a case at the same point as the Joint Committee had begun its consideration of cases under the previous arrangements was taken with the agreement of the Lord Chief Justice. But on reflection I accept the conclusion of the Divisional Court that there are strong arguments for carrying out this consultation exercise as soon as practicable following the imposition of a discretionary life sentence.

Following consultation with the Lord Chief Justice it has been agreed that the most satisfactory way of obtaining the judicial view is to ask the trial judge to write to me, through him, in every case where a discretionary life sentence is passed giving his view on the period necessary to meet the requirements of retribution and deterrence. This view will be related to the determinate sentence that would have been passed but for the element of mental instability and/or public risk which led the judge to pass a life sentence and will also take account of the notional period of the sentence which a prisoner might expect to have been remitted for good behaviour had a determinate sentence been passed. The date of the first formal review by the Parole Board machinery will then be fixed in accordance with the judicial view on the requirements of retribution and deterrence; and the review will, as before, normally take place three years before the expiry of that period. I have agreed with the Lord Chief Justice that this procedure will be introduced with effect from 1 October 1987.

Arrangements have also been made to consult the judiciary about those discretionary life sentence cases where the first formal review has not yet been set, with a view to fixing the date as soon as possible. In addition, I will arrange for a review to be undertaken of all discretionary life sentence cases with a first formal review date of January 1988 or later. Where account has been taken of factors other than the judicial view on the requirements of retribution and deterrence in fixing the date, the date will be adjusted to bring it into line with the judicial view.

Although the issues before the Divisional Court related only to prisoners serving discretionary life sentences, I have decided that the date of the first formal review of the cases of prisoners serving mandatory life sentences should also be fixed as soon as practicable after conviction and sentence. The procedure under which the views of the trial judge and the Lord Chief Justice about the requirements of retribution and deterrence are obtained will be the same as that proposed for discretionary life sentence cases, and will be introduced at the same time. A similar exercise will also be carried out to fix the first review date in outstanding mandatory life sentence cases where this has not already been done. In view of the large number of cases involved (around 750) this will inevitably take some time.

In cases of prisoners serving life sentences for murder, where the sentence is not at the discretion of the Court, the question of the notional equivalent determinate sentence does not arise. I shall continue to take into account the view of the judiciary on the requirements of retribution and deterrence in such cases as a factor amongst others (including the need to maintain public confidence in the system of justice) to be weighed in the balance in setting the first review date. I shall ensure that the timing of the first formal review in such cases is fixed in accordance with my overall policy for ensuring that the time served by prisoners serving sentences for the worst offences of violence fully reflects public concern about violent crime.

As indicated in the November 1983 statement, the setting of the first review date under these arrangements will enable a life sentence prisoner to be released within three years of that date if the Parole Board so recommends, subject to the policy announced in reply to a Question by the Rt Hon and learned Member for Warrington South (Mr Mark Carlisle QC) on 1 March 1985 that no life sentence prisoner will be detained for more than seventeen years without a formal review of his case even where the period thought necessary to meet requirements of retribution and deterrence exceeds twenty years. Ministers will continue to review every case where a life sentence prisoner has been detained for ten years. However, as was made clear by the Divisional Court, the release of a life sentence prisoner is solely at my discretion and it is for me to decide, after receiving the Parole Board's recommendation and after consulting the judiciary as required by section 61(1) of the Criminal Justice Act 1967, when actual release should take place.

Tuesday, 27 July 1993

QUESTION: To ask the Secretary of State for the Home Department, how he intends to implement the House of Lords judgments in *R v Secretary of State for the Home Department, ex parte Smart, Pegg, Doody and Pierson* given on 24 June 1993.

REPLY: From the Home Secretary, Michael Howard.

The current procedures governing the release of persons convicted of murder and sentenced to mandatory life imprisonment are described in statements made in 1983 and 1987 by two of my predecessors as Secretary of State, the Rt Hon Sir Leon Brittan and my Rt Hon Friend, the Member for Witney, respectively. Under those procedures, shortly after a person has received a mandatory life sentence, the Secretary of State invites the judiciary to give their views on the period to be served to satisfy the requirements of retribution and deterrence. The judiciary's views presently comprise the advice of the trial judge and the Lord Chief Justice. Their advice is one factor amongst others which the Secretary of State considers before he sets the date for the first review by the Parole Board of the case for releasing the prisoner on licence. This review is timed to take place three years before the expiry of the minimum period which the Secretary of State considers necessary to satisfy the requirements of retribution and deterrence or, where that period is twenty years or more, seventeen years after sentence.

At present, a prisoner is not told the contents of the judicial recommendation, nor the length of the period which the Secretary of State has determined to be the minimum necessary to satisfy the requirements of retribution and deterrence. However, where the period so determined is less than twenty years, the prisoner can deduce its length by adding three years to the date which he is given for his first review; and where it is twenty years, he can deduce its length from the terms of the notice informing him that his first review will take place seventeen years after sentence. But where the period is more than twenty years, the prisoner is not able to establish its total length.

The House of Lords judgment requires me to inform the prisoner of the recommendations made by the judiciary as to the period necessary to satisfy the requirements of retribution and deterrence and of the substance of any opinions expressed by the judiciary which are relevant to my decision as to the appropriate minimum period to be served to satisfy those requirements. In addition, I am required to afford to the prisoner the opportunity to submit written representations. Although I am not required to adopt the judicial advice, I must give reasons where I, or a Minister under my authority, decide to depart from it.

I propose to give effect to this judgment by informing all persons who are now serving a mandatory life sentence and any persons who may subsequently be so sentenced, as soon as is reasonably practicable, of the substance of the judicial recommendations which were made in their cases as to the period to be served by them in order to satisfy the requirements of retribution and deterrence. I am consulting the Lord Chief Justice about the precise way in which this will be done.

In addition, I have decided to disclose to both existing and future mandatory life sentence prisoners the Secretary of State's decision, taken after consideration of the judicial advice, on the appropriate period in question.

In accordance with the judgment, reasons will be given to the prisoner for any departure from the judicial view.

As the judgment makes clear, successive Secretaries of State have been, and I continue to be, willing to consider any written representations by prisoners as to the minimum period to be served by them to satisfy the requirements of retribution and deterrence. In future, prisoners will be afforded the opportunity to submit such written representations at the beginning of the sentence and before I have formed a view as to the minimum period for retribution and deterrence.

I take this opportunity to emphasise that the view which I, or a Minister acting under my authority, take, at the beginning of a mandatory life sentence, of the period necessary to satisfy the requirements of retribution and deterrence is an initial view of the minimum period necessary to satisfy those requirements. It therefore remains possible for me, or a future Secretary of State, exceptionally to revise that view of the minimum period, either by reducing it, or by increasing it where I, or a successor in my Office, conclude that, putting aside questions of risk, the minimum requirements of retribution and deterrence will not have been satisfied at the expiry of the period which had previously been determined.

Before taking a decision to increase this minimum period, the Secretary of State would inform the prisoner that he was minded to take this action and afford him the opportunity to submit written representations as to why the period should not be increased. Any such representations would then be taken into account before any new decision was made. If it were decided to increase the period in question, the prisoner would be informed of the length of the new period and given the reasons for the increase.

Finally, I wish to state that a mandatory life sentence prisoner should not assume that once the minimum period fixed for retribution and deterrence has been satisfied he will necessarily be released if it is considered that he is no longer a risk. In this respect, the position of a prisoner subject to a mandatory life sentence is to be contrasted with that of a prisoner serving a discretionary life sentence. As the then Minister of State, the Rt Hon Member for Mitcham and Morden, stated in the House on 16 July 1991 (cols 311–12) during debates on the Criminal Justice Bill:

In a discretionary case, the decision on release is based purely on whether the offender continues to be a risk to the public. The presumption is that once the period that is appropriate to punishment has passed, the prisoner should be released if it is safe to do so. The nature of the mandatory sentence is different. The element of risk is not the decisive factor in handing down a life sentence. According to the judicial process, the offender has committed a crime of such gravity that he forfeits his liberty to the State for the rest of his days—if necessary, he can be detained for life without the necessity for subsequent judicial intervention. The presumption is, therefore, that the offender should remain in custody until and unless the Home Secretary concludes that the public interest would be better served by the prisoner's release than by his continued detention. In exercising his continued discretion in that respect, the Home Secretary must take account, not just of the question of risk, but of how society as a whole would view the prisoner's release at that juncture. The Home Secretary takes account of the judicial recommendation, but the final decision is his.

I wish to make it clear that, in so far as the judgment of the House of Lords considered that there was an inconsistency between the practice established by Sir Leon Brittan in 1983 and the above quoted statement by the Rt Hon Member for Mitcham and Morden, I wholly endorse the latter as a description of the way I currently exercise my discretion to release mandatory life sentence prisoners and intend to do so in future.

Accordingly, before any such prisoner is released on licence, I will consider not only, (1) whether the period served by the prisoner is adequate to satisfy the requirements of retribution and deterrence and, (b) whether it is safe to release the prisoner, but also (c) the public acceptability of early release. This means that I will only exercise my discretion to release if I am satisfied that to do so will not threaten the maintenance of public confidence in the system of criminal justice.

Everything that I have said about the practice of the Secretary of State in relation to mandatory life sentence prisoners applies equally to persons who are, or will be, detained during Her Majesty's Pleasure under section 53(1) of the Children and Young Persons Act 1933, as well as to persons who have been, or will be, sentenced to custody for life under section 8 of the Criminal Justice Act 1982.

Thursday, 4 November 1993

QUESTION: To ask the Secretary of State for the Home Department, pursuant to his Answer of 27 July 1993 (Official Report, Cols 863–5), whether he can now provide further information about his proposals for implementing the House of Lords judgment of 24 June 1993 in the case of *Smart, Pegg, Doody and Pierson.*

REPLY: From the Home Secretary, Michael Howard.

The judgment is concerned with the disclosure to prisoners serving mandatory life sentences of information about the minimum period of custody that they will be required to serve in order to satisfy the requirements of retribution and deterrence. *Inter alia*, it requires that the prisoner should be told the gist of the judicial advice which the Secretary of State receives on this subject, the Secretary of State's decision and the reasons for any departure from the judicial view.

In my Reply to my Hon and learned Friend on 27 July, I announced that I was consulting the Lord Chief Justice about the precise way in which the judgment would be implemented in respect of those prisoners who had already been sentenced. Those consultations have now been completed. Disclosure of the matters required by the judgment has already been given to four prisoners immediately affected by the judgment and to another four, in respect of whom there were extant judicial review proceedings.

Following this consultation, I propose now to commence a programme of disclosure to all mandatory life sentence prisoners. There are two categories of such prisoners. First, there are approximately 100 prisoners who were sentenced either shortly before, or after, the House of Lords judgment, for whom a minimum period of detention has not yet been considered by a Minister. In accordance with my previous Answer, they will, as soon as is practicable, be informed of the relevant judicial recommendations in their cases so that they may, if they wish, submit written representations before that period is set. Any such representations will be considered by me or by a Minister acting on my behalf; and the prisoner will be informed of the decision with reasons for any departure from the judicial view.

Second, there is a much larger number of some 2,600 prisoners whose cases have already been considered by Ministers, often some years ago, and who have already been notified of the date when their case would be first reviewed by the Local Review Committee prior to consideration by the Parole Board. My officials will now begin the process of disclosure to them of the gist of the relevant judicial recommendations and advice, and of the decision by the Secretary of State of the day as to the minimum period which must be served for retribution and deterrence together, in appropriate cases, with a statement of the reasons why a recommendation from the judiciary was not followed. These prisoners will also be able to submit written representations. They will be considered and a response will be provided.

It will inevitably take some time to clear the backlog of cases represented by this second group, given the limited resources available in my Department for the task. Taking account of the need to consider and respond to prisoners' representations, it will probably be some twelve months before every mandatory life sentence prisoner has been considered. Priority will be given to prisoners who have first Local Review Committee dates in the calendar years 1994–1996 inclusive, in the order of those dates. In fairness to all, and to ensure maximum efficiency, cases will not normally be taken out of turn.

Wednesday, 7 December 1994

QUESTION: To ask the Secretary of State for the Home Department, what changes have been made in the review procedures in cases of persons sentenced to life imprisonment.

REPLY: From the Home Secretary, Michael Howard.

Two of my predecessors as Secretary of State, the Rt Hon Sir Leon Brittan and my Rt Hon Friend the Member for Witney, made statements in 1983 and 1987, respectively, about the review arrangements for life sentence prisoners. Under those arrangements, the first review by the Parole Board takes place three years before the expiry of the period thought necessary to satisfy the requirements of retribution and deterrence (commonly referred to as the tariff). However, no life sentence prisoner is detained for more than seventeen years without a Parole Board review of his or her case, even where the period in question exceeds twenty years. The Secretary of State also reviews the case of every life sentence prisoner who has been detained for ten years.

From now on all life sentence prisoners will have a Parole Board review three years before the expiry of their tariff. Since all prisoners will now know the length of their tariff and also the date of this review, I consider that the automatic review at the seventeen year point will therefore be discontinued, save in respect of those existing prisoners for whom such a review has already been fixed.

This means that the review three years before the expiry of the tariff will be the first review for all prisoners. The setting of a review at this point is intended to allow sufficient time for preparing the release of those life sentence prisoners who may be considered an acceptable risk. This is subject, in the case of mandatory life prisoners, to the question of public acceptability of early release.

In recent years, successive Secretaries of State recognised that for the majority of life sentence prisoners, a period in open conditions is generally vital in terms of testing the prisoner's suitability for release and in preparing him or her for a successful return to the community. It is, therefore, now normally the practice to require the prisoner to spend some time in open conditions before release and to arrange a further review while the prisoner is in an open prison for a formal assessment of his or her progress. I intend to continue with this practice and the first Parole Board review will therefore normally serve the purpose of assessing the prisoner for open conditions.

The purpose of the ten year Ministerial review is to consider whether there are any grounds for bringing forward the date of the first review by the Parole Board. This review is now redundant as far as discretionary life sentence prisoners are concerned since their cases are dealt with in accordance with the arrangements introduced by Part II of the Criminal Justice Act 1991. However, the ten year Ministerial review will continue to take place for mandatory life sentence prisoners.

In addition I have decided that for those life sentence prisoners for whom it is decided that the requirements of retribution and deterrence can be satisfied only by their remaining in prison for the whole of their life, there will in future be an additional Ministerial review when the prisoner has been in custody for twenty-five years. The purpose of this review will be solely to consider whether the whole life tariff should be converted to a tariff of a determinate period. The review will be confined to the considerations of retribution and deterrence. Where appropriate, further Ministerial reviews will normally take place at five yearly intervals thereafter. Existing prisoners who fall into this category and who have already served twenty-five years or more in custody will not be disadvantaged. Their cases will be reviewed by Ministers as soon as is practicable and after any representations they may wish to make.

As I announced in reply to a Question by my Hon and learned Friend the Member for Burton on 27 July 1993 (Cols 863–5), successive Secretaries of State have been, and I continue to be, willing to consider any written representations by life sentence prisoners about their tariff. They will also continue to be afforded the opportunity to submit such written representations at the beginning of the sentence and before I have formed a view as to the appropriate period in question.

Monday, 10 November 1997

House of Lords Judgments

Ms Jennifer Jones: To ask the Secretary of State for the Home Department how he intends to implement the House of Lords judgment in *Regina v Secretary of State for the Home Department ex parte Pierson* given on 24 July.

Mr Straw: This judgment concerned the discretion of any holder of my office to increase a tariff once set for an adult convicted of murder. The majority of the House found that it is lawful for the Secretary of State to increase a tariff previously set, as set out in the reply given by my predecessor, the then Right Hon and learned Member for Folkestone and Hythe, Mr Howard, on 27 July 1993, Official Report, cols 863–5. However, one of that majority found that the statement did not purport to apply to a decision to increase a tariff set before 27 July 1993, and so a different majority found that the increase of the tariff in the *Pierson* case was unlawful.

So far as the procedures for setting and reviewing tariffs of adult murderers are concerned, I am continuing the practice of my predecessor, as described in his answer of 27 July 1993, Official Report, cols 861–4 and 7 December 1994, Official Report, vols 234–5. In particular, before setting the tariff, I am continuing to take the advice of the trial judge and the Lord Chief Justice, informing the prisoner of the substance of that advice and inviting representations about it, and giving reasons for any departure on my part from the judicial review.

With regard to the discretion to alter tariff, I reiterate that the view which I take (or a Minister acting under my authority takes) at the beginning of a mandatory life sentence of the period necessary to satisfy the requirements of retribution and deterrence is an initial view of the minimum period necessary to satisfy those requirements. It therefore remains possible for me, or a future Secretary of State exceptionally to revise that view of the minimum period, either by reducing it, or by increasing it where I, or a successor in my office, conclude that, putting aside questions of risk, the minimum requirements of retribution and deterrence will not have been satisfied at the expiry of the period which had previously been determined. The procedure for considering any increase of a tariff once set will include the opportunity for the prisoner to make representations after being informed that the Secretary of State is minded to increase tariff and to be given reasons for any subsequent decision to increase it.

So far as the potential for a reduction in tariff is concerned, I shall be open to the possibility that, in exceptional circumstances including for example, exceptional progress by the prisoner whilst in custody, a review and reduction of the tariff may be appropriate. I shall have this possibility in mind when reviewing at the twenty-five year point the cases of prisoners given a whole life tariff and in that respect will consider issues beyond the sole criteria of retribution and deterrence described in the answer given on 7 December 1994. Prisoners will continue to be given the opportunity to make representations and to have access to the material before me.

I intend to apply these policies in respect of all tariffs for adult murderers, whether or not they were originally set before 27 July 1993 and whether or not they were originally fixed by me personally, or a Minister acting on my behalf, or by or on behalf of a previous holder of my office. In the *Pierson* case, where the tariff has now been quashed, I intend to invite representations from the prisoner before re-setting tariff at a level which I consider appropriate.

I take the opportunity to confirm that my approach on the release of adults convicted of murder once tariff has expired will reflect the policy set out in the answer given on 27 July 1993. In particular, the release of such a person will continue to depend not only on the expiry of tariff and on my being satisfied that the level of risk of his committing further imprisonable offences presented by his release is acceptably low, but also on the need to maintain public confidence in the system of criminal justice. The position of a prisoner subject to a mandatory life sentence continues to be distinct from that of a prisoner serving a discretionary life sentence, a decision on whose final release is a matter for the Parole Board alone.

Everything in this answer about my practice in relation to mandatory life sentence prisoners applies equally to persons who are, or will be sentenced to custody for life under section 8 of the Criminal Justice Act 1982. For present purposes, a life sentence imposed under section 2 of the Crime (Sentences) Act 1997 is treated as a discretionary life sentence.

Thursday, 9 July 1998

QUESTION: To ask the Secretary of State for the Home Department if he intends to make changes to the review procedures in cases of persons sentenced to life imprisonment.

REPLY: From the Home Secretary, Jack Straw.

Under the present arrangements announced by previous Home Secretaries, most recently on 7 December 1994, Official Report, columns 234–35, by the Right Hon and learned Member for Folkestone and Hythe (Mr Howard), the first Parole Board review in the case of a life sentenced prisoner begins three years before the expiry of tariff. The purpose of this review is normally to enable the prisoner to be assessed for, and, where appropriate, transferred to, open conditions (category D) where he or she may be tested in conditions of lower security, fully assessed by staff and prepared for release. A further Parole Board review is then held to determine whether the level of risk is low enough to enable the prisoner to be safely released on life licence. Where the level of risk is considered to be acceptable, the objective is to release the prisoner on or very shortly after tariff expiry.

The need for two or more reviews and the average time of eight and a half months to complete each one make it very difficult for this objective to be achieved. Of the 109 life sentenced prisoners who were released on life licence between April 1997 and March 1998, only one was released on tariff expiry. A further 31, who could have been safely released at or close to tariff expiry, were released within 12 months. I have therefore decided to make some adjustments to the review timetabling arrangements to reduce delays by enabling prisoners whom it is safe to release but who are currently being released within 12 months of tariff expiry to be released on tariff or shortly afterwards.

In future, the first Parole Board review for mandatory and discretionary life sentenced prisoners will be brought forward by six months to start three and a half years before tariff expiry, but normally only where the prisoner has been in category C prison conditions for 12 months or more at that point. Cases falling just outside the 12 month criterion, and cases where exceptional circumstances exist, will be considered for early review on their merits.

In addition, reviews for all mandatory life sentenced prisoners who are in open conditions will commence 18 months after arrival rather than after two years as is now the practice. I am satisfied that this will still allow ample time (at least two years) in open prison for the prisoner to be fully tested, assessed and prepared for release. This change will bring the timetable for the review of mandatory life sentenced prisoners into line with that for discretionary cases in which there is a statutory entitlement to a further review on the second anniversary of the conclusion of the previous one. In order to avoid disrupting the scheduled offending behaviour programmes and pre-release preparatory work for those already in open conditions, this new arrangement will apply to those transferring to open conditions from 1 August.

The statement of 7 December 1994 also announced the abolition in discretionary life sentence cases of the ten year Ministerial review to consider whether there were any grounds for bringing forward the date of the first Parole Board review. The purpose of that review had been to identify any special circumstances or exceptional progress which might justify bringing forward the date of the first Parole Board review. I have decided that this review should also be abolished in mandatory life sentence cases. Those convicted of murder are now fully informed about the tariff-setting process and may make representations at any time about the length of their tariff. In addition, they may at any time make representations for their tariff to be reduced to take account of exceptional circumstances, including exceptional progress in prison. Those sentenced to be detained during Her Majesty's pleasure have an annual review of tariff by officials and a Ministerial review at the halfway point. In these circumstances, the ten year review is now redundant.

APPENDIX 11

Framework Document for the Prison Service

FOREWORD

The Prison Service was established as an executive agency of the Home Office on 1 April 1993. The launch of this revision of the framework document concludes the five-yearly review of the Prison Service which has also included an evaluation of the performance of the agency and a re-examination of the case for agency status.

The years since agency status have been demanding ones for the Prison Service. The prison population has increased dramatically over the period, putting pressure on the estate and staff alike. Against this background, I endorse the conclusion of the evaluation report that the performance of the Service as a whole has been remarkable and I warmly congratulate every member of the service for this impressive achievement.

The conclusion of the Prior Options report, which the Government has accepted, was that agency status should be re-confirmed. Drawing on the findings of both these reports, this framework document defines a new relationship between the Prison Service, Ministers and the rest of the Home Office. It has been drawn up taking into account the views of the trade unions, with whom Ministers and the Prison Service are committed to work constructively in partnership.

This document reflects changes we have made since the General Election in May 1997 and, in particular, the steps we have taken to ensure proper Ministerial responsibility and accountability to Parliament for the work of the Prison Service. The roles of the principal players and bodies, including a Prison Service Strategy Board to be chaired by the Prisons and Probation Minister, are set out within a framework of responsibilities and accountabilities.

Other important changes have come about as a result of the Comprehensive Spending Review. A new tripartite system has been introduced to improve the management of the criminal justice system as a whole. New joint aims, objectives and targets and an integrated planning process have been devised for the system as a whole. Work is also in hand on the future organisation of the probation services and to ensure greater joint working between the Prison and Probation Services. These changes will improve the performance of every part of the criminal justice system but they demand that in future its constituent parts must take greater account of the needs of the wider system in their plans and operations.

I have every confidence that the Prison Service will rise to this new challenge and that the arrangements which are set out in this framework document will facilitate that task. I wish the Director General and his staff every success in the period which lies ahead.

Jack Straw
Home Secretary

Contents

Foreword by the Home Secretary

Annexes

1 Introduction

1.1. HM Prison Service for England and Wales is an executive agency of the Home Office established on 1 April 1993. Agency status was re-confirmed following a quinquennial review in 1998.

1.2. The Agency's title is 'HM Prison Service'. It is referred to as 'the Prison Service' in this Framework Document.

1.3. The Prison Service is responsible for providing prison services in England and Wales, both directly and through contractors. Its main statutory duties are set out in the Prison Act 1952 and rules made under that Act.

1.4. The Prison Service is a major component of the wider criminal justice system and contributes, alongside other partners, to achieving the system's overall aims and objectives. As the responsible Minister, the Home Secretary accounts to Parliament for the Prison Service and shares Ministerial responsibility and accountability for the criminal justice system as a whole with the Lord Chancellor and the Attorney General. The Director General is the Chief Executive of the Prison Service.

2 Role and Task

2.1. The Prison Service is a part of the criminal justice system which works to two overarching aims:
- to reduce crime and the fear of crime, and their social and economic costs;
- to dispense justice fairly and efficiently, and to promote confidence in the rule of law.

These aims and their associated targets are set out in the Public Service Agreement for the Criminal Justice System.

Aim

2.2. Deriving from these overarching aims, the Prison Service works within the Home Office to the following specific aim and associated targets set out in the Home Office Public Service Agreement:

- effective execution of the sentences of the courts so as to reduce re-offending and protect the public.

Objectives

2.3. In support of that aim the objectives set for the Prison Service are:

- to protect the public by holding in custody those committed by the Courts in a safe, decent, and healthy environment;
- to reduce crime by providing constructive regimes which address offending behaviour, improve educational and work skills and promote law abiding behaviour in custody and after release.

Principles

2.4. In support of the specified aim and objectives is a statement of the ways in which the Prison Service works towards them and the conduct expected from staff:

In undertaking our work, all members of the Prison Service will:

- deal fairly, openly, and humanely with prisoners and all others who come into contact with us;
- encourage prisoners to address offending behaviour and respect others;
- value and support each other's contribution;
- promote equality of opportunity for all and combat discrimination wherever it occurs;
- work constructively with criminal justice agencies and other organisations;
- obtain best value from resources available.

Statement of purpose

2.5. The objectives of the Service and the principles by which it operates are encapsulated in the following Statement of Purpose for all staff:

Her Majesty's Prison Service serves the public by keeping in custody those committed by the courts.

Our duty is to look after them with humanity and help them lead law-abiding and useful lives in custody and after release.

Key performance indicators

2.6. The Prison Service's performance is monitored against a wide range of measures and indicators which derive from the aims of the Home Office and the criminal justice system. The suite of key performance indicators has changed over the years both to reflect new priorities and to remove indicators in areas where problems have been eradicated. The current indicators are set out at Annex A. Indicators will be developed which measure the success of the Prison Service in achieving high quality outputs within a framework of efficiency and economy consistent with the Home Office Public Service Agreement.

3 MANAGEMENT AND ACCOUNTABILITY

Home Secretary and Home Office Ministers

3.1. As the responsible Minister, the Home Secretary is accountable to Parliament for the Prison Service in England and Wales.

3.2. The Home Secretary sets the strategic direction of the Prison Service and specifies the outputs and targets which it is required to achieve and allocates resources to it accordingly. These are set out in detail in the Service's Corporate Plan.

3.3. The Home Secretary determines this strategic direction in the context of wider Ministerial planning for the criminal justice system as a whole and within the Home

Office in the context of overall policy for correctional matters and greater collaborative working between the Prison and Probation Services. The Home Secretary will designate a Minister in the Home Office to provide support to him on prison matters (the Designated Minister).

3.4. The Designated Minister will chair a Prison Service Strategy Board with membership of the Director General, other executive directors of the Prison Service as agreed between the designated Minister and the Director General, the Director, Sentencing and Correctional Policy, and non-executive directors appointed by the Home Secretary. The Board will provide a forum for discussing the strategic direction of the Service and Prison Service plans and performance.

3.5. The Home Secretary will agree annually a Corporate Plan submitted to him by the Director General following discussion by the Prisons Strategy Board. The Director General will provide quarterly reports on performance against the targets in the Corporate Plan and ensure that the Prison Service keeps Ministers informed of matters likely to generate public or Parliamentary concern.[1] The Home Secretary publishes and lays before both Houses of Parliament the Prison Service Annual Report. The Director General has the right of direct access to the Home Secretary on any matter affecting the Prison Service.

Permanent Secretary

3.6. The Permanent Under-Secretary of State for the Home Office (the Permanent Secretary) advises the Home Secretary on all matters relating to the Home Office ('the Department') as a whole and in particular: the overall contribution of the Department and its services to the wider criminal justice system; the performance of the Department in delivering Home Office aims; and, the allocation of resources across the aims. The Permanent Secretary is responsible for advising the Home Secretary on Home Office plans, targets and performance, including those of the Prison Service.

The Home Office Management Board

3.7. The Home Office Management Board exists to ensure that the Home Office, and through their framework documents, its executive agencies, achieve the aims set by Ministers. The Board will monitor progress in delivering the aims as a whole including where appropriate the contribution to the aims provided by the work of the Prison Service. The Board assists the Permanent Secretary in advising Ministers in strategic planning and in the setting of objectives and allocation of resources.

3.8. The Director General is a member of the Home Office Management Board.

Director General

3.9. The Director General has, in accordance with this framework document, delegated authority for the day to day management of the Service. The Director General is responsible to the Home Secretary for the Prison Service and, in particular, for its performance against the corporate plans and targets. The Director General is also the principal adviser to the Home Secretary on matters relating to the activities of the Prison Service. The Director General's responsibilities include:

- preparing draft corporate plans, including key targets, and following consideration by the Prison Service Strategy Board and the Permanent Secretary submitting them to the Home Secretary for approval;
- achieving the Prison Service's key targets;
- managing the Prison Service's resources efficiently, effectively and economically;
- attending quarterly performance meetings chaired by the Home Secretary or Designated Minister and providing quarterly reports on performance for the Home Secretary and Prison Service Strategy Board;

- contributing to Home Office Management Board consideration of progress against the Home Office aims in general;
- submitting an Annual Report to the Home Secretary;
- ensuring that effective procedures for handling complaints about the Agency are established and publicised. This includes replying to complaints personally if they cannot be resolved satisfactorily at a local level.

3.10. The Director General has delegated authority on financial and personnel matters which are set out in later sections of this document.

3.11. The Director General is appointed by the Home Secretary with the approval of the Prime Minister.

3.12. The Director General will be supported in his day to day responsibilities by a Prison Service Management Board which will comprise the executive directors. The Director General may appoint ex-officio members as required.

The Director, sentencing and correctional policy

3.13. Within the Department the Director, Sentencing and Correctional Policy advises Ministers on matters relating to correctional policy as a whole, including the implications for correctional policy and for other parts of the criminal justice system of the work of the Prison Service. The Director, Sentencing and Correctional Policy is designated as aim owner on the Management Board for Home Office aim four (set out at paragraph 2.2 above) and is responsible for the overall coordination of the programmes which contribute to the aim. The Director General is responsible for delivery of the output of aim four with regard to the Prison Service.

Non-executive directors

3.14. The non-executive directors will be appointed by the Home Secretary on the advice of the Director General and will be members of the Prison Service Strategy Board. The role of the non-executive directors will be to contribute to collective discussions on the future strategy and performance of the Prison Service drawn from a range of perspectives and views. The non-executive directors will also have the right of access to the Home Secretary and the Permanent Secretary on major matters affecting the Prison Service.

Accounting Officer responsibilities

3.15. The Permanent Secretary as the principal Accounting Officer is responsible for the overall organisation, management and staffing of the Home Office and for ensuring a high standard of financial management in the Department as a whole.

3.16. Within the single Home Office Departmental Expenditure Limit, money is voted to the Prison Service within a separate Vote. The Director General is appointed by the Treasury as an additional Accounting Officer in the Home Office with responsibility for this vote. However, from 2000–2001 with the expected introduction of Resource Accounting and Budgeting the Permanent Secretary will sign a single consolidated account. The implications of the new arrangements for the maintenance of a separate Prison Service Vote will be considered in the light of the planned legislation.

3.17. The Director General is responsible for ensuring that proper procedures are followed for securing the regularity and propriety of expenditure on the Vote, that the public funds for which he or she is responsible are properly and well managed and that the requirements of Government Accounting are met, that the Prison Service observes any general guidance issued by the Treasury or the Cabinet Office, and for putting into effect any recommendations accepted by Government of the Public Accounts Committee, other Parliamentary Select Committees or other Parliamentary authority.

The respective responsibilities of the principal Accounting Officer and the additional Accounting Officer are set out in more detail in a financial memorandum. The Director General and the Permanent Secretary are both liable to be summoned before the Public Accounts Committee in connection with their respective responsibilities. It is for the Home Secretary to decide who should appear at Departmental Select Committee hearings but, in practice, the Director General will normally appear unless the interest of the Committee lies in the systems of financial management of the Department as a whole.

Contracted out prisons

3.18. The Director General is also accountable to the Home Secretary for the performance of contracted out prisons. The performance of these establishments contributes to the suite of Key Performance Indicators. The performance of the Contracted Out Prisons is monitored by a Prison Service Controller in each establishment to ensure their compliance with relevant statutes and their contractual obligations. The Controller is also responsible for adjudicating on disciplinary charges brought against prisoners and investigating allegations against staff.

3.19. Contracted out prisons are subject to the same arrangements for Parliamentary, independent and public scrutiny as applies to directly managed prisons. These arrangements are set out below.

Members of Parliament

3.20. Parliamentary Questions on all prison matters will be answered by Ministers. Members of Parliament will be encouraged to write direct to the Director General on matters for which the Director General has delegated responsibility. The Home Secretary will normally ask the Director General to reply to correspondence from Members of Parliament on such matters.

Parliamentary Commissioner for Administration

3.21. The Prison Service is subject to the jurisdiction of the Parliamentary Commissioner for Administration. The Permanent Secretary is the Principal Officer of the Department for this purpose but will normally delegate to the Director General responsibility for replying on any matters concerning the Prison Service.

Her Majesty's Chief Inspector for Prisons

3.22. The Home Secretary receives reports from Her Majesty's Chief Inspector of Prisons on inspections of prison establishments. The Director General will act in accordance with the protocol about the handling of the Chief Inspector's reports agreed between the Prison Service and the Chief Inspector and endorsed by Ministers.

Prisons Ombudsman

3.23. The Prisons Ombudsman is appointed by the Home Secretary to consider grievances from prisoners once all internal procedures have been exhausted. The Home Secretary receives annual reports from the Prisons Ombudsman. The Director General will respond to recommendations from the Prison Ombudsman in respect of particular complaints.

Boards of Visitors

3.24. The Home Secretary appoints a Board of Visitors for every prison establishment to provide an independent assessment on the state of prison premises, the administration of prisons and the treatment of prisoners. The Home Secretary receives an annual report from Boards of Visitors. The Designated Minister will respond to such reports after taking advice from the Prison Service.

4 PLANNING, FINANCE AND SUPPORT SERVICES

Planning framework

4.1. Plans for the Prison Service will be drawn up and approved by Ministers in the context of the wider criminal justice system. In particular, planning will take place in the context of the tripartite planning for the criminal justice system, joint planning for the Prison and Probation Services, and planning for the delivery of Home Office aims and the targets in the Home Office Public Service Agreement and the Output and Performance Analysis.

4.2. Each year, the Director General will submit the draft Corporate Plan to the Prison Service Strategy Board, and then to the Home Secretary for approval. The Plan will cover the following three years and include a more detailed plan for the first year of the planning period and will be published before the start of the financial year to which it applies. The Plan will include:

- Prison Service objectives in support of Home Office aims together with key performance indicators and targets;
- the strategies which it intends to follow to achieve its objectives;
- operating assumptions about the prison population and planned capacity;
- information about its sensitivity to variations in those assumptions;
- how the resources and assets will be deployed, consistent with totals and outputs agreed;
- plans for securing agreed efficiency improvements, including through public private partnerships.

4.3. If there are major unforeseen changes to the Prison Service's operating assumptions the plan may need to be revised in the course of the year. Proposals to this effect made by the Director General require the approval of the Home Secretary who will be advised by the Permanent Secretary on the impact of any changes on the delivery of wider Home Office or criminal justice system aims.

Financial provision

4.4. The Prison Service is financed as part of the overall Home Office Departmental Expenditure Limit voted by Parliament. The Agency operates within gross running costs control. As part of Corporate Planning, the Director General puts forward proposals to the Home Secretary for current and capital expenditure to meet its projected needs, as part of the cycle of Departmental and Government-wide resource planning.

Accounting responsibilities

4.5. Each year the Director General produces and signs[2] an Appropriation Account for the Prisons' Vote, which is prepared in accordance with Treasury guidance. This vote Account is subject to external auditing by the Comptroller and Auditor General. The Annual Report and Accounts are submitted by the Director General to the Home Secretary and are laid before Parliament, published and placed in the libraries of both Houses. The Prison Service will plan to lay the Accounts before the summer Recess each year. Accrual Accounts will be produced in accordance with Treasury 'direction' issued under Section 5 of the Exchequer and Audit Department Act 1921 and will be audited by the Comptroller and Auditor General. These will reflect the requirements of parliamentary accountability and the nature of management needs of the business. The Director General will provide a reconciliation of the Appropriation Account and the Accruals Accounts. The Director General acts as accounting officer in accordance with the

Financial Memorandum at Annex B. Under resource accounting and budgeting, and subject to Parliamentary approval, there will be a single resource Estimate and account for each Department, composed of one or more Requests for Resources. Future arrangements will be made in accordance with the guidance contained in DAO (RAB) 1/98 or other guidance in place at the time.

Internal audit and other services

4.6. The Director General is responsible for making arrangements for the provision of an internal audit service to be conducted in accordance with best commercial practice and the objectives and standards set out in the Government Internal Audit Manual. The Director General is also responsible for making arrangements for consultancy, inspection and review services. Home Office Internal Audit will have access to the Prison Service as necessary to perform any work required by the principal Accounting Officer as part of his or her responsibility for ensuring a high standard of financial management in the Department as a whole.

Financial delegations

4.7. The Director General acts as accounting officer for the resources allocated to the Prison Service in accordance with the Financial Memorandum at Annex B. These arrangements will be reviewed in the light of the forthcoming introduction of resource accounting. The Director General will delegate responsibility for expenditure, consistent with the needs of financial control and propriety.

Departmental Investment Strategy

4.8. Prison Service capital expenditure forms part of the overall Home Office Investment Strategy. The Prison Service will ensure that capital is managed and invested in such a way as to contribute to the Home Office aim set out at paragraph 2.2 while achieving value for money for the taxpayer.

Press and publicity

4.9. The arrangements for press and publicity are set out in Annex E.

Support services

4.10. Annex F sets out the support services currently performed by the Prison Service for the rest of the Department or vice-versa. Any changes in these arrangements will be made in consultation with the other party. These arrangements would normally be supported by service level agreements which will include, where it is cost effective, charges for the services provided.

Information Technology

4.11. In order to assist the Prison Service and the rest of the Home Office in working both autonomously and together, and to communicate efficiently using Information Technology, in some cases common systems and standard interfaces will be required. Arrangements to support these systems and interfaces are set out in an IT Memorandum at Annex G.

5 PERSONNEL MATTERS

General

5.1. Prison Service staff will continue to be civil servants employed in the Home Office on civil service terms, conditions and pension arrangements. Variations may be made subject to the approval of the Treasury and Cabinet Office as necessary.

5.2. Authority on most personnel matters is delegated to the Director General. These delegations, together with the principles under which they are exercised, are set out in detail in a memorandum of understanding at Annex C. In exercising delegated personnel responsibility the Director General will have regard to:

- the delivery of Home Office aims and the Prison Service role in that;
- the need to facilitate interchange of staff in the interests of the Home Office as a whole.

5.3. The Director General may, where appropriate, negotiate or consult with the recognised trade unions on matters affecting staff pay and conditions.

Industrial relations

5.4. The Director General is responsible for ensuring that managers work with trade unions with a view for ensuring the maintenance of good industrial relations throughout the Prison Service. The Whitley Committee structures will continue to operate, although—and in consultation with the relevant trade unions—their scope and role may be changed.

6 Review and Variation of Framework Document

6.1. The Prison Service is subject to five yearly review which will consider: the performance of the agency; structural options; and, if agency status is reconfirmed, the need for amendments to the Framework Document. The Home Secretary may approve amendments to the Framework Document at any time in the light of experience or changed circumstances having taken advice from the Permanent Secretary and the Director General and having consulted the Cabinet Office and The Treasury. The views of the relevant trade unions would also be sought. Copies of this Framework Document and any subsequent amendments will be published and placed in the libraries of both Houses of Parliament and in prison libraries.

6.2. The Home Secretary may approve amendments to the annexes to this Framework Document having taken advice from the Permanent Secretary and the Director General.

Annexes

Annex A—Prison Service Key Performance Indicators (KPIs)

Annex B—HM Prison Service: Financial Memorandum

Annex C—Memorandum of Understanding between the Prison Service and the Corporate Resources Directorate on Personnel Issues

Annex D—Circumstances in which Reports will be required by Ministers on Prison Matters

Annex E—Press and Publicity Arrangements

Annex F—Provision of Support Services

Annex G—Memorandum of Understanding on IS/IT

NOTES

[1] The matters on which reports will be always be required are listed at Annex D.

[2] The Director General will produce an appropriation account for 1999–2000. From 2000–2001 onwards the Department as a whole will have a single Resource Account: a separate appropriation account for the Prison Service will no longer be necessary.

BIBLIOGRAPHY

Books

AIDS Advisory Committee, *The Review of HIV and AIDS in Prison* (London, 1995).

Amnesty International, *Prisoners Without a Voice: Asylum Seekers in the United Kingdom* (London, 1995).

Ashworth, A and B Mitchell, *Rethinking English Homicide Law* (Oxford: OUP, 2000).

Bailey, S, D Harris, and B Jones, *Civil Liberties: Cases and Materials* (3rd edn, London: Butterworths, 1991).

Brazier, M, *Medicine, Patients and the Law* (2nd edn, London: Penguin, 1992).

Buergentahl, T, *International Human Rights* (St Paul, Minn: West Publishing, 1988).

Burns, Henry, *Correctional Reform: Britain and the USA Compared and Contrasted* (1978).

Clayton, R and H Tomlinson, *The Law of Human Rights* (Oxford: OUP, 2000).

Clements, L, N Mole, and A Simmons, *European Human Rights: Taking a Case under the Convention* (2nd edn, London: Sweet & Maxwell, 1999).

Craig, P, *Administrative Law* (4th edn, London: Sweet & Maxwell, 1999).

DiIulio, J, 'The Old Regime and the Ruiz Revolution: The Impact of Federal Intervention on Texas Prisons' in J DiIulio (ed), *Courts, Corrections and the Constitution* (New York: OUP, 1991).

Ditchfield, J, *Control in Prisons: A Review of the Literature* (London: Home Office Research Study 118, 1990).

Dobash, R, R Dobash, and S Gutteridge, *The Imprisonment of Women* (Oxford: Blackwell, 1986).

Downes, D, *Contrasts in Tolerance: Post War Penal Policy in the Netherlands and in England and Wales* (Oxford: Clarendon, 1988).

Emmerson, B, QC and A Ashworth QC, *Human Rights and Criminal Justice* (London: Sweet & Maxwell, 2001).

Evans, M and R Morgan, *Preventing Torture: A Study of the European Convention for the Prevention of Torture and Inhuman or Degrading Treatment or Punishment* (Oxford: Clarendon Press, 1998).

Fitzgerald, M and J Sim, *British Prisons* (2nd edn, Oxford: Blackwell, 1982).

Flynn, N and D Price, *Education in Prisons: A National Survey* (London: Prison Reform Trust, 1995).

Fordham, M, *Judicial Review Handbook* (3rd edn, Oxford: Hart Publishing, 2001).

Forsythe, W, *Penal Discipline, Reformatory Projects and the English Prison Commissioners 1895–1939* (Exeter: Exeter University Press, 1990).

Garland, D, *Punishment and Welfare* (Aldershot: Gower, 1985).

Gray, C, *Remedies in International Law* (Oxford: Clarendon Press, 1987).

Gunn, J, T Madden, and M Swinton, *Mentally Disordered Offenders* (London: HMSO, 1992).

Harding, C, B Hines, R Ireland, and P Rawlings, *Imprisonment in England and Wales: A Concise History* (London: Croom Helm, 1985).

Harding, R, *Private Prisons and Public Accountability* (London: OUP, 1997).

Harper, R, *Medical Treatment and the Law* (Bristol: Family Law, 1999).

Harris, D, M O'Boyle, and C Warbrick, *Law of the European Convention on Human Rights* (London: Butterworths, 1995).

Hart, HLA, *Punishment and Responsibility: Essays in the Philosophy of Law* (Oxford: Clarendon, 1957).

Howard League, *Lost Inside: The Imprisonment of Teenage Girls* (London, 1997).

Hunt, M, *Using Human Rights Law in English Courts* (Oxford: Hart Publishing, 1997).

Jackson, G, *Blood in my Eye* (London: Penguin, 1972).

Jacobs, J, *Stateville: The Penitentiary in Mass Society* (Chicago, Ill: Chicago University Press, 1977).

James, A, A Bottomley, A Liebling, and E Clare, *Privatising Prisons: Rhetoric and Reality* (London: Sage, 1997).

Joseph, S, J Schultz, and M Castan (eds), *The International Covenant on Civil and Political Rights: Cases, Materials and Commentary* (Oxford: OUP, 2000).

Justice, *Justice in Prisons* (London, 1983).

Justice, *Providing Protection: Towards Fair and Effective Asylum Procedures* (London, 1997).

Klug, F, K Starmer, and S Weir, *Three Pillars of Liberty* (London: Routledge, 1996).

Lewis, Derek, *Hidden Agendas: Politics, Law and Disorder* (London: Hamish Hamilton, 1997).

Liebling, A, *Suicides in Prison* (London: Routledge, 1992).

Loucks, N (ed), *Prison Rules: A Working Guide* (London: Prison Reform Trust, 1993).

——*Anything Goes: The Use of the 'Catch-all' Disciplinary Rule in Prison Service Establishments* (London: Prison Reform Trust, 1995).

Loughlin, M, *Public Law and Political Theory* (Oxford: Clarendon, 1992).

Macdonald, I and F Webber, *Macdonald's Immigration Law and Practice* (5th edn, London: Butterworths, 2001).

Manderaka-Sheppard, A, *The Dynamics of Aggression in Women's Prisons in England* (Aldershot: Gower, 1986).

Matrix Media and Information Group, *Privacy and the Media: The Developing Law* (London, 2002).

McColgan, A (ed), *Discrimination Law Handbook* (London, 2002).

McConville, Sean, *A History of English Prison Administration* (London: Routledge and Keegan Paul, 1981).

Morgan, R and M Evans, *Combating Torture in Europe – The work and standards of the European Committee for the Prevention of Torture* (Council of Europe, 2001).

Morison, J and P Leith, *The Barrister's World* (London: Open University Press, 1991).

NACRO, *Women Prisoners: Towards a New Millennium* (London, 1996).

Padel, U, *HIV, AIDS and Prisons* (London: Prison Reform Trust, 1988).

Penal Affairs Consortium, *An Unsuitable Place for Treatment: Diverting Mentally Disordered Offenders from Custody* (London, 1998).

Prison Health Policy Unit and Task Force, *Prison Health Handbook* (London, 2000).

Reynaud, A, *Human Rights in Prisons* (2nd edn, Strasbourg: Council of Europe, 1987).

Rodley, N, *The Treatment of Prisoners in International Law* (Oxford: Clarendon, 1999).

Rose, Gordon, *The Struggle for Penal Reform* (London: Stevens & Sons, 1961).

Salmond, *The Law of Torts* (15th edn, London: Sweet & Maxwell, 1969).

Sieghart, P, *The International Law of Human Rights* (Oxford: Clarendon, 1983).

Sim, J, *Medical Power in Prisons* (Buckingham: Open University Press, 1990).

Simor, J and B Emmerson, *Human Rights Practice* (London, 2000).

Sparks, R, A Bottoms, and W Hay, *Prisons and the Problem of Order* (Oxford: Clarendon, 1996).

Stern, V, *Bricks of Shame: Britain's Prisons* (London: Penguin, 1987).

Thomas, David, *Current Sentencing Practice* (London: Sweet & Maxwell, 1982).

Thompson, EP, *Whigs and Hunters* (London: Penguin, 1977).

Tomasevski, K, *Prison Health: International Standards and National Practices in Europe* (Helsinki: HEUNI, 1992).

Unger, R, *Knowledge and Politics* (New York: Free Press, 1975).

Van Dijk, P and G Van Hoof, *Theory and Practice of the European Convention on Human Rights* (3rd edn, Dewenter: Kluwer, 1998).

Van Zyl Smit, D, *South African Prison Law and Practice* (Durban: Butterworths, 1992).

Vogler, R, *Germany: A Guide to the Criminal Justice System* (London: Prisoners Abroad, 1989).

Wallace, R, *International Human Rights: Text and Materials* (London: Sweet & Maxwell, 1997).

Wasik, M, *Emmins on Sentencing* (4th edn, London: Blackstone, 2001).

Weber, L, *Deciding to Detain* (University of Cambridge Institute of Criminology, 2000).

Yackle, L, *Reform and Regret: The Story of Federal Judicial Involvement in the Alabama Prison System* (New York: OUP, 1989).

Articles in books

Bank R, 'Country Oriented Procedures under the Convention Against Torture: Towards a New Dynamism' in P Alston and J Crawford (eds), *The Failure of UN Human Rights Treaty Monitoring* (Cambridge: CUP, 2000).

Blom Cooper, Sir Louis, 'The Centralisation of Government Control of National Prison Services with special reference to the Prison Act 1877' in J Freeman (ed), *Prisons Past and Future* (London: Heinemann, 1978).

Bottoms, A, 'The Philosophy and Politics of Punishment and Sentencing' in C Clarkson and R Morgan (eds), *The Politics of Sentencing Reform* (Oxford: Clarendon, 1995).

Boyle, K, 'Practice and Procedure on Individual Applications in the European Convention on Human Rights' in H Hannum (ed), *Guide to International Human Rights Practice* (2nd edn, Philadelphia, Penn: University of Pennsylvania Press, 1994).

Bronstein, A, 'Criminal Justice: Prisons and Penology' in N Dorsen (ed), *Our Endangered Rights* (New York: Pantheon, 1984).

Farer, T, in D Harris and S Livingstone (eds), *The Inter-American System of Human Rights* (Oxford: Clarendon, 1998).

Fawcett, J, 'Applications to the European Convention on Human Rights' in M Maguire, J Vagg, and R Morgan, *Accountability and Prisons: Opening up a Closed World* (London: Tavistock, 1986).

Fitzgerald, E, 'Prison Discipline and the Courts' in M Maguire, J Vagg, and R Morgan (eds), *Accountability and Prisons: Opening Up a Closed World* (London: Tavistock, 1986).

Fordham, M and T de la Mare, 'Identifying the Principles of Proportionality' in J Jowell and J Cooper (eds), *Understanding Human Rights Principles* (Oxford: Hart, 2001).

Foucault, M, 'Two Lectures' in *Power/Knowledge: Selected Interviews and Other Writings 1972–77* (New York: Pantheon, 1980).

Gearty, C, 'The Prisons and the Courts' in J Muncie and R Sparks (eds), *Imprisonment: European Perspectives* (London: Sage, 1991).

Grounds, A, 'Mentally Disordered Prisoners' in E Player and M Jenkins (eds), *Prisons After Woolf: Reform through Riot* (London: Routledge, 1994).

Hayes, L, 'Custodial Suicide: Overcoming the Obstacles to Prevention' in A Liebling (ed), *Deaths in Custody: Caring for People at Risk* (London: Whiting and Burch, 1994).

Hood, R and S Shute, 'The Changing Face of Parole in England and Wales—A Story of Well-intentioned Reforms and Some Unintended Consequences' in C Prittwitz et al (eds), *Festschrift für Klaus Luderssen* (Baden-Baden, 2002).

Liebling, A, 'Prison Suicide: What Progress Research?' in A Liebling (ed), *Deaths in Custody: Caring for People at Risk* (London: Whiting and Burch, 1994).

—— 'Risk and Prison Suicide' in H Kaushall and J Pritchard (eds), *Good Practice in Risk Assessment and Risk Management* (1997).

Livingstone, S, 'Prisoners' Rights' in D Harris and S Joseph (eds), *The International Covenant on Civil and Political Rights and United Kingdom Law* (Oxford: Clarendon, 1995).

McHale, J and A Young, 'Policy, Rights and the HIV Positive Prisoner' in S McVeigh and S Wheeler (eds), *Law, Health and Medical Regulation* (London: Routledge, 1992).

Morgan, R and M Evans, 'CPT Standards: An Overview' in R Morgan and M Evans (eds), *Protecting Prisoners: The Standards of the European Committee for the Prevention of Torture in Context* (Oxford: OUP, 1999).

Neal, D, 'Prison Suicides: What Progress Policy and Practice' in A Liebling (ed), *Deaths in Custody: Caring for People at Risk* (London: Whiting and Burch, 1994).

Neale, K, 'The European Prison Rules: Contextual, Philosophical and Practical Aspects' in J Muncie and R Sparks, *Imprisonment: European Perspectives* (London: Sage, 1991).

Opsahl, T, 'Settlement based on respect for Human Rights under the European Convention on Human Rights' in *Proceedings of the Sixth International Colloquy about the European Convention on Human Rights* (Dordrecht: Martinus Nijhoff, 1988).

Player, E, 'Women's Prisons After Woolf' in Player (ed), *Prisons After Woolf: Reform through Riot* (London: Routledge, 1994).

Richardson, G, 'Prisoners and the Law: Beyond Rights' in C McCrudden and G Chambers (eds), *Individual Rights and the Law in the United Kingdom* (Oxford: Clarendon, 1993).

Simon, J and M Feeley, 'True Crime: The New Penology and Public Discourse on Crime' in T Blomberg and S Cohen (eds), *Punishment and Social Control: Essays in Honor of Sheldon L Messinger* (New York: Aldine de Gruyter, 1995).

Taylor, L, 'Bringing Power to Particular Account: Peter Rajah and the Hull Board of Visitors' in P Carlen and R Collinson (eds), *Radical Issues in Criminology* (Oxford: Martin Robertson, 1980).

Van Swaaningen, R and G de Jonge, 'The Dutch Prison System and Penal Policy in the 1990s: From Humanitarian Paternalism to Penal Business Management' in V Ruggiero, M Ryan, and J Sims (eds), *Western European Penal Systems* (London: Sage, 1995).

Journal articles

Arnott, H, 'HIV/AIDS, prisons and the Human Rights Act' [2001] European Human Rights L Rev 71.

Baker, E and CMV Clarkson, 'Making Punishments Work? An Evaluation of the Halliday Report on Sentencing in England and Wales' [2002] Crim LR 81.

Beloff, M, QC and H Mountfield, 'There is no alternative' [1999] JR 143.

Bennion, F, 'What Interpretation is 'Possible' under Section 3(1) of the Human Rights Act 1998?' [2000] PL 77.

Bershad, B, 'Discriminatory Treatment of the Female Offender in the Criminal Justice System' (1985) 26 Boston College L Rev 389.

Bossuyt, M, 'The Development of Special Procedures of the United Nations Commission on Human Rights' (1985) 6 Human Rights LJ 179.

Bradley, A, 'Judicial Review by Other Routes' [1988] PL 169.

Branthwaite, M, 'Deaths in Custody – Causes and Legal Consequences' (2001) 69 Medico-Legal J 107.

Bratza, N and M O'Boyle, 'The Legacy of the Commission to the New Court Under the Eleventh Protocol' [1997] European Human Rights L Rev 211.

Brazier, M, 'Prison Doctors and their Involuntary Patients' [1982] PL 283.

Buckley, RA, 'Liability in Tort for Breach of Statutory Duty' [1984] LQR 204.

Cassese, A, 'The New Approach to Human Rights: The European Convention for the Prevention of Torture' (1989) 83 AJIL 128.

Clarkson, CMV, 'Beyond Just Deserts: Sentencing Violent and Sexual Offenders' (1997) 36 Howard J 284.

Clements, L, 'Striking the Right Balance: The New Rules of Procedure for the European Court of Human Rights' [1999] European Human Rights L Rev 266.

Coles, D, and H Shaw, 'Deaths in prison and their investigation: a critical overview' (2001) 138 Prison Service J 15-19.

Collins, H, 'Capitalist Discipline and Corporatist Law' (1982) 11 ILJ 78.

Craig, P, 'Common Law, Reasons and Administrative Justice' [1994] CLJ 282.

——'The Courts, the Human Rights Act and Judicial Review' (2001) 117 LQR 589.

——and S Schonberg, 'Substantive Legitimate Expectations after *Coughlan*' [2000] PL 684.

Cram, I, 'Interfering with Gaol Mail: Prisoners' Legal Letters and the Courts' [1993] LS 356.

Ditchfield, J and D Duncan, 'The Prison Disciplinary System: Perceptions of its Fairness and Adequacy by Inmates, Staff and Members of Boards of Visitors' (1987) 26 Howard J 122.

Drzemczewski, A, 'The International Organisation of the European Court of Human Rights: The Composition of Chambers and the Grand Chamber' (2000) European Human Rights L Rev 233.

——and J-M Ladewig, 'Principal Characteristics of the New ECHR Control Mechanism' (1994) 15 Human Rights LJ 81.

Ekland-Olson, S and S Martin, 'Organizational Compliance with Court-Ordered Reform' (1988) 22 L and Society Rev 359.

Elliott, M, 'The HRA 1998 and the Standard of Substantive Review' (2001) 60 CLJ 301.

Emmerson, B, 'This Year's Model: Options for Incorporation' [1997] European Human Rights L Rev 313.

Evans, Malcolm and Rod Morgan, 'The European Convention for the Prevention of Torture: Operational Practice' (1992) 41 ICLQ 590 and 'The European Convention for the Prevention of Torture 1992–7' (1997) 46 ICLQ 663.

Feeley, M and J Simon, 'The New Penology: Notes on the Emerging Strategy of Corrections and its Implications' (1992) 30 Criminology 449.

Fordham, M, 'Convention Case-Law: Judicial Warnings' [2000] JR 139.

——and T de la Mare, 'Anxious Scrutiny, the Principle of Legality and the HRA' [2000] JR 48.

Ghandi, P, 'The Human Rights Committee and Articles 7 and 10 of the International Covenant on Civil and Political Rights 1966' (1990) 13 Dalhousie LJ 758.

Gowan, H, 'The United Kingdom's Second Periodic Report under the UN Torture Convention' [1996] European Human Rights L Rev 34.

Greenberg, D and F Stender, 'The Prison as a Lawless Agency' (1972) 21 Buffalo L Rev 799.

Henderson, A, 'Readings and Remedies: Section 3(1) of the HRA and Rectifying Construction' [2000] JR 258.

Higgins, R, 'Derogation Under Human Rights Treaties' (1976–77) 48 British Yearbook of Intl L 281.

Hirschkop, B, and D Milleman, 'The Unconstitutionality of Prison Life' (1969) 55 Virginia L Rev 795.

Jackson, M, 'The Right to Counsel in Prison Disciplinary Proceedings' (1986) 20 U of British Columbia L Rev 221.

Johnston, J, 'The Meaning of "Public Authority" under the Human Rights Act' [2001] JR 250.

Jowell, J, 'Beyond the Rule of Law: Towards Constitutional Review' [2000] PL 671.

Keene, J, 'Drug Misuse in Prison: Views from Inside: A Qualitative Study of Prison Staff and Inmates' (1997) 36 Howard J 28.

Kennedy, I, 'Note' (1995) 3 Medical L Rev 189.

Kidd, C, 'Disciplinary Proceedings and the Right to a Fair Criminal Trial Under the European Convention on Human Rights' (1987) 36 ICLQ 856.

Klug, F, K Starmer, and S Weir, 'The British Way of Doing Things: The United Kingdom and the International Covenant on Civil and Political Rights 1976–94' [1995] PL 504.

Knop, K, 'Here and There: International Law in Domestic Courts' (2000) 32 New York U J of International L and Politics 501.

Leigh, I, 'Taking Rights Proportionately: Judicial Review, the Human Rights Act and Strasbourg' (2002) PL 265.

——and L Lustgarten, 'Making Rights Real: the Courts, Remedies and the Human Rights Act' (1999) 58 CLJ 509.

Lester, A, 'The Art of the Possible – Interpreting Statutes under the Human Rights Act' [1998] European Human Rights L Rev 665.

——'UK Acceptance of the Strasbourg Jurisdiction: What Really went on in Whitehall in 1965' [1998] PL 237.

Lewis, C, 'The Exhaustion of Alternative Remedies in Administrative Law' [1992] CLJ 138.

Liebling, A, 'Suicide in Prison: Ten Years On' (2001) 138 Prison Service J 35-41.

Light, R and K Mattfield, 'Prison Disciplinary Hearings: The Failure of Reform' (1988) 27 Howard J 266.

Livingstone, S, 'Prisoners and Board of Visitors Hearings: A Right to Legal Representation After All?' (1987) 38 Northern Ireland LQ 144.

——'Prisoners Have Rights, But What Rights' (1988) 51 MLR 525.

——'Designing a New Framework for Prison Administration: The Experience of the Canadian Corrections and Conditional Release Act 1992' (1994) 24 Anglo-American L Rev 426.

—— 'Article 14 and the Prevention of Discrimination in the European Convention on Human Rights' [1997] 1 European Human Rights L Rev 25.

Logan, C, 'Well Kept: Comparing Quality of Confinement in Public and Private Prisons' (1992) 83 J of Criminal L and Criminology 577.

Mackay, R and D Machin, 'The operation of section 48 of the Mental Health Act 1983: an empirical study of the transfer of remand prisoners to hospital' (2000) 40 British J of Criminology 727.

Malloch, M, 'Caring for drug users? The experiences of women prisoners' (2000) 39 Howard J 354.

Manknell, D, 'The Interpretative Obligation under the Human Rights Act' [2000] JR 109.

Markus, K and M Westgate, 'Unilever and Hargreaves: A Cross-Analysis' [1997] JR 220.

Marshall, G, 'Two Kinds of Compatibility: More about section 3 of the Human Rights Act 1998' [1999] PL 377.

Martinson, R, 'What Works? Questions and Answers About Prison Reform' (1974) 35 Public Interest 22.

McDougall, C, '"The Alchemist's Search for the Philosopher's Stone": Public Authorities and the Human Rights Act (One Year On)' [2002] JR 23.

Melzer, D, 'Prisoners with psychosis in England and Wales: a one-year national follow-up study' (2002) 41 Howard J 1.

Morgan, R, 'More Prisoners Denied Lawyers' Help' (1987) 91 New Society 1283.

Morgan, Rod, 'Prisons Accountability Revisited' [1993] PL 314.

Mowbray, A, 'The European Court of Human Rights Approach to Just Satisfaction' [1997] PL 647.

Moyle, P, 'Separating the allocation of punishment from its administration: theoretical and empirical observations' (2001) 41(1) British J of Criminology 77.

Neenan, C, 'Is a Declaration of Incompatibility an Effective Remedy?' [2000] JR 247.

Note, '"Mastering" Intervention in Prisons' (1979) 88 Yale LJ 1062.

Nowicki, M, 'NGOs before the Commission and Court of Human Rights' (1996) 14 Netherlands Q of Human Rights 289.

O'Bryan, S, 'Closing the Courthouse Door: The Impact of the Prison Litigation Reform Act's Physical Injury Requirement on the Constitutional Rights of Prisoners' (1997) 83 Virginia L Rev 1189.

O'hAdhmaill, P, 'Sexual Apartheid in the Prison System' (1994) 28 Prison Report 26.

Oliver, D, 'The Frontiers of the State: Public Authorities and Public Functions under the Human Rights Act' [2000] PL 476.

Olley, K, 'Alternative Remedies and the Permission Stage' [2000] JR 240.

Owen, Tim, 'Prisoners and Fundamental Rights' [1997] JR 81.

Padel, U, 'It's Not Just a Visit' (1998) 43 Prison Report 18.

Quinn, P, 'Reflexivity Run Riot': The Survival of the Prison Catch-all' (1995) 34 Howard J 354.

Raz, J, 'The Rule of Law and Its Virtue' (1977) 93 LQR 195.

Reidy, A, F Hampson, and K Boyle, 'Dealing with Gross Violations of Human Rights: Turkey and the ECHR' (1997) 15 Netherlands Q of Human Rights 161.

Rhodes, S, 'Prison Reform and Prison Life: Four Books on the Process of Court Ordered Change' (1992) 26 L and Society Rev 189.

Richardson, G and M Sunkin, 'Judicial Review: Questions of Impact' [1996] PL 79.

Robbins, I and M Buser, 'Punitive Conditions of Prison Confinement: An analysis of *Pugh v Locke* and Federal Court Supervision of State Penal Administration Under the Eighth Amendment' (1977) 29 Stanford L Rev 892.

Robertshaw, P, 'Providing Reasons for Administrative Decisions' (1998) 27 Anglo-American L Rev 29.

Schermers, H, 'The Eleventh Protocol to the European Convention on Human Rights' (1994) 20 European L Rev 367.

—— 'Adoption of the Eleventh Protocol to the European Convention on Human Rights' (1995) 20 European L Rev 559.

Schone, JM, 'The Short Life and Painful Death of Prisoners' Rights' (2001) 40 Howard J of Criminal Justice 70.

Smith, C, 'Federal Judges Role in Prisoner Litigation: What's Necessary? What's Proper?' (1986) 70 Judicature 144.

Stern, Vivien, *Bricks of Shame* (London, 1987).

Steyn, Karen, 'Substantive Legitimate Expectations' [2001] JR 244.

Sturm, S, 'Resolving the Remedial Dilemma: Strategies of Judicial Intervention in Prisons' (1990) 138 U of Pennsylvania L Rev 805.

—— 'The Legacy and Future of Corrections Litigation' (1994) 142 U of Pennsylvania L Rev 639.

Tchaikovsky, C, 'Mixed Prisons: Misogynistic and Misguided' (1991) 16 Prison Report 12.

Teers, J, 'Testing for Drugs in an Open Prison' (1997) 40 Prison Report 12.

Tettenborn, AM, 'Prisoners' Rights' [1980] PL 74.

Thomas, DA, 'Sentencing Legislation—The Case for Consolidation' [1997] Crim LR 406.

—— 'The Crime (Sentences) Act 1997' (1998) Crim LR 83.

Thomas, P, 'AIDS/HIV in Prisons' (1990) 29 Howard J 1.

Toube, David, 'Requiring Reasons at Common Law' [1997] JR 68.

Treacey, V, 'Prisoners Rights Lost in Semantics' (1989) 28 Howard J 27.

Treves, T, 'The UN Body of Principles for the Protection of Detained or Imprisoned Persons' (1990) 84 AJIL 578.

Valette, D, 'AIDS behind bars: prisoners' rights guillotined' (2002) 41(2) Howard J 107.

Wadham, J, 'The Human Rights Act: One Year On' [2001] European Human Rights L Rev 620.

Zellick, G, 'The Forcible Feeding of Prisoners: An Examination of the Legality of Enforced Therapy' [1976] PL 153.

—— 'The Prison Rules and the Courts' [1981] Crim LR 602.

—— 'The Prison Rules and the Courts: A Postscript' [1982] Crim LR 575.

—— 'The Rights of Prisoners and the European Convention on Human Rights' (1975) 38 MLR 683.

INDEX

Please note that all references are to paragraph numbers except for references to the Appendices which are by page number